GROLIER
ENCYCLOPEDIA
OF KNOWLEDGE

Grolier Incorporated
Danbury, Connecticut

1993 Printing

ISBN 0-7172-5300-7 (complete set)
ISBN 0-7172-5308-2 (volume 8)

Printed and manufactured in the United States of America.

This publication is an abridged version of the *Academic American Encyclopedia.*

3 4 5 6 7 8 9 10

Foss, Lukas [faws]   Lukas Foss, b. Aug. 15, 1922, is a Berlin-born American composer, conductor, and pianist who received his early training in Berlin and Paris. In 1937 he went to the United States and studied at the Curtis Institute in Philadelphia; he also attended Serge Koussevitzky's conducting classes at the Berkshire Music Center, where he later taught. He was conductor of the Buffalo Philharmonic Orchestra from 1963 to 1970 and subsequently became conductor of the Brooklyn Philharmonic (1971–90) and the Milwaukee Symphony (1981–86). His works include ballets, cantatas, chamber music, concertos, operas, and orchestral pieces.

fossa [fahs'-uh]   The fossa, *Cryptoprocta ferox*, the largest carnivore of Madagascar, is a member of the civet family, Viverridae. It grows to a length of about 140 cm (55 in), including a tail of approximately 66 cm (26 in). Its coat is dense, soft, and reddish brown. When annoyed, the fossa discharges an odorous scent from its anal glands. The fossa is nocturnal and preys on lemurs and small domestic animals.

The physical characteristics of the fossa are a mixture of those found in the cat, civet, and mongoose.

Fosse, Bob   American director and choreographer Robert Louis Fosse, b. Chicago, June 23, 1927, d. Sept. 23, 1987, choreographed or staged shows and films including *Pajama Game* (1954; film, 1957), *Damn Yankees* (1955; film, 1958), and his own *Sweet Charity* (1966; film, 1969), which he directed. He performed in *Kiss Me, Kate* (1953) and twice took the title role in revivals of *Pal Joey* in the 1960s. On Broadway Fosse first directed *Redhead* (1959) and thereafter directed and choreographed *Pippin* (1972), his own *Chicago* (1975), and *Dancin'* (1978), among others. He also directed the films *Cabaret* (1972), *Lenny* (1975), and the semiautobiographical *All That Jazz* (1979).

Fossey, Dian   Dian Fossey, b. San Francisco, Jan. 16, 1932, d. 1985, was a zoologist known for her field studies of the rare mountain gorilla in east central Africa. From 1963 until her death, she carefully observed the gorillas in their native habitat with little outside assistance. Fossey's book *Gorillas in the Mist* (1983) chronicles her observations of three generations of mountain gorillas and urges the preservation of this endangered species. Fossey was found murdered on Dec. 27, 1985, at the Karisoke Research Center in Rwanda, which she established in 1967.

fossil fuels   see COAL AND COAL MINING; ENERGY SOURCES; NATURAL GAS; PETROLEUM

fossil record   Fossils are remains of prehistoric organisms. Preserved by burial under countless layers of SEDIMENTARY ROCKS, they are a record of the history of life beginning approximately 3.5 billion years ago, the study of which is called PALEONTOLOGY.

Some fossils are abundant in the strata of the Earth's crust. The CHALK cliffs of Dover, England, and the Niobrara Chalk of Kansas are composed of complex platelets of algae so small that millions fill a cubic millimeter. Shells of invertebrate marine animals, such as brachiopods, bryozoans, clams, snails, corals, and echinoderms, are preserved in many beds of limestone, and the bones and teeth of vertebrates are sometimes so numerous that they form deposits called "bone beds." In other sedimentary rocks, such as the majority of the world's red SANDSTONES, shells and bones are rarely found, although tracks and burrows may be abundant. Fossils are uncommon in sedimentary rocks of Precambrian age (see GEOLOGIC TIME), although some rocks of the latter part of that era have yielded a moderately diverse assemblage known as the EDIACARAN FAUNA.

Entire or partial bodies of organisms are referred to by paleontologists as body fossils. In contrast, marks left in rock by the activities of organisms are called trace fossils.

When this fish died, its body settled to the ocean bottom and became covered by calcareous sediments. The organic material of the fish decayed; the skeleton, which contained large amounts of calcium phosphate, was well preserved.

These include artifacts, burrows, feces, tracks, and trails. Microscopic spores, pollen grains, and cysts, useful for POLLEN STRATIGRAPHY, are extracted from sediment by acid treatment (see PALEOBOTANY).

How and Where Fossils Form

The Earth is teeming with life, all of it searching for food—organic compounds of hydrogen and carbon. As a result very little digestible organic matter escapes destruction, and indigestible skeletal material, such as shells, bones, and teeth, has a much better chance of burial and preservation. Shell material is typically composed of calcium carbonate, as are mollusk shells; teeth and bones are composed of calcium phosphate; sponge spicules and diatom and radiolarian skeletons are composed of opaline silica. The highly indigestible organic jackets of spores and pollen grains also commonly escape destruction. Such materials form most of the body fossils common in layered rocks.

Much rarer are accumulations of sediment in settings from which scavengers are excluded and in which the bodies of plants and animals, carried in from outside, may retain their general form. Although few such occurrences are preserved and discovered, they are of greatest value to the paleontologist because they give the most comprehensive view of past life.

In contrast to such occurences, most of the fossil record is composed of remains recovered from ordinary sediment, in a cliff or quarry or roadcut, or from wells drilled deep into the ground. These remains may be preserved as the original material, as hollows (molds) formed by dissolving the original matter to leave only an imprint, or as replacement material, with a mineral such as quartz or pyrite having replaced the original bone or shell.

Fossils and Earth History

Toward the end of the 17th century, the naturalist Robert HOOKE turned his attention to spectacular marine fossils found in his native England. Determining that these must be the remains of once-living animals, he noted that they did not resemble any living species then known, causing him to believe that life might have changed at some time in the past and that fossils might be a chronological guide to geologic history. Hooke also noted that these fossils looked more like tropical shells than species then living on British shores and wondered whether Britain's geographic latitude had also changed since the time these animals lived. The first suggestion was verified a century later, and the second three centuries later with the discovery of CONTINENTAL DRIFT.

The Earth's sedimentary rock strata first form as layers of sediment (see SEDIMENT, MARINE), each covering an old-

A theoretical section through the Earth's surface shows strata containing fossils. A glacier (1) may contain bodies of mammoths and other recently extinct animals. Quaternary limestone (2) contains shells of mollusks (A), such as Glycimeris (center). Entire insect bodies (B) are preserved in amber, which occurs with lignite (3). Tertiary sandstone (4) contains shells of the crab Xanthopsis (C). Such ammonites as Euhoplites (D) occur in Cretaceous limestone (5). Deer antlers (E) may be found in caves (6). Jurassic rocks (7) contain such remains as a jaw of Ichthyosaurus (F), a marine reptile. A bark impression of the treelike club moss Lepidodendron (G) may be found in Upper Carboniferous limestone (10). Fossils of such corals as Aulophyllum (H) occur in Lower Carboniferous rock (11). Cambrian rocks (12) contain fossils of such trilobites as Conocoryphe (I). Oil (8) and water (9) deposits and volcanic rock (13) are also shown.

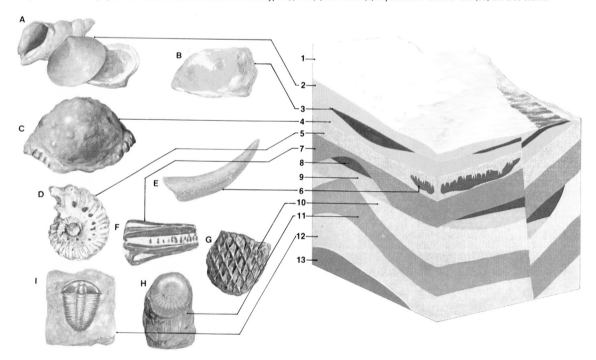

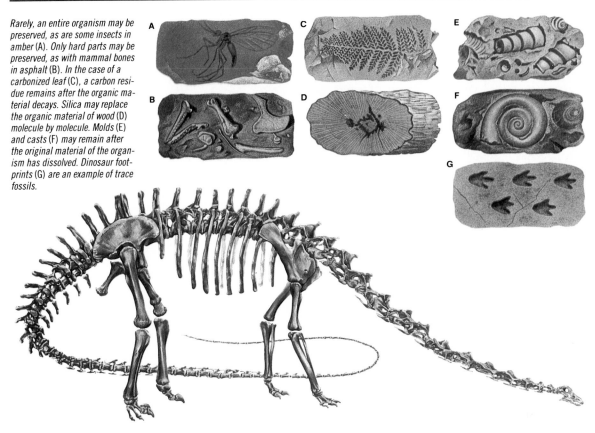

Rarely, an entire organism may be preserved, as are some insects in amber (A). Only hard parts may be preserved, as with mammal bones in asphalt (B). In the case of a carbonized leaf (C), a carbon residue remains after the organic material decays. Silica may replace the organic material of wood (D) molecule by molecule. Molds (E) and casts (F) may remain after the original material of the organism has dissolved. Dinosaur footprints (G) are an example of trace fossils.

Diplodocus, considered the longest land animal ever to walk the Earth, lived in North America at the end of the Jurassic Period. It measured more than 25 m (82 ft) in length and weighed 20 tons or more. This illustration shows a reconstruction of its skeleton, which became fossilized as the minerals in groundwater slowly permeated the bones.

er stratum and being covered, in turn, by a younger one (see STRATIGRAPHY). They form, in this manner, a historical sequence, and the fossils that they contain can be arranged in time, by what has come to be known as the law of superposition. Early in the 1800s, William SMITH, in England, noted that fossils were characteristic of individual beds or groups of beds in such sequences of strata, and that distinctive assemblages of fossils could be traced cross-country. Geologists soon discovered that the sequences of fossils in England could be matched with similar sequences elsewhere in the world.

Any given area contains a stratigraphic record of only some part of Earth history. By combining information from many different areas, geologists can determine a global history. Nearly two centuries of such efforts have resulted in ever more detailed classification of the more fossiliferous part of Earth history—the last 600 million years (see EARTH, GEOLOGICAL HISTORY OF). The fossil record of this 600-million-year span yields a relative chronology, whereas RADIOMETRIC AGE-DATING yields an absolute one.

The Progression of Prehistoric Life

The earliest megafossils, some 1 to 3.5 billion years old,

are STROMATOLITES, calcareous masses formed in shallow water by blue-green algae. Microfossils from CHERT AND FLINT this old include a variety of BLUE-GREEN ALGAE and other bacterial forms. By about 1 billion years ago, a wider variety of microscopic one-celled organisms had appeared, perhaps including some, called eukaryotes, that had nuclei. In deposits approximately 600 million years old, imprints of soft-bodied invertebrates are found. In Cambrian sediments 570 million years old, the first hard-shelled invertebrates appeared—MOLLUSKS, BRACHIOPODS, and TRILOBITES. The appearance of these invertebrates, in rocks deposited at the beginning of the Paleozoic Era, coincided with the first widespread signs of burrowing. In rocks of the Ordovician Period (500–425 million years ago), researchers have found fossil animal burrows that are evidence of the earliest known land animals. Most of the modern groups of marine invertebrates, as well as OSTRACODERMS (the first fish), were represented by this time. In the Silurian Period (425–400 million years ago) landmasses were colonized by rapidly evolving higher plants, whose supporting structures and water-conducting vessels now made life on dry land possible. In the Devonian Period (400–345 million years ago) the main groups of

Fossils that character-ize particular geologic strata are known as index fossils; ideally, they are abundant and have a wide geographic distribution within a limited geologic time. Although evidence of bacterialike life exists in rocks up to 3.5 billion years old, multicellular organisms do not become numerous in the fossil record until the Paleozoic Era. Index fossils of the Paleozoic include trilobites in the Cambrian Period, graptolites in the Ordovician, crinoids in the Silurian, fishes in the Devonian, land plants in the Carbonif-erous, and certain brachiopods in the Permian. Mesozoic Era strata contain reptile footprints in the Triassic Period, ammo-nites in the Jurassic, and sea urchins and sand dollars in the Cretaceous. Shells of foraminifera are common in Cenozoic marine deposits.

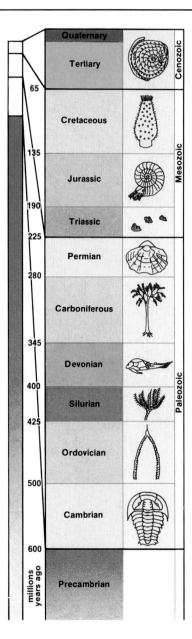

SAURS) and BIRDS, as well as MAMMALS, appeared during the Jurassic Period (190–135 million years ago). On land, forests of CONIFERS and CYCADS had largely replaced the lycopod- and seed-fern-dominated forests of the Pa-leozoic Era. In the sea, one-celled, calcite-armored, pho-tosynthetic organisms called coccolithophorids appeared, and massive calcium carbonate (chalk) deposition began in the deeper oceans. The Cretaceous Period (135–65 million years ago) is the time of origin of two great groups of organisms—the flowering plants (ANGIOSPERMS) on land and the plantlike, planktonic DIATOMS in water. Flowering plants changed the face of the Earth in many ways and triggered a great wave of EVOLUTION among the insects. At the end of Cretaceous time, the extinction of dinosaurs resulted in the spectacular evolution of terrestrial mam-mals, and giant sharks and marine mammals replaced large reptiles in the sea.

The group of mammals known as the PRIMATES—now represented by lemurs, monkeys, apes, and humans—dates back to the beginning of the Cenozoic Era (65 mil-lion years ago to the present), but humanlike creatures (see PREHISTORIC HUMANS) are known only from the last few million years, the Pliocene and Pleistocene epochs. *Homo sapiens*, modern humans, appeared in the Old World during the Pleistocene but did not reach the Amer-icas until the latter part of the epoch.

Fossils record the progressive evolutionary diversifica-tion of living things, the progressive colonization of habi-tats, and the development of increasingly complex organ-ic communities. The development of new species and such larger groups of species as genera and families has gone on throughout time, but so also has the loss of spe-cies by EXTINCTION. The rate of extinction at some times in Earth history greatly exceeded the rate of speciation, and the faunas and floras of the world became reduced.

Fossils and Evolution

The fossil record corresponds to the general theory of or-ganic evolution, and any group of plants or animals can be seen to change through the record of strata. The smallest general unit of classification is the species, rec-ognized in the fossil record by great similarity of form. Most species are seen to have an existence that is short in terms of Earth history—usually one to several million years, more rarely tens of million years, and very rarely hundreds of million years. Most genera (groups of related species) can be traced through time spans of tens of millions of years; larger units of this classification system, or taxono-my, tend to persist through longer time spans. The majority of the classes and phyla of invertebrate animals, for exam-ple, have records beginning early in the Paleozoic Era.

Fossils suggest that evolution has resulted mainly from the tendency of all species to experiment with new ways of living, thereby to exploit new opportunities as they arose in an ever-changing world, gaining a new foothold in one place and losing one in another. With Charles DARWIN's theory of evolution in the mid-1800s came the expectation that the fossil record would provide unbroken evolutionary sequences, in which species after species would be seen to emerge gradually from its ancestors and

FISH—COELACANTHS, LUNGFISH, SHARKS, bony fish, and the extinct arthrodires—were differentiated. Forests and the first primitive INSECTS appeared on land, as did AMPHIBIANS. The Carboniferous Period (345–280 million years ago), known for its great coal deposits, witnessed the develop-ment of REPTILES, the first animals having an amniote egg, which enables the embryo to develop on dry land.

The Mesozoic Era (225–65 million years ago) is known particularly for the evolution of gigantic reptiles, both in the sea (ICHTHYOSAURS, PLESIOSAURS, and MOSA-SAURS) and on land (DINOSAURS). Flying reptiles (PTERO-

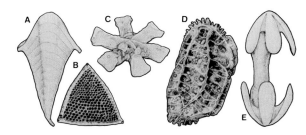

Pelagic microfossils, remains of open-sea microorganisms, are found in ocean-floor deposits. Pteropods (A), small snails with calcite shells, often occur in Atlantic and Mediterranean sediments. Diatoms (B), single-celled algae with siliceous shells, are abundant in cool seas. Coccolithophorids (C) are photosynthetic plankton, covered by calcite plates, which accumulate in deep-sea sediments. Ostracods (D) are minute, bivalved crustaceans with calcite shells. Siliceous spicules (E) remain from skeletons of certain glass sponges.

pass, equally gradually, into its descendants. Most species, however, are seen to appear abruptly, to maintain their typical form for most of their history, and to vanish as suddenly as they appeared. This failure to trace coherent lineages of ancestors and descendants does not prevent recognition of changes in larger groups of animals: horses are seen to have developed through Cenozoic time from small to large, from five-toed to one-toed, and from short- to long-toothed, but complete fossil records of the transition from one species to another have not been found. This caused some paleontologists to doubt Darwin's belief that evolution proceeds by the gradual accumulation of small changes.

One of the most difficult problems in evolutionary paleontology has been the almost abrupt appearance of the major animal groups—classes and phyla—in full-fledged form, in the Cambrian and Ordovician periods. This must reflect a sudden acquisition of hard parts by the various groups, in itself a problem. Paleontologists are not certain whether the soft-bodied forms of the Precambrian Ediacarian fauna are in fact ancestral to modern groups; in any case, the lack of well-documented animal remains in older rocks indicates that differentiation of the major groups occurred more rapidly than did their subsequent evolution.

Fossils and Ancient Landscapes

The fossil record contains a history of the evolution of life on Earth and provides geologists with a detailed and widely applicable chronology. It also contains much information about the geographical–ecological changes that have occurred in the course of geologic time.

Using the fossil record, ancient environments can be reconstructed. For example, strata of Tertiary age in the oil-bearing "transverse basins" of California, such as the Los Angeles and Ventura basins, contain many microfossils of the protozoan group called FORAMINIFERA. These were studied because they provided a means of tracing strata from one oil well to another, in accumulations of sediment thousands of meters thick. This sedimentary sequence began with stream deposits in the Oligocene Epoch, passed through a long marine phase in the Mio-

cene and Pliocene, and reverted to mammal-bearing alluvial deposits in the Pleistocene Epoch. In order to learn something about the conditions under which the oil-bearing marine portion was deposited, paleontologists compared the fossil assemblages with the depth range of the same species or the most closely related species living today off the California coast. Interpreted in this manner, environmental change from continental, through shallow near-shore, into deep-water (more than 1,500 m/5,000 ft), back through the shallow water, and into alluvial was revealed. This history has been confirmed by the study of fossil fish scales. Although sardine scales are found throughout the marine parts, angler fish and other species of the bathyal zone are found only in association with deep-water foraminifera.

This is one example of the field of study that is called PALEOECOLOGY. Palynologists studying pollen grain assemblages from lake beds and peat bogs have determined the shifting of forests and grasslands that occurred in the later stages of the Pleistocene ICE AGE and in the interval since then and are establishing a much-needed history of climates, which can be related directly to the historical record (see POLLEN STRATIGRAPHY). Study of the foraminifera in marine cores enables scientists to chart the distribution of OCEAN CURRENTS and water masses during the height of the last glaciation, 18,000 years ago, in an effort to understand the Ice Age and its cause.

Fossil chemistry is another area of research for paleoecologists. Many elements occur in two or more atomic forms that differ from each other in weight—ISOTOPES. Thus, oxygen occurs as O^{16} and O^{18}, O^{16} being by far the most abundant. When an organism such as a foraminifera builds a skeleton of calcium carbonate ($CaCO_3$), it incorporates O^{16} and O^{18} in a proportion that depends on the ratio in which they occur in the ambient water, and on the temperature of the water. The higher the temperature, the less O^{18} is put into the skeleton. If the ratio of the iso-

This microphotograph of fossil wood (artificially stained) shows the preservation of structural detail. The original wood material was replaced molecule by molecule, in this case by the mineral francolite. This fossil was found in Lower Cretaceous rocks of the eastern Netherlands.

topes has remained constant in the oceans, then the ratios of such isotopes in a foraminiferal shell are a direct indication of temperature. The isotopic composition of SEAWATER, however, has not remained constant, and the ratios in the shells can be disturbed by chemical changes after burial. But paleoecologists have demonstrated, for example, that the thermal structure of the oceans in Cretaceous times was much different from what it is today, with much warmer midwater masses.

Fossils and Paleogeography

The distribution of plant and animal species in the world today reflects the interplay between the physical environment, which, for example, restricts polar bears to the high latitudes, and geographical barriers to migration, which, for example, have kept polar bears from invading the Antarctic and keep the marine snakes of the Pacific side of Panama from invading the Caribbean Sea. Such barriers divide the world into biogeographic provinces. The fossil record enables paleontologists to reconstruct such provinces for the past and to study their history. South America, for example, was joined to Africa during most of the Mesozoic Era, as its Triassic and Jurassic reptile faunas demonstrate. When it broke away, in mid-Cretaceous time, with the opening of the South Atlantic Ocean, the dinosaurs of South America succumbed to the Cretaceous crisis, and the mammals took their place as the dominant land animals, forming a very different kind of mammalian fauna that evolved independently of the Eurasian-American fauna. Australia underwent similar changes except that it remained isolated, and its indigenous mammalian fauna (a marsupial one) has evolved to its modern state. South America became linked with North America during the Pliocene Epoch, and the two very different mammalian faunas invaded each other's territories, pitting species against species for existence. Eventually, North America assimilated some South American mammals (ground sloths, armadillos, opossums, and porcupines), but the majority of South American species became extinct.

The fossil record also shows that the Caribbean and eastern Pacific marine faunas were essentially identical in Miocene times, diverging only since the Panamanian land bridge closed in Pliocene time. The question of whether to build a Panamanian sea-level canal has focused attention on what would happen to present faunas if communications were to be reestablished. Would the Pacific sea snakes, for example, invade the Caribbean to the detriment of fisheries there?

Overview

The fossil record spans three-quarters of Earth history but forms a coherent whole only since the time that animals with hard parts appeared at the beginning of the Cambrian Period. Both the origin of life and the origin of the major groups of animals remain unknown. The seafloor became heavily populated with animals in Cambrian time, and the lands were colonized in the Silurian Period. Organic communities have become more complex through geologic time, but not in a linear fashion. Extinction of species is normally counterbalanced by speciation,

but at times it has prevailed, and during the great biotic crises some communities were reduced to low levels throughout the world, and major groups of organisms, such as the dinosaurs and AMMONITES, were lost. That part of the record is a reminder that organisms exist at the tolerance of the ENVIRONMENT, and that this environment, throughout geologic time, has exhibited variations of a nature and magnitude outside the realm of human experience.

Foster, Abigail Abigail Kelley Foster, b. near Amherst, Mass., Jan. 15, 1810, d. Jan. 14, 1887, was an American crusader for the abolition of slavery and for women's suffrage. A teacher in Quaker schools, she married (1845) a radical abolitionist, Stephen S. Foster (1809–81). Foster was one of the first women to deliver speeches before sexually mixed audiences.

Foster, Stephen Stephen Collins Foster, b. Lawrenceville, Pa., July 4, 1826, d. Jan. 13, 1864, was an American composer of songs whose words and music have become associated with the American South. Among his best-known songs are "Camptown Races" (1850), "Old Folks at Home," also known as "Swanee River" (1851), "My Old Kentucky Home" (1853), "Jeanie with the Light Brown Hair" (1854), and "Old Black Joe" (1860).

Ironically, Foster was born in the North and never lived in the South. He was reluctant to have his name associated with songs of his that were written in a stage Negro dialect. Such music was popularized by minstrel shows, especially that of Edwin P. CHRISTY, for whom Foster wrote many songs. The greater number of Foster's more than 200 songs, however, were written for family singing at home.

Although his songs were immensely popular, Foster never gained great financial reward from their sale because he usually accepted a flat sum from his publisher for each song. Toward the end of his life, Foster drank heavily and lived in virtual poverty. He died in New York City.

Foster, William Z. William Zebulon Foster, b. Taunton, Mass., Feb. 25, 1881, d. Sept. 1, 1961, was for many years head of the Communist party in the United States. He joined the Communist party about 1921 and quickly rose within its ranks. He was the presidential candidate on the Communist ticket in 1924, 1928, and 1932 and a candidate for governor of New York in 1930. In 1948 he was indicted under the Smith Act with 11 other top American Communists but was not tried with them because of his ill health.

foster care see ADOPTION AND FOSTER CARE

Foucault, Jean [foo-koh'] Jean Bernard Léon Foucault, b. Sept. 19, 1819, d. Feb. 11, 1868, a French physicist, took the first photograph of the Sun in 1845, measured the velocity of light in the laboratory using a rapidly rotating mirror, and showed that the brain combines separate color images from the two eyes into a single image. His name is also associated with important developments in telescope mirrors, lenses, prisms, and arc lamps, but most of all with the gyroscope and the FOUCAULT PENDULUM, with which he demonstated, rather than deduced, the rotation of the Earth for the first time.

Foucault, Michel

The French cultural historian Michel Foucault, b. Oct. 15, 1926, d. June 25, 1984, examined the codes and theories of order by which societies operate and the "principles of exclusion" through which they define themselves: for example, the sane and the insane, the innocent and the criminal, the insider and the outsider. His works include *Madness and Civilization* (1961; Eng. trans., 1965), *The Order of Things* (1966; Eng. trans., 1971), *The Archeology of Knowledge* (1969; Eng. trans., 1972), *Discipline and Punish: The Birth of the Prison* (1975; Eng. trans., 1977), and *The History of Sexuality*, vol. 1 (1976; Eng. trans., 1978).

Foucault pendulum

A Foucault pendulum, named for its inventor, Jean FOUCAULT, who first demonstrated it in 1851, is a long, simple pendulum mounted so that it can be driven to maintain constant amplitude without influencing its direction of swing. Such a pendulum maintains a fixed plane of oscillation with respect to the stars. Consequently, if one were mounted at the North Pole, the Earth would rotate under it, and the plane of the pendulum would appear to rotate through 360° in 24 hours. At a latitude of θ, the plane rotates through $360° \sin\theta$ in 24 hours. The Foucault pendulum furnishes proof of the Earth's rotation.

Fouché, Joseph

[foo-shay'] Joseph Fouché, b. probably on May 21, 1760, d. after 1816, was a Jacobin leader during the FRENCH REVOLUTION and minister of police under NAPOLEON I. He was elected (1792) to the National Convention and voted to execute King Louis XVI. A spokesman for the radical Jacobins, Fouché is best known for his ruthless suppression (1793) of counterrevolutionaries in Lyon. For supporting the atheistic movement, Fouché was expelled from the Jacobin club by Maximilien ROBESPIERRE, but he in turn helped overthrow Robespierre on July 27, 1794.

Under the DIRECTORY, Fouché served as ambassador in Milan (1798) and The Hague (1799). He supported the coup by Napoléon Bonaparte (later Napoleon I) and was retained as minister of police under the newly established Consulate. Fouché's elaborate police system was highly efficient, especially at internal spying. His involvement in political maneuvering against Bonaparte, however, led to his dismissal in 1802. Reinstated in 1804, he was created duc d'Otrante (1809) but was again ousted in 1810 after intriguing with the British. He was appointed governor of Rome and, in 1813, administrator of Illyria.

After Napoleon's first abdication (1814), the restored Bourbons rejected Fouché's services. When Napoleon returned in 1815, the opportunistic Fouché was reappointed minister of police, but he secretly corresponded with the Allies to assure his future. After Napoleon's defeat at Waterloo, he became president of the provisional government. The law proscribing those responsible for the death of Louis XVI forced Fouché into exile in 1816, and he died in obscurity.

foundation, building

A foundation supplies the base for a structure such as a building, bridge, dam, or breakwater, transmitting the load of the superstructure to the supporting soil or rock in such a way as to prevent the settling or slippage of the structure.

The construction of a foundation is preceded by a study of the material on which the structure is to be built, includ-

A modern method of sinking deep foundations for high-rise buildings involves casting concrete piles in place. After excavation of the ground to the desired level, interlocking steel sheets are driven around the site perimeter (1), and a hole is driven through the soft clay into hard rock (2). The base of the hole is widened with a special tool (3), and a cylindrical steel liner (4) is sunk into the hole, along with a reinforcing steel grid (5). Concrete (6) is poured into the hole and allowed to set; the steel liner (7) is then withdrawn. The concrete pile (8) is continued up into the building, and the floor (9) and sheet-steel walls are concreted in. The number of such deep-set concrete piles that are used in a foundation will depend on the condition of the ground, the depth of the rock layer, and the planned height of the building.

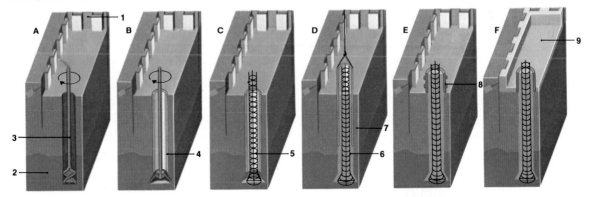

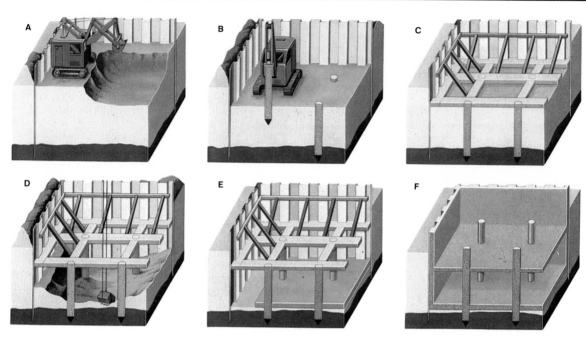

In constructing buildings in areas of soft, waterlogged clay and gravel, support foundations are often of piles sunk in solid bedrock and strengthened with a hollow concrete box structure. Such foundations transmit the weight of the building directly to the bedrock. Interlocking sections of steel sheeting are first driven into the bedrock to form a watertight casing; then part of the ground is excavated (A). Precast, steel-tipped, concrete piles are driven into the bedrock (B) to a predetermined level. Concrete crossbeams are cast on top of the piles to keep the casing upright (C), and the remainder of the earth is removed down to the bedrock (D). A concrete base is cast on the bedrock (E), a concrete platform is laid over the crossbeams, and the box structure is completed with concrete (F).

ing test pits and borings to determine the type of soil and the depths at which rock or water are encountered.

Foundations fall into two general classifications: spread and deep. A common type of spread foundation is the footing, a slab, block, or pedestal that forms an enlargement of the bottom of an individual pier or bearing wall and distributes the load to a broader area of the underlying material. Another type, the mat or raft foundation, is used for heavier, more widely distributed loads. It consists of a number of footings combined into a single, thick reinforced-concrete slab beneath the entire structure. A third kind of spread foundation, which is used in soils that may settle or slide, is the floating foundation, a boxlike underground construction with a weight equal to or slightly exceeding that of the excavated soil.

There are two principal types of deep foundations, piles and CAISSONS. Piles, which can be made of timber, concrete, or steel, are driven by hammers into the ground. End-bearing piles are sunk to the bearing stratum (the depth at which soil resistance can support the weight of the structure), or sometimes to bedrock. Friction piles, which are rough-surfaced and tapered, transfer their load to the adjacent soil along the length of the pile through friction and adhesion. Caissons are hollow boxlike or cylindrical structures.

Bridge foundations (see BRIDGE, engineering) were once constructed by using a cofferdam, an enclosure to exclude water. The invention in the 1850s of the pneumatic cais-

son made possible much deeper foundations. Deep water and swift currents often create special problems.

In DAM foundations, poor soil characteristics are countered by measures such as grouting (piping in a cement curtain), building cutoff trenches, excavating drainage wells, or building a concrete drainage blanket under the dam on the upstream side.

Harbor installations such as breakwaters and docks are built on caissons or piles. Modern quay design often calls for steel sheet-piling, consisting of flat sections with interlocking grooves.

foundations and endowments Foundations are organizations that distribute private wealth for the public good, usually by making grants to other nonprofit organizations and individuals engaged in social welfare, educational, charitable, or religious activities. Some private foundations use the words *fund, trust,* or *endowment* in their names, but this implies no difference in function or law.

Operating foundations make few if any grants; they plan and carry through programs managed by their own staffs. *Community foundations* derive their principal funds from many donors, generally make grants only in their own metropolitan areas, and are governed by boards broadly representative of the community. *Company-sponsored foundations* derive their funds from profit-making companies but are legally independent. *Federal-govern-*

ment foundations make grants in science, the arts, and humanities usually from tax money appropriated by Congress. Other organizations that use the word *foundation* in their names employ their resources to further a particular point of view or cause or to aid only a specified institution.

The general-purpose foundation, whose broad charter enables its trustees to address any problem affecting the general welfare worldwide, is an American innovation that emerged in the late 19th and early 20th century. In practice, general-purpose foundations have limited their programs to a few broad fields of interest.

Regulation of Foundations

Private foundations are defined and regulated principally by provisions of the Tax Reform Act of 1969. The crucial distinction between the status of a private foundation and that of other charitable organizations is the amount of private financing received from a single source. Congress assumed that although publicly supported organizations are subject to the discipline of public opinion, institutions drawing their funds from one source are not subject to this corrective influence and should be regulated in some other way. Therefore, special rules for private foundations were added to the Internal Revenue Code in 1969. These regulate the relations between wealthy persons and the foundations with which they are involved, minimum expenditures to charities by foundations and maximum administrative costs, foundation ownership and control of private business, foundation investments, and the use of foundation money for noncharitable purposes. An annual 2 percent (originally 4 percent) excise tax on net investment income is levied on private foundations to support auditing and other administrative expenses incurred by the Internal Revenue Service.

Proponents of a limited life for foundations fear that the dead hand of a wealthy donor may perpetually bind funds to be used for whatever purposes the donor chooses, even when those purposes are or become of little or no value. Counterarguments cite the remedy of cy pres, legal proceedings by which the courts may alter a will or trust outmoded by changing social needs. Professional staffing and independent boards also serve as insurance against donor control.

Extent of Foundation Activity

There are about 25,000 foundations in the United States, many of them concentrated in the Northeast. Most U.S. foundations are funds of fewer than $1 million, but their combined assets exceed $50 billion, and together they give away more than $4 billion each year. Education has always ranked highest in grants received, followed by health, science, welfare, humanities, international activities, and religion. Among the largest foundations are the FORD FOUNDATION, MACARTHUR FOUNDATION, MELLON FOUNDATION, ROCKEFELLER FOUNDATION, Carnegie Foundations, Duke Endowment, Robert Wood Johnson Foundation, Kellogg Foundation, Kresge Foundation, Lilly Endowment, and the Pew Memorial Trust. Small foundations in many communities make grants for local projects and services.

The Council on Foundations in Washington, D.C., is a membership organization of grant makers promoting responsible and effective grant making and fostering the growth of the field. The Foundation Center in New York compiles and makes available current information about foundations to the general public including those seeking foundation grants.

Among the largest foundations outside the United States are the Nuffield (England), Donner Canadien, Volkswagenwerk (Germany), Gulbenkian (Portugal), Agnelli (Italy), and Toyota (Japan) foundations.

foundry   see CASTING; FORGE; METALLURGY; TOOL AND DIE MAKING

---

fountains   Fountains, which are channels or spouts through which water is directed under pressure for decorative or cooling effects, have been an important feature of cities, GARDENS, and private houses throughout history. The earliest fountains were natural springs, but the artificial harnessing of water power dates back to the first Egyptian and Babylonian cvilizations. The ancient Greek custom of regarding springs as sacred sources of life was perpetuated by the Romans, who devised the *nymphaeum*, a structure enclosing a pool. Fountains decorated the villas and gardens of wealthy Romans, but also served a practical function in cities as sources of public water supply. The most elaborate waterwork of this period was constructed (AD 118–34) in the gardens of HADRIAN'S VILLA.

In the Middle Ages, the *Fontana Maggiore* (1278) in Perugia, Italy, built by Nicola and Giovanni PISANO, was the first to display the decorative effect of water cascading from a central spout. Italian architects and sculptors of the RENAISSANCE exploited the movement and sound of water in such works as Giovanni da BOLOGNA's *Neptune Fountain* (1563–67) in Bologna and the immense series of cascades constructed at the Villa d'Este near Rome by Pirro Ligorio (c.1510–1583). Fountains became a crucial element in Italian LANDSCAPE ARCHITECTURE; natural undulations in the land were used to create water pressure, as in the Boboli Gardens (begun 1560) of the PITTI PALACE in Florence, or Giacomo Barozzi da VIGNOLA's Villa Farnese (begun 1559) at Caprarola.

Unlike their Oriental and Indian counterparts, who have used water to induce calm contemplation, European architects and sculptors have generally been attracted by the theatrical effects of jets and cascades, as in Giovanni Lorenzo BERNINI's *Fountain of the Four Rivers* (1648–51) and Nicola Salvi's TREVI FOUNTAIN (1732–62), both in Rome. The Italian formal garden, where fountains formed the focal points of radiating avenues, was emulated in France, where Marie de Médicis ordered the building of the Jardins de Luxembourg, Paris (1611–20), and André LE NÔTRE planned (c.1660) the vast gardens of VERSAILLES.

Garden and city designers, in the 20th century have made use of modern materials and engineering techniques. Alexander CALDER's *Water Ballet* (1954) at the General Motors Company building in Detroit, Mich., consists of 21 jets that rise 12 m (40 ft) into the air and are illuminated at night in red, blue, and green. At the IBM headquarters in Armonk, N.Y., Isamu NOGUCHI's electronically controlled fountain celebrates the spirit of scientific inquiry.

Fouquet, Jean

Fouquet, Jean [foo-kay'] Jean, or Jehan, Fouquet, c.1420–1481, was the most important French painter of the 15th century. As a result of a trip to Italy about 1443–47, he assimilated characteristics of Italian Renaissance art with his native French style. He is known to have been in Rome before 1447 because he was asked to paint a portrait of Pope Eugene IV (now lost). By 1448, Fouquet was working in his native Tours for King Charles VII; he was appointed court painter by Louis XI in 1475. His most famous work is a manuscript he illustrated for Étienne Chevalier about 1452, of which only fragments survive (Musée Condé, Chantilly). Another widely known work is *Virgin and Child Surrounded by Angels* (c.1450; Antwerp Museum). Several panel paintings have been attributed to Fouquet, among which are portraits of Charles VII (c.1445) and of Juvenal des Ursins (c.1455), both in the Louvre in Paris.

Fouquet, Nicolas

Fouquet, Nicolas [foo-kay'] Nicolas Fouquet, b. January 1615, d. Mar. 23, 1680, was an adept French judge-administrator and lavish patron of the arts. Fouquet became Cardinal MAZARIN's trusted agent during the FRONDE, attaining the post of *procureur general* in the parlement of Paris in 1650 and the superintendency of finance in 1653.

Irregular financial methods, including personal loans, kept the treasury afloat and made him fabulously wealthy, but they also allowed his rival Jean Baptiste COLBERT to discredit him with LOUIS XIV. The king, determined to be his own prime minister, was wary of Fouquet's independent power. He had Fouquet arrested in 1661, subjected him to an irregular trial that lasted three years, then changed the sentence from banishment to perpetual imprisonment.

four-color theorem

four-color theorem The four-color theorem, first proposed about 1850 by Francis Guthrie, states that four colors suffice to color any map, given the requirement that any two countries with a contiguous boundary should have different colors. In 1879, A. B. Kempe published a proof of this conjecture, but some years later the proof was found to be incomplete. Only in 1976 did Kenneth Appel and Wolfgang Haken of the University of Illinois prove this conjecture with the aid of a modern large-scale computer. They proved that instead of considering infinitely many maps, one could reduce the problem to considering only a finite number of maps. Using a computer they developed a catalog of 1,936 "unavoidable configurations," of which any map must contain at least one, and showed that each of these could be reduced to four colors. Thus, the assumption that there exists a map that cannot be colored by four colors leads to an absurdity.

four-eyed fish

four-eyed fish The four-eyed fish, *Anableps anableps,* is found in muddy streams in southern Mexico, Central America, and northern South America. It seldom exceeds 30 cm (12 in) in length. Because each of its two eyes is divided horizontally by a band of tissue, the fish appears to have four eyes. The upper half of each eye is adapted for seeing above the water and the lower half for seeing below, the fish cruising just below the surface with the upper half of its eyes protruding. Light passes through the oval-shaped lens of each eye at different angles in the upper and lower halves, giving each half the required different focal lengths for vision in air and water.

Each male has a sex organ that can be moved only to the right or only to the left. Each female's genital aperture opens either only to the right or only to the left. Consequently, a "right-handed" male can mate only with a "left-handed" female, and vice versa.

The four-eyed fish, a freshwater fish of Central America and parts of South America, has eyes that divide at the water line, enabling it to see above and below the surface simultaneously.

Four Freedoms

Four Freedoms The Four Freedoms was a list of basic human rights formulated by President Franklin D. Roosevelt on Jan. 6, 1941. In his State of the Union message to Congress, Roosevelt identified them as freedom of speech and expression, freedom of worship, freedom from want, and freedom from fear. Later that year they were in large part incorporated into the ATLANTIC CHARTER, a joint British and U.S. statement of aims for a peaceful world. The Four Freedoms were criticized by some as being too vague to serve as a practical guide.

4-H program

4-H program The 4-H program was founded in 1900 to provide local educational clubs for rural youth from ages 9 to 19. Designed to teach better home economics and agricultural techniques and to foster character development and good citizenship, the program, administered by the Cooperative Extension Service of the U.S. Department of Agriculture, state land-grant universities, and county governments, emphasizes projects that improve the four H's: head, heart, hands, and health. The 4-H pledge reflects these concerns: "I pledge my Head to clearer thinking, my Heart to greater loyalty, my Hands to larger service, and my Health to better living, for my club, my community, my country, and my world."

The 4-H program, expanded to include urban and suburban youth, has nearly 5 million members in the United States, and about 80 other countries also have some type of 4-H club program. Each year a national meeting of the clubs is held in Chicago to demonstrate improvements in such fields as livestock breeding, food cultivation, canning, and handicrafts.

Four Horsemen of the Apocalypse In the New Testament, the Four Horsemen of the Apocalypse are the allegorical figures of the sixth chapter of the Book of REVELATION (sometimes called the Apocalypse). Riding a white, a red, a black, and a pale horse, the horsemen are generally understood to symbolize power or conquest, violence or war, poverty or famine, and death. The rider on the white horse is sometimes interpreted as representing Jesus Christ. The four horsemen are frequent symbols in works of art and literature. Albrecht Dürer's *Apocalypse* (1498), for example, is a series of woodcuts representing the horsemen.

Four Quartets *Four Quartets,* a suite of meditative poems written by T. S. ELIOT, concerns the interaction of time and timelessness. Each poem is named for a place—"Burnt Norton" (1936), "East Coker" (1940), "The Dry Salvages" (1941), and "Little Gidding" (1942). Each is centered on one of the medieval elements—air, earth, water, and fire. "Little Gidding," for example, describes wartime bombings. *Four Quartets* employs Eliot's idiosyncratic style of musical free verse, the form of a quartet, and personal mixed with literary allusions.

Fourier, Charles [foor-yay', sharl] François Marie Charles Fourier, b. Apr. 7, 1772, d. Oct. 10, 1837, was a French social theorist whose vision of the ideal society centered on the phalanstery, a small cooperative agricultural community. After inheriting an income, Fourier devoted himself to writing. He first set forth his ideas in the *Theory of the Four Movements and of the General Destinies* (1808). The basis of the phalanstery would be mutual cooperation and personal fulfillment, with all members sharing both the work and the profits. Communities based on Fourier's ideas were founded in Red Bank, N.J., and at BROOK FARM in Massachusetts (1841–46). After his death his work was continued by his disciple, Victor Considérant.

Fourier analysis [foor-yay'] Fourier analysis is a branch of mathematics that is used to analyze repeating, or periodic, phenomena. Many natural and artificial phenomena occur in cycles that repeat constantly. These phenomena—such as alternating currents, business cycles, high and low tides, the orbits of planets and artificial satellites, and the vibrations of electromagnetic waves—can be described by a mathematical concept called a FUNCTION. Since these phenomena are periodic, their functions are called periodic functions. In general, a function is said to be periodic if its graph is a repeating pattern.

The basic goal of Fourier analysis is to represent periodic functions in terms of series of particular, and generally simpler, periodic functions. Most of the simpler functions occur in TRIGONOMETRY and are therefore called trigonometric functions. They are often used in Fourier analysis to expand a given function. If the function does possess a Fourier series, the coefficients—which are called Fourier coefficients—can be calculated by certain rules involving integral calculus. Fourier analysis was first developed in the 1820s by Jean Baptiste Joseph Fourier (1768–1830), a French mathematician, and has subsequently been highly elaborated. Fourier's work laid the foundation for later work on trigonometric functions.

Fourteen Points The Fourteen Points were a program announced by U.S. President Woodrow WILSON before a joint session of Congress on Jan. 8, 1918, as the basis for a just peace settlement following World War I. Although many of Wilson's suggestions had been made before, in total effect the speech represented a radical departure from the old diplomacy and called upon future victors and vanquished to liberalize their diplomacy and ideology.

The first 5 points included the following: open covenants, openly arrived at; freedom of the seas; removal of economic barriers in international trade; reduction of national armaments to the lowest point consistent with domestic safety; and adjustment of all colonial claims on the basis of the self-determination of peoples. Points 6 through 13 dealt with specific territorial settlements. The 14th point became most important to Wilson: a general association of nations for the purpose of providing mutual guarantees of political independence and territorial integrity for all nations.

The address at once gave Wilson moral leadership of the Allies and became a powerful diplomatic and propagandist weapon. The Allies generally accepted it as a statement of war aims, and when Germany sued for peace it was on the basis of the Fourteen Points.

At the PARIS PEACE CONFERENCE (1919–20) the second point was quickly repudiated by Britain, and several others were modified or compromised in spirit by territorial agreements. On the whole, however, the final settlement was nearer the Fourteen Points than Wilson and his major advisors had at first thought possible. Out of the 14th point came the LEAGUE OF NATIONS.

14th Amendment Although the 14th Amendment to the CONSTITUTION OF THE UNITED STATES, ratified in 1868, was designed to restrain state governments from abridging the rights of former slaves after the Civil War, it has been used to extend virtually all of the personal liberties and rights granted in the BILL OF RIGHTS to protection against infringement by state governments. The amendment itself defines citizenship and restrains states from abridging the privileges or immunities of a citizen, requires DUE PROCESS of law and EQUAL PROTECTION OF THE LAWS for persons under its jurisdiction, reduces representation in Congress for states that deny voting rights, disqualifies for office certain officials of the Confederacy, and invalidates any war debts of the Confederate states.

In *Lochner* v. *New York* (1905) the Court interpreted the due-process clause of the 14th Amendment to invalidate state legislation regulating working conditions, hours, and minimum-wage laws. This decision was reversed in 1937. In 1925 in *Gitlow* v. *New York* the Court used the due-process clause of this amendment to incorporate a provision of the Bill of Rights by extending the 1ST AMENDMENT protection of freedom of speech to persons against abridgment by state action. By 1937 all of the 1st Amendment protections were binding on the states. The Court has gradually included all amendments of the Bill of Rights except the 2d, 3d, 7th, 10th, and the requirement of grand jury indictment in the 5th Amendment in its "selective incorporation doctrine," protecting individual rights from state encroachment. The due-process clause has also been used to acknowledge the right to privacy (ROE V. WADE, 1971).

The equal-protection clause has been used to limit racial discrimination (BROWN V. BOARD OF EDUCATION OF TOPEKA, KANSAS, 1954), maintain fair legislative apportionment (*Baker* v. *Carr*, 1962), and to forbid the use of rigid quotas in public EQUAL OPPORTUNITY programs (UNIVERSITY OF CALIFORNIA V. BAKKE, 1978).

See also: CIVIL RIGHTS; FREEDOM OF THE PRESS; FREEDOM OF SPEECH; PLESSY V. FERGUSON.

4th Amendment   see BILL OF RIGHTS; CONSTITUTION OF THE UNITED STATES

fourth dimension   see RELATIVITY

Fourth Estate   *Fourth Estate* is a term used to describe the press—the journalistic profession or its members. Thomas Carlyle wrote that the British statesman Edmund Burke (1729–97) called the reporters' gallery in the English Parliament "a Fourth Estate more important by far" than the other three estates of Parliament—the peers, bishops, and commons. Similarly, Thomas Babington MACAULAY, in his essay *On Hallam's Constitutional History* (1828), refers to the reporters' gallery as a "fourth estate of the realm." In the United States this role of the press as the watchdog of government has ranged from self-enforced censorship during World War II to investigative reporting.

Fourth Republic   see FRANCE, HISTORY OF

Fowler, H. W.   [fow'-lur]   Henry Watson Fowler, b. Mar. 10, 1858, d. Dec. 26, 1933, was an English lexicographer who is best known for *A Dictionary of Modern English Usage* (1926; rev. ed. by Sir Ernest Gowers, 1965), a commentary on English style and usage conceived with his brother, Francis George Fowler (1870–1918), and completed by H. W. Fowler after Francis's death. He also collaborated with his brother on *The*

King's English (1906) and *The Concise Oxford Dictionary of Current English* (1911).

Fowles, John   [fowlz]   John Fowles, b. Mar. 31, 1926, is an English writer whose first two novels, *The Collector* (1963; film, 1965)—a thriller—and *The Magus* (1966; film, 1968), explored unusual psychological states and philosophical themes. In *The French Lieutenant's Woman* (1969; film, 1981), Fowles used an experimental framework to contrast contemporary and Victorian attitudes toward sex. *Daniel Martin* (1977), considered his finest novel, has a theme common to all Fowles's work: the search for where individuals—and, by extension, Western civilization—went astray and how the future can be salvaged. His other books include *The Aristos* (1965), a "self portrait in ideas"; the novel *The Ebony Tower* (1974); a revised version of *The Magus* (1978); and the novel *Mantissa* (1982).

Fox   Members of this Algonquian-speaking North American Indian tribe call themselves *Meskwakihuk* or *Mesquakie* ("Red Earth People"), but they have become generally known by the name Fox, derived from the name of the first Mesquakie clan that French explorers encountered, the *Wagosh* ("Red Fox"). Originally from central Michigan, the Fox migrated to Wisconsin sometime before 1670. They settled along the Fox and Wisconsin rivers where they attempted to disrupt trade between the French and their enemies the Sioux. Extremely individualistic and warlike, the Fox precipitated a series of wars in the Great Lakes area through the first half of the 18th century.

Their power was eventually broken by an alliance of French, Ottawa, Potawatomi, Sioux, and Menominee. Their population had been greatly reduced when they amalgamated with the SAUK tribe and moved into Illinois and Iowa. Assigned (1842) to a reservation in Kansas, the tribe later returned (1859) to Iowa. There they sold their pony herds and purchased lands near Tama, on the Iowa River. They have since enlarged their land holdings; today tribal enrollment is about 1,050.

fox   The fox is the smallest member of the dog family, Canidae. Foxes are agile predators that usually weigh less than 7 kg (15 lb). They scavenge carrion and wild fruits and hunt small rodents, rabbits, birds, and invertebrates. Because they hunt small prey sufficient to feed only one animal, foxes are solitary predators and do not hunt in packs.

Foxes are a diverse group of canids containing 14 species and occupying almost all continents. The best-known foxes are the forest, chaparral, and farmland species. This group contains the gray fox, *Urocyon cinereoargenteus,* of North America, and the red fox, *Vulpes vulpes,* of North America, Europe, Asia, and North Africa.

A pair of red foxes normally occupies a territory of 2.6 to 7.8 km^2 (1 to 3 mi^2), which they defend against other

The red fox has been widely represented in fables and stories as a clever and sly creature. This fox ranges throughout temperate and warm regions of the Northern Hemisphere.

foxes. The male and female mate during midwinter, and four to seven young are born after an average gestation period of 51 days. The dog fox brings food to the vixen while she is nursing; later both parents feed the pups. By midsummer the young foxes begin to hunt on their own and are self-sufficient by autumn. During early winter the family group breaks up, and the young leave the territory.

Some fox species show clear adaptations to the special environments they inhabit. For example, the sand foxes, such as the kit fox, *V. macrotis*, of the U.S. Southwest, have evolved a sandy-colored coat, dense fur, dark eyes as protection against the sun, and the ability to go without water for long periods. Their large ears disperse body heat without water being lost through panting or sweating.

Fox, Charles James   Charles James Fox, b. Jan. 24, 1749, d. Sept. 13, 1806, was perhaps the ablest leader in the history of the British WHIG PARTY. A son of the influential 1st Baron Holland, he could easily have ascended the conventional ladder of Whig political preferment after entering Parliament in 1768. Instead, Fox openly opposed GEORGE III during the American Revolution. In 1783, Fox further alienated the king by allying

The English Whig statesman Charles James Fox spent most of his political career in opposition, detested by King George III. Challenging the policies of William Pitt the Younger, Fox became known as a champion of individual liberties.

with his old enemy Lord NORTH to lead a coalition ministry. George himself brought the ministry down, in December 1783, by securing parliamentary defeat of its bill to reform the government of India.

Except during the last months of his life, when he was a member (1806) of the wartime "ministry of all the talents," Fox spent the rest of his career in opposition. He espoused many liberal causes, including parliamentary reform, the repeal of the laws restricting Roman Catholics and dissenters, and the abolition of slavery. He was the only major British politician to approve the French Revolution.

Fox died a few months after the death of his great rival, William PITT the Younger, and a few months before the slave trade was abolished. Though often reviled in his lifetime for his political opportunism and his supposedly scandalous private life, Fox kept alive a spirit of reform that later determined the direction of the Whig party.

Fox, George   George Fox, b. July 1624, d. Jan. 13, 1691, was an English preacher who founded the Society of Friends (Quakers; see FRIENDS, SOCIETY OF). The son of a Puritan weaver, he learned to read and write, although there is no record that he had any formal education. His personal religious experience led him to conclude that Christianity should stress the inner life of the soul illumined by Christ, rather than the externals of religion. He began to preach in 1647, making converts mostly in the north of England. The Friends spread rapidly, with major concentrations in London and Bristol by 1654. By 1660 there were Quakers in America, Ireland, and the West Indies. Fox and Margaret Fell, whom he married in 1669, coordinated the missionary activity.

After the RESTORATION (1660) of the monarchy, Fox was imprisoned many times. He proclaimed the right of women to full spiritual equality and, in 1660, insisted that Friends should not participate in war.

In 1671–72, Fox journeyed to North America, visiting Quaker meetings. By the time of Fox's death in 1691, the Quakers in England had become a respected denomination.

Fox, Virgil   Virgil Keen Fox, b. Princeton, Ill., May 3, 1912, d. Oct. 25, 1980, established the modern organ as a concert instrument and was renowned for his blazingly fast and impeccable organ-pedal technique. Fox studied at Peabody Conservatory and with Marcel Dupré in Paris, and he first performed in London and New York in 1933. He was head (1938–42) of the organ department at Peabody Conservatory and organist (1946–65) of Riverside Church in New York City.

fox terrier   The fox terrier is one of the oldest English working terriers, known before 1800 for its use in flushing foxes and other animals both above and below ground. There are two varieties of fox terrier, smooth and wirehaired, distinguished by coat, but identical in all oth-

The wirehaired fox terrier was originally bred as a hunting dog in England. Quick intelligence, an energetic disposition, and a smart appearance have earned the wirehaired terrier top honors in competition.

er respects. Fox terriers are small dogs with V-shaped drop ears and an erect, docked tail. Males stand up to 40 cm (15½ in) high at the shoulder and weigh 8 kg (18 lb); females are slightly smaller. Fox terriers should be predominantly white in color, although they frequently have brindle, red, fawn, or liver markings.

Foxe, John   John Foxe, b. 1516, d. Apr. 18, 1587, was an English clergyman who wrote the famous Protestant martyrology. While in religious exile in Basel he began to write a history of the persecutions of Christians, which was later expanded and published (1563) as the *Acts and Monuments of These Latter and Perillous Dayes.* The work, known almost immediately as the *Book of Martyrs,* extolled the heroism of the Protestant martyrs of the Reformation. Foxe described their sufferings in vivid terms. The book contains much information about 16th-century England unobtainable elsewhere.

foxglove   Foxglove is the common name for about 20 to 30 species of summer-flowering biennial or short-lived perennial herbs in the genus *Digitalis,* family Scrophulariaceae. They are native to Europe and northwest Africa to Central Asia. The common foxglove, *D. purpurea,* grows to

The common foxglove bears spikes of bell-shaped, speckled flowers. The dried leaves are used to produce digitalis, a drug that stimulates the heart.

a height of 150 cm (5 ft). Its leaves are alternate, lance shaped, up to 30 cm (1 ft) long, and hairy above with soft white hairs below. Leaves are tapered at the base to form winged stalks. The flowers droop on erect racemes, and the fruit are capsules with numerous seeds.

Common foxglove is found in clearings, in burned areas, and in hilly dry pastures, and it is often grown as an ornamental. Many varieties have been originated through breeding, with flowers varying from white to deep rose in color. The dried leaves, the source of the drug DIGITALIS used for heart trouble, have been used medicinally since the 13th century.

foxhound   see AMERICAN FOXHOUND; ENGLISH FOXHOUND

fox-trot   The fox-trot is a syncopated ballroom dance in 4/4 time consisting of an ordinary walk, quarter turns, sideward slides of the feet, and alternating fast and slow steps. By adding rapid trotting steps to the one-step for his act in the Ziegfeld Follies in 1913, Harry Fox created Fox's Trot. After Oscar Duryea standardized a less strenuous form of the dance, the fox-trot's simple execution and many, uncomplicated variations assured its lasting success.

Foxx, Jimmie [fahx]   Baseball Hall of Fame member James Emory Foxx, b. Sudlersville, Md., Oct. 22, 1907, d. July 21, 1967, known as "Double X," was a power-hitting first and third baseman during the Babe Ruth era. He hit 58 home runs in 1932, only 2 short of Ruth's best seasonal total. Foxx spent 11 years with the Philadelphia Athletics (1925–35), then went to the Red Sox, Cubs, and Phillies before retiring (1945). He hit at least 30 home runs in 12 straight seasons and accumulated 100 or more runs batted in for 13 straight seasons. American League Most Valuable Player 3 times (1932–33, 1938), Foxx had a lifetime batting average of .325 with 534 home runs.

Foyt, A. J. [foyt]   Anthony Joseph Foyt, Jr., b. Houston, Tex., Jan. 16, 1935, is one of American auto racing's most versatile drivers, having won major championships on the stock-car circuit, the USAC (U.S. Auto Club) tour, the Indianapolis 500, and Le Mans. Foyt won the USAC driving title seven times and the Indy 500 a record four times (1961, '64, '67, '77). Less than two weeks after winning the 1967 Indy 500, he teamed with Dan Gurney to win at Le Mans, France, for one of the greatest double victories ever achieved in the sport. He became the first and only driver to win 100 USAC-sponsored races—in sprint, stock, midget, and championship classes.

fractal   see GEOMETRY, FRACTAL

fraction   A fraction is the quotient of two integers: one integer, called the numerator, divided by another, non-zero integer, called the denominator. Where *a* represents the numerator and b the denominator, a fraction can be written $a \div b$, a/b, or $\frac{a}{b}$.

Often different symbols are used to represent the same ratio. For example, 1/2, 2/4, and 3/6 all represent the same ratio, so they are called equivalent fractions. Two fractions a/b and c/d are equivalent if $a \cdot d = b \cdot c$. Since for any fraction there are infinitely many equivalent fractions, there is a need for a preferred form of a fraction to represent a given ratio. Called a reduced fraction, this is the fraction that results when all common factors have been divided out of the numerator and denominator.

Addition and subtraction of any fractions a/b and c/d are defined by

$$\frac{a}{b} + \frac{c}{d} = \frac{ad + bc}{bd} \text{ and } \frac{a}{b} - \frac{c}{d} = \frac{ad - bc}{bd} .$$

When fractions have a common denominator, addition and subtraction are done by adding or subtracting the numerators and retaining the same denominator.

Multiplication is the easiest operation to perform on two fractions. For any fractions a/b and c/d,

$$\frac{a}{b} \cdot \frac{c}{d} = \frac{a \cdot c}{b \cdot d} = \frac{ac}{bd} .$$

Division by zero is undefined in any number system; therefore, it is also undefined for fractions. Zero, however, can be divided by another number, and the quotient is always zero. For any fractions a/b and c/d with c not equal to zero,

$$\frac{a}{b} \div \frac{c}{d} = \frac{a}{b} \cdot \frac{d}{c} = \frac{ad}{bc} .$$

fractionation [frak-shun-ay'-shuhn]   Fractionation is a process that separates a mixture of chemical substances into individual fractions, or components. The term most often refers to fractional distillation, which involves the volatilization, or boiling, and subsequent condensation and collection of volatile liquids with different boiling points. This is the first step in petroleum refining (see PETROLEUM INDUSTRY). Other methods include fractional crystallization, ION EXCHANGE, CHROMATOGRAPHY and solvent EXTRACTION, and field-flow fractionation.

Each method takes advantage of differences in properties of the components involved. The effectiveness of fractional crystallization, for example, depends on slight differences in the solubility of the different compounds. The least soluble solutes crystallize first and are removed in sequence from the remaining solution, or mother liquid. Ion exchange is based on the selective absorption of anions or cations from solution by passage through certain finely divided solid materials that are capable of exchanging their component ions for other ions. In chromatography, differential absorption of substances occurs at different positions along materials held in a column or tube. The fractions can then be withdrawn from the column by selective use of solvents. Field-flow fractionation is used in separating materials in the macromolecular and colloidal size range. It resembles the technique of chromatography except that separation of components is induced by an electrical, magnetic, thermal, or other field applied to the flow of materials.

The concept of fractionation is also involved in the separation of isotopes from one another. Lasers may be used in such separations.

fracture (medicine)   In medicine, a fracture is a break in a bone. In normal bones, fracture results from injury or from violent stress. In bones weakened by disease, fractures can occur spontaneously under ordinary stresses, a condition called pathological fracture. The susceptibility of a bone to fracture under stress depends on its brittleness, which in turn is determined by its mineral content, or degree of calcification. The bones of infants and young children have low calcification and are therefore softer and more flexible than those of older persons, whose bones are highly calcified (see OSTEOPOROSIS). A fracture in which bone fragments protrude through the skin is called an open, or compound, fracture; one in which the skin is not broken is called a closed, or simple, fracture.

Fractures of the skull or spinal column can result in permanent damage if bone fragments penetrate nerve tissue. Only a trained professional should move or transport an individual who might have a broken neck or a broken back.

Signs of a limb fracture may include pain and swelling in the overlying tissues, skin discoloration, distortion, impaired or complete loss of function, and a grinding sensation in the limb during movement. The injured person should not be moved unless the limb has been immobilized with splints.

Fractures are treated by aligning the ends of broken bones and holding them in place for several weeks in plaster casts or splints; metal wires or screws may be needed for smaller bone fragments. Healing begins with formation of special tissue called callus. This grows in excess of need, so that a bone is permanently thicker in the vicinity of a healed fracture. A polymer has also been developed that is absorbed by the body as it holds bones in place without metal fixtures.

fragile X syndrome   Fragile X syndrome is the general term for cases of MENTAL RETARDATION that are linked with a genetic defect called "fragile X," at the tip of the X chromosome (see GENETIC CODE). Infants with the syndrome sometimes have minor structural abnormalities and may later exhibit hyperactivity and a range of learning disabilities. Males with the defect are about three times more likely than females to display symptoms, and may also show AUTISM. Perhaps 1 out of every 1,500 persons in the general population is affected to some degree. The pattern of inheritance of the syndrome is not yet well understood.

Fragonard, Jean Honoré [frah-goh-nar']   Jean Honoré Fragonard, b. Apr. 5, 1732, d. Apr. 22, 1806,

The voluptuous nudes of the Bathers, *by the French rococo artist Jean Honoré Fragonard, are painted in a luminous, fluid, and spontaneous style. (Louvre, Paris.)*

was the last great French painter of the rococo period (see ROCOCO STYLE). "Frago," as he was known, was born in Grasse and moved with his family to Paris in 1738. About 1748, Fragonard was apprenticed to the painter J. B. S. CHARDIN; after only six months, however, he joined the studio of François BOUCHER. From 1756 to 1761 he was a student at the French Academy in Rome. While in Italy he developed an interest in landscape drawing and produced some of the most luminous and majestic nature studies ever made. Although some of Fragonard's later works foreshadow 19th-century romanticism, for the most part he adhered to the subjects and style of the rococo, even after they had become outmoded.

The character of the society in which Fragonard's art flourished is epitomized in such works as *The Swing* (c.1767; Wallace Collection, London) and the four paintings originally constituting the *Progress of Love* suite (1771; Frick Collection, New York). *The Swing* was commissioned by the Baron de Saint-Julien, who directed Fragonard to depict his mistress on a swing and the baron himself in a position to glimpse her legs beneath her skirts as she swings above him. The Frick canvases, created for Madame du Barry, are a playful narration of the theme of pursuit and conquest. Fragonard's facile and confident brushwork is particularly evident in these works. The *Bathers* (c.1765; Louvre, Paris) is almost a sketch, brushed in rapidly with broad strokes. The speed and bravura of which Fragonard was capable are also revealed in his fantasy portraits, for example, *Portrait of a Man,* or *The Warrior* (c.1769; Clark Art Institute, Williamstown, Mass.), which he is said to have painted in only one hour.

France France is the largest European nation (excluding the USSR) and the center of a large but diminishing overseas administration. Shaped like a hexagon, the country is bounded by the English Channel on the north-

west, the Atlantic Ocean and Bay of Biscay on the west, and the Mediterranean Sea on the southeast. The remaining sides are mostly mountainous and are shared by seven European neighbors—Belgium and Luxembourg on the northeast; Germany, Switzerland, and Italy on the east; and Spain and tiny Andorra on the south. France's eighth neighbor is Monaco, located on the Mediterranean coast near Nice and entirely surrounded by French territory.

The frontiers of France have changed relatively little since the close of the Middle Ages. The name of the country is derived from the Latin *Francia*, meaning "the country of Franks," a Germanic people who occupied the territory during the 5th century.

Since its formation, France has played a major role in European and world events. In the mid-20th century it has emerged from the ruins of World War II to become an important world supplier of agricultural and industrial products and a major partner in the EUROPEAN COMMUNITY.

Today, the term *metropolitan France* refers to the mainland departments and CORSICA, a large island located in the Mediterranean Sea off the coast of Italy. France has four overseas departments—FRENCH GUIANA in South America; GUADELOUPE and MARTINIQUE in the West Indies; and RÉUNION, an island in the Indian Ocean—and two overseas collective territories—MAYOTTE, an island formerly part of the Comoros, located in the Indian Ocean, and SAINT PIERRE AND MIQUELON, islands off the east coast of Canada. In addition, France has numerous small possessions called overseas territories. These include a group of widely scattered islands in the South Pacific, known collectively as FRENCH POLYNESIA; FRENCH SOUTHERN AND ANTARCTIC TERRITORIES; NEW CALEDONIA and WALLIS AND FUTUNA ISLANDS; and many small islands in the southern oceans, including the Kerguelen and Crozet archipelagos, and the islands of St. Paul and Amsterdam (Indian Ocean).

Land and Resources

France may be divided into two regions by an imaginary line joining BIARRITZ in the southwest and Luxembourg in the northeast. Broad plains with low hills predominate north and west of this line, and elevated plateaus and high mountains, including Mont BLANC (4,807 m/15,771 ft), the highest point in France and in Europe (outside of the USSR), are found south and east of the line. Linking the two types of terrain are several wide valleys and gaps, including the Belfort Gap, the Saône valley, the upper Rhône valley, the combined Rhône-Saône corridor south of LYON, and the gaps at Carcassonne and TOULOUSE.

The three major types of European landforms—sedimentary basins and lowlands, worn-down Hercynian mountain blocks, and younger, folded mountain belts—are all well represented in France. The principal sedimentary basin is the Paris Basin, which forms a vast, saucer-shaped lowland composed of alternating layers of hard and soft rocks. The smaller Aquitaine Basin, also sedimentary, lies to the southwest. Other lowlands include several narrow plains that run north-south, including the Alsace Plain west of the Rhine and the Rhône-Saône corridor, and coastal plains, including the Languedoc Plain, along the Mediterranean.

AT A GLANCE

FRENCH REPUBLIC

Land: Area: 543,965 km² (210,026 mi²). Capital and largest city: Paris (1988 est. pop., 2,057,000).

People: Population (1990 est.): 56,400,000. Density: 103.7 persons per km² (268.5 per mi²). Distribution (1990): 73% urban, 27% rural. Official language: French. Major religion: Roman Catholicism.

Government: Type: republic. Legislature: Parliament— National Assembly and Senate. Political subdivisions: 22 regions subdivided into 96 metropolitan departments, 4 overseas departments, 4 overseas territories, 2 collective territories.

Economy: GNP (1988): $939.2 billion; $16,800 per capita. Labor distribution (1987): services—61.5%; industry—31.3%; agriculture—7.3%; unemployed— 10.7%. Foreign trade (1989): imports—$192.5 billion; exports—$178.8 billion. Currency: 1 franc = 100 centimes.

Education and Health: Literacy (1990): 99% of adult population. Universities (1988, State Teaching and Research Units): 72. Hospital beds (1987): 574,000. Physicians (1988): 138,859. Life expectancy (1990): women—82; men—73. Infant mortality (1990): 6 per 1,000 live births.

The Hercynian mountain blocks are remnants of ancient mountains formed during the Hercynian orogeny (a mountain-building period during the Carboniferous and Permian periods, 340 to 230 million years ago) and subsequently worn down before being uplifted during the Tertiary Period (65 to 2 million years ago). The principal uplands are the MASSIF CENTRAL, in south central France, the VOSGES, in eastern France, and the ARDENNES, the main portion of which lies in Belgium and Luxembourg. The soils in all the Hercynian uplands are usually thin and developed on underlying granite and crystalline rocks.

The two principal mountain chains in France are the PYRENEES, on the border with Spain, and the ALPS, which form most of the border with Switzerland and Italy. The Pyrenees are difficult to cross because of their high altitude—several summits exceed 3,000 m (10,000 ft)— and the absence of low passes. The French Alps, the western end of the European Alpine chain, are also high and rugged, with elevations of 3,500 m (11,500 ft), but they are broken by several important river valleys along the Rhône, Isère, and Durance rivers. The JURA, a mountain range on the Swiss border, are lower and less rugged components of the Alpine chain.

France's coastline is 3,427 km (2,129 mi) long, including 644 km (400 mi) on Corsica. The character of the coastline ranges from sandy and straight, as in LANGUEDOC on the Mediterranean, to deeply indented capes and bays, as in BRITTANY, the CÔTE D'AZUR, and Corsica.

Climate. Four climatic types prevail in France. A true temperate maritime climate, near the western coasts, is exemplified at BREST, where winters are mild (7° C/45° F in January), summers are cool (16° C/61° F in July), and rainfall is frequent (800 mm/32 in) during 180 days of the year. A mid-latitude continental climate prevails in the interior of the country, with hotter summers (average July temperature of 18° C/64° F in PARIS) and colder winters (average January temperature of 2° C/36° F in Paris), and rain falls on fewer days of the year.

A mountain climate prevails at high elevations, where winters are generally bitterly cold. Precipitation increases with elevation and occurs in the form of snow in winter, many villages in the high valleys receiving more than 50 days of snow each year. Briançon, in the Alps, has a mean temperature of –2° C (28° F) in January, and 17° C (63° F) in July; annual precipitation there averages 587 mm (23 in). A Mediterranean type of climate is found in a zone about 20 to 60 km (12 to 35 mi) wide along the Mediterranean coast. It is characterized by hot, dry summers, mild and humid winters, and a small number of rainy days during the year. In MARSEILLE, 550 mm (22 in) of rain falls during 60 days of the year, and the sun shines for over 3,000 hours yearly. The average temperature is 7° C (45° F) in January and 23° C (73° F) in July.

Drainage. The SEINE, the best-known French river, drains the Paris Basin. It is 780 km (485 mi) long, and its major tributary is the MARNE River. The LOIRE, with a length slightly more than 1,000 km (620 mi), is France's

FRANCE

| Major Urban Area |
| Railroad |
| Canal or Waterway |
| + Spot Elevation or Depth |

National capitals are underlined

City type size indicates relative importance

Meters	Feet
Above 4000	Above 13124
2000	6562
1000	3281
500	1640
200	656
0	0
200	656
Below 2000	Below 6562

0 50 100 150 km
0 50 100 mi

Scale 1:6,892,000

© 1980, 1991 Rand McNally & Co.
A-550900-772 -2- -2

largest river. Its major tributaries are the Sarthe, Loir, Vienne, Cher, and Allier. The RHÔNE—the deepest river, with the largest volume of flow—has a length of only 523 km (325 mi) in France and receives, among its major tributaries, the SAÔNE, ISÈRE, and Durance rivers. The Ga-

ronne and Dordogne rivers join below BORDEAUX to form the Gironde.

Vegetation and Animal Life. Because of centuries of intensive agricultural and pastoral activity, the forests that once covered the whole country have been largely de-

This view of Paris, capital of France and the country's economic and cultural center, is taken from the Eiffel Tower, the landmark that was built for the International Exposition of 1889. The 300-m (984-ft) tower directly overlooks the Champ-de-Mars.

stroyed. Since the end of the 19th century, however, programs to protect the natural environment have been implemented, particularly in the national and regional parks. Conifers have been planted in reforestation programs, and forests now cover 25% of France's land area.

Brown bears, wild boars, alpine hares, eagles, and falcons are in the Pyrenees and in the Alps; smaller animals such as foxes, weasels, badgers, and otters can be found in the lower-lying regions.

Resources. Although diverse, the natural resources of France are relatively limited in quantity. France has some coal, iron ores, bauxite, and uranium, but the coal veins are deep and difficult to work. Iron ores are of a low grade, and the uranium ore is found only in small quantities. Hydroelectric production, although well-developed, does not meet France's needs. On the other hand, high-quality soils cover almost half the country's surface, giving France an agricultural advantage over other European countries.

People

The modern French population is largely native-born and represents a fusion of many peoples of Celtic, Germanic, Latin, and Slavic origins. Twentieth-century immigrants include an estimated four million foreigners—mainly Portuguese, Spanish, and Italians—and many French citizens, a large number of them Arabs, who have recently entered France from former French colonies in Algeria and sub-Saharan Africa.

The French language is understood and spoken by virtually the entire population, although other languages and dialects persist; they include BASQUE, Alsatian, Corsican, Breton, Provençal, Catalan, and Flemish. About 80% of the population nominally belong to the Roman Catholic church, although only a minority of these participate regularly in church activities. Protestants constitute less than 2% of the population; Jews, about 1%; Muslims, who have entered France recently from former North African colonies, over 3%.

Demography. In 1801, France, with a population of 27 million, was the most populous country in Europe; by 1850, the population had grown to 36 million. During the late 19th and early 20th centuries, however, the French birthrate dropped to levels lower than those in the rest of Europe, and at the end of World War II the population was only 40 million. After 1946, however, the birthrate rose. The last few decades have witnessed an unprecedented expansion of the population that added millions of people to France's schools and, later, to the labor force and consumer markets.

This unusual demographic evolution explains why population densities in France today are only one-half to one-third that of other Western European nations. Within France, the population distribution is uneven and closely reflects levels of economic development. The regions with the largest populations are the great centers of economic activity: the industrial north; Lyon, where industry is important; along the Côte d'Azur, which depends on tourism; and especially Paris, where diverse economic activities are concentrated.

An agricultural laborer unloads freshly harvested wine grapes. France and its neighbor Italy are the world's largest producers of wine. France is distinguished for its prestigious specialty wines—including Champagne, Bordeaux, and Burgundy—which are named for their regions of origin.

Since 1950, France has experienced rapid urbanization. Almost all cities have increased in size, at the expense of the rural population. In the late 1980s about three-quarters of the country's population lived in cities. France has, therefore, now largely caught up with the rest of Europe in its urbanization. Metropolitan Paris, with almost 9 million people, is the largest urban agglomeration in Europe outside the USSR. Other French cities are small by comparison, the largest being the metropolitan areas of Lyon and Marseille, each with between 1 and 2 million people, and Bordeaux and Nice, each with metropolitan areas of about 800,000.

Education and Health. Education is compulsory for all children between the ages of 6 and 16, who may attend either free public schools or fee-charging private schools run mostly by the Roman Catholic church. About one-sixth of schoolchildren attend the private schools. More than 2.5 million children are also enrolled in optional preschool programs. After primary schools, students proceed at age 12 to secondary schools, called *lycées* and *collèges.* Work in the secondary schools is divided into a compulsory first cycle for ages 12 to 16, after which a student may leave school or take an optional second cycle of courses; students who wish to pursue higher education take the second cycle to prepare for the difficult *baccalauréat* exam, which is the minimum university entrance requirement. Students who will pursue a technical career take a short course that offers practical training.

Lyon, the capital of Rhône department, is the third largest city in France. The city became a major commercial center at the beginning of the Christian era because of its location at the confluence of the Rhône and Saône rivers.

Beginning in 1980 the Mitterrand government introduced greater local control and a more flexible curriculum into the formerly highly centralized school system. A plan to extend state control over private schools was abandoned because of widespread public opposition.

Higher education is free to qualified students. Nearly one million students, or five times as many as a generation ago, now continue their studies after secondary school in 72 universities, and in technological institutes and *grandes écoles* (prestigious schools that prepare students for high-ranking careers in business and government).

France has a state-subsidized medical system. Doctors and dentists establish private practices, and patients, who are free to choose their own doctors and dentists, are reimbursed by the state for up to 85% of medical costs. Hospital facilities, although greatly expanded since World War II, are still considered inadequate. Doctors tend to be concentrated in the cities and are in short supply in some rural areas.

The Arts. French literature includes a roster of world-famous novelists, poets, playwrights, and philosophers. Many of the new art movements of the 19th and 20th centuries, including IMPRESSIONISM and CUBISM, began in France. A ministry of culture was established in 1959 to preserve this rich cultural heritage and to make it more widely available outside of Paris. (See FRENCH ART AND ARCHITECTURE; FRENCH LITERATURE; and FRENCH MUSIC.)

Economic Activity

By the 18th century France was one of the world's richest nations. Industrialization began promisingly at the end of the 18th century, but unlike England, France failed to maintain the momentum of its early industrial start and was still primarily agricultural at the end of the 19th century. Industry expanded behind protective trade barriers in the early 20th century, but most growth has occurred since the end of World War II. France now ranks among the world's most economically advanced nations.

A distinctive feature of the postwar French economy has been national economic development plans. The first, the Monnet Plan (named for Jean MONNET, who conceived it), ran from 1947 to 1953. Railways were nationalized in 1937, and many other sectors of the economy, including coal, natural gas, electricity, banking, and transportation (Renault and Air France), came under state control shortly after World War II. Other major industries were nationalized in the early 1980s. The increasing state control of production has been matched by a partial removal of protective trade tariffs and membership in the European Community.

Manufacturing. In the late 1980s manufacturing employed about 22% of the labor force. The principal industrial concentrations are around Paris, in the Pas du Nord and Lorraine coalfields, in the Lyon and SAINT-ÉTIENNE complex of the Rhône valley, and in the new industrial centers of DUNKERQUE and LE HAVRE and the Mediterranean industrial complex at Fos (west of Marseille).

The leading manufacturing industries are metallurgy, mechanical and electrical engineering, chemicals, and textiles. In 1987, France ranked third in Europe (exclud-

Hayange is the oldest iron-working center in the Lorraine region of northeastern France. Lorraine, where much of the nation's heavy industry is concentrated, contains sizable deposits of coal, iron ore, and potash.

ing the USSR) in steel production (after West Germany and Italy) and third (after West Germany and Norway) in aluminum output. These and imported metals are fabricated into a wide range of mechanical and electrical equipment marketed throughout the world. French locomotives, turbines, electronics equipment, nuclear power plants and submarines, and television systems are famous for their innovative design, as are French automobiles, such as Citroën, Peugeot, Simca, and Renault, and French aircraft, such as Caravelle, Mirage, and Concorde. A wide range of chemicals, including perfumes, pharmaceuticals, nitric acid, sulphuric acid, and fertilizers, are also produced. The French textile and garment industry has long been known for its high fashion.

Mining. Only about 0.5% of the labor force are engaged in mining. Coal production has been declining—it was 21.8 million metric tons in 1981, but only 13.5 million metric tons in 1987. Two principal coalfields are the Lorraine coalfield near METZ, and the Nord/Pas de Calais coalfield around Lille. In Lorraine the largest iron-ore deposits in Europe outside the USSR are found, but they have a low iron content and are in less demand than higher-grade imported ores. Large bauxite deposits (from which aluminum is produced) are mined in the south; in 1987, France ranked fourth in Europe in bauxite production. Potash deposits, used in the chemical industry, are

extensive in the vicinity of Mulhouse. Natural-gas deposits have been worked since 1951 near PAU, close to the Spanish border. The gas has a high sulfur content, which is extracted at Lacq; France is a major European supplier of this mineral. Small amounts of petroleum are produced at the Parentis oilfield in the southwest, and the search for petroleum deposits continues off the coast of Brittany and in the Bay of BISCAY.

Power. France's fuel resources are inadequate, and it must import petroleum to meet its requirements. In 1984 thermal power plants provided about 20% of all electricity, 22% was derived from hydroelectric plants, and nuclear power plants provided nearly 60%. France is the world's second largest supplier of nuclear power after the United States. A tidal power plant is located on the Rance River in Brittany. A major engineering triumph, it is expected to spur other projects in areas where TIDAL ENERGY can be harnessed. In 1977 the world's first solar generating plant integrated into a national electricity-producing grid was opened at Odeillo, in the Pyrenees.

Agriculture and Fishing. France is the leading agricultural nation in Europe (excluding the USSR). Since the end of World War II, modernization of agriculture has included mechanization of farms, raising productivity per hectare, and consolidating numerous holdings into larger, more efficient farms.

Sixty percent of France's farm income comes from livestock raising. Cattle are raised mainly in the north and west; sheep and goats in the south and east, and pigs and chickens throughout the country. France is Europe's (excluding the USSR) leading producer of beef, veal, poultry, and cheese and a major producer of milk and eggs.

Crops contribute about 40% of farm income, with cereals and sugar beets the most important products. Wheat is widely grown in the Paris Basin, and France ranks fifth in world wheat production. Other grains grown are barley, corn, and oats, which, with sugar-beet factory residues, are used primarily for livestock feed; some rice is grown under irrigation in the Rhône delta. Wine is a major crop throughout the country, both the *vin ordinaire*, or everyday wine, of the region and the *appellation contrôlée*, or quality-controlled, wines of such regions as BURGUNDY, CHAMPAGNE, Bordeaux, and Alsace (see ALSACE-LORRAINE). In recent years the government has tried to discourage overproduction of wine. Flowers are grown for perfume at Grasse, and a wide variety of fruits and vegetables are raised in the warm Mediterranean region.

Fishing, unlike agriculture, occupies only a modest place in the economy; France ranked sixth in Europe (excluding the USSR) in total fish caught in 1987. Fishing is locally important along the coast of Brittany, on the Bay of Biscay, and in the English Channel.

Transportation. Major efforts have been made since World War II to improve and modernize the extensive French transportation system and to lessen its historical focus on the Paris metropolitan area. Train service, provided by the state, is fast and efficient, especially on the more than 10,000 km (6,200 mi) of electrified track. In 1981 a new railroad speed record was set by the French National Railways' Train de Grande Vitesse (TGV, "high

Terraced farmland surrounds an alpine village in northern Provence, a historical region in southeastern France adjacent to Italy.

speed train"), which traveled at 377 km/h (235 mph) between Paris and Lyon. Airlines are also state run; Air France is one of the world's largest airlines.

The road system, which in 1988 included 6,570 km (4,105 mi) of expressways, provides access to all parts of the nation. Three principal waterways carry much of the nation's bulk freight: the Seine between Le Havre and Paris, the Rhine, and the canalized section of the Moselle below Metz.

Trade and Tourism. France has the fourth largest trading volume in the world. The two major ports are Marseille on the Mediterranean and Le Havre at the mouth of the Seine on the English Channel. Major imports are petroleum and petroleum products, machinery, food, chemicals, motor vehicles, raw materials, iron and steel, and textile yarns. The major exports are machinery and motor vehicles, chemicals, and iron and steel. Most trade is conducted with other members of the EC. In 1988 over 38 million tourists visited France.

Government

The present constitution, adopted in 1958 and revised in 1962, established the Fifth Republic and provided for a powerful president, originally Charles DE GAULLE, and a bicameral legislature with less power than it had in the past. The president is elected by direct popular vote for a seven-year term. He appoints the prime minister and may dissolve the National Assembly.

The legislature consists of a 304-member Senate elected indirectly by an electoral college, and a politically more important 577-member, directly elected National Assembly. The overseas departments and territories are represented in the National Assembly. Senate members serve nine-year terms, and the National Assembly is elected every five years. The minimum voting age is 18 years.

The four leading French political parties are the Socialist party; the conservative Rassemblement pour la république (RPR), founded by Charles de Gaulle and led by Jacques CHIRAC since 1974; the Union pour la démocratie française (UDF), the party of former president Valéry GISCARD D'ESTAING; and the French Communist party, headed by Georges Marchais. François MITTERRAND, leader of the Socialist party, was elected president in May 1981, giving the Fifth Republic its first socialist government. When a UDF-RPR coalition won a majority of seats in the parliamentary election of 1986, Mitterrand had to call on opposition leader Chirac to form a government, marking another first for the Fifth Republic—a "cohabitation" arrangement in which the president and the prime minister were of different parties. The Chirac government modified many of the socialist reforms introduced earlier by Mitterrand. When Mitterrand was elected to a second term in 1988, he was able to replace Chirac with Michel ROCARD, a Socialist.

France, history of   Modern French institutions and people are derived from 2,000 years of contacts with diverse cultures and peoples. Into the area now defined as France came the Celts, Romans, Franks, and other peoples, producing a mixture of practices and races. Since 1500 the French have formed a relatively unified territorial state in which diversity nevertheless persists.

The conquest of France (ancient Gaul) by Julius Caesar during the Gallic Wars (58–51 BC) marked the beginning of 500 years of Roman rule. The Pont du Gard, a Roman aqueduct spanning the Gard River, is a product of Gallo-Roman culture.

Ancient Gaul

When Julius CAESAR invaded GAUL in 58 BC, he found a population of possibly 10 million without either homogeneous roots or unified rule. Several centuries earlier, the CELTS had surged from their Danubian homeland and mingled with the native Ligurians of the Alps, Iberians of the Pyrenees, and other folk of Phoenician, Greek, or Roman stock.

The Celts. Celtic rule in Gaul was decentralized. The Gauls (Latin for Celts) were grouped as members of clans that sometimes functioned separately and sometimes formed into one over 400 tribes, which in turn often joined into one of the 70 or so nations. Thus the Gauls had no single leader, and except for Marseille and Nice, they had no cities or towns either. Most lived in scattered mud huts generally surrounded by a stockade. Hunting, fishing, and pastoral pursuits supplied basic needs. Gallic religious life too was localized and pluralistic, with pantheistic worship of rivers, woods, and other elements of nature. The most widespread but not universal cult was that of the DRUIDS, centered in Brittany.

Roman Conquest. Roman legions marched into Gaul in 58 BC not only to protect the Roman republic's Mediterranean holdings but also to promote Julius Caesar's personal ambitions. The Gauls contributed to their own subjugation by their tribal rivalries and inability to resist the infiltration of trans-Rhenish barbarians and the Swiss (Helvetii). Caesar's speedy success in stopping the barbarians was followed by the conquest of all Gaul.

Five hundred years of Roman rule produced striking consequences for Gaul. Politically, the idea was planted of citizenship of a common state with a single set of laws and administrators and a more or less unified tax system. The Gauls also derived economic advantage from their connection with imperial Rome. Security against barbarians and bands of brigands encouraged the Gauls to clear more forests and farm more lands. Better roads, bridges, and communications fostered greater trade. Towns and villages began to appear in place of the mud-hut habitations.

Culturally, a taste for learning Latin and Greek was cultivated in rudimentary educational institutions in cities like Marseille, Bordeaux, and Lyon. Old Celtic paganism and Druidism continued to prevail in outlying regions despite the spread of Christianity. As missionaries crisscrossed Gaul to convert the pagans and to organize the church, other Christians clustered in monasteries to pray and to establish islands of learning. When the Roman Empire collapsed, the surviving Roman church proved crucial for the retention of Gallic-Roman forms and practices.

Frankish Kingdom

The 5th-century decline of Rome was disastrous for Gaul's political unity, economic development, and cultural life. An accelerated flow of barbarian invasions by groups of FRANKS, GOTHS, and Burgundians began the process of splintering Gaul. However, as the Romans and Gauls had become assimilated, so too did the Gallo-Romans and the barbarians adopt each other's ways. The France that emerged by the year 1000 was thus a combination of Celts (Gauls), Romans, and barbarians (Franks, Teutons, Visigoths, Burgundians, Vandals, Vikings, and others).

Merovingians. From the 5th to the 11th century, the church and the successive dynasties of the MEROVINGIANS (431–751) and the CAROLINGIANS (c.747–987) supplied links of continuity. The founder of the Frankish kingdom was CLOVIS (r. 481–511), a Merovingian. He first overwhelmed the Gallo-Roman forces at Soissons in 486, and then extended Frankish rule over Burgundy and the whole southern region to the Pyrenees by defeating the Visigoths. A convert to Christianity in 496, Clovis found that his services to the church helped his own status in and beyond his new capital, PARIS.

Upon Clovis's death in 511, the Frankish kingdom was parceled out among his four sons, whose heirs subdivided their holdings and waged bitter wars against one another and outsiders. In the last century of Merovingian rule, aristocratic landowners whittled away at royal power in administrative, legal, military, and tax matters. Agriculture and trade were in disarray with the countryside ravaged by feuding chiefs and barbarian bands, and towns and villages dwindled as commerce ebbed. The only institution that retained influence was the church, with bishops protecting townsmen and monastic orders maintaining some semblance of culture. Finally, at the beginning of the 8th century, the Carolingians, who had served as palace mayors (or advisors), secured the reins of power.

Carolingians. Even before a Carolingian, CHARLEMAGNE, became king of the Franks in 768 and emperor in 800, his grandfather CHARLES MARTEL had amassed sufficient power to "save" Europe from the Moors at Tours in 732. Martel's talents and military forces were passed on to Charlemagne's father, PEPIN THE SHORT, whose aid to the missionary Saint BONIFACE was compensated by the pope's endorsement of Pepin and his sons as the legitimate dynasty of the Frankish kingdom. Upon these foundations, Charlemagne waged innumerable wars and gained all Europe from the Pyrenees to the Vistula. His rule left a strong imprint upon France and also foreshadowed the feudal system, which was already being born.

Within the Frankish state, the vigorous and attractive Charlemagne extended royal power and financial resourc-

The Carolingian king Charlemagne, crowned emperor of the West by Pope Leo III in 800, is depicted on this silver coin. During his reign trade routes were expanded, and coins bearing his image have been found throughout Europe.

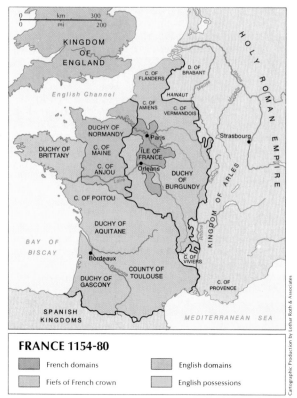

FRANCE 1154-80

▨ French domains	▨ English domains
▨ Fiefs of French crown	▨ English possessions

This map shows the extensive English land holdings in France during the 12th century. With the marriage of Eleanor of Aquitaine and Henry II of England, the area of France under English control was greater than that under French king Louis VII.

held an ever-weakening grip over the kingdom against invading Vikings—who, as NORMANS, established the duchy of Normandy—and predatory lords.

Capetian Kingdom (987–1328)

For nearly 1,000 years the house of Capet furnished France with kings, first as direct-line CAPETIANS and later through the branch families of Valois and Bourbon. The line was literally cut by the guillotining of Louis XVI in 1792, although his brothers Louis XVIII and Charles X and his distant cousin Louis-Philippe served as monarchs after Napoleon I.

Between Hugh Capet's coronation in 987 and the succession of the Valois in 1328 or the inception of the Hundred Years' War in 1338, the feudal system became crystallized along with the concept of French kingships. Cities and towns revived, peopled by bourgeois citizens engaged in a resurgent trade. A cathedral-building boom satisfied the religious spirit and supplied jobs. The Crusades absorbed the energies of kings, counts, clergy, and commoners. And the Norman conquest of England established the centuries-long connection and rivalry with that island kingdom.

FEUDALISM, rooted in land grants of Charlemagne and the subsequent breakdown of his empire, became almost inevitable when weak kings failed to check the Viking incursions of the 9th and 10th centuries. Feudalism developed as a contractual arrangement between lord and king, and MANORIALISM came to determine the relationship between lord and peasant. As warriors for the king, the lords were bound to render military service at their own cost. In return, they received hereditary titles to land and the right to tax, oversee, and judge their inhabitants. To-

The chronicles of Jean Froissart recorded the history of western Europe from the early 1300s to 1400, a period that covered the first half of the Hundred Years' War. This miniature shows the attack (1373) on Brest by the English.

es. In exchange for extensive but nonhereditary land grants and the right to levy local taxes, lords of manors furnished military and judicial services to the king, and the lower classes provided labor on road and other public works. As a check on the local notables, Charlemagne sent out teams of *missi dominici* (usually a bishop and a count) to inspect the districts. Two assemblies were held each year, possible forerunners of the States-General (parliament).

In his capital at AACHEN (Aix-la-Chapelle) and in other towns, Charlemagne rekindled intellectual life by gathering scholars and literary figures like ALCUIN. Works of Greek and Latin were copied and analyzed in new schools founded by churchmen. Charlemagne's encouragement of learning had perhaps more long-range significance for French and Western civilization than his military and political ventures.

The Carolingian decline after Charlemagne followed the same pattern as the Merovingians' after Clovis. The partition of lands, formalized in the Treaty of Verdun in 843 (see VERDUN, TREATY OF), resulted in the area roughly equivalent to medieval France being assigned to the Frankish emperor CHARLES II. He and his descendants

Huguenots (French Protestants) are shown under attack by French soldiers after the revocation of the Edict of Nantes in 1685. The edict, which granted toleration to the Huguenots, had been promulgated (1598) by King Henry IV to bring to an end the prolonged Wars of Religion of the 16th century.

ward their subjects, the lords owed protection and the preservation of order; from them, they were due loyalty, rents, fees, and other obligations.

The local lords' power was demonstrated in the election of HUGH CAPET to the kingship in 987. As kings, the Capetians were in actual possession of only their family lands of central France—the Île de France—situated around Paris and Orléans. It was long a question how much authority would be allowed the kings of France in the lands of the dukes or counts of NORMANDY, AQUITAINE, BURGUNDY, and FLANDERS. An outstanding example was the case of the dukes of Normandy. Duke William's conquest of England in 1066 and his ascent to the English throne, as WILLIAM I, obviously made the subsequent dukes of Normandy–kings of England awesome competitors to their feudal overlords, the kings of France. The English kings extended their French holdings even further when ELEANOR OF AQUITAINE, after the annulment of her marriage to the Capetian LOUIS VII, married (1152) the future HENRY II of England.

Shrewd Capetian kings frequently encouraged and linked up with the new middle class, whose urban and commercial interests often clashed with the warrior and rural concerns of the feudal lords. Churchmen too could be wooed to the king's side with his patronage for cathedrals and schools. French participation in the CRUSADES stimulated a spirit of national rather than local pride, tied the church more closely to the monarchy, and created contacts with Italy and the Middle East for French merchants and scholars.

Of unquestionable vitality in this medieval era was the cultural expression. In monasteries and universities, churchmen and laymen studied, discussed, and debated theological tracts, Greek and Latin works, and a spate of literature beginning to appear in the vernacular French language.

Consolidation of Royal Power (1328–1715)

Such Capetians as Hugh Capet, PHILIP II, LOUIS IX, and PHILIP IV succeeded in upholding and enlarging the royal prerogative beyond their family lands; other Capetians failed. The VALOIS branch (1328–1589), after a dreary start and before a whimpering end, drove the English out of France, consolidated the kingdom, asserted royal authority, launched expeditions into Italy, and ushered in a cultural Renaissance. What the Valois left undone was completed by the BOURBONS.

From the Hundred Years' War to the Wars of Religion. The expulsion of the English involved the French in the HUNDRED YEARS' WAR (1338–1453), a conflict of intermittent intensity. One highlight of the war was the contribution of Saint JOAN OF ARC. Inspired by visions instructing her to go to the Dauphin (later CHARLES VII) and free Orléans, she in turn inspired the Dauphin, his advisors, and the public. Although she was burned at the stake in 1431, her mission was accomplished within a generation. Relieved of the English presence, the French monarchs, notably LOUIS XI (r. 1461–83), finished the task of consolidating the kingdom. They then began to seek extension of their power beyond the boundaries of France. CHARLES VIII invaded Italy in 1494, launching the ITALIAN WARS and a long dynastic rivalry with the HABSBURGS of Austria and Spain.

Sixteenth-century France was blessed by two strong kings, FRANCIS I and HENRY II, and cursed by three weak ones, the sons of Henry II by CATHERINE DE MÉDICIS. French prosperity was also spoiled by the Wars of Religion (see RELIGION, WARS OF) after 1560. Catholics battled Calvinist HUGUENOTS, each faction aspiring to control the monarchy. The assassination of HENRY III in 1589 paved the way for the first Bourbon, HENRY IV, leader of the Huguenots, to both fight and compromise his way to the

The grandiose temperament of Louis XIV is captured in this portrait (1694). Known as "Le Roi Soleil" (The Sun King), Louis established an absolute monarchy and expanded French territorial holdings. His Palace at Versailles is a lasting testimony to the grandeur of his long reign (1643–1715). (Prado, Madrid.)

EXPANSION OF FRANCE UNDER LOUIS XIV

France in 1661	Acquired by Treaty of Ryswick (1697)
Acquired by Treaty of Aix-la-Chapelle (1668)	Acquired by Treaty of Utrecht (1713)
Acquired by Treaty of Nijmegen (1678)	Ceded to Savoy (1696-1713)

The military campaigns of Louis XIV expanded French territorial control. Shaded areas indicate France as it was in 1661 and its territorial gains in subsequent years.

throne by 1598. He satisfied Huguenots by the tolerant Edict of Nantes in 1598 (see NANTES, EDICT OF) and mollified Catholics by his own conversion so as to enter the Paris he considered "worth a Mass."

Bourbon Reconstruction. By tact, persuasion, and force, Henry IV reduced religious tensions, stimulated commerce and manufacturing, and curbed the nobility. The last process was vigorously pursued by cardinals RICHELIEU and MAZARIN, the de facto rulers of France under Henry's weak son LOUIS XIII.

It was LOUIS XIV, however, who truly tamed the aristocracy, turning the nobles into powerless courtiers, forced to attend him in the new Palace of Versailles (see VERSAILLES, PALACE OF). The grandeur of Versailles, imitated by so many European monarchs, was not merely architectural and social in value. It was also a focal point from which emanated favors and patronage for artists, writers, and scientists.

In this period the bourgeoisie was the beneficiary of mercantilist policies (see MERCANTILISM) developed most notably by Jean Baptiste COLBERT. The interests of the royal treasury often coincided with subsidies for manufacturing and for expanded internal, colonial, and foreign trade.

French influence abroad rose as the secular-minded Cardinal Richelieu engaged Catholic Frenchmen as allies with Protestant princes against the Holy Roman emperors, the German Catholic princes, and Spain in the THIRTY YEARS' WAR, after which France gained Alsace by the Peace of Westphalia (1648). Louis XIV further expanded French territory in Europe and overseas and placed his grandson on the Spanish throne as PHILIP V—all through wars, diplomacy, and marriage.

The Old Regime and the Enlightenment (1715–89)

After Louis XIV's death, the kingdom remained powerful and prosperous: it was Europe's most populous, single, unified state, endowed with the greatest military and economic resources. France even extended its boundaries by the acquisition (1766) of Lorraine. Colonially, however, the story was different. The FRENCH COLONIAL EMPIRE that had come into being in the 17th century was largely lost to Britain as a result of the SEVEN YEARS' WAR (1756–63).

Revival of the Nobility. LOUIS XV and LOUIS XVI retained, in principle, divine right and absolute sovereignty, but in practice these kings failed to exercise that power. Consequently the nobility of old feudal blood (nobility of the sword) and of the purchased variety (nobility of the robe) moved to displace the bourgeoisie and fill the functions of state, in the provinces, army, and church. The first two estates—clergy and nobility—aimed to dominate France and keep their many privileges. This "reinfeudation" displeased the third estate—the rest of the population. The bourgeoisie, although increasingly prominent in

The provinces of France as they were during the ancien régime before the Revolution.

PROVINCES OF FRANCE BEFORE THE FRENCH REVOLUTION

RULERS OF FRANCE

Carolingians		Valois		Second Empire	
Pepin (the Short)	751–68	Philip VI	1328–50	Napoleon III	1852–70
Carloman	768–71	John II (the Good)	1350–64	**Third Republic** (presidents)	
Charlemagne	768–814	Charles V (the Wise)	1364–80	Louis Jules Trochu (provisional)	1870–71
Louis I (the Pious)	813–40	Charles VI (the Mad	1380–1422	Adolphe Thiers	1871–73
Charles II (the Bald)	843–77	or Well-Beloved)		Patrice de MacMahon	1873–79
Louis II (the Stammerer)	877–79	Charles VIII (the Well-Served)	1422–61	Jules Grévy	1879–87
Louis III	879–82	Louis XI	1461–83	Sadi Carnot	1887–94
Carloman	879–84	Charles VIII	1483–98	Jean Casimar-Périer	1894–95
Charles the Fat	884–87	Louis XII	1498–1515	Félix Faure	1895–99
Odo, or Eudes	887–98	Francis I	1515–47	Émile Loubet	1899–1906
(non-Carolingian)		Henry II	1547–59	Armand Fallières	1906–13
Charles III (the Simple)	898–922	Francis II	1559–60	Raymond Poincaré	1913–20
Robert I (non-Carolingian)	922–23	Charles IX	1560–74	Paul Deschanel	1920
Rudolf (of Burgundy;	923–36	Henry III	1574–89	Alexandre Millerand	1920–24
non-Carolingian)		**Bourbons**		Gaston Doumergue	1924–31
Louis IV (d'Outremer)	936–54	Henry IV	1589–1610	Paul Doumer	1931–32
Lothair	954–86	Louis XIII	1610–43	Albert Lebrun	1932–40
Louis V	986–87	Louis XIV	1643–1715	**Vichy Government**	
Capetians		Louis XV	1715–74	Henri Philippe Pétain,	1940–44
Hugh Capet	987–96	Louis XVI	1774–92	chief of state	
Robert II (the Pious)	996–1031	**First Republic**		**Provisional Government** (presidents)	
Henry I	1031–60	National Convention	1792–95	Charles de Gaulle	1944–46
Philip I	1060–1108	Directory	1795–99	Félix Gouin	1946
Louis VI (the Fat)	1108–37	Consulate	1799–1804	Georges Bidault	1946
Louis VII (the Young)	1137–80	**First Empire**		Léon Blum	1946
Philip II Augustus	1180–1223	Napoleon I	1804–15	**Fourth Republic** (presidents)	
Louis VIII	1223–26	**Bourbons** (restored)		Vincent Auriol	1947–54
Louis IX (St. Louis)	1226–70	Louis XVIII	1814–24	René Coty	1954–59
Philip III (the Bold)	1270–85	Charles X	1824–30	**Fifth Republic** (presidents)	
Philip IV (the Fair)	1285–1314	**House of Orléans**		Charles de Gaulle	1959–69
Louis X (the Stubborn)	1314–16	Louis Philippe	1830–48	Georges Pompidou	1969–74
John I	1316	**Second Republic**		Valéry Giscard d'Estaing	1974–81
Philip V (the Tall)	1316–22	Louis Napoléon, president	1848–52	François Mitterrand	1981–
Charles IV (the Fair)	1322–28				

economic life, found itself excluded from political posts.

Enlightenment. The most illustrious aspect of the Old Regime was the work and influence of its philosophers of the ENLIGHTENMENT. From the essays, tracts, encyclopedias, novels, plays, and letters of such thinkers as Denis DIDEROT, MONTESQUIEU, VOLTAIRE, Caron de BEAUMARCHAIS, and Jean Jacques ROUSSEAU, there flowed a penetrating critique of humankind and society.

Revolutionary and Napoleonic Era (1789–1814)

The FRENCH REVOLUTION has been attributed to many causes. The challenging ideas of the philosophers subverted the Old Regime. Agricultural disaster and depression in commerce, finance, and manufacturing sharpened class tensions. Conflicting political aims separated aristocratic, bourgeois, and popular elements, and presiding over the nation in this troubled state was the inept Louis XVI.

The Revolution. All of these and other factors contributed to the drama unfolded in 1788 and 1789. Inflated by aid to the American Revolution, the French public debt reached crushing proportions. Aristocrats, fearful of losing their privileges and desirous of an even larger share in national policy-making, boldly forced the king to call the STATES-GENERAL in 1789. In disuse since 1614, the States-General was expected to sit and vote by estate, by

order. However, the deputies of the third estate were incensed at the prospect of being outvoted by the first two estates. Their forcing of the king to accept voting by head resulted in the transformation of the States-General into a National Assembly by June 1789. Workers and peasants soon entered the fray by storming the hated BASTILLE in Paris on July 14, 1789.

Between 1789 and 1792, a new France was born, characterized by a declaration of rights, the end of the feudal system, the drafting of a constitution, reform of the church, and reorganization of local government. On paper, the Old Regime was dead—hereditary privilege was terminated, as was the absolutism of the king and the hold of the church.

The Revolution became more radical after 1792 with the guillotining of the "treasonable" king, the outbreak of civil war at home, the FRENCH REVOLUTIONARY WARS abroad, and the lower classes' militancy for political and other advantages. The Reign of Terror (1793–94), a period of brutal dictatorship under the leadership of Maximilien ROBESPIERRE, was ended by the Thermidorean Reaction of July 1794. Thereafter, France was ruled by a DIRECTORY until the victorious general Napoléon Bonaparte established the CONSULATE in 1799. He crowned himself emperor as NAPOLEON I in 1804.

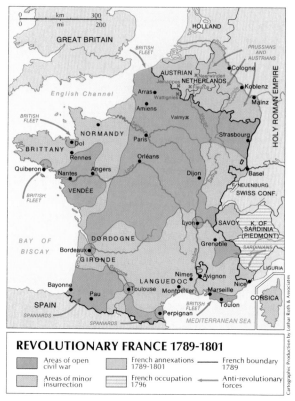

REVOLUTIONARY FRANCE 1789-1801

| | Areas of open civil war | | French annexations 1789-1801 | —— French boundary 1789 |
| | Areas of minor insurrection | | French occupation 1796 | ←— Anti-revolutionary forces |

This map illustrates the turbulent conditions in France during the years 1789–1801. The country was beset internally by civil unrest and insurrection while undergoing antirevolutionary attacks from foreign powers during the French Revolutionary Wars.

Cartographic Production by Lothar Roth & Associates

Napoleon I. Napoleon's initial reforms incorporated much of the revolutionary decade's intentions and helped pacify France internally. Internationally, his conquests had already created an extended French empire in Europe by 1802. Setbacks in Spain and defeat in Russia in 1812 turned the tide against him. After defeat in 1814 he was forced to abdicate, and the Bourbon dynasty was restored in the person of LOUIS XVIII. Although Napoleon briefly seized power again in 1815, the NAPOLEONIC WARS were concluded by his defeat in the Battle of WATERLOO (June 1815).

A Succession of Regimes (1814–70)

The search for permanent political forms hypnotized the French from 1814 to 1870. The conservative CHARLES X, Louis XVIII's brother and successor, became increasingly despotic. His Restoration regime was supplanted by the constitutional Orléanist monarchy of LOUIS PHILIPPE in the July Revolution of 1830. Initially welcomed by the business and professional classes, the new ruler eventually lost their favor as his government slid into corruption, subversion of parliamentary power, suppression of civil liberties, and economic mismanagement. The February REVOLUTION of 1848 dislodged Louis Philippe and established the Second Republic.

The Second Republic elected Louis Napoléon (subsequently NAPOLEON III), nephew to Napoleon I, as president. He transformed the republic into the Second Empire in 1852 and ruled in an authoritarian fashion. Napoleon III's participation in the CRIMEAN WAR and the Italian wars of unification brought only faint luster to France. The bungled effort of the emperor to extend French influence abroad by placing Archduke Maximilian (see MAXIMILIAN, EMPEROR OF MEXICO) on the Mexican throne further eroded the country's international prestige. Moreover, Napoleon III was no match for the Prussian chancellor Otto von BISMARCK's diplomatic and military maneuvers of

Louis XVI, the last king of France, before the Revolution, is portrayed with the French explorer Jean François La Pérouse. Louis, who was condemned by the Convention and guillotined in 1793, was incapable of resolving the social and political upheavals that led to the Revolution and ended the absolute monarchy.

Recognized throughout Europe for his military acumen and leadership of French forces, Napoléon Bonaparte was crowned emperor in 1804. The legendary spirit of his heroism is preserved in this portrait (1800) by Jacques Louis David.

the 1860s. The defeat of the French in the FRANCO-PRUSSIAN WAR (1870–71) led to the proclamation of the Third Republic.

This plethora of regimes was produced by many elements. Political issues of restrictive suffrage and office-holding alienated the lower and middle social classes from the monarchical form. On the other hand, the wealthy bourgeois joined church and nobility in abhorring the anticlericalism of republicans. Political divisions were multiplied, too, by the social tensions stemming from industrialization, socialist movements, and trade unionism.

Despite its poor political record, France did move ahead economically, building railroads and factories, opening mines, actively trading at home and abroad, and modernizing the city of Paris. Intellectual and cultural life too was at a peak as painters, sculptors, and writers displayed their talents in the ages of romanticism and realism.

The Republics since 1870

Since 1870 the French have experienced the survival of republican forms, the traumas of two world wars and several colonial ones, modernization of the economy, transformation of societal structure and mores, and more than lingering attention to intellectual and cultural questions.

Third Republic. The organic laws of the Third Republic of 1870 were formulated by 1875. Repression of the COMMUNE OF PARIS in 1871 and facing down the monarchists gave the republic respectability by 1880. The par-

liament had gained ascendancy over the executive branch of president and cabinet, and republican forces wrested control over the educational system away from the church in the 1880s, finally separating the church from the state in 1905. The republic was shaken by scandals over presidential abuses, parliamentary bribery in the projected building of the Panama Canal, and the court-martial of the Jewish army captain Alfred Dreyfus as an alleged spy. The ultimate effect of the long, drawn-out DREYFUS AFFAIR, however, was to discredit further the remnants of antirepublican aristocrats, army officers, and clergy and to solidify the republic.

Industrialization proceeded rapidly, although at a slower pace than in Germany or Britain. Along with other major European powers, France engaged in a burst of imperialism, adding substantial holdings in Africa and Asia by 1914. By 1914, French diplomats had forged a system of alliances including a defensive military pact with Russia (1894) and an Entente Cordiale with Britain (1904; see TRIPLE ENTENTE). Paris in the pre-1914 era—indeed until 1940—was the center for French and foreign artistic and literary figures.

World Wars. When WORLD WAR I began in August 1914, the French anticipated a brief conflict in which they could recover both the territory (Alsace-Lorraine) and prestige lost in 1871. In fact, French troops marched into a long war of attrition and suffered greater casualties than other belligerents. The Treaty of Versailles temporarily restored French ascendancy, but the Great Depression of the 1930s and the challenge of Nazi Germany spelled disaster for France by 1940.

At home, Socialist premier Léon BLUM's Popular Front of Socialists, Communists, and Radical-Socialists in 1936–37 preserved the republic against the threat of fascist groups, such as the ACTION FRANÇAISE, and enacted a wide range of social and economic reforms. A foreign policy of appeasement of Adolf Hitler, however, failed to maintain international peace, and WORLD WAR II began in September 1939.

Guided by an antiquated military strategy, the French armies suffered blitzkrieg defeat by Hitler's panzers in May 1940. From the rubble rose the collaborationist VICHY GOVERNMENT under Marshal Henri Philippe PÉTAIN, the Free French movement of Charles DE GAULLE, and the resistance movement within France. Allied victory brought liberation in 1944 and had ushered in the Fourth Republic by 1946.

Fourth Republic. Until 1947 the Communist, Socialist, and liberal Catholic parties worked together to deal with the reconstruction of the country. In 1947, however, the Communists moved into the opposition, and the rise of the Gaullist right in the form of the *Rassemblement du peuple français* placed the Socialists and center parties in the quandary of forming fragile coalitions to preserve the republic against the left and right challengers.

The Fourth Republic nationalized several large banks and insurance companies, enfranchised French women, and expanded the previously feeble warfare benefits. Under Jean MONNET's plan, and with U.S. aid, the republic also built the substructure for a modern economy, tied in with the EUROPEAN COMMUNITY. To meet the Soviet threat in the cold war, France joined (1949) the NORTH ATLANTIC TREATY ORGANIZATION (NATO) but began to develop its own nuclear arsenal. Hostility from the Communist left and the Gaullist right weakened the republic and its ability to cope with the colonial wars in Indochina and Algeria (see also VIETNAM WAR).

Fifth Republic. On the verge of civil war over the Algerian question in 1958, the French called de Gaulle out of retirement. His price was the right to draft a new constitution to be submitted to a referendum, and so the Fifth Republic was born, with the election (December 1958) of de Gaulle as president. The new republic gave more power to the executive than to the previously dominant parliament. Having liquidated the Algerian War in 1962 and introduced prosperity and stability, de Gaulle faced a large-scale student-worker revolt in 1968 and left office the following year. The Gaullist party dominated politics through the 1970s under de Gaulle's successors, Georges POMPIDOU and Valéry GISCARD D'ESTAING. An energy crisis contributed to rising inflation and unemployment in the 1970s.

The general elections of 1981 produced a dramatic change. Socialist François MITTERRAND became president, and Socialists gained a solid majority in the parliament.

Paris was liberated from the Germans by the Free French troops of General Charles de Gaulle and other Allied forces on Aug. 15, 1944. De Gaulle served as head of the provisional government until the Fourth Republic was established by 1946.

This map illustrates the division of France between the Vichy Government and German occupying forces in World War II. In July 1940, Marshal Henri Philippe Pétain set up Vichy as an autonomous regime. The Germans occupied all of France in 1942.

VICHY FRANCE 1940-44

Occupied by Germany in 1940
Occupied by Germany Nov. 1942
French-Italian demilitarized zone
- - - - - Demarcation line

Mitterrand immediately proposed measures to create new jobs, shorten working hours, and extend welfare benefits. He also took steps to nationalize several large banks and selected industries. In foreign affairs the new president reaffirmed France's commitment to NATO and took a more critical stance toward the USSR than had his predecessor. In 1982 and 1983 a deteriorating economy forced Mitterrand to curtail his social-welfare programs and adopt unpopular austerity measures. When the Socialists lost their parliamentary majority in 1986, he had to appoint Gaullist leader Jacques CHIRAC as premier. This marked the beginning of a "cohabitation" system in which the president shared power with his prime minister. Over Mitterrand's opposition, Chirac lowered taxes and pushed through a privatization plan, selling off many of the previously nationalized banks and industries. After Mitterrand was reelected to the presidency in 1988, his party regained enough strength in parliament for him to oust Chirac in favor of a Socialist, Michel ROCARD.

France, Anatole [frahns, ah-nah-tohl'] Anatole France, the pseudonym of Jacques Anatole François Thibault, b. Apr. 16, 1844, d. Oct. 12, 1924, was a French novelist, poet, and critic. An erudite man who wore his learning lightly and wrote in a melodious style, France was the most respected writer of his age by the time of his election to the Académie Française in 1896. He was awarded the Nobel Prize for literature in 1921. His reputation was founded on numerous books, which include an early volume of poems in the PARNASSIAN manner, *Poèmes Dorés* (Golden Verses, 1872); the successful novels *The Crime of Sylvestre Bonnard* (1881; Eng. trans., 1906) and *At the Sign of the Reine Pédauque* (1893; Eng. trans., 1913); and an exquisite collection of short stories, *The Mother-of-Pearl Box* (1892).

After the turmoil of the DREYFUS AFFAIR, France wrote his satiric allegory of civilization, *Penguin Island* (1908; Eng. trans., 1909), but his historical novel of the French Revolution, *The Gods Are Athirst* (1912; Eng. trans.,

1913), preserves a skeptical balance between political extremes.

France's literary achievement was founded on his penetrating irony and his appreciation of classical art and 18th-century French literature. He held sway over the writers of his time through his weekly critical essays, published in the Paris newspaper *Le Temps* between 1887 and 1893.

Franche-Comté [frahnsh-kohn-tay'] The Franche-Comté (Free County of Burgundy) is a historic province in eastern France that constitutes one of the country's 21 administrative regions. BESANÇON is the traditional capital. The region was occupied (4th century BC) by the Celtic Sequani tribe and was taken (52 BC) by Julius Caesar. The Burgundians had settled there by the 5th century AD. During the 9th century the area was unified with Transjurane BURGUNDY, which in turn became (933) part of the united Kingdom of Burgundy. All of Burgundy was integrated into the Holy Roman Empire in 1032. The name *free county* was acquired during the 12th century when the local count refused to pay homage to the German king. In 1556, the Franche-Comté passed to the Spanish Habsburgs. France annexed the province in 1678 by the Peace of Nijmegen. In 1790, during the administrative reorganization of France, the Franche-Comté was divided into the departments of Doubs, Haute-Saône, and Jura. Farming, particularly dairying and viticulture, remains the chief economic activity.

---

franchise (business) [fran'-chyz] A franchise, in law and business, is a privilege or right, granted by a government entity or sold by a business, that allows the recipient to carry on commercial activity under protected, or monopoly, conditions. The legal concept dates from the Middle Ages, when a lord could grant a knight or an abbot the right, or franchise, to govern part of his domain.

In the United States since the mid-19th century, municipalities and states have granted monopoly franchises to utility and public-transportation companies in return for the right to regulate the firms' activities. The franchisees undertake certain obligations (to provide electrical service throughout a town, for example), and the rates charged for the services are controlled by the government, usually through expert commissions.

The term *franchise* today, however, is most closely associated with the business arrangement that allows a distributor or retailer exclusive rights to sell a product or service within a specified area. The franchising company grants its franchisees the use of a well-known, nationally advertised name, standardized designs for buildings and furnishings, financial assistance, and other business aids.

franchise (political) see SUFFRAGE

Francia, José Gaspar Rodríguez de [frahn'-syah, hoh-say' gahs-par' roh-dree'-gays day] José Gaspar Rodríguez de Francia, b. Jan. 6, 1766, d. Sept. 20, 1840, was a dictator of Paraguay who established that country's independence. Francia participated in the bloodless revolution against Spain in 1811 and was a member of the junta that took control of the government. In 1814, however, he established himself as the sole ruler. Thereafter, Francia, who became known as El Supremo, ruled as undisputed dictator until his death. Assuming direction of the church, he broke the power of the clergy and upper classes. He also promoted agricultural and industrial development.

Francis, Sam Samuel Lewis Francis, b. San Mateo, Calif., June 25, 1923, is an abstract expressionist painter who, by 1947, was creating works influenced by Jackson POLLOCK, Mark ROTHKO, and Clyfford STILL. Francis spent much time from 1950 to 1957 in Paris at the studio of the cubist master Fernand LÉGER. During the 1950s, crucial years in the development of contemporary art, he made prolonged sojourns in Europe and the Orient that resulted in his gaining more fame abroad than at home. Ebullient color, smooth weightless shapes, and infinite space characterize his major commission, *Basel Triptych* (1956–58; a portion of which is *Basel Mural II*, Stedelijk Museum, Amsterdam).

See also: ABSTRACT EXPRESSIONISM.

Composition *(1960) by Sam Francis, an American abstract expressionist, combines vivid patches of color and large areas of bare canvas. (Galérie Jacques Dubourt, Paris.)*

Francis of Assisi, Saint [uh-see'-zee] Saint Francis, b. Assisi, Italy, c.1182, d. Oct. 3, 1226, was the founder of the FRANCISCANS. The son of a rich merchant named Pietro di Bernardone, he was very worldly in his early years and was recognized as a leader in the escapades of the town's youth. Dissatisfied with his life, he turned to prayer and service to the poor, and in 1206 he publicly renounced his father's wealth.

A detail from Giotto's panel painting (c. 1300) of the life of Saint Francis of Assisi portrays the saint preaching to the birds.

Francis began to live as a hermit and soon attracted followers. He preached the necessity of a poor, simple life-style based on the ideals of the Gospels. Pope Innocent III approved his way of life, gave him and his disciples permission to preach on moral topics, and had Francis ordained a deacon. The followers increased and were called friars minor by Francis, that is, the lesser brethren. With the collaboration of Saint CLARE, Francis founded (1212) a branch of his order for women, called the Poor Clares. Later, he established (1221) another branch for lay men and women, called the Third Order. In 1219, during the Fifth Crusade, Francis made his famous but fruitless attempt to convert the sultan al-Kamil while the crusaders laid seige to Damietta in Egypt.

Francis was not adept at day-to-day organization. Under the influence of more practical men, such as Cardinal Ugolino, the future pope GREGORY IX, and Brother Elias, Francis retired from the government of the order to a life of contemplation, during which he received the STIGMATA, the imprint of the wounds of Christ in his own body, and composed his famous poem, the *Canticle of Brother Sun*. He was canonized in 1228. Feast day: Oct. 4.

Francis de Sales, Saint [duh-sahl'] Francis de Sales, b. Aug. 21, 1567, d. Dec. 28, 1622, was a French bishop and one of the Doctors of the Church. In 1602 he was consecrated bishop of Geneva, where he promoted the measures for reform that were part of the COUNTER-REFORMATION. He is remembered today for his writings, especially the spiritual classic *Introduction to a Devout Life*, and for the various orders and congregations founded under his patronage. He was canonized in 1665 and was designated the patron saint of writers by Pius XI in 1923. Feast day: Jan. 24 (formerly Jan. 29).

Francis Joseph, Emperor of Austria Francis Joseph, b. Aug. 18, 1830, d. Nov. 21, 1916, began his long reign as emperor of Austria in the revolutionary turmoil of 1848; he died in the midst of World War I, which was to destroy the Austrian empire. He succeeded his feebleminded uncle FERDINAND I to the throne, mainly on the advice of Minister-President Felix Schwarzenberg (see SCHWARZENBERG family).

The new emperor and Schwarzenberg called in a Russian army to suppress the REVOLUTION OF 1848 in Hungary. In 1851 they inaugurated a program of centralized absolutism designed to modernize the empire along German lines. This regime antagonized the other nationalities of the empire, and after the Austrian defeat by Sardinia and France in 1859, it gave way to the February Patent of 1861, which provided a moderately liberal constitution. After the defeat by Prussia in the SEVEN WEEKS' WAR of 1866, Francis Joseph was compelled to grant Hungary autonomy and full parity with Austria in the Compromise of 1867. Henceforth the empire was known as AUSTRIA-HUNGARY. Francis Joseph ruled both constitutionally with parliaments elected by the propertied classes and dominated by the Germans and the Magyars.

Francis Joseph's reign saw remarkable economic and cultural progress, but the clashes of nationalities and economic conflicts generated such turmoil that after 1900 parliamentary majorities were increasingly rare and rule by imperial decree common.

The emperor suffered much personal tragedy: the execution of his brother MAXIMILIAN in Mexico in 1867; the suicide of his son RUDOLF at Mayerling in 1889; the assassination of his wife, Empress Elizabeth, in 1898; and in 1914 the assassination of his heir apparent, FRANZ FERDINAND, which precipitated World War I. Through all vicissitudes he maintained an austere personal life, a lofty concept of duty, and a sober, realistic view of statecraft.

Francis Joseph is portrayed here at the beginning of his long reign (1848–1916) as Austrian emperor. Despite economic and cultural progress, his reign was marked by increasing conflict among the empire's many nationalities. (Castle Schönbrunn, Vienna.)

Saint Francis Xavier, one of the original seven members of the Society of Jesus, or Jesuits, was ordained a priest in 1537 and began missionary journeys to the Far East in 1541. His work in India, the East Indies, and Japan resulted in his canonization in 1662.

Francis Xavier, Saint

Francis Xavier, Saint [zay'-vee-ur]   Francis Xavier, b. Apr. 7, 1506, d. Dec. 3, 1552, was a Spanish-Basque Jesuit missionary called the Apostle of the Indies and of Japan. In 1534, IGNATIUS LOYOLA, Xavier, and five others bound themselves by vow to the work of preaching the gospel in non-Christian areas of the world. After his ordination to the priesthood, Xavier worked with Loyola in Italy, where they drew up the rules for the new order, called the Society of Jesus (see JESUITS).

In 1541, Xavier left for India. After working for seven years in Goa, Travancore, Malacca, the Molucca Islands, and Ceylon (now Sri Lanka), he went (1549) to Japan. After he had learned the local language, he spent the next two years setting up missions. During this time, he also translated a catechism. Xavier returned (1552) to Malacca and then to Goa, but he was there only a few months before departing for China. He died in Sancian (Shangchuan), an island not far from Guangzhou (Canton). His body, found to be undecayed after two months of burial, was later taken to Goa. Because of his zeal and success as a missionary, he is considered the patron saint of the Orient and of missionaries. He was canonized in 1662. Feast day: Dec. 3.

See also: MISSIONS, CHRISTIAN.

Francis I, Emperor of Austria

Francis I, Emperor of Austria   see FRANCIS II, HOLY ROMAN EMPEROR

Francis I, King of France

Francis I, King of France   Francis I, b. Sept. 12, 1494, d. March 31, 1547, the autocratic king who ruled France from 1515 to 1547, personified the splendors of the Renaissance. The son of Charles of Angoulême and Louise of Savoy, he married (1514) Claude, daughter of ANNE OF BRITTANY and his predecessor, LOUIS XII.

In July 1515, seven months after his accession, Francis led an army across the Alps and conquered Milan with his victory at Marignano. Four years later his rivalry with the house of HABSBURG intensified when he became a candidate for the imperial crown in Germany. The election was won by the Habsburg king of Spain, who became Holy Roman emperor as CHARLES V. Francis's subsequent war against Charles ended in total defeat at the Battle of PAVIA (1525), in which Francis himself was captured. Francis sought alliances with the German Protestant princes and the Turkish sultan, and he fought further wars against Charles V in 1536–38 and 1542–44.

Like his elder sister, Margaret of Angoulême, the king became a patron of the arts and learning. He founded (1529) the Collège de France, brought Leonardo da Vinci to Amboise, and built magnificent châteaus, such as FONTAINEBLEAU.

Francis's concordat with the papacy at Bologna in 1516 gave him control of church appointments. Until 1534, the king was tolerant of Protestantism, but in that year a series of extremist Protestant placards gave him personal offense. Persecution increased toward the end of his reign.

At the same time, the royal court was divided into factions under the influence of Francis's favorites and his mistress, the duchesse d'Étampes. War and patronage so strained the royal resources that Francis had to adopt such devices as the sale of government offices. By the time of the king's death, the early glamour of his reign had become tarnished.

Francis I of France began his reign with the conquest of Milan in 1515 and was at war with his Habsburg rival, Emperor Charles V, for much of the ensuing 32 years.

Francis II, King of France   Francis II, b. Jan. 19, 1544, d. Dec. 5, 1560, king of France, was the oldest son of HENRY II and CATHERINE DE MÉDICIS. Francis married MARY, QUEEN OF SCOTS, in April 1558. After succeeding to the throne in 1559, Francis came under the influence of Mary's powerful GUISE relatives, who sought to destroy the French Protestants, or HUGUENOTS. The ensuing persecution provoked the Huguenot Conspiracy of Amboise (1560), a plot to abduct Francis and arrest his Guise mentors. The plan was discovered and the incipient rebellion bloodily crushed, but Francis's death curtailed Guise influence.

Francis I, Holy Roman Emperor   Francis I, b. Dec. 8, 1708, served as Holy Roman emperor from Sept. 13, 1745, until his death on Aug. 18, 1765. The second son of Leopold, duke of Lorraine, he ruled over his native duchy from 1729 to 1736. On Feb. 12, 1736, he married the Habsburg heiress, MARIA THERESA, and as part of a diplomatic compromise that ended the War of the POLISH SUCCESSION (1733–35) Francis transferred Lorraine to STANISŁAW I, the deposed king of Poland, in return for the Italian state of Tuscany. When Maria Theresa inherited the Habsburgs' central European domains in October 1740, a coalition of powers contested the succession in the War of the AUSTRIAN SUCCESSION, and the imperial election went to the Bavarian candidate, CHARLES VII rather than Francis. Only on Charles's death in 1745 did Maria Theresa secure the crown for her husband. A weak ruler, Francis left government in the hands of his wife.

Francis II, Holy Roman Emperor   Francis II, b. Feb. 12, 1768, d. Mar. 2, 1835, was the last Holy Roman emperor (1792–1806) and, as Francis I, the first emperor of Austria (1804–35). Succeeding his father, LEOPOLD II, in 1792, he was confronted with the war declared by Revolutionary France in the west and by a Polish crisis in the east. Successive defeats by France in the FRENCH REVOLUTIONARY WARS and NAPOLEONIC WARS compelled him to accept a series of treaties that destroyed the Holy Roman Empire and shrank the new Austrian Empire to its core lands.

Francis's greatest achievement was Austria's recovery. This was accomplished first by allying with NAPOLEON I, who married Francis's daughter, Marie Louise, in 1810, and then by joining (1813) the coalition that defeated him. Francis then served as host to the Congress of Vienna (1814–15; see VIENNA, CONGRESS OF), where his brilliant minister, METTERNICH, recovered Austria's territorial position and its old preeminence in central Europe.

In domestic policy Francis favored his uncle JOSEPH II's centralized administration but lacked the latter's enlightened ideals. His rule, like his personal life, was austere, disciplined, and aimed at stability. At his death, Austria was allied to Prussia and Russia in a common cause to suppress change. Francis was succeeded by his son FERDINAND I.

Franciscans   [fran-sis'-kuhnz]   The Franciscans are members of a religious order that follows the rule of Saint FRANCIS OF ASSISI. The first Franciscans, called the Order of Friars Minor, followed an ideal of total poverty; they possessed nothing in common or individually. Forbidden to accept money, they lived from day to day by working and begging. When they began studying and living at universities, however, they had to modify their strict ideal of poverty. By the time Saint Francis died (1226), the order had spread from Italy to England, the Holy Land, and all of Europe. The friars were known as the people's preachers. They wore a gray tunic with a white cord at the waist; hence, their English name Grey Friars.

From the beginning, there were disagreements about the direction the order would take. The Franciscan minister general, Saint BONAVENTURE, sought a balance between the Conventuals, who wanted to adapt their poverty to the needs of the time, and the Spirituals, who wanted a strict poverty. The quarrel intensified during the 14th century when some of the Spiritual Franciscans, known as the Fraticelli, were condemned (1317–18) by Pope JOHN XXII. Disagreements about the ideal of poverty brought a permanent division in the 15th century between the Friars Minor Conventual (O.F.M. Conv.) and the Order of Friars Minor (O.F.M.). In the 16th century, the Order of Friars Minor Capuchin (O.F.M. Cap.) established a stricter independent branch of Franciscans.

Preaching, teaching, foreign missions, and parish work remain the work of the Franciscans today. The Poor Clares, Franciscan nuns, are the second order. The Third Order comprises lay men and women who combine prayer and penance with everyday activity. Many sisters, brothers, and priests follow the Franciscan ideal in communities affiliated with the Third Order. There are Franciscan communities in the Roman Catholic church and the Anglican (or Episcopalian) churches.

francium   [fran'-see-uhm]   Francium, or eka-cesium, is a radioactive chemical element, one of the alkali metals of Group IA of the periodic table. Its symbol is Fr and its atomic number is 87. The atomic weights of Fr isotopes range widely; the stablest isotope is ^{223}Fr, also called actinium-K, with a half-life of about 21 minutes. Mendeleyev postulated the existence of element 87, but francium was not identified until 1939, when Marguerite Perey discovered it as a product of actinium decay. Francium occurs in such minute amounts in nature that it cannot be isolated. Many francium isotopes, all radioactive, are artificially produced.

Franck, César   [frahnk, say-zar']   César Auguste Franck, b. Dec. 10, 1822, d. Nov. 8, 1890, was a Belgian composer, organist, and teacher. From 1858 until his death he was organist at the Church of Sainte-Clotilde in Paris, where his pupils, friends, and admirers gathered to hear him improvise on the organ. As professor of organ at the Paris Conservatory from 1872, Franck had a great influence on the younger generation of French musicians. A kind, warmhearted man, he was much loved and revered by his pupils.

As a composer, however, Franck suffered long years of neglect. In 1879 he completed his oratorio, *The Beatitudes,* although it was not publicly performed until 3 years after his death. He composed his only symphony (in D minor) at age 66; unappreciated at its first performance in 1889, it has become a standard work in the orchestral repertoire. In his last year, Franck wrote his *Three Chorales* for organ, which are considered among the most important organ works of the 19th century. In addition to his popular symphony, he is best known for the *Violin Sonata in A* (1886), the *Symphonic Variations* (1885) for piano and orchestra, and the *Prelude, Chorale, and Fugue* (1884) for piano solo. He also wrote chamber music, operas, songs, symphonic poems, and much organ, piano, and religious music. Franck was fond of cyclic form, in which the same theme appears in more than one movement of a composition.

Franck, James [frahnk] The German physicist James Franck, b. Aug. 26, 1882, d. May 21, 1964, is known for his contributions to quantum mechanics. In 1911, Franck and Gustav Hertz began experiments on the collisions of electrons with atoms, for which they shared the Nobel Prize for physics in 1925. When Adolf Hitler came to power Franck moved to the United States, where he became a professor at the Johns Hopkins University and later at the University of Chicago. During World War II he worked on the Manhattan Project and prepared the "Franck Report," which urged President Harry Truman to demonstrate the bomb before authorizing its use.

Franco, Francisco [frahn'-koh, frahn-sees'-koh] Generalissimo Francisco Franco, b. Dec. 4, 1892, led the Nationalist forces in the SPANISH CIVIL WAR (1936–39) and ruled Spain as dictator until his death, on Nov. 20, 1975. In 1912 he volunteered for the Moroccan war and quickly distinguished himself as a courageous and intelligent officer. He was personally sober, quiet, serious, and aloof, qualities that gained him much respect but few friends. In 1923 he became commander of the Spanish Foreign Legion, and in 1925 he led the attack on Alhucemas Bay that brought victory over the Moroccan leader Abd el-Krim. In 1926 he became Spain's youngest general, and two years later he was named director of the General Military Academy in Saragossa.

Franco gained the admiration of conservatives and the hatred of the left by his repression of a miners' revolt in Asturias in 1934. In 1935 a conservative government appointed him chief of the general staff. In 1936 the Popular Front government exiled him by making him military commander of the Canary Islands, but there he joined a growing military and conservative conspiracy.

On July 18, 1936, when the Nationalist rebellion broke out, Franco flew to Morocco, where he took over the

General Francisco Franco of Spain established his authoritarian regime in 1939, after leading the Nationalist forces to victory in the Spanish Civil War. His rule, somewhat liberalized during the 1950s and '60s, saw increased industrial and economic development.

Spanish garrison. His forces then invaded southern Spain and advanced on Madrid, and by September 1936 the country was divided between government and Nationalist territories. On Oct. 1, 1936, the Nationalists appointed Franco head of state and commander in chief. In the ensuing conquest of Loyalist Spain he was cautious in strategy, cunning in diplomacy, reactionary in politics, and heartless toward his enemies. The war ended on Apr. 1, 1939.

During World War II Franco kept Spain neutral, although his fascist regime was pro-Axis. By a referendum in 1947 the regime turned itself into a monarchy, with Franco as regent, given the power to choose the next king.

In the 1950s, Franco modified his fascist image into a more moderate anti-Communist one, thereby gaining the approval of the United States, with which he concluded a military bases agreement in 1953. An improving economy and increasing contacts with Western nations led to a gradual liberalization of the regime. In 1955, Spain joined the United Nations and the following year pulled out of northern Morocco. In the last decade of his life, Franco allowed further mild liberalization and delegated greater powers to his ministers. Yet he never faltered in his conviction that he alone had saved Spain from anarchy and revolution. In 1969 he chose JUAN CARLOS, grandson of Alfonso XIII, as his successor.

Franco-Prussian War The Franco-Prussian War of 1870–71 brought on the fall of the Second French Empire and created the situation that enabled Otto von BISMARCK to establish the German Empire. It was the first European war in which both principal adversaries used railroads, the electrical telegraph, rifles, and rifled and breech-loading artillery—technological innovations that revolutionized warfare in the 19th century.

Causes. The two nations went to war nominally over the candidacy of a HOHENZOLLERN prince for the Spanish throne but actually over Prussia's growing power in Germany, which NAPOLEON III saw as a threat to French security. In 1870, Bismarck, anxious to complete the unification of Germany begun in 1866, undertook to use the issue of the Spanish succession to provoke France into an act of war that would frighten the south German states into alliance with Prussia. On July 13 the Prussian king (later Emperor WILLIAM I) sent a message to Napoleon III reporting a fairly innocuous meeting with the French ambassador. Bismarck, however, edited this Ems Telegram to suggest that the meeting consisted of an exchange of insults. He thus maneuvered the French government into a position where it had either to accept a diplomatic defeat or go to war. Napoleon III's government, judging the former course to be politically dangerous at home, declared war on Prussia on July 19, 1870.

Course of the War. When hostilities began, the French armies, outnumbered and outgeneraled, fell back from the frontier—one army to Metz, where it was besieged, the other to Sedan, where it was surrounded. The emperor surrendered the army of Sedan and himself to Bismarck on Sept. 2, 1870. When this news reached Paris on September 4, republicans proclaimed the Third Republic and established the Government of National Defense to carry on the war. The government remained in Paris but established a delegation in Tours, under Léon GAMBETTA, to direct the war effort in the provinces.

From September 23 to January 28, Paris was besieged and for the last 23 days was bombarded by German artillery. In the Loire Valley, Gambetta carried on the war for five months, but he failed to relieve Paris. On January 28 the government concluded an armistice with Bismarck. French elections in early February returned a large

A grenadier of the French imperial guard (left) *shares a drink with a* franc-tireur (right), *one of the guerrilla, or partisan, soldiers who aided in the defense of France during the Franco-Prussian War. Because the francs-tireurs were not affiliated with the national army of France, they were considered spies and were executed when captured by the Prussians. The franc-tireur carries an 11-mm chassepot rifle, a weapon adopted by French armed forces in 1866.*

The map indicates major battle sites and the routes of German invasion during the Franco-Prussian War of 1870–71. This conflict resulted in the defeat of France, which was forced to relinquish Alsace and Lorraine, and led to the creation of the German Empire.

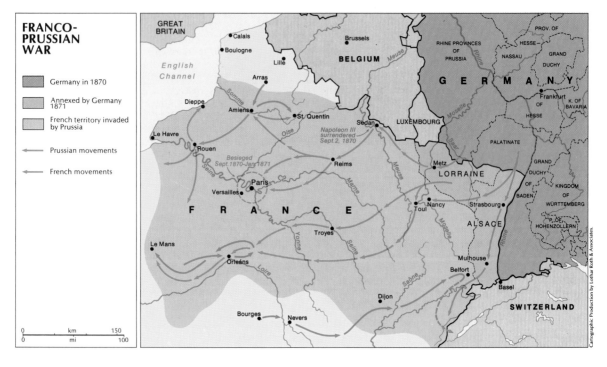

Although the Prussian-led army that invaded France in 1870 was composed of units from more than a dozen German states, most of the troops wore similar uniforms. Infantrymen from Württemberg (left), Prussia (center), and Bavaria (right) are distinguished chiefly by their headgear and regimental insignia.

majority in favor of ending the war, and a peace was quickly concluded. By the Treaty of Frankfurt (May 10, 1871), France was required to cede Alsace and part of Lorraine to Germany and to pay an indemnity of unprecedented size—5 billion francs.

Results. At the outbreak of war the south German states joined their forces with those of Prussia, and Bismarck soon persuaded all the German rulers to join in forming the new German Empire with the king of Prussia as the German emperor. The empire was formally proclaimed on Jan. 18, 1871. It was to survive only until Germany's defeat in World War I, when Germany became a republic and France recovered its lost territories.

Franconia [frang-kohn'-ee-uh]   Franconia consists of the central German lands in the MAIN RIVER valley and forms the northern segment of the state of BAVARIA in Germany. Its strategic importance lies in its being the geographical connection between north and south Germany.

It derived its name from the FRANKS who settled there early in the Middle Ages. After the Carolingian collapse, Franconia became one of the five tribal duchies of Germany, and one duke became German king as Conrad I (r. 911–18). Emperor OTTO I suppressed and partitioned the duchy in 939. The nominal duchies of Eastern and Western Franconia emerged, but ecclesiastical princes—notably the archbishops of Mainz and the bishops of Würzburg, Bamberg, and Speyer—later dominated the area. The city of Nuremberg was also important. From Western, or Rhenish, Franconia came the Salian, or Franconian,

dynasty of the HOLY ROMAN EMPIRE. In the 16th century the empire was divided into administrative areas called *Kreis* ("circles") one of which was the Franconian Circle, including most of the territories of Eastern Franconia. Most of this area passed to Bavaria on the dissolution of the empire in 1803–06.

Frank, Anne   Anne Frank, b. June 12, 1929, d. March 1945, was a young Jewish girl who kept a diary while hiding from Nazi persecution in the Netherlands during World War II. She and her family lived in a secret apartment in Amsterdam for two years before being discovered. Anne died in a German concentration camp. Her poignant diary was published in 1947, and an annotated edition was brought out by the Dutch in 1989.

Frank, Jacob   Jacob Frank, b. Galicia, 1726, d. Dec. 10, 1791, was the Polish-Jewish founder of a messianic sect called the Frankists. He claimed to be a reincarnation of SABBATAI ZEVI, founder of the Sabbateans. The followers of Frank rejected the Torah, claiming exemption from the moral law, and practiced sexually promiscuous rites.

Frank became deeply involved with extremist Sabbateans during a visit to Salonika in 1753. After his deportation to Turkey he became (1757) a Muslim. Frank and his followers returned to Poland in 1759 and accepted Christian baptism en masse. But their clannish behavior led to prosecution by the Inquisition, and Frank was imprisoned from 1760 to 1773. After his death his daughter was unable to hold the sect together, and it eventually disappeared.

Frank, Robert   Robert Frank, b. Switzerland, Nov. 9, 1924, a photographer and filmmaker, is best known for *The Americans* (1959), a book of photographs with text by Jack Kerouac. In the United States from 1947, Frank worked as a fashion photographer for *Harper's Bazaar*. On a 1955–56 Guggenheim fellowship he traveled America, producing the ironic pictures that make up his famous work. He subsequently made a series of films, including *Pull My Daisy* (1959), a short classic on the authors of the beat generation.

Frankel, Zacharias [frahng'-kul, zak-uh-ry'-uhs]   Zacharias Frankel, b. Sept. 30, 1801, d. Feb. 13, 1875, was a German-Jewish rabbi and scholar. He accepted accurate scholarly ("positive") investigation of Judaism while retaining the ritual and spirit of traditional ("historical") Judaism. Frankel's "positive-historical Judaism" became the central thrust of the Conservative Jewish seminary at Breslau, created at his urging. He was named director at its foundation in 1854.

Unlike the Reform party, Frankel opposed rejection of messianic belief and elimination of Hebrew from Jewish services. Yet he was not acceptable to the Orthodox party, because he favored consideration of modern and advanced positions. He is claimed as an ancestor by the Conservative movement in American Judaism.

Frankenstein [frank'-en-stine]   *Frankenstein; or, The Modern Prometheus* (1818), one of the most famous horror stories ever composed, was the first novel of Mary Wollstonecroft SHELLEY. It was written in 1816 as a result of a contest among Mary Shelley, her husband (Percy), Lord Byron, and Byron's physician (Polidori) to write a ghost story. The tale concerns Frankenstein, a German student scientist who learns how to breathe life into dead flesh and who thus creates a nameless monster. Physically ugly but innately good, the monster turns evil when Frankenstein refuses to accept and nurture him. After the monster kills Frankenstein's wife and brother, the scientist pursues him to the North Pole, where they both perish. In his "Preface," Shelley warned against interpreting his wife's book as an attack on romantic philosophy; rather, it attacks romantic isolation. Numerous films were based on the story, including a popular 1931 version with Boris KARLOFF as the monster.

Frankenthaler, Helen [frank'-en-thahl-ur] The American painter Helen Frankenthaler, b. Dec. 12, 1928, is one of the inventors of a style of abstract art termed COLOR-FIELD PAINTING. After studying at Bennington

Helen Frankenthaler's Blue Territory (1955) is typical of the vivid colors and lyrical moods of her work during the 1950s. With her invention of the "soak-stain" technique, Frankenthaler became an innovator among American abstract color-field painters. (Whitney Museum, New York City.)

College in Vermont she returned to her native New York and, through her relationship with art critic Clement GREENBERG, was exposed to ABSTRACT EXPRESSIONISM in the 1950s. She was influenced by the work of Arshile Gorky, Willem de Kooning, Jackson Pollock, and the cubist painters.

Frankenthaler developed an innovative staining technique in which acrylic pigment is poured directly onto unsized canvas. The result is both an expressive, personal image and a sumptuous surface of vivid color. Her *Mountains and Sea* (1952; Metropolitan Museum of Art, New York City) influenced the mature styles of the artists Morris Louis and Kenneth Noland. Since 1961, Frankenthaler's works have tended to become larger, simpler, and more geometric in form. *Guiding Red* (1967), one of her largest works, measures 9.1×4.9 m (30×16 ft).

Frankfort [frank'-furt]   Frankfort (1990 pop., 25,968) is the capital of Kentucky and the seat of Franklin County. Located in the north central part of the state on the Kentucky River, it is in the center of the famous bluegrass region noted for Thoroughbred horses. Surrounded by fertile farmland, the city is a trade and distribution center for corn and burley tobacco. Its industries include a bourbon distillery and manufacturing plants for automobile parts, furniture, shoes, and candy.

Frankfort was chosen as the capital in 1786, six years before Kentucky became a state. The Old Capitol, built (1827–29) of native limestone, now houses a historical museum.

Frankfurt am Main [frahnk'-foort ahm mine'] Frankfurt am Main, the largest city of the German state of Hesse, is located on the Main River about 32 km (20 mi) east of its confluence with the Rhine. Its name is derived from *Frankonovurt* ("the ford of the Franks"). The city has a population of 618,500 (1987 est.).

Frankfurt is one of Germany's oldest cities. Recent archaeological findings indicate that a Roman post occupied the site as early as the 1st century. The original "Old Town" was built on the right bank of the river and was enclosed by walls in the 12th century. The "New Town" was added in the 14th century and was ringed by still more fortifications. Most of these walls, however, were razed as the city expanded. The most conspicuous remnant is the Eschenheimer Tor, a 47-m (155-ft) tower dating from the 15th century. The historic center of Frankfurt is the Römerberg, a square surrounded by medieval houses.

Situated at a convenient crossroad between south and north Germany, Frankfurt developed into one of Germany's most important commercial, industrial, and transportation centers. Manufactures include chemicals, pharmaceuticals, leather goods, and electrical equipment. The city annually holds two great trade fairs, one in the spring (initiated in 1330) and one in the fall (held since 1240). It is a major railroad junction as well as an important river port. Its airport is one of the busiest in Europe.

Frankfurt am Main, a major manufacturing city and river port, is one of Germany's oldest commercial centers. Founded by the Romans during the 1st century AD, Frankfurt has hosted annual trade fairs since 1240 and is today a leading financial city.

Charlemagne held his imperial assembly in Frankfurt in 794. Emperor Louis I chose the city as his headquarters and had a large palace erected there in 822. In 843, Frankfurt became the capital of the East Frankish kingdom. The Golden Bull of 1356 designated Frankfurt as the seat for the election of the Holy Roman emperors, and beginning in 1562 they were crowned in the city's Gothic cathedral. In 1815 the city became the capital of the German Confederation. During the Revolutions of 1848 it hosted the Frankfurt Parliament, which met in the city's St. Paul Church to draft a liberal German constitution. In 1866, however, Frankfurt was occupied by the Prussian army and incorporated into Prussia, thus losing its cherished free-city status. In 1871 the peace treaty ending the Franco-Prussian War was signed there and came to be known as the Treaty of Frankfurt.

Frankfurt Parliament The Frankfurt Parliament was the popularly elected German national assembly that convened during the REVOLUTIONS OF 1848 with the purpose of creating a unified Germany. On Mar. 31, 1848, liberal leaders met in Frankfurt am Main and called on all the German states to elect delegates by universal male suffrage to a national assembly. On May 18 about 600 duly elected delegates gathered at Frankfurt; after lengthy debates, they adopted a constitution in March 1849. It provided for the union of the German states (excluding Austria) under a federal government, with a popularly elected parliament and a hereditary emperor. The crown was offered to FREDERICK WILLIAM IV of Prussia, but he refused it (April 1849), asserting that he would accept only a crown offered by the German princes. The Frankfurt Parliament soon dispersed. Its constitution later formed the basis for Otto von BISMARCK's constitution for the North German Confederation in 1867.

Frankfurter, Felix [frank'-furt-ur, fee'-liks] Felix Frankfurter, b. Vienna, Austria, Nov. 15, 1882, d. Feb. 22, 1965, was a justice of the U.S. Supreme Court known for his scholarship and his belief in judicial re-

straint. He came to the United States from Austria in 1894, studied at the College of the City of New York and in 1906 received a law degree from Harvard. During World War I he was legal advisor to Secretary of War, Newton D. Baker. He was an advisor to President Woodrow Wilson at the Paris Peace Conference in 1919. A liberal and a Zionist, Frankfurter helped found (1920) the American Civil Liberties Union. In 1927 he gained public attention by publishing a critique of the SACCO AND VANZETTI CASE. During the 1930s, Frankfurter became influential in the New Deal. President Franklin Roosevelt appointed him to the Supreme Court in 1939, where, despite his reputation as a liberal, Frankfurter turned against some liberal positions, notably in his narrow interpretation of rights under the 1st Amendment. He also believed that in a complex society the courts should be slow to interfere with acts of legislatures.

Felix Frankfurter, an American jurist, was active in several liberal causes, including the founding of the American Civil Liberties Union, before his appointment to the Supreme Court in 1939.

frankincense [frank'-in-sens] Frankincense is an aromatic gum resin from trees of the genus *Boswellia*, which grow in Somalia and in the southern Arabian peninsula. It was used in the ancient world for religious and medicinal purposes; today it is an ingredient of incense, fumigants, and perfumes. Frankincense is obtained by making a deep incision in the trunk of the tree, which exudes a milky juice that on exposure to air hardens into semiopaque lumps. From ancient times through the Middle Ages, frankincense was a principal Arabian trading commodity.

See also: MYRRH; RESIN.

Frankl, Viktor   Viktor E. Frankl, b. 1905 in Vienna, is the originator of the psychotherapeutic school of logotherapy. Frankl was professor of neurology and psychiatry in Vienna. He was imprisoned for several years during World War II in the concentration camps at Auschwitz and Dachau, and partly through that experience came to the central premise of logotherapy: that a human being's most fundamental motive is to find meaning in life.

Franklin, Aretha   The leading SOUL singer of the 1960s and early 1970s, Aretha Franklin, b. Detroit, Mich., Mar. 25, 1942, is the daughter of a prominent black minister. Her earliest musical training was in GOSPEL singing, and at age 14, she was a soloist in her father's choir. At 18 years of age she began singing blues professionally, and by the mid-1960s her records—including many songs that she wrote and produced herself—had achieved sales in the millions. Franklin's intensity, her flawless technique, four-octave range, and deep conviction place her, along with Sarah Vaughan and Ella Fitzgerald, among the greatest contemporary singers.

Franklin, Benjamin   In his many careers as printer, moralist, essayist, civic leader, scientist, inventor, statesman, diplomat, and philosopher, Benjamin Franklin became for later generations of Americans both a spokesman and a model for the national character.

He was born in Boston on Jan. 17, 1706, into a pious Puritan household. His parents raised a family of 13 children. In honoring them and in a lifelong affection for New England ways, Franklin demonstrated the lasting impact of his Puritan heritage.

The Bookman. With less than two years of formal schooling, Franklin devoured books by John Bunyan, Plutarch, Daniel Defoe, and Cotton Mather at home, and, after being apprenticed to his brother James, printer of *The New England Courant,* he read virtually every book that came to the shop. He generally absorbed the values and philosophy of the English ENLIGHTENMENT.

At the age of 16, Franklin wrote some pieces for the *Courant* signed "Silence Dogood," in which he satirized the Boston authorities and society. In one essay he argued that "hypocritical Pretenders to Religion" more injured the commonwealth than those "openly Profane." At one point James Franklin was imprisoned for similar statements, and Benjamin carried on the paper himself.

Benjamin Franklin, an 18th-century American statesman, inventor, and writer, figured prominently in the governmental organization of the emerging American nation. He made invaluable contributions to the Declaration of Independence and the U.S. Constitution.

Having thus learned to resist oppression, Benjamin refused to suffer his brother's own domineering qualities and in 1723 ran away to Philadelphia.

Though penniless and unknown, Franklin soon found a job as a printer. After a year he went to England, where he became a master printer, sowed some wild oats, astonished Londoners with his swimming feats, and lived among the aspiring writers of London. Returning to Philadelphia in 1726, he soon owned his own newspaper, the *Pennsylvania Gazette,* and began to print POOR RICHARD'S ALMANACK (1732). His business expanded further when he contracted to do the public printing of the province, and established partnerships with printers in other colonies. He also operated a book shop and became clerk of the Pennsylvania Assembly and postmaster of Philadelphia. In 1748, Franklin, aged 42, retired to live comfortably off the income from his business, managed by others, for 20 years.

The Civic Leader and Scientist. In 1727, Franklin began his career as a civic leader by organizing a club of aspiring tradesmen called the Junto, which met each week for discussion and planning. They aspired to build their own businesses, insure the growth of Philadelphia, and improve the quality of its life. Franklin thus led the Junto in founding a library (1731), a fire company (1736), a learned society (1743), a college (later the University of Pennsylvania, 1749), and an insurance company and a hospital (1751).

Franklin began yet another career when in 1740 he invented the Pennsylvania fireplace, later called the Franklin stove, which soon heated buildings all over Europe and North America. He also read treatises on electricity and began a series of experiments with his friends in Philadelphia. Experiments he proposed, first tried in

France in 1752, showed that lightning was in fact a form of electricity. Later that year his famous kite experiment, in which he flew a kite with the wire attached to a key during a thunderstorm, further established that laboratory-produced static electricity was akin to a previously mysterious and terrifying natural phenomenon. When the Royal Society in London published these discoveries, and the lightning rods he soon invented appeared on buildings all over America and Europe, Franklin became world famous. He was elected to the Royal Society in 1756 and to the French Academy of Sciences in 1772. His later achievements included formulating a theory of heat absorption, measuring the Gulf Stream, designing ships, tracking storm paths, and inventing the bifocal lens.

The Politician and Provincial Agent. In 1751, Franklin was elected to the Pennsylvania Assembly, thus beginning nearly 40 years as a public official. In 1754 he presented the Plan of Union to the ALBANY CONGRESS; in it he proposed partial self-government for the American colonies. A year later Franklin supported the ill-fated expedition of Gen. Edward BRADDOCK to recapture Fort Duquesne, and he persuaded the Quaker-dominated Pennsylvania Assembly to pass the colony's first militia law. He himself led a military expedition to the Lehigh Valley, where he established forts to protect frontiersmen from French and Indian raiders. As Franklin helped the empire fight for its life, however, he saw that colonial and ministerial ideas of governing the colonies were far apart. When he went to England in 1757 as agent of the Pennsylvania Assembly, he was alarmed to hear Lord Granville, president of the Privy Council, declare that for the colonies,

Poor Richard, 1733.

AN

Almanack

For the Year of Chrift

1733,

Being the Firft after LEAP YEAR:

And makes fince the Creation	Years
By the Account of the Eastern *Greeks*	7241
By the Latin Church, when ☉ ent. ♈	6932
By the Computation of *W. W.*	5742
By the *Roman* Chronology	5682
By the *Jewish* Rabbies	5494

Wherein is contained

The Lunations, Eclipfes, Judgment of the Weather, Spring Tides, Planets Motions & mutual Afpects, Sun and Moon's Rifing and Setting, Length of Days, Time of High Water, Fairs, Courts, and obfervable Days.

Fitted to the Latitude of Forty Degrees, and a Meridian of Five Hours Weft from *London*, but may without fenfible Error, ferve all the adjacent Places, even from *Newfoundland* to *South-Carolina*.

By *RICHARD SAUNDERS*, Philom.

PHILADELPHIA:

Printed and fold by *B. FRANKLIN*, at the New Printing-Office near the Market.

The frontispiece to Benjamin Franklin's Poor Richard's Almanack (1732–57) indicates that the almanac contained all the meteorological and astronomical information common to the genre. In addition, Franklin's compendium was peppered with the original aphorisms that made his work enormously popular.

the king's instructions were "the *Law of the Land:* for the King is the Legislator of the Colonies."

In England from 1757 to 1762, Franklin worked to persuade British officials to limit proprietary power in Pennsylvania. While in England he was presented honorary doctor's degrees by the universities of St. Andrews (1759) and Oxford (1762).

At home from 1762 to 1764, Franklin traveled throughout the colonies, reorganizing the American postal system. He also built a new house on Market Street in Philadelphia—now reconstructed and open to visitors—and otherwise provided for his family, which included the former Deborah Read, his wife since 1730; their daughter Sally, who married Richard Bache and had a large family of her own; and his illegitimate son, William. Though he was appointed governor of New Jersey in 1762, William became a Loyalist during the American Revolution, completely estranged from his father.

As an influential politician, Franklin opposed the bloody revenges of frontier people against innocent Indians after PONTIAC'S REBELLION (1763) and helped to defend Philadelphia when the angry pioneers threatened its peace. In 1764 he lost his seat in the assembly in an especially scurrilous campaign. However, his party sent him to England in 1764 to petition that Pennsylvania be taken over as a royal colony.

The Defender of American Rights. The crisis precipitated by the STAMP ACT (1765) pushed that effort into the background and propelled Franklin into a new role as chief defender of American rights in Britain. At first he advised obedience to the act until it could be repealed, but news of violent protest against it in America stiffened his own opposition. Later he opposed the TOWNSHEND ACTS (1767) because such "acts of oppression" would "sour American tempers" and perhaps even "hasten their final revolt." When the British Parliament passed the Tea Act (1773), which hurt the colonial merchants, Franklin protested in a series of finely honed satirical essays. As these satires circulated in England, Franklin wrote his sister: "I have held up a Looking-Glass in which some of the Ministers may see their ugly faces, and the Nation its Injustice."

In 1773, Franklin's friends in Massachusetts, against his instructions, published letters by Gov. Thomas HUTCHINSON that Franklin had obtained in confidence. Apparently exposed as a dishonest schemer, Franklin was denounced before the Privy Council in January 1774 and stripped of his postmaster general's position. He continued to work for conciliation, but the Boston Tea Party and Britain's oppressive response to it doomed such efforts. In March 1775, Franklin sailed for home.

From April 1775 to October 1776, Franklin served on the Pennsylvania Committee of Safety and in the Continental Congress, submitted articles of confederation for the united colonies, proposed a new constitution for Pennsylvania, and helped draft the Declaration of Independence. He readily signed the declaration, thus becoming a revolutionist at the age of 70.

The Diplomat. In October 1776, Franklin and his two grandsons sailed for France, where he achieved an amazing personal triumph and gained critical French aid for the Revolutionary War. Parisian literary and scientific circles hailed him as a living embodiment of Enlightenment virtues. Wigless and dressed in plain brown clothes, he was called *le Bonhomme Richard.* Franklin was at his best creating the legend of his life among the ladies of Paris, writing witty letters, printing bagatelles, and telling anecdotes.

He moved slowly at first in his diplomacy. France wanted to injure Britain but could not afford to help the American rebels unless eventual success seemed assured. Franklin thus worked behind the scenes to send war supplies across the Atlantic, thwart British diplomacy, and make friends with influential French officials. He overcame his own doubts about the possibly dishonest dealings of his fellow commissioner Silas DEANE in channeling war materials to American armies, but the third commissioner, Arthur Lee (1740–92), bitterly condemned both Deane and Franklin. Despite these quarrels, in February 1778, following news of the American victory at Saratoga, the three commissioners were able to sign the vital French alliance.

Franklin then became the first American minister to France—and generally the main representative of the new United States in Europe. Though nearly 80 years old, he oversaw the dispatch of French armies and navies to North America, supplied American armies with French munitions, outfitted John Paul JONES—whose famous ship the *Bonhomme Richard* was named in Franklin's honor—and secured a succession of loans from the nearly bankrupt French treasury.

After the loss at Yorktown (1781) finally persuaded British leaders that they could not win the war, Franklin made secret contact with peace negotiators sent from London. In these delicate negotiations he proposed treaty articles close to those finally agreed to: complete American independence, access to the Newfoundland fishing grounds, evacuation of British forces from all occupied areas, and a western boundary on the Mississippi. Together with John JAY, Franklin represented the United States in signing the Treaty of Paris (Sept. 3, 1783), by which the world's foremost military power recognized the independence of the new nation.

Franklin traveled home in 1785. Though in his 80th year and suffering from painful bladder stones, he nonetheless accepted election for three years as president of Pennsylvania and resumed active roles in the Pennsylvania Society for Promoting the Abolition of Slavery, the American Philosophical Society, and the University of Pennsylvania. At the Constitutional Convention of 1787, although he was too weak to stand, Franklin's good humor and gift for compromise often helped to prevent bitter disputes.

Franklin's final public pronouncements urged ratification of the Constitution and approved the inauguration of the new federal government under his admired friend George Washington. Cheerful and optimistic to the last, Benjamin Franklin died in Philadelphia on Apr. 17, 1790.

Franklin, Sir John   British Rear Admiral Sir John Franklin, b. Apr. 16, 1786, d. June 11, 1847, discov-

After two overland expeditions in northern Canada, British Rear Adm. Sir John Franklin set out in 1845 to find the Northwest Passage. After the entire party had disappeared, searchers uncovered evidence that he had found the passage but that he and his crew were dead.

ered the NORTHWEST PASSAGE but disappeared in the course of the exploration. Between 1819 and 1822, Franklin followed the Coppermine River and traced the shoreline east of Coronation Gulf along the Arctic coast of Canada. In a second expedition (1825–27) he descended the Mackenzie River and explored the region west of the river's mouth. In recognition of these services, he was knighted in 1829.

In 1845, Franklin was sent in search of the Northwest Passage. His ships, *Erebus* and *Terror,* were last seen in Baffin Bay on July 25 or 26, 1845. When nothing was heard from the party, no fewer than 40 expeditions were sent to find him. In 1859 a search vessel outfitted by Lady Franklin discovered a cairn that revealed the date and place of Sir John's death and that he had, in fact, found the Northwest Passage.

Franklin, John Hope   John Hope Franklin, b. Rentiesville, Okla., Jan. 2, 1915, an American historian, taught at the University of Chicago from 1964 to 1982, when he went to Duke University. He earned his doctorate from Harvard in 1941 and has written extensively on blacks in the United States. His books include *From Slavery to Freedom* (1947; 5th ed., 1980), *The Militant South, 1800–1861* (1956), and *Racial Equality in America* (1976).

Franklin, State of   Franklin was a short-lived state established after the Revolutionary War in what is now eastern Tennessee. North Carolina claimed jurisdiction over the area and offered to cede it to the federal government in 1784. Its inhabitants retaliated by forming their own state, with land speculator John SEVIER as governor. The United States refused to recognize Franklin, and when Sevier's term expired in 1788 and no successor was chosen, North Carolina resumed control.

franklinite   Franklinite is a zinc and iron-manganese OXIDE MINERAL, $Zn(FeMn)_2O_4$, that occurs abundantly only at Franklin, N.J., where, associated with zincite and willemite, it has been mined as an ore of zinc. A member of the SPINEL group, franklinite forms brilliantly metallic, iron-black octahedral crystals, rounded grains, and granular masses.

Franks The Franks were a group of GERMANIC PEOPLES inhabiting the lower and middle Rhine Valley by the 3d century AD, when they are first mentioned by classical authors. Identified by these writers as the Salians, the Ripuarians, and the Chatti, they are said to have shared the same language and to have had many similar laws and customs.

Toward the middle of the 3d century the Franks began penetrating the Roman frontier around Mainz. They were driven back by Emperor Probus. In 358, JULIAN THE APOSTATE handed over Toxandria, the region between the Meuse and the Scheldt rivers, to the Salian Franks, who became Roman allies and provided troops for the imperial army.

The Salian Franks were divided into several groups led by chiefs (*reguli*). One of these groups, the MEROVINGIANS,

This 14th-century miniature portrays the coronation of the Merovingian ruler Clovis, founder of the Frankish kingdom during the early Middle Ages. After ending Roman domination in Gaul (486), Clovis gained control and unified most of Gaul.

which took its name from the chief Merovech (Merowen), was particularly successful. Merovech and his successor, Childeric (d. 481), extended Salian domination to the south, perhaps as far as the Somme River. Childeric aided the Romans, but after the death (461) of Emperor Majorian he sought to overthrow Aegidius, the imperial governor in northern Gaul. Aegidius forced Childeric into exile among the Thuringians, but he returned after a few years and, in alliance with some Saxons, defeated the Romans.

Syagrius, Aegidius's son and successor, kept Childeric from moving his people south of the Somme, but another *regulus* took control of Le Mans. Cambrai and Thérouanne were also held by Salian *reguli*. CLOVIS, Childeric's son, conquered most of Gaul and unified the Franks under the Merovingian dynasty. Clovis also converted to Christianity.

The Ripuarian Franks and the Chatti raided across the middle Rhine frontier during the first quarter of the 5th century. In the wake of the Hunnic invasion of Gaul, a band of Ripuarians gained control of Cologne. By c.470, Trier was in Ripuarian hands, and thereafter Metz, Toul, and Verdun fell to the Franks. The CAROLINGIAN dynasty, which succeeded the Merovingians, is considered to have been of Ripuarian origin.

Under the Carolingians, the Franks formed a vast empire that reached its pinnacle in the reign (768–814) of CHARLEMAGNE. This empire was divided in the mid-9th century, from it emerging the West Frankish kingdom (France) and the East Frankish kingdom (Germany).

This map illustrates the expansion of the Frankish kingdom from its founding by Clovis (r. 481–511) through the reign of Charlemagne. It was under the Carolingian Charlemagne, who was crowned emperor by the pope in 800, that the Frankish empire reached its height.

EXPANSION OF FRANKISH POWER, 481-814

- ■ Territory in 481
- ■ Conquests of Clovis, 486-511
- ■ Conquests, 531-768
- ■ Conquests of Charlemagne, 768-814

Franz Ferdinand, Austrian Archduke [frahnts fair'-dee-nahnt] Franz Ferdinand, b. Dec. 18, 1863, was the Austrian archduke whose assassination by a Serbian nationalist at Sarajevo on June 28, 1914, sparked WORLD WAR I. A nephew of Emperor FRANCIS JOSEPH, he became heir apparent after the suicide (1889) of Archduke RUDOLF. The Emperor, however, disapproved of his marriage (1900) to a Czech commoner, Sophie Chotek, and their children were barred from the succession. Although reactionary, Franz Ferdinand for a time favored the reorganization of AUSTRIA-HUNGARY to create a third

Archduke Franz Ferdinand, heir to the Austro-Hungarian thrones, and his wife, Sophie Chotek, were assassinated by a Serbian nationalist while visiting the Bosnian city of Sarajevo in 1914. Their deaths resulted in Austria's declaration of war against Serbia, marking the opening hostilities of World War I.

kingdom of Croatia. This was one reason for his assassination by the Serbian nationalist Gavrilo Princip.

Franz Josef   see FRANCIS JOSEPH, EMPEROR OF AUSTRIA

___

Franz Josef Land [frans joh'-zef]   Franz Josef Land, an archipelago of about 187 islands in the northern part of the Barents Sea, is the northernmost possession of the USSR. The land area is about 20,700 km² (8,000 mi²) and is divided into three main island groups. Most of the terrain includes elevated plateaus that are covered by ice. The area was discovered by an Austro-Hungarian expedition in 1873 and was named after the Austrian emperor; in 1928 the USSR claimed the region.

___

Fraser, Dawn   The Australian Dawn Fraser, b. Sept. 4, 1937, became the first swimmer to win the same event in the Olympic Games three different times. She was the greatest sprinter in women's history, winning the 100-meter freestyle event in the 1956, 1960, and 1964 Olympics; she held the record in that event for 16 years. She was the first woman to break 1 minute for 100 meters, a record she broke 9 successive times. She set 27 individual records plus many relay records before her suspension for a prank at the 1964 Olympics.

___

Fraser, J. Malcolm   John Malcolm Fraser, b. Melbourne, May 21, 1930, was appointed prime minister of Australia on Nov. 11, 1975, by Gov.-Gen. Sir John KERR after Kerr had dismissed the incumbent prime minister, Gough WHITLAM. Fraser called a general election in December 1975, which his party won with ease.

Fraser was elected to Parliament in 1955, later serving as minister for the army (1966–68), for education and science (1968–69, 1971–72), and for defense

(1969–71). He was elected leader of the Liberal party in March 1975.

As prime minister, Fraser reduced government expenditures, cut back public services, reorganized the health administration to reduce the government's role, and reduced inflation while cutting the income tax. His austere strategies were not popular, however. His Liberal-Country party coalition, which won a huge majority in the general election of December 1977, was returned with a much-reduced majority in October 1980 and was decisively defeated by the Labor party, led by Robert HAWKE, in March 1983.

J. Malcolm Fraser was prime minister of Australia from 1975 to 1983. Although he was able to curb inflation and attract foreign investment to develop Australia's natural resources, his conservative economic policies and the lifting of the ban on the mining and exporting of uranium aroused widespread opposition.

___

Fraser, James Earle   James Earle Fraser, b. Winona, Minn., Nov. 4, 1876, d. Oct. 11, 1953, created some of the best-known sculpture in the United States. Fraser modeled the reliefs of a buffalo and an Indian's head for the nickel issued in 1913. His famous *The End of the Trail* (Cowboy Hall of Fame, Oklahoma City, Okla.), made for the 1915 Pacific Panama Exposition in San Francisco from a smaller version done in 1894, portrays a beaten warrior on a broken pony and symbolizes the fate of the Plains Indians. Fraser's bronze equestrian statue (1923–40) of Theodore Roosevelt stands in front of New York City's Museum of Natural History.

___

Fraser, Simon   Simon Fraser, b. Bennington, Vt. (then N.Y.), 1776, d. Apr. 18, 1862, was a Canadian fur trader and explorer. He moved to Canada with his mother after his father, a Loyalist, died in prison during the American Revolution. In 1792 he joined the NORTH WEST COMPANY, and in 1805 he took charge of the company's expansion west of the Rockies. In 1808, believing it to be the Columbia, he explored to its mouth the dangerous river that today bears his name. Fraser's epic journey proved that the river was unsuitable for transporting goods and furs.

Later taking charge of his company's Red River department, Fraser was one of the Nor'westers charged with complicity in the massacre of Seven Oaks, when an armed band attacked the RED RIVER SETTLEMENT in 1816. Fraser retired soon after and settled in Upper Canada (now Ontario).

Fraser River The Fraser, a major river in British Columbia, Canada, rises at Yellowhead Pass, Alberta, on the western slopes of the Rocky Mountains. It flows northwest in the Rocky Mountain Trench to Prince George, British Columbia, then south to the Strait of Georgia near Vancouver. The river drains a huge, scenic area of 217,800 km² (84,100 mi²), receiving the Nechako, Quesnel, Thompson, and Chilcotin rivers as well as numerous smaller streams along its 1,369-km (850-mi) course. The Fraser is navigable to Yale, approximately 145 km (90 mi) from its mouth, through the cliffs of Fraser Canyon. Hydroelectric development is prohibited to protect the river's valuable salmon-spawning runs.

fraternal societies Fraternal societies are private, voluntary associations of persons with shared interests. Nonprofit organizations, they serve a social function but also often have civic or benevolent purposes—in the tradition of their 16th-century forerunners, the English "friendly societies," which provided members with sickness and death benefits. Many are SECRET SOCIETIES, like the Freemasons. Some, such as B'NAI B'RITH and the KNIGHTS OF COLUMBUS, have religious backgrounds. Fraternal groups may also be esoteric (the ROSICRUCIANS) or political (TAMMANY HALL).

An early U.S. group, the Independent Order of Odd Fellows, formed in 1819, declared its independence from its English parent in 1842. Other notable U.S. fraternal benevolent life insurance groups began during and after the Civil War, including the Knights of Pythias (1864), the Benevolent and Protective Order of Elks (1868), and the Loyal Order of Moose (1888).

fraternities and sororities Fraternities and sororities are organizations that bring together men and women, respectively, for social, honor, service, or recognition purposes. Social fraternities and sororities, usually known by their Greek letters, are commonly found on American college campuses and may be national, with branches at many colleges, or on one campus only. PHI BETA KAPPA, the first honor society, or fraternity, was established in 1776.

History. Most social fraternities began in semisecrecy, possibly in imitation of FREEMASONRY, and bore the initials of Greek letters. Kappa Alpha at Union College was the first (1825). Adelphean at Wesleyan College, Georgia, was the first sorority, established in 1851. Fraternities grew rapidly after 1840. Divisiveness and controversy existed from the beginning, and animosity resulted from the fraternities' and sororities' choosing only the more socially favored as members, and then encouraging an intense-

ly conformist style of thought and behavior among those selected. By 1898 a large minority of male American college students were fraternity members. Fraternities and sororities had developed into established national organizations, run by their alumni, and operating local chapters on many campuses. Separate fraternities and sororities were formed by black students, who were excluded from white societies; and fraternities and sororities for people of various ethnic groups and in certain academic disciplines were also established.

Recent Trends. During the late 1960s and early 1970s, as college students became involved in politics and alternative life-styles, fraternities and sororities temporarily lost favor. Certain societies had already been under attack for discriminating against nonwhite students. Some chapters closed, and many had trouble filling their available spaces. Between 1965 and 1972 fraternities nationally lost 20 percent of their undergraduate members, so that by 1972 the number of students who became fraternity members was fewer than 4 percent of the male college population. At this time there were 4,407 national fraternity chapters, with an average of 34 undergraduates in each chapter. Since the late 1970s fraternities and sororities have experienced a steady revival despite occasional resistance, such as Amherst College's abolition of its fraternities in 1984.

fraud Courts have distinguished two types of fraud, actual fraud and constructive fraud. Actual fraud is intentional criminal deception for the purpose of inducing another to part with something of value, to acquire something of less than apparent value, or to surrender a legal right. Schemes specifically intended to cheat someone, such as selling shares in nonexistent plots of land, are actual frauds. Constructive frauds are words, acts, or omissions that tend to mislead or deceive someone or violate a confidence but that are not necessarily of malicious intent. Selling a house while forgetting to mention a chronically malfunctioning heating system is an example of constructive fraud. In civil law fraud is an element in the TORT of deceit (fraudulent representation). To collect DAMAGES or to void a fraudulent contract, the plaintiff must usually show that the defendant knowingly made false statements and deliberately tricked the plaintiff into doing something the plaintiff would not have done if in possession of the facts.

Some examples of fraud include confidence games, EMBEZZLEMENT, FORGERY, the use of stolen credit cards, and impersonation. Other common practices are investment frauds in which swindlers sell worthless securities. Government attempts to prevent fraud led to the creation (1934) of the Securities and Exchange Commission, disclosure laws such as the Truth in Lending Act (1968), and other forms of consumer protection.

Fraunhofer lines [frown'-hoh-fur] In astronomy, Fraunhofer lines are the numerous dark lines that appear in the SPECTRUM of the Sun and other stars. Although they were first observed and mentioned by the British physicist William H. Wollaston in 1802, the lines are named for Joseph von Fraunhofer, the German optician who made the first detailed study of them, starting in about 1814. Approximately 25,000 Fraunhofer lines have been mapped in the Sun's spectrum. The lines are due to atoms (not molecules) in the star's lower atmosphere that selectively absorb light at the same wavelengths that, under different conditions, they would emit. Thus the presence of a given element in the star may be proved by demonstrating the existence of Fraunhofer lines in the same positions as in that element's emission spectrum. Fraunhofer designated the more prominent lines by letters, a system still in use.

Frazer, Sir James   The Scottish anthropologist and classicist Sir James George Frazer, b. Glasgow, Jan. 1, 1854, d. May 7, 1941, is best known for his masterpiece, The *Golden Bough* (2 vols., 1890; 3d ed., 12 vols., 1911–15; abr. 1 vol. ed., 1922), a monumental study in comparative myth and religion. Written in an eloquent style, the influential work is especially important for its insight into the nature of MAGIC and its examination of Europe's pagan past. Frazer was educated at the universities of Glasgow and Cambridge and was a fellow of Trinity College, Cambridge. His other writings include *Totemism and Exogamy* (1910) and *Folk-lore in the Old Testament* (1918).

Frazier, Edward Franklin   Edward Franklin Frazier, b. Baltimore, Md., Sept. 24, 1894, d. May 17, 1962, was an African-American sociologist whose overall concern was the progress, organization, and function of the black family. He wrote *The Negro Family in the United States* (1939), in which he analyzed the destructive effects of slavery and prejudice on the black family, and *Black Bourgeoisie* (1957). Frazier was chairman of Howard University's sociology department (1934–59).

Frazier, Joe   Joseph Frazier, b. Beaufort, S.C., Jan. 12, 1944, an American boxer who became heavyweight champion, is best known for his bouts with Muhammad Ali, which were enormous competitive and financial successes. Frazier turned professional after winning the 1964 Olympic heavyweight title, then emerged with the world title after Ali was stripped of it in 1967. Frazier continued undefeated and eventually defeated Ali in 1971. He lost the title to George Foreman in 1973 but fought and lost to Ali two more times and to Foreman once more before retiring with a 32–4 record in 1976.

freckle   Freckles are small, yellowish or brownish spots on the skin caused by an accumulation of the skin pigment melanin. The pigment cells respond unevenly to sunlight. Freckles appear in susceptible, usually fair-skinned persons as a result of exposure to sunlight and

may become permanent. Freckles can sometimes be minimized by the use of sunscreen lotions containing para-aminobenzoic acid (PABA).

Frederick   Frederick is an agricultural center in north central Maryland. The seat of Frederick County, it was settled in 1733 and has a population of 40,148 (1990). The city is the site of Hood College, a state school for the deaf, and Fort Detrick Army Research Laboratory. Frederick's historical attractions include the grave of Francis Scott Key and the home of Barbara Fritchie, a legendary Civil War heroine.

Frederick I, Elector of Brandenburg   Frederick I, elector of Brandenburg, b. 1371?, d. Sept. 20, 1440, was the first HOHENZOLLERN ruler in Berlin, where his descendants reigned until 1918. By his many services as *Burggraf* (count) of Nuremberg, Frederick won the gratitude of the German king Sigismund, who rewarded him with the office of administrator of Brandenburg (1411) and then elector (1417). Frederick's chief tasks were to curb the fractious nobility, restore order, repel external foes, and recover alienated properties. He unsuccessfully schemed (1421–24) to acquire the Polish crown and feuded with the Teutonic Knights.

Frederick III, King of Denmark   Frederick III, b. Mar. 18, 1609, d. Feb. 9, 1670, king of Denmark and Norway, established the most thoroughly absolute monarchy in Europe. A younger son of CHRISTIAN IV, he grew up in Germany as administrator of Bremen and Verden. In 1644 these territories were conquered by Sweden.

Frederick succeeded his father to the throne in 1648, his older brother having died in 1647. War with Sweden in 1657–60 made him popular for his defense of Copenhagen. It also gave him control of an army, which he used in 1660 to establish a completely absolute royal regime that survived for 200 years. His son, Christian V, succeeded him.

Frederick IV, King of Denmark   Frederick IV, b. Oct. 11, 1671, d. Oct. 12, 1730, was king of Denmark and Norway during the Great NORTHERN WAR. He succeeded his father, Christian V, in 1699. The wars against Sweden in 1700 and 1709–20 gave him control of the Swedish satellite, Holstein-Gottorp (also called ducal Schleswig), on Denmark's southern border. Frederick reformed Danish education, the national militia, and the status of peasants. He sponsored one of the earliest foreign missions from Protestant Europe—to India. Unhappily married, he twice became a bigamist. He was succeeded by his son, Christian VI.

Frederick VI, King of Denmark   Frederick VI, b. Jan. 28, 1768, d. Dec. 3, 1839, was the last Danish king to rule Norway as well as Denmark. In 1784 he led a bloodless coup that made him the actual ruler, though his insane father, Christian VII, remained king until 1808. Frederick and his advisors carried through reforms to establish an independent landowning peasantry and universal education in Denmark. Allying with France in 1807, he lost Norway when Napoleon I was defeated in 1814. Immensely popular, Frederick was succeeded by his cousin's son, Christian VIII.

Frederick VII, King of Denmark

Frederick VII, b. Oct. 6, 1808, d. Nov. 15, 1863, king of Denmark, ended absolute monarchy in his country. He became king in 1848 when his father, Christian VIII, died. Facing disturbances, he signed the constitution of 1849, establishing parliamentary government. This act and his congeniality made him tremendously popular. He recognized CHRISTIAN IX as his successor but left his kingdom on the verge of war with Prussia and Austria over SCHLESWIG-HOLSTEIN.

Frederick I, King of Germany and Holy Roman Emperor

(Frederick Barbarossa)   Frederick I, or Frederick Barbarossa, b. probably 1122, d. June 10, 1190, German king and Holy Roman emperor, was one of the outstanding medieval German rulers. An intelligent statesman, he entertained an exalted concept of his dignity as Roman emperor and introduced the use of the word *Holy* in the title. This was intended to reflect a mystical association between himself and the destiny of Christianity.

Frederick was the nephew of the German king CONRAD III, whom he was elected to succeed in 1152. His HOHENSTAUFEN dynasty had its base in Swabia and Franconia; Burgundy came into his hands by his marriage (1156) to its heiress, Beatrix.

Frederick I (Barbarossa), German king (1152–90) and Holy Roman emperor (1155–90), is shown flanked by his sons, the future emperor Henry VI (left) and Frederick, duke of Swabia. Barbarossa was a powerful statesman and believer in his mystical destiny as emperor.

Frederick's concept of government was feudal and hierarchical. He created the rank of *Reichsfürst,* prince of the empire, for his chief vassals. His major rival was the Welf, or Guelph, HENRY THE LION. To placate Henry, Frederick in 1154 confirmed his rights as duke of both Saxony and Bavaria. When Henry later refused military service, Frederick in 1180 broke his power and seized his duchies.

Anxious to assert his imperial power in Italy, Frederick undertook six expeditions across the Alps. On his first expedition (1154–55) he overthrew the republican ARNOLD OF BRESCIA in Rome and was crowned (1155) by the pope. Later his chief foe was the Lombard League, supported by Pope Alexander III. The Lombards defeated Frederick at Legnano in 1176, but the Treaty of Constance (1183) acknowledged his sovereignty over Lombardy while reducing his actual control.

In 1186, Frederick arranged the marriage of his son, the future HENRY VI, to Constance, heiress of Sicily; this brought the Norman kingdom of Sicily into Hohenstaufen hands. Joining the Third CRUSADE, Frederick led his army across Europe into Anatolia, where he drowned.

Frederick II, King of Germany and Holy Roman Emperor

Frederick II, b. Dec. 26, 1194, d. Dec. 13, 1250, German king (1212–20), king of Sicily (1197–1250), and Holy Roman emperor (1220–50), was a fascinating personality. He was a Renaissance man with a broad cultural outlook and intellectual gifts, but his policies irrevocably weakened the German monarchy.

The son of Emperor HENRY VI and Constance of Sicily, Frederick grew up in Sicily as the ward and vassal of Pope INNOCENT III. When Henry VI died (1197), his son was recognized as king of Sicily, but in Germany PHILIP OF SWABIA and OTTO IV were elected rival kings. In 1212, Pope Innocent persuaded Frederick to go north to assert his hereditary rights. First, however, Frederick promised to resign his Sicilian kingdom, for the pope feared the loss of his own freedom should both kingdoms be held by the same man.

The Battle of Bouvines (1214) made Frederick master of Germany, where he stayed until 1220. With the permission of Pope Honorius III, he then exchanged Germany for Sicily as the kingdom he could retain, assigning Germany to his infant son Henry. His policy toward Germany was to make any concession necessary to avoid controversy. He gave away one royal prerogative after another and compelled his unwilling sons, Henry and CONRAD IV, to acquiesce.

Frederick preferred the greater freedom of the Norman kingdom of Sicily, whose government he organized into unparalleled centralized efficiency. The Constitutions of Melfi (1231) are his outstanding pieces of legislation. He quarreled with the Lombard towns and the popes, however. Honorius III excommunicated him in 1227 for violating his vow to go on crusade. Frederick then recovered Jerusalem from the Muslims by diplomacy. Already married (1225) to Isabel of Brienne, queen of Jerusalem, he crowned himself king of Jerusalem in 1229. In 1239, Pope GREGORY IX excommunicated Frederick on charges of heresy, and INNOCENT IV induced the Council of Lyon (1245) to declare him deposed. Frederick continued to fight both the popes and Lombards with mixed success until his death.

Frederick III, King of Germany and Holy Roman Emperor

Frederick III, b. Sept. 9, 1415, d. Aug. 19, 1493, German king from 1440, was the first HABSBURG to be crowned Holy Roman emperor by the pope and the last emperor to be crowned in Rome (1452). Aware of the limitations of his authority within Germany, he concentrated his energies on family matters.

Frederick helped force dissolution of the Council of Basel, which was asserting conciliar (see CONCILIARISM) supremacy over the popes. His secretary, Aeneas Sylvius Piccolomini (later Pope PIUS II), first brought Renaissance influences to Germany. Frederick's greatest dynastic achievement was to arrange the marriage (1477) of MARY OF BURGUNDY to his son Maximilian (later Emperor MAXIMILIAN I), which set the stage for the Habsburg domination of Europe.

Frederick I, King of Prussia

Frederick I, b. July 11, 1657, d. Feb. 25, 1713, the first king of PRUSSIA, was the son of FREDERICK WILLIAM, the Great Elector, whom he succeeded as elector of Brandenburg in 1688.

The one substantial political achievement of his largely undistinguished reign came at the outset of the War of the SPANISH SUCCESSION. By agreeing to support the claims of the Austrian Habsburgs to the territorial possessions in Spain, Frederick received approval from Emperor LEOPOLD I to assume a royal title, and on Jan. 18, 1701, proclaimed himself "king in Prussia." His new crown was an immediate source of prestige for the HOHENZOLLERN dynasty and served as a symbol of unity for the rising state of Brandenburg-Prussia.

Frederick II, King of Prussia

(Frederick the Great)   Frederick II, b. Jan. 24, 1712, d. Aug. 17, 1786, known to posterity as Frederick the Great, ruled the kingdom of PRUSSIA from 1740 to 1786. His early interest in literature and music brought him into conflict with his authoritarian father, FREDERICK WILLIAM I, who imposed a rigidly structured military upbringing upon the crown prince. In 1730, Frederick tried to escape his father's tyranny by fleeing the court. He was soon captured, however, and imprisoned in the fortress of Küstrin, where his father forced him to witness the execution of his close friend Lieutenant Katte.

Determined to regain his father's trust, Frederick immersed himself in administrative duties. As a reward Frederick William allowed him to spend his leisure hours studying philosophy, playing the flute, writing poetry, and corresponding with famous intellectuals, most notably Voltaire.

Succeeding his father on May 31, 1740, Frederick immediately invaded SILESIA, a possession of the Austrian

Frederick II, King of Prussia (1740–86), called Frederick the Great, successfully pursued a course destined to aggrandize Prussia. A brilliant general whose wars secured Silesia for Prussia, "Old Fritz" also instituted important legal and administrative reforms.

Habsburgs. He spent the next 23 years defending this valuable conquest. Illustrious campaigns in the War of the AUSTRIAN SUCCESSION (1740–48) and the SEVEN YEARS' WAR (1756–63) demonstrated his military talents and enabled him to consolidate Prussia's position as a leading European power.

To preserve his gains, Frederick followed a peaceful course after 1763. He negotiated the first partition of Poland with Austria and Russia in 1772 (see POLAND, PARTITIONS OF), and through diplomacy he acquired all of West Prussia except the cities of Danzig (Gdánsk) and Thorn (Toruń). His major preoccupation, however, was with the rehabilitation of his war-ravaged domains. Referred to by his subjects as "Old Fritz," he implemented far-reaching reforms that made his regime a model of 18th-century enlightened despotism.

Frederick abolished torture, except for crimes such as murder and treason, and permitted some freedom of speech and press. His religious toleration extended to Jesuits, but not to Jews, whom he viewed as "useless to the state." Frederick also improved Prussia's judicial system.

In social policies Frederick was less progressive, defending traditional distinctions of rank and privilege. He relieved the burdens of peasants who lived on his own lands but did little to ameliorate the lot of serfs tied to the private estates of JUNKERS.

Frederick's economic policies were influenced by MERCANTILISM. Hoping to turn Prussia into a self-sufficient state, he limited the export of raw materials, erected tariff barriers against foreign goods, and removed many internal tolls. He subsidized the metallurgy and textile industries, granted monopolies for products such as porcelain, silk, and tobacco, and introduced scientific methods of cattle breeding and crop rotation from western Europe. He also drained swamps in the Oder and Vistula river valleys, initiated reforestation projects, and settled approximately 300,000 immigrant farmers in sparsely populated areas.

No monarch ever worked harder than Frederick the Great. He maintained a vigorous schedule that customarily started at six in the morning. Unwilling to delegate authority, he wanted all important governmental business to pass across his desk at the palace of Sans Souci near Potsdam. He depended upon written reports from his ministers and personal inspection tours in his supervision of every branch of his administration. Although he stifled initiative and independence, Frederick raised professional standards in his civil service by treating corruption and mismanagement with the utmost severity.

By the time of "Old Fritz's" death, Prussia's population was approaching 6,000,000 and its army numbered 200,000 men. He left his successor, FREDERICK WILLIAM II, a full treasury and a smoothly operating, disciplined bureaucracy. Unfortunately, his system of government required able leadership, and those who followed him lacked his energy, intelligence, and dedication.

Frederick III, Emperor of Germany

Frederick III, b. Oct. 18, 1831, d. June 15, 1888, emperor of Germany, reigned for only 99 days in 1888. The son of WILLIAM I, king of Prussia and emperor of Germany, Frederick married (1858) Victoria, eldest daughter of Queen Victoria of Britain. As crown prince, he served in the Franco-Prussian War (1870–71) and was a patron of the arts. Frederick was considered a liberal, and his death, from cancer, disappointed many who had looked forward to his rule. He was succeeded by his son WILLIAM II.

Frederick III, Elector of Saxony

(Frederick the Wise)   The Saxon ruler Frederick III, b. Jan. 17, 1463, d. May 5, 1525, sheltered Martin LUTHER when he was under attack by the pope and Holy Roman Emperor CHARLES V. Frederick succeeded as elector of Saxony in 1486. Called "the Wise" because of his reputation for good advice, he founded (1502) the university at Wittenberg where Luther and Philipp Melanchthon taught. After the Diet of Worms (1521) placed Luther under an imperial ban, Frederick took him into custody and won an exemption for Saxony from the Edict of Worms outlawing Lutheran teachings.

Frederick V, Elector Palatine

(the Winter King)   Frederick V, b. Aug. 26, 1596, d. Nov. 29, 1632, elector palatine (1610–20) and king of Bohemia (1619–20), called the Winter King, was largely responsible for the outbreak of the THIRTY YEARS' WAR.

A member of the Calvinist Palatine branch of the house of WITTELSBACH, Frederick V was the nephew of MAURICE OF NASSAU, virtual ruler of the Netherlands. In 1613 he married Elizabeth, daughter of JAMES I of England. The couple shared religion, personal charm, ambition, and political incompetence. In 1619 the rebellious Bohemians elected Frederick king. Failing to receive support from his powerful relatives, Frederick was defeated in 1620 by the armies of the Holy Roman emperor and the Catholic League and fled. The emperor then bestowed the Upper Palatinate and the electorate on Frederick's distant relative, MAXIMILIAN, duke of Bavaria.

Frederick Henry, Prince of Orange

Frederick Henry, b. Jan. 29, 1584, d. Mar. 14, 1647, prince of Orange and count of Nassau, established by his military victories the general territorial limits of United Provinces of the Netherlands. The youngest son of WILLIAM I (William the Silent), founder of the Dutch republic, he followed his half-brother MAURICE OF NASSAU as stadholder (governor) of the five principal provinces in 1625 and also of Groningen in 1640. As captain- and admiral-general, Frederick Henry halted the renewed Spanish offensives against the republic and captured numerous cities from Spain between 1627 and 1645. During his reign the golden age of Dutch art flourished.

Frederick William, Elector of Brandenburg

(the Great Elector)   Frederick William, b. Feb. 16, 1620, d. May 9, 1688, elector of BRANDENBURG and duke of PRUSSIA, is known as the Great Elector because of his critical contributions to the early development of the HOHENZOLLERN state. He succeeded his father, George William, in 1640, inheriting widely dispersed northern German territories ravaged by the THIRTY YEARS' WAR (1618–48).

By the time of his death the Great Elector had built a standing professional army of 30,000 men to defend his poverty-stricken lands against outside invasion and a unified administration capable of levying taxes. In asserting his authority over the local estates, Frederick William diminished the independence of the JUNKER aristocracy and enlisted their service as army officers. He sought to increase the prosperity of Brandenburg-Prussia by promoting agriculture, industry, and commerce, and by encouraging Polish Jews, French Huguenots, and other religious refugees to settle within his domains.

By the Peace of Westphalia, which ended the Thirty Years' War, the Great Elector received Eastern Pomerania and other territories. In the Little Northern War (1655–60) he fought against Poland in alliance with Sweden until 1657 and then allied with Poland against Sweden. By the Peace of Oliva (May 3, 1660) he won formal recognition of his sovereignty over ducal Prussia, formerly held as

Frederick William, elector of Brandenburg (1640–88), known as the Great Elector, laid the foundations of the Prussian state. A man of superb organizational ability, he created a centralized administration for his scattered lands, built up the army, and fostered commerce and industry.

a fief of the Polish crown. Later, Frederick William also conquered Western, or Swedish, Pomerania but was compelled to surrender it by the peace settlements. His victory over the Swedes at Fehrbellin (June 18, 1675) was the first demonstration of the superiority of the new Prussian army.

Frederick William I, King of Prussia

Frederick William I, b. Aug. 15, 1688, d. May 31, 1740, succeeded his father, FREDERICK I, as king of Prussia in 1713. He devoted his reign to the building of the military power of his small state. He first centralized governmental administration and organized an efficient bureaucracy that more than doubled annual income. Then he expanded his peacetime army to 83,000 men, transforming it into one of the best-trained military establishments in Europe. To strengthen the economy, he nurtured industry and agriculture through mercantilistic policies, and by avoiding wars. Frederick William left to his son, FREDERICK II, a treasury of 7,000,000 thalers.

Frederick William II, King of Prussia

Frederick William II, b. Sept. 25, 1744, d. Nov. 16, 1797, king of Prussia, succeeded his uncle FREDERICK II in 1786. From the outset the new king revealed an incompetence that threatened the political achievements of the HOHENZOLLERN dynasty.

From the Polish partitions of 1793 and 1795, Prussia acquired Danzig (Gdánsk) and other extensive territories. Frederick William's mismanaged involvement in the War of the First Coalition (1792–97) against Revolutionary France, however, foreshadowed Prussia's disastrous defeat by Napoleon I at the Battle of Jena in 1806.

See also: FRENCH REVOLUTIONARY WARS; POLAND, PARTITIONS OF.

Frederick William III, King of Prussia

Frederick William III, b. Aug. 3, 1770, d. June 7, 1840, king of Prussia (1797–1840), lived through more turbulence than almost any other member of the HOHENZOLLERN dynasty. The son of Frederick William II, he had an appealing middle-class simplicity and dedication. His main personal achievement was the emancipation of peasants on the royal estates. After 1806, Frederick William put through the administrative reforms proposed by K. A. HARDENBERG and H. F. K. STEIN.; he also promised a constitution, but never granted it. The ZOLLVEREIN, or customs union, of 1834 was the major accomplishment of his later years.

The king's foreign policy was marked by caution. Prussia remained neutral in the NAPOLEONIC WARS until 1806, when it allied with Russia and Austria. Immediately defeated by the French in the Battle of Jena, it signed the humiliating Treaty of Tilsit (1807; see TILSIT, TREATIES OF). In 1813, however, Prussia's reorganized army played a major role in the final defeat of Napoleon I. As a result it gained much territory at the Congress of Vi-

enna (1814–15; see VIENNA, CONGRESS OF). Frederick William was an original signatory of the HOLY ALLIANCE (1815).

Frederick William IV, King of Prussia

Frederick William IV, b. Oct. 15, 1795, d. Jan. 2, 1861, the king who gave Prussia its first constitution, was artistically and intellectually gifted but lacked the simple realism of his father, Frederick William III. On succeeding to the throne in 1840, he recalled many professors dismissed by his father. In 1847 he summoned an all-Prussian diet, and, initially acceding to the demands made in the REVOLUTIONS OF 1848, he granted a constitution in 1848.

In 1849, however, Frederick William refused the German imperial crown proffered by the FRANKFURT PARLIAMENT. He also amended (1850) the Prussian constitution to favor the rich by introducing a three-class voting system and increasingly relied on conservative cronies instead of ministers. Ironically, the reign of this backward-looking romantic also saw extensive railroad construction and industrial development. In 1857 the king's mental disability necessitated a regency under his brother, William (later German emperor as WILLIAM I), which lasted until the king's death.

Frederick William IV, king of Prussia (1840–61), refused the crown of a united Germany offered (1849) by the Frankfurt Parliament. His own plan for German unification under Prussian domination was abandoned in the face of Austrian opposition.

Fredericksburg

[fred'-riks-burg] Fredericksburg (1990 pop., 19,027) is a city in northeast Virginia, located within Spotsylvania County but politically independent. It is located on the Rappahannock River, at the fall line, and is a commercial center for the surrounding agricultural area. Fredericksburg was founded in the 1720s and named for Prince Frederick Louis, the father of George III. During the Civil War several important battles were fought at or near Fredericksburg.

Fredericksburg, Battle of

The Battle of Fredericksburg, an engagement of the U.S. Civil War, was fought at Fredericksburg, Va., on Dec. 13, 1862. Gen. Ambrose E. BURNSIDE, who had just replaced Gen. George B. McClellan in command of the Union Army of the Potomac, attacked the heavily fortified lines of Robert E. LEE preparatory to a drive on Richmond, Va. All through a bloody day federal ranks surged against Lee's lines, melted away, reformed, surged, and melted again. Burnside lost 12,500 men, and his defeat ended federal activity in Virginia until the spring of 1863.

Fredericton [fred'-rik-tuhn] Fredericton, a Canadian city of 44,352 (1986), is the capital of New Brunswick and seat of York County. Located on the Saint John River, it was the site of the French Fort Nachouac (1692) and the Acadian settlement of Saint Anne's Point (1731). Between 1783 and 1785, United Empire Loyalists settled the area, naming it for Frederick, the son of King George III. The city manufactures canoes, footwear, lumber products, and handicrafts and is the provincial headquarters for the Royal Canadian Mounted Police. The University of New Brunswick (founded 1785, reorganized 1859) and St. Thomas University (1910), which shares the University of New Brunswick campus, are in the city.

Fredonian Rebellion [free-dohn'-yuhn] The Fredonian Rebellion, in December 1826, was an early and abortive attempt by American settlers in Texas to gain independence from Mexico. A gang of 30 men captured the town of Nacogdoches, declared the independence of the Republic of Fredonia, imprisoned the *alcalde* (mayor), and signed a pact with representatives of the Cherokees promising the Indians half of Texas in return for their support. The uprising was short-lived: most settlers, Americans as well as Mexicans, scorned participation with the renegade Fredonians and Cherokees, and more responsible Indian leaders rejected the pact. When Mexican troops and militia from Stephen AUSTIN's colony arrived to suppress the rebellion, the Fredonian leaders fled.

free enterprise system see CAPITALISM

free fall Free fall is motion determined solely by gravitational forces. For example, an object dropped or thrown into the air is in free fall at every point in its trajectory. An object in space, although influenced by the gravitational fields of many celestial bodies, is always in free fall, despite the fact that it may not actually be "falling" toward any of them.

A person inside a vessel that is falling freely is also in free fall and experiences the phenomenon of WEIGHTLESSNESS. Because gravitational effects are the same on both the person and the vessel, no acceleration is felt relative to the vessel.

A parachutist experiences free fall for a brief period before the parachute opens, but the force of air resistance against the person's body soon becomes significant and

he or she no longer falls freely. In fact, a terminal velocity (maximum speed) is reached of about 180 to 250 km/h (110 to 155 mph). An aircraft can simulate free-fall conditions for about a minute by flying a particular parabolic trajectory, thereby subjecting its occupants to temporary weightlessness.

free port A free port or a free zone within a port (also called a foreign-trade zone) is an area where foreign goods may be landed, processed, or manufactured and then reshipped without payment of customs duties. If, however, the goods are sold within the country in which the free port or zone is located, customs duties must be paid.

Free ports flourished in medieval Europe during the time of the HANSEATIC LEAGUE, when German towns such as Hamburg and Bremen became famous as ports for the transshipment of goods. The first free port in the United States was established in 1939 in New York harbor and was followed by the creation of free ports in New Orleans (1947), San Francisco (1948), and Seattle (1949). Other Western Hemisphere ports that have free zones include Salina Cruz, Mexico, and Colón, Panama, and Asian free ports include Hong Kong, Singapore, and Macao. Major international airports also have free zones, where duty-free goods can be bought and sold.

free radical In chemistry, a free radical is an uncharged atom or molecule that has an odd number of electrons; that is, one electron is unpaired. Free radicals are highly reactive and thus have only a temporary existence. They may be formed by cleavage of a covalent bond when both new products retain one electron of the original shared pair. Cleavage of the chlorine molecule Cl_2 yields two chlorine free radicals (chlorine atoms). Free radicals react to yield other free radicals, which can similarly react, causing a chemical CHAIN REACTION. Fire is propagated by this mechanism, as are many polymerization reactions. In biology, superoxides—free radicals that contain the O_2^- molecule—are the main cause of the lethal effect that oxygen has on obligate ANAEROBES. The product of many biochemical reactions in the human body, superoxides can injure or kill cells and may contribute to the effects of cancer, heart attacks, strokes, and emphysema.

free schools Free schools are designed to foster noncompetitive, nonauthoritarian attitudes in pupils. Often informal and antibureaucratic, they use OPEN CLASSROOMS and emphasize individualized instruction. Some free schools try to develop political awareness, sensitivity to the feelings of others, and antiracist sentiments. Although free schools such as SUMMERHILL are half a century old, the American movement began to grow in the mid-1960s. Private free schools were formed both in poor neighborhoods and in middle-class communities. Some were established in public school systems as alternative schools.

free silver   Free silver was the battle cry used in late-19th-century America by advocates of unlimited coinage of silver. The cause was especially popular among silver miners, farmers, and debtors. Until the post–Civil War era the United States had been a bimetallist nation—that is, the value of its currency was based on both gold and silver—but the silver standard was abandoned in 1873

A severe depression in the mid-'70s and the sudden decline in silver's market price that followed expanded production in the western United States made the concept of free silver increasingly popular. Silverites believed that free coinage of silver would produce inflation and alleviate their financial woes. Both the BLAND-ALLISON ACT of 1878 and the Sherman Silver Purchase Act of 1890 included concessions to silverites.

In 1893, in the midst of another national depression and with discontented farmers mobilizing through the POPULIST PARTY, President Cleveland successfully brought about repeal of the Sherman Silver Purchase Act. Repeal strengthened the conviction of many that opposition to free silver was part of a class war by bankers and industrialists on the common people, a conviction exemplified by William Jennings BRYAN's oratorical cry: "You shall not crucify mankind upon a cross of gold!" But Bryan's defeats for the presidency (1896, 1900), plus the return of prosperity and passage of the Gold Standard Act (1900), dealt a death blow to the free-silver crusade.

In this late-19th-century political cartoon, Uncle Sam is "blind" to the silver controversy. Free-silver advocates were unable to convince the federal government to mint unlimited quantities of silver coins.

I AM SILVER BLIND
PLEASE ASSIST ME

Free-Soil party   The Free-Soil party was organized in 1848 to oppose the extension of slavery into the territories newly acquired by the United States from Mexico. Among its leaders was Salmon P. CHASE. The Free-Soil forces, composed of former Liberty party members, antislavery Whigs, and certain New York Democrats known as Barnburners, chose former president Martin VAN BUREN as their presidential candidate in 1848. Although they failed to carry a single state, the substantial Free-Soil vote in New York helped the Whigs defeat the Democrats in that state and thereby win the presidency for Zachary Taylor. They did, however, elect a number of congressmen. The party weakened in the 1852 election; most of its members later joined the new Republican party.

free trade   Free trade refers to commerce that is relatively unrestricted and unaided by government regulations, such as TARIFFS, quotas, and subsidies. The concept of free trade was first delineated as a reaction against MERCANTILISM by the French PHYSIOCRATS of the 18th century and, later, by the classical economists, especially Adam SMITH and David RICARDO. Extending LAISSEZ-FAIRE principles to international trade, they asserted that nations should specialize in producing and exporting goods that they were most efficient at manufacturing and import goods that they were less efficient in producing. All nations would benefit by this economic law of comparative advantage if there were no barriers to the exchange of goods.

The practice of free trade received its initial impetus in Great Britain with the repeal (1846) of the CORN LAWS and the subsequent sweeping tariff reductions under William GLADSTONE. The Anglo-French Treaty of 1860 and later free trade treaties introduced the concept of MOST-FAVORED-NATION STATUS, which greatly expanded international trade. Developing nations, however, such as the United States and many European countries, tended to favor high-tariff policies to protect young industries from foreign competition. The United States remained protectionist until the 1930s, when the Reciprocal Trade Agreements Act of 1934 revived interest in free trade. An increased desire for free trade was reflected in the BRETTON WOODS CONFERENCE (1944); the GENERAL AGREEMENT ON TARIFFS AND TRADE, after World War II; and organizations like the EUROPEAN FREE TRADE ASSOCIATION and the EUROPEAN COMMUNITY. The unified European market set for 1992 has raised fears that foreign goods will face tariff barriers and has also prompted movement toward other regional free-trade zones, such as the U.S.-Canada-Mexico free-trade zone proposed by the United States in 1991.

free verse   see VERSIFICATION

free will   see WILL (philosophy)

Freedmen's Bureau   The Freedmen's Bureau was a U.S. government agency set up at the end of the Civil War to aid refugees and ex-slaves. A branch of the armed forces, the bureau was headed by a commissioner—Gen. Oliver O. HOWARD—and military officers. Its purpose was to provide food, shelter, seeds, and agricultural equipment to white Civil War refugees and the thousands of newly freed blacks, to superintend the camps in which the freedmen had gathered, and to administer lands abandoned by Confederate sympathizers in such a way as to provide employment to ex-slaves. The bureau also supervised the transition from slavery to freedom in the South, helping employers and employees draw up labor contracts and settle disputes. So long as state courts enforced BLACK CODES or did not adequately protect freedmen's rights, the commissioner set up courts to hear civil and criminal cases involving African Americans.

Bureau officials often came into conflict with Southern whites, who felt the bureau was too sympathetic to blacks and encouraged labor unrest. Most bureau activities were discontinued in 1869, after new state constitutions had been adopted in the South in accordance with the congressional RECONSTRUCTION plan.

Freedom of Information Act The Freedom of Information Act of 1966 requires that the records of U.S. government agencies be made available to the public. Records include all books, papers, maps, photographs, or other documentary material. Information must be made available promptly—within ten working days as a rule—to the person requesting it. The law exempts, however, nine classes of information related to national security or involving trade secrets, investigatory files, material exempted from disclosure by statute, reports prepared for use in regulating financial institutions, and other matters considered confidential. In 1982, President Ronald Reagan signed an executive order increasing the amount of security-classified material. The Freedom of Information Act is supplemented by the Privacy Act of 1974, which requires federal agencies to provide individuals with any information in their files relating to them and to amend incorrect records.

---

freedom of the press Freedom of the press is the right to gather and publish information or opinions without governmental control or fear of punishment. It applies to all types of printed and broadcast material, including books, newspapers, magazines, pamphlets, films, and radio and television programs. Historically, freedom of the press has been bound up with the question of CENSORSHIP. In countries where censorship is extensive, the right to publish news, information, and opinions is usually tightly restricted. Even in the United States, however, where censorship is light, the right to publish is not absolute.

Historical Basis

Governments have restricted the right to publish in two ways: by restraining the press from publishing certain materials and by punishing those who publish matter considered seditious, libelous, or obscene. The first kind of restriction, often called prior restraint, is rare in the United States and in most other democratic countries. One of the first attacks on prior restraint can be found in John Milton's essay *Areopagitica* (1644), which was directed against the English licensing and censorship laws enacted in 1534 under Henry VIII. These laws were abolished in England in 1695, but the government was still able to take action on grounds of "seditious libel" against those who published material—whether true or false—that criticized government policies.

In the American colonies prosecutions of this kind were made more difficult by a jury's decision in the Zenger case of 1735. John Peter ZENGER, a New York newspaper publisher, had been charged with libel because he had published articles criticizing the policies of the colonial governor. The jury acquitted Zenger on the ground that his charges were true and could therefore not be considered libelous. Not until 1868 did the truth of the published material become an accepted defense in England.

Freedom of the press was protected in the Constitution of the United States by the adoption (1791) of the 1st AMENDMENT, which states: "Congress shall make no law... abridging freedom of speech or of the press." This restraint on the federal government was later made binding on state governments in 1931 by the Supreme Court's interpretation of the DUE PROCESS clause of the 14th AMENDMENT. Restrictions on the press have always occurred during times of national emergency. The extensive censorship during World War I led to the first clear articulation of the limits to FREEDOM OF SPEECH, with which free-press issues are closely tied. Justice Oliver Wendell HOLMES, Jr., enunciated (in SCHENCK v. UNITED STATES, 1919) the concept that abridgment of free speech was justified only if the words used constituted "a clear and present danger." During World War II freedom of the press was greatly curtailed, but the press proved eager to comply with censorship restrictions. Besides wartime restrictions, freedom of the press has also been traditionally limited in the area of obscenity and PORNOGRAPHY.

Recent Issues

The bounds of freedom of the press in the United States in recent years have been determined in the courts on a case-by-case basis.

Defamatory Libel and Public Figures. The Zenger case had established the precedent that truthful statements were not to be considered libelous; the obvious corollary was that damages could be collected for false statements. In *New York Times Company* v. *Sullivan* (1964), however, the Supreme Court held that public officials are entitled to win damages only if they can show that a statement defaming them was made "with `actual malice'— that is, with knowledge that it was false or with reckless disregard of whether it was false or not." Other court rulings have extended the principle to include public figures who are not in government office but who are involved in public controversy. These rulings, which essentially protect the press, have inevitably led to difficulties in defining just who is a public figure.

National Security. Other than in time of war, censorship for national security reasons has been carefully limited. In 1971 the U.S. government attempted to halt publication of the PENTAGON PAPERS on the grounds that their publication could endanger national security. The Supreme Court ruled in *New York Times Company* v. *United States* that this case of prior restraint was unconstitutional. Recent cases involving national security have concerned attempts to censor or halt publication of books about the Central Intelligence Agency. In March 1979 a court injunction prohibited a magazine for six months from publishing instructions on making a hydrogen bomb. In 1983, when U.S. troops invaded the Caribbean island of Grenada, the press was initially barred from the island. These restrictions were thought to be unprecedented in

U.S. practice and generated much controversy, as did press restrictions during the ground war phase of the Gulf war in early 1991.

Privileges of the Press. The privileges of the press have had to be constantly weighed against such other considerations as the rights to privacy and to a fair trial. In 1976, for example, the Supreme Court ruled that so-called gag orders by trial courts forbidding the press to publish certain information about a defendant were unconstitutional. Several court decisions in 1978, however, appeared to narrow the right of newspaper reporters to withhold information given them in confidence. In 1979, in a controversial effort to curb prejudicial pretrial publicity, the Court ruled (*Gannet* v. *DePasquale*) that judges have the authority to bar the press and the public from criminal proceedings. In other cases, however, courts have allowed televised proceedings.

Global Status

Freedom of the press is generally limited to the United States, Great Britain and the Commonwealth nations, Western Europe, parts of Latin America, and Japan. Even these countries differ to some extent in the amount of freedom. In Great Britain and Canada, for example, Official Secrets Acts make it a crime to disclose government documents without permission. Britain also has strict libel laws, and the press is barred by potential contempt-of-court penalties from commenting on any case before the courts.

Until the advent of GLASNOST (openness) under Soviet leader Mikhail Gorbachev, freedom of the press in Communist countries was almost nonexistent. In other dictatorial governments various types of control restrict what the press can print.

----

freedom of religion   Freedom of religion is a political principle that forbids government constraint on people in their choice of beliefs. Religious freedom requires also that one be free to act upon those beliefs. It therefore includes the freedom to worship, to print instructional material, to train teachers, and to organize societies for their employment. Thus, freedom of religion is closely conjoined with other freedoms, such as freedom of speech, freedom of the press, and freedom of assembly. It is recognized (as are the other freedoms) in a provision of the 1ST AMENDMENT to the Constitution of the United States:

> Congress shall make no law respecting an establish ment of religion, or prohibiting the free exercise there of....

In Western Europe and North America, freedom of religion is almost universally enjoyed. In some other parts of the world freedom of religion is either severely circumscribed by state action or limited by social pressure.

History of Religious Freedom

For centuries people have been persecuted for their religious beliefs. Tolerance for Christians and Jews under the early Roman Empire depended on the attitudes of emperors and local governors; in Christian Europe Jews, Muslims, and heretics were generally persecuted during the Middle Ages. During the Reformation pitched battles occurred between Catholics and Protestants; later, nonconforming Protestant sects were harrassed by established Protestant churches. Persecution of Jews, atheists, and agnostics continued into the 20th century, while Protestant-Catholic conflict has persisted to this day in Northern Ireland. Until recently, Communist countries were mostly officially atheistic and made religious practice difficult.

Before the 18th century, instances of religious toleration were rare. Proliferating Hindu and Buddhist sects created a form of religious freedom in India, Japan, and China, and limited religious liberty was permitted under the Islamic caliphate. In Europe the Roman emperor Constantine issued (AD 313) the Edict of Milan granting freedom to practice the religion of one's choice; within a few years, however, Christianity had become the only legal religion. In 1598 the promulgation of the Edict of Nantes by Henry IV of France enabled the Huguenots to obtain a certain degree of religious freedom.

Religious freedom developed in the English-speaking world mainly for pragmatic reasons. In the 16th and 17th centuries efforts were made by the state to regulate totally the Church of England and to stamp out or severely constrain Catholics and Protestant sects that did not conform to the Church of England. The Puritans came to power after the English Civil War (1642–48). They in turn suppressed Catholics. The reestablishment of the Church of England brought about the CLARENDON CODE (1661–65), which persecuted non-Anglicans. There was, however, an increasing realization that religious oppression was deleterious not only to domestic tranquility but to commerce and trade as well. The Act of Toleration (1689) opened the way to fuller development of religious freedom.

Escape from religious persecution was one reason for emigration to the New World, but early settlers were themselves generally unwilling to grant religious liberty for differing beliefs. By 1786, however, Thomas Jefferson, James Madison, and George Mason had produced the Virginia Statute of Religious Liberty, which firmly set forth principles that separated state power from church affairs, a position that reflected the one taken almost a century before by John Locke in his *Letter Concerning Toleration* (1689). Madison drew heavily on this experience in fashioning the Bill of Rights, proposed in 1789.

Religious Freedom in the United States

The concept of separation of church and state is used to describe the legal and institutional nature of freedom of religion in the United States. It is not a widespread concept, nor does it necessarily indicate the presence or absence of religious freedom. England, Scotland, and Sweden, for example, have officially established churches but enjoy religious freedom.

It has been difficult literally to separate church and state in the United States. Churches are required to conform to building codes, fire regulations, and sanitation laws. Government is expected to decide whether a group claiming to be religious should be exempt from property taxes or whether the claim is fraudulent. The 1st Amendment pledges the federal government neither to favor nor to be hostile, but to be "neutral." The struggle of the courts to be truly neutral in judging disputes has long been the hinge of religious freedom in the United States. Courts have had to weigh the requirements of the "free exercise" and "establishment" clauses of the 1st Amendment against certain legal, social, and religious needs of society. Laws against polygamy, for example, were declared constitutional in 1878 despite Mormon religious claims based on the "free exercise" clause. The same clause, however, has protected prisoners' freedom of worship. The "establishment" clause has been interpreted at various times to mean either that government cannot show preference to any particular religion or that there must be complete separation of church and state.

Large areas of dispute exist, and litigation is constantly in progress over such issues as government assistance to religiously sponsored schools, devotional practices in public schools, and the treatment of sectarians whose religious convictions are not easily accommodated by local law. In education the Supreme Court has held that state reimbursement to parents for money spent to transport their children to parochial schools on the public bus system does not constitute an establishment of religion. Public school boards may furnish secular textbooks for the use of children in religious schools. Public schools may cooperate administratively with churches concerned for the religious education of children, but public property may not be used, public funds may not be directly appropriated, and religion itself may not be promoted. In public schools a period of silence may be observed in which children may pray if they wish, but the schools may not enter the field of religious instruction. The "equal access" law of 1984, however, gives students the right to hold religious meetings in public high schools outside class hours.

freedom of the seas   see SEAS, FREEDOM OF THE

---

freedom of speech   Freedom of speech is the liberty to speak and write without fear of government restraint. It is closely linked to FREEDOM OF THE PRESS. In the United States both freedoms—commonly called freedom of expression—are protected by the 1ST AMENDMENT to the Constitution, which provides that "Congress shall make no law abridging the freedom of speech, or of the press." The practice of free speech is consistent only in the United States and in the democracies of Western Europe, English-speaking countries, and Japan. All countries, however, limit manifestations of free speech that are regarded as threatening the civil order or as obscene or slanderous.

History of Freedom of Speech

Until the 17th century various forms of CENSORSHIP of free speech were common and contested principally within the framework of larger issues of political and religious conflict. In England in the 17th century, however, freedom of speech began to assume its own importance. John Milton wrote in his *Areopagitica* (1644): "Give me the liberty to know, to utter, and to argue freely according to conscience, above all liberties." Other philosophers such as John LOCKE, VOLTAIRE, and, later, John Stuart MILL took up the cry. Beginning with the British Bill of Rights (1689) and the adoption of the French Declaration of the Rights of Man (1789) and the U.S. BILL OF RIGHTS (1791), freedom of speech became an integral part of constitutional law even in countries that do not in reality permit free speech.

Free Speech in the United States

In the United States freedom of speech and the constitutional limits to it have been defined, in practice, by rulings of the Supreme Court. Originally the free-speech guarantee of the 1st Amendment applied only to acts of Congress. In the 20th century, however, the Supreme Court began to interpret the DUE PROCESS clause of the 14TH AMENDMENT to mean that the states as well as the federal government are bound by the provisions of the 1st Amendment. Restrictions on freedom of speech have occurred most often in time of war or national emergency. The ALIEN AND SEDITION ACTS of 1798 were the first incursions by Congress on this freedom. These laws were never tested in the courts and were allowed to expire after several years.

Clear and Present Danger. The first clear-cut test came over the Espionage Act (1917) passed by Congress during World War I; this act made it illegal to interfere with the recruitment or drafting of soldiers or to do anything adversely affecting military morale. In SCHENCK V. UNITED STATES the Court upheld the conviction of a socialist indicted under the act on the ground that freedom of speech is not absolute. Justice Oliver Wendell HOLMES, Jr., delivering the Court's unanimous opinion, argued: "The most stringent protection of free speech would not protect a man in falsely shouting fire in a theatre and causing a panic....The question in every case is whether the words used are used in such circumstances and are of such a nature as to create a clear and present danger that they will bring about the substantive evils that Congress has a right to prevent."

Bad Tendency. The "clear and present danger" doctrine became one of the tests the Court applied to subsequent cases involving freedom of speech. Another test, which placed more restrictions on individual expression, was whether an expression had a tendency to lead to results that were bad for the public. In *Gitlow* v. *New York* (1925) the Court held that "a State in the exercise of its police power may punish those who abuse this freedom by utterances inimical to the public welfare, tending to corrupt public morals, incite to crime, or disturb the public peace...." Gitlow had been indicted under a New York State law prohibiting the advocacy of the overthrow of the government by force or violence.

Society's Interests. In 1940, Congress enacted the SMITH ACT, which declared it unlawful to advocate overthrowing the government by force or violence. Eleven leaders of the Communist party were convicted under the act and appealed on the ground that it was unconstitutional. The Court upheld the act's constitutionality in *Dennis* v. *United States* (1951) but not on the ground of "clear and present danger." Instead, the majority adopted a standard put forward by Judge Learned HAND: "...whether the gravity of the `evil,' discounted by its improbability, justifies such invasion of free speech as is necessary to avoid the danger." This standard has been called the "clear and probable danger" test.

Preferred Freedoms and the Absolute Approach. The preferred freedoms approach has been important in constitutional law since World War II. This approach stresses that the civil liberties have a preferred position among other constitutional values since they are requisite to a democracy. Under this concept the burden lies largely with the government to prove that clear and present danger exists when a freedom is exercised.

Some justices have tended to see freedom of speech as nearly an absolute right. The difficulty of the absolute approach to free speech issues was shown (1977–78) when American Nazis sought to hold a rally in Skokie, Ill. They were denied a permit on the ground that a Nazi rally would incite hostility in the largely Jewish population. Lawyers for the AMERICAN CIVIL LIBERTIES UNION (ACLU) represented the Nazis, arguing that the Skokie laws limiting public demonstrations were unconstitutional. A U.S. court of appeals agreed with the ACLU, but many Americans were outraged at the defense of those they considered the enemies of free speech.

The judicial interpretation of the right of free speech has yet to produce a clear definition of what is permissible. Insofar as seditious speech is concerned, the courts have held language permissible so long as it does not tend to incite the violent overthrow of the government. In other free-speech areas, such as obscenity and PORNOGRAPHY, "fighting words," picketing or demonstrating, symbolic speech (for example, wearing armbands or burning the flag), and loyalty oaths, the courts have also had to consider the various interests of society and the requirements of the Constitution.

freeholder *Freeholder,* a term derived from feudal law, refers to a landowner with an inheritable life title to his or her land. In some American colonies only freeholders had the right to vote and hold office. In contemporary New Jersey, a freeholder is an elected county official.

freemasonry [free'-may-suhn-ree] Freemasonry refers to the principles, institutions, and practices of the fraternal order of the Free and Accepted Masons. The largest worldwide society, freemasonry is an organization of men based on the fatherhood of God and the brotherhood of man, using builders' tools as symbols to teach basic moral truths generally accepted by persons of good will. It is religious in that a belief in God is the prime requirement for membership, but it is nonsectarian in that

This 19th-century lithographic print shows the initiation ceremony of a Mason. Freemasonry emphasizes the brother- and sisterhood of humankind, and the principal activities of its lodges are related to social and charitable works.

no religious test is used. The purpose of freemasonry is to enable men to meet in harmony, to promote friendship, and to be charitable. Its basic ideals are that all persons are the children of one God, that all persons are related to each other, and that the best way to worship God is to be of service to people.

The basic unit of freemasonry is the lodge, which exists under a charter issued by a grand lodge exercising administrative powers. The lodge confers three degrees: Entered Apprentice, Fellow Craft, and Master Mason. Additional degrees are conferred by two groups of advanced freemasonry, the York Rite and the Scottish Rite. In the United States and Canada members have formed a large number of groups to enable them to expand their social and charitable activities. The best known of these groups is the Shriners, who hold festive parades and support hospitals for crippled and burned children. There are also the Order of the Eastern Star for Master Masons and their wives; the Order of De Molay for boys; and the Order of Job's Daughters and the Order of Rainbow for girls.

Freemasonry is generally believed to have evolved from the medieval guilds of the stonemasons. Its present organizational form began on June 24, 1717, when a grand lodge was formed in London. Since that time lodges have spread all over the world. Lodges first appeared in America in Philadelphia (1730) and Boston (1733).

At various times and places freemasonry has met religious and political opposition. Religious opponents, especially the Roman Catholic and Eastern Orthodox churches, have traditionally claimed that freemasonry is a religion and is a secret organization. Freemasons hold that the organization is religious but not a religion, and that it is not a secret organization since it works openly in the community. Freemasonry has always been suppressed in totalitarian states.

There are more than 5,000,000 Freemasons around the world, with about three-quarters of them in the United States. Many notable men in history have been Freemasons, including Benjamin Franklin, George Washington, Mozart, Henry Ford, Will Rogers, and Douglas MacArthur.

Freer, Charles Lang [freer]   Charles Lang Freer, b. Feb. 25, 1856, d. Sept. 25, 1919, was the Detroit industrialist whose important Oriental art collection forms the nucleus of the Freer Gallery of Art, which is part of the Smithsonian Institution in Washington, D.C. He bequeathed his entire collection to the U.S. government in 1906, along with funds and plans for constructing a museum and endowing future acquisitions and study of Far Eastern art.

The Renaissance-style gallery, completed in 1921, houses some of the nation's finest examples of Chinese and Japanese art as well as Freer's extensive collection of paintings by such artists as Winslow Homer, John Singer Sargent, and James McNeill Whistler.

freesia [free'-zhuh]   Freesia is a genus of about 19 species of South African bulbous plants in the iris family, Iridaceae. They are usually grown for cut flowers. The flowers are very fragrant, typically white or yellow, and are borne in spikelike racemes.

Freesia F. refracta, an elegant greenhouse plant, produces arched rows of exquisitely scented flowers. It is becoming increasingly popular for cut floral arrangements.

freethinker   see DEISM

Freetown   Freetown is the capital and largest city of Sierra Leone in West Africa. It has a population of 469,776 (1985). A busy Atlantic port, it is located on the shore of a rugged peninsula that shelters a large natural harbor. Freetown is the shipping, commercial, and industrial heart of Sierra Leone. Its various industries in-

clude diamond cutting, food processing, and petroleum refining.

The city was settled in the late 1780s under British auspices by freed slaves from England and the New World; they mingled with the indigenous population to produce a new language, Krio, and a society known as Sierra Leone Creole. Today the city is a blend of Western and African in which Muslims outnumber Christians. The city's university incorporates colleges founded as early as 1827.

freeze-drying   Freeze-drying is a FOOD PRESERVATION technique in which food is first frozen into a solid state; then, with the application of heat, the frozen moisture content is vaporized—a phenomenon known as sublimation (see SUBLIMATION, chemistry). Freeze-dried foods, most often liquids or small foods such as bamboo sprouts, lose at least 90 percent of their water content through this process. They regain a very close approximation of their original shape, texture, and flavor when reconstituted with the addition of water.

freezing point   The freezing point (also called fusion point or melting point) is the temperature at which a substance's solid and liquid forms can coexist indefinitely.

At a pressure of one atmosphere, the freezing (or melting) point of water is 0° C (32° F); that of hydrogen is −259.2° C. Among high-melting substances, tungsten (used in light-bulb filaments) melts at 3,370° C, and diamonds, above 3,500° C.

Impurities always lower freezing points. Salt water freezes at a lower temperature than pure water, which is why salt is often spread on icy streets. Certain metals can be mixed to produce low-melting alloys, such as solder and type metal. Freezing and melting points can be used to test a substance's purity. Every mole (6.022×10^{23} particles) of impurity in 1,000 grams of water lowers water's freezing point 1.86° C. Conversely, freezing points can be used to determine molecular weights and degrees of dissociation of substances in solution.

Increasing the pressure on a substance that expands on melting raises its melting point. Conversely, for substances such as water that expand on freezing, increasing the pressure lowers the freezing point. Under a pressure of 2,000 atmospheres, liquid water (density 1 g/cm^3) freezes to ordinary ice (density 0.92 g/cm^3) at −22° C. Under a pressure of 20,000 atmospheres, however, liquid water freezes to compact ice VIII (density 1.7 g/cm^3) at about 81° C.

Frege, Gottlob [fray'-geh, gawt'-lohp]   Gottlob Frege, b. Nov. 8, 1848, d. July 26, 1925, a German philosopher and mathematician, was one of the founders of modern symbolic LOGIC. He received his education at the universities of Göttingen and Jena and then taught at Jena in the department of mathematics.

Frege's writings on the philosophy of logic, philosophy of mathematics, and philosophy of language are of seminal importance. He was the first to fully develop the main thesis of logicism, that mathematics is reducible to logic. His works *The Foundations of Arithmetic* (1884; Eng. trans., 1950) and *The Basic Laws of Arithmetic* (1893; Eng. trans., 1964) are devoted to this project. He was a major influence on Bertrand RUSSELL.

Frei Montalva, Eduardo [fray mohn-tahl'-vah, ay-dwar'-doh]

Eduardo Frei Montalva, b. Jan. 16, 1911, d. Jan. 22, 1982, was president of Chile from 1964 to 1970. Political interests led him in 1938 to help form the reformist-conservative National Falange party, which became (1957) the Christian Democratic party. He was minister of roads and public works from 1945 to 1949. Elected president in 1964, Frei instituted a program that included nationalization of the copper industry, land reform, and expenditures on public health and education. When his party was defeated in 1970 by Salvador ALLENDE, he became an opposition spokesman.

Freiburg im Breisgau [fry'-boork im brys'-gow]

Freiburg im Breisgau is a cultural and commercial center in Baden-Württemberg, southwestern Germany, located on the Dreisam River at the western edge of the BLACK FOREST, about 30 km (18 mi) southwest of Stuttgart. It has a population of 186,200 (1987 est.). The city's industries produce wood and paper products, chemicals, glass, textiles, and precision instruments. Tourism is also important.

Freiburg was established in 1120 by the duke of Zähringen as the capital and free-market town of the Breisgau area. It passed to the Habsburgs in 1368 and was the scene of a major victory (1644) by the French over the Austrians and Bavarians in the THIRTY YEARS' WAR. Captured by the French in 1677 and again in 1744, Freiburg became part of Baden in 1805.

During World War II many of the city's older buildings were destroyed, but the Gothic cathedral (begun *c.*1200)—with its lacework steeple, magnificent stained-glass windows, and altar paintings by Hans BALDUNG-GRIEN, Lucas CRANACH the Elder, and Hans HOLBEIN the Younger—was unharmed.

Frelinghuysen, Frederick Theodore [free'-ling-hy-zen]

Frederick Theodore Frelinghuysen, b. Millstone, N.J., Aug. 4, 1817, d. May 20, 1885, served in the U.S. Senate from 1866 to 1869, and again from 1871 to 1877, and in 1881 was appointed by President Chester A. Arthur to succeed James G. Blaine as secretary of state. Frelinghuysen reversed Blaine's policies, withdrawing from a modest diplomatic intervention in the War of the Pacific; urging abrogation of the Clayton-Bulwer Treaty with Great Britain, rather than modification; and, also, taking back invitations Blaine had extended to the Latin American nations to attend a Pan-American Conference in Washington.

John C. Frémont, an American military leader and explorer, led several expeditions into the Far West, eventually participating in the conquest of California during the Mexican War.

Frémont, John C. [free'-mahnt]

John Charles Frémont, b. Savannah, Ga., Jan. 21, 1813, d. July 13, 1890, was an American explorer, soldier, and politician, best known as "the Pathfinder" for his western explorations of 1842–44. Following military training, he was assigned (1842) to survey the OREGON TRAIL up the Platte River to South Pass.

It was during his second expedition in 1843–44 that Frémont made the contributions that were to secure his fame. On this expedition he made a massive circle of the least-known parts of the West: from the Colorado Rockies north to the South Pass, northwest to the Columbia, south along the Cascade and Sierra Nevada ranges into California, and southward before turning east across the desert to the vicinity of Salt Lake and thence east across the Colorado Rockies. He returned to St. Louis in August 1844, after proving the existence of Salt Lake and a vast region of interior drainage (the Great Basin), dispelling the myth of the San Buenaventura River (supposed to flow from the Rockies to California), and demonstrating that the South Pass was the best route across the mountains.

In 1845, Frémont returned to California, where he encouraged the American settlers to revolt against Mexican rule and establish (June 1845) the Bear Flag Republic. In the ensuing dispute over command between Commodore Robert STOCKTON and Gen. Stephen KEARNY, Frémont supported the former and was consequently courtmartialed for insubordination.

Frémont resigned from the army in 1847, served as U.S. senator from California in 1850–51, and in 1856 was defeated in the presidential election as the first candidate of the Republican party. At the start of the Civil War he was made commander of the Western Department, but he was removed after ordering emancipation of the slaves in Missouri on his own authority. He was then given command of the Mountain Division (1862) but resigned when subordinated to John POPE. Later business failures left Frémont a near-pauper; Congress finally granted him a pension only three months before his death.

French, Daniel Chester

Daniel Chester French, b. Exeter, N.H., Apr. 20, 1850, d. Oct. 7, 1931, was America's unsurpassed sculptor of public monuments. For his first commission, the rugged *Minute Man* (1873–

Daniel Chester French's Minute Man *(1873–75), a bronze created to commemorate the Battle of Concord in 1775, is a naturalistic representation of an idealized American patriot.*

75; Concord, Mass.), which commemorates the first New Englanders to fall in the American Revolution, French used the pose of the Apollo Belvedere, invigorating the surfaces with the details of the colonial garments. He rapidly gained a reputation as a creator of monumental personifications of national sentiments and ideals. In his *Mourning Victory* (1906–08; Sleepy Hollow Cemetery, Concord, Mass.), a memorial to the North's Civil War dead, a half-bared figure emerges from the marble block past a shrouding flag that surrounds her with flowing Art Nouveau curves. The gigantic seated *Abraham Lincoln* (1911–22) for the Lincoln Memorial in Washington, D.C., climaxed French's career.

French, John, 1st Earl of Ypres John French, b. Sept. 28, 1852, d. May 22, 1925, was a British field marshal who commanded the British forces in Belgium and France in the early stages of World War I. He served in the South African War (1899–1902) and was chief of the imperial general staff (1912–14). Given command of the British Expeditionary Force (BEF) in August 1914, he failed to coordinate with the French armies, and the BEF suffered huge casualties at the first and second battles of Ypres and at Loos. In December 1915 he was replaced by Gen. Douglas Haig.

French Academy see ACADÉMIE FRANÇAISE

French art and architecture The earliest artistic remains in France date from Paleolithic times (see PREHISTORIC ART). The periods of Celtic culture from the late 5th century BC to the 1st century AD and of Roman occupation to the 5th century AD saw the building of towns (see CELTIC ART; ROMAN ART AND ARCHITECTURE). It is not possible, however, to speak of a nationally distinct French art before the mid-5th century AD, when the Merovingian

and Carolingian dynasties established authority over this region.

Merovingian and Carolingian Period

After the decline of the Roman Empire, Christianity spread, leading to the foundation of abbeys and monastic communities in the 5th to the 7th century. Few survive from the Merovingian period (see MEROVINGIAN ART AND ARCHITECTURE); the most notable is the baptistery of Saint Jean at Poitiers, dating from the 7th century.

In the 8th century, under the authority of Charlemagne—the first king to create a unified realm—a great building campaign began (see CAROLINGIAN ART AND ARCHITECTURE). Carolingian churches were intricately decorated with pictorial murals, mosaics, goldwork, and tapestries.

Charlemagne's Palace Chapel at Aachen, West Germany, or Aix-la-Chapelle (top), was designed by Odo of Metz and dedicated in 805. Based on the design of the church of San Vitale at Ravenna, the chapel plan is essentially octagonal, with a 16-sided structure forming aisles (1) and galleries (2) and the alternating sides of the polygon converging on eight massive stone piers (3). Unlike the expansive interior of San Vitale, the interior space of the chapel is clearly defined by its heavy stone masonry with superimposed arches (4) and its Roman columnar supports (5). The clerestory (6) illumines the mosaics of the central vault. Turreted stairwells (7) flanking the entrance later developed into the elaborate western facade. The entire palace complex (bottom), of which only the chapel remains, consisted of the royal hall (8), gatehouse (9), and chapel flanked by annexes (10, 11). The whole was linked by an enclosed corridor (12).

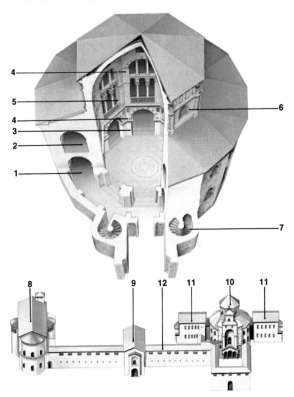

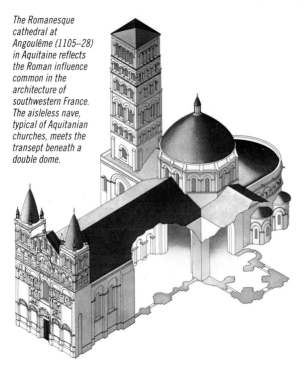

The Romanesque cathedral at Angoulême (1105–28) in Aquitaine reflects the Roman influence common in the architecture of southwestern France. The aisleless nave, typical of Aquitanian churches, meets the transept beneath a double dome.

The richness of Carolingian church interiors was equaled by the ILLUMINATED MANUSCRIPTS created at the monasteries of Reims, Tours, Metz, and Paris. The best preserved of Carolingian churches is the Chapel of Charlemagne (796–804) at Aachen (Aix-la-Chapelle).

Romanesque Period

Architecture. Two forces affected the development of church architecture in France from the 10th to the 12th century. One was the growth of large, wealthy monastic orders, and the other was a rapid increase in the number of religious pilgrimages to holy shrines. The largest and most important Romanesque structure (see ROMANESQUE ART AND ARCHITECTURE) was the Benedictine monastery church at CLUNY in Burgundy (begun in 1088 and destroyed in the 19th century). Cluny was the center of the Benedictine order in France. The massive monastery church, crowned with a stone vault (see ARCH AND VAULT), contained five aisles, two transepts, a chevet (an ambulatory with chapels radiating from the apse), an imposing westwork, and a narthex. The pattern established at Cluny was imitated by Benedictine churches throughout France.

Sculpture. The principal fulfillment of the devout medieval Christian was a pilgrimage to Rome, or to one of the many European shrines that contained holy relics, and churches were built along the well-traveled pilgrimage routes. Romanesque sculpture developed as decorations in these pilgrimage churches and is characterized by its highly stylized depictions of natural forms. The most prominent location for religious sculpture was in the TYMPANUM over the main west door leading to the center

aisle of the church. A fine example of such a carved tympanum survives at the church of Saint Pierre in Moissac. Sculpture also adorned columns, capitals, wells in cloisters, and crypts.

Enamelwork. The ancient art of enamelwork (see ENAMEL), which had continued to develop in France throughout the Merovingian and Carolingian periods, reached unprecedented heights in the 11th and 12th centuries, when the technique of *champlevé* came into general use. LIMOGES was a center of production, and its enamelwork was prized throughout Europe.

Gothic Period

The Gothic style grew out of the Romanesque in a surge of activity that began in the mid-12th century (see GOTHIC ART AND ARCHITECTURE). It evolved in northern France and spread throughout Europe, becoming the universal style from the 13th through the 16th century. Although the influence of Romanesque architecture had spread beyond France, Gothic was the first French style to dominate Europe.

Architecture. Gothic architecture began with the construction of cathedrals in Noyon (begun c.1150–70) and Laon (begun c.1160) and of the abbey church of SAINT-DENIS (1137–44), the most important achievement of early Gothic architecture. The Abbot SUGER intended to make Saint-Denis a showplace in keeping with its function as the royal abbey church of France and burial place of French kings.

In order to make these Gothic churches larger, the ribbed vault, capable of spanning large areas, was devised. To bear the greater stress of these taller, broader interiors, and to create larger window areas, a system of

The abbey church of Saint Denis (1137–44) began the Gothic style, with its integration of the pointed arch, ribbed vault, and flying buttress in one unified structure. Although all these elements appeared separately in Romanesque architecture, Saint Denis was the first structure in which they were brought together in one cohesive system. The combination resulted in a soaring vertical design and increased interior space, evoking the spiritual uplift and awe characteristic of Gothic architecture.

The upper chapel of the Sainte-Chapelle, Paris, one of the finest achievements of High Gothic, was built by Louis IX between 1243 and 1248 as a shrine for sacred relics. The chapel wall, relieved of its support function by ribbed vaults and buttresses, was filled with large stained-glass windows rivaling in beauty those of Chartres.

external supports or flying buttresses (see BUTTRESS) was developed. As the builders became more sophisticated, they were able to achieve ever grander effects at NOTRE DAME DE PARIS (begun 1163), CHARTRES CATHEDRAL (1145; rebuilt after a fire begun 1194), REIMS CATHEDRAL (begun 1210), Amiens Cathedral (begun 1220), and the SAINTE-CHAPELLE in Paris (begun after 1243, completed 1248). The windows were enlarged not to lighten the interiors but rather for extensive use of STAINED GLASS, which attained the height of its development in the late 12th and 13th centuries at Chartres and the Sainte-Chapelle.

Sculpture. Both the exteriors of these churches and certain interior elements were decorated with elaborate sculpture. Facades were populated with large figures of kings; portals were flanked by pillar-statues, called jamb figures, of saints, angels, and apostles; and other parts of the building were encrusted with decorative cusps, finials, and grotesque GARGOYLES. Gothic sculptors took a revolutionary step beyond their Romanesque predecessors in their conception of the figures as independent, almost free-standing statues rather than as reliefs. One of the finest 14th-century creations is the refined and mannered figure of the Virgin that stands in the south transept of Notre Dame de Paris.

Renaissance Period

The Italian RENAISSANCE began to influence French art in the last decade of the 15th century, when Charles VIII returned (1496) from his conquest of Naples accompanied by several Italian artists. Italian styles first appeared in the chateaux of the Loire Valley and became predominant during the reign (1515–47) of Francis I. Initially, however, Italian decorative elements were superimposed on Gothic principles. The earliest example is the Château d'Amboise (*c*.1495), where LEONARDO DA VINCI spent his last years. The marriage of Gothic structure and Italianate ornament progressed in the work of Italian architects

such as Sebastiano SERLIO, who was engaged after 1540 at the Château de FONTAINEBLEAU.

The climate of active royal and aristocratic patronage encouraged many talented artists and architects, including Philibert DELORME and Giacomo VIGNOLA. One of the finest surviving monuments of the French Renaissance is the southwest interior facade of the Cour Carrée of the Palais du LOUVRE in Paris, designed by Pierre Lescot and covered with exterior carvings by Jean GOUJON. Strong regional schools appeared in Lorraine as the arts continued to flourish under the reigns of Henry II and Henry III.

Baroque Period

The reign of Henry IV (1589–1610) was a period of competent and enlightened government. The Place des Vosges (1605), then called the Place Royale, and the Place Dauphine (1607) were planned and built. In Paris a second generation of artists—called the second school of Fontainebleau—was trained or inspired by Italian painters to perpetuate the Italianate tradition under the patronage of Henry IV.

Architecture. In the second and third quarters of the century, during the ministries of Cardinal Richelieu to Louis XIII and of Cardinal Mazarin to the child-king Louis XIV, France became a great European power. The architects Jacques LEMERCIER—builder of Richelieu's Palais Cardinal (begun 1633), now site of the the the Palais Royale, and of the Church of the Sorbonne (begun 1635)—François MANSART, and Louis LE VAU adapted the Italian baroque style to French needs (see BAROQUE ART AND ARCHITECTURE). During the personal reign of Louis XIV (1661–1715), under the direction of the powerful minister of commerce and of royal works, Jean Baptiste COLBERT, the Louvre was enlarged, and the palace of VERSAILLES (*c*.1669–90) was built as a fitting residence for the powerful king of France. The leading architect of the latter half of the 17th century was Jules HARDOUIN-MANSART, who designed parts of the palace of Versailles, the Orangerie, and numerous squares and public buildings in Paris.

Nicolas Poussin's The Childhood of Bacchus *(c. 1629), with its warm palette, free brushwork, and spontaneous drama, reflects the influence of Titian on the artist's early work. (Louvre, Paris.)*

Painting. Italy played a fundamental role in the redirection of French painting in the 17th century. Some French artists, notably Nicolas POUSSIN and Claude LORRAIN, created new modes of painting while living in Italy. Other artists, such as Simon VOUET, fostered a native French baroque style. Colbert founded the Royal Academy of Painting and Sculpture (1663) to protect this group of artists and enlist their services for the state. Charles LE BRUN was named first painter to the king. Under his leadership, artists celebrated the triumphs of the Sun King in MURAL PAINTINGS, altarpieces, tapestry CARTOONS, and other large-scale narrative works.

Recognizing that Italy was the great school of both classical and Renaissance art, Colbert founded the French Academy in Rome in 1666, to which gifted French artists and architects were sent at the expense of the crown.

Jacques Louis David's portrait Madame Recamier *(1800) exhibits the typically cool, crisp line of French neoclassicism. (Louvre, Paris.)*

The Eighteenth Century

On the death of Louis XIV in 1715, his 5-year-old great-grandson, Louis XV, became king. The realm was guided until 1723 by a regent, Louis XIV's nephew Philippe d'Orléans. During the regency, the single-minded direction given the arts by Louis XIV was relaxed in favor of individualism.

Painting and Sculpture. During the first half of the 18th century, the French became enamored of the small genre subjects of 17th-century Holland and of the mythological scenes of the Italian baroque. Decorative arts and interior design were transformed by the growing popularity of the ROCOCO STYLE, a light-hearted and elegant style based on asymmetrical natural forms. Public attention shifted from the courtly taste set at Versailles to the fashion set by the

nobility and wealthy bourgeoisie in their private Parisian residences, called *hôtels*. This new spirit received its finest expression in the brilliant work of the Flemish painter Antoine WATTEAU, whose scenes of revelers in contemporary dress, inhabiting a mythological realm of pleasure, changed the direction of private patronage in France. Artists such as François BOUCHER were inspired to create ravishing combinations of color and graceful forms. This development was encouraged by the court of Louis XV, who adopted the taste of Paris as his courtly style.

In the last quarter of the century, a generation of artists emerged who were devoted to high principles of art and the service of the state. Most famous of these was the painter Jacques Louis DAVID, pioneer of a pure classicizing

The Panthéon (c.1755–90) in Paris, originally the church of Sainte Geneviève, was designed by Jacques Germain Soufflot, one of the leading neoclassical architects of France. Neoclassical architecture reacted against baroque and rococo ornateness and emulated the massive form and restrained line of antique architecture. Soufflot integrated many Gothic elements into the structure of the Panthéon: the vaulting, for example, increased strength and interior lightness while preserving classical form. Corinthian columns support both the portico (1), based on the Roman Pantheon, as well as the saucer domes (2) within the roof of each arm of the building, which is constructed in the form of a Greek cross. The central dome (3), whose three shells resemble the triple-constructed dome of Wren's Saint Paul's Cathedral, is supported by four slender piers, later thickened and strengthened by Rondelet. The windows (4) were eventually eliminated and the towers (5) removed to emphasize the austere, rigid classicism popular at the beginning of the 19th century. During the French Revolution the building was renamed the Panthéon and secularized as a memorial to French heroes.

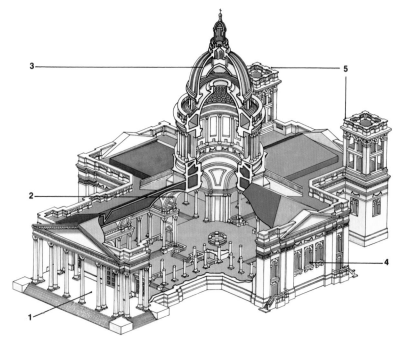

Théodore Géricault's Officer of the Imperial Guard (1812) was one of only three works exhibited during his lifetime. The officer's struggle against a turbulent nature epitomizes an ideal of romantic heroism that Géricault's paintings helped establish. (Louvre, Paris.)

Edgar Degas's pastel Blue Dancers (1890) shows the preparations of ballet dancers waiting in the wings. Degas shared a concern for immediacy with the other impressionists, but his composition foreshadows postimpressionism. (Louvre, Paris.)

style. A wide divergence existed between the didactic art of David and the courtly taste of Louis XV and his grandson, Louis XVI, who preferred artists such as Jean Honoré FRAGONARD and Hubert ROBERT. Consequently, a healthy variety characterized the art of late-18th-century France.

Architecture. French architecture of the 18th century continued the classicizing tendencies of the 17th century in France. Restrained ornament, delicate carved limestone details, and the sophisticated play of volume and lighting give the domestic and public architecture of the period a sense of calm grandeur. Among the architectural gems of the reign of Louis XV is the Petit Trianon (1762) by Ange Jacques Gabriel, a leisure retreat in the park at Versailles.

Late-18th-century architecture was affected by a neoclassical revival comparable to that in painting. NEOCLASSICISM was particularly well suited to monumental buildings, such as Jacques Germain Soufflot's Saint-Geneviève, now called the Panthéon, in Paris.

The Nineteenth Century

The 18th-century interest in sentiment and emotion led to an interest in extremes of sensibility in the romantic art of the following century (see ROMANTICISM, art).

Jean Auguste Dominique Ingres's Turkish Bath (1863) shows his sensitive modeling of bodily contours. Although he often appealed to the exotic romanticism of his day, Ingres perfected the linear style and polished surface of the neoclassical ideal. (Louvre, Paris.)

Painting. The greatest practitioners of romantic painting in France were Théodore GÉRICAULT, Eugène DELACROIX, and Jean Auguste Dominique INGRES. Géricault's *Raft of the Medusa* (1818–19; Louvre, Paris), a depiction of the victims of a shipwreck, exposed the full range of human emotions from despair to exhilaration. Delacroix's *Death of Sardanapalus* (1827; Louvre) explored the potential of color and vibrant brushwork as a means of heightening the sensations aroused by a dramatic narrative episode. In harem scenes such as *The Great Odalisque* (1814; Louvre) Ingres reflects 19th-century European fascination with the life of the senses and exotic cultures.

By the mid-19th century the self-indulgence of romanticism was tempered by the changing relationship of the artist to the subject matter. Gustave COURBET's paintings of peasants, such as *Funeral at Ornans* (1850; Louvre), caused a scandal, but his powerful depiction of nature found other exponents in Jean François MILLET and Honoré DAUMIER (see REALISM, art).

The new conception of art as an activity that was worthwhile for its own sake, regardless of its subject matter or allegiance to institutional values, was a necessary precondition for the emergence of IMPRESSIONISM, a movement in painting that concentrated on the effects of light and color. The favored subjects of Claude MONET, Pierre Auguste RENOIR, and Camille PISSARRO were coastal and river scenes in which light dissolves form and softens focus. The loosely associated impressionist group also included Edgar DEGAS, whose interior scenes challenged conventional theories of formal composition and subject matter.

POSTIMPRESSIONISM, a general term for the work of such painters as Paul CÉZANNE, Paul GAUGUIN, Vincent VAN GOGH, Georges SEURAT, and Pierre BONNARD, evolved in reaction to the neutrality of subject matter and dissolution of form inherent in impressionism. These artists had few qualities in common, but their individual styles did much to determine the directions that painting would take in the 20th century.

The Paris Opéra, designed by Charles Garnier in 1861 and completed in 1875, was initiated as part of Napoleon III's replanning of Paris between 1853 and 1868 and was designed to glorify the Second Empire. The monumental structure, based upon precepts of the École des Beaux-Arts, broke with neoclassical restraint in an exuberant revival of the baroque. Garnier's eclectic facade, employing elements from Renaissance architectural tradition, is elaborately ornamental. The sumptuous interior focuses upon a central domed auditorium (1) with tiered balconies and a large stage house (2). Private entrance wings for the emperor (3) and house patrons (4) flank the auditorium. The showpieces of the Opéra, however, are the frankly ostentatious gilt foyers and the immense staircase of multicolored marble.

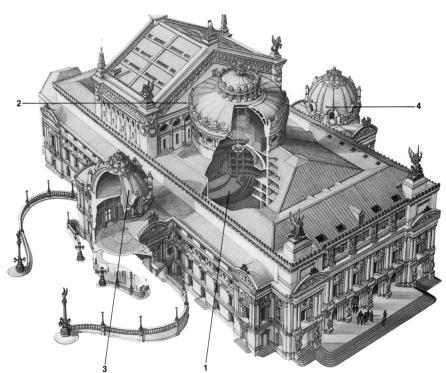

Sculpture. In sculpture, the 19th century tended to be conservative. The romantic sculpture of François Rudé, Jean Baptiste CARPEAUX, and Antoine Louis BARYE stands out. Auguste RODIN revitalized sculpture by returning to the direct study of the human form.

Paul Cézanne's The Card Players (c.1892), with its distortion of figures and its unifying color motifs, illustrates the artist's transition from representational impressionism to abstract art. (Courtauld Institute Galleries, London.)

Architecture. In architecture, the neoclassicism of the late 18th century was perpetuated by monumental forms serving the political ambitions of the Second Empire (1852–70) of Napoleon III. The work of architects trained at the ÉCOLE DES BEAUX-ARTS, such as Jean Louis Charles GARNIER's spectacular Paris Opéra (1861–75), played an important role in Baron HAUSSMANN's modernization of the city. New industrial materials and construction techniques were investigated by such pioneers as Alexandre Gustave Eiffel, whose EIFFEL TOWER (1889) has become a symbol of Paris.

The Twentieth Century

Painting and Sculpture. The course of 20th-century art was shaped from Paris by the Spaniard Pablo PICASSO, the Russian Wassily KANDINSKY, the Romanian Constantin BRANCUSI, and many lesser figures. The history of 20th-century expressionist art (see EXPRESSIONISM, art) descends from van Gogh and other postimpressionists through the Fauve group (see FAUVISM) that formed around Henri MATISSE, one of the most influential French artists of the 20th century. Picasso and Georges BRAQUE changed the direction of painting through their experiments with CUBISM. The last influential Parisian artistic movement was SURREALISM, a literary and artistic movement devoted to the exploration of irrational and subconscious states of mind.

Architecture. In architecture, France was at the forefront of the creation of a new 20th-century aesthetic. At

Georges Braque's Still Life with Playing Cards (1913) isolates specific aspects of form, color, and texture from their constituent objects and re-creates the table, grapes, apple, and cards through superimposed patches. Braque's collaboration with Picasso brought about the development of cubism. (Musée National d'Art Moderne, Paris.)

the turn of the century, the experiments of ART NOUVEAU led to the creation of graceful decorative motifs based on natural forms. The Swiss architect Charles Édouard Jeanneret, called LE CORBUSIER, pioneered in France a philosophy of functionalism in architecture. His theory and practices, reinforced by those of the BAUHAUS in Germany, became the fundamental principles of the INTERNATIONAL STYLE, typified by Le Corbusier's Villa Savoire (1929–31; Poissy-sur-Seine). Major achievements of French art since World War II include the paintings of Jean DUBUFFET, the brilliantly colored paper cutouts of Matisse, and Le Corbusier's Pilgrim Church of Notre Dame at Ronchamp (1950–55).

See also: ARCHITECTURE; ART; ART DECO; CATHEDRALS AND CHURCHES; DADA; DIRECTOIRE STYLE; EMPIRE STYLE; FURNITURE; INTERIOR DESIGN; PAINTING; SCULPTURE; TAPESTRY; TEXTILES.

Henri Matisse's Dance (1910) conveys a delight in color and a love of undulating line. Throughout his career Matisse sought simplicity of expression. (Hermitage, Leningrad.)

French bulldog   The French bulldog is a small but massive breed, reaching only 30 cm (12 in) high at the shoulder but weighing up to 13 kg (25 lb). It is low-set and smooth-coated, with a blunt, heavy head and relatively high, batlike ears. The tail is naturally short, not docked. Coat colors are brindle, fawn, white with brindle patches, or solid white. The breed's exact origin is uncertain. The English claim that it originated from miniature English bulldogs brought to France about the middle of the 19th century. The French claim that the breed is an old native one. Although the breed probably did originate from small English bulldogs, its development was French and its preservation the result of efforts by American breeders. The French Bulldog Club of America was founded in 1898.

The French bulldog, smaller than the English bulldog, is distinguished by its batlike ears. This nonsporting breed reached its greatest popularity in the early 1900s.

French colonial empire   From its beginnings in the early 1600s through the great expansion of the late 19th century, the French overseas empire was formed more by the agencies and stimulation of the state, church, and armed forces than by the initiation of the business community. Merchants, financiers, and manufacturers did engage in and profit from French imperial ventures, but generally they had to be prodded into participation by monarchical or republican officials. In this the French colonial empire differed from its chief rival, the BRITISH EMPIRE.

Before the French Revolution, Henry IV, Louis XIV, the latter's minister Jean Baptiste COLBERT, and many missionaries, explorers, and merchants helped acquire Canada, Louisiana, several West Indian islands, and parts of India. In 1763, at the end of the SEVEN YEARS' WAR, the French lost Canada and India to the British, and in 1803, Napoleon I sold the Louisiana Territory to the United States. By 1815 only the West Indian sugar islands and some scattered African and Asian posts remained French.

The foundations of a second French colonial empire were laid between 1830 and 1870, when Louis Philippe's forces penetrated Algeria and Napoleon III seized Cochin China in southeastern Asia. Along with other European powers, France rode the post-1870 wave of new imperialism. By 1914, France had amassed an empire

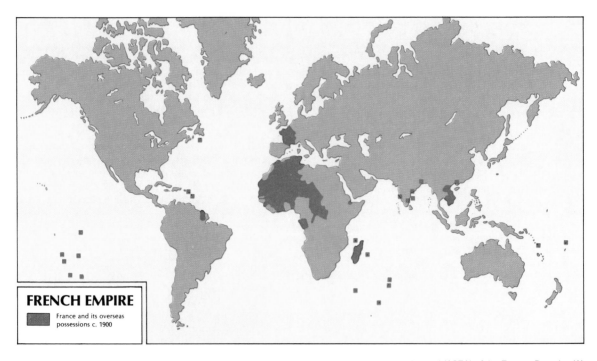

FRENCH EMPIRE

France and its overseas
possessions c. 1900

A global map shows France and its colonial possessions in 1900. During the period between the end (1871) of the Franco-Prussian War and the onset (1914) of World War I, the French colonial empire expanded greatly, notably in Africa and the Far East.

incorporating over 10,000,000 km² (4,000,000 mi²) and 60 million people. In Southeast Asia the French pieced together the colony of INDOCHINA by 1893, adding Laos, Cambodia (now Kampuchea), Annam, and Tonkin to Cochin China. Tunisia and Morocco became protectorates. France's vast African empire also included FRENCH EQUATORIAL AFRICA, FRENCH WEST AFRICA, French Somaliland (now Djibouti), and the islands of Madagascar and the Comoros.

The motives for this overseas penetration ranged from the search for markets, raw materials, investments, and cheap labor to the drive for glory, prestige, strategic advantage, and manpower. Prominent, too, was the *mission civilisatrice,* the urge to implant Roman Catholicism and French culture.

The governance of the empire followed two patterns, sometimes intertwined: assimilation and association. Where there prevailed long traditions of organized political life and a common culture, the French tended to rule indirectly through existing local authorities, as in Tunisia and Morocco. In less structured societies like those of West Africa, the French imposed direct rule. More than the British, the French intermixed with the indigenous population.

The French colonial empire survived World War I, but World War II led to its reorganization as the French Union in 1946. This new entity, in which citizenship rights were extended to natives of former French dependencies, was replaced by a looser French Community in 1958. Since

many member states chose full sovereignty in the 1960s, however, the community was gradually dissolved.

See also: COLONIALISM; EAST INDIA COMPANY, FRENCH; FRANCE, HISTORY OF; VIETNAM WAR.

French East India Company   see EAST INDIA COMPANY, FRENCH

French Equatorial Africa   French Equatorial Africa was a former (1910–59) administrative grouping of four French territories in west central Africa. It comprised Chad, Ubangi-Shari (Central African Republic), Gabon, and the Middle Congo (Congo). Brazzaville, Congo, served as the capital.

French foreign legion   The *Légion Étrangère* ("foreign legion") is a French military corps founded originally to serve in the French colonies. It is now an elite corps in the French army. The legion was first raised by King Louis Philippe in 1831. Garrisoned in Algeria until that country achieved independence in 1962, the legion was not permitted in France during peacetime. Since 1962, however, it has been headquartered at Aubagne, near Marseille. Although the majority of its officers are French, the legion consists mainly of foreign volunteers.

The French foreign legion has captured the popular imagination as a subject of romance, epitomized in the classic American film *Beau Geste* (1939; based on the novel by P. C. Wren). During World War I its *régiment de marche* was France's most decorated army unit. After World War II the legion fought in Indochina, in Algeria, in Zaire (1978), and in Chad in the late 1970s and again in 1983. It has 8,000 men. The Spanish army has a similar corps, the *Legión Extranjera*, formerly stationed in Spanish Morocco, and now in the Canary Islands.

French Guiana [gee-ah'-nuh]

French Guiana is an overseas department of France—an administrative status that renders it an integral part of the French Republic. It is located on the northern coast of South America and is bordered on the west by Suriname, on the south and east by Brazil, and on the north by the Atlantic Ocean. Its total land area is 86,504 km^2 (33,399 mi^2), and the estimated population in 1990 was 97,781. The capital, CAYENNE (1982 pop., 37,097), is a port on the north coast and the country's only important urban center. There are a number of small, rocky islands along the coast, the most famous of which is DEVIL'S ISLAND, long a French penal colony.

Land and Economy

The coastal strip of French Guiana was once the center of a prosperous sugar industry and still grows small quantities of sugarcane as well as rice and corn. The densely forested interior, almost totally undeveloped, rises gradually to the mountains along the Brazilian border in the south.

The climate is tropical, with an annual average temperature of 27° C (80° F); rainfall is heavy, averaging 3,200 mm (126 in) a year at Cayenne. A dry season, however, lasts from August to November. Agricultural activities along the coast have been in decline since the abolition of slavery in 1848 made plantation agriculture uneconomic. For many years the principal economic activity centered on the penal colony on Devil's Island. With the closing of the prison in 1945, however, this source of income disappeared. The French government provides many jobs at French-scale wages and substantial aid. Fisheries are being developed, especially for shrimp. Exports of fish and fish products account for about two-thirds of total revenue. Forestry is also important, and the sawmill industry is being expanded. Most of the labor force, however, works in services, government, and commerce.

Extensive mineral resources are known to exist, including iron ore, copper, silver, lead, platinum, diamonds, and gold, but they remain unexploited. The rain forests that cover nearly 90% of the country are an abundant resource of tropical hardwoods. In the 1960s the de Gaulle government established the Guianan Space Center at Kourou, northwest of Cayenne, primarily because its proximity to the equator makes it a favorable site for the launching of space vehicles. The European Space Agency's rocket Ariane is launched from the center. Overall French investment has declined, however, and in the 1970s and '80s the economy has tended to stagnate. One of the greatest problems is unemployment, especially among young people.

People

Most of the people of French Guiana are Creoles—people of mixed European and African descent. There are small minorities of Europeans (mostly French), American Indians, Chinese, and Laotians. In recent decades there has been some migration of people of mixed African-European ancestry from Haiti, Martinique, and Guadeloupe. In the interior, small groups of blacks descended from escaped slaves have reverted to an African tribal form of life. French Guiana's dominant religion is Roman Catholicism, and the official language is French.

History

The first permanent French settlement was effected in 1604. Cayenne was taken by the Dutch in 1676 and held for a year. The Portuguese occupied the town from 1808 to 1817. The region was long neglected and development was hindered by the establishment of the penal colony. In 1946, when most of the penal colonies had been closed, French Guiana was made an overseas French department with representation in the French parliament.

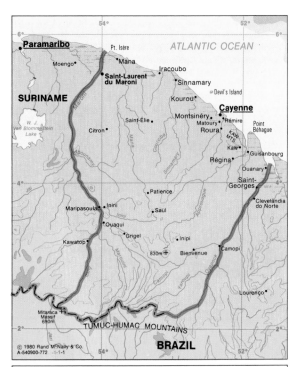

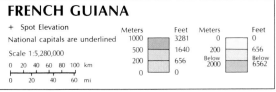

FRENCH GUIANA

+ Spot Elevation
National capitals are underlined

Scale 1:5,280,000

	Meters	Feet	Meters	Feet
	1000	3281	0	0
	500	1640	200	656
	200	656	Below 2000	Below 6562
	0	0		

0 20 40 60 80 100 km

0   20   40   60 mi

French horn The French horn (so called to distinguish it from the ENGLISH HORN, a member of the OBOE family) is the developed European orchestral member of the true horn family. The instrument is classified technically as a lip-vibrated aerophone (see MUSICAL INSTRUMENTS), characterized by a conical bore and funnel-shaped mouthpiece, as opposed to the cylindrical bore and cup-shaped mouthpiece of the TRUMPET family.

Descended from primitive animal-horn prototypes (for example, the biblical SHOFAR), short, curved horns were used in medieval Europe primarily as signal instruments. By the late 17th century in France the *cor de chasse* ("hunting horn") emerged with a wide, flaring bell and a coiled tube length of up to 4.37 m (14 ft), the obvious prototype of the modern instrument. Responsive to a greatly increased number of its natural overtones, the *cor de chasse* possessed a wide enough range of pitches for use in the orchestra of the early 18th century.

The addition of "crooks" (curved extensions to the tubing of various lengths) and the technique—attributed to the Dresden virtuoso Anton Joseph Hampel—of altering the pitch by stopping the bell with the hand made the horn still more complete melodically in its middle ranges. Also at this time (the late 18th century) the cup-shaped, trumpetlike mouthpiece was abandoned for the funnel-shaped mouthpiece of the modern horn, resulting in a smoother, less raucous sound.

In 1818, Heinrich Stölzel and Friedrich Blühmel in Berlin added patented valves to vary the playing length of the tube, yielding an instrument virtually chromatic (proceeding by semitones) throughout its range. The modern French horn is usually pitched in F, and has three valves

The modern French horn evolved from the hunting horn developed during the 17th century. The "double horn" shown here, a late-19th-century invention, is a combination F horn and B-flat horn; a valve operated by the thumb allows the player to switch from one key to the other. Three other valves provide a full chromatic range. The player's right hand is inserted in the bell to modulate the open tone.

and a tube length of about 3.75 m (12 ft). In the "double horn" a separate set of coils for a horn in B-flat is added to a horn in F, a fourth valve acting as a switch between the two sets of coils.

French and Indian Wars The French and Indian Wars were a series of armed conflicts between England's colonies in North America on the one side and rival European colonies on the other during the period 1689–1763. Each conflict was part of a larger war in Europe and on the high seas.

By the 1680s, Spain held Florida, France occupied Canada (NEW FRANCE), and England possessed a chain of colonies along the Atlantic seaboard from New England to the Carolinas. West of the Appalachians lay a vast extent of territory open to international competition and strife. Inevitably involved on both sides were the various tribes of Indians, whose own deep-seated rivalries meshed with the rivalries of the Europeans. The IROQUOIS LEAGUE, often known as the Five (later Six) Nations, was a particularly influential and powerful group of Indians occupying the area south and east of Lake Ontario, thereby dominating the fur-trading routes leading both to French Montreal and English Albany, N.Y. In general, the Iroquois tended to support the English against the French, but increasingly they found advantage in playing one side off against the other.

During these wars in North America the English always enjoyed a tremendous preponderance of population. In 1689, New France had only about 12,000 inhabitants, while the English colonists numbered over 200,000. By 1760 the population of New France may have reached 60,000, but at the same time the British colonies swarmed with nearly 1.6 million people. (These figures do not include unassimilated Indians.)

King William's War

In May 1689, England, under its new Dutch king, WILLIAM III, entered the War of the GRAND ALLIANCE against France. That summer in America an Iroquois raiding party struck hard at the French settlement of Lachine near Montreal. Soon a new French governor, the comte de FRONTENAC, arrived in New France and initiated a counteroffensive against the English frontier, carried out in 1690 by mixed parties of French and Indians. Their ferocity and destructiveness established a pattern of savagery in border warfare for the next century.

Recognizing that Quebec on the St. Lawrence River was the heart of New France, English colonial leaders decided to attempt its capture. A land army was to advance down the Champlain Valley toward Montreal, while a fleet commanded by Sir William PHIPS was to proceed from Boston to the St. Lawrence and up to Quebec. The failure of the land army to get within a hundred miles of Montreal enabled Frontenac to shift troops from that town to Quebec. Phips took Port Royal (now Annapolis Royal, Nova Scotia), but by the time he reached Quebec in October 1690, that city was too strongly defended to be taken. The New Englanders had to withdraw in humiliation, losing Port Royal to the French again in 1691.

Thereafter, the war was characterized by sporadic, small-scale raiding activity against isolated frontier settlements. In Europe both sides were growing weary of the struggle, and a peace was arranged at Ryswick in September 1697, ending the war indecisively.

Queen Anne's War

The French then resumed their expansion into the region of the Great Lakes and the Mississippi Valley, causing the English to fear that the whole trans-Appalachian West would come under the French flag. When Louis XIV of France secured the Spanish throne for his grandson, Philip V of Spain, the War of the SPANISH SUCCESSION broke out in Europe in 1701. England entered the conflict in May 1702, this time declaring war on both France and Spain. Thus in the American theater, where the war was named for the English monarch Queen Anne, the English colonies now faced enemies to the south as well as to the north.

In 1702 the Carolinas sent an expedition against the Spanish settlement of Saint Augustine. After an unsuccessful siege the Carolinians returned home, but Florida was too weak to retaliate, and in subsequent years the Carolinians ravaged the Apalachee region with impunity. In the meantime, New England again was struggling to cope with French and Indian raiders along its lengthy and ill-defended frontier. Various settlements in Maine were attacked, and early in 1704 a party of French and Indians surprised Deerfield, Mass., killing many of the inhabitants and taking others into captivity.

England sent military and naval assistance to New England in 1710, with the result that Port Royal, and with it ACADIA, was seized by the British in that year. In 1711 the Tuscarora Indians of North Carolina rose up against the English, beginning an Indian war that ended two years later with the defeat of the Tuscaroras. That tribe then migrated northward and became the sixth nation of the Iroquois League.

By 1712, France and Spain were eager for peace, and an international agreement was reached at Utrecht in the spring of 1713. Spain retained Florida, but France was forced to relinquish Acadia to the British, and it became

The map indicates major troop movements of the French and the British, forts, and significant battle sites of the French and Indian War (1754–63). During this conflict both colonial powers competed for the loyalties of powerful Indian tribes, whose affiliations are also shown.

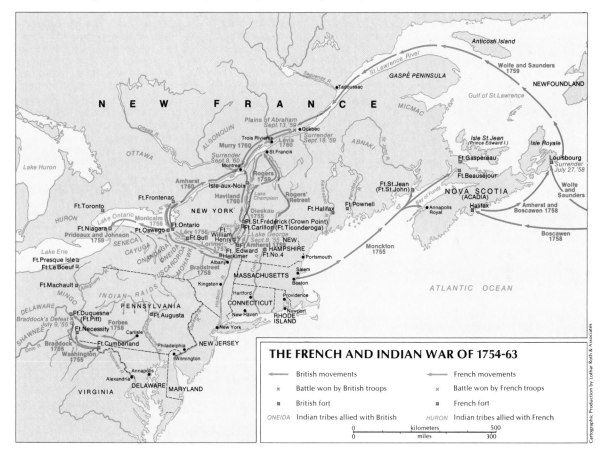

THE FRENCH AND INDIAN WAR OF 1754-63

← British movements		→ French movements
✕ Battle won by British troops		✕ Battle won by French troops
▣ British fort		▣ French fort
ONEIDA Indian tribes allied with British		*HURON* Indian tribes allied with French

Cartographic Production by Lothar Roth & Associates

the new British colony of Nova Scotia. Britain also secured Newfoundland.

The Treaty of Utrecht (see UTRECHT, PEACE OF) introduced a period of uneasy peace that lasted just 26 years in North America. During this time Britain sought to strengthen the southern flank of its colonies by founding the colony of Georgia (1733) under James OGELTHORPE.

War of the 1740s

Commercial rivalry between Britain and Spain produced the War of Jenkins' Ear—named for the alleged mutilation of an English sea captain by the Spanish—in 1739. This gave Oglethorpe an opportunity to lead Carolinians and Georgians against Saint Augustine in 1740, but he had to abandon the siege after several weeks. In 1742 he thwarted a Spanish invasion of Georgia, making the war in the south a standoff.

New England's relative security ended in 1744 when France entered the war as an ally of Spain in what was to become known as King George's War. After their loss of Nova Scotia in 1713, the French had constructed the large fortress of LOUISBOURG on Cape Breton Island at the southern entrance to the Gulf of St. Lawrence. From Louisbourg, French sea raiders could prey upon New England shipping. In 1745 a New England army led by William PEPPERRELL of Maine, with the assistance of a squadron from the Royal Navy, forced the surrender of Louisbourg.

Since 1731 the French had also had an advance base at Crown Point on Lake Champlain whence they could send parties of French and Indian raiders south to attack the frontiers of New England and New York. During the War of the 1740s, such raids did considerable damage and discouraged the British colonists in the area, who lacked the means and the will to attempt the capture of Crown Point.

With neither side close to a decisive victory either in North America or in the War of the AUSTRIAN SUCCESSION at home, the European powers again needed peace. In 1748 the Treaty of Aix-la-Chapelle was reached; its terms required that Louisbourg be given back to France.

French and Indian War

In the continuing colonial rivalry, attention soon focused on the Forks of the Ohio River, a strategically crucial area claimed by both the British and the French but effectively occupied by neither. In 1754 the OHIO COMPANY of Virginia, a group of land speculators, began building a fort at the Forks only to have the workers ejected by a strong French expedition, which then proceeded to construct FORT DUQUESNE on the site. Virginia militia commanded by young George WASHINGTON proved no match for the French and Indians from Fort Duquesne. Defeated at Fort Necessity (July 1754), they were forced to withdraw east of the mountains.

The British government in London, realizing that the colonies by themselves were unable to prevent the French advance into the Ohio Valley, sent a force of regulars under Gen. Edward BRADDOCK to uphold the British territorial claims. In July 1755, to the consternation of all the English colonies, Braddock's army was disastrously defeated as it approached Fort Duquesne.

Again the British looked to the Iroquois League for assistance. As usual, the Iroquois responded but without much enthusiasm. Other tribes, impressed with French power, either shifted allegiance to the French or took shelter in an uneasy neutrality. In 1755 the British forcibly deported virtually the entire French peasant population of Nova Scotia (Acadia) to increase the security of that province. But it was not until May 1756, nearly two years after the outbreak of hostilities on the Virginia frontier, that Britain declared war on France. For the time being Spain remained uncommitted in the conflict, which was part of the larger SEVEN YEARS' WAR.

Under the effective generalship of the marquis de MONTCALM, New France enjoyed victory after victory. In 1756, Montcalm forced the surrender of the British fort at Oswego on Lake Ontario, thereby breaking the British fingerhold on the Great Lakes. A year later he destroyed Fort William Henry at the south end of Lake George, dashing British hopes for an advance through the Champlain Valley to Crown Point. The northern frontier seemed to be collapsing in upon the British colonies.

William PITT (the Elder), Britain's new prime minister, had adopted a policy of drastically increasing aid to the American colonies. France, in contrast, found itself unable to maintain large-scale support of its colonies. As a result, by 1758 the period of French ascendancy was coming to an end. The British began gaining important victories under the military leadership of Jeffrey, Lord AMHERST.

In 1758 a British expedition forced the surrender of Louisbourg, and another expedition advancing west from Philadelphia caused the French to abandon the Forks of the Ohio. This latter victory, in turn, convinced many Indians that Britain would prevail after all, accelerating a shift of tribal support away from the French. Only at TICONDEROGA, south of Crown Point, did British arms suffer a major defeat.

For the British, 1759 proved to be a year of stunning successes in America. One British expedition took Niaga-

Gen. James Wolfe, commander of the British army that captured the French city of Quebec in 1759, lies dying from wounds received in battle. The painting (1770) is by Benjamin West. (National Gallery of Canada, Ottawa.)

ra. Another, led by Amherst himself, seized both Ticonderoga and Crown Point, thereby opening the way to Montreal. A third, commanded by young Gen. James WOLFE, sailed up the St. Lawrence and, after much difficulty, defeated Montcalm on the Plains of Abraham just outside Quebec. The surrender of Quebec itself soon followed. In 1760, Amherst completed the conquest of Canada with a successful three-pronged offensive against Montreal.

War-weary by 1763, the belligerent nations negotiated the decisive Treaty of Paris. Britain gained all of North America east of the Mississippi River, including Canada and Florida, so that a bright future for its colonists seemed assured. With the French and Spanish menace now removed from their frontiers and the Indians deprived of foreign support in their resistance to British expansion, the inhabitants of the coastal colonies could feel less dependent on Britain and better able to fend for themselves. Their experience with British regular forces during the war, moreover, had generated mutual dislike. At the same time, Britain's costly struggle with France had depleted the British treasury, a fact that soon would lead Parliament to seek additional revenue by taxing the American colonies. Clearly, then, conditions arising from the French and Indian Wars helped set the stage for the AMERICAN REVOLUTION.

French language see ROMANCE LANGUAGES

French literature French literature has been for centuries an impressive facet of French civilization, an object of national pride, and a principal focus for feelings of national identity. Several European literary trends have originated in France, and the continuing prestige of literature there is evidenced by the innumerable private societies devoted to individual authors and the many literary prizes awarded each year.

The Middle Ages

French literature began when writers started using the dialects that had evolved from the Latin spoken in the parts of the Roman Empire that would become France. Eventually, the dialect in use around Paris gained supremacy and by the 10th century was vying with Latin for prestige. The 11th century witnessed the emergence of numerous epic poems called CHANSONS DE GESTE, which told of the heroic deeds of knights fighting with or against Charlemagne. Of the more than 80 *chansons* remaining, the masterpiece is the *Chanson de Roland* (12th century).

The *chansons* were followed in the second half of the 12th century by the *romans courtois*, or tales of COURTLY LOVE, written in verse and intended to be read aloud before aristocratic audiences. Celebrating knights fighting in honor of their ladies, many of these poems are set at King Arthur's court and steeped in the Celtic mythology of Brittany, Cornwall, and Wales. Of particular importance was the Tristan and Iseult cycle with its semimystical evocation of a love as strong as death. The greatest poet in this tradition was CHRÉTIEN DE TROYES, author of *Erec, Lancelot*, and *Perceval*. The *lais* were very short *romans*

courtois, a genre to which MARIE DE FRANCE contributed. The most significant medieval poem was Le ROMAN DE LA ROSE, whose first 4,000 lines were written about 1230 by Guillaume de Lorris in the courtly tradition; about 40 years later, Jean de Meung added 18,000 lines in a realistic, satirical vein.

Outside aristocratic circles a different type of literature flourished. The FABLIAUX were short verse narratives, earthy and bantering in tone, sparing no one, least of all women or clergy. FABLES, allegorical stories in which animals were used to satirize human characteristics or advance a moral point, were equally popular, the most celebrated being REYNARD THE FOX.

The greatest French poet of the late medieval period was François VILLON—thief, murderer, and prison inmate—whose alternately bitter, amusing, and deeply moving *Testament* (1461; Eng. trans., 1924) sounds a strangely modern note. In it are many examples of the BALLADE and the *rondeau*.

The Middle Ages also saw the development of history as a prose genre, especially in Jean FROISSART's *Chronicles* (Eng. trans., 1523–25), which vividly evoke the barbarities of the Hundred Years' War. The *Memoirs* (1489–90, 1497–98; Eng. trans., 1596) of Philippe de Commynes, dealing with the reigns of Louis XI and Charles VIII, reveal a truer historian, more concerned with the hidden causes of events than with mere chronicling.

The French Renaissance

By the 1530s, François RABELAIS, in one of the great comic works of world literature, gave pointed expression to the feeling of rebirth then being experienced by the European intellectual community. In *Gargantua* (1534) his giant hero reports to his son Pantagruel on the amazing intellectual progress that has occurred in just one generation, thanks to the revival of the literature and thought of antiquity. Behind the rollicking carnivallike story the incoherence, the coarse humor, and the symbolic exaggerations of *Gargantua* and the associated *Pantagruel* volumes (1532, 1556; Eng. trans. of Rabelais's *Works*, 1653–94) lie an immense learning and understanding of contemporary problems.

In religion HUMANISM found expression in Protestantism, whose chief voice in France was the great Genevan reformer John CALVIN. His *Institutes of the Christian Religion* (1541; Eng. trans., 1813) conquered for the French language the ability to discuss religious subjects that had previously been reserved for Latin.

Humanism was perhaps best exemplified by Michel de MONTAIGNE, who in the second half of the 16th century invented the genre of the familiar ESSAY. Although inspired by an enormous number of quotations, his *Essays* (1580, 1588; Eng. trans., 1603) are nevertheless profoundly original and together constitute one of the most honest and ingratiating self-examinations ever conducted.

The break with the past was even more pronounced in poetry. New forms like the sonnet imported from Italy, as well as Greek and Latin odes, enjoyed popularity. But in 1549 the poet Joachim du Bellay wrote a manifesto calling for the enrichment of the French language to ensure

Pierre Corneille (1606–84)   *Molière (1622–73)*   *Jean Racine (1639–99)*

its parity with ancient tongues. The prince of Renaissance poets, however, was Pierre de RONSARD, the uncontested leader of the constellation of poets called La PLÉIADE.

The Triumph of Classicism

France's position as the most powerful nation in Europe during the reign of Louis XIV was reflected in the preeminence French literature attained. In 1635, Cardinal Richelieu created the ACADÉMIE FRANÇAISE to regulate the language. The conflict between two literary tendencies—one toward greater creative freedom, later called "baroque," and the other toward an acceptance of literary rules—had been resolved in favor of CLASSICISM by 1660. Its components were codified by Nicolas BOILEAU-DESPRÉAUX, the founder of French literary criticism, in his *Art of Poetry* (1674; Eng. trans., 1683), in which reason, proportion, and harmony were defined as the outstanding values.

France's two greatest dramatists emerged during this period. Pierre CORNEILLE, whose tragic masterpiece *The Cid* (1637) concerns the conflict between duty and passion, wrote over 30 plays, most of them in accordance with the Aristotelian unities of time, place, and action. He was surpassed in popularity and critical esteem only by Jean RACINE, whose simpler style and more realistic characters and plots, as in *Andromache* (1667; Eng. trans., 1675) and *Phaedra* (1677; Eng. trans., 1776), reveal a world of ferocious passions beneath a veneer of elegant poetry. In comedy, MOLIÈRE, ranging from the farcical to sharp explorations of social, psychological, and metaphysical questions, created a body of plays as fresh today as when first produced. His masterpieces are *Tartuffe* (1664; Eng. trans., 1670) and *The Misanthrope* (1666; Eng. trans., 1709).

The French novel, which in the first part of the 17th century was long, diffuse, and full of improbable adventures (*L'Astrée*, 1607–28, for instance), also came of age. In *The Princess of Clèves* (1678; Eng. trans., 1925), a concise psychological analysis of a moral problem in married life, the comtesse de LA FAYETTE fashioned a perfect model of the novel of character.

Minor literary forms were ennobled by such brilliant practitioners as Madame de SÉVIGNÉ, in her correspondence; the duc de LA ROCHEFOUCAULD, in his *Maxims* (1665; Eng. trans., 1694); and Jean de LA BRUYÈRE, whose *Characters* (1688; Eng. trans., 1699) anticipated the liberal, scientifically oriented tendencies of the 18th century. The poet Jean de LA FONTAINE achieved lasting fame with his successive volumes of *Fables* (1668, 1678, 1694; Eng. trans., 1734), a genre he made his own by combining sophisticated "morals" with a deliberately archaic and deceptively simple style. The memoir assumed a new power and subtlety when composed by such participants in historical events as the duc de SAINT-SIMON, La Rochefoucauld, and Cardinal de Retz.

The enormously influential *Discourse on Method* (1637) not only established its author, René DESCARTES, as the first modern philosopher but set the precedent for that clarity and precision with which French thinking and writing would be associated. Another philosopher admired as much for the perfection of his prose as for his thought was Blaise PASCAL. His *Lettres provinciales* (1656–57; Eng. trans., 1816) demonstrated the effectiveness of simplicity informed by intelligence and wit, whereas the *Pensées* (1670; Eng. trans., 1688) directed the reader to faith in the Christian God through a combination of reason, passion, and insight. More grandiloquent, and representative of 17th-century orthodoxy, were the sermons and funeral orations of the preacher and polemicist Jacques Bossuet. His quietist opponent François de FÉNELON combined the interests of a classicist with a new critical spirit in his didactic novel *Télémaque* (1699; Eng. trans., 1743).

The French Enlightenment

With the decline in the authority of the French monarchy, all social and political institutions came under question and, eventually, attack. Ideas assumed sovereign power as, one by one, traditional bastions were subjected to the scrutiny of the PHILOSOPHES. Probably no other country or century has witnessed such a concentration of intellectual talent as that represented by the French EN-LIGHTENMENT.

Pierre BAYLE, a Protestant philosopher turned freethinker, set the tone of the century with his *Dictionnaire historique et critique* (1697; rev. 1704–06; Eng. trans., 1709), which foreshadowed the aggressive religious and social criticism of VOLTAIRE's *Dictionnaire philosophique* (1764; Eng. trans., 1765). Voltaire wrote classical tragedies, histories, deistic poetry, and light verse. He is chiefly remembered, however, for his philosophical tales, such as *Zadig* (1747; Eng. trans., 1749) and *Candide* (1759; Eng. trans., 1759); his *Letters concerning the English Nation* (1733), comparing English with French institutions; and his *Essai sur les moeurs et l'esprit des nations* (1769; partially trans. as *The General History and State of Europe*, 1754), an anthropologic comparative history of national characteristics.

MONTESQUIEU also adopted the method of comparative analysis, producing in his masterpiece *The Spirit of the Laws* (1748; Eng. trans., 1750) a profound study of the different types of government. In this treatise he expounded the doctrine of the separation of powers, which helped mold the U.S. Constitution.

The biggest weapon leveled against prejudice and tradition, however, was the *Encyclopédie*, published in 35 volumes between 1751 and 1780 and incorporating the materialist, skeptical, and antireligious ideas of the day. This was a collective enterprise directed by Denis DIDEROT to which the best minds contributed: Jean d'ALEMBERT, Baron d'HOLBACH, Étienne de CONDILLAC, Anne Robert Jacques TURGOT, Montesquieu, Voltaire, and Jean Jacques ROUSSEAU.

Rousseau asserted the principle of the collective sovereignty of the people in *The Social Contract* (1762; Eng. trans., 1764); in *Émile* (1762) he expressed progressive pedagogical theories. His novel *La Nouvelle Héloïse* (1761), a compendium of the major intellectual questions of the time, was a forerunner of ROMANTICISM through which he popularized the "return to nature" and the natural morality he believed would flow from such a state. Rousseau's *Confessions* (1781, 1788) and *Rêveries*

(1782; Eng. trans. for both, 1783) were daring autobiographical works that helped to develop the romantic taste for the public display of the inner self.

The novel and the play contributed to the new sensibility. Alain René LESAGE's (1668–1747) picaresque romance *Gil Blas* (1715, 1724, 1735; Eng. trans., 1749) opened the way to the novels of "sentimental education." In *Manon Lescaut* (1731; Eng. trans., 1738), the Abbé PRÉVOST presented passion triumphing over every obstacle but death, while in *Les Liaisons dangereuses* (1782), Pierre Choderlos de Laclos (1741–1803) analyzed the psychology of a cynical seducer. From the plays of Pierre de MARIVAUX came the term *mari vaudage*, meaning the style in which the psychological components of love and dalliance are portrayed. Toward the end of the century BEAUMARCHAIS's popular comedies *The Barber of Seville* (1775; Eng. trans., 1776) and *The Marriage of Figaro* (1784; Eng. trans., 1785) also conveyed a subtly rebellious political message.

Poetry in the 18th century suffered from the desiccating influence of rational analysis, but one great poet emerged. André CHÉNIER, inspired by the harmonies of classical Greek models and a love of liberty, became after his execution during the Terror an important influence on the romantic school.

The Nineteenth Century

The Vicomte de CHATEAUBRIAND ushered in the 19th century with an aggressive defense of Catholicism, *Le Génie du christianisme* (1802; trans. as *The Beauties of Christianity*, 1815). His *Mémoires d'outre-tombe* (Eng. trans., 1902), composed between 1811 and 1841, is considered a classic of autobiographical writing. Madame de STAËL, notable as a literary critic, became the champion of German romantic literature in her *De L'Allemagne* (1813; trans. as *Germany*, 1913). Her influence can be seen in Benjamin CONSTANT's novel *Adolphe* (1816; Eng. trans., 1817), analyzing the waning passion of a young man for an older woman.

Alphonse de LAMARTINE, with his *Méditations poétiques* (1820; Eng. trans., 1839), became the first in a

Voltaire (1694–1788)   *Honoré de Balzac (1799–1850)*   *Victor Hugo (1802–85)*

Charles Baudelaire (1821–67)

Émile Zola (1840–1902)

Marcel Proust (1871–1922)

line of romantic poets that included Alfred de VIGNY, who came to prominence with his *Poèmes antiques et modernes* (1826); Alfred de MUSSET, known alike for his Byronic poetry and his affair with George SAND, herself a romantic novelist and early feminist; and Victor HUGO, who for 65 years amplified every possible poetic theme and reigned as chief spokesman and practitioner of the romantic credo.

The first break with romanticism was made by Théophile GAUTIER, whose art-for-art's-sake credo announced the PARNASSIANS, poets infatuated with formal perfection and objectivity and hostile to the romantics' effusions. Led by Charles Marie LECONTE DE LISLE in the 1860s, the Parnassians saw their ideals best realized in the sonnet collection *Les Trophées* (1893; Eng. trans., 1897) of José María de Heredia.

Influenced by the Parnassians but determined to create beauty even out of the horrors of life, Charles BAUDELAIRE in *The Flowers of Evil* (1857; Eng. trans., 1909) sounded a new note—obsessive, morbid, presenting the poet as an accursed being. Arthur RIMBAUD, in *A Season in Hell* (1873; Eng. trans., 1932) and *Illuminations* (1886; Eng. trans., 1932), reached an absolute of revolt, experimenting with mixtures of verse and prose, with rhythms, and with the juxtaposition of unrelated words. His older friend and lover Paul VERLAINE brought to French poetry a musical, melodic quality seen especially in his collection *Jadis et naguère* (Once Upon a Time and Not Long Ago, 1884). Stéphane MALLARMÉ, whose most celebrated poem is *Afternoon of a Faun* (1876; Eng. trans., 1951), guided poetry toward even more abstruse paths and, as the leader of SYMBOLISM in the 1880s and '90s, exercised an enormous influence.

Madame George Sand, exemplifying romanticism in its most individualistic form, in *Lélia* (1833; Eng. trans., 1978) championed the ultimate moral claim of passion over convention. STENDHAL, who also portrayed the dominant role of passion as a motivating force, nevertheless injected into his two great novels *The Red and the Black* (1830; Eng. trans., 1916) and *The Charterhouse of Parma* (1839; Eng. trans., 1901) an ironic tone and analytical power. Victor Hugo, in *The Hunchback of Notre Dame* (1831; Eng. trans., 1833), an evocation of medieval Parisian life, and Alexandre DUMAS père, in a whole series of adventures covering high points of the 16th, 17th, and 18th centuries in France, established the historical novel. Hugo's later work, *Les Misérables* (1862; Eng. trans., 1862), recounting the redemption of a convict emerging from the lower depths, successfully merged high drama with questions of social morality.

The colossus of 19th-century French novelists, however, was Honoré de BALZAC, whose prodigious, multivolume *Human Comedy* (1842–48; Eng. trans., 1895–98), encompassing more than 2,000 characters from every rank and walk of life and sweeping imaginatively over 40 years of French history, brilliantly delineated a society in flux.

REALISM triumphed in Gustave FLAUBERT's *Madame Bovary* (1857; Eng. trans., 1886), the story of a provincial adulteress whose bleak life ends in tragedy. A disciple of Flaubert, Guy de MAUPASSANT, excelled in the sparely told, often ironic short story, as in such collections as *La Maison Tellier* (1881; Eng. trans., 1910) and *Mademoiselle Fifi* (1882; Eng. trans., 1917). Influenced by contemporary determinist thought, Émile ZOLA sought to make the novel a more scientific reflection of reality. His 20-volume fictional examination of every level of social life during the Second Empire, *Les Rougon-Macquart* (1871–93), with its emphasis on the sordid and the depressing, remains the outstanding exemplar of NATURALISM.

History and criticism also came to maturity during the 19th century. Jules Michelet's immense 17-volume *History of France* (1833–43, 1855–67; Eng. trans., 1882–87) exemplified the romantic narrative tradition. Alexis de TOCQUEVILLE, in his *Democracy in America* (1835, 1840; both trans. the same years), offered analyses of American politics and character largely still valid. Charles Augustin SAINTE-BEUVE, in his study *Port-Royal* (1840–59) and his in-depth analyses of French literary figures, gave a new

Colette (1873–1954)

Jean Paul Sartre (1905–80)

Albert Camus (1913–60)

importance to literary criticism. Applying his erudition as Hebrew scholar and philologist to religion in *The Origins of Christianity* (7 vols., 1863–83; Eng. trans., 1888–89), Ernest RENAN established modern critical methods in France, and the philosopher and historian Hippolyte TAINE, seeking a scientific explanation for historical and cultural phenomena, professed to discover in the interplay of physical and psychological factors the cause of national and individual variations.

The French theater was at first dominated by the romantic dramas of Hugo, whose *Hernani* (1830; Eng. trans., 1830) liberated playwrights from past traditions, and by those of Dumas père. These were followed in popularity by the "well-made plays" of Eugène SCRIBE, Victorien SARDOU, and Alexandre DUMAS fils, who also defended social theses.

The Twentieth Century

In 20th-century poetry, symbolism continued to inspire without stifling new departures. Paul CLAUDEL, dramatist and poet, injected a mystical Catholicism into his masterpiece, *Five Great Odes* (1904–10; Eng. trans., 1967). Paul VALÉRY's delicate poems were at once meditative, musical, and rich in imagery. Guillaume APOLLINAIRE not only coined the term *surrealist* but in *The Breasts of Tiresias* (1918; Eng. trans., 1966) produced the first surrealist play. Under the leadership of André BRETON, SURREALISM aimed for a complete revolution in poetry and the visual arts through an exploration of the subconscious. A rejuvenator of poetic imagination, surrealism launched, among others, the poet and novelist Louis ARAGON.

Anatole FRANCE kept the tradition of political satire alive with his allegorical spoof, *Penguin Island* (1908; Eng. trans., 1909). Romain ROLLAND, with his 10-volume *Jean-Christophe* (1904–12; Eng. trans., 1910–13), followed later by Jules ROMAINS, with his even larger *Men of Good Will* series (27 vols., 1932–47; Eng. trans. in 14 vols., 1933–46), continued the *roman-fleuve*, or cyclical novel. André GIDE, from *The Immoralist* (1902; Eng.

trans., 1930) through *The Counterfeiters* (1926; Eng. trans., 1927), championed the individual at war with conventional morality. France's greatest 20th-century novelist, however, was Marcel PROUST. In the multivolume, multilevel *Remembrance of Things Past* (1913–27; Eng. trans., 1922–31), Proust sought to recapture the essence of lost time, for him a spiritual reality, through reconstructing the external shape or sensations of the past.

Working on a smaller canvas, COLETTE produced short novels that shrewdly analyzed the complexities of intimate relations, while François MAURIAC addressed the eternal battle between spirit and flesh. Two of the freshest voices in the decade before World War II belonged to Louis Ferdinand CÉLINE, whose cynical, often scurrilous *Journey to the End of Night* (1932; Eng. trans., 1934) and *Death on the Installment Plan* (1936; Eng. trans., 1938) spoke for the fascism to come, and to the then politically radical adventurer-writer André MALRAUX in *Man's Fate* (1933; Eng. trans., 1934) and *Man's Hope* (1937; Eng. trans., 1938).

Philosophical EXISTENTIALISM dominated literature in postwar France. Jean Paul SARTRE, leader of the movement, had explained its tenets—the human freedom to choose and to forge one's own values—in the novel *Nausea* (1938; Eng. trans., 1949), the play *No Exit* (1944; Eng. trans., 1946), and a trilogy of novels dealing with World War II. Its themes were echoed by Albert CAMUS in *The Stranger* (1942; Eng. trans., 1946) and *The Plague* (1947; Eng. trans., 1948), which stress the meaninglessness of life. Simone de BEAUVOIR, Sartre's lifelong friend and disciple, also dealt with existentialist problems in her novels but is best known for her massive treatise on the status of women, *The Second Sex* (1949; Eng. trans., 1952).

The dominant trend since the 1950s has been the new novel, or antinovel, as represented by Nathalie SARRAUTE, Michel BUTOR, and Alain ROBBE-GRILLET. These authors all reject plot and verisimilitude, each inventing a personal technique of expression.

The French theater illustrates the literary revolution that has swept France since the days of Edmond ROSTAND's flamboyant *Cyrano de Bergerac* (1897; Eng. trans., 1937). The poetical plays of Jean GIRAUDOUX, especially the astringent *Madwoman of Chaillot* (1945; Eng. trans., 1947), continued to appeal, as did the productions of Jean ANOUILH, some smiling, some ferocious. But with Eugéne IONESCO's *The Bald Soprano* (1950; Eng. trans., 1958), an altogether new drama, called the THEATER OF THE ABSURD came into being. Samuel BECKETT best exemplified both the strengths and limits of this theater in *Waiting for Godot* (1953; Eng. trans., 1954) and *Endgame* (1957; Eng. trans., 1958), in which the sets, characters, and language itself disintegrate. The plays of Jean GENET, such as *The Balcony* (1956; Eng. trans., 1958) and *The Blacks* (1958; Eng. trans., 1960), also aim at destruction, but in a fuller, more sacramental way.

Maurice Ravel, an important French composer of the first half of the 20th century, became a leading exponent of musical impressionism. Ravel's most famous works include the ballet Daphnis et Chloë (1909–11) and his orchestral masterpiece, Boléro (1928).

French music The term *French* is used here in its broadest cultural sense to include all geographical areas within the influence of the French language and some composers of non-French origin who worked in France.

The earliest French influence on Western music is found in the plainsong of the Christian Church. It is believed that Gregorian chant as it is known today is an 8th- or 9th-century Gallican interpretation of Roman chant, but it is difficult to distinguish the Gallican ornamentation from its Roman basis. It has been suggested that the basic idea of the trope (an interpolation in a preexistent chant) is Gallican.

During the later Middle Ages, France led in the development of European music in all its forms. Some of the earliest manuscripts containing organum (the earliest form of polyphony) are found from the 10th century in Chartres, Montpellier, Fleury, Tours, and other French cities. Especially important was the group of musicians active during the 10th and 11th centuries at the Abbey of St. Martial in Limoges. In the late 12th century, Leonin, Perotin, and other composers associated with the cathedral of Notre Dame in Paris composed some of the earliest motets as well as a number of theoretical treatises on music.

This French miniature portrays Guillaume Dufay and Giles Binchois, two of the most influential European composers of the 15th century.

The poet-musicians called troubadours and trouvères flourished from the late 11th until the 13th century. ADAM DE LA HALLE and others created such musical forms as the *lai* and the *ballade*. The jongleurs were roving minstrels who performed the courtly love lyrics of the troubadours.

The music of the 14th century took its name, *Ars Nova*, from a treatise by Philippe de Vitry (1291–1361). Vitry is credited by some scholars with the invention of the isorhythmic motet, an important musical form. Guillaume de MACHAUT (c.1300–1377), master of all 14th-century forms and the leading poet of his time, brought the medieval motet to its peak.

With the beginning of the Renaissance style in the 15th century, the center of musical activity shifted from Paris to Burgundy, then a separate state, where Guillaume DUFAY, Gilles Binchois, and the Englishman John Dunstable wrote motets and cyclic masses in a new, expressive style.

By the late 15th century musical leadership shifted to Flanders. Many French composers were active during the Renaissance—for example, Jean Mouton (c.1475–1522) and Pierre Certon (c.1510–72)—but their music was overshadowed by that of the Flemish and Italians. The most important French contribution to the Renaissance was the CHANSON, a secular, polyphonic song, usually light in style.

The Reformation in France took the form of Calvinism, which allowed only the singing in unison of metrical French translations of the Psalms. The tunes composed by Louis Bourgeois (c.1510–c.1561) and others went with the Calvinist Psalter to Scotland and found their way into English hymnody where several still exist.

Opera was the ruling 17th-century form. Beginning with Balthasar de Beaujoyeaux's *Ballet comique de la reine* (1580), French composers combined elements of opera, ballet, and spoken drama in a form sometimes called opera-ballet. The arias were simple and songlike, in contrast to the long, florid arias of Italian music. The foremost French operas in the 17th century were those of Jean Baptiste LULLY and in the 18th century those of Jean Philippe RAMEAU. Ballet, spoken dialogue, and the absence of the Italian-style recitative-aria remained characteristic of French *opéra comique* through the 19th century.

At the close of the 19th century, musical impressionism found its fullest expression in the compositions of Claude Debussy. Debussy developed an improvisatory style, evoking subtle ranges of mood and color in his music.

French harpsichord music of the baroque period consisted mostly of suites of dance movements and short character pieces rather than the longer forms cultivated by the Germans. Representative composers were Jacques Champion de Chambonnières, Louis Couperin, François Couperin, and Rameau. All influenced the development of keyboard technique. Rameau wrote treatises that still influence the teaching of music theory.

The Paris Conservatory and the national opera were established amid the turmoil of the Revolution and the Napoleonic Wars. In the early 19th century, Paris was a center for musicians from other countries, such as Frédéric Chopin and Franz Liszt. Hector Berlioz, the greatest of the French romantics, expanded the orchestra and influenced Richard Wagner, but was little appreciated in his home country.

In the late 19th century, Camille Saint-Saëns worked for the establishment of a French instrumental style based on the classical tradition, and César Franck helped restore the quality of French organ and church music. The works of Georges Bizet, Charles Gounod, and Jules Massenet brought a new spontaneity and color to French opera. IMPRESSIONISM, whose subtle coloristic effects are exemplified in the music of Claude Debussy and the early

works of Maurice Ravel, blossomed toward the end of the century. The movement, inspired by the work of French impressionist painters and poets, attempted to give music a more improvisatory character with subtle and understated coloristic effects. An outstanding body of songs was produced by Debussy, Ravel, Gabriel Fauré, and Henri Duparc.

Between the two world wars, French music—such as the later work of Albert Roussel—was often written in simple, direct, "neoclassical" style. A group of young musicians gathered around the composer Erik Satie and were known as "Les Six": Arthur Honegger, Darius Milhaud, Francis Poulenc, Georges Auric, Germaine Tailleferre, and Louis Durey.

The eclectic aspect of contemporary French music, which uses SERIAL MUSIC, ELECTRONIC MUSIC, and ALEATORY techniques, as well as Oriental and other non-Western modes, is largely due to the influence of composer Olivier Messiaen, who taught many of the major postwar composers, most notably Pierre Boulez.

French Polynesia   French Polynesia is an overseas territory of France. It comprises about 130 islands, with a total land area of 3,885 km^2 (1,500 mi^2), in the south central Pacific Ocean. More than half the total population of 192,000 (1989 est.) live on the island of TAHITI. The capital is PAPEETE, Tahiti.

Land, People, and Economy. There are five major island groups: the SOCIETY ISLANDS; Tuamotu Archipelago; Tubuai (Austral) Islands; MARQUESAS ISLANDS; and Gambier Islands. The French government conducts nuclear tests on Mururoa Atoll, in the Tuamotu Archipelago. The islands are mainly mountainous and generally of volcanic origin, except for the coral atolls of the Tuamotu islands. The high islands (those with volcanic peaks) are heavily eroded and frequently marked by deep valleys. Mount Oroheno on Tahiti rises to a height of 2,237 m (7,339 ft). The high islands are forested, with areas of dry grassland. Coconut and pandanus trees abound on the flat atolls and the coastal plains of the high islands.

Southeast trade winds create equable temperatures (an annual average of about 24° C/76° F) and bring higher rainfall to the windward sides of the islands. Average annual rainfall at Papeete is 1,905 mm (75 in), but on the windward coasts it can reach as much as 3,050 mm (120 in). Although the atolls lack natural streams, the high islands frequently have drainage systems of short, rapid-flowing streams.

The population consists mainly of the indigenous Polynesians or part Polynesians (called Demis), with minorities of Asians (mostly Chinese), Europeans, and Americans. The official language is French, but eastern Polynesian languages are widely spoken. The predominant religions are Protestantism (47%) and Roman Catholicism (40%). Most people live along the coast. Greatest population densities occur on Tahiti. Education is primarily in government-aided mission schools; the population is 95% literate.

Village agriculture is at a subsistence level and is

Pierre Boulez, a composer, pianist, and conductor, emerged at the forefront of the post–World War II avant-garde in European music. He became musical director of the New York Philharmonic in 1971 but returned to Paris in 1979 to head the Beaubourg's experimental music laboratory.

based on root crops, fruits, and coconut. Commercial crops, such as copra, vanilla, coffee, and mother-of-pearl, are in decline, and tourism is on the rise. Economic ties with France remain strong. In addition to its modern port, Papeete has an international airport with air services to several outer islands.

History and Government. European exploration continued from the late 16th to the early 19th century. Tahiti became a French protectorate in 1844, and the other islands were gradually annexed. In 1946 the islands became a French overseas territory—a status confirmed in 1958 by vote of the islanders. The people are French nationals and have representation in the French parliament.

See also: OCEANIA.

French Revolution   The French Revolution (1789–99) violently transformed France from a monarchical state with a rigid social hierarchy into a modern nation in which the social structure was loosened and power passed increasingly to the middle classes.

Causes

There is considerable controversy over the causes of the Revolution. Marxist scholars emphasize material factors: as the population increased, food supplies grew short; land had become divided into such small parcels that most Frenchmen lived close to the subsistence level. Marxists also maintain that commercial prosperity had stimulated the growth of a monied middle class that threatened the position of the established landed aristocracy. Other social historians emphasize the importance of the growing discrepancy between reality and the legally defined social structure, which distinguished men by hereditary or acquired rank and recognized corporate rather than individual rights.

Political historians usually regard the weakness of the monarchy as a crucial factor. Nominally, the benevolent

Two figures representing the French clergy and nobility blithely crush the life out of a peasant symbolizing the social injustice tolerated by the French monarchy under the ancien régime. *These conditions helped precipitate the French Revolution.*

LOUIS XVI (r. 1774–92) was the absolute ruler of a united country. Actually, so many rights, or privileges, were retained by provinces, towns, corporate bodies, the clergy, and the nobility that the king had little freedom of action. Moreover, since offices in the legal and administrative system—and the noble rank that went with them—could be purchased and bequeathed as property, a new aristocracy of ennobled officials had developed. These men were able to frustrate royal reforms and to prevent the monarchy from raising taxes. Some writers contrast the arbitrariness of the old regime with the desire, stimulated by the ENLIGHTENMENT and the example of America, for reforms and more participation in government; curiously, few historians have attached much importance to the gradual growth of national consciousness.

The expense of the French participation in the AMERICAN REVOLUTION made fiscal reform or increased taxation imperative after 1783. Since no further revenue could be raised from a peasantry already overburdened by taxes and manorial dues, the royal ministers—particularly Charles Alexandre de CALONNE—attempted to tax all landowners regardless of privileges. When this plan met with resistance in the law courts and provincial assemblies, the ministers tried to replace those bodies with more representative ones. In 1788 this led to the Aristocratic Revolt, which compelled the ministers to convene the STATES-GENERAL for the first time since 1614.

The Course of the Revolution

The Revolution of 1789. The first phase of the Revolution was marked by moral and physical violence. The States-General met in 1789 in Versailles but were paralyzed by the refusal of the Third Estate (the Commons) to meet separately as a distinct, inferior body. On June 17 the Commons took the crucial revolutionary step of declaring their assembly to be the National Assembly, thereby destroying the States-General. This first assertion of the sovereign authority of the nation soon inspired a popular rising in Paris, marked by the storming of the BASTILLE on July 14. Concurrently, urban and rural revolts occurred throughout France. The peasants pillaged and burned the châteaus of the aristocracy—an episode known as the *Grande Peur* ("Great Fear")—destroying the records of their manorial dues.

The National Assembly established a new legal structure by abolishing privileges, venality, and "feudal" obligations (August 4); formulating a Declaration of Rights (August 26); and specifying basic constitutional principles that left the king as the chief executive but deprived him of any legislative power except a suspensive veto. Louis's reluctance to sanction these decrees led to a second Parisian uprising, the so-called March of the Women. On October 5 a mob marched to Versailles and forced the king, who had to be protected by the revolutionary national guard under the marquis de LAFAYETTE, to capitulate. Louis and his queen, MARIE ANTOINETTE, were moved to Paris, followed by the Assembly. France thus became a constitutional monarchy, and legal distinctions between Frenchmen disappeared; but the king was practically a prisoner, and many people became alienated by the pre-

Louis XVI accepts the laws of the people in a painting produced during the early phase of the Revolution. From 1789 to 1791 France was governed by the National Assembly, which issued the Declaration of Rights and drafted the Constitution of 1791, establishing a constitutional monarchy. Within a year the constitution had collapsed, and Louis XVI and his queen, Marie Antoinette, were executed in 1793.

tensions of the Assembly and the prevailing disorder.

The Reconstruction of France. In 1789–91, a comparatively peaceful period, the National Assembly did much to modernize France. Despite the Declaration of Rights, the reformed franchise still excluded the poor; but the public maintained its faith in freedom and unity, as shown in the first Festival of Federation, a celebration of national unity on July 14, 1790. Bankruptcy was averted by the confiscation of ecclesiastical land, and the church and law courts were reconstructed to conform with a rational and uniform system of local government by elected councils. Dissension nevertheless developed as several drastic changes, such as the reorganization of the church by the Civil Constitution of the Clergy (1790), followed in rapid succession. In 1791 the call for a clerical oath of loyalty crystallized the conflict between the new sovereignty and traditional loyalties and split the whole country.

When King Louis tried to escape from Paris (the flight to Varennes, June 20, 1791), civil war seemed imminent. The Assembly, however, retained control. A Parisian crowd, which had assembled to demand a republic, was dispersed by force on July 17, and Louis was reinstated after he had accepted the completed Constitution of 1791. The Revolution was then believed to be over, and the National Assembly was dissolved on September 30.

The Revolution of 1792. In 1791–92 the hard-won constitution collapsed. On Apr. 20, 1792, the new Legislative Assembly declared war on Austria, which it believed to be instigating counterrevolutionary agitation and thus launched the FRENCH REVOLUTIONARY WARS. Louis, who looked to Austria for succor, vetoed emergency measures, and Austrian and Prussian forces invaded France. Insurrection broke out in Paris. On August 10 the palace was stormed, and Louis was imprisoned by a new revolutionary Commune of Paris. The Legislative Assembly, reduced to a "patriotic" rump, could only dispute the Commune's

pretensions and order the election by manhood suffrage of a National Convention. Meanwhile, the invaders took Verdun, and alleged counterrevolutionaries were massacred in the prisons of Paris.

Foundation of the Republic. Born of this second revolution and briefly favored by military victory, the National Convention horrified Europe by establishing a republic (Sept. 22, 1792), inaugurating a policy of revolutionary war, and sending the king to the guillotine on Jan. 21, 1793. It also appalled France by its own furious disputes. A militant minority, the Montagnards, who spoke for Paris and the left-wing club called the JACOBINS, demanded vigorous revolutionary measures. Their opponents, the GIRONDIST leaders of the amorphous majority, looked to the provinces and hoped to consolidate the Revolution. In the spring of 1793, as the military and economic situation deteriorated and a savage royalist rising began in the Vendée region of western France, the Montagnards gained ground. Emergency bodies such as the Committee of Public Safety and the Revolutionary Tribunal were then established, but unified leadership was lacking until the Parisian insurrection of June 2 compelled the Convention to expel the Girondists and accept Montagnard control.

The Reign of Terror, 1793–94. The Montagnard Convention then had to contend with invasion, royalist civil war, and widespread provincial revolts against "the dictatorship of Paris." Initially, Georges DANTON tried to placate the provinces, and the democratic Constitution of 1793 was approved by plebiscite and celebrated at a Festival of Unity (August 10). After July, however, Maximilien ROBESPIERRE's influence prevailed, and armies were sent to subdue rebellious cities. When the city of Toulon voluntarily surrendered to the British, a demonstration in Paris compelled the National Convention to establish (September 5) the repressive regime known as the Terror. A fearful time ensued: the Committee of Public Safety strove to organize the economy and the war effort; the Revolutionary Tribunal sent state prisoners, including the Girondists, to the guillotine; and agents of the Convention known as Representatives of the People enforced bloody repression throughout France. A campaign of dechristianization, marked by a new Revolutionary Calendar computed from Sept. 22, 1792 (1 Vendémiaire, Year I), led to the closing of all churches on 3 Frimaire,

Georges Danton, who became minister of justice in France's revolutionary government in 1792, was instrumental in organizing resistance against the invading Prussian and Austrian armies. His popularity antagonized the more radical revolutionary leaders, and in 1794 he was denounced and executed.

Maximilien Robespierre separates money from his fellow citizens in this satirical cartoon. As the dominant figure of the Committee of Public Safety from July 1793, Robespierre was largely responsible for the Reign of Terror.

Year II (Nov. 23, 1793).

From December 1793, when republican armies began to prevail, both at home and abroad, the Terror became identified with ruthless but centralized revolutionary government. Because dissidence was now classified as counterrevolutionary, moderate Montagnards such as Danton and extremists such as Jacques René HÉBERT, a leader of dechristianization, were guillotined early in 1794. The work of the Revolutionary Tribunal was expedited by the draconian Law of 22 Prairial (June 10). Robespierre's insistence on associating Terror with Virtue and his efforts to make the republic a morally united patriotic community led to endless bloodshed. Finally, after a decisive military victory over the Austrians at Fleurus

(June 26), Robespierre was overthrown by a conspiracy of certain members of the National Convention on 9 Thermidor (July 27, 1794). After trying in vain to raise Paris, the Robespierrist deputies and most members of the Commune were guillotined the next day, July 28.

The Thermidorian Reaction. During the ensuing period (1794–95) of the Thermidorian Reaction, anarchy and runaway inflation almost overwhelmed the republic. In the southeast the royalists conducted a "white terror," and in Paris gangs of draft-dodgers, called *la jeunesse dorée* ("gilded youth"), persecuted the patriots. Twice, in Germinal and Prairial (April and May, 1795), there were desperate risings demanding "Bread and the Constitution of 1793." Without the Montagnards and Jacobins, however, the *sansculottes* ("those without kneebreeches," the name given to extreme republicans) could achieve nothing, and the Convention broke the popular movement with the aid of the army. The death (1795) of the imprisoned dauphin (titular King LOUIS XVII) and an unsuccessful royalist landing in Brittany also checked the reaction toward monarchy, enabling the Convention to complete the Constitution of 1795. This liberal settlement was approved by plebiscite, and it took effect after a reactionary rising in Vendémiaire (Oct. 5, 1795) had been suppressed by General Napoléon Bonaparte (the future Emperor NAPOLEON I) with what he described as "a whiff of grapeshot."

The Directory, 1795–99. The Constitution of 1795 established an executive DIRECTORY, two assemblies, and a property owners' franchise. Many provisions, including the initial derivation of two-thirds of the deputies from the Convention, guarded the republic against any reversion to either democratic Terror or monarchy. The only attempt to renew violent revolution, François BABEUF's communistic Conspiracy of Equals (May 1796), was easily thwarted.

(Bottom left) The National Convention arrested the radical leader Maximilien Robespierre on 9 Thermidor (July 27, 1794) and ordered his execution the following day. Robespierre's fall marked the end of the Terror and the beginning of the Thermidorian Reaction, a period in which the repressive manifestations of the Revolution were discarded. (Bottom right) In this allegorical painting, a figure representing the victorious forces of Reason pays homage to various symbols of the French Revolution.

In 1799 a three-man governing body called the Consulate was established. The first consul, Napoléon Bonaparte, is shown here flanked by his nominal colleagues, Jean Jacques Régis de Cambacérès (left) and Charles François Lebrun (right).

In 1797 the directors purged the parliament ruthlessly, branding many deputies as royalists and sentencing them to the penal colony of French Guiana (called "the dry guillotine"). This coup d'état of Fructidor (September 1797) was a devastating blow to all moderates. Thereafter, although administration improved and French power increased in Europe, coups against conservative or radical revivals occurred annually until 1799, when the Abbé SIEYÈS, determined to strengthen central authority, enlisted the aid of Bonaparte to effect the coup d'état of Brumaire (November 9–10).

The Consulate, 1799–1804. The Constitution of 1799 established the CONSULATE with Bonaparte as First Consul. He used his power to effect a remarkable reorganization of France, most notably reestablishing centralized control and restoring Catholicism by the Concordat of 1801. Constitutional controls and republican institutions were nonetheless steadily eroded until the creation of the First Empire (1804–15) ended the revolutionary period.

Consequences

The most concrete results of the French Revolution were probably achieved in 1789–91, when land was freed from customary burdens and the old corporate society was destroyed. This "abolition of feudalism" promoted individualism and egalitarianism but probably retarded the growth of a capitalist economy. Although only prosperous peasants were able to purchase land confiscated from the church and the emigrant nobility, France became increasingly a land of peasant proprietors. The bourgeoisie that acquired social predominance during the Directory and the Consulate was primarily composed of officials and landed proprietors, and although the war enabled some speculators and contractors to make fortunes, it delayed economic development. The great reforms of 1789–91 nevertheless established an enduring administrative and legal system, which was subsequently incorporated in the NAPOLEONIC CODE.

Politically, the revolution was more significant than successful. Since 1789 the French government has been either parliamentary and constitutional or based on the plebiscitary system that Napoleon inherited and developed. Between 1789 and 1799, however, democracy failed. Frequent elections bred apathy, and filling offices by nomination became commonplace even before Napoleon made it systematic. The Jacobins' fraternal—and Jacobin-controlled—community expired in 1794, the direct democracy of the *sansculottes* was crushed in 1795, and the republic perished in 1804; as ideals, however, they continued to inspire and embitter French politics and keep right and left, church and state, far apart.

The Revolution nevertheless freed the state from the trammels of its medieval past, releasing such unprecedented power that the revolutionaries could defy, and Napoleon conquer, the rest of Europe. Moreover, that power acknowledged no restraint: in 1793 unity was imposed on the nation by the Terror. Europe and the world have ever since been learning what infringements of liberty can issue from the concepts of national sovereignty and the will of the people.

See also: FRANCE, HISTORY OF; NAPOLEONIC WARS.

French Revolutionary Wars   The "French Revolutionary Wars" is the name given to the campaigns fought between France and the other European powers from 1792 to 1802, the first decade of conflicts that followed the FRENCH REVOLUTION. In their subsequent phase, from 1803 to 1815, these conflicts are known as the NAPOLEONIC WARS. The French Revolutionary Wars were fought from the Caribbean to the Indian Ocean, but the principal encounters occurred in the Low Countries, the Rhineland, and Lombardy.

Between 1789 and 1792 traditional antagonisms between France and its neighbors, particularly Austria, were greatly aggravated by ideological differences. Every conflict of interest became a confrontation with French democrats and their belief that the will of the sovereign people transcended treaties. Exaggerated fear of Austrian support for an armed assembly of emigrant French nobles at Coblentz consequently led France to declare war on Austria and Prussia in April 1792.

Initially, France was almost overwhelmed. Disorganized advances ended in mutinous retreats, and soon the Prussian army threatened Paris. Halted at Valmy (Sept. 20, 1792), the Prussians retired, and the French defeated the Austrians at Jemappes (Nov. 6, 1792) and overran the Austrian Netherlands (Belgium). Britain, Holland, Sardinia, and Spain then aligned themselves against France, and when in 1793 a French invasion of Holland was repelled at Neerwinden (March 18), this First Coalition attacked France on every frontier. Suppressing civil war at home by the Reign of Terror, the revolutionary republic raised the first national conscript army, and in 1794 its forces were successful everywhere. After the Battle of Fleurus (June 26, 1794), the Low Countries were conquered. In 1795, Prussia became neutral, and Holland and Spain accepted treaties making them virtual French satellites. Austria, too, was compelled to make

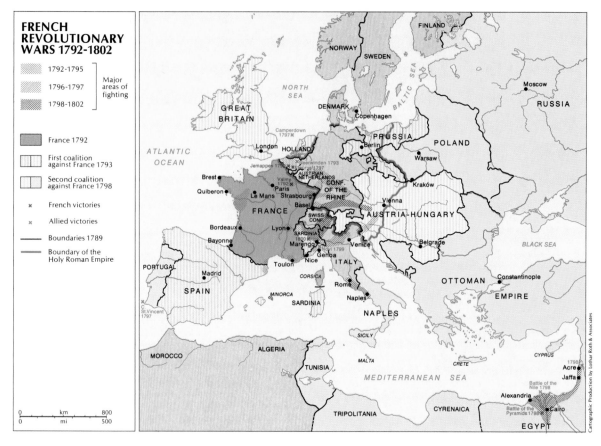

FRENCH REVOLUTIONARY WARS 1792-1802

1792-1795
1796-1797 } Major areas of fighting
1798-1802

France 1792
First coalition against France 1793
Second coalition against France 1798
× French victories
× Allied victories
—— Boundaries 1789
—— Boundary of the Holy Roman Empire

Nations allied against France during the French Revolutionary Wars, as well as the major areas of conflict, are identified. France, aided by the levée en masse of 1793, which created the first national army raised by universal conscription, faced successive coalitions.

peace at Campo-Formio (October 1797), after the brilliant Italian campaign (1796–97) of Napoléon Bonaparte (later NAPOLEON I).

Britain was now isolated and exposed to invasion. The French fleet, however, had been greatly weakened by the British victory called the Glorious First of June (1794), and in 1797 the Royal Navy defeated the Spanish fleet off Cape St. Vincent (February 14) and the Dutch at Camperdown (October 11), thus ending the threat of a naval combination. In 1798 the French DIRECTORY approved Bonaparte's plan to conquer Egypt. His victories there, however, were nullified by Horatio NELSON's destruction of his fleet in the Battle of the Nile (Aug. 1, 1798) and by the Turks' defense of Acre.

In Bonaparte's absence, a Second Coalition, consisting of Britain, Austria, Russia, and Turkey, was created. Once again, however, the French Republic triumphed. In 1799, Russian armies under Aleksandr SUVOROV swept across Lombardy only to be held at Zurich (September 25) and forced to retreat through the Alps in midwinter. Exposed, the Austrians retired from the Rhine, and an Anglo-Russian landing in Holland then had to be withdrawn. Returning from Egypt, Bonaparte, as first consul,

defeated the Austrians at Marengo (June 14, 1800). A further defeat by Jean Victor MOREAU at Hohenlinden (Dec. 3, 1800) forced the Austrians to make peace at Lunéville on Feb. 9, 1801. Isolated for a second time, Britain disrupted a new maritime combination by bombarding the Danish fleet at Copenhagen (Apr. 2, 1801) and destroyed Bonaparte's Egyptian army at Alexandria (August 1801). In March 1802, Britain sought an experimental peace by the Treaty of AMIENS.

Strikingly illustrative of the power of one militant nation in arms, these wars were nonetheless inconclusive: revolutionary republicanism had not dominated Europe, but Napoleonic imperialism had still to be encountered.

French Southern and Antarctic Territories

The French Southern and Antarctic Territories form an overseas territory of France, established in 1955, that consists of several groups of rugged, volcanic, uninhabited islands in the southern Indian Ocean and a sector of Antarctica that is claimed by France. The Antarctic territory, called Adélie Coast (Terre Adélie), includes the area between 136° and 143° east longitude south of the Antarctic Circle. The island components include the Kerguelen Islands, the Crozet Islands, St. Paul Island, and Amsterdam Island (Nouvelle-Amsterdam).

French West Africa French West Africa was a federation of French territories in West Africa established in 1895 and dissolved in 1958. The constituent territories were Dahomey (Benin), Ivory Coast, French Guinea (Guinea), Senegal, French Sudan (Mali), Mauritania, Niger, and Upper Volta (Burkina). Dakar, in Senegal, was its capital.

French West Indies see GUADELOUPE; MARTINIQUE

Freneau, Philip [freh-noh'] Philip Morin Freneau, b. New York City, Jan. 2, 1752, d. Dec. 18, 1832, was one of the most significant early American poets. His poem "The Power of Fancy" (1770), although neoclassical in style, anticipates the romantics in its awareness of nature. His topical poetry, both patriotic and critical of the British, as in "The British Prison Ship" (1781), earned him the sobriquet "Poet of the American Revolution." In the early 1790s, before the Federalists swept to power, Freneau, in his *National Gazette,* was one of the first political journalists to actively support Jefferson.

Freon [free'-ahn] Freon is a trademark of E. I. du Pont for a series of chlorinated and fluorinated hydrocarbons. The parent hydrocarbons are methane, CH_4, and ethane, C_2H_6; a few Freons contain a bromine atom.

The Freons are chemically stable, nontoxic, and nonflammable. Other useful properties are high density, low boiling point, and low viscosity. These characteristics make the Freons especially suited for use as refrigerants. They have also been used as propellants in aerosol cans, as solvents, and to expand polyurethane insulating foams. Freons are FLUOROCARBONS, the substances that have been implicated in the depletion of the OZONE LAYER. In 1988 the du Pont company pledged to phase out production of fluorocarbons, and substitutes are being developed.

---

frequency Frequency is one of the primary characteristics of a wave (see WAVES AND WAVE MOTION). It refers to all kinds of waves and is the number of times the wave varies through a complete cycle in a given unit of time. Frequency is denoted by either the symbol f or the Greek letter nu (v) and is commonly expressed in hertz (Hz); 1 Hz equals 1 cycle per second. The frequency of a sound wave determines its pitch; that of a light wave determines its color.

---

frequency allocation TELECOMMUNICATIONS makes use of a limited frequency range in the electromagnetic spectrum (see ELECTROMAGNETIC RADIATION). The available frequencies must be assigned, or allocated, in a way that minimizes interference between the transmitted signals. In each country, frequencies are allocated by a controlling government agency; in the United States, it is done by the FEDERAL COMMUNICATIONS COMMISSION. Each transmitting service is allocated a certain band, or range of frequencies. The standard band for AM radio broadcasting is 535 to 1,605 kHz. Other forms of RADIO, such as FM broadcasting, citizen's band (CB) radio, and maritime and aviation communications, are also allocated bands, as are TELEVISION and RADAR. Frequencies are classified as follows:

Very low frequency (VLF)	10–30	kHz
Low frequency (LF)	30–300	kHz
Medium frequency (MF)	300–3,000	kHz
High frequency (HF)	3–30	MHz
Very high frequency (VHF)	30–300	MHz
Ultrahigh frequency (UHF)	300–3,000	MHz
Superhigh frequency (SHF)	3,000–30,000	MHz

---

frequency modulation Frequency modulation (FM) is a method of MODULATION in which the frequency of a wave is varied in response to a modulating wave. The method was developed (1925–33) by Edwin Howard ARMSTRONG. The wave in which the frequency is varied is called the carrier, and the modulating wave is called the signal. Frequency modulation requires a higher-frequency carrier wave and a more complex method for transmitting information than does AMPLITUDE MODULATION (AM), although FM has an important advantage. Because a frequency-modulated electromagnetic wave has constant amplitude, it is much less susceptible to interference from both natural and artificial sources of ELECTROMAGNETIC RADIATION. Such sources cause STATIC in an amplitude-modulated radio or a telephone receiver. Both types of modulation, however, are used in radio broadcasting, whereas only FM is used for television. FM radio is a popular source of high-fidelity music.

---

fresco painting [fres'-koh] Fresco (an Italian word meaning "fresh") is a technique of durable wall painting used extensively for murals (see MURAL PAINTING). In pure, or *buon,* fresco, a fresh wet layer of plaster is applied to a prepared wall surface and painted with pigments mixed with water. The pigments soak into the plaster, which, when dry, forms a permanent chemical bond fusing paint and wall surface. Another type of fresco, painting on a dry *(secco)* surface with adhesive binder flakes, is not permanent. All fresco is susceptible to humidity.

Magnificent examples of this technique survive from the MINOAN ART of Crete in the 2d millennium BC. Whereas few Greek frescoes survive, examples of Roman frescoes (prior to AD 79) from HERCULANEUM and POMPEII are preserved. The early Christians (AD 250–400) decorated the Roman CATACOMBS with simple frescoes. The Byzantine era (AD c.500–1300) produced frescoes in the USSR, Yugoslavia, and Crete (see BYZANTINE ART AND ARCHITECTURE). Knowledge of the technique was not restricted to Europe: AJANTA, India (200 BC–AD 700), and Gansu, China (AD 400–800), have vast wall frescoes.

This detail from The Defeat of Khusrau *was created by the Italian artist Piero della Francesca as part of his fresco cycle (1452–66) in the Church of San Francesco in Arezzo, Italy. Fresco painting proliferated in Italy during the Renaissance and culminated during the 15th century.*

The origins and development of fresco are unclear as only pieces of early monuments survive. The most sustained use of fresco occurred in Italy between 1300 and 1800, hence the Italian terminology for fresco techniques.

Most frescoes painted between 1250 and 1400 were *buon*. Because this type of fresco requires wet plaster, plaster was applied only to an area that could be finished in one work session. For the next session fresh plaster was applied to new areas. The juncture between one "patch" and another is called *giornata*, or "one day's work." Most early frescoes were first sketched in red chalk or ocher wash called *sinopia* (see CARTOON, art). As the artists worked, they covered the section of the *sinopia* about to be painted with a second layer of plaster called *intonaco*. New techniques for restoring frescoes permit *intonaco* to be peeled off so that the *sinopia* can be studied.

In the early 15th century, painters began to experiment with new techniques to shorten work time and allow greater flexibility. Longevity was often sacrificed in the experiments; for example, LEONARDO DA VINCI's *Last Supper* (1495–*c.*1497) in Milan is now all but lost. Artists began to eliminate the *sinopia* by working out their ideas in large-scale cartoons that could be transferred onto the wet *intonaco* by either tracing or *pouncing* (dusting through perforations).

Innumerable treasures in Italian fresco survive. Notable examples from the late 13th through the early 14th century include CIMABUE's work in Assisi, GIOTTO DI BONDONE's unparalleled cycles in Padua and Florence; and Pietro and Ambrogio Lorenzetti's and Simone MARTINI's work in Assisi. The later 14th century saw frescoes by Taddeo Gaddi (see GADDI family) in Florence. Altichiero and Vitale da Bologna rank among important non-Tuscan fresco masters.

The early 15th century witnessed important contributions by the revolutionary painters MASACCIO and Paolo UCCELLO. Fra Filippo LIPPI, Fra ANGELICO, Benozzo GOZZOLI, and Andrea del Castagno furnished Florence with highly decorative frescoes, while PIERO DELLA FRANCESCA created

astonishingly powerful cycles in Arezzo and Rimini. Later in the century Andrea MANTEGNA worked in Mantua while Alesso Baldovinetti, Domenico GHIRLANDAIO, Sandro BOTTICELLI, and Luca SIGNORELLI painted major frescoes in Florence, Rome, and Orvieto.

The 16th century saw the great achievements of RAPHAEL's Stanze frescoes and MICHELANGELO's ceiling and *Last Judgment* for the SISTINE CHAPEL in Rome, perhaps the most famous frescoes ever painted. These achievements provided the impetus for ROSSO FIORENTINO, ANDREA DEL SARTO, Jacopo PONTORMO, Giorgio VASARI, and BRONZINO working primarily in Florence, and for Domenico Beccafumi working in Siena and CORREGGIO in Parma. Toward the end of the century Paolo VERONESE established a new fresco tradition in Venice. Rome was the major center of patronage in the 17th century; in the 18th century the fame of the Venetian Giovanni Battista Tiepolo (see TIEPOLO family) won him commissions in Italy, Germany, and Spain.

During the 19th century fresco fell into disuse; it was revived in the 20th century by the Mexican painters Diego RIVERA, José OROZCO, and David SIQUEIROS for their murals. During the Depression of the 1930s many U.S. artists, such as Thomas Hart BENTON and others, produced fresco murals under the auspices of the Works Progress Administration.

—

Frescobaldi, Girolamo [fres-koh-bahl'-dee, jee-roh'-lah-moh]   Girolamo Frescobaldi, b. Sept. 1583, d. Mar. 1, 1643, was the most important composer for the harpsichord and the organ of the early Baroque period. In 1597 he moved from his native Ferrara to Rome, where he held several posts as church organist, culminating in positions at Saint Peter's Basilica and at the pope's Julian Chapel, which he held beginning in 1608. He remained in Rome, except for a sojourn in Florence from 1628 to about 1634, during which time he served the Medici grand duke Ferdinando II. His numerous Italian students spread his influence throughout the peninsula, and Johann Jakob Froberger and Johann Kaspar Kerll passed on Frescobaldi's influence to succeeding generations of northern Europeans.

Frescobaldi's works for the keyboard include dance suites; variations; improvisational, often sectional, toccatas; and strictly composed, contrapuntal ricercares and canzonas. His best-known collection, the *Fiori musicali* (1635), consists of toccatas, ricercares, and capriccios intended to be played during the Mass.

—

Fresnel, Augustin Jean [fray-nel', oh-goo-stan' zhawn]   The French physicist Augustin Jean Fresnel, b. May 10, 1788, d. July 14, 1827, made fundamental contributions to theoretical and applied optics. Partially anticipated by Thomas YOUNG, Fresnel rejected the view derived from Newton that light consists of material particles and established the wave theory on a firm mathematical-experimental basis. He devised a new lens and other improvements in lighthouse illumination.

Fresno [frez'-noh] Fresno, a city in central California, is the seat of Fresno County and the principal commercial center of the agriculturally rich San Joaquin Valley. In 1990 there were 354,202 residents within the city and 667,490 in the metropolitan area. Grapes for wine and raisins, figs, cotton, and vegetables are grown, processed, and marketed. Local industries manufacture paper containers, sheet and optical glass, vending machines, agricultural machinery, fertilizers, and plastics.

Educational institutions include California State University at Fresno and Fresno City College. Founded in 1872 as a station on the Central (later Southern) Pacific Railroad, Fresno (Spanish: "ash tree") became an agricultural center when irrigation was introduced in the 1880s.

Freud, Anna [froyd] Anna Freud, b. Dec. 3, 1895, d. Oct. 10, 1982, was an internationally renowned Austrian-English psychoanalyst and the daughter of Sigmund Freud. When she became a teacher in Vienna her interests in education and psychoanalysis led to the publication of *Introduction to Psychoanalysis for Teachers* (1930; Eng. trans., 1931). She was a pioneer in, and a substantial contributor to, the development of psychoanalysis of the child and is especially noted for her *Introduction to the Technique of Child Psychoanalysis* (1927; Eng. trans., 1928). Other writings include *Normality and Pathology in Childhood* (1965), *The Ego and the Mechanisms of Defence* (1936; Eng. trans., 1937), which has become a psychoanalytic classic, and her collected papers in seven volumes, *The Writings of Anna Freud.*

Anna Freud stressed the function of the ego in coping with the outside world and setting up defenses, and in so doing added new directions to her father's emphasis on the id and sexual influences. She devoted considerable effort to the welfare of children. After leaving Vienna for London with her family in 1938, she founded the Hampstead War Nurseries, and after World War II she established the renowned Hampstead Child Therapy Course and Clinic.

Freud, Sigmund Sigmund Freud, b. May 6, 1856, d. Sept. 23, 1939, the creator of PSYCHOANALYSIS, was the first person to explore the human unconscious mind scientifically; his ideas profoundly influenced the shape of modern culture by altering man's view of himself. Freud was born in Freiberg, Moravia (now Příbor, Czechoslovakia), the oldest child of his father's second wife. Before Freud was 4 years of age, the family moved first to Leipzig, Germany, and then to Vienna, where Freud remained for most of his life. Freud's father, Jakob, a struggling Jewish merchant, encouraged his intellectually precocious son and passed on to him a tradition of skeptical and independent thinking. Jakob's passive acceptance of anti-Semitic insults, however, troubled the young Freud: his feelings toward his father were ambivalent. Freud shared his mother's attention with seven younger brothers and sisters, but he nevertheless maintained a close attachment to her. Amalie Freud had high hopes for her oldest son.

At 8 years of age Freud was reading Shakespeare and, despite the recognizable influence of an education in Greek, Latin, French, and German classics, he later spoke of "the works of the men who were my real teachers—all of them English or Scotch," referring to their "sober industriousness" and "stubborn feeling for justice." Freud's literary gifts and insights into human motives and emotions were first apparent in letters he wrote during adolescence. He considered studying law but decided in-

The Austrian physician Sigmund Freud founded psychoanalysis. Freud used the term to describe both his theories of personality and his method of treating mental illness. Freud's work revolutionized modern psychiatry and strongly influenced 20th century Western theories of child rearing and education, art, literature, and culture. Shown at the right is the study in his London home, where he lived during the last year of his life.

stead on a career in medical research in response to an essay on nature attributed to Goethe. Guided by contemporaries such as Ernst von Brücke and Theodor Meynert, Freud began on a promising research career; his later monographs on aphasia and on infantile cerebral paralysis were both the culmination of his neurological research and a harbinger of his burgeoning psychological insight.

In 1886 he married Martha Bernays. In order to support a wife he turned from research to the clinical practice of neurology. By that time Freud's interest in hysteria had been stimulated by Josef Breuer's successful use of therapeutic hypnosis and by Freud's studying with the famous neurologist Jean Martin CHARCOT in Paris. Freud took up Breuer's "cathartic method," and they published their findings in *Studies in Hysteria* (1895), which outlined their "talking cure" and is generally regarded as the beginning of psychoanalysis. Breuer lost interest when sexuality emerged as central to Freud's view of neurosis.

Freud, devoting himself to the new science, discarded authoritarian and cumbersome hypnosis by enlisting his patients' cooperation in "free association." This enabled him to notice the unconsciously motivated resistance of a patient to revealing repressed thoughts and memories, especially sexual ideas. The central discovery of this approach was transference, or the unconscious shift of feelings associated with persons in the patient's past to the therapist. Breuer's defection and the death (1896) of Freud's father precipitated a crisis for Freud to which he reacted by entering a period of self-analysis. Leaning for emotional support on his friend Wilhelm Fliess, Freud explored his dreams and fantasies for clues to his childhood sexual passions—his Oedipus complex.

A comprehensive exposition of the new science of psychoanalysis, *The Interpretation of Dreams* (1900), was regarded by Freud as his greatest book. At first the book was all but ignored; gradually, however, a number of interested persons gathered around Freud to study and apply his revolutionary discoveries. Of his early followers, Alfred ADLER and C. G. JUNG defected to form their own schools of psychology, largely because they could not accept infantile sexuality as pivotal.

Freud's creativity continued undiminished for almost four more decades, during which he developed the technique for psychoanalytic treatment of neuroses and established the guiding principles of psychoanalysis. Freud's method investigates a human's internal world through controlled methods of introspection and empathy. His ideas aroused considerable hostility during his time, particularly among his medical colleagues. A regular weekly meeting of friends at Freud's home for the purpose of discussing his discoveries grew into the Vienna Psychoanalytic Society and eventually into the International Psycho-Analytical Association. In 1909, Freud was invited by Clark University in Worcester, Mass., to deliver a series of lectures; this was his only visit to the United States.

Shortly after World War I, Freud learned that he had cancer of the jaw, to which he would succumb after nearly 17 years of chronic pain and disability and 33 surgical operations. Throughout this period, however, he remained

productive. Although recognition from the scientific community had not yet come, he was honored in 1930 with the Goethe Prize for Literature, and in 1936 he was elected to the Royal Society. When the Nazi occupation of Austria threatened his life and work, he moved to England. He died there on Sept. 23, 1939.

With psychoanalysis, Freud added psychological treatment methods to the biological basis of PSYCHIATRY. Beyond that, Freudian concepts—such as the powerful influence of the unconscious mind on conscious thought and behavior and the equally powerful influence of the apparently forgotten past on the present—have become part of western culture.

Frey [fray]   In Norse mythology, Frey was the god of fertility, peace, and prosperity. He was one of the Vanir gods, who were responsible for wealth, and the brother of Freya. Among his magical possessions was a sword that he gave to Skirnir, who in return obtained him Gerda, the most beautiful woman in the world, as his wife.

Freya [fray'-ah]   In Norse mythology, Freya, or Freyja, was the goddess of beauty and love. A beautiful, blonde, blue-eyed young woman, she was the sister of Frey and in later traditions the wife of ODIN. Freya claimed half of the heroes slain in battle, carrying them to her realm of Folkvang in ASGARD. Most of her myths concern attempts by the giants to abduct her. In Teutonic mythology, she was fused with the goddess FRIGG. Friday is named for her.

Freyre, Gilberto [fray'-ruh, jeel-bair'-too)   Gilberto Freyre, b. Mar. 15, 1900, d. July 18, 1987, pioneered sociological studies in his native Brazil. His most famous work, *The Masters and the Slaves* (1933; Eng. trans., 1946), examined the relationships of Brazil's Portuguese colonizers and their African slaves. It inspired other studies of African contributions to Brazilian society. Also well known among his 120 books is *The Mansions and the Shanties* (1936; Eng. trans., 1963), which examines the rise of urbanization in 19th-century Brazil and the decline of the rural social structure.

Frick, Ford   Although Ford Christopher Frick, b. Wawaka, Ind., Dec. 19, 1894, d. Apr. 8, 1978, was a sportswriter who never played professional baseball, he served as president of the National League for 17 years and as commissioner of baseball from 1951 to 1965. As president of the league he vigorously supported Jackie Robinson's entrance (1947) as the first black player in the major leagues and was instrumental in the formation (1936) of the Baseball Hall of Fame. As commissioner, Frick aided in the inception of national television coverage.

Frick, Henry Clay   Henry Clay Frick, b. West Overton, Pa., Dec. 18, 1849, d. Dec. 2, 1919, was an indus-

Henry Clay Frick, an American industrialist and philanthropist, managed (1889–1900) and expanded the Carnegie Steel Company and served as director of the U.S. Steel Corporation. His art collection, bequeathed to the public, is housed in his New York residence.

trialist and a philanthropist. As head of a company that supplied coke to the steel mills of Pittsburgh, Pa., he became a millionaire at the age of 30. In 1889, Andrew Carnegie made him chairman of his steel company. While attempting to break the 1892 HOMESTEAD STRIKE at Carnegie's Homestead, Pa., plant, Frick was shot and stabbed by Alexander Berkman, an anarchist. Frick participated in the formation (1901) of J. P. Morgan's U.S. Steel Corporation, of which he became a director. Over the years he amassed a valuable art collection (later known as the Frick Collection) that he bequeathed to New York City. He also gave sums to hospitals, educational institutions, and the city of Pittsburgh.

friction   Friction is the universal force between surfaces that opposes sliding motion. When surfaces of two bodies are in contact, the interactive force at the surface may have components both perpendicular and tangent to the surface. The perpendicular component is called the normal force, and the tangential component is called the friction force. If there is relative sliding at the surface, the friction force always acts in the opposite direction of this motion.

Most dry surfaces behave approximately according to Coulomb's friction law, which states that when the surfaces slide relative to one another, the friction force is proportional to the normal force and is independent of both the contact area and the speed of sliding. The ratio of the tangential force to the normal force during sliding is called the coefficient of friction and depends on the nature of the two surfaces.

In order to initiate sliding against friction, it is necessary to apply a tangential force at least as great as the product of the coefficient of friction and the normal force; before the onset of motion the force is resisted by the equal and opposite force of static friction. The force required to overcome static friction is usually greater than the force needed to sustain uniform sliding motion.

Friction is essential for the success of many operations, such as tires gripping roadways, the driving of pulleys and belts, and even walking. It is the lack of significant friction that makes it difficult to walk on ice. In many machine parts friction is undesirable, causing wear and unwanted heat and requiring additional power.

Friedan, Betty [free-dan']   Betty Friedan, b. Peoria, Ill., Feb. 4, 1921, an American writer who was trained as a psychologist, became the "founding mother" of contemporary feminism in the United States after publishing *The Feminine Mystique* (1963). In this influential work she isolated the "housewife syndrome" and stated that women must have opportunities for fulfillment beyond those provided by marriage and motherhood. In 1966, Friedan helped found the NATIONAL ORGANIZATION FOR WOMEN (NOW) and since then has been active in the formation of other feminist groups. Her book *It Changed My Life* (1976) is an account of her years in the women's movement. In the controversial *The Second Stage* (1981), Friedan called for a return to the family.

Betty Friedan's best-selling book, The Feminine Mystique (1963), was instrumental in reviving the women's movement in the United States. Friedan, a psychologist and political activist, helped found (1966) the National Organization for Women.

Photo Jill Krementz © 1976

Friedman, Milton   The economist Milton Friedman, b. Brooklyn, N.Y., July 31, 1912, is the leading exponent of the conservative, free-enterprise point of view in modern economics identified with the University of Chicago. His practical proposals are often radical in their implications. Friedman's MONETARY POLICY approach to economics offers a major alternative to the FISCAL POLICY of the Keynesians.

In *A Monetary History of the United States, 1867–1960* (1963), written with Anna J. Schwartz, and in other works, Friedman argues that John Maynard KEYNES incorrectly minimized the role of money and greatly exaggerated the efficacy of government taxing and spending policies in determining the level of national income (see INCOME, NATIONAL) and EMPLOYMENT. According to mone-

Milton Friedman is America's foremost conservative economist. An opponent of Keynesian economics, he has argued for limiting federal manipulation of the money supply. Friedman, a professor of economics at the University of Chicago, won the Nobel Prize for economic science in 1976.

tarist theory, the level of economic activity is largely determined by the quantity of money in the system.

Another of Friedman's important contributions is his argument for a negative income tax in *Capitalism and Freedom* (1962). Payments to the poor would be made automatically when their incomes fell below a certain level.

Friedrich, Caspar David

The German romantic painter Caspar David Friedrich, b. Sept. 5, 1774, d. May 7, 1840, was one of the greatest exponents in European art of the symbolic landscape. Friedrich's landscapes, based entirely on those of northern Germany, are beautiful renderings of trees, hills, harbors, morning mists, and other light effects based on a close observation of nature.

Some of Friedrich's best-known paintings are expressions of a religious mysticism. In 1808 he exhibited one of his most controversial paintings, *The Cross in the Mountains* (Gemäldegalerie, Dresden), in which—for the first time in Christian art—an altarpiece was conceived in terms of a pure landscape. The cross, viewed obliquely

In The Polar Sea *(1824), the 19th-century German romantic landscape painter Caspar David Friedrich reconstructed an actual episode in an Arctic expedition: a wrecked ship crushed by mountainous slabs of ice. (Kunsthalle, Hamburg.)*

from behind, is an insignificant element in the composition. More important are the dominant rays of the evening sun, which the artist said depicted the setting of the old, pre-Christian world. A landscape showing a ruined abbey in the snow, *Abbey with Oak Trees* (1810; Schloss Charlottenburg, Berlin), can be appreciated on one level as a bleak, winter scene, but the painter also intended the composition to represent both the church shaken by the Reformation and the transitoriness of earthly things.

Friends, Society of

The Society of Friends, commonly called Quakers, is a body of Christians that originated in 17th-century England under George Fox. Quakers unite in affirming the immediacy of Christ's teaching; they hold that believers receive divine guidance from an inward light, without the aid of intermediaries or external rites. Meetings for worship can be silent, without ritual or professional clergy, or programmed in which a minister officiates.

Although their antecedents lie in English PURITANISM and in the ANABAPTIST movement, the Society of Friends was formed during the English Civil War. Around 1652, George Fox began preaching that since there was "that of God in every man," a formal church structure and educated ministry were unnecessary. His first converts spread their faith throughout England, denouncing what they saw as social and spiritual compromises and calling individuals to an inward experience of God. In spite of schism and persecution, the new movement expanded. By openly defying restrictive legislation, Friends helped achieve passage of the Toleration Act of 1689.

In colonial America, enclaves of Quakers existed in Rhode Island, North Carolina, Pennsylvania, and western New Jersey. In Pennsylvania, founded by William PENN as a refuge for Quakers and as a "holy experiment" in religious toleration, Friends maintained an absolute majority in the assembly until 1755 and remained a potent force until the American Revolution. Between 1754 and 1766, Friends throughout America strengthened their commitment to pacifism and began to denounce slavery. After the Revolution, Friends concentrated on a wide variety of reform activities: Indian rights, prison reform, temperance, abolition, freedmen's rights, education, and the women's movement.

In a conflict over theology that was complicated by social tensions, the Society underwent a series of schisms beginning in 1827 and ending with the formation of three major subgroups: Hicksites (liberal), Orthodox (evangelical), and Conservative (quietist). During the 20th century, however, Friends have attempted to heal their differences.

frieze

see ARCHITECTURE

frigate

[frig'-uht] The ultimate derivation of the word *frigate* is unknown, but in 16th-century usage the equivalent term in the major Mediterranean languages indicated a small, fast, oared warship with sails for extended cruising. The generic meaning, a swift warship used for

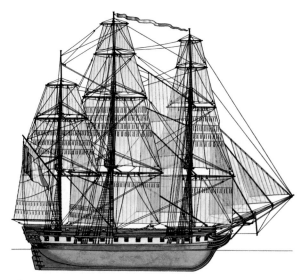

Frigates, such as this French man-of-war (c.1800), were three-masted warships second in size only to ships of the line. Their speed, maneuverability, and heavy armament made them ideal for conducting raids and escorting merchant fleets.

reconnaissance and for raiding, survived and was applied to a specific class of warship in the 18th and early 19th centuries: the largest class of warship below the ship of the line. It was a three-masted, square-rigged vessel with 24 to 50 guns on two decks (one covered). Frigates could usually outrun whatever ships they could not outfight and outfight the ships they could not outrun. During World War II the term *frigate* was extended to mean an antisubmarine escort vessel intermediate in size between a destroyer and a corvette. The term is used in this sense today, although no clear-cut criteria of size apply.

frigate bird Frigate bird is the common name for birds of the family Fregatidae, which reside in the tropics and subtropics. Their long, pointed wings, which have more surface area per unit of body weight than those of any other bird, give them a unique lightness and grace in flight. Although they are water birds, they seem never voluntarily to enter water, swooping or hovering to take food from the surface of the sea and sometimes robbing other birds. Frigate birds are large (79–104 cm/31–41 in) and mostly dark colored and have long, hook-tipped bills and deeply forked tails. In the male, the bare throat becomes greatly inflated during the breeding-season display. The magnificent frigate bird, *Fregata magnificens*, breeds in the American tropics, but it regularly wanders north to Florida and the Gulf Coast and, on occasion, strays far to the north of its normal range.

(Right) The frigate bird, the largest species of the family, lives along the coasts of tropical America. The female (left) is white breasted and is usually larger than the male. During courtship, the male inflates a brilliant red throat patch.

Frigg In Scandinavian mythology, Frigg was the supreme goddess and the principal wife of ODIN. She was goddess of the sky and, like the Greek Hera and the Roman Juno, presided over marriage. The myths portray her as very wise and very silent. In Teutonic mythology she was fused with the goddess FREYA.

frigidity *Frigidity* is an obsolete term for several forms of sexual dysfunction in women that preclude sexual gratification through intercourse. An imprecise term, it has been used to refer both to a total absence of sexual desire and to difficulties in experiencing orgasm during sex. Mental health professionals stopped using the term because of its imprecision and because it was felt to be derogatory to women.

Preferred alternatives to the term *frigidity* include: hypoactive sexual disorder—a lack of desire for sex; female sexual arousal disorder—a lack of physical arousal during sex; and inhibited female orgasm—persistent delay or lack of orgasm during sex.

See also: IMPOTENCE.

Friml, Rudolf [frim'-ul] Rudolf Friml, b. Prague, Dec. 7, 1879, d. Nov. 12, 1972, was an American composer of operettas. He was best known for *The Firefly, Rose Marie, The Vagabond King,* and *The Three Musketeers.* Jeanette MacDonald and Nelson Eddy starred in film versions of his operettas.

Frisbee A Frisbee (trademark of the Wham-O Corp.) is a circular plastic disk used for a variety of athletic, usually informal recreational activities involving tossing and catching. Emerging during the mid-1950s in the United

States, the pastime is now the single most popular form of U.S. athletic activity: it is estimated that more Frisbees are sold each year than baseballs, basketballs, and footballs combined. There are local, state, national, and international competitions.

Frisch, Karl von [frish]   The Austrian zoologist Karl von Frisch, b. Nov. 20, 1886, d. June 12, 1982, contributed greatly to early studies of ANIMAL BEHAVIOR with his research on direction finding and communication among bees. He found that bees can infer the position of the Sun from polarized light and that they use special "waggle" dances to inform other members of the hive of the direction and distance of a food source. He also found, in earlier work, that fish can discriminate colors. He and two other pioneer researchers in animal behavior, Konrad Lorenz and Nikolaas Tinbergen, shared the 1973 Nobel Prize for physiology or medicine. His writings included *The Dancing Bees* (Eng. trans., 1955) and *A Biologist Remembers* (Eng. trans., 1967).

Frisch, Max   The Swiss dramatist and novelist Max Rudolf Frisch, b. May 15, 1911, d. Apr. 4, 1991, was noted for plays that offered a grimly pessimistic view of modern society. His first successful play, *Santa Cruz* (1944), took up a theme that was to prove central to his work: the shaping of individual destiny and behavior by social pressures. Frisch's friendship with Bertolt Brecht profoundly influenced Frisch's dramatic technique of surrealistic fable, effectively used in his play *The Chinese Wall* (1946; Eng. trans., 1961). His disturbing conception of Western society is fully realized in his two best-known plays, *Biedermann und die Brandstifter* (1958; trans. as *The Firebugs,* 1963) and *Andorra* (1961; Eng. trans., 1962). The former points to the failure of European societies to prevent the rise of Nazism and other totalitarian creeds but also suggests that the basis of political failure is individual weakness. Frisch's moral concerns continued in such notable novels as *Montauk* (1975; Eng. trans., 1976) and *Man in the Holocene* (1979; Eng. trans., 1980).

Frisian Islands [frizh'-uhn]   The Frisian Islands are a chain of low-lying islands off the coasts of the Netherlands, Germany, and Denmark, in the North Sea. They are separated from the European mainland by a narrow, shallow channel ranging from 5 to 32 km (3 to 20 mi) in width. The islands are divided into the West Frisians, belonging to the Netherlands and consisting of five main, inhabited islands and other uninhabited ones; the East Frisians, belonging to Germany; and the North Frisians, which are divided between Germany and Denmark. Farming, fishing and the raising of sheep and cattle are the main industries. The islands' beaches attract tourists in the summer.

Frisian language   see GERMANIC LANGUAGES

Frith, William   The English painter William Powell Frith, b. Jan. 9, 1819, d. Nov. 2, 1909, became famous for his scenes of Victorian life. He began painting sentimental scenes from history and literature, which were well received. His *Ramsgate Sands* (Royal Collection) was exhibited at the Royal Academy in 1854 and was bought by Queen Victoria. He continued in this successful vein with *Derby Day* (1858; Tate Gallery, London), *The Railway Station* (1862; Royal Holloway College, Egham), and *Private View Day at the Royal Academy* (1883). All are marked by a careful attention to detail, for which he used photographs, and a multiplicity of incident, humorous and moralizing. They provided a popular mirror image for a self-confident Victorian era.

Friuli-Venezia Giulia [free-oo'-lee-vay-net'-seeuh jool'-yah]   Friuli-Venezia Giulia is a region in northeastern Italy, bordered by the Austrian Alps on the north, Yugoslavia on the east, and the Adriatic Sea on the south. It has a population of 1,210,242 (1988 est.) and an area of 7,846 km^2 (3,029 mi^2). TRIESTE is the capital city, principal port, and commercial center.

Once part of the Roman Julian region, Friuli-Venezia Giulia was subsequently controlled by the Byzantines. Venice and Austria shared control of the area from the 15th century to 1815, when the entire region came under Austria. Italy took most of the area in 1866, although, after World War II, Trieste passed to Yugoslavia. In 1954 the city was returned to Italy, and in 1963 the region was given limited autonomy.

Frobisher, Sir Martin [froh'-bish-ur]   Martin Frobisher, b. c.1539, d. Nov. 22, 1594, was a well-known Elizabethan navigator and explorer. He made two voyages to Africa as a youth. Becoming convinced of the existence of a NORTHWEST PASSAGE, he secured support for three voyages in search of it.

On the first voyage in 1576, Frobisher found an inlet in Baffin Island, now known as Frobisher Bay, that he believed to be the Northwest Passage. He brought back ore that was mistakenly identified as gold, attracting many investors to the Company of Cathay, organized by Frobisher's partner, Michael Lok. A second voyage in 1577 and a third in 1578 found no gold, but in July 1578, Frobisher sailed up what he called the "Mistaken Strait," later named Hudson Strait.

After the collapse of Lok's company Frobisher had various commands, including that of vice-admiral in Sir Francis Drake's 1585–86 expedition to the West Indies. He served honorably in the defense against the Spanish Armada in 1588 and was knighted. He died from a wound received while fighting the Spanish on the coast of France.

Froebel, Friedrich Wilhelm August [frur'-bul, freed'-rik vil'-helm ow'-gust]   Friedrich Wilhelm August

Froebel, b. Apr. 21, 1782, d. June 21, 1852, was a German educator who created and developed the kindergarten. Influenced by the Swiss educator Johann PESTALOZZI, he viewed infant education as the basis of educational reform. He opened his first kindergarten (1841) and attracted ardent disciples, who helped spread his idea. His major educational work, *The Education of Man* (1826), stated his belief that the purpose of education was to help children understand the oneness of life. This led him to advocate cooperation rather than competition in education, manual training to unite hand and brain, a thorough study of nature, and the use of play as an aid to the harmonious expression of all human faculties. His work was a major inspiration for child-centered PROGRESSIVE EDUCATION.

See also: EDUCATION; PRESCHOOL EDUCATION.

—

frog   The typical frog has long hind legs, a large head, a short body, and no tail; it may live entirely in water or may spend much of its life on land. Frogs are found on every continent except Antarctica. They are thought to have evolved from a tailed, four-limbed, amphibious ancestor.

Classification. The classification of frogs above the family level is currently debated. It is usually determined by characteristics of skeletal and muscular structures in larvae and adults, features of the frogs' life histories, and certain genetic and biochemical components. One current theory states that the Leiopelmatidae of New Zealand and the Ascaphidae of the Pacific Northwest are the most primitive living frogs. The Discoglossidae of Europe, Anatolia, China, northwestern Africa, and the Philippines are also considered primitive.

The family Pipidae of South America and of Africa south of the Sahara is a highly specialized group; the African clawed toad, *Xenopus laevis,* is a member of this family. The southern Mexican Rhinophrynidae, with its single species, may be related to pipids. The Microhylidae of the Americas, Southeast Asia, and Africa constitute a separate group.

The Pelobatidae, spadefoot toads of Europe, North America, and Southeast Asia, are part of a large group of related families that includes the successful family Ranidae—the true frogs, such as the leopard frog and bullfrog. Ranids occur in North and South America, Europe, Asia, and northern Australia. Ranid relatives include the following: the Sooglossidae, two genera on the Seychelles Islands and Madagascar; the Hyperoliidae of Africa, Madagascar, and the Seychelles; and the Rhacophoridae of Africa, Southeast Asia, and the Philippines.

The Bufonidae, or true toads, inhabit all landmasses except Australia, New Zealand, New Guinea, and Greenland. The Atelopodidae, Allophrynidae, and Brachycephalidae of Central and South America are closely related to bufonids. The Heleophrynidae of South America and the Myobatrachidae of Australia and New Guinea have affinities with the Leptodactylidae of the New World. Also related are the Hylidae, widespread only in the Americas but with one genus, *Hyla,* occurring nearly worldwide; the Pelodryadidae of Australia; the arrow poison frog, Dendrobatidae, and the green-boned frogs, Centrolenidae, of Central and South America; and the Pseudidae of South America. The status of the Rhinodermatidae of Chile is undecided.

Habitat. Frogs live in diverse habitats. Pipid frogs and many other types spend their entire lives in ponds and streams in the tropics. Other species require only the moisture found on leaves or under rocks or logs to survive. Desert-dwelling spadefoot toads live buried in sand much of the year and emerge to breed only when it rains. They lay their eggs in puddles, and tadpole metamorphosis must be completed before the puddle dries up. Frogs are widely distributed from lowland tropics to high mountains and high latitudes, and from very wet to seasonally dry habitats.

Structure and Function. Frogs may be easily identified and classified into species by various external characteristics. These include the proportions of the head, body, and limbs; color patterns; placement of the tympanum, or eardrum; toe webbing and shape; and such ornamentation as cranial crests, the so-called claws, and skin structures.

Frogs, like other amphibians, are cold-blooded (poikilothermic). Thus, if the environmental temperature stays within an acceptable range, a frog's body temperature will correspond to it. In winter, frogs must escape freezing; in summer, they avoid high temperatures.

Frogs have several unique attributes. Vocalization occurs as inspired air is directed into pockets in the floor of the mouth, then forced through the larynx at various rates and frequencies. The inner ear of a vocalizing frog has specialized cells that perceive sound at specific frequencies.

The adaptation of long hind limbs has resulted in various locomotor patterns. Temperature, body weight, body proportions, and resistance of the medium all affect the method and rate of locomotion.

There are two types of feeding: tongueless and tongued. Tongueless aquatic species feed by gulping prey into their mouths; tongued forms extend the tongue to capture prey. The end of the tongue has glands that secrete a viscous material that holds the prey on contact. The tongue and prey are then withdrawn into the mouth.

Life Cycle. The frog's life cycle is complex. Courtship in many species is highly stylized, involving specific calls or prescribed turns and positions before mating occurs. Most frogs practice external fertilization; the female lays eggs and the male sheds sperm over them. Some females lay several hundred eggs and abandon them. Other frog species lay fewer eggs and protect the developing young in a variety of ways, including direct development—laying eggs on land, which then develop through METAMORPHOSIS without the larval (tadpole) stage—and maternal retention of developing young.

In aquatic development, the tadpole's mouthparts develop at hatching, gills are covered by the operculum, and the tail structure is finned. Tadpoles are of different body shapes, depending on their habitat, and their mouthparts also vary. At metamorphosis, limbs develop, hindlegs first; the tail begins to resorb; the shape of the head changes; jaws modify; the intestine shortens, and a host of biochemical changes takes place. During metamor-

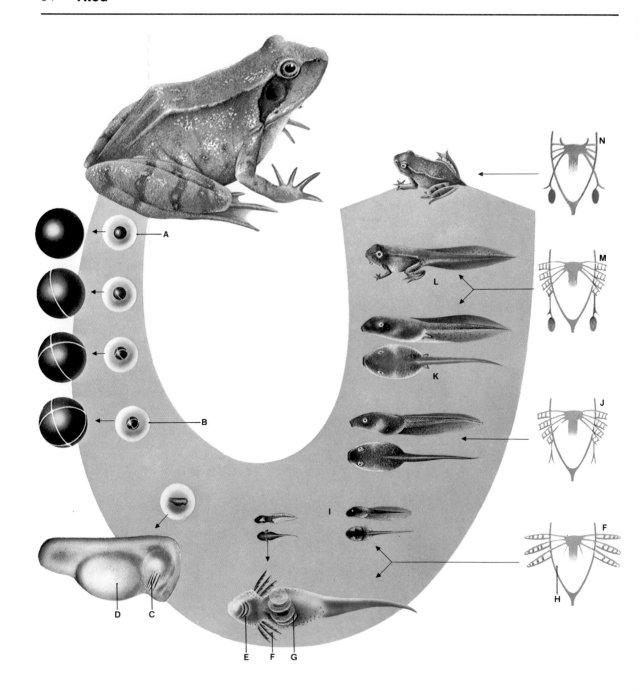

The common European frog lays a mass of black eggs at the end of winter. They become surrounded by a protective jellylike material (A). Each egg cleaves into 2, 4, and 8 cells (B) and so on until a ball of cells forms as the embryo. At the tail-bud stage organs and gill arches (C) are present, and internal yolk (D) supplies nutrient. After 21 days the embryo wriggles out of its jelly capsule and attaches to a weed by its cement gland (E). External gills (F) with branches to (blue) and from (red) the circulatory system (H) supply the body with oxygen. After 4 days horny jaws (I) and a long-coiled intestine (G) equip the larvae for its diet of weeds. External gills are replaced by internal gills (J). Five weeks after hatching the hind limbs develop (K), followed by the forelimbs (L). The mouth widens, horny jaws disappear, lungs begin to develop (M), and about 11 weeks after spawning, the adult frog with fully developed lungs (N) leaves the water.

phosis the tadpole is vulnerable to predators, and it cannot feed while its body is reorganizing.

Importance of Frogs Frogs are significant predators in their ecosystems. Human actions have caused a reduction of numbers of some frogs, and this has had a detrimental effect in many areas. Frogs continue to be in great demand as test animals for studies in biology.

Froissart, Jean [fwah-sahr'] Jean Froissart, c.1337–c.1405, was a French historian and poet whose *Chronicles* (c.1369–1400) provides a lively, if often biased, account of European affairs during the Hundred Years' War. He traveled widely in Europe and enjoyed the patronage of Queen Philippa of England, wife of Edward III, and several European noblemen. Despite its many inaccuracies, his *Chronicles*, which covers events from 1325 to 1400, remains a major source for the period and its concepts of chivalry. Froissart also wrote *Méliador,* a verse romance, and lyric poetry.

Fromm, Erich [frawm] Erich Fromm, b. Frankfurt am Main, Germany, Mar. 23, 1900, d. Mar. 18, 1980, was a psychoanalyst, philosopher, and anthropologist. Fromm stressed the role of culture in the formation of personality; in this he parted company with traditional psychoanalysis. In industrial society, Fromm maintained, people have become estranged from themselves, and he proposed that society should fulfill human needs.

Fromm received his Ph.D. from the University of Heidelberg in 1922 and trained as a psychoanalyst at the Berlin Psychoanalytic Institute. In 1934 he moved from Nazi Germany to the United States, teaching at several schools before becoming (1951) professor of psychoanalysis at the National University of Mexico and later (1961) professor of psychiatry at New York University. Fromm's description of the authoritarian personality has become an important concept in the psychological study of personality.

Fronde [frohnd] The Fronde (1648–53) was a series of major revolts in France during the minority of LOUIS XIV. They temporarily blocked the continuation by the regent ANNE OF AUSTRIA and her able but hated advisor, Cardinal MAZARIN, of the harsh policies of Louis XIII and Cardinal Richelieu. Merchants, artisans, and peasants disliked the spiraling taxation caused by the Thirty Years' War, the PARLEMENTS and taxing bureaus resented loss of their functions to the intendants (financial administrators), and nobles were frustrated by erosion of their powers.

During the first, or parlementary, Fronde (1648–49) the Parlement of Paris, joined by more specialized Parisian tribunals and backed by street rioting (Days of Barricades, August 1648), forced the regent to abolish most intendancies, many taxes not registered with parlements, and arbitrary detention. A brief winter siege of Paris by the royal army of Louis II, prince de Condé (see CONDÉ family), ended inconclusively.

The second, or princely, Fronde (1650–53) began as an unsuccessful military uprising in Normandy and Guienne by noble followers of Condé; Condé himself had been imprisoned for seeking to assume Mazarin's powers. In 1651 a coalition of Condé's party, the Parlement of Paris, and a rival noble faction under Cardinal de Retz (1613–79) obtained Condé's release and Mazarin's exile abroad. Rivalry between Condé and Retz, however, as well as basic political differences between the cautious, legalistic judges of the Parlement and the bolder warrior-nobles, allowed Mazarin to return. Condé, although defeated by the vicomte de TURENNE in July 1652, established a brief dictatorship over Paris, but he abandoned the city in October to join the Spanish troops that he had invited into the country. The rebellion soon collapsed, and Mazarin overturned most of the reforms of 1648.

Louis XIV, reacting to the rebellion and his subjects' yearning for order, made his long personal reign the high point of royal absolutism. He took into account the Frondeurs' grievances, however, by making his financial administrative machinery more efficient and less burdensome than Louis XIII's.

Frondizi, Arturo [frohn-dee'-see] Arturo Frondizi, b. Oct. 28, 1908, was president of Argentina from 1958 to 1962. Member of the lower house of the Congress in 1946, he became an opponent of Juan PERÓN, who was ousted in 1955. As president, Frondizi encouraged development of Argentine petroleum resources by foreign companies. He allowed the *peronistas* to enter the 1962 elections in order to gain their support, but their impressive victories led conservative elements in the military to arrest Frondizi and nullify the elections. He was released in 1963.

front A front is a boundary between AIR MASSES having different temperature and humidity. Fronts move in the same direction as the denser, colder air. Thus the leading edge of an advancing cold-air mass demarcates a cold front, whereas the retreat of cold air from the air-mass boundary is a warm front. In a stationary front the winds in the cold air blow parallel to the division. Occluded fronts occur when a cold front catches up to a warm front and forces the intermediate and less dense (warm) air aloft. At the surface, a number of weather indicators determine frontal location: a wind-shift line, a pressure trough, and temperature and dew-point temperature discontinuities, as well as changes in pressure (falling or rising, and how quickly), visibility, precipitation type, and cloud amount across the frontal zone.

CLOUDS and precipitation result when warmer air associated with these fronts is forced to rise over the colder air. Such active fronts are usually associated with well-developed extratropical cyclones (see CYCLONE AND ANTICYCLONE). On the other hand, if the winds in the warmer air mass slide down and push ahead of the frontal boundary, subsidence and therefore clear skies result, and the front is said to be inactive. Most of the inclement weather in the middle and northern latitudes is a result of active frontal zones. Because of frictional drag on the moving air mass, active cold fronts tend to be steeper (and have a narrower region of inclement weather) than an active warm front with the same magnitude of horizontal temperature contrast.

See also: ATMOSPHERE; WEATHER FORECASTING.

Frontenac, Louis de Buade, Comte de [frohn-tuh-nak', lwee duh boo-ahd']   Louis de Buade, comte de Frontenac et de Palluau, b. May 22, 1622, d. Nov. 28, 1698, was twice governor-general of New France. He is known as French Canada's foremost 17th-century military defender as well as the architect of French expansion into the North American interior. Born at St. Germain-en-Laye near Paris, Frontenac spent more than 30 years as soldier in Europe and as an extravagant, irascible, and pretentious courtier.

His appointment (1672) as governor-general enabled him to defer repayment of enormous debts in France, to profit personally from the fur trade, and to indulge his vanity by holding vice-regal court at Quebec. This first term (1672–82) was marked by Frontenac's quarrels with subordinate officials over jurisdiction and with the Jesuits over moral questions. However, he promoted the western fur trade by sponsoring the endeavors of the sieurs de LA SALLE and DULUTH, Nicolas PERROT, and Henri de TONTY and by the carefully disguised appeasement of English and Iroquois rivals.

War with the Anglo-American colonies and their Iroquois allies dominated his second term (1689–98). Following his haughty rejection of Sir William PHIPS's demand for the surrender of Quebec in 1690, Frontenac successfully defended New France by means of a guerrilla war of attrition. By building many new fortified posts in the west and southwest, albeit for personal gain, he not only expanded the French fur trade but also laid the groundwork for strategic control of the lands west of the Appalachians.

See also: FRENCH AND INDIAN WARS.

Louis de Buade, comte de Frontenac, was appointed governor of New France in 1672. Recognized as one of the major builders of New France, Frontenac sponsored much exploration and expanded the fur trade.

frontier   In American history, the frontier was the westernmost area of settlement at any given time in the expansion of the nation. Historians assume that the process of extending the frontier westward began in 1607 with the settlement of Jamestown and ended around 1890, when there was no longer any new land for homesteaders. Many of the attitudes and principles associated with this process—rugged individualism, conquest and progress, law and order, free enterprise, and the right to bear arms—reinforce American ideas and myths.

Charles Russell captures the spirit of cowboy life in his painting A Tight Dally and a Loose Latigo. *From the 1860s on, the romantic cowboy image came to symbolize the taming of the frontier.*

The Westward Movement

Frontier settlers moved from the Atlantic coast across 3,000 miles (more than 4,800 km) of wilderness, deserts, and mountains until they were finally stopped by the Pacific Ocean. This advance averaged 10 mi (16 km) a year, but in actuality movement progressed by successive waves and at a very uneven rate. Geography and hostile Indians generally determined the boundaries of a particular frontier region. The fall line—the junction of the tidewater region and the piedmont—marked the frontier of the 17th century. Within the next 100 years, pioneers pushed the settlement line to the base of the Alleghenies. During the American Revolution, many settlers crossed the mountains into Kentucky and Tennessee and from there ventured into the Old Northwest and Old Southwest. Pioneers poured through the Cumberland Gap and down the Ohio in ever-increasing numbers. By 1820 all the lands east of the Mississippi had been carved into separate states or territories.

During the next three decades, a wave of settlers moved beyond the Mississippi to the edge of the arid plains. Near the 98th meridian, the forested area gives way to rolling prairies, and beyond that the prairies merge with the Great Plains. As the elevation increases, the annual rainfall gradually drops below that amount necessary for conventional agriculture. For this reason settlement halted for a long time at the bend of the Missouri and along the eastern boundary of Indian Territory (Oklahoma), Nebraska, and Kansas. Long after Missouri, Arkansas, and Iowa had been admitted to statehood, Minnesota and Wisconsin to the north still retained their frontier characteristics.

The discovery of gold in California in 1848 altered the pattern of westward migration, as hordes of settlers and prospectors joined the GOLD RUSH and passed through the Great Plains, Rocky Mountains, and Great Basin to the very edge of the Pacific Ocean. By 1860, the line separating the settled region from the unoccupied zones had moved back to the Rockies. For all practical purposes, the last remaining frontier—excluding Alaska—now lay be-

tween the mountains to the west and the prairies to the east, bordered on the north by Canada and on the south by the Rio Grande.

During the post–Civil War years, cattlemen moved onto the Great Plains from Texas, and farmers, or nesters, poured in from the Mississippi Valley. By 1880 the settled area included northern Michigan, Wisconsin, Minnesota, and the Black Hills, and the remainder of the nation's heartland was quickly being inhabited. Frontier expansion was effectively over by the end of the decade, when the superintendent of the census stated that the

This map illustrates the expansion of the American frontier west of the Mississippi during the 19th century, showing the major trails and railroads and settlements.

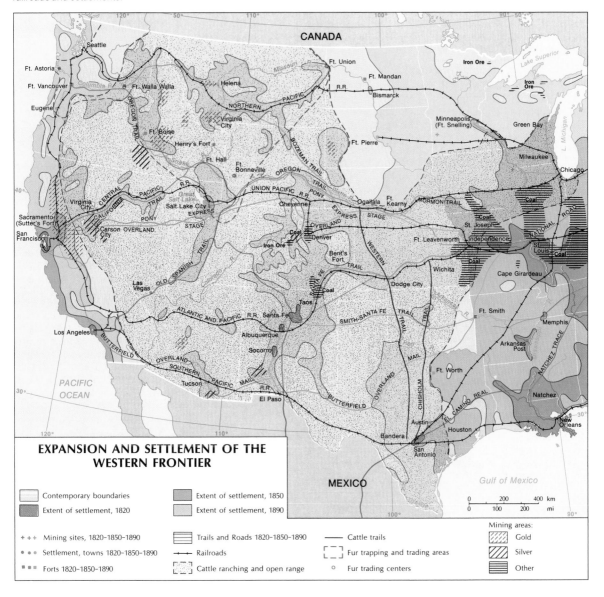

EXPANSION AND SETTLEMENT OF THE WESTERN FRONTIER

settlements of the West "now lie so scattered over the western half of the United States that there no longer can be said to be a frontier line."

Frontier Life

The myth of the American frontier as a bucolic place where one could do as one pleased continues to influence popular attitudes. In reality, the process of opening a wilderness region and wresting a living from the land took a heavy toll. Pioneer women suffered especially, as the stories of Hamlin GARLAND and other writers so poignantly reveal. The incessant burden of hard work, childbearing, and sickness, as well as fear of Indian attacks, caused most women to grow old before the age of 40. Worse yet was the stupefying loneliness brought on by the lack of social contact with friends or neighbors for months at a time. Nevertheless, the works of these pioneer women were crucial to taming the frontier, a reality that is now finally being recognized.

Characteristics. The raw frontier experience also fostered boisterous politics, rude manners, disregard for conventions, contempt for intellectual and cultural pursuits, mobility of population, unmitigated waste, and the exploitation of natural resources. The predominant spirit was to take while the taking was good, and frontier history includes many accounts of individuals who carved out empires and acquired great wealth within a few years. But the cattle kings, railroad and town builders, lumber barons, and mineowners sometimes lost fortunes as quickly as they made them. Still, there was always another tomorrow; for whatever faults frontier people possessed, they were usually ready to start again.

Small-mindedness and petty thievery were rare among frontier people. A stranger was considered honest until proved otherwise, and it was taken for granted that any traveler stopping at a farmhouse was welcome to have supper and to spend the night; an offer to pay for such hospitality would have been taken as an insult. Locks symbolized an impeachment of public honesty and integrity, and frontier people frequently did not secure the doors of their homes or even their places of business. A

The discovery of gold in 1848 at Sutter's Mill in California began a series of gold and silver rushes. Although few were successful in their search, the miners remained and contributed greatly to the economic growth of California and the west.

Texas historian declared that there was not one lock on a single building or office in the town of Colorado City throughout the 1880s.

Similarly, a man's word on the frontier was held to be as good as his bond. The owners of various mercantile enterprises at the crossing of Red River near present-day Vernon, Tex., sold supplies and clothing on credit, or advanced money without collateral, to literally hundreds of cowboys and total strangers between 1874 and 1894 without losing a dime. Some customers rode hundreds of miles out of their way to settle accounts as soon as they had the money. Like the miners in California, frontiersmen might shoot or hang a thief or murderer in short order, but they would rarely deceive him.

An admirable characteristic of Americans has been their ability to organize themselves smoothly and swiftly into a body politic. But the very ease with which town charters could be drawn up, laws passed, and officials elected sometimes fostered too much self-confidence in the community or lulled the political conscience of the ordinary person. The simplicity of frontier governmental apparatus made it easy for lawless elements to seize what government there was. When this happened, local leaders formed VIGILANTE groups to apprehend and punish the guilty and to put their weak governments back in order. But the primary danger of frontier vigilantism was that some continued to take the law into their own hands after

During the early 1800s, fur trappers and traders explored the American frontier in the Rocky Mountains. Known as mountain men, two of these buckskin-clad traders are portrayed in this 19th-century drawing by Frederic Remington.

During the American Revolution, state governments issued land grants, such as this one to General George Rogers Clark, to recruit troops.

Settlers of the Great Plains built their homes, called "soddies," out of earth. The influx of farmers following the 1862 Homestead Act limited the previously "open" range and led to the decline of the great cattle ranches.

regular judicial processes had been instituted.

Most frontier people were friendly, hard working, and just, and for every act of violence during the frontier period, there were thousands of acts of kindness, generosity, and sacrifice. People usually worked together harmoniously for the good of the community. The majority literally practiced the biblical adage and served as their brother's keeper. They gave their time, money, and sometimes their lives in behalf of friends or total strangers in moments of misfortune or extreme danger. If a neighbor lost his crop or if sickness prevented him from planting at the proper time, the whole neighborhood donated part of their harvest or time. If a bank threatened to foreclose a mortgage or an official tried to seize a man's livestock or tools because he could not pay his taxes, friends and neighbors frequently banded together to prevent it.

The Frontier Heritage. The transition from rural to urban society has long been accomplished, but the frontier remains very much a part of the American heritage. For example, many Americans continue to keep and sometimes revere guns, even though guns have not been survival necessities for more than three generations. American folklore tends to support the image of tough, aggressive, and unafraid heroes who tamed the wild frontier. This has contributed to the commonly expressed philoso-

In this 19th-century sketch by Seth Eastman, pioneers defend against attack by Comanche Indians. Wagon trains transported people and goods during the westward expansion.

phy that winning is everything, whether on the football field, in the used-car lot, or in the board room of a large corporation.

Perhaps this explains why frontier types such as the COWBOY, MOUNTAIN MAN, and OUTLAW have endured so long in American literature and legend. They went out and got what they wanted with their own two hands, frequently by violent means. Their deeds, real and imaginary, have served as a cultural metaphor of how Americans view themselves. However, in terms of actual frontier life, the emphasis is misleading. In many respects it is remarkable that the American frontier was settled in as orderly a fashion as it was.

Turner's Frontier Thesis

The best-known interpretation of the American frontier experience was proposed by Frederick Jackson TURNER. As a little-known historian from the University of Wisconsin, Turner read a paper, "The Significance of the Frontier in American History," at the annual meeting of the American Historical Association in Chicago in 1893. According to the 32-year-old professor, "The existence of an area of free land, its continuous recession, and the advance of American settlement westward explain American development." Turner enunciated what has been called the "safety valve" theory of U.S. history: "Whenever social conditions... tended to press upon labor, or political restraints to impede the freedom of the mass, there was this gate of escape to the free conditions of the frontier.... Men would not accept inferior wages and a permanent position of social insubordination when this promised land of freedom and equality was theirs for the taking." He also concluded that the frontier decreased American dependence on England and that the true point of view in American history of the United States "is not the Atlantic Coast, but the West."

Turner's hypothesis altered the course of American historical scholarship, which at that time was focused almost exclusively on New England and the East. Among other things, Turner suggested that in the course of the westward movement forces were created or released that shaped American ideas of government and contributed to the evolution of its economic and social institutions. He

Life on the frontier was rugged and, on occasion, violent. In California, for example, a period of lawlessness, characterized in part by "claim-jumping," followed the 1848 discovery of gold.

also observed that the open frontier was already an environment of the past and that Americans should of necessity move on to another chapter of history. Regardless of the validity of his thesis as a whole, few will quarrel with his assertion that the American frontier experience will never be repeated.

frontier literature   see WESTERNS

▬

frost   Frost is a light deposit of ice that is formed by the condensation of water vapor on a surface whose temperature is below freezing (0° C/32° F) at sea level. Knowledge of when and where frost may occur is of great importance in agriculture, ecology, energy conservation, and the construction industry.

Within SOILS, the movement of a frost front, and the opposite process, thawing, are complex cases of heat transmission, or conduction. At the boundary of solid and liquid, the latent heat of fusion (the additional heat at the melting point that is required to fuse a substance, approximately 80 cal/g for ice) is released if frost is forming; the latent heat is absorbed if frost is thawing.

Radiation frost, a local phenomenon, is most likely to occur during calm, clear, dry nights when rapid, long-wave radiation to the sky results in great heat loss from the surface or object. Advection frost is the result of a cold AIR MASS moving into an area, which often produces a hard freeze. HOARFROST (white frost) is caused by the SUBLIMATION of ice crystals on objects at temperatures below freezing, whereas black frost (often called dry frost or killing frost) forms on vegetation when air is dry but at temperatures below the freezing point.

See also: FROST ACTION; PERMAFROST.

▬

Frost, Robert   Robert Lee Frost, b. San Francisco, Mar. 26, 1874, d. Boston, Jan. 29, 1963, was one of America's leading 20th-century poets and a four-time winner of the Pulitzer Prize. An essentially pastoral poet of-

ten associated with rural New England, Frost wrote poems whose philosophical dimensions transcend any region. Although his verse forms are traditional, he was a pioneer in the interplay of rhythm and meter and in the poetic use of the vocabulary and inflections of everyday speech.

After the death of Frost's father in 1885, the family left California and settled in Massachusetts. Frost entered Dartmouth College but remained less than a semester. Returning to Massachusetts, he taught school and worked in a mill and as a reporter. In 1894 he sold "My Butterfly: An Elegy" to *The Independent*, a New York literary journal. A year later he married Elinor White, with whom he had shared valedictorian honors at Lawrence (Mass.) High School. From 1897 to 1899 he attended Harvard College as a special student but left without a degree. Over the next ten years he wrote (but rarely published) poems, operated a farm in Derry, N.H., and taught at Derry's Pinkerton Academy.

In 1912 he sold the farm and took his family to England, where he could devote himself entirely to writing. *A Boy's Will* was accepted by a London publisher and brought out in 1913, followed a year later by *North of Boston*. Favorable reviews on both sides of the Atlantic resulted in American publication of the books.

As part of his determined efforts on his own behalf, Frost had called on several prominent literary figures soon after his arrival in England. One of these was Ezra Pound, who wrote the first American review of Frost's verse for Harriet Monroe's *Poetry* magazine. (Later, Frost was instrumental in obtaining Pound's release from long confinement in a Washington, D.C., mental hospital.) Frost was more favorably impressed with the so-called Georgian poets Lascelles Abercrombie, Rupert Brooke, and T. E. Hulme, whose rural subjects and style were more in keeping with his own.

The Frosts sailed for the United States in February 1915 and landed in New York City two days after the U.S. publication of *North of Boston*. Sales of this book and of *A Boy's Will* enabled Frost to buy a farm in Franconia, N.H.; to place new poems in literary periodicals and publish a third book, *Mountain Interval* (1916); and to embark on a long career of writing, teaching, and lecturing. In 1924 he received a Pulitzer Prize in poetry for

One of America's most widely read and critically acclaimed poets, Robert Frost received numerous honors for his verse, among them four Pulitzer Prizes and two unanimous resolutions of praise from the U.S. Senate.

New Hampshire (1923). He was lauded again for *Collected Poems* (1930), *A Further Range* (1936), and *A Witness Tree* (1942).

Frost's importance as a poet derives from the power and memorability of particular poems. "The Death of the Hired Man" (from *North of Boston*) combines lyric and dramatic poetry in blank verse. "After Apple-Picking" (from the same volume) is a free-verse dream poem with philosophical undertones. "Mending Wall" (also published in *North of Boston*) demonstrates Frost's simultaneous command of lyrical verse, dramatic conversation, and ironic commentary. "The Road Not Taken" and "Birches" (from *Mountain Interval*) and the often studied "Stopping by Woods on a Snowy Evening" (from *New Hampshire*) exemplify Frost's ability to join the pastoral and philosophical modes in lyrics of unforgettable beauty.

frost action   Frost action is the WEATHERING process caused by repeated cycles of freezing and thawing. GROUNDWATER confined in pores of rock or SOIL expands almost 9 percent in volume upon freezing, exerting great pressure on the surrounding material and causing frost heaving in soil and frost wedging in rock.

When groundwater freezes in soil, an ice crystal grows, pushing soil particles upward. More rapid heat loss under rock fragments results in greater growth of ice crystals beneath the fragments and causes them to surface. In PERMAFROST areas, uneven freezing produces mounds or other irregularities, called patterned ground, that protrude above the surface and are surrounded by circular or polygonal accumulations of large particles that have slid off.

Frost heaving occurring along a slope produces soil creep because particles rise perpendicular to the slope as the ice crystal grows, but they sink vertically upon thawing. Thawing of frozen groundwater produces a soft, spongy soil.

The expansion of water upon freezing can also cause rocks to split if the water has been confined in joints and crevices, or shatter if it has been confined in the pores. Large block fields are produced by frost wedging. When frost wedging occurs on a slope, an accumulation of rock debris, called talus, forms along or at the base of the slope.

frostbite   Frostbite is the freezing of tissues, which may damage skin, muscle, blood vessels, and nerves. The damage is probably caused both by the formation of ice crystals in tissues and by drastic reduction of blood flow in the frozen areas. The numbing effect of cold may allow frostbite to occur without warning. The skin in the frostbitten area is hard, numb, and yellowish-white. Frostbite may be superficial or deep. If it is superficial, redness and blisters appear after thawing; if it is deep, EDEMA appears under the skin after thawing and persists for a day or two, after which GANGRENE may develop. During healing, a black crust develops over the frostbitten area, but it

later peels off. Superficially frostbitten tissue may be thawed immediately by body heat, but it should not be exercised or rubbed with snow. Deep frostbite should be thawed with warm (not hot) water as soon as possible. Most victims recover but may have persistent numbness, sensitivity to cold, and a tendency to repeated frostbite. Severe cases may require amputation.

frozen food   Although weather freezing is an ancient technique for preserving foods in cold climates, science and engineering principles have been applied to the freezing of foods only since the late 1920s. Much of the work has been directed toward perfecting methods for the fast freezing of foods, since fast freezing retains texture and flavor characteristics better than do slow-freezing methods, which result in the growth of large crystals and the concentration of solutes. Three quick-freezing methods exist: air-blast freezing; immersion freezing, using such refrigerants as brine, or cryogenic liquids or gas (liquid nitrogen, carbon dioxide); and indirect-contact freezing, using chilled plates. Some vitamin loss takes place during processing, varying according to the food, the type of process, and the type of packaging. Freezing may also cause a slight loss of minerals, some denaturation of protein, and some oxidation of fats. These losses may occur during the preparation, in storage, or during the thawing of the product prior to consumption.

Extensive quality-control measures ensure the freshness and optimal texture, color, and taste of the product. Freezing is not a sterilization process. Even extreme cold does not prevent the growth of bacteria, yeasts, and molds or the activity of enzymes. Extreme cold does, however, slow down the growth of microorganisms, and frozen foods, if prepared in a sanitary manner and unthawed before use, are as wholesome as fresh foods.

fructose   Fructose, $C_6H_{12}O_6$, is an important MONOSACCHARIDE, or simple sugar, found in most fruits and in honey. It is also found in sugarcane and sugar beets, where it is chemically combined with GLUCOSE to form the disaccharide sucrose. Fructose (also called levulose) is the sweetest sugar, and like other CARBOHYDRATE molecules it can provide the body with energy. Although broken down in the body more slowly than glucose, fructose has essentially the same nutritional value.

fruit fly   Fruit fly is the common name for a large number of small insects whose larvae typically eat their way through fruits. Vinegar, or pomace, fruit flies, classified in the family Drosophilidae, typically feed on fungi (yeasts) found on decaying fruit. All other fruit flies, members of the family Tephritidae, feed directly on fruit; many are highly destructive and serious agricultural pests. One species of vinegar fruit fly—*Drosophila melanogaster*—played an important part in the development of theories of heredity and is still used for research in genetics.

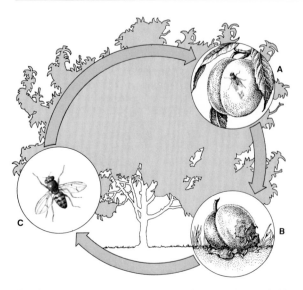

The life cycle of a fruit fly begins when an adult female lays her eggs inside the skin of an overripe fruit still on a tree (A). Larvae hatch (B) and feed on the fruit, which drops to the ground. A developing larva leaves the rotting fruit and bores into soil, where it pupates and emerges as a mature fly (C).

The apple maggot, *Rhagoletis pomonella*, attacks apples, crab apples, pears, and plums. Females deposit their eggs under the skin of fruit. The eggs hatch into white maggots that tunnel their way through the fruit, drop to the ground, and pupate. New flies emerge in the spring. Adults, about 6 mm (0.2 in) long, have dark bodies with light bands on the abdomen and dark-patterned wings. Cherry fruit flies, *R. congulata* and *R. fausta*, are similar.

The Mediterranean fruit fly, or Medfly, *Ceratitus capitata*, is a major pest of citrus and other fruits. To some extent, Medflies can be kept under control by releasing sterile males to interfere with the normal reproductive cycle. Large outbreaks, such as occurred in California in 1990, have been fought by extensive—and controversial—aerial spraying of the pesticide malathion.

▬

fruits and fruit cultivation   Fruit is the ripened ovary of any flowering plant, or ANGIOSPERM, and usually contains one or more seeds.

Classification of Fruit

By definition, fruit refers to such edibles as tomatoes, string beans, corn, peas, and mustard, as well as to nuts, acorns, oranges, peaches, and others. Tomatoes, string beans, and peaches, for example, are fruits that are eaten whole. Peas, corn, and mustard are the seeds, or fertilized ovules, of fruits. Flour is ground from the fruit of the wheat plant, and coffee is made from the seeds of the coffee fruit, or bean.

Some fruits, called accessory fruits, are partly derived from flower structures other than the ovary. Most accessory fruits, such as bananas, cucumbers, and gooseberries, are fleshy throughout and are thus called false berries. Apples and pears are accessory fruits called pomes; the edible part is the fleshy exterior, and the true fruit forms the core.

Fruits promote seed dispersal and seed germination. Animals that eat fleshy fruits may spit out or expel undigested seeds with the feces and deposit them in a new location. Dry fruits, such as nuts, may be carried about by animals such as the squirrel and left in some forgotten hiding place. Fruits with burrs, hooks, or wing blades may be scattered widely by the wind or, clinging to the pelt of a passing animal, be transported to other locations. Fruits that fall to the ground eventually decay, aiding seed development by enriching the soil.

The nutritional value of fruits varies. Many have few calories because they are composed largely of water: a ripe tomato, for example, may be 97 percent water. Such fruits are valued in the human diet primarily for their vitamin content and their distinctive tastes and textures. Soybeans and peanuts, on the other hand, have high protein and caloric content, and valuable oils are obtained from olive and sunflower fruits and castor-oil seeds. Cereal grains are humankind's major food, contributing more than two-thirds of the world production of edible dry matter and half of the world's protein.

Simple Fruits

A simple fruit consists of a single ripened ovary and may be either dry or fleshy. With ripening, the walls of a simple dry fruit become leathery, papery, or woody. At maturity the walls may be dehiscent, opening to shed the seeds, or indehiscent, remaining closed and usually containing only one seed. Dehiscent fruits are further classified as follicles, legumes, or capsules. The follicle dehisces along one side only. Examples include milkweed and peony fruits. Such legumes as the pea dehisce along two sides.

The capsule develops from a compound pistil, which is two or more carpels (inner flower parts) fused together. The poppy fruit is a capsule from which the seeds are released through a distal ring of pores. The large single seed of the horse-chestnut fruit, however, is released only when the thick, spiny, three-valved capsule falls apart at maturity.

Dry, Hard Fruits. Indehiscent dry fruits include the achene, grain, samara, and nut. The achene—for exam-

When the proper levels of juice, sugar, and acid are reached, oranges are harvested by clipping them from the trees or by pulling them from the stems, as is done in this Florida orange grove.

Apples may be harvested by hand, as in this orchard in Virginia. When the apples reach the proper size and color, they are harvested by twisting them so that the stem breaks away from the branch without damaging the tree.

ple, of the dandelion or buttercup—contains a single seed that almost fills the fruit cavity but is separable from the ovary wall, or pericarp. Because of their small size, achenes are frequently mistaken for seeds. The grain, or caryopsis, is the characteristic fruit of the grass family, including the cereals. It differs from the achene in that the thin seed coat is fused with the pericarp. The samara also is usually one-seeded and has a winglike outgrowth of the pericarp that facilitates its dispersal by wind. Examples are the fruits of elm and maple trees.

A nut is a drupe, which is a one-seeded fruit with a thickened pericarp that hardens upon ripening. Examples are the fruits of hazel, oak, beech, chestnut, and walnut.

The term *nut* is popularly misused, often when referring to individual seeds. The so-called Brazil nut is a seed, one of 12 to 20 borne in a globular, thick-walled capsule. The peanut fruit is a legume containing edible seeds, or peanuts, and the edible parts of almonds and walnuts are the seeds of drupes.

Fleshy Fruits. Fruits in which all or most of the fruit wall is fleshy at maturity are classified as simple fleshy fruits. They are further classified as berries, drupes, false berries, and pomes. The seeds escape as a result of the decomposition of the fleshy tissues. The entire ovary wall of the berry ripens into a fleshy, usually edible, pericarp. Berries include the fruits of the tomato, grape, date, aubergine, avocado, and red pepper. There may be a single seed, as in the date, or many, as in the tomato. Citrus fruits are modified berries in which the pericarp forms the peel and the edible part consists of saclike outgrowths of the carpel walls.

The pericarp of a drupe has three parts: an outer exocarp, which is often a thin skin; the fleshy mesocarp; and the endocarp, which is a stone or pit enclosing the seed. Drupes include the olive, cherry, and peach. In the coconut fruit the exocarp and mesocarp form the fibrous husk, while the familiar nut is a single seed enclosed in the woody endocarp.

Compound Fruits

A compound fruit is classified either as aggregate or as multiple. An aggregate fruit is a cluster of ripened ovaries produced by a single flower. The individual fruits of raspberry, for example, are tiny drupes that separate as a unit

Fleshy simple fruits consist of a single mature ovary with a fleshy or mostly fleshy wall, or pericarp. They are classified as berries, drupes, or pomes. Berries (left) have seeds embedded in fleshy tissue. True berries such as tomatoes and grapes have entirely fleshy pericarps. Pepos are berries with a hard rind, including watermelons and cucumbers. Hesperidiums such as oranges have leathery rinds and internal segmentation. Drupes (center) have a hard pit surrounding a single seed; the outer part of the pericarp forms a thin skin. Drupes include peaches, olives, cherries, and certain nuts. Pomes (right), such as pears and apples, have papery central cores containing several seeds.

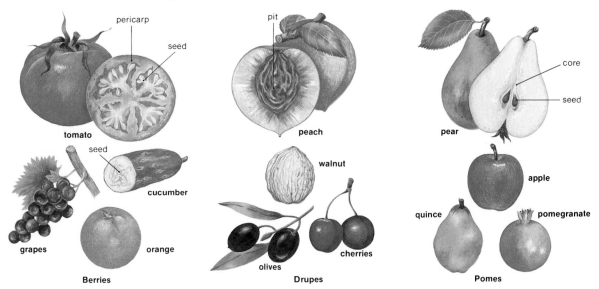

The seed follicles of dehiscent dry fruits may open along one edge (milkweed); legume follicles split along both edges (pea). The poppy sheds its seeds through pores in its seed capsule. Indehiscent dry fruits include the chestnut, an achene, which has a thin, separable pericarp. The fruit of the ash tree is a samara, with a wing-shaped pericarp. Wheat is a caryopsis, with the pericarp and seed coat fused.

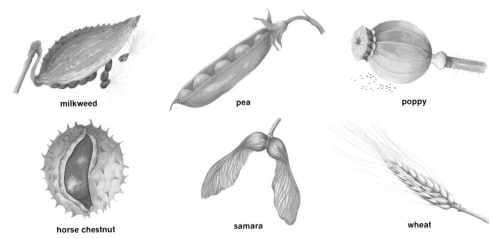

milkweed

pea

poppy

horse chestnut

samara

wheat

from the receptacle. The strawberry, however, is both aggregate and accessory: the individual fruits are achenes, commonly called the seeds, while the fleshy edible part is the receptacle.

A multiple fruit is formed from a number of flowers grouped closely together as an inflorescence, rather than from a single flower. Each flower produces a fruit, and the fruits remain together at maturity. The best example is the pineapple, which comprises fruits derived from several hundred individual flowers fused together. The fig, breadfruit, and mulberry are also multiple fruits.

Commercial Fruit Crops

Horticulturally, fruit is defined as the seed-bearing product of a perennial plant. The botanical fruits of annual plants, such as the tomato, melon, or bean, are classified as vegetables for horticultural purposes.

Geographical Distribution of Fruit Crops. Fruits are grown commercially throughout the temperate and tropical areas of the world. Tropical fruits, the banana and pineap-

ple, for example, are mostly evergreen and are seriously damaged or killed by freezing temperatures. Those of the subtropics are also mostly evergreen, but possess some resistance to freezing injury, and benefit from seasonal changes. Commercial citrus culture, for instance, is concentrated in regions where night temperatures in winter approach freezing.

In warm-temperate regions most fruit species are deciduous, with exceptions such as the evergreen olive. Almost all warm-temperate fruits can resist temperatures down to −7° C (19.4° F) during winter DORMANCY. These species must experience a short period of low temperature in order to flower. Because a long, warm growing season is necessary for satisfactory productivity and quality, however, they cannot be cultivated commercially in cooler regions. The grape is grown in warm-temperate areas, as are figs, olives, members of the genus *Prunus* (apricot, peach, plum, almond), and filbert, walnut, and pistachio nuts.

The cool-temperate species are characteristically decid-

Aggregate fruits consist of a number of mature ovaries from a single flower; each ovary forms a complete fruit. Many so-called berries are aggregates. Each "seed" of a strawberry is a small achene. Raspberries and blackberries consist of clusters of small, individual drupes.

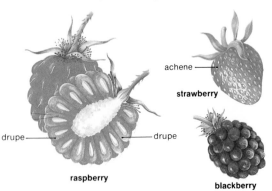

drupe

drupe

achene

strawberry

raspberry

blackberry

Multiple fruits consist of a number of mature ovaries produced by a cluster of flowers. The pineapple is produced by hundreds of flowers; each of its segments is an individual fruit. Each "seed" of a fig is also a fruit. The mulberry consists of a cluster of tiny drupes.

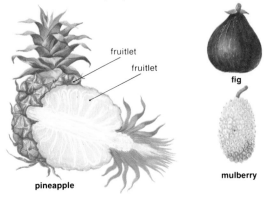

fruitlet

fruitlet

fig

pineapple

mulberry

uous and can withstand temperatures as low as -20° C (-4° F). Among the important cool-temperate fruits are species of apple, pear, cherry, strawberry, raspberry, and currant.

Fruit Ripening and Storage. The onset of ripening, which marks the end of the growth of the fruit and the start of its senescence, is controlled by hormones. The fruit tissues soften as cell-wall materials break down, stored starches are converted to sugar, and characteristic pigment changes take place. Ripening fruits produce minute quantities of the gas ethylene, which is used commercially to accelerate ripening of citrus and other tree fruits. Fruits that are to be harvested early are sprayed with an ethylene compound. Other chemicals can be used to retard ripening and thus to extend the harvesting season.

Harvested fruits continue to carry on most of the life processes that were predominant just before harvest. They respire, using oxygen; give off carbon dioxide; and generate heat. Respiration consumes food and water stored in the fruit and leads to the breakdown of tissues, causing perishability. Respiration and tissue breakdown can be delayed by refrigeration. Fruits may also be stored in refrigerated storage rooms, where the oxygen content of the atmosphere is reduced and the carbon dioxide level is increased. In this controlled atmosphere, respiration is reduced still further.

Drying or dehydration of fruits also prolongs edibility. It is commonly used for dates, figs, prunes, and apricots. Freezing and canning are used to preserve the more perishable berries. Most nuts, though far less perishable than shell-less fruits, are subject to mold and rancidity and are often kept in controlled-atmosphere storage.

See also: FLOWER; HORTICULTURE; TROPICAL FRUIT.

Frumentius, Saint [froo-men'-shuhs] Saint Frumentius, *c.*300–*c.*380, is known as the "Apostle of the Abyssinians." A youth from Tyre, he was attacked and shipwrecked, with Saint Aedesius, on the Ethiopian coast. They were taken as captives to the royal Abyssinian court at Aksum, where they engaged in missionary work and eventually became court officials. About 340, Frumentius was consecrated a bishop at Alexandria, Egypt, by Saint Athanasius. Feast day: Aug. 1 (Ethiopian); Dec. 18 (Coptic); Nov. 30 (Greek); Oct. 27 (Roman).

Frunze [froon'-zeh] Frunze (1988 est. pop., 626,000) is the capital of Kirghizia, in the Central Asian USSR. Situated at an altitude of 755 m (2,480 ft), it lies at the foot of the Kirghiz Mountains, a range of the Tian Shan system. Frunze is a manufacturing city and the center of the Chu Valley, the most densely settled area of the predominantly mountainous republic. Its factories, which yield about half of the republic's industrial output, produce machinery, textiles, and food products. Seized (1862) by the Russians in their conquest of Central Asia, it was known as Pishpek until 1926, when it was renamed for Mikhail V. Frunze, an early Bolshevik military leader who was born there.

frustration Frustration is the blocking of a person's active movement toward a goal. In psychology the term is generally applied to the emotional state that results from such blocking. Frustration is inevitable in daily life, because people must continually overcome large and small obstacles.

Frustration may result from the attempt to reach incompatible goals. Attractive but mutually exclusive goals cause a type of inner conflict known as approach-approach conflict. Such a conflict occurs, for example, when a person chooses one of two equally attractive jobs. In an approach-avoidance conflict, a person may simultaneously wish for and fear an action: if both tendencies are equal in strength—if, for instance, a person wishes to get married but also fears the responsibilities of marriage—he or she may become immobilized, incapable of any action. Avoidance-avoidance conflict occurs when two equally unpleasant consequences are confronted, and avoiding one leads to the other: for example, a person may wish to avoid being fired, but at the same time dislike the boring job.

For some people the reaction to frustration is anger, often leading to aggression. Anger vented against a safe, albeit inappropriate, target is called displaced aggression. Another reaction to frustration is withdrawal into fantasy (psychologists call this withdrawal "reaction repression"), or regression to methods of adjustment that were successful in childhood.

Several compensatory reactions to frustration also exist. Failure in one area of activity may result in an intense effort to succeed in another area.

See also: DEFENSE MECHANISMS.

Fry, Christopher Christopher Fry, b. Dec. 18, 1907, is an English playwright whose verse dramas, though failing to revive poetry in the theater, were greatly successful in their time and include several minor classics. Fry began his career in the theater as an actor and a director. His first success was the one-act *A Phoenix Too Frequent* (1946). Three full-length poetic comedies followed: *The Lady's Not for Burning* (1948), *Venus Observed* (1950), and *The Dark Is Light Enough* (1954). Of his several religious plays, *A Sleep of Prisoners* (1951) was the most widely produced. Fry's other writing includes translations of the French playwrights Jean Anouilh and Jean Giraudoux and film scripts for *The Beggar's Opera* (1953), *Ben-Hur* (1959), *Barabbas* (1962), and *The Bible* (1966).

Fry, Elizabeth Elizabeth Fry, b. May 21, 1780, d. Oct. 12, 1845, was an English prison reformer and philanthropist. She became a Quaker in 1798; devoted to serving the poor, she was recognized as a minister. In 1813 she started investigating prison conditions and began visiting jails to read the Bible and preach to the inmates. Appalled at the treatment of female prisoners in Newgate prison, London, she publicized abuses—asking

Elizabeth Fry, a British prison reformer, Quaker minister, and philanthropist, campaigned throughout Great Britain and Europe to improve prison conditions.

for separation of the sexes, classification of prisoners, more food and clothing, and better supervision. She organized an association that supported religious and secular instruction for the inmates and provided clothing and other necessities for prisoners. Fry wrote tracts, testified before parliamentary committees, and visited monarchs in Europe to advocate prison reform.

Fry, Roger   Roger Eliot Fry, b. Dec. 14, 1866, d. Sept. 9, 1934, was an English art critic and artist. In 1894, Fry began to lecture on art and quickly became an influential critic and author. His initial exposure to Paul Cézanne's paintings in 1906 made him an enthusiastic champion of the postimpressionists, and in November 1910 he organized a successful exhibition of their works at the Grafton Gallery, London. From 1905 to 1910, he was curator of paintings at the Metropolitan Museum of Art, New York City. Fry wrote on individual artists, but was at his best in more general aesthetic studies, such as *Vision and Design* (1920) and *Reflections on British Painting* (1934).

Frye, Northrop   Herman Northrop Frye, b. Sherbrooke, Quebec, Canada, July 14, 1912, d. Jan. 23, 1991, was a literary critic known for his studies of the relationships of literature, myth, and society. His first major work, *Fearful Symmetry: A Study of William Blake* (1947), which explores myth and mysticism in Blake's works, is a pioneering study in the "mythical" school of modern criticism. In his best-known work, *Anatomy of Criticism* (1957), Frye, who was ordained a minister in 1936, introduced a critical system built on the analysis of recurrent literary archetypes, especially the Judeo-Christian myths of the quest, redemption, and fall. Frye also wrote extensively on Shakespeare, Milton, and the English Romantics. His theories are further explored in *Spiritus Mundi* (1976), *The Great Code: The Bible and Literature* (1982), and *Words with Power: Being a Second Study of "The Bible and Literature"* (1990).

FSH   see HORMONE, ANIMAL; PITUITARY GLAND

Fu-Shou-Lu   see FUSHOULU

Fu-shun   see FUSHUN

Fuad I, King of Egypt [foo-ahd']   Fuad I, b. Mar. 26, 1868, d. Apr. 28, 1936, was the first king of modern Egypt. A son of ISMAIL PASHA, he succeeded his brother Hussein Kamil as sultan in 1917 and became king on his country's independence in 1922. His reign was marked by continued British influence in politics and by the king's struggle against the Wafd party.

Fuchs, Sir Vivian   Sir Vivian Fuchs, b. Feb. 11, 1908, is a British geologist and Antarctic explorer. After serving as an officer in World War II he headed a survey of the Falkland Islands (1947–50). During the International Geophysical Year (1957–58) he led the 12-man Commonwealth Trans-Antarctic Expedition, the first land crossing of Antarctica. Using snow tractors and dog teams, and supported by aircraft, the team made its way from the Filchner Ice Shelf to McMurdo Sound in 99 days, a feat for which Fuchs was knighted.

fuchsia [fue'-shuh]   Fuchsias, genus *Fuchsia*, are small shrubs or trees belonging to the evening-primrose family, Onagraceae. They are native to New Zealand, Tahiti, and regions in Central and South America. The sizes of various species range from 46 cm (18 in) to more than 600 cm (20 ft) in height. Many species have hanging flowers that are brilliant red, purple, or pink in color. Hardy fuchsia, *F. magellanica*, and honeysuckle fuchsia, *F. triphylla*, are two well-known ornamentals, and their hybrids are often grown in hanging baskets and even, in warm climates, planted as hedges.

Honeysuckle fuchsia is a decorative shrub that is native to the West Indies. Its tubular, showy flowers are borne in hanging clusters. It reaches about 60 cm (2 ft) in height.

fuel Fuel is any substance used to produce heat energy through a chemical or nuclear reaction. The energy is produced by the conversion of a portion of the fuel's mass.

Origin of Fuels

The fuels used today as ENERGY SOURCES fall into two general categories: those which are photosynthetic in origin (fossil fuels) and those which make use of atomic nuclei (nuclear fuels). The process of photosynthesis harnesses SOLAR ENERGY to produce the chemical reactions that convert carbon dioxide and water into carbohydrates, leading to the growth of plants, which can be burned directly as fuel. Alternatively, the plants may be eaten by animals, which in turn produce waste products that can be burned directly or processed.

Fuel derived from photosynthesis is also produced through the accumulation of decaying animal and vegetable matter over long periods of time. PEAT, for example, accumulates in suitable boggy areas.

Fossil Fuels. Economically more important is the formation of fossil fuels. Vegetable matter is converted into coal (see COAL AND COAL MINING). The initial step is the formation of a peatlike deposit. Over the course of time, hydrogen becomes attached to carbon, forming hydrocarbons, and coal is formed. Oil (see PETROLEUM; NATURAL GAS), another key fossil fuel, is formed from the decay of marine plankton.

Nuclear Fuels. Nuclear fuels (see NUCLEAR ENERGY) can be made from some heavy atomic nuclei, particularly ura-

By 1890 coal had supplanted wood as the primary fuel in the United States; coal in turn had been superseded by petroleum and natural gas by 1950. In the future the United States may once again rely on coal, along with nuclear energy, as primary sources.

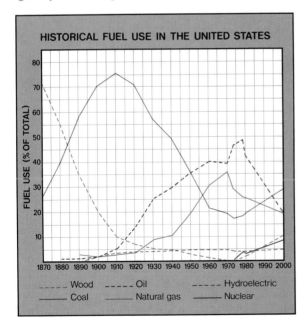

nium-235 and plutonium-239. Energy is also released in nuclear fusion—nuclear reactions between very light nuclei that combine to form a heavier atom. (See FUSION, NUCLEAR; FUSION ENERGY.)

History of Fuel Use

The historical development of fuel use in the industrialized nations shows a gradual decline in the use of WOOD as fuel. By the 17th century, wood was used to produce another fuel, CHARCOAL, for smelting. Next, wood was replaced by coal, and charcoal by COKE. By the late 19th century, the use of oil became feasible.

All the Western nations were greatly affected by the sharp price rise in petroleum products in the 1970s (see PETROLEUM INDUSTRY). The United States initiated a SYNTHETIC-FUELS program (see SHALE, OIL). Other experimental fuels include ethanol (see ETHYL ALCOHOL) and methanol (see METHYL ALCOHOL), produced by conversion of biomass (see GASOHOL), and METHANE.

See also: BUTANE; GASOLINE; KEROSENE; POWER, GENERATION AND TRANSMISSION OF; PROPANE.

fuel cell A fuel cell is a device that continuously converts chemicals into direct-current electricity through electrochemical reactions. In a typical fuel cell hydrogen gas combines with hydroxyl ions at one electrode to produce water and electrons. The electrons perform electrical work by flowing through an external circuit to the other electrode, where they recombine with oxygen and water to produce hydroxyl ions. The overall reaction is $2H_2 + O_2 \rightarrow 2H_2O$. The fuel cell differs from a BATTERY in that its reactants must be supplied from an outside source. Fuel cells can theoretically convert fuel to electricity with nearly 100% efficiency. By contrast, burning fuel to produce steam for electricity is 40% to 50% efficient, and internal-combustion engines are only 10% to 20% efficient.

History. The first attempt to obtain electricity directly from a fuel was probably made in 1802 by Sir Humphry Davy, who described a cell with a carbon anode and aqueous nitric acid as the cathodic reactant. The first hydrogen-oxygen cell (reported 1839) was composed of two platinum strips immersed in acidified water; the upper part of one was exposed to hydrogen, the other to oxygen. Numerous attempts were made to develop efficient fuel cells that used carbon, because a galvanic cell that produced electrical energy directly from carbon and oxygen would be an inexpensive source of energy.

Types. The most common fuel cells have used oxygen and hydrogen gas with potassium hydroxide as an electrolyte. The water produced by the reaction is carried out by circulating gases and condenses externally.

Considerable research has been done on fuel-cell systems that use the direct oxidation of hydrocarbons. One promising model, the solid-oxide (or monolithic) cell, passes fuel through a ceramic honeycomb structure that resembles corrugated cardboard. The solid-oxide cell (so-called because it contains electrolytes of yttria-stabilized zirconium oxide) produces electrical energy from almost any hydrocarbon fuel, including gasoline. Moreover, it

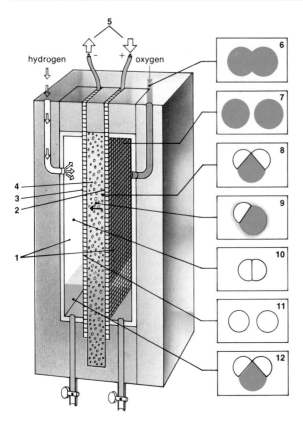

The 20th-century Mexican writer Carlos Fuentes uses the contemporary postrevolutionary period of his native country as a background for his writings.

A fuel cell produces electricity from a chemical reaction of hydrogen and oxygen. The chemical reaction forms water as a by-product. This cell is made up of two gas chambers (1), a platinum-coated wire cathode (2) and anode (3), and a very thin electrolyte-saturated membrane (4) that can pass ions but not atoms or molecules. As molecular oxygen (6) entering the cell contacts the cathodic platinum, it is split into atoms (7), which combine with electrolyte water (8) and cathode electrons to form hydroxyl ions (9), which move to the anode. At the anode, molecular hydrogen (10) is split into atoms (11) similarly. These atoms combine with the hydroxyl ions to produce water (12), which is drained periodically, and electrons, which flow through the external circuit (5) as an electric current.

produces little pollution and maintains high efficiency even at low operating levels.

Fuel cells are at present used chiefly in space vehicles and for limited military purposes. A 4.8-megawatt plant was put into operation in Tokyo in 1984, however. In the United States it is anticipated that similar electricity-producing and cogeneration plants will eventually be on-line. Even cars may someday be powered by economical fuel cells.

fuel injection   SEE CARBURETOR

Fuentes, Carlos [fwayn'-tays]   Carlos Fuentes, b. Nov. 11, 1928, one of Mexico's leading writers, is known for his experimental novels and social criticism. A lawyer by training, Fuentes published his first work, the collec-tion of surrealist short stories *Los días enmascarados* (The Masked Days), in 1954. In his first novel, *Where the Air Is Clear* (1958; Eng. trans., 1960), he portrayed a cross section of Mexico City's people and what they had lived through since the 1910 revolution. In *The Good Conscience* (1959; Eng. trans., 1961), he examined the provincial background of a character in his first novel in a more direct way. *Aura* (1962) is a novella in the manner of Henry James. *The Death of Artemio Cruz* (1962; Eng. trans., 1964) brought Fuentes international recognition. Two symbolic novels, *A Change of Skin* (1967; Eng. trans., 1968) and *Cumpleaños* (Birthdays, 1969), combined the persistent Fuentes themes of myth and history. Recent novels include *Terra Nostra* (1975; Eng. trans., 1976) and *Distant Relations* (Eng. trans., 1982). The author of two absurdist plays, Fuentes has also published *Casa con dos puertas* (House with Two Doors, 1970) and *Tiempo mexicano* (Mexican Time, 1971), essay collections on American and Mexican writing and art. Influenced by the philosopher Octavio Paz and the poet José Gorostiza, Fuentes first focused on the betrayal of the ideals of the Mexican Revolution; his later works present a more universal examination of the human condition.

Fugard, Athol [foo'-gard]   Athol Fugard, b. June 11, 1932, is South Africa's finest producing playwright. Almost all his plays are about South Africa's black population, praising the human spirit's tenacity in the face of misery and humiliation. His best plays include *Nogogo* (1960); *The Blood Knot* (1961); *People Are Living There* (1968); *Boesman and Lena* (1970; film, 1972), which won a 1972 Obie Award; and a trilogy that includes *The Island* and *Sizwe Banzi Is Dead* (both 1973) and *Statements after an Arrest under the Immorality Act* (1974). Among his recent plays are *Master Harold… & the Boys* (1982), *The Road to Mecca* (1984), and *My Children, My Africa* (1989). Fugard has described his work in *Notebooks 1960–1977* (1983).

Fugger (family) [fug'-ur]   The Fuggers of Augsburg, Germany, were the most successful family of merchants, mineowners, and bankers of the 16th century. Jacob

Fugger (1459–1525) took control of the family firm in 1485. In return for loans to the counts of Tyrol and the Habsburg emperors, Fugger obtained monopoly concessions for the mining of Tyrolese silver, Hungarian copper, and Spanish mercury. For a time both the firm's profits and the loans to the Habsburgs rose by more than 50 percent each year, and the business became a vital part of imperial finances. Gradually the Habsburgs ruined the Fuggers by failures to repay loans. The firm was finally closed in the mid-1600s.

fuging tune [fueg'-ing] The fuging tune was a short religious vocal composition that opened with a section in chordal style and concluded with an imitative passage, usually repeated, in which all voices entered at different times with the same thematic material. It was common in 17th- and 18th-century England and 18th- and early 19th-century America. The fuging tune was not an attempt to create a fugue in miniature, but a device to bring variety to the homophonic (chordal) psalm tune. William BILLINGS is the best-known American composer of fuging tunes; others were Lewis Edson, Daniel Read, and Oliver Holden.

Fugitive Slave Laws The U.S. Congress legislated separate Fugitive Slave Laws in 1793 and 1850 that provided for return between states of escaped slaves. The first act was largely ineffective. As slavery was abolished in the Northern states and antislavery sentiment increased, enforcement in the North became lax. Several Northern states passed personal liberty laws that allowed fugitives a jury trial; others prohibited state officials from cooperating in the capture and return of fugitives.

As a concession to the South, Congress legislated a more stringent Fugitive Slave Law as part of the COMPROMISE OF 1850. Violent disorders broke out during the 1850s, however, when slaveholders attempted to capture runaways in the North. Northern states rendered the law useless by passing more sweeping personal liberty laws. The dispute over the Fugitive Slave laws was an important cause of conflict between North and South. On June 28, 1864, during the Civil War, Congress repealed both acts.

Fugitives and Agrarians The Fugitives, also called the Agrarians, were a group of American poets and critics based at Vanderbilt University. The group included John Crowe RANSOM, Allen TATE, and Robert Penn WARREN. They defended the aristocratic heritage of the South, an agrarian society they felt was being destroyed by industrialization. They expressed these views in *I'll Take My Stand* (1930), their manifesto. They published the poetry magazine *The Fugitive* (1922–25) and contributed to the *Southern Review,* the *Sewanee Review,* and the *Kenyon Review.*

fugue [fueg] The fugue (from the Italian *fuga,* flight) is the most highly developed form of imitative COUNTERPOINT;

it came to prominence in the late 17th century as the successor to the ricercar and canzona. The fugue has no strict form; rather, it is a contrapuntal style distinguished by its texture. It is written for a given number of parts, from two to normally no more than five or six. The fugue's theme, or "subject," is introduced as a solo melody. Fugues often end with an overlapping "stretto," in which each entry of the subject begins before the previous one has completed its statement. Then a second part sounds the subject in counterpoint with a "countersubject" in the first part, and so on until all the parts have entered with the subject, completing an "exposition." Lighter-textured "episodes" are inserted between later entrances of the subject.

The subject of a fugue may be modified by one or more of the following devices: augmentation, in which the subject is presented in longer notes; diminution, in which the note values are halved or quartered; inversion, in which the subject is sounded upside down; and retrograde, in which it is sounded backward.

The rules of fugue were formulated by Johann Joseph Fux in his *Gradus ad Parnassum* (1725), which served as a counterpoint text until well into the next century. Johann Sebastian BACH brought the fugue to its peak of development in both instrumental and vocal music.

Fuji, Mount [foo'-jee] Mount Fuji (Japanese: Fujiyama) is a dormant volcano located 112 km (70 mi) southwest of Tokyo in south central Honshu island. The highest mountain in Japan, it rises in near perfect symmetry from a base 126 km (78 mi) in circumference to a height of 3,776 m (12,388 ft). Five interconnecting lakes, formed during earlier lava flows, ring its base. One of these lakes, Kawaguchi, is famous for the inverted image of the mountain reflected in its water. Long held sacred by Japanese Buddhists, Fuji has inspired artists and poets for centuries.

Legend maintains that Fuji was created during an earthquake in 286 BC. Geologists believe that it and the rugged peaks that stretch across Honshu from the Sea of Japan to the Pacific Ocean were created during the Tertiary Period (65–2 million years ago). The elliptical crater, now approximately 610 m (2,000 ft) in diameter, was formed during the Quaternary Period, when great quantities of lava flowed from its center. The last eruption occurred in 1707. The slopes of Fuji are seriously eroded, and rock and sand slides occur frequently. Thousands of hikers and pilgrims climb to the summit during July and August. Mount Fuji is located in Fuji-Hakone-Izu National Park.

Fujian (Fukien) [foo'-kee-en] Fujian, a province in southeastern China, lies on the Formosa Strait across from Taiwan. The population of Fujian is 27,824,000 (1987 est.), and the province covers an area of about 121,000 km^2 (46,718 mi^2). FUZHOU is the capital and leading port. With the exception of an irregular coastal strip and the long Min River valley, most of the area is mountainous. The Wui Shan reach 1,800 m (6,000 ft) in the east. Rice, fruits, sugarcane, and tea are cultivated at lower elevations. Coal, iron, copper, and other minerals are mined, and timber is an important resource.

Fujian became part of China during the 2d century BC. From the 17th through the 19th century, Fujian was the departure point for many of China's emigrants to Southeast Asia.

Fukien   see FUJIAN

Fukuoka [foo-koo'-oh-kah]   Fukuoka, the capital of Fukuoka prefecture, Japan, is located on Hakata Bay in the northern part of Kyushu island, about 100 km (62 mi) north-northeast of Nagasaki. The city has a population of 1,203,729 (1988 est.).

Fukuoka is near the western end of the east-west Tokaido megalopolis, a huge urban-industrial region. One of the leading commercial, industrial, and political centers of Kyushu, it manufactures iron and steel, chemicals, ceramics, machinery, textiles, and processed food. Agriculture in the surrounding area is also important to the city's economy. The city is the home of Kyushu University, one of the five imperial universities of Japan, established in 1910.

Fulani [foo-lahn'-ee]   The Fulani, also called Fulbe or Peul, are an African people widely dispersed through West Africa, from Senegal eastward to Chad and western Sudan. They number more than 7,000,000 and speak a language in the Atlantic subgroup of the Niger-Congo stock of African languages. Nomadic Fulani live in bands, move about with their herds, and are essentially egalitarian; they are pagans or indifferent Muslims. Town-dwelling Fulani live mainly by farming, trade, and the extensive production of crafts; they are ardent Muslims and are often stratified into social classes. Both types of Fulani traditionally kept slaves. Fulani descent and residence are traced through the male line. Marriage is predominantly polygynous, with co-wives living in separate houses.

A Muslim people since the 11th century, the Fulani have played a major role in the history of West Africa. During the 1600s they became leaders in an Islamic spiritual renaissance and, beginning in the 1700s, proselytized widely in the Sudan. In 1804–10, USMAN DAN FODIO led a *jihad* (holy war) in which the Hausa states of northern Nigeria were conquered and governed by Fulani fief-holders until British conquest in 1903.

Fulbright, J. William   James William Fulbright, b. Sumner, Mo., Apr. 9, 1905, served for 30 years as U.S. senator from Arkansas. A Rhodes scholar and a lawyer, he was elected to the U.S. House of Representatives as a Democrat in 1942 and entered the Senate in 1945. In 1946 he sponsored the Fulbright Act, which provided

J. William Fulbright, a U.S. senator from Arkansas, served as chairman of the powerful Senate Foreign Relations Committee and was a chief congressional critic of American involvement in the Vietnam War. He advocated increased congressional participation in the formulation of foreign policy.

government grants for the international exchange of students and teachers.

During the cold-war period following World War II, Fulbright advocated accommodation with the Communist world but at the same time pushed for a powerful nuclear deterrent and a strong alliance with Western Europe. As chairman of the Senate Committee on Foreign Relations (1959–1974), he took issue with the use of executive power in determining foreign policy and argued that Congress should have greater control of decisions involving foreign aid and American military commitments overseas. He was often critical of U.S. foreign policy. Fulbright was defeated for renomination in 1974.

Fuller, Alfred Carl   Alfred Carl Fuller, b. Nova Scotia, Canada, Jan. 13, 1885, d. Dec. 4, 1973, was the first "Fuller Brush man." In 1903 he moved to Boston and worked as a salesman for a brush company. Fuller started his own company in Hartford, Conn., in 1906, making the twisted-wire brushes himself and selling them door to door. In 1913 the firm was incorporated as the Fuller Brush Company, and its nationwide direct-sales organization eventually made Fuller products so famous they needed little advertising.

Fuller, Loie   One of the instigators of modernism in the theater, the American dancer Loie Fuller (originally Mary Louise Fuller), b. Fullersburg, Ill., Jan. 22, 1862, d. Jan. 21, 1928, created a furor with her novel use of theatrical techniques in the dance. She first appeared in 1892 in Paris. With her innovative ideas (above all, the manipulation of long, diaphanous skirts under continually changing lights), she helped to create an atmosphere in which such experimental dancers as her fellow American Isadora Duncan could flourish. Popular with theatergoers, she also became a cult figure for many of the artists and writers of her time.

Fuller, Margaret   The American writer and intellectual Sarah Margaret Fuller, b. near Boston, May 23, 1810, d. July 19, 1850, is generally regarded as one of America's first major woman journalists and authors and, along with Edgar Allan Poe, the best literary critic of her day.

Fuller, the first of nine children, was committed to a complete and rigorous education, and her precocious intellect soon brought her into contact with young thinkers at Harvard and around Cambridge in the late 1820s. In 1836 she met Raloh Waldo EMERSON and by 1839 had become a prominent member of the transcendentalists and had published her translation of Johann Eckermann's *Conversations with Goethe* (1839). She edited the *Dial* from 1840 to 1842 and in Boston began holding her famous Conversations, or intellectual discussions. In 1844, Fuller published the accounts of her travels to the midwest in *Summer on the Lakes, in 1843*, and that same year she went to New York to join Horace Greeley's *Tribune* as literary critic. While in New York she published *Woman in the Nineteenth Century* (1845), probably the most impressive early American feminist work, and *Papers on Literature and Art* (1846).

In 1846 she went to Europe as America's first woman foreign correspondent. While in Italy she began living with Count Giovanni Angelo Ossoli, ten years her junior. The couple had a child in 1848 and were married in 1849. Fuller became a partisan of the Roman republic led by Mazzini, a popular revolt against the dominance of the Papal States, and began to write a history of the revolution. In 1850 she sailed for America to escape the upheavals in Italy, but she and her family died in a shipwreck off the coast of Fire Island, N.Y.

Fuller, Melville Weston   As the eighth chief justice of the United States (1888–1910), Melville Weston Fuller, b. Augusta, Maine, Feb. 11, 1833, d. July 4, 1910, left no distinctive legal mark. An advocate of strict construction of the Constitution, Fuller's most important opinions invalidated the Income Tax Act of 1893. He was popular, however, and a great friend of Oliver Wendell Holmes, Jr. He helped to settle the Venezuela Boundary Dispute (1899) and served on the Permanent Court of Arbitration at The Hague.

Fuller, R. Buckminster   The futurist Richard Buckminster Fuller, b. Milton, Mass., July 12, 1895, d. July 1, 1983, achieved an international reputation as an inventor, designer, and philosopher. Fuller had no patience with the profit motive and was interested in developing new products and designs only as long as technical problems remained challenging. He worked from the premise that humankind's creative intelligence is limitless. Therefore, technological progress can, if unhampered by outmoded traditions and conventions, give all human beings a rich and satisfying life. The Earth's limited resources, in his view, can be overcome by inventions that provide ever-greater amenities while using ever-decreas-

The American architect and inventor Buckminster Fuller devised some of the most original and practical designs of modern technology. He was perhaps best known for his ecologically conservative geodesic domes, derived from his system of vectorial geometry.

ing amounts of materials. Because Fuller was persuaded that humans' geographical mobility should also be limitless, many of his major inventions were designed to reduce or eliminate barriers to mobility. The first of these, the Dymaxion House of 1927—entirely self-contained and readily movable—hung from a central core, thereby greatly reducing its use of materials, its weight, and its cost. His Dymaxion Car of 1933 brought similar economies to the automobile. His GEODESIC DOME (first perfected in 1947) encloses a greater volume with less material than any alternative form and may well be the most significant structural innovation of the 20th century. Fuller's many design credits include the U.S. Pavilion at the Montreal World's Fair (1967).

Fuller held more than 2,000 patents and was the author of about 25 books, including *Operating Manual for Spaceship Earth* (1969). From 1959 until his death he was a professor at Southern Illinois University.

Fulton   Fulton (1990 pop., 10,033), located about 160 km (100 mi) west of St. Louis in east central Missouri, is the seat of Callaway County. Fulton serves as the commercial center for the surrounding agricultural region. Firebrick manufacturing is the principal industry, although machinery and shoes are also produced. In 1946, Sir Winston Churchill made his famous Iron Curtain speech there at Westminster College (1851). Fulton was laid out in 1853.

Fulton, Robert   The American inventor, artist, and engineer Robert Fulton, b. Fulton County, Pa., Nov. 14, 1765, d. Feb. 24, 1815, is known for his pioneer work in the development of the STEAMBOAT, even though others had built steamboats before him. In the mid-1780s he worked as an artist in Philadelphia, and in 1786 he went to London to study painting under Benjamin West. By the early 1790s, however, his interests had shifted to science and engineering. In 1794 he received a British patent for a double inclined plane, which was used to raise and lower canal boats from one level to another.

Fulton moved to France in 1797 and submitted proposals to the French government for a submarine. His submarine, the *Nautilus*, was launched in 1800; although it proved workable, he could not obtain any government support and abandoned the project. In the meantime Fulton agreed (1802) to design and build for Robert R. Livingston a steamboat that would operate on the Hudson River. His first steamboat was successfully tested on the Seine River in 1803. Fulton returned to the United States in 1806, and in 1807 his steamboat was launched in New York harbor. The boat, which eventually was called the CLERMONT, proved the commercial feasibility of steamboats.

---

fumarole [fue'-muh-rohl]   A fumarole (from the Latin word for "smoke hole") is a small hole, vent, or fissure in the earth from which gases and vapors escape. Most fumaroles are found in areas of recent volcanic activity, where ground temperatures are still very high. Recently erupted LAVA contains various dissolved gases that react with engulfed organic material to form water vapor, hydrogen, hydrogen fluoride, and hydrogen sulfide. In old volcanic areas where temperatures are lower, the gases given off are mostly carbon dioxide, methane, nitrogen, and oxygen. Fumaroles laden with sulfurous vapors are called solfataras.

A different type of fumarole—essentially a nearly dried-up HOT SPRING—emits mostly steam and water vapor. This kind forms in areas that are not necessarily associated with active VOLCANOES, such as Yellowstone National Park.

Funchal [foon-shahl']   Funchal (1981 pop., 48,638) is the capital city of Portugal's Madeira Islands in the Atlantic Ocean. Situated on the south shore of Madeira Island it is a center of commerce, communications, and industry. It is also a scenic port and a winter resort. The city was founded in 1421 by Portuguese explorers. In the old sector is the Se, a 15th-century cathedral.

---

function   The concept of a function is basic to almost all parts of mathematics and its applications. A specific kind of mathematical relation, it can be considered as a way of associating with each element of a set A one and only one element of a set B. For example, if A is the set {1, 2, 3} and B is the set of squares of elements of A, {1, 4, 9}, then one can associate each element of set A with its square in set B. This function, called f, can be pictured as shown below.

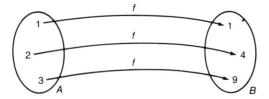

The elements of set A are called the independent variables, and the elements of set B are the dependent variables.

Functions are often called "mappings." Mathematicians use the terminology "f maps 1 in A into 1 in B," "f maps 2 in A into 4 in B," and "f maps 3 in A into 9 in B." Given an element a in A, the element b in B determined by f is designated by f(a) (read "f of a") and is called a functional value. Thus, for this example, $f(1) = 1$, $f(2) = 4$, and $f(3) = 9$.

The set A that is being mapped by f is called the domain of f, and the set B, which is the set of all f(a) for a in A, is called the range of f. Thus, in the example the domain of f is {1, 2, 3}, and the range of f is {1, 4, 9}.

Functions are frequently defined by EQUATIONS. Thus, one can write the function of the example as $x \rightarrow x^2$, or as the function f: $f(x) = x^2$, or as the function f such that $f(x) = x^2$.

Other examples of functions are the following: C: $C(r) = 2\pi r$ (the circumference of a circle of radius r); s: $s(t) = 490t^2$ (the distance in centimeters that a freely falling body will travel in t seconds); and r: $r(x) = \sqrt{x}$ (length of the side of a square whose area is x). For the functions C and r the domain would be taken to be the set of all positive numbers. For the function s the domain would be taken to be the set of all nonnegative numbers, that is, positive numbers and zero.

See also: SET THEORY.

---

functionalism (in design)   Functionalism is the concept or doctrine that the design and form of an object should be determined by consideration of its intended function or use. Although functionalism has been a significant concept in all design since prehistoric times, it has been particularly important in the development of MODERN ARCHITECTURE. In the 19th century the American artist Horatio GREENOUGH and the French architect Eugène Emmanuel VIOLLET-LE-DUC developed in their writings the theory that architecture should express directly the structural functions of the parts of a building. The theoretical basis was thus provided for overcoming eclecticism in architecture (see ECLECTICISM, art)—the predominant tendency of the 19th and early 20th century to use historic forms to decorate most architecture. In 1896 the American architect Louis SULLIVAN formulated the statement "form follows function," which served as a unifying thesis for the modern movement until the 1960s.

---

functionalism (in social science)   Functionalism is a general social theory that stresses the interdependence among the institutions and customs of any particular society. Functional analysis explains how social order is achieved by the functions that institutions—the state, religion, the family, schools, and markets—perform. For example, in complex societies, like that of the United States, religion and the family support values that function to reinforce the operations of political democracy and a market economy. In simpler, tribal societies, participation in religious rituals functions to sustain social solidarity among groups related by kinship. Although basic to the writings of major 19th-century European social theorists, especially Émile DURKHEIM, functionalism was explicitly developed as a theory by the sociologists Talcott PARSONS and Robert MERTON in the 1950s. This theory was the leading influence in Anglo-American sociology as well as in the other social sciences into the 1970s. Somewhat earlier than Parsons and Merton, Bronislaw MALINOWSKI and A. R. Radcliffe-Brown, working separately, had developed a version of functionalist theory designed specifically for research in anthropology and focused on the study of small-scale, non-Western societies. Since the 1970s functionalism has been modified to deal more adequately with the dynamics of social conflict.

—

fund-raising   The purpose of fund-raising is to encourage voluntary monetary contributions to such entities as educational and religious institutions and public-interest and social-welfare organizations. Many organizations seek their funds from FOUNDATIONS AND ENDOWMENTS and business corporations rather than individuals. Although organized giving takes place throughout the world, it assumes a special importance in the United States, where government plays a relatively small role in supporting services. Subject to restrictions introduced in 1986, charitable donations may be deducted from federal income tax.

In 1988, U.S. residents donated $104.3 billion to charitable causes, 17% of which was given by foundations, bequests, and corporations. About 46% of the total was donated to religious organizations. Education accounted for about 9% of total donations in 1988. The health-care field also received about 9%, with giving in this area dominated by foundations rather than private individuals. Social-welfare groups received almost 10% of the total, the largest single portion going to local agencies through the United Way.

About 7% of all donations went to arts and humanities groups. Public radio and television stations periodically broadcast their fund-raising campaigns and often receive matching grants from foundations. Civic and public groups, such as the Sierra Club or the National Association for the Advancement of Colored People (NAACP), received about 3% of the total.

Many large organizations, such as the American Cancer Society, conduct nationwide campaigns and often employ professional fund-raising staffs. Most local fund-raising, however, is organized by nonprofessionals in behalf of such vital local services as the fire and police departments.

—

fundamental interactions   All known physical interactions of matter occur through the agency of four basic, or fundamental, kinds of forces: gravitation, electromagnetism, the strong nuclear force, and the weak nuclear force. The first two are well known; because they act over long distances, it is easy to observe their effects.

Strong and weak nuclear forces, on the other hand, were not discovered until the 20th century. The range of their effects is limited to subatomic distances (see FUNDAMENTAL PARTICLES); therefore, they can be studied only by using the special techniques of NUCLEAR PHYSICS. A major goal of physicists is to develop a single description of forces (UNIFIED FIELD THEORY) that will relate the four types of interactions.

Each force has a characteristic strength. If the strong nuclear force between two protons is assigned a strength of 1, then the electromagnetic, weak nuclear, and gravitational forces between the same two protons have relative strengths of 10^{-2}, 10^{-5}, and an incredibly small 10^{-40}. Thus the effect of gravity on interactions among particles of atomic size is negligible.

Gravitation. The most pervasive interaction is GRAVITATION. Every particle of matter seems to attract every other particle with a force that is proportional to the mass of each and inversely proportional to the square of their separation. This relationship was first proposed by Isaac NEWTON. Gravitational force becomes appreciable only when at least one of the attracting masses is very large, typically of planetary size. Newton's theory of gravitation is fundamental, in the sense that all motion due to the gravitational forces exerted on all objects can be described as a result of the same force. Several slight deviations from the predictions of Newton's theory are observed and are explained by Albert EINSTEIN's general theory of RELATIVITY, a more fundamental and sweeping theory that reproduces the Newtonian results as a first approximation. A few scientists have hypothesized a fifth force—a weak, repelling force that would work against gravity—but this notion has gained little favor among physicists in general.

Electromagnetic Force. Electromagnetic forces (see ELECTRICITY; MAGNETISM) exist among particles bearing electric charge or intrinsic magnetic moments or both. These particles need not be stable, but their net electrical charge must be conserved throughout any reaction they undergo. All of chemistry, hence all of biology, is a direct consequence of the electromagnetic interaction of atoms and molecules.

Strong and Weak Forces. When isolated, the neutron, a fundamental particle with no electric charge and a slightly larger mass than the proton, decays very slowly, by means of a weak nuclear interaction, into a proton plus an electron-neutrino pair. Weak nuclear forces are similarly involved in many nuclear decay processes and in all interactions that involve neutrinos. On the other hand, neutrons and protons are themselves bound together over distances of the order of 10^{-12} cm by short-range strong nuclear forces to make up the nuclei of all atoms. Disintegration and transmutation of radioactive nuclei (see RADIOACTIVITY) depend on the details of the strong, weak, and electromagnetic interactions between bound nuclear particles.

Unification Attempts. Beginning in the early 20th century scientists sought to unify, in theory, the fundamental forces. The first successful attempt was the electroweak theory, which unified the electromagnetic and weak nuclear forces. Formulated in the late 1960s, it was confirmed in 1983 when experimenters observed the appropriate electroweak vector BOSONS. Present attempts (as yet unsuccessful) to unify the strong, weak, and electromagnetic forces are called GRAND UNIFICATION THEORIES.

Fundamental Orders Settlers from the first permanent Connecticut River valley towns of Hartford, Wethersfield, and Windsor met in Hartford in 1639 and adopted the Fundamental Orders of Connecticut, a written body of laws by which they would govern themselves. Thomas HOOKER and Roger LUDLOW played key roles in framing this document, sometimes called the first written constitution. It provided for a system of government similar to that of Massachusetts, except that church membership was not specified as a qualification for suffrage and the general court (legislature) could assemble without a call by the governor. Most of its principles were confirmed by the royal charter granted to Connecticut in 1662.

fundamental particles Scientists of every period have believed that certain objects are fundamental and that others are derived, in the sense that the latter are composed of the former. In one version of this distinction, the fundamental objects are particles, or points of matter carrying such properties as mass. Although the view of which objects qualify as fundamental particles has changed several times, the notion that the world is ultimately made of such material points, moving through space, has endured in some form ever since the theory of ATOMISM was first proposed by the Greeks LEUCIPPUS and DEMOCRITUS in the 5th century BC.

The atomic theory languished until the 18th and early 19th centuries, when physicists and chemists revived it to explain the properties of gases and some of the facts of chemistry. In these theories the fundamental particles, the ATOMS, remained indivisible points. The discovery in the late 19th and 20th century that atoms were composite, rather than indivisible, set the stage for modern discoveries.

History of Modern Particle Physics

The history of modern particle physics has gone through four stages. In the first stage Sir Joseph J. THOMSON discovered (1897), by studying electricity passing through gases, that all atoms contain certain particles, called ELECTRONS, that carry a negative electric charge. Because atoms are electrically neutral, there must be balancing positive charges somewhere in the atom. Based on a series of experiments by Hans Geiger and Ernest Marsden, Ernest RUTHERFORD proposed (1911) that these positive charges are concentrated in a very small volume, called the atomic nucleus, at the center of the atom.

In the second stage scientists recognized, through an analysis of isotopes of elements, that all atomic nuclei could be thought of as composed of two types of particles: the PROTON, which carries both mass and electric charge, and the NEUTRON, which has about the same mass

as a proton but is electrically neutral. This model was confirmed through the discovery (1932) of free neutrons by Sir James Chadwick.

The third stage of modern particle physics came with the recognition that protons, neutrons, and electrons—the constituents of ordinary matter—were but three of a vast number of similar particles, which differed only in a few properties, such as their mass and their stability against spontaneous decay. Experiments with particle ACCELERATORS indicated that these many subatomic particles could be readily produced from protons and neutrons, provided that enough energy was available to produce the additional mass of the new particles predicted by the rules of Albert Einstein's RELATIVITY theory. These discoveries in the 1940s and '50s indicated that the proton and neutron were not really fundamental particles and that they would have to be understood as part of a much larger family of similar objects.

In the fourth stage physicists found a successful explanation for the large number of particles. The prevailing theory is that many of these particles are combinations of QUARKS.

Properties of Particles

Subatomic particles carry two kinds of properties: those which can vary for a given particle, such as total energy, and those which remain the same for one type of particle, such as mass, spin, electric charge, and color. The combination of the latter four properties serves to define each particle type and to distinguish the particles from each other.

Mass. The mass of an object, originally thought of as an independent property of matter, is now recognized as a measure of the energy content of the object when it is at rest, according to Einstein's equation $E = mc^2$. The rest energy of a fundamental particle ranges from zero to many millions (MeV) or billions (GeV) of electron volts.

Spin. Many fundamental particles behave as if they are spinning on an internal axis, as the Earth does. According to the theories of QUANTUM MECHANICS, the angular momentum related to this spin can take on only certain values: either zero or an integer or half-integer multiple of the constant $h = 1.04 \times 10^{-27}$ erg-seconds. Each particle has a specific and unchanging value of spin.

Electric Charge. All known electric and magnetic effects originate from the property of electric charge, which is carried by certain subatomic particles. All particles of one type, such as electrons, have the same charge. Further, all observed particles have either charge zero or a positive or negative integer multiple of the proton's charge, symbolized by e. Quarks, which have not been directly observed, are thought to have charges $2/3$ e and $-1/3$ e.

Color. Quarks carry another property, known as color, which, like electric charge, remains constant in any particle reaction. Three forms of color exist, and each quark bears one of these. A quark of one color can convert into one of another color by emission or absorption of a type of gauge particle called a GLUON, which also must carry the color property in order that the total color remain constant.

Interactions and Classification of Particles

Fundamental particles exhibit several characteristic forms of behavior that have enabled physicists to find patterns among the particles and to make successful theories of their internal structure. The most remarkable thing that particles do is to change into one another, either by the decay of a single particle into several others (see RADIOACTIVITY) or in a collision between two particles from which several new ones may emerge. Quantum mechanics allows only the probabilities of these transformations to be predicted.

Fundamental Interactions. Because fundamental particles change into one another, the old notion of a force—an influence that produces physical change—is insufficient to describe their behavior. Instead physicists speak of a FUNDAMENTAL INTERACTION—any influence that causes a collection of particles to undergo some change. A measure of the strength of the interaction is the rate at which such changes take place. If other conditions are equal, then the stronger the interaction, the less time is needed for a change to occur.

Using this measure, physicists have discovered four fundamental interactions, known, in decreasing order of strength, as the strong nuclear, the electromagnetic, the weak nuclear, and the gravitational forces (see ELECTRICITY; GRAVITATION; MAGNETISM; NUCLEAR PHYSICS). Each type of fundamental particle participates in a specific subset of the four interactions. The HADRONS—which comprise MESONS, whose spin is an integer multiple of ℏ, and BARYONS, whose spin is a half-integer multiple of ℏ—can undergo all four types of interaction. Another type of particle, the charged LEPTON, can undergo all of the interactions except the strong nuclear. Uncharged leptons, or NEUTRINOS, undergo only weak-nuclear and gravitational interactions and are little affected by other matter.

The four known interactions are generated by the exchange of gauge bosons, also called gauge particles. PHOTONS are the carriers of electromagnetic interactions, gluons carry strong interactions between quarks, and W and Z particles (first observed in the early 1980s) generate weak interactions. All of these gauge bosons have one unit of spin. The still-hypothetical graviton, which carries the gravitational force, would be a gauge boson with two units of spin.

Conservation Laws. The four interactions differ not only in strength but also in their detailed behavior, especially regarding which quantities are conserved (see CONSERVATION, LAWS OF) when the interaction operates. A quantity is said to be conserved in a process when its value remains the same throughout the process. In reactions involving fundamental particles, such quantities as energy, linear momentum, angular momentum, and electric charge are always conserved.

Until recently, scientists believed that the number of baryons in a reaction is also always conserved. This law would forbid a proton from decaying into lighter particles, and indeed such decays have never been seen. Some scientists, however, have suggested that protons do decay, if rarely, and are testing this hypothesis.

There are also conservation laws that apply for some interactions but not others. Some of the hadrons, such as the sigma-plus particle (Σ^+), are produced by strong interactions but decay only by weak interactions. Because of these circumstances, these particles, termed *metastable*, exist between production and decay for enough time (10^{-10} seconds) to leave an observable track in a detection device (see DETECTOR, PARTICLE). The fact that metastable hadrons do not decay by strong interactions suggests that some law inhibits the decay. Because the decay does occur by weak interactions, the latter must not obey this law. Physicists assign a property called strangeness to several metastable hadrons. Strangeness is conserved in strong and electromagnetic interactions but not in weak interactions. Several other properties of particles that obey such partial conservation laws are also recognized, each with its own set of metastable particles.

Antimatter. Another important criterion for classification is the division into particles and antiparticles (see ANTIMATTER). This distinction was first theorized for electrons by Paul DIRAC in 1930 and was later extended to all other particles. According to the principles of relativity and quantum mechanics, for every type of particle there exists a corresponding antiparticle with the same spin and mass but with opposite electric charge. Such particles as the photon, whose electric charge, baryon number, and strangeness are all zero, are identical to their antiparticles. Antiparticles for most of the known particles have been detected, beginning with the antielectron, or POSITRON, detected by Carl David ANDERSON in 1932. The preponderance of matter over antimatter is a result of little-understood processes that occurred very early in the history of the universe (see COSMOLOGY).

Quarks and Gluons. In addition to the metastable hadrons, there are hundreds of known hadrons that are unstable and will decay by strong interactions. These unstable hadrons typically have lifetimes of 10^{-20} seconds or less. The properties of hadrons have been explained with some success by the quark-gluon theory of strong interactions. According to this theory, hadrons are composed of combinations of the various types of quarks. The quarks are held together by unbreakable bonds resulting from gluon exchange between the quarks. Baryons are each composed of three quarks; mesons are composed of a quark and an antiquark. Six different types of quarks are theorized to exist, each of which can be any of the three colors.

The quark-gluon theory also explains why quarks and gluons are never observed alone but rather in combinations such as the three quarks that make up a baryon. Gluon exchange induces a force between quarks, and between the gluons themselves, that remains strong even when the particles involved are relatively far apart. Because of this, it is not possible to separate the quarks and gluons of a single hadron far enough from each other so that they can be observed in isolation. This phenomenon is referred to as confinement of quarks and gluons. Certain combinations of quarks and gluons are color neutral, just as some combinations of electric charges are charge neutral. These color-neutral systems are the observed hadrons. It follows from the mathematical theory of the quark-gluon interaction that color neutrality can be achieved with three quarks or with a quark and an antiquark.

Advanced Theories

Many aspects of fundamental particles remain to be understood. Although the photon and the W and Z particles have similar properties, their masses are very different. Theories accounting for this in terms of a breakdown of an underlying SYMMETRY have been partially successful, but it is unknown whether this breakdown arises from the interaction of W and Z with undiscovered spin-zero particles called Higgs bosons, or from some other mechanism (see HIGGS PARTICLE).

Many physicists are uncomfortable with the large number of particles. Some have devised theories describing particles as tightly bound combinations of a small number of more fundamental particles. According to the so-called Standard Model, only three foursomes, or "generations," of particles exist, each consisting of two quarks and two leptons. The first, consisting of up and down ·quarks, the electron, and the electron neutrino, constitutes ordinary matter. The second consists of charmed and strange quarks plus the muon and muon neutrino, while the third consists of top and bottom quarks plus the tau and tau neutrino. Experiments have supported this theory.

Another approach involves a mathematical description of particles in which close relationships are found between particles of different spin. These so-called supersymmetry theories imply the existence of many yet-undiscovered particles, such as spin-zero quark analogues. Many physicists think that the rest energies of such particles would be about one trillion electron volts (TeV). To produce them, accelerators of much higher energy than existing ones are needed. In order to create the hypothesized particles, accelerators would require thousands of superconducting magnets, as well as rings that are 100 km (62 mi) in circumference. It is proposed that the collisions of protons accelerated to such energies might yield the new fundamental particles (see UNIFIED FIELD THEORY).

fundamentalism   *Fundamentalism* is a term popularly used to describe strict adherence to Christian doctrines based on a literal interpretation of the Bible. With some differences among themselves, fundamentalists insist on belief in the inerrancy of the Bible, the virgin birth and divinity of Jesus Christ, the vicarious and atoning character of his death, his bodily resurrection, and his second coming as the irreducible minimum of authentic Christianity. This minimum was reflected in such early fundamentalist declarations as the 14-point creed of the Niagara Bible Conference of 1878 and the 5-point statement of the Presbyterian General Assembly of 1910.

Two immediate doctrinal sources for fundamentalist thought were MILLENARIANISM and biblical inerrancy. Millenarianism, belief in the physical return of Christ to establish a 1,000-year earthly reign of blessedness, was a doctrine prevalent in English-speaking Protestantism by the 1870s. At the same time, powerful conservative forces led by Charles Hodge and Benjamin Warfield opposed the growing use of literary and historical criticism in biblical studies, defending biblical inspiration and the inerrant authority of the Bible.

The name fundamentalist was coined in 1920 to designate those "doing battle royal for the Fundamentals." Also figuring in the name was *The Fundamentals*, a 12-volume collection of essays written in the period 1910–15 by 64 British and American scholars and preachers. Three million copies of these volumes and the founding of the World's Christian Fundamentals Association in 1919 gave sharp identity to fundamentalism as it moved into the 1920s. Leadership across the years ranged from such men as A. T. Pierson and A. J. Gordon to A. C. Dixon, William Jennings BRYAN, and J. G. Machen.

The caricature of fundamentalism arising from the SCOPES TRIAL (1925), the popularization of the liberal response, well-publicized divisions among fundamentalists themselves, and preoccupations with the Depression of the 1930s and World War II curtailed fundamentalism's appeal. By 1950 it was either isolated and muted or had taken on the more moderate tones of EVANGELICALISM. In

FUNDAMENTAL PARTICLES

Quarks	Symbol	Mass (GeV)	Charge	Leptons	Symbol	Mass (GeV)	Charge
Up	u	.378	+2/3	Electron	e	0.511	−1
Down	d	.336	−1/3	Electron neutrino	ν_e	<4.6 10^{-5}	0
Strange	s	.540	−1/3	Muon	μ	105.66	−1
Charmed	c	1.5	+2/3	Muon neutrino	ν_μ	<0.52	0
Bottom (or Beauty)	b	4.72	−1/3	Tau	τ	1784.2	−1
Top (or Truth)	t	30–50	+2/3	Tau neutrino	ν_τ	<250	0

Hadrons (examples)	Symbol	Quark Composition	Charge	Gauge Particles (Bosons)		Mass (GeV)	Charge
Proton	p	uud	+1	Gluon		0	0
Neutron	n	udd	0	Photon		0	0
Lambda	Λ	uds	0	W⁺		79.5	+1
Omega⁻	Ω⁻	sss	−1	W⁻		79.5	−1
Pion	π°	u̅u or d̅d	0	Z°		90	0
J/ψ	J,ψ	cc̄	0	Graviton		0	0

the 1970s and '80s, however, fundamentalism again became an influential force in the United States. Promoted by popular television evangelists (see RELIGIOUS BROADCASTING) and represented by such groups as the MORAL MAJORITY, the new politically oriented "religious right" opposed the influence of liberalism and secularism in American life. The term *fundamentalist* has also been used to describe members of militant Islamic groups.

—

Fundy, Bay of [fuhn'-dee] The Bay of Fundy is a 240-km-long (150-mi) arm of the Atlantic Ocean that separates the Canadian provinces of Nova Scotia and New Brunswick and runs in a northeasterly direction. The bay is noted for its swift and exceptionally high tides of up to 21 m (70 ft). Serious attempts are being made to harness the tide as an alternative energy source, particularly in the Minas Basin area, where the wide bay necks sharply down to a 50-km (30-mi) width. The Petitcodiac River exhibits a TIDAL BORE, or upstream wave, and the falls at St. John are reversed as a result of the force of the tide. St. John, New Brunswick, is the largest city on the bay.

—

funeral customs Funeral customs are the ceremonies connected with the disposition of the dead. Anthropologists have found that formal procedures exist for insuring proper treatments of the deceased in virtually every society, regardless of how primitive or remote. Like birth and marriage, death seems universally to be regarded as a socially significant event, marked by rituals and beliefs that dictate how the dead are to be dealt with and how the survivors are to mourn. This fact has led anthropologists to view funeral customs as the final *rite de passage* (see PASSAGE, RITES OF) in an individual's life span.

Rites of Separation and Transition. Funeral ceremonies generally involve events that symbolize the separation of the deceased from his or her former status, a transitional phase, and the deceased's final assumption of a new role in the afterlife. A ritual cleansing of the corpse is the typical form of expression for the rite of separation. Among many groups this involves washing the corpse in holy water and dressing the deceased in special garb; it may sometimes also include EMBALMING procedures. Like all funerary rites, these ceremonies are intimately related to the religious beliefs of the specific society in which they are practiced.

The transitional phase, after the corpse has been prepared or cleansed but prior to its final disposition, is of variable length. Some societies will permit a relatively brief period to elapse, generally in the form of a WAKE. For one or more nights close relatives and friends will gather to watch the closed or open coffin into which the body of the deceased has been placed. These may be solemn or joyous occasions; often this period is accompanied by prayers. In many cases disposition is delayed for prominent persons; in Korea, for example, a delay of up to three months is permitted. Among certain groups the corpse is allowed to decompose in a shallow grave, within a tree, or upon a scaffold, thereby enabling the soul or spirit to emerge from the body. After the appropriate period of time has elapsed the corpse is recovered, prayers are said, and the remains are buried in an ordinary grave.

Modes of Disposition. Following the rites of separation and transition is the final phase of permanent disposition of the body. As with the other phases, great diversity of methods exists for disposing of the corpse. The most common form of disposition is BURIAL. The body may be interred in a simple pit or beneath a large earthen mound. The corpse may be wrapped in cloth, placed in a coffin, or buried directly in the earth. The grave may contain the body of a single deceased individual or large numbers of corpses. The dead may be placed in symbolically important positions, such as facing a given direction or in a flexed position. Segmented burials may occur in which the skull is buried separately from the rest of the body.

CREMATION is also used by numerous groups to dispose of the dead. In its simplest form, the deceased is incinerated on a pyre or in a crematory, and the ashes are disposed of ritually. Sometimes the body of the deceased is placed in a house, on a raft, or on a boat, and the entire

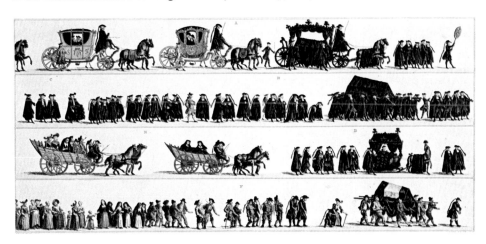

The funeral procession, in which mourners escort the body to the place of interment, reflects, in either its elaboration or its simplicity, the social status of the deceased. Subdued colors are traditional expressions of mourning.

Bali's Hindu culture prescribes cremation as the standard method for disposal of the dead. Here, mourners twist the tower supporting the deceased to prevent evil forces from ascending the structure before cremation is complete.

structure is ignited. Other methods used to dispose of the dead include placing the corpse in a sarcophagus, which in turn is housed in a vault, mausoleum, or other type of TOMB. Sinking the corpse in water or permitting it to drift down a river or out to sea are other methods found.

Funeral customs reveal much about a culture's structure, values, and religion. In an egalitarian society all funerals generally involve the same degree of elaboration. In societies stratified on the basis of wealth or rank, burial in large vaults for the rich or the nobility contrasts with less ornate practices for the lower classes. The inclusion of many personal possessions, like those found in the sumptuously furnished pyramid tombs of the ancient Egyptians, often reveals the nature of the afterlife anticipated by the members of a given society.

In many societies, especially in the past, funeral ceremonies were intended to ensure that the spirit of the deceased is properly treated so that it will gain admission to its final resting place. The fear that spirits of the dead will return to the living world to bestow tragedy or death upon those who do not venerate them in the prescribed manner has been the major motivation for elaborate funeral arrangements in many societies. Before it was banned in 1829, an extreme manifestation of this was found in the Hindu rite of SUTTEE, in which the widow of the deceased would voluntarily perform an act of self-immolation by throwing herself onto the funeral pyre of her husband. Should she refuse, relatives and friends of her husband often forced her to do so lest plague or death come to the village.

Mourning. Many customs of mourning have been observed around the world, including isolation or marking of the bereaved (such as by the wearing of black in many Western cultures); taboos on speaking the name of the deceased; use of ritual specialists such as priests or undertakers in funeral ceremonies; and final funeral ceremonies that terminate the mourning period weeks, months, or even years after a death.

Prehistoric Evidence. Archaeological research indicates that funeral customs have been practiced for many thousands of years. The earliest known evidence of ritual associated with death dates back to some 60,000 years ago at Shanidar cave in Iraq. A pollen analysis of the soil revealed that hyacinths, hollyhocks, and daisies had been strewn over the grave site of a NEANDERTHALER buried within the cave.

At La Ferassie, an archaeological site in the Dordogne area of France that dates back at least 50,000 years, a skeleton of a boy 15 or 16 years old was found laid out with a beautifully fashioned stone ax near his hand. With the body were charred wild cattle bones, perhaps the remnants of a funeral feast. Near the same site, graves of three other children and two adults, interred together in what may have been a family plot, were also discovered.

---

funeral industry   The funeral industry is concerned with the handling and BURIAL of the dead and, often, with arrangements for the conduct of funerals. The industry is sizable, earning an annual gross income of $4 billion and employing 45,000 persons who are licensed funeral directors or embalmers and work primarily through the 22,000 funeral homes in the United States. (Many Western countries handle funerals through institutions analagous to those in the U.S.; in other parts of the world FUNERAL CUSTOMS differ widely.) For a fee that is decided on in negotiations between the bereaved family and the funeral home, the home undertakes to remove the body of the deceased from the place of death, to prepare the body for burial, to provide rooms where mourners can meet and where a service may be held, and to make the burial arrangements. Often the corpse will be embalmed (see EMBALMING) and cosmetic attention paid to the face. The home also supplies the coffin, or "casket."

Every state enforces its own regulations governing the practices of funeral homes and the disposition of corpses. Nevertheless, over the past decade the industry has been the subject of investigation both by private groups and by government agencies, notably the Federal Trade Commission (FTC). In 1982 the FTC issued a regulation, which became effective in mid-1983, requiring funeral directors to disclose their prices and to offer customers their choice of services.

In recent years increasing use is being made of CREMATION rather than burial.

---

fungi [fuhn'-jy]   The fungi constitute a large and diverse group of organisms that share some characteristics with both lower plants (algae) and lower animals but are not closely related to either. They contain true mitochondria and membrane-enclosed nuclei, lack chlorophyll and chloroplasts, and reproduce by both asexual and sexual means. Most fungi grow as branched tubular systems, or mycelia, whose individual filaments, or hyphae, are surrounded by rigid cell walls containing chitin, cellulose, or both, and other polysaccharides. All fungi lack photosynthetic ability and therefore require preformed organic compounds. They exist throughout the world.

Industrial Uses

The microfungi are most often used commercially because of their rapid growth. Brewer's yeast was used for brewing beer, fermenting grapes and other substances to produce wines, and starting mashes for distilled spirits long before the process of FERMENTATION was scientifically understood. Alcohol, the product of fermentation, also has chemical and medical uses. Baker's yeast is equally important in the baking industry. Camembert cheese derives its flavor from *Penicillium camemberti*, and Roquefort from *P. roqueforti*. Soy sauce is fermented with *Aspergillus oryzae* or *A. soyae*.

ANTIBIOTICS were first produced (1929) using penicillin from *P. notatum*. A huge antibiotic industry has since developed. Only a few of the many antibiotics now available, however, are of fungal origin: the penicillins, the cephalosporins, and gresiofulvin, which is one of the few effective antifungal antibiotics. Various fungi are used to produce a number of organic acids—gluconic, itaconic, and citric acids, for example—and in other chemical processes. Fungi are also grown for the production of enzymes such as the acid proteases, which are used for meat tenderizing and bread making.

Classification of Fungi

Prior to the development of the microscope in the 1600s, the only fungi described were the higher fungi that have large fruiting structures, such as MUSHROOMS, morels, and puffballs. The first scientific description of fungi was given by Piér Antonio Micheli, an Italian botanist, in his work *Nova Plantarum Genera* (1729). In 1836 the study of fungi was termed MYCOLOGY. Because fungi and bacteria were for many years considered more similar to plants than to animals, mycology has traditionally been a branch of botany.

Evolution. Fossil records reveal that fungi occurred in the early periods; however, the record is sparse, and most phylogenetic speculations have been based on comparisons of living species. As a result, the evolutionary relationships are still not clear. It is generally accepted that fungi arose as more than one phylogenetic branch from flagellated protistan ancestors.

Taxonomy. Groups of fungi are classified according to their methods of sexual reproduction, types of life cycle, growth forms, and methods of asexual propagation. Because the fossil record is inadequate, no single classification scheme is accepted by all mycologists; changes continue to be made, particularly at the lower levels. It is now generally agreed, however, that the major fungi groups should be classified in a kingdom Fungi (Mycetae), separate from plants and animals. Most mycologists

Many species of fungi reproduce asexually. This photomicrograph of the aquatic fungus Hesseltina vesiculosa shows specialized hyphae, or elongated filaments, that bear reproductive structures called sporangia—spheres in which the spores are produced.

group plasmodial organisms in the division Myxomycota (or Gymnomycota) and all others in either one division, the Eumycota (true fungi), or in two divisions, the Mastigomycota (with flagellate spores) and Amastigomycota (with nonflagellate spores). The simpler, two-division system is followed below.

Division Myxomycota

The organisms in this division grow as multinucleate amoeboid plasmodia and produce motile uninucleate amoebas as well as biflagellate cells.

Members of the class Plasmodiophoromycetes of this division parasitize the roots of plants, and some species may infect the hyphae of aquatic fungi. *Plasmodiophora brassicae* causes a disease of cabbages called clubroot.

The class Myxomycetes comprises the true, free-living plasmodial SLIME MOLDS, which range from microscopic species to those which produce very large and conspicuous plasmodia. Starvation induces the plasmodia to convert to sporangia, in which nonmotile spores form. They typically grow under moist conditions in or on decaying wood or other vegetation.

Division Eumycota

The so-called true fungi are placed in this division. There are five subdivisions.

Mastigomycotina. In the subdivision Mastigomycotina, which comprises two classes, the fungi produce motile spores, called zoospores, with one or two flagella.

The class Chytridiomycetes (the chytrids, or water molds) includes three orders of fungi that produce asexual zoospores with a single posterior whiplash flagellum in a sporangium, or, more specifically, a zoosporangium. Most species are microscopic, and many grow as parasites within the cells of algae, other fungi, or higher plants. The cells are coenocytic (multinuclear) and enclosed in rigid walls containing chitin, except for some that grow as plasmodia within their host. The chytrids characteristically grow as sac-shaped cells with tapering, rootlike extensions, called rhizoids, that penetrate the substratum or its host. In asexual reproduction part or all of the cell body is converted into zoosporangia, or sporangia-producing zoospores. Sexual reproduction leads to a thick-walled, often dormant resting spore.

The class Oömycetes of the subdivision Mastigomycotina is a group of fungi (water molds and fish molds) that typically occur in freshwater streams and ponds or as parasites of higher plants. Many are saprobes, living off decayed matter. Others cause damping-off or rotting of seedlings; downy mildews of many plants, such as potato blight; and fish diseases. Oömycetes reproduce asexually by motile biflagellate zoospores with one whiplash and one tinsel flagellum. Pathogenic species such as *Phytophthora infestans* (the cause of potato blight) produce zoospores on specialized branches of the mycelium. The zoosporangia break free and are carried by wind or water to new hosts, whereupon zoospores may be released to initiate new infections or, under dry conditions, the sporangia may directly produce a mycelium.

Zygomycotina. The subdivision Zygomycotina has a single class, Zygomycetes. This class includes fungi (bread molds or pin molds) that typically produce an abundant and rapidly growing aerial, coenocytic mycelium and are common causes for the decay of foods and other rich sources of organic material. The cell walls contain chitin as a primary component. The cells reproduce asexually by means of nonmotile spores (sporangiospores) produced in sporangia formed on branches (sporangiophores) of the mycelium. In some species, such as *Rhizopus nigricans*, the sporangia arise in clusters with rhizoids at the base and hyphal strands (stolons) interconnecting the clusters. The spores are released by breakdown of the sporangial wall and dispersed by air or water currents.

Sexual reproduction may occur between different parts of the same mycelium or between two self-sterile but cross-fertile strains of opposite mating type. The latter is regulated by a single pair of genes, or alleles. One gene is said to be of the plus mating type and the other of the minus mating type. The gametangia, or sex organs, fuse to form a dormant, thick-walled, pigmented, and often sculptured zygote called the zygospore. The mature zygospores eventually germinate to produce a new haploid mycelium.

Ascomycotina. The subdivision Ascomycotina (formerly the class Ascomycetes) includes all true fungi in which sexual reproduction results in ascospores, produced within a specialized cell called an ascus. In many ascomycetes, male structures (antheridia) and female structures (ascogonia) are produced. The antheridia donate nuclei to the ascogonia by fusion with a receptive filament, the trichogyne. In others the same function may be accomplished by conidia (asexual spores that can also serve as fertilizing elements) or by hyphal fusion.

The parental nuclei unite in the ascogonium and enter hyphal branches that grow out from it within a developing fruiting body, the ascocarp. The paired parental nuclei divide synchronously (conjugate division) in specialized hyphae with binucleate cells (ascogenous hyphae). The tip cells of the ascogenous hyphae form a hook in which the haploid parental nuclei fuse to produce a diploid zygote nucleus. The zygote nucleus undergoes meiotic divisions to produce four haploid nuclei in the enlarging cell,

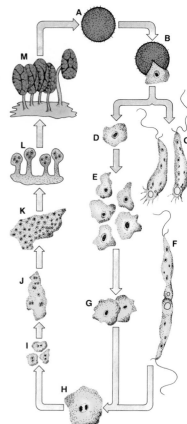

The life cycle of a slime mold begins when the adult fungus (A) produces spores. Upon germination (B), spores of plasmodial slime molds release one to four swarm cells (C); spores of cellular slime molds produce one to four amoebalike organisms (D), which, like the swarm cells, may then divide (E). Pairs of swarm cells (F) or amoebas (G) fuse to form binucleate zygotes (H), which then undergo mitotic cell division. Zygotes of plasmodial slime molds (I) fuse (J) to form a multinucleate plasmodium (K), in which individual cells are not differentiated. Zygotes of cellular slime molds aggregate to form a similar mass called a pseudoplasmodium, in which individual cells do not fuse. Both masses eventually form sporangia (L), which, when they mature (M), produce new spores.

called the ascus at this stage of development. In most cases a mitotic nuclear division then doubles the number of nuclei per ascus, after which each nucleus is enclosed in a cell wall to form the ascospores.

Other major features of the fungi of this subdivision are that the cell walls contain chitin; the hyphae have simple, washer-shaped septa with a central pore; and asexual reproduction occurs by formation of nonmotile spores (conidia, oidia, arthrospores, and others) that are usually produced on specialized branches called conidiophores.

Several classes of ascomycetes exist. The class Hemiascomycetes includes the YEASTS; these may be unicellular or mycelial, but all lack ascogenous hyphae and fruits. Most yeasts are saprobic, commonly occurring on plant parts, in soil, and in other locations with adequate moisture and organic material. A small group is parasitic on the leaves, twigs, and branches of vascular plants, causing leaf curl and witches'-broom (tufts of branchlets resulting from repeated branching).

Another class of ascomycetes, Plectomycetes, includes several economically important fungi that form their asci in small, simple, closed, fruiting structures (cleistothecia). The powdery MILDEWS—so named from the powdery appearance of infected leaves—are all obligate

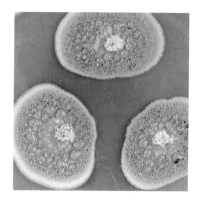  

(Left) *Penicillin is produced by* Pencillium chrysogenum (shown) *and the related* P. notatum. (Center) Geastrum *fungi are called earthstars because they burst into a star shape when releasing spores.* (Right) Meripilus giganteus *grows in rosettelike clusters.*

parasites of higher plants and are largely host-specific. The fungus grows on the surface as a white, cottony mycelial mat and produces many simple conidiophores and ellipsoidal spores (conidia). The surface cells of the host are invaded by special extensions called haustoria. The conidia give rise to new sites of infections by germination on the surface and haustorium formation. The cleistothecia become brown or black at maturity, bear a number of characteristically shaped external appendages—hook-shaped or spearlike, for example—and overwinter on the fallen leaves.

A second major group of plectomycetes includes the commercially utilized genera *Aspergillus* and *Penicillium*, as well as important pathogens of plants and humans. Sexual reproduction is relatively rare among species of *Aspergillus* and *Penicillium*. *Aspergillus* produces chains of pigmented, asexual conidia on the surface of an inflated region of a branch, called a conidiophore. Conidium formation is similar in *Penicillium*, but the conidiophore is branched to form a brushlike structure (penicillus) instead of having an inflated vesicle. The conidia are connected in chains on the conidiophores but are readily dispersed by air currents. The green, black, yellow, and gray colors of the colonies of these common microfungi are the result of the color of the huge number of pigmented conidia produced on the surface.

In addition to their roles in the decay of plant and animal residues and in food spoilage, these fungi are of great significance to humans in other ways. *Aspergillus fumagatus*, a common inhabitant of heated compost, can cause respiratory disease in humans, and a number of related species may produce aflatoxin, a tumor-inducing alkaloid, in poorly stored, moldy grain. Species of both *Penicillium* and *Aspergillus* are used extensively in commercial fermentations. This class also includes other species that cause disease in humans, animals, and plants; for example, the fungus *Ceratocystis ulmi* is responsible for Dutch elm disease, other species cause a wilt disease in oaks, and still others reduce the quality of lumber.

All fungi in the class Pyrenomycetes produce asci and ascospores as an organized hymenial layer in a fruiting body called a perithecium. The perithecium is a small, flask-shaped structure with a thin wall that surrounds a basal tuft of asci; the opening at the top is called an ostiole. The ascospores are typically discharged violently from the tips of the asci as they sequentially protrude through the ostiole. This class includes many saprobes that grow on dung or cellulosic materials such as tree stumps and logs. Other species cause diseases of higher plants. They include *Claviceps purpurea*, which causes the disease ERGOT of rye.

The TRUFFLES, cup fungi, earthtongues, and morels are ascomycetes in the class Discomycetes. The fertile hymenial layer of asci is exposed at maturity in all but the truffles, which are produced below ground. This layer lines various surfaces of the fruiting bodies, or apothecia; it occurs on the inner surface of cup fungi, within channels in the closed fruits of the truffle, on the outer surface in earthtongues, and on the surfaces lining the pits on the caps of morels. Parasitic species such as *Monilinia fructicola*, the cause of brown rot in peach, may produce numerous conidia, but many saprobic species do not. The morel, *Morchella esculenta*, produces rather large, tan brown, stalked fruits with a roughly conical cap that is lined with shallow pits separated by ridges. The fungi of this species are considered excellent for eating, as are other, related species, but the false morel, genus *Gyromitra*, is poisonous. Truffles, genus *Tuber*, are a popular delicacy in Europe. These fungi form dark, warty, potato-like fruits below the surface of the ground and are found in association with the roots of oak and beech trees.

The ascomycetes of the class Loculoascomycetes include those fungi whose asci lie within a cavity (locule) in a tightly knit mass of hyphae called a stroma. These differ from stromatic species in the class Pyrenomycetes in that the fertile cavities do not have their own distinct wall layers. Ascostromatic fungi also produce asci with a double wall. The group includes a number of fungi that are saprobes or pathogenic on plants; some of them parasitize insects. The fruits may be very small and may contain either a single locule or a number of locules with individually separated asci. The ascospores are discharged through a pore formed by lysis of stromatic cells between the cavity and the surface of the stroma.

Basidiomycotina. True fungi of the subdivision Basidiomycotina produce haploid sexual spores (basidiospores) on a specialized cell called the basidium. All these fungi produce a "primary" haploid mycelium (the monokaryon); also, as a result of crossing, a "secondary" mycelium (the dikaryon) results, which contains pairs of parental nuclei that replicate by conjugate division. This group includes the rust and smut fungi, as well as mushrooms, puffballs, and related forms.

The rusts and smuts in the class Hemibasidiomycetes of basidiomycetes all produce basidia that are divided, or septate. A thick-walled spore (teliospore) is produced on the secondary mycelium; it is this cell that produces the basidium and basidiospores. Rusts and smuts are parasites of many higher plants. They do not produce fruiting bodies but develop the teliospores in or on the tissues of the host.

The subdivision Basidiomycotina also includes the classes Hymenomycetes and Gasteromycetes, which comprise the mushrooms, toadstools, puffballs, and related species. They are the most advanced groups of fungi and produce the largest fruiting bodies. In the Hymenomycetes the basidia occur in a hymenium that lines the surface of gills, pores, or spines and is exposed before the basidiospores are produced. In the Gasteromycetes (puffballs) there may or may not be a true hymenial layer, and the basidiocarps either remain closed or else open after the basidiospores have been produced. Both groups lack specialized structures for sexual mating, but they have complex genetic systems that regulate sexual compatibility by means of hyphal fusion between monokaryons. Many species are edible, but others are deadly poisonous.

Deuteromycotina. The subdivision Deuteromycotina includes all fungi that lack known sexual reproductive structures and thus cannot be otherwise classified. Many soil fungi, plant pathogens, and industrially useful species are included in this group.

See also: PARASITIC DISEASES.

---

fungus diseases　About 30 human diseases caused by fungi are known. Such fungi usually reside in soil and enter the body through a skin puncture or the lungs, but some spread between humans or from animals to humans. The INFECTIOUS DISEASES, called mycoses, develop slowly and are sometimes difficult to treat. Even diagnoses can be complicated, because few laboratory tests are specific for the organisms.

Dermatophytoses. These are mycoses of the skin, hair, or nails, but never of internal organs. Common names include RINGWORM, athlete's foot, jock itch, and nail fungus. Medically they are called tinea (Latin for "worm"); thus, tinea capitis is scalp ringworm, and so forth. About two dozen species of fungi cause ringworms. Ringworms—except certain nail infections—respond well to medication; little resistance, however, develops to reinfection.

Systemic Mycoses. These fungi can invade the internal organs, bones, and eyes. Some may exist as both spores (the infectious particles) and yeasts (the parasitic stage). The mycoses range from transient infections to fatal diseases, but the latter are rare and are usually seen in patients debilitated by other diseases such as cancer. Several drugs are effective in many cases, but diagnosis must be certain beforehand because of the drugs' varying toxicity.

About four species of *Aspergillus* can cause the lung disease called aspergillosis in debilitated persons, in whom the disease can be fatal. Another potentially fatal mycosis, CANDIDIASIS, is unique in being acquired from *Candida* yeasts that are normal inhabitants of the gastrointestinal tract. The term actually covers a spectrum of diseases, ranging from white patches in the mouth (thrush) to persistent vaginal infections to invasions of almost any organ.

COCCIDIOIDOMYCOSIS, or "valley fever," infects up to 90 percent of the inhabitants of the southwestern United States and northern Mexico. Usually after an influenza-like episode the patient gains protection against reinfection, but in a few cases the fungi infect internal organs, often fatally. The agent, *Coccidioides immitis*, lives in desert soils.

Cryptococcosis is caused by a yeast found worldwide in pigeon droppings. It probably enters the body through the lungs, and in rare instances a fatal brain disease called cryptococcal MENINGITIS results. Cryptococcosis is usually seen in debilitated persons. HISTOPLASMOSIS is caused by *Histoplasma capsulatum*, which occurs in bird droppings or bat guano. It is found worldwide. Most people inhaling the spores develop lifelong immunity, but in rare cases the organism invades white blood cells and becomes a parasite of the reticuloendothelial system, the only mycosis to do so. In some instances, histoplasmosis is fatal.

Mycotoxicosis. This is not a mycosis but, instead, the ingestions of toxins produced by any of several fungi. Such fungi occur worldwide, usually as saprophytes on vegetation. Aflatoxin, for example, comes from *Aspergillus flavus* infections of corn. ERGOT, a disease of rye and other grains, is caused by *Claviceps* fungi and was once a serious problem for humans. Some mycotoxins are lethal in extremely small amounts.

Funston, Frederick [fuhns'-tuhn]　Frederick Funston, b. New Carlisle, Ohio, Nov. 9, 1865, d. Feb. 19, 1917, was an American general who, on Mar. 23, 1901, captured Emilio AGUINALDO, leader of the Filipino insurrection against U.S. occupation. After fighting from 1896 in the Cuban rebel army opposing Spanish rule, Funston was given command of a Philippines-bound regiment when the Spanish-American War began in 1898. During the subsequent Filipino insurrection he won a Medal of Honor for bravery. For capturing Aguinaldo, Funston was transferred to the regular army as a brigadier general. In 1914 he commanded the U.S. troops sent to occupy Veracruz, Mexico, and then commanded the troops on the Mexican border from 1914 to 1917.

fur   Fur is the soft, hairy coat of an animal that is processed into a pelt used for wearing apparel. By definition, a true fur, such as mink, is made up of a soft, thick, insulating layer called underfur, and a top layer of longer, lustrous guard hairs. Furs such as Persian lamb lack guard hairs, however, whereas others such as monkey fur lack an underlayer.

Fur Sources

Although some fur-bearing species such as beaver and seal are hunted or trapped, many popular furs are produced from animals that have been raised on fur farms or ranches.

Wild Furs. Commercial furs from wild sources constitute at most half of the total trade. In recent years, regulations designed to prevent the extinction of certain wild species have reduced the number of fur pelts taken in the wild. Furs such as those from the leopard, cheetah, and jaguar may no longer be hunted in the countries where they are indigenous, and many other countries forbid their importation. The Federal Endangered Species Act prohibits the sale of these furs in the United States. In addition, special laws protect certain North American species. The killing of North Pacific fur seals, which precipitated the Bering Sea Controversy, has been regulated by international agreement. A 1972 agreement regulates the hunting of Antarctic seals.

In the United States, those wild animals which may still be legally taken are also protected by various federal and state laws.

Fur Farming. As an industry, fur farming—the breeding and rearing of wild species for their pelts—is relatively new. The first experimental farms in the United States and Canada were established in the 1920s in order to develop techniques for breeding mink and silver fox. Breeding techniques have improved to the point where breeders are now able to develop fur mutations with specific desirable characteristics.

Since the 1930s, mink ranching has grown into a thriving industry in the United States. In addition to mink and fox, other wild species raised on fur ranches include chinchilla and nutria. Various species of sheep are reared for lamb pelts.

Fur Marketing

Regularly scheduled sales for fur dealers and brokers are held, primarily in the large fur-marketing centers of New York, Montreal, London, and Leningrad. There are also specialized markets for specific furs.

Fur Manufacturing

Dressing. In the dressing process, pelts are cleaned of animal greases and tanned to make the skin more pliable. (See LEATHER AND HIDES for a description of the tanning process.) Some furs may have the guard hairs plucked out and the underfur sheared closer to the skin, as in sheared beaver and raccoon, to create a different texture. Some furs are bleached to achieve a lighter color. The final dressing process is glazing, where the fur is combed, the oils in the skin are brought to the surface with a padded iron, and a glazing substance, such as a liquid vegetable gum, is brushed on to increase the fur's sheen.

Garment Making. In the production of a fur garment the dressed furs are matched for uniformity. The waste parts are cut away. In mink and other costly furs an additional process called letting-out is employed, whereby the skin of the pelt is cut down the center, and each half is sliced into narrow diagonal strips ranging in width from 1.5 to 13 mm ($\frac{1}{16}$ to $\frac{1}{2}$ in). These strips are resewn to produce a longer, narrower pelt.

The skin pieces left over from the letting-out process are matched and sewn together into plates that are used to make other garments.

In the skin-on-skin process, used primarily for small furs such as muskrat, raccoon, and rabbit, whole skins are trimmed and sewn together, with the seams hidden under the fur.

The Fur Industry

Of all the apparel industries, fur is probably the most sensitive to changing economic and social trends. After a sharp decline in the late 1960s and the 1970s, due in large part to increased environmental concerns, the industry rebounded in the early 1980s. High-priced coats—Russian sable and lynx, silver fox, and mink made by American craftspeople and with prestigious designer labels—sold well. Asia has developed its own fur industry, which captured more than one-quarter of the U.S. market in the mid-1980s. By the end of the 1980s partisans of animal rights had convinced many potential buyers that the wearing of furs was morally wrong, and the fur industry dived into another decline.

fur seal   see SEAL

fur trade   The fur trade in North America profoundly influenced the economic life, exploration, and diplomacy of the United States and Canada. The scarcity of fur-bearing animals in Europe by the 17th century encouraged English, French, and Dutch traders to look to their nations' colonies as sources of valuable animal skins. Several factors favored the development of the fur trade in the New World: the great abundance of animals in the American woodlands; the presence of Indians skilled in trapping and in the processing of pelts; and, above all, the possibility of tremendous profit.

French Trade. The French were particularly fortunate, for in the colony of NEW FRANCE, the St. Lawrence River and Great Lakes gave them access to inland forests teeming with animal life. Only the land along the St. Lawrence was suited for farming, so the fur trade became the mainstay of the colony's economy. To tap the region's potential, the French explored the area around the Great Lakes and the valleys of the Ohio and Mississippi rivers and negotiated commercial and military alliances with the Hurons, Ottawas, Illinois, and many other Indian tribes.

Indians either brought furs into the settlements of Quebec, Montreal, and Three Rivers or traded with the *coureurs de bois*, Frenchmen who often would live among the Indians for months at a time. The Indians' reliance upon European utensils, weapons, and blankets revolutionized their way of life and made them increasingly dependent on those supplying these goods. To protect French interests, the French constructed a series of military posts and towns: Niagara, Detroit, Mackinac (Michilimackinac), Kaskaskia, Natchez, New Orleans, Mobile, and others. By 1715 the French had established a widespread fur-trading empire that was highly profitable, but one that faced increasing competition from the English colonies.

British Trade. Although all English colonies on the Atlantic coast engaged in fur trading, the enterprise was especially important in South Carolina, Pennsylvania, and, above all, New York. There the Hudson and Mohawk rivers allowed easy transport of furs from Lake Erie to the trading center of Albany and the port of New York. In the 18th century, French supremacy in the fur trade was challenged by the HUDSON'S BAY COMPANY in northeastern Canada and by New York traders in alliance with the confederation of Iroquois Indians. Bitter competition in western New York and the upper Ohio Valley led directly to the FRENCH AND INDIAN WAR of 1754–63, in which Britain wrested from France control of Canada and all the land east of the Mississippi River.

U.S. Trade. After the United States won its independence in the American Revolution, the British Hudson's Bay Company and NORTH WEST COMPANY continued to operate in Canada and in the Pacific Northwest. The U.S. government tried to discourage trade with Indians except by its own agents, but private firms eventually dominated the field. John Jacob Astor's AMERICAN FUR COMPANY controlled Great Lakes trade and later operated in the northern Rocky Mountains and far Northwest. The heyday of the trans-Mississippi fur trade began with William ASHLEY and Andrew Henry in 1822 and 1823. Ashley and Henry soon inaugurated the rendezvous system by which MOUNTAIN MEN who lived in the wilds year-round met in the mountains with representatives of trading companies each summer to exchange animal skins for goods.

While trapping proved an economic boon for the market centers of the fur trade, particularly St. Louis, Mo., and Taos, N.Mex., its impact on the national economy was not great. Far more important was the exploration of the Rocky Mountains, Great Basin, and Pacific coast by such mountain men as Jedediah SMITH, James BRIDGER, and Thomas FITZPATRICK in their search for animals. Settlers on their way west were soon taking advantage of the trappers' detailed knowledge of the mountains and plains.

By 1840 bitter competition among trappers had severely reduced the beaver population in the West. This decline in supply, along with the growing popularity of the silk hat in Europe, meant the end of the golden age of the fur trade although some trappers and Indians continued to bring skins to trading posts on the Great Plains.

Furies [fyur'-eez] In Greek mythology, the three Furies—Tisiphone, Megaera, and Alecto—were goddesses

of vengeance. Their function was to punish crimes that had escaped detection or public justice. Although their usual abode was HADES, they also pursued the living, as in the story of ORESTES. In appearance they were ugly, bat-winged, serpent-haired creatures born of the blood of URANUS when he was mutilated by the sickle of CRONUS. In the afterlife, the Furies dispensed justice from the netherworld, where, armed with scourges, they meted out the torments of remorse and other punishments. The Furies, also known as Erinyes, were called the Eumenides in later Greek literature.

furnace [fur'-nis] Furnaces are closed devices in which FUEL is burned to produce high temperatures. They are usually lined with fire-resistant brick insulation and metal and are not to be confused with ovens, which operate at lower temperatures.

Furnaces were known as long ago as 3000 BC, during the BRONZE AGE. With the advent of the IRON AGE, furnaces became more highly developed to reach the higher temperatures required to separate iron from its ores and to forge articles of commerce and war. Today highly specialized furnaces include the BLAST FURNACE, the ELECTRIC FURNACE, the open-hearth furnace, and the reverberatory furnace (see IRON AND STEEL INDUSTRY). The term "furnace" has also been applied to the forced-air furnace widely used in in-home HEATING SYSTEMS.

High-pressure, or gun-type, oil burners are used to heat many homes. Oil pumped under pressure through a nozzle is atomized into a fine mist, mixed with air, and burned in a refractory fire pot, or chamber, after ignition by a high-voltage spark generated by a transformer.

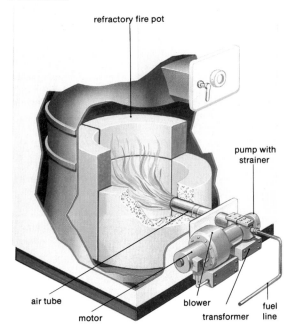

refractory fire pot

pump with strainer

air tube

motor

blower

transformer

fuel line

Basic Principles

If the gaseous products of fossil-fuel combustion in a furnace are in direct contact with the gaseous, liquid, or solid substance to be heated, the furnace is said to be direct fired. If the heat from the products of combustion is transferred through a partition or HEAT EXCHANGER, the furnace is said to be indirect fired.

The direct-fired furnace is preferred whenever possible because it is cheaper to construct, operate, and maintain.

Indirect-fired furnaces protect the heated substance from direct contact with the flue gases by a wall division or heat exchanger.

Types

Furnaces may be classified according to the kind of fuel that they use.

Solid-fuel furnaces burn their fuel on a grate, where the primary combustion occurs. Heat created by this combustion is tranferred to the substance to be heated.

Liquid fuels are much easier to use than solid fuels. Refineries make fuel oils in several different grades. Diesel engines and home furnaces burn the light oils. Ships and power plants use a heavy residual oil.

Solid fuels such as coal and coke may be powdered and burned like liquid fuels (see COAL AND COAL MINING).

Gas is the best possible fuel for furnaces because it burns the cleanest and is the easiest to control.

---

furniture Furniture originated as utilitarian, functional objects: something to sit on, something to sleep in, something in which to store things. Then, at some time so remote that it cannot be pinpointed, groups arose whose members desired objects that were both utilitarian and attractively decorated, or, in short, decorative furniture.

Decorative Furniture

The first sophisticated cultures of which there is any knowledge—the Chinese, the Egyptians, the Greeks, the Romans—all had highly developed forms of decorative furniture. The styles and techniques manifested in these pieces could only have been the end result of a long period of development.

Origins of Decorated Furniture. Decoration in furniture is part of the general artistic development of society, although almost certainly a later manifestation. That is, the society that has developed elaborately decorated furnishings invariably will also have a highly sophisticated tradition of painting and sculpture.

All early art, whether a rock painting or a carved chief's stool, served a ritual, magical purpose. Even in this century the painted or carved headmen's seats of Africa and the Pacific islands were clearly understood within the society to be more than attractive pieces of furniture. They were symbols of power, and it is safe to assume that all decoration initially was intended to reinforce this purpose—to propitiate the gods, to bring luck, or to ward off evil. Only with the development of a cultural level in which people perceive themselves as having some

control over their destiny does true decoration—art for its own sake, for pleasure—begin to appear. The role of the artist-decorator-designer is directly related to the way in which people view the resultant work.

Types and Techniques. What is called decorative furniture is found in every part of the world. In certain regions, such as the Pacific islands and the desert areas of the Near East, custom and climate have militated against the use of many types of furniture; yet those forms which do exist—small chests and low tables in Persia, for example—may be plain and functional in form but elaborately decorated.

Decoration varies from country to country. Carving is certainly one of the earliest techniques employed, and at certain times, such as during the European Gothic period, it was predominant. Painting or staining is equally pervasive. On the other hand, certain sophisticated techniques have had more limited application. The use of wood veneer and marquetry (wood inlay in contrasting light and dark patterns), ormolu (the application of gilt-bronze mounts), and the use of lacquerwork imply a technical development limited primarily to the more advanced cultures of Asia and Europe. Yet in the societies where these advanced techniques do appear they are frequently of great age. Veneering and inlaying with semiprecious stones, ivory, metal, and mother-of-pearl were practiced in Egypt as long ago as the Early Dynastic Period (c.3100–2613 BC).

Egyptian Furniture. Egypt, in fact, was one of the earliest centers for the making of decorative furnishings. The tombs of the Nile Valley have yielded a rich store of chests, tables, stools, and beds. Chairs were often painted a dead white, whereas storage chests were boldly stained with bands of geometric decoration. Gilding was used extensively. Varnishes and waxed finishes were also applied to the wood, and carving was common. Chair and table legs were usually carved in the shape of a curved animal leg terminating in a bull hoof or lion paw.

Greek and Roman Furniture. Greece, between 1200 and 300 BC, produced an even greater variety of decorative furniture. Native olive, yew, and cedar wood were turned, carved, painted, and inlaid with precious stones. Cast bronze legs in animal form were attached to chairs and tables whose forms were low and curvilinear. Chests were covered with a rich gilt and inlaid with ivory, and the heavily carved couches of the period resembled elongated thrones. As in Egypt, the way of life dictated light, mov-

This Egyptian folding stool (4th century BC), carved of acacia, exhibits the simple, lightweight design characteristic of much Egyptian furniture. (Metropolitan Museum of Art, New York City.)

able pieces; most furniture was portable or even collapsible, as illustrated by the folding X or scissors chair, a form still popular today.

A far greater variety of forms developed in ancient Rome, in part because the Romans freely adopted and modified the furnishings of Greece and Egypt. Carving was of great importance to the Roman artisan, who cut chair and settee backs to imitate the heads of mules or horses and who used the curving cabriole or animal leg freely. Many other techniques were also utilized. Beds and couches were mounted on lathe-turned legs, painted in bright colors or inlaid in contrasting woods, and mounted with brass fittings. A great many different types of chairs, tables, stools, and pedestals were created, and every type of decorative technique known at the time was employed in their manufacture.

Chinese Furniture. China was the great Eastern cabinetmaking center. No one knows when the first pieces were made, but miniature furniture found in tombs of the Han dynasty (202 BC–AD 220) included chairs, cupboards of several sizes, tables, and chests. These differ from occidental examples in several ways. They have a sophisticated flowing line, and decoration is by most standards limited. Chinese furniture is made almost exclusively of rich, fine-grained hardwoods such as ebony, rosewood, or sandalwood, polished to a high natural-color finish. Carving, when used, is generally confined to small areas; and such fittings as locks and drawer pulls (generally of brass or iron) are of much greater visual importance. Inlay in brass, copper, pewter, or marble is applied to flat surfaces but never in the quantity found on Roman and Egyptian furniture.

Lacquerwork is traditionally associated with Chinese taste; in fact, however, the process of applying a lacquer finish (involving the painting on and polishing of countless layers of shellac) was so time-consuming and expensive that only in palaces would one find suites of lacquer furniture. Similarly, teak, regarded by many as the traditional Chinese furniture wood, was rarely used prior to the 19th century, and only then in pieces intended for export

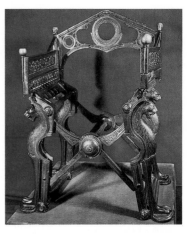

The Throne of Dagobert (early 9th century; back added 11th century), a Carolingian seat of honor crafted in bronze, follows the design of the folding stool used centuries earlier by Roman dignitaries. (Louvre, Paris.)

to Europe. The bulk of Chinese furniture continued to be made of the traditional materials and in traditional ways well into the 20th century.

Byzantine Furniture. Roman crafts had reached a high degree of sophistication well before the birth of Christ, but following the collapse of the Western Roman Empire in the 5th century, much of this skill was lost to Europe. It persisted, however, in the Eastern Roman Empire, commonly called the Byzantine Empire. Constantinople, the capital, flourished until 1453, and Byzantine furniture forms had a profound influence on the styles of Italy and, indeed, on all of western Europe. The Byzantine style was essentially a mixture of Greco-Roman and Oriental elements, and nearly all the surviving finer furniture made in this manner was intended for royal or ecclesiastical use. The general form was Roman, but superimposed upon this was profuse ornamentation in the Eastern mode—that is, an emphasis on curvilinear and geometric forms with much mosaic inlay in gold, glass, and stone. Human and animal figures were less often incorporated, and decorative elements tended to be stiff and conventionalized rather than fluid.

Medieval European Furniture. Although its influence waned with time, Byzantine taste was dominant in the eastern Mediterranean until the 15th century. Farther west, however, furniture, decorated or not, became an uncommon luxury during the so-called Dark Ages in Europe. Very little has survived from the Merovingian (c.500–750), Carolingian (c.750–950), and Ottonian (c.950–1050) periods. The bronze chair known as the Throne of Dagobert (early 9th century; Louvre, Paris), the best-known example of Carolingian furniture, clearly reveals its Roman ancestry.

What style there was came in the Romanesque period (beginning c.1050), also reflecting its origin in a debased Roman style. Furniture forms were few—primarily, chests, tables, and stools—and decoration was almost exclusively carved, chiefly in the form of primitive, vigorous floral motifs. The wood of choice was oak, and furnishings were crude and heavy, reflecting the limited technical knowledge of the time.

Gothic Furniture. By the 12th century, however, condi-

A Ming dynasty testered bed with an alcove (c. 15th–16th century), of fine rosewood, illustrates the plain, boxlike design typical of Ming furniture. Chinese cabinetmakers used such decorative elements as inlay and carving very sparingly, maximizing instead the beauty of the wood through highly polished forms.

This 16th-century French choir stall demonstrates the influence of Renaissance decorative motifs, seen in the back carving, upon a predominantly Gothic ecclesiastical form. (Philadelphia Museum of Art.)

tions in western Europe had begun to improve. The dominant factor in this era—which came to be known as the Gothic—was the church, and the dominant masters were the architects and stonemasons. Building on the existing Romanesque style, architects in France and later in the rest of western Europe began to construct massive churches whose form influenced nearly everything else made during the period. Gothic furniture is essentially rectilinear in concept, and its decorative motifs—round or pointed arches, carved tracery, pillars and buttresses—are taken directly from church architecture.

Carving remained the preferred method of embellishment, with native plant forms such as grape and maple leaves, wild cress, and parsley dominating the foliage; figural subjects, primarily birds and animals or humans in grotesque forms, were also used. Oak and walnut, both of which lend themselves to carving, were the preferred timbers, and carving and molding often almost entirely covered the surface of a piece. Toward the end of the period painted decoration became popular, but sophisticated techniques such as inlay were almost entirely absent in furniture; nor was there a great variety of forms. The greatest decorative skill was lavished on chests and coffers, but stools, benches, tables, and a very few chairs were also made. Befitting their dominant position, the clergy had a somewhat greater range of furnishings. Altars, screens, and desks (often embellished with the layered "linenfold" carving characteristic of the period) were found in churches and monasteries.

Renaissance Furniture. The Gothic mode, although exceedingly popular in northern Europe, made little headway in Italy, and by 1400 a new style was rapidly developing there. This was the Renaissance style, a mixture of native Greco-Roman forms and Eastern ideas derived from Constantinople. Renaissance decoration, far more elaborate than its Romanesque predecessor, was imposed upon furniture, which was constructed by cabinetmakers who were becoming artists.

The widespread use of mill-sawed and lathe-turned wood led to the making of lighter, well-constructed furnishings, while the range of timbers employed was expanded to include walnut, pine, ebony, and other woods. Decoration became varied and complex. To the catalog of Gothic decorative motifs were added those of the East: stars, crescents, and the intertwining scrollwork known as the arabesque. From the East also came intarsia, the inlay in wood of bone, shell, and metal. Gilding became popular again, as it had been in Roman times; famous painters of the day, such as PIERO DI COSIMO, vied for the opportunity to decorate the storage chests and cupboards of their royal patrons.

A great variety of new furnishings appeared at this time including, in Italy, the *cassone*, a very large storage chest, and, in Spain, a framed drop-front desk, the *vargueno*, which was carved, inlaid, and painted with the greatest care. Also in Spain iron and leather were first used extensively in the construction and decoration of furniture.

Baroque Furniture. By the middle of the 16th century a new style, the baroque, was emerging, first in Italy and later in France where, under Louis XIV, cabinetmaking became a recipient of royal patronage and subject to royal control. The first *ébéniste du roi* (cabinetmaker to the king) was André Charles Boulle, appointed in 1672; his furniture epitomized the baroque style.

Baroque furniture is characterized by strong emphasis on decoration and a reduced concern with form. Scale is deliberately distorted, and carving grows lavish with deep moldings, sinuous twisted scrollwork, and pediments of gigantic proportions in relation to the pieces they crown.

Carving was the most important decorative technique employed in the baroque style. Veneering was also popular, however, and marquetry was practiced, as was inlay in gilt, bronze, and marble; marble inlay was used exten-

A Louis XVI commode, designed by J. H. Riesener, exhibits the heavy proportions and elegant, symmetrical ornamentation characteristic of early neoclassical furniture. (The Frick Collection, New York City.)

A lady's dressing table, attributed to the 18th-century cabinetmaker Jean François Oeben, displays the delicate curves, slender proportions, and detailed ornament of the Louis XV style. (National Gallery of Art, Washington, D.C.)

sively for tabletops made in Italy and exported. Chairs, the forms of which were now many and varied, were also carved and frequently covered with stamped and gilded leather studded with nailheads in the Spanish manner.

Rococo Furniture. The disenchantment with form continued during the following period, the rococo (1700–75). The term *rococo* is derived from *rocaille*, the French word for shellwork in garden grottoes. Rococo furniture is typically light in weight and feeling with curving, asymmetrical forms lushly decorated with floral and animal motifs. Surface decoration, including gilding, painting, carving, and application of gilt bronze ornaments, almost totally dissolves the outline of individual furniture pieces.

The greatest patron of the ROCOCO STYLE was Louis XV of France; French decorative furniture in the Louis XV style is scarce and costly and is considered by many to be among the finest ever made. There is no question that it is extraordinary in execution and in form. New forms, such as the slant-front desk, were invented; old forms changed their appearance, as the curved cabriole leg was applied to tables and chairs and chests of drawers assumed swelling bombé, or bulging, serpentine fronts.

In England a more conservative mode prevailed in the baroque and rococo periods, typified by the QUEEN ANNE STYLE—with cabriole legs, graceful curves, and opulent carving, as in the work of Grinling GIBBONS. Publication of Thomas CHIPPENDALE's *Gentleman and Cabinet Maker's Directory* (1754) heralded the birth of a style that owed much to the influence of imported Chinese furnishings.

The German style of baroque and rococo furniture achieved its own exuberant flowering, especially in Munich in the work of François CUVILLIÉS for the Bavarian

royal family. His *Reiche Zimmer* (Rich Rooms, *c.*1750) in the Munich Residenz and his furnishings for the Amalienburg Pavilion (1734–40) in the park of NYMPHENBURG PALACE are considered the highest achievements of the German rococo style.

Neoclassic Furniture. In time the lush decoration and irregular form of the rococo went out of fashion, and after 1770 cabinetmakers sought new inspiration, which they found in the recently discovered Roman ruins at Herculaneum and Pompeii, first excavated in 1748, and in the general interest in antiquity called NEOCLASSICISM. From the architectural forms and wall paintings found in Pompeii such designers as Robert ADAM in England and David Roentgen in Germany developed a new style—the neoclassic (1770–1810).

Carving and curvilinear form, so popular in the two previous periods, now nearly disappeared, to be replaced by strong vertical and horizontal lines, combined with delicate construction and flat panels decorated with contrasting veneers or painted designs. Furniture legs became long and slim with a square taper or a reeded form. Fluting and grooving emphasized the verticality of the pieces, and moldings and feet took the forms of the capitals and bases of Greek and Roman columns. Decorative devices were used more sparingly, and those employed were classical in form, such as the oak leaf, the urn, and the Greek palm. Brass and gilt continued to be used but only in delicate, small-scale fittings.

Empire Furniture. Neoclassicism came late to France and was soon replaced, first by the DIRECTOIRE STYLE and soon after by Napoleon's version of the classic revival, known appropriately as the EMPIRE STYLE. Empire furniture is characterized by absolute symmetry, heavy proportions, and wide, flat surfaces, sparse molding and decoration, and veneering. Carving, except on chair arms and table legs, is rare, and ormolu is used with a certain restraint. Motifs and forms were inspired by Egyptian, Greek, and Roman furniture. The Empire style was enthusiastically adopted in England and particularly so in

This Louis XV armchair (c.1770), composed entirely of curving forms, epitomizes the delicate grace of French rococo furniture. It is characterized by such features as the slender frame, carved molding, and floral ornamentation. (National Gallery of Art, Washington, D.C.)

the United States, as in the work of Lambert Hitchcock and Duncan PHYFE. In Germany and Austria the Empire style formed the basis for the pervasive BIEDERMEIER style, an even simpler and heavier version of Empire.

Victorian Furniture. The Victorian era, spanning the reign of the British queen Victoria (1837–1901), spawned the greatest proliferation of decorative furniture ever seen. This was in part due to the eclectic nature of design during the era. Rather than working within a single, dominant style as had previously been the custom, furniture makers borrowed and adapted elements from numerous previous eras, using them interchangeably in bewildering combinations. The proliferation of Victorian furniture was also made possible by the mechanization of furniture manufacture, which took place in the 1840s. The development of mechanical presses and veneer-cutting machinery allowed for the rapid and inexpensive (if not always artistic) creation of decorative furniture. Moreover, improvements in transportation made the finest and most exotic woods—mahogany, rosewood, teak, ebony, and the like—readily available throughout the world in quantity. As a consequence, a great variety of decorative furniture was produced.

Stylistic adaptations hark back to other eras. Victorian Gothic is carved to imitate 14th-century church furnishings, while Renaissance Revival pieces show a strong, if archaic, Italian influence. The Victorian era's final flowering was in the style called ART NOUVEAU, related to the rococo style and directly inspired by the ARTS AND CRAFTS MOVEMENT. Art Nouveau furniture is characterized by sinuous, flowing lines and rich contrasts of light and shadow, as in the desks, tables, and chairs designed by the French architect Hector GUIMARD.

In spite of all the eclectic revivals of the 19th century, certain important advances were made: the American John Belter created laminated wood furniture beginning about 1845, and in 1841, Michael Thonet of Vienna patented the bentwood process. These new techniques had a profound influence on later furniture design and manufacture.

Meanwhile, taste was changing once again, with a reaction to Victorian decorative excesses. Under the in-

The classical revival of the late 18th century returned linearity and monumentality to furniture forms. This 18th-century roll-top desk, designed by one of the leading cabinetmakers of the time, David Roentgen, exemplifies the neoclassic style. (Metropolitan Museum of Art, New York City.)

fluence of the ARTS AND CRAFTS MOVEMENT in England, led by William Morris, and in the United States, led by such designers as Elbert Hubbard, a new style emerged. Mission, as it was called in the United States, emphasized square-cut oak furniture upholstered in leather and decorated with hand-hammered copper cutouts. Popular for the first two decades of the 20th century and subsequently denigrated for its bulkiness, Mission is now undergoing a revival of interest.

Scandinavian and Bauhaus Furniture. Early in this century, designers in Scandinavia began to employ wood and steel in a large repertoire of what is now called "modern" furniture. Such designer-architects as Alvar AALTO of Finland and Arne JACOBSEN of Denmark set style precedents that are still followed. However, the strongest influence on modern furnishings was the Paris *Exposition Universelle des Arts Decoratifs et Industriels Modernes* of 1925, at which the BAUHAUS architects Ludwig MIES VAN DER ROHE and Marcel BREUER showed the first modern nickel-plated steel furniture as well as adaptations and updated versions of Thonet's bentwood furniture. These

The Empire style of the early 19th century combined classical austerity with Napoleonic grandeur. This couch (c.1810) is derived from the form of a Roman triclinium, or banquet couch. (Ford Museum, Dearborn, Mich.)

The sinuous lines of Art Nouveau appeared in the decorative as well as in the graphic arts toward the end of the 19th century. The French designer Hector Guimard's pearwood side table (c.1908) reflects the forms and motifs of Art Nouveau. (Museum of Modern Art, New York City.)

This parlor from the Colonel Robert J. Milligan house, in Saratoga, N.Y., exemplifies the Victorian style of mid-19th-century America. The curvilinear rococo was one of the most prevalent of the various revived styles popular during the Victorian era. (Brooklyn Museum, N.Y.)

pieces, severely elegant and simple, became 20th-century classics that influenced all subsequent designers.

The Paris Exposition also launched the style now called ART DECO, which had its roots in the Viennese SECCESSION MOVEMENT of the first decade of the 20th century. Art Deco furniture, like its architecture, is sleek, streamlined, and decorated with geometric designs and abstracted natural forms. This style was in vogue until 1939 and then experienced a revival of interest in the 1960s and '70s.

Contemporary Furniture. Many 20th-century furniture designers have been architects, including Frank Lloyd WRIGHT, Eero SAARINEN, Charles EAMES, and Charles and Henry Greene in the United States. Their furniture was usually designed for their own buildings, but much of it was capable of mass manufacture, such as Saarinen's pedestal chair of molded plastic and the so-called Eames chair (in fact designed by Eames and Saarinen) of molded plywood upholstered in leather. New synthetic materials have been adopted rapidly in furniture design and manufacture. However, the basic trend set in 1925 continues unchanged. Line is all-important, and decoration as it existed in the 19th century and before has effectively ceased to exist. Gone are ormolu, lush carving and paint, inlay, and elaboration. In part this is a matter of taste, but it also reflects the fact that artisans are no longer trained to do this sort of work.

Furniture Manufacture

Furniture making remained a handicraft until the early 19th century, when water- and steam-powered tools came into widespread use. Powered saws could cut and shape wood pieces quickly and in quantity, and large steam-driven presses made it possible to stamp decorative patterns on wood instead of laboriously carving them by hand. These labor-saving devices also reduced the role of the individual artisan.

Early Factory Systems. The chair factory established (1818) by the American furniture maker Lambert Hitchcock was typical of the early factory systems. Situated on the Barkhamsted River in Connecticut, the factory was almost completely water powered, and the individual pieces of each chair were sawed, planed, and turned by machine. Assembly, painting, and the elaborate stenciling that became a Hitchcock trademark were done by hand but on a production line.

In the United States industrialization was accelerated by the expansion of migration to the West. The thousands of new settlers in the frontier territories created a huge new market for inexpensive furniture. In Grand Rapids, Mich., and in other cities on the fringes of settlement, a number of factories began to pour out furniture in unprecedented volume.

By the end of the 19th century, furniture handicrafts that had once flourished were now used only by custom shops making expensive furniture to order or by people interested in the arts-and-crafts revival.

Influence of Technology on Design. Throughout the 19th century, factory-made furniture imitated traditional styles. It was not until the early 20th century that designers began to consider the potential offered by mass-production techniques. In Germany the Bauhaus School (founded 1919) attempted to design objects that were attractive, simple, and reproducible in quantity, although perhaps expensive. In the United States the modernist movement achieved wide recognition beginning only in the 1930s, with designers such as Charles Eames, Paul McCobb, T. H. Robsjohu-Gibbings, and Eero Saarinen. Their designs eventually transformed the manufacture of furniture, allowing the introduction of simple, undecorated surfaces, functional shapes, and a range of new materials: glass, chrome, steel, aluminum, and plastic.

Contemporary Manufacture. Contemporary wood furniture frequently uses a combination of wood with such composite materials as Masonite and plywood. Wood surfaces are usually made of a thin veneer laid over a less expensive wood. Veneers may be made of plastic or plastic-covered wood.

Mass-produced furniture parts are machine cut and machine sanded and assembled with powered hand tools or with mechanically applied glues. The parts of flat-surfaced furniture, such as chests and tables, are often spray painted on a moving belt, in a completely automatic process. Complicated or expensive pieces are stained and varnished by hand.

The development of quick-setting, permanent-bonding glues and of new techniques in lamination and high-pressure processes has encouraged the creation of new furniture forms. A one-piece molded chair body, for example, can be produced by gluing many layers of thin wood veneer together, then molding the veneer block into a chair

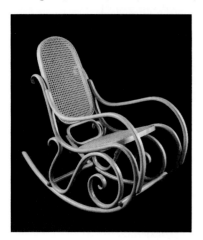

(Left) *Michael Thonet's bentwood rocking chair (c. 1860) foreshadowed the clean lines and functionalism of 20th-century furniture.*

(Right) *The comfortable sculptural designs of Charles Eames are typified by the Eames chair and ottoman, among the most imitated works of the 20th century.*

(Below) *Two examples of contemporary furniture illustrate the great range of modern design. The red leather chair is by German designer Till Leeser, who exhibits his work as art. A table by American designer George Nakashima is typical of his use of solid wood— the natural profile of a cut of timber dictates the shape of the piece.*

(Above) *Ludwig Mies van der Rohe's Barcelona chair (1929) epitomizes the spare, functional Bauhaus designs.*

shape in a heat press. Plastic furniture shapes are molded or cast, and molded plastic or fiberglass is also used—instead of wood—for the skeletons of furniture to be covered by upholstery.

The cushions used on contemporary styles are usually filled with sponge rubber or plastic foam. For traditional chairs and sofas, however, traditional handicrafts are still used. Coiled steel springs are tied in a lacing of burlap webbing and attached to the furniture frame. The springs are embedded in a bulky filling material, such as foam rubber, and covered with a soft padding layered to the desired shape of the piece, then finished with upholstery fabric. The use of mechanical knives to cut many layers of fabric into the necessary shapes and the replacement of upholsterer's tacks by air-driven staples are the only modern innovations in the upholstering process.

Knockdown and Do-It-Yourself Furniture. A variety of new forms have become popular in recent years. A knockdown chest of drawers, for example, can be purchased disassembled and packed in a flat box and can be put together with glue and a few screws. These new furniture categories have been made possible because modern machining methods can produce furniture components to precise size tolerances, and because joining and finishing techniques have been simplified to the point where an amateur can easily build an attractive chair or table from precut components.

See also: ANTIQUE COLLECTING; INDUSTRIAL DESIGN; INTERIOR DESIGN.

Furtwängler, Wilhelm [foort'-veng-glur] Wilhelm Furtwängler, b. Jan. 25, 1886, d. Nov. 30, 1954, was perhaps the outstanding German conductor of the 20th century. He studied with Max von Schillings and Josef Rheinberger and held conducting posts in Zurich, Strasbourg, Lübeck, Mannheim, and Frankfurt am Main before succeeding Arthur Nikisch in 1922 as director of the Berlin Philharmonic and Leipzig Gewandhaus orchestras. He also became closely associated with the Vienna Philharmonic Orchestra and appeared as guest conductor with the New York Philharmonic for three seasons (1925–27). An opponent of the Hitler regime, he nonetheless remained in Germany during the Nazi years. An Allied tribunal found him innocent of collaboration.

Furtwängler was renowned for his individual yet scrupulous performances of the German repertory. His grasp of the immense musical structures of Richard Wagner and Anton Bruckner was unequaled.

furze [furz] Furze, or gorse, is the common name for a genus, *Ulex*, of about 25 species of shrubs in the pea family, Leguminosae. Furze is native to Europe and is widely cultivated; its dense branches are dark green and spiny. The principal species is *U. europaeus*, which grows up to 1.2 m (4 ft) tall or more in sunny areas with sandy or gravelly soil. Its yellow flowers are showy and are pro-

duced continuously in mild climates. The plants are sometimes used to stabilize dry banks.

fuse The electrical fuse is a device placed in an electrical circuit to avoid overload. It usually contains a thin strip of metal that melts and breaks when a current above a certain amperage passes through it. It is important that a fuse or other circuit breaker control an overloaded circuit in order to avoid damage to the system.

Fuseli, Henry [fue'-zil-ee] Henry Fuseli, b. Zurich, Feb. 6, 1741, d. Apr. 16, 1825, was an artist and art historian. The son of a painter, he was educated as a theologian at the Collegium Carolinum in Zurich. His early literary and theological training remained a decisive factor throughout his career. His subject paintings were frequently drawn from a wide range of literature; Shakespeare was his favorite writer. In his choice of subjects he showed a preference for the fantastic and the horrific (for an example, see FAIRY). Much romantic art is literary in origin, and in this respect Fuseli was a key romantic painter (see ROMANTICISM, art). His paintings, although highly imaginative, were sometimes technically inept; his ideas often appear less stilted, however, in the freshness of his many drawings. He also produced paintings and drawings of women in elongated forms, sometimes with fantastic hairstyles.

As professor of painting at the Royal Academy in London from 1799 to 1805, and again from 1810 until his death, Fuseli gave the best series of discourses since those of Sir Joshua Reynolds. He started to compile the first history of Italian art in the English language and revised the standard dictionary on art of the time.

Fushoulu (Fu-Shou-Lu) [foo-shoh'-loo] In Chinese mythology, the Fushoulu are the three so-called stellar gods: Fu Xing, god of happiness; Shou Xing, god of longevity; and Lu Xing, god of prosperity. The most revered of the three is Shou Xing, who is believed to determine the life span of each individual. The other two gods are deified historical figures.

Fushun (Fu-shun) [foo'-shoon] Fushun (1988 est. pop., 1,290,000) is a city in China on the Hun River in the highly industrialized Liaoning province of Manchuria. The area's high-quality coal deposits are exploited chiefly by open-cut methods, and the mines, which extend for 16 km (10 mi), are among the largest in the world. The shale oil overlying the coal is processed in large refineries there. Fushun also has iron and steel mills, as well as aluminum-processing and chemical plants.

Fushun was settled by the 8th century but did not grow until 1905, when the Russians began to mine coal. Industrial development, expanded by the Japanese during the 1930s, has continued to grow under the present Chinese regime.

fusion, nuclear   Nuclear fusion is a type of nuclear reaction in which two atomic nuclei combine to form a heavier nucleus, releasing energy. For a fusion reaction to take place, the nuclei, which are positively charged, must have enough kinetic energy to overcome their electrostatic force of repulsion. This can occur either when one nucleus is accelerated to high energies by an accelerating device or when the energies of both nuclei are raised by the application of very high temperatures. The latter method, referred to as thermonuclear fusion, is the source of the Sun's energy. If a proton is accelerated and collides with another proton, these nuclei can fuse, forming a deuterium nucleus (one proton and one neutron), a positron, a neutrino, and energy. Such a reaction is not self-sustaining, because the released energy is not readily imparted to other nuclei. Thermonuclear fusion of deuterium and tritium (one proton and two neutrons) will produce a helium nucleus and an energetic neutron that can help sustain further fusion. This is one basis of the HYDROGEN BOMB, which employs a brief, uncontrolled thermonuclear fusion reaction. A great effort is now under way to harness thermonuclear fusion as a source of power (see FUSION ENERGY).

Thermonuclear fusion depends on high energies, and the possibility of low-energy, low-temperature nuclear fusion has generally been discounted. Early in 1989, however, two electrochemists startled the scientific world and aroused great public interest when they declared that they had achieved room-temperature fusion in a simple laboratory experiment. The scientists, Stanley Pons of the University of Utah and Martin Fleischmann of the University of Southampton, England, described their experiment as involving an electrochemical cell in which palladium and platinum electrodes were immersed in heavy water (see DEUTERIUM). They claimed that the cell produced more heat than could be accounted for by a chemical reaction alone and that they had observed certain typical fusion by-products in the course of the process. According to their theory, deuterium was absorbed by the palladium electrode and fused there, releasing the extra heat.

In nuclear fusion two light nuclei unite to form a heavier nucleus. The fusion of deuterium and tritium, for example, yields helium and a neutron and releases tremendous energy. The energy produced by the hydrogen bomb and by the Sun and stars results from fusion reactions.

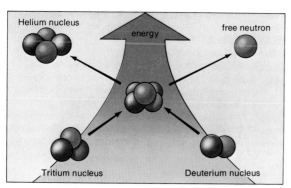

Helium nucleus

energy

free neutron

Tritium nucleus

Deuterium nucleus

Various laboratories around the world tried to duplicate the process, with conflicting but generally negative results. Scientists nevertheless continued to explore this possibility of "cold" fusion.

fusion energy   A fusion reaction is one in which two atomic nuclei merge to form a heavier nucleus and, in most cases, an accompanying product such as a free nucleon. In almost all types of fusion reactions between light nuclei, a portion of their rest mass is converted into kinetic energy of the reaction products or into gamma rays. Stars produce energy through a variety of fusion reactions. In main-sequence stars such as the Sun the net effect of these reactions is to convert hydrogen nuclei (protons) into helium nuclei. The kinetic energy and gamma rays released in the process heat the stellar interior, maintaining it at the very high temperatures (greater than 10 million K) required to continue the fusion. Such conditions, where the thermal energy of the nuclei drives them together in spite of their electrostatic repulsion, are called thermonuclear.

This process, which has been driving the stars for billions of years, has clear potential as a power source on Earth, and scientists have worked for decades toward the goal of employing thermonuclear fusion reactions to produce useful power. The two fusion reactions that are by far the most promising involve the heavier isotopes of hydrogen: deuterium (composed of one proton and one neutron) and tritium (composed of one proton and two neutrons). Deuterium occurs naturally as a minor constituent in all hydrogen-containing materials—such as water—in quantities sufficient to meet all the energy needs of societies for many billions of years. Tritium can be bred from lithium by a neutron-induced reaction in a blanket that could conceivably surround a fusion reactor. The western United States contains large lithium deposits in the salts of dry lake beds, and much larger quantities are dissolved in the sea. The reaction that occurs with the greatest probability and at the lowest temperatures involves the fusing of a deuterium nucleus with a tritium nucleus to form a helium (He^4) nucleus and a neutron. The products contain 17.6 million electron volts (MeV) of released kinetic energy. The second promising reaction, involving the fusing of two deuterium nuclei, has two branches that occur with about equal probability. One leads to a He^3 nucleus, a neutron, and 3.2 MeV of kinetic energy; the other produces a tritium nucleus, a proton, and 4.0 MeV. While the deuterium-deuterium reaction is the one that could furnish power beyond even the expected lifetime of the Sun, it is the somewhat more easily produced deuterium-tritium reaction, which would itself be sufficient for many thousands of years, that will provide most of the energy in the next generation of research devices.

Fusion reactions can be induced easily by using a charged particle accelerator (see ACCELERATOR, PARTICLE) to bombard a solid or gaseous tritium target with energetic deuterium nuclei. This technique consumes power rather than producing it, however, because most of the acceler-

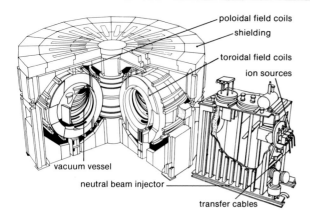

poloidal field coils
shielding
toroidal field coils
ion sources
vacuum vessel
neutral beam injector
transfer cables

Major components of the TFTR tokamak at Princeton University are shown. The toroidal field coils produce the strong (up to 50 kG) toroidal magnetic field, which, along with the poloidal field produced by the plasma current, confines the plasma. The equilibrium field coils control the plasma position. The plasma is heated by beams of energetic atoms produced from ions accelerated in the ion sources.

ated nuclei lose their energy through elastic collisions with electrons and nuclei, without producing fusion reactions. A net energy gain is obtained only by mimicking the Sun and producing starlike thermonuclear conditions. Because a reactor must be much smaller than a star and must operate in a limited time frame, however, it must have a much higher power density and be several times hotter than the center of the Sun. At thermonuclear temperatures, matter can exist only in the plasma state, consisting of electrons, positive ions, and very few neutral atoms (see PLASMA PHYSICS). To achieve ignition, when the energy deposited within the plasma by fusion reactions equals or exceeds the energy being lost, a plasma must be confined and heated. Obviously, a plasma at millions of degrees is not compatible with an ordinary confining wall, but the effect of this incompatibility is not the destruction of the wall, as might be expected. Although the temperature of a thermonuclear plasma is very high and the power flowing through it may be large, a thermonuclear plasma is self-limiting because any significant contact with the vessel housing it causes its extinction within a few thousandths of a second.

Magnetic Confinement. Since the early 1950s most fusion research has used magnetic fields to confine the charged particles that constitute a plasma. The density required in magnetic-confinement fusion is much lower than atmospheric density, so the plasma vessel is evacuated and then filled with the hydrogen-isotope fuel at 0.000001 times the density of the atmosphere. Magnetic-field configurations fall into two types: open and closed. In an open configuration the charged particles, which are spiraling along magnetic field lines maintained by a SOLENOID, are reflected at each end of a cell by stronger magnetic fields. In this simplest type of mirror machine, many particles that have most of their velocity parallel to the solenoidal magnetic field are not reflected

and can escape. Present-day mirror machines retard this loss by using additional plasma cells to set up electrostatic potentials that help confine the hot ions within the central solenoidal field.

In closed configurations, the magnetic-field lines along which charged particles move are continuous within the plasma. This closure has most commonly taken the form of a torus, or doughnut shape, and the most common example is the TOKAMAK. In a tokamak the primary confining field is toroidal and is produced by coils surrounding the vacuum vessel. Other coils cause current to flow through the plasma by induction. This toroidally flowing current engenders a poloidal magnetic field, at right angles, that wraps itself around the plasma. The poloidal field and the stronger toroidal field, acting together, yield magnetic-field lines that spiral around the torus. This spiraling ensures that a particle spends equal amounts of time above and below the toroidal midplane, thus canceling the effects of a vertical drift that occurs because the magnetic field is stronger on the inside of the torus than on the outside.

Plasma Heating. Tokamak plasmas can be heated to temperatures of 10–15 million K by the current flowing in the plasma. At higher temperatures the plasma resistance becomes too low for this method to be effective, and heating is accomplished by injecting beams of very energetic neutral particles into the plasma. These ionize, become trapped, and transfer their energy to the bulk plasma through collisions. Alternatively, radiofrequency waves are launched into the plasma at frequencies that resonate with various periodic particle motions. The waves give energy to these resonant particles, which transfer it to the rest of the plasma through collisions.

Current Drive. Experiments are also under way in which radio-frequency waves are used to push electrons around the tokamak to maintain the plasma current. Such noninductive current drive allows the tokamak pulse to outlast the time limits imposed by the fact that, in a transformer-driven tokamak, the plasma current lasts only as long as the current in the secondary coils is changing. When the secondary coils reach their current limits, confinement is lost, and the plasma terminates until the transformer can be reset (a matter of at least seconds). Although the plasma in an inductively driven tokamak is pulsed, the electricity produced would not be, because the thermal inertia of the neutron-capturing blanket would sustain steam generation between pulses. By allowing longer pulse or steady-state plasma operation, however, radio-frequency current drive could lessen the thermal stresses in the fusion reactor.

Inertial Confinement. Another approach to fusion, pursued since about 1974, is termed inertial confinement. Its aim is to compress a solid pellet of frozen deuterium and tritium to very high temperatures and densities in a process analogous to what occurs in a thermonuclear (hydrogen) bomb. The compression is accomplished by bombarding the pellet from all sides, simultaneously, with an intense pulse of LASER light, ions, or electrons. The outer pellet mass vaporizes and, by mechanical reaction, imparts inwardly directed momentum to the remaining pellet core. The inertia of the inwardly driven pellet material must be sufficient to localize the resulting fusion plasma for the approximately 10^{-9} seconds required to get significant energy release. In 1988 it was learned that the U.S. government, which secretly had been using underground nuclear tests in Nevada to study inertial-confinement fusion, had achieved such fusion in 1986 by this means.

Progress toward Energy Production. The minimum confinement condition necessary to achieve energy gain in a deuterium-tritium plasma—the so-called Lawson criterion—is that the product of density in ions per cm^3 and energy containment time in seconds must exceed 6×10^{13}. This was attained in 1983 for the first time in a hydrogen plasma at the Massachusetts Institute of Technology. Further advances have since been made at other fusion laboratories, such as the Joint European Torus at Culham Laboratory near Oxford, England. The temperature required to ignite a fusion reactor is in the range of 100–250 million K, several times the temperature of the center of the Sun. Much research remains to be done before fusion power reactors can become a reality.

The goal of fusion—in effect, to make and hold a small star—is daunting. That it is pursued nevertheless is an indication of the magnitude of the benefits that success could bring. In addition to providing an almost inexhaustible fuel supply, fusion is environmentally benign: the resulting ash is harmless helium and hydrogen, and the afterheat in the reactor structure would be much less than in a fission reactor and would be distributed through a greater thermal mass. In addition, because fusion is not a chain reaction, it cannot run out of control, and any perturbation would cause the plasma to extinguish itself. It would also be far more difficult to produce nuclear-weapons materials surreptitiously at a fusion plant than at a fission plant; because no fissionable material should ordinarily be present, it would be a simple matter to detect characteristic gamma rays. Present levels of support for research are aimed at building the first demonstration fusion power plant in the early 21st century.

Fust, Johann   see GUTENBERG, JOHANN

Futuna Islands   see WALLIS AND FUTUNA ISLANDS

▬

Future Farmers of America   Future Farmers of America, founded in 1928, has as its primary objective the development, through practical experience, of leadership abilities among young people preparing for careers in agriculture and agribusiness. The organization provides training programs for agricultural students in high school and publishes the bimonthly *National Future Farmer Magazine* from its headquarters in Alexandria, Va.

▬

futures   Futures are contracts describing the sale of a "commodity" scheduled to occur at a later date. No

money changes hands between the buyer and seller when a trade is made, but both must post collateral ("margin") to demonstrate their good faith to fulfill their future obligations. Initial margin deposits range between 5% and 15% of contract value.

Futures contract markets are an important part of the financial system. They let businesses shift the risk of losing money to others more willing to bear such a risk. In doing so, the futures markets provide information about the value of the items traded.

Futures markets are organized by commodity-futures exchanges. An exchange standardizes the terms of all contracts, oversees trading, and coordinates all payments. Members of an exchange gather in a "pit" or "ring" on the exchange floor and trade contracts by shouting and using hand signals.

Until the 1970s virtually all futures contracts were written for agricultural commodities, such as wheat. Now some of the largest futures markets trade contracts on financial instruments, such as currencies, government and corporate debt, and stock indexes. In 1982 exchanges organized markets for put and call options on futures contracts (see OPTION TRADING).

The two largest U.S. futures exchanges are the Chicago Board of Trade and the Chicago Mercantile Exchange. Both have important agricultural and financial-futures markets. Some other exchanges are located in New York City, Kansas City, London, Tokyo, and Paris. In the United States the Commodity Futures Trading Commission regulates all futures trading.

▬

futurism   Futurism, a movement in early-20th-century Italian painting and sculpture, was initiated by the literary manifesto of Filippo Tommaso MARINETTI, published in the French newspaper *Le Figaro* in February 1909. Marinetti extolled the dynamic energy of the modern machine,

Gino Severini's Danseuse bleue (1912) exemplifies the dynamic movement sought by the adherents of futurism. Severini was one of the movement's founders and leading figures, and was also closely associated with cubism. (Mattiolo Collection, Milan.)

declared that classical art was less beautiful than the automobile, and proposed that art should celebrate the violence of speed and war. He simultaneously decried conventional artistic taste and its preference for the achievements of the Italian past over recent innovations of technology. In the following year a group of young painters led by Umberto BOCCIONI produced a technical manifesto that applied Marinetti's ideas to painting. Boccioni and his fellow signatories, Giacomo BALLA, Carlo CARRÀ, Gino SEVERINI, and Luigi Russolo, sought to represent the sensations of movement and used the word *dynamism* to describe the relationship between a moving object and its surroundings, as when a vehicle, speeding along a street, sets up vibrations that shake surrounding buildings.

In order to represent the movement of machines and human figures, the futurists resorted to the techniques of French CUBISM, which used fragmented images consisting of intersecting planes to impart a sense of motion to their work. Marcel DUCHAMP's celebrated *Nude Descending a Staircase* (1912; Philadelphia Museum of Art) reveals the shared characteristics of the two movements. Through a series of similar forms distributed in jerky sequence across the canvas, Duchamp finds a concrete equivalent for the idea of descent. Like Duchamp, the futurists moved toward abstraction, striving to represent the noises of a construction site, as in Boccioni's *The City Rises* (1910–11; Museum of Modern Art, New York City), or the patterns of sound made by music, as in Russolo's *Music* (1911; private collection, London).

In a second manifesto of 1912, Boccioni applied futurist doctrine to the three-dimensional medium of sculpture, suggesting that a work of art might be set in motion by a motor, and that sculpture might incorporate readymade objects of common use. His ideas, which he did not live to put into practice, were later brought to fruition by KINETIC ART, and in the COLLAGES and assemblage of Pablo PICASSO and Duchamp.

The futurist movement lost momentum when, in 1915, many of its members joined the army. The death of Boccioni in 1916 deprived the futurists of their guiding spirit. His theories did, however, find expression in the architecture of Antonio Sant'Elia, who designed futurist cities and technical installations, perpetuating an interest in the aesthetic beauty of the machine age. Thereafter the aims of futurism were disseminated and absorbed by other movements and can be discerned in the designs of ART DECO, in VORTICISM, and in DADA.

---

futurology   Futurology is the study of long-term trends in society in order to develop and promote alternative ways of dealing with future events or conditions. With the capacity to alert both governments and private industries to future problems and future opportunities, futurology is directed toward assisting in intelligent decision making. The terms *futures research, future studies,* and *forecasting* are also used to describe this field of study.

World War II was the turning point for research on the future. In 1944, Henry Harley ARNOLD, a general in the

U.S. Air Force, initiated the first technological forecasting project, and in 1946 he was instrumental in establishing the RAND Corporation as a THINK TANK. The development and application of technological forecasting techniques accelerated in the late 1940s, '50s, and '60s, and other important future-oriented think tanks, such as the Stanford Research Institute (1946) and the Hudson Institute (1961), were created. In recent decades the writings of such futurists as Daniel Bell and Alvin Toffler (1928–) have dealt with the period of transformation to a highly complex, technological, global society, and the works of Buckminster FULLER and Herman Kahn (1922–83) have forecast their views of future life-styles and conditions.

Widely diverse methods are used by futurists to make forecasts, ranging from simple, informed hunches to complex computer analyses. Because futurists recognize the unavoidable uncertainty inherent in forecasting, much of their work focuses on "what-if" examinations of alternatives rather than on precise prediction. Two general types of forecasting methods exist, exploratory and normative. Exploratory forecasts, which begin with the past by examining historical data and move into the future by projecting probability outcomes, are labeled the "can do" type. Examples of exploratory forecasts are trend extrapolations and growth models. Normative forecasts, which include market analyses and relevance trees, imagine a desired future in order to facilitate the making of decisions that will achieve a predicted, or preferred, future.

Two other popular methods that cannot be strictly classified are Delphi, an iterative and anonymous questioning process used to obtain the judgment of a panel of experts, and scenario writing, which uses a narrative to present an image of a future.

Pitfalls in forecasting include reliance on a single method, invalid underlying assumptions, and basing the forecast only on the very recent past (thus missing overriding long-term trends).

Fuzhou (Foochow) [foo-joh']   Fuzhou is the capital and largest city of Fujian (Fukien) province, China. It is located near the mouth of the Min River, about 55 km (34 mi) from the Taiwan Strait and has a population of 1,240,000 (1988 est.). Fuzhou is also known by its traditional name, Yongcheng (Banyan City), because its humid tropical climate favors the growth of banyan trees. Major manufactures include machinery, paper, chemicals, and textiles. In addition the city is noted for its traditional handicraft industries such as lacquer ware and sculpture. A railroad linking it to the main Chinese rail system was opened in 1958.

Fuzhou was founded in the late 6th century. It was one of the five earliest treaty ports opened (1842) to international trade as a result of the OPIUM WARS, and was particularly important for its export of tea, but it declined after 1880 as a result of silting of the river and the decreasing demand for China tea. In the hills around the city are many historic temples, and the 14th-century Bridge of Ten Thousand Ages crosses the Min River. Educational institutions include Fuzhou University.

GERMAN-GOTHIC	RUSSIAN-CYRILLIC	CLASSICAL LATIN	EARLY LATIN	ETRUSCAN	CLASSICAL GREEK	EARLY GREEK	EARLY ARAMAIC	EARLY HEBREW	PHOENICIAN

G *G/g* is the seventh letter of the English alphabet. Both the form of the letter and its position in the alphabet were derived from the Latin, which in turn derived it from the letter C of that alphabet by the addition of a stroke to the lower limb. In English, *G/g* is pronounced as a hard *g*, as in *get* and *go*, and is the voiced counterpart of voiceless *k*; or as soft g, with the sound of *dzh* as in *gem*, and is the voiced counterpart of *ch* (*tsh*). This second sound of *G/g* is partly shared by the letter j, as in the spellings *gaol* and *jail*, which are pronounced the same. In words recently borrowed from French the sound *dzh* of *G/g* has become *zh*, as in *gendarme*.

gabbro [gab'-roh] Gabbro is a dark-colored plutonic IGNEOUS ROCK composed mainly of coarse grains of calcium-rich plagioclase FELDSPAR and PYROXENE. In addition, the rock may contain olivine, hornblende, biotite, garnet, rutile, apatite, zircon, magnetite, ilmenite, and chromite. Chemically and mineralogically, gabbro is equivalent to BASALT. Gabbros may occur as border rocks around granitic and other plutons, or as small individual plutons or DIKES. Their most common occurrence is in the lower parts of large, layered complexes. Most gabbros appear to intrude the rocks surrounding them and so are thought to be of igneous origin, although some may also be produced by metamorphic processes.

Gabin, Jean [gah-ban'] The tough-tender hero of many French film melodramas, Jean Gabin, b. May 17, 1904, d. Nov. 15, 1976, surprisingly failed to find an international audience, perhaps because he was more at home suggesting action than demonstrating it. He is remembered for his roles in *Pépe le Moko* (1936), *Grand Illusion* (1937), *Port of Shadows* (1938), *The Human Beast* (1938), and *Daybreak* (1939). He gave his most remarkable postwar performance in *A Monkey in Winter* (1962).

Gable, Clark Such was the brash charm of American film actor Clark Gable, b. Cadiz, Ohio, Feb. 1, 1901, d. Nov. 16, 1960, that for 30 years he was the undisputed king of Hollywood. As a fast-talking he-man, he was noted for the force of his personality more than for acting talent. Gable appeared in such classic films as *Red Dust* (1932);

The American actor Clark Gable captivated film audiences with his straightforward and charismatic style of acting. He appears here in his role as Rhett Butler, with actress Vivien Leigh, in a scene from the Civil War epic Gone with the Wind (1939).

It Happened One Night, for which he won an Academy Award (1934); *Mutiny on the Bounty* (1935); *San Francisco* (1936); and, most notably, as Rhett Butler in *Gone with the Wind* (1939). His postwar films were popular but far less memorable. He died during the filming of *The Misfits* (1961).

Gabo, Naum [gah'-boh, nowm] The Russian-American sculptor, painter, and architect Naum Gabo, b. Naom Pevsner in Bryansk, Russia, Aug. 5 (N.S.), 1890, d. Aug. 23, 1977, was one of the chief initiators of the abstract-art movement CONSTRUCTIVISM. Shortly after the outbreak of World War I, Gabo fled to Oslo, Norway, where he made (1915) his first "constructions." These were figurative heads and abstract forms influenced by synthetic CUBISM, and composed of intersecting planes of plywood or cardboard.

Gabo returned to Russia in March 1917, following the first Russian Revolution. He won the approval of the Communist government for his art and taught at the Moscow State Art School while engaged in a series of projects such as Serpuchov radio station (1919), which attempted to synthesize the arts of painting, sculpture, and architecture. In 1920, Gabo began to study the aesthetic properties of movement, an interest he shared with the members of the Italian futurist movement (see FUTURISM), and constructed his *Kinetic Sculpture*. This work was followed by the *Design for Kinetic Construction* (1922) and *Monument for the Institute of Physics and Mathematics* (1925).

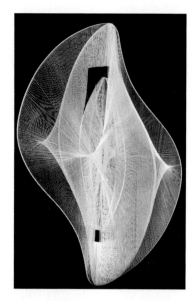

Naum Gabo's Linear Construction, Number 2 (*1949*), *a delicate structure of plastic and nylon thread, exemplifies his mature style. Industrial materials are inherent to constructivism, a movement that Gabo helped found. (Municipal Museum, Amsterdam.)*

From 1926 to 1927 he collaborated with his brother, Antoine Pevsner, in designing stage sets for Serge DIAGHILEV. In 1946, Gabo became a permanent U.S. resident; from 1953 to 1954 he taught architecture at Harvard University and executed several architectural commissions, including the U.S. Rubber Company building, New York City (1956). Notable examples of his painting and sculpture may be seen in New York's Museum of Modern Art.

Gabon [gah-bohn']   Gabon is a country on the west coast of Africa that straddles the equator. It is bounded on the south and east by the Congo, on the north by Cameroon, and on the northwest by Equatorial Guinea. Located on its 885-km (550-mi) Atlantic coastline is the capital and principal port, LIBREVILLE.

Land and Resources

Gabon has a coastal plain that varies from 32 to 160 km (20 to 100 mi) in width. In the north and east are rugged plateaus, 300–610 m (1,000–2,000 ft) in elevation. Beyond the plateaus, to the east, mountain ranges rise to over 914 m (3,000 ft), with Mount Iboundji of the Chaillu Mountains, the highest point in the country, reaching 1,575 m (5,167 ft).

Gabon has an equatorial climate with continually high humidity and an average annual temperature of about 27° C (81° F). Rainfall occurs all year, except along the coast, where the cold Benguela Current cools and dries the air to produce two dry seasons—one from May to September, when almost no rain falls, and one from mid-December to mid-January. In the north, about 3,810 mm (150 in) of rain falls annually.

The rough terrain and heavy rainfall produce many rivers that have the potential for hydroelectric development. The largest is the Ogooué, draining the southern half of the country. About 75% of Gabon is covered by dense tropical rain forests; occasional areas of savanna interrupt the forest along the coast and in the south.

People

Waves of migrating Negroid peoples from the northeast displaced much of the earlier Pygmy population, and today the major groups are the FANG, Adouma, Eshiras, and Okande. French is widely spoken, although the country's peoples also speak eight separate tribal languages. More than 50% of the people are Roman Catholics and Protestants, but traditional African religions prevail outside the larger towns.

Gabon is sparsely populated; most of the people live near the coast or along the river banks. Libreville is the largest city. Other urban centers include Port-Gentil, Lambaréné (the site of Albert SCHWEITZER's famous mission hospital), the mining centers of Franceville and Moamba, and the new port at Owedo, near Libreville. Education is free and compulsory between the ages of 6 and 16. Improved medical facilities have lowered the very high death rate that, until recently, caused Gabon's population to decline.

Economic Activity

In recent decades Gabon has experienced rapid economic growth, primarily because of its extensive mineral re-

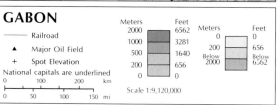

GABON

	Meters	Feet	Meters	Feet
Railroad	2000	6562	0	0
	1000	3281		
▲ Major Oil Field	500	1640	200	656
+ Spot Elevation	200	656	Below 2000	Below 6562
National capitals are underlined	0	0		

0   100   200   km
0   50   100   150   mi

Scale 1:9,120,000

AT A GLANCE

GABONESE REPUBLIC

Land: Area: 267,667 km^2 (103,347 mi^2). Capital and largest city: Libreville (1987 est. pop., 352,000).

People: Population (1990 est.): 1,068,240. Density: 4.0 persons per km^2 (10.3 per mi^2). Distribution (1986): 41% urban, 59% rural. Official language: French. Major religions: Roman Catholicism, traditional religions, Protestantism.

Government: Type: republic. Legislature: National Assembly. Political subdivisions: 9 provinces.

Economy: GDP (1989): $3.2 billion; $3,200 per capita. Labor distribution (1983): agriculture—65%; industry and commerce—30%; government and services—5%. Foreign trade (1989): imports—$760 million; exports—$1.14 billion. Currency: 1 C.F.A. franc = 100 centimes.

Education and Health: Literacy (1990): 62% of adult population. Universities (1991): 2. Hospital beds (1985): 5,516. Physicians (1984): 300. Life expectancy (1990): women—56; men—50. Infant mortality (1990): 106 per 1,000 live births.

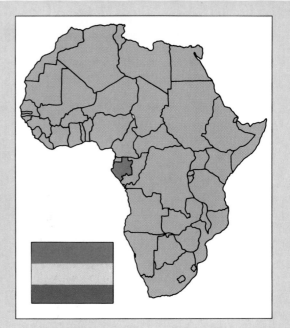

sources. It now has one of the highest per capita incomes in Africa. Petroleum production represents more than 80% of the country's export earnings. Gabon has about 25% of the world's known deposits of manganese, particularly in the Moamba region. Uranium and iron ore are also mined, and there are deposits of lead, zinc, phosphate, and other minerals.

More than half of the work force engage in subsistence farming. Less than 1% of the land is cultivated, and nearly 90% of all foodstuffs are imported. Forest products, which once provided more than 75% of all export earnings, now provide less than 10%. Manufacturing is limited.

Rivers remain important means of internal transportation. The first two stages of the Trans-Gabon railroad, opened in 1983 and 1986, link Libreville to Franceville and open the interior jungle to logging, mining, and other activities. Despite a continuing foreign-trade surplus, the nation is burdened with a large foreign debt and has introduced reforms to reduce public spending.

History and Government

In 1839, France signed a treaty with local chiefs that gave it powers over the southern coastal regions of Gabon. The Berlin Conference of 1885 awarded all of the territory discovered by Pierre de Brazza to France. This area was organized (in 1910) into French Equatorial Africa, and the separate colonies of Gabon, Congo, Chad, and Ubangi-Shari were formed. Gabon achieved its independence from France in 1960. Leon M'ba was the first president of the republic. At his death in 1967, Omar Bongo succeeded to the presidency; he introduced a one-party system in 1968. In 1990 popular protests forced constitutional revisions to legalize multiple parties, with Bongo to remain president until at least 1993.

Gaborone [gah-buh-roh'-nee] Gaborone (formerly Gaberones) is the capital of Botswana in south central Africa. In 1965, the year before Botswana received independence, the city replaced Mafeking, South Africa, as the country's administrative headquarters. It has a population of 111,000 (1988 est.) and is situated on the Cape-Zimbabwe railroad, close to the South African border. Primarily an administrative center with a university and national museum, it lacks a modern urban-industrial economy.

Gabriel (angel)   The angel Gabriel, an important figure in the Bible, appears first in the Book of Daniel (chapters 8 and 9) as a messenger and revealer. In the New Testament he announces the births of John the Baptist and Jesus Christ (Luke 1), and in the Book of Enoch, part of the pseudepigrapha, he is one of the seven archangels who stand close to God. Later Christian tradition made him the trumpeter of the Last Judgment. A popular figure in art, Gabriel is often pictured appearing to Mary or with trumpet raised. In Islam he is Jibril, the principal of many tales, who revealed the Koran to Muhammad.

Gabriel (family)   During the 17th and 18th centuries, the Gabriel family produced a dynasty of architects that enjoyed the favor of French royalty. Two members of the family had unusually distinguished careers. **Jacques V Gabriel**, b. Apr. 6, 1667, d. June 23, 1742, was appointed first architect to the king in 1734. His most notable commissions were the royal squares at Rennes (after 1720) and Bordeaux (1735–55). With Jean Aubert, he created one of the outstanding private houses of the period, the Hôtel de Biron, Paris (1728–31; now the Rodin Museum).

Ange Jacques Gabriel, b. Oct. 23, 1698, d. Jan. 4, 1782, succeeded his father as first architect to the king in 1742. To fulfill Louis XV's desire for a more intimate architectural scale than the grandiose style preferred by Louis XIV, Gabriel took responsibility for the modernization and extension of the royal residences: the Palace of VERSAILLES (Grand Projet, 1742–75; Opéra, 1748–70); Château de FOUNTAINEBLEAU (Gros Pavillon, 1749–50); and Château de Compiègne (begun 1751). Public buildings commissioned from Gabriel by the crown included the École Militaire (1751–58) and the Place de la Concorde (designed 1753–55 as Place Louis XI), both in Paris.

Ange Jacques Gabriel's chief architectural triumphs were his small, blocklike structures, chastely decorated, such as the king's hunting lodges and the pleasure houses of the king's mistress, Madame de Pompadour. His masterpiece is the Petit Trianon (1762–68), at Versailles. The "Style Gabriel" was essentially conservative, but its chiseled features and small-scale decoration represent the ultimate refinement of French classical tradition.

Gabriel (slave)   Gabriel, sometimes called Gabriel Prosser, b. c.1776, d. Oct. 7, 1800, was a black slave who led an abortive uprising near Richmond, Va., in 1800. Having sought in vain to develop a broad base of support, Gabriel and his followers nevertheless made plans to assault Richmond on August 30. The plot was discovered, and James Monroe, then governor of Virginia, called out the militia. Gabriel fled but was brought back and hanged, along with some 35 others.

Gabrieli (family) [gah-bree-ay'-lee]   The Gabrielis were a Venetian family, two of whose members, Andrea and Giovanni, were among the most important composers of the 16th and early 17th centuries.

Andrea Gabrieli, b. c.1520, d. 1586, was a pupil of Adrian Willaert at St. Mark's Basilica, Venice. He was appointed (1566) second organist of St. Mark's, later succeeding (1584) Claudio Merulo as first organist. His compositions include settings of Latin psalms, masses, and motets; several books of madrigals; and instrumental music, mostly for organ.

Giovanni Gabrieli, b. c.1554–57, d. Aug. 12, 1612, was a nephew and pupil of Andrea. In 1586 he succeeded his uncle as first organist of St. Mark's, and he held the post until he died. He had many pupils, of whom Heinrich Schütz was the most celebrated. His compositions include motets, madrigals, many pieces for ensembles of brass instruments, and organ works.

The Gabrielis' progressive, innovative style led directly to the operatic idiom of the 17th century. Andrea was a master of the art of setting texts to music. He was the first composer to pit groups of instruments against contrasting vocal groups, and the first to write pieces designated as "sonatas." Giovanni further developed the style of his uncle, exploiting dynamic (loud and soft) contrasts as well. His concertos, works for opposing forces of voices and instruments, initiated the concerto concept that dominated much of baroque music.

Gaddi (family) [gahd'-dee]   The Gaddi family, which included Gaddo, Taddeo, and Agnolo Gaddi, was prominent in Florentine painting for more than a century. **Gaddo Gaddi**, c.1250–1330, a contemporary of Giotto di Bondone, has been credited with several Florentine mosaics that reveal the influence of CIMABUE. Gaddo's son **Taddeo**, c.1300–66, was one of Giotto's most accomplished pupils and collaborators. In Taddeo's fresco cycle on the life of Mary (1332–38) in Santa Croce, Florence, he elaborated upon his master's monumental style, giving a greater sense of spatial illusion. His mature work, complex in figural detail, is well represented by his altarpiece of the *Madonna and Child with Saints* (1353) in the Cathedral of Pistoia.

Taddeo's son **Agnolo**, fl. 1369–96, also painted in the tradition of Giotto. His major works include frescoes on the *Legend of the True Cross* in the choir of Santa Croce, Florence (c.1388–93). His highly decorated manner anticipates the style of his pupil Lorenzo Monaco.

Gaddis, William [gad'-is]   The American author William Gaddis, b. New York City, Dec. 29, 1922, published two long novels, *The Recognitions* (1955) and *JR* (1975), whose complicated plots and loose narrative structure allowed ample opportunities for digressions into philosophy, theology, and social comment. *Carpenter's Gothic*, a shorter novel, was published in 1985.

gadolinium [gad-uh-lin'-ee-uhm]   The chemical element gadolinium is a lustrous, magnetic metal of the rare earth LANTHANIDE SERIES, Group IIIB of the periodic table. Its symbol is Gd, its atomic number is 64, its atomic weight is 157.25, and its valence is +3. It is often found in association with other rare earths. Gadolinium oxide was isolated in 1880 by the French chemist J. C. G. de Marignac from the mineral gadolinite, for which the element is named. Seven gadolinium isotopes occur in nature. At least one, ^{152}Gd, is radioactive, with a half-life of 1.1×10^{14} years. With the highest neutron-absorption CROSS-SECTION of any known element, gadolinium is used in control rods in some nuclear reactors. It is also used in noise filters, in phosphors for color television, and to increase the strength and conductivity of some other metals.

Gadsden [gadz'-den] Gadsden (1990 pop., 42,523), the seat of Etowah County in northeastern Alabama, is situated on the Coosa River about 95 km (59 mi) northeast of Birmingham. Iron, manganese, coal, and limestone are mined in the surrounding Appalachian foot hills, and Gadsden's steel industry is the second largest in the South. Other industries manufacture rubber and electronic devices. Founded in 1846 as Double Springs, the town was renamed in 1853 for James Gadsden, who negotiated the Gadsden Purchase.

Gadsden Purchase The Gadsden Purchase is the name given to a strip of land, now the southern part of Arizona and New Mexico, purchased by the U.S. government from Mexico. On Dec. 30, 1853, American diplomat James Gadsden (1788–1858) signed a treaty whereby Mexico ceded a rectangular strip of about 76,760 km^2 (29,640 mi^2), in the Mesilla Valley south of the Gila River, for $10 million. Negotiated by the Democratic administration of President Franklin Pierce, the treaty offered Southerners a route for a railroad to the Pacific. Before such a project could be undertaken, however, the Civil War intervened.

Gaea [jee'-uh] In Greek mythology Gaea (or Gaia) was the goddess of Earth and the daughter of CHAOS. She was regarded as the mother of all creation, preceding Zeus and the other Olympian gods. She gave birth to URANUS, the sky, and with Uranus she produced the TITANS. Other offspring followed, of whom some were such frightful monsters, like the CYCLOPS, that Uranus decided to imprison them in the depths of the Earth. Gaea took vengeance by instigating Uranus's castration. In Roman mythology, she was identified with Tellus and Terra.

Gaelic language see CELTIC LANGUAGES

gag rules The gag rules were procedural rules first adopted by the U.S. House of Representatives on May 25–26, 1836, to prevent debate of the slavery question. In the 1830s ABOLITIONISTS presented thousands of petitions to Congress, calling for abolition of slavery in the District of Columbia, an end to the slave trade, and refusal of admission to the Union of more slave states. In response, a coalition of Southerners and Northern Democrats in the House secured passage of rules to stifle debate on this issue. Opposition to the rules was led by former President John Quincy Adams, who deplored the infringement of the right to petition. With the rise of antislavery sentiment in the North, he was finally able to secure repeal of the rules on Dec. 3, 1844.

Yuri Gagarin, a Soviet cosmonaut, became the first man in space on Apr. 12, 1961, when his Vostok 1 spaceship orbited the Earth once and made a successful reentry.

Gagarin, Yuri [gah-gah'-rin, yoo'-ree] The Soviet cosmonaut Yuri Gagarin, b. Mar. 9, 1934, d. Mar. 27, 1968, was the first man in space. Gagarin, an air force jet pilot, was chosen with the first group of Soviet cosmonauts in March 1960. On Apr. 12, 1961, he was launched into orbit in the VOSTOK 1 spaceship. It reached a maximum altitude of 327 km (203 mi) and circled the Earth once before landing near the Volga River. After a series of triumphant world tours, Gagarin was assigned as training director of the brief women-cosmonaut program (1961–63) and later returned to flight status for the SOYUZ program. When he was killed in the crash of a MIG trainer jet in 1968, he was given a state funeral, and his ashes were interred in the Kremlin Wall. A prominent crater on the back of the Moon is named for him.

Gage, Thomas Thomas Gage, b. 1719 or 1720, d. Apr. 2, 1787, was a British general in North America during the years preceding the outbreak of the American Revolution. He first came to America to serve in Edward BRADDOCK's expedition of 1755, and he was subsequently active in several campaigns against the French. Appointed (1760) governor at Montreal, he went to New York in 1763 as commander-in-chief of the British forces. In 1774 he became governor of Massachusetts, where he attempted to quell agitation and enforce the INTOLERABLE ACTS. It was Gage who ordered the troops to Lexington and Concord in April 1775. After the Battle of BUNKER HILL, he was recalled to England.

Gaines, Edmund Pendleton Edmund Pendleton Gaines, b. Mar. 20, 1777, d. June 6, 1849, was a U.S. military commander of the pre–Civil War period. Born in Virginia, he was a grandnephew of Revolutionary leader Edmund Pendleton. His success against the British at Fort Erie, Ontario, during the War of 1812 won him the rank of brigadier general. He fought in the Black Hawk and Seminole Wars and was censured for insubordination in the Mexican War.

Gainsborough, Thomas [gaynz'-bur-oh] Thomas Gainsborough, b. 1727, d. Aug. 2, 1788, was one of the most accomplished English painters of the 18th century, excelling in both landscapes and portraits. A Suffolk cloth merchant's son, Gainsborough went to London in 1740 to work as an assistant to the French engraver Hubert Gravelot, who had been a pupil of the rococo painter François BOUCHER. He also worked as a restorer of paintings for art dealers and thus became acquainted with work of such 17th-century Dutch landscape artists as Jacob van RUISDAEL. Gainsborough's debt to the light-hearted artificiality of the ROCOCO STYLE was tempered by his admiration for the Dutch landscape tradition and its direct observation of nature.

In 1748, Gainsborough settled in Ipswich, where he established a reputation as a portraitist. His early, small-scale works depict their unpretentious, even homely, subjects in a setting that is often stylized but sometimes naturalistic—as in *Robert Andrews and Mary, His Wife* (c.1748; National Gallery, London), who sit in a verdant landscape bordering on a cornfield. Gainsborough's early portraits of prosperous English families continue a tradi-

Thomas Gainsborough, best known for his portraits of 18th-century British aristocrats, painted The Morning Walk, *a portrait of Mr. and Mrs. William Hallett, in 1785. (National Gallery, London.)*

tion that was begun by the conversation pieces of William HOGARTH.

Throughout his life Gainsborough painted and drew landscapes, but he was obliged to devote most of his time to portraiture, which was more esteemed and better remunerated. Demand for Gainsborough's portraits steadily increased when, in 1759, he moved to the fashionable spa town of Bath. There his mature style developed in numerous portraits of the aristocracy: elegantly dressed men and women depicted full-length against idyllic imaginary landscapes. His most celebrated work, *The Blue Boy* (1770; Henry Huntington Art Gallery, San Marino, Calif.), dates from this period.

In 1768, Gainsborough became a founding member of the Royal Academy of Arts in London, where he moved in 1774, and established a large portrait practice in rivalry with his great contemporary, Sir Joshua REYNOLDS. Gainsborough now numbered members of the royal family among his patrons, but many of his finest works of these years are informal portraits of his friends from the world of music and the theater.

In 1780, Gainsborough began to paint what Reynolds called his "fancy pictures." These arcadian landscapes populated with bucolic figures realized his talents in a complex synthesis. In Gainsborough's landscape drawings, discovered after his death, John CONSTABLE found encouragement for his own studies of natural scenery.

Gaiseric, King of the Vandals [gy'-sur-ik] Gaiseric, also known as Genseric, d. 477, was the founder of a 5th-century Vandal kingdom based in North Africa. Succeeding his brother Gunderic as king of the VANDALS and Alans in 428, Gaiseric led (429) his people from Spain to North Africa, which he gradually conquered from the Romans over the next 10 years. He then built a powerful fleet, with which he dominated the western Mediterranean, capturing and looting Rome in 455. At the time of his death he was ruler of what are now Tunisia, and parts of Algeria and Libya, along with Sicily, Corsica, Sardinia, and the Balearic Islands. The dynasty established by Gaiseric lasted until 533.

Gaitskell, Hugh [gayts'-kul] Hugh Todd Naylor Gaitskell, b. Apr. 9, 1906, d. Jan. 18, 1963, was leader (1955–63) of the British Labour party. Entering Parliament in 1945, he served as minister of fuel and power (1947–50), minister of economic affairs (1950), and chancellor of the exchequer (1950–51). In 1955, Gaitskell succeeded Clement ATTLEE as leader of the party, then in opposition. A moderate, he faced strong left-wing dissension, which contributed to Labour's defeat in the 1959 election. He finally reunited the party but died before his work bore fruit in Labour's electoral victory of 1964.

galactosemia [guh-lak'-tuh-see'-mee-uh] Galactosemia is an inherited inability to fully metabolize the sugar galactose, a major component of milk, to glucose. The defect occurs due to the absence of one of the enzymes that act in the conversion of galactose, which can build up to toxic levels in the body. Manifestations appear early; if untreated, an infant fails to grow and usually develops brain and liver damage and cataracts. Another sugar should then be substituted for galactose in the diet.

galago

galago [guh-lay'-goh] Galagos, or bush babies, family Galagidae, order Primates, are small, agile African primates related to the lorises but placed in a distinct separate family. They are found throughout Africa south of the Sahara wherever trees are present. They spend much of their time in trees and can jump swiftly from branch to branch or across open grasslands. Their rapid hopping locomotion is aided by two elongated ankle bones. The larger galagos have bushy tails that aid in balancing.

The needle-clawed bush baby, or galago, is a primitive primate that nests communally in the forests of western Africa and feeds on insects and fruit. It looks more like a squirrel than a primate and has large eyes and ears, a long, bushy tail, and thick silky fur.

Galahad, Sir

Galahad, Sir [gal'-uh-had] In the Arthurian legends Galahad was a knight of the Round Table who succeeded in the quest for the Holy GRAIL through his unexcelled spiritual purity. Galahad was the son of LANCELOT and Elaine the Fair of Astolat. He gradually replaced PARSIFAL as the hero of the Grail legends in the 13th century, when they became invested with Christian symbolism. Galahad was the king of Sarras when he died. He was taken into heaven with the Holy Grail.

See also: ARTHUR AND ARTHURIAN LEGEND.

Galápagos Islands

Galápagos Islands [guh-lahp'-uh-guhs] The Galápagos Islands are a group of 13 main volcanic islands and numerous islets in the Pacific Ocean about 965 km (600

The map indicates the location of the Galápagos Islands, a volcanic archipelago in the Pacific Ocean that is administered by Ecuador.

mi) off the coast of South America. The islands constitute a province of Ecuador, and their official name is Archipiélago de Colón. They have a total area of 7,845 km^2 (3,029 mi^2) and a population of 9,243 (1989 est.). The capital is San Cristóbal.

Because they are located in the path of the cold Peru Current, the islands have a climate that is generally cool and dry for islands that lie on the equator. The coastal zones are desolate, but the upper slopes of the high volcanic mountains (some reaching 1,525 m/5,000 ft) receive heavy precipitation and support a dense vegetation.

The islands are noted for their distinctive life forms, including giant land tortoises, flightless cormorants, and marine iguanas. In 1985 a fire charred Isabela Island and drew attention to the fact that increasing numbers of settlers (and tourists) and attendant development are threatening the ecological balance of the islands. Conservationists are also trying to control the species introduced by humans and to stop the poaching of protected species.

Discovered by the Spanish in 1535, the Galápagos (Spanish, meaning "tortoises") sheltered buccaneers and whalers until Ecuador annexed and settled the islands in 1832. The naturalist Charles DARWIN used his observations of the islands in 1835 in constructing his evolutionary theory. In 1991 drowned older islands of the group were discovered on the nearby seafloor.

Galatea

Galatea [gal-uh-tee'-uh] In Greek mythology Galatea was a nymph, noted for her great beauty, who was loved by the Cyclops POLYPHEMUS. Another Galatea was a statue loved by PYGMALION, king of Cyprus. He prayed to Aphrodite that the statue might be given life. His prayer was answered, and Pygmalion and Galatea were married. The story was the model for George Bernard Shaw's play *Pygmalion* (1913), which in turn was the basis for the musical *My Fair Lady* (1956).

Galatia

Galatia [guh-lay'-shuh] Galatia was an ancient territory of central Anatolia, now part of Turkey. It was named for its early inhabitants, a branch of an Indo-European tribal confederation called CELTS or Galli (Gauls). These tribes crossed into Anatolia in 278 BC at the invitation of Nicomedes I of Bithynia, who sought their aid in war.

Thereafter they began to ravage and plunder on their own. By 275 the Seleucid king Antigonus I had defeated and settled them in an area stretching from southwest to northeast through the central Anatolian plateau, the area that subsequently bore their name.

Always warlike, the Galatian tribes were employed as mercenaries and fought both against and for the Hellenic kingdoms of Anatolia. Galatia became a Roman protectorate in 85 BC. In 25 BC the Romans created a larger province of Galatia, administered from Ancyra (modern Ankara), that enclosed the Galatians between Cappadocia and the province of Asia on the west. Saint Paul's Epistle to the Galatians addressed the Christian churches founded there.

Galatians, Epistle to the [guh-lay'-shuhnz]   The Epistle to the Galatians is one of the books of the New Testament. It was written by Saint Paul in answer to opponents who were trying to convince the Galatian Christians that circumcision was necessary for salvation. The letter, written about AD 54–55, is the fourth epistle in the collection of Pauline letters in the Bible.

The Galatians lived in north central Anatolia. Their faith evidently had been disturbed by the insistence of some Jewish Christians on close ties to Judaism even for gentile converts to Christianity. Paul replied by developing the theme of the efficacy of salvation in Jesus Christ. This epistle and the Epistle to the Romans served as prime sources for the Reformation teaching on justification by faith.

galaxies   see EXTRAGALACTIC SYSTEMS

Galaxy, The [gal'-uhk-see]   The galaxy in which we live, usually referred to simply as the Galaxy, or the Milky Way—which is actually only the portion visible to the naked eye—is a giant spiral assemblage of several billion stars, including our Sun. Its true shape, size, and nature were not discovered by astronomers until the 20th century. It is now known to be an immense disk-shaped object, far larger than most of the galaxies in its immediate neighborhood (the LOCAL GROUP OF GALAXIES). Its visible disk has a diameter of approximately 100,000 light-years and a height above its principal plane of about 1,000 light-years, although some kinds of objects, such as globular CLUSTERS, extend much farther above the galactic plane.

The total mass of the Galaxy can be measured by studying the motions of individual stars and clouds of hydrogen gas in different parts of the Galaxy and by applying CELESTIAL MECHANICS to calculate a total mass that will account for the observed motions. The mass can also be determined from the motions of the Galaxy's small satellite galaxies, especially the nearby dwarf elliptical galaxies and globular clusters. Computations by both methods agree that the Galaxy's mass is possibly 1,000 to 2,000 billion times the mass of the Sun. As the Sun's mass is about average for a star in the Galaxy, the total number of stars must also be of this order. Most of these stars are invisible from the Earth, however, because the solar sys-

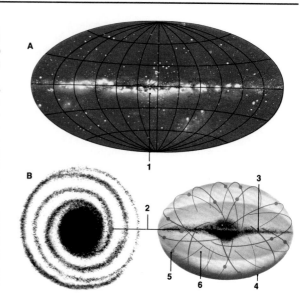

From the Earth, the Milky Way, which lies along the plane of the Galaxy, appears as a circular band of light around the sky, which contains dust and gas, as well as stars (A). The dust is sufficiently dense to prevent visual observation of the Galaxy's center (1) in Sagittarius. A view of the Galaxy from above (B) reveals a spiral-shaped structure with the Sun (2) about 30,000 light-years from the center. An edge-on view shows a hubbed disk (3) surrounded by a spherical halo region (4) containing globular clusters (5) and high-velocity stars, and by an intermediate region (6) containing planetary nebulae.

tem lies in the dense plane of the Galaxy, where interstellar dust obscures all but its nearer parts.

The Sun lies a little more than 30,000 light-years from the center of the Galaxy. From our vantage point, the Galaxy appears thicker toward its center, in the direction of the constellation Sagittarius, and somewhat thinner in other directions. Because of the obscuration by dust, however, which limits our view in all directions, it is difficult to realize from observation that we are not near the center of the system.

Determination of Galactic Structure

Until the 1920s it was thought that the system of stars outlined by the Milky Way was the entire universe; early attempts to understand the structure of the Galaxy were thought of as studies of the universe itself. In 1784, Sir William Herschel concluded that we live in the central region of a flat, round arrangement of stars that extends far along the Milky Way.

A much more accurate view of the Galaxy resulted from Harlow Shapley's studies of globular clusters, begun in 1914. By determining the size of the system of globular clusters that lie above and below the obscuration of the Milky Way plane, he determined that the Galaxy is about ten times larger than previously thought, that the Sun is a considerable distance from the center, and that the clusters make up a thin, spherical halo that surrounds a bright, flat disk. The detailed structure of the disk was difficult to discover because of the dust. An important breakthrough occurred in 1951, when Harvard scientists Harold Ewen and Edward Purcell made the first radio detection of the 21-cm emission line of neutral hydrogen gas in the Milky Way. By 1954, Dutch and Australian radio astronomers were ready to assemble a radio map of the Galaxy. Since radio waves pass through the dust unimpeded, this map was far more accurate than those based on visual observations. The result clearly showed a complex and beautiful spiral structure, very much like that of the giant galaxy Messier 101 or the Whirlpool Galaxy, Messier 51.

Our present view of the Galaxy is based on highly detailed radio maps of neutral atomic hydrogen gas and other sources, including hot gas clouds and gas-dust complexes that emit radiation from various molecules and parts of molecules, such as water (H_2O), carbon monoxide (CO), and hydroxyl (OH). The Galaxy consists of a slightly warped, scalloped disk of heavy-element–rich stars, gas clouds, and dust, surrounded by a tenuous spherical halo of old, heavy-element–poor stars and star clusters. The halo extends 85,000 light-years from the center and is enveloped by a corona extending to at least 200,000 light-years.

In recent years astronomers have begun to examine the core of the Milky Way in other wavelengths (see INFRARED ASTRONOMY; RADIO ASTRONOMY; X-RAY ASTRONOMY). Infrared studies have revealed a small number of fast-moving red supergiant stars within 5 light-years of the center. Strong radio and X-ray emissions from the same area suggest that a BLACK HOLE may exist in that region and that it may be generating the extremely hot gases spiraling around the galactic center at speeds of up to 700,000 kilometers per hour. Heavy-metal synthesis, which accompanies the formation of new stars, is also thought to occur in that region. Farther out are dramatic radio-wave-emitting filaments perpendicular to the galactic plane; these arcs of matter, approximately 150 light-years long, suggest that a huge magnetic field exists around the galactic core. Unrelated to these arcs are three bizarre, threadlike structures, uniformly bright and about 1 light-year wide and more than 100 light-years long, that cut across the central galactic regions. These threads remain unexplained.

This panoramic map of the celestial sphere was drawn at the Lund Observatory in Sweden on the basis of many photographs. The map illustrates 7,000 stars, the Milky Way, the Magellanic Clouds, the Andromeda galaxy, and several nebulae. The galactic center is in the Sagittarius region at the center of the map. The Great Rift, a dark cloud of interstellar dust, extends from the constellation Sagittarius to the constellation Cygnus at left center. The number of stars decreases from Sagittarius to Auriga, shown at both ends, and toward the galactic poles at top and bottom.

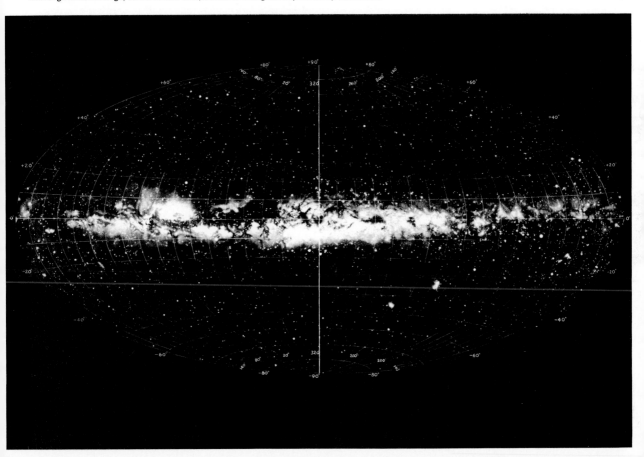

Composition of the Galaxy

Our galaxy, like most well-studied spiral galaxies, chiefly consists of stars, gas, and dust. Studies of its visible disk indicate that most of the mass is in the stars, with only about 2% gas (mostly hydrogen) and about 0.01% dust.

The Galaxy's stars have been divided into Population I and Population II. Population I stars, prevalent in the spiral arms, include stars of all ages. They contain elements heavier than helium, in ratios comparable to those found in the Sun. Population II stars occur in the bulge around the galactic nucleus and in the spherical halo, including its globular clusters. Population II stars are about 12 to 15 billion years old and are deficient in heavy elements. These are the Galaxy's oldest inhabitants, and they are frequently offered as evidence that the Galaxy itself is 15 billion years old.

The total amount of stars, gas, and dust observed to exist in the Galaxy does not quite equal the total measured mass, suggesting that the Galaxy contains matter in some invisible form, such as neutrinos, molecular hydrogen, black holes (collapsed large stars), or meteoroids. Recent investigations, however, suggest that the "missing mass" may be found in the corona, the composition of which is unknown; the corona may contain between 100 and 200 billion solar masses.

Dynamics of the Galaxy

In 1927, Jan H. Oort of the Netherlands showed that the motions of stars in different parts of the Milky Way could be used to derive the properties of the rotation of the Galaxy, including the velocity of the Sun through space. When modern values are used in Oort's equations, it is found that the Sun's velocity is approximately 250 km/sec in its orbit around the galactic center. The velocities for stars at larger distances from the center are lower than in the inner part of the Galaxy. These velocity differences cause differential rotation in the disk, and they may be the primary cause of the spiral shape of the arms (and also, incidentally, of the rotation of the bodies in the solar system, including the Earth).

The dynamics of the spiral arms are still only imperfectly understood. Differential rotation will make spiral arms out of almost any structural feature in a galaxy, but the arms should last only a fraction of the age of the galaxy. It would lead to a rapid winding-up of the arms in the 50 or so rotations that have occurred since the Galaxy was formed.

Determinations have been made of the Galaxy's movement as a whole, relative to the rest of the universe. For example, high-altitude measurements were made of the universe's BACKGROUND RADIATION, the residual glow of the so-called "big bang" that is assumed to have occurred in the first moments of the universe (see COSMOLOGY). The measurements indicated that the Galaxy is moving, relative to the universe, in the same direction as the constellation Leo lies relative to the Earth, and with a velocity of more than 600 km/sec (373 mi/sec). The Galaxy is also moving at about 100 km/sec (62 mi/sec), relative to the center of mass of the local group of galaxies. The local group, in turn, is moving at a comparable velocity relative to the supercluster of galaxies to which it belongs. This large-scale flow of galaxies is apparently directed toward a huge, distant region of space that has been called the Great Attractor. The cause of this flow is one of the major problems occupying modern cosmology.

See also: EXTRAGALACTIC SYSTEMS; STELLAR EVOLUTION.

Galba, Roman Emperor [gal'-buh]   Galba, 3 BC–AD 69, was Roman emperor from AD 68 to 69. Respected by Augustus and Tiberius, he governed Aquitania, served (33) as consul, commanded Roman forces in Gaul, and governed (60) Hispania Tarraconensis (Hither Spain). When Nero committed suicide in 68, Galba's praetorian guards supported him as caesar, and he marched to Rome with Otho, governor of Lusitania. Galba was noted for his integrity and extreme thriftiness. When he adopted a successor, Otho was enraged and conspired with the praetorians. Galba was murdered, and Otho assumed the imperial title.

Galbraith, John Kenneth [gal'-brayth]   John Kenneth Galbraith, b. Ontario, Canada, Oct. 15, 1908, is a U.S. economist whose provocative theories have stirred national interest and debate. Galbraith taught economics at Harvard University from 1949 to 1975. He was U.S. ambassador to India from 1961 to 1963 and has also served as an economic advisor to John F. Kennedy, Adlai Stevenson, and other major political figures.

The impact of the large industrial CORPORATION on modern society has been a continuing concern in Galbraith's writing. In *American Capitalism* (1952) he suggested that the restraints on large corporations came not from competitors on the same side of the market but from "countervailing powers" on the opposite side of the market, such as large labor unions. Subsequent books, including *The Affluent Society* (1958; 4th ed., 1984) and *The New Industrial State* (1967; 4th ed., 1985), described American industrial structure. In Galbraith's view, the large corporation insulates itself from market forces, manages consumer demand through advertising, and emphasizes growth of output above profit maximization. A

The American economist John Kenneth Galbraith, an advisor to such political figures as Adlai Stevenson and John F. Kennedy, has exerted considerable influence over the nation's long-range economic planning.

versatile stylist, Galbraith's other books include *Ambassador's Journal* (1969), *Economics and the Public Purpose* (1973), *The Voice of the Poor* (1983), and *Economics in Perspective* (1987).

Galen [gay'-len]   The Greek physician Galen, AD 130–200, did notable work in the field of human anatomy despite being confined to dissecting animals such as pigs, dogs, and goats. He identified numerous muscles for the first time and showed the importance of the spinal cord, noting the resulting paralysis when the cord was cut at different levels. Galen was also the first to consider the pulse a diagnostic aid. His physiological theories include concepts of blood formation, digestion, and nerve function. His written treatises survived as the medical authority until the 16th century, when Andreas Vesalius and, later, William HARVEY amended Galen's theories.

galena [guh-leen'-uh]   Galena, a lead sulfide, PbS, is the most important ore mineral of lead. Its metallic, lead-gray cubic crystals (isometric system) and cubic, perfectly cleavable masses are distinctive and characteristic. Hardness is 2½, streak lead gray, and specific gravity 7.4–7.6. Galena is a widespread mineral deposited by hydrothermal solutions as irregular masses in dolomitized limestones and in zones of contact metamorphism (see METAMORPHIC ROCK), and as veins in volcanic rocks. It often contains enough silver to be mined as an ore.

See also: ORE DEPOSITS; SULFIDE MINERALS.

Galena is a common, soft, dark gray or black lead sulfide mineral. The major commercial source of lead, it is usually found in metal-bearing veins as cubic crystals or as granular masses.

Galerius, Roman Emperor [guh-lir'-ee-uhs]   Gaius Galerius Valerius Maximianus, b. AD c.242, d. May 311, was Roman emperor from 305 to 311. From 293 a junior member (caesar) of the tetrarchy established by DIOCLETIAN, Galerius improved his status with a decisive victory over the Persians in 297–98, and when Diocletian and Maximian retired in 305, he became the senior emperor (augustus) in the East. He was an able administrator who managed to hold together an empire divided by civil war in the West. Just before his death, he issued an edict of toleration that granted freedom of worship and opened the way for the legalization of Christianity by CONSTANTINE I.

Galicia (Central Europe) [guh-lish'-ee-uh]   Galicia was the name given to the southern Polish territories annexed by Austria in the 1st and 3d Partitions of Poland (1772, 1795). The region was regained by POLAND in 1918–19. In 1939, East Galicia was annexed to the USSR; it remained part of the USSR after World War II (see UKRAINE).

The official Austrian name for the region—Kingdom of Galicia and Lodomeria—derived from the medieval principality of Galich (Polish, Halicz). The region was under Mongol rule before becoming part of Poland in 1340. The Hungarians had earlier laid claim to it, and the Austrian Habsburgs, who inherited the Hungarian crown, used this claim as a legal pretext for taking these lands in 1772.

Galicia had a population of 7,316,000 in 1910; 59% spoke Polish, 31% Ukrainian, and 10% Yiddish. Ukrainians predominated in eastern Galicia and Poles in western Galicia. Poor soil, lack of significant industry, and rural overpopulation led to massive emigration around the turn of the century. In 1868, Galicia was accorded limited self-government, with Polish education and administration. Thus it was the only part of partitioned Poland in which Polish political and cultural life could develop freely. The concurrent development of Ukrainian national consciousness later provided the pretext for the Soviet annexation of eastern Galicia.

See also: AUSTRIA-HUNGARY; POLAND, PARTITIONS OF.

Galicia (Spain) [gah-leeth'-ee-ah]   Galicia is a historic region and former kingdom in the northwestern corner of Spain; it is bounded by the Bay of Biscay on the north, the Atlantic Ocean on the west, and Portugal on the south. LA CORUÑA is the principal industrial city, and SANTIAGO is the religious and cultural center. The population speaks a dialect closely related to Portuguese. Today the region comprises the provinces of La Coruña, Lugo, Orense, and Pontevedra. During the 6th century BC the region was settled by the Celtic Gallaeci tribe for whom the region was named. In 137 BC, Galicia was conquered by Rome. It was the independent kingdom of the Suevi tribe from AD 410 until 585, when it was conquered by the Visigoths. Occupied briefly (718–57) by the Moors, it was soon retaken and in 914 became part of the kingdom of Asturias. In the 13th century Galicia was part of Castile.

Galilee [gal'-i-lee]   Galilee was the northern province of ancient Palestine. Located east of the Sea of Galilee and the Jordan River, with the plain of Acre on the West, Galilee is roughly coextensive with the boundaries of northern Israel. The province is known as both a cultural melting pot and a major farming region because of its position on the major trade route between Egypt and Syria and its fertile land.

Jesus Christ, known as "the Galilean" (Matthew 26: 69), was raised in the Galilean city of NAZARETH and spent

most of his life there. Galilee, especially the city of TIBE-
RIAS, became the center of rabbinic learning after the fall
of Jerusalem in AD 70; the Mishnah was codified and
the Talmud produced there. Many 1st-century ruins of
Galilean synagogues have since been excavated.

Galilee, Sea of

The Sea of Galilee, or Sea of Tibe-
rias (Hebrew: Yam Kinneret; Arabic: Bahr Tabariya), is a
lake in northeastern Israel. It is 21 km (13 mi) long, by
12 km (7.5 mi) at its widest point and has an area of 166
km² (64 mi²). It lies 212 m (696 ft) below sea level and
has a maximum depth of 48 m (157 ft). Of the several
towns and villages on its shores, TIBERIAS, on the west
bank, is the largest. Agricultural settlements ring the
lake, which is the source of irrigation carried by canal and
tunnel as far as the Negev in southern Israel. It is also
important as a fishing ground and tourist attraction.

Basalt ridges flank the basin—part of the GREAT RIFT
VALLEY—that holds the Sea of Galilee, and alluvial plains
are to the north and south. The lake is fed principally by
the JORDAN RIVER, which also provides drainage from its
southern end.

The Sea of Galilee features prominently in the New
Testament, since Jesus Christ worked and preached in
the towns surrounding it and is reputed to have walked on
its water.

Galileo

[gal-i-lee'-oh]   Originally known as the Jupiter
Orbiter and Probe, *Galileo* is the first spacecraft designed
to orbit the planet JUPITER and send a probe into its atmosphere. After repeated delays over a period of several
years, *Galileo* was finally launched from a Space Shuttle
on Oct. 18, 1989. Its six-year flight will take it past Venus once and Earth twice and will include fly-bys of two
asteroids, Gaspra and Ida, before reaching Jupiter in December 1995. While in orbit around the planet, *Galileo*
will take closer looks at the moons Io, Ganymede, Callis-
to, and Europa. The spacecraft contains an electric generator powered by a plutonium isotope.

Galileo Galilei

[gal-i-lay'-oh gal-i-lay'-ee]   Galileo
Galilei, b. near Pisa, Italy, Feb. 15, 1564, d. Jan. 8,
1642, was a pioneer of modern physics and telescopic
astronomy. In 1581 he entered the University of Pisa as a
medical student, but he soon became interested in mathematics and left without a degree in 1585.

After teaching privately at Florence, Galileo was made
professor of mathematics at Pisa in 1589. There he is
said to have demonstrated from the Leaning Tower that
Aristotelian physics was wrong in assuming that speed of
fall was proportional to weight; he also wrote a treatise on
motion, emphasizing mathematical arguments. In 1592,
Galileo became professor of mathematics at the University of Padua, where he remained until 1610. He devised a
mechanical calculating device now called the sector,
worked out a mechanical explanation of the tides based
on the Copernican motions of the Earth, and wrote a trea-

Galileo Galilei built the first astronomical telescope in 1609 and with it made observations sup-porting his belief in the Copernican model of the solar system, a view he was later forced to deny. Galileo also overturned an accepted precept of Aristotle when he stated that falling bodies accelerate uniformly.

tise on mechanics showing that machines do not create
power, but merely transform it.

In 1602, Galileo resumed his investigations of motion
along inclined planes and began to study the motion of
pendulums. By 1604 he had formulated the basic law of
falling bodies, which he verified by careful measurements.

Late in 1604 a supernova appeared, and Galileo became involved in a dispute with philosophers who held
(with Aristotle) that change could not occur in the heav-
ens. Applying the mathematics of PARALLAX, Galileo found
the star to be very distant, in the supposedly unchange-
able regions of the cosmos, and he attacked Aristotelian
qualitative principles in science. Returning to his studies
of motion, he then established quantitatively a restricted
inertial principle and determined that projectiles moved
in parabolic paths. In 1609 he was writing a mathematical treatise on motion when news arrived of the newly invented Dutch telescope. He was so excited at the possible
scientific applications of such an instrument that he put
all other work aside and began to construct his own telescopes.

The Telescope and the Copernican Theory. By the end of
1609, Galileo had a 20-power telescope that enabled
him to see the lunar mountains, the starry nature of the
Milky Way, and previously unnoted "planets" revolving
around Jupiter. He published these discoveries in *The
Starry Messenger* (1610), which aroused great controversy until other scientists made telescopes capable of confirming his observations. The Grand Duke of Tuscany
made him court mathematician at Florence, freeing him
from teaching to pursue research. By the end of 1610 he
had observed the phases of Venus and had become a firm
believer in the Copernican HELIOCENTRIC WORLD SYSTEM. He
was vigorously opposed in this belief because the Bible
was seen as supporting the opposite view of a stationary
Earth. Galileo argued for freedom of inquiry in his *Letter
to the Grand Duchess Christina* (1615), but despite his
argument that sensory evidence and mathematical proofs
should not be subjected to doubtful scriptural interpretations, the Holy Office at Rome issued an edict against
Copernicanism early in 1616.

Trouble with the Church. In 1623, Maffeo Barberini, long friendly to Galileo, became pope as Urban VIII, and Galileo obtained his permission to write a book impartially discussing the Ptolemaic and Copernican systems. This became Galileo's famous *Dialogue* (1632), for which he was called to Rome for trial by the Inquisition on the grounds that in 1616 he had been personally ordered never to defend or to teach Copernicanism. In June 1633, Galileo was condemned to life imprisonment for "vehement suspicion of heresy." His *Dialogue* was banned, and printers were forbidden to publish anything further by him or even to reprint his previous works. Outside Italy, however, his *Dialogue* was translated into Latin and was read by scholars throughout Europe.

Galileo's sentence was swiftly commuted to house arrest, at first under custody of the friendly archbishop of Siena and then at his own villa in Arcetri, near Florence. There Galileo resumed and completed his Paduan studies on motion and on the strength of materials, published at Leiden as *Discourses and Mathematical Demonstrations Concerning Two New Sciences* (1638). He rightly regarded this as containing the elements of a new physics that would be carried further by his successors.

See also: PHYSICS, HISTORY OF.

Gall [gawl] Gall, b. *c.*1840, d. Dec. 5, 1894, called Pizi in the Lakota Siouan language, was a famous SIOUX warrior who fought in the Battle of the LITTLE BIGHORN (1876) in which George Armstrong CUSTER and the 7th Cavalry were killed by Indian forces. He was a leader in the Hunkpapa section of the Sioux encampment, which was the focal point of Custer's attack. With SITTING BULL and CRAZY HORSE, Gall had led Indian attempts to thwart the construction of forts and roads through the Lakota Sioux buffalo country. In late 1876, after the Little Bighorn encounter, Gall and Sitting Bull retreated into Canada. Gall returned to the United States with part of the Hunkpapa band in early 1881. After a brief battle with Gen. Nelson A. MILES, he was taken as a prisoner to Fort Buford. He was released (June 1881) to the Standing Rock Indian Reservation in South Dakota, where he converted to Christianity, cultivated land, and attempted to live up to treaty agreements.

gall see DISEASES, PLANT

Gall, Franz Joseph see PHRENOLOGY

Gallatin, Albert [gal'-uh-tin] Albert Gallatin, b. Geneva, Switzerland, Jan. 29, 1761, d. Aug. 12, 1849, was a distinguished diplomat and U.S. financier of the early national period. He emigrated to America in 1780 and settled in Fayette County, Pa., where he acquired substantial landholdings. In 1790 he entered the state legislature, where he worked to secure reform of the penal code, the abolition of slavery, and the creation of a public educational system. He displayed notable financial ability and devised a plan for the liquidation of the state debt.

Albert Gallatin, the U.S. secretary of the Treasury (1801–14) under Presidents Jefferson and Madison, reduced the national debt by half in the years before the War of 1812. He excelled not only as a financial expert but as a diplomat.

Distrustful of centralized government, Gallatin helped organize the Republican, or Democratic-Republican, party in Pennsylvania. As a member of the House of Representatives (1795–1801), he rendered outstanding service to the party. Jefferson named him secretary of the treasury in 1801, a post he held until 1814. By stringent governmental economy, Gallatin was able to reduce the national debt by one-half before the War of 1812. In 1814 he served as peace commissioner at Ghent and then, until 1823, as minister to France. As minister to Britain in 1826 he was successful in renewing existing agreements and arranging for the joint occupation of Oregon.

Keenly interested in the study of the American Indians, Gallatin published (1836) *A Synopsis of the Indian Tribes in North America.* Often called the father of American ethnology, he was instrumental in founding the American Ethnological Society in 1842.

Gallaudet (family) [gal-uh-det'] **Thomas Hopkins Gallaudet**, b. Philadelphia, Dec. 10, 1787, d. Sept. 10, 1851, was an American who made important contributions to the education of the DEAF. He went to England to study the oral method of teaching the deaf but preferred the sign method, which he learned at the Institut Royal des Sourds-Muets (Royal Institute for Deaf-Mutes) in Paris. He returned to the United States and established the first free school for the deaf, the American Asylum for Deaf-Mutes, in Hartford, Conn. His older son, **Thomas Gallaudet** (1822–1902), an Episcopal minister, founded a church for the deaf in New York City. His younger son, **Edward Miner Gallaudet** (1837–1917), helped establish (1864) Gallaudet College (now Gallaudet University) for the deaf.

Gallaudet University Established in 1864, Gallaudet University, in Washington, D.C., is the only liberal arts institution in the United States devoted to educating the deaf and teachers of the deaf. The library contains works dating from 1546 on the subject of deafness. On campus are an elementary and a secondary school for the deaf. In 1988, under pressure from student protests, the board of trustees appointed the institution's first deaf president.

gallbladder [gawl'-blad-ur]   The gallbladder, in humans, is a small, pear-shaped sac that stores bile, or gall, a yellowish brown or green fluid, secreted by the liver, that aids in the digestion of dietary fat. Upon stimulation by the hormone cholecystokinin, the gallbladder contracts and discharges the bile into the small intestine.

Bile contains bile salts, cholesterol, mucus, fat, lecithin, cells, cellular debris, and the breakdown products from hemoglobin. The bile salts, sodium glycocholate and sodium taurocholate, emulsify fats, facilitating their absorption by cells lining the passage of the small intestine.

Cholecystokinin is produced in the wall of the duodenum, the initial segment of the small intestine, and is released into the bloodstream when the duodenum lining is stimulated by fat coming from the stomach.

Cholecystitis (inflammation), generally caused by GALLSTONES, may require the removal of the gallbladder, by either traditional or laparoscopic surgery, which uses a much smaller incision and has a faster recovery time. In the absence of the organ, bile passes directly from the liver to the small intestine.

See also: DIGESTION, HUMAN.

Gallegos, Rómulo [gah-yay'-gohs, roh'-moo-loh]
The Venezuelan novelist, educator, and political leader Rómulo Gallegos, b. Aug. 2, 1884, d. Apr. 4, 1969, used methods acquired during his formative modernist period to portray Venezuelan rural life with a comprehensiveness and clarity that won international acclaim. In his novels, set in the various areas of Venezuela, the landscape became a principal force. His prolific production began with *El último solar* (The Last Manor, 1920), and he secured his reputation with *Doña Bárbara* (1929; Eng. trans., 1931). Other major novels include *Cantaclaro* (Chanticleer, 1934) and *Canaima* (1935), concerning an evil spirit, "Canaima," that lurks in the tropical forest. Gallegos was elected president of Venezuela on Dec. 14, 1947, but was ousted in a coup on Nov. 24, 1948.

galleon [gal'-ee-uhn]   The galleon was a large, 3- or 4-masted ship developed during the 15th and 16th centuries as a merchant vessel and warship. During the late 1500s it was the standard vessel of European navies (see NAVAL VESSELS). Galleons were more slender than previous sailing ships, their lines resembling those of the oared GALLEY; and they were built without the earlier overhanging forecastle that had made sailing to windward almost impossible. Sir John HAWKINS streamlined the English galleons ever further, and it was his light, maneuverable fleet that defeated the heavier ships of the SPANISH ARMADA.

With the development of the galleon naval battle tactics were revolutionized. Where earlier ships had to use

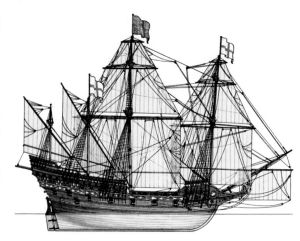

The galleon, a large, three-masted sailing vessel, was developed as a warship but was commonly used as an armed merchantman. Its size and armament capacity made it the dominant warship of the late 16th century.

oarsmen to bring them within boarding range of the enemy, the galleon could hold its position into the wind and use its broadside banks of cannon to shell enemy ships lying at a distance.

galley   Galleys were warships that were driven by oars in battle and equipped with sails for cruising (see NAVAL VESSELS). In use for over two millennia, the galley was the standard European battle vessel until the late 16th century, when the sail-powered, more heavily armed GALLEON began to replace it.

The earliest galleys about which much is known were Greek and Phoenician warships of early classical times. The largest of these were biremes, which had two banks of oars. By the time of the Persian Wars, the Greeks were

This Venetian galley (c.1545), a merchantman, was equipped with a single lateen sail in addition to the single bank, or row, of oars on either side.

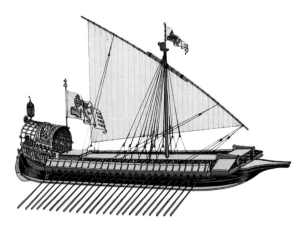

also using triremes, galleys with three banks of oars.

A different kind of trireme became the dominant type of late medieval galley. In this type, three oarsmen, each having his own oar, shared the same bench. Instead of piercing the hull along three levels, the oars passed over the wales along the same level in clusters of three. Early modern galleys typically had about 24 banks of oars; their hulls were 36–39 m (120–130 ft) long and just over 6 m (20 ft) wide.

Beginning about 1550 the trireme was replaced by galleys in which four or more oarsmen on the same bench pulled a single large oar. This change accompanied a shift from predominantly free oarsmen to convicts and slaves. Sometimes as many as eight oarsmen were used on each bench. In the Battle of Lepanto (1571), the last great galley fight, some galleys had over 200 oarsmen.

Gallic Wars [gal'-ik]

Julius CAESAR's campaigns in GAUL (58–51 BC) are collectively termed the Gallic Wars. In 58 BC, Gallic agitation against the Suevi, a German tribe that had recently conquered territory in Gaul, and the threat of invasion by the Helvetii, a Celtic tribe from the area that is now Switzerland, gave Caesar a pretext to advance his career through war. Lack of cavalry support almost caused Caesar's defeat by the Helvetii at Bibracte, but his legions rallied and forced the Helvetii to withdraw (58). In the same year Caesar's army defeated and killed the Suevi's leader Ariovistus in Alsace after a hard campaign.

In 57, Caesar successfully met the attacks of the Gallic Belgae and Nervii and established Roman control over what is now Belgium and northern France. The following year he conquered the Atlantic coast and massacred the German Usipites and Tencteri, who had entered Belgium. His invasions of Germany (55) and Britain (55 and 54) accomplished little.

The winter of 54 and most of 53 were spent suppressing sporadic revolts in northern Gaul. The biggest threat came in 52 when a coalition of tribes in central Gaul under Vercingetorix rose against the Romans. Caesar finally besieged and defeated Vercingetorix at Alesia. Except for minor uprisings in 51 BC, serious Gallic resistance had ended.

The Gallic Wars provided Caesar with wealth, a trained loyal army, and enormous popularity to use against his rivals at Rome.

Gallicanism [gal'-i-kuhn-izm]

Gallicanism is the name commonly given to a complex of theological doctrines and political positions that emphasized the relative independence from the PAPACY of the Roman Catholic church in France and the French king. The Gallican theorists argued that the decisions of ecumenical councils had supremacy over the pope (see CONCILIARISM), that all bishops were of divine institution, and that the French kings were absolutely independent of Rome in all temporal questions. A more radical form, called parliamentary Gallicanism, also argued that the church must be subordinated to the state and that the state could intervene in the church's financial and disciplinary problems. Although Gallicanism can be traced back at least to the 14th century, it reached its fullest manifestation during the 17th and 18th centuries and was best enunciated in the Four Articles, approved by LOUIS XIV in 1682.

Gallieni, Joseph Simon [gahl-lee-ay'-nee]

Joseph Simon Gallieni, b. Apr. 24, 1849, d. May 27, 1916, was a French general who worked to integrate France's colonial conquests into the FRENCH COLONIAL EMPIRE. In the course of his military and administrative career he served in the Upper Niger area, Martinique, French Sudan, Indochina, and Madagascar. In Madagascar he introduced compulsory labor as part of his policy to have the natives raise their own standard of living.

In 1911, Gallieni declined the position of supreme commander of the French army because of ill health and age. He was appointed military governor of Paris in August 1914 and raised troops to drive back the Germans in the First Battle of the Marne. He served as minister of war from 1915 to 1916 and was made a marshal of France posthumously.

gallinule [gal'-uh-nool]

Gallinule is the common name for several birds of the RAIL family, Rallidae. Like the closely related coots, gallinules are often mistaken for ducks but have cone-shaped bills. They prefer marshes with openings of shallow water congested with aquatic vegetation. Their long toes permit them to appear at times to be walking on water; actually, they are supported by lily pads and other surface growth. The common gallinule, *Gallinula chloropus,* is slate gray and drab except for a bright red forehead and red and yellow bill. It is distributed over most of the temperate regions of the world. The

The gallinule, or moorhen, is an aquatic bird common everywhere except Australasia. Its head shield is similar to the coot's.

colorful purple gallinule, *Porphyrula martinica,* of warmer regions of the New World, is deep purple with a green back, pale blue forehead plate, and red and yellow bill.

Gallipoli campaign   see WORLD WAR I

▬

Gallipoli Peninsula   The Gallipoli Peninsula in western Turkey is a narrow, hilly projection that separates the Aegean Sea from the DARDANELLES. It was known as the Thracian Chersonese in classical times. About 80 km (50 mi) long, this remote area is separated from the rest of Turkey by the Garros Hills, which rise to a height of 915 m (3,000 ft). The port of Gallipoli, which was once an important post on the Dardanelles, is now a small fishing center and military garrison. During WORLD WAR I the peninsula was the scene of the Gallipoli campaign (1915).

▬

gallium [gal'-ee-uhm]   The chemical element gallium is a bluish metal of Group IIIA in the periodic table. Its chemical symbol is Ga, its atomic number is 31, and its atomic weight is 69.72.

Gallium is a relatively rare metal that has become important in the manufacture of SEMICONDUCTOR electronic devices. Its existence was originally detected spectroscopically; it was isolated for the first time from zinc sulfide ore in 1875 by the French chemist Lecoq de Boisbaudran, who named it after *Gallia,* the Latin name for France. Later the same year, Dmitry Mendeleyev showed that gallium was the missing Group IIIA element below aluminum and above indium predicted in his theory of chemical periodicity.

Gallium is present in the earth's crust in an average abundance of 5–15 ppm. It often occurs in small amounts as Ga_2S_3 in the sulfide ores of zinc and germanium, and it is a minor component in all aluminum ores. No important mineral deposits contain a high percentage of gallium.

Most of the world's gallium is produced in the United States. The metal is recovered by controlled electrolysis of the concentrated alkaline liquors that are by-products of the extraction of aluminum and zinc from their ores. Ultrapure gallium for electronics is obtained by repeated fractional crystallization of the metal. Gallium is relatively expensive because of its low concentration in most minerals and because the metal must be extremely pure for most applications.

The pure metal has a slight bluish luster resembling that of zinc. Its melting point (29.78° C) is unusually low, and the boiling point (about 2,250° C) is not precisely known because the metal is highly active at high temperature. Molten gallium expands in volume by 3.2% on freezing; among all the other elements only bismuth shares this property.

Gallium normally forms compounds in the trivalent state. A +1 state also exists, but it is easily oxidized to gallium(III). A rare +2 state has been reported, but all gallium(II) compounds are unstable. At room temperature the metal is kept from corroding in air by a protective oxide film of Ga_2O_3. Hot molten gallium forms alloys with most other metals.

The most important gallium compounds are the semiconductors, formed with the elements phosphorus, arsenic, and antimony. The most widely used and studied compound is gallium arsenide, GaAs, which has important applications in solid-state microwave generators and photoelectric cells. It is also used in LASERS, because the light emitted from GaAs diodes (electroluminescence) is coherent and has a narrow frequency bandwidth. Gallium compounds have no known biological function, and ordinary gallium salts have very low toxicity.

▬

Galloway, Joseph [gal'-oh-way]   Joseph Galloway, b. West River, Md., *c.*1731, d. Aug. 29, 1803, was a prominent loyalist during the American Revolution. He was speaker of the Pennsylvania Assembly from 1766 to 1775. As a delegate to the First Continental Congress (1774), he tried to avert the imminent break with Britain. He proposed a scheme for self-government to the colonies while maintaining allegiance to the mother country, suggesting that all legislation affecting the colonies be approved both by Parliament and by a council representing the American states. The plan was rejected, and when war came Galloway sided with the British. He went to England in 1778.

▬

gallstone [gawl'-stohn]   Gallstones, or cholelithiasis, are hard masses of stonelike material found in the GALLBLADDER or the bile duct (see LIVER). They are composed mainly of CHOLESTEROL, as well as calcium bilirubinate, calcium carbonate, or a mixture of all three. Their mechanism of formation is unknown and probably varies with their chemical nature. Predisposing factors include heredity, obesity, certain diseases, and drugs.

Surgical removal of gallstones—usually by removal of the gallbladder as well—effects a cure in 95 percent of all cases. In elderly patients or those in poor health, stones may be removed nonsurgically by widening the bile duct with an ENDOSCOPE. Depending on the type of stone, the gallbladder may also be flushed with various solvents. The nonsurgical method called lithotripsy, used in breaking up KIDNEY STONES, has been modified in several ways for the more difficult internal location of the gallbladder.

▬

Gallup [gal'-uhp]   Gallup (1990 pop., 19,154), the seat of McKinley County in northwestern New Mexico, is situated on the Puerco River. Founded in 1880 as a supply base for the Atlantic and Pacific Railroad, it later flourished as a commercial center for a timber and ranching region; today coal and uranium are mined in the area. It is a major market for neighboring Indian reservations. Fort Wingate, an army ordnance depot, is nearby.

Gallup, George George Horace Gallup, b. Jefferson, Iowa, Nov. 18, 1901, d. July 26, 1984, pioneered the development of techniques for measuring PUBLIC OPINION. He helped make the OPINION POLL one of the most characteristic institutions of 20th-century America. While director of research at New York's Young and Rubicam advertising agency, a position he held from 1932 to 1947, he founded (1935) the American Institute of Public Opinion. Gallup used market research methods to sample opinion on behalf of clients in government, business, universities, and the news media.

Galsworthy, John [gawlz'-wur-thee] John Galsworthy, b. Aug. 14, 1867, d. Jan. 31, 1933, was an English novelist, short-story writer, essayist, and playwright who won the Nobel Prize for literature in 1932. He is chiefly remembered for THE FORSYTE SAGA, a series of novels adapted for television in the late 1960s. Galsworthy was educated at Harrow and New College, Oxford, and trained as a lawyer. His works reflect a privileged background but also show a desire to analyze contemporary society and document its changes from the late Victorian period to that following World War I. Novels such as *The Island Pharisees* (1904), *Fraternity* (1909), and *The Freelands* (1915) reveal these interests, but *The Forsyte Saga,* collectively published in 1922, best achieved his objectives. This sequence of novels includes *The Man of Property* (1906), *In Chancery* (1920), and *To Let* (1921), and had two sequels, *A Modern Comedy* (1929) and *End of the Chapter* (1931–32). Other works about the Forsytes include *On Forsyte 'Change* and *Soames and the Flag* (both 1930).

Galsworthy's plays also reflect his interest in social documentation. They include *Strife* (1909), which led to prison reform; *The Skin Game* (1920), in which the old landed class confronts the new industrial aristocracy; and *Loyalties* (1922), which deals with racial hatred. His collections of essays include *A Sheaf* (1916), *Castles in Spain* (1927), and *Glimpses and Reflections* (1937).

Galt, Sir Alexander Tilloch [gawlt] Alexander Tilloch Galt, b. London, Sept. 6, 1817, d. Sept. 19, 1893, was a political leader of the English-speaking community of Canada East (Quebec) before Confederation and a pioneer Canadian diplomat. He became a clerk and later the commissioner of the British American Land Company, settling the Eastern Townships of Quebec.

Galt was a member of the Legislative Assembly of United Canada (1849–50, 1853–67) and then of the Canadian House of Commons (1867–72). He was active in railway promotion, especially for the Grand Trunk Railway, and he was also an early advocate of a transcontinental union for British North America. Minister of finance in Conservative administrations from 1858 to 1862 and 1864 to 1866, he was a prominent participant in the financial part of the discussions that resulted in Confederation (July–October 1867). He served as the first federal minister of finance (1867–68) in the administration of John A. MACDONALD but retired from politics in 1872. He was the first Canadian high commissioner in Great Britain (1880–83).

Galton, Sir Francis [gawl-tuhn] Francis Galton, b. Feb. 16, 1822, d. Jan. 17, 1911, was an Englishman who investigated mental differences between individuals, using new statistical methods. His work stimulated interest in heredity patterns and the potential of selective parenting in the early part of the 20th century (see EUGENICS). He developed the correlation method and was an early proponent of statistical analysis as applied to mental and behavioral phenomena. He also made important contributions to the fields of meteorology, anthropometry, and physical anthropology.

Interest in the role of heredity led Galton to introduce the method of twin studies to examine the different contributions of nature and nurture. He also inquired into racial differences and was one of the first to employ questionnaire and survey methods, which he used to investigate mental imagery in different groups. Galton was knighted in 1909.

The British novelist and dramatist John Galsworthy, recipient of the 1932 Nobel Prize for literature, is remembered chiefly for his three trilogies tracing the history of the fictional Forsyte family. In these and other works, Galsworthy examines the mores of late Victorian and Edwardian society.

The British scientist Sir Francis Galton, who pioneered the use of statistical methods for studying human heredity and intelligence, is now best remembered as the founder of modern eugenics. He also worked out the basic principles of fingerprint classification.

Galvani, Luigi [gahl-vah'-nee]   The Italian physician Luigi Galvani, b. Sept. 9, 1737, d. Dec. 4, 1798, is best known for his experiments on "animal electricity," which led Alessandro VOLTA to the discovery of current ELECTRICITY. Galvani was trained at the medical school at Bologna and after graduation practiced medicine and surgery, conducted physiological research, and taught medicine at Bologna. In 1780 he undertook carefully planned and executed experiments on the effects of static electricity on nerves and muscles. Using prepared frogs, Galvani observed continual muscle contractions when the spinal cords were connected by brass hooks to an iron railing. Galvani took this as confirmation of the theory that animal nerve and muscle tissue contained an electric fluid. Volta, however, later demonstrated that the electricity did not come from the animal tissue but from the different metals—brass and iron—coming into moist contact with each other.

galvanometer [gal-vuhn-ah'-muh-tur]   A galvanometer, a device named for Luigi GALVANI, is an instrument that measures the amount of electrical current by converting electrical energy into the physical displacement of a coil, which in turn moves a pointer or light beam. The direct-current ammeter is a type of calibrated galvanometer that measures larger currents; a calibrated galvanometer may also be used as a direct-current voltmeter, which measures direct voltage using Ohm's law. Galvanometers are currently being replaced by modern digital instruments.

Galveston [gal'-ves-tuhn]   Galveston, a city in southeast Texas, lies on the northeastern end of Galveston Island at the entrance to Galveston Bay, an inlet of the Gulf of Mexico. The seat of Galveston County, it has a population of 59,070 (1990). The city is a deepwater port of entry whose economy is based on oil refining, shipbuilding, dry-cargo export, and food processing. Tourists are attracted by the mild climate and the resort facilities along its beaches. Galveston is the site of the University of Texas Medical Branch, Galveston Community College, a Coast Guard base, and Texas Maritime Academy.

Visited by Spanish and French explorers and buccaneers, Galveston was founded and laid out in 1836 by Michel B. Menard. During the Civil War it was a major Confederate supply port. Over 5,000 lives were lost and much of the city was destroyed by a hurricane that struck on Sept. 8, 1900. A massive seawall was then built to protect the city.

Galway (city) [gawl'-way]   Galway (Gaillimh), the seat of County Galway on the west central coast of Ireland, is on the River Corrib at the head of Galway Bay. It has a population of 47,104 (1986). Iron foundries, fisheries, and a black-marble quarry form the major industries. University College was founded in 1849. The earliest settlement dates from a fortification built there in 1124; Anglo-Normans took the city in 1232. The fishing village of Claddagh is across the river, and Salthill, a popular resort, is nearby.

Galway (county)   Galway is a county in western Ireland on the Atlantic coast in the historic province of Connacht. The town of Galway is the county seat. The county has a population of 178,552 (1986) and covers 5,940 km^2 (2,293 mi^2). Galway is bisected from north to south by Lough Corrib. To the west the mountains of Connemara district reach 730 m (2,400 ft); silver, lead, and copper are mined there, and marble is quarried. To the east, oats, wheat, and root crops are grown, and sheep and cattle are raised. Tourism, textile manufacturing, and fishing are also important. Galway has the largest percentage of Gaelic speakers of any county in Ireland.

Galway, James   The popular Irish flute virtuoso James Galway, b. Dec. 8, 1939, took up the flute, which his father played, after briefly studying the violin. At the age of 15 a scholarship permitted him to attend the Royal College of Music and the Guildhall School in London; later he enrolled at the Paris Conservatory. After playing in various London orchestras, he became principal flutist of the London Symphony and the Royal Philharmonic, and from 1969 to 1975 was first flutist of the Berlin Philharmonic. Galway has since pursued a highly successful soloist's career, giving concerts and making several television appearances.

Gama, Vasco da [gah'-mah, vahs'-koh dah]   The Portuguese navigator Vasco da Gama, b. Sines, Portugal, c.1460, d. Dec. 24, 1524, led an expedition at the end of the 15th century that opened the sea route to India by way of the Cape of Good Hope. Entering the service of the Portuguese king John II, he helped to seize French ships in Portuguese ports in 1492.

Many years of Portuguese exploration down the West African coast had been rewarded when Bartolomeu DIAS rounded the Cape of Good Hope in 1488. The Portuguese then planned to send a fleet to India for spices and to outflank the Muslims in Africa. Vasco da Gama was placed in command of the expedition and carried letters to the legendary PRESTER JOHN and to the ruler of Calicut, on India's Malabar coast.

Four ships left Lisbon on July 8, 1497—the *São Gabriel,* on which da Gama sailed, the *São Rafael,* the *Bérrio,* and a storeship. They stopped in the Cape Verde Islands, reaching the Cape of Good Hope region on November 7. The expedition rounded the cape on November 22 and reached Mozambique on Mar. 2, 1498. There the sultan of Mozambique supplied them with pilots. They stopped in Mombasa and Malindi before sailing to the east. They crossed the Indian Ocean in 23 days, aided by the Indian pilot Ibn Majid, and reached Calicut on May 20, 1498. Unfortunately, the Arabs who dominated trade in the

Vasco da Gama, the Portuguese navigator who in 1497–98 opened a maritime trade route from Europe to India, appears in a contemporary drawing. (Bibliothèque Nationale, Paris.)

Indian Ocean region viewed the Portuguese as rivals. As a result, da Gama was unable to conclude a treaty or commercial agreement in Calicut. After one further stop on the Indian coast, the Portuguese set out to return with a load of spices. They took three months to recross the Indian Ocean, however, and so many men died of scurvy that the *São Rafael* was burned for lack of a crew. The expedition made a few stops in East Africa before rounding the Cape of Good Hope on Mar. 20, 1499. The ships were separated off West Africa in a storm and reached Portugal at different times. Da Gama stopped in the Azores and finally reached Lisbon on Sept. 9, 1499.

Da Gama's success led to the dispatch of another Portuguese fleet, commanded by Pedro Álvares CABRAL. Some of the men Cabral left in India were massacred, so King Manuel I ordered da Gama to India again. He was given the title of admiral and left Portugal in February 1502 with 20 ships. The Portuguese used their naval power on both the East African and Indian sides of the Indian Ocean to force alliances and establish their supremacy. Da Gama's mission was a success, and the fleet returned to Lisbon in October 1503.

Da Gama then settled in Portugal, married, and raised a family. He may have served as an advisor to the Portuguese crown and was made a count in 1519. King John III sent him to India in 1524 as viceroy, but he soon became ill and died. Vasco da Gama's first voyage to India linked that area to Portugal and opened the region to sea trade with Europe. On that foundation the Portuguese soon built a great seaborne commercial empire, with colonies in India and the Spice Islands.

Gamaliel of Jabneh [guh-may'-lee-ul jab'-nee]
Gamaliel of Jabneh succeeded JOHANAN BEN ZAKKAI in the leadership of Jewry toward the end of the 1st century AD. A great-grandson of HILLEL the Elder, he was head of the

SANHEDRIN at Jabneh, a leading center of Judaism after the siege of Jerusalem in AD 70. Gamaliel is credited with organizing the synagogue service. He also standardized the Jewish calendar, assigning fixed dates to festivals.

Gambetta, Léon [gahm-be-tah', lay-ohn']   Léon Gambetta, b. Apr. 2, 1838, d. Dec. 31, 1882, was a French statesman who helped to found the Third Republic. A lawyer, he gained fame for his defense of a revolutionary agitator in 1868 and was elected to the Legislative Assembly in 1869. As war minister during the FRANCO-PRUSSIAN WAR (1870–71), he worked vigorously to avert the French defeat. After NAPOLEON III surrendered at Sedan, Gambetta made a dramatic escape by balloon from besieged Paris and directed a "people's war" against the Germans from southwest France.

Gambetta left office in 1871 when the National Assembly accepted Germany's humiliating peace terms. After the radical COMMUNE OF PARIS was crushed later that year, he returned to politics to help consolidate the new Third Republic. He wrote articles supporting the republic in his paper *La République française* and worked to unite various groups of republicans. In 1877, when President Patrice MACMAHON, who was a monarchist, arbitrarily dissolved the Chamber of Deputies, Gambetta campaigned to ensure a republican majority in the elections. After MacMahon's resignation (1879) Gambetta became president of the Chamber.

He became premier in 1881, but his attempt to end factionalism among republicans made him appear to be an aspiring dictator. He sought to institute voting reforms, press freedoms, and laws for the separation of church and state. If successful, Gambetta might have changed the Third Republic's system to resemble Great Britain's parliamentary government, but he was voted out of office in 1882.

Gambia [gam'-bee-uh]   Gambia (or The Gambia) is a tiny coastal republic of West Africa. Totally surrounded by Senegal except for its Atlantic coast, the country occupies the lower and central Gambia River valley and is one of Africa's smallest nations. Its narrow strip of land is only about 24 to 48 km (15 to 30 mi) wide and stretches eastward from the Atlantic Ocean for 475 km (295 mi). Gambia gained independence from Britain in 1965.

Land, People, and Economy

Gambia occupies a river valley and is thus a low-lying country. In the west the land adjacent to the river is very low and dominated by dense mangrove swamps. At Elephant Island, 130 km (80 mi) inland, this terrain gives way to higher riverbanks and cliffs punctuated by marshes.

North and south of this riverine strip are higher flats called *banto faros,* a Mandingo phrase meaning "beyond the swamp." Near the Atlantic the flats are often flooded with salt water. Beyond the *banto faros,* toward the northern and southern borders, lies higher, better-drained land that supports the cultivation of sorghum and rice, the major subsistence crops, and peanuts, Gambia's most

AT A GLANCE

REPUBLIC OF THE GAMBIA

Land: Area: 11,295 km² (4,361 mi²). Capital and largest city: Banjul (1983 pop., 44,536).

People: Population (1990 est.): 848,147. Density: 75 persons per km² (194.5 per mi²). Distribution (1985): 20% urban, 80% rural. Official language: English. Major religion: Islam.

Government: Type: republic. Legislature: House of Representatives. Political subdivisions: 6 districts, Banjul.

Economy: GDP (1989 est.): $195 million; $250 per capita. Labor distribution (1986 est.): agriculture—75%; industry, commerce, and services—19%; government—6%. Foreign trade (1989): imports—$105 million; exports—$133 million. Currency: 1 dalasi = 100 butut.

Education and Health: Literacy (1985): 25% of adult population. Universities (1991): none. Hospital beds (1981): 756. Physicians (1981) 66. Life expectancy (1990): women—50; men—46. Infant mortality (1990): 140 per 1,000 live births.

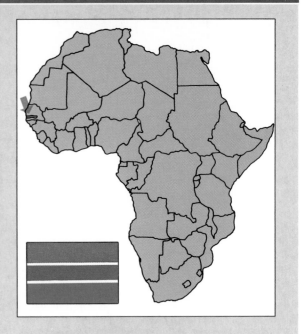

important export. The highest point in the country, near the eastern border, rises to only 49 m (160 ft).

The climate is tropical, with a rainy season that lasts from June to October. Average annual temperatures range from 25° C (77° F) in the west to 28° C (82° F) in the east. On the coast, annual precipitation averages 1,295 mm (51 in); in the interior it averages 1,090 mm (43 in).

The peoples of Gambia may be divided into five major groups whose languages fall into two categories. The dominant Mandingo agriculturalists and the Seranuleh traders speak West Atlantic languages; Mande speakers include the pastoralist Foula as well as the Wolof and Jola cultivators. Although each people has its own language, Mandingo serves as a lingua franca, and English is the official language. About 90% of the country's inhabitants are Muslim. BANJUL is the capital and largest city.

The Gambian economy is heavily dependent on peanuts and peanut by-products, which provide nearly 90% of export earnings. Agriculture was adversely affected by drought during much of the 1980s, and the country suffers from a chronic trade deficit and relies on extensive foreign aid.

History and Government

Attracted by the river, most peoples of Gambia emigrated from neighboring parts of today's Senegal. By the 15th century, Mandingo settlers associated with the Mali empire had settled in the valley, founding a cluster of kingdoms that controlled trade along the river. Muslim religious wars in the 19th century resulted in the more complete Islamicization of the region and brought further immigration.

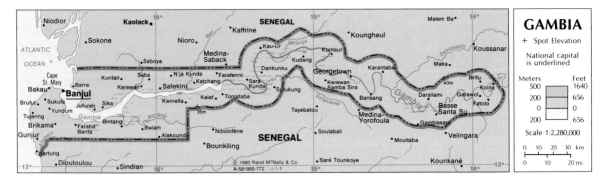

The Portuguese first reached the Gambia River in 1455 and sold trading rights to the British in 1618. In 1660 the British established a fort on Fort James Island. During the 18th century, Britain and France struggled for supremacy in the area. The British established a trading post at Bathurst at the mouth of the river in 1807 and carved out a zone of influence. In 1889, its present boundaries were settled with France, and Gambia became a crown colony. Slavery was abolished there in 1906. In 1965 the colony became independent.

According to the constitution of 1970, Gambia is a republic headed by a president; Dawda K. Jawara and his People's Progressive party have ruled since independence. On Feb. 1, 1982, in the wake of a 1981 coup attempt put down with the aid of Senegalese troops, Gambia and Senegal inaugurated the Confederation of Senegambia. Each nation would retain its sovereignty, but their armed forces would be integrated, their foreign and domestic policies coordinated, and monetary and economic union created. Deteriorating relations between the two nations led to the formal dissolution of the confederation on Sept. 30, 1989.

Gambia River   The Gambia River, an important trade artery in West Africa, rises in the Fouta Djallon highlands of Guinea, West Africa. It flows north and west through Senegal and Gambia, meeting the Atlantic Ocean at Cape St. Mary, near Banjul. The middle course of the river has numerous islands, the largest being Elephant and MacCarthy islands. The river is 1,125 km (700 mi) long and navigable to large oceangoing vessels from its mouth to Kuntaur, 242 km (150 mi) upstream.

gambling   Gambling is the wagering of money or other valuables on the outcome of a game or other event. Gambling has been known throughout recorded history. Dice carved from antelope bones have been found in prehistoric tombs and burial caves. The ancient Egyptians played atep, a game of guessing the number of fingers held up. The classical Greeks are known to have played with astragals, the forerunner of dice, and Jews in biblical Israel gambled by throwing dice.

Although few societies have ever wholly approved of gambling, none has been able to eradicate it completely. Today the United Kingdom appears to have the most liberal gambling laws, but legal gambling can be found in many other places, among them Macao, Monaco, Puerto Rico, Scandinavia, and Yugoslavia. In the United States the forms of gambling that have been legalized vary from state to state. By the late 1980s a majority of U.S. states ran LOTTERIES.

The games most closely associated with gambling usually involve a heavy element of chance. Whereas POKER, for instance, requires skill to play well, the outcome of the game is determined primarily by the distribution of the cards. Many casino games, such as ROULETTE and craps (see DICE GAMES), are dictated solely by chance. Betting on the outcome of sporting events—especially on

HORSE RACING—or on a lottery is perhaps the most widespread legal form of gambling, and in many countries, some wagering is sponsored by the government.

Illegal gambling—in the United States and elsewhere—constitutes one of the largest "businesses" in existence, and its "gross" has been estimated to exceed that of its legal counterpart.

Today, as throughout history, gambling is not confined to any economic stratum. Compulsive gambling is recognized as a sickness, and such organizations as Gamblers Anonymous exist for the purpose of providing help.

game management   Game management is the branch of wildlife management concerned with animals that people hunt for sport and food. It takes the form of laws that control FISHING and HUNTING activities. It may also involve programs for maintaining a good balance between predators and prey in a given area, for establishing game preserves and WILDLIFE REFUGES, and for stocking or restocking areas with desired game species.

The first forms of game control were those established in different areas to protect the hunting rights of leaders and aristocrats. Such efforts were exercises in privilege rather than attempts to manage game in the modern sense of the term. Wide concern about preservation of game stocks arose only with the rapid expansion of settled areas in the 19th century and the near or total extermination of various species by overhunting (see ENDANGERED SPECIES). From mid-century onward, various governments have enacted increasingly stringent game laws and management programs, establishing hunting seasons and setting kill limits. The U.S. game conservation program is directed by the Fish and Wildlife Service.

Good game management requires the use of all available resources of biological and environmental information (see ECOLOGY). Thus even establishment of game preserves may offer hazards of ecological imbalance, once threatened species begin breeding in number.

game theory   The theory of games might be called the mathematics of competition and cooperation. It analyzes situations in terms of gains and losses of opposing players. It is applied widely in economics, operations research, military science, political science, organization theory, and the study of bargaining and negotiation. First formulated in the 1920s by the mathematician John VON NEUMANN, it did not become well known until the publication (1944) of the monumental work *Theory of Games and Economic Behavior* by von Neumann and the economist Oskar Morgenstern. Since then many others have joined in extending and applying the theory.

Although the terminology of players, moves, rules, and payoffs might suggest a preoccupation with sports or recreation, the theory of games has seldom been of practical use in playing real games. This may be because the theory is based on idealized players who have clear motives and unlimited skill and calculating ability. Nevertheless, familiar parlor games can be used to illustrate certain aspects of game theory. CHESS is a typical "game of perfect information." Because there are no hidden moves, it is possible in principle to determine whether each board position is a win for White, a win for Black, or a draw; this is the "minimax value" of the position and is discussed below. Moreover, for each player there exists an "optimal pure strategy"—a complete plan of action that guarantees the player the minimax value of the starting position regardless of how opponent plays. Poker, in contrast, is a game of "imperfect information" because decisions must be made without knowing the identity of the concealed cards. As a result, good play usually demands the use of purposely randomized behavior, or "mixed strategies." For example, certain situations call for a bluff—not based on certainty but on a small probability. Poker also illustrates how there may be no universally best way to play, even in principle. Indeed, when there are more than two players the theory predicts only a "noncooperative equilibrium," in which each player's best strategy depends on the strategies adopted by the other players.

The mathematical cornerstone of game theory is the Minimax Theorem, discovered by von Neumann in 1928. It asserts that every finite, zero-sum, two-player game has a minimax value if mixed strategies are allowed. This means that every such game has a solution (an optimal strategy); it may, however, be difficult to find the solution. In this theorem, "zero-sum" means that any gain in payoff for one player represents an equal loss for the other. Many parlor games are zero-sum, but the "games" that are found in economics or in operations research usually are not, since wealth may be created or destroyed.

The Minimax Theorem does not apply to nonzero-sum games or to games with more than two players. Nevertheless, such games do have a weaker form of solution, a noncooperative equilibrium in which no player, acting on the assumption that the other players' strategies are fixed, can gain anything by changing his or her own strategy. This theorem was proved in 1950 by John Nash, and these solutions are often called Nash equilibria.

The theory of cooperative games provides another approach to games with more than two players. It is concerned primarily with "coalitions"—groups of players who coordinate their actions and perhaps even pool their winnings. A cooperative game can often be put into the form of a characteristic function, $v(S)$, which expresses for each set of players S the amount they can get if they form a coalition excluding the other players. In an economic context, $v(S)$ might represent the gross product achievable by an arbitrary subset of the national economy, or, in an industry model, the prospective profit of each set of firms acting as a cartel. In a political context, $v(S)$ could be defined to be 1 for sets of legislators that have enough votes to pass a bill and 0 for sets that do not. Often, however, a single characteristic function $v(S)$ is not enough to describe the essential worth of a coalition, and more complex mathematical forms must be employed.

More than a dozen solution concepts for cooperative games have been introduced, serving different analytical purposes. One of them, introduced by Donald Gillies and

Lloyd Shapley in 1953 and named the "core," is defined as the set of outcomes of the game that are "socially stable," in that no coalition has the power to force an improvement for its members. This means that if there is a characteristic function v, then the total payoff to each set of players S must be at least $v(S)$. Unfortunately, if coalitions are too strong the core may fail to exist, and if the coalitions are too weak, the core may include a great variety of different outcomes and not provide a satisfactory solution of the game. In many important economic applications, however, the core does give a sharp solution that is closely related to the classical equilibrium of supply and demand. For this reason, core theory has become a useful theory in the field of mathematical economics.

___

Gamelin, Maurice Gustave [gah-muh-lan', mohr-is gue-stahv'] Maurice Gustave Gamelin, b. Sept. 20, 1872, d. Apr. 18, 1958, was the French commander of Allied forces on the Western Front in the early stages of World War II. Commissioned in the French Army in 1893, he was a divisional commander in World War I. A believer in the MAGINOT LINE, he became (1938) chief of staff of national defense and assumed field command in late 1939. In May 1940 he was unable to resist the German invasion of France and was replaced by Maxime WEYGAND on May 19. He was later tried by France's Vichy government and interned (1943–45) in Germany.

___

games Games are models of real-life situations in which—unlike real life—the issues are quite simply drawn and the participants can become engaged without all the confusions that surround everyday action and decision making. Typically, games simulate the more intense human experiences: physical combat, intellectual contest, and the expectancy and excitement involved in random occurrences.

Details of many games may be found in separate articles on individual games (for example, MONOPOLY). Games

This board-and-tile game is based on a gaming board excavated from a royal tomb in the ancient city of Ur. The board, which dates from the 4th millennium BC, is believed to be the forerunner of backgammon.

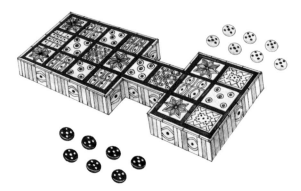

of physical skill that have become organized sports are discussed under their separate names (BASEBALL, FOOTBALL, and so on) and in the article SPORTS, HISTORY OF.

Games of Physical Skill. Games of physical skill are those in which the outcome is determined by the athletic abilities of the players. At the simplest level such games may not even involve competition. In some very simple cultures there are no competitive games. In these groups one is more likely to find group-effort games: a ball is kept up in the air cooperatively by all the players, or the players, holding hands, whirl around in a circle while trying not to fall over. These games are not unlike those played in early childhood in Western society.

Perhaps the most universal game in societies that have only competitive physical-skill games are those involving spear throwing through a target rolled between two teams.

In modern society the simplest physical-skill games are such contests as races, archery, and darts. Most modern games, however, are combinations of physical skill and strategy. This combination is most apparent in the many varieties of ball games, such as American football.

Games of Chance. Until fairly recently, with the growth of state-sponsored lotteries, pure games of chance were not particularly welcome in the United States. Today, however, more money is spent on them and on GAMBLING than on any other types of games. The simplest games of chance usually involve some form of dice or other random number selection that determines the outcome, as in bingo or the lottery.

Games of chance, however, have been increasingly combined with strategy, so that real knowledge helps to determine the outcome. In Monopoly, for example, chance combined with strategy leads by cumulative steps to a winner who can buy out everyone else in the game.

Games of Strategy. Games of strategy, either by themselves (chess) or in combination with chance (poker) or with physical skill (ice hockey), are the characteristic games of the 20th century. A game of strategy is defined by the fact that its outcomes must be determined by rational decision making.

In the history of civilization, games of strategy seem to have emerged when societies increased in complexity to such an extent that there was need for diplomacy and strategic warfare. In the Asian game of wiqi, or go, where the players attempt to surround each other's pieces, one has the experience of a blockading kind of warfare. The Indoeuropean game of chess, by contrast, has been seen as a battle between different social orders, with the status of each member—from king to pawn—being carefully stated.

Word Games and Solitary Games. The original word game is undoubtedly the riddle, which is essentially a strategic contest over information. The player must be able to untangle the riddle's linguistic deceits in order to discover the answer.

The arrival of printing in the 15th century, and the spread of the ability to read, enormously increased the number of word games. Today, some word games involve the guessing of enacted meanings, as in charades. Others

With rules simple enough for children to learn, go is Japan's most popular board game. Players try to surround points on the board, as well as their opponent's pieces, with their own pieces.

require the guessing of correct answers based on information provided by different systems of clues, such as geography or twenty questions.

Many modern word games can be enjoyed solitarily. Just as literacy allowed people to become solitary through reading, in a way that had never before been possible, it also gave them the tools to play solitary games. These games now include mathematical puzzles, logical puzzles, and most important, word games such as crossword puzzles.

Video Games. The video game is not simply a game of physical skill, chance, or strategy, but combines all of these to produce something completely new. There is physical skill in adjusting perceptually to the immense amount of visual information provided on the screen, which must be adapted to quickly. Many video games are programmed to allow seemingly random events to occur, so they are also games of chance. In most games, however, decisions must be made on the basis of perceived changes or recognizable logical sequences, so strategy is also involved.

Fantasy Games. It has taken some time for purely imaginative games to develop. The best known is Dungeons and Dragons, in which the players act out a scenario often derived from science fiction or fantasy stories. The game is a drama in which the outcomes are dependent on the fantasies of the players, as well as on the rolls of the dice that determine how far a player may go toward the goal, whether or not his or her character has the ability to perform certain feats, and what kind of luck will accompany each move.

Children's Games. The first teachers of children's games are likely to be parents, and the first games are usually face games, where parents attract their infant's attention by making funny faces. In the second half of the first year the parents play hand and body games, such as "this little piggy went to market."

By the second year of life toddlers are able to mimic each other in the same way as they have mimicked their parents. By three and four years of age the child plays simple collaborative games with larger groups. By five and six years children begin to play recognizably traditional games. At the root of these games one can see the major oppositions in both animal and human culture, namely chase and escape, and attack and defense.

From seven and onward children gradually begin to play games that have less to do with symbolic survival and more to do with achievement. In general girls are less competitive than boys and play games where there is more defined turn-taking, such as jacks, hopscotch, and jump rope. Boys begin quite early to be organized into smaller-sized versions of the sports of their fathers (Little League baseball). This difference between the play of girls and boys is often repeated in the differences between men's and women's attitudes toward play, where women seem to prefer play that is more informal, spontaneous, and collaborative, while men seek play that is organized and competitive. Whether these differences are the result of genetic patterning or learned behavior is an issue that now occupies psychologists and other scientists.

gamma globulin   see BLOOD

---

gamma-ray astronomy Gamma-ray astronomy opens another window through which astronomers can observe the universe. Gamma rays (γ rays) are photons, or quanta, of extremely high-energy electromagnetic radiation having much shorter wavelengths than X rays (see X-RAY ASTRONOMY). They are produced by nuclear processes such as fission and fusion reactions and radioactive decay. Thus γ-ray astronomy provides a means for studying the most energetic processes taking place in the universe. Conversely, however, the production of γ rays by unshielded Soviet nuclear reactors in Earth orbit is proving a significant hindrance to such studies. The existence of these reactors has been publicly known since at least 1978 and their effects on γ-ray astronomy have been observed by scientists since 1980, but for unclear reasons the U.S. government kept the information classified until 1988.

Studies of γ rays can help explain the origin of the very high energy particles called cosmic rays, the composition of material throughout the galaxies, and the way in which stars begin to form deep within interstellar clouds of dust and gas. By measuring the gravitational RED SHIFT in the γ-ray region of celestial spectra, astronomers can learn more about the properties of NEUTRON STAR surfaces, QUASARS, galactic cores, and the theoretically existing BLACK HOLES.

Development. The science of γ-ray astronomy did not get started until well into the 20th century. In 1972 the first certain detection of celestial γ rays was made with equipment aboard the U.S. OSO-3 satellite (see OSO). In that same year another satellite, OSO-7, was used to detect γ-ray emission lines in the Sun's spectrum. Thereafter, knowledge of the γ-ray universe grew rapidly by means of such satellites as the U.S. *SAS-2* (1972–73) and the European *COS-B* (1975–82). These and other devices have found γ rays to be more intense in regions corresponding to the structures of our galaxy, probably

arising from the interaction of cosmic rays with interstellar gas.

Three pulsars within our galaxy, two in or near the CRAB NEBULA and the other in the constellation Vela, are emitting γ rays in fractional-second pulses. The largest discrete source of γ rays (as well as other high-energy rays) yet discovered in our galaxy is the binary star system Cygnus X-3. Gamma rays originating from outside our galaxy have been detected emanating from Supernova 1987A. Other discrete sources thus far identified include radio and Seyfert galaxies and quasars. Unexplained bursts of low-energy γ rays have also been observed, each lasting for roughly ten seconds, at intensities that fluctuate even at the shortest resolvable time intervals. No explanation has been found for the "bursters," although one theory posits that they originate in the universe's BACKGROUND RADIATION.

Instruments. Devices for detecting γ rays include assemblies of scintillators of various types. More complicated techniques use large area detectors that, in effect, supply pictures of the tracks produced by the charged particles produced by high-energy photons. These SPARK CHAMBER telescopes make it possible to distinguish γ-ray events and determine the arrival direction of each γ ray individually.

Higher-energy γ rays can produce detectable flashes of light in the atmosphere, through the Cherenkov effect of bombarded particles being caused to move at speeds faster than that at which light moves through the atmosphere (see CHERENKOV RADIATION). These flashes can be observed by suitably equipped ground-based telescopes and by high-altitude balloons. The Gamma Ray Observatory, devoted solely to the study of γ rays, was launched in 1991 from the Space Shuttle.

---

gamma rays Gamma radiation is a form of ELECTROMAGNETIC RADIATION, first detected as emissions from natural radioactive substances such as uranium, radium, and thorium. The Greek letter γ (gamma) is used to denote this phenomenon. Gamma radiation does not carry any electric charge or mass; it is a penetrating radiation. Its properties are similar to those of X rays; the distinction is made on the basis of origin. The sources of gamma rays are nuclear processes, whereas those of X rays are atomic. Gamma rays travel with the speed of light, 2.997925×10^{10} cm/sec.

There are several different sources of gamma radiation. After the emission of an alpha or beta particle from a parent nucleus, the daughter nucleus formed may have more energy than it would have in its normal state. The nucleus then deexcites by the emission of gamma rays carrying the excitation energy. Gamma radiation is also produced in a nuclear reaction such as the combination of a neutron with a proton to form a deuteron. When a particle such as an electron combines with its antiparticle, in this case a positron, they annihilate each other and give rise to gamma radiation.

Gamma radiation undergoes many diverse interactions with matter. Different interactions are observed at differ-

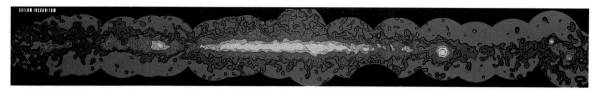

The emission of gamma rays in our Galaxy is shown in this chart by the use of colors indicating different intensities of emission. The regions of lowest intensity are in blue, ranging upward through green, red, orange, dark and pale yellow, to white regions of highest intensity. Galactic center is one such high-intensity region, as is the Vela pulsar at the middle right.

ent energy ranges. Low-energy gamma radiation may be totally absorbed by an atomic electron that is then emitted. The ejected electron is known as a photoelectron, and the process is known as the PHOTOELECTRIC EFFECT. Gamma radiation can also interact with an atomic electron, sharing its energy and giving rise to the COMPTON EFFECT, in which the gamma radiation is scattered away with reduced energy and the electron is ejected. This electron is known as a Compton electron. Gamma radiation of sufficiently high energy can also interact with the electric field of the positively charged nucleus producing an electron and a positron. This phenomenon is known as pair production. When a beam of gamma radiation passes through matter, its intensity after emergence has diminished, principally as a result of the above three processes. Very high energy gamma radiation can also cause nuclear disintegration and can eject a nuclear particle such as a neutron or a proton. Mesons can also be produced by gamma radiation of extremely high energy in its interaction with atomic nuclei.

See also: RADIOACTIVITY.

Gamow, George [gam'-ahf]

The Russian-born American physicist George Gamow, b. Mar. 4, 1904, d. Aug. 19, 1968, contributed significantly to increasing the knowledge of nuclear reactions within stars. After graduating (1928) from the University of Leningrad, he traveled in Europe. Gamow worked with Niels Bohr and Ernest Rutherford before coming to the United States in 1934. He taught at George Washington University until 1956; thereafter he was a professor at the University of Colorado.

During his early years at George Washington University, Gamow collaborated with Edward Teller in the field of nuclear physics. Gamow's elaboration of the ideas of Hans BETHE led him to important conclusions about STELLAR EVOLUTION, particularly that stars tend to become hotter as their hydrogen is depleted.

Gamow strongly supported the now generally accepted BIG BANG THEORY of the origin of the universe, first expressed by Georges Lemaître, as opposed to the steady-state theory advanced by Fred Hoyle. In the field of biochemistry, Gamow proposed (1954) that nucleic acids carry genetic code.

Gamow was noted for his popularization of science, as exemplified by his books *The Birth and Death of the Sun* (1940), *Biography of the Earth* (1941), *One Two Three... Infinity* (1947), and *A Star Called the Sun* (1964).

Gance, Abel [gahns, ah-bel']

The French filmmaker Abel Gance, b. Oct. 25, 1889, d. Nov. 10, 1981, began his career as a poet and dramatist. He entered the film industry in 1910, and within five years had established himself as a screenwriter and director: *La Folie du Docteur Tube* (1915) is a fascinating example of the use of distorting lenses and mirrors for subjective effect, and *J'accuse* (1919)—Gance's first major work—is a pacifist protest against war. Films on such subjects as the end of the world and the death of Christ show the sweep of his imagination. *La Roue* (1922) is an epic story of family life and tragedy. Even more ambitious is his epic film on Napoleon, released after three years' effort as *Napoléon vu par Abel Gance* (1927; reconstructed by Kevin Brownlow, 1980). Here he found scope for his overwhelming enthusiasm, striking technical skills, and desire to extend the limits of the film screen.

Ganda [gan'-duh]

The Ganda are a Bantu-speaking people who constitute the largest population group in Uganda, numbering more than 1,000,000. In their traditional kingdom of Buganda, the patrilineal Ganda developed a civil administration that was centralized and elaborately hierarchical. When the Europeans arrived, Buganda was the largest and most powerful of the region's great states. The capital, KAMPALA, became politically and commercially the most important town in the British Protectorate (established 1894) and later in the independent nation of Uganda. Under a law known as the 1900 Agreement, the Protectorate administration gave most of the fertile land in Buganda in freehold to individuals. This led to a series of struggles between landlords and Ganda peasants who grew cotton and later coffee as cash crops. Although the Ganda practiced no complex ritual cycle of traditional seasonal celebrations, religion and politics have been closely meshed in the often violent factional struggles that have pitted groups of Christian Ganda against each other and against Muslims.

Gander [gan'-dur]

Gander (1986 pop., 10,207) is a town in Newfoundland, Canada. Its airport, one of the largest in North America, served as an air force base during World War II. Until the early 1960s it was a refueling station for transatlantic flights.

Gandhara [guhn-dahr'-uh] Gandhara was a semi-independent kingdom that flourished from the 3d century BC to the 5th century in what is now northern Pakistan. It extended from present-day Rawalpindi through the Peshawar Valley to Kabul. The region was invaded by Persian rulers in the 6th century BC. It came under Alexander the Great in 327 BC and soon after was captured by Chandragupta Maurya; subsequently it fell to the Saka dynasty (Scythians) in 95 BC, the Kushans in AD 48, and finally to the Muslims in the 7th to the 8th century. Its main city was Taxila. Gandhara is best known for its cultural achievements, particularly its Greco-Buddhist school of sculpture.

Gandhi, Indira [gahn'-dee, in-dir'-uh] Indira Gandhi, b. Nov. 19, 1917, d. Oct. 31, 1984, became India's first woman prime minister in 1966. The only child of Jawaharlal NEHRU, India's first prime minister, she married Feroze Gandhi (no relation to Mahatma), a lawyer who died in 1960. She was made president of the ruling INDIAN NATIONAL CONGRESS party in 1959. After her father's death in 1964, Gandhi became minister of information and broadcasting, and she succeeded Lal Bahadur Shastri as prime minister in 1966. After India's decisive victory over Pakistan in 1971 (see INDIA-PAKISTAN WARS), she won an overwhelming electoral victory.

Gandhi, however, was accused of violating election laws, and her position as prime minister was threatened. These developments, and growing domestic unrest, led her to declare (June 1975) a state of emergency. She postponed elections from 1976 to 1977, suspended civil liberties, and arrested thousands of political opponents. In the March 1977 elections her party suffered a sweeping defeat at the hands of the opposition Janata (People's) party, an uncongenial coalition of six different groups, headed by her long-time challenger Morarji DESAI. Gandhi lost her own seat along with the premiership. In 1978 she returned to Parliament as head of a Congress party faction. Although she was found guilty of contempt of Parliament in 1978, she and her Congress (I) party won an overwhelming electoral victory in 1980.

Gandhi maintained close ties with the Soviet Union but continued her father's policy of nonalignment. During her last years in office, power became increasingly concentrated in the hands of the central government, and there was growing communal strife. In June 1984 she ordered the invasion of the Golden Temple at AMRITSAR by Indian troops to quell well-armed Sikh extremists in their heavily fortified headquarters there. Later that year she was assassinated by Sikh members of her own security force.

Gandhi, Mahatma [muh-haht'-muh] Mohandas Karamchand Gandhi, b. Porbandar, India, Oct. 2, 1869, d. Jan. 30, 1948, leader of the Indian nationalist movement and known in his later life as Mahatma ("great soul"), was one of the greatest national leaders of the 20th century. His methods and philosophy of nonviolent confrontation, or civil disobedience, not only led his own country to independence but influenced political activists of many persuasions throughout the world.

Gandhi's father was a chief minister for the maharaja of Porbandar, but the family came from the traditional caste of grocers and moneylenders (the name *Gandhi* means "grocer"). His mother was a devout adherent of Jainism, a religion in which ideas of nonviolence and vegetarianism are paramount.

Married by arrangement at 13, Gandhi went to London to study law when he was 18. He was admitted to the bar in 1891 and for a while practiced law in Bombay. From 1893 to 1914 he worked for an Indian firm in South Africa. During these years Gandhi's humiliating experiences of overt racial discrimination propelled him into agitation on behalf of the Indian community of South Africa. He assumed leadership of protest campaigns and gradually developed his techniques and tenets of nonviolent resistance known as *satyagraha* (literally, "steadfastness in truth").

Returning to India in January 1915, Gandhi soon became involved in labor organizing. The massacre of AMRITSAR (1919), in which troops fired on and killed hundreds of nationalist demonstrators, turned him to direct political protest. Within a year he was the dominant figure in the INDIAN NATIONAL CONGRESS, which he launched on a policy of noncooperation with the British in 1920–22. Although total noncooperation was abandoned, Gandhi continued to organize protest marches against unpopular British measures, such as the salt tax (1930), and boycotts of British goods.

Gandhi was repeatedly imprisoned by the British and resorted to hunger strikes as part of his civil disobedience. His final imprisonment came in 1942–44, after he had demanded total withdrawal of the British (the "Quit India" movement) during World War II.

Together with his struggle for political independence, Gandhi fought to improve the status of the lowest classes of society, the casteless UNTOUCHABLES, whom he called

Indira Gandhi, the daughter of India's first prime minister, Jawaharlal Nehru, dominated Indian politics for nearly two decades. She was prime minister from 1966 to 1977 and again from 1980 until her assassination in 1984.

Mahatma Gandhi, an Indian political and spiritual leader, developed the tactics of nonviolent disobedience that forced Great Britain to grant independence to India in 1947.

In his first year as prime minister of India, Rajiv Gandhi was praised for signing accords to end strife in Punjab and Assam, but as communal violence in these and other areas later increased he was charged with a failure to provide India with strong leadership. In 1987, he signed an accord with neighboring Sri Lanka designed to end violence between that country's Sinhalese majority and Tamil minority. In 1991 he was assassinated in Tamil Nadu state.

harijans ("children of God"). He was a believer in manual labor and simple living; he spun the thread and wove the cloth for his own garments and insisted that his followers do so too. He disagreed with those who wanted India to industrialize.

Gandhi was also tireless in trying to forge closer bonds between the Hindu majority and the numerous minorities of India, particularly the Muslims. His greatest failure was his inability to dissuade India Muslims, led by Muhammad Ali JINNAH, from creating a separate state, Pakistan. When India gained independence in 1947, after negotiations in which he was a principal participant, Gandhi opposed the partition of the subcontinent with such intensity that he launched a mass movement against it. Ironically, he was assassinated in Delhi by a Hindu fanatic who mistakenly thought his antipartition sentiment was pro-Muslim and pro-Pakistan.

Gandhi, Rajiv   Rajiv Gandhi, b. Aug. 20, 1944, d. May 21, 1991, succeeded his mother, Indira Gandhi, as prime minister of India on Oct. 31, 1984. Rajiv grew up in the home of his distinguished grandfather, Jawaharlal Nehru, and earned (1965) a degree in mechanical engineering. He became his mother's unofficial assistant after the 1980 death of his brother, Sanjay. In 1981 he resigned from his job to contest, and win, Sanjay's former seat in the Lok Sabha (the lower house of India's parliament); in 1983 he became a general secretary of the Congress (I) party. Appointed prime minister following his mother's assassination by Sikh extremists, he led his party to victory in 1984. Subsequently, he faced mounting opposition that was exacerbated by rising communal tensions, economic problems, and corruption charges and called new elections in November 1989. Congress lost its majority, and Gandhi resigned, becoming leader of the

opposition. He was assassinated during the 1991 elections, in which he hoped to regain power.

Gang of Four   Chinese moderate leaders, including DENG XIAOPING, used the name Gang of Four (Ssu-jen Pang) to refer to a group of leaders of the CULTURAL REVOLUTION who attempted to seize power after the death of ZHOU ENLAI in 1976. The four were arrested in September 1976, shortly after the death of MAO ZEDONG. They have since been blamed for the excesses of the Cultural Revolution and for China's backwardness in general and were brought to trial in 1980.

The four, all members of the politburo of the Chinese Communist party at the time of their arrest, were JIANG QING, Mao's widow; Zhang Chunqiao, a deputy premier; Wang Hungwen, second vice-chairman of the party; and Yao Wenyuan. They were brought to trial in November 1980 on 48 charges, including attempting to overthrow the state. Both Jiang Qing and Zhang Chunqiao refused to plead guilty, claiming that their actions had been at Mao's behest, but in January 1981 they were sentenced to death (later commuted to life imprisonment). Wang Hungwen and Yao Wenyuan were sentenced to imprisonment for life and 20 years respectively. Jiang Qing was released in 1987.

Ganges River   [gan'-jeez]   The Ganges (Ganga) River, the most sacred river of Hinduism, flows across northern India and through Bangladesh. It is 2,507 km (1,557 mi) long and drains an area of 1,035,000 km^2 (409,000 mi^2). The two main headstreams of the Ganges—the Alaknanda and Bagirathi—rise in the Himalayas near Nanda Devi. Flowing south-southeast, they join northwest of Kanpur and flow southeast and east across the heavily

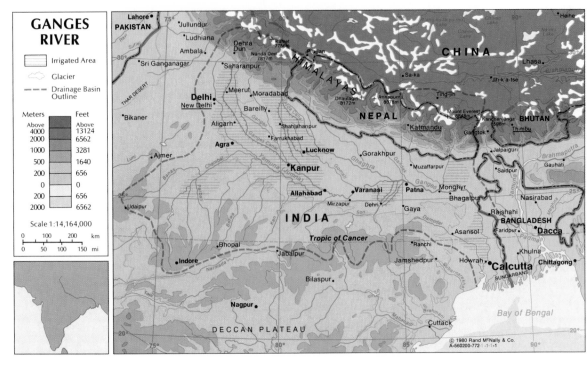

GANGES RIVER

Irrigated Area
Glacier
Drainage Basin Outline

Meters Above	Feet Above
4000	13124
2000	6562
1000	3281
500	1640
200	656
0	0
200	656
2000	6562

Scale 1:14,164,000

0   100   200   km
0   50   100   150   mi

© 1980 Rand McNally & Co.
A-560200-772 1-1-1

farmed plains of Uttar Pradesh, Bihar, West Bengal, and Bangladesh, entering the densely populated delta region 320 km (200 mi) from the sea. The Ganges and Jamuna (part of the BRAHMAPUTRA RIVER) join below Dhaka to form the Padma River, which then enters the Bay of Bengal through several mouths just west of Chittagong.

Major cities on the Ganges include the sacred city VARANASI; the commercial center ALLAHABAD; industrial KANPUR; and Patna, a rice center. Crops grown in the river basin include rice and other grains, sugar, cotton, and lac trees; cattle are also raised.

gangrene [gayn'-green]   Gangrene is the destruction of living tissue due to obstruction of its blood (and therefore oxygen) supply. Once such obstruction occurs, the gangrenous process is often caused by infection by such bacteria as *Clostridium* (gas gangrene) or a combination of streptococci and staphylococci (Meleney's synergistic gangrene).

Another common form of gangrene, diabetic gangrene, results from arteriosclerosis due to diabetes. The infection has a strong tendency to spread because the bacteria produce powerful toxins that destroy adjacent healthy tissues, making them highly susceptible to further invasion. Treatment involves antibiotics and the surgical removal of all affected tissue.

gannet [gan'-et]   Gannet is the common name for the birds of the genus *Morus*, family Sulidae, that migrate over the seas of the middle and upper latitudes of both the Northern and the Southern Hemisphere. Gannets are much larger (89–102 cm/35–40 in) than any of the gulls and have long, narrow, pointed wings, pointed tails, and cone-shaped bills. They are gregarious, nesting in large colonies on rocky shores and promontories. Spectacular divers, they plunge from heights of 15 m (50 ft) or more and often swim to great depths in pursuit of fish. In adult

The northern gannet, or solan goose, dives for fish from up to 30 m (100 ft) above the water. Air sacs beneath the skin protect it from the shock of impact.

plumages, the North Atlantic species, *M. bassanus*, is white with black wing tips and a yellow bill. Gannets are related to the boobies, genus *Sula*, of tropical seas.

Gannett, Frank E. [gan-net'] Frank Ernest Gannett, b. Bristol, N.Y., Sept. 15, 1876, d. Dec. 3, 1957, was an American NEWSPAPER publisher. He began to build a newspaper chain during the 1920s; concentrating on New York State, Gannett eventually owned more than 20 newspapers and 7 radio stations. In 1990 the Gannett Company—the largest U.S. newspaper group—owned 83 dailies (including *USA Today*), as well as a number of television and radio stations.

Gansu (Kansu) [gan'-soo] Gansu, a province in northwestern China, is bounded on the north by the Republic of Mongolia. Gansu has an area of 366,500 km² (141,500 mi²) and a population of 21,034,000 (1988 est.). Ninety percent of the people are Chinese, and the remainder consists of Tibetan, Mongol, Turkic, and Chinese Muslim minorities. The capital, LANZHOU, is a trading, industrial, and refining center.

Gansu lies on a high plateau, which has an average elevation of about 1,830 m (6,000 ft). The eastern part of the province is the principal center of earthquakes in China. Gansu has very little arable land (less than 10%), and its most valuable resources are petroleum, coal, and iron. New road and railroad systems have been built in the last decades. The region became a part of the Chinese territory in the 3d century BC. An ancient route, the Gansu corridor for centuries provided the link between China and Central Asia.

Ganymede [gan'-ee-meed] Ganymede, a satellite of the planet JUPITER, is the largest satellite in the solar system. It was discovered by Galileo in 1610. With a diameter of 5,276 km (3,278 mi), it is larger than the planet Mercury. Its average distance from Jupiter's center is 1,070,000 km (665,000 mi), and it takes a little more than a week to complete one orbit of the planet. Ganymede's density is not quite twice that of water, so the satellite probably has a rocky core and thick icy mantle.

Parts of Ganymede's surface are dark and heavily cratered. Interspersed are lighter regions filled with bands of parallel grooves a few hundred meters deep and several kilometers apart. Some grooves extend for thousands of kilometers, and the bands sometimes intertwine with other bands in complicated patterns. Although less heavily cratered than the dark areas, the bands are sufficiently cratered to indicate that they formed fairly early in the satellite's history. The grooves are thought to be cracks that formed as areas of the old, dark crust pulled apart.

gar Gars are long, slender, predaceous fish, characterized by a long, tooth-studded jaw and a tough, armored skin of linked, diamond-shaped scales. They belong to

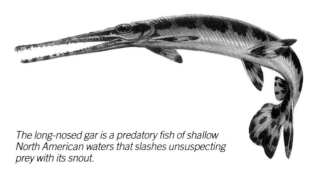

The long-nosed gar is a predatory fish of shallow North American waters that slashes unsuspecting prey with its snout.

the family Lepisosteidae, order Lepisosteiformes. The approximately eight species of this primitive fish inhabit placid fresh waters of the New World. As adults, they feed on small fish. The largest species, the only one eaten by humans, is the giant, or tropical, gar, *Lepisosteus tristoechus*, of Mexico, Central America, and Cuba. It may reach 3.7 m (12 ft) in length. The alligator gar, *L. spatula*, of the southeastern United States, grows to 3 m (10 ft) in length. The long-nosed gar, *L. osseus*, which often reaches 1 m (3.3 ft), is abundant in the Florida Everglades but ranges northward to Canada.

The gar's swim bladder is highly vascular and can function as a lung. This accounts for the gar's ability to survive in large numbers in often stagnant waters.

Garbo, Greta [gahr'-boh, gret'-uh] Greta Garbo, b. Greta Lovisa Gustafsson in Sweden, Sept. 18, 1905, d. Apr. 15, 1990, was brought to Hollywood in 1925. MGM turned her into a beautiful, queenly actress whose ambitious films always made headlines, even if they sometimes lost money. She was known for her shyness, and her sudden retirement in 1941 enhanced the air of mystery that surrounded her for most of her life. *Flesh and the Devil* (1927) is the best of her silent melodramas. Her first talkie was *Anna Christie* (1930). Other notable films include *Mata Hari* (1932), *Grand Hotel* (1932), *As You Desire Me* (1932), *Queen Christina* (1933), *Anna Karenina* (1935), *Camille* (1936), *Conquest* (1937), *Ninotchka* (1939), and *Two-Faced Woman* (1941).

Greta Garbo, a Swedish actress, became one of Hollywood's first major romantic idols. In such films as Flesh and the Devil *(1927) and* Anna Christie *(1930), Garbo projected an aura of mystery and sensuality that established her as an international celebrity.*

García Lorca, Federico [gahr-thee'-ah lohr'-kah, fay-day-ree'-koh] Federico García Lorca, b. June 5, 1898, d. Aug. 19, 1936, was 20th-century Spain's most illustrious poet and dramatist. Since his death in the Spanish Civil War, his influence even beyond the Spanish-speaking world has been enormous.

The eldest son of a wealthy landowner, García Lorca studied literature and law at the University of Granada before turning to writing. A trip through Castille in 1918 inspired the prose sketches *Impresiones y paisajes* (Impressions and Landscapes, 1918). In 1919 he went to Madrid, planning to devote himself to art, music, folklore, literature, and the theater; there he met such avant-garde as Salvador Dalí, Rafael Alberti, Luis Buñuel, Juan Ramón Jiménez, and Pablo Neruda. García Lorca's first play, *El Maleficio de la mariposa* (The Evildoing of the Butterfly, 1920), was neither a commercial nor an artistic success. More in tune was his first volume of verse, *Libro de poemas* (Book of Poems, 1921).

By 1925, García Lorca was the center of a group of poets known as the Generation of 1927 because in that year they honored the baroque poet Luis de Góngora on the 300th anniversary of his death. The year also saw the production of *Mariana Pineda*, a historical play, and the publication of another book of poetry, *Canciones* (Songs). The most famous of his poems, *Romancero gitano* (trans. as *Gypsy Ballads*, 1953), followed in 1928; using the rhythms of the traditional Spanish ballad form, it dealt with the closed, marginal society of Andalusian gypsies and was largely responsible, along with *Poema del Cante Jondo* (1931), for making García Lorca famous throughout the Spanish-speaking world.

During a six-month visit to New York in 1929, García Lorca completed several works influenced by surrealism, including a book of poems, *Poet in New York* (1940; Eng. trans., 1955), which evoked the anomie and disgust he

The Spanish poet and dramatist Federico García Lorca established his reputation as one of Spain's finest poets with the lyrical Gypsy Ballads *(1928). Using rhythm and vivid imagery, he infused his work with a radiant and violent beauty evocative of his native Andalusia.*

experienced there, and the play *If Five Years Pass* (1931; Eng. trans., 1941). Back in Spain García Lorca took an active role in the theater productions sponsored by the new Republican government; in 1932 he toured Spain as codirector of the La Barraca troupe. He also began to enjoy success with his own plays, of which the trilogy *Blood Wedding* (1933; Eng. trans., 1939), *Yerma* (1934; Eng. trans., 1941), and *The House of Bernarda Alba* (1936; Eng. trans., 1947) is his masterpiece. He also wrote such farces as *The Shoemaker's Prodigious Wife* (1930; Eng. trans., 1941), *The Love of Don Perlimplín with Belisa in the Garden* (1931; Eng. trans., 1941), and *Doña Rosita, the Spinster* (1935; Eng. trans., 1941).

When Gen. Francisco Franco's rebellion began on July 18, 1936, García Lorca returned to Granada. Although never affiliated with any party, he was known for his Republican sympathies, and soon after the rebels took control of the city he was arrested, imprisoned, and three weeks later shot by a firing squad and buried in a large unmarked grave.

The moving *Lament for Ignacio Sánchez Mejías* (1935; Eng. trans., 1939) serves as a microcosm of his mastery of the Spanish language.

García Márquez, Gabriel [gahr-see'-ah mahr'kays, gah-bree-el'] Gabriel García Márquez, b. Mar. 6, 1928, is a major Colombian novelist and short-story writer who was awarded the Nobel Prize for literature in 1982. His masterpiece, *One Hundred Years of Solitude* (1967; Eng. trans., 1970), is a family saga that mirrors the history of Colombia. Like many of his works, it is set in the fictional town of Macondo, a place much like García Márquez's native Aracataca. Mixing realism and fantasy, the novel is both the story of the decay of the town and an ironic epic of human experience.

García Márquez began as a reporter for *El Espectador,* for which he wrote (1955) a series of articles exposing the facts behind a Colombian naval disaster. The articles won him fame and were published as *Relato de un náufrago* (The Account of a Shipwrecked Person, 1970). His novel *The Autumn of the Patriarch* (1975; Eng. trans., 1976) again explores the theme of decay, depicting with typical exaggeration and ironic humor the barbarism, squalor, and corruption of the reign of a Latin American military dictator. Other works include collections of short stories (*No One Writes to the Colonel*, 1968; *Leaf Storm*, 1972; and *Innocent Erendira*, 1978) and the novels *In Evil Hour* (1968; Eng. trans., 1979), *Chronicle of a Death Foretold* (1981; Eng. trans., 1983), and *Love in the Time of Cholera* (1985; Eng. trans., 1988).

Garcilaso de la Vega [gahr-thee-lah'-soh day lah vay'-gah] The Spanish Golden Age poet Garcilaso de la Vega, b. 1501, d. Oct. 14, 1536, changed the course of Spanish poetry by adapting such Italian lyrical forms as the SONNET, the ECLOGUE, the 11-syllable line, and the rhyming stanza that he called the *lira*. His important and influential works were published posthumously along with those of his friend Juan Boscán in 1543.

Garcilaso was a Renaissance humanist and courtier who served Emperor Charles V as a diplomat and soldier. His brief life ended in a battle near Fréjus, in southern France, when he was crushed by a rock hurled from a battlement. Garcilaso's abiding love for the married Portuguese lady Isabel Freire informs much of his poetry, where she appears as the shepherdess Galatea or Eliza. Although Garcilaso molded his poetry into Italinate forms, there is a strong aura of traditional Spanish courtly verse about his work.

Garda, Lake [gahr'-dah]   Lake Garda, the largest lake in Italy, lies in the Piedmont region of northern Italy, 105 km (65 mi) east of Milan. Fed by the Sarca River at its narrow, mountain-guarded northern end, it is drained by the Mincio River to the south. It covers an area of 370 km^2 (143 mi^2) and has a maximum width of 18 km (11 mi) and a maximum depth of 346 m (1,135 ft). Many resorts line its shores.

garden   People cultivate gardens either to produce food or for aesthetic reasons—to create pleasant surroundings harmonizing flowers, shrubs, and trees within the landscape. Gardens in the second sense comprise plants, water, natural land formations, and architectural elements. The use of these ingredients of garden design developed differently in the Islamic world, the West, and the Far East.

In the Middle East, gardens have been important as a retreat from the intense heat of the natural environment. The Persian garden is divided into two crossed axes making four quadrants, symbolizing the belief that the universe is divided by four great rivers. Irrigation provides formal pools and gentle dripping fountains to add a musical dimension. High walls and flowers create a shady oasis. This pattern is restated in the Mogul gardens of

The gardens at Marly, a château built for the French king Louis XIV, were designed (1679–86) by André Le Nôtre in the mode that became the standard of palatial landscape design.

The garden at Sissinghurst Castle in England was laid out in the 1930s by diplomat Harold Nicolson and his wife, the novelist and poet Victoria Sackville-West. A compartmental garden, divided by paths, walls, and hedges, it shows the influence of both English and continental design.

India, most notably that surrounding the TAJ MAHAL at Agra, and in the magnificent Moorish gardens of the ALHAMBRA and Generalife palaces at Granada, Spain.

In western tradition—Italian, French, and English styles—water and architectural elements fuse into dynamic forms that dramatize human control over nature. Italian gardens, beginning in the 16th century, combined balustrades, colonnades, and terraces with elaborate fountains. At the Villa Lante in Bagnaia, the water source, a woodland spring in a natural setting, culminates in a formal pool. The gardens of the Villa d'Este, famous for its FOUNTAINS, those of the Villa Medici in Rome, and of the Villa Farnese at Caprarola are other notable examples of the Italian Renaissance style.

In France garden design is linked with the name André LE NÔTRE, creator of the gardens of the Palace of VERSAILLES. Two principles of the Italian garden, the axial plan and the parterre (scalloped or geometric beds with clipped shrubs forming the perimeter), were adapted in France to allow formal arrangement of the great vistas. Broad avenues were lined with symmetrical plantings of trees. The parterre developed into the *parterre de broderie*—hedges planted in elaborate "embroidered" patterns—and fountains spewed jets of water into pools shaped like the parterres. Human beings were reduced to miniature in this setting.

Many formal gardens show the influence of Versailles: those at the NYMPHENBURG PALACE, near Munich, and Schönbrunn Palace, near Vienna, are examples, as is the summer palace (Peterhof) outside Leningrad, with its gilded statues, built for Peter the Great by Alexandre Le Blond.

The cottage-style garden with free-wheeling perennial borders is the look most associated with the English style.

The Tofuku-ji garden in Kyoto, Japan—like the nearby Ryoan-ji—is an example of Kare-sansui, or dry landscaping. In such gardens the raked gravel often represents water, and the rocks symbolize mountains.

The graceful shaping of the English landscape is the result of centuries of garden design fluctuating between stylized continental gardens and attempts to adhere to nature. This can be seen at Blenheim Palace in Oxfordshire, where a "natural" park designed by Capability BROWN contrasts with the formal east and west parterres. Another example is the 18th-century garden at Stourhead in Wiltshire, which features lakes, rolling hills, and classical temples. In the Victorian garden at Chatsworth, in Derbyshire, Joseph PAXTON constructed a large greenhouse in which he produced out-of-season fruits and vegetables and exotic, floral bedding plants.

Today numerous fine private English gardens developed in the early 1900s are open to the public, including Hidcote in Gloucestershire, Sissinghurst in Kent, Exbury in Hampshire, and Crathes Castle near Aberdeen, Scotland. All were influenced by William Robinson and Gertrude Jekyll, who advocated dense plantings of familiar, indigenous species.

In the United States, Longwood Gardens in Pennsylvania and nearby Winterthur in Delaware reproduce this English style in a different setting. Examples of 18th- and 19th-century American gardens can be seen at Monticello and Williamsburg in Virginia and at the Hermitage, near Nashville, Tenn.

In the East Asian garden, no grandiose architectural implants or imposing water contrivances impinge on nature's setting. Little waterfalls, quiet streams and pools surround pavilions that shimmer in reflected light. Rocks and stones are purposefully arranged. The most significant difference between eastern and western gardens is scale: in the gardens of China and Japan the goal is the re-creation of nature in miniature.

Japan learned from China as early as the 7th century, when Japanese envoys visited the Western Park, the garden of the Sui dynasty emperor Yang Ti at Lo-Yang. As grand as Versailles, it had four lakes, one over 21 km (13 mi) long. From the beginning oriental gardens concentrated on harmony with nature. Lakes, islands, and rocks—elements in landscape painting as well—were aligned to stress verticality. Spiritual influences—Taoism and Buddhism in China, Shinto and Buddhism in Japan—are essential to an understanding of the Far Eastern garden. Zen Buddhism influenced the development of Kare-sansui, or dry landscaping. The Ryoan-ji garden near Kyoto, with its 15 rocks arranged in a bed of raked tiny stone, is a study in tension and balance.

Gardens today often reflect a synthesis of eastern and western aesthetics, as in the case of the BROOKLYN BOTANIC GARDEN AND ARBORETUM.

See also: LANDSCAPE ARCHITECTURE.

Garden, Mary   Mary Garden, b. Aberdeen, Scotland, Feb. 20, 1877, d. Jan. 3, 1967, was a celebrated operatic soprano. She went to the United States as a child and studied voice in Chicago. She worked with Mathilde Marchesi and was encouraged by the singer Sibyl Sanderson, who introduced her to the director of the Opéra-Comique, where she made a triumphant debut in the title role of Gustave Charpentier's *Louise*. She was chosen by Claude Debussy to sing the female lead in *Pelléas and Mélisande*. After 1907, Garden often sang in the United States and scored a sensation at the Manhattan Opera House in Richard Strauss's *Salome*. She became director of the Chicago Opera for its last season in 1921–22. A glamorous and controversial artist, Garden was as well known for her acting as for her singing.

---

garden city   The garden city movement of the early 20th century was inspired by the ideas and work of the English urban theorist Sir Ebenezer Howard. Howard's idea of a garden city was a meticulously planned self-supporting and community-owned urban center contained by a deep circle of undeveloped land called a greenbelt.

The 19th-century utopianism of the reformers Robert OWEN and Charles FOURIER provided the intellectual impetus behind the garden city movement. Howard's innovations included the establishment of the greenbelt to limit its spread; the founding of satellite cities; the return to the community of any unearned profit from the growth and prosperity of the city; community ownership and control of land; limitation of population to a predetermined size; and inclusion, within each city, of industry capable of supporting the greater part of its population.

By 1903, Howard had enough ideological and financial support to test his theories, and he started the town of Letchworth in Hertfordshire. In the next 50 years, garden cities and NEW TOWNS were developed throughout Europe and the Western Hemisphere. In the United States such developments include the town of Radburn, N.J. (1929), and the greenbelt towns (organized 1936–38) of Greenhills, Ohio, and Greenbelt, Md.

See also: URBAN PLANNING.

Garden of Eden   see EDEN, GARDEN OF

The gardenia, an evergreen shrub from China, produces glossy white flowers.

gardenia [gahr-dee'-nee-uh] The genus *Gardenia* comprises several species of flowering shrubs or small trees that belong to the madder family, Rubiaceae. Their flowers are sweet-scented. Gardenias are native to subtropical regions of the Eastern Hemisphere, where they grow outdoors, but they are also grown extensively indoors in greenhouses. Because of their need for warm, moist conditions, gardenias do not thrive as houseplants. Cape jasmine, *G. jasmimoides*, is a bushy shrub up to 1.8 m (6 ft) tall with glossy evergreen leaves and waxy-white, heavily scented flowers with nine petals each.

gardening   The ancient art of gardening—the raising of one's own flowers, shrubs, fruits, and vegetables within a limited area—is enjoying a contemporary renaissance as millions of Americans discover the satisfactions inherent in working the soil. Almost everyone who has access to a bit of ground raises a few flowers, and it is estimated that perhaps half of all American families maintain vegetable gardens. The HOUSEPLANT business is booming, and plant nurseries and florists have enjoyed record sales. (The garden and its history as a formal art are discussed in GARDEN.)

Soil. Soil must contain the essential nutrients to feed growing plants, and it must have a structure capable of holding air and moisture without becoming waterlogged. Soil analysis reveals nutritional deficiencies that may be remedied through the use of FERTILIZERS, which add the minerals necessary for plant growth. Analysis also indicates the pH, or acidity-alkalinity index, of the soil. On a scale of 1 to 14, acid to alkaline, a pH rating of 7 is neutral—neither acid nor alkaline. Most garden plants thrive best at a pH of 6 to 7, although certain plants, such as blueberries and rhododendrons, need a higher acid level. Overacidity, the more usual problem, can be decreased by adding ground limestone. Overalkaline soils, which may cause yellowing in plants, can be treated by adding sulfur or gypsum.

In general, soil structure is classified as sandy, clay, or loam, although most garden soils are mixtures of the three in varying proportions. A sandy soil is very loose and will not hold water. A clay soil is dense and heavy, sticky when wet, and almost brick-hard when dry. Loam is a mixture of sand and clay soils, but it also contains large quantities of HUMUS, or decayed organic material, which loosens and aerates clay soil and binds sandy soil particles together. In addition, humus supplies nutrients. Soil structure can be improved by digging in COMPOST, MANURE, PEAT MOSS, and other organic matter.

A good soil can be kept in good condition, year after year, by digging in decaying organic materials and by adding the recommended amounts of fertilizer, usually a compound commercial mixture sold at garden centers. Fertilizers should be applied only as recommended and never in excess.

Bright red and yellow tulips bloom beside a path in a flower garden in Williamsburg, Va. Called a mixed border, this informal arrangement of spring-blooming flowers will gradually be replaced by summer varieties as the season changes.

This small backyard vegetable garden, seen in early summer, will soon provide its owners with an abundance of fresh vegetables. The tomatoes at the rear of the garden will not produce for another month or so, but beans, beets, carrots, and cauliflower are almost ready to harvest, and the green pepper plants already bear small fruits.

State agricultural experiment stations test soil samples. The report shows what fertilizer or other material is required to make the soil suitable for growing plants.

Not every plant will thrive in every type of soil, nor are sunlight requirements the same for all plants. In general, however, a garden should not be situated near large trees, which not only shade the area but also draw large amounts of water and nutrients out of the soil. Areas open to the wind are to be avoided, as well as areas at the bottom of slopes, because the ground there tends to retain too much water.

Annuals and Perennials. Most garden VEGETABLES are annuals—plants with a life span of a single growing season—or biennials—plants that are picked and eaten during their first year, although they have a two-season life span.

The FLOWER garden may contain a mixture of annuals, biennials, and perennials, plants that live more than two years. Annuals are usually easier to grow, and they produce more colorful flowers in greater abundance than do biennials and perennials. They may be planted from seed in the beds where they are to grow, or raised in seedbeds or in flats (see Seeds and Seedlings section below) and transplanted when they have grown into small plants, or seedlings. Biennials are planted either as seeds or as year-old transplants, and may not bloom during their first year in the garden. Perennials, the most difficult flowering plants to grow from seed, are usually set out as seedlings or as divisions of older plants that have become too large. Once perennials are established, they flower for several years. Although not classed as perennials, ferns and flowers grown from bulbs also live for extended periods.

Seeds and Seedlings. Although the seeds of many flowers and vegetables may be sown directly into well-cultivated soil, some plants are better started indoors in shallow boxes, or flats. A controlled indoor environment aids seed germination, and plants started in flats, when spring weather is still too cold to allow outdoor planting, will be well advanced by the time they are set out. Many heat-sensitive vegetables (lettuce, broccoli, and cauliflower, for example) grow far better when they are planted as seedlings and can reach maturity before the heat of midsummer.

A cold frame is a boxlike wooden frame covered with a movable glass sash. Positioned to face south for the best exposure, the cold frame gathers and conserves sunlight and heat and acts as a miniature greenhouse in which seeds may be sown outdoors in late winter and early spring. Some cold frames have an electric heating cable buried slightly below the surface of the soil so that seedlings may be started even when outdoor temperatures are well below freezing.

Plant Cultivation. If the soil furnishes sufficient nutrients and contains enough humus to hold air and water, the basic necessities for successful plant growth are present. Instructions for sowing seed or setting out transplants will be found in gardening guides, in seed catalogs, or on the seed packets themselves. Thinning instructions are also given.

Many gardeners use a mulch to discourage weed growth and to help conserve soil moisture. Straw is a fine mulch for vegetable gardens; in flower beds a less noticeable mulch, such as peat moss or wood chips, is often used. Mulchless gardens require regular weeding so that weeds can be eliminated while they are small.

In dry periods the garden should be watered on a regular schedule. Morning is the best time for watering; the Sun's afternoon heat may evaporate moisture too quickly, and watering at sunset may encourage development of fungal diseases.

Plant Pests and Diseases. Many varieties of disease-resistant plants are available and are listed as such in garden catalogs. Plant diseases can be avoided by watering at the proper times; by weeding; and by removing dead plants, leaves, and other debris that often harbor injurious insects. Chemical HERBICIDES and pesticides (see PESTICIDES AND PEST CONTROL) are available but should be used sparingly and with care, for many will also destroy beneficial insects and garden plants. Chemical residues left on vegetables can be harmful if they are ingested.

Organic Gardening. Organic-vegetable gardeners do not use inorganic chemical pesticides or fertilizers but depend on composts and manures for soil enrichment and for maintaining a healthy garden environment. Organic gardeners encourage beneficial insects such as the lady-bug, which eats plant aphids. They use natural insecticides, such as sprays made from garlic juice, whose odor and antiseptic properties are reported to repel insects. They cluster together plants that are believed to have mutually beneficial effects: marigolds planted between tomatoes, for instance, are supposed to prevent infestation of certain harmful insects and may even repel rabbits.

See also: FRUITS AND FRUIT CULTIVATION; GRAFTING; PLANT PROPAGATION; separate articles on individual flowers and vegetables.

The American writer John Gardner's background as a medievalist and classicist surfaced in such novels as Grendel *(1971) and* The Sunlight Dialogues *(1972). Gardner was head of the creative writing program at the State University of New York at Binghamton at the time of his death in a motorcycle accident in 1982.*

Photo Jill Krementz © 1977

Gardiner, Stephen   Stephen Gardiner, b. *c.*1482, d. Nov. 12, 1555, was an English bishop at the time of the Reformation. Although he assented to King Henry VIII's declaration of royal supremacy over the English church, he nevertheless remained doctrinally conservative. He was probably the author of Henry VIII's *Six Articles*, which reasserted Catholic doctrines such as transubstantiation in the Eucharist and practices such as celibacy of the clergy. After Edward VI became king in 1547, Gardiner was imprisoned. When the Catholic Queen Mary I ascended the throne in 1553, Gardiner was reinstated as bishop of Winchester and was made lord chancellor. He once more accepted papal supremacy over the Church of England.

Gardner, Erle Stanley   The detective novelist Erle Stanley Gardner, b. Malden, Mass., July 17, 1889, d. Mar. 11, 1970, the best-selling author of his time, was the creator of Perry Mason, a Los Angeles lawyer-sleuth who appeared in Gardner's first book, *The Case of the Velvet Claws* (1933). Gardner began to practice law in 1911, specializing in the defense of indigent Mexicans and Chinese but became a full-time writer in 1933 after the phenomenal success of his magazine stories. Under the pseudonym A. A. Fair he also wrote a series of comic novels centered on the detective Bertha Cool.

See also: MYSTERY, SUSPENSE, AND DETECTIVE FICTION.

Gardner, John   The American novelist, scholar, and critic John Champlin Gardner, Jr., b. Batavia, N.Y., July 21, 1933, d. Sept. 14, 1982, was best known for his voluminous and well-crafted works of fiction. His books characteristically pose metaphysical problems in fabulous and ingenious forms. The novel *Grendel* (1971) retells the Beowulf legend from the monster's point of view. His other works include the short-story collection *The King's Indian* (1974) and the novels *The Wreckage of Agathon* (1970), *The Sunlight Dialogues* (1972), *Nickel Mountain*

(1973), and *October Light* (1976), which won the 1977 National Book Critics Circle Award for fiction. Gardner also produced scholarly works on the age of Chaucer; volumes of poetry; and the posthumously published *On Becoming a Novelist* (1983) and *The Art of Fiction* (1984).

Gardner, John W.   John William Gardner, b. Los Angeles, Oct. 8, 1912, founded the nonpartisan citizens' lobby COMMON CAUSE and headed it from 1970 to 1977. An educator who became an administrator, he worked (1946–65) for the Carnegie Corporation, serving as its president from 1955. President Lyndon Johnson appointed Gardner, a Republican, as secretary of Health, Education, and Welfare (1965–68), a position from which he resigned to become head (1968–70) of the National Urban Coalition.

Gardner, Martin   Martin Gardner, b. Tulsa, Okla., Oct. 21, 1914, is best known for his mathematical games and puzzles, which he published in a regular column in *Scientific American* from 1956 to 1983, as well as in a continuing series of books. In books such as *In the Name of Science* (1952)—republished as *Fads and Fallacies in the Name of Science* (1957)—and *Science: Good, Bad and Bogus* (1981) he has sought to distinguish between science and pseudoscience. He has successfully explained many difficult aspects of science to the nonspecialist; for example, relativity is treated in *Relativity for the Million* (1962), and *The Ambidextrous Universe* (1964; rev. ed., 1978) discusses symmetry and aspects of astronomy.

Garfield, James A.   James Abram Garfield became the 20th president of the United States in 1881 and was assassinated later that year. He had been an influential member of the House of Representatives for the period

AT A GLANCE

JAMES ABRAM GARFIELD
20th President of the United States (1881)

Born: Nov. 19, 1831, Orange Township, Cuyahoga County, Ohio

Education: Western Reserve Eclectic Institute (now Hiram College); Williams College (graduated 1856)

Profession: Teacher, Public Official

Religious Affiliation: Disciples of Christ

Marriage: Nov. 11, 1858, to Lucretia Rudolph (1832–1918)

Children: Eliza A. Garfield (1860–63); Harry A. Garfield (1863–1942); James R. Garfield (1865–1950); Mary Garfield (1867–1947); Irvin M. Garfield (1870–1951); Abram Garfield (1872–1958); Edward Garfield (1874–76)

Political Affiliation: Republican

Writings: *Diary, 1848–1874* (2 vols., 1967), ed. by H. J. Brown and F. D. Williams

Died: Sept. 19, 1881, Elberon, N.J.

Buried: Lake View Cemetery, Cleveland, Ohio

Vice President: Chester A. Arthur

1863 to 1880, but his presidency was too short to confirm the indications that he would have been the moderate, successful leader that the Republican party required in the 1880s. Garfield is now remembered mostly as the last chief executive to be born in a log cabin and as a dark-horse candidate for the Republican presidential nomination in 1880.

Early Life. Garfield was born on Nov. 19, 1831, in Cuyahoga County, Ohio. After an impoverished childhood he attended what became Hiram College and graduated from Williams College in 1856. In 1858 he married Lucretia Rudolph; two of their children, James Rudolph and Harry Augustus, gained national distinction.

Intensely religious as a youth (he was a member of the Disciples of Christ and a lay preacher), Garfield moved toward secular and political concerns in the 1850s. He studied law, became a Republican, and was elected to the Ohio Senate in 1859. When the Civil War began, he joined and helped recruit the 42d Ohio Volunteer Infantry. He fought at Shiloh and Chickamauga, rose to major general, and, as chief of staff of the Army of the Cumberland, displayed impressive talents as a planner and organizer.

Elected to Congress in 1862, Garfield began his legislative service in December 1863. For the next 17 years he concentrated on economic issues on the Appropriations and Ways and Means committees. He voted with Radical Republicans on Reconstruction but did not endorse the more stringent measures of that bloc. He was a mild protectionist in Ohio tariff politics, and he opposed greenbacks and other inflationary ideas. Scandal touched him only slightly when his modest dealings with the CRÉDIT MOBILIER company became public.

Early in 1880 the Ohio legislature elected Garfield to the Senate to succeed John SHERMAN, and he then served as Sherman's campaign manager in the race for the Republican presidential nomination. At the convention Garfield worked skillfully to block the candidacies of James G. BLAINE and Ulysses S. GRANT. In the process his appeal as a compromise candidate outshone Sherman's lackluster personality and record. By the 35th ballot a Garfield tide was running through the hall, and on the next ballot he received the nomination.

Presidency. With Chester Alan ARTHUR as his running mate, Garfield faced a difficult race against Winfield Scott HANCOCK, the Democratic nominee. The narrow victory that Garfield achieved testified to the stalemated condition of politics in the Gilded Age. His majority in the electoral college was 214 to 155, but his plurality in the popular vote was under 7,500. The Republicans won because of superior organization, a new emphasis on the tariff issue, and Democratic errors. Garfield's deft speeches at his home in Mentor, Ohio, foreshadowed the "front porch" campaigns of Benjamin Harrison and William McKinley.

Divisions within the Republican party made Garfield's cabinet and patronage choices the primary issue between his election and assassination. He named James G. Blaine secretary of state and gave greater recognition to Blaine's Half-Breed faction than to the Stalwarts led by Sen. Roscoe CONKLING of New York. Once in office, Garfield nominated an enemy of Conkling's as collector of the New York port and pushed hard to secure the appointee's Senate confirmation. As defeat became likely, Conkling resigned his Senate seat and sought vindication and reelection from the New York legislature. When that body seemed ready to reject Conkling's bid, Garfield's ascendancy as president appeared assured.

On July 2, 1881, Garfield went to Washington's railroad station to begin a family trip. There Charles J. GUITEAU, an insane Stalwart and disappointed office seeker, shot him. Garfield lived for 11 weeks in increasing pain and failing strength and died in Elberon, N.J. on Sept. 19, 1881. Garfield quickly faded from public and historical memory. The circumstances of his assassination facilitated passage of the Pendleton Civil Service Act in 1883. His death left the Republican party confused and leaderless throughout much of the 1880s and helped delay its emergence to majority status for 15 years.

Garfield, John   An antiestablishment American film hero of the 1930s, John Garfield, b. Julius Garfinkle in New York City, Mar. 4, 1913, d. May 21, 1952, was a stage actor who brought a taste of New York's Lower East Side to the Hollywood fantasy factories. He became a star in one of his first films, *Four Daughters* (1938). His rather sullen manner, however, kept him out of the top rank, despite good performances in *They Made Me A Criminal* (1939), *Pride of the Marines* (1945), *Body and Soul* (1948), and *Force of Evil* (1949).

Gargantua and Pantagruel   see RABELAIS, FRANÇOIS

gargoyle [gahr'-goyl]   Gargoyles are grotesque stone figures most commonly found on Gothic buildings at the roof or eaves. Originally the term meant the unadorned spout that extended outward from a rain gutter or parapet; the gargoyle allowed water to fall free of the building, preventing seepage and damage to masonry. Eventually the spout became a carved head or body with grotesque features. Superstition held that the gargoyle frightened away evil spirits while serving its practical function. After the introduction of the lead drain pipe in the 16th century, gargoyles primarily served a decorative function.

Garibaldi, Giuseppe [gahr-ee-bahl'-dee]   Giuseppe Garibaldi, b. Nice, July 4, 1807, d. June 2, 1882, was Italy's most brilliant soldier of the RISORGIMENTO. While serving (1833–34) in the navy of the Kingdom of Sardinia-

Guiseppe Garibaldi was the leading general in the Risorgimento, the movement that unified Italy during the 19th century. With 1,000 volunteers, the "Red Shirts," Garibaldi conquered Sicily and Naples for King Victor Emmanuel II in 1860.

Piedmont, he came under the influence of Giuseppe MAZZINI, the prophet of Italian nationalism. He took part in an abortive republican uprising in Piedmont in 1834.

Under a death sentence, he managed to escape to South America, where he lived from 1836 to 1848. He fought in Brazil and helped Uruguay in its war against Argentina, commanding its small navy and, later, an Italian legion at Montevideo. The handsome warrior achieved international fame through the publicity of the elder Alexandre DUMAS.

Wearing his colorful gaucho costume, Garibaldi returned to Italy in April 1848 to fight in its war of independence. His exploits against the Austrians in Milan and against the French forces supporting Rome and the Papal States made him a national hero. Overpowered at last in Rome, Garibaldi and his men had to retreat through central Italy in 1849. Anita, his wife and companion-in-arms, died during this retreat.

Garibaldi again escaped abroad, where he lived successively in North Africa, the United States, and Peru. The "hero of two worlds" could not return to Italy until 1854. In 1859 he helped Piedmont in a new war against Austria, leading a volunteer Alpine force that captured Varese and Como.

In May 1860, Garibaldi set out on his greatest venture, the conquest of Sicily and Naples. This time he had no governmental support, but Premier CAVOUR and King VICTOR EMMANUEL II dared not stop the popular hero. Sailing from near Genoa on May 6 with 1,000 Redshirts, Garibaldi reached Marsala, Sicily, on May 11 and proclaimed himself dictator in the name of Victor Emmanuel. At the Battle of Calatafimi (May 30) his guerrilla force defeated the regular army of the king of Naples. A popular uprising helped him capture Palermo.

Garibaldi crossed the Strait of Messina on August 18–19 and in a whirlwind campaign reached Naples on September 7. On October 3–5 he fought another battle on the Volturno River, the biggest of his career. After plebiscites, he handed Sicily and Naples over to Victor Emmanuel, and then retired to his home on Caprera, off Sardinia. Nevertheless, he continued to plot to capture the Papal States. In 1862 the Italian government intercepted him at Aspromonte, and when he led another private expedition toward Rome in 1867, French troops halted him at Mentana. Subsequently, during the FRANCO-PRUSSIAN WAR (1870-71), Garibaldi led a group of volunteers in support of the new French republic.

Without Garibaldi, the unification of Italy could not have taken place when it did. A gifted leader and man of the people, he knew far better than Cavour or Mazzini how to stir the masses, and he repeatedly hastened the pace of events. In later life he declared himself a socialist. He died at Caprera.

Garland, Augustus Hill [gahr'-luhnd] Augustus Hill Garland, b. Tipton County, Tenn., June 11, 1832, d. Jan. 26, 1899, was an American lawyer and politician best known for his role in the 1867 Supreme Court case *Ex parte Garland*. The case arose because an 1865 law barred from law practice in the United States those, like Garland, who had served in the Confederate government during the Civil War. Garland argued successfully that the law was EX POST FACTO and thus unconstitutional.

Garland, Hamlin A significant early American realistic writer, Hannibal Hamlin Garland, b. West Salem, Wis., Sept. 14, 1860, d. Mar. 4, 1940, is best known for his short-story collections *Main-Travelled Roads* (1891) and *Other Main-Travelled Roads* (1910) and for the novel *Rose of Dutcher's Coolly* (1895), all notable for their grim portrayal of midwestern rural life. Garland's two autobiographical novels are *Son of the Middle Border* (1917) and *A Daughter of the Middle Border* (1921), which won the 1922 Pulitzer Prize for biography or autobiography.

Garland, Judy Judy Garland, originally named Frances Gumm, b. Grand Rapids, Minn., June 10, 1922, d. June 22, 1969, was one of America's most notable sing-

Judy Garland's distinctive singing and dancing talents made her a star of Hollywood musicals during the 1940s.

ers and entertainers. She began her career at age four singing with the Gumm Sisters in her father's theater and touring in vaudeville. In 1935, Garland joined MGM, gained popularity in the Andy Hardy film series, and in 1939 won a special Academy Award for her rendition of the song *Over the Rainbow* from the film The WIZARD OF OZ. Her later films include *Babes in Arms* (1939), *Strike Up the Band* (1940), *Meet Me in St. Louis* (1944), *Easter Parade* (1948), *A Star Is Born* (1954), and *Judgment at Nuremburg* (1961). Between illnesses and breakdowns said to have originated from her early exhaustion as a young star, and her resulting dependence on alcohol, she performed in concerts throughout the world and exuded a magnetism and courage that endeared her to an international audience.

garlic Garlic, *Allium sativum*, a perennial herb related to the onion, is a pungent bulb composed of cloves surrounded by a thin white or purplish sheath. It is among the most ancient of cultivated plants and has long been used as a food flavoring, as a medicine, and as a germicide, since its juice contains the antibiotic oil allicin. Because seed is rarely produced, garlic is propagated by planting individual cloves. When the green tops ripen and fall over, the bulbs are pulled. Garlic can be stored for several months if kept dry and cool.

Originating in central Asia, garlic today grows wild in southern Europe and the east central United States. It is cultivated for its bulb, containing up to 20 cloves, which are used to flavor many Mediterranean and Asian cuisines.

Garner, John Nance John Garner, b. Red River County, Tex., Nov. 22, 1868, d. Nov. 7, 1967, was a Texas politician who served (1933–41) as the 32d vice-president of the United States. A conservative Democrat, he served (1903–33) in the House of Representatives and was speaker from 1931 to 1933. In 1932, Franklin D. Roosevelt chose Garner as his running mate. Garner was not sympathetic to the NEW DEAL, however, and became estranged from Roosevelt. He challenged Roosevelt for the 1940 presidential nomination and, after losing, retired to his ranch in Texas.

garnet　The garnets are a family of common and widespread SILICATE MINERALS found in METAMORPHIC and some IGNEOUS ROCKS. The generalized chemical formula of garnets is $X_3Y_2(SiO_4)_3$, with X indicating a divalent cation, such as iron, magnesium, calcium, or manganese, and Y a trivalent cation, such as aluminum, iron, or chromium. The SiO_4 indicates silica tetrahedra—a silicon ion surrounded by four oxygen ions. The various cations are packed between the tetrahedra.

Garnet CRYSTALS belong to the ISOMETRIC SYSTEM and commonly occur in well-formed dodecahedral or trapezohedral shapes. Because their atoms are so tightly packed, garnets are relatively hard and dense.

Iron-rich almandine, the most common garnet, is widespread in metamorphic rocks such as SCHISTS and GNEISSES and in granitic igneous rocks. The magnesium garnet, which tends to form under high pressure, is found in deep-seated magnesium-rich metamorphic rocks and may be an important constituent of the mantle of the Earth (see EARTH, STRUCTURE AND COMPOSITION). Spessartine is found in manganese-rich gneisses and in coarsegrained PEGMATITES.

Grossular, containing calcium and aluminum, is found in clay-rich limestones that have been metamorphosed to marble and in some contact-metamorphic deposits, or skarns, formed when an igneous rock intrudes and reacts with limestone. The calcium-iron garnet andradite and the rare calcium-chromium garnet uvarovite are also usually found in skarns.

Garnet is commonly cut as a GEM. The dark red, Victorian garnet jewelry was made from pyrope garnets mined in Bohemia, a section of Czechoslovakia. Hessonite is an attractive, cinnamon brown variety of grossular, and demantoid, the green variety of andradite, is rare and highly prized. Synthetic yttrium-aluminum garnet, or YAG, is used to imitate diamond as a gem. Garnet is also mined for use as an abrasive.

Clear garnet stones (left) suitable for gems characteristically have 12 or 24 faces and are found in all colors except blue. A polished gem (right) is usually cut with a brilliant top and stepped facets.

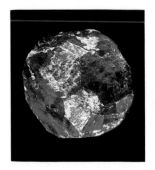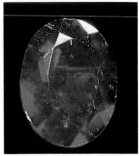

Garnet, Henry Highland　Henry Highland Garnet, b. 1815, d. Feb. 13, 1882, was an African-American abolitionist clergyman. Born a slave in Maryland, he escaped (1824) to New York where he obtained an education and became a Presbyterian pastor. In 1843 he called upon slaves to rise up and kill their masters, but he lost support because of his radicalism. In 1881 he was named U.S. minister to Liberia, where he died.

Garnier, Jean Louis Charles　The work of the 19th-century French architect Jean Louis Charles Garnier, b. June 11, 1825, d. Aug. 3, 1898, epitomizes the exuberant ornamentation of the Second Empire style. In 1861, in competition with the most eminent architects of the time, he was chosen to design the Paris Opéra (completed 1875). The opéra was intended as, and remains, the focal point of Baron HAUSSMANN's replanning of Paris and the city's most conspicuous example of the ornate French neobaroque style. The Casino at Monte Carlo (1878–81) displays a similar graceful opulence, but on a smaller scale, and provided a model for resort architecture.

garnishment　see ATTACHMENT (law)

Garonne River [gah-ruhn']　The Garonne River rises in the Maladeta massif on Spain's Pyrenees Mountains and flows northeast and then northwest 503 km (312 mi) through southwest France. It reaches the Atlantic Ocean 26 km (16 mi) north of Bordeaux through the 72-km-long (45-mi) Gironde Estuary. Its principal tributaries include the Ariège River in the Pyrenees and the Tarn, Lot, and Dordogne rivers in France. Although the river is navigable only on its lower course, the Canal du Midi links it at Toulouse with the Mediterranean. The Garonne Lateral Canal, which is 193 km (120 mi) long, runs parallel to the river from Toulouse to Castets.

Garrett, Pat　Patrick Floyd Garrett, b. 1850, d. 1908, was the New Mexico sheriff who tracked down and shot (1881) Billy the Kid (William H. Bonney). Born in Alabama, Garrett was a buffalo hunter, cowboy, horse rancher, Texas Ranger, and twice a sheriff—once in 1880 and again in 1897. The circumstances of his death in 1908 have never been resolved.

Garrick, David [gair'-ik]　David Garrick, b. Feb. 19, 1717, d. Jan. 20, 1779, was the greatest English actor and stage manager of the 18th century. He raised the practice of acting to a true art form and introduced a number of scenic improvements, such as hidden stagelighting, to the English stage.

Rejected by the managers of Drury Lane and Covent Garden theaters, he acted at Goodman's Fields Theatre, where as Richard III in 1741 he launched a triumphant career. He was especially noted for his expressive features

David Garrick, one of the great performers of the English stage, became manager of the Drury Lane Theatre, where his innovative productions revived interest in the plays of Shakespeare.

and his naturalistic acting style, which determined the direction of acting technique. His great tragic roles included Hamlet, Macbeth, and Lear. His famous comedy parts included Benedick in *Much Ado About Nothing*, Able Drugger in *The Alchemist*, and Bayes in *The Rehearsal*. Garrick had a strong temper and a reputation for vanity, snobbishness, and parsimony.

As the manager of Drury Lane from 1746 to 1766, Garrick prompted significant advances in representational scene design, ended the practice of audience seating on the stage, and renewed the popularity of Shakespeare's plays, which he often emended. His own plays include *Lethe* (1740) and *Miss in Her Teens* (1747), which were published along with his others in 1768. He was buried in Westminster Abbey.

▬

Garrison, William Lloyd [gair'-i-suhn] William Lloyd Garrison, b. Dec. 12, 1805, d. May 24, 1879, became to many of his time the personification of the American ABOLITIONIST movement. On Jan. 1, 1831, he

published the first issue of the *Liberator*, declaring slavery an abomination in God's sight, demanding immediate emancipation, and vowing never to be silenced. The *Liberator*, published weekly through 1865, always served as a personal sounding board for Garrison's views, but it was also an authoritative voice of radical Yankee social reform in general.

In 1833, Garrison presided over the meeting that organized the American Anti-Slavery Society. A believer in "moral suasion," Garrison insisted that slavery would be abolished only when the mass of white Americans experienced a revolution in conscience. Therefore, he aimed to convert grass-roots public opinion in favor of emancipation and race equality.

Until the late 1830s, Garrison cooperated easily with most other major abolitionists, but by 1840 important figures like James G. Birney and Elizur Wright, Jr., had broken with him. Garrison's espousals of anticlericalism, perfectionism, radical pacifism, and women's rights drove these individuals from the American Anti-Slavery Society. Others, however, such as Wendell Phillips and Lydia Maria Child, defended Garrison's radical doctrines and took over the society. In 1842, Garrison took the even more controversial position that Northerners should disavow all allegiance to the Union, since the Constitution protected slavery. Throughout this decade, however, he and most of his associates upheld pacifist creeds and insisted that slavery should not be ended violently.

During the 1850s, Garrison became less opposed to violence as a means for ending slavery. He condoned violent resistance to the 1850 Fugitive Slave Law, hailed John Brown's 1859 raid on Harper's Ferry, and in 1861 announced his support for war against the seceding Southern states. Throughout the Civil War, Garrison agitated for rapid and complete emancipation of the slaves; after the war he continued to insist on race equality and the creation of freedman aid programs.

▬

garter snake Garter snakes, genus *Thamnophis*, family Colubridae, are the most common snakes in North America. The 12 to 19 species are found from the Atlantic to the Pacific coasts and from Costa Rica north to the Yukon. Their habitats range from low-lying swamps to altitudes of 4,000 m (13,000 ft). Terrestrial forms feed largely on earthworms and insects; aquatic forms, mainly on amphibians. Garter snakes are slender and about 0.6

William Lloyd Garrison, perhaps the most outspoken champion of the abolitionist cause, published the first issue of the Liberator *in 1831 and continued to use its pages to agitate for reform for the next 35 years.*

The 60-cm (2-ft) common garter snake, widely distributed throughout North America, is the only snake found as far north as Alaska.

m (2 ft) long. Some forms lack stripes, but the predominant pattern consists of dark brown, black, or reddish upper sides, with one to three stripes and a checkerboard pattern of blotches running the length of the body. Garter snakes generally mate in early spring. The female bears 12 to 70 living young in late summer.

Garvey, Marcus [gahr'-vee]   Marcus Mosiah Garvey, b. Jamaica, Aug. 17, 1887, d. June 10, 1940, organized the African-American nationalist movement of the 1920s in the United States. Garvey went to New York City in 1916 and recruited followers for his Universal Negro Improvement Association. Its program was to unite all black peoples through the establishment in Africa of a country and government of their own. Garvey was a magnetic speaker who dressed in a resplendent uniform and led his followers in parades through Harlem. In 1921 he claimed nearly 1 million followers.

Garvey's newspaper, *Negro World*, carried his views to all parts of the United States. He preached economic independence, pride of race, and the need for African Americans to return to Africa. Garvey organized a steamship company, the Black Star Line, to provide a commercial link among all the black peoples of the world. His methods of selling stock in the line, however, led to his conviction (1923) for using the U.S. mails to defraud. After serving nearly 3 years of a 5-year sentence, he was pardoned by President Coolidge and deported to Jamaica in 1927. Although he died in obscurity, Garvey is remembered as a national hero in his native Jamaica.

Marcus Garvey, the leader of a black separatist movement early in the 20th century, wears a uniform signifying the presidency of his hoped-for African republic. Although Garvey anticipated the later emphasis on black culture and racial pride, in the early 1920s he alienated many by advocating separate political and economic institutions.

Gary [gar'-ee]   A port on Lake Michigan in the northwest corner of Indiana, Gary is the state's third largest city, with a population of 116,646 (1990). A principal city in the great Calumet industrial region adjacent to Chicago, it is also one of the nation's major steel centers.

The United States Steel Corporation purchased land there in 1905, and soon a steel mill and a new city emerged from the coastal sloughs and sand dunes. The city was chartered in 1906 and named for Judge Elbert H. Gary, then the company's chairman of the board. The Gary plan of education, developed in the city's public schools between 1908 and 1915, was widely adopted in other parts of the United States.

Gary, Romain [gah-ree', roh-man']   Romain Gary, b. Romain Kacew in Vilnius, Lithuania, May 8, 1914, d. Dec. 2, 1980, was a French writer whose first novel, *A European Education* (1945; Eng. trans., 1960), described the Polish resistance during World War II. *The Roots of Heaven* (1956; Eng. trans., 1958), about a Frenchman imprisoned in a German concentration camp, won Gary the Prix Goncourt (1956). His later works include the autobiographical *Promise at Dawn* (1960; Eng. trans., 1961). After Gary's suicide it was revealed that he had written several works under the pseudonym Émile Ajar, including *La vie devant soi* (1975; trans. as *Momo*, 1978).

gas   see GASEOUS STATE

gas chamber   A gas chamber is an airtight room in which persons are killed with poison gas. As a method of executing condemned prisoners it was first used in Nevada in 1924 (see CAPITAL PUNISHMENT). The prisoner is strapped in a chair, and sodium cyanide pellets are dropped into a bucket of acid. If the prisoner breathes deeply, death comes almost at once.

The infamous concentration camp gas chambers used in Nazi Germany's program of genocide were disguised as bathhouses. Naked prisoners were herded into them, and lethal carbon monoxide or hydrocyanic gas fumes were pumped in.

gas laws   In chemistry and physics, the behavior of gases under varying conditions of temperature, pressure, and volume may be described and predicted by a set of equations, or gas laws. These laws were determined by measurements of actual gases and are valid for all substances in the GASEOUS STATE.

The first quantitative measurements of gases were published by Robert BOYLE in 1660. He observed that if an enclosed amount of gas is compressed until it is half its original volume (V) while the temperature is kept constant, the pressure (P) will be doubled. Quantitatively, Boyle's law is PV = constant, where the value of the constant depends on the temperature and the amount of gas present.

Jacques CHARLES studied (1787) the relationship between the temperature and volume of a gas while maintaining constant pressure. Charles observed that for every degree Celsius rise in temperature, the gas volume increased by 1/273 of its volume at 0° C. Charles's observations led to the concept of the absolute temperature scale, or KELVIN SCALE, because the gas would have zero volume at −273° C. The absolute temperature scale was defined so that ABSOLUTE ZERO equals −273° C. This new temperature scale allowed Charles's law to be written V/T = constant, where V is the volume of the gas, T is the temperature on the absolute scale, and the constant depends on the pressure and the amount of gas present. Joseph GAY-LUSSAC studied the relationship between pressure and temperature and in 1802 formed an additional law: P/T = constant. About this time John DALTON formulated his law of partial pressures: the pressure of a mixture of gases is the sum of the pressures of the constituent gases.

Boyle's, Charles's, and Gay-Lussac's laws may be combined to express a generalized gas law, PV/T = constant, where the value of the constant depends on the amount of gas present and T is the absolute (or Kelvin) temperature. This law, combined with AVOGADRO'S LAW, led to the relation known as the ideal gas law, $PV = nRT$, where n is the number of moles of gas and R is known as the gas constant. The gas constant can be evaluated experimentally as $R = 0.082$ liter-atmospheres per Kelvin-mole. Knowing R, the fourth variable can be evaluated if any three are known.

The laws are valid for most gases at moderate temperatures and pressures. At low temperatures and high pressures, gases deviate from the above laws because the molecules move slowly at low temperatures and they are closer together on the average at higher pressures (see KINETIC THEORY OF MATTER). Both of these effects increase the attractive forces between the molecules that cause the deviations (see INTERMOLECULAR FORCES).

___

gas mask Invented during World War I to protect combatants' eyes and lungs from poison gas, gas masks are used today to filter many airborne substances—dust, asbestos fiber, vaporized paint—as well as some gases used in chemical warfare. The protective gas mask cleans the breathed air by means of a filter of chemically impregnated fibers over a bed of adsorbent material—usually activated charcoal. Another type, the closed-system rebreathing mask, uses a chemical such as sodium peroxide to react with the carbon dioxide and water from exhaled air, regenerating oxygen for breathing.

___

Gascoigne, George [gas-koyn']   George Gascoigne, b. c.1539, d. Oct. 7, 1577, was an innovative English playwright, poet, and prose writer. His drama *The Supposes* (1566), an adaptation of Ariosto's *I Suppositi*, was the first English prose comedy. *Jocasta* (1573), which Gascoigne wrote with Francis Kinwelmersh and based on Euripides' *Phoenician Women*, was one of the earliest English blank-verse tragedies. After a scandalous youth, during which he was imprisoned for debt, he became a member of Parliament (1557–59) and fought in the Low Countries (1572–74). His *A Hundred Sundry Flowers* (1573), containing his dramas and poems, was expanded to *The Posies of George Gascoigne* (1573), which includes the earliest treatise on English prosody, "Certain Notes of Instruction." *The Steele Glass* (1576), in blank verse, is considered the first true English satire.

___

Gascony [gas'-kuh-nee]   Gascony (French: Gascogne) is a historic region of southwestern France bordered by Béarn on the southwest, Guienne on the north, Languedoc on the east, Foix on the southeast, and Spain on the south. The name is derived from the Vascones (BASQUES), who settled here after crossing the Pyrenees from Spain in the 6th century.

The Landes, the coastal region in the west, is flat, barren, sandy country planted with pine forests. In the south the peaks of the Pyrenees exceed 3,050 m (10,000 ft). The mountain slopes are used for the summer grazing of cattle and sheep. In the fertile, populous valleys, wheat, peaches, apricots, and grapes are grown, and tourism is increasingly important. Armagnac, in the far north, produces fruit, cereals, and a brandy that rivals cognac. In the Armagnac area is the town of Auch, the traditional capital of Gascony.

Known as Novempopulana in Roman times, Gascony became a semiautonomous duchy under Frankish suzer-

A modern military gas mask protects the wearer's face, eyes, and lungs from poisonous gases. Air (blue arrows) is drawn in through a valve in the air-purifying canister, which contains a filter for removing particles and an activated charcoal layer that absorbs and removes harmful gases. Exhaled air exits through a valve at the front of the mask.

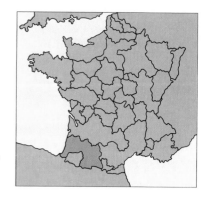

The map indicates the location of Gascony, a historic region of southwestern France. An independent duchy during part of its history, it was divided into several departments in 1790.

ainty in the 7th century and remained a separate entity until it was joined to AQUITAINE in the mid-11th century. It came under English rule in 1154 and continued so until it was annexed by the French crown in 1453. Today Gascony corresponds to the departments of Landes, Gers, and Hautes-Pyrénées, and parts of Haute-Garonne, Tarn-et-Garonne, Lot-et-Garonne, Ariège, and Pyrénées-Atlantiques.

gaseous state [gash'-uhs]

The gaseous state is one of three basic physical states of matter. In contrast to the liquid or solid states, a gas when unconfined tends to expand indefinitely, and a gas in a container always fills the container completely. This is because gas molecules have sufficient kinetic energy to overcome basic intermolecular forces of attraction. If liquids or solids are given enough energy, as by heating, their molecules will overcome such forces and will change to the gaseous state. This is called boiling or EVAPORATION in the case of liquids and SUBLIMATION in the case of solids.

Empirical studies by chemists of the properties of gases led to a series of GAS LAWS that are of use today. These laws have been verified and modified by theoretical chemists (see KINETIC THEORY OF MATTER).

Much of the behavior of gases, as determined by observation, is explained or predicted by statistical THERMODYNAMICS. In this treatment, the mechanical behavior of a single gas molecule is calculated, and then all molecules moving in the same manner are counted. This leads to expressions for the gas pressure and kinetic energy as a whole. It also leads to estimates of thermal conductivity, viscosity, and diffusion. All gas molecules have translational energy, and molecules with more than one atom also have rotational and vibrational energies. Not all the molecules in a given gas sample have the same energy, but methods of statistical mechanics can produce a probable energy distribution among the molecules at a given temperature. Temperature is essentially a measure of average kinetic energy of the gas. For each gaseous substance there is a certain temperature, called the critical temperature, above which the gaseous molecules cannot be liquefied by increasing pressure.

Gaskell, Elizabeth Cleghorn [gas'-kul]

The English author Elizabeth Cleghorn Stevenson Gaskell, b. London, Sept. 29, 1810, d. Nov. 12, 1865, was an influential novelist whose works focus on social and economic themes. Her first novel, *Mary Barton* (1848), attacked the callousness of manufacturers. In 1853 she published *Ruth*, a condemnation of sexual hypocrisy, and *Cranford*, a series of sketches of provincial life based on her years in the small Cheshire village of Knutsford. *North and South* (1855), often considered her finest novel, contrasted the socioeconomic conditions in the urban north and rural south of England. A meeting with Charlotte Brontë in 1850 led to friendship, and, on Brontë's death Gaskell wrote *The Life of Charlotte Brontë* (1857). Her later novels *Sylvia's Lovers* (1863), *Cousin Phillis*

(1865), and the posthumously published and incomplete *Wives and Daughters* (1866) showed continuing concern with social problems and a deepening awareness of the levels of the human personality.

gasohol [gas'-uh-hawl]

Gasohol is a mixture of gasoline and the alcohol ethanol (or, more rarely, methanol) used as a motor fuel. Commercial quantities of ethanol can be obtained by the fermentation of agricultural wastes. During the gasoline shortages of the late 1970s gasohol was often available to U.S. motorists, but few U.S. car owners now use it. Although gasohol burns more slowly, coolly, and cleanly than gasoline and provides greater octane, in concentrated amounts it can damage the plastics and synthetic rubbers used in engines. The U.S. Environmental Protection Agency allows the addition of only 10 percent ethanol by volume (or 3 percent methanol) to unleaded gas.

gasoline [gas-uh-leen']

Gasoline, known as petrol in England, is a petroleum hydrocarbon fuel used principally to power internal-combustion engines. Composed primarily of the ALKANES hexane, heptane, and octane, it may contain molecules with between 4 and 12 carbon atoms. It is liquid at ordinary ambient temperatures but evaporates easily in air to form a flammable mixture.

Production. Gasoline is produced by the distillation of crude oil and also by the cracking, or breaking up, of heavier distillation products. This cracking can be either by thermal means—that is, by maintaining heavy-oil fractions at elevated temperatures and pressures, when they break up into smaller units—or by catalytic cracking (see PETROLEUM INDUSTRY).

In catalytic cracking, the oil is fed in a stream of steam into a reaction vessel containing a catalyst—such as fine particles of Fuller's Earth (a hydrated aluminosilicate)—suspended in a fluidized bed. A reaction occurs in which large molecules are broken down into smaller ones. Some carbon is deposited on the catalyst, which therefore loses some of its effect and has to be regenerated in a second fluidized bed, where the carbon is burned off in a stream of air. The resultant carbon dioxide is released into the atmosphere.

Composition and Use. The burning properties of gasoline depend on the composition of the sample. One property particularly important for automobile-engine applications is the tendency for hydrocarbons in the gasoline range to ignite spontaneously under the high temperature and pressure conditions inside an engine cylinder. This preignition leads to a characteristic knocking in the engine. The antiknock properties of the gasoline are measured by its octane number.

In the past, tetraethyl lead was often added to increase octane ratings and improve fuel efficiency. In 1985 the Environmental Protection Agency ruled that gasoline lead content be reduced by over 90 percent, resulting in a dramatic drop in airborne lead emissions. To control the levels of other polluting emissions from automobile exhaust, engines must now be equipped with various emission-control devices. The most effective is the CATALYTIC CONVERTER, which cannot operate efficiently when leaded gasoline is used.

Gaspé Peninsula [gahs-pay'] The Gaspé Peninsula, also known as Gaspésie, is a rugged, remote area of eastern Quebec, Canada, which projects into the Gulf of St. Lawrence between Chaleur Bay and the mouth of the St. Lawrence River. It is about 240 km (150 mi) long and 115 to 135 km (70 to 85 mi) wide. Famous for its scenic views, the peninsula has a mountainous, thickly forested interior, with many lakes and rivers. Its highest peak is Mount Jacques Cartier (1,268 m/4,160 ft), in the Shickshock (Chic Choc) Mountains. Important towns include Matane, Gaspé, and Percé. The inhabitants, most of whom are French speaking, live primarily by fishing, although some maintain marginal farms on the rocky soil. Lumbering and tourism are additional sources of income.

Gasperi, Alcide de   see DE GASPERI, ALCIDE

Gass, William H. [gas] The American author William Howard Gass, b. Fargo, N.Dak., July 30, 1924, is a leading exponent of so-called innovative fiction, maintaining that words themselves—not characters, themes, and ideas—make up fiction. This philosophy is articulated in *Fiction and the Figures of Life* (1970) and supported in the essay collections *The World within the Word* (1978) and *The Habitations of the Word* (1984). Gass's fiction includes *Omensetter's Luck* (1966), his first novel; *In the Heart of the Heart of the Country and Other Stories* (1968); and *Willie Masters' Lonesome Wife* (1968).

gastritis   see GASTROINTESTINAL TRACT DISEASE

gastrointestinal tract disease [gas'-troh-in-tes'tin-ul] Diseases of the gastrointestinal system are major causes of illness and death. In developing nations malnutrition and poor sanitation predispose the populations to bacterial and parasitic infections. In industrialized nations a shorter life expectancy is associated with an increase in the incidence of gastrointestinal cancer.

Congenital or Acquired Structural Lesions. Congenital pyloric stenosis is a genetically determined disorder that is more common in male infants. Thickening of the circular muscle at the pylorus, the opening from the stomach to the duodenum (first portion of the small intestine), causes gastric obstruction accompanied by vomiting and dehydration. A pyloromyotomy—surgical division of the circular pyloric muscle—corrects this condition. Diverticula and strictures are the most commonly acquired structural lesions (defects). A diverticulum is a localized outpouching of the gut caused by a high pressure in the lumen (cavity) and a localized weakness of the muscle layers. Diverticula extending from the pharynx or lower

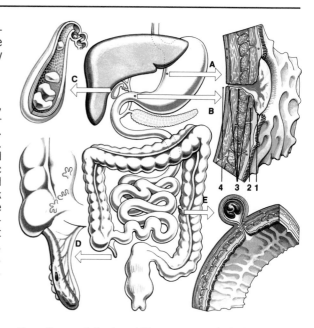

Ulcers often occur in the stomach (A) or, more commonly, the duodenum (B). They erode the mucous membrane (1) and may invade the submucous (2) and muscle (3) layers; complete perforation (4) through the wall of the gut requires treatment to prevent inflammation of the peritoneum, the membrane that lines the abdominal cavity. Gallstones (C), formed from bile pigment and cholesterol, may cause obstruction or inflammation in the gall bladder. Appendicitis, an acute inflammation of the appendix (D), requires surgical removal of that organ. Diverticulosis, or the formation of saclike diverticula (E), occurs in the colon and may lead to inflammation.

esophagus may collect food and secretions and interfere with normal swallowing. Bacteria in small-intestine diverticula may cause malabsorption. Diverticula in the colon may perforate to form abscesses and cause inflammation (diverticulitis).

Abnormalities of Motor Function. The normal contraction and relaxation of the muscle layers of the gastrointestinal tract mixes food with digestive secretions, propels the intestinal content by peristaltic contraction, and prevents regurgitation. Disorders of intestinal movements may be due to neurological disease or muscle abnormalities.

Mucosal Injury. Mucosal injury may arise due to physical or chemical agents. Two chemical agents, hydrochloric acid in the stomach and bile salts secreted into the duodenum, may cause mucosal injury. The cells that line the surface of the normal stomach protect it from acid injury. If these cells are damaged (for example, by aspirin) the acid within the stomach may leak back into the mucosa and cause erosions, or ULCERS. ANTACIDS are usually effective in relieving ulcer symptoms and in promoting ulcer healing.

The rapidly proliferating cells lining the gastrointestinal tract are sensitive to irradiation and to drugs that are used to treat cancer (chemotherapy). In the esophagus, injury may cause pain, or difficulty in swallowing; in the intestine, injury may lead to diarrhea; in the colon, radiation COLITIS may cause bleeding.

Viral, Bacterial, and Parasitic Infections. "Intestinal flu" is a common epidemic viral infection of the small bowel mucosa, causing a brief febrile (fever-present) illness with vomiting or diarrhea or both. "Traveler's diarrhea" is usually caused by bacteria (*Escherichia coli*) that stimulate intestinal secretion of fluid. CHOLERA, caused by *Vibrio cholerae* bacteria (usually due to water contamination), is a more severe diarrhea because the bacteria produce toxins.

Certain bacteria, including *Salmonella* and *Shigella*, invade the mucosa of the small bowel or colon to produce enteritis or DYSENTERY. Parasitic diseases, such as SCHISTOSOMIASIS, are a major worldwide public-health problem.

Maldigestion and Malabsorption. Digestion is impaired in the case of pancreatic insufficiency when there is a lack of the major pancreatic digestive enzymes and bicarbonate. When the concentration of bile salts is depressed by hepato-biliary disease or by resection of the distal small bowel (the normal site of bile acid reabsorption and conservation), malabsorption of fat and fat-soluble vitamins causes diarrhea and deficiency of vitamins A, D, and K.

Diseases of the intestinal mucosa may cause malabsorption of many nutrients. In the tropical malabsorption syndrome (tropical sprue), mucosal damage may be due to bacterial infection, which is corrected by antibiotic therapy.

Immunological Diseases. Deficiencies of certain immunological agents can promote intestinal infection by bacteria and parasites. Sensitivity to dietary antigens, such as cow's-milk proteins, may cause local allergic reactions within the intestine, which subsequently cause diarrhea, bleeding, or leakage of plasma protein. The atrophic gastritis of pernicious anemia appears to be an autoimmune disease.

Neoplastic Disease. Benign (nonmalignant) polyps are relatively common in the colon and in the stomach. Patients with a family history of multiple polyps have a high risk of developing CANCER of the colon at an early age.

Vascular Lesions. Vascular malformations, with thin, dilated blood vessels in the mucosa, may cause bleeding from the stomach, small intestine, or cecum. Mesenteric vascular disease may be arterial or venous. Blockage of one of the main abdominal arteries by ATHEROSCLEROSIS or by blood clot may cause tissue death (necrosis) in the small bowel.

Gastritis. Gastritis is an inflammation of the stomach lining that can be caused by many factors, including irritation by agents such as drugs, alcohol, and corrosive chemicals; bacterial and viral infections; and allergies. The symptoms, including nausea and loss of appetite, usually subside after identifying and dealing with the causative agent.

Advances in Treatment. Patients with impaired gastrointestinal tracts can starve to death, because the method of feeding—intravenous sugar—can supply only 500 to 600 calories per day. A technique called intravenous hyperalimentation can supply up to 3,000 calories per day, plus vitamins, amino acids, and minerals. The food is pumped into a large vein, the superior vena cava. Used while patients recover from illness, surgery, or severe burns, the technique is also used to give the bowels a chance to heal in severe inflammatory disease, eliminating the need for surgery.

gastronomy   see COOKING

gastropod   see MOLLUSK

gastroscope   see ENDOSCOPE

Gates, Horatio   Horatio Gates was an American general who won the Battle of SARATOGA, perhaps the most significant engagement of the AMERICAN REVOLUTION. Born in England on July 26, 1727, he entered the British army and served in America during the French and Indian War (1754–63). Retiring on half pay, he immigrated to America in 1772 and bought a Virginia plantation.

Gates became adjutant general of the Continental Army in 1775. Promoted to major general in 1776, he was placed in command of the northern army. On Oct. 17, 1777, Gen. John BURGOYNE surrendered his army to Gates at Saratoga after two fierce battles. Saratoga proved to be a turning point in the war, for it convinced France to become America's ally.

Gates was appointed president of the board of war in 1777. The alleged object of the CONWAY CABAL of that year was to replace Washington with Gates as commander in chief, but there is little evidence of a real conspiracy. Taking command of the southern army in 1780, Gates was disastrously defeated at Camden, S.C., on August 16 by Gen. Charles Cornwallis. Retiring to his Virginia plantation, Gates returned to active duty in 1782 at Newburgh, N.Y. Leaving the army in 1783, he moved eventually to Manhattan Island, where he died on Apr. 10, 1806.

Horatio Gates, a military commander during the Revolutionary War, led an American army to victory over a British force under Gen. John Burgoyne at Saratoga (1777) in one of the pivotal engagements of the war.

Gates, Sir Thomas   Sir Thomas Gates, d. 1621, was the English governor of the Virginia colony and one of the original investors in the LONDON COMPANY that founded Virginia. Before his involvement with the company,

Gates was an adventurer on the high seas, sailing (1585) with Sir Francis Drake in a raid on the Spanish and commanding his own expeditions in the 1590s. In 1609, Gates was made second in command to Lord De La Warr, first governor of Virginia. When he set sail for Virginia, his ship was wrecked at Bermuda—an incident that allegedly inspired Shakespeare's *The Tempest*—but he finally reached JAMESTOWN in May 1610. He was about to evacuate the few colonists who had survived the bitter winter when De La Warr arrived and insisted that the settlers remain. Gates later brought in new settlers and livestock and governed the colony, after De La Warr's return to England, from 1611 to 1614.

gating circuit   see COMPUTER

Gatling, Richard Jordan [gat'-ling]   The American inventor Richard Gatling, b. Maney's Neck, N.C., Sept. 12, 1818, d. Feb. 26, 1903, is best known for his crank-operated MACHINE GUN, patented in 1862. The son of a North Carolina planter, Gatling made a fortune before the Civil War from his agricultural inventions, among them a steam-powered plow. His gun was capable of firing 350 rounds a minute through its rotating multiple barrels. Although there is evidence that the Gatling was used during the war, it did not become official U.S. Army weaponry until 1866. It remained in use until 1911, when the introduction of smokeless powder made possible the gas-operated Maxim gun. *Gat*, the slang term for pistol, is derived from Gatling's name.

GATT   see GENERAL AGREEMENT ON TARIFFS AND TRADE

Gaudí, Antonio [gow-dee']   The Catalan architect Antonio (Antoni) Gaudí i Cornet, b. June 25, 1852, d. June 7, 1926, was one of the most eccentric and original geniuses in the development of modern art. His extremely personal style evolved without any perceptible contemporary influence, and he arrived independently at an equivalent of the international ART NOUVEAU style.

In the Palau Güell (1885–89), a town mansion for his patron Eusebio Güell, Gaudí forecast his ultimate fantastical style, especially in the highly original forms of the ironwork and in the sculptural roofscape of chimneys and cornices. Güell also sponsored the spectacular Parque Güell (1900–14), a hilly site in the heart of Barcelona that Gaudí dotted with biomorphic pavilions and galleries and linked serpentine benches surfaced with mosaics.

In 1884, Gaudí began the monumental task that occupied him until his death and that remains unfinished, the vast Expiatory Temple of the Holy Family—the Sagrada Familia—in Barcelona. Gaudí at first continued in the Gothic Revival style set by his predecessor Francisco del Villár (1845–1922). As the building progressed, however, Gaudí revised the plans until, by 1900, the building designs were entirely without precedent, as seen in the four colossal openwork spires—outer pair, 98.4 m (323 ft); inner pair, 107 m (351 ft)—of the completed entrance

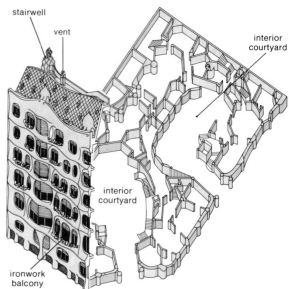

The remarkable Casa Milá apartment house in Barcelona, designed by the Spanish architect Antonio Gaudí, embodies the curvilinear Art Nouveau style. Despite its fluid and organic appearance, the building is constructed of cut stone and roofed with marble slabs. Two courtyards flow into the interior with the same rhythmic pattern characteristic of the exterior. Spiraled chimneys and ironwork balconies ornament the facade.

facade. Two other important works are the Casa Batlló (1905–07) and the Casa Milá (1905–10) in Barcelona.

Gaudí had no influence whatever beyond Barcelona until decades after his death, when his innovative forms and constructed environments were reflected in avant-garde architecture, painting, and sculpture.

Gaudier-Brzeska, Henri [goh-dee-ay'-bur-zes-kah']   Henri Gaudier-Brzeska, b. Oct. 4, 1891, d. June 5, 1915, was a French sculptor whose considerable fame rests on a relatively small number of works produced in London between 1912 and 1914. Gaudier-Brzeska rapidly assimilated the influence of Auguste RODIN and contemporary CUBISM, and, like many other artists of his time, admired primitive African and Asian wood carving and stone carving. From 1911 he lived in London and associated with the vorticist group of artists and writers (see VORTICISM). Gaudier-Brzeska worked in wood, marble, stone, and bronze, forming heads, figures, and animals—many of which are almost miniature in size.

Gauguin, Paul [goh-gan'] Paul Gauguin, b. Paris, June 7, 1848, d. May 8, 1903, was one of the leading figures in postimpressionist French art of the 1880s and '90s (see POSTIMPRESSIONISM). Both his personality and his principles of coloring and composition exerted a strong influence on modern painting.

Gauguin was essentially a "Sunday" painter, pursuing his art on weekends and in the summer, until he met Camille PISSARRO in 1875 and began to work with him to improve his drawing and painting. After the financial crash of 1882–83, he abandoned his wife and five children in Denmark and returned to France to become a full-time artist.

Prior to this time Gauguin's painting displayed the marks of his gradual assimilation of the principles and techniques of IMPRESSIONISM. Now he began experimenting with ceramics and sculpture, and he moved rapidly toward a firmness of composition and a concern for rhythm and mass in painting. In 1888, in Brittany, Gauguin painted *Vision after the Sermon* (1888; National Gallery of Scotland, Edinburgh), in which Breton women returning from church see a vision of the biblical struggle between Jacob and the angel, about which the priest has just preached. The use of bold color and strongly defined forms, together with a subject that combines the visionary and the real in one composition, marked a decisive breakthrough for him. After spending a few months at Arles with Vincent VAN GOGH at the end of 1888, Gauguin passed the next few years in Brittany, where he continued to paint the local people and their way of life and simple faith, and in Paris, where he established contact with the leading writers and theorists of the symbolist movement. Although Gauguin called the style he developed in 1888 *synthetism*, he now instilled into his work qualities of mystery and suggestiveness that may be compared with symbolism in literature.

Early in 1891, Gauguin left for Tahiti, where he began a series of paintings that depict the physical beauty of the people and the myths underlying their traditional religion. The series evokes the Tahitian cycle of existence from birth through maturity to old age and death. Plagued increasingly by ill health and poverty, he attempted suicide in 1898 after completing, by way of a last testament to his vision of Tahiti, *Where Do We Come From? What Are We? Where Are We Going?* (1897–98; Museum of Fine Arts, Boston). The paintings of his final years project an idealized vision of native life, removed from both time and actuality in its conception of Tahitian culture.

The French post-Impressionist painter Paul Gauguin revitalized his art by directly experiencing primitive culture. This portrait of Tahitian Women *(1891) was painted during his first year in Tahiti. Despite the exotic dress and setting, the heavy, monumental forms of these women reveal Gauguin's classical heritage. (Louvre, Paris.)*

Gaul [gawl] Gaul (from the Latin *Gallia*) was the ancient name for an area roughly equivalent to modern France, Belgium, Luxembourg, and Germany west of the Rhine. The CELTS, whom the Romans called Galli, began to cross the Rhine into Gaul *c.*900 BC and by the 5th century BC had established a fairly uniform culture typified by the art of LA TÈNE. Along the Mediterranean, Greek civilization was introduced with the founding of Massilia (now Marseille) *c.*600 BC.

To protect its ally Massilia and ensure communications with Spain, Rome in 121 BC annexed a strip of territory between the Cévennes and the Alps roughly equivalent to the modern Provence. Julius CAESAR conquered the rest of Gaul during his GALLIC WARS (58–51 BC). Three new Roman provinces eventually emerged: Belgica, Lugdunensis, and Aquitania.

Emperor CLAUDIUS I, who was born at Lugdunum (now Lyon), admitted Gallic nobles to the Roman Senate in AD 48. He also ordered the suppression of the DRUIDS, the Celtic priests. Native deities were amalgamated with Roman counterparts, and emperor worship was encouraged. By the 4th century AD, however, Christianity predominated and weakened Celtic culture further by using Latin in worship.

In the 1st and 2d centuries AD, Gaul flourished through the export of food, wine, and pottery. In the 3d century it suffered devastating barbarian raids, however, and the Roman emperors' ineffective defense led to the creation *c.*260 of a short-lived kingdom of the Gauls. Beginning in 406 various Germanic tribes, especially VANDALS, ravaged Gaul. The Visigoths (see GOTHS), nominally Roman allies, settled in Aquitaine, where they cooperated with the Roman general Flavius AETIUS to defeat (451) the HUNS. By 478 the Visigoths had also acquired Narbonensis. Meanwhile, the FRANKS took over northern Gaul, and the Alemanni and Burgundians settled in the east. The last Roman territory in Gaul fell to CLOVIS, king of the Franks, in 486.

See also: FRANCE, HISTORY OF; ROME, ANCIENT.

Gaulle, Charles de   see DE GAULLE, CHARLES

Gauss, Carl Friedrich [gows]   Carl Friedrich Gauss, b. Apr. 30, 1777, d. Feb. 23, 1855, was a German mathematician who dominated the mathematical community during and after his lifetime. While still attending Caroline College (1792–95), Gauss formulated the least-squares method, and in 1799 he gave the first proof of the fundamental theorem of algebra. In 1801, Gauss published a treatise on number theory, which contained his solutions to many outstanding problems. In the same year he computed the orbit of Ceres, using an improved theory, and predicted where and when the asteroid would reappear. When the prediction was proved correct, Gauss's fame spread far and wide. He subsequently accepted a financially secure position as astronomer at the Göttingen Observatory.

The mathematician Carl Friedrich Gauss calculated the orbit of the asteroid Ceres after only three observations. He published his work in number theory in Disquisitiones arithmeticae *and later made contributions in differential geometry and topology.*

To fulfill his sense of civic responsibility, Gauss undertook a geodetic survey of his country and did much of the field work himself. During the 1820s, with the collaboration of the physicist Wilhelm Weber, he explored many areas of physics, including magnetism, mechanics, acoustics, and optics. In 1833 he constructed the first telegraph. Gauss's publications were polished and finished works that opened new paths for investigation and contained the seeds of much future work. To date, 12 volumes have been published.

Gautama, Siddhartha   see BUDDHA

Gautier, Théophile [goh-tee-ay', tay-oh-feel']
Théophile Gautier, b. Aug. 30, 1811, d. Oct, 23, 1872, was one of the finest and most versatile French romantic writers. His gifts for picturesque imagery and unusual diction, apparent in *Albertus* (1832) and *Comedy of Death* (1838), reached their highest level in *Enamels and Cameos* (1852). Gautier's sensitivity to beauty and insistence on formal perfection inspired Charles Baudelaire and the PARNASSIAN movement.

After 1835, Gautier earned his living as a journalist, novelist, and travel writer. His first important novel, *Mademoiselle de Maupin* (1835), was prefaced by a provocative manifesto of the doctrine of "Art for Art's sake." A prolific body of prose writing followed, including *Young France* (1833), an affectionate satiric portrait of the excesses of his contemporaries; "The Dead Lover" (1836; Eng. trans., 1903), a ghost story of incomparable skill; and *The Romance of the Mummy* (1856; Eng. trans.,

1863), a historical novel of ancient Egypt. Gautier traveled extensively in order to write *A Romantic in Spain* (1845; Eng. trans., 1926); *Journeys in Italy* (1852; Eng. trans., 1902); *Constantinople of Today* (1853; Eng. trans., 1854); *Voyage en Russie* (Travels in Russia, 1867); and a novel set in England, *La Belle Jenny* (1865). He also wrote two plays, but these were less successful than his two ballet scripts *Giselle* (1841) and *La Péri* (1843).

Gavarni, Paul [gah-vahr-nee'] Paul Gavarni was the pseudonym of Guillaume Sulpice Chevalier, b. Jan. 13, 1804, d. Nov. 24, 1866, French lithographer and caricaturist. Trained as a copperplate engraver, Gavarni became a fashion illustrator during the late 1820s. His elegant and witty portrayals of the fashionable Parisians of his day, appearing in satirical publications such as *Caricature* and *Charivari*, were popular in both France and England. He drew directly on the lithographic stones without using sketches or preparatory drawings; the resulting images of servant girls, courtesans, boulevardiers, and middle-class couples display an immediacy and intimacy. Gavarni's later work increasingly portrayed the darker side of life, but without the mastery of his great contemporary Honoré DAUMIER.

gavial [gay'-vee-ul] The gavial, *Gavialis gangeticus*, or gharial, is a crocodilian originally found in a number of river systems, including the Indus River of India and Pakistan, Ganges and Brahmaputra rivers of India and Bangladesh, and the Kaladan River of western Burma. Gavials are the sole living member of the family Gavialidae. They are one of the largest crocodilians, reaching adult lengths of 3.5 to 4.5 m (12 to 15 ft), with a recorded maximum of 6.5 m (21.5 ft). Their snout is more slender than that of any other crocodilian, an adaptation that allows them to rapidly slash sideways in the water to catch fish, which constitute the bulk of their diet. Gavials occasionally eat birds and small mammals, but they are not known to attack humans. Gavials have been brought to the edge of extinction due to dam building, hide hunting, and net fishing. It is thought that no more than 100 survive in the wild.

Gawain, Sir [gah'-win] In the Arthurian legends Sir Gawain was King Arthur's nephew, the son of King Lot of Orkney and Morgawse. *Sir Gawain and the Green Knight*, a 14th-century romance, is the most famous legend about him. His name and some of his attributes suggest that he was identified with or related to the Celtic sun deity.

See also: ARTHUR AND ARTHURIAN LEGEND.

Gay, John A leading poet and playwright of the English AUGUSTAN AGE, John Gay, b. June 30, 1685, d. Dec. 4, 1732, is best known for *The Beggar's Opera* (1728).

A former schoolmate helped Gay publish his first poem, "Wine," in 1708, and thereafter he rose quickly to notice. By 1711 he had become friendly with Sir Richard Steele, Joseph Addison, and Alexander Pope. With Pope and Jonathan Swift he founded the Scriblerus Club (1714). He later held a government sinecure and in his last years enjoyed the patronage of the duke of Queensbury.

Gay's major works treat low realistic subjects and parody traditional forms and styles. *The Shepherd's Week* (1714) parodies pastoral poetry, especially *The Shepheardes Calendar* (1579) by Edmund Spenser; *The What D'Ye Call It* (1715) burlesques contemporary tragedy; *Trivia, or the Art of Walking the Streets of London* (1716) imitates the *Georgics* of Vergil by describing city scenes in the same manner Vergil described the country. *The Beggar's Opera* ludicrously mingles elements of ballad and Italian opera in a satire on Sir Robert Walpole, England's prime minister. Its vehicle is opera, but its characters are criminals and prostitutes. Gay's other works include *Rural Sports* (poem, 1713), *Three Hours After Marriage* (stage comedy, with Pope and John Arbuthnot, 1717), and *Fables* (2 vols., 1727 and 1738).

The Indian gavial is a large crocodilian. Measuring 4 to 5 m (13 to 16 ft), it has a narrow, elongated snout adapted for catching fish by quick sideways movement.

John Gay, an English dramatist of the 18th century, is remembered chiefly for his satire of social and literary conventions. Gay's most durable work, The Beggar's Opera *(1728), lampooned genteel Italian opera.*

gay activism   Gay activism is the effort to eliminate all forms of prejudice and discrimination against homosexual women and men. It may be viewed as part of the broad cultural reevaluation of traditional male and female roles that has been fostered by the women's movement and by human potential and self-help groups.

The impetus for gay activism came from social movements of the 1950s and '60s that demanded full individual and human rights for members of racial, religious, and ethnic minorities, and from the insistence by members of these groups on the right to cultural diversity and self-determination. Though it also coincided with the so-called sexual revolution, most gay activists have emphasized human rights and dignities more than sexual freedom.

The use of the term *gay activism* since the early 1970s was sparked by riots outside a New York homosexual bar in June 1969, in which groups of gay men and women for the first time resisted police harassment. Within three years the number of gay groups in the United States grew from fewer than 20 to about 1,200, and similar groups emerged in Western Europe, Latin America, Canada, Australia, and Japan. The primary aim of U.S. organizations was the passage of civil rights laws similar to those forbidding discrimination on the basis of race, religion, ethnic origin, and sex. They also worked for the repeal of all laws criminalizing any form of private sexual behavior between consenting adults.

By 1986 more than 50 U.S. county and local governments and one state had enacted civil rights protection for homosexuals. Openly gay political candidates had been elected to office, ranging from city councils to the House of Representatives. Newspapers frequently carried accounts of individual homosexuals seeking rights: to adopt children, to serve in the military, or to be ordained in the ministry.

In response to the AIDS crisis, gay-activist efforts since the 1980s have largely concentrated on protecting persons with AIDS from discrimination in jobs, housing, or health care.

See also: CIVIL RIGHTS; HOMOSEXUALITY.

Gay-Lussac, Joseph Louis [gay-loo-sahk']   One of the leading scientists of his generation, the Frenchman Joseph Louis Gay-Lussac, b. Dec. 6, 1778, d. May 9, 1850, made his chief contributions in physical and inorganic chemistry. His earliest investigations led to the formulation of the law, sometimes credited to his countryman J. A. C. Charles, that all gases expand by equal amounts when subjected to equal increments in temperature. Subsequently he announced another fundamental generalization, that gases combine chemically in simple proportions by volume. Seized upon by the Italian physicist Amedeo Avogadro, this law helped pave the way for the modern atomic-molecular theory of matter.

Gaza [gah'-zuh]   Gaza is the principal city in the so-called Gaza Strip. It lies in the coastal plain north of the Sinai Peninsula about 5 km (3 mi) east of the Mediterranean Sea and about 80 km (50 mi) southwest of Jerusalem. It has a population of 120,000 (1979 est.).

An important settlement along ancient trade routes, Gaza has been fought over since before the 15th century BC. It was one of the five cities of the Philistine League (see PHILISTINES) and is mentioned frequently in the Bible, notably as the site of the Philistine temple that Samson brought down on himself and his enemies (Judges 16). Since its capture by Arabs in the 7th century, it has been inhabited by Muslims. A part of Palestine, it was occupied by Egypt in the Arab-Israeli War of 1948 and became a main center of Palestinian refugee concentration. Gaza was captured by Israel in the Six-Day War of 1967 and remains under Israeli administration.

Gaza Strip   The Gaza Strip is a narrow band of desertlike land along the western Mediterranean coast. It is about 42 km (26 mi) long and 6.5 to 8 km (4 to 5 mi) wide and has a land area of 363 km^2 (140 mi^2). From 1917 to 1948 the Gaza Strip was part of the British mandate of Palestine. Since the Arab-Israeli War of 1948 the political status of Gaza has been unresolved, with its Palestinian residents seeking autonomy. Egypt controlled it (except for a brief period of Israeli occupation in 1956–57) until the Six-Day War of 1967, when it was occupied by Israel. The Egyptian-Israeli peace treaty of 1979 provided for negotiations concerning the strip's status, but little progress was made. In December 1987 frustrated Palestinians in the West Bank and Gaza Strip launched an *intifadah* (uprising) to end Israeli occupation.

The Gaza Strip is very densely populated, with a youthful and rapidly growing population of 615,575 (1990 est.). More than 99% of the residents are stateless Palestinian Arabs. More than 60% are refugees from Israel, most of whom have lived in refugee camps since 1948. Gaza is the administrative center. The economy centers on agriculture, livestock raising, fishing, and small industry. Nearly 60% of the labor force commuted to menial jobs in Israel before the 1991 GULF WAR which devastated the local economy.

gazebo [guh-zee'-boh]   A gazebo is a small decorative building or garden house, usually open on all sides, offering an excellent view of the surrounding landscape. The term, a facetious combination of the word *gaze* and the Latin suffix *-ebo*, meaning "I shall," first appeared in *New Designs for Chinese Temples* (1752) by the English architect William Halfpenny.

gazelle [guh-zel']   Gazelles, genus *Gazella*, are slender, graceful ANTELOPES belonging to the family Bovidae, order Artiodactyla. There are about 12 species and 50 recognized forms. The largest gazelle is the dama, or red-necked, gazelle, *G. damaruficollis*, of northern Africa, which stands slightly less than 1 m (3 ft) tall at the shoulder. Other species are 51 to 86 cm (20 to 34 in)

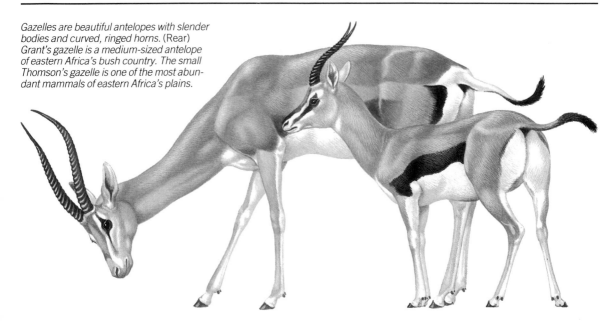

Gazelles are beautiful antelopes with slender bodies and curved, ringed horns. (Rear) Grant's gazelle is a medium-sized antelope of eastern Africa's bush country. The small Thomson's gazelle is one of the most abundant mammals of eastern Africa's plains.

tall. Gazelles have long, thin legs with two-toed hooves. Both sexes have beautiful, black-ringed, 25- to 38-cm-long (10- to 15-in) horns, except for the Persian, or goitered, gazelle, only the bucks of which have horns. Grant's gazelle, *G. granti*, of eastern Africa, has 81-cm (32-in) horns—as long as the animal is tall. Gazelles have brown or fawn-colored coats, usually with black and white markings around the face and neck, white undersides and rump, and often a horizontal band of dark color along the flanks. The ears are long and narrow. The tail is short. The large, luminous black eyes are a striking feature. Many gazelles are fast runners, and Grant's gazelle has been clocked at 80 km/h (50 mph).

Gazelles inhabit open plains from Mongolia and India to Egypt and Morocco and into tropical eastern and central Africa. Several species have become threatened because of overhunting. Gazelles graze in herds numbering from four or five to several hundred. Central and eastern African gazelles often mingle with herds of other herbivores. Like other antelopes, gazelles are ruminants, or cud-chewers.

Gdańsk [guh-dahnsk'] Gdańsk (Danzig), a port city in Poland, has a population of 469,100 (1988 est.). The city lies at the mouth of the VISTULA RIVER on the Baltic Sea; the surrounding land is low lying, and both water defenses and dock basins were easily carved from the soft alluvium.

The ports of Gdańsk and its twin city, the port of Gdynia to the north (1988 est. pop., 249,500), are operated under a single port authority. Gdańsk's industries include shipbuilding, engineering, food processing, and chemical manufacturing. In postmedieval times, Gdańsk spread outside the original walls and extended to the east, beyond the Motława, a tributary of the Vistula. The city was severely damaged during World War II but has been rebuilt and the old city restored to its former splendor.

A settlement existed there during the 10th century, but the commercial city grew up during the 12th and 13th centuries with the development of the HANSEATIC LEAGUE and Baltic trade. It became the major port of the Vistula basin and attained its greatest prosperity during the 16th and 17th centuries, when it was the principal grain market in Europe. Although Gdańsk underwent a decline during the 18th century, it remained the region's leading port until the 1920s.

In the second Partition of Poland (1793), Gdańsk was absorbed into Prussia. After World War I, Gdańsk was not given to the reconstituted Polish state because of its largely German population. Instead, it was constituted a free city under the sovereignty of the League of Nations. Although it was intended that Gdańsk should serve the needs of Poland, increasing difficulties with the German population led Poland to establish (1924) a new port at Gdynia in the POLISH CORRIDOR. Germany's claim to annex the city was an important factor in causing World War II. At the end of the war the city was fully incorporated into Poland and was repopulated largely by Polish refugees from further east. The city was a major center of opposition to Poland's Communist government during the 1980s.

Gdynia see GDAŃSK

gear A gear is a toothed wheel or, less commonly, an object of some other shape with teeth cut into it, for example, a cylinder or cone. Gears are usually fastened to axles or shafts and are used to transmit rotational motion from one shaft to another. In doing this gears change the

Gears are toothed wheels that are used to transmit motion from one shaft to another. Spur gears (A) have teeth cut parallel to the axis of rotation and connect shafts that are parallel to each other. Ordinary cone-shaped bevel gears (B) have straight teeth and are used to transmit power between shafts whose axes intersect. Hypoid gears (C), or bevel gears with straight teeth cut at an angle to the shaft axis, can transmit power between shafts whose axes cross each other in different planes. Spiral bevel gears (D) have teeth cut in a spiral, resulting in a larger area of contact between meshing teeth and permitting larger torques to be transmitted. In a worm gear (E) a spirally threaded worm drives a spiral-toothed gear at right angles to its own axis. Double helical gears (F) have two opposing helices cut in the same gear in order to cancel the sideways thrust generated by single spiral gears and thus reduce gear wear.

direction of the force applied and may also change the magnitude of the force. They thus function as a machine. In fact, they are often considered a form of the wheel and axle, one of the basic SIMPLE MACHINES.

When two gears are arranged so that the teeth of one mesh, or mate, with the teeth of the other, the turning of one gear will cause the other one to turn also. If the two gears have the same number of teeth, they will turn at the same rate of rotation (angular velocity), and the applied force and turning effort (TORQUE) are changed in direction but not in magnitude. If the gears have different numbers of teeth, however, the magnitude of the torque and the angular velocity are also changed.

A small gear (one with fewer teeth) that drives a larger one (with more teeth) will increase the torque and reduce the speed of the driven gear. The opposite arrangement (a larger gear driving a smaller gear) will decrease the torque while increasing the speed. As with other machines these effects can be described in terms of the mechanical advantage of the system, which is the ratio of the torque of the driven shaft to that of the driving shaft.

Geber (Jabir ibn Hayyan) [jee'-bur]   Jabir ibn Hayyan, known in the West as Geber, is the reputed author of an extensive body of Arabic writings significant for their codification of alchemical knowledge and their transmission of Greek philosophy (see ALCHEMY). The writings date from the late 8th and early 9th centuries; some may actually have been written by Jabir, but most others are the works of an Arabic school. The Latin alchemical writings under the name of Geber are of separate origin.

gecko [gek'-oh]   Geckos are nocturnal, arboreal, generally stoutly built, insect-eating lizards found in warmer regions throughout the world. This diverse group is divided into about 75 genera and more than 400 species, constituting the family Gekhonidae. Most geckos are somber browns or grays, but some, such as the brilliant green day geckos, *Phelsuma*, are brightly colored. Geckos are commonly 10 to 15 cm (4 to 6 in) in total length, with a few reaching 30 cm (12 in)—for example, the to-

The banded gecko, a nocturnal desert lizard, is one of the few species with movable eyelids.

kay gecko, *Gekko gecko*, can grow to 35.5 cm (14 in). Some of the dwarf geckos, *Sphaerodactylus*, barely exceed 2.5 cm (1 in).

Geckos have large eyes, and most species do not have movable eyelids; in these, the eyes are covered with a protective, transparent scale. Except for the primitive types, which have rounded pupils, geckos have vertical-slit pupils, which may be straight-sided or lobed. The toes of geckos vary from simple claw-bearing digits to those equipped with expanded pads and concealed claws. The pads, which enable the gecko to cling even to smooth surfaces, consist of rows of plates covered with thousands of microscopic hooklike projections that can catch into any minute surface irregularity. Geckos are the only lizards that can produce more than a hiss or other simple sound; vocalizations range from squeaks and clicks to croaks and barks. With rare exceptions geckos lay eggs.

Gedda, Nicolai [ged'-ah]   Nicolai Gedda, b. July 11, 1925, is a Swedish-Russsian tenor admired for his impeccable musicianship and linguistic abilities. He made his debut (1952) at the Royal Opera in Stockholm. That same year he recorded the role of Dimitri in Mussorgsky's *Boris Godunov* and soon achieved international recognition. Gedda made his Metropolitan Opera debut (1957) as Faust in Gounod's opera; he also sang the part of Anatol in the world premiere (1958) of Samuel Barber's *Vanessa* there. His other roles include Don Ottavio in Mozart's *Don Giovanni* and Hoffmann in Offenbach's *The Tales of Hoffmann*.

Geddes, Sir Patrick [ged'-es]   The British biologist and sociologist Sir Patrick Geddes, b. Oct. 2, 1854, d. Apr. 17, 1932, established a considerable reputation based on his contributions to theories of URBAN PLANNING. He pioneered in recognizing the need for comprehensive preliminary planning surveys of cities that would take into account historical, biological, sociological, economic, aesthetic, and geographic factors. His resultant plans for Dunfermline, Scotland, and for dozens of cities in India, remain models of rational solutions to persistent urban problems. Geddes founded the Collège des Écossais (Scots College) near Montpellier, France, in 1924.

Gehrig, Lou [gair-ig]   Hall of Fame member Henry Louis Gehrig, b. New York City, June 19, 1903, d. June 2, 1941, nicknamed the "Iron Horse," played in a record 2,130 consecutive major league baseball games. A star athlete at Columbia University, Gehrig then played his entire career (1923–39) for the New York Yankees. Gehrig's offensive statistics are among the most impressive in baseball history. Despite playing in the shadow of Babe Ruth, the first baseman led the American League in home runs three times (career: 493) and in runs batted in five times (career: 1,991—3d all time). His lifetime batting average was .340, and slugging average, .632 (3d all time). He played in seven World Series, of which the Yankees won six; he was the 1936 AL Most Valuable Player; and his 23 lifetime grand slam home runs is still the major league record. Gehrig was stricken fatally with amyotrophic lateral sclerosis, often called Lou Gehrig's disease.

Geiger, Abraham [gy'-gur]   Abraham Geiger, b. May 24, 1810, d. Oct. 23, 1874, was a German rabbi who played an important part in the early development of Reform Judaism. He called the first conference of Reform rabbis together in 1837 and participated actively in the conferences of 1845 and 1846. Advocating a Judaism fully integrated into European culture, Geiger argued that Judaism should be considered as a religious community exclusively, without nationalistic or racial distinctiveness.

Geiger counter   The Geiger counter, also known as the Geiger-Müller counter, is an instrument used to detect and measure the intensity of radiation, such as beta particles and cosmic rays. The device, which takes its name from the German physicists Hans Geiger and Wilhelm Müller, may be used as a laboratory instrument, in mineral exploration, as a thickness gauge for continuous sheet materials, and as a stock level gauge in blast furnaces. It is also employed in diagnostic medical work.

The heart of the Geiger counter is the ionization tube, which may be metal, or glass with a metalized interior, and a central conductor maintained at a high positive potential with respect to the outer enclosure. The tube may contain air, argon, or other gas at or below atmospheric pressure. When the tube is exposed to nuclear radiation the gas is ionized. Negative ions or electrons are attracted to the center conductor, and positive ions are attracted to the negative enclosure. If the voltage on the tube is in the Geiger range (800–1,500 volts), each ionizing event will cause an electron avalanche (gas amplification) and will result in a large output pulse. This pulse may be received

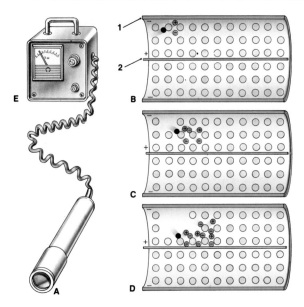

A Geiger counter detects charged particles. It consists of a metal-sheathed glass tube (A) that encloses a negatively charged metal cylinder, or anode (1), and a positively charged wire, or cathode (2). When a high-energy particle (black) enters the tube (B), which is filled with neon gas at low pressure (gray), it knocks an electron (blue) out of a neon atom, leaving a positively charged neon ion (red). The electron is attracted to the anode and the ion to the cathode. Both liberate more electrons by further collisions with neon atoms (C, D). The resulting flow of electrons is registered on a meter (E).

audibly in headphones or recorded electronically through counting devices.

Geisel, Ernesto [gy'-sel]   Ernesto Geisel, b. Aug. 3, 1908, was president of Brazil from 1974 to 1979. A career army officer, Geisel was instrumental in planning the military coup that removed leftist president João GOULART in 1964. From 1969 to 1974 he directed the government-owned Petróleo Brasileiro (Petrobras). His expansion of the oil industry was an important factor in Brazil's spectacular economic growth. As president, Geisel attempted to liberalize the military junta's authoritarian rule.

geisha [gee'-shuh]   In Japanese society a geisha is a young woman professionally trained to entertain men, especially businessmen at restaurant parties. The conception of the geisha as a prostitute is false; the name means "artistic person," and many geisha dance, sing, or play musical instruments. Their chief function, however, is to provide light conversation. Traditionally, geisha were like indentured servants, bonded by their parents to geisha houses that boarded, clothed, and trained them. Many modern geisha are unionized, although the profession as a whole has declined in numbers since World War II. Geisha must retire when they marry; those who retire without marrying often become teachers of music or dance.

gel [jel]   A gel is a solid or semisolid colloidal system, exemplified by the jelly that forms when a mixture of about 5% gelatin in hot water is allowed to cool. Although a gel is usually classed as a solid because it does not flow and is elastic, it is typically not as rigid as a conventional solid. It could, in some cases, properly be regarded as a supercooled liquid. In other colloidal systems one component forms discrete particles within a continuous, dispersing medium; in gels, however, both the solid and the liquid can be continuous, the liquid filling the interstices between the network of molecules of the solid. The liquid content in typical gels is above 90%, and it may be greater than 99% in some instances. Pectins and agar are well known for their gel-forming ability; pectins are used to make fruit jellies, and agar is used in bacteriological work. Gels formed from silica are widely used in laboratories and industry as fillers and supports for catalysts.

See also: COLLOIDAL STATE.

Gela [jay'-lah]   Gela is a city in Caltanissetta province in southern Sicily, Italy, on the Mediterranean Sea. A fishing port and seaside resort, it is the center of a cotton-growing region and has a petroleum-refining industry and a population of 74,789 (1981). Founded by Greek colonists from Crete and Rhodes about 688 BC, Gela itself sent out colonists to found Acragas (now AGRIGENTO) about 582 BC. Gela was sacked by Carthaginians in 405 BC and destroyed by Mamertini in 281 BC. Refounded by Holy Roman Emperor Frederick II in the 1230s, it was called Terranova di Sicilia until 1928. A landing point (July 1943) for the Allies' World War II invasion of Sicily, Gela is also known for its important Greek archaeological remains.

gelatin [jel'-uh-tin]   Gelatin is a protein obtained from the skin, tendons, and bones of animals. It is used in food products and pharmaceuticals, in many industrial processes, and for cooking. Derived from COLLAGEN, a constituent of animal skin and bone, it is extracted by treating hides and bone with lime or acid; boiling, filtering, and concentrating the material; and then drying and grinding it to produce commercial gelatin, in the form of transparent, odorless, and tasteless granules. Gelatin dissolves in hot water and congeals to form a gel as the solution cools.

Gelatin is an incomplete protein lacking the essential amino acid tryptophan, but as a food supplement it supplies several amino acids lacking in the protein of wheat, barley, and oats. Free of antigens, it does not cause allergic reactions.

Isinglass is a form of gelatin produced from the bladders of fish, and AGAR is a gelatinous seaweed extract used as a laboratory culturing medium and as a gelling agent in foods.

Gell-Mann, Murray [gel-mahn']   Murray Gell-Mann, an American theoretical physicist, b. New York City, Sept. 15, 1929, is known for his discovery of a classification

Murray Gell-Mann, an American theoretical physicist, won the Nobel Prize for physics in 1969 for devising a predictive classification of subatomic particles. Gell-Mann's system of particle types led him to postulate fundamental particles called "quarks" as the constituents of all nuclear particles.

scheme for nuclear particles and their interactions, for which he was awarded the 1969 Nobel Prize for physics. The son of an Austrian immigrant, Gell-Mann worked briefly at the Institute for Advanced Study in Princeton, N.J., before joining the faculty of the University of Chicago in 1952. In 1955 he went to the California Institute of Technology, where he became a full professor in 1956.

In 1953, Gell-Mann proposed that certain subatomic particles were characterized by an invariant property that he called "strangeness." He showed that strangeness was conserved in strong and electromagnetic interactions but not in weak interactions. This new conservation law was the foundation of later SYMMETRY schemes for classifying strongly interacting particles, including the so-called SU(3) symmetry introduced by Gell-Mann and, independently, by the Japanese physicist Kazuhiko Nishijima in 1961.

One of the consequences of SU(3) symmetry, also known as the "Eight-Fold Way," was the predicted existence of a new particle, the omega minus. The discovery of this particle, by N. P. Samios and R. P. Schutt in 1964, was a crucial test for Gell-Mann's theory and a turning point in particle physics. In 1963, Gell-Mann and, independently, George Zweig, a colleague at the California Institute of Technology, introduced QUARKS—particles carrying fractional electric charges—into FUNDAMENTAL PARTICLE theory to explain the organization of particle families.

gem cutting   Gem cutting is the art of cutting and polishing rough GEMS in order to transform them into

Tools used to cut gemstones include an aluminum dop, or gem holder (1), for cabochon cutting; a hardwood dop (2), for faceting; and a steel cleaving knife (3), for splitting stones. In cabochon cutting, corners and edges are first removed (4) by bruting, or rotating a diamond against the stone. The process is continued until the desired polished cabochon dome (5) is obtained. In brilliant cutting of a diamond, the edge of a pyramid cut is rounded by bruting (6); then facets are ground and polished, yielding a finished gem (7–11). Stones engraved and carved with an array of diamond-tipped tools (12) include a cameo (13), a signet ring (14), and a jade pendant (15).

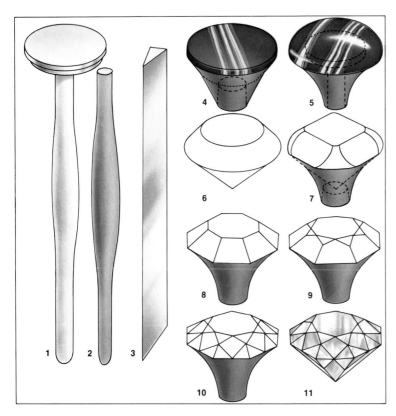

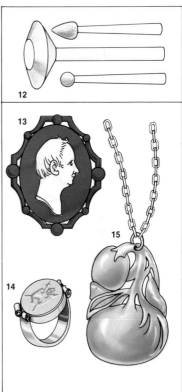

rounded or faceted gems suitable for jewelry. The expert cutting of a gem greatly enhances its value by giving it harmonious proportions and by bringing out to the fullest its luster, brilliancy, color, and fire. An artisan who cuts gems is called a lapidary.

The two major gem cuts are the cabochon cut and the facet cut. The cabochon cut is usually reserved for gems that are opaque (such as turquoise), translucent, chatoyant (having a changing color, as does opal), or asterism (reflecting a star-shaped light, as does star sapphire). A cabochon-cut gem has smooth, curved surfaces. Most gems that can produce a high degree of brilliancy, color, or fire—for example, diamonds, aquamarines, and sapphires—receive a facet cut. Facet cutting uses smooth, flat faces, which are cut into the gem at precise angles so that the greatest amount of light is refracted. Some facet-cut gems may have more than 100 facets. The two main facet cuts are the brilliant cut and the step (or trap) cut. The brilliant cut, with its kite-shaped facets, is often used on gems that are round in form, and is almost always used on diamonds. The step cut, which has trapezoidal facets, is reserved for gems that are square in form, such as emeralds and rubies.

A lapidary cuts a gem by shaping it against a grinding wheel, or lap, that is sprinkled with an abrasive powder. Especially hard gems are cut and polished on metal laps that use diamond powder as the abrasive. Diamond faceting was probably developed during the 15th century in the Low Countries; the full brilliant cut was perfected in Venice in the 17th century. Antwerp and Amsterdam have been leading diamond-cutting centers for more than three centuries. Tel Aviv and New York City have also become important centers.

Gemayel, Amin

Gemayel, Amin [juh-my'-uhl] Amin Gemayel, b. 1942, a Lebanese Maronite Catholic and son of Pierre Gemayel, the founder of Lebanon's Phalangist party, succeeded his brother Bashir as that country's president when the latter was assassinated by political opponents in 1982. He concluded a security agreement with Israel in 1983 but was forced to repudiate it a year later under Syrian and Lebanese Muslim pressure, and his power continued to erode. When the legislature failed to agree on a successor by the time his term expired on Sept. 23, 1988, Gemayel appointed an interim military cabinet headed by Christian Gen. Michel Aoun and went into exile in France.

Gemini

Gemini [jem'-in-y] Gemini, the Twins, a constellation of the Zodiac, is seen best in the Northern Hemisphere. The two brightest stars, Castor and Pollux, are named for the twin sons of Leda in Greek mythology. Pollux is a first-magnitude star. Castor, a second-magnitude star, is a triple star, and each of its components is a double star—making six stars in all. Gemini is located by extending an imaginary line from the two bottom stars in the Big Dipper's bowl away from the handle.

Gemini program

Gemini program The Gemini program was a series of piloted U.S. spaceflights in the mid-1960s. The series was authorized by Congress in 1961 as an intermediate step, between the MERCURY PROGRAM and the APOLLO PROGRAM, in the U.S. effort to land on the Moon. It was called Gemini, which means "twins" in Latin, because each piloted flight carried two astronauts into orbit.

The earlier Mercury program had demonstrated that a trained astronaut could fly in orbit for up to 34 hours. The National Aeronautics and Space Administration (NASA) next had to determine whether trained crew members could endure the weightlessness of orbital free fall long enough to survive a journey to the Moon and back. This was one important objective of the Gemini program; others were to develop rendezvous and docking techniques needed for the lunar mission and to train personnel in their use.

A highly maneuverable spacecraft was required, with an elaborate life-support system that could maintain a crew for up to 14 days. A NASA team, including James A. Chamberlain and André J. Meyer, designed a two-person spacecraft, and NASA awarded the chief contract to the McDonnell Aircraft Corporation of St. Louis, Mo., on Dec. 7, 1961. Within five years the program had achieved all of its objectives at a cost of $1,283,400,000. The flight series used the global tracking and communications network established in Project Mercury.

Gemini 7 was only 2.7 m (9 ft) away when this photograph was taken from Gemini 6 during the historic rendezvous of the spacecraft on Dec. 15, 1965. By maneuvering their craft to within 0.3 m (1 ft) of Gemini 7, the astronauts demonstrated that a rendezvous of moving vehicles in space would be possible.

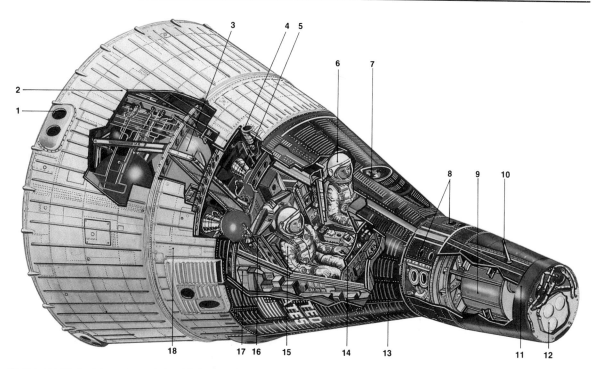

The two-man U.S. Gemini capsule was designed for longer and more complex missions than its predecessor, the Mercury capsule. Numbers indicate attitude control thrusters (1); equipment module (2); fuel, oxidant, and pressure tanks (3); maneuver thrusters (4); retro-rockets (5); command pilot (6); window (7); reentry attitude thrusters (8); landing parachute stowage (9); docking bar (10); rendezvous radar (11); drogue parachute storage (12); reentry module (13); instrument panels (14); pilot and extravehicular activity (EVA) astronaut (15); ejection seat (16); electrical equipment (17); and retrograde section (18), with four braking rockets of 930 kg (2,050 lb) thrust each.

Gemini Hardware

The Gemini capsule was a scaled-up version of the bell-shaped, blunt-ended Mercury capsule. It had 50 percent more cabin space and weighed more than twice as much, about 3,640 kg (8,000 lb). Including its reentry, retrograde, and adapter sections, the vehicle was about 5.8 m (19 ft) long and 3 m (10 ft) wide at its base. The reentry module consisted of the cabin, which contained two couches side by side, and a cylindrical nose containing the docking mechanism and parachutes. Behind it was the retrograde section, which contained an array of four retro-rockets to be fired in quick succession to decelerate the spacecraft for reentry. The adapter section at the rear contained the 16 engines of the Orbital Attitude and Maneuvering System (OAMS), the fuel-cell electric-power supply, and reserve oxygen. The retro-rockets and adapter were jettisoned at reentry.

The Gemini spacecraft were launched by the TITAN 2 ICBM, a two-stage rocket that was more powerful than the Atlas ICBM used in the Mercury program. To reenter, the crew separated the forward, or reentry, section from the adapter section and fired four retro-rockets of 11,100 newtons (1,100 kg/2,500 lb) of thrust each. The capsule, which was stabilized by an eight-thruster reentry control system (RCS), was designed to have lift in the high atmo-

sphere. The pilot could control the landing point within a limited area by rolling the vehicle. The final descent was made by parachute.

Gemini Missions

The first piloted Gemini mission, *Gemini 3*, was flown by Air Force Maj. Virgil I. "Gus" GRISSOM and Navy Lt. Comdr. John W. YOUNG for three orbits on Mar. 23, 1965. Five days earlier, the Soviet cosmonaut Aleksei Leonov had spent ten minutes outside VOSKHOD *2* in the first demonstration of extravehicular activity (EVA) during orbital flight. This feat was duplicated on June 3, 1965, by Air Force Maj. Edward H. White II on the four-day, 62-orbit flight of *Gemini 4* (June 3–7). The American space-endurance record was extended to eight days on the flight of *Gemini 5* (Aug. 21–29, 1965) by Air Force Lt. Col. Leroy Gordon COOPER, Jr., and Navy Comdr. Charles Conrad, Jr.

Walter M. Schirra piloted his *Gemini 6* craft to within one foot of *Gemini 7* on Dec. 15, 1965—the first successful rendezvous in space. *Gemini 7* remained in orbit to prove that trained personnel could endure a round trip to the Moon. On its 220 orbits of the Earth, *Gemini 7* flew approximately 20 times the distance to the Moon.

Rendezvous and docking with an AGENA target rocket was achieved on March 16, 1966, during the mission of *Gemini 8*, by civilian Neil A. ARMSTRONG and Air Force

Maj. David R. Scott. The mission was abruptly terminated, however, when a malfunction in the Gemini OAMS thrusters forced the crew to undock and make an emergency landing in the western Pacific Ocean. Docking was also achieved on the flights of *Gemini 10*, *11*, and *12*.

See also: SPACE EXPLORATION.

Geminiani, Francesco [jay-meen-ee-ahn'-ee]
Francesco Geminiani, b. Dec. 5?, 1687, d. Sept. 17, 1762, was one of the great violin virtuosos of his day and a composer of violin music. Most of his career was centered in London during George Frideric Handel's time there. A student of Arcangelo Corelli, Geminiani at first imitated his teacher's style, then cultivated a more up-to-date *galant* idiom. Geminiani's *Rules for Playing in a True Taste on the Violin, German Flute, Violincello, and Harpsichord* (1745) and *Art of Playing on the Violin* (1751) reveal much about performing practices of his time.

---

gems Gemstones are unusually bright, colorful, or transparent minerals found in the rocks of the Earth. Pearl, coral, amber, ivory, shell, jet, and similar materials are also often considered gemstones, although, unlike minerals, they are the end products of organic processes.

Gemologists use several different tests to identify gemstones. A specially designed gem refractometer determines the refractive index—a measure of light-bending ability equal to the sine of the angle of incidence divided by the sine of the angle of REFRACTION. Each species of gem has its own particular refractive index. The detection under a microscope of foreign inclusions and the determination of hardness by tiny test scratches made with special hardness pencils are usually sufficient additional tests. Density determination, or, more rarely, sophisticated methods of X-ray diffraction (see MINERAL) and chemical analysis, are sometimes also required.

The cutting of gems is both a craft and an art (see GEM CUTTING). The finest pieces of rough gem material are converted primarily into patterned, faceted stones. Various combinations of flat faces or facets have been devised, all designed to bring out of the gem the greatest brilliance or color display possible. EMERALDS and other attractively colored gems have different kinds of cuts, usually with large flat table facets, to display the interior color at its best.

What Makes a Gem Desirable

In various cultures throughout history, certain preferences have developed for one kind of gemstone over another. These preferences, reflected in commercial price levels for gems, are based on several factors: beauty, durability, rarity, and the current fashion. DIAMOND or the finest JADE come as close as any gemstones to meeting all these requirements. Some gemstones meet only a minimum of these requirements; for example, TURQUOISE is beautiful and fashionable but neither particularly rare nor durable.

The beauty of a gemstone, usually revealed to its fullest only after cutting and polishing, may depend on the natural color, transparency, or some other more unusual optical effect. Most important gemstones are allochromatic; that is, the color of an individual stone depends on very slight differences in composition. Those whose color does not depend on these compositional impurities are idiochromatic. Some gemstones, because of their chemical and physical nature, are always opaque. The beauty of turquoise can be seen only by light reflected from polished surfaces. Other gems are quite transparent, transmitting light easily. The value of transparent gemstones may be greatly diminished, however, if they contain internal flaws or bits of foreign material, blemishes that are clearly visible. Totally clean, high-quality gemstones are exceedingly rare, because minerals are usually formed in nature under stress or from relatively impure materials.

REFRACTION, DISPERSION, DIFFRACTION, and REFLECTION are other important optical effects that produce beauty in gemstones. Different colors, or wavelengths of light, are bent, or refracted, by different amounts as they travel from the air into a cut gem. When white light, a mixture of all wavelengths, enters certain gems, its colors are dispersed or spread by differential refraction and are then reflected back out of the gem as separate color flashes. This phenomenon is quite familiar in diamond, which has excellent dispersion. Colors are also separated by diffraction, an optical process that depends on the orderly internal array of gemstone atoms or groups of atoms (see CRYSTAL).

Simple reflection of light from internal flaws and inclusions in gems can also cause some remarkable and beautiful effects. Star sapphires and rubies, for example, contain thousands of needlelike foreign particles that line up uniformly in the three major directions of atomic structure for these species. Light reflecting from these three sets of needles produces asterism, a bright six-rayed, starlike reflection. If the needlelike inclusions line up in only one direction, as they sometimes do in the mineral species chrysoberyl, the reflection is in only a single ray, giving a CAT'S-EYE effect, or chatoyancy.

The durability of a gemstone depends on its toughness (its freedom from a tendency to break, cleave, or otherwise separate) and its hardness (its resistance to scratching and general abrasion). Jade is tough but only moderately hard; diamond, on the other hand, is hard but only moderately tough. Gemstones usually exceed 6 on Mohs' scale of hardness (see HARDNESS, MINERAL) and often exceed 7 or more. No comparable established standard scale for toughness exists.

The rarity of gemstones depends on two factors. Some mineral materials, such as alexandrite, just do not exist in nature in large quantities. Others, such as opal, are common, but only a small number have the quality and beauty to be considered gems.

Fashion is one of the least predictable factors determining gemstone desirability and value. Popularity may depend on the availability and price of gems, or perhaps on a volatile fadlike preference. Diamond, ruby, sapphire, emerald, and pearl are traditionally considered precious stones, the other gems semiprecious.

diamond (brilliant cut)

ruby

sapphire (baguette cut)

blue star sapphire

star ruby (pink)

pearl

emerald (typical emerald cut)

topaz

amethyst (quartz)

opal

chrysoberyl cat's eye

alexandrite (natural light)

alexandrite (artificial light)

garnet

peridot (olivine)

lapis lazuli

malachite

American turquoise

heliotrope

rhodonite

moss agate

carnelian

sunstone (aventurine feldspar)

aquamarine (beryl)

moonstone (adularia feldspar)

golden zircon

Popular Gems

The most popular and therefore the most important commercial gems are DIAMOND, RUBY, SAPPHIRE, EMERALD, and PEARL. A typical jewelry store may also carry several other kinds of gems: blue to bluish green aquamarine, pink to peach morganite, and other varieties (including those colored yellow green to green) of beryl; the complex borosilicate TOURMALINE, which may be pink to red (rubellite), blue (indicolite), bright green or several other colors; the aluminosilicate TOPAZ, which may be sherry or muscatel wine colored, pink, green, blue, or brown; QUARTZ (silicon dioxide), whose gem varieties include AMETHYST (purple), chrysoprase (green), citrine (yellow to brown), rock crystal (colorless), and rose quartz; and OPAL, a stone valued for its brilliant flashes of color.

Less common gems include the beryllium aluminate CHRYSOBERYL, especially its cat's-eye variety and fascinating alexandrite variety, which appears green in daylight and red in artificial incandescent light; GARNET, such as the red Bohemian pyropes and Indian almandines; PERIDOT, a yellow green variety of the mineral species OLIVINE, a magnesium-iron silicate; the magnesium-aluminate SPINEL, in its ruby red and mauve varieties; tanzanite, a sapphire blue variety of the mineral species zoisite, a calcium-aluminum hydroxy silicate; and spodumene, in its green to yellow-green varieties or the beautiful lavender lilac kunzite variety.

Synthetics

Synthetic gemstones are manufactured, rather than created by nature. Emerald, ruby, sapphire, and spinel are made commercially in large quantities. Gem-quality diamonds can also be synthesized, but at prohibitive expense. Synthetic gemstones are superior in quality to their natural counterparts. Synthetic ruby and sapphire were first successfully made in the late 1800s by the French chemists Edmund Fremy (1814–1894) and Auguste Verneuil (1856–1913). The latter devised the flame-fusion method of ruby synthesis that is still used extensively today. In recent years the science of crystal growth has advanced greatly and permitted the synthesis of new gems that have no natural counterparts. The most successful of these at the moment are strontium titanate, a series of synthetic garnets, and cubic zirconia. Of the synthetic garnets, the yttrium aluminum garnet and gadolinium gallium garnet are among the most useful. Cubic zirconia so well matches diamond in brilliance and color dispersion that a well-cut gem of this material is difficult to distinguish as being synthetic.

gemsbok [gemz'-bahk]   The gemsbok (or gemsbuck), *Oryx gazella*, is a large ANTELOPE, belonging to the family Bovidae, order Artiodactyla. Gemsbok are 120 to 210 cm (4 to 7 ft) tall at the shoulder and may weigh more than 200 kg (about 450 lb). They have horns up to 120 cm (4 ft) in length and a coat of brown and black. Gemsbok live in deserts of southern Africa.

The gemsbok, a southern African antelope with straight or slightly curved horns that measure up to 120 cm (4 ft) in length, resembles the gazelle in both facial markings and behavior.

gene   The gene is the unit of HEREDITY. Along with many other such units, it is transmitted from parents to offspring. Each gene, acting either alone or with other genes, determines one or more characteristics of the resulting organism. The totality of genes that make up the hereditary constitution of an organism is called a GENOME.

Genes occur in strands of genetic material called chromosomes (see GENETICS). In most cells each gene occupies a particular position within a specific chromosome. Chromosomes can break, however, and some of their genes may be transferred either to other places on the same chromosome or to other chromosomes. When this happens, new combinations (recombinants) of the genes are formed. Genes can also change in chemical composition. In their altered recombinant or chemically varied form, they produce different effects from those of the unaltered genes (see MUTATION). Depending on the characteristic transmitted by the gene, the environment may also play an important role in determining the extent to which the gene's potential effect is realized (see GENE BANK).

The Nature of the Gene

The subdivision of genetics concerned with the structure and functioning of genes at the molecular level is called molecular genetics. Since the term *gene* was first proposed in 1909, concepts of the nature of the gene have undergone great modification. Current understanding of gene structure and function at the molecular level began in 1944, with the work of Oswald T. AVERY, Colin M. MacLEOD, and Maclyn McCARTY, who showed that bacterial genes are composed of the chemical compound called deoxyribonucleic acid, or DNA. This was later found to be true of the genes of most other organisms.

A further advance was made in 1953, when James D. WATSON and Francis CRICK presented their model of the structure of DNA. The DNA molecule was shown to consist of two chains of chemical compounds called polynu-

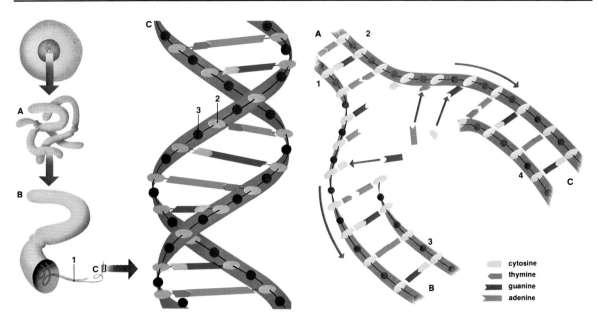

(Left) *In each type of organism, the cell nucleus contains a set number of chromosomes* (A), *each of which* (B) *consists of a threadlike complex of DNA and protein* (1) *coiled into a tightly packed structure. Each DNA molecule* (C) *consists of a backbone of two chains—composed of the sugar deoxyribose* (2) *and phosphate molecules* (3)—*linked by purine-pyrimidine base pairs. DNA has four bases: thymine* (magenta) *always pairs with adenine* (green), *and cytosine* (yellow) *with guanine* (purple). *The order of the bases in each chain forms the genetic code. The entire DNA molecule twists to form a double helix.* (Right) *When the DNA molecule* (A) *replicates, the two strands* (1, 2) *uncoil and the base pairs separate. Free bases in the cell nucleus form bonds with corresponding bases of the DNA strands—that is, cytosine bonds with guanine and adenine with thymine. Sugar and phosphate molecules attach to the new bases and form new backbones* (3, 4) *of two new double-stranded DNA molecules* (B, C). *Each original strand thus serves as a template for the formation of a complementary new strand, a process known as semiconservative replication. DNA replication occurs in cells during the period between cell divisions.*

cleotides, the chains being twisted into a coil, or double helix. Subsequently, scientists determined the GENETIC CODE: the relationship between the composition of DNA and that of the proteins produced by genes. It later became clear that another nucleic acid—ribonucleic acid, or RNA—also carries out protein synthesis.

At first it was thought that all genes functioned in an identical manner to produce the various characteristics of an organism. Three different classes of genes, however, are now recognized. One class consists of the structural genes, whose genetic codes determine the sequences of AMINO ACIDS that go to make up proteins or the smaller molecules known as polypeptides, including many hormones. Another class of genes has genetic codes that specify molecules that function in the processes involved in PROTEIN SYNTHESIS. The third gene class consists of regulatory genes, which are noncoding. They act solely as "recognition" sites for enzymes and other proteins involved in controlling protein synthesis (see OPERON).

Some genes have a region called the leader that precedes the coding segment, and a region called the trailer that follows it. In addition, the coding segment may be broken into sections, with intervening noncoding sequences called introns between coding portions called exons.

A far-reaching advance in gene study was made in 1973, when scientists showed that certain enzymes, called restriction endonucleases, could be used to cut a DNA molecule at certain specific sites. This produced a series of segments with identical free ends, which could join with other free ends having the appropriate complementary configuration. The result was the reestablishment of a fully functional DNA double helix. Using this procedure, called gene splicing (see GENETIC ENGINEERING), it became possible to take a gene from a human cell and transfer it to a bacterium, mouse, rat, or pig, where the human gene functioned as it would in a human being. One projected use of this procedure is to transfer appropriate normal human genes to cells of people suffering from GENETIC DISEASES, thus providing a possible cure.

DNA

DNA occurs as the genetic material in most viruses and in all cellular organisms. Some viruses, however, have no DNA. Instead, their genetic material is in the form of RNA.

Depending on the particular DNA-containing organism, most DNA is found either in a single chromosome, as in bacteria, blue-green algae, and DNA viruses, or in several chromosomes, as in all other living things. In addition to its presence in chromosomes, DNA is also found in many CELL organelles, such as plasmids in bacteria, chloroplasts in plants, and mitochondria in both plants and animals.

Structure. DNA molecules consist of a linked series of units called nucleotides. Each DNA nucleotide is composed of three subunits: a 5-carbon sugar called deoxyribose, a phosphate group that is joined to one end of the sugar molecule, and one of several different nitrogen-containing bases linked to the opposite end of the sugar molecule. The four bases that predominate in DNA are adenine and guanine (double-ringed purine compounds), and thymine and cytosine (single-ringed pyrimidine compounds). Four different types of DNA nucleotides can be formed, depending on the base involved.

The phosphate group of each nucleotide bonds to one of the carbon atoms of the sugar molecule in the adjacent nucleotide. This forms a so-called polynucleotide chain. The DNA of most organisms consists of two polynucleotide chains that are coiled to form a double helix. The backbone, or outside margin, of each chain consists of the sugar-phosphate sequence. The bases project inward from this backbone, into the helix. The bases of one chain are attracted to bases on the other chain by means of hydrogen bonds. This holds the double helix together. Exceptions to this structure are found in some viruses with genetic material consisting of a single DNA chain.

In a DNA double helix the pairing between bases of the two chains is highly specific. That is, adenine is always linked to thymine by two hydrogen bonds, and guanine is always linked to cystosine by three hydrogen bonds. This arrangement—a purine linked to a pyrimidine—results in a molecule of uniform diameter. Because of this specific way in which DNA nucleotides are paired through certain pairs of bases, the base sequence of the two strands in the helix is said to be complementary. This means that the base sequence of either strand may be converted to that of its partner by replacing adenine by thymine or thymine by adenine, and replacing guanine by cytosine or cytosine by guanine.

Functions. The genetic material DNA has two specific functions. It provides for protein synthesis and hence for the growth and development of an organism. It also furnishes all descendants of the organism with protein-synthesizing information by replicating itself and passing a copy to each offspring. This information, known as the genetic code, lies in the sequence of bases of DNA, which specifies the sequence of amino acids in a protein. DNA does not act directly in the process of protein synthesis. Instead, it acts through the formation of a particular type of RNA called messenger RNA.

DNA replication depends on the principle of complementarity mentioned above. During the process of replication, the two strands of the DNA double helix separate from one another. As separation occurs, each base on each strand attracts, from free bases in the cell nucleus, its complementary base-containing nucleotide, to which it becomes attached by hydrogen bonds. For example, adenine attracts and bonds to free thymine. As the complementary nucleotides are fitted into place, an enzyme called DNA polymerase binds the phosphate of one nucleotide to the sugar molecule of the adjacent nucleotide, forming a new polynucleotide chain. The new strand of DNA remains hydrogen-bonded to the old one, and together they form a new double-helix molecule.

Viruses, which contain single-stranded DNA, replicate by a slightly more complicated process. When a virus enters a cell, it makes a complementary copy of itself, to which it remains attached. A virus in this condition is said to be in its replicative form (RF), temporarily becoming a double-stranded DNA virus. The two chains separate during replication, but only the recently formed strand attracts complementary nucleotides. These newly attracted nucleotides are joined together by the enzyme DNA polymerase, their base sequence being exactly the same as that of the original DNA virus. The newly formed polynucleotide chain is then released and functions alone.

Mutations. Many physical and chemical environmental factors can alter the structure of a DNA molecule. A mutation occurs when such alterations lead to a permanent change in the base sequence of a DNA molecule. Mutations in turn result in an inherited change in protein synthesis. Most mutations tend to be harmful. Certain self-repair mechanisms exist to deal with the damage done to DNA by environmental factors.

RNA

Ribonucleic acid, or RNA, is needed in all organisms in order for protein synthesis to occur. It is also the genetic material of some viruses, called RNA viruses (see VIRUS).

As in DNA, all RNA molecules consist of nucleotides and each RNA nucleotide consists of three subunits. One is a 5-carbon sugar called ribose, the second is a phosphate group that is attached to one end of the sugar molecule, and the third is one of several different nitrogen-containing bases linked to the opposite end of the sugar molecule. Four bases predominate in RNA: adenine and guanine (double-ringed purines), and uracil and cytosine (single-ringed pyrimidines).

Structure. RNA differs from DNA in two aspects of its organization. First, the sugar in RNA is of the ribose type; the second carbon molecule in the ring has a hydroxyl (OH) group attached to it. (In DNA the second carbon in the ring has only a hydrogen [H] atom—hence the prefix *deoxy*, meaning "lacking oxygen," in the DNA sugar deoxyribose.) Second, the base uracil is present only in RNA. (Thymine, the base comparable to uracil, is present only in DNA.)

The nucleotides of RNA are joined in a polynucleotide chain by means of bonding the phosphate of each nucleotide to a carbon atom of the adjacent nucleotide's sugar subunit. In RNA viruses the RNA is in the form of either a double or a single polynucleotide chain. In double-stranded RNA viruses, the geometric arrangement of the two polynucleotide chains is similar to that of double-stranded DNA, and the pairing between bases of the two RNA chains is highly specific. Adenine is always linked to uracil by two hydrogen bonds, and guanine is always linked to cytosine by three hydrogen bonds. Again as in DNA, the specific pairing of RNA nucleotides according to the base concerned indicates that the base sequence of the two RNA strands is complementary.

Functions. Replication of double-stranded RNA follows the pattern described for DNA. The RNA chains separate, and each base attracts an RNA nucleotide carrying the complementary base, to which it is attached by hydrogen

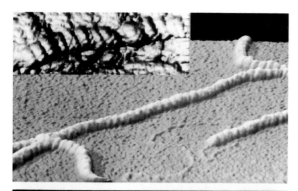

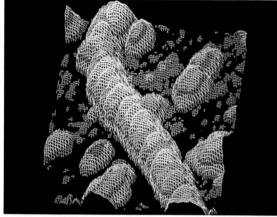

Scientists can view nucleic acids with a scanning tunneling microscope. In the lower and main upper views, a DNA strand in its protein envelope has been coated with metal to enhance the images. In the upper insert of an uncoated DNA-protein strand, individual molecules are visible.

bonds. As the complementary nucleotides are fitted into place, an enzyme called RNA replicase binds the nucleotides together, forming a new polynucleotide chain.

Single-stranded RNA viruses fall into two classes. The first group includes the polio virus that attacks the nerve cells of humans and other primates. When this type of virus enters a cell, the virus makes a complementary copy of itself, to which it remains attached. In this stage the virus is again said to be in its RF, temporarily becoming a double-stranded RNA virus. During replication, although the two chains separate, only the recently formed strand attracts nucleotides with complementary bases. The newly attracted nucleotides are joined together by the enzyme RNA replicase. In their base sequence they are exactly the same as the original RNA virus. The newly formed chain is then released to function independently.

The second group of single-stranded RNA viruses contains some that cause tumors in animals, such as mouse leukemia virus and mouse mammary tumor virus. Upon entering a cell, this type of virus makes a complementary strand of itself. This newly formed chain, however, is composed of DNA nucleotides. The single strand of DNA in turn makes a complementary DNA strand of itself,

forming a DNA double helix. The newly formed DNA double helix becomes incorporated into one of the chromosomes of the host cell, where it is replicated along with the host DNA. While in the host cell, the RNA-derived viral DNA produces single-stranded RNA viruses that leave the host cell and enter other cells. The enzyme involved in making a DNA complement of RNA is called RNA-directed DNA polymerase, or reverse transcriptase—a name based on the action of reversing the transcription process. Such viruses are also referred to as RETROVIRUSES.

Types of RNA. RNA involved in protein synthesis is single stranded. There are three types: ribosomal RNA (rRNA), transfer RNA (tRNA), and messenger RNA (mRNA). A cell's rRNA is associated with protein, forming bodies called RIBOSOMES, which are the sites of protein synthesis. Transfer RNA, also called soluble RNA or adapter RNA, is a group of small molecules, each of which has a specific attraction for one of the amino acids. The function of each type of tRNA is to bring its specific amino acid to a ribosome for possible inclusion in the particular protein being synthesized.

Messenger RNA acts as an intermediary between the genes in the chromosomes and the ribosomes in the cytoplasm. As its name implies, mRNA carries the genetic code contained in the sequence of bases in the cell's DNA. DNAs from various organisms differ only in the sequence of their bases, and mRNA from the organisms must reflect this difference in base sequence. The synthesis of mRNA, called transcription, involves the formation of an RNA chain that is complementary to one of the two strands of a DNA double helix.

RNA as an Information Molecule. RNA, which acts as the carrier of genetic messages in all organisms, is the simplest molecule known that has the capacity to store and transmit information.

Initially, evidence that RNA can also act as a catalyst of reactions centered on the enzyme called ribonuclease P, which consists of protein and RNA. It is involved in the process that transforms the precursor molecules of tRNAs into their fully functional forms. Geneticists have since discovered that the RNA component of this enzyme, acting alone, can perform the catalytic activity of the enzyme, whereas the protein alone cannot. More recently, investigations have concentrated on the ribosomal-RNA specifying gene of the protozoan *Tetrahymena thermophila*. This gene consists of a noncoding sequence, or intron, between two coding portions, or exons. After transcription, the precursor RNA molecule has to have the intron-transcribed segment removed before the ribosomal-RNA molecule can become functional. The intron-specified segment snips itself out of the precursor molecule and splices the loose ends together to form the functional molecule.

gene bank   *Gene bank* is a popular term used to describe repositories for GENES of living organisms. It is commonly used in the context of PLANT BREEDING, as discussed below, but it also applies to the freezing and storage of animal sperm and embryos for use in ANIMAL HUSBANDRY (see also ARTIFICIAL INSEMINATION).

Genetic variation is the raw material for the plant breeder, who must often select from primitive and wild plants, including related species, in the search for new genes. The appearance of new diseases, pests, or new virulent forms of existing disease-causing organisms makes it imperative that plant variation be preserved, because it offers a potential for the presence of disease-resistant genes not present in cultivated varieties. Also, there are demands for new characters, for example, high protein, improved nutritional factors, and fertility restoration. As a result, plant breeders require a large and diverse gene pool to meet ever-changing demands.

An understanding of crop origins and variations is necessary in assembling genetic diversity in plant crops. In certain geographical areas there has existed a rich source of variability in crop plants, but the encroachment of civilization has reduced the natural variability inherent in primitive plant forms and related species of crop plants. Agricultural progress, as a result of new breeding programs, has reduced rather than increased crop variability as improved cultivars, or varieties, are planted in wider and wider areas and old cultivars, which may contain valuable genes, are lost. Crop failures, which result in a smaller gene pool, have also led to an increased awareness of the need to preserve genetic diversity in plants.

Efforts are under way to increase collections of plant materials in various forms. Usually these are preserved as seeds, but living plants, pollen, and cell cultures may also be used. In most gene banks, seeds are usually preserved under conditions of low temperature and humidity. These collections must be periodically renewed by growing the plants and producing new seeds. Increasing emphasis is also being placed on preserving living collections of asexually propagated crops, such as fruit and nut species.

See also: GENETIC ENGINEERING; GENETICS; SEED.

gene therapy   see GENETIC DISEASES

---

genealogy [jen-ee-ahl'-uh-jee] Genealogy is the study of ancestry, or family lineage. Genealogists trace lines of family ancestry and usually show their findings by means of pedigree charts, or genealogical trees. Their studies may be relevant to history, law, sociology, or eugenics, or their appeal may be more personal, providing people with a sense of continuity and of belonging.

Primitive societies, which are usually organized in tribes or clans, have often sought to trace clan ancestry to gods, legendary heroes, or animals. Clans can thus bolster their identity and strive for divine protection. Lineages were originally transmitted by oral tradition, but later literate societies began to write them down. Notable early Western examples include the genealogies of the tribes of Israel (recorded in the Bible), the Greeks, and the Romans. Genealogies assumed particular importance in connection with the principle of inheritance—of power, rank, and property. Lists of hereditary kings were compiled by the ancient Sumerians, Babylonians, Egyptians, Indians, and Chinese. In medieval Europe feudal landholders kept records for the transference of rank and land. Concern with descent, and thus rank, was also reflected in heraldic developments (see HERALDRY).

In modern times, social status has depended less on pedigree, but genealogy remains of interest to many people other than scholars. The United States, for example, has numerous genealogical societies that trace people's descent. The Mormon church has collected an enormous bank of genealogical data (official registers of births, marriages, and deaths and related documents), probably the greatest such collection in existence. Church members use these records to bring their ancestors posthumously into the church (see MORMONISM). Popular interest in genealogy was stimulated by the television dramatization of Alex HALEY's ROOTS (1976); in researching this book Haley had traced his ancestry back to his African forebears.

General Accounting Office   As the auditing authority of the U.S. Congress, the General Accounting Office (GAO) examines the finances of almost all federal government agencies. It has statutory authority to investigate all matters relating to the receipt, disbursement, and application of public funds. It also reviews the accounting systems used by federal agencies, determines whether expenditures conform to law, and settles claims made against the United States by individuals or governments. In recent years Congress has broadened the scope of the GAO's responsibilities to include analysis of program management and policy decisions by the executive branch in diverse fields ranging from defense to health. The GAO also assists the Congress in carrying out its legislative and oversight responsibilities. The GAO, created in 1921, is headed by the comptroller general of the United States, who is appointed by the president with the consent of the Senate for a term of 15 years.

General Agreement on Tariffs and Trade   The General Agreement on Tariffs and Trade (GATT) is a treaty that has been signed by 95 nations and Hong Kong and recognized on a de facto basis by 30 others as of 1987. It took effect on Jan. 1, 1948. GATT lays down a code of conduct for international trade, based on the principles that trade should be conducted without discrimination (the MOST-FAVORED-NATION principle); that domestic industry should be protected only through customs tariffs and not through quantitative restrictions or other measures; that tariffs should be reduced through multilateral negotiations; and that member countries should consult to overcome trade problems. GATT also established (1964) the International Trade Center, operated jointly with the United Nations Conference on Trade and Development, to assist developing nations in the promotion of their export trade. GATT is administered by a secretariat from a headquarters in Geneva.

Since the inception of GATT a total of eight "rounds" of trade negotiations held under its auspices have brought about far-reaching reductions in tariffs and other trade barriers. The latest round began in September 1986 with a ministerial conference at Punta del Este, Uruguay, in which representatives agreed to hold talks over the next 3 to 4 years. During the course of the Uruguay Round, progress was made toward the reduction of barriers on service industries such as banks, insurance, and telecommunications. (Previous rounds had been limited to discussion of manufactured goods.) The Soviet Union was also given observer status in 1990. Negotiations were suspended for a time when the United States and the member countries of the European Community reached an impasse over the issue of state subsidies to agriculture.

General Services Administration
As the United States government's property manager and procurement agent, the General Services Administration (GSA), with 11 regional offices, operates much like a large corporation. Its activities are divided among four separate services—the Public Buildings Service, Federal Supply Service, Information Resources Management Service, and Federal Property Resources Service. Among its major functions are the construction and operation of federal buildings; the distribution of supplies, services, and personal property to federal agencies; the management of transportation and travel services, and the operation of federal motor pools; and the handling of telecommunications and automated data processing and the operation of Federal Information Centers. The GSA also utilizes and disposes of government-owned real property and handles the National Defense Stockpile of strategic and critical materials.

general staff
A general staff is a group of officers who assist the commanding officer of a national ARMY in administration, planning, and coordination. The term is also used less frequently to refer to those assisting the commander of a large field unit. Staff officers have no authority to command but act as agents of the chief of staff.

The general staff concept began to develop in the 16th and 17th centuries with the growth of national armies. A prototype was created by Napoleon I, but the system was brought to its full development by the Prussian Army under Helmuth von MOLTKE, chief of the Prussian General Staff (1857–88). Moltke realized that the need to mobilize and deploy men and equipment on railroads at the onset of war required careful preparation by a trained staff during peacetime. His efforts were crowned by the crushing victories of his armies in the Seven Weeks' War (1866) and the Franco-Prussian War (1870–71).

In the United States a general staff, consisting of the chiefs of various administrative bureaus in the Department of War, was created by Congress in 1813. At the urging of Secretary of War Elihu ROOT, the modern general staff was introduced into the U.S. Army in 1903 with the establishment of a general staff corps and a chief of staff. (The British army general staff was created in 1906.) In 1920, under Gen. John J. PERSHING, the general staff was organized into five sections: personnel (G-1), intelligence (G-2), operations and training (G-3), supply (G-4), and the War Plans Division (later renamed the Operations Division). Numerous reorganizations have occurred since then, and the navy and air force have acquired their own general staffs. The U.S. Army general-staff positions are designated as: chief of staff; vice chief; director; commander general, Army Strategic Defense Command; and deputy chiefs for operations and plans, personnel, logistics, and intelligence.

general strike
A general strike is a stoppage of work by most workers in a number of different industries at the same time. It may be employed to obtain economic goals, to protest specific policies adopted by a government, or to force political concessions (see SYNDICALISM). It sometimes begins in one industry and spreads to others. General strikes in the United States have occurred only on a local basis, but in Europe some have been nationwide. In Britain in 1926 strikes in sympathy with the coal miners grew into a general strike involving three million workers. The strike failed and led to the Trade Disputes and Trade Union Act of 1927, which limited unions' strike powers. In the years after World War II general strikes were sometimes used to protest government policies in Belgium, France, and Italy. A spontaneous general strike occurred in France in May 1968 when widespread student protests sparked a walkout by workers that threatened the the de Gaulle government and led to economic concessions and educational reforms. In the autumn of 1989 the general strike again proved its effectiveness when used by opponents of the Communist government of Czechoslovakia to bring about democratic changes in that country.

generator
A generator is a machine that converts mechanical energy into electrical energy by rotating an armature, which contains conductors, through a magnetic field. A voltage is induced in the moving conductors by an effect called ELECTROMAGNETIC INDUCTION. In order for voltage to be generated, relative motion must exist between the conductors and the magnetic field. An ENGINE, MOTOR, TURBINE, or other source of mechanical energy is used to turn the armature shaft. Generators are built in many sizes. Most electricity used today in cars, in homes, and by industry is produced by generators.

The development of the electric generator began in 1831, when Michael FARADAY in England and Joseph HENRY in the United States proved that a magnet could be made to produce an electric current. In a classic experiment, Faraday connected a sensitive galvanometer across a coil and found that as a magnet was moved into the coil, a current flowed in the coil. As the magnet was withdrawn, a current flowed through the coil in the opposite direction.

Faraday's experiment proved that voltage can be produced by magnetism when three conditions exist. First, a conductor must exist in which the voltage will be induced. Second, a magnetic field must be close to the conductor. Third, relative motion must occur between the magnetic field and the conductor. The conductor must be moved so as to cut across the magnetic field, or the magnetic field must be moved so that it is cut by the

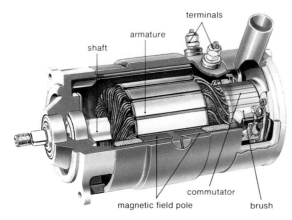

An automobile generator consists of a shaft on which is mounted an armature, composed of wires coiled around slots in a soft-iron core that is rotated between magnetic field poles and connected to a commutator for delivering direct current to external terminals.·

conductor. When the conductor or magnetic field moves, electrons within the conductor are forced in one direction or the other, creating a voltage.

Types. The two main types of generators are direct-current (DC) generators and alternating-current (AC) generators, or alternators. The DC generator rotates the conductors in a stationary magnetic field. The alternator rotates a magnetic field that is cut by the stationary conductors. Current induced in the conductors of all generators is an alternating current. The current taken from the generator, however, may be AC or DC, depending on how the generator is constructed.

The strength of the voltage induced in the conductor depends on its speed and on the strength of the magnetic field. The magnetic field may be furnished by a permanent magnet or by current flowing through field coils to form an electromagnet. When the ends of the conductor are connected to form a complete circuit, the induced voltage causes a current to flow in the external circuit.

Components. The principal components of a DC generator are the armature, commutator, field poles, brushes and brush rigging, yoke or frame, and end bells or end frames. Other components found on some DC generators are interpoles, compensating windings, and various controls and devices for regulating the generated voltage and current output.

DC generators have a commutator mounted on one end of the armature shaft. The commutator rectifies or changes the alternating current in the conductors into direct current. Brushes mounted in holders ride on the rotating commutator bars and carry the direct current from the commutator to the external load circuit.

In an alternator the armature coils, or stationary conductors, are held in place in slots in the alternator frame. The field coils are wound on poles or slots around the rotating shaft. The assembly that contains the stationary conductors is called the STATOR. The assembly that includes the rotating poles and field coils is called the rotor.

Most alternators use brushes and slip rings on the rotor to pass direct current to the revolving field windings. Some alternators do not use any type of brushes or slip rings.

Genesis, Book of [jen'-i-sis]   Genesis, the first book of the Bible, is so named because it opens with an account of the creation of the world (see CREATION ACCOUNTS). The first 11 chapters, which are heavily indebted to Mesopotamian tradition, trace the gradual expansion of humankind and the development of human culture. But they show the ambiguity of this development by incorporating stories about the sin of ADAM and EVE and about the DELUGE, both of which illustrate humankind's growing alienation from God and one another.

Following the call of ABRAHAM in chapter 12, this universal outlook appears to be lost; the focus narrows to one man and his family. Yet the traditions about Abraham, ISAAC, JACOB, and Jacob's 12 sons are linked to the earlier chapters by God's promise to bless the whole world through Abraham's descendants. Furthermore, the COVENANT established with Israel through the promise made to Abraham (22:15–18) is fundamentally the same as the covenant established with all of humankind through NOAH (9:1–17).

Although Moses has traditionally been considered the author of Genesis, modern scholars generally agree that the book is a composite of at least three different literary strands: J (10th century BC), E (9th century), and P (5th century). The interpretation of the book has led to many controversies. One of the most difficult problems has been distinguishing historical fact from symbolic narration intended to convey a religious message.

Genêt, Edmond (Citizen Genêt) [zhuh-nay']   Edmond Charles Édouard Genêt, b. Jan. 8, 1763, d., July 15, 1834, was a French diplomat who served as minister to the United States in 1793. He entered the diplomatic service through the patronage of Queen Marie Antoinette and was (1789–92) chargé d'affaires in St. Petersburg. His staunch republicanism led the revolutionary government to appoint him minister to the United States. Arriving in Charleston, S.C., in April 1793, Genêt was given a warm popular welcome but was coldly received by President George Washington, who disapproved of the radicalism of the French Revolution. Mistakenly believing he enjoyed popular support, Genêt defied the president's ban on outfitting privateers and threatened a direct appeal to the people. Washington requested his recall in August 1793. Fearing reprisal, Genêt never returned to France. He married a daughter of Gov. George Clinton of New York and died near Albany.

Genet, Jean [zhuh-nay']   The French writer Jean Genet, b. Dec. 19, 1910, d. Apr. 15, 1986, was a novelist and exponent of the THEATER OF THE ABSURD. Discovered and championed by the existentialist Jean Paul Sartre, Genet was an orphan, a thief, and a homosexual who

Jean Genet, painted by the film actor Jean Marais, was one of the most prominent figures of contemporary French literature and a vital contributor to the theater of the absurd. (Collection Viollet, Paris.)

had spent most of his youth in prison. There he developed his credo: to harden himself against pain. Reversing the Christian mystic's ascent toward a state of holiness, Genet in the 1930s embarked on a satanic pilgrimage toward the lowest possible state of evil. *The Thief's Journal* (1949; Eng. trans., 1964) is his record of this journey in which no suffering, sordidness, or degradation was spared him. While still in prison, Genet wrote his first novel, *Our Lady of the Flowers* (1943 and 1951; Eng. trans., 1963), a transposition and sublimation of the elements of his life. Likewise, in *Miracle of the Rose* (1943 and 1951; Eng. trans., 1966) his heroes—monsters and saints—represent aspects of men he knew in prison, as well as extensions of himself: rootless, troubled personalities in revolt.

Genet's plays are the finest products of his art, mature reappraisals of the themes treated in his novels. In *The Maids* (1947; Eng. trans., 1954), *Deathwatch* (1949; Eng. trans., 1954), *The Balcony* (1956; Eng. trans., 1957), *The Blacks* (1958; Eng. trans., 1960), and *The Screens* (1961; Eng. trans., 1962) are seen conflicts between illusion and reality, life and death, good and evil, the strong and the weak, the old and the young, the conscious and the unconscious. Although hedonistic and ostensibly amoral, these plays nevertheless approach religious ritual and can best be understood as sacred drama through which the audience's deepest feelings are aroused by sharing in the theatrical ceremony.

---

genetic code   The genetic code is the chemical equation by which hereditary information is translated from genes into PROTEINS such as hemoglobin, insulin, and pepsin. Some proteins serve as structural material for the body, whereas others, namely ENZYMES and polypeptide HORMONES, regulate the chemical reactions of the body.

The chromosomes, located in the nucleus of the CELL, contain the nucleic acid DNA (deoxyribonucleic acid), which is the hereditary material of most organisms. The chromosome is divided into units called genes, each gene being responsible for a particular trait (see GENETICS). In biochemical terms, each gene is responsible for the manufacture of the particular protein that is involved in the development of a trait. PROTEIN SYNTHESIS takes place in the cytoplasm of the cell, so the transfer of genetic information must occur across the nuclear membrane. The constancy of the genetic code in all past and present members of the species permits the genes to have the same effects on their carriers from generation to generation.

The Code in Operation

Both DNA and ribonucleic acid (RNA) are large chemical compounds that consist of a sequence of units called nucleotides. Each nucleotide consists of three smaller chemical compounds: a phosphate, a sugar, and a base. Four types of bases occur in DNA: adenine (A), guanine (G), thymine (T), and cytosine (C). In RNA the bases are adenine, guanine, cytosine, and uracil (U). The key that unlocks the genetic code is the way in which the bases are arranged in sequence along the one chain of single-stranded DNA and RNA, or along one of the two chains of double-stranded DNA or RNA (see GENE).

A specific sequence formed by 3 bases is called a codon. There are 64 possible combinations of 3 bases in sequence, or 64 codons. This is more than enough code words for the 20 different amino acids found in proteins. Most of the amino acids have more than a single codon.

During the manufacture of proteins the transfer of the information contained in genes takes place in two steps, transcription and translation. In transcription the organism's hereditary material acts as a template on which messenger RNA (mRNA) forms. The messenger RNA is so called because it carries the genetically coded information from nucleic acids in the cell's nucleus to ribosomes in the cytoplasm.

During translation the mRNA becomes attached to the cell's ribosomes, which are the sites of actual protein synthesis. The sequence of the mRNA's codons determines the sequence of the amino acids in a protein. Each amino acid is carried to the ribosome by a molecule of transfer RNA (tRNA), which contains among its nucleotides a sequence of three nucleotide bases called an anticodon. The anticodon is complementary to some particular codon of the mRNA. An attraction and temporary hydrogen bonding occurs between the tRNA and mRNA. During this bonding the particular amino acid is transferred from the tRNA to the growing polypeptide chain.

In order for the nucleic acid chain to be divided into genes, each carrying a specific message, signals must be present that indicate where a message begins and where it ends. The mRNA contains special nucleotides at both ends of the message—one that initiates and one that terminates the translation of the code.

The codon for methionine (AUG) is the initiator codon for protein synthesis. When first formed, all polypeptide chains have methionine as their first amino acid. Three nonsense codons, or terminators—UAA, UAG, and UGA—do not code for any amino acid but function as punctuation marks in the message. When any of these appears in an mRNA chain, the translation process stops.

Characteristics of the Genetic Code

The genetic code has certain characteristics, described below, that determine how and under what conditions the sequence of nucleotide bases of a gene are read.

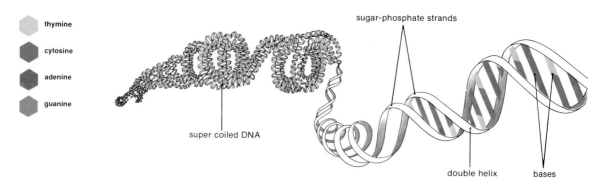

thymine

cytosine

adenine

guanine

sugar-phosphate strands

super coiled DNA

double helix

bases

Chromosomes found in the cell nucleus of higher organisms (eucaryotes) are tightly packed structures that include various proteins and the long molecule DNA in a supercoiled form. When unraveled, the eucaryotic DNA has a ladderlike, spiral structure often called the double helix. Two strands of the double helix—each containing a sugar-phosphate sequence—are held together by bonds between two pairs of bases. One pair, the purine compound adenine and the pyrimidine thymine, bind only to each other, as do the purine guanine and pyrimidine cytosine.

Degeneracy of the Code. Even though most of the 20 amino acids found in proteins have at least two codons, some have as many as six. Any code in which two or more different code words have the same meaning is a degenerate code. The ability to use more than one codon to specify a particular amino acid requires as many different tRNAs for a particular amino acid as there are triplets for it in the genetic code.

The degeneracy of the genetic code appears to have a pattern. For all amino acids that have two, three, or four synonym codons, the first two bases of the relevant triplets are identical. It is only in the third base that the codons vary. For example, all codons that specify glycine start with GG, and so on. This flexibility probably minimizes the potentially deleterious effects of a mutation or an error in translation.

Nonoverlapping Code. Although each amino acid is specified by one or more triplets, a question arises as to whether adjacent bases overlap in the formation of codons. For example, the sequence AUGUGG would, in a nonoverlapping code, specify two amino acids: methionine (AUG) and tryptophan (UGG). In an overlapping code, however, AUGUGG could specify four amino acids: methionine (AUG), cysteine (UGU), valine (GUG), and tryptophan (UGG).

A number of serious problems can arise with an overlapping genetic code. For example, asparagine is specified by codons AAU and AAC. If the genetic code were overlapping, asparagine could never follow methionine in a protein because the overlapping codon that results, UGA, is a terminator codon. In many proteins, however,

When genetic information is transferred from DNA to messenger RNA (mRNA), the pyrimidine compound thymine is replaced by another pyrimidine, uracil. By means of the genetic code, the mRNA regulates the sequences of amino acids that will be bound together in a polypeptide chain to form a protein. The basic unit of the code, called a codon or triplet, consists of three bases. Each codon specifies a particular amino acid. Because there are 64 codons but only 20 amino acids, some amino acids are coded for by more than 1 codon. The table shows the amino acid (represented by its abbreviation) that is specified by each triplet. The codon AUG that specifies the amino acid methionine (met) also functions as the initiator codon for protein synthesis. The word term in the table signifies the terminators, or nonsense codons, that end the amino acid chain. Four examples of codons and their corresponding amino acids are shown in the column to the right of the table. Thus (from top), GGU codes for glycine (gly); GUC codes for valine (val); AAG codes for lysine (lys); and UGC codes for cysteine (cys).

uracil   cytosine   adenine   guanine

first letter	second letter				third letter
	U	C	A	G	
U	phe	ser	tyr	cys	U
	phe	ser	tyr	cys	C
	leu	ser	term	term	A
	leu	ser	term	trp	G
C	leu	pro	his	arg	U
	leu	pro	his	arg	C
	leu	pro	gln	arg	A
	leu	pro	gln	arg	G
A	ile	thr	asn	ser	U
	ile	thr	asn	ser	C
	ile	thr	lys	arg	A
	met	thr	lys	arg	G
G	val	ala	asp	gly	U
	val	ala	asp	gly	C
	val	ala	glu	gly	A
	val	ala	glu	gly	G

gly

val

lys

cys

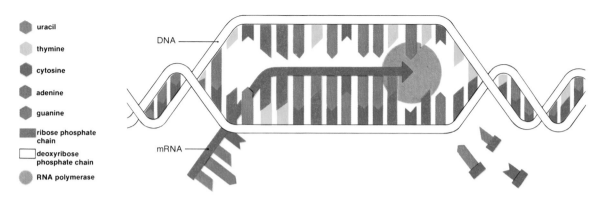

uracil

thymine

cytosine

adenine

guanine

ribose phosphate chain

deoxyribose phosphate chain

RNA polymerase

DNA

mRNA

In transcription, messenger RNA (mRNA) is synthesized along a DNA template in the cell nucleus. The enzyme RNA polymerase initiates the process. Nucleotide bases of one of the two DNA strands attract a complementary sequence of bases, which form the RNA molecule. The RNA strand remains attached to the single DNA strand for a short distance; as it separates from the DNA, the double DNA strand reforms. Because the mRNA is a complementary copy of the DNA molecule, it can carry the genetic code from the DNA to the cell cytoplasm.

asparagine does follow methionine. The same is true for all amino acids whose code letters form mutually exclusive sequences. Geneticists have therefore concluded that the genetic code is nonoverlapping.

Although the genetic code is nonoverlapping, instances are found where the same nucleotide bases form parts of more than one gene. This has been observed in viruses where the number of amino acids composing the various viral proteins exceeds the number of mRNA triplets that code for the proteins. In these situations, the same sequence of bases is read from different starting points. For example, the base sequence AUGAAUGUGUGG. . . can code for one polypeptide chain by starting with the first base at the left, but the same base sequence can simultaneously code for a second polypeptide chain by starting with the fifth base from the left. Under these conditions, terminator codons will also occur at different points of the mRNA. The resulting proteins will differ from each other in length, amino acid composition, and function. In these situations, the base sequence of one gene may overlap that of another, or one gene may even be included within the base sequence of another gene.

Universality of the Code. A particular codon was once thought to specify the same amino acid in all organisms, but exceptions have been found. In human mitochondria, exceptions to the genetic code table are as follows: UGA specifies *trp* instead of *term* (terminator); AGA and AGG specify *term* instead of *arg*; and AUA specifies *met* instead of *ile*. Mitochondria of other species have different, although equally few, variations in their genetic codes. In the case of some ciliated protozoans, UAA and UAG specify *glu* instead of *term*, and only UGA serves as a terminator codon. Although the origin of the genetic code is unknown, its widespread existence among the vast majority of organisms suggests that its formation occurred more than 3 billion years ago.

Transfer RNA (tRNA) Identity. Each tRNA molecule has two crucial roles to play in the translation process. First, it has to become attached to a particular amino acid. Second, it has to place that amino acid in its proper place in

a protein. For both tasks some recognition site must exist on the tRNA that will serve to accomplish the task.

Geneticists have known for some time that the anticodon on each tRNA is the complement of a particular messenger RNA (mRNA) codon that specifies one of the amino acids in the genetic code. Identification of the recognition site that determines which amino acid will be coupled to the tRNA has not been simple, however, because a pattern, or "code," does not seem to be involved. The most efficient arrangement would be to have one recognition site that serves both functions and hence establishes the identity of the tRNA molecule for both tasks. The most clear-cut situation would be to have the anticodon of the tRNA also act as the recognition site for selecting the proper amino acid. This appears to be the case for more than half of the tRNAs, where any change in the anticodon of the tRNA is accompanied by a change in the amino acid selected for attachment to the tRNA.

There are other tRNAs, however, in which the amino-acid recognition site is located elsewhere in the tRNA molecule. It has been tempting to look for a "second genetic code" that would decipher the tRNA recognition sites for amino acids, but such a code does not appear to exist.

Mutation. If by any means the base sequence of the DNA chain is altered, the code of one or several genes is read differently, resulting in the manufacture of different proteins. This alteration, called a mutation, sometimes results in a change in the appearance or metabolism of the organism. A mutation can be minor and relatively insignificant, or it can cause serious deformity or metabolic deficiency in the organism. On the other hand, mutations are theoretically one of the causes of changes in a species that lead to EVOLUTION.

Such an alteration may be the substitution of one base for another (base-substitution), resulting in the transformation of that particular codon. Another type of mutation entails adding or deleting one or more nucleotides from the DNA chain, thereby changing the number of nucleotides in a gene. Frame shift mutation is an addition-deletion type of mutation, in which bases along the entire

If a molecule of DNA is irradiated by ultraviolet light, damage can be caused to the molecule by the fusion (A) of adjacent thymine bases. This could potentially change the triplet sequences in the genetic code and result in the manufacture of a mutated protein. This problem can be avoided through the action of a repair mechanism, which begins when an enzyme called endonuclease severs the sugar-phosphate chain (B) near the fused thymines. An exonuclease enzyme removes a small region (C) containing the thymine dimer. DNA polymerase synthesizes the missing segment (D), using the complementary strand as a template. The final gap is closed by another enzyme, DNA ligase (E). The repair of the DNA thus maintains the integrity of the genetic information.

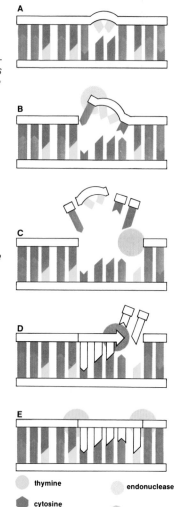

thymine

cytosine

adenine

guanine

deoxyribose phosphate chain

endonuclease

exonuclease

DNA polymerase

DNA ligase

that protein. The entire gene is transcribed from DNA to mRNA; enzymes then cleave the intron-originating portions from the molecule and string the exon-originating portions together. Geneticists believe that the value of having the genetic code in segments is to reduce even further the possibility of extensive mutation.

genetic diseases   Genetic diseases are inherited disorders reflecting gene MUTATIONS or abnormalities in chromosome structure or number and resulting in functional or anatomical changes. Common genetic diseases include deformities, such as cleft lip; metabolic disorders, such as phenylketonuria; and albinism. The frequency of chromosome abnormalities in the United States is 1 in about 150 live births. Approximately 40% of all recognized spontaneous abortions are chromosomally abnormal. Six in every 100 stillbirths have chromosome abnormalities, and 6 in every 100 neonatal deaths are associated with chromosome defects.

Gene Transmission in Families

Gene transmission, or HEREDITY, in families is most often identified by the function of an altered GENE; its expression in a family or kindred may be charted by a family pedigree. A pedigree chart is a schematic outline of individuals in a family throughout several generations, including the sex, age, and presence or absence of a specific genetic characteristic or disease in each individual. The pedigree chart is used to determine how a particular trait or disease is transmitted.

The term *allele pair* means a pair of genes that determines a certain trait. Any number of variations in each gene of the pair can occur. For an individual to have blue eyes, for example, the alleles of the gene pair must be identical, both specifying blue eyes. A person having identical alleles for that characteristic is said to be homozygous. If the gene pair is not identical—for example, one allele specifies blue and the other brown—the individual is heterozygous for that trait. The allele for blue eyes is said to be recessive, and for brown eyes, dominant. A heterozygous individual having the two different alleles in the gene pair will have brown or mixed-color eyes but never blue.

Genetic diseases can be inherited in a manner similar to that of normal traits. These diseases include single-gene disorders that are autosomal dominant, autosomal recessive, sex-linked dominant, or sex-linked recessive. They also include multifactorial disorders, resulting from more than one gene often interacting with environmental factors. Autosomal means that the gene pair is present in a chromosome pair other than the sex chromosomes.

Single-Gene Disorders

Disorders caused by the mutation of a single gene are often called inborn errors of metabolism because they reflect alterations of a biochemical pathway. As a result of the mutation of a single gene, the final gene product normally manufactured is absent or is present in low amounts. Therefore, either an important end product is

gene sequence are so displaced that new triplets are formed. This displacement leads to a sequence of different triplets in the mRNA transcribed from the mutated portion of the gene and is reflected in a changed amino acid sequence in the polypeptide chain produced, which may, in fact, be entirely different from the polypeptide produced by an unmutated DNA chain.

Researchers have discovered that, instead of having an entire gene contained in an unbroken DNA molecule, as in bacteria and other lower organisms, a typical gene in higher organisms is segmented. The DNA coding segments, called exons, are connected by sections of DNA, called introns, that do not code for any amino acids of not synthesized in sufficient quantity, or an excessive accumulation of intermediate products that may be toxic occurs. Many inborn errors of metabolism are fatal in early childhood or make maintenance of proper body function difficult if not impossible.

Autosomal Dominant Genes. Autosomal dominant genes, of which more than a thousand are fully identified, are expressed in both heterozygous and homozygous individuals. Many are lethal when the individual is homozygous. Dominant traits are usually expressed equally in both the male and the female. If one parent is affected, therefore, each pregnancy involves a 50% risk of recurrence. The pedigree usually reflects at least one affected member in each generation. The sex of the parent contributing the gene can also play a role in the course of the disease. An example is HUNTINGTON'S CHOREA.

Autosomal Recessive Genes. Autosomal recessive traits, of which 600 are fully identified, are expressed phenotypically only in homozygotic individuals. Most of these traits, if not all, result from a single-gene mutation affecting a single step in a biochemical pathway. Most autosomal recessive traits are expressed to some extent in heterozygotic individuals, although their physical appearance and general health are normal. These people are known as carriers because they can transmit the gene to their children, who manifest the disease. Usually, affected children will have unaffected carrier parents. Frequently, parents who are closely related transmit autosomal recessive disorders. The recurrence risk for heterozygous parents is 25% for each pregnancy. COOLEY'S ANEMIA, GALACTOSEMIA, PHENYLKETONURIA, SICKLE-CELL DISEASE, and TAY-SACHS DISEASE are examples of autosomal recessive disorders.

Sex-Linked Dominant Genes. Only a few disorders with sex-linked dominant inheritance are known, such as vitamin D–resistant RICKETS. Mutations occur on the X chromosome, so if the female carries the mutation, recurrence risks are 50% for both female and male progeny; if the male has the disorder, no sons but all of the daughters will be affected.

Sex-Linked Recessive Genes. In most cases of sex-linked recessive traits, of which 125 are fully identified, the mother is heterozygous but unaffected—she is a carrier. She has a 50% chance of producing affected sons through transmission of an X chromosome carrying the gene mutation. Her daughters have a 50% chance of being heterozygous like the mother. If an affected male is able to reproduce and marries a homozygous normal female, none of his children will be affected, but all of his daughters will be heterozygous for the sex-linked gene. His sons do not inherit the disease. HEMOPHILIA and MUSCULAR DYSTROPHY are representative sex-linked recessive disorders.

Multifactorial Inheritance

Disorders that reflect the activity of several genes rather than one are known as multifactorial traits. In most cases the environment, especially during pregnancy, plays an important role in determining the severity of the disease in the child. Several relatively common disorders fall into this category; for example, cleft lip and palate, pyloric stenosis (obstruction of the stomach), and SPINA BIFIDA (defect of the bony spinal column). In general, the recurrence risk for parents who have an affected child is in the range of 3–5%. If one parent is affected, the risk for any pregnancy is also in the 3–5% range.

Chromosome Abnormalities

Chromosome abnormalities are detected with increasing frequency in birth defects. The most common type is a change in total chromosome number. In general, reduction of the total number of autosomes is incompatible with life. An infant with an extra chromosome involving virtually any autosome pair also has a limited life span, with multiple physical abnormalities and mental retardation.

The most common chromosomal abnormality is DOWN'S SYNDROME, or mongolism, which involves the chromosome designated as number 21. This defect is termed Trisomy 21 because all cells in the infant's body carry an extra number 21 chromosome. Other trisomies in humans are Trisomy 13 (Patau's syndrome) and Trisomy 18 (Edwards' syndrome).

Like autosomal abnormalities, aberrations of the sex chromosomes may result in impaired or absent fertility. For example, one abnormality is known as 45X, or Turner's syndrome. Individuals with this condition, who are classified as female, most commonly are short in stature and show impaired development of female genitalia and of such secondary sex characteristics as the breasts and the distribution of body hair; they are also sterile. Another abnormality, called KLINEFELTER'S SYNDROME, occurs when the individual has 47 chromosomes in the cells of the body, with an XXY sex-chromosome composition. The individual is male in appearance, tall in stature, has sparse hair distribution over the body, and is sterile.

Gene Therapy

One goal of recombinant-DNA technology (see GENETIC ENGINEERING) is the cure of human genetic diseases. A first step toward the use of gene-altered cells for this purpose has been proposed by researchers at the U.S. National Institutes of Health, in connection with an experimental cancer therapy that uses the patient's own cancer-fighting cells.

When a tumor forms, it is invaded by a special type of white blood cell called tumor-infiltrating lymphocyte (TIL). These cells can be obtained from a tumor, cultured in the laboratory to obtain large numbers of them, and then infused back into the patient. This procedure is effective in about half the patients, causing the tumor to regress by 50% or more. It is not known, however, why the treatment fails to work in other patients. Planning to use a RETROVIRUS as a vector, the researchers want to add to the TIL cells, as a marker while they are cultured, a bacterial gene that codes for resistance to the antibiotic neomycin. This will permit them to identify the marked cells and monitor their fate after they are returned to the patient, by periodically sampling the TIL cells in the tumor. In principle, this procedure would be identical to the ones intended for use in curing human genetic diseases through gene therapy. If successful, this project will represent the first step toward achieving that goal.

In 1990, for the first time, two gene therapies gained U.S. approval. One treats children with adenosine deaminase deficiency, the other deals with advanced malignancies.

Gene Mapping and Analysis

In the late 20th century, libraries of gene probes are being developed and genes are being sequenced and characterized in detail (see GENOME). The use of gene probes permits pedigree analysis with precision; genetic risks can be assigned without the need to know the gene product. Through recombinant DNA technology and DNA-probe analysis, prenatal diagnosis is available for such disorders as Huntington's chorea, phenylketonuria, cystic fibrosis, adult-onset polycystic kidney disease, retinoblastoma, hemophilia A and B, hemoglobinopathies, and Duchenne muscular dystrophy. Such technology also promises important information on such disorders as ALZHEIMER'S DISEASE and MANIC-DEPRESSIVE PSYCHOSIS. Various types of cancer, diabetes mellitus, and disorders associated with hypercholesterolemia may also become available to diagnosis in this way.

Genetic Counseling

Genetic counseling is a service available to couples who desire information or advice concerning the probability of bearing children with a genetic disease. The counselors are usually physicians; some hospitals have teams that include counselors specifically trained in genetic disease, a pediatrician, a high-risk obstetrician, a nurse, a social worker, and consultants such as a neurologist.

Couples should seek genetic counseling if they already have a defective child, if a close relative is known to have a hereditary disease, or if the mother is approximately 35 years of age or older, because women in this age group run a higher-than-average risk of bearing children with Down's syndrome and certain other chromosomal abnormalities.

The genetic counselor usually begins by obtaining a family history, performing a physical examination, and ordering appropriate laboratory tests. The counselor will want to determine whether or not the problem is genetic, and if so, the mode of inheritance. A test may disclose such defects as the presence of an extra chromosome, as in Down's syndrome; the presence of abnormal hemoglobin, as in sickle-cell anemia; or the absence of a particular blood-clotting factor, as in hemophilia.

Every couple faces about a 3% risk with each birth that the child will be born with a major defect of some kind. Against this background, the genetic counselor, after concluding various studies, may predict that the couple who produced a defective child face a high recurrent risk. This risk may be 25% to 50% in the case of single-gene defects, as high as 100% for certain chromosome disorders, or as low as 5% for the more common multifactorial conditions.

A defective fetus may be identified by AMNIOCENTESIS, a procedure in which a sample of the amniotic fluid surrounding the fetus is withdrawn through a hollow needle. The fluid can be studied for chromosomal or chemical abnormalities and may indicate the presence of certain birth defects. More than 100 hereditary diseases can be identified by amniocentesis. The sex of the fetus can also be determined. Sometimes, knowledge of the sex of the fetus rules out a hereditary disorder: hemophilia, for example, occurs almost always in males, and therefore a female fetus will not be likely to have this disease.

One problem with amniocentesis is that the woman must wait until the 15th or 16th week of pregnancy before sufficient fluid has accumulated for sampling. A more recent, experimental approach is to sample placenta tissue itself, through a catheter, a process called chorionic villous sampling. This can be done as early as the ninth week of pregnancy.

Two new techniques exist for identifying fetuses carrying particular genes. One uses so-called restriction enzymes, which cut DNA only at specific "recognition sites." These sites may vary among families, yielding DNA fragments that characterize a particular lineage. If the gene causing a disease in one parent's family line happens to be located within a unique DNA fragment, the presence of such a fragment in a fetus identifies it as having the gene for the disorder. The second test involves the use of a previously obtained fragment of DNA that has been made radioactive. Such a fragment is called a probe, and it will be attracted specifically to the DNA at the site of the gene of interest. If the probe contains a normal form of the gene and the fetus contains a mutated, disease-causing form of the gene, little binding will take place between the DNA sections and very little radioactivity will be detected at the site.

Genetic Testing

Much of the suffering and cost of genetic diseases could be prevented if an affected child could be identified early enough to start adequate treatment. An example is the enzyme-deficiency disease phenylketonuria, one of many metabolic disorders that can be detected by the screening of blood and urine samples from newborns. Immediate dietary reduction of the amino acid phenylalanine will prevent severe mental retardation. An earlier approach is to identify parents at risk before they produce an affected child. For example, parents who are carriers for genes causing Tay-Sachs disease or sickle-cell anemia can be detected by blood tests and informed about the risks of producing affected offspring.

While offering much hope, however, genetic testing also raises difficult ethical questions. For example, does a patient with Huntington's chorea or other late-developing hereditary disorders have a right to the traditional doctor-patient confidentiality? What is the responsibility (and liability) of physicians for warning family members at risk for inheriting the disease? At what age should persons be told that they are destined to be affected? Can workers who are genetically susceptible to harm from particular substances in the workplace be excluded from certain jobs? Ethical questions such as these are emerging as society begins to grapple with the field of genetic testing.

genetic engineering

Genetics is the science that studies all aspects of inherited characteristics. Genetic engineering is the application of the knowledge obtained from genetic investigations to the solution of such problems as infertility, diseases, food production, waste disposal, and improvement of a species. Included in genetic-engineering techniques are a wide range of procedures that alter the reproductive and hereditary processes of organisms. Depending on the problem, the procedures used may involve ARTIFICIAL INSEMINATION, CLONING, in vitro fertilization, species hybridization, or the direct manipulation of the genetic material itself by the recombinant-DNA technique.

Nonmolecular Examples

Genetic engineering has been effectively practiced in ANIMAL HUSBANDRY, HORTICULTURE, and agriculture for thousands of years. CORN has been selectively bred for food production for 7,000 years. More recently, a comparable program, involving wheat and rice, called the GREEN REVOLUTION has done much to meet the world's increasing need for food (see PLANT BREEDING). Cattle and pigs had been domesticated by 8,000 years ago and through selective breeding have become two main meat sources in the human diet.

For human diseases, successful application of a number of discoveries in the field of immunology has until recently been limited by the need for large amounts of particular types of antibodies, each specific to a given virus, protozoan, or kind of cell. In 1975 a cancer cell was fused to a spleen cell that was producing antibodies against a specific antigen. The hybrid cell (hybridoma) continued to produce the single type of antibody of its spleen-cell parent and continued to grow and divide like its cancer-cell parent. Such monoclonal antibodies are now produced in large amounts against specific microorganisms and even against the malignant cells of some children with acute lymphocytic leukemia.

Fifteen percent of all human couples encounter various fertility problems. If the woman is fertile but the man is sterile, artificial insemination, using the sperm of another man, permits the woman to conceive. If the man is fertile but the woman has blocked fallopian tubes, eggs

Genetically altered bacteria are sprayed on a field of strawberries to give the plants greater protection against frost.

may be withdrawn from her ovary, fertilized by his sperm in vitro (outside the body), and later inserted into the woman's uterus for completion of development and subsequent birth.

Recombinant DNA

Technique. Recombinant-DNA formation, also known as GENE splicing, is a procedure whereby segments of genetic material from one organism are transferred to another. The basis of the technique lies in the use of special enzymes (restriction enzymes) that split DNA strands wherever certain sequences of nucleotides occur. This process results in a series of donor DNA fragments that can combine with similarly formed DNA fragments from other organisms. In most experimental situations the donor DNA fragments are combined with viruses or with plasmids (small rings of self-replicating DNA found within cells). The virus or plasmid vectors carry the donor DNA fragments into cells. The combined vector and donor DNA fragment constitutes the recombinant-DNA molecule. Once inside a cell, referred to as a host, this mole-

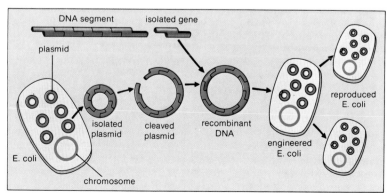

In a typical recombinant-DNA procedure, a plasmid found in E. coli, a common intestinal bacterium, carries the foreign DNA into an E. coli host. The isolated plasmid and the donor DNA are cleaved by the same restriction enzyme at the same sequence of nucleotides. (Other restriction enzymes would produce different fragments for insertion in plasmids similarly formed.) The donor DNA fragment matches up with the cleaved plasmid. The recombinant-DNA molecule is then introduced into the host cell and reproduced when the cell divides. Repeated divisions produce a clone of E. coli, containing the recombinant-DNA molecule, which may encode a useful protein, such as insulin.

Bacteria that colonize plant roots are altered to turn blue in the presence of certain chemicals. Such bacteria, when altered for testing, are easy to track and monitor.

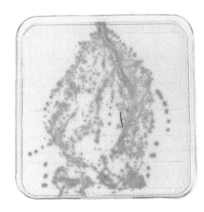

cule is replicated along with the host's DNA each time the host divides. These divisions produce a clone of identical cells, each having a copy of the recombinant-DNA molecule and the potential to translate the donor DNA fragment into the protein it encodes.

Applications. The use of bacteria as host cells in recombinant-DNA experiments has yielded important information on gene regulation. By using donor DNA fragments, the location and action of the controlling units that govern the expression of particular genes have been identified.

Recombinant-DNA procedures involving bacteria and donor DNA fragments that translate into proteins have led to the increased availability of such medically important substances as INSULIN (for diabetes), INTERFERON (for viral infections and some forms of cancer), and growth hormone (for dwarfism).

Another important medical application of the recombinant-DNA procedure has been the production of vaccines against a number of diseases. Heretofore, vaccination against a disease has involved the injection of killed or weakened microorganisms into a person, with the subsequent production of ANTIBODIES by the individual's immune system. This procedure has always carried the risk of there being live, virulent pathogens in the vaccine because of some error in the vaccine-producing process. Research has shown that it is the microorganism's outer surface that serves as the ANTIGEN that stimulates antibody formation. Through the recombinant-DNA procedure, it is now possible to transfer the genes that control a pathogen's surface characteristics to a harmless microorganism and use it as a vaccine against the particular disease.

Bacteria with altered genomes, or genetic informational contents, may also be used in waste disposal. Such organisms could decompose many forms of garbage; one such strain can break down oil slicks.

Plant cells can also be used as hosts, which could have important consequences for food production. If the genes that code for the nitrogen-fixing system of certain bacteria could be transplanted into the cells of crop plants, the world's food production would dramatically increase and fertilizers would become unnecessary. Not only can plant cells act as hosts for bacterial genes, they

can also serve as recipients of animal genes. In one such gene-splicing experiment involving the firefly, which is capable of BIOLUMINESCENCE, the gene that produces the enzyme needed for light production was transferred to a tobacco plant. Subsequently, when the roots of the plant were immersed in a solution containing the necessary ingredients, the plant began to emit light.

Recombinant-DNA procedures have been used to study the genes of extinct animals. A zebralike animal called the quagga, for example, became extinct in the 19th century, but some quagga skins with underlying muscle tissues have been salt-preserved in museums. Enzymes were used to release DNA from these muscle cells, yielding DNA fragments representing parts of different genes. These fragments were transferred to the plasmids of bacteria, where they were replicated along with the bacterial DNA. They were then retrieved, analyzed, and compared to corresponding DNA segments of closely related living animals.

Controversy. Questions have been raised by a number of scientists and lay people on the advisability and ethics of recombinant-DNA research. It was feared that the insertion of a disease-causing, antibiotic-resistant, or cancer-causing virus or plasmid into a bacterium such as *Escherichia coli*, which lives in the human intestinal tract, could cause a deadly epidemic in the general population upon accidental release. Since 1973, however, when the recombinant-DNA technique was first demonstrated, genetic material has been transferred thousands of times without any of the feared catastrophes occurring.

In 1987, after four years of legal challenges, the recombinant-DNA Advisory Committee (RAC) of the NIH gave final approval for a series of experiments involving the spraying of plants with genetically engineered bacteria to protect the plants from light frost. The bacteria

The world's first patented animal is a mouse whose genetic material has been altered, for research purposes, to include a gene known to cause breast cancer in humans. The historic patent was issued in April 1988.

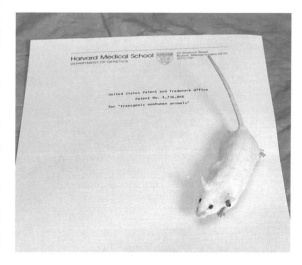

Human recombinant beta interferon is being produced in quantity in these fermentation vats. Before the advent of genetic engineering techniques, a number of biochemicals were available for medical research only in very small and costly amounts. The new techniques gave birth to a rapidly growing biotechnology industry.

commonly found on these plants secrete a protein that initiates the formation of ice crystals when the temperature drops to freezing. In the genetically modified bacteria, the gene that codes for the protein has been deleted. Without the protein, ice formation does not occur until the temperature falls well below the freezing point. The first field test of the genetically modified bacteria was conducted on a plot of strawberry plants. Similar experiments on other crops have followed. The results showed that the gene-spliced bacteria were effective.

The objection raised to the experiments, and to any method of increasing food production through the release of genetically altered microbes, is that such organisms might spread and upset the ecosystem of the area.

Antisense DNA and Antisense RNA

In a double-stranded DNA molecule, geneticists originally thought that only one strand—the "sense" strand—contained the actual genes transcribed into RNA. The other, "antisense" strand was believed to function only in replication. At least in some cases, however, both DNA strands are transcribed, and therefore if a gene's nucleotide base sequence is known, the antisense DNA strand can be synthesized. Such strands can then be introduced into cells, where they attach themselves to the complementary sense DNA strands, thereby depressing transcription of these genes. This has been done successfully, in cell culture, for the cancer-causing gene that produces human larynx squamous carcinoma.

If a duplicate copy of a gene is inserted into a chromosome in reverse orientation to the normal gene, the antisense DNA strand of this gene is transcribed. This yields an antisense messenger RNA strand that is complementary to the mRNA strand transcribed for the normal gene. The two RNAs, being complementary, bind to one another, thereby preventing the translation of the

normal RNA strand. Antisense RNA has been used to block the translation of the tomato plant mRNA for the enzyme polygalacturonase, which is responsible for fruit softening. Tomatoes with greatly reduced amounts of this enzyme can be shipped without refrigeration and still retain their flavor and consistency.

Forensic DNA

When DNA is subjected to restriction endonuclease enzyme activity, fragments of various sizes are formed (see GENE). Except for identical twins, the pattern of sizes of the fragments from an individual is unique and can serve as a "DNA fingerprint" of that person. This fact has been crucial in identifying assailants in a number of specific instances of violent crime where the victims were unable to do so. In these cases, bloodstains or semen stains on clothing, sperm cells found in a vaginal swab taken after a rape, or root hairs of the assailant were available for analysis. Extraction of DNA from dried blood or from one of the other sources, followed by enzymatic digestion, resulted in an unambiguous match of DNA fragments with DNA obtained from cells of the accused.

genetics   Genetics is the area of biology concerned with the study of inheritance, the process by which certain characteristics of organisms are handed down from parent to offspring. Modern genetics began in 1865, when the Austrian monk Gregor MENDEL demonstrated the inheritance patterns of the garden pea, *Pisum sativum,* and provided a new way of looking at HEREDITY. Mendel's theories were based on hereditary factors, or GENES, the existence of which he deduced without seeing them. His work went unnoticed until 1900, when it was rediscovered by three scientists, who performed similar experiments and arrived at the same conclusions reached by Mendel. It is now known that genes dictate the characteristic structures and functions of all organisms and that these characteristics are passed on from parent to offspring. It is also known that the variety of hereditary traits are caused by variations in the genes themselves.

Mendel's Experiments

Mendel studied seven characteristics of the garden pea and obtained experimental results that suggested a similar hereditary mechanism for all. For example, he obtained a line of pea plants that always produced tall plants and a line that always produced short plants. He crossed the two lines by transferring pollen from one plant to another. The progeny (the first filial, or F_1, generation) were all tall. Mendel then allowed these to self-pollinate and produce another generation of progeny (the F_2 generation), three-quarters of which were tall and one-quarter short.

From these results, Mendel deduced an explanation for the mechanism of inheritance and assumed certain principles (three of which are now called Mendel's laws) to be true: (1) hereditary factors (genes) must exist; (2) two factors exist for each characteristic; (3) at the time of sex-cell formation, the hereditary factors of a pair sepa-

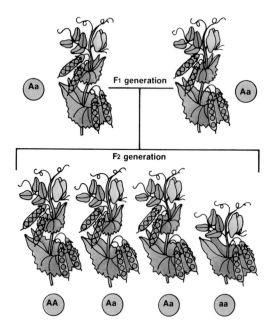

Mendel's crossing of a tall pea plant (AA) with a short plant (aa) yielded all tall F₁ offspring; these, in turn, produced F₂ progeny in the ratio of 3 tall:1 short. He assumed that alleles (A or a) separate during gamete formation and recombine randomly in offspring. According to the law of dominance, plants with AA and Aa genotypes display the dominant trait; those with aa are short.

rate equally into the gametes (law of segregation); (4) the gametes bear only one factor for each characteristic; (5) hereditary factors for different traits sort independently of one another at gamete formation (law of independent assortment); and (6) gametes join randomly, irrespective of the factors that they carry. The characteristic that appeared in the F₁ plants seemed to dominate over the one that did not appear. Mendel called tallness a dominant trait and shortness recessive; this phenomenon was referred to as the law of dominance.

A capital letter, such as *A*, is now usually used to represent the gene that determines the dominant character, and a small *a* for one that determines the recessive character. When a pair of hereditary factors, or genes, are of the same type (*AA* or *aa*), the condition is said to be homozygous for that character. On the other hand, if the two members of a pair are different (*Aa*), the condition is called heterozygous.

The F₂ plants of Mendel's experiment were composed of one-quarter *AA*, one-half *Aa*, and one-quarter *aa*. Since tallness is dominant, *AA* and *Aa* both appear tall, accounting for the three-quarter:one-quarter ratio of tall to short. The alternate forms of a gene, known as alleles, combine to produce different genetic types, or genotypes. Mendel demonstrated that the three-quarter:one quarter ratio existed for all seven characteristics of peas that he studied; he also showed that the gene pairs for the seven traits behaved independently of each other during gamete formation.

Chromosomes

It is now believed that genes behave as they do because of their location on chromosomes (see GENETIC CODE), structures in the nucleus of each CELL of an organism. Chromosomes are not all the same length, and, when stained, each may show characteristic bands, thickenings, or constrictions.

The cells of each species contain a fixed and characteristic number of chromosomes. Some organisms, such as fungi and single-celled algae, have only a single set, or haploid number (*n*), of chromosomes in their cell nuclei. The somatic cells of most higher organisms, including humans, contain two sets, or a diploid number (*2n*), of chromosomes. Still other organisms, such as mosses, ferns, and horsetails, alternate between diploid and haploid during different stages of their life cycles.

Meiosis. In diploid cells, gene pairs are located at specific sites (loci) on each chromosome. These gene pairs can be composed of either two identical genes or two alleles. A diploid cell therefore contains two genes for each hereditary characteristic. The gametes (sex cells) of diploid organisms, however, contain only a haploid (*n*) number of chromosomes; the union of two gametes, one from each parent, produces a diploid (*2n*) zygote, from which the offspring develops.

The process of cell division by which such gametes are produced is called meiosis. It takes place in the testes and ovaries of animals, in the anthers and ovaries of higher plants, and in the sporophyte (*2n*) stage of organisms that alternate between haploid and diploid. In meiosis a single diploid cell divides into two haploid cells, each of which divides into two more haploid cells. During this process, the two sets of chromosomes separate, thereby separating the members of the gene pairs. Each of the four resulting gametes therefore contains only one gene for each characteristic, and different gametes from the same parent may carry different alleles.

Mendel's postulates may therefore be restated in physical terms as follows: (1) genes are located on chro-

This microphotograph shows a polytene chromosome from the salivary gland of the fruit fly Drosophila hydei. *Polytene, or many-stranded, chromosomes duplicate without cell division. The enlarged, nonbanded areas, called puffs, are associated with protein synthesis.*

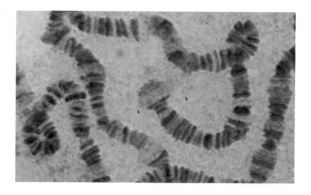

mosomes; (2) genes occur in pairs, occupying specific loci on a chromosome pair; (3) the first meiotic division separates the chromosome pairs, producing an equal separation of the members of a gene pair in the product cells; (4) since there are two cell divisions and only one replication of chromosomes, the chromosome number is halved; (5) different gene pairs on separate chromosome pairs behave independently of each other; and (6) collision of egg and sperm is a chance process.

Linkage and Crossing-Over. In the early 1900s, Thomas Hunt MORGAN used the fruit fly *Drosophila melanogaster* to test a situation that Mendel did not encounter, namely, that in which two gene pairs are located on the same chromosome pair. In this case they do not behave independently, since genes on the same chromosome tend to stay together during meiosis. This is called linkage. The combinations can be separated by the simultaneous breaking of homologous chromosomes during the first meiotic division, and the joining of the broken segments from each chromosome to the homologous broken segments. This process, called crossing-over, occurs regularly during meiosis and randomly between any chromosome pair in a bundle of four. Crossovers can be detected genetically if they involve two heterozygous gene pairs (the alleles producing distinct gene products). Under a microscope, they appear as cross-shaped structures called chiasmata.

Mapping. Crossing-over can be used to produce a chromosome map showing the relative positions of the loci of the known gene pairs. Two organisms having homozygous gene pairs are bred, and the offspring (F_1) has heterozygous gene pairs (AaBb):

$$\frac{A\ B}{A\ B} \times \frac{a\ b}{a\ b} = \frac{A\ B}{a\ b}(F_1)$$

This heterozygote is then crossed with a tester strain of the genotype *aabb*, a standard tool known as a testcross. The progeny of a testcross are screened for the appearance of the genotype *Aabb* and *aaBb*, which can only arise from crossovers. The frequency of these types is a standard measure and is assumed to be proportional to the distance between the two loci on their chromosome.

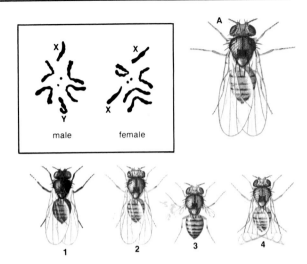

male   female

Geneticists often use the fruit fly Drosophila melanogaster (A) *in experiments: it is small (about 2 mm/0.08 in long), it reproduces every 10 to 15 days, and its cells contain 4 pairs of large chromosomes* (upper left). *The chromosome complements shown are those of male and female fruit flies. A female has 2 x-chromosomes, but no y-chromosome. Genetic damage at specific positions, or loci, on the chromosomes produces certain mutations, including black bodies* (1), *bar-shaped eyes* (2), *vestigial wings* (3), *and curled wings* (4).

Using different combinations of gene pairs, an internally self-consistent map can be constructed in which the number of map units is defined as the percentage of progeny in a testcross derived from a crossover.

The Role of Chromosomes. It is now known that genes are lengths of a threadlike chemical called deoxyribonucleic acid (DNA) and form a continuous string that constitutes the chromosomes. Several researchers have attempted to explain the significance of the long assemblages of genes in chains, or chromosomes. First, some combinations of genes have adaptive value and need to be inherited as a package. Having them linked closely on one chromosome is one way of ensuring this. Second, genes with related functions often need to be activated simultaneously; their proximity allows them to be activated by one common switch mechanism. Third, the packaging of genes into units facilitates the orderly production of daughter cells in cell division.

Crossing-over and independent assortment of genes result in combinations of genes in progeny that are different from the parental arrangements. This process, called recombination, is believed to be an important mechanism for generating new genotypes. Recombination most frequently occurs among genes widely separated from each other.

Polygenes and Gene-Environment Interaction

Mendel explained the phenomenon of discontinuous hereditary variation, which is expressed in separate and distinct phenotypes that are associated with a particular kind of allele, such as tall versus short or wrinkled versus smooth. Continuous variations occur in many phenotypes, however, such as length or weight. This phenomenon, known as polygenic inheritance, results from the complex

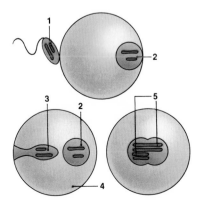

The sperm nucleus contains a haploid set of chromosomes, two of which are shown (1), *as does the egg nucleus* (2). *During fertilization, the sperm nucleus, in a fertilization cone* (3), *passes through the egg cytoplasm* (4) *toward the egg nucleus. The two nuclei fuse, and homologous chromosomes pair up* (5).

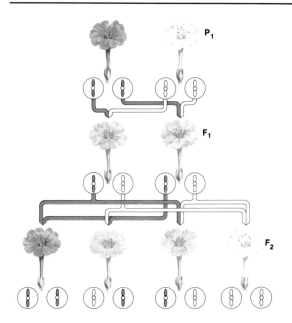

Flowers of four-o'clock plants, Mirabilis jalapa, *illustrate the principle of incomplete dominance: heterozygous offspring expresses an intermediate character rather than the dominant trait. The crossing of a four-o'clock containing red alleles with a plant containing white alleles yields plants with pink flowers (F_1 generation). If the pink four-o'clocks are crossed, the alleles combine to produce offspring (f_2) that are red, pink, and white in the ratio of 1:2:1. In the case of complete dominance, the comparable ratio would be 3 red:1 white in the F_2, while the F_1 would have been all red.*

interaction among a set of genes. Human skin color, in shades ranging from dark brown to pinkish white, is a good example of a trait determined by polygenes.

The phenotype of an organism is shaped not only by its genotype but also by the interaction of that genotype with the environment. It is often difficult to determine the relative contribution of genetic and environmental factors to a particular phenotype.

Sex Determination

The sex of an organism is usually an inherited phenotype. In haploid forms, alleles of one gene pair can determine sex, but in higher organisms sex is often associated with a special pair of chromosomes called sex chromosomes. For example, human cells contain 22 pairs of autosomes, or nonsex chromosomes, and one pair of sex chromosomes. Women possess two identical sex chromosomes (X and X), and men possess two different sex chromosomes (X and Y). The presence or absence of the Y chromosome determines sex in humans.

In humans, the X chromosome bears genes that affect traits having nothing to do with the sex. Because they are located on the X, however, they show a special inheritance pattern different from autosomal gene inheritance; the Y chromosome apparently has no counterpart. Red-green color blindness and hemophilia are two traits determined by X-linked genes.

The Nature of the Gene

The genetic material of most organisms, DNA, is a double-stranded helix comprising a long chain of nucleotide bases with a sugar-phosphate backbone.

During mitotic cell division, chromosomal replication produces two daughter cells, each of which contains identical DNA, assuring the stability of the hereditary material.

Genes of the DNA in eukaryotic organisms (RNA in some viruses) control phenotype by coding for the structure of PROTEINS, which are the main structural and catalytic molecules in an organism. During PROTEIN SYNTHESIS, the order of the nucleotide pairs in DNA dictates the corresponding order of amino acids that give proteins their specific shape and function.

In humans the DNA in each cell contains about 3 billion base pairs, distributed among 22 sets of autosomal chromosomes and one set of sex chromosomes in the nucleus as well as one set of chromosomes in each mitochondrion. Only about 2 percent of a person's DNA forms the actual genes, as well; the rest constitutes either noncoding "spacer" regions between genes or noncoding "intron" regions within genes.

Mutation

MUTATION is the process by which genes change from one form to another. Mutations may be caused by such mutagens as X rays, ultraviolet rays, nitrous acid, ethyl methane sulfonate, and nitrosoguanidine; less frequently, mutations may occur spontaneously as a result of accidental changes in the chemistry of the cell. Because mutation is random, haphazard change, most mutants contain damaged genes that are nonfunctional. Mutants usually do not live long in nature.

A mutation in DNA usually results in an altered nucleotide sequence, either by substitution, addition, deletion, or insertion, which is translated into an altered amino-acid sequence that usually produces a change in normal body function.

All humans carry quite a large number of deleterious and lethal mutant genes that are recessive. Each mating is a kind of a lottery, in which the offspring reveal whether or not the parents' mutations are at identical loci. For

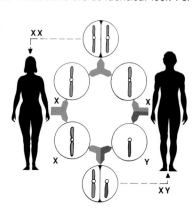

Human cells contain one pair of sex chromosomes, XX in females and XY in males. Ova contain only the X chromosome; spermatozoa possess either X or Y. At fertilization, the chance of an XX or XY pair being formed is about equal. Sex-linked characteristics arise from genes on the X chromosome, which have no counterpart on the Y chromosome.

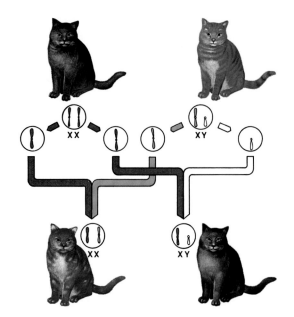

The X chromosome (but not the Y) carries genes for coat color in cats, which accounts for the observation that nearly all tortoiseshell cats are female. If a female carrying a black gene on each X chromosome is crossed with a male carrying a ginger gene on its X chromosome, only the female (XX) offspring can possess both types of genes; their coats have a black-and-ginger "tortoiseshell" pattern. Male offspring are black because their X chromosome carries a black gene; the Y chromosome lacks a corresponding gene for coat color.

example, if both parents are heterozygous (*Aa*) for a gene pair in which the recessive allele is deleterious, then ¼ of their children will show GENETIC DISEASE of the kind controlled by that locus.

Movable Genes

In 1951, Barbara McClintock presented evidence that genetic elements in corn could change locations among chromosomes. One of these elements, the Dissociation locus (*Ds*), upon insertion next to the gene responsible for pigment production, caused the gene to stop functioning; that is, it acted as the equivalent of a mutation. Any subsequent movement of *Ds* to another location resulted in the restoration of the pigment-producing gene to its normal function. Similar movable elements, now called TRANSPOSONS, have since been discovered in bacteria, yeasts, protozoans, and fruit flies and are presumed to exist in all organisms, humans included.

Genes in Development

Most organisms start life as single cells (zygotes) and grow into massive multicellular bodies with cells of considerable differences in form and function. This process, which involves growth and differentiation, is called DEVELOPMENT. Although skin cells, liver cells, brain cells, and so on are highly differentiated, they are all derived from the original zygote as a result of the high-fidelity copying

of DNA during mitotic division. Cell specialization is achieved by a complex process whereby different genes are active in different tissues.

The best examples of gene regulation are found in bacteria, where genes of related function are grouped on the chromosome together with a special class of regulatory genes to form an operon, which is a kind of control unit. Regulatory genes, usually responding to environmental cues, either assist or prevent the passage of the mRNA synthesis enzyme along the operon, thereby controlling gene activity.

Genes in Cytoplasmic Organelles

Although most genes are found in the chromosomes of the nucleus, certain genes exist in cytoplasmic structures: chloroplasts, mitochondria, and other cell bodies (flagella and centrioles) contain DNA that determines some of their traits. Phenotypes determined by these genes are inherited through the female parent. This uniparental type of inheritance is called non-Mendelian inheritance. It has taken on increasing importance since cytoplasmic chromosomes, called PLASMIDS, were discovered in bacteria. The plasmids control such traits as resistance to antibiotics. It has also been found that genetic material from other species of organisms, human beings included, can be inserted into the plasmids of bacteria, and the bacteria will then proceed to produce the proteins of the foreign species.

Mitochondrial genes also code for proteins involved in the production of adenosine triphosphate (ATP), the key energy molecule of cells. Recently it has been discovered that people suffering from Leber's hereditary optic neuropathy (LHON) have a defect in a mitochondrial gene that codes for a protein involved in the first step of ATP production. LHON is a rare disease that causes the optic nerve to degenerate in young adults, leading to blindness. It has been hypothesized that other maternally inherited genetic diseases exist that are caused by mutations in mitochondrial DNA.

Genes in Populations

Mendelian genetics can predict the inheritance patterns within families, but one should not expect to see similar

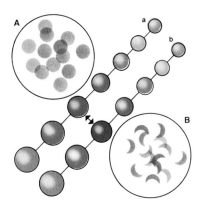

Normal red blood cells (A) depend on a gene that controls the production of normal hemoglobin (a), a protein containing chains of amino acids (colored disks). A mutant form of the gene causes a change of one amino acid in the protein chain (b), leading, in homozygotes, to the sickle-shaped red blood cells (B), resulting in sickle-cell disease.

patterns and ratios in populations, which are complex mixtures of different families. A different approach, called POPULATION GENETICS, is used to analyze genetic distribution in populations.

In order to understand the analytical procedures involved in population genetics, assume that a chromosome locus contains two alleles (*A* and *a*) of one gene. The gene pool of a population is derived by considering each diploid individual to be one cell bearing two genes at that locus. The total number of *A* and *a* genes in a population is calculated and an allele frequency for each is obtained. Usually, the frequency of *A* is called *p*, and the frequency of *a* is called *q*, where *p* + *q* = 1 (or 100%). The allele frequencies are the main determinants of the genetic structure of populations. If mating is random, for example, there will be p^2 of *AA*, 2 *pq* of *Aa*, and q^2 of *aa*. This distribution, which is stable if all other factors are constant, is named Hardy-Weinberg equilibrium for its discoverers. At its most fundamental level, evolution is little more than a change in relative allele frequencies.

The actual values of *p* and *q* at each locus are determined by the complex interaction of many forces, including mutations, chance fluctuation due to small populations, and natural selection for or against certain genotypes. In turn, selection can be directional, ultimately eliminating one allele from the population, or stabilizing, favoring intermediate genotypes and tending to maintain several alleles and phenotypes in an interbreeding population, a phenomenon called genetic polymorphism.

Modern Genetics

Genetics is an important aspect of many areas of pure and applied biology. Viral genetics, microbial genetics, plant genetics, animal genetics, and human genetics focus research on specific types of organisms. Research in molecular genetics involves studies on chemical structure and function; cytogenetics, on location of the genetic material in cells and on cell division; developmental genetics, on the genetic function in embryological phenomena; behavior genetics, on the role of the gene in regulating behavior; and population genetics, on the evolutionary process.

At the applied level, genetics is of direct use in understanding genetic diseases and environmental mutation. It is used in plant and animal breeding to improve the quality and quantity of food. It also is a tool in basic research by which complex biological processes can be analyzed.

This map shows the distribution of the human blood group gene B throughout the world. The highest frequency (25% to 30%) of gene B occurs in Central Asian populations. The incidence of the gene generally decreases as distance from this center increases. Such maps can be used to study past migrations of populations.

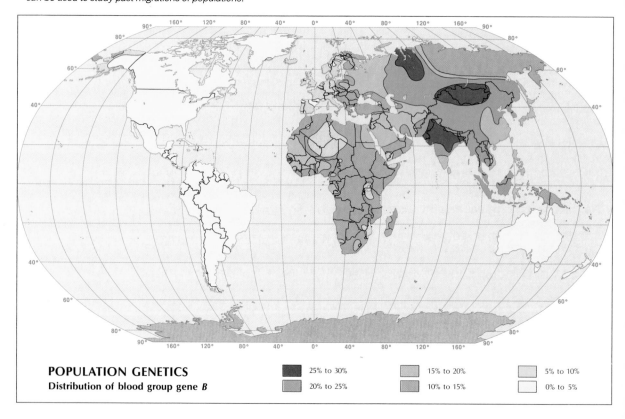

POPULATION GENETICS
Distribution of blood group gene *B*

25% to 30%   15% to 20%   5% to 10%
20% to 25%   10% to 15%   0% to 5%

Geneva [juh-neev'-uh]   Geneva (French: Genève; German: Genf) is the third largest city in Switzerland and capital of the canton of Geneva, in the western part of the country. The population of the city is 161,473 (1988 est.). Located at the southwest tip of Lake Geneva, it is known for its view of the Mont Blanc massif.

The city of Geneva is the intellectual and economic center of the French-speaking area of Switzerland and has many contacts with nearby France. It still retains its early importance as a transportation center, but its economy is based primarily on service industries, especially international organizations, finance, watchmaking, printing, and the manufacture of electrical machinery, jewelry, and handicrafts.

Contemporary City. Geneva is famous for having been the seat of John CALVIN in the 16th century. In the 19th and 20th centuries, Geneva blossomed into an international city; international and ecumenical organizations ranging from the International Red Cross to the World Health Organization and the World Council of Churches have their headquarters there. Between the two world wars it was the seat of the League of Nations. The international flavor of the city has also facilitated Geneva's rise as an international banking center and given the city a unique character. A rich cultural life is provided by the University of Geneva, several museums, theaters, a conservatory, and the Orchestre de la Suisse Romande.

History. Geneva was founded by a Celtic tribe, the Allobroges, who settled in the 1st century BC at the tip of Lake Geneva, at one of the few convenient crossings of the Rhône River. Geneva was Christianized under the Romans, and trade developed along routes across the mountains to France and Italy. During the Middle Ages the bourgeoisie resisted the power of resident bishops supported by Burgundy and turned to the counts of Savoy, who began appointing the bishops in the 15th century.

The city adopted Protestantism in 1535; this led to war with Savoy. In 1536, Calvin established theocratic rule that lasted well past his death in 1564. He made Geneva a political and religious center and involved the city in several religious wars. The dukes of Savoy were ultimately repulsed in 1602. The atmosphere in Geneva gradually became more tolerant, and in the 18th century many radical thinkers were drawn there. Following French occupation (1798) and forced membership in Napoleon I's Helvetic Republic, Geneva joined the Swiss Confederation in 1815.

Geneva, Lake   Lake Geneva (French: Lac Léman; German: Genfersee) is a crescent-shaped lake that lies in the Alps of southwestern Switzerland and southeastern France. The largest of the Alpine lakes, it has an area of 580 km^2 (224 mi^2). The lake is 72 km (45 mi) long, 14 km (8.5 mi) wide, and 310 m (1,017 ft) deep; its mean depth is 152 m (500 ft).

Lake Geneva is essentially a widening of the RHÔNE RIVER, which enters the lake at its eastern end and exits at the city of Geneva in the extreme west. Fluctuations, called seiches, probably caused by changes in atmospheric pressure, cause the entire lake to rock rhythmically from shore to shore. Its deep, clear waters support about 20 species of indigenous fish. The Alps, to the east and south, and the Jura Mountains, to the west and north, provide dramatic mountain backgrounds. Lakeside resorts include Montreux and Vevey in Switzerland and Évian-les-Bains in France.

Geneva conferences   Geneva, Switzerland, the home of the League of Nations and of some branches of the United Nations, as well as numerous other interna-

Geneva, a canton capital in western Switzerland, is a center of international banking and finance. Attracted by the city's location and by Switzerland's traditional neutrality, many international organizations, including the European offices of the United Nations and the International Red Cross, have established their headquarters in Geneva.

tional organizations, has been the site of many international conferences. Among the most significant meetings held there have been the World Disarmament Conference of 1932–37 and the conference of 1954 to effect a settlement of the war in Indochina.

Disarmament Conference. The World Disarmament Conference was the last effort to achieve armaments limitation in the period before World War II. DISARMAMENT had been a major objective of the LEAGUE OF NATIONS since its establishment after World War I, but the reluctance of certain powers, most notably France, to disarm without adequate security guarantees had blocked agreement.

The Disarmament Conference opened in Geneva in February 1932 with 60 nations represented. Because delegates could not agree on either the budgetary limitations proposed for air, land, and naval forces or the categories of weapons to be restricted, the conference made no headway. Various plans were suggested, including one by U.S. president Herbert HOOVER that proposed a one-third reduction in the defense components of armed forces, but to no avail. France remained insistent on security and Germany on its right to equality with the other powers. After adjourning in March 1933, the representatives met again the following October. Germany, now the Nazi government of Adolf Hitler, withdrew, however, from both the conference and the league. This move destroyed any chances for success, and although the conference continued to meet sporadically until April 1937, it reached no agreement.

Indochina Conference. The Geneva Conference of 1954 was called to settle the war between France and the Communist-backed VIET MINH in Indochina. Since 1946, when French forces returned to Vietnam after World War II, the French had been unable to overcome the opposition to their rule. French losses in the Battle of DIEN BIEN PHU (March–May 1954) led the United States, Britain, the USSR, and France to call the Geneva Conference. Representatives of those powers, as well as of the Indochinese nations, Communist China, and North and South Korea, met from April until July 1954.

The French, Vietnamese, Cambodian, and Laotian representatives agreed to draw a cease-fire line along the 17th parallel, effectively dividing Vietnam into two countries: Communist in the north and French-backed in the south. The agreement to reunify Vietnam by holding elections within two years was not honored by South Vietnam, and the Geneva Accords became the subject of later controversy (see VIETNAM WAR).

Geneva conventions   The Geneva conventions are a series of international agreements to provide for the humane treatment of the wounded, prisoners of war, and civilians in time of war. The first Geneva convention "for the amelioration of the condition of the wounded and sick of armed forces in the field" was signed in Geneva, Switzerland, in August 1864. Representatives of 16 countries pledged to respect the neutrality of civilians and medical personnel and of hospital ships bearing the emblem of the RED CROSS and to treat the war wounded humanely.

Other conventions were added in 1899, 1907, and 1929, covering such things as maritime warfare and treatment of prisoners of war. Four more conventions in 1949 extended and codified the laws of war. They recognized the fact that warfare had become total, thus erasing the distinctions between the civilian home front and the war front.

The fourth convention of 1949 sought to broaden the protection of civilians menaced by saturation bombings and other manifestations of total war. It forbade such abuses as deportation, the taking of hostages, torture, collective punishment and reprisals, and racial, religious, national, or political discrimination.

See also: HAGUE CONFERENCES; WAR CRIMES.

Genghis Khan, Mongol Emperor [jeng'-gis kahn] The MONGOL leader Genghis Khan, b. c.1167, d. Aug. 18, 1227, was one of the great conquerors in the history of the world. He was the son of Yesügei, leader of a small tribe in northeastern Mongolia, in an area adjacent to the modern border with the Soviet Union. Yesügei was poisoned when Temüjin (Genghis Khan's name as a youth) was about 10 years old, and the orphaned boy later entered the service of Toghril Khan, the most powerful Mongol ruler of the time. Struggle and bloodshed characterized the succeeding years until 1206, when Temüjin united the warring Mongol tribes and was proclaimed Genghis Khan ("universal ruler") of the Mongol chieftains. (The name also appears as Jenghiz Khan.)

In 1207, Genghis Khan led the Mongols on the first of the series of destructive, bloody invasions that would result in the conquest of much of the Asian mainland. After defeating the JIN empire in northern China, the Mongols

Genghis Khan, the Mongol leader who conquered a vast Asian territory that stretched from the Pacific in the east to the Black Sea in the west, appears in this 13th-century Chinese illustration. After uniting the hostile nomadic tribes of Mongolia, Genghis Khan created one of the largest land empires in history. (National Palace Museum, Taipei.)

occupied Beijing in 1215. Extending their expeditions to the shores of the Caspian Sea, the Mongol warriors penetrated the steppes of Russia and totally defeated the Russian army by 1223. They did not, however, follow up their victory with a conquest of the cities to the west; instead they returned eastward. The empire established by Genghis Khan eventually extended from the Pacific Ocean to the Black Sea and from Siberia to the northern borders of mainland Southeast Asia.

Genghis Khan's success as soldier, conqueror, and ruler resulted largely from his military organization, strategy, and mobility, all of which gave him a consistent advantage over opponents who were often weaker and less well organized. Although he never learned to read, he left behind a system of law that probably represented more than a mere codification of existing practices.

Gennep, Arnold van [je-nep']   Arnold van Gennep, b. Apr. 23, 1873, d. May 7, 1957, was a French ethnographer and folklorist noted for the influential work *The Rites of Passage* (1909; Eng. trans., 1961). In it he theorized about the significance of ceremonies marking the transition of individuals or groups from one status in society to another (see PASSAGE, RITES OF).

Genoa [jen'-oh-uh]   Genoa (Italian: Genova) is the capital of Genoa province and the Liguria region in northwestern Italy. It has a population of 722,026 (1988 est.) and is located about 120 km (75 mi) south of Milan on the Gulf of Genoa. Genoa is Italy's most important seaport and one of the largest in Europe.

Contemporary City. Genoa's economy is dominated by its port activities and by the rail, air, and highway transportation systems that service the shipping industry. Genoa is the major embarkation point for the products of northern Italy and much of central Europe. It is also a leading passenger port on the Mediterranean. In addition to shipping, important industries include shipbuilding,

iron and steel production, and the manufacture of textiles, munitions, paper products, chemicals, locomotives, cement, and aircraft supplies. Genoa is also an important banking, commercial, and insurance center.

Genoa is noted for its medieval, Renaissance, and baroque palaces, including the Ducal Palace (begun 1291). The Doria Tursi Palace (16th century) is now used as the city hall. Genoa has several museums and the University of Genoa (founded 1243) is a major learning center.

History. By the 5th century BC, Genoa was already an important trade center of the Ligurians, a pre-Roman people of northern Italy. The city flourished under Roman rule, which began in the 3d century BC; although it was destroyed by Carthage, it was quickly rebuilt. After the fall of Rome the city suffered numerous Germanic and Arab invasions. It became a free commune, or republic, in the 12th century, and its maritime power increased. In the 13th century it gained control of Sardinia and Corsica and also held possessions in the Greek Islands and in the Black Sea, defeating its rival, Pisa, in 1284. The Crusades brought Genoa great wealth, and for a time it was Venice's chief rival in trade with the East until its defeat in the War of Chioggia (1378–80).

Beginning in the 14th century Genoa went through a long period of foreign domination, although its nominal independence was preserved. France, Milan, Spain, and Austria all controlled the city at various times. In 1796 the French ousted the Austrians, and Genoa's formal independence came to an end. It became part of the Ligurian Republic, and in 1805, Napoleon I annexed it to France. At the end of the Napoleonic era, the Congress of Vienna (1815) gave the city to the Kingdom of Sardinia. In 1861 the city was absorbed into the newly unified Kingdom of Italy. The city prospered as part of the new kingdom. During World War II, it was a center of underground resistance to the Axis.

---

genocide [jen'-uh-syd]   Genocide (Greek *genos*, "race," and Latin *cide*, "killing") is the persecution or

Genoa, a provincial capital in northwestern Italy, is the nation's busiest seaport. The city's highly developed harbor facilities have been a major source of revenue since the Middle Ages.

destruction of a national, racial, or religious group. Years before the word *genocide* was coined by the Polish-American scholar Raphael Lemkin in 1944, genocide was practiced by the Russians in their pogroms against the Jews and by the German Nazis, who systematically killed ethnic groups including Jews, Poles, and Gypsies. A more recent example is the slaughtering (1972–79) of various tribal groups by the former president of Uganda Idi AMIN DADA. The tribunal at the NUREMBERG TRIALS (1945–46) of Nazi war criminals declared that persecution of racial and religious groups was a crime under international law. In 1948 the General Assembly of the United Nations approved the Convention on the Prevention and Punishment of the Crime of Genocide, which took effect in 1951. The nations that ratified the convention agreed that genocide was a matter of international concern, even if committed by a government within its own territory. The United States ratified the Genocide Convention in 1986.

genome   The genome of an organism is the totality of genes making up its hereditary constitution. In the late 1980s, two research projects were proposed concerning the human genome. The goal of one would be to determine the exact location of all the genes—50,000 to 100,000, plus regulatory elements—on their respective chromosomes (see GENETICS). The goal of the other would be to establish the sequence of nucleotides—estimated to be about 3 billion pairs—of all the genes (see GENETIC CODE). Both goals are possible and would be of great medical benefit, but they would take at least a decade to complete at an estimated cost of $3 billion. The U.S. National Institutes of Health (NIH) and Department of Energy are mainly involved in the projects, with the assistance of the National Science Foundation and the Howard Hughes Medical Institute.

genre [zhawn'-ruh]   Genre, a French word rendered in English as "type," "kind," or "form," is a term that describes works of literature according to their shared thematic or structural characteristics. The attempt to classify literature in this way was begun by ARISTOTLE in the *Poetics*, where he distinguishes TRAGEDY, EPIC, and COMEDY and recognizes even more fundamental distinctions between DRAMA, epic, and LYRIC poetry. Classical genre theory, established by Aristotle and reinforced by HORACE, is regulative and prescriptive, attempting to maintain rigid boundaries that correspond to social differences. Thus tragedy and epic are concerned exclusively with the affairs of the nobility, comedy with the middle or lower classes.

Modern literary criticism, however, does not regard genres as dogmatic categories, but rather as aesthetic conventions that guide writers and are also led by them. The unstable nature of genres does not reduce their effectiveness as tools of critical inquiry, which attempts to discover universal attributes among individual works and has since classical times evolved theories of the NOVEL, ODE, ELEGY, PASTORAL, SATIRE, and many other kinds of writing. A dominant contemporary genre theory is that of Northrop FRYE, whose *Anatomy of Criticism* (1957) presents a comprehensive literary typology.

genre painting   Genre painting (from the French word *genre*, meaning "type" or "kind") is a term applied to works that depict secular scenes of everyday domestic work or recreation. The term is commonly used to distinguish such paintings from works of a religious, historical, or ceremonial character, which tend to elevate their subjects above the mundane level of ordinary existence. Genre painting, which is characterized by realism (see REALISM, art), first appears as an element in early Renaissance art and northern European 15th-century religious painting. Genre scenes play a far larger part in the work of Albrecht DÜRER and Pieter Bruegel (see BRUEGEL family), which led to the full flowering of genre painting in 17th-century Holland. Among the Dutch masters of the form were Gabriel METSU, Jan STEEN, Jan VERMEER, and Adriaen van Ostade. Their work, as distinct from the closely related forms of conversation piece and portraiture, was informal and anecdotal, depicting anonymous figures engaged in familiar activities.

gentian [jen'-shuhn]   Gentian is the common name for any of some 350 species of mostly perennial herbs of the genus *Gentiana*, family Gentianaceae. Gentians are found throughout the world except in Africa and occur chiefly in cool temperate or mountainous regions. Species range in height from about 10 cm (4 in) to more than 3.5 m (12 ft). The tubular white, yellow, blue, or purple flowers occur singly or in small clusters. They show an increasingly specialized adaptation to different types of insects. Simpler forms are rather open, with their nectar readily accessible to short-tongued insects. Intermediate forms are longer; their nectar is taken by certain kinds of bees. The most advanced forms have deeply tubular flowers whose nectar is obtainable only by long-tongued butterflies.

The gentian, native to southern Europe, is a herbaceous plant that bears showy, trumpet-shaped flowers. When dried, its roots yield the drug gentian, which is used as a tonic and as a stimulant to digestion.

Gentile, Giovanni [jayn'-tee-lay]   Giovanni Gentile, b. May 30, 1875, d. Apr. 15, 1944, was the self-proclaimed philosopher of Italian FASCISM and a major figure in the rise of Hegelian thought in Italy. As minister of education in Benito MUSSOLINI's first cabinet, he presided over a purge of liberals and democrats from Italian education.

Gentile's works develop a philosophy that he called "actual idealism." While denying that any philosophy can transcend actual human experience, he defended the view that such experience is fundamentally mental or spiritual and finds its fulfillment in the creation and defense of the state.

Gentile da Fabriano [jayn'-tee-lay dah fahb-ree-ah'-noh]   Gentile da Fabriano, c.1370–1427, born Gentile di Nicolò di Giovanni di Massio, was one of the major Italian painters of the early 15th century who worked in the International Gothic style. Among his many works now lost were important frescoes in the basilica of Saint John Lateran in Rome, which were completed by Antonio PISANELLO after Gentile's death.

The Adoration of the Magi *(1423), by Gentile da Fabriano, an Italian master of the International Gothic style, was painted for the church of Santa Trinità in Florence. The painting is considered the finest of the artist's extant works. (Uffizi, Florence.)*

His most famous works are two large altarpieces: *Adoration of the Magi* (1423; Uffizi, Florence), commissioned by the wealthy Florentine Palla Strozzi for his family chapel in the sacristy of Santa Trinità in Florence; and a large polyptych, *Quaratesi Polyptych* (1425), made for the Quaratesi family in Florence; its panels are now dispersed in museums in London, Florence, Rome, and Washington, D.C.

The *Adoration of the Magi* is generally considered the quintessential International Gothic style painting. The work is characterized by sinuous lines and elegant decorative effects, with little concentration on volume or depth.

Gentile's style is often contrasted with the monumental style of his Florentine contemporary MASACCIO. Gentile's influence, which was extensive, can be seen in the works of his followers Jacopo Bellini (see BELLINI family) and Pisanello, among others.

Gentileschi (family) [jen-tee-les'-kee]   Orazio Gentileschi and his daughter Artemisia were Italian painters inspired by Michelangelo CARAVAGGIO's naturalism, which they transformed into their own personal styles.

Orazio Gentileschi, c.1563–c.1639, was trained by his half brother Antonio Lomi in Florence and went to Rome in the late 1570s. Little is known of his early work

The Lute Player (1626), a late work by the Italian baroque painter Orazio Gentileschi, modifies Caravaggio's realistic, chiaroscuro style by infusing it with a Florentine delicacy and attention to detail. The grand gesture and monumental composition reflect Orazio's Roman Renaissance heritage. (National Gallery, Washington.)

there. He knew Caravaggio, whose influence can be seen in Orazio's paintings done between about 1605 and 1615, such as the *Judith* (*c*.1610; Wadsworth Atheneum, Hartford, Conn.). At this time he also painted in fresco, collaborating with Agostino Tassi. The brighter, more elegant compositions of his later period, such as his *Rest on the Flight into Egypt* (*c*.1626; Louvre, Paris), appealed to such painters as Philippe de CHAMPAIGNE. In 1626, Orazio went to London and became court painter to Charles I, for whom he executed numerous works.

Artemisia Gentileschi, *c*.1593–1651, first studied painting with her father and then with his colleague Agostino Tassi. In 1612, Tassi was accused of raping Artemisia, but the case was dismissed. Artemisia left Rome (1621) for Florence, where she established a reputation for her paintings of biblical and mythological heroines. In *Judith with the Head of Holofernes* (*c*.1625; Detroit Institute of Arts), a composition that she repeated several times, the impact of Caravaggesque CHIAROSCURO is pronounced. Her role in the dissemination of Caravaggesque realism was significant: she influenced the French painter Simon VOUET in Rome and inspired such artists as Bernardo Cavallino and Massimo Stanzione in Naples.

Gentz, Friedrich von [gents]   Friedrich von Gentz, b. May 2, 1764, d. June 9, 1832, was a German political theorist, publicist, and statesman remembered for his opposition to revolutionary movements in early 19th-century Europe. Although he was a supporter of the popular movement that culminated in the French Revolution, in his masterpiece, *On the Sources and Character of the Wars against the French Revolution* (1801), he sounded the conservative themes that were increasingly to characterize his career. A powerful figure in Austrian and European politics, he was secretary at the congresses of Vienna (1814–15), Aix-la-Chapelle (1818), Troppau (1820), Laibach (1821), and Verona (1822). His clear, objective writings are regarded as significant sources for the understanding of his times.

---

geocentric world system [jee-oh-sen'-trik]   The geocentric world system was the Earth-centered view of the universe systematized by ARISTOTLE in the 4th century BC, elaborated by PTOLEMY in the 2d century AD, and universally accepted until the HELIOCENTRIC WORLD SYSTEM was expounded by COPERNICUS in the 16th century. The geocentric system of hierarchical spheres is prominent in Dante's *Divine Comedy*.

---

geochemistry [jee-oh-kem'-is-tree]   Geochemistry is the application of chemistry to geologic problems. Its primary focus is the distribution and migration of the elements (particularly the rarer ones) in Earth materials. It most often refers to a method of prospecting for buried ore deposits by analyzing soil, water, and vegetation. Geochemistry also touches upon mineralogy, petrology, oceanography, and economic geology.

Differentiation of Earth Materials

On a planetary scale the most striking chemical feature of the Earth is that its material is separated into three distinct layers: a core extending out from the center about halfway to the surface, primarily composed of metallic iron; a mantle making up most of the rest of the Earth, composed in large part of compounds containing the four elements iron, magnesium, silicon, and oxygen; and a thin outer crust, variegated in composition but far richer in compounds of sodium, potassium, aluminum, silicon, and oxygen than the materials beneath it (see EARTH, STRUCTURE AND COMPOSITION). Outside the solid crust are the oceanic liquid water and the atmospheric gases.

Chemical changes have occurred in the crust and upper mantle all through the Earth's 4½-billion-year history and continue today. Through such plate tectonic processes as SEAFLOOR SPREADING and subduction, new material is constantly being added to the continents. One result is that elements typical of GRANITE (sodium, potassium, aluminum, silicon) are removed from BASALT, and the basalt's iron and magnesium are returned to the mantle. The reactions occurring today represent a late stage in the long history of differentiation of the Earth's original materials. The continents are islands of silicon-rich scum, or slag, accumulated on top of a huge circulating system of heavier materials rich in iron and magnesium. The process's chemistry is similar to the operation of a blast furnace, in which silicon-rich slag forms on top of molten iron, although more complex.

The Rock Cycle

Granite is formed by the solidification of molten rock at great depths, but slow movements in the solid crust eventually bring much of it to the surface, where, exposed to air and water, it undergoes slow chemical changes called WEATHERING. Aluminum minerals are very slowly changed to CLAYS, making the rock soft and vulnerable to disintegration. Iron in the granite's minor, dark-colored minerals is oxidized, giving the yellow and brown iron-oxide stains common on rock surfaces. Much of the sodium, potassium, and calcium is dissolved in rainwater and carried into streams and ultimately into the ocean. Only the very resistant minerals, especially QUARTZ (silicon dioxide), are left as the weathered rock disintegrates; these, moved by wind and water, are worn down to form grains of sand. Part of the clay and sand accumulates on the granite surface to form SOIL, part is carried by streams and deposited as layers of sediment (see SEDIMENT, MARINE) on plains or in the ocean. Such layers eventually harden into SEDIMENTARY ROCKS.

Through EROSION AND SEDIMENTATION, granite's original chemical constituents become separated and then redeposited to form new kinds of rock. As sedimentary layers (strata) pile up on one another in a GEOSYNCLINE, the lowest part of the pile may sink to great depths and become chemically altered to METAMORPHIC ROCK by high pressure and temperature. Ultimately, some of this material may begin to melt. Metamorphism and partial melting take place on a large scale in sedimentary piles (eugeosynclines) near certain continental margins, where subduction, the movement of the seabed under a continent, crumples the sedimentary layers and drags them down, with basalt, into the mantle. The sediment and basalt form new granite melt, completing what is known as the rock cycle.

Seas, Air, and Life

Geochemistry is concerned not only with these transformations in the Earth's solid materials but also with the envelopes of water and atmospheric gases that surround the planet. The water and gases have come primarily from the Earth's interior, probably mostly in the early part of geologic history, and have undergone continual chemical changes. Material dissolved from the land has poured into the ocean, forming seawater salt, and much of this material has precipitated out of the water as marine sediment. Long ago a balance was reached, the addition of each element to the ocean being compensated by its deposition in sediment, so that for much of GEOLOGIC TIME the composition of SEAWATER has remained nearly constant. The composition of air, however, has changed profoundly (see ATMOSPHERE).

The original atmosphere is thought to have consisted mainly of carbon dioxide, nitrogen, and water vapor. Complex organic molecules could have been formed from these gases by lightning discharges, ultraviolet light from the Sun, or simply the heat of molten rock from volcanoes. If such molecules were to dissolve in the warm water of shallow seas, a type of molecule might form that was capable of duplicating itself, thereby giving rise to the first living organisms.

Once life established itself, the geochemistry of the Earth's surface changed slowly but profoundly. Of particular importance was PHOTOSYNTHESIS in green plants, by which carbon dioxide was converted into organic compounds and free oxygen released to the air. Operating over 2 billion years, this activity could have removed most of the atmosphere's carbon dioxide and replaced it with oxygen. The Earth's present oxygen-rich atmosphere is unique in the solar system. It has permitted development of the higher forms of animal life and makes oxidation a major part of the weathering of rocks and minerals.

Living creatures also have a strong influence on the chemistry of sedimentary rocks. Many marine organisms use the dissolved calcium carbonate of seawater to build shells of CALCITE; others use SILICA. Remains of these organisms have accumulated in enormous quantities to form beds of LIMESTONE and CHERT. When dead plants and animals have been buried in airless environments, the organic matter slowly changes to simpler compounds. Coal, petroleum, and natural gas accumulate from such changes.

Applications of Geochemistry

During all chemical changes involving the major elements of the Earth's crust and upper mantle, the minor elements partly follow the major elements and partly separate from them. Geochemists study the processes of separation in order to understand how some of the rare elements are concentrated into ORE DEPOSITS. During the cooling of a granite intrusion, for example, the last liquid remaining as MAGMA crystallizes is a water-rich solution, part of the water coming from the molten granite and part from surrounding rocks. In this hot water are dissolved elements such as copper and gold, the atoms of which do not fit easily into the crystal structures of the major granite minerals. Movement of the water into surrounding cooler rocks can form VEIN DEPOSITS of these valuable metals.

Not only the distribution of elements, but the distribution of ISOTOPES as well, has become a major subject of geochemical research. Isotopes of a few light elements are slightly separated in ordinary geochemical processes, and the subtle variations in their distribution often shed light on the origin and history of rocks and minerals. The isotopes of elements produced by radioactive decay have a special interest because analyses for these isotopes make possible the RADIOMETRIC AGE-DATING of geologic materials.

One branch of geochemistry has proved useful to the mining industry. This is a technique, called geochemical prospecting, for finding ore deposits hidden by soil, vegetation, or thick sediments. For example, if a copper deposit exists beneath a layer of soil, the soil may look no different from soil elsewhere, and the deposit would be missed by ordinary prospecting methods. The soil above the deposit may, however, contain copper from weathering of the ore, and sensitive analysis can detect it. The hidden deposit may also become evident through abnormal copper concentrations in nearby vegetation, or in the water and sediments of streams that drain the area.

Geochemistry plays a growing role in environmental health as more is learned about how human and animal well-being depends on trace elements in plants, soil, and water. Some of the rarer elements—mercury is an example—are toxic in even minute quantities. Others, like selenium and fluorine, are essential for life in trace amounts but toxic in larger amounts. Deficiencies or excesses of a number of elements must be remedied, and geochemical knowledge of their distribution and mobility is necessary.

See also: EARTH, HEAT FLOW IN; OCEANIC MINERAL RESOURCES; PLATE TECTONICS.

geode [jee'-ohd]   Geodes are slightly flattened spherical mineral bodies that contain layers of inwardly radiating crystals surrounded by a layer of cryptocrystalline QUARTZ. New crystal layers frequently grow on the terminations of old layers, often nearly or completely filling the geode. Most geodes range in size from less than 5 cm (2 in) to more than 30 cm (12 in) in diameter. The crystals usually are composed of quartz. They also may be composed of the CARBONATE MINERALS calcite, dolomite, aragonite, and ankerite; of the OXIDE MINERALS hematite and magnetite; or of the SULFIDE MINERALS pyrite, chalcopyrite, and sphalerite.

Geodes occur in LIMESTONE and volcanic rock, where they form when mineral-bearing waters percolate into cavities in the rock, depositing crystals on the cavity wall.

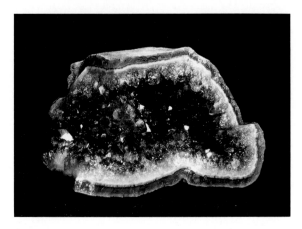

Geodes are rock cavities partially lined with layers of tiny crystals along their inner walls. Geodes of quartz, dolomite, and calcite are common. Many resemble rough, rocky balls until they are opened to reveal their crystalline interiors.

Subsequent periods of crystallization may follow, leaving the characteristic layers of crystals.

geodesic dome [jee-oh-des'-ik dohm]   The geodesic dome was developed by the American designer R. Buckminster FULLER after World War II as a low-cost and efficient method of space-frame, modular construction. Fuller employed standardized parts, usually spherical forms with triangular or polygonal facets made of bamboo, wood, plastic, aluminum, or any other material from cardboard to prestressed concrete. The architectural significance of these domelike structures made of interconnected, self-supporting members lies in their high structural efficiency, in which a large area may be enclosed without internal supports, a minimum of material is required, and construction time is brief. The principle has been widely adopted in the United States by industry and the military sector. During the 1960s, geodesic domes, which can be insulated and are suitable for all climates, became popular as an alternative, or "people's," technology. They have been used as exhibition halls, as in the

The U.S. pavilion at Montreal's Expo '67, a 60-m-high (200-ft) structure designed by R. Buckminster Fuller, is a geodesic dome constructed of interlocking steel struts and plexiglass panels.

U.S. pavilions at the Seattle World's Fair (1962) and at Expo '67 in Montreal. The dome's design principles also have been utilized for sports arenas and greenhouses.

Geoffrey of Monmouth   Geoffrey of Monmouth, d. 1155, bishop of Saint Asaph in Wales, wrote the *Historia Regum Britanniae* (1135–39), which introduced the Arthurian legend (see ARTHUR AND ARTHURIAN LEGEND) into Western literature. Shakespeare's *King Lear* is based on Geoffrey's work, which was essentially folklore.

geographical linguistics   Geographical linguistics, the study of variations in language within a geographical area, is concerned primarily with dialectal variations and therefore is also called dialect geography or dialectology. Geographical linguistics overlaps SOCIOLINGUISTICS and HISTORICAL LINGUISTICS. In the former, differences in dialect or language within an area often correlate with social differences. In the latter, the variations encountered at a particular time are the product of historical developments, and investigation of these developments can shed light on the current situation.

Idiolects and Dialects. No two individuals speak in exactly the same way; everyone has a unique form of speech, or idiolect. Nevertheless, for communication to be possible each speaker's idiolect must generally correspond to the idiolects of others who speak the same language. To the extent that people are in close communication, their idiolects will tend to be similar. When communication is more limited because of geographical separation or other reasons, however, differences between forms of speech become more numerous. In such cases one group of people will have common speech characteristics that another group does not share, even though the groups speak the same language. Any variety of a language that distinguishes one group from another is called a dialect.

In areas that have been settled for centuries and where most of the inhabitants rarely travel far, each village can have its own dialectal peculiarities. Even where there is a much higher degree of population mobility, regions may differ in dialectal features. A line on a map that separates an area where a specific linguistic feature is typically found from other areas where it is absent or occurs only infrequently is called an isogloss. A set of maps of this sort—each dealing with a different linguistic feature of a language area—is a linguistic atlas.

Linguistic Atlases. Compiling a linguistic atlas is time-consuming and expensive. Many years may separate inception from completion. This was the case with the earliest such enterprise, founded by Georg Wenker in 1876. He mailed a questionnaire to schoolteachers in more than 40,000 localities throughout Germany and asked them to translate a set of sentences into their local dialects. The *Deutscher Sprachatlas*, based on Wenker's data, first began publication a half century later, in 1926.

Another pioneering work was the *Atlas linguistique de la France* of Jules Gilliéron, which appeared between

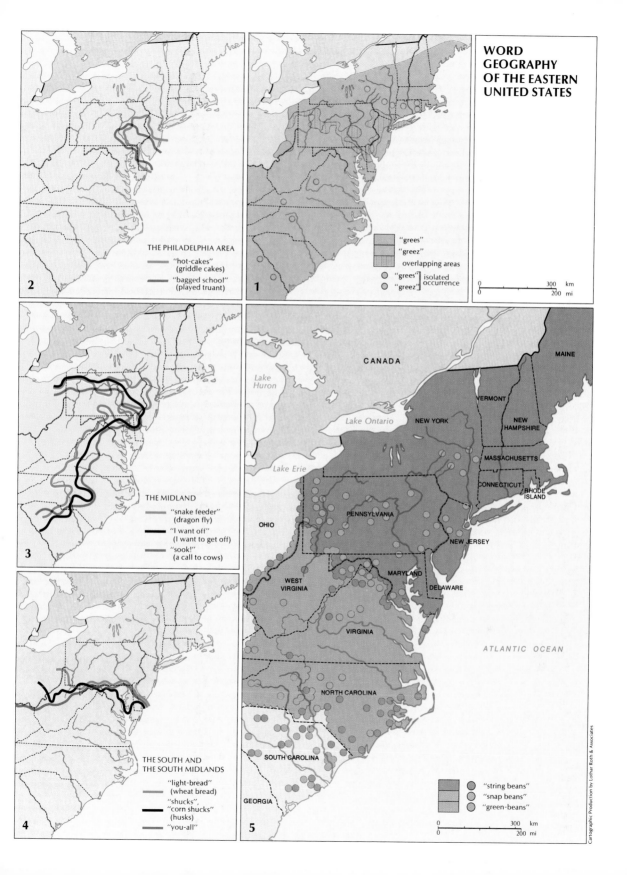

WORD GEOGRAPHY OF THE EASTERN UNITED STATES

2

THE PHILADELPHIA AREA

— "hot-cakes" (griddle cakes)
— "bagged school" (played truant)

1

"grees"
"greez"
overlapping areas
○ "grees" ⎫ isolated
○ "greez" ⎭ occurrence

0 300 km
0 200 mi

3

THE MIDLAND

— "snake feeder" (dragon fly)
— "I want off" (I want to get off)
— "sook!" (a call to cows)

4

THE SOUTH AND THE SOUTH MIDLANDS

— "light-bread" (wheat bread)
— "shucks", "corn shucks" (husks)
— "you-all"

5

CANADA

Lake Huron
Lake Ontario
Lake Erie

MAINE
VERMONT
NEW YORK
NEW HAMPSHIRE
MASSACHUSETTS
CONNECTICUT
RHODE ISLAND
PENNSYLVANIA
NEW JERSEY
OHIO
MARYLAND
WEST VIRGINIA
DELAWARE
VIRGINIA
ATLANTIC OCEAN
NORTH CAROLINA
SOUTH CAROLINA
GEORGIA

○ "string beans"
○ "snap beans"
○ "green-beans"

0 300 km
0 200 mi

Cartographic Production by Lothar Roth & Associates

1902 and 1910. Gilliéron relied on the fieldwork of one carefully trained investigator, Edmond Edmont, who traveled to 639 selected locations scattered throughout France, presenting a questionnaire to informants and taking down their answers.

Isoglosses: Analysis of Speech Patterns. Certain patterns are noticeable when the maps of a linguistic atlas are compared. Often a set of isoglosses radiates from a single focal area. This is generally a center of prestige, whether political, economic, or cultural, from which characteristic features of speech have been adopted by the surrounding population.

Features of speech in a focal area may spread throughout a region until only the outskirts preserve the older forms, called relics. In the pronunciation of Boston and the neighboring port cities, the sound of *r* in such words as *far* and *farm* was lost. This pronunciation came to characterize most of New England east of the Connecticut River.

Sometimes a bundle of isoglosses follows approximately the same course. Such a bundle, for example, delimits the Midland area of the eastern United States, including most of Pennsylvania and dividing the western mountain region of Virginia and the Carolinas from the rest of the South. This bundle reflects earlier patterns of population migration because more settlers in the Southern highlands came from Pennsylvania than from the coastal South.

Isoglosses may also coincide with political boundaries, as, for example, the Southern use of *you-all* as the plural of *you*, which extends only up to the Mason-Dixon Line. Isoglosses run along such lines because, like natural barriers such as mountain ranges, political boundaries can constitute long-term obstacles to communication or to the extension of influence from centers of prestige.

Because isoglosses often crisscross one another, reflecting competing influences, assigning a particular locality to a single dialect area is sometimes difficult. Most of West Virginia, for example, would go with the South on the basis of *you-all* or the pronunciation of the vowel in words like *time*. It would, however, belong with Pennsylvania as part of the Midland region if the greatest weight were given to the retention of the sound of *r* in *far* and *farm* or to such vocabulary items as *green beans* instead of the Southern *snap beans* or the Northern *string beans*.

Isoglosses are much less clear-cut in the western United States than in the East, bearing out the principle that dialect differences are more striking in older, established areas. Nevertheless, differences are observable in the West; one instance is the more Northern pronunciation of *egg* with a short *e* in San Francisco and Los Angeles, whereas in the surrounding nonurban areas *egg* rhymes with *vague*.

Sociological Factors. As the last example indicates, language variation has a social as well as a geographical dimension and often reflects the contrast between urban and rural populations and differences in age, sex, class, or ethnic identity. Furthermore, the same speaker may command several registers or styles of language. People will not necessarily use the same vocabulary, grammar, or pronunciation at a job interview as when talking to friends. In many parts of the world the difference between the informal and formal varieties is so great that learning the latter is comparable to learning another language.

Local dialects are forms of a language that are just as authentic as the standard form. Standard languages always originated as local dialects, or amalgams of such; they became more widely used, not for any inherent qualities, but because of the dominant position of their speakers. Thus Standard English developed out of the speech of London, Standard French out of that of Paris, and Standard German out of the fusion of dialects employed by the bureaucracies in the central and southern German seats of power in the Holy Roman Empire of the 14th to 16th centuries.

Bilingualism. In diglossia, two closely related forms of speech serve distinct functions within a community; the same can be true of two or more different languages as well. In India, for example, an educated person may use English with professional colleagues, Hindi with merchants, and a regional language radically different from both, such as Bengali or Marathi, with friends and family.

Such bilingualism or multilingualism can lead to changes in one or more of the languages. In extreme cases the outcome may be a PIDGIN, a form of speech with simplified grammar and reduced vocabulary that evolves as a means of intercommunication among speakers of mutually incomprehensible languages. Even without such explosive transformations, multilingualism can lead to the spread of linguistic features over a group of otherwise dissimilar languages spoken in the same geographical area.

▬

geographical societies Numerous privately and governmentally sponsored geographical societies function in countries around the world. Basically, their goals are to encourage, sponsor, and, in some cases, financially support worthwhile geographic research. The results are printed and disseminated in the various journals published by the societies. The International Geographical Union (1923) is a worldwide organization of geographers. In the United States, the American Geographical Society of New York (founded 1852) and the Association of American Geographers (1904) are of particular interest to the geographer. The NATIONAL GEOGRAPHIC SOCIETY (1888) in Washington, D.C., however, is better known by the public because of its monthly magazine, its maps, and the programs it produces for television. In Britain the Royal Geographical Society (1830) has made invaluable contributions, sponsoring many expeditions of exploration.

▬

geography Geography is the study of spatial variation on the Earth's surface and of humankind's relationship to its environment. Of essential concern to the geographer are spatial patterns and the interrelationships of climate, landforms, vegetation, soils, population, economic activities, and political units, either on a global scale or in a more limited area. Geography is thus an exceedingly complex discipline that can be subdivided into numerous

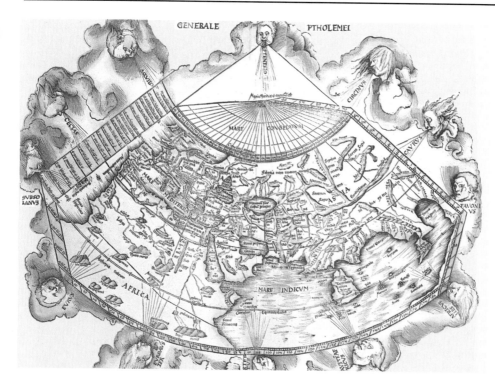

GENERALE   PTHOLEMEI

This 15th-century map of the known world was, like many others of its period, based on an atlas compiled by the Greco-Egyptian cartographer Claudius Ptolemy during the 2d century. Ptolemy's Geography, derived from earlier Phoenician sources, listed the latitudes and longitudes of thousands of places in Europe, Asia, and Africa. Despite numerous substantial errors, Ptolemy's work remained the standard cartographic text until the 16th century.

specialized areas. The geographer seeks to explain the location of various elements in the environment and to describe and establish the spatial patterns of these elements. The processes that form and change these patterns are also analyzed. One principal means to this end is the map, which for the geographer is an indispensable research tool as well as a visual representation (see MAPS AND MAPMAKING).

History and Evolution of Geography

Early Geographers. Many consider geography one of the oldest academic disciplines. Its antecedents may be traced to ancient Greece. Most of the ancient Greek geographers, such as THALES OF MILETUS (6th century BC) and HERODOTUS (5th century BC), were actually philosophers or historians. Much of their geographic writings described their physical environment. Indeed, the word *geography* is derived from the Greek, meaning "Earth description."

The Greeks also observed the planet as a whole. ARISTOTLE (4th century BC) is most often credited with conceiving the Earth as a sphere, a conclusion he arrived at by using philosophical reasoning and astronomical observations. His speculation about the Earth's shape was seconded by ERATOSTHENES, who calculated the circumference of the Earth based on a limited, measured arc of longitude. The astronomer HIPPARCHUS of Rhodes (2d century BC) developed a location system of lines on the surface of the Earth, the forerunners of latitude and longitude. STRABO (c.63 BC–AD 21) wrote *Geography,* a 17-volume work that describes through firsthand observation the world known to him. He is considered the father of regional geography because he substituted divisions based on natural boundaries (such as mountain ranges and drainage systems) for the less permanent and artificially drawn political units. PTOLEMY of Alexandria (fl. AD 121–51), perhaps the most famous ancient geographer, further systematized the geographical study of areas by classing regions in terms of size and detail. He drew a map of the then-known world that is remarkably accurate. His eight-volume *Guide to Geography* consisted of a list of all known places tabulated according to longitude and latitude, a system he devised himself.

After the collapse of the Roman Empire the heritage of Greek geography was preserved in the Arab world, and the Arabs made important contributions to a more profound knowledge of the world. In the 12th century al-IDRISI devised a refined system of climate classification. The great 14th-century explorer IBN BATTUTA found, on his travels through Africa and Asia, concrete evidence that refuted Aristotle's thesis that hot regions of the world would be too warm for human habitation. In the same century IBN KHALDUN wrote an important historical-geographic treatise.

Age of Discovery. Although the Crusades had stimulated European interest in the outside world, it was not until the Renaissance, when the voyages of Bartolomeu DIAS, Vasco da GAMA, and Christopher COLUMBUS in the late 15th century ushered in the so-called age of discovery, that there was a concomitant renewal of interest in world exploration, geographic description, and mapping.

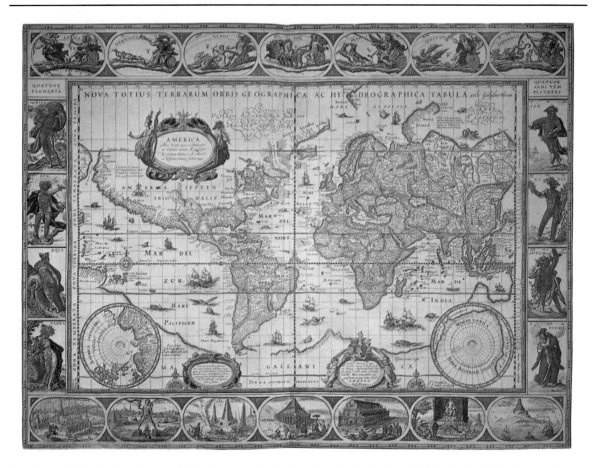

A world map by the Dutch cartographer Willem Blaeu employs the technique devised by Gerardus Mercator in 1569 for transferring the curved meridians of a globe to a two-dimensional chart with straight meridians.

As early as 1507 the German cartographer Martin Waldseemüller (*c.*1470–*c.*1521) produced a map of the world that clearly indicated both North and South America. It was on this map that the term *America* was first applied to any part of the New World. Fifteen years later Ferdinand MAGELLAN's party circumnavigated the Earth, thereby confirming its global shape. This information allowed for greatly increased accuracy of measurements and observations. Gerardus MERCATOR, a Dutchman, published a series of maps that in terms of accuracy surpassed anything previously produced. This included his famous navigation chart (1569), which introduced the map projection bearing his name, with its parallels and meridians at right angles.

Geography as an academic discipline was rejuvenated by Bernhardus Varenius (1622–50), who, in his *Geographia Generalis* (1650), established the concepts of topical geography and regional geography. This work may be said to have dominated the field for the following 150 years. By the 19th century the discipline was closely identified with GEOLOGY.

Founders of Modern Geography. During the 19th century there was a renewed effort to develop geography as a descriptive science. Contributions toward that end were made by the German geographers Alexander von HUMBOLDT, Carl Ritter, and Friedrich RATZEL. The first two have sometimes been called the founders of modern scientific geography, although neither was trained as a geographer. Humboldt laid the foundations of plant geography. Ritter, whose interest in geography was stimulated by Humboldt, is credited with introducing humankind into geographical studies, particularly humanity in relationship to its environment. Ratzel took Ritter's human geography still further, subdividing it into anthropogeography and political geography. He is best known for his organic theory of the state, in which he compares the evolution of the state to that of a living organism.

In the United States, geography was not pursued by university scholars until the end of the 19th century and the first part of the 20th century—about the same time that the United States emerged as a world power. Many of the early American geographers, such as Ellen Churchill

Semple, were former students of Ratzel in Germany.

German and French Schools. This period in the history of geography was marked by the development in the 19th century of the geographic philosophy referred to as determinism, environmentalism, or the German school of thought. Determinism held that the environment was the deciding factor in a person's way of living and his or her economic development. One American geographer, Ellsworth Huntington, expressed the idea that the climate determined the extent and character of a people's capacity for physical work and intellectual development.

Determinism began to decline during the 1930s and was eventually discredited. Earlier in the century, however, another geographical philosophy had emerged. This French school of thought, called possibilism, held that people had a choice in determining their development within the physical environment. Thus, although neither humans nor their environment existed in isolation, neither was able to control the other, and humans, therefore, were the ultimate master of their destiny. Paul Vidal de la Blache was a notable proponent of this theory.

Quantitative Revolution. During the 1960s a major change took place in the methodology of geographic research. The desire to make geography more scientific, or at least more intellectually acceptable as a discipline, led to the adoption of statistical methods as a major research technique. Location (or spatial) analysis, as this new aspect of geography is called, seeks to analyze and explain the factors that control humankind's spatial organization,

This infrared satellite photograph taken over southwestern Arizona shows the Colorado River (center, lengthwise) *and farmland, which appears as patches of red.*

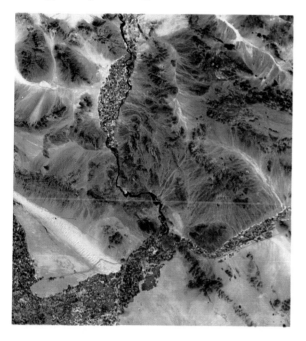

specifically by statistical methods and models. Mathematically constructed models became tools useful to the geographer in coping with rapidly accumulating knowledge, and they could also be used to predict future trends or spatial patterns.

This was not the first time statistics had been used for geographical research. As early as the 1920s and '30s, Torsten Hägerstrand in Sweden and Walter Christaller in Germany had used statistical techniques. Only in the 1960s, however, did significant growth in statistical methodology occur.

Since the late 1960s other new techniques have aided the analysis of geographic information. Two developments have been most significant: the electronic computer and remotely sensed imagery of the Earth from satellites.

Approaches to Geography

Two principal approaches to the study of geography have developed: topical, or systematic, and regional. Regional and topical geography are often pursued in combination. Topical geography is the study of the spatial organization or locational distribution of a specific phenomenon and its relationship to human presence. Medical geography, an example of topical geography, studies the distribution of disease-causing organisms.

Regional geography concerns all aspects of a relatively small area and compares that area with other areas. A region can be defined by physical criteria or by sociopolitical criteria. For example, a region may be an area receiving 100 mm (4 in), or less, of rainfall annually, or an area where more than 50% of the population are under the age of 15.

Branches of Geography

Physical Geography. Physical geography studies the natural conditions and processes on the Earth's surface and the resulting spatial structures; it includes several subdisciplines.

1. Geomorphology studies landforms, or the Earth's relief features, and examines their origins and evolution. The field is a bridge between geography and geology.
2. Biogeography, or ecogeography, is the study of plant and animal distribution. Plant geography, or phytogeography, and zoogeography are allied with ECOLOGY, which studies the relationships of plants and animals to their habitat.
3. Climatology examines the distribution of weather patterns, their seasonal changes, and what shapes the patterns.

Human (or Social) Geography. Human geography studies the changing spatial distributions of people and their activities and their interaction with the natural environment. It draws on the knowledge of the related social sciences but is particularly concerned with spatial analysis and description.

1. Cultural geography examines the distribution of cultural groups or of specific cultural traits such as religions, languages, architecture, place names, or burial rites.

2. Population geography studies the numbers and distribution of people and the changing patterns of distribution.

3. Economic geography deals with the location of economic activities and analyzes the reasons for location. Included are such subdivisions as agricultural geography, manufacturing geography, and transportation geography.

4. Historical geography is concerned with the local or regional environments of humankind as they existed in the past. This involves assessing both historical events and the role of the natural environment.

5. Political geography is the study of governmental units as observed on the landscape. This can involve the regional study of a specific political unit or the effect of political phenomena on an area.

6. Urban geography analyzes the origin and growth of cities as well as the spatial arrangement within cities. Many of the new statistical methods used in modern geography were introduced by urban geographers.

See also: EXPLORATION; GEOPOLITICS; REMOTE SENSING.

---

geologic time   One of the most important discoveries of modern science has been the age of the Earth and the vast length of time encompassed by its history. The scale of this history, in the millions and billions of years, is recognized as geologic time.

Most cultures incorporate some form of creation mythology, for example, the biblical Book of Genesis. In the mid-17th century an Irish churchman Bishop James USSHER added the years in the biblical genealogies and concluded that the Earth was created in 4004 BC. This idea persisted for a long while, although the 18th-century French scientist Georges Louis Leclerc, comte de Buffon, reasoned that the Earth cooled from an originally molten body and that this would have required at least 75,000 years.

Buffon had to recant, but development of the principle of UNIFORMITARIANISM in the late 1700s and early 1800s provided geologists with new grounds for arguing that the Earth is far older than anyone had imagined.

Similarly, in 1859, Charles DARWIN recognized that millions of years were necessary for small evolutionary changes to accumulate and produce the variety of life we see today. Because they lacked definitive, precise data, however, 19th-century geologists could only guess at the age of the Earth. In the meantime, an accurate, relative geologic time scale had been developed, which placed the main events of geologic history in proper sequence.

The Relative Time Scale

The relative time scale, developed on the basis of the FOSSIL RECORD, comprises four major intervals, called eras. The oldest, or Precambrian, includes ancient rocks whose only fossils are microorganisms and the layered mounds (stromatolites) built by BLUE-GREEN ALGAE. The next era, the Paleozoic, was dominated by marine invertebrate life, although arthropods, mollusks, vertebrates, and plants that invaded land later in the era began rapidly to expand. After many forms of marine life had become extinct,

the Mesozoic Era began with a new radiation of marine life and the dominance of reptiles on land. This era also closed with a number of EXTINCTIONS, particularly among the reptiles, such as the dinosaurs, and some marine groups.

Finally, the Cenozoic, or present, Era is characterized by the dominance of mammals, insects, and flowering plants on land, and still another radiation of marine life.

During the late 19th and early 20th centuries, scientists, in an attempt to determine the Earth's age, measured the present rates of physical processes and tried to extrapolate these rates to the past. The English physicist Lord KELVIN reasoned that the Earth and Sun had been formed at the same time, and that, given conventional energy sources, the Sun could have emitted energy at its present rate for only about 40 million years. Geologists and biologists familiar with the geologic and fossil records regarded such figures as being far too low, but they lacked the quantitative data necessary to refute Kelvin.

Absolute Age Dating

In the first decade of the 20th century, an American chemist, B. B. Boltwood, found that in the radioactive decay of uranium (U) to lead (Pb), the ratio Pb:U was consistently greater the older the rock containing these elements. Thus if the rate of radioactive decay could be determined, it could be used to calculate absolute ages for the geologic time scale. Utilizing RADIOACTIVITY, the techniques of RADIOMETRIC AGE-DATING, involving the decay of ISOTOPES of uranium to lead, rubidium to strontium, potassium to argon, or carbon to nitrogen, were developed for determining the age of rocks. With the exception of the carbon isotope C^{14}, all of these have half-lives long enough so that they can be used to determine the Earth's great age. Carbon^{14}, which has a short half-life, is useful only for dating substances in the late Quaternary Period. Several techniques devised in recent years substantiate the earlier dates, as well as increase the variety of datable materials.

Radiometric dating techniques have shown that the oldest rocks are approximately 3.8 billion years old, that the Paleozoic Era began about 570 million years ago and the Mesozoic Era about 230 million years ago, and that the Cenozoic Era has occupied the last 65 million years. In addition, meteorites (which are probably material left over from the formation of the solar system; see METEOR AND METEORITE) and rocks from the Moon (the surface of which has not been altered by atmospheric WEATHERING and EROSION or by tectonic processes) indicate that the Earth and the remainder of the SOLAR SYSTEM originated 4.65 billion years ago. (See also: EARTH, GEOLOGICAL HISTORY OF.)

Most radioactive elements occur in IGNEOUS and METAMORPHIC ROCKS, whereas nearly all fossils, on which the relative time scale is based, occur in SEDIMENTARY ROCKS. If igneous rock such as a lava flow or an ash bed is intercalated in a sequence of sedimentary strata, the assignment of a radiometric date to the sediments is relatively easy. In other instances, geologists must analyze regional relationships in an attempt to relate radiometrically dated crystalline rocks and sedimentary strata. For example, if a

GEOLOGIC TIME SCALE				
Era	Period	Epoch	Approximate Duration (millions of years)	Approximate Beginning (millions of years ago)
Cenozoic	Quaternary	Holocene	10,000 years ago to the present	
		Pleistocene	1.7	1.7
	Tertiary	Pliocene	9	12
		Miocene	14	26
		Oligocene	12	38
		Eocene	16	54
		Paleocene	11	65
Mesozoic	Cretaceous		70	135
	Jurassic		55	190
	Triassic		35	225
Paleozoic	Permian		55	280
	Carboniferous – Pennsylvanian		40	320
	Carboniferous – Mississippian		25	345
	Devonian		55	400
	Silurian		25	425
	Ordovician		75	500
	Cambrian		100	600
Precambrian – Proterozoic			3,200	
Precambrian – Archeozoic				3,800

sedimentary formation is cut by an igneous intrusion that is 250 million years old, the geologist knows that the strata are older than this, but not how much older. If the intrusion is truncated by an overlying sedimentary formation, the geologist knows that these strata are less than 250 million years old but not how much less. But if this second sedimentary formation is intruded by a second igneous body dated at 200 million years, the second set of strata must be between 200 and 250 million years old. Thus, geologists can continue to refine the calibration of radiometric and relative time scales.

geology Geology, derived from the Greek *geo*, "earth," plus *logos*, "study," deals with the study of the planet Earth—the materials of which it is made, the pro-

cesses that affect Earth materials, the products formed in the Earth, and the history of the planet and its inhabitants since its origin.

Geologists study the composition of Earth materials and the various geological processes in order to locate and exploit the Earth's mineral resources. They also investigate earthquakes, volcanoes, and other geologic hazards in order to predict and minimize the damaging effects of these natural phenomena. Geologists study geologic history to determine the former positions of the continents and oceans, to ascertain the nature of ancient climates, and to trace the evolution of life as revealed in the FOSSIL RECORD.

Geology draws heavily from other sciences; EARTH SCIENCE and the basic sciences overlap in many areas of investigation. For example, chemistry is used to analyze the

A geologist observes at close hand the active Kilauea crater of Hawaii's Mauna Loa volcano. The scientific study of volcanic activity, which extends back to the days of ancient Rome, has been essential to the growth of geologic knowledge.

rocks and minerals of the Earth's crust. Biology aids in understanding the nature of prehistoric organisms. Thus, botany provides information about ancient plants, and a knowledge of zoology is essential to the understanding of prehistoric animals. Physics helps to explain the various physical forces that affect the Earth and how Earth materials respond to these forces. Findings from astronomy reveal where the Earth fits into the universe, and astronomers have also attempted to explain the origin of the Earth.

Subfields

Because of its broad scope, geology has been divided into two major divisions: physical geology and historical geology. Physical geology deals with the composition of the Earth, its structural arrangement, the movements within and on the Earth's crust, and the myriad geologic processes by which the Earth is, or has been, changed. The principal subfields of physical geology include mineralogy, the study and classification of MINERALS; PETROLOGY, dealing with the origin, structure, occurrence, and history of rocks; and structural geology, which has to do with the deformation of rocks and their structural attitude or arrangements. GEOMORPHOLOGY is concerned with the general configuration of the Earth's surface and the origin, development, and classification of landforms. Economic geology has to do with geologic processes and materials that can be utilized by humans, and GEOPHYSICS and GEOCHEMISTRY rely on data derived from the study of the physics and chemistry of the Earth. More specialized subfields of physical geology include seismology (the study of EARTHQUAKES and the Earth's interior), volcanology (the study of VOLCANOES and volcanic phenomena), glaciology (the study of GLACIERS and glacial phenomena), environmental geology (geological studies related to human environmental concerns), engineering geology (the application of the geological sciences to engineering practice), and marine geology, or geological oceanography (that aspect of the study of the ocean which deals specifically with the ocean floor and with the ocean-continent margins; see OCEAN AND SEA).

Historical geology is concerned with the evolution of the Earth and its inhabitants from their origin to the present day. Subfields include STRATIGRAPHY, dealing with the study, interpretation, and correlation of sedimentary ROCK strata, and PALEONTOLOGY, the study of prehistoric plants and animals as revealed by their fossils and related to the chronology of the Earth's history. Geochronology is the study of time in relationship to the history of the Earth, and PALEOGEOGRAPHY deals with the physical geography of all or part of the Earth's surface at some time in the geologic past. More specialized are PALEOCLIMATOLOGY (the study of climates of the geologic past), PALEOECOLOGY (the study of the relationship between ancient organisms and their environment), PALEOMAGNETISM (the study of the Earth's magnetic field over geologic time), and micropaleontology (the study of microscopically small fossils).

History of Geology

Although geology is a relatively young science, humans have long been interested in the Earth. Prehistoric people utilized stones as tools and weapons, formed clay into pottery, and sought shelter in rocky caves. But their knowledge of the Earth was restricted to the ground beneath their feet or the limited areas that they could explore on foot.

Ancient Greek and Roman Beliefs. As early as the 4th century BC, ARISTOTLE taught that the Earth was a sphere. He also believed that streams originated from springs and that minerals were formed from "exhalations" of the Earth. He said that earthquakes were caused when "pent-up" winds burst to the surface after being trapped in subterranean channels.

Other ancients pondered the origin of fossils. In the 5th century BC, ANAXIMANDER of Miletus noted fossil fish well above sea level and concluded that fish had been the ancestors of all living things, including humans. XENOPHANES of Colophon (5th century BC) found fossils of marine organisms far inland and correctly inferred that they represented the remains of sea-dwelling animals.

Medieval Thought. There were few attempts to solve the Earth's mysteries during the Middle Ages. No distinction was made between rocks, minerals, and fossils as the terms are now understood. Early in the 11th century, however, AVICENNA, a Persian physician and Islamic scholar, perceived basic geologic processes that were not to be understood for centuries. He recognized water and wind as erosional agents, flooding of the land by prehistoric seas, the development of solid rock from soft, water-deposited sediment, the formation of soils, and fossils as the remains of ancient animals.

The Renaissance: An Awakening. Interest in the Earth was rekindled early in the Renaissance by LEONARDO DA VINCI. He recognized the true nature of fossils and refuted the then-popular notions that fossils were freaks of nature or devices that Satan had put in the rocks to lead people astray. His approach to the study of the Earth was modern in that he explained features in the rocks in the light of natural processes that could still be observed.

In the mid-16th century Georg Bauer, a German writing under the name of Georgius AGRICOLA, wrote on the origin of mountains, minerals, and underground water. Two of his books, *De natura fossilium* (1546) and *De re matallica* (1556), laid the foundations for mineralogy and mining geology.

The 17th Century. In 1667, Nicolaus Steno, a Danish physician and theologian, published the first true treatise on geology. He wrote on processes of sedimentation, the origin of rocks, the formation of crystals and fossils, and the interpretation of rock strata. His *Prodromus* (1669) established criteria for differentiating between freshwater and marine sediments. He was the first to recognize the principle of superposition—that the lower layers in a sequence of rock strata must be older than those deposited above them. He also stated that rock layers were formed from beds of sediment that were originally laid down in a nearly horizontal position—the principle of original horizontality. Steno was also the first to note that the CRYSTAL faces of a given mineral always have the same angle with respect to each other. This is now known as the law of constancy of interfacial angles.

Despite advances in the 17th century, however, the concept of GEOLOGIC TIME was not understood. The creation of the Earth and the geologic record were still explained in terms of biblical chronology. Accordingly, the creation was believed to have taken place in 4004 BC, a date based on the calculations of James USSHER, a mid-17th-century Irish bishop.

18th- and 19th-Century Advances. Modern geologic thought began to develop in the 18th century and expanded steadily in the 19th. Benoit de Maillet, a French consul to Egypt, was probably the first to note that older rocks contain fewer fossil species than do younger rocks.

Two major geological controversies emerged during the late 18th century, both of which were largely resolved by Scottish geologist James HUTTON. The first centered around the neptunism/plutonism debate. Proponents of neptunism, led by German mineralogist Abraham Gottlob WERNER, held that all bedrock had been precipitated in an ancient universal sea. Accordingly, fossils were seen as victims of Noah's flood, and granite and basalt were believed to be the oldest deposits of an ancient sea. Proponents of plutonism, led by Hutton, acknowledged that sedimentary build-up occurred, but held that most rock had solidified from an original molten mass. Neptunism was eventually discounted when granite and basalt were proven to be IGNEOUS ROCKS.

The second controversy involved CATASTROPHISM, a then widely held doctrine that the Earth's major physical features were caused by periodic, worldwide catastrophes. Hutton shared the belief that the Earth had undergone

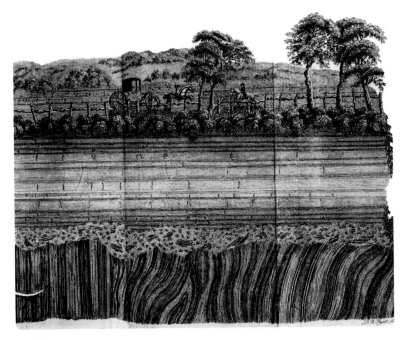

An engraving (left) *from James Hutton's* Theory of the Earth *(1795) shows horizontal rock strata resting on inclined layers. Hutton attributed such unconformities to gradual folding and erosion together with deposition of surface strata. A modern field geologist (below) uses methods similar to those used by Hutton.*

great changes, but he saw no concrete evidence for catastrophism. He proposed that all past geologic events were somehow connected, that the most important events occurred over immense time periods, and that they continue to occur in the present. Hutton's concepts, which became known as UNIFORMITARIANISM, established the significance of geologic time and provided the cornerstone of future geologic thought.

Field studies and mapmaking burgeoned in the 19th century. William SMITH, an English civil engineer, observed that each layer of rock contained fossils characteristic of that particular stratum, and that such strata might be identified by their fossils and thus correlated over wide areas. He laid the foundation for stratigraphical paleontology and published the first geologic map of England. William Maclure, a Scottish geologist who settled in Virginia, published the first maps of what was then the United States in 1809.

Near the end of the 19th century, geologists began to abandon a 6,000-year age for the Earth, and many came to believe that the Earth was at least tens of millions of years old. In 1896 RADIOACTIVITY was discovered by Henri BECQUEREL, a French physicist. This paved the way for the 20th-century development of RADIOMETRIC AGE-DATING, which has been used to determine the age—3.8 billion years—of the Earth's oldest rocks.

Geology in the 20th Century. With an understanding of geologic time and with Hutton's concept of uniformitarianism to guide them, 20th-century geologists began to forge geology as it is known today. Increasing knowledge of radioactive minerals, rates of decay, and decay products led to the development of the long-awaited "geologic clock," which suggests that the Earth is at least 4.6 billion years old.

In 1912, Alfred WEGENER, a German meteorologist, put forth his theory of CONTINENTAL DRIFT. This was followed 50 years later by the theory of SEAFLOOR SPREADING, which along with advances in paleomagnetism, led to the theory of PLATE TECTONICS. According to this important and now widely accepted theory, the Earth's crust is divided into a number of slowly moving plates that form by volcanic activity at the oceanic ridges and are destroyed in great seafloor trenches at the margins of the continents.

Deep-sea cores recovered by research vessels have confirmed seafloor spreading and yielded much information about the composition and geologic history of the ocean floor. Studies of the CONTINENTAL SHELVES have provided clues to valuable deposits of oil and natural gas. Radar and infrared imagery from high-altitude aircraft and satellites (see REMOTE SENSING) are being used to study volcanoes and potential earthquake FAULTS and to locate accumulations of valuable mineral deposits. In the laboratory, COMPUTER MODELING is now used in solving geological problems, and MASS SPECTROMETRY, the scanning electron microscope, and computerized axial tomography are probing rocks, minerals, and fossils.

geomagnetism   see EARTH, GEOMAGNETIC FIELD OF

geometry   Geometry is a mathematical system that is usually concerned with points, lines, surfaces, and solids. All mathematical systems are based on undefined elements, assumed relations, unproved statements (postulates and assumptions), and proved statements (theorems); different sets of assumptions give rise to different geometries.

Historical Development

Geometric figures first appeared more than 15,000 years ago in both practical and decorative forms such as shapes of buildings and pottery and in cave paintings. The word *geometry* is derived from the Greek words for "Earth" and "measure." In this context geometry was used at least 5,000 years ago by Egyptian surveyors who reestablished the boundaries of fields after the annual flooding of the Nile River.

PYTHAGORAS OF SAMOS (fl. *c.*540 BC) tried to explain all aspects of the universe in terms of counting numbers, which he frequently represented by sets of objects arranged in geometric shapes. For example, there were the triangular numbers 1, 3, 6, 10, 15,..., $(1/2)n(n+1)$; square numbers 1, 4, 9,..., n^2; and so forth. Magnitudes—measures of quantities that could not be represented by counting numbers—were represented by lengths of line segments.

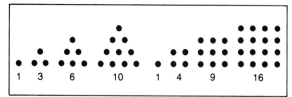

TRIANGULAR NUMBERS AND SQUARE NUMBERS

PLATO (fl. *c.*400 BC) emphasized geometry in his Academy and used the five regular POLYHEDRONS to explain the scientific phenomena of the universe. ARISTOTLE, a pupil of Plato, developed the laws of logical reasoning. The mathematics taught in Plato's Academy was structured by EUCLID (fl. *c.*300 BC) into a logical system. For 2,000 years the geometry of Euclid's *Elements* was assumed to be the one true geometry. Despite doubts about Euclid's parallel postulate, all attempts to derive it from his other four postulates or to develop other geometries without it were futile until the 19th century.

Types of Geometries

Euclidean Geometry. The most common geometry is Euclidean geometry, which appears to explain the universe in which humans live. One of its postulates assumes the existence of one and only one line that is both parallel to a given line *m* and contains a given point that is not a point of the line *m*. The two non-Euclidean geometries were developed from efforts to prove Euclid's parallel postulate and are based on alternatives to it.

Other Approaches. Spherical geometry, the geometry of points and lines on a sphere, can be easily visualized. Because the Earth is approximately spherical, this geometry has practical applications in navigation and surveying. The surface of a given sphere is a two-dimensional space because each point may be located by two coordinates. For example, points on the Earth may be identified by latitude and longitude. On this two-dimensional surface the shortest distance between two points is measured along a spherical line called a great circle, the intersection of the sphere and a plane that contains its center.

Angles formed by spherical lines have the same measures as the angles formed by the planes that determine the spherical lines in the model. SPHERICAL TRIGONOMETRY is the study of triangles on a sphere, or spherical triangles.

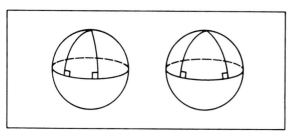

SPHERICAL TRIANGLES

If a geometry requires that two distinct lines have at most one common point, then spherical geometry is excluded, and the only geometries possible are Euclidean geometry and the two NON-EUCLIDEAN GEOMETRIES (elliptic geometry and hyperbolic geometry).

Coordinates, which were first used by APOLLONIUS OF PERGA (fl. *c.*225 BC) to identify points on a conic section and developed further by Oresme (fl. AD *c.*1360), René DESCARTES (1596–1650), and Pierre de FERMAT (1601–65), are used extensively today in the study of geometries. They are usually called Cartesian coordinates, in recognition of Descartes's work on coordinate systems (see COORDINATE SYSTEMS, mathematics). Because ordered sets of coordinates can be handled algebraically for any number of coordinates, geometries of any number of dimensions may be considered algebraically. Algebraic geometry is the study of geometry in terms of coordinates and algebraic representations of figures.

After Renaissance artists began to use PERSPECTIVE in their work, artists and mathematicians developed PROJECTIVE GEOMETRY. Efforts to represent three-dimensional figures by plane figures led to the development of descriptive geometry.

ARCHIMEDES (287–212 BC) used small elements of volume to derive a formula for the volume of a sphere. The use of such small elements (infinitesimals) led to the development of analysis (see CALCULUS) and DIFFERENTIAL GEOMETRY.

Many geometries may be considered studies of properties that are invariant (unchanged) under a group of transformations. A hierarchy of geometries may be obtained by considering the effect of removing various assumptions from Euclidean geometry. From this point of view, Euclidean geometry is a study of congruent figures, figures that have the same area and the same shape. If only the requirement that area be preserved is removed (while retaining the requirement that the shape remain the same), the geometry of similar figures (similarity geometry) is obtained. If only the requirement that shape be preserved is removed, equiareal geometry is obtained. If both requirements are removed, affine geometry is obtained.

Affine geometry is the geometry used by artists when a horizon (ideal) line is added to the Euclidean plane. In Euclidean geometry, lines correspond to lines, and parallel lines correspond to parallel lines. In affine geometry, any two lines that have a point of the horizon line in common are regarded as parallel lines. The study of lines that are allowed to correspond to linear continua (curves) is called TOPOLOGY. Two-dimensional topology is sometimes loosely referred to as "rubber sheet geometry" because it does not allow cutting apart or sealing together, but deformations are permitted. Topology is the most general geometry in the hierarchy of the branches of geometries shown in the accompanying figure.

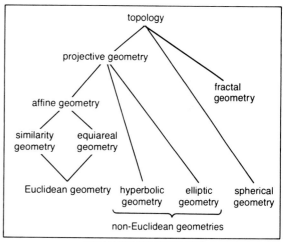

BRANCHES OF GEOMETRY

Logical Structure

Each of the 13 books of Euclid's *Elements* opens with a statement of the definitions required in that book. In the first book the definitions are followed by the assumptions (postulates and common notions) that are to be used. There follows a set of propositions (theorems) with proofs. The logical structure of the exposition of the proofs has influenced all scientific thinking since Euclid's time. This logical structure is essentially as follows:

1. A statement of the proposition.
2. A statement of the given data (usually with a diagram).
3. An indication of the use that is to be made of the data.

4. A construction of any additional lines or figures.
5. A synthetic proof.
6. A conclusion stating what has been done.

Modern refinements of logical procedure have long since shown that Euclid's work needs modification. The recently developed fractal geometry (see GEOMETRY, FRACTAL), for example, requires a more abstract, general definition of dimension than Euclid's. Furthermore, mathematicians today recognize that any logical system must contain some undefined terms (see GÖDEL, KURT).

—

geometry, fractal   A modern mathematical theory that radically departs from traditional Euclidean geometry, fractal geometry describes objects that are self-similar, or scale symmetric. This means that when such objects are magnified, their parts are seen to bear an exact resemblance to the whole, the likeness continuing with the parts of the parts and so on to infinity. Fractals, as these shapes are called, also must be devoid of translational symmetry—that is, the smoothness associated with Euclidean lines, planes, and spheres. Scaling symmetry without translational symmetry yields nonstandard scaling—a rough, jagged quality maintained at every scale at

A computer can use the concept of fractals to generate a wide range of complex shapes. Here, for example, a basic plane is repeatedly subdivided into smaller and smaller self-similar triangles. This same process can be continued to the limits of the capacity of the computer. The resulting network can be manipulated by adding random factors to produce a desired simulation of a complex terrain.

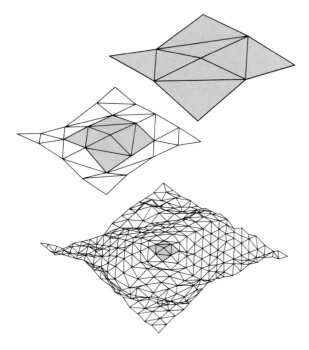

which an object can be examined. The quintessential nature of fractals is reflected in their etymology. The word was coined by mathematician Benoit B. Mandelbrot from the Latin verb *frangere*, "to break," and the related adjective *fractus*, "irregular and fragmented."

The simplest fractal is the Cantor bar (named for the 19th-century German mathematician Georg CANTOR). One may be constructed by dividing a line in 3 parts and removing the middle part. The procedure is repeated indefinitely, first on the 2 remaining parts, then on the 4 parts produced by that operation, and so on, until the object has an infinitely large number of parts, each of which is infinitesimally small.

Fractals are not relegated exclusively to the realm of mathematics. If the definition is broadened a bit, such objects can be found virtually everywhere in the natural world. The difference is that "natural" fractals are randomly, statistically, or stochastically rather than exactly scale symmetric. The rough shape revealed at one length scale bears only an approximate resemblance to that at another, but the length scale being used is not apparent just by looking at the shape. Moreover, there are both upper and lower limits to the size range over which fractals in nature are indeed fractal. Above and below that range, the shapes are either rough (but not self-similar) or smooth—in other words, conventionally Euclidean.

Whether natural or mathematical, all fractals have particular fractal dimensions. These are not the same as the familiar Euclidean dimensions measured in discrete whole integers—1, 2, or 3—but a different kind of quantity. Usually noninteger, a fractal dimension indicates the extent to which the fractal object fills the Euclidean dimension in which it is embedded. A natural fractal of fractal dimension 2.8, for example, would be a sponge-like shape nearly 3-dimensional in appearance. A natural fractal of fractal dimension 2.2 would be a much smoother object that just narrowly misses being flat.

Background. The roots of fractal geometry can be traced to the late 19th century, when mathematicians started to challenge Euclid's principles (see GEOMETRY). Fractional dimensions were not discussed until 1919, however, when the German mathematician Felix Hausdorff put forward the idea in connection with the small-scale structure of mathematical shapes. His work, as completed by the Russian mathematician A. S. Besicovitch, was a forerunner of fractal dimensionality. Other mathematicans of the time considered such strange shapes as "pathologies" that had no significance.

This attitude persisted until the mid-20th century and the work of Mandelbrot, a Polish-born French mathematician who moved to the United States in 1958. In 1961 he studied similarities in large- and small-scale fluctuations of the stock market. A 1967 paper on the length of the English coast showed that irregular shorelines are fractals whose lengths increase with increasing degree of measurable detail. By 1975, Mandelbrot had developed a theory of fractals, and publications by him and others made fractal geometry accessible to a wider audience. The subject began to gain importance in the sciences.

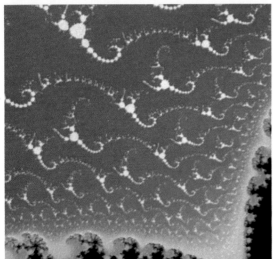

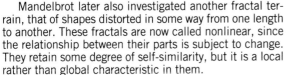

Computer graphics produced these striking fractal images derived from a mathematical set known as the Mandelbrot set, named for Benoit Mandelbrot, the founder of modern fractal geometry. The set's major element of stability is a budlike shape. As the set is magnified, however, through a repeating process known as a Julia set, its unpredictability increases. The result is a potentially infinite variety of geometrical patterns that can be colored by the computer to produce such images as those seen here. The Mandelbrot set has become popular for its beauty, but it also represents an important contribution to dynamical system theory.

Mandelbrot later also investigated another fractal terrain, that of shapes distorted in some way from one length to another. These fractals are now called nonlinear, since the relationship between their parts is subject to change. They retain some degree of self-similarity, but it is a local rather than global characteristic in them.

Impact on the Sciences. Scientists have begun to investigate the fractal character of a wide range of phenomena. Researchers are interested in doing so for the practical reason that behavior on a fractal shape may differ markedly from that on a Euclidean shape. Physics is by far the discipline most affected by fractal geometry. In condensed-matter, or solid-state, physics, for example, the so-called "percolation cluster" model used to describe critical phenomena involved in phase transitions and in mixture of atoms with opposing properties is clear-

ly fractal. This has implications, as well, for a host of attributes, including electrical conductivity. The percolation cluster model may also apply to the atomic structure of glasses, gels, and other amorphous materials.

Mathematical physics, for its part, has a particular interest in nonlinear fractals. When dynamical systems—those which change their behavior over time—become chaotic, or totally unpredictable, physicists describe the route they take with such fractals (see CHAOS THEORY). Called strange attractors, these objects are not real physical entities but abstractions that exist in "phase space," an expanse with as many dimensions as physicists need to describe dynamical physical behavior. One point in phase space represents a single measurement of the state of a dynamical system as it evolves over time. When all such points are connected, they form a trajectory that lies on the surface of a strange attractor.

Although not concerned with fractals to the same extent as physics, other sciences have also discovered them, including biology, geology, and meteorology.

Finally, on the interface of science and art, specialists in COMPUTER GRAPHICS, using a recursive splitting technique, have produced striking new fractal images of great statistical complexity. Landscapes made this way have been used as backgrounds in many motion pictures; trees and other branching structures have been used in still lifes and animations.

geomorphology [jee-oh-mohr-fahl'-uh-jee]   Geomorphology, from Greek words for *earth* and *form*, is the study of landforms and landscapes, particularly from the standpoint of origin. Unlike physiography, a branch discipline restricted to classifying landscapes, geomorphology seeks to relate specific landforms to the formative processes that operate in different environments (see LANDFORM EVOLUTION).

geophysics [jee'-oh-fiz-iks]   Geophysics, one of several EARTH SCIENCES, is the application of the principles and techniques of physics to the study of the Earth and its environment. It encompasses not only studies of the solid Earth but also of the oceans and atmosphere.

Studies of the solid Earth's shape, composition, physical properties, and fields are the subjects of several disciplines. Geodesy is concerned with the shape of the Earth, its gravity field, and its orbital parameters, and with changes in the shape of the Earth brought about by tidal and tectonic forces (see EARTH, SIZE AND SHAPE OF; EARTH, GRAVITATIONAL FIELD OF).

Seismology, the study of EARTHQUAKES and related phenomena, involves earthquake prediction as well as investigation of their mechanisms, modes, and locations of occurrence. This overlaps with the field of tectonophysics, which is concerned with deformations in the Earth, ranging from the small ones produced by TIDES to PLATE TECTONICS and mountain building. Central to this field is the science of rock mechanics, the study of the physical processes responsible for the deformation of rock under the high temperatures and pressures of the Earth's interior.

Geomagnetism and PALEOMAGNETISM relate to the nature of the Earth's magnetic field and the geological history of this field (see EARTH, GEOMAGNETIC FIELD OF). The study of VOLCANOES—their origin, behavior, and mode of occurrence—is the subject of volcanology. This science, especially with regard to the origin of the MAGMAS that generate volcanoes, overlaps with the fields of GEOCHEMISTRY, PETROLOGY, and mineralogy (see MINERAL).

Investigation of the fluid envelopes of the Earth, both liquid and gaseous, have more in common with each other than with solid-earth geophysics. METEOROLOGY is concerned with the behavior of the lower ATMOSPHERE. The study of the oceans is usually broken into chemical, biological, and physical branches; only the latter, physical OCEANOGRAPHY, is considered a branch of geophysics. The study of the HYDROSPHERE of the Earth—water that is not only in the oceans and atmosphere but on land, in lakes, rivers, and under ground—is the domain of the HYDROLOGIC SCIENCES. In studies of the HYDROLOGIC CYCLE, hydrology merges with both oceanography and meteorology; other areas are GROUNDWATER hydrology and LIMNOLOGY (the study of lakes).

The Earth's magnetic field forms a repulsive sheath about 100,000 km (62,000 mi) in diameter, called the MAGNETOSPHERE, that extends beyond the upper limits of the atmosphere. Magnetospheric physics studies the changes in this sheath arising from interaction with the SOLAR WIND. The study of the upper atmosphere, called aeronomy, includes phenomena such as AURORAS and the VAN ALLEN RADIATION BELTS.

Geophysics depends on data-gathering systems of global extent, such as seismograph networks and weather satellites. Operation of such systems is dependent, in turn, on international agreements. The success of the first fully international cooperative venture, the INTERNATIONAL GEOPHYSICAL YEAR (IGY) of 1957–58, paved the way for a growing number of cooperative programs.

See also: EARTH, GEOLOGICAL HISTORY OF; OCEAN-ATMOSPHERE INTERACTION.

geopolitics [jee-oh-pahl'-i-tiks]   Geopolitics is the study of the influence of geography, along with economics and demography, on the politics of a nation. Geopolitics helps in understanding forces that affect the politics of national states, especially foreign relations.

Geopolitics had its beginnings in the early 20th century in the work of the Swedish political scientist Rudolf Kjellén, a follower of the German geographer Friedrich RATZEL. The British geographer Sir Halford J. MACKINDER maintained that the Euro-Asian "heartland" (comprising most of the USSR) was of strategic importance; he warned that a resurgence of German power after World War I might lead to world dominance if Germany were to control Europe and Russia. Karl Haushofer's German school of geopolitics in the 1920s promoted similar ideas that were used by the Nazis to justify their *Lebensraum* program of territorial expansion. MANIFEST DESTINY was a geopolitical theory promoted in the United States during the 19th century.

George, David Lloyd   see LLOYD GEORGE, DAVID

George, Henry   Henry George, b. Philadelphia, Sept. 2, 1839, d. Oct. 29, 1897, was an American social reformer whose *Progress and Poverty* (1880) won him in-

The 19th-century American social reformer Henry George advocated a single-tax solution for the inconsistencies of existing tax laws. In his treatise, Progress and Poverty *(1880), he outlined a plan aimed at abolishing all forms of taxation except land taxes.*

ternational fame. In it he asserted that working the land was a natural right and that landlords were not entitled to reap the profits from it. He advocated a tax on land equal to its total economic rent—that is, the amount by which its value exceeded the value of land in other, less productive uses. Such a tax, he said, would eliminate the need for other taxes. His exposition of the SINGLE TAX theory made George a much-sought-after lecturer. In 1886 he ran for mayor of New York City; he was defeated, although he ran ahead of Theodore Roosevelt.

George, Lake   Lake George, a long (51 km/32 mi), narrow (up to 6 km/4 mi wide) glacial lake, lies in the foothills of the Adirondack Mountains in northeastern New York. It has a depth of 120 m (400 ft) and drains into Lake CHAMPLAIN to the north through a series of falls and cascades. Located in a region of great natural beauty, Lake George mainly serves recreational purposes. Named for George II in 1755, it was the site of several important battles in the French and Indian War and the American Revolution.

George, Saint   Saint George, the patron saint of England, may have been a martyr in Palestine before AD 300, but no actual details of his life are known. The legend that he saved a Libyan princess by killing a dragon arose in the 12th century, possibly from the myth of PERSEUS, who slew a sea monster near the site of George's supposed martyrdom. His status as patron of England probably originated with the foundation of the Order of the Garter under his patronage about 1347. George is also patron of Portugal, Aragon, Catalonia, and Lithuania. Feast day: Apr. 23.

George, Stefan   [gay'-ohr-ge, shtef'-ahn]   Stefan George, b. July 12, 1868, d. Dec. 4, 1933, was one of Germany's great lyric poets in the romantic-symbolist tradition. In Paris he met the French symbolist poets Stéphane Mallarmé and Paul Verlaine, and by his early twenties he had already produced such collections of lyrical, but often esoteric, poems as *Hymns* (1890), *Pilgrimages* (1891), and *Algabal* (1892). George was influenced by Friedrich NIETZSCHE, and by age 24 he had attained sufficient stature to found his own elitist literary society, "The George Circle." In 1892 the group, which included some of the most influential writers and critics, founded a journal, *Blätter für die Kunst* (Pages for Art). Following a book of historical costume-poems, *Die Bücher der Hirten* (Books of the Shepherds, 1895), George composed some of his finest verse in *Das Jahr der Seele* (The Year of the Soul, 1897).

In 1903, during a difficult time in his life, George became infatuated with a 15-year-old boy, "Maximin," and sublimated the experience into a poetic, even mystical, encounter, *Der siebente Ring* (The Seventh Ring, 1907), celebrating Maximin as a new god. *Der Stern des Bundes* (The Star of the Covenant, 1913) continued the notion of

a select league or circle. George's last book, *Das neue Reich* (The New Kingdom, 1928), prophesied an era in which Germany would become a new Greece.

George of Poděbrady, King of Bohemia   [pawd'-yuh-brah-dee]   George of Poděbrady, b. Apr. 23, 1420, d. Mar. 22, 1471, was the last national monarch of Bohemia (1458–71). After becoming the leader of the moderate HUSSITES (Utraquists) in 1444, George represented the main source of stability in Bohemia. He was elected king in 1458, but his continued allegiance to Hussitism brought him papal excommunication, as well as the military intervention of MATTHIAS CORVINUS of Hungary, who conquered Moravia (1468) and was elected king (1469) by the Catholic nobility. George died in the midst of this struggle, after naming Vladislav II (1471–1516), the son of CASIMIR IV of Poland, as his successor. George embodied the religious and national aspirations of his people, and his proposal for a league of princes to deal with general European problems made him an early champion of European unity.

George Town   see PENANG

George Washington Bridge   The George Washington Bridge links the island of Manhattan, New York City, with Fort Lee, N.J., across the Hudson River. It has a clear span of 1,067 m (3,500 ft), which made it the world's longest suspension bridge (see BRIDGE, engineering) when it was completed (1931). Designed by the famous bridge engineer O. H. AMMANN, and with a second deck and stiffening trusses added in 1959–62, the bridge now carries 14 lanes of traffic on the two decks, which are suspended from four main cables, each 0.9 m (3 ft) in diameter and built up of 26,474 parallel wires. Because of notable innovations in its erection, the bridge may be regarded as the first bridge to use modern methods of cable spinning.

George Washington University   George Washington University, in Washington, D.C., was established as Columbian College in 1821 by a group that included President James Monroe. George Washington had planned for the university, but the shares he left to endow it turned out to be worthless. It is a private university with graduate schools of law, medicine, and international affairs.

George I, King of England, Scotland, and Ireland   George I, b. March 28, 1660, d. June 12 1727, elector of Hanover, succeeded to the British throne on the death of Queen ANNE in 1714. The succession was determined by the Act of SETTLEMENT of 1701, which passed over the legitimate but Roman Catholic representatives of the STUART line in favor of the Protestant house of HANOVER, descended from the daughter of James I.

Born in Hanover, George was well educated in the

George I, the founder of the Hanoverian dynasty of British monarchs, succeeded Queen Anne in 1714. A German prince, he spoke no English and took little interest in Britain's domestic affairs. As a result, the power of his ministers, most notably Robert Walpole, grew enormously.

military and diplomatic arts. He became elector in 1698. After succeeding to the British throne, he remained staunchly German in his attachments and objectives. His constant aim was the aggrandizement of Hanover, and it was due largely to his use of the British fleet that he successfully completed the acquisition of Bremen and Verden for Hanover in the Great NORTHERN WAR. In England George caused much controversy by his uncompromising support for the WHIG PARTY against the Tories and by his tendency to take advice on matters of state from his Hanoverian counselors. The uprising of the JACOBITES in 1715, several Jacobite conspiracies, and the SOUTH SEA BUBBLE in 1720 all presented threats to the security of his dynasty.

George quarreled both with his wife, Sophia Dorothea (1666–1726), whom he divorced and incarcerated (from 1694 until her death) in punishment for her alleged infidelity, and with his son, Prince George, who consorted with his political opponents. The prince succeeded to the throne as George II upon his father's death.

George II, King of England, Scotland, and Ireland   George II, b. Nov. 10, 1683, d. Oct. 25, 1760, succeeded to the British throne and the electorate of Hanover on the death of his father, George I, in 1727. Born in Hanover, he remained largely Hanoverian in his interests, although, unlike his father, he learned fluent English. He visited the electorate regularly and sometimes utilized his position as king of England to the advantage of his German territory.

Although George has been represented as a king manipulated by his own ministers—notably Sir Robert WALPOLE and the duke of NEWCASTLE—and by his highly intelligent wife, Queen Caroline (1683–1737), he was by no means a weak monarch. He played a larger part in the direction of foreign and military policy than most contemporaries suspected, and at Dettingen (1743), in the War of the AUSTRIAN SUCCESSION, was the last British monarch to appear in person on the battlefield. His reign witnessed the final collapse of the JACOBITES after their uprising of 1745 and closed with Britain's brilliant successes in the

SEVEN YEARS' WAR (1756–63) under the leadership of William PITT the Elder. George had long detested Pitt, but he eventually came to recognize his merits.

George's son, Frederick, predeceased him, so when George II died, he was succeeded by Frederick's son, George III.

George III, King of England, Scotland, and Ireland   George III, b. June 4, 1738, d. Jan. 29, 1820, was the longest reigning of male British monarchs. The son of Frederick, prince of Wales, and the grandson of George II, he succeeded his grandfather in 1760, his father having died in 1751.

George had high but impractical ideas of kingship. On his accession he sought to banish corruption from political practice, and to abandon the Hanoverian preoccupations of his predecessors. He chose the 3d earl of Bute (1713–92), an unpracticed politician, to implement his new system, but the result was 10 years of ministerial instability. In 1770, George appointed the able and congenial Frederick, Lord NORTH, as chief minister.

Although not autocratic, George III was always a powerful monarch. He viewed the concession of independence to America in 1783 with such detestation that he considered abdicating his throne. He also fought a personal feud with the Whig leader Charles James Fox, and his intervention brought the fall of the Fox-North ministry in 1783. He then found another minister, William PITT, the Younger, who suited him. In 1801, however, he forced Pitt to resign rather than permit CATHOLIC EMANCIPATION, a measure that he considered contrary to his coronation oath to uphold the Church of England.

George III's later years were made wretched by a mental instability that ultimately compelled him to submit to the establishment of a formal REGENCY in 1811. The regent was his oldest son, the future George IV, one of 15 children borne him by his wife, Queen Charlotte.

George III was bitterly criticized by Whig historians of his own and later days. But 20th-century scholarship has somewhat redressed the balance, and he is now seen as a strong-minded but public-spirited monarch. A conserva-

George III saw a great expansion of Britain's commercial empire during his lengthy reign (1760–1820) despite the loss of the American colonies. The latter years of his rule were marred by a rare metabolic disorder known as porphyria, which ultimately cost him his sanity and his sight.

tive statesman, he brought to the court a sense of public duty and private morality that proved popular in a society already being transformed by the evangelical revival. His personal reputation stood the Hanoverian house in good stead during the disastrous reign of his son George IV.

George IV, King of England, Scotland, and Ireland

George IV, b. Aug. 12, 1762, d. June 26, 1830, who served as prince regent from 1811 to 1820 (see REGENCY) before succeeding his father, George III, to the throne, brought the standing of the British monarchy lower than at any other time in its modern history. As a young man he consorted with his father's parliamentary opponents, including Charles James Fox. In 1785 he illegally married Mrs. Maria Fitzherbert. He subsequently denied the marriage in order to secure Parliament's payment of his debts, and in 1795 he married Princess Caroline of Brunswick, whom he later attempted to divorce on his accession as king. Although long an ally of the Whigs, he declined to bring them into power when he became regent, and he was thereafter associated with deeply conservative causes, especially the maintenance of official discrimination against Roman Catholics and Protestant dissenters. His personal profligacy and his treatment of Queen Caroline brought him great unpopularity. He spent extravagant sums on the arts. Some of the richest portions of the royal collection and, above all, the Royal Pavilion at Brighton remain as monuments to his cultural interests. He was succeeded by his brother, WILLIAM IV.

Appointed (1811) prince regent because of the mental instability of his father, George III, George IV finally succeeded to the throne in 1820. During his 10-year reign, the prestige and political influence of the monarchy suffered a steady decline.

George V, King of England, Scotland, and Ireland

George V, b. June, 1865, d. Jan. 20, 1936, succeeded his father, EDWARD VII, to the British throne in 1910. He pursued a naval career until the death (1892) of his older brother made him second in line to the throne of his grandmother, Victoria. In 1894 he married Princess Mary of Teck.

At the beginning of his reign George was involved in two crises—one over reform of the House of Lords

George V, king of Great Britain from 1910 until 1936, was held in deep affection by the British people. He relinquished his German titles in 1917 and changed the name of the royal house from Saxe-Coburg-Gotha to Windsor.

(1910–11) and the other over Irish HOME RULE (1912–14). His conduct in these and, later, his choices of Stanley BALDWIN as prime minister in 1923 and Ramsay MacDONALD as head of the national government in 1931 generated some controversy. Nonetheless, he won popular affection, despite his gruff personality, by his visits to the troops during World War I and later by his Christmas radio broadcasts. During the war he changed the name of the royal family to WINDSOR. He was succeeded by his oldest son, EDWARD VIII.

George VI, King of England, Scotland, and Ireland

George VI, b. Dec. 14, 1895, d. Feb. 6, 1952, succeeded to the British throne on the abdication of his brother, EDWARD VIII, in 1936. He was the second son of George V. In 1923 he married Lady Elizabeth Bowes-Lyon.

A shy man, George VI struggled successfully to overcome a speech defect and won wide respect for his dedication and courage. During World War II, to encourage

George VI assumed the British throne in 1936, when his elder brother, Edward VIII, abdicated. During World War II, George VI concentrated on bolstering public and military morale by visiting battle fronts and severely bombed areas.

morale, he risked his life visiting war zones and recently bombed cities. He also created the George Cross for civilian gallantry, awarding it to the people of Malta for heroism under air attack. He and his consort, Queen Elizabeth, made notable state visits to France (1938), Canada and the United States (1939), and South Africa (1947). The king's frail health was weakened, and his life probably shortened, by his determination to carry on with his public duties despite serious illness. He was succeeded by his elder daughter, ELIZABETH II.

George I, King of Greece

George I, b. Dec. 24, 1845, d. Mar. 18, 1913, succeeded OTTO I on the Greek throne in 1863. The second son of King CHRISTIAN IX of Denmark, he was nominated as king of the Hellenes by Britain, France, and Russia and then elected by the Greek National Assembly. During his reign the territory of Greece was considerably extended by the cession of the Ionian Islands by Britain (1864) and the acquisition from Turkey of Thessaly and Arta (1881) and, later, of Epirus, Macedonia, and Crete (1913). The last territories were won in the First BALKAN WAR, at the end of which George was assassinated.

George II, King of Greece

The eldest son of King CONSTANTINE I, George II, b. July 20, 1890, d. Apr. 1, 1947, was king of the Hellenes from 1922 to 1924 and again from 1935 to 1947. He went into exile after the British and French forced his father to abandon the throne in June 1917. Constantine returned in late 1920, and when he was compelled to abdicate after Greece's defeat by Turkey in Asia Minor, George became king on Sept. 27, 1922. In the aftermath of an abortive military revolt (October 1923) involving proroyalist officers, republicans in military and civilian circles pressed George into leaving Greece. In the early spring of 1924, a republic was declared.

The republic fell when ardent royalists engineered the restoration of the monarchy in the autumn of 1935. George II returned in November 1935, hoping to reconcile opposing factions. When moderate methods failed to improve conditions, he approved the establishment of a dictatorship under Ioánnis METAXÁS in August 1936. The German invasion of Greece in the spring of 1941 drove George into exile. A plebiscite on Sept. 27, 1946, approved his return, but he died soon after.

Georgetown

Georgetown is the capital of Guyana. Situated at the mouth of the Demerara River on the northeastern coast of South America, its port handles Guyanan sugar and rice products, gold, and bauxite. The population (1985 est., 200,000) is mixed East Indian, African, and European. The first English settlement, called Georgetown, was occupied (1784) by the Dutch, who changed the name to Stabroek; it was renamed Georgetown in 1812. With wide avenues and canals, this tropical city contains some of the best-preserved British colonial architecture in the Caribbean. The University of Guyana is there.

Georgetown University

Established in 1789 and operated by the Jesuits, Georgetown University, in Washington, D.C., is the oldest Roman Catholic institution of higher learning in the United States. Among its professional schools are the School of Foreign Service (1919), the first school in the country for the training of diplomats, and the School of Languages and Linguistics (1949).

Georgia (United States)

Georgia is the largest state east of the Mississippi River. Its territorial domain extends from the Sea Islands on the Atlantic shore to the forested mountains of the southern Appalachians. Georgia is bounded on the east by South Carolina and the Atlantic Ocean, on the west by Alabama, on the north by Tennessee and North Carolina, and on the south by Florida.

A distinctive feature of Georgia is the paradox of old and new—often side by side. The forces generating change throughout the American South can readily be seen in Georgia. The state has experienced major economic growth in recent years, and Atlanta has emerged as the major urban center of the southeastern United States. In 1976 a native Georgian, Jimmy Carter, was elected president of the United States, the first southerner to occupy the nation's highest office since Reconstruction.

Land and Resources

Five physiographic regions are identifiable within Georgia: the CUMBERLAND PLATEAU, BLUE RIDGE MOUNTAINS, Ridge and Valley Region, PIEDMONT PLATEAU, and Coastal Plain. Lookout Mountain and Sand Mountain in the northwest corner of Georgia are remnants of the modest synclinal structure associated with the Cumberland Plateau. The surface elevations of these plateau remnants are 450 to 550 m (1,500 to 1,800 ft). The Blue Ridge Mountains extend into northern Georgia from adjacent Tennessee and North Carolina; the highest elevations in the state are found there. The narrow valleys and forested mountains are a major recreational resource. Springer Mountain (1,164 m/3,820 ft) is the southwestern terminus of the APPALACHIAN TRAIL. The Ridge and Valley Region extends across northeast Georgia from Alabama to Tennessee. A group of low and open valleys 150 to 250 m (500 to 825 ft) above sea level are separated by ridges that extend 200 to 250 m (675 to 825 ft) above the valley floors.

The Piedmont is the rolling upland plain south of the mountains. The northern margin of the Piedmont has an average elevation of 360 m (1,200 ft). The Piedmont's southern margin, which follows a line from Columbus to Augusta, is at an elevation of 150 m (500 ft). Local relief on the Piedmont is normally not more than 30 to 60 m (100 to 200 ft), but several MONADNOCKS exist with elevations that make them distinctive on the rolling Piedmont surface, such as Mount Yonah at 967 m (3,173 ft).

The fall line is associated with the point at which the unconsolidated materials of marine origin forming the

AT A GLANCE

GEORGIA

Land: Area: 153,953 km² (59,441 mi²); rank: 24th. Capital and largest city: Atlanta (1990 pop., 394,017). Counties: 159. Elevations: highest—1,458 m (4,784 ft), at Brasstown Bald; lowest—sea level, at Atlantic coast.

People: Population (1990): 6,508,419; rank: 11th; density: 42 persons per km² (108.9 per mi²). Distribution (1990): 63.2% urban, 36.8% rural. Average annual change (1980–90): +1.9%.

Government (1993): Governor: Zell Miller, Democrat. U.S. Congress: Senate—1 Democrat, 1 Republican; House—7 Democrats, 4 Republicans. Electoral college votes: 13. State legislature: 56 senators, 180 representatives.

Economy: State personal income (1989): $103.3 billion; rank: 12th. Median family income (1989): $33,529; rank: 24th. Agriculture: income (1989)—$3.87 billion. Fishing: value (1989)—$20 million. Lumber production (1991): 2.5 billion board feet. Mining (nonfuel): value (1988)—$1.37 billion. Manufacturing: value added (1987)—$33.7 billion. Services: value (1987)—$25.7 billion.

Miscellany: Statehood: Jan. 2, 1788; the 4th state. Nicknames: The Empire State of the South, Peach State; tree: live oak; motto: Wisdom, Justice, and Moderation; song: "Georgia on My Mind."

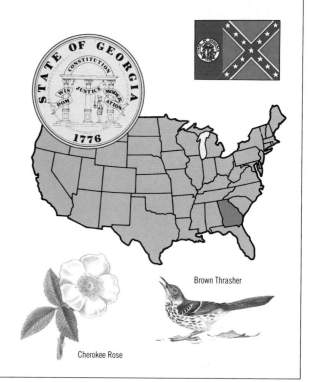

Brown Thrasher

Cherokee Rose

Coastal Plain overlap with the geologically older rocks of the Piedmont. In Georgia the fall line extends through the cities of Macon, Columbus, Milledgeville, and Augusta. The border area is marked by low hills—the Sand Hills—that contrast with the low relief of the Coastal Plain. The outer, or Atlantic, edge of the Coastal Plain is composed of offshore islands—including St. Simons, Jekyll, St. Catherines, Sapelo, and Cumberland—and tidal marshes and low marine terraces. One such poorly drained terrace is occupied by the OKEFENOKEE SWAMP, a national wildlife refuge.

Soils. Georgia's soils are varied. The slopes of the three mountain regions prohibit their soils from being used for cropland agriculture. The valley soils of the Ridge and Valley Region, which are formed from limestone, are highly productive, however. Piedmont soils range from sandy loams to clay, but the rolling character of the Piedmont, in combination with the practice of intensive row cropping, has contributed to extensive and severe erosion damage. During the past five decades much of the Piedmont has been converted to grassland or forest, and the potential for continued resource destruction has been greatly reduced. The soils of the Coastal Plain are light, deep, and sandy.

Climate. A humid subtropical climate with mild winters and hot moist summers is characteristic of most of Geor-

gia. The average annual precipitation varies from about 1,015 mm (40 in) in central Georgia to more than 1,900 mm (75 in) in northeast Georgia. One of two annual precipitation maxima occurs in February or March, when between 100 and 150 mm (4 and 6 in) of rain may be expected because of the high seasonal incidence of cyclonic activity over the southeastern United States. The second maximum occurs in June and July, when precipitation from thunderstorm activity may bring 100 to 180 mm (4 to 7 in) monthly.

The number of summer days when the temperature exceeds 32° C (90° F) is high, but in the mountain areas and the hilly Piedmont cool evenings bring welcome relief. Winters are mild, but significant variation occurs from south to north in Georgia. Snow cover lasting more than one or two days or exceeding 50 mm (2 in) occurs only in the mountainous fringe of north Georgia. The great day-to-day variability in winter weather is caused by the interaction of polar and subtropical air masses. Atlanta's extreme low temperatures are rarely below −10° C (14° F).

Vegetation and Animal Life. Forest, Georgia's most common landscape component, covers nearly 70% of the state. Complexes of longleaf and slash pines cover most of the Coastal Plain, and loblolly and shortleaf pines forest the Piedmont. A forest of oak and pine is dominant on the upper Piedmont, changing to oak and hickory forest

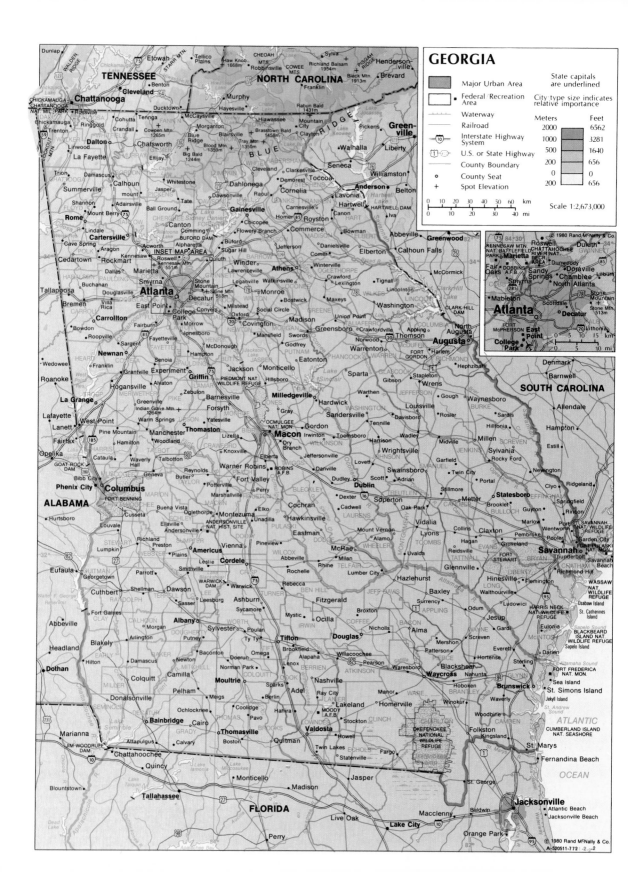

GEORGIA

in the mountains. The declining acreage for cropland has allowed extensive forest regrowth of pine.

Georgia has a thriving wildlife population. Bears are limited mainly to the mountain regions and Okefenokee Swamp, but deer, squirrel, raccoon, and bobcat are numerous throughout the state. Many of the rivers, reservoirs, and coastal bays and thousands of farm ponds are available for recreational purposes. Lake Sidney Lanier, northeast of Atlanta, is the largest water body in the state. Bass, crappie, bream, and catfish are sought by freshwater-fishing enthusiasts.

Drainage. Most of Georgia's major river systems have headwaters in the uplands of north Georgia. The Savannah River follows much of Georgia's eastern boundary, and the Altamaha system drains eastern Georgia to the Atlantic. The CHATTAHOOCHEE and Flint rivers join the Appalachicola after draining much of western Georgia. Numerous dams have been constructed for power, flood control, and recreational purposes. Large areas of the Coastal Plain experience poor drainage, and rivers crossing this area are generally sluggish. In southwestern Georgia AQUIFERS underlay the soil and make irrigation possible.

People

Georgia's population was 6,508,419 in 1990. Between 1980 and 1990 the population increased by 19.1%. Although the state's overall population density is 42 persons per km^2 (108.9 per mi²), it is considerably lower in most areas of the south Georgia plains and the northern mountains.

In 1990, 63.2% of Georgia's population lived in urban areas. ATLANTA, with a population of 394,017 (1990), is the largest city and functions as the state capital, as a wholesale and retail center, and as the southeastern regional commercial center. Growth in the Atlanta area has been rapid for several decades. More than two-fifths of the total population of the state live within Atlanta's metropolitan area (1990 pop., 2,833,511). AUGUSTA, COLUMBUS, and MACON—the fall-line cities—each has a metropolitan population of more than 240,000. SAVANNAH (1990 pop., 137,560) is Georgia's oldest city and has managed to retain its historic charm even while functioning as a major Atlantic port. The following smaller cities serve as regional centers: ALBANY, ATHENS, Gainesville, Rome, Valdosta, and Waycross.

In 1990 there were 1,746,565 blacks in Georgia, which constituted 27% of the total population. The Baptists constitute the largest religious denomination; Methodists, Presbyterians, and Roman Catholics are other religious groups with significant memberships.

Education. A system of statewide elementary and high schools is supported with state and local tax funds. Beginning in 1985 the state required that high school students pass a standardized test of minimum skills in order to graduate. Public higher education is organized as the University System of Georgia and includes junior colleges, 4-year colleges, and universities. The two largest universitites in the system are the University of Georgia (1785) at Athens, the oldest state-chartered university in the United States, and Georgia State University (1913) at Atlanta.

Tourism and Recreation. Tourism is becoming a major economic activity. Georgia has numerous historic sites: Savannah, an early settlement center; Atlanta and environs, the site of major Civil War battles; and the coastal zone with its relics of former plantation systems. Automobile traffic that crosses the state en route to Florida adds to the tourism income. The mountains and the Sea Islands are contrasting environments for the many summer vacationers from Georgia and surrounding states.

Georgia's growth and progress in the past two decades

Okefenokee Swamp, extending from the southeastern part of Georgia into northern Florida, is the largest preserved freshwater swamp in the United States. A sizable portion of the swamp, designated the Okefenokee National Wildlife Refuge, is a sanctuary for such threatened species as the American alligator and numerous varieties of migratory waterfowl.

(Above) *A high-relief carving in the granite face of Stone Mountain is a memorial to Confederate leaders—Jefferson Davis (left), Robert E. Lee, and Stonewall Jackson (not shown).*

(Right) *Stone Mountain, which rises 513 m (1,683 ft) above the surrounding plain, is one of the largest granite monadnocks in the world.*

is nowhere seen more sharply than in Atlanta and its environs. The city now has a symphony orchestra; boasts major league baseball, football, and basketball teams; and has become a major convention and cultural center. Atlanta's location at the junction of several interstate highways at the southern end of the Appalachians makes it a crossroads city, benefiting from exchange and interaction with other regions. The folk art and culture of the mountain people have fostered crafts fairs and handwork exhibits, often in conjunction with music festivals.

ETOWAH MOUNDS, near Cartersville in northwestern Georgia, are remnants of prehistoric Indian constructions. To the west President Franklin D. Roosevelt's Little White House in WARM SPRINGS is now a national shrine. Tybee Lighthouse, still standing at the mouth of the Savannah River, was built in 1736 by James Oglethorpe; it was reconstructed after the Civil War in 1867. STONE MOUNTAIN, with its Confederate memorial, is east of Atlanta.

Georgia's communications needs are served by daily and weekly newspapers. Numerous television and radio stations broadcast from within the state.

Economy

Manufacturing and wholesale and retail trade account for about 60% of all nonfarm employment in Georgia. Although agriculture no longer dominates employment in Georgia, many workers still are engaged in industries related to farming and farm products. Poultry production is a major industry, with most processing plants centered in Gainesville in north Georgia. The mean per capita income in Georgia is slightly below the national average.

Agriculture. Georgia agriculture is modern and mechanized, and the former strong economic dependence on cotton has been replaced with a diversified agricultural economy based on the production of soybeans, corn, peanuts, tobacco, poultry, cattle, and horticultural and or-

chard crops. Much of Georgia's crop production is concentrated on the Inner Coastal Plain. The Piedmont, once an established farming region, is now characterized by farmers who operate small part-time cattle farms but who earn most of their income from employment in towns and cities.

Forestry. The extensive pine forests of the state are the basis for an important sector of the economy. Sawtimber and pulpwood for paper manufacturing are produced in large quantity. Georgia's forests are also sources of tars and resins.

Mining. Georgia ranks among the leading U.S. states in the value of its nonfuel mineral production. Granite and marble are quarried throughout the state. Kaolin, a fine-grained clay found in central Georgia, is a major export.

Manufacturing. In the post–World War II years Georgia has undergone an economic revolution. The growth of textile manufacturing, begun in the late 19th century, continues, particularly the carpet industry of northwest Georgia. Apparel manufacturing has become a leading Georgia industry and is primarily located in the many small towns and cities of rural areas. Other industries include transportation equipment, pulp and paper, food processing, and electrical machinery.

Transportation. The first settlements in the state developed along the waterways leading from the coast; after a decline, water transport is again gaining importance. Railroad and truck transportation serve the bulk of the state's transit needs. Airlines, primarily in the Atlanta area, provide access to all major national cities.

Energy. The Tennessee Valley Authority power system does not serve the state, so Georgia must import fuel. Its proximity to the Appalachian coalfield is advantageous. Hydroelectric plants along rivers contribute 20% to the power needs of Georgia; coal and natural gas fuel the remaining steam generators.

(Above) *Tobacco, Georgia's second most valuable cash crop, dries outside a barn near Waycross.*

(Left) *Georgia leads all states in the production of peanuts, a crop that contributes more than $500 million annually to the state economy.*

Government and Politics

Georgia's ninth state constitution became effective in 1977 and provides for a government composed of legislative, executive, and judicial branches. The executive branch is headed by a governor who holds office for a 4-year term. Legislative power is granted to a General Assembly that is composed of the Senate and House of Representatives. The judicial system includes a supreme court, a court of appeals, and superior courts. Local government is vested in cities and counties. Georgia is divided into 159 counties. Georgia has been a Democratic state since the period following Reconstruction. Local and state politics remain overwhelmingly Democratic, but on the national level extremely liberal Democrats have been rejected by the basically conservative Georgia voters.

History

The earliest known inhabitants of present-day Georgia are thought to have been MOUND BUILDERS, predecessors of the CHEROKEE and CREEK Indians inhabiting the area at the time of European arrival. Hernando DE SOTO crossed Georgia in 1539–40, vainly searching for precious metals and gems.

Savannah, the first European settlement in Georgia, was established in 1733 by James OGLETHORPE—a British general and member of parliament. King George II of England granted a charter to Oglethorpe in order to provide a new home for the poor of England. In 1752 the trustees turned over control of the colony to the royal government. Georgia became actively involved in the AMERICAN REVOLUTION in 1778 when the British captured Savannah. This seizure was followed by the eventual British seizure of all Georgia except for Wilkes County, northwest of Augusta.

Settlement had first expanded along the coastal zone and Sea Islands. Interior settlement occurred later, between 1770 and 1840, when settlers moved southwestward from Virginia and the Carolinas. That it took nearly seven decades after 1770 to complete the settling process of the state was in no small part due to the resistance of the Creek and Cherokee Indians. In a series of land cessions the Creeks were pushed westward from river to river, until by 1826 all Creek Indian lands had been seized. During the following 12 years the Cherokee Indians of north Georgia were also deprived of their territory. In 1838 the federal government forcibly removed the Cherokee people to lands in western territory, an exodus that would come to be known as the "trail of tears." Portions of Georgia, such as the Pine Barrens of southeast Georgia and the southwest, remained sparsely populated until well after the Civil War. Along the coast and on the Sea Islands a black culture known locally as "Gullah" developed among the slaves tending the cotton and rice fields.

The advance of settlement between 1780 and 1840 was encouraged by improved cotton-ginning technology and the increased markets for cotton in Europe. The corollary of this was an intense demand for land, for slaves, and for the removal of Indians. The expansion of the planter system not only set distinctive demographic patterns but also established a social, economic, and political structure that prevailed in the state well into the 20th century.

The CIVIL WAR was a period of disruption and destruction in Georgia. The Union army of General William Tecumseh SHERMAN crossed the state in 1864. After burning Atlanta in November of that year, he and his 60,000 men moved eastward, reaching Savannah in 29 days and leaving devastation in their wake. During RECONSTRUCTION the Georgia legislature's refusal to ratify the 14th AMENDMENT placed the state under military rule. Georgia was readmitted to the Union in 1870. Although slavery was declared illegal, planters and ex-slaves adopted a tenancy system that kept many blacks and whites in poverty until the system's demise after World War II.

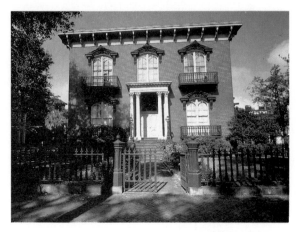

A restored home in Savannah reflects an Italian Renaissance revival in the antebellum South. An important port city on the Atlantic coast, Savannah was the site of the first English settlement in Georgia.

During the 1920s agriculture declined rapidly in the state, when boll-weevil infestations destroyed the cotton crops, forcing workers off the land. The out-migration from the farms and from the state as a whole exceeded any movement into Georgia, but the population continued to increase because of a high birthrate. The great northward migration during this century, however, reduced the black population from 47% in 1900 to 27% in 1990.

The post–World War II era has been one of economic development and new social attitudes—amounting to an economic and social revolution. Business has greatly expanded, and many new jobs have been attracted to Georgia, especially to Atlanta and its environs. The state continued to prosper through the 1980s. The CIVIL RIGHTS movement and its achievements in the 1960s have particularly altered urban life in Georgia. Blacks have united to become a political force in Georgia's cities and, in turn, a vocal element in the state and in the nation.

Georgia, Republic of   Georgia, formerly one of the 15 constituent republics of the USSR, became independent in December 1991. Located in Transcaucasia, on the Black Sea, the country borders Turkey, Armenia, and Azerbaijan in the south, and Russia in the north and west. Its area is 69,700 km^2 (26,900 mi^2), and the population is 5,464,200 (1991 est.). The capital is TBILISI (1989 pop., 1,260,000).

The topography of Georgia consists of the Greater CAUCASUS MOUNTAINS in the north, a central valley, and the uplands of the Lesser Caucasus to the south. The climate varies from semiarid in the interior, where vineyards dominate, to humid-subtropical along the coast.

The Georgians, who constitute 69% of the population, are a Caucasian language group with a distinct alphabet; they adhere to the Eastern Orthodox religion.

Georgia is climatically suitable for the cultivation of warm-weather crops. It supplies tea, citrus, wines, and fruits to the former Soviet republics. Tbilisi and Kutaisi are centers for the nation's silk-textile and automobile industries. Important manganese deposits are mined at Chiatura.

Georgia encompasses 3 areas, based on separate ethnic groups. The Abkhaz Autonomous Republic in the northwest (1989 pop., 537,000) is based on a Caucasian ethnic group. The Adzhar Autonomous Republic (393,000), on the Turkish border, contains mostly Turkicized Georgians known as Adzhars. South Ossetia (99,000), in the Greater Caucasus, is composed primarily of Ossetians of Iranian-language stock. In 1990, South Ossetia tried to secede from Georgia, and warfare erupted. In 1992 a joint Russian-Georgian peacekeeping force was deployed in the region. Meanwhile, similiar fighting erupted in the Abkhaz.

Known to the Greeks and Romans as COLCHIS (western Georgia) and Iberia (eastern Georgia), the region adopted Christianity in the 4th century. Between inroads by the Arabs, Mongols, Turks, and Persians, Georgian states flourished briefly in the Middle Ages and in the second half of the 18th century before union with Russia in 1801. The overthrow of the tsar in 1917 brought independence before the Bolsheviks assumed control in 1921. In late 1991 violent strife occurred between supporters and opponents of Georgia's first freely elected president, Zviad Gamsakhurdia. In March 1992 ex-Soviet foreign minister Eduard SHEVARNADZE became head of the government.

Georgian Bay   Georgian Bay, in south central Ontario, Canada, is an inlet of Lake HURON, from which it is separated by the Bruce (or Saugeen) Peninsula and Manitoulin Island. It is 190 km (120 mi) long and 80 km (50 mi) wide and is the site of Georgian Bay Islands National Park. First explored (1615) by Samuel de Champlain, it was named for King George IV by an English naval officer.

Georgian style   *Georgian* is the term applied to the architectural and decorative art styles that flourished in England during the reigns of the first four Georges (1714–1830). The period began with the revived Palladianism (see PALLADIO, ANDREA) of Richard Boyle, earl of BURLINGTON (Chiswick House, London; begun 1725), and the baroque style of William KENT. Toward 1750 the style lightened under the influence of the ROCOCO STYLE, although the rococo was never completely accepted in England. Its spirit encouraged outré styles such as Gothic and Chinese; all three can be seen in the furniture designs (published 1754–62) of Thomas CHIPPENDALE. The rococo had virtually disappeared from the furniture designs (published 1788) of George HEPPLEWHITE, but from 1760 onward Robert ADAM's influential and increasingly refined neoclassical style appeared (see NEOCLASSICISM, art). Refinement is also seen in Thomas SHERATON's delicate and rectilinear furniture designs (1791–94). The ages of walnut and mahogany were succeeded by that of satinwood. From 1800 the influences of Louis XVI and

EMPIRE STYLE furniture, together with the archaeological Greek, Roman, and Egyptian designs of Thomas Hope (1769–1831), produced the REGENCY STYLE (until about 1840); it was accompanied in architecture by the GREEK REVIVAL. The style coarsened until, by 1835, the decline of the classical tradition made Victorian eclecticism possible.

GEOS GEOS (Geodetic Earth Orbiting Satellite) is a series of satellites developed for the National Aeronautics and Space Administration (NASA) as part of its overall program to study the Earth's surface, shape, and gravitational field. *GEOS 1* (also known as EXPLORER *29*) was launched on Nov. 6, 1965, from (then) Cape Kennedy by a DELTA vehicle. The satellite carried an optical and radio Doppler beacon, range and range-rate transponder, and 322 small prisms to reflect laser beams from Earth. *GEOS 2* (also known as *Explorer 36*) was launched on Jan. 11, 1968; *GEOS 3* was launched on Apr. 9, 1975. The GEOS series added greatly to the knowledge of the Earth's true shape. A balloon satellite similar to Echo and known as PAGEOS (Passive Geodetic Satellite) was not officially a part of the GEOS series but accomplished similar objectives.

geosyncline [jee-oh-sin'-klyn] A geosyncline is a large, usually elongate depression in the crust of the Earth in which, as it subsided, great thicknesses (thousands of meters) of sedimentary, and usually also volcanic, rocks accumulated.

The German geologist Wilhelm Hans Stille (1876–1966) introduced the terms *eugeosyncline* and *miogeosyncline* to distinguish deep, rapidly subsiding depressions (eugeosynclines) from more slowly subsiding, shallow-water depressions (miogeosynclines). A eugeosyncline contains extensive volcanic deposits, and even though it accumulates the thickest deposits, not enough sediment reaches its depths to keep pace with subsidence. A miogeosyncline, which usually stands between the eugeosyncline and the craton (the central, relatively stable CONTINENTAL SHIELD), contains virtually no volcanic deposits, and sedimentation rates here are almost always sufficient to keep up with subsidence.

The development cycle of geosynclines has been a subject of intense interest since the mid-20th century. The general pattern is first for sediments to accumulate in the subsiding geosynclinal trough along a cratonic margin, with volcanic materials and deep-water sediments accumulating in the peripheral eugeosyncline. Next come folding, deformation, and overthrusting centered in the eugeosyncline, often displacing eugeosynclinal deposits over the miogeosyncline. Third, metamorphism and placement of large intrusive IGNEOUS ROCK masses occurs, particularly in the eugeosyncline. This is followed by uplift of the eugeosyncline and the formation of mountains and marginal troughs, with renewed sedimentation. The compressive stresses then relax, and trough basins form within the mountains, often accompanied by outpourings of basaltic lava. EROSION then completes the cycle.

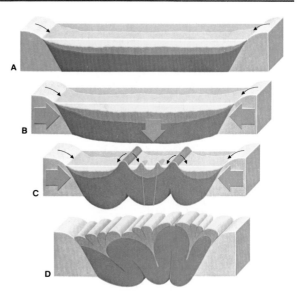

Geosynclines are long, narrow, seafloor depressions where thick layers of sediment from the adjoining crustal blocks accumulate (A) *as the sea bottom subsides* (B). *As the crustal blocks move together, large masses of sedimentary layers are squeezed together, folded, and uplifted to form geanticlines, or ridges* (C), *which, if above the water, divide the geosyncline into separate basins. The crustal blocks eventually move so close together that compressive forces fold and raise the sediment between them into mountain ranges* (D).

Modern research has concentrated on identifying contemporary geosynclines and reconciling the geosynclinal cycle with PLATE TECTONICS. Here American and European investigators tend to diverge. The New World model for the modern geosyncline is usually the marginal deposits of the Gulf of Mexico and the Atlantic coast. These reach geosynclinal thicknesses and show most of the characteristics of the miogeosyncline, but without the eugeosynclinal elements (deep-water sediments and volcanic rocks). Old World geologists have looked more to the deep-ocean trenches and the associated island-arc systems for a modern analogue of the ancient geosyncline (see OCEANIC TRENCHES).

Recognizing the profound differences among continental margins, British geologists have attempted a synthesis of continental margins, geosynclines, and plate tectonics, identifying five situations where contemporary geosynclines are forming. Among these, the most important distinction is the presence or absence of a deep-ocean trench, or subduction zone. The Atlantic-type continental margin has no subduction zone; it is the trailing edge of a continent adjacent to a spreading ocean. The edge of the continent receives miogeosynclinal deposits, while deep-water sediments accumulate off the edge of the continent on the continental rise. The Atlantic-type margin corresponds to the earliest stages in the geosynclinal cycle. The Pacific-type continental margin has an active subduction zone in which ocean crust is consumed either immediately adjacent to the continent (west coast of Central and South America) or at some distance from shore (northwest Pacific). Fully developed eugeosynclinal activity, including active volcanism and intense deformation, is attained with the development of the Pacific-type margin, as exemplified by the RING OF FIRE that encircles the Pacific.

geothermal energy   Geothermal energy is the heat energy that occurs naturally within the Earth. The molten interior contains vast quantities of thermal energy; although some diffuses upward to the surface and is dissipated, temperatures within the Earth remain fairly constant, apparently maintained by the decay of radioactive material. Geothermal energy therefore represents a potentially inexhaustible source of energy, which has been tapped by humans for centuries but, until recent years, only on a small scale (see ENERGY SOURCES).

In some regions of the world, particularly in the zone of tectonic activity surrounding the Pacific Ocean, MAGMA may occur at depths of only a few kilometers. GROUNDWATER trickling down to the hot rocks overlying the magma chambers can be heated to temperatures as high as 205°–260°C (400°–500°F). Where topography permits, the heated water may rise to the surface as HOT SPRINGS. In a few areas where the water is prevented from reaching the surface, some of it may turn to steam. Energy also can be derived from heated rocks in the absence of groundwater.

Heating Use. Geothermal fluids may be used directly for heating homes and greenhouses and for industrial purposes if they occur near populated areas. Iceland is the most notable example. About 65% of its homes and much of its greenhouse produce depend on groundwater heat. Parts of Budapest, some Paris suburbs, and several communities in the Soviet Union are also heated in this way. In the United States most of Klamath Falls, Oreg., and parts of Boise, Idaho, depend on geothermal heating. Examples of the industrial use of geothermal fluids are found in Iceland and New Zealand. In addition, such countries as Denmark and Sweden are experimenting with the use of geothermal fluids in heat-pump installations that also burn sewage.

Power Generation. The greatest potential for large-scale use of geothermal energy is in the generation of electric power. Geothermal steam has been used in Larderello, Italy, since 1904 to produce power. Other nations with geothermal power plants include China, Indonesia, Japan, Kenya, Mexico, New Zealand, the Philippines, and the Soviet Union. The largest plant in the world is in the United States, near Geyserville, Calif. (north of San Francisco), where steam has been used to produce power since 1960. The present generating capacity there is about 1,140 megawatts (MW), and the potential capacity is estimated to range up to 4,000 MW. Drilling into the steam pockets is a difficult process, however, and the steam itself is corrosive and contains dissolved gases, particularly hydrogen sulfide, that are difficult to remove.

No other region in the United States is known to possess geothermal steam in sufficient quantities, although the Pacific Northwest is under study. Sources of geothermal hot water are much more numerous, particularly in

such western states as California, Nevada, New Mexico, and Utah. Much of this water has a temperature of only 95°–150° C (200°–300° F), too low for economic power generation by conventional methods. When the temperature is above 200° C (400° F), however, the water may be partially "flashed" into steam by reducing the pressure on it, and the steam can be used to drive turbines. Cooler water may be used to boil a secondary fluid, such as isobutane, whose vapor may then be used in special turbines. The efficiency of this so-called binary process may be increased by placing the heat exchangers at depth. The use of geothermal water for power production is still in the development stage.

Also being studied is the use of hot rocks themselves to heat water for power production. Hot dry rock is found almost everywhere, but hotter rocks closer to the surface are more common in geologically active areas, such as the U.S. western mountain regions.

Outlook. Estimates of what proportion of U.S. electric-power supply will be produced from geothermal energy by the year 2000 range from approximately 1% by the U.S. Bureau of Mines to at least 15% by some proponents of geothermal energy. The rapid growth anticipated in the 1980s, however, has been hampered both by lack of funding and by technological problems.

See also: EARTH, HEAT FLOW IN.

Gera [gay'-rah]   Gera (1987 est. pop., 132,939) is a city in Germany, located along the White Elster River about 55 km (35 mi) southwest of Leipzig. It is a rail and industrial center, producing machinery, tools, furniture, leather products, textiles, and musical instruments. Gera was first mentioned in written sources in 995. From 1564 to 1918, it served as the capital of the Reuss princes, whose castle (built 1686–1735) still stands. Gera was almost completely destroyed by fires in 1639, 1686, and 1780.

geranium [juh-rayn'-ee-uhm]   *Geranium* is the generic name of the cranesbills, or true geraniums, and is also

Florists' geraniums, genus Pelargonium, *are hardy houseplants. The Martha Washington geranium* (left) *and the common geranium* (right) *are two popular varieties.*

commonly applied to the showy garden and greenhouse plants of the genus *Pelargonium.* Both genera are members of the geranium family, Geraniaceae.

The cranesbills include more than 300 species distributed throughout the cooler regions of the north temperate zone and the mountains of the Southern Hemisphere. Most are annual or perennial herbs with erect to spreading stems; deeply lobed, opposite leaves; and flowers with five sepals, five overlapping petals alternating with small glands, and ten stamens. Some are commonly cultivated.

The storksbills, or florists' geranium, genus *Pelargonium,* include about 280 species of mostly succulent perennial herbs, subshrubs, and vines native to southern Africa. Although similar to *Geranium,* the flowers of *Pelargonium* are irregular; two petals differ from the others in size, structure, or markings and lack glands between them.

gerbil [jur'-bul]   Gerbils, family Cricetidae, are soft-furred, burrowing rodents inhabiting arid regions in Africa and Asia. They have elongated hind legs, with which they can make kangaroolike leaps, and, usually, long tails. The 100 or more species are grouped into 10 or 12 genera. The fur is usually of sand or earth colors, and the larger species, *Rhombomys,* may reach 200 mm (nearly 8 in) in body length. The popular American pet is the Mongolian gerbil, *Meriones unguiculatus.* Some species are called jirds, and one species, *Pachyuromys duprasi,* with a short, thick tail, is also called the fat-tailed mouse.

The large, naked-soled gerbil, like other gerbils, is adapted to life in arid regions and rarely drinks water, obtaining almost all of the water it requires from the foods that make up its diet.

geriatrics [jair-ee-at'-riks]   Geriatrics is the branch of medicine that treats the problems of AGING. Medical treatment of elderly persons presents a challenge, because many of them have numerous physical problems that complicate and interfere with diagnosis and treatment of any single illness. Diseases of one organ system place stress on other systems; furthermore, some diseases do not produce the symptoms in the elderly that are usually seen in younger persons. Many older people also have nutritional deficiencies because of limited incomes,

poor dental status, and other problems (see NUTRITIONAL-DEFICIENCY DISEASES). In addition, the elderly run increased risks of complications from surgery, and convalescence takes longer because damaged tissues recover more slowly; the longer periods of bedrest can also lead to pneumonia, bedsores, and circulatory disorders. Drugs are metabolized more slowly, as well, and their effects are prolonged in the body.

Some diseases that occur in younger people become increasingly common among persons over the age of 65. Among them are CARDIOVASCULAR DISEASES, including ATHEROSCLEROSIS, angina, other HEART DISEASES, and STROKE. The elderly have a higher incidence of CANCER. Chronic diseases that develop earlier in life also often present severe health problems in the elderly because the metabolism becomes slower with age. For example, gangrene of the foot occurs in elderly persons with DIABETES mellitus because of poorer circulation in the extremities.

Some BONE DISEASES are of special concern in the elderly. Decrease in bone mass, or OSTEOPOROSIS, mainly affects women after menopause; the bones become brittle and may easily fracture. Also limited to the elderly is PAGET'S DISEASE, the slowly progressive deformation of bone. Osteoarthritis (see ARTHRITIS) affects all elderly persons to some degree. It can also cause joint deformities, swelling, and pain. When the weight-bearing joints are affected, instability can result; this is a common cause of falling and FRACTURES. Some degenerative neurological diseases such as PARKINSON'S DISEASE occur almost exclusively among the elderly, as does accidental HYPOTHERMIA, the sudden drop in body temperature in response to cooler air temperatures.

Mental disorders of physical or other origin are also a problem of old age. Senile dementia (see SENILITY) is a progressive deterioration of personality and intellect that can occur in the seventh and eighth decades of life. ALZHEIMER'S DISEASE, caused by deterioration of brain cells, has similar symptoms but begins in the fifth or sixth decades of life. In addition, DEPRESSION in the elderly can have symptoms almost identical to senile dementia; loss of interest in life, memory lapses, and living in the past are common in both conditions.

Géricault, Théodore [zhay-ree-koh', tay-oh-dohr']
Best known for his painting *The Raft of the Medusa,* Jean Louis André Théodore Géricault, b. Sept. 26, 1791, d. Jan. 26, 1824, was one of the most gifted French artists of the 19th century. Géricault was deeply impressed by the impassioned military paintings of Antoine Jean GROS; he exhibited *The Charging Chasseur* (Louvre, Paris) in 1812 and *The Wounded Cuirassier* (Louvre) at the Salon of 1814.

Géricault drew many classical subjects (for example, *Centaur Abducting a Nymph*; Louvre) in a crude and rugged style, but he also sketched contemporary subjects. After witnessing the annual race of the riderless horses during the Roman carnival, Géricault began developing this theme in numerous studies for a monumental masterpiece, but he never carried this project through.

The Raft of the Medusa *(1819), Théodore Géricault's interpretation of a disaster, was initially acclaimed more for its political implications than for its artistic merit. (Louvre, Paris.)*

In 1819, Géricault caused a sensation with his *Raft of the Medusa* (Louvre), an enormous canvas depicting survivors of a shipwreck that the government had been blamed for mishandling. He turned this event into a monumental history painting, a heroic scene of ghastly suffering and Michelangelesque nude figures.

In England he sketched English street life and painted *Racing at Epsom* (1821; Louvre). He continued to paint genre scenes in the restrained manner he developed there, and sometimes portrayed everyday scenes with a bleak grandeur (*The Lime Kiln,* 1822; Louvre). At the instigation of the psychiatrist Dr. Georget, Géricault painted a haunting yet objective series of portraits of the insane in 1822–23 (for example, *The Kleptomaniac,* Museum of Ghent).

Gerlache de Gomery, Adrien de, Baron [zhair-lahsh' duh gohm-ree', ah-dree-an' duh]   A Belgian naval officer, Adrien Victor Joseph de Gerlache, b. Aug. 2, 1866, d. Dec. 4, 1934, led a scientific expedition to Antarctica in 1897–99. When its ship, *Belgica,* got trapped in pack ice for 13 months, the party—which included Roald AMUNDSEN—became the first to spend a winter in Antarctica. Gerlache subsequently conducted oceanographic research in the Arctic and helped plan Ernest SHACKLETON's British Imperial Trans-Antarctic Expedition (1914–17).

germ warfare   see CHEMICAL AND BIOLOGICAL WARFARE

Germain, Lord George [jur'-muhn]   George Sackville Germain, 1st Viscount Sackville, b. Jan. 26, 1716, d. Aug. 26, 1785, was British secretary of state for the American colonies during the American Revolution. He was known as Lord George Sackville until 1770 and then as Lord George Germain until he became Viscount Sackville in 1782.

Entering the British army, he was wounded and captured at Fontenoy (1745) in the War of the AUSTRIAN

SUCCESSION; later he served in the SEVEN YEARS' WAR.

Germain virtually directed the Revolutionary War in America as secretary of state for the colonies—a position he held from 1775 to 1782. Many critics charged him with the British errors of strategy, but recent scholarship suggests that he was blamed too much. Germain had conflicts with Generals William Howe, Guy Carleton, and Henry CLINTON, and he favored John BURGOYNE and Charles CORNWALLIS. His efforts to control the conduct of the war too strictly from London contributed to Britain's ultimate defeat.

German art and architecture   German art and architecture refers to the artistic production of the many principalities and kingdoms that were united into a single German state in 1871. The art and architecture of Austria, although they share the same German cultural heritage, are treated in AUSTRIAN ART AND ARCHITECTURE.

The Carolingian and Ottonian Periods

Although the beginnings of German art can be traced back to pre-Christian times, it was not until the Carolingian age (8th and 9th centuries AD) that a significant artistic and architectural style began to emerge in the German lands. The Frankish king Charlemagne, whose realm included much of present Germany, sought to revive the glories of the Roman Empire in both the political and the cultural spheres. He gathered scholars and artists at his court and imported entire libraries from Italy and Byzantium. Byzantine influence can be seen in Charlemagne's Palatine Chapel (790–805) in Aachen, which is probably based on the church of San Vitale in Ravenna; classical influence is visible in the Carolingian Gatehouse at Lorsch, inspired by the Arch of Constantine in Rome (see CAROLINGIAN ART AND ARCHITECTURE). In the art of manuscript illumination, the *Godescalc Gospels* (781–83; Bibliothèque Nationale, Paris) shows how German artists of the period strove to integrate classical forms with their native tradition (see ILLUMINATED MANUSCRIPTS).

After the breakup of Charlemagne's empire, Emperor Otto I and his successors (the Saxons, or Ottonians) reestablished stability in Germany in the 10th century. Ottonian architects and artists, though not entirely independent of Carolingian and Roman-Byzantine models, developed a vernacular style of their own (see OTTONIAN ART AND ARCHITECTURE). This style is apparent in perhaps the most important ecclesiastical structure of the period, Saint Michael's church at Hildesheim (1001–31). It has a Roman basilican nave with symmetrical towers at the east and west ends, but it also has an additional transept and is entered from the north and south. The figures on the bronze doors (1015) of this church were cast in a single piece for the first time since ancient Rome. The wooden *Gero Cross* (969–76) expresses the suffering of the crucified Christ far more viscerally than any Carolingian or Early Christian work of art. Such dramatic expression is often found as well in the manuscripts of the period, as the *Gospel Book of Otto III* (983–1002; Bayerische Staatsbibliothek, Munich) illustrates.

The Cathedral at Worms (1110–81) is typical of German Romanesque architecture, which was centered in the Rhineland during the 11th and 12th centuries. Seen in this view of the exterior are the eastern and western apses, with twin circular towers containing staircases, an octagonal tower with pointed roof crossing the nave, double bays and rib vaulting supporting the nave, and a small polygonal choir that was added in 1234. The scale of the cathedral, which dwarfed other churches, was meant to symbolize the church's power. The height of the towers serves as an expression of the relationship between the Church and the spirit.

twin towers flanking eastern apse

octagonal tower

north transept

south transept

western apse   nave

The soaring verticality and multiplicity of form displayed in the façade of Cologne Cathedral are typical of Gothic architecture. This, the largest Gothic church in northern Europe, was begun in 1248, but the nave and the two spires shown here, each 157 m (515 ft) high, were built between 1842 and 1890, from the original specifications.

The Romanesque Period

Following the death of the last Ottonian ruler in 1024, the Salian dynasty came to power, marking the beginning of the Romanesque period in Germany. Perhaps the most important achievement of the era was the development of the groin vault, which allowed architects to construct masonry ceilings that could both admit light and resist the fires that destroyed many pre-Romanesque structures with their flat, timber roofs. Speyer Cathedral (1082–1106) is one of the earliest fully vaulted Romanesque churches, and its innovations made possible the later expansion of the Mainz and Worms cathedrals. Like most other Romanesque structures, it is blocky in appearance, and its exterior surface, in contrast to that of its Ottonian predecessors, is richly articulated, reflecting the cathedral's interior organization.

Other architectural developments of the period show the influence of the Cluniac and Cistercian orders spreading from France into Germany in the 12th and 13th centuries. Not only churches, but also chapter houses, dormitories, and other types of monastic buildings began to receive advanced architectural treatment.

Although elsewhere in Europe outdoor stone sculpture underwent a revival in the Romanesque period, this did not happen in German territories. The highest quality sculpture could be found instead on church furnishings such as choir screens, tombs, baptismal fonts, and reliquaries and in the form of small ivory carvings. With the enlargement of windows in Romanesque cathedrals, stained glass became a more important art form. Among the most impressive remaining examples—and the only one still in its original location—is the cycle of five prophets in Augsburg Cathedral (*c.*1120–30).

The Gothic Period

It was not until the second half of the 13th century that German cathedrals began to lose their Romanesque character. Two of the major examples of German Gothic architecture, Strasbourg Cathedral (nave begun 1235) and Cologne Cathedral (begun 1248), reflect the influence of French structures, the former of Saint-Denis and the latter of Amiens. (See GOTHIC ART AND ARCHITECTURE.)

Yet the Germans did make two unique contributions to European Gothic. In the north, the lack of sandstone necessitated the use of brick in the construction of Gothic

The Four Horsemen of the Apocalypse *(1498) is one of a series of 15 woodcuts by the German Renaissance painter and graphic artist Albrecht Dürer. In Dürer's imagination, God's final judgment falls on terrified humanity in the form of three soldiers who ride with Death.*

architecture, precluding the intricate detailing of Gothic sandstone cathedrals and thereby imposing an austerity and clarity of overall design. The *Hallenkirche* (hall church), probably of French origin, was developed most fully in the large urban centers of Germany; as is illustrated by Saint Elizabeth at Marburg (1233–83), the aisles of these hall churches rise to the same height as the nave.

Early Gothic German sculpture also reflected French influence. Both the *Bamberg Rider* (late 13th century), mounted on a pier in Bamberg Cathedral, and the sober *Ekkehart and Uta* (*c*.1250–60), from the choir of Naumburg Cathedral, illustrate the growth of realism during the 13th century. While Renaissance idealism flourished in Italy in the latter 15th century, contemporaneous Gothic German sculpture, particularly in the accomplished, yet very different hands of Tilman RIEMENSCHNEIDER and Veit STOSS, remained tied to the realistic late Gothic mode.

In the field of painting, the most important development was the evolution of painting on wood panels in the 14th century, and later on canvas. Though the influence of the Sienese dominated in the 14th and early 15th centuries, by 1450, Netherlandish sources were equally important. In the north, Stephen Lochner (1400–51) joined the influence of Jan van Eyck with the tradition of the International Style to produce what is sometimes referred to as a "soft" or flowing style, quite unlike the blocky, "hard" forms of Konrad Witz in the south. Martin SCHONGAUER was probably the century's most skilled northern master of the new technique of copper engraving, which was developed in the 1430s and widely replaced the woodcut by the second half of the century.

Renaissance and Baroque

The greatest of the German Renaissance artists was unquestionably Albrecht DÜRER, who synthesized the realis-

The Zwinger (1711–22) of the Dresden Palace is an open-air arena for ceremonies such as tournaments and festivals. This rare example of secular high baroque architecture in northern Germany was built by Matthäus Popplemann. The view on the right is of the West Pavilion, with sculptural decorations by Balthasar Permoser. On the left is the ground plan of the Zwinger, showing single-story galleries and stone pavilions arranged around a court with fountains and pools.

The church of the Benedictine Abbey at Ottobeuren, Bavaria, typifies the south German rococo style of architecture. Designed by Johann Michael Fischer, it achieves a dynamic effect by decoration rather than structure.

tic and expressive German with the more idealized, humanistic Italian tradition. Hans HOLBEIN the Younger was a particularly accomplished portraitist; other German Renaissance artists of great accomplishment were Albrecht ALTDORFER, Lucas CRANACH the Elder, Hans BALDUNG-GRIEN, and Matthias GRÜNEWALD.

The German Renaissance was remarkably short lived, for by 1530 the Reformation had effected an almost complete halt in the production of religious imagery, and painters in Protestant regions thereby lost the patronage of the church. It was not until well after the Thirty Years' War (1618–48) that a new generation of German artists could contribute to international artistic developments. This occurred above all in the field of architecture. Among the remarkable examples of the late baroque-rococo style that flourished in Catholic Bavaria are Johann Balthasar NEUMANN's Vierzehnheiligen church near Bamberg (begun 1743), and the Ottobeuren Abbey church (1748–62) by Johann Michael Fischer. Perhaps the greatest frescoes of the period were executed by the Italian painter Tiepolo in the Würzburg Residenz (1751–53). (See BAROQUE ART AND ARCHITECTURE.)

Neoclassicism and Romanticism

Neoclassicism taught that the arts should serve an edu-cational function, and the foundation of many German museums in the 19th century as well as academies of art in Berlin, Munich, Düsseldorf, and Dresden, owed much to the impact of neoclasical theory. The leading architect of the period was Karl Friedrich Schinkel, whose many buildings in Berlin include the Schauspielhaus (1821) and the Altes Museum (1824–28). Leo von Klenze had a similar impact on Munich through his city planning, as did Gotfried Semper in Dresden.

Paralleling the growth of neoclassicism was an interest in romantic themes and styles, particularly among painters. Artists such as Caspar David Friedrich, as well as the Nazarenes, all rejected the academic and classical direction and pursued an art based on either landscape or literary and biblical themes. Painters of the middle and late 19th century, including Max Liebermann, became increasingly interested in a realistic aesthetic, though some, such as Anselm Feuerbach, continued to paint in a classicizing vein.

The Twentieth Century

A number of regional expressionist groups developed early in the 20th century. Composed of Wassily Kandinsky, Franz Marc, and Paul Klee, among others, Der Blaue Reiter (The Blue Rider) society was established in Munich, its ideaistic purpose being to rejuvenate society through

The German Romantic painter Caspar David Friedrich painted Landscape on the Island of Rügen in 1818. The human figures in the foreground are dwarfed by the grandeur of the white cliffs and sea. (Sammlung Oskar Reinhart, Winterthur.)

(Right) *A pioneering example of modern architecture, the Fagus shoe last factory (1911) at Alfeld-an-der-Leine, Germany, was the first structure built with the metal and glass curtain walls that became standard in the later International Style. It was designed by Walter Gropius and Adolf Meyer; Gropius went on to become (1919) the founder of the Bauhaus.*

(Below) *Max Beckmann's* The Night *(1918–19) expresses the fear and confusion of the German people during World War I. (Kunstsammlung Nordrhein-Westfalen, Düsseldorf.)*

a spiritual art based on the intimate relationship of man and animal to nature. In contrast, Die Brucke (The Bridge) painters—ERNST LUDWIG KIRCHNER, EMIL NOLDE, Erich HECKEL, and Karl SCHMIDT-ROTTLUFF, among them—pursued a more intense, directly expressive art similar in sensibility to the primitive objects from which it drew inspiration.

Also predominant in the early decades of the 20th century was an interest in the applied arts. This movement has its roots in the Jugendstil (style of youth) of the 1890s, with its taste for organic, curvilinear forms of both the fine and decorative arts. The rapid industrialization of Germany soon found expression in the Werkbund movement, which involved the creation of an expressly modern and functional design vocabulary that might be applied to the products of machine technology.

The applied art movement reached its fullest expression in the BAUHAUS (house of building), founded in Weimar in 1919 and subsequently located in Dessau and Berlin. Led by architects Walter GROPIUS, Ludwig MIES VAN DER ROHE, and Marcel BREUER, and by painters and sculptors such as Oskar SCHLEMMER, László MOHOLY-NAGY, Lyonel FEININGER, and Josef ALBERS, the Bauhaus sought to apply the most advanced, and generally geometric, for-

mal concepts to the arts. It became the 20th century's most influential school of architecture and design.

A more cynical response to World War I and modern culture was expressed by the Berlin Dada group. Politically motivated, and responding to the militarism associated with the war, artists such as George GROSZ and Otto DIX assaulted the Weimar government through their polemical art. The post–World War I period also produced a number of great yet essentially independent artists, among them Max ERNST and Kurt SCHWITTERS and the expressionist Max BECKMANN.

All these progressive movements were brought to a standstill by the rise of Nazism in the early 1930s. After the work of Germany's most accomplished vanguard artists was exhibited in the notorious Entartete Kunst (degenerate art) exhibition in Munich in 1937, many artists and architects emigrated to France or the United States. Under Hitler's direction, the avant-garde was replaced by a highly political form of neoclassical painting, sculpture, and architecture, much of which was destroyed at the conclusion of World War II.

Since 1960, influential work has again been produced on German soil, particularly in the form of expressionist painting. Notable among contemporary German architects is Gottfried Böhm.

German and Austrian music From medieval times until the mid-20th century composers working in the German-speaking countries of central Europe created a rich and varied literature that has come to be regarded as the backbone of the Western art music tradition. The classical style—a proportioned approach to organizing thematic and harmonic materials that informs the sonatas and symphonies at the core of today's concert repertoire—was largely developed in the German musical centers (especially Vienna) in the late 18th and early 19th centuries. As this classicism unfolded into romanticism, with its grander structures, the Germans and Austrians retained the historical initiative, and they held it firmly into the 20th century.

The Middle Ages

Although today Germany and Austria are two separate countries, historically they form a single cultural region, whose location in the center of Europe made it a cross-roads for cultural ideas.

In its origins, the German musical tradition was influenced by those of the ancient Romans, the Magyars, the Slavs, and the early Germanic peoples themselves. The Gregorian chant, or PLAINSONG, flourished at monastic centers in Salzburg and elsewhere in the 8th century.

By the 10th and 11th centuries, German monks were compiling musical treatises by the dozen, some of these addressing the subject from a purely philosophical point of view, others dealing with practical concerns. The German monks introduced variants into the traditional plain-song formulas, in the hope of highlighting the chants' expressive qualities. This led to freer, inspired compositions, such as the extraordinary sequences, hymns, and songs of the Abbess Hildegard von Bingen (1098–1179).

Outside the abbeys and monasteries, religious music was taking another form. A folk-music tradition had slowly emerged in Germany, and as it developed, German missionaries turned it to sacred use, creating a parallel literature of sacred folk songs, sung in the vernacular rather than in Latin.

The vernacular tradition in court music, from the 11th through the 14th century, was reflected in the art of the minnesinger. Influenced by the French troubadours and trouveres, the minnesingers composed chivalric epics of courtly love, usually in a monodic style (one melody line, accompanied instrumentally). Among the greatest of the minnesingers were WALTHER VON DER VOGELWEIDE, Neidhardt von Reuenthal, and Heinrich von Meissen (known as Frauenlob, c.1255–1318). The minnesingers were supplanted in the 14th century by the MEISTERSINGERS—primarily middle- and lower-class artisans—who established musicians' guilds and schools. The meistersingers cultivated a conservative style, devoid of the polyphony that composers of other countries were exploring.

The Renaissance and Early Baroque Periods

Polyphony began making headway in 15th-century Germany in the compositions of the Netherlands-born composers Heinrich Isaac and Roland de LASSUS (Orlando di Lasso). Instrumental music also came of age at this time; dance music was played in the home, and in the church, performance on the organ was more highly developed in Germany than anywhere else in Europe. Town governments employed musicians for civic purposes.

In the 16th century the Protestant Reformation had a strong effect on the music of the German cities that came under Martin Luther's influence. The primary musical expression of Luther's reformed church was the CHORALE—a polyphonic setting of a simple sacred hymn, sung in the vernacular. The newly invented printing press, which had been turning out music books in Germany as early as 1511, mass-produced Luther's hymnals. In Austria, Lutheranism and its church music reigned only briefly: by 1600 the chorale tradition there was in decline.

One of the few Germans whose sacred music did not rely heavily on the chorale was the 17th-century composer Heinrich SCHÜTZ, the first to compose works that fully reflected the developments of the Netherlands and Italian composers of the time. Consequently, his distinctive and vital choral settings (usually on biblical texts) came to be renowned throughout Europe. Many 17th-century German works have remained in the active repertoire. Michael PRAETORIUS composed vivid dance and instrumental works, and composers such as Johann Jacob Froberger (1616–67), Johann PACHELBEL, Jan Reincken (1623–1722), and Dietrich BUXTEHUDE brought refinements to the art of solo keyboard writing.

The Later Baroque

These composers were the immediate predecessors of Jo-

Johann Sebastian Bach (left) *was the greatest German composer of the baroque period, but his genius was recognized only after his death. Wolfgang Amadeus Mozart* (center) *and Ludwig van Beethoven* (right) *were celebrities in their own lifetimes.*

hann Sebastian BACH, who as a young man studied their works and probably heard some of them play. For posterity, the figure of Bach dominates the first half of the 18th century; in his own time, he was more highly regarded as a keyboard virtuoso than as a composer, primarily because he devoted himself to perfecting the ornate contrapuntal style of his predecessors, at a time when younger composers—including his own sons, Johann Christian BACH and Carl Philipp Emanuel BACH—were developing the more streamlined *stil galant* (elegant style), which pointed the way to the classic era.

From today's perspective, Bach's music stands not only as the culmination of the polyphonic style that began in the Renaissance, but also as the foundation of Western classical music in the 19th and 20th centuries. Generations of keyboard players have studied the 48 preludes and fugues of his *Well-Tempered Clavier*, chorale preludes for organ, and other works; violinists, cellists, flutists, and others have their Bach sonatas, partitas, and suites. Bach's mass in B minor, Passion settings, cantatas, orchestral suites and concertos, and THE ART OF FUGUE have been an inspiration to audiences, composers, and theoreticians alike.

George Frideric HANDEL left Germany fairly early, traveling through Italy and finally settling in England, where he composed his best-known orchestral works, operas, and oratorios. George Philipp TELEMANN, who held a variety of posts in Germany and Poland before settling in Hamburg, was the most prolific of them all: among his works are 40 operas, 600 orchestral suites, 44 Passion settings, 700 cantatas, and countless concertos and sonatas. Telemann wrote in a simpler style than Bach or Handel, reflecting the public's preference for light dance music and unadorned but emotionally direct sacred works. This change in taste reflected a change in the social structure of music making. As the resources of the German towns were depleted by the Thirty Years' War, the municipally supported guilds gave way to amateur, but highly polished, ensembles of part-time players.

The Classic Era

In the 1740s, Berlin, Dresden, and Mannheim emerged as centers where orchestras (and orchestral music) grew and flourished. In Berlin, Frederick the Great (Frederick II of Prussia)—a composer himself—brought together an orchestra that included C. P. E. Bach, the flute virtuoso and theorist Johann Joachim QUANTZ, and other brilliant players. He also established an opera house there. Mannheim, too, was known for its large and brilliantly polished orchestra, which its composers—among them Johann Stamitz (see STAMITZ family) and Franz Xaver Richter (1709–87)—exploited in a unique symphonic style that used dramatic dynamic contrasts.

By the end of the 18th century the front line of musical development shifted to Austria, where Franz Joseph HAYDN, beginning in the 1760s, experimented freely with forms and ensemble deployments; as a result, he was able to shape the string quartet, symphony, and sonata into their modern forms. Expanding on the *stil galant* no-

tion of contrasting themes, for instance, he wrote works that were the embodiment of the sonata form—essentially a two-theme, three-part symmetrical structure containing an exposition, a development section, and a recapitulation. All told, he composed 104 symphonies, plus chamber works, operas, and oratorios.

Wolfgang Amadeus MOZART was one of music's most brilliant prodigies. Under the tutelage of his father, Leopold, he learned the basics of composition as well as keyboard and violin performance, and before he was ten years old he had astounded Europe's royalty with his abilities and composed his first symphonies. Mozart excelled at every genre he essayed, from chamber music to solo piano sonatas, orchestral works, and opera. In opera, he competed with Italian composers in works such as *Le nozze di Figaro* (The Marriage of Figaro, 1786) and *Don Giovanni* (1787), and he also developed the singspiel, a German-language genre that combines the spoken dialogue of the comic theater with musical interludes and arias. Works such as *Die Zauberflöte* (The Magic Flute, 1791) paved the way for the more ambitious forms of German opera that would evolve during the following century.

Haydn and Mozart began a revolution in music that was brought to fruition in the works of Ludwig van BEETHOVEN. Born in the Rhineland, Beethoven moved to Vienna to study with Haydn and spent the rest of his life there. These were heady times: in literature and art, the age of romanticism was dawning; in the political world, revolution was in the air. Although his patrons were members of Vienna's aristocracy, Beethoven made it clear that he considered himself their equal (or perhaps their better) by virtue of his talents.

Beethoven's early works show an affinity for the style of Haydn—but also an impatience with the constraints of the classic style. In 1804 (by which time he was almost entirely deaf), he embarked on what he called "a new way," unveiling his Third Symphony (the *Eroica*)—a work

This drawing by Erald Kaiser, done in 1847, portrays Robert and Clara Schumann. Inspired by the German romantic school of poetry, both Schumann and his wife composed piano music and vocal songs renowned for their elegance and melodic clarity.

This caricature silhouette depicts the 19th-century composer Richard Wagner as a giant surrounded by tiny critics. Criticism persisted from 1843 in reaction to Wagner's operatic reforms and musical innovations. His genius was fully recognized only during the 20th century.

of enormous proportions, for the time. Thereafter, many of his works seemed to deal with idealized, lofty concepts, and in the spirit of the romantic literature he was reading (particularly the works of Goethe), he heightened the dramatic contrasts of his musical language. His output was much smaller than Bach's, Haydn's, or Mozart's. There were only 9 symphonies, 5 piano concertos, 1 violin concerto, a single opera (*Fidelio*, recast several times between 1803 and 1814, and never entirely successful), 32 piano sonatas, and chamber music (including 16 progressively brilliant string quartets).

The Romantic Age

The German and Austrian composers who ventured forth in Beethoven's shadow found that while he had pointed the way toward the expressive romantic style, he had by no means explored all the available routes. Working in Vienna, Franz SCHUBERT composed music that, while less stormy than Beethoven's, was equally passionate. Schubert expressed these passions through his sweetly harmonized chamber works, symphonies, and piano sonatas. The medium he excelled in, however, was the song, or lied, of which he composed some 600. Using the sparest of performing forces—a solo voice, with piano accompaniment—Schubert set lengthy cycles of poems in a way that made the cycle's organic development clear while delving into the fine shades of emotion that each phrase in each poem was meant to convey.

In Germany, meanwhile, Felix MENDELSSOHN composed an array of orchestral, choral, and chamber works that were as exquisitely melodic as Schubert's, while Robert SCHUMANN expressed himself most successfully through his idiosyncratic piano music. Schumann's wife, Clara Wieck (1819–96), was also a talented composer, although she made her reputation primarily as a pianist.

Besides composing, Schumann published a journal of musical criticism and philosophy, wherein he appraised the work of his predecessors and contemporaries. One young composer he was particularly impressed with was Johannes BRAHMS, a native of Hamburg whose conserva-

tive inclinations led him to compose works that looked back at classical structural models while taking full advantage of the large-scale romantic orchestra, with all its thunder and coloration. His four symphonies are extensions of what he considered a Beethovenian ideal, as are his finely crafted chamber works. In the intimate setting of his songs and later piano pieces, Brahms anticipated harmonic ideas of the 20th century.

German Music Drama

In *Der Freischutz* (1821) and *Euryanthe* (1823), Carl Maria von WEBER took a crucial step beyond the limits of the singspiel tradition by giving the orchestra an unprecedented importance in expressing the works' drama and emotionality. Beyond that, he pioneered the use of leitmotiv, a brief, recurring musical theme that represents a specific character, object, emotion, or trait.

Richard WAGNER expanded the use of the leitmotiv considerably. His rich orchestration (which required powerful voices to rise above it) and his unbridled use of harmonic chromaticism gave the music an almost mystical aura. Many of his operas, most notably the four-part Ring cycle (1848–74), are grandly nationalistic works that revolve around episodes, characters, and legends of the distant Teutonic past.

Since no one could out-Wagner Wagner, Richard STRAUSS adopted a more sensationalistic approach in *Salome* (1905) and *Elektra* (1908), shocking audiences with both his plot choices and his evocative, chromatic music. On the other hand, in works such as *Der Rosenkavalier* (1911), *Intermezzo* (1924), and *Capriccio* (1942), he struck an interesting balance between his modern tonal language and orchestral texturing, and an almost neoclassical sense of elegance and proportion. Strauss's earlier symphonic poems, such as *Till Eulenspiegel's Merry Pranks* (1895), *Also Sprach Zarathustra* (1896), and *Ein Heldenleben* (A Hero's Life, 1898), are orchestral precursors to the operas.

This portrait of Gustav Mahler dates from the 1890s, when he was conducting in Hamburg and writing his early symphonies. His music's grandiose quality is leavened by folk elements and the German romantic spirit. Mahler's later symphonies brought the romantic era to a close.

On the lighter side, Johann Strauss, Jr. (see STRAUSS family), an Austrian orchestra leader, became reknowned for his lavish, colorfully orchestrated waltzes and his operetta *Die Fledermaus* (1874). The Hungarian-born Franz LEHAR, composer of *The Merry Widow* (1905), helped to sustain the art of Viennese operetta into the 20th century.

The Twentieth Century

In Austria, Anton BRUCKNER and Gustav MAHLER expanded the scope of the symphony (and, in Mahler's case, the orchestrally accompanied song cycle) to epic lengths. Their sprawling canvases embody a searing emotional intensity and a sense of self-revelation. They mark the zenith of the expressive romantic style.

Arnold SCHOENBERG composed his early works, including the massive *Gurrelieder* (1901–13) and the dark, mysterious string sextet *Transfigured Night* (1899), in a style that seemed the outgrowth of Brahms's and Mahler's romantic aesthetic. By 1920, however, he had developed a method of composition in which he arranged the 12 tones of the scale in a series, and then used the permutations of the series as the thematic material on which he based his works (see SERIAL MUSIC). Serialism, as Schoenberg saw it, was a tool whereby composers could find fresh material, free from the constraints of major and minor tonalities. Later composers serialized not only pitches but rhythms, tone colors, and dynamics.

Schoenberg, along with his two greatest disciples—Alban BERG and Anton von WEBERN—worked in Vienna, and were the central figures in what is known as the Second Viennese School. Schoenberg adapted his method to the traditional chamber and orchestral forms, while Webern left a body of compact, concise miniatures and Berg—in many ways the most enduring of the three—composed two full-scale operas, *Wozzeck* (1921) and *Lulu* (1935),

The Austrian composer Arnold Schoenberg began to work on atonal music during the early 1900s. This work led him to formulate his 12-tone technique, a form of serial music.

plus a gorgeously romantic violin concerto (1935) and a handful of songs and chamber works.

The advent of the Nazis brought an end to Germany's dominance of the musical world. The music of Schoenberg and his followers was declared "decadent"—as was the much more popularly based theatrical music of Kurt WEILL, and the neobaroque and neoclassical music of Paul HINDEMITH, a prolific and practical composer who rejected the serial approach. Schoenberg, Weill, and Hindemith fled to the United States, as did hundreds of other composers, performers, authors, and artists from Germany, Austria, and other European countries that came under German domination in the 1930s.

Leading figures in the gradual postwar recovery of German music include Karlheinz STOCKHAUSEN, an influential composer of electronic music and of works combining electronic tape and conventional instruments, and Hans Werner HENZE whose operas, symphonic scores, and chamber works run the stylistic gamut from avant-garde to almost neoromantic.

German Confederation   The German Confederation was a loose grouping of German states created (1815) by the Congress of Vienna (see VIENNA, CONGRESS OF) to replace the Holy Roman Empire. The confederation was rendered largely ineffective by the rivalry between Austria and Prussia, and it was dissolved after the Prussian defeat of Austria in the SEVEN WEEKS' WAR (1866).

German Democratic Republic   see GERMANY

German East Africa   German East Africa was a former German colony comprising the areas of most of Rwanda, Burundi, present-day Tanzania, and part of Mozambique. The Germans controlled the region from 1884 until World War I, after which most of the area was mandated to Great Britain.

German language   see GERMANIC LANGUAGES

German literature   German literature, which comprises the literatures of Germany, Austria, and part of Switzerland, has always tried to integrate foreign influences, especially those of classical antiquity and France. Thus the concept of a German literary tradition did not emerge before the 17th century.

Early and Medieval German Literature

Among the earliest extant poems, the *Song of Hildebrand* (*c*.800; Eng. trans., 1906), an alliterative verse fragment, is genuinely pagan in its emphasis on fate, whereas the *Heliand* (*c*.830), an epic poem about the life of Christ, attempts to synthesize old and new. Otfried von Weissenburg's *Evangelienbuch* (Book of Gospels, completed *c*.870) set the precedent for a new Christian literature consisting of biblical paraphrases. This work, the first by an identifiable German author, introduced end rhyme into

German poetry. Secular Latin works included *Waltharius Manufortis* (*c*.930; trans. as *Walter of Aquitaine,* 1950), which introduced classical hexameter; *Ecbasis Captivi* (*c*.940), the earliest extant German beast fable; and *Ruodlieb* (*c*.1050; Eng. trans., 1959), the adventures of a young hero. Hroswitha von Gandersheim (fl. after 950), the first known German woman writer, was a nun who used the Roman playwright Terence as a model for her morality plays.

During the Middle High German period (*c*.1050–*c*.1300), secular culture, perpetuated by minstrels (see MINSTRELS, MINNESINGERS, AND TROUBADOURS), now became the concern of the knights who celebrated COURTLY LOVE in complex lyrics. Among the minnesingers who, influenced by Provençal troubadours, produced an abundance of songs, WALTHER VON DER VOGELWEIDE turned away from empty gallantry to express powerful emotions of love and transformed the short poem of proverbial wisdom into a political weapon of satire and patriotism.

King ARTHUR AND ARTHURIAN LEGEND, popular in contemporary French literature, also formed the basis of German heroic poetry. The idealized world of chivalry was counterbalanced by religious restraint in the work of Hartmann von Aue, especially in *Der arme Heinrich* (*c*.1195; trans. as *Henry the Leper,* 1905). GOTTFRIED VON STRASSBURG glorified sensual passion in his unfinished *Tristan and Isolde.* WOLFRAM VON ESCHENBACH's *Parzival* (*c*.1210; Eng. trans., 1956) symbolizes in the quest for the Holy Grail the search for eternal salvation. In the NIBELUNGENLIED (*c*.1200; Eng. trans., 1904) an anonymous author tried to combine the archaic legends of popular tradition with the refinement of the age by describing the exploits of the warrior Siegfried in the setting of courtly love and chivalry.

Late Middle Ages and Sixteenth Century

The high style of chivalry was frequently parodied, and

Friedrich Schiller, a dramatist, poet, and philosopher, profoundly influenced the direction of German literature. His early historical dramas, such as The Robbers *(1781), focus on the issue of political freedom; his later historical dramas, such as* Wilhelm Tell *(1804), explore the question of moral freedom.*

human folly satirized, by such writers as Sebastian BRANT and Johann Baptist Fischart. The many plays, legends, and tales of Hans SACHS exemplify the coarse humor of this period, as do the adventures of the prankster Till Eulenspiegel. The FAUST legend appeared in several versions at this time.

In the hands of the MEISTERSINGERS, poetry degenerated into a mechanical practice of matching rhymed lines. Prose writing, however, acquired stylistic refinement and expressive quality. The mystics Meister ECKHART and Johannes TAULER contributed, as did Johannes von Tepl in *The Bohemian Plowman* (*c*.1400; Eng. trans., 1958). Martin LUTHER's German translation of the Bible and his beautiful religious songs had a considerable effect. Some of the greatest literary works, however, were written in Latin by the humanists Ulrich von HUTTEN and Johannes Reuchlin (1455–1522).

Johann Wolfgang von Goethe, one of the principal figures in German literature, influenced the development of the late-18th-century Sturm und Drang period and the classicism of the early 19th century.

Rainer Maria Rilke is considered one of the foremost lyric poets of 20th-century German literature. In such works as New Poems (1907–08), he used symbolism and skillfully manipulated language and rhythm to evoke the essence of his subject.

The Seventeenth Century

During the 17th century, Academies (*Sprachgesell-schaften*) were founded to establish a pure language and correct grammar. The rules of literary neoclassicism were first formulated (1624) by Martin Opitz. Seneca was the model for the tragedies of Andreas GRYPHIUS and Daniel Caspar von Lohenstein, whereas the Jesuits developed their own religious theater in Latin. In poetry the sonnet and alexandrine verse were the preferred forms. Among the many poets, Paul Fleming (1609–40), Gryphius, and Christian Hofmann von Hofmanns-Waldau (1617–79) are outstanding. Among the voluminous novels of the period, only the ribald humor and colorful realism of Hans GRIM-MELSHAUSEN survive. The visionary Jakob BÖHME profoundly influenced mystics.

The Eighteenth and Nineteenth Centuries

Gotthold LESSING replaced courtly tragedy with bourgeois drama. His *Minna von Barnhelm* (1767; Eng. trans., 1930) remains the unsurpassed masterpiece of German comedy; his *Nathan the Wise* (1779; Eng. trans., 1955) is a stirring call for religious tolerance.

Christoph Martin WIELAND added grace and playfulness to the language and flavored his verse and prose with subtle irony. *Oberon* (1780; Eng. trans., 1798) is his best-known epic poem; *The History of Agathon* (1766; Eng. trans., 1773) emphasizes the psychological growth of character. Friedrich Gottlieb KLOPSTOCK created in his *Odes* (1771; Eng. trans., 1848) a new poetic language of dynamic expression.

Sturm und Drang (1770–85). The STURM UND DRANG movement praised original genius, demanded a poetry of strong passions, and found models in Shakespeare and simple folk songs. Johann Gottfried von HERDER disseminated these ideas among youthful writers, who included Johann Wolfgang von GOETHE and Johann Christoph Friedrich von SCHILLER. The first novel of this movement, Goethe's *The Sorrows of Young Werther*, spread the tenets of ROMANTICISM. In later works, however, Goethe endowed his creations with self-discipline, as in the BILDUNGSROMAN *Wilhelm Meister's Apprenticeship* (1795; Eng. trans., 1824).

The Second Golden Age. In Weimar during the early 19th century Goethe and Schiller tried to integrate the ancient classical tradition into German romanticism. In Jena, August Wilhelm and Friedrich von SCHLEGEL, the mystic NOVALIS, and the poet Ludwig TIECK formed the first romantic circle. This was followed by other groups in Berlin and Heidelberg whose members included Clemens BRENTANO; Joseph, Freiherr von EICHENDORFF; Achim and Bettina von Arnim; and Ernst Theodor Amadeus Hoffmann. Jacob and Wilhelm GRIMM stimulated interest in early Germanic literary traditions. Friedrich HÖLDERLIN's poems achieved a synthesis of ancient Greek forms and modern sensibility, and Heinrich von KLEIST expressed his

The literature of modern Germany reflects the influence of Nietzche, Freud, and politics in its concern with philosophy, psychology, and the complexities of 20th-century society. Bertolt Brecht (left) developed his drama into terse and moving studies of the politics of the human condition. Thomas Mann (center) and Hermann Hesse (right), both of whom received Nobel Prizes for literature, used character studies to explore intellectual and philosophical arguments.

chaotic view of the world in passionate dramas and powerful short stories.

Postromanticism. After 1830 the so-called BIEDERMEIER poets reacted by withdrawing into the realm of the family and idyllic nature. This resignation was replaced in the poems of Heinrich HEINE by new political directions and a realistic outlook. Many progressive writers had to go into exile after the revolution of 1848, among them Karl MARX and Carl SCHURZ. Annette Elisabeth von DROSTE-HÜLSHOFF and Eduard MÖRIKE were the leading poets; Franz GRILLPARZER and Christian Friedrich Hebbel, the dramatists; Gottfried KELLER, Theodor STORM, Jeremias Gotthelf, Conrad Ferdinand Meyer, Wilhelm Raabe, and Adalbert Stifter, the storytellers. Far ahead of his time was Georg BÜCHNER, who rejected bourgeois values in such plays as *Woyzeck* (1850; Eng. trans., 1957). Friedrich Wilhelm NIETZSCHE rejected the idealistic philosophy of Georg Wilhelm Friedrich HEGEL and Arthur SCHOPENHAUER.

The Twentieth Century

NATURALISM was introduced after 1885 by Gerhart HAUPTMANN and Arno Holz. Arthur SCHNITZLER, a contemporary of Sigmund Freud's, added a Viennese flavor to his erotic, melancholy plays. SYMBOLISM was introduced as a reaction to naturalism about 1900 by the poets Stefan GEORGE, Rainer Maria RILKE, and Hugo von HOFMANNSTHAL.

Expressionism is a collective term for the style of certain poets and dramatists active between 1910 and 1925. Before the war such poets as Gottfried BENN, Georg Trakl, and Georg Heym created apocalyptic visions or experimented with style. Toward the end of World War I and during the early years of the German republic, dramatists, notably Georg KAISER and Ernst TOLLER, tried to revolutionize the theater. Meanwhile the novel gradually developed from the refined realism of Theodor FONTANE, the chronicler of Prussian aristocracy and Berlin's lower middle class, to the epic canvases of Hermann BROCH, Alfred DÖBLIN, Thomas MANN, and Robert MUSIL.

Literature under the Nazis. Most writers had to go into exile after 1933. After the war Germany was a cultural vacuum. A writer who had been known only as author of a few minor prose sketches—Franz KAFKA—appeared as a great novelist. Bertolt BRECHT, who had written his best plays in exile, also became recognized. His theory of EPIC THEATER and alienation was applied by the Swiss dramatists Friedrich DÜRRENMATT and Max FRISCH.

German Literature since World War II. The West German postwar literary resurgence was organized around GRUPPE 47, to which belonged the novelists Heinrich BÖLL, Günter GRASS, and Uwe JOHNSON. Other authors now widely read include the poets Paul CELAN and Ingeborg Bachmann; the playwrights and novelists Peter WEISS and Peter HANDKE; and the East German novelist Christa WOLF.

German measles

German measles, or rubella, is a contagious but mild viral disease common in children and young adults. Early symptoms, similar to those of the common cold, are often followed by a skin rash that first appears on the face and neck and then rapidly spreads to the trunk and extremities. Lymph nodes on the neck become swollen and tender. Symptoms usually disappear without complication in about a week. Many people have had German measles without knowing it, because a skin rash is not always present. Natural infection apparently produces lifelong immunity. Pregnant women who become infected have a high risk of giving birth to a baby with serious defects, including blindness, cardiovascular disorders, or mental retardation. Vaccination is therefore recommended before the childbearing age, although the immunity provided is weaker than that from natural infection.

German music   see GERMAN AND AUSTRIAN MUSIC

German shepherd

The German shepherd dog, known as the Alsatian in Britain, is one of the most widely known and popular breeds of purebred dogs in the world. The breed is a descendant of earlier German herding and farm dogs. Today's German shepherd was developed in the latter part of the 19th century by methodical breeding. German shepherds are commonly selected to be army dogs, police dogs, or guide dogs for the blind. They are medium-sized, powerful animals; the males can be up to 65 cm (26 in) in height and weigh 38.5 kg (85 lb); the females are slightly shorter and weigh a little less. The dense coat may be black and tan, gray, or solid black.

The German shepherd, or Alsatian, is a powerful, intelligent dog with a long body and short fur. Although shepherds are often pale or white, breeders prefer the characteristic tan-and-black coloring.

German shorthaired pointer

The German shorthaired pointer, or kurzhaar, was developed in the late 19th century by German hunters interested in an all-purpose sporting breed. The older, heavier German pointers, descendants of Spanish pointers and various hounds, were mated with English pointers and possibly other gundogs to produce the desired animal. The German shorthaired pointer can scent and point game and retrieve on both land and water. The breed was recognized by the American Kennel Club in 1930.

The German shorthaired pointer was bred from the pointer, blood-hound, foxhound, and other breeds. Considered one of the finest all-purpose sporting dogs, it is an excellent pointer and has a highly developed sense of smell.

German shorthairs resemble pointers. Males stand to 62.5 cm (25 in) high at the shoulder and weigh about 32 kg (70 lb). The tail is docked at about two-fifths of its length. The smooth coat is light or dark brown, with or without grayish white or dark-brown to liver-colored patches.

German wirehaired pointer   The German wire-haired pointer, or drahthaar, resembles the German shorthaired pointer in all ways except for the coat. The wirehaired pointer has a two-layered coat: the undercoat is a soft, dense insulating covering, and the outercoat is straight, harsh, and wiry. The wirehaired pointer was developed in Germany, during the last half of the 19th century, from the German shorthaired pointer and several

The German wirehaired pointer is an all-around hunting dog similar to the German shorthaired pointer in its general shape and abilities. The wirehair, however, has a double-layered coat that provides protection against jagged underbrush.

other pointing breeds, including the pudelpointer. The breed very quickly became popular in its native land. Introduced into the United States in the 1920s, it was officially recognized by the American Kennel Club in 1959.

Germanic languages   Germanic languages, a sub-family of INDO-EUROPEAN LANGUAGES, are spoken by 540 million people all over the world but chiefly in Europe and North America. Traditionally, the Germanic languages comprise three major branches: West Germanic, North Germanic, and East Germanic.

The Germanic languages broke away from other Indo-European languages before 500 BC. A more-or-less regular series of sound changes, described by GRIMM'S LAW, was one of the distinguishing features of this separation. The Dane Karl Adolf Verner posited a further rule, Verner's Law, to explain later developments among Germanic consonants.

East, North, and West Germanic

Today no general agreement exists as to the correctness of the traditional division into East, West, and North Germanic subgroups, which took place after the Proto-Germanic period and was completed by the time of Christ (5th to 1st century BC). The West Germanic grouping in particular is questioned because it is apparent that language elements of German, English, Netherlandic, and Frisian go back to three groups of which the Ingvaeones are most frequently named.

East Germanic. The oldest surviving Germanic literary text—fragments of a Bible translation made by Ulfilas, bishop of the West Goths (d. *c.*385)—was written in Gothic. Since the Goths had no written language, Ulfilas took the Greek uncial alphabet, added to it a few Latin and runic letters, and thus created an alphabet for his translation.

North Germanic. The North Germanic languages all descend from Old Norse and share several distinctive features. Old Norse separated into West Nordic and East Nordic. West Nordic comprises Old Icelandic (12th–15th century), which became Icelandic; Old Norwegian, which became Landsmål, now called Nynorsk (modern Norwegian); and Faeroese, also called Faeroic. East Nordic comprises Old Swedish, which evolved into Swedish, and Old Danish, which became modern Danish.

West Germanic. All West Germanic languages doubled consonants except *r* before *i* or *j* after short vowels and sometimes before *l, r,* and *w*—a process called gemination. West Germanic shared with North Germanic the changes of *z* to *r* and *ē* to *ā*. English and Netherlandic also share several sound characteristics.

Anglo-Frisian (Ingvaeonic in the broadest sense) includes English and Frisian. The bases for English are the dialects of the Angles, Saxons, and Jutes, who emigrated to England from Schleswig-Holstein about AD 450. Anglo-Saxon or Old English existed until the 12th century, Middle English until 1450, and New English since then. (See ENGLISH LANGUAGE.)

The German-Netherlandic group includes Low German

and High German. Low German splits into Low Franconian, which becomes Netherlandic (Dutch and Flemish), and Low Saxon, which has a three-stage evolution: Old Saxon or Old Low German (AD 800–1200) becomes Middle Low German (1200–1600), which in turn becomes modern Low German or Plattdeutsch since 1600. High German subdivides into Middle German and Upper German.

The dividing line between Low German and High German (the Benrath line) is located near the Düsseldorf-Magdeburg parallel. The set of sound changes that took place in the High German area, but not Low German, English, or Dutch areas, is called the High German Sound Shift.

Writing and Spelling

Aside from Gothic, for which Ulfilas invented an alphabet, before the year 600, no written Germanic existed except for a few single words and short sentences in runic characters. More of these have been found in Scandinavia and Britain than in Germany. After 600, when Christian monks tried to write the Germanic languages in Latin characters, they experienced many difficulties because Latin and Germanic sounds do not resemble each other very closely.

Written Dutch is fairly uniform in spelling, grammar, and vocabulary, but spoken Dutch has a number of dialects as well as an official spoken form. Written Dutch evolved from the Flemish spoken in Flanders and Brabant in the 15th century; modern spoken Dutch, however, grew out of the vernacular of the province of Holland.

Afrikaans arose from the Dutch spoken by the Boers, who emigrated from the Netherlands to South Africa in the 17th century. Its written form dates only from the mid-19th century. Its basic Dutch vocabulary has been greatly expanded with native African and English borrowings.

Yiddish, though not a national language, is spoken by Jews all over the world. It arose (c.1100) out of a blend of a number of German dialects in the ghettos of Central Europe and from there spread to other parts of the world. Phonetically, Yiddish is closer to Middle High German than is modern German. Its vocabulary is basically German, but it has been enlarged by borrowings from Hebrew, Slavic, Romance languages, and English.

Vocabulary

Only about 25 percent of the vocabulary of modern Germanic languages can be traced through West and North Germanic to Indo-European. The pronouns (I, my, you), nouns of kinship (father, mother, brother), parts of the body (eye, ear, arm), domestic animals (hound, ox, steer), and common activities (build, bite, go, stand, sit, know) are such words.

Latin vocabulary and grammar have influenced the Germanic languages extensively. The most important Latin influences occurred during the Reformation and the rise of humanism (15th and 16th centuries). Many Greek words were also borrowed then. The great influence of French on English after the Norman invasion (1066) produced a hybrid language West Germanic in grammar and basic vocabulary but French in most words of five letters or more.

Morphology

The Germanic languages have two adjective declensions, strong and weak. Weak forms are used generally after articles, demonstrative pronouns, and possessive adjectives; the strong are used independently. These forms are reduced greatly in Danish, Swedish, and Netherlandic and are absent in English. The comparison of adjectives and adverbs in Germanic differs from that in the Romance languages. Generally, -r and -st endings are added: long, longer, longest; Swedish, lång, längre, längst.

The eight cases of Indo-European nouns, adjectives, and pronouns were reduced to four, and sometimes even fewer, in Germanic. Free stress (accent) became recessive, and precise accent rules became dominant, with the first root syllable in Germanic carrying the stress. Umlauting, a process of modifying vowel sounds, took place extensively (woman, women; foot, feet). A system of strong verbs developed as the result of vowel alternation (ablaut), as in sing, sang, sung, and a unique way of forming the past tense using weak verbs (jump, jumped) was created.

Germanic law Early Germanic law was the unwritten, customary law of the GERMANIC PEOPLES from their entry into recorded history until the end of the early Middle Ages. It was not the law of a unified people or state. Early Germanic law had three characteristics. It was customary law, not statute law or the work of a legislator. The law seemed to live in the consciousness and conviction of each individual. It was attached to people, not to territory, and it was regarded as unalterable. It was unwritten law, transmitted orally. Legal rules were expressed simply, formally, and directly. Legal acts, moreover, had to be visible or audible; requirements were established for specific formalities, for witnesses or even for an assembly, and for the use of legal symbols.

Under the influence of the Roman and Christian cultures of the lands they conquered, the Germanic peoples began to reduce their customs to writing. By the time this occurred, the kings had begun to make law; indeed, the Visigoths (see GOTHS) and LOMBARDS made no outward distinction between old customary and new kingly law.

The first written collections of Germanic law date from about the 5th century. For the Visigoths the comprehensive *Codex Euricianus* (c.475) is the earliest collection and shows the considerable influence of ROMAN LAW. Shortly thereafter, however, in 506, Alaric II promulgated the *Lex Romana Visigothorum* ("Breviary of Alaric"), a compilation based on Roman sources for the Romans living in his territories. Then, for the Goths alone, Leovigild (d. 586) issued a revised *Codex*. The important *Lex Visigothorum* (c.654) of King Reccesvinth once again applied to both Visigoths and Romans and contained Germanic customary law.

The Burgundians had the *Lex Burgundionum* (501), promulgated by King Gundobad. It applied to Germans and in disputes between Romans and Germans. The same king issued (506) a separate code for Romans, the

Lex Romana Burgundionum, but this seems to have had no practical importance.

Collections of Lombard laws began with King Rothair's Edict of 643, distinguished by clear systematization and exactness of expression. Of all Germanic laws, Lombard law alone was subjected to scholarly treatment.

Germanic peoples

Germanic peoples   Classical writers were aware of localized tribes of Germans (speakers of a Germanic language) perhaps as early as 600 BC. Substantial political contact, however, did not occur until the late 2d century BC when the Cimbri and Teutons attacked Italy. Julius CAESAR and TACITUS in his *Germania* (AD 98) provide most of the available information about the early Germans. Groups such as the Treveri, Nervii, and Tencteri were important during the mid-1st century BC. Later, the Frisians, Marcomanni, Quadi, GOTHS, VANDALS, and LOMBARDS are mentioned. The FRANKS, SAXONS, Alamans (also called Suevi), and Burgundians became more important in the West, and small groups such as the Heruli, Rugii, and Turcilingi are mentioned only briefly in the sources.

For most of the period through the late 5th century what is known about the Germanic peoples comes from classical writings of this era. Much has also been learned about the developing Iron Age culture of these peoples from archaeological evidence. Additional written sources became available with the appearance of GERMANIC LAW codes in the late 5th and early 6th centuries and the histories of writers like Jordanes and Gregory of Tours in the 6th century and BEDE in the early 8th century.

The Germanic peoples are generally credited with or blamed for destroying the Roman Empire and bringing an end to classical civilization. From the 2d to the 11th century various Germanic peoples, including VIKINGS, invaded, ravaged, and devastated great parts of Western Europe. Much wealth was consumed in defending the "civilized world" from these "barbarians," and countless lives were lost in these conflicts. Although they contributed to the fall of the Roman Empire, they also played an important role in building a new society within the framework of the Roman fortified *civitates,* the Christian religion, and Latin culture.

The Germanic contribution to the new medieval culture was largely that of human resources and military vitality. After having been absorbed in what is today France by the dominant Romance-Christian culture, these peoples proceeded to convert the less Romanized peoples east of the Rhine and educate them to the values of ancient civilization.

Germanicus Caesar

Germanicus Caesar   [jur-man'-i-kus see'-zur]   A popular Roman general, Germanicus Caesar, b. May 24, 15 BC, d. Oct. 10, AD 19, was a member of the DRUSUS family and the nephew of TIBERIUS who adopted him in AD 4.

He fought under Tiberius in Pannonia and Dalmatia (AD 7–9) and on the Rhine (AD 11). Consul in 12, Germanicus was appointed commander in Germany and Gaul. After Augustus's death (14) he suppressed a mutiny in Lower Germany and from 14 to 16 waged a series of inconclusive campaigns against the German leader ARMINIUS. Recalled by Tiberius (now emperor), he celebrated a triumph in 17 and served a second consulship in 18. Sent to the east, Germanicus subdued Cappadocia and Commagene, organizing them into provinces. He died suddenly at Antioch, the probable victim of poisoning. Germanicus's children included CALIGULA (r. 37–41) and AGRIPPINA II, mother of the emperor NERO (r. 54–68). Germanicus's brother also reigned (41–54) as CLAUDIUS I.

germanium

germanium   [jur-mayn'-ee-uhm]   The chemical element germanium, a semimetal of Group IVA in the periodic table, is of central importance in the manufacture of SEMICONDUCTOR materials and devices. Its symbol is Ge, its atomic number is 32, and its atomic weight is 72.59. The German chemist Clemens A. Winkler first isolated the element in 1886 from the mineral argyrodite, a mixed sulfide of silver and germanium, and named it after his homeland. Germanium is widely distributed in the Earth's crust, with an average abundance of about 7 grams per metric ton. The element is usually found as a minor component in sulfide ores of copper, zinc, tin, lead, and antimony.

Germanium has a brittle metallic appearance, a melting point of 937.4° C, and a boiling point of 2,830° C. It crystallizes in a cubic structure similar to diamond but has a hardness of only 6 on Moh's scale (diamond is 10). The ultrapure element is an intrinsic semiconductor, which accounts for its major use in solid-state electronics. It forms compounds in the +2 and +4 oxidation states. The +2 state is both easily reduced to the element and easily oxidized to Ge(IV), so that tetravalent germanium compounds are the most common. The chloride and oxide, $GeCl_4$ and GeO_2, are the most important compounds because of the role they play in the production of the pure element.

Ultrapure germanium can be produced in near-crystalline perfection more easily than other semiconductors. For this reason alone, the electronic properties of germanium have been studied more than those of any other solid. The earliest semiconductor research was done with this element, and William Shockley used germanium to make the first transistor in 1948.

Germanium is recovered by treating enriched wastes and residues from zinc sulfide ores, pyrometallic ores, and coal with hydrochloric acid to form the volatile liquid $GeCl_4$, which is extracted with carbon tetrachloride and purified by distillation. The tetrachloride is treated with demineralized water to precipitate the dioxide GeO_2, which is then reduced to germanium with hydrogen. The ultrapure element is obtained by zone refining, a selective fusion-recrystallization process that concentrates impurities in the melt.

Germanium dioxide is finding increasing use in special optical materials. Fused GeO_2 glasses have transmission characteristics greatly superior to quartz (SiO_2) glasses in the infrared portion of the spectrum.

AT A GLANCE

GERMANY

Land: Area: 357,042 km² (137,854 mi²). Capital and largest city: Berlin (1988 est. pop., 3,307,021); seat of the government: Bonn (1987 est. pop., 278,180).
People: Population (1990 est.): 78,475,370. Density: 220 persons per km² (569 per mi²). Distribution (former West Germany, 1987): 85% urban, 15% rural; (former East Germany, 1989): 77% urban, 23% rural. Official language: German. Major religions: Protestantism, Roman Catholicism.
Government: Type: Federal republic. Legislature: Federal Parliament. Political subdivisions: 15 states.
Economy: GDP (former West Germany, 1989 est.): $945.7 billion; $15,300 per capita. GNP (former East Germany, 1989 est.): $159.5 billion; $9,679 per capita. Labor distribution, former West Germany (1988): manufacturing and mining—27%; agriculture—4.2%; services—14.4%; public administration—13.7%; trade—11%; construction—5.6%; transport and communication—4.8%; other—19.3%; former East Germany (1987): manufacturing and mining—40.6%; agriculture—10.8%; trade—10.3%; transport and communication—7.4%; construction—6.6%; services and public administration—24.3%. Foreign trade, former West Germany (1988): imports—$251 billion; exports—$323 billion; former East Germany (1988): imports—$31 billion; exports—$31 billion. Currency: 1 Deutsche Mark = 100 pfennige.
Education and Health: Literacy (1990): 100% of adult population. Universities (1989): 46. Life expectancy, former West Germany (1990): women—81; men—73; former East Germany (1990): women—77; men—71. Infant mortality, former West Germany (1990): 6 per 1,000 live births; former East Germany (1990): 7 per 1,000 live births.

Germany   From 1945 until its reunification in 1990, Germany was divided into two states, the Federal Republic of Germany (West Germany) and the German Democratic Republic (East Germany). Located in central Europe, the country is bordered on the north by the North Sea, Denmark, and the Baltic Sea; on the east by Poland, Czechoslovakia, and Austria; on the south by Austria and Switzerland; and on the west by France, Luxembourg, Belgium, and the Netherlands.

Following Germany's defeat at the end of World War II, the country was divided into four zones of occupation by the Allies—France, Great Britain, the United States, and the USSR. In 1949, West Germany was created from the combined British, French, and U.S. zones, and East Germany was soon created from the Soviet-occupied zone. BERLIN, the capital of Germany, was also divided into occupation sectors after the war and subsequently partitioned. Throughout the postwar period West Germany was

allied with the West, whereas East Germany was a Communist state, closely tied to the USSR and the other Soviet-bloc nations.

In March 1990, East Germany held its first free elections in more than half a century. The electorate voted the Communist government out of office and endorsed union with West Germany. With the agreement of the United States, the USSR, Britain, and France, East Germany became part of the Federal Republic of Germany on Oct. 3, 1990, and Berlin became the capital of the reunified state.

Land and Resources

Five major physiographic regions may be differentiated in Germany: the North German Lowlands, the Southern Transitional Borderlands, the Central Uplands (Mittelgebirge), the Alpine Foreland, and the Alps.

The hilly North German Lowlands extend south from the Baltic Sea coast. The plain was covered by Quaternary deposits, which are partially of glacial origin. Because

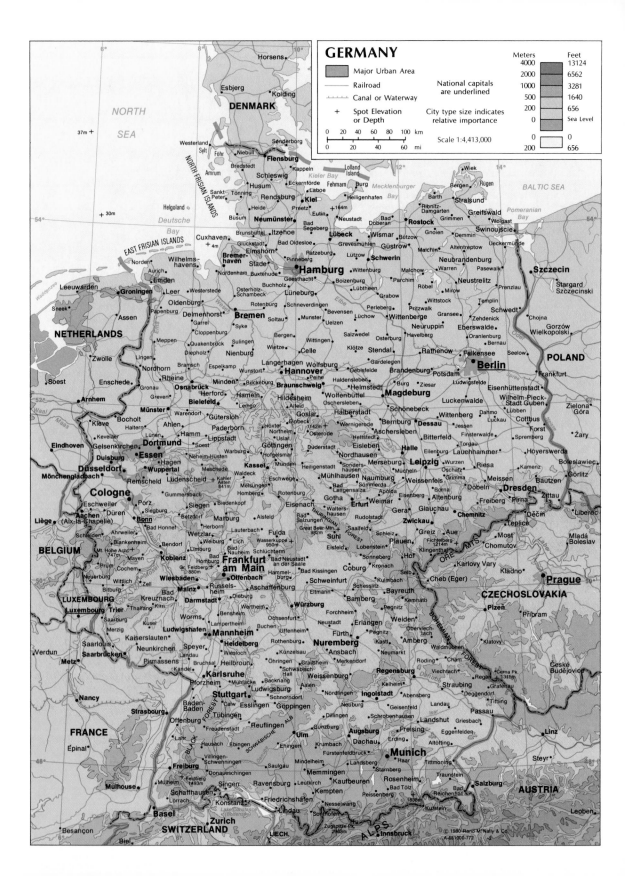

coastal waters are shallow the area is deficient in natural harbors. The infertile soils require intensive tillage and fertilization.

The Southern Transitional Borderlands form a transitional belt of thinly layered morainic material with highly fertile loess soil. Most of the country's coal and lignite deposits are located in this region. The Mittelland Canal is a vital artery.

A faulted area composed of worn-down fragments of the late Paleozoic system, the Central Uplands are heavily forested and consist of inactive volcanoes, plateaus, and granite massifs. The highland areas include the scarplands of Swabia and Franconia in the southwest; the HARZ Mountains, Thuringian Forest, and Saxon Uplands in the north and east; and the Bohemian Forest in the southeast. Of the many valleys of the region, the most picturesque is the valley of the Middle Rhine River, which flows in an 80-km-long (50-mi), often-narrow, steep gorge from Bingen to Bonn.

Alpine Foreland and the Alps. The Alpine Foreland, located to the northeast of the Alps, has the appearance of a broad plain. Rivers rise in the Alps and cross the foreland in broad, marshy valleys. Only the Danube is navigable. A small part of the ALPS lies within Germany, in the extreme south. Germany's highest mountain peak, the Zugspitze (2,963 m/9,721 ft) is located south of Munich.

Drainage. Germany has an extensive network of rivers, most of which drain into the Baltic and North seas. The major exception is the DANUBE RIVER, which flows to the Black Sea. The RHINE RIVER is navigable throughout Germany. The MOSELLE (German: Mosel) and the MAIN rivers are its chief tributaries. Chief tributaries of the Danube are the INN, Isar, and Naab rivers. Other important rivers are the ELBE, ODER, SPREE, Weser, Ems, and Saale. Lake CONSTANCE, Germany's largest lake, is located in the Alps.

Climate. Germany's climate is generally temperate. Because of warm winds from the Atlantic, the west has mild winters and summers. The average annual temperature in northwestern Germany is about 10° C (50° F); in the southwest it averages 12° C (53° F) yearly. The east has a more continental climate with cold winters and short, hot summers. Annual temperatures average about 2° to 4° C (3.6° to 7.2° F) lower than in the west. Baltic Sea harbors are frequently closed by ice during the winter.

Precipitation is evenly distributed throughout Germany, with the heaviest rainfall—from 864 to 1,016 mm (34 to 40 in)—occurring in the highlands. The coast has an annual average precipitation of 762 mm (30 in), and the east receives from 406 to 508 mm (16 to 20 in).

Flora and Fauna. More than one-quarter of the land is

(Left) *Neuschwanstein Castle, located in the Bavarian Alps and begun in 1869, was inspired by three operas—*Lohengrin, Parsifal, *and* Tannhäuser—*by the German composer Richard Wagner.*

(Below) *The Schwarzwald, or Black Forest, is a mountain range in southwestern West Germany. The range, a resort area with many rivers and lakes, extends approximately 145 km (90 mi) roughly parallel with the Rhine.*

The tower of the Kaiser Wilhelm Gedächniskirche, damaged during World War II, looms above the recently constructed memorial church along the Kurfürstendamm, Berlin's major commercial boulevard. The older church has been preserved in its ruined state as a reminder of the city's sufferings during World War II.

still under forest cover, mostly in highland regions. Coniferous trees constitute two-thirds of the timber stands; deciduous species include birch, beech, chestnut, oak, and walnut. Vines flourish in the Rhine, Moselle, and Danube River valleys.

Wild fauna are limited in number and variety. Red and roe deer and wild boars inhabit some forested areas, and the bear, wolf, fox, wildcat, otter, and badger can be found in remote areas.

The harmful effect of pollutants on Germany's forests has become a major concern. Former East Germany, particularly its southern part, is one of the worst polluted areas in Europe.

People

Language and Religion. The German language has been distinguished by its many regional varieties. The standard language, *Hochdeutsch* (High German), is taught in school, but despite the influence of radio and television, most people still speak their own dialects (see GERMANIC LANGUAGES). Schleswig-Holstein has a small Danish minority, and there is also a small Slavic minority of Sorbs (or Wends) east of Berlin, near the border with Poland.

Most Germans are Protestants and belong to several Evangelical and Lutheran churches. About 45% of the population of former West Germany are Catholics. Of the population of former East Germany, 47% were Protestants, 7% were Catholics, and 46% were unaffiliated in 1987. Under the Communist rule, church membership declined, but the Evangelical church became a haven for dissidents during the 1980s. Jews, once a large minority, today constitute less than 1% of the population.

Demography. The postwar influx of refugees and expel-

lees from Eastern Europe and East Germany resulted in a rapid growth of West German population, which increased by about 13 to 14 million between 1950 and 1980. Thereafter the combination of a decline in immigration and a lowered birth rate caused the population to level off and decrease slightly. In the last several decades, the former East Germany had a zero growth rate.

The territory of the former West Germany has the third highest population density in Europe (after Netherlands and Belgium), but the former East Germany, particularly in the north, is sparsely settled. The unification in 1990 has not redressed this imbalance, but rather the contrary: from October 1989 to early 1991, almost 600,000 people, mostly young, moved westward.

The largest city, and since late 1990 the capital of the unified Germany, is Berlin; other large cities in former West Germany, in order of size are HAMBURG, MUNICH, COLOGNE, FRANKFURT AM MAIN, DORTMUND, DÜSSELDORF, and STUTTGART. The former West German capital, BONN, is still the seat of the government. The largest city in former East Germany, apart from Berlin, is LEIPZIG; other major cities are DRESDEN, CHEMNITZ, MAGDEBURG, and ROSTOCK.

Education and Health. The population is virtually 100% literate. Educational and cultural matters are the reponsibility of the individual states. In former West Germany, school attendance is compulsory for nine to ten years (depending on the state) and is free. Kindergarten, which originated in Germany, is for children ages three to six. After four years of primary school, children can go either to a nine-year GYMNASIUM (which is required for university admission), to a five-year vocational secondary school (the *Hauptschule*), or to an intermediate technical school (*Realschule*). A new comprehensive school (*Gesamts-*

chule) combines the curricula of all three types of traditional schools.

In former East Germany, the educational system was based on a 10-year basic polytechnical school, stressing science and technology. Secondary education was provided in professional and vocational schools and in specialized adult institutes. As in all other Communist countries, education was strictly supervised to conform to the official ideology of Marxism-Leninism.

The oldest German university is at HEIDELBERG (founded 1386), followed by that at Leipzig (1409). The linguist and philosopher Wilhelm von HUMBOLDT (1767–1835) is considered the father of the university system as it developed in the 19th century, when German universities set a new world standard by a skillful and successful combination of teaching and research.

In both parts of Germany, health standards are quite high. Compulsory health-insurance programs cover health, disability, unemployment, and accident costs.

Economic Activity

Germany experienced an industrial revolution following its political unification in 1871. Soon it exceeded other European countries in production and trade. Despite its defeat and territorial losses during World War I, Germany continued its economic progress until World War II. Then the country split, and each part followed a different economic course. With the help of MARSHALL PLAN aid from the United States, West Germany's economy quickly revived, and in the early 1950s the standard of living exceeded the prewar level. Meanwhile, East Germany had to pay REPARATIONS in the form of shipments of entire factories and industrial goods to the USSR. As in other Communist countries, centralized planning was introduced, industrial enterprises were nationalized, and agriculture was collectivized. By the 1980s, East Germany had become the leading industrial nation in Eastern Europe, but the full extent of its economic backwardness was revealed only after the unification in 1990. The estimates of the cost of economic rebuilding of former East Germany have been steadily rising.

Manufacturing. The former West Germany is one of the world's great industrial powers. Steel and chemicals are the leading products, and other major goods include automobiles, transportation equipment, heavy machinery, diverse small consumer goods, and precision instruments.

The former East Germany has built a large industrial sector, producing iron and steel, machine tools and engineering equipment, optics, and precision equipment. Former East Germany's industrial standing seemed quite high as long as it was compared to the other Soviet-bloc economies, but following the unification of Germany in 1990 it has become obvious that its industry is supremely inefficient and far below West German Standards. By early 1991 the East German manufacturing sector was collapsing, with many enterprises closing down and unemployment reaching up to 50% in some areas.

Mining and Energy. Coal, potash, and lignite are the basic mineral resources of former West Germany; other minerals include iron ore, lead, zinc, and copper. The

Berlin's Alexander Platz, one of the city's largest public squares, contains department stores, hotels, and the World Clock, which indicates the time in national capitals around the world.

RUHR VALLEY is the center of rich coking coal and other types of coal, with the Saar and the region near Aachen contributing the remainder. Lignite deposits, concentrated in the Cologne vicinity, occur in thick deposits close to the surface. Hard-coal production has declined significantly since 1970, while lignite production has undergone a moderate increase.

The former West Germany is independent in coal requirements, but has to import most of its needed petroleum (small quantities of petroleum are extracted from the North Sea). Domestic natural gas is produced in areas bordering the Netherlands and the North Sea. About one-third of its electric power is nuclear generated.

The former East Germany is mineral poor and until its unification with West Germany depended almost exclusively on Soviet raw materials. Potash, lignite, and a small natural-gas industry constituted most of the mining sector. Small amounts of iron, copper, tin, silver, and salt are also mined. Before unification about 10% of East Germany's energy was nuclear generated.

Agriculture, Forestry, and Fishing. Only a small minority of the labor force in former West Germany is engaged in agriculture, forestry, and fishing. In former East Germany, 95% of the farmland was collectivized, which hindered the performance of the agricultural sector, particularly during the 1950s. Both parts of Germany have been net importers of food. The envisioned privatization of agriculture in former East Germany will require a major readjustment.

The major food crops are oats, barley, wheat, rye, and

potatoes. In former West Germany, barley is of special importance for the brewing of beer. Well-developed animal husbandry has produced meat and dairy products for export. Industrial crops include hemp, flax, tobacco, and sunflowers.

The North Sea is the main fishing ground, and cod is the most important fish landed, but fishing accounts for only a minor portion of the GDP.

About 27% of former East Germany and 29% of former West Germany is covered by forests, much of it regarded as wood producing. Afforestation programs have been implemented in both parts of the country.

Trade. Free Trade within the EC (see EUROPEAN COMMUNITY) has played a major role in increasing former West Germany's foreign commerce. Food constitutes about one-tenth of its total imports; raw materials account for about a quarter and include sizable quantities of natural rubber, petroleum, and ores. Additional imports include such manufactured goods as machinery and automobiles. Exports include a wide range of industrial goods, raw materials and fuels, and food items.

Major export markets besides the EC are the United States, the non-EC European nations, and Japan. Since the 1970s, West Germany has been the leading Western trading partner of most East European countries.

During the period of Communist rule, most of East Germany's trade was with the other Communist nations, but trade with West Germany gained in importance in the 1970s and '80s and East Germany was sometimes called a "shadow partner" of the EC. East Germany's main exports were machinery, precision and optical instruments, chemicals, and textiles and clothing. Following the unification of Germany and the collapse of COMECON (see COUNCIL FOR MUTUAL ECONOMIC ASSISTANCE), the trade pattern of former East Germany began to change drastically.

Transportation. In former West Germany, the most important means of transportation is the federal railways; the rail network of nearly 70,000 km (20,000 mi) is 35% electrified. Road traffic has been growing rapidly and competing with the railroads; four-fifths of passenger transportation is by private car. West Germany has 7,400 km (4,600 mi) of express highways, called autobahns.

The East German transportation network will undergo changes as a result of its union with West Germany. The roads, railways, airports, and telecommunications are so rundown that a West German report described them as "wholly inadequate for rapid development of the five new federal states."

The canals and navigable rivers in both parts of Germany are important for bulk transport. The Rhine-Main-Danube Canal, to be completed in 1992, will enable vessels to travel from the North Sea to the Black Sea.

The former East German airline, Interflug, is to be dissolved in 1991; Lufthansa is the national West German airline.

Tourism and Services. In former West Germany, the service sector—including finance, trade, and public employees—engages a large portion of the labor force. West

Wearing traditional knickers and vest, members of a brass band give a concert in their town square. Germans from all regions of the country have perpetuated local traditions.

Diners enjoy a meal at a sidewalk cafe in the Marienplatz, the center of the old city of Munich. Munich historically has been the most important city of Bavaria.

(Left) *Karl Marx Platz, Neubrandenburg's central square, blends traditional and modern architectural styles. The city, located in Germany's northeastern lowlands, served as capital of the duchy of Mecklenburg-Stargard during the 14th and 15th centuries.* (Right) *Factories in the Ruhr River valley have been producing large quantities of iron and steel since the 19th century. Heavily bombed during World War II, the Ruhr was rebuilt and is now the center of Germany's steel, chemical, and petroleum-products industries.*

Germany's tourist industry is economically important. Popular areas include the Alps, the Rhine valley, coastal resorts, and the BLACK FOREST.

In former East Germany, the tourist industry was relatively small. Most of the foreign tourists visiting the country came from other Communist-bloc countries.

Government and Politics

The federal constitution of Germany, the Basic Law, was put into effect at a constitutional convention in 1949. The constitution provides for a president, a largely ceremonial post. The legislative branch consists of two houses: the Bundestag, or House of Representatives, and the Bundesrat, or Federal Council. The federal chancellor is the head of the government. Cabinet ministers are nominated by the chancellor and approved by the president.

Individual state governments have considerable power—the right to levy taxes, to establish educational and cultural policies, and to maintain police forces. Each state's chief official is a president elected by popular vote. Each state has its own parliament. The ten original states (*Länder*) were Baden-Württemberg (see BADEN; WÜRTTEMBERG), BAVARIA, BREMEN, HAMBURG, Hessen (see HESSE), Lower Saxony (see SAXONY), North Rhine-Westphalia (see WESTPHALIA), Rhineland-Palatinate (see RHINELAND; PALATINATE), Saarland, and SCHLESWIG-HOLSTEIN. In October 1990 these were joined by the five states of East Germany (which had been reestablished in July 1990): BRANDENBURG, MECKLENBURG–West Pomerania (see POMERANIA), Saxony, Saxony-Anhalt, and THURINGIA.

Germany has three main political parties—the Chris-

tian Democrats, with whom the Christian Social Union in Bavaria is closely associated (CDU/CSU); the Social Democratic party (SPD); and a smaller party associated with the CDU/CSU in the present government, the Free Democratic party (FDP).

The valleys and plateaus of Germany's Central Uplands are dotted with small farms, which produce a variety of grains and other crops. The heavily forested hills are a major source of timber, which is used primarily for paper.

(Above) *The Rhine-Main-Danube Canal, under construction in the 1980s, flows through the fertile river valleys of south central Germany. The canal links the tributaries of the Rhine with those of the Danube, providing a waterway from Rotterdam to the Black Sea.* (Below) *These women are assembling electronic instruments in a Berlin factory. The East German economy expanded rapidly after the 1960s, making the nation the most highly industrialized country of the Eastern European bloc.*

Following the toppling of the Communist leadership in East Germany in the fall of 1989, political parties were reconstituted and on Mar. 18, 1990, the first free multiparty elections took place. The East German Christian Democratic Union (CDU) and its allies won the largest share (48%) of the vote and formed a coalition government. In July the two Germanies formed an economic union extending the Federal Republic's free-market system to the East, and Chancellor Helmut KOHL won Soviet agreement to a reunited Germany within the NATO alliance.

On Oct. 3, 1990, the five reestablished East German states became part of the Federal Republic of Germany. Just before the unification the East and West German CDUs merged, and in December 1990, Kohl's CDU/CSU-FDP coalition was victorious in the first all-German elections since 1932.

See also: GERMAN ART AND ARCHITECTURE; GERMAN AND AUSTRIAN MUSIC; GERMAN LITERATURE.

Germany, history of German history has been marked by two major features. First, important political, social, and religious divisions have repeatedly raised questions about whether Germany can be thought of as a single entity. The second major feature is Germany's exposed geographical position. Without natural boundaries and often overshadowed by more powerful neighbors, Germany has been a frequent battleground. This has made Germans highly conscious of the need for security.

Ancient Germany

When the Romans first attempted to conquer the German lands late in the 1st century BC, they found them inhabited by a variety of GERMANIC PEOPLES, comprising perhaps 4 million individuals. These tribes had probably migrated from Scandinavia and the territory between the Elbe and Oder rivers between 1000 and 100 BC, displacing the CELTS as they did so. The ancient Germans lived in simple log houses grouped into villages, and the nearby fields were owned and tilled communally. Tribal government was primitively democratic, and assemblies of freemen made all important decisions, except in times of war, when elected kings temporarily held unlimited power. These ancient people worshiped a variety of gods and goddesses, and made human and other sacrifices to propitiate them.

The Romans, for all their efforts to conquer Germany between 12 BC and AD 16, met with only limited success. In AD 9, German forces under ARMINIUS annihilated three Roman legions in the Battle of Teutoburg Forest. The Romans avenged that defeat but then fell back to a 4,800-km (3,000-mi) fortified border, called the *limes,* which extended from the Rhine to the Danube.

The fact that most of Germany experienced little or no contact with the civilizing influences of Greco-Roman culture had far-reaching effects. Political allegiances remained with local leaders and traditional customs and were not transferred to a common state with unified laws and administration.

Charlemagne, the subject of this 9th-century bronze statue, extended Frankish rule as far east as the Elbe. The division of his empire by his grandsons eventually created (870) two Frankish realms: the East Frankish kingdom (Germany) and the West Frankish kingdom (France).

The Frankish Kingdom and Empire (481–919)

As the German tribes overran the Roman Empire in the 5th century, one tribe, the FRANKS, expanded from its base in northwest Germany until it controlled territories stretching from the Atlantic Ocean in the west to Bavaria and Thuringia in the east. The first great leader of the Franks, CLOVIS (r. 481–511), established the MEROVINGIAN dynasty, which lasted until 751. Clovis forged his empire by combining conquest, murder, and intrigue with conversion to Christianity. Once allied with the church it was only natural for him and his successors to sponsor the activities of missionaries in the eastern reaches of his realm. Thus the Frankish kingdom began the merger of Roman, German, and Christian elements that was the foundation of medieval German culture.

Charlemagne. The decline of the Merovingian dynasty in the 8th century placed power in the hands of royal officials, one of whom, CHARLES MARTEL (r. 714–41), established a new line of Frankish kings. This CAROLINGIAN dynasty was named after its greatest figure, Charles I (r. 768–814), better known as CHARLEMAGNE. Charlemagne conquered still more lands in Germany, including Bavaria in the east and Saxony in the north. To the SAXONS, particularly warlike and unruly, he gave the choice of death or conversion to Christianity.

Charlemagne made additional conquests in Italy and Spain, and when the pope crowned him emperor in 800, he was recognized as master of a revived Roman Empire in the West. This partial restoration and extension of political order was accompanied by a rebirth of interest in learning, which has been called the Carolingian Renaissance. To his palace at AACHEN in northwest Germany, Charlemagne brought scholars from all over Europe for the purpose of setting educational standards for the empire's monastery schools. The most important of these scholars, ALCUIN, had left his native England to supervise Charlemagne's own palace school. One of Alcuin's Frankish pupils, Einhard (c.770–840), wrote a biography of his emperor that is a major source of knowledge of the period (see CAROLINGIAN ART AND ARCHITECTURE).

Civil War and Disruption. These promising developments were reversed after Charlemagne's death. He himself had stipulated that his lands should be divided among his heirs after his death, according to the long-standing German tradition. The result was almost a century of civil war among the heirs and the eventual emergence (870) of two Frankish kingdoms, that of the West Franks (France) and that of the East Franks (Germany). The general chaos of these decades was complicated by invasions of barbarian VIKINGS and MAGYARS. FEUDALISM took hold in most of Germany as a means of preserving a modicum of law and order.

Medieval Germany (911–1517)

The last Carolingian king of the East Franks was Louis the Child (r. 899–911). On his death (911), LOTHARINGIA (Lorraine) was the only East Frankish duchy to transfer its allegiance to the Carolingian king of the West Franks. The dukes of BAVARIA, FRANCONIA, SAXONY, and SWABIA—the other so-called stem duchies—initially elected the duke of Franconia king of Germany as Conrad I. In 919, however, they turned to the house of Saxony as their best defense against the Magyars.

Otto I (left) founder of the Holy Roman Empire, presents Jesus with a model of Magdeburg Cathedral in this 10th-century plaque. As German king (936–73; emperor from 962), Otto extended German power into eastern Europe. (Metropolitan Museum of Art, New York.)

Frederick I kneels in submission to Pope Alexander III after Frederick's army was routed by the Italians in 1176. Frederick acknowledged Alexander as the true pope and abandoned his attempts to assert authority in Italy.

Saxon, Salian, and Hohenstaufen Dynasties. The first two Saxon kings, HENRY I and his son, OTTO I, were able to reassert the strength of a centralized monarchy. They stopped the Magyar onslaught and expanded German holdings into Eastern Europe—the so-called DRANG NACH OSTEN. They also established effective administrative machinery that succeeded in keeping the ambitious rival German dukes in line. Equally important in controlling the other dukes was the Saxon kings' claim to the title of Holy Roman emperor. When Otto I founded the HOLY ROMAN EMPIRE in 962, he gained both a powerful ally in the papacy and new sources of taxes in northern Italy.

Early in the 11th century, the Saxon line of monarchs died out, and the German princes began to elect a series of Salian (Franconian) kings. Of these, HENRY III (r. 1039–56) brought imperial control over the church to its pinnacle, deposing three rival popes in 1046 and nominating four popes in succession. His successor, HENRY IV, however, faced a resurgent papacy, which not only resisted lay control of the church but also allied with the German princes, who sought to win back the powers taken from them by the kings. This struggle, usually called the INVESTITURE CONTROVERSY, ended in 1122, essentially in victory for the papacy and the German nobility.

The HOHENSTAUFEN dynasty increased the power of the monarchy briefly. First elected to the throne in 1138, the

Hohenstaufens held it, despite vigorous challenge from the rival WELF family, until 1254. The dynasty's greatest figure, FREDERICK I (r. 1152–90), known as Barbarossa, chose to work within the feudal structure as a partner of the great princes. His successors were overwhelmed by a resurgent papal-aristocratic alliance and by French and English intervention. Only the brilliant FREDERICK II (r. 1212–50) was able to restore a measure of order, but he was so absorbed in Italian affairs that he neglected Germany. Hence, Germany fell once more into the hands of regional princes.

There were sufficient intervals in this turbulent age to permit some economic progress and cultural achievement. Cities and commerce made a solid resurgence, and impressive Romanesque cathedrals were built. The early 13th century was also the peak of the medieval German court epic, represented most notably by WOLFRAM VON ESCHENBACH, and of *Minnesang*, or lyric love poetry, whose great genius was WALTHER VON DER VOGELWEIDE.

Consolidation of Princely Rule. The period immediately following Frederick's death—the so-called Interregnum—was one of particular chaos. During this time the Hohenstaufens were finally extinguished, and foreign princes contested for the imperial title. In 1273, RUDOLF I of the house of HABSBURG was elected king. The German princes were suspicious of Habsburg territorial ambitions, however, and elected a series of kings from other dynasties in

The map indicates the political divisions and dynastic holdings within the Holy Roman Empire about 1176, the year in which the Hohenstaufen emperor Frederick I (Barbarossa) was defeated by the Lombard League in the Battle of Legnano.

GERMANY c.1176

- Welf territories
- Hohenstaufen territories
- Ascanian territories

—— Boundary of the Holy Roman Empire

0   km   300
0   mi   200

Holy Roman Emperor Maximilian I extended the power of the Habsburg dynasty by his own marriage to the Burgundian heiress Mary and his son's marriage into the Spanish royal house. Throughout his reign (1493–1519), Maximilian strove to curtail the power of the Valois dynasty, which ruled France.

Rise of the Habsburgs. The imperial title remained valuable to the ambitious Habsburgs as a symbol of sovereignty. From 1438, members of the ruling dynasty of AUSTRIA were elected Holy Roman emperors, with only one short break (1740–45) until the empire's dissolution in 1806. The ablest of the early Habsburgs, MAXIMILIAN I (r. 1493–1519), decreed "Eternal Peace" in 1495 in order to control the unruly imperial knights. He also created an imperial court of justice (Kammergericht) to help enforce his decrees.

The German princes responded by demanding an imperial governing council (Reichsrat) to control imperial policies. As constituted in 1500, it included several of the great princes and representatives of the imperial free cities, but it did not evolve into an effective organ of representative government. The additional divisions generated by the Reformation overwhelmed the council and left Germany as fragmented as ever.

Political fragmentation, however, did not retard growth in other areas. Germany's economic advances and its recovery from the calamity of the Black Death (1347–50; see BUBONIC PLAGUE) were reflected in the prosperity of the great northern trading cities that banded together into the HANSEATIC LEAGUE. The economic expansion was paralleled by technological developments, most notably the invention of movable type, attributed to Johann GUTENBERG of Mainz. The printing press had a major impact on the succeeding era, which was also distinguished by the achievements of artists such as Albrecht DÜRER, Hans HOLBEIN the Younger, Lucas CRANACH, and Matthias GRÜNEWALD.

succession to Rudolf. One of these kings, LOUIS IV (r. 1314–46) of the Bavarian house of WITTELSBACH, rallied the support of the German princes for his 1338 declaration asserting the authority of these princes to elect the emperor without confirmation by the pope.

CHARLES IV (r. 1347–78) of the house of Luxemburg formally acknowledged the principle of elective monarchy with the GOLDEN BULL of 1356, which regularized elections by naming seven electors: the archbishops of Mainz, Trier, and Cologne, the duke of Saxony, the margrave of Brandenburg, the count palatine of the Rhine, and the king of Bohemia. The Golden Bull thus confirmed the political realities of an age in which unified monarchy had become impossible in Germany.

Religion and Absolutism (1517–1789)

On Oct. 31, 1517, Martin LUTHER nailed to a church door in Wittenberg his 95 theses condemning the sale of INDULGENCES by the Roman Catholic church. This event is

Holy Roman Emperor Charles V (center), whose dynastic holdings included Spain, the Netherlands, and portions of Italy, as well as the traditional Habsburg territories of Austria, personally presided over the Diet of Augsburg (1530), convened in an attempt to reconcile differences between Catholics and Protestants in Germany. (Bibliothèque Nationale, Paris.)

usually taken to mark the beginning of the Protestant REFORMATION.

The Reformation. Luther's revolt soon became entangled in larger political and social issues. The peasants of much of Germany drew some unwarranted political conclusions from Luther's religious independence and rose in the PEASANTS' WAR in 1524. The revolt was suppressed, with Luther's help, but religious and social radicalism lived on in the ANABAPTIST sects.

Still more important were the political uses to which the German princes put LUTHERANISM. Emperor CHARLES V (r. 1519–56) found himself confronted simultaneously with a revolt by the Lutheran princes and free cities, organized into the League of Schmalkald, and a massive Turkish invasion of southeastern Europe. After a long and desperate struggle, the religious wars ended in a stalemate with the Peace of Augsburg (1555), which in effect recognized Lutheranism as the religion of most of northern and central Germany. Although the settlement was a great victory for Protestantism, it helped perpetuate and intensify Germany's political disintegration.

Thirty Years' War. The Peace of Augsburg did not solve Germany's basic political and religious problems. Luthe-

ranism and CALVINISM, a rival Protestant sect, continued to make progress, but the Habsburg emperors had not given up their goal of making the Holy Roman Empire into a modern, unified state.

These conflicting developments produced the THIRTY YEARS' WAR (1618–48), a series of four related wars. In it the Protestant states barely held their own, although they were aided by the Swedes and the French. When hostilities were ended by the Treaty of Westphalia (1648; see WESTPHALIA, PEACE OF), devastated Germany was still torn hopelessly apart, a collection of more than 300 virtually sovereign states without effective central government.

Rise of Brandenburg-Prussia. The state that was ultimately to unify Germany arose from unpromising beginnings. BRANDENBURG, in origin a small march (military frontier) state created on lands conquered from the Slavs on the north German plain in the 13th century, began to expand under its vigorous HOHENZOLLERN rulers in the 17th century. Its most important early acquisition was the duchy of PRUSSIA, which had been conquered by the TEUTONIC KNIGHTS in the 13th century and secularized in 1525. The territories of Brandenburg were further augmented by the Treaty of Westphalia.

The map of central Europe indicates the major territorial acquisitions formalized by the Treaty of Westphalia (1648), which concluded the Thirty Years' War. This conflict (1618–48), in which the German Protestant principalities in alliance with Denmark, Sweden, and France fought imperial, Spanish, and Bavarian forces to a standstill, left Germany physically devastated and politically fragmented.

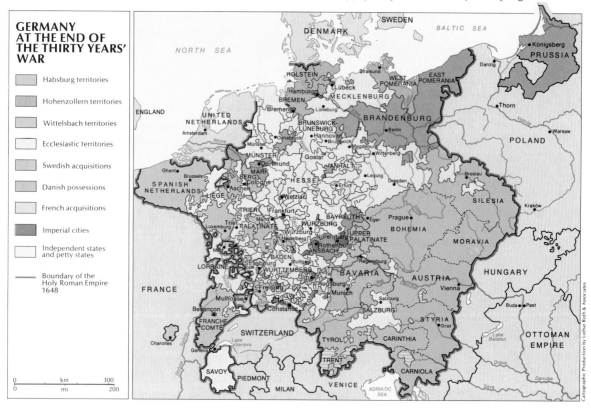

Frederick II (the Great) of Prussia used the efficient army created by his predecessors to challenge the dominance in Germany of Habsburg Austria. He seized Silesia from Austria in the War of Austrian Succession (1740–48) and retained it through the Seven Years' War (1756–63).

The most prominent of the early Hohenzollern rulers were FREDERICK WILLIAM, elector of Brandenburg (r. 1640–88), and his grandson FREDERICK WILLIAM I (r. 1713–40), king of Prussia (the rulers of Brandenburg-Prussia had assumed the title "king in Prussia" in 1701). They built an army that was far larger than those of other states of comparable population. Their purpose was originally defensive, but King FREDERICK II (r. 1740–86), later called the Great, used the army to expand Prussia's borders. As a result of the war of the AUSTRIAN SUCCESSION (1740–48) and the SEVEN YEARS' WAR (1756–63), Frederick won the valuable province of SILESIA from Austria. He also participated (1772), with Russia and Austria, in the first of three successive partitions of Poland (see POLAND, PARTITIONS OF). Like the other so-called enlightened despots of the 18th century, Frederick used authoritarian methods to modernize his government and society.

When Frederick died, Prussia was the largest and most significant state in Germany. Austria, with its imperial Habsburg dynasty, was still considered the dominant German state. However, its wars with Prussia had revealed serious weaknesses, and the reforms of MARIA THERESA and her son, emperor JOSEPH II, antagonized some of the Habsburgs' subjects.

These often chaotic years of religious and dynastic struggles caused German economic and cultural life to decline, although the astronomy of Johannes KEPLER and the novel *Simplicissimus* (1669; Eng. trans., 1924) by Hans Jakob von GRIMMELSHAUSEN were significant exceptions. Partial recovery during the 18th century helped to produce magnificent BAROQUE ART AND ARCHITECTURE and the equally monumental baroque and classical music of Johann Sebastian BACH, Wolfgang Amadeus MOZART, and Franz Josef HAYDN.

Nationalism and Unification (1789–1871)

During the wars of the French Revolution and the Napoleonic period, Germany was conquered by the French,

which instilled a sense of unity and nationalism in the German people. Even before that, Johann Gottfried von HERDER had urged Germans to cast off their servile imitation of the French. Prussia, although defeated by NAPOLEON I, carried out drastic military and social reforms and ultimately led the other German states in the victorious War of Liberation against the French in 1813. (See FRENCH REVOLUTIONARY WARS; NAPOLEONIC WARS.)

German Confederation. The dreams of German patriots were smashed by the peacemakers at the Congress of Vienna (1814–15; see VIENNA, CONGRESS OF). German states were bound loosely together in the GERMAN CONFEDERATION, which was dominated by the Habsburgs, who now called themselves emperors of Austria. For the time being, Prussia contented itself with instituting (1834) the ZOLLVEREIN, a tariff union that included most of the German states.

In the following decades the forces of conservatism, personified by the Austrian foreign minister Klemens von METTERNICH, were increasingly challenged by liberal ideas and by nationalism. During the REVOLUTIONS OF 1848, liberal concessions were granted in virtually all the German states, and representatives were elected to a national convention, the FRANKFURT PARLIAMENT, to unite Germany. However, divisions among the revolutionaries and the opposition of conservative Prussia, whose king, FREDERICK WILLIAM IV, refused to rule over a united German constitutional monarchy, caused the revolution to collapse in 1849.

Bismarck's Unification of Germany. The cause of German nationalism was taken up again in 1862 by Prussia's

The Revolutions of 1848 were aimed at securing constitutional government in the various German states and a united Germany. More radical republican groups, such as the one shown meeting here in Berlin, played a peripheral role.

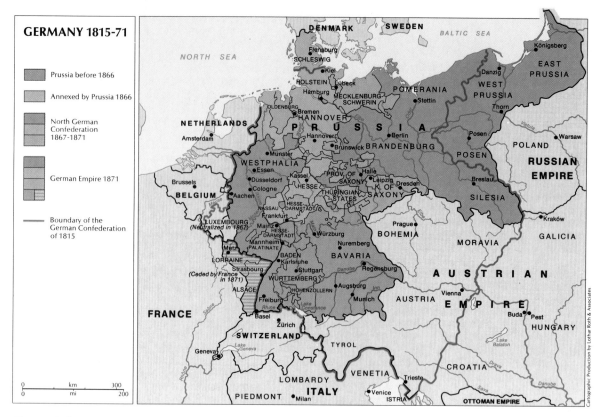

GERMANY 1815-71

Prussia before 1866

Annexed by Prussia 1866

North German Confederation 1867-1871

German Empire 1871

Boundary of the German Confederation of 1815

The map indicates the stages of German unification during the 19th century. The German Confederation, created in 1815, collapsed when Prussia defeated Austria in 1866. The North German Confederation united the northern states under a government dominated by Prussia. During the Franco-Prussian War (1870–71) the southern states joined the federation to form the German Empire.

new minister-president, Otto von BISMARCK. A conservative Prussian patriot, he was determined to steal the nationalist issue from the liberals and assure Prussian leadership in a united Germany. In a series of three wars, he eliminated first Danish, then Austrian, and finally French influence from Germany. From the Danes he gained SCHLESWIG-HOLSTEIN, and in the SEVEN WEEKS' WAR (1866) he defeated Austria. Bismarck then formed (1867) the North German Confederation, uniting the northern German states under a federal government dominated by Prussia. Three years later, during the FRANCO-PRUSSIAN WAR (1870–71), the southern German states joined the federation, and on Jan. 18, 1871, the Prussian king WILLIAM I was crowned emperor of a new German Reich at Versailles. With "blood and iron" tactics, Bismarck had thus succeeded where the German liberals had failed.

The years of growing German national consciousness were also great ones for German culture. Classical idealism reached its highest expression in the poetry and drama of Johann Wolfgang von GOETHE and the music of Ludwig van BEETHOVEN. Lasting influence on the development of philosophy was exerted by G. W. F. HEGEL, while romantic music found two of its geniuses in Robert SCHUMANN and Richard WAGNER.

Imperial Germany (1871–1918)

The German Empire, organized on a federal basis, retained the constitution Bismarck had created for the North German Confederation. It provided for a democratically elected parliament, the REICHSTAG, but granted it only limited powers. Real power lay with the Prussian king, who was also the German emperor (*Kaiser*), and his advisors.

Bismarck's Rule. Bismarck at first allied with his former foes, the liberals, to encourage the growth of industrial and commercial capitalism in Germany. Simultaneously, he fought the large Roman Catholic minority and its political arm, the Center party, as enemies of the new state. This campaign, known as the Kulturkampf, produced only short-term benefits since the Catholics resisted doggedly.

Bismarck ended the Kulturkampf in 1878 because he had concluded that the best way to deal with a severe economic depression was to protect German industry and agriculture with tariffs, a policy more acceptable to conservative than to liberal minds. The enemy, too, changed. This time it was Germany's mildly Marxist party, the Social Democratic party (SPD), that represented the growing industrial working class. In the 1880s, Bismarck had the SPD outlawed and tried to win over the German workers with the world's first comprehensive social security sys-

The rise of German industrialism was delayed by the lack of a strong central government. During the 1850s, however, the German states more than doubled their industrial output, creating the favorable economic conditions that led to the formation of a powerful, unified Germany.

tem. However, he was no more successful in suppressing the socialists than he had been with the Catholics. In 1890 the new emperor compelled him to resign.

Bismarck's foreign policy was far sounder than his domestic politics. Convinced that Germany had all the territory it needed, he promoted European stability by isolating France and diverting its attention to colonial expansion overseas. He won important allies for Germany by the TRIPLE ALLIANCE with Austria and Italy (1882) and the Reinsurance Treaty with Russia (1887). He endorsed German colonial expansion only half-heartedly, mainly to secure support for his domestic policies from nationalists and from industrial and commercial interests.

William II's Policies. William I was succeeded briefly by his son FREDERICK III and then by his grandson WILLIAM II (r. 1888–1918). The young William appreciated neither Bismarck's assumption that only Bismarck could govern

Germany nor his heavy-handed attempts to bludgeon minorities into submission. After forcing the Iron Chancellor to retire (1890), the new emperor attempted to dominate German politics himself. In order to conciliate the German working class, he dropped the anti-socialist laws and extended the social security system. The idea of political democracy did not appeal to him, however, and he resisted demands by the SPD and liberals for reform of Prussia's old, undemocratic constitution. The growth of reform sentiment and outrage over William's frequent blunders produced all the ingredients for a constitutional confrontation on the eve of World War I.

Not the least of the reformers' complaints concerned William II's inept foreign policy, in which he was guided by the foreign office official Friedrich von HOLSTEIN and by Bernhard von BÜLOW, who became foreign secretary in 1897 and chancellor in 1900. The emperor let the Rein-

King William I of Prussia is proclaimed German emperor at Versailles in 1871. The architect of this triumph and the whole process of German unification was Otto von Bismarck, who stands at the foot of the dais in a white uniform.

A famous British cartoon, "Dropping the Pilot," satirizes the dismissal of Bismarck by Germany's ruler, Emperor William II, in 1890. The emperor's reckless militarism and personal ambitions contributed to Germany's disastrous participation in World War I.

surance Treaty with Russia lapse in 1890. Four years later, France concluded an alliance with Russia. William then launched a naval arms race with Britain, and plunged into colonial adventures, thus further antagonizing both Britain and France. By 1909, when Bülow was succeeded as chancellor by the more sober Theobald von BETHMAN-HOLLWEG, Germany had only one reliable ally, Austria-Hungary.

These flaws were less apparent at the time because of imperial Germany's economic, scientific, and cultural achievements. Encouraged by government subventions, Germany experienced a dazzling economic growth between 1870 and 1910. German science and technology, supported by a sophisticated university system, came to be regarded as the world's best. At the same time, the early novels of Thomas MANN, the late romantic music of Johannes BRAHMS and Richard STRAUSS, and the apocalyptic philosophy of Friedrich NIETZSCHE helped maintain Germany's reputation as a major cultural center.

World War I. Eager to support its ally Austria in a dispute with Russia over Serbia, Germany helped precipitate WORLD WAR I in 1914 by sending an ultimatum to Russia and, when it was rejected, declaring war on both Russia and France, in accordance with the rigid war plan devised by Alfred von SCHLIEFFEN. Most Germans, even the SPD, supported the war effort at first, but their mood began to change when no swift victory could be won and terrible food shortages developed. When, in November 1918, it was obvious that Germany had to sue for peace, the German people rose in revolt against their leaders. Even the German generals pressed for the emperor's abdication. William went into exile in the Netherlands, and the Social Democrats took over the government, proclaimed a republic, and brought the war to an end.

Weimar and Nazi Germany (1918–45)

It is one of the great tragedies of modern history that Germany's first encounter with democratic government was associated with defeat and misery. The Social Democrats suppressed several Communist revolts, including the re-

Members of the Spartacus League, a revolutionary socialist group, march through the streets of Berlin during the "Spartacist Revolt" of January 1919. This Communist uprising was ruthlessly suppressed.

gime of Kurt EISNER in Bavaria. Early in 1919 a freely elected constituent assembly met in Weimar to write a constitution giving direct governing power to the Reichstag. SPD leader Friedrich EBERT was named president of the new Weimar Republic, and Philipp SCHEIDEMANN formed a coalition government of the SPD, the Center party, and a liberal group. This government soon resigned rather than sign the Treaty of Versailles, imposed by the PARIS PEACE CONFERENCE. However, Germany really had no choice. In June 1919 the Weimar Assembly voted to comply with the treaty, which deprived Germany of large amounts of land, people, and natural resources and forced it to pay enormous REPARATIONS.

Crisis and Recovery. The attempt to root parliamentary democracy in Germany was beset from the beginning by grave problems. There were too many political parties to form stable coalitions for effective government. Militant minorities—the Communists on the far left and monarchists and racists on the opposite extreme—sometimes resorted to force. Notable among these efforts was the MUNICH PUTSCH of 1923, in which the tiny National Socialist party led by Adolf HITLER made a somewhat farcical attempt to seize power in Bavaria.

The payment of reparations placed an enormous strain on a country already bankrupted by more than four years of war. As inflation mounted Germany suspended payment in 1922, provoking the French to occupy the Ruhr area in January 1923. Workers in Ruhr mines and factories resisted by striking, but such resistance contributed to inflation, which brought on economic collapse. The situation was saved in November 1923 when the ablest of Germany's republican politicians, Gustav STRESEMANN, introduced a new currency and improved Germany's relations with the western nations.

During the later 1920s, therefore, the German economy revived, and politics settled down. Also, during those years, a remarkable avant-garde culture blossomed in Germany, extending from the epic theater of Bertolt BRECHT, to the BAUHAUS school of functional art and architecture, to the relativity physics of Albert EINSTEIN, and to the existential philosophy of Martin HEIDEGGER.

This new Germany was cut down in its infancy by the onset of the DEPRESSION OF THE 1930S and the Nazi seizure of power. Depression conditions once more radicalized politics and so divided the parties in the Reichstag that parliamentary government became all but impossible. The main beneficiary of these developments was Hitler's National Socialist party, which had the twin attractions of appearing to offer radical solutions to economic problems while upholding patriotic values. By 1932 it was the largest party in the Reichstag, and the following year President Paul von HINDENBURG appointed Hitler chancellor.

Nazi Dictatorship. Most Germans who supported Hitler during his rise to power did so out of desperation, scarcely knowing what he planned to do. They received much more than they had bargained for. After half-persuading, half-coercing the Reichstag to grant him absolute power, Hitler lost no time in founding a totalitarian state, known unofficially as the THIRD REICH—supposedly in the tradi-

EXPANSION OF GERMANY 1933-42

- Germany in 1933
- Re-militarized in 1936
- Annexed *before* Sept.1, 1939
- Annexed *after* Sept.1, 1939
- Allied with Germany
- Occupied by Germany
- Boundary of Greater Germany in 1942 (The Reich)

The map of Germany (1933–42) shows, in chronological progression, how Hitler conducted his campaign to expand the Third Reich. Not appearing on the map are the extensive areas in North Africa and the Soviet Union controlled by the military forces of the Reich and its Axis allies.

tion of the Holy Roman Empire and the unified German Empire set up by Bismarck. When confronted by demands from Storm Trooper (SA) leader Ernst ROEHM and others for a second revolution that would make good on

Nazi claims to socialist ideals, Hitler purged Roehm and his associates on the weekend of June 30, 1934. Four years later, he forced out two of the top generals on trumped-up charges in order to assure himself of full control of the expanding German armed forces. Thanks to a ruthless secret police (the GESTAPO) and a CONCENTRATION CAMP system under the direction of SS (Schutzstaffel) leader Heinrich HIMMLER, known enemies of Nazism were put away and potential ones terrorized. (See also NAZISM.)

Hitler's virulent racism gave rise to a cruel system of anti-Semitism. The Nuremberg Laws of September 1935 deprived Jews of most civil rights, and official anti-Semitism later culminated in a policy of deliberate extermination during World War II, taking the lives of approximately 6 million European Jews. More immediately, however, a state program of ending unemployment with public works projects and a restoration of business confidence produced remarkable economic recovery. Joseph GOEBBELS's efficient propaganda ministry controlled the media to assure that Hitler would be viewed as a genius and Nazi Germany as the best of all possible worlds. Given this combination of coercion, achievement, and thought control, it is perhaps not surprising that there was little resistance.

World War II. Hitler's foreign policy goals were determined by his belief that Germany was overpopulated and needed to conquer Europe in order to secure *Lebensraum* (living space) in Poland and Russia. The 1936 remilitarization of the Rhineland, from which troops had been banned by the Versailles treaty; the annexation of Austria (the so-called Anschluss) in 1938; and the dismemberment of Czechoslovakia in 1938–39 (initiated at the MUNICH CONFERENCE) were all accomplished without interference by the other European powers.

When Britain and France finally declared war (Sept. 3,

(Below) *Adolf Hitler assumed leadership of the National Socialist German Workers' (NAZI) party after Germany's defeat in World War I. Using his position as chancellor, and later as führer, Hitler transformed the nation into a militarist Fascist state.* (Left) *Hitler delivers one of his charismatic orations at a rally in Nuremberg.*

1939) after the German invasion of Poland, Hitler found himself involved in war on a much larger scale than he had expected. A series of initially successful *Blitzkriege* (lightning campaigns) against Poland (1939), western Europe (1940), and the USSR (1941) made him temporary master of most of Europe. But, unable to destroy Britain and Russia, Hitler found himself confronted by an overwhelmingly powerful enemy coalition, including (after December 1941) the United States. The German collapse began in mid-1944, and when Hitler committed suicide in Berlin in April 1945, Germany was largely in ruins and at the mercy of the countries it had ravaged. (See WORLD WAR II.)

History since 1945

After the German capitulation the Allies—the United States, France, Great Britain, and the USSR—divided Germany into four occupation zones, and tried the major Nazi war criminals before an International Military Tribunal at Nuremberg (see NUREMBERG TRIALS). Berlin, located within the Soviet zone, was at first jointly administered by the four powers, each occupying a sector of the city. According to the terms of the POTSDAM CONFERENCE (August 1945), Germany lost its territory east of the Oder and western Neisse rivers (see ODER-NEISSE LINE) to Poland and a major part of Prussia to the USSR. Together the lands totaled about 25 percent of the former German Reich. Subsequently 5.5 million ethnic Germans were expelled from Poland, and 3.5 million Sudeten Germans were forced to leave Czechoslovakia. Perhaps another 4 million Germans left their ancestral homes in Romania, Yugoslavia, and Hungary, and most of them settled in areas that became West Germany.

Meanwhile, tensions between the USSR and the Western allies grew into the COLD WAR. In March 1948 the USSR left the Allied Control Council and between June of that year and September 1949 blockaded West Berlin. The U.S. and British air fleets supplied the city through the huge "Berlin Airlift," and the USSR was finally forced to reopen its access routes.

On Sept. 21, 1949, the Western powers established the Federal Republic of Germany, and the following month the Soviet zone of Germany was proclaimed the German Democratic Republic. Konrad ADENAUER (Christian Democratic Union, or CDU) was elected the first West German chancellor, and Walter ULBRICHT became the leader of East Germany.

Under Adenauer (1950–63), West Germany was transformed from a defeated enemy to a valuable partner. With the help of the MARSHALL PLAN, the German "economic miracle" took place, and on May 5, 1955, full sovereignty was restored when the Western powers eliminated the occupation regime. West Germany became a member of the NORTH ATLANTIC TREATY ORGANIZATION (NATO) in 1955 and in 1958 it was one of the founding members of the EUROPEAN COMMUNITY.

The regime in East Germany developed differently. It was firmly controlled by the Communist party (formally known as the German Socialist Unity party, or SED), which had been formed in 1946 by a forced merger be-

tween the Communist and Social Democratic parties. An anti-Soviet uprising in June 1953 was easily crushed by Soviet troops. During the 1950s, East Germany became a member of the WARSAW TREATY ORGANIZATION and the COUNCIL FOR MUTUAL ECONOMIC ASSISTANCE (COMECON).

Many East Germans fled to West Berlin and West Germany, and the East German government decided to put a stop to this continuing exodus by constructing a barbed-wire fence along its entire border and finally creating the Berlin Wall in August 1961. By then about 3.5 million people had left East Germany.

Soon after that, Chancellor Adenauer was forced to resign (1963); his economics minister, Ludwig ERHARD, replaced him. Erhard won the 1965 election, but differences within his party forced his resignation in 1966. With Erhard's resignation, a grand coalition was formed by the CDU and its Bavarian affiliate, the Christian Social Union (SCU), and the SPD (Social Democratic party) with Kurt Georg Kiesinger as federal chancellor and Willi BRANDT as foreign minister.

In 1969 a new party coalition was formed between the SPD and the Free Democratic party (FDP), with Brandt as chancellor. The new government established an entirely new policy for relations with East Germany and the USSR, known as *Ostpolitik*. An important change took place in East Germany as well. In 1970, the hard-line Stalinist Walter Ulbricht was replaced by a more pragmatic Erich HONECKER, who later became the first East German head of state to visit West Germany. West Germany signed a series of treaties with the Soviet-bloc countries, including a 1972 treaty between East and West Germany in which the two states recognized each other's borders and sovereignty.

In May 1974, Chancellor Brandt resigned following the exposure of an East German spy on his staff. He was succeeded by Helmut SCHMIDT (SPD). In 1982 the FDP switched its support to the CDU/CSU, enabling that party to return to power under Helmut KOHL. The Kohl government won a secure majority in the election of March 1983 and won a second but closer victory in January 1987.

By that time Mikhail GORBACHEV had been in power in the USSR for two years, and his "new thinking" in foreign policy was opening the doors for democratic reform in Eastern Europe. Poland and Hungary were the first countries that began to dismantle their Communist regimes, and by the summer of 1989 popular demand for change rose in East Germany. Beginning in the summer of that year, nearly a quarter of a million East Germans fled to the West through Hungary and Czechoslovakia, provoking a crisis that forced the resignation of Honecker. In rapid succession there followed the opening of the Berlin Wall (November 9), the first free elections in East Germany (March 1990), the monetary union between East and West Germany in July 1990, and the accession of East Germany to the Federal Republic on Oct. 3, 1990.

germination [jur-min-ay'-shuhn]   Germination is the resumption of growth of a plant seed, spore, or bud after a period of DORMANCY. The main feature of germination is the increased rate of respiration, that is, the biologic "burning," or oxidation, of carbohydrate to provide energy for metabolism and growth. The viability, or the ability to germinate after prolonged periods of time, varies greatly among different species. The spores of mosses and other lower plants reputedly remain viable for thousands or even millions of years, but this belief has not been substantiated. Among the best-documented spore survivals are those of slime molds, which may remain viable for more than 50 years. Some seed plants, however, have shown remarkable viability. The seeds of toadflax, *Spergula arvensis*, found in Denmark, sprouted after 1,700 years. The record for dormancy is held by the Arctic lupine, *Lupinus arcticus*, whose seeds were found in the frozen permafrost layer of earth in the Yukon, Canada, in 1954 and were determined by the radiocarbon method to be at least 10,000 and possibly as much as 15,000 years old. These seeds germinated in a laboratory in 1966.

Geronimo, a leader of the Chiricahua Apaches, conducted a series of raids against both Mexican and American settlements in the Southwest. In 1876 the tribe was confined to Arizona's San Carlos Reservation, but Geronimo and his followers repeatedly escaped. After eluding federal troops for nearly a year, Geronimo finally surrendered in 1886.

Gernsback, Hugo [gurnz'-bak] Editor, publisher, and inventor Hugo Gernsback, b. Luxembourg, Aug. 16, 1884, d. Aug. 19, 1967, is best known for his founding of *Amazing Stories* (1926), the first magazine devoted to "scientifiction" (as Gernsback called it)—a new genre of fiction based loosely on science laced with a good deal of fantasy. Other, rival magazines quickly followed, and eventually SCIENCE FICTION became an established field of imaginative writing. The annual Hugo Award, given to the best new science fiction of the year is named in Gernsback's honor.

Gérôme, Jean Léon [zhay-rohm'] The French painter and sculptor Jean Léon Gérôme, b. May 11, 1824, d. Jan. 10, 1904, was one of the most notable academic artists of the second half of the 19th century. He achieved immediate acclaim for his *Cockfight* (1847; Louvre, Paris), which has remained his most famous painting.

Following his appointment (1863) as professor at the École des Beaux-Arts and his election (1865) to the Institut de France, he concentrated on meticulously drawn and highly finished depictions of historical episodes from ancient times, such as *Pollice verso*, or *Thumbs down* (1874; Phoenix Art Gallery, Ariz.) and *The Death of Caesar* (1867; Walters Art Gallery, Baltimore, Md.). From about 1878, Gérôme turned his attention to sculpture, often innovatively combining marble with bronze, precious stones, and ivory.

Geronimo [jur-ahn'-i-moh] Geronimo, b. 1829 in southern Arizona, d. Feb. 17, 1909, was an APACHE war leader noted for his guerrilla raids against Mexican and later U.S. troops in the American Southwest. A member of the Deindai band of the Chiricahua Apache, he was called *Goyathlay* (meaning "one who yawns") in Apache.

In 1850 the ambush killing of his first wife and children kindled in Geronimo an undying hatred of Mexicans. As leader of the avenging Apache at Arispe in Sonora, he performed such daring feats that the Mexicans singled him out with the sobriquet *Geronimo* (Spanish for "Jerome"). Some attributed his numerous raiding successes to powers conferred by supernatural beings, including a reputed invulnerability to bullets.

Geronimo's war career was linked with that of his brother-in-law, Juh, a Chiricahua chief. Although he was not a hereditary leader, Geronimo appeared so to outsiders because he often acted as spokesman for Juh, who had a speech impediment. In 1875, U.S. authorities branded Geronimo the chief opponent of the policy to consolidate all Apache and called for his hanging to end the disruption. When the Chiricahua were forcibly removed (1876) to arid land at San Carlos, in eastern Arizona, Geronimo fled with a band of followers into Mexico. He was soon arrested and returned to the new reservation. For the remainder of the 1870s, he and Juh alternated between raiding attacks and a quiet life on the reservation, but with the slaying of an Apache prophet in 1881, they returned to full-time hit-and-run raiding activities from a secret camp in the Sierra Madre Mountains.

Three times during the next five years Geronimo surrendered to the army, only to lead his people to escape from the reservation. After he surrendered to Gen. Nelson MILES on Sept. 4, 1886, the government breached its agreement and transported Geronimo and nearly 450 Apache men, women, and children to Florida for confinement in Forts Marion and Pickens. In 1894 they were removed to Fort Sill in Oklahoma.

Geronimo became a rancher, appeared (1904) at the Louisiana Purchase Exposition in St. Louis, sold Geronimo souvenirs, and rode in President Theodore Roosevelt's 1905 inaugural parade.

gerontology SEE GERIATRICS; MEDICINE

Gerry, Elbridge [gair'-ee, el'-brij] Elbridge Gerry, b. Marblehead, Mass., July 17, 1744, d. Nov. 23, 1814, was a signer of the U.S. Declaration of Independence, a congressman, governor of Massachusetts, and vice-president of the United States (1813–14). He graduated from Harvard College in 1762 and became an early advocate of American independence. Gerry served in the Massachusetts Provincial Congress (1774–75) and the Continental Congress (1776–80, 1783–85). He was a delegate to the Constitutional Convention of 1787, but refused to sign the Constitution because it did not agree with his ideas on republicanism.

Gerry was elected to the House of Representatives in 1789, after declaring that he would support the Constitution. In 1797 President John Adams appointed him a member of the mission to France that became involved in the XYZ AFFAIR, during which he was at odds with his fellow negotiators, John MARSHALL and Charles C. Pinckney (see PINCKNEY family). Gerry was elected governor of Massachusetts in 1810 and in 1812 signed into law a redistricting bill designed to ensure continued majorities for his party, the Democratic-Republicans; this political maneuver was named the gerrymander for him. That year he was elected vice-president under James MADISON.

gerrymander [jair'-ee-man-dur] A gerrymander is an election district whose boundaries have been redrawn by the party in power for its own political advantage, usually by excluding areas in which the opposing party is strong or including areas in which it is weak. The word originated in 1812, during Elbridge Gerry's second term as governor of Massachusetts, when the legislature redistricted the state so as to give the Democratic-Republicans an advantage in state senatorial elections. One of the new senatorial districts was particularly sprawling. An artist jokingly added wings, claws, and teeth to its outline, prompting the suggestion that it resembled a salamander. Benjamin Russell, a staunchly Federalist newspaper editor, gave it the name *Gerrymander*, referring to the Democratic-Republican governor.

The U.S. Supreme Court has ruled that legislative dis-

In1812 the Massachusetts legislature rearranged the senatorial districts to favor the dominant Democratic-Republican party. One strangely shaped district in Essex County was caricatured as a salamander and was soon dubbed a "gerrymander," after Gov. Elbridge Gerry.

tricts must contain roughly equal numbers of people, but legislatures are still permitted to draw district lines so as to give a particular party or faction an electoral advantage.

Gershwin, George and Ira [gur'-shwin] The composer of *Rhapsody in Blue* and PORGY AND BESS, George Gershwin, b. Brooklyn, N.Y., Sept. 26, 1898, d. July 11, 1937, was one of America's most versatile and popular songwriters. With his brother Ira, b. Dec. 6, 1896, d. Aug. 17, 1983, he was also the creator of the first musical comedy to win the Pulitzer Prize for drama, *Of Thee I Sing*. A talented pianist, George left school at age 15 to become a "song plugger" in New York's Tin Pan Alley. His brother Ira fared poorly at the piano but compensated for this deficiency years later by writing the words to most of George's songs.

The American composer George Gershwin gained renown for his popular Broadway musicals of the 1920s. He began his career as a jazz pianist and created a landmark in American music with Rhapsody in Blue (1924), in which the style of the piano concerto is blended with symphonic jazz.

"Swanee" (1919), popularized by Al Jolson, was Gershwin's first hit song. From 1920 to 1924 he wrote songs for the *George White's Scandals* revues and met Paul Whiteman, who commissioned him to write a jazz piece for a concert at Aeolian Hall in New York City. The result, *Rhapsody in Blue* (1924), was orchestrated by Ferde Grofé and first performed, with Gershwin as piano soloist, with great success. The conductor of the New York Symphony, Walter Damrosch, asked Gershwin for a symphonic work, and the composer complied with his *Concerto in F* (1925). After further studies in composition, Gershwin wrote other classical-oriented works such as *An American in Paris* (1928) and *Second Rhapsody* (1931). Meanwhile, with his brother Ira as lyricist, he had also composed the musical shows *Lady Be Good* (1924), *Strike up the Band* (1927), *Girl Crazy* (1930), and *Of Thee I Sing* (1931).

One of Gershwin's deepest ambitions was the creation of an American opera, and this ambition he achieved with *Porgy and Bess* (1935), based on the book by DuBose Heyward and with lyrics by Heyward and Ira Gershwin. The opera was Gershwin's last major work. He died of a brain tumor two years later in Hollywood, where he and Ira had been writing songs for films.

Gerson, Jean le Charlier de [zhair-sohn'] Jean le Charlier de Gerson, b. Dec. 13, 1363, d. July 12, 1429, was a French theologian and chancellor of the University of Paris who was instrumental in ending the Great SCHISM (1378–1417), a period during which the Christian church was divided by rival claimants to the PAPACY. He played a leading role at the Council of CONSTANCE (1414–18), advocating CONCILIARISM.

Gerson devoted his last ten years to a life of asceticism. His most important work is *Montagne de contemplation* (The Mountain of Contemplation, 1397), in which he proposed mystical teachings.

Gersonides see LEVI BEN GERSHON

Gestalt psychology [ge-shtahlt'] Gestalt psychology was a movement in experimental psychology that originated just prior to World War I and that made significant contributions to the study of PERCEPTION and PROBLEM SOLVING. German researchers such as Kurt KOFFKA, Wolfgang KÖHLER, and Max WERTHEIMER began studying the way in which percepts are determined by context, configuration, and meaning, instead of by the accumulation of separable sensory elements. (*Gestalt* translates from German as "configuration.") They identified several new perceptual phenomena.

The focus on meaning and "seeing as" also informed the Gestalt psychologist's studies of higher mental processes, which laid the foundations for later work in COGNITIVE PSYCHOLOGY. These were step-by-step accounts, notably those of Wertheimer and Karl Duncker, of how chimpanzees and human beings approach puzzling situations.

Since the 1950s the term *Gestalt* has been adopted to describe certain psychotherapies. Gestalt psychotherapies, pioneered by Fritz PERLS, assume that the human organism responds holistically to life events—that separation of mind and body is artificial. The theory emphasizes awareness and the accurate perception of oneself, of one's needs, and of the world. Experience can become unbalanced when the person avoids awareness of unpleasant events—the holistic response or Gestalt is then broken and incomplete. Incomplete or unfinished Gestalten may be carried with an individual and may interfere with later experiences of a similar nature.

Gestapo [ge-stah'-poh] The Geheime Staatspolizei (Secret State Police), known as the Gestapo, was, together with the SS (Schutzstaffel, or Black Shirts), the mainstay of power of the German National Socialists under Adolf HITLER. Originally formed (1933) by Hermann GOERING as a political police unit in the state of Prussia, it gradually came under the control of Heinrich HIMMLER. The day-to-day operations of the Gestapo were handled by Heinrich Müller, supervised by Reinhard Heydrich, and after January 1943 by Ernst Kaltenbrunner, under the overall authority of Himmler as leader of the SS. At its height, in 1943–45, the Gestapo had 40,000 to 50,000 employees.

The Gestapo's task was to suppress opposition to the regime inside Germany and, after World War II began, in the occupied territories. One of its six sections dealt with the Jews and was headed by the notorious Adolf EICHMANN. Its methods included savage interrogation techniques, torture, outright murder, and imprisonment in CONCENTRATION CAMPS. The Gestapo, with the help of the SS, put about 4 million Jews in these camps for extermination and murdered an additional 2 million Jews as well as many others in the wake of the advancing German armies.

gestation [jes-tay'-shuhn] Gestation is the process by which the females of viviparous animals—those which give birth to live young—carry the young internally from conception to birth. In mammals it is synonymous with pregnancy (see PREGNANCY AND BIRTH). The gestation period, or interval between fertilization and birth, varies considerably among the different mammalian species. Examples, given as mean length in days, are Syrian hamster 16, mouse 20, rabbit 31, dog 61, cat 63, pig 113, sheep 148, human 267, cattle 284, horse 337, Indian elephant 645. The period is obviously related to the size of the adult, but there may also be a complementary adaptive adjustment to the time of the mating season, so that the young are born when food is abundant. The young of marsupials are born in a very immature state, and the period of gestation is generally shorter. It is said to be only 12 days in the Virginia opossum.

VIVIPARITY occurs in some species of many classes of animals, including coelenterates, insects, fish, and reptiles, as well as mammals. It is an adaptation that safeguards the young during the early and highly vulnerable stages of development, but at the cost of reduced numbers of progeny and greatly increased physiological demands on the females.

The fetus is nourished internally through a placenta, which connects fetus and mother. In addition to supplying nutrition, the placenta performs the fetal respiratory and excretory functions by exchanging substances between the blood of the mother and that of the fetus.

The initiation and termination of gestation are signaled, and its maintenance regulated, by hormones produced principally in the pituitary gland, the ovaries, the chorion, and the placenta. Details vary greatly, even between closely related species. The maintenance of pregnancy appears, however, to depend on a continuous supply of a progestogen, which in most species investigated is the SEX HORMONE progesterone.

Gesualdo, Carlo [jay-zoo-ahl'-doh] Carlo Gesualdo, prince of Venosa, b. *c.*1560, d. Sept. 8, 1613, was one of the leading Italian MADRIGAL composers of the Renaissance. He was born into a noble family of Naples; his uncle was Saint Charles Borromeo. He was already a noted composer when in 1590 he ordered the murder of his wife and her lover, which caused a scandal that spread throughout Italy. His first four books of madrigals were published (1594–96) in Ferrara, were he lived with his second wife. Two other books of madrigals and three volumes of sacred music followed. Gesualdo's late works, in which contrapuntal and homophonic elements mingle freely, are remarkable for the intensity of their musical expression. Their daring harmonic progressions and striking chromaticism anticipate the music of Richard Wagner.

Gethsemane [geth-sem'-uh-nee]   Gethsemane is the place on the Mount of Olives near Jerusalem where Jesus Christ was betrayed by Judas Iscariot and arrested while praying with his disciples after the Last Supper. The name (Matt. 26:36; Mark 14:32) may have meant "oil vat," suggesting a stand of olive trees. John's Gospel (18:1) refers to the site as a garden; hence, the composite designation, the Garden of Gethsemane. Despite several conjectures, the site is not precisely identifiable today.

Getty, J. Paul [get'-ee]   Jean Paul Getty, b. Minneapolis, Minn., Dec. 15, 1892, d. June 6, 1976, amassed an enormous fortune estimated at more than a billion dollars. With backing from his father, an oil tycoon, Getty entered the oil business in Oklahoma. By the time he was 23 he had made his first million dollars. During the depression years of the 1930s he put together a network of companies through stock purchases. The Tidewater, Skelly, and Getty companies were the primary links in his vast domain. He lived most of his life in hotel rooms, and his chief indulgence was collecting art. He owned a 16th-century estate (Sutton Place) in England and established the Getty Museum in Malibu, Calif. Among his books were *My Life and Fortunes* (1963), *How to Be Rich* (1966), and *As I See It* (1976).

Getty Museum   The J. Paul Getty Museum was founded in 1954 by the oil magnate and art collector on his estate overlooking the Pacific Ocean in Malibu, Calif. The collections, originally displayed in a Spanish-style villa, are now housed in a sumptuous and meticulously researched re-creation of the Villa of the Papyri (begun 2d century BC) in Herculaneum, buried by the eruption of Mount Vesuvius in AD 79. Opened in 1974, the museum and its gardens were designed to enhance Getty's Greek and Roman art collection. The museum also houses important Renaissance and baroque paintings and a superlative collection of French decorative arts from about 1670 to 1790. Getty bequeathed (1976) the museum an endowment in excess of $700 million, which had appreciated to $1.1 billion by the time the funds were actually transferred in 1982. The museum is thus by far the richest in the world.

Gettysburg [get'-eez-burg]   Gettysburg, site of the great Civil War battle (July 1–3, 1863) is situated in rolling fruit-orchard country in southern Pennsylvania. The borough has a population of 7,025 (1990) and is the seat

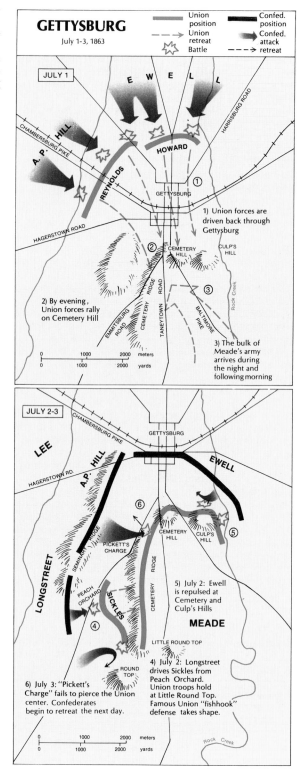

GETTYSBURG
July 1-3, 1863

Union position | Confed. position
Union retreat | Confed. attack
Battle | retreat

JULY 1

EWELL

HARRISBURG ROAD

CHAMBERSBURG PIKE

A. P. HILL

HOWARD

REYNOLDS

GETTYSBURG

HAGERSTOWN ROAD

1) Union forces are driven back through Gettysburg

CEMETERY HILL   CULP'S HILL

Rock Creek

2) By evening, Union forces rally on Cemetery Hill

EMMITSBURG ROAD   CEMETERY RIDGE ROAD   TANEYTOWN ROAD   BALTIMORE PIKE

3) The bulk of Meade's army arrives during the night and following morning

0   1000   2000   meters
0   1000   2000   yards

JULY 2-3

CHAMBERSBURG PIKE

GETTYSBURG

LEE

A. P. HILL

EWELL

HAGERSTOWN RD.

SEMINARY RIDGE

PICKETT'S CHARGE

CEMETERY HILL   CULP'S HILL

LONGSTREET

PEACH ORCHARD

SICKLES

CEMETERY RIDGE

5) July 2: Ewell is repulsed at Cemetery and Culp's Hills

MEADE

LITTLE ROUND TOP

ROUND TOP

4) July 2: Longstreet drives Sickles from Peach Orchard. Union troops hold at Little Round Top. Famous Union "fishhook" defense takes shape.

6) July 3: "Pickett's Charge" fails to pierce the Union center. Confederates begin to retreat the next day.

0   1000   2000   meters
0   1000   2000   yards

Rock Creek

of Adams County. It has been a college community since before the Civil War, the seat of a theological seminary and of Gettysburg College. The town has iron mines and granite quarries, but most important to its economy is the 1,380-ha (3,409-acre) National Military Park, which draws thousands of visitors every year. Adjoining the battlefield is the farm of Dwight D. Eisenhower. The borough was founded in the 1780s and named for James Gettys, to whom William Penn originally granted the land.

Abraham Lincoln was asked to deliver a speech at the ceremony dedicating a national cemetery at the site of the Civil War battle at Gettysburg, Pa. His brief remarks on Nov. 19, 1863, known as the Gettysburg Address, contain one of the most concise and eloquent definitions of democracy.

Gettysburg, Battle of The Battle of Gettysburg, one of the most important battles of the U.S. Civil War, was fought at Gettysburg, Pa., on July 1–3, 1863. Gen. Robert E. LEE invaded Pennsylvania for strategical and logistical reasons. His army of about 75,000 encountered the Union Army of the Potomac, about 90,000 strong, under Gen. George G. MEADE on the outskirts of Gettysburg on July 1. In a battle of considerable movement, Lee tested first the Union right (July 1) and then, in an assault led by Gen. James LONGSTREET, the left (July 2). On July 3, Gen. George PICKETT led perhaps the most famous charge in American military history against the Union center. Only 5,000 of his original force of 15,000 survived the repulse.

Lee watched the survivors return and confessed, "It is all my fault." Gettysburg, a military and logistical disaster for the South, cost Lee 20,000 men (killed and wounded) and 30,000 arms. Meade lost almost as many men. The battle had considerable psychological effect on both North and South, calling forth President Lincoln's Gettysburg Address. Occurring in the same week that Vicksburg fell to Gen. Ulysses S. Grant, Gettysburg put the Confederates on the defensive in the east.

Gettysburg Address On Nov. 19, 1863, President Abraham Lincoln dedicated a national cemetery on the battlefield at Gettysburg, where a few months earlier over 7,000 men had died. Although Lincoln's address received little attention at the time, it has since come to be esteemed as one of the finest speeches in the English language.

Fourscore and seven years ago our fathers brought forth on this continent a new nation, conceived in liberty and dedicated to the proposition that all men are created equal. Now we are engaged in a great civil war, testing whether that nation or any nation so conceived and so dedicated can long endure. We are met on a great battlefield of that war. We have come to dedicate a portion of that field as a final resting-place for those who here gave their lives that that nation might live. It is altogether fitting and proper that we should do this. But in a larger sense, we cannot dedicate, we cannot consecrate, we cannot hallow this ground. The brave men, living and dead who struggled here have consecrated it far above our poor power to add or detract. The world will little note nor long remember what we say here, but it can

never forget what they did here. It is for us the living rather to be dedicated here to the unfinished work which they who fought here have thus far so nobly advanced. It is rather for us to be here dedicated to the great task remaining before us—that from these honored dead we take increased devotion to that cause for which they gave the last full measure of devotion—that we here highly resolve that these dead shall not have died in vain, that this nation under God shall have a new birth of freedom, and that government of the people, by the people, for the people shall not perish from the earth.

geyser [gy'-zur] A geyser is a HOT SPRING that periodically throws hot water and steam into the air, sometimes to a great height and for a considerable length of time. The word *geyser,* which means to "gush forth," comes from Iceland, where there are about 30 active geysers. By far the most spectacular and the largest number, some 200, are in YELLOWSTONE NATIONAL PARK.

Geysers are located near geologically recent (within the last 1 million years) volcanic activity, especially in regions where precipitation is heavy. Yellowstone National Park is a huge collapsed VOLCANO, or caldera, that erupted about 600,000 years ago; geysers in New Zealand, Iceland, and Kamchatka, USSR, are all located near active volcanoes.

In order to function, a geyser must have a source of heat, a reservoir where water can be stored until it reaches an unstable temperature, an opening through which to eject hot water and steam, and underground channels for replenishing the supply of fresh water after an eruption. A geyser erupts when some of its hot water expands explosively into steam, growing a thousandfold in volume. Water under pressure can remain liquid at temperatures above its normal boiling point. In a geyser, the weight of the upper water exerts pressure on the lower water, permitting the latter to reach much higher temperatures than the upper water before turning to steam. As the deep water becomes hotter and lighter, a blob of superheated water forms, sud-

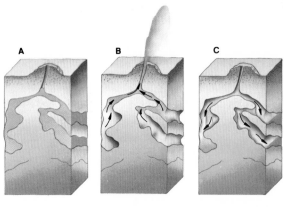

A geyser results from the superheating of pressurized water in contact with hot volcanic rocks in deep, interconnecting chambers (A). As the superheated water expands, it drives out some of the water above it, which reduces the pressure. The superheated water immediately flashes into steam, which violently drives out a column of water and steam through the surface opening (B). Groundwater then flows back into the chambers (C).

denly rises to the surface, and explodes into steam. The explosion churns up all the water in the geyser reservoir, triggering renewed upward movement of hot water, and further explosions. The geyser is then in full eruption.

A complete cycle of eruption may take minutes, hours, days, or years. Some geysers erupt regularly, others spo-

"Old Faithful," in Yellowstone Park, is so named because it has sent, for more than 100 years, a column of hot water and steam to a height of about 50 m (165 ft) for periods of 2 to 5 minutes at intervals of 30 to 90 minutes.

radically; some are active briefly, then become inactive, only to rejuvenate at a later time; new geysers come into being while others become dormant. Many of the changes in eruption patterns are associated with changes in barometric pressure, earthquake activity, and variations in the gravitational pull of the Sun and the Moon on the Earth. OLD FAITHFUL, the most famous geyser in Yellowstone Park, plays a column of hot water and steam into the air for 2 to 5 minutes, reaching a height of about 50 m (165 ft), at intervals of 30 to 90 minutes. Steamboat Geyser (also in Yellowstone), now the largest active geyser in the world, unexpectedly erupted in March 1978 after 9 years of dormancy. Water was thrown to heights of 150 m (500 ft) for nearly 15 minutes, and steam gushed forth for about 40 hours. Grand Geyser, perhaps the most magnificent in Yellowstone, now erupts about three times a day, although it too has had dormant periods.

Geyser water is usually heavily laden with dissolved SILICA MINERALS, which precipitate out when the discharged water cools. This produces huge (up to 5 m/15 ft high) cones and terraces of SINTER, the nozzles and pools so common in geyser basins.

Gezer   Gezer (modern Tell Jezer) is a large mound located 11 km (7 mi) southeast of Ramla in present-day Israel. Guarding a major strategic crossroads, it was one of the most important Canaanite cities. Occupied since the 4th millennium BC, Gezer was first fortified during the Middle Bronze Age (c.1900–1550 BC) with a massive stone wall 16 m (52 ft) wide. Just inside were placed, slightly later, ten enormous standing stones set on a north-south line; they were intended as a religious installation. Under Solomon the city became a major stronghold. Numerous inscriptions have been found, including an early Hebrew calendar dating from the 10th century BC and six Roman boundary stelae recording the name *Gezer*.

Ghana [gah'-nuh]   Ghana is an independent country of West Africa located on the Gulf of Guinea of the Atlantic Ocean. It is bounded on the west by Ivory Coast, on the north by Burkina Faso, and on the east by Togo. Its capital city is ACCRA. Ghana, formerly the British colony of the Gold Coast, was the first black-African colony to receive independence (Mar. 6, 1957). The country takes its name from the medieval empire that was located to the northwest of the present state.

Land and Resources

Most of Ghana is composed of lowlands; more than half the country has an elevation less than 150 m (500 ft). Along the eastern border of the country are the Akwapim Hills, which include Mount Afadjato (885 m/2,905 ft), the highest point in the country. The 550-km (340-mi) coastline is mostly sandy beaches backed by plains and saltwater lagoons. Stretching inland from the coast and covering about one-third of the country is the forest belt. North of the forest belt are the savanna and plains at elevations from 120 to 400 m (400 to 1,300 ft).

AT A GLANCE

REPUBLIC OF GHANA

Land: Area: 238,539 km² (92,100 mi²). Capital and largest city: Accra (1988 est. pop., 949,100).

People: Population (1990 est.): 15,165,243. Density: 63.6 persons per km² (164.7 per mi²). Distribution (1990): 32% urban, 68% rural. Official language: English. Major religions: traditional religions, Christianity, Islam.

Government: Type: military rule. Legislature: Parliament (suspended). Political subdivisions: 8 regions, Greater Accra.

Economy: GNP (1988): $5.2 billion; $400 per capita. Labor distribution (1986): agriculture—55%; trade, government, and services—27%; manufacturing—18%. Foreign trade (1987): imports—$988 million; exports—$977 million. Currency: 1 cedi = 100 pesawas.

Education and Health: Literacy (1985): 53% of adult population. Universities (1990): 3. Hospital beds (1981): 20,582. Physicians (1984): 1,900. Life expectancy (1990): women—56; men—52. Infant mortality (1990): 89 per 1,000 live births.

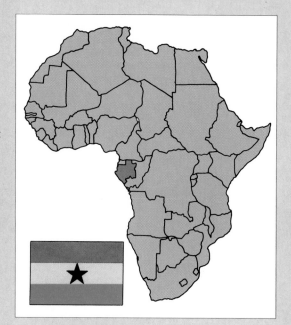

Ghana has a tropical climate influenced by the hot, dry, dust-laden continental air mass from the Sahara in the north and the warm, humid marine air mass from the Atlantic in the south. Consequently, rainfall varies from more than 2,025 mm (80 in) in the southwest to less than 1,000 mm (40 in) in the north, where the Saharan influence is strongest. The annual average temperature is about 25° C (78° F).

The VOLTA RIVER basin covers all but the southwestern third of the country. Artificially created Lake VOLTA extends 400 km (250 mi) along the river behind the Akosombo Dam. The Tano and Pra rivers drain directly into the sea.

Natural vegetation in Ghana is tropical rain forest in the southwest and savanna—mostly grasslands with scattered trees—in the drier north and extending south to the coast around Accra. Much of the tropical forest has been cleared for agriculture, and the formerly rich African fauna has been depleted because of human population pressure.

People

Of the more than 75 ethnic groups in Ghana, the AKAN, EWE, Ga, and Mole-Dagbani are the largest. Although broad cultural similarities exist, ethnic groups are separated by varying rules of descent systems and residence patterns. Languages fall into the Gur or Kwa groups of the Niger-Congo family, but each ethnic group is associated with a separate dialect, and the larger groups sometimes speak several dialects. English is the official language

and is taught in the schools.

About 21% of the population maintain traditional animistic beliefs. Christianity is the religion of some 63% of the population.

Urban centers are experiencing rapid growth, and nearly one-third of the population now live in cities. The largest cities, in descending order, are Accra, Kumasi, Tamale, Tema, and SEKONDI-TAKORADI. Many Ghanaians work in neighboring countries. High population densities are found in the south and the northeast, along the border with Burkina Faso. Elsewhere population densities are low, reflecting the extensive (rather than intensive) agricultural methods.

In 1974 free, mandatory, primary and middle-school education was introduced in state schools and in government-supported missionary schools. The resulting education system is considered one of the best in black Africa. The University of Ghana (1948) at Legon, near Accra, is the country's leading university.

Life expectancy and infant mortality rates are close to the average for Africa. Hospitals and clinics are provided by the government and by Christian missions.

The arts are closely allied to traditional religions. The visual arts are dominated by wood carving, especially masks, and the most important performing arts are dancing and music.

Economic Activity

At independence, in 1957, Ghana was the world's largest

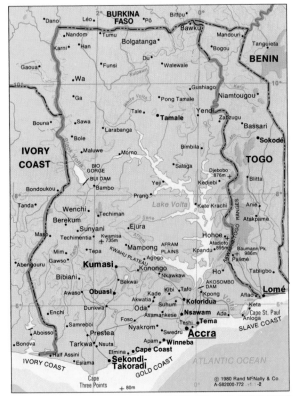

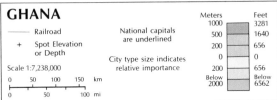

GHANA

————— Railroad

+   Spot Elevation or Depth

Scale 1:7,238,000

0   50   100   150   km

0   50   100   mi

National capitals are underlined

City type size indicates relative importance

Meters	Feet
1000	3281
500	1640
200	656
0	0
200	656
Below 2000	Below 6562

Akosombo Dam (operational 1966) accounts for 99% of Ghana's electricity production. The Volta Aluminum Company at Tema generally uses more than 60% of the electricity generated there to smelt imported alumina.

Cacao dominates the cash-crop production and accounts for about 45% of the country's exports. The principal food crops are cassava and other root crops, corn, and sorghum; few cattle are kept due to the presence of the disease-carrying tsetse fly. Logs and sawn timber account for 6% of exports by value, and gold, diamonds, manganese, and bauxite for another 18%. Offshore oil deposits are being exploited for domestic use. There is some fishing in Lake Volta and along the coast.

Ghana's railroads are concentrated in a triangle connecting Kumasi with Sekondi-Takoradi and Accra. Roads are located mostly in the southern third of the country. Ghana is heavily dependent on imported food, petroleum, consumer goods, and capital equipment.

History

Medieval Ghana, the empire that flourished from the 9th to the 13th century, was centered slightly north of the headwaters of the Senegal and Niger rivers in present-day Mali and should not be confused with the modern state of Ghana. The name "Ghana" was chosen for the Gold Coast with the assumption that migrants from the ancient kingdom settled the coastal region.

Initial contact with Europeans occurred when the Portuguese reached West Africa in the early 1400s. They soon established trade relations with the people of the Gold Coast. The West African slave trade began in the mid-1400s, when the Portuguese transported some Africans to meet their own labor shortage. The Portuguese built Elmina Castle on the coast in 1482. The Dutch, seeing the profits of slave trading, conquered the Portuguese bases in West Africa, and by 1642 they controlled the Gold Coast forts. Between 1500 and 1870 an estimated 10 million slaves left Africa, about 19% of them from the Gold Coast.

The British, who from about 1660 were the chief competitors of the Dutch, greatly increased their involvement in the Gold Coast between 1850 and 1874, by which time they had practically broken the authority of traditional African rulers. By 1898 the boundaries of the British Gold Coast were established. The British developed the infrastructure of the colony in an effort to lure British private investments to the area.

The very developments that improved the economic status of the colony eventually led to the rise of nationalism and the end of colonialism. The expanded economy required skilled African labor for subordinate positions. The emergence of an educated African elite, combined with a changed world opinion, ultimately led to independence. In 1947 the British- and American-educated Kwame NKRUMAH organized a nationalist party, and ten years later the colony attained full independence, with Nkrumah as president. His one-party state, however, suffered from inefficiency and corruption and was overthrown by the army in 1966. The military ruled the nation

producer of cacao and had substantial cash reserves. In an effort to create a socialist state as rapidly as possible, large sums of money were spent on industrialization, state farms, and public-works projects, and by 1966 the country was badly in debt. Governmental programs have since been considerably curtailed. Aging trees, low prices paid to growers, and adverse weather conditions contributed to a decline in vital cacao production during the 1970s and '80s. Government attempts to revitalize the cacao industry have met with little success, and the overall lack of economic growth has led many Ghanaians to seek employment outside the country.

The small-scale production of consumer goods such as processed foods, textiles, beverages, cigarettes, plywood, and furniture is important to the economy. Large manufacturing enterprises, however, are often underutilized and unprofitable due to chronic shortages of imported raw materials and spare parts. The hydroelectric plant at the

Accra is the capital, most populous city, and principal port and transportation center of Ghana. The site was long occupied by the Ga ethnic group, and by the late 17th century European traders had constructed fortified trading posts there.

until 1979, when elections were held to return the country to civilian rule. Hilla Limann, who became president, was deposed in December 1981. The coup leader, former flight lieutenant Jerry RAWLINGS, worked to reverse the nation's economic decline.

Ghana's third constitution, promulgated in 1979, was suspended following the 1981 military coup. The country is governed by a provisional national defense council which rules by decree; the chairman of the council is head of state.

Ghats [gahts]   The Ghats (Hindi, "steps") are two mountain ranges bordering the Deccan Plateau in southern India. The Western Ghats, average height 915 to 1,525 m (3,000 to 5,000 ft), extend about 1,600 km (1,000 mi) along the coast of the Arabian Sea. They are the watershed for the Godavari, Kistna, and Cauvery rivers; the Palghat Gap is their only break. The Eastern Ghats, a discontinuous series of hills, average height 610 m (2,000 ft), extend about 1,450 m (900 mi) from the Mahanadi Valley to the Nilgiri Hills along the Bay of Bengal.

Ghazali, al- [gaz-ah'-lee, ahl]   Abu Hamid Muhammad al-Ghazali, b. 1058, d. Dec. 18, 1111, a theologian, mystic, and apologist, is one of the most revered personalities in the Muslim world. His spiritual autobiography, *al-Munqidh min al-Dalal* (The Deliverer from Error), describes the great crisis that forced him in 1095 to abandon his brilliant professional career in Baghdad and to search for an inner, direct knowledge of the reality of God. He adopted the life of a wandering ascetic and mystic, visited Damascus, Jerusalem, and Mecca, and lived with some disciples in his birthplace, Tus (in present-day Iran), before he was persuaded to return (1106) to his teaching career.

Ghent [gent]   Ghent (Flemish: Gent; French: Gand) is the capital of the province of East Flanders in northwestern Belgium and the second largest city in the country. The population is 232,620 (1988 est.). Its location at the junction of the Scheldt and Lys rivers made it a trading center early on. It remains Belgium's second largest port after Antwerp.

Called the "city of flowers" because of its nurseries, Ghent is also known for its textiles. Other industries include oil refining and the manufacture of steel, chemical dyes, and paper. Ghent is a major tourist center; attractions include the castle of the counts of Flanders (reconstructed 1180), the medieval belfry and town hall, the cathedral of Saint Bavon (12th–16th centuries), and scenic quays. Among the city's many art masterpieces is the *Adoration of the Holy Lamb,* a polyptych altarpiece by Hubert and Jan Van EYCK.

Ghent's weaving industry was prominent by the 13th century and influenced its politics for years. The strong middle class retained a degree of independence despite the nominal rule of the counts of Flanders and dukes of Burgundy. The city pursued an independent policy under the leadership of the Artevelde family during the Hundred Years' War and resisted Habsburg rule during the 16th century. Its economy later declined but was revived when the region was occupied by French Revolutionary armies. Europe's first cotton-spinning mill was built there in 1800, and cotton-textile manufacture soon replaced wool cloth as the dominant industry.

Ghent, Treaty of   see WAR OF 1812

Gheorghiu-Dej, Gheorghe [gay-ohr'-gue-dayzh, gay-ohr'-gay]   Gheorghe Gheorghiu-Dej, b. Nov. 8, 1901, d. Mar. 19, 1965, was the first postwar Romanian Communist party leader. He joined the outlawed Communist party in 1930 and in 1933 was sentenced to 12 years in prison. Escaping in 1944, he became (1945) the party's general secretary and served in the Communist-led coalition government that established the People's Republic in 1947. After an intraparty struggle, Gheorghiu-Dej made himself premier in June 1952. He resigned that office in 1955 but in 1961 assumed the equivalent post of president of the state council.

ghetto [get'-oh]   The ghetto was originally a separate area of a city for JEWS. Some of the earliest ghettos were voluntarily established by Jewish communities in the cities of Europe and the Middle East in which they settled during the DIASPORA. From the 12th century on, however, Jews were often required by law to live apart from Christians in sections that were sometimes walled and accessible only through controlled portals. Jews dwelt freely in most parts of the Muslim world until the 18th century, after which they were often confined to special areas away from mosques and other holy places. This was especially characteristic of Persia, Yemen, and Morocco, where remnants of the old ghettos still exist. In Western Europe, the last ghetto (Rome) was abolished in 1870. In the 1930s and '40s, however, the Nazis revived the enforced ghettoizing of Jews, but only as a temporary step in their plan for exterminating European Jewry.

Ghetto culture, often oversimplified by depictions of 19th-century Jewish life in the *shtetls* (Jewish towns) of Eastern Europe, was in fact highly varied. Professionals, artisans, merchants, and laborers, as well as Talmudic scholars, were usually found within the gates. Almost all enjoyed a certain amount of autonomy. They ran their own political, social, and economic affairs through religious and secular councils, often with the consent, and sometimes at the insistence, of the external authorities. At times ghetto dwellers performed special functions for the world outside, such as lending money to government officials or members of the aristocracy in lands where such activity was forbidden to Christians, collecting taxes, or peddling soft goods and hardware in other parts of the city and to peasants in the hinterland. Their limited contacts, specialized occupations, and unusual garb set them apart and often reinforced the prejudices of those who used the ghetto-dwelling Jews as scapegoats for the ills of society. As scapegoats, ghetto Jews in Tsarist Russia were the target of government-organized riots called POGROMS.

In recent years the word *ghetto* has been extended to any area of confinement or voluntary residence of minority populations, and especially to the black, Puerto Rican, and Chicano ghettos of the United States. (Hispanic ghettos are often called *barrios*.) In these areas one finds many of the characteristics associated with Jewish quarters: evidence of discrimination and "second-class citizenship"; dual allegiances created by the fact that the ghetto dwellers are subject to but not of the dominant society; communal bonds created out of a need for insulation against the outer world; and, sometimes, local insti-

tutions to help care for group members. The most famous black ghetto is Harlem, in New York City.

See also: ANTI-SEMITISM; HOLOCAUST; INNER CITY.

Ghibellines   see GUELPHS AND GHIBELLINES

Ghiberti, Lorenzo [gee-bair'-tee]   The creator of some of the most admired sculpture of the Renaissance, Lorenzo Ghiberti, b. Florence, *c.*1381, d. Dec. 1, 1455, is best known for his bronze doors for the Baptistery in Florence. Sharing the Renaissance ideals of humanism with his contemporary artists, Ghiberti based his art on close study of nature and the classical tradition. After early work as a painter he was mainly occupied with sculptural commissions from Florentine guilds for two buildings: the Florence Baptistery and the church of Or

Lorenzo Ghiberti's Gates of Paradise (1425–52) *were greatly admired by Michelangelo and are among the masterpieces of Early Renaissance art. The ten reliefs show scenes from the Old Testament (Baptistry, Florence.)*

"The Story of Jacob and Esau" is one of the ten reliefs constituting Lorenzo Ghiberti's Gates of Paradise. *The elegantly draped figures were first modeled in wax, then cast in bronze. Despite their swirling Gothic drapery, these bronzes mark the Renaissance's true beginning.*

the careful observation and representation of visual reality that characterized early Renaissance painting. Ghirlandaio worked almost exclusively in Florence except for a trip to Rome (1481–82) to paint frescoes in the SISTINE CHAPEL. In Ghirlandaio's paintings, figures, architecture, landscape, and still-life elements are all represented with precise and prosaic reality. His works generally avoid effects that might be termed dramatic, imaginative, or poetic; his beautiful color, technical excellence, clear expression of narrative content, and compositional balance make his paintings masterpieces.

Ghirlandaio's greatest accomplishments are the decorative narrative schemes that he devised for Florentine family chapels. Those in the Sassetti Chapel at Santa Trinità (1483–86) and the Tornabuoni Chapel at Santa Maria Novella (1485–90) survive virtually intact. These decorative ensembles exalt Ghirlandaio's patrons and their friends, as well as life in 15th-century Florence in general. Ghirlandaio's panel paintings demonstrate his absorption of the Flemish oil technique, which allowed him to achieve ever more impressive naturalistic effects. His realistic style lent itself especially well to portraiture.

San Michele. For the Baptistery door commission (1403), Ghiberti's *Abraham and Isaac* bronze relief (Bargello, Florence) won the competition over Filippo BRUNELLESCHI, Jacopo della Quercia, and others. Between 1403 and 1424, Ghiberti worked on the 28 bronze high reliefs for his first set of doors. The earlier reliefs show some characteristics of the Late Gothic (see GOTHIC ART AND ARCHITECTURE) or International Style, blended with innovative Renaissance features. During this period he also cast the larger-than-life bronze figures for Or San Michele: *St. John* (1414–46), *St. Matthew* (1419–22), and *St. Stephen* (1425–28).

In 1425, Ghiberti was commissioned to do the second pair of doors for the Baptistery. This consisted of ten pictorial reliefs, numerous figures and busts, and a festooned frame. The reliefs were cast by 1437 and finished, gilded, and installed by 1452.

According to Giorgio VASARI, Ghiberti was the first to imitate antique art. He also revived the technique of casting large-scale figures. His illusionistic reliefs *Jacob and Esau* and *Solomon and Sheba*, for the "gates of paradise," exemplify the Renaissance style in their perfection of design, their variety within harmonious balance, and the decorum of the individual figures.

In his concern for classical nobility and grace, Ghiberti's style in general is an illustration of the Renaissance preoccupation with visual and intellectual harmony. Ghiberti was also a writer on art and is the author of the earliest surviving autobiography by an artist.

See also: BRONZES, ITALIAN ART AND ARCHITECTURE; RENAISSANCE ART AND ARCHITECTURE; SCULPTURE.

Ghirlandaio, Domenico [geer-lahn-dah'-ee-oh]   The naturalistic style of the Florentine painter Domenico Ghirlandaio, 1449–94, is the culminating expression of

Domenico Ghirlandaio, the last important Florentine painter of the Early Renaissance, painted the famous portrait Old Man with His Grandson *(1480), which shows scrupulous attention to painterly detail. (Louvre, Paris.)*

Ghose, Aurobindo   see AUROBINDO, SRI

---

ghost   A ghost is the spirit of a dead person capable of making itself seen or heard by the living. Belief in, and worship of, ghosts was common in ancient societies and is still found today (see ANCESTOR WORSHIP). In Europe belief in ghosts dates back to ancient times and was widespread during the Middle Ages. The belief declined somewhat in the ensuing centuries, but was revived in the 19th century when SPIRITUALISM came into vogue.

The forms ghosts are believed to take differ from culture to culture. They can include the solid or transparent likeness of the deceased, strange lights, or a disembodied voice. Poltergeists are disruptive ghosts who move or break objects. There is no scientifically accepted evidence of the existence of ghosts.

---

ghost dance   The ghost dance refers to a type of messianic movement that arose (1870–78) among Indians of the western Great Basin and later (1887–95) spread to Plains Indians. It expressed a desperate longing for the restoration of the past—a return to a life free of hunger, epidemic disease, and the bitter warring and divisiveness that accompanied the Indians' subjugation by whites. Prophets "died," visited God, and returned with the message that the dead would soon join the living in a world where game was plentiful and all lived happily together in the old way. Followers were admonished to purify themselves, speak the truth, and love one another. The ghost-dance belief began among the PAIUTE of Nevada with the revelations of the shaman Tävibo in 1870. Between 1887 and 1889 the prophet WOVOKA "died" and returned with a ritual dance to hasten the renewal of the world and return of the ancestors.

During the battle at WOUNDED KNEE (1890), in which hundreds of Sioux warriors, women, and children were massacred, many wore "ghost shirts" emblazoned with eagle, buffalo, and morning-star decorations. They believed that these symbols of powerful spirits would protect them from the soldiers' bullets. The tragedy at Wounded Knee effectively put an end to the ghost dance, although some Plains tribes performed it until 1895 or incorporated aspects of the ritual into their culture, as in the ghost-dance handgame of the PAWNEE.

---

ghost towns   Ghost towns are settlements that have been abandoned by their inhabitants. Because of their rapidly changing economic fortunes, many frontier towns of the American West underwent spectacular fluctuations in population. A few thousand persons might be attracted to a mining camp in the course of a few months and just as quickly leave again.

Because of the value of building materials, departing settlers usually stripped an abandoned town of everything they could carry, and only rarely can a true ghost town of empty, decaying buildings be found. St. Elmo, Colo., is one.

Many communities called ghost towns restored saloons, corrals, hotels, and stores to become "true West" tourist attractions; for example, Virginia City, Nev., and Tombstone, Ariz.

G.I. Bill of Rights   The G.I. Bill of Rights is the popular name for a series of U.S. programs that provide educational and economic assistance to veterans of World War II, the Korean War, and the Vietnam War. Congress passed the first G.I. Bill, called the Servicemen's Readjustment Act, in 1944. It was designed to assist healthy soldiers in reentering the civilian world by helping them procure job training or an education.

All veterans who had served at least 90 days and been honorably discharged were eligible for educational benefits. The duration of the benefits depended on the length of service, ranging from one year of full-time education or vocational training for veterans who had served 90 days, up to a maximum of 48 months. The government paid the tuition costs and standard educational fees and provided a tool allowance for veterans training for skilled occupations. It also provided a living allowance. With some variations, the program was reinstated for veterans of the Korean and Vietnam wars. The existing education-benefits program was terminated in 1976, although eligible Vietnam veterans could use benefits until 1989. In 1987, after a three-year trial period, Congress voted to make a voluntary educational-benefits program available to all following military service, with beneficiaries paying a small share toward the benefits.

More than 7.8 million veterans of World War II took advantage of the educational provisions of the G.I. Bill, and by the late 1980s well over 20 million veterans of the three wars had received training or educational assistance under the various G.I. Bills. In meeting the needs of World War II veterans , often different from the needs of prewar students, American universities furthered the democratization of U.S. higher education.

Giacometti, Alberto [jah-koh-met'-tee]   The Swiss sculptor Alberto Giacometti, b. Oct. 10, 1901, d. Jan. 11, 1966, was primarily concerned with reporting the precise visual perception of objects and their relationship to the enveloping space.

In 1925, Giacometti opened his own studio and began to sculpt in a cubist manner (see CUBISM). Under the influence of Henri LAURENS, Jacques LIPCHITZ, and the primitive art of Africa and Oceania, he developed compact pieces, such as *The Couple* (1926; Museum of Fine Arts, Zurich). He also created open cagelike forms, which are exemplified by the *Palace at 4 A.M.* (1932; Museum of Modern Art, New York City), which he executed during his affiliation (1929–35) with the surrealist movement (see SURREALISM, art).

After working for a decade (1925–35) almost exclusively from his imagination, Giacometti became discontented and turned to figuration. His mature sculpture is typified by attenuated bronze figures with scarred or

Giacometti's Walking Man II *(1960) is surrealistic in visual effect. Its proportions and scale derive, however, from his study of Egyptian, archaic Greek, and primitive art. (Rijksmuseum Kroller Muller, Otterlo, Netherlands.)*

eroded surfaces. In *Composition with Seven Figures and a Head or The Forest* (1950; Reader's Digest Association, Pleasantville, N.Y.) Giacometti confronted the relationship of the figure to the space around it. The result is a group of isolated figures placed in a void, a space that becomes an obstacle to communication between individuals. The psychological implications of compressed space and the indistinctness caused by the frenetic surface handling is apparent in the painting *Head of a Man* (1961) and in the sculpture *Monumental Head* (1960), both in the Hirshhorn Museum and Sculpture Garden, Washington, D.C. These works assert humanity's universality and are the culmination of Giacometti's relentless examination of spatial phenomena.

Giamatti, A. Bartlett [jee-uh-mah'-tee] Angelo Bartlett Giamatti, b. Boston, Apr. 4, 1938, d. Sept. 1, 1989, became commissioner of baseball in April 1989.

Although he had served (1986–89) as president of the National League and was a lifelong baseball fan, Giamatti's choice had been considered somewhat unlikely. A medieval and Renaissance scholar, he taught (1966–78) English and comparative literature at Yale and served (1978–86) as its president.

Giambologna   see BOLOGNA, GIOVANNI DA

Giannini, Amadeo Peter [jah-neen'-nee, ah-muh-day'-oh] Amadeo Peter Giannini, b. San Jose, Calif., May 6, 1870, d. June 3, 1949, founded the Bank of America and controlled the world's largest private banking system at the time of his death. The son of an Italian immigrant, at 13 he went to work in the produce business in San Francisco. Giannini became a partner in the firm but sold his interest in 1901 to go into banking. His Bank of Italy, founded in 1904, survived the earthquake and fire of 1906 and then grew rapidly and was renamed (1930) the Bank of America.

giant schnauzer   see SCHNAUZER

---

giant toad The giant toad, *Bufo marinus*, in the family Bufonidae, grows to 23 cm (9 in) in length. Adult males are brown in color; adult females and young are yellowish with brown spots. The species is found from south Texas to the Amazon Basin of South America, ranging from sea level to elevations of about 1,500 m (5,000 ft). A single female can produce 35,000 eggs a year. Giant toads were introduced into many tropical islands to help control insects, but the plan backfired because they also devour beneficial native fauna.

The giant toad lives in a wide range of habitats throughout Central and South America. Secreted by parotid glands in the skin, its poison is highly toxic to small animals.

giantism   see ENDOCRINE SYSTEM, DISEASES OF THE

---

giants In folklore and mythology, giants are primeval creatures of immense size, usually humanlike but evil and cruel. In Greek mythology the Gigantes were a race born from the blood of URANUS after the latter had been castrated by his son CRONUS. They rebelled against Zeus and the Olympian gods but were defeated—symbolizing the triumph of civilization over barbarism—and were buried in the Earth. Thus they were thought to cause earthquakes and volcanic eruptions. In Norse mythology, the Mountain Giants were also represented as powers of the Earth, and the Frost Giants were associated with winter storms. Like their Greek counterparts, the Norse giants were the enemies of the gods; the giants and most of the gods were to destroy each other at the great final battle of RAGNAROK.

In European folklore giants usually appear as cannibalistic ogres whose stupidity makes it possible to defeat them by trickery. Examples in English folklore include Cormoran and Blunderbore, who were mastered by Jack the Giant Killer. In the mythologies of peoples of the Western Hemisphere, giants often have the form of birds or other animals. The Indians of the North American Great Plains believed that giants were the first race of people on Earth.

Belief in giants was often related to the myth that men had degenerated to their present condition from a golden age in which they had been taller and stronger. This myth was inspired, in part, by fossil bones of huge extinct animals and by massive prehistoric mounds and stone circles and alignments such as Stonehenge.

Giant's Causeway The Giant's Causeway is a promontory on the northern coast of Northern Ireland. It is composed of thousands of basalt columns, mostly irregular hexagons, and is divided into three sections—the Little, Middle, and Grand causeways—the last extending more than 200 m (about 700 ft). The causeway was formed when a lava flow cooled quickly and contracted to form the hexagonal pattern. The columns reach a maximum diameter of 50 cm (20 in) and a maximum height of 6 m (20 ft). Seen from above, the causeway resembles a giant checkered pavement.

The Giant's Causeway is a prismatic basalt formation of volcanic origin located on the northeastern coast of Ireland. Legend states that the formation was created by giants as part of a road to the island of Staffa, where a similar formation occurs.

Giap, Vo Nguyen   see VO NGUYEN GIAP

Giardia [jee-ahr'-dee-uh] Giardia, genus *Giardia*, are any of several flagellated PROTOZOA of the small intestine in humans and other vertebrates. Found worldwide, Giar-

dia are not fatal, but *G. intestinalis* may cause diarrhea, cramps, and nausea. This condition is highly contagious. The organism has two nuclei and four pairs of flagella. (See PROTOZOAL DISEASES.)

gibberellins   see HORMONE, PLANT

gibbon [gib'-uhn] Gibbons are long-armed APES of the order PRIMATES, family Hylobatidae, which also includes the SIAMANG. They live in rain forests from northeastern India to Borneo. There is one genus, *Hylobates*, and four to six species are recognized. Gibbons stand 40 to 64 cm (16 to 25 in) high and weigh up to 8 kg (about 17 lb). The coat is dense and shaggy and ranges from black to brown or gray, varying greatly even within a species. They have relatively the longest legs of any apes and can run with agility, holding their even longer arms in the air. They are best known for their speed and grace in swinging from limb to limb through the trees, using the movement called brachiation in which the hands serve only as hooks. Gibbons live in small groups and feed mainly on fruit.

A lar gibbon swings easily from tree to tree as it makes a loud whooping sound. A screaming troop of lar gibbons can be heard for several kilometers. Such troops consist of up to about 15 family members. Each troop maintains its own territory within a forest, but during the day several troops may gather and feed peacefully in regions between territories.

Gibbon, Edward   Edward Gibbon, b. Apr. 27, 1737, d. Jan. 16, 1794, considered one of the greatest English historians, was the author of *The History of the Decline and Fall of the Roman Empire*. This work, published in six vol-

Edward Gibbon, the great 18th-century English historian, produced in his work The History of the Decline and Fall of the Roman Empire *(1776–88) both a broad historical interpretation and a literary master-piece.*

Gibbons, James   James Gibbons, b. Baltimore, July 23, 1834, d. Mar. 24, 1921, was an American Roman Catholic archbishop and the second American to be named a cardinal. As the principal leader of American Catholicism during the period of its greatest growth, Gibbons's vocal patriotism and his endorsement of the separation of church and state helped to overcome traditional Protestant hostility. His concise exposition of Catholic doctrine, entitled *The Faith of Our Fathers* (1876) was widely read by non-Catholics. Conversely, he defended the American church-state relationship at the Vatican and prevented a papal condemnation of the unionizing efforts of the KNIGHTS OF LABOR movement. In 1889, Gibbons became the first chancellor of the Catholic University of America.

James Gibbons, Roman Catholic archbishop of Baltimore and a cardinal, was a key leader of the American Catholic church during its years of enormous growth in the late 1800s.

umes from 1776 to 1788, is a masterpiece of both history and literature. Its breadth of treatment, accuracy of detail, and elegant style are among its strong points. However, Gibbon's negative treatment of Christianity and his bitter irony also made the work a subject of controversy.

Gibbon was born at Putney, near London. Although a sickly youth, Gibbon went to Magdalen College, Oxford, in 1752. Fourteen months later, however, he became a Roman Catholic and was expelled from the university. His father then sent him to Lausanne, Switzerland, where he studied French literature and the Latin classics, thus laying the foundation of his vast erudition. He was also reconverted (1754) to Protestantism. Although he left Lausanne in 1758, he was to return many times.

Between 1763 and 1765 Gibbon toured Europe. While he was in Rome, "musing amidst the ruins," as he later described it, the idea of writing the history of the later Roman Empire came to him. He spent the next 20 years at the task. From 1774 to 1783 he was also a member of Parliament. His *Miscellaneous Works*, which included his memoirs, was published posthumously (1796).

Gibbons, Grinling   Grinling Gibbons, b. Apr. 4, 1648, d. Aug. 3, 1721, the leading English woodcarver of the late 17th and early 18th centuries, was celebrated for astonishingly naturalistic carvings of birds, flowers, fruit, and foliage, which rivaled the finest European decorative sculpture of the period. In 1671, Gibbons's work came to the attention of Charles II, who later commissioned him to execute a considerable amount of ornamental woodwork. He subsequently worked for William and Mary in the royal palaces of Kensington and Hampton Court. By the 1690s, Gibbons was the most famous craftsman among the many builders and decorators employed by Sir Christopher Wren at SAINT PAUL'S CATHEDRAL, London. Gibbons's work at Saint Paul's included the intricately carved ornaments of the choir stalls, organcase, and bishop's throne.

Gibbons, Orlando   The celebrated English composer Orlando Gibbons, baptized Dec. 25, 1583, d. June 5, 1625, is best known for his madrigals and music for the Anglican church. In 1605 he was appointed organist of the Chapel Royal, a post he held until his death. He was named (1619) virginalist to the king, and in 1623 he became organist of Westminster Abbey.

In 1612, Gibbons published *The First Set of Madrigals and Motets of 5 Parts*, which includes the well-known "The Silver Swan." As a group, his madrigals are more austere than those of his contemporaries. Examples of his excellent chamber music are found in *Fantasies of Three Parts* (c.1610) for viols. His keyboard works include six pieces printed in *Parthenia* (1611), a collection (including pieces by William Byrd and John Bull) of music for the virginal. Gibbons composed about 40 anthems, some of which are choral throughout (full anthems), and some (verse anthems) that include sections for one or more solo voice parts with accompaniment, as in *This is the Record of John*. He also composed a poignant fantasia for voices and viols based on the traditional cries of London street peddlers.

Gibbons v. Ogden   The case of *Gibbons* v. *Ogden* (1824) resulted in the United States Supreme Court interpretation of the so-called commerce clause of the U.S. Constitution and was one of Chief Justice John MARSHALL's most important decisions. The New York legislature had granted exclusive rights to navigate New York's waterways by steam vessels to the inventors and entrepreneurs Robert Fulton and Robert Livingston. In turn Aaron Ogden obtained permission from the holders of the franchise to navigate between New York and New Jersey but was confronted by competition from Thomas Gibbons, a citizen of New Jersey who ran steamboats between Elizabethtown and New York City.

Chief Justice Marshall invalidated the New York monopoly on the grounds that the state law was in conflict with the act of Congress under which Gibbons had been granted a license. He maintained that commerce includes navigation, that the government's power to regulate it includes the power to "prescribe the rule by which commerce may be governed," and that Congress may deal with commerce wherever it exists, including within a state, when it is connected with interstate or foreign commerce.

Gibbs, James   The Scotsman James Gibbs, b. Dec. 23, 1682, d. Aug. 5, 1754, was the most important London church architect of the early 18th century. His first important commission, St. Mary-le-Strand Church, London (1714), is an example of his early, individual, neobaroque manner. His most distinguished achievements are St. Martin-in-the-Fields, London (1721–26), whose design became the prototype for many parish churches in England and the United States, and the Radcliffe Camera of Oxford University (1739–49).

James Gibbs's Radcliffe Camera (1739–49), a library at Oxford University, is a monumental tribute to the dome, reflecting the diverse influences of Mannerist and baroque styles. The exterior is an eclectic synthesis typical of Italian Mannerism. The interior, which articulates the building's two concentric cylinders by means of a strongly linear ornamentation, suggests the restraint of Christopher Wren's baroque style.

Gibbs's eclectic architectural style reflects the influence of Sir Christopher WREN, but he later took up the popular Palladian manner (see PALLADIO, ANDREA), especially in St. Martin-in-the-Fields, an original combination of a steeple with a portico facade. The originality of the Radcliffe Library lies in Gibbs's use and understanding of the Mannerist style.

Gibbs's designs were influential because they were published in books. *A Book of Architecture* (1728) and *Rules for Drawing the Several Parts of Architecture* (1732) were widely used in both England and the American colonies.

Gibbs, Josiah Willard   The theoretical physicist and chemist Josiah Willard Gibbs, b. New Haven, Conn., Feb. 11, 1839, d. Apr. 28, 1903, was one of the founders, along with Ludwig BOLTZMANN, of statistical mechanics. Gibbs graduated from Yale in 1863 and taught there until his death. In the early 1870s, Gibbs began his studies in thermodynamics. His first scientific paper, "Graphical Methods in the Thermodynamics of Fluids," discussed the relationships among entropy, energy, temperature, pressure, and volume in thermodynamic systems. He used a geometric (graphical) approach in diagraming the system in two dimensions. Another paper published later the same year extended his geometry to three dimensions. Gibbs's longest and most important paper, "On the Equilibrium of Heterogeneous Substances," appeared in 1876–78. This study incorporated into a single thermodynamic system chemical, elastic, surface, electromagnetic, and electrochemical phenomena. The application of these ideas to chemistry led to a better understanding of chemical equilibrium in systems composed of several phases.

Gibraltar   [juh-brawl'-tur]   Gibraltar is a British territory located on a peninsula 6 km^2 (2.25 mi^2) in area that extends 5 km (3 mi) into the Mediterranean Sea from southeastern Spain and dominates the Strait of Gibraltar, which connects the Mediterranean to the Atlantic Ocean. The peninsula consists of the Rock of Gibraltar, a high ridge of limestone and shale rising 426 m (1,396 ft) above sea level, and a low-lying isthmus, 1.6 km (1 mi) long, connecting it to the mainland. The northern and eastern sides of the rock are steep cliffs, but its southern and western sides slope more gradually in a series of terraces. The city of Gibraltar, which contains two-thirds of the territory's 30,127 people (1988 est.), is situated on the lowest of these terraces. Summer temperatures average about 22° C (71° F), and annual rainfall averages 865 mm (34 in). Tourism and services to shipping are the main industries.

Gibraltar and Mount Abyla, which is located across the strait on the Moroccan coast, have long been known as the Pillars of Hercules. According to classical myth, Hercules created the Strait of Gibraltar by forcing apart Gibraltar and Mount Abyla in order to let water into the Mediterranean.

The Rock of Gibraltar is an imposing promontory dominating the surrounding peninsula. Strategically located at the gateway between the Mediterranean Sea and the Atlantic Ocean, Gibraltar is a valuable military base and the subject of a long dispute between Spain and Great Britain.

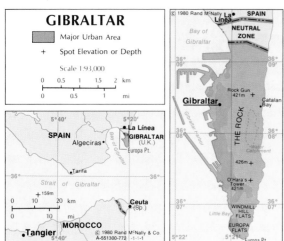

GIBRALTAR

Major Urban Area

+   Spot Elevation or Depth

Scale 1:93,000

0   0.5   1   1.5   2 km

0   0.5   1 mi

Government. Gibraltar is administered by a governor appointed by the British crown. The governor commands the British garrison that runs the large naval base, airfield, and artillery emplacements in the territory and is responsible for all defense and internal-security matters. Since 1969 control of municipal affairs has been vested in a board of ministers that is responsible to a 15-member elected House of Assembly. All Gibraltarians (those who can trace residency on Gibraltar through the male line back to before 1925) may vote, as may those with special British residency permits.

History. Because of the strategic value of its location and topography, Gibraltar has always been a prized military possession. It was conquered by the successive Mediterranean empires of the Phoenicians, Carthaginians, Romans, Vandals, and Visigoths. In 711 it was taken by

Muslim Moorish forces, who built (725) a massive castle that partly remains today. It was retaken by the Spanish in 1462. In 1704 it was captured by the British, to whom Spain formally ceded it in the Treaty of Utrecht (1713). When the Suez Canal opened in 1869, Gibraltar became even more important as a military and supply link on the Mediterranean route from Great Britain to India. It was a strategic naval base during the two world wars.

In 1967 the residents of Gibraltar voted by referendum to remain a British crown colony, and a new constitution was adopted in 1969. In the latter year, the Spanish government closed the border between Spain and Gibraltar. The border was partially (1982), then totally (1985), reopened, but Spain still pressed its claim to the peninsula.

Gibraltar, Strait of   The Strait of Gibraltar is the 60-m-long (36-mi) channel that separates Europe (Spain) from Africa (Morocco) at the western end of the Mediterranean Sea. The strait is 13 km (8 mi) across at its narrowest point. Its current is two-layered; the upper layer moves east into the Mediterranean, carrying oxygen and nutrients, and the lower, saline layer moves west, or outward. The strait is deepest in the east; the relative shallowness of the western end (320 m/1,050 ft) causes it to retain the warmth of the Mediterranean's water. The strait is named for the Spanish promontory that was once named Jebel Tariq or Mount Tariq in honor of the Berber leader who began the Muslim conquest of Spain in 711.

Gibran, Kahlil [juh-brahn', kah-leel'] A Lebanese poet who emigrated to the United States, Kahlil Gibran, b. Jan. 6, 1883, d. Apr. 10, 1931, is best known for his poetic parables and aphorisms, contained in such works as *The Prophet* (1923) and *Sand and Foam* (1926). Gibran was influenced by Nietzsche but was also highly religious and dealt with such abstractions as God, love, and woman. He also wrote Arabic poetry and was a skillful artist, producing drawings similar in style and feeling to those by the English poet-illustrator William Blake.

Gibson, Althea   Althea Gibson, b. Silver, S.C., Aug. 25, 1927, was the first black person to win major titles in tennis. She won the Italian championship in 1956 and again in 1957, a year in which she also won Wimbledon and the U.S. championship. She repeated her singles victories at Wimbledon and Forest Hills in 1958 and ranked number one in the world among women players in both 1957 and 1958. Gibson's strength as a tennis player was her powerful serve and volley. She later became a moderately successful professional golfer.

Gibson, Bob   Robert Gibson, b. Omaha, Nebr., Nov. 9, 1935, was an American baseball pitcher who won 251 games in the 1960s and '70s and was outstanding for his strikeout records. He also had a brief basketball career with the Harlem Globetrotters. Gibson joined the St. Louis Cardinals, the only team he played for in the major leagues, in 1959. He pitched the Cardinals to World Series triumphs in 1964 and 1967, and in the 1968 series, which the Cardinals lost, he struck out 35 men, including 17 in one game. He had 3,117 strikeouts in his career. Gibson won the Cy Young Award as the National League's best pitcher in 1968 and 1970, retired in 1975, and was inducted into the Hall of Fame in 1981.

Gibson, Charles Dana   A popular American illustrator, Charles Dana Gibson, b. Roxbury, Mass., Sept. 14, 1867, d. Dec. 23, 1944, was widely known for his pen-and-ink drawings of the "Gibson Girl," which influenced fashions and publications for 20 years. This Victorian "glamour girl," born on his drawing board in the early 1890s, and his sentimental, humorous, and sometimes gently satirical pictures of social life appeared in many publications, including the old humor magazine *Life*. His books include *The Education of Mr. Pipp* (1899), another popular Gibson character.

Gibson, Josh   Joshua Gibson, b. Buena Vista, Ga., Dec. 21, 1911, d. Jan. 20, 1947, was considered the greatest hitter of the black baseball leagues in the United States before blacks were allowed to play in the major leagues. Called the "Black Babe Ruth," Gibson hit about 800 home runs in the 17 years he played, including 75 in the 1931 season.

Although statistics were often undocumented in the Negro National League, Gibson was the leading hitter four times and had a lifetime batting average of .347. A catcher, he played for teams in and around Pittsburgh. He died suddenly in 1947, the year Jackie Robinson became the first black player in the major leagues. Gibson was inducted into the Hall of Fame in 1972.

Gide, André [zheed]   André Gide was one of the major French literary figures of the first half of the 20th century. In awarding him the Nobel Prize for literature in 1947, the Nobel jury spoke of his works—a lifelong study of mind and soul, beginning with the confessional *Cahiers d'André Walter* of 1891—as a major contribution to humanism.

Gide, b. Nov. 22, 1869, d. Feb. 19, 1951, was the son of a Sorbonne professor who died when André was 11. He was brought up in a strict Protestant atmosphere bounded by women: his mother, her English companion, his grandmother in Provence, and cousins in Normandy. He married his cousin Madeleine in 1895, but the union proved tragic.

Gide's early works, of the 1890s, were influenced by symbolism. A trip to North Africa and his discovery of a homosexuality free of shame set him in open rebellion against his family and polite society. He waged his war against conformity in prose pieces, plays, the press, and lectures. *Fruits of the Earth* (1897; Eng. trans., 1949) preached Nietzschean paganism in musical and visually evocative language. *Strait Is The Gate* (1909; Eng. trans., 1924) depicted the folly of denying the flesh, although in *The Immoralist* (1902; Eng. trans., 1930), perhaps his best-known work, he had already demonstrated the evils of sensual indulgence.

Although the tone of Gide's books is usually serious, *Lafcadio's Adventures* (1914; Eng. trans., 1927) proved he could use humor effectively. Its whimsical young hero, Lafcadio, is equally capable of risking his life to rescue someone from a burning building and of pushing a stranger off a fast-moving train. The heroine of *The Pastoral Symphony* (1919; Eng. trans., 1931) is another sort of innocent, a blind girl victimized by a Swiss pastor whose love for her exceeds Christian charity.

Lafcadio and the pastor were still on Gide's mind when he composed what could be considered his greatest novel, *The Counterfeiters* (1925; Eng. trans., 1927), a comprehensive summary of his views on life and art. As head of the eminent *Nouvelle Revue Française*, Gide fostered the best in French writing, publishing works by Proust, Claudel, Valéry, and Giraudoux.

The French author André Gide, writing during the first half of the 20th century, influenced the development of modern literature with his introspective writing and experimental narrative techniques.

Gideon [gid'-ee-uhn]   Gideon was the biblical judge and warrior who saved the Israelites from the annual raids of the nomadic Midianites. Because of his opposition to the worship of Baal and his dramatic victories, he was offered the kingship of Israel. But he refused it because he believed that God was Israel's only king. The Gideon tradition is related in Judges 6–8.

Gielgud, Sir John [geel'-gud]   The English actor Arthur John Gielgud, b. Apr. 14, 1904, is the grand-nephew of actress Ellen Terry and is one of the foremost actors of the English-speaking stage. He made his debut in 1921 with the Old Vic theater and achieved his first popular success in the play *Richard of Bordeaux* in 1932. His speaking voice is remarkable for its diction and tone, which enable him to sustain the melody of a poetic line without losing its drama.

Gielgud's most notable roles include Hamlet (1934), Jack Worthing in Oscar Wilde's *The Importance of Being Earnest* (1939), Benedick in *Much Ado About Nothing* (1952), and Spooner in Harold Pinter's *No Man's Land* (1975). He is also a producer and director and has appeared in a number of films. He was knighted in 1953.

Sir John Gielgud, British director, producer, and one of the finest Shakespearean actors of his time, was knighted in 1953 for his contributions to the British theater.

Gierek, Edward [gyair'-ek]   Edward Gierek, b. Jan. 6, 1913, was the political leader of Poland from Dec. 20, 1970, when he succeeded Władysław Gomułka as first secretary of the Polish United Workers' party, to Sept. 6, 1980. Previously a coal miner and first secretary of the party organization in Silesia, Gierek took office at a time of serious unrest over food prices. Under his leadership Poland expanded its trade with the West and undertook a costly effort to industrialize and to make consumer goods more available. Gierek acquiesced in the visit (1979) of Pope John Paul II to Poland, the first visit by a pope to a Communist country. New food price increases sparked worker demonstrations in 1976 and a wave of strikes beginning in July 1980. Gierek's dismissal came after the strikes forced him to concede the rights of workers to strike and to form independent unions.

gifted, education of the   see SPECIAL EDUCATION

Gigli, Beniamino [jeel'-yee, ben-yah-meen'-oh]   The Italian tenor Beniamino Gigli, b. Mar. 20, 1890, d. Nov. 30, 1957, was known for his powerful and expressive voice. He made his opera debut as Enzo in Ponchielli's *La Giaconda* in 1914. He made his American debut (1920) at the Metropolitan Opera as Faust in Boito's *Mefistofele* and remained with the company for 12 years. Although Gigli was admired especially for his Verdi and Puccini, he also shone in French and German roles. He returned (1939) to Italy and remained there during World War II; returning to the United States in 1955, he gave a series of highly successful concerts.

Gila monster [hee'-luh]   The Gila monster, *Heloderma suspectum*, and its close relative, the beaded lizard, *H. horridum*, the only poisonous lizards in the world, make up the family Helodermatidae. The venom is produced by glands in the lower jaw and is conducted by grooves in the upper and lower teeth. The bite is rarely fatal to humans but is extremely painful. The Gila monster acquired its name from the Gila Basin of Arizona; the beaded lizard, from its scales, which in this family do not overlap but merely adjoin one another, like rows of beads. The Gila monster, found from southern Utah and Nevada to Mexico, grows to about 50 cm (20 in) in overall length and is blackish brown with irregular, pinkish or orangish areas. The beaded lizard, found in western Mexico, grows to about 81 cm (32 in) overall and is black and yellow. The thick, blunt tail of both species serves for fat storage. This enables the lizards to go for long periods without food. Their diet consists mainly of eggs, young birds, small mammals, and lizards.

The venomous Gila monster is not dangerous unless carelessly handled. It hunts at night and if necessary can go without food for months, living on the fat stored in its tail.

Gila River The Gila River rises in southwestern New Mexico and flows about 1,015 km (630 mi) west and southwest to join the COLORADO RIVER at Yuma, Ariz. Its main tributaries include the San Francisco, San Pedro, Santa Cruz, Salt, Agua Fria, and Hassayampa rivers. Many dams along its course, including Coolidge and Painted Rock, impound its waters for flood control, hydroelectricity, and irrigation projects in the otherwise arid region. The remains of prehistoric Indian dwellings can be seen in the river's valley at Gila Cliff Dwellings (New Mexico) and Casa Grande (Arizona) national monuments.

Gilbert, Cass Cass Gilbert, b. Zanesville, Ohio, Jan. 28, 1858, d. May 17, 1934, designed some of the most important commercial and civic landmarks in New York City. He established his reputation by winning two important architectural competitions, for the Minnesota State Capitol in St. Paul (1896) and the U.S. Customs House in New York City (1905). Gilbert was particularly successful with the Gothic verticality of his most famous skyscraper, the WOOLWORTH BUILDING (1913). He was also chief architect of the GEORGE WASHINGTON BRIDGE (1927), whose magnificent steel towers he originally planned to cover with stonework in medieval style.

Gilbert, Sir Humphrey Sir Humphrey Gilbert, b. c.1539, d. Sept. 9, 1583, was an English soldier and colonizer who failed in his attempt to establish the first permanent English colony in North America. After studying military science at Oxford, Gilbert joined the army and was wounded in France (1563). In 1566 he wrote *Discourse*, in which he expressed his belief in the existence of a NORTHWEST PASSAGE. He fought in Ireland from 1566, eventually attaining the rank of colonel. He crushed the Munster rebellion there in 1569 and was knighted the next year.

In 1571 he served in Parliament for Plymouth. The next year he commanded an expedition to aid the Dutch Revolt against the Spanish. His plans for colonization, originally applied to Ireland, were transferred to the New World. He set sail in 1579, but his fleet broke up, and he was forced to return to England. A second colonizing expedition reached St. John's Bay, Newfoundland, in August 1583. After one ship was lost, the remainder of the expedition headed for England. Gilbert's ship, the overloaded *Squirrel*, sank en route.

Gilbert, William The English physician William Gilbert (also known as William of Colchester), b. May 24, 1544, d. Dec. 10, 1603, is known for his early studies on electricity and magnetism. His *De magnete* (1600) propounded the theory that the Earth was a giant lodestone with north and south magnetic poles. His theory that the Earth exerted a magnetic influence throughout the solar system was a precursor to the modern conception of gravity as an attracting force between masses. Gilbert was among the first to divide substances into electrics (spar, glass, amber) and nonelectrics.

Gilbert, Sir William S. see GILBERT AND SULLIVAN

Gilbert Islands see KIRIBATI

Gilbert and Sullivan Gilbert and Sullivan were a highly successful librettist-composer team. Their OPERETTAS are enjoyed for their satirical wit, comic plots and characters, and tuneful music.

Before their collaboration, William Schwenk Gilbert, b. Nov. 18, 1836, d. May 29, 1911, wrote drama criticism, verse, and stage pieces. Arthur Seymour Sullivan, b. May 13, 1842, d. Nov. 22, 1900, had composed hymns, cantatas, oratorios, piano pieces, songs, and orchestral works.

Sullivan's early ventures into comic opera, with writer F. C. Burnand, resulted in *Cox and Box* and *The Contrabandista,* in 1867. But his work with Gilbert brought out the best in each man: from Gilbert a waggish wit and pungent satire, from Sullivan an almost inexhaustible lyricism and musical wit.

Their first collaboration, *Thespis, or the Gods Grown Old* (1871), was unsuccessful. *Trial by Jury* (1875), though not a success at first, was unusual in being a one-act operetta without spoken dialogue. *The Sorcerer* (1877) began their public acclaim, as well as their asso-

The musical collaboration of the composer Sir Arthur Sullivan (left) and the librettist Sir William Gilbert (right) resulted in 14 comic operas that satirized Victorian manners. Works such as H.M.S. Pinafore *(1878) and* The Mikado *(1885) have delighted audiences throughout the world.*

ciation with Richard D'OYLY CARTE's company, which was organized for their productions. *H.M.S. Pinafore* (1878) and *The Pirates of Penzance* (1879) brought them to the peak of their fame, which extended to the United States. *Patience* (1881), *Iolanthe* (1882), *Princess Ida* (1884), and especially *The Mikado* (1885) consolidated their success and were followed by *Ruddigore* (1887), *The Yeomen of the Guard* (1888), and *The Gondoliers* (1889). A quarrel between them temporarily halted (1890–93) their collaboration, to the public's dismay. Reconciled, they attempted two more operettas, *Utopia Limited* (1893) and *The Grand Duke* (1896), but without their earlier deftness.

Knighted in 1883, Sullivan tried to compose more serious works, including his grand opera *Ivanhoe* (1891) and five more operas, and died exhausted. Gilbert was knighted in 1907. At age 74 he died trying to save a drowning woman.

Gilbreth, Frank and Lillian [gil'-breth]   A husband and wife engineering team, Frank Bunker Gilbreth, b. Fairfield, Maine, July 7, 1868, d. June 14, 1924, and Lillian Moller Gilbreth, b. Oakland, Calif., May 24, 1878, d. Jan. 2, 1972, developed the time and motion study to increase the efficiency and output of industry. Married in 1904, the Gilbreths launched an industrial consulting firm in Providence, R.I., which they later moved to Montclair, N.J. In 1911, Frank Gilbreth published *Motion Study,* which was followed by a series of books on INDUSTRIAL ENGINEERING, written in collaboration with his wife.

See also: INDUSTRIAL MANAGEMENT.

Gilded Age   The Gilded Age is a term used to describe the post-Civil War period in U.S. history. A satirical novel, *The Gilded Age* (1873), by Mark Twain and Charles Dudley Warner gave the period its name. The era, one of rapid industrialization, was characterized by the ruthless pursuit of profit, government corruption, conspicuous consumption, and vulgarity in taste.

Gilead [gil'-ee-ad]   In the Bible, Gilead is the name of the fertile region east of the Jordan and northeast of the Dead Sea. An area of rugged highlands, it was known for its pastures, vineyards, olive groves, and especially for the proverbial "balm of Gilead," a medicinal resin. It was at Gilead that David took refuge during the rebellion of Absalom.

Gilels, Emil   Known for his interpretations of Beethoven, Russian pianist Emil Grigoryevich Gilels, b. Oct. 19 (N.S.), 1916, d. Oct. 14, 1985, made his debut at the age of 13. He studied with Yakov Tkatch and Berthe Ringold at the Odessa Conservatory. Upon graduation in 1935 he studied with Heinrich Neuhaus at the Moscow Conservatory. Gilels won three major international piano competitions: 1st prize at Moscow in 1933, 2d prize in Vienna in 1936, and 1st prize in Brussels in 1938. He

performed in recital and as orchestra soloist throughout Europe and in the Far East and appeared frequently in the United States. When he made his U.S. debut in 1955, he was the first Soviet artist to perform in the United States since Sergei Prokofiev in 1921.

Gilgamesh, Epic of [gil'-guh-mesh]   The Epic of Gilgamesh is a long Akkadian poem on the theme of human beings' futile quest for immortality. A number of earlier Sumerian stories about Gilgamesh, the quasi-historical hero of the epic, were used as sources, but the Akkadian work was composed about 2000 BC.

In the story, Gilgamesh and his friend Enkidu seek immortality through fame, but when Enkidu dies, Gilgamesh finds fame hollow. Unable to accept the finality of death, he goes to Utnapishtim, the Babylonian counterpart of the biblical NOAH, to learn the secret of his immortality. Utnapishtim explains that he received it due to the unique circumstances of the flood, but he consoles the dejected Gilgamesh with news about a plant of life. A snake swallows the plant before Gilgamesh can use it, however, and he finally returns home, reluctantly accepting death as inevitable.

gill   see FISH

Gillespie, Dizzy [guh-les'-pee, diz'-ee]   John Birks "Dizzy" Gillespie, b. Cheraw, S.C., Oct. 21, 1917, is a jazz trumpeter-composer-bandleader most noted for creating BEBOP along with Charlie Parker and Thelonious Monk. Early musical training from his father led Gillespie to formal study and a long career in jazz. He was one of Cab Calloway's featured soloists in the early 1940s and played in several other prominent big bands, including that of Earl Hines. A fine musician and a superb technician, by 1945 he had helped evolve the complex and difficult bop mode. One of the most popular of present-day jazz artists, Gillespie has led his own groups—from big bop bands to small combos—in tours throughout the United States and much of the rest of the world.

Gillette, William H. [juh-let']   William Hooker Gillette, b. Hartford, Conn., July 24, 1853, d. Apr. 29, 1937, was an American playwright and actor who was noted for his portrayal of cool, unruffled men of action. He rose to stardom in his plays *Held by the Enemy* (1886) and *Secret Service* (1895). Gillette's most famous play, *Sherlock Holmes,* was first produced in New York in 1899, with Gillette in the title role. He revived the play many times in the United States and England. He also played the lead in one silent film, *Sherlock Holmes* (1916).

Gillray, James [gil'-ray]   James Gillray, b. Aug. 13, 1756, d. June 1, 1815, was the outstanding English caricaturist of the golden age of British political satire. He entered the Royal Academy in 1778 and also studied under Francesco Bartolozzi, gaining a sound printmaking technique. At first he produced a variety of engravings, but by the mid-1780s he had become a specialist in political cartoons, inventing his own subjects and producing his own plates. Everyone and everything became a target for his devastating burlesques: George III, William Pitt the Younger, Napoleon, Whigs, and Tories were all victims of his savage wit. During his industrious career he produced nearly a thousand prints, but his activity ended in insanity in 1810.

Gilson, Étienne [zheel-sohn', ay-tee-en'] Étienne Gilson, b. June 13, 1884, d. Sept. 19, 1978, was a French historian and proponent of Thomism, the philosophy of Thomas Aquinas. Among his many works are *Descartes' Concept of Liberty and Theology* (1913), *Moral Values and the Moral Life* (1925), *The Spirit of Medieval Philosophy* (1936), and *The Philosopher and Theology* (1960). According to Gilson, there have been only three great metaphysicians: Plato, Aristotle, and Aquinas; by balancing faith and reason, religion and science, the philosophy of Aquinas can fill the dangerous void left by the failures of modern philosophy.

gin [jin] Gin is an alcoholic beverage made by distilling fermented mixtures of grains and flavoring the resulting alcohol with juniper berries. The name is derived from the French word *genièvre* (juniper). First made in 17th-century Holland, the manufacture and popularity of gin spread quickly throughout Europe, and variations began to appear. Today Holland gin is a comparatively heavy-bodied, lower-proof beverage; London gin is drier and more potent; Plymouth gin is a sweeter variety. Sloe gin is flavored and tinted with sloe berries, the fruits of the blackthorn tree, and is sweetened by the addition of sugar. Other fruits, herbs, or spices may also be used to flavor gin. Gin is rarely drunk by itself, but is used as the alcoholic base for such mixtures as the martini (gin and vermouth) and the gin-and-tonic.

In 1689 the English, who had previously imported distilled liquors, began to encourage the domestic manufacture of spirits from English grain. Gin, which could be cheaply made and sold, rapidly became the solace and the scourge of the nation's poor. By the 1740s gin consumption had reached 20 million gallons annually. Appalled by the steeply rising mortality rate—attributable, in part, to urban alcoholism—and by the disastrous effects of widespread public drunkenness, Parliament passed the Gin Act in 1736. Although the act imposed heavy duties on both distillers and retailers of gin, its effect was minimal because the production of bootleg gin was impossible to control. It was only with the imposition of stiff excise taxes on gin production and the rigid control of its retail sale through a series of laws regulating public houses that the kind of mass inebriation depicted by Hogarth (*Gin Lane*, 1751) disappeared from the English scene.

See also: WHISKEY.

gin rummy see RUMMY

Ginastera, Alberto [hee-nah-stay'-rah] Alberto Evaristo Ginastera, b. April 11, 1916, d. June 25, 1983, was the foremost Argentine composer of his generation. At first he was closely identified with Argentine musical nationalism, embodied in such works as *Argentine Dances* (1937), for piano; *Estancia* (1941), a ballet; and *Pampeana* no. 3, "Symphonic Pastorale" (1954), for orchestra. In the 1950s, however, Ginastera gradually withdrew from musical nationalism. In the 1960s he won acclaim for his operas *Don Rodrigo* (1964) and *Bomarzo* (1967). *Bomarzo* seemed to have everything to attract a modern audience: sex, violence, perversion, death, serialism (see SERIAL MUSIC), and aleatoric devices (see ALEATORY MUSIC). The opera was a sensation, as was its successor, *Beatrix Cenci* (1971). In 1962, Ginastera organized and became director of the Latin American Center for Advanced Musical Studies in Buenos Aires.

ginger [jin'-jur] Ginger is the spice made from the rhizome, or enlarged underground stem, of the herbaceous perennial plant *Zingiber officinale*. Native to southern Asia, ginger is widely cultivated in Africa, India, the Orient, and the West Indies.

The plants grow 60 to 90 cm (2 to 3 ft) high, with long, narrow leaves and pale green flowers. The plant is vegetatively reproduced by planting its rhizome segments. The fleshy, aromatic rhizomes are commonly referred to as roots; they are harvested when the plant is about a year old and are washed, dried, bleached by liming or by the sun, and then shipped, peeled or unpeeled.

The rhizomes are processed in several different ways. Preserved ginger is made by boiling tender rhizomes in a sugar solution and packing them in syrup or in a sugar coating. Unpeeled rhizomes may be scalded in boiling water before drying to make black ginger; without scald-

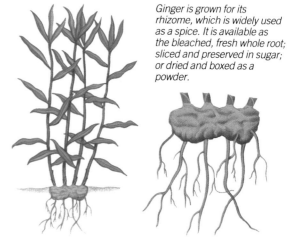

Ginger is grown for its rhizome, which is widely used as a spice. It is available as the bleached, fresh whole root; sliced and preserved in sugar; or dried and boxed as a powder.

ing, the product is green ginger. When parboiled, peeled, and bleached, the rhizomes are marketed as white ginger. Fresh gingerroot and dried, ground ginger are the most common commercial forms.

___

gingham [ging'-uhm]   A yarn-dyed fabric identified by woven-in plaids, checks, or stripes of two or more colors, gingham was originally of cotton, but it now may contain synthetic fibers as well. (In yarn-dying, threads are dyed before the cloth is woven, in contrast to a print, in which the color is printed on the fabric after weaving.) Gingham has been a common fabric for generations. Its name may be derived from a Malay word, *genggang,* meaning "striped." Combed gingham has fine, even yarns, and is used for better grades of women's and children's dresses, aprons, men's shirts, pajamas, and curtains; carded gingham is a medium-grade fabric used for apparel and household textile goods.

gingivitis   see DENTISTRY

___

ginkgo [ging'-koh]   The ginkgo, or maidenhair tree, *Ginkgo biloba,* is the only living species of the family Ginkgoaceae, which were GYMNOSPERMS that thrived about 175 to 200 million years ago. It is a medium-sized, deciduous tree, growing up to 36 m (120 ft) in height. Its fan-shaped leaves have two lobes and parallel veins. Male ginkgo trees bear cones and female trees bear pairs of ovules, or seeds, at the end of each flower stalk; when ripe, the fleshy seeds fall to the ground and emit a strong, unpleasant odor.

Native to southeastern China, ginkgoes are now distributed worldwide. They are hardy in moderate climates

and are commonly planted in Europe and North America as ornamentals or to line streets. For centuries the ginkgo was used to landscape monastery and temple grounds in China and Japan. The Chinese also used ginkgo extracts for medicinal purposes, and U.S. scientists have synthesized a compound found in ginkgoes that may be used to treat asthma and other ailments.

The exact ancestry of the ginkgo is uncertain, but it is thought to have originated from seed ferns, which are extinct groups of gymnosperms.

___

Ginsberg, Allen [ginz'-burg]   Allen Ginsberg, b. Newark, N.J., June 3, 1926, is an American poet and leading apostle of the BEAT GENERATION. His first published work, *Howl and Other Poems* (1956), sparked the San Francisco Renaissance and defined the generation of the 1950s with an authority and vision not seen in the United States since T. S. Eliot captured the anxiety of the 1920s in *The Waste Land.* Ginsberg's bardic rage against material values, however, was very different from Eliot's scholarly mourning for the loss of the spirit. In his second major work, *Kaddish* (1961), a poem on the anniversary of his mother's death, Ginsberg described their anguished relationship. In the 1960s, while participating in the anti–Vietnam War movement, he published several poetic works, including *Reality Sandwiches* (1963) and *Planet News* (1969). *The Fall of America* received the National Book Award for 1974. *Collected Poems, 1947–80* contains all his important work. Ginsberg sees himself as part of the prophetic tradition in poetry begun by William Blake in the 18th century and continued by Walt Whitman in the 19th. He names his contemporary influences as William Carlos Williams and his friend Jack Kerouac.

The ginkgo, native to southeastern China, is the remaining species of a tree family that existed 175 to 200 million years ago. The tree bears fan-shaped leaves and clusters of tiny flowers. Its fruit yields a sweet, nutlike seed prized as a delicacy in China.

Allen Ginsberg became a prophet of the Beat Generation with Howl *(1956), an assault in verse on American materialism. A cultural rebel, Ginsberg has proclaimed his outrage in books of poetry and in public readings and performances.*

Photo Jill Krementz © 1972

___

ginseng [jin'-seng]   Ginseng is a perennial herb of the genus *Panax.* The root of the ginseng has for centuries been reputed to be a panacea for cancer, rheumatism,

The American ginseng grows wild in North American woodlands. It stands up to 60 cm (2 ft) tall, has leaves up to 15 cm (6 in) long, and bears greenish white flowers.

diabetes, sexual debility, and aging. The claims date back to ancient China, and the root was long of great value there; Europe did not hear of it, however, until 1642, when the explorer Alvaro Samedo returned with a report of the restorative properties of Oriental ginseng (later named *P. pseudoginseng*).

In 1718 an almost identical species, *P. quinquefolius*, was found in North America. Millions of pounds were uprooted, dried, and exported in the China trade. Eventually the slow-maturing plant, native to cool woods from Quebec to Oklahoma, was almost extinct. Cultivation began in the late 19th century, but the Chinese market balked at the cultivated American product, and many investments were lost.

Today China and Korea export ginseng to the West, where its popularity has grown in recent years. Soviet scientists claim to have found substances in ginseng that stimulate endocrine secretions and act as a tonic to the cardiovascular system. Medical research in the West, however, has failed to substantiate these claims.

Ginzberg, Asher   see ACHAD HA-AM

Ginzberg, Louis [ginz'-burg] The Jewish scholar Louis Ginzberg, b. Lithuania, Nov. 28, 1873, d. Nov. 11, 1953, was one of this century's foremost authorities in rabbinic literature. He emigrated to the United States in 1899 and was a professor at New York's Jewish Theological Seminary from 1902. His best-known work is the monumental 7-volume *Legends of the Jews* (1909–38), in which he compiled the folklore scattered throughout the Midrash and Talmud, tracing the stories to their sources.

Giolitti, Giovanni [joh-lit'-tee, joh-vahn'-nee] Giovanni Giolitti, b. Oct. 27, 1842, d. July 17, 1928, was one of the ablest Italian political leaders of the modern era. A member of Parliament from 1882 until his death, he was premier five times between 1892 and 1921. Under his leadership, Italy prospered, the suffrage was democratized, and social security was introduced. Giolitti guided Italy into the ITALO-TURKISH WAR over Libya in 1911 but opposed entry into World War I. His reputation, however, remains controversial; some of his electoral victories were linked with corruption. He accepted the support of the Catholics after 1904 and the Fascists after World War I. At first, he supported the government of Benito MUSSOLINI, thinking he could tame it, but after November 1924 he withdrew his support.

Giordano, Umberto [johr-dahn'-oh] Umberto Giordano, b. Aug. 27, 1867, d. Nov. 12, 1948, was an Italian composer of VERISMO operas. Giordano's first success, *Mala vita* (1892), identified him with the new school of blood-and-thunder melodrama. His fourth opera, *Andrea Chénier* (1896), was a triumph, and on it his fame largely rests. *Fedora* (1898) is also still performed. Among Giordano's 12 operas, *Siberia* (1903) and *La Cena della Beffe* (1924) also bear mentioning.

Giorgione [johr-john'-ay] The Italian painter Giorgione, b. Castelfranco, Veneto, c.1477, played a pivotal role in the development of the High Renaissance in early-16th-century Venetian painting. Little is known of his career, however, and few of his paintings have been authenticated. In 1508 he worked on frescoes on the facade of the Fondaco dei Tedeschi and on a group portrait of the Council of Ten in Venice (now lost). It can be inferred from 16th-century descriptions of Venetian collections that Giorgione also executed commissions for numerous private patrons. He died of the plague in September or October 1510.

Modern scholars are restrictive and generally unanimous in accepting as Giorgione's the following works: the *Castelfranco Madonna* (c.1500; cathedral, Castelfranco, Veneto); *Judith* (c.1504; Hermitage, Leningrad); *Portrait of a Youth* (Staatliche Museum, Berlin); *The Tempest* (c.1503; Accademia, Venice); *Venus*, finished by TITIAN (c.1507; Gemäldegalerie, Dresden, Germany); *Portrait of a Young Woman* (1506; Kunsthistorisches Museum, Vienna); and *The Three Philosophers*, finished by SEBASTIANO DEL PIOMBO (Kunsthistorisches Museum, Vienna). This group of paintings has established a sense of Giorgione's style against which numerous other paintings attributed to him have been measured. Strongly argued attributions include *Self Portrait of David* (Herzog Anton-Ulrich Museum, Brunswick, Germany); *Christ Carrying the Cross* (Isabella Stewart Gardner Museum, Boston); *The Knight of Malta* (Uffizi Gallery, Florence); *Portrait of a Man* (Fine Arts Gallery, San Diego, Calif.); *Portrait of an Old Woman* (Accademia, Venice); and *Adoration of the Shepherds* (National Gallery, Washington, D.C.).

Giorgione was a musician and poet as well as a painter, and he moved in the most cultivated circles of Venice;

The Tempest (c.1503), celebrated for the mysterious, sensual associations of its subject, is one of the few unquestioned works of Giorgione. (Accademia, Venice.)

his painting deals with subjects also treated by contemporary writers. While history or narrative painting was the Renaissance artist's major concern, Giorgione produced nonnarrative "mood scenes" such as The Tempest or The Pastoral Concert, developing open forms with soft contours defined by warm light and creating a subtle balance between the highlights and transparent shadows. Giorgione's influence on his contemporaries was profound, particularly on Titian. Because Giorgione diminished the importance of subject matter and emphasized the purely expressive content of his paintings, recent critics have claimed that he anticipated much of modern art.

Giotto di Bondone [joht'-toh dee bohn-doh'-nay]

The leading Florentine painter of his generation, Giotto di Bondone, b. c.1267, d. Jan. 8, 1337, created a revolution in painting that set Italian Renaissance art on the course it would follow for centuries. Giotto broke free of the flat, ethereal Byzantine manner of his Italian predecessors by painting convincing human figures with the semblance of weighty pieces of sculpture placed within a convincing illusion of space. Giotto dramatized religious narratives with a keen comprehension of human behavior in a way that later artists seldom equaled or surpassed.

Little of Giotto's career has been documented. A late tradition claims that he was trained by his most famous Florentine predecessor, CIMABUE. Dante's Purgatorio not-

ed in the early 14th century that Giotto's reputation soon surpassed Cimabue's. In Giotto's lifetime his most famous work was the mosaic Navicella (c.1300; Saint Peter's, Rome), which is now all but destroyed.

Giotto's major extant works and the touchstone of his artistic personality are found in Padua, where he frescoed (c.1305) almost the entire inner surface of the Arena Chapel for the wealthy Enrico Scrovegni. At the bottom of a depiction of the Last Judgment covering the entrance wall, Scrovegni is shown presenting the chapel, in the form of a model, to the Virgin. On the other walls, three ranges of paintings narrate the life of the Virgin and of Christ. In each incident Giotto, like a skilled stage director, arranges his "actors" across the surface of each scene and within a shallow stagelike space so that the drama attains a climactic visual focus. In the well-known scene of the Lamentation, somber, blocklike figures surround the body of Christ within the space while all glances and gestures and even the diagonal line of the hill draw the eye to Mary's embrace of her dead son.

Giotto's works in Florence include the Ognissanti Madonna (c.1310; Uffizi Gallery, Florence), a large wooden panel painting. In the 1320s he also painted frescoes in the chapels of the Bardi and Peruzzi families in the church of Santa Croce. These later frescoes have a broader format than his earlier Paduan paintings.

In 1334, Giotto was made director of public works for Florence and designed the cathedral's bell tower (campanile). He influenced almost all Florentine painters in the first half of the 14th century. MASACCIO in the early

The iconography of Giotto's Betrayal (c.1305), from his fresco cycle in the Arena Chapel, Padua, follows a typical medieval pattern. The artist, however, has introduced a kind of psychology of relationships in his representation of faces and bodily movement.

15th and MICHELANGELO in the early 16th century are the true heirs to Giotto's style of weighty figures and dramatic narration.

See also: FRESCO PAINTING; ITALIAN ART AND ARCHITECTURE; RENAISSANCE ART AND ARCHITECTURE.

Giovanni, Nikki [joh-vah'-nee] Nikki Giovanni, b. Knoxville, Tenn., July 6, 1943, is an American poet known for her exploration of the attitudes toward black consciousness that became current in the 1960s. Some of her poems are portraits of individuals, such as "Aretha Franklin" and "Angela Davis" (from *Black Feeling/Black Talk/Black Judgment*, 1970) or those in her later volume, *The Women and the Men* (1975). Among her other works are an autobiography, *Gemini* (1971), and *A Poetic Equation: Conversations between Nikki Giovanni and Margaret Walker* (1974).

Giovanni da Montecorvino Giovanni da Montecorvino, 1247–1328, was an Italian Franciscan friar who founded the earliest Roman Catholic missions in India and China. After missionary work in Armenia and Persia, he was commissioned (1289) by Pope Nicholas IV to travel east carrying papal letters to the rulers of the East. Setting out from Persia in 1291, he went to India, where he stayed a year, and reached the Mongol court in Beijing, China, in 1294. Working mainly alone, he made numerous converts and translated the New Testament into Uighur.

Giovanni di Paolo Giovanni di Paolo, baptized Nov. 19, 1403, d. between January and Mar. 27, 1482, was an eclectic yet distinctive Sienese painter whose special gift for depicting narratives is evident both in his panel paintings and in illuminated manuscripts. Many fragments of the altarpieces he painted from 1426 on for churches in Siena are now dispersed in various European and American collections. Indifferent to his Florentine contemporaries' preoccupation with perspective, Giovanni created fantastic, seemingly endless vistas that were uniquely his own, such as that in *St. John Entering the Wilderness* (n.d.; Art Institute of Chicago). Giovanni's *Purification of the Virgin* (1447–49; Pinacoteca, Siena) resembles a painting of the same subject by Ambrogio Lorenzetti more than 100 years earlier (1342; Uffizi Gallery, Florence). Here, as throughout his work, however, the style is unmistakably Giovanni's: decorative, sometimes even dainty, but also agitated and expressionistic to a degree unparalleled in his sources.

giraffe [juh-raf'] The giraffe, *Giraffa camelopardalis*, family Giraffidae, order Artiodactyla, is the tallest of all animals, as much as 5.5 m (18 ft) high. A series of valves in the vessels of the vascular system ensures a blood supply to the head. The shoulder height may be up to 3.7 m

The giraffe is the tallest animal in the world, reaching heights up to 5.5 m (18 ft). The giraffe can run as fast as 48 km/h (30 mph).

(12 ft), and the weight 1,400 kg (3,000 lb). There are usually three skin-covered horns, two on top of the head and one between the eyes. Sometimes an additional pair of hornlike knobs is also present on the back of the head. Patterns and shades of dark patches on the tawny coat, which help conceal the animals when they stand in the shade of trees, vary among the subspecies. The long tongue is used for plucking leaves from trees. Giraffes live on tree-dotted grasslands south of the Sahara in Africa. Their chief foods are acacia and mimosa leaves. When startled, a giraffe can gallop up to 48 km/h (30 mph) for a moderate distance. The female gives birth to a single young, rarely twins. The life span is from 15 to 20 years.

Girard, Stephen [jur-ahrd'] Stephen Girard, b. near Bordeaux, France, May 20, 1750, d. Dec. 26, 1831, an American entrepreneur and banker, began his career at sea and eventually owned a fleet of ships. In 1812 he established the Bank of Stephen Girard and in 1813 underwrote the sale of government war bonds. He played a key role in setting up the Second Bank of the United States in 1816, underwriting most of its capital stock. The bulk of his fortune went to establish Girard College in Philadelphia, Pa., a preparatory school for boys that opened in 1848.

Girardon, François [zhee-rahr-dohn'] The French sculptor François Girardon, b. Mar. 17, 1628, d. Sept. 1, 1715, was a key figure in the classical movement that dominated 17th-century French art. In 1657 he was admitted to the French Academy of Painting and Sculpture, which under the autocratic leadership of Charles Le Brun had become the supreme arbiter of artistic taste in France. Girardon made significant contributions to Le Brun's aesthetic program, which stressed the primacy of reason and the faithful emulation of classical models. After collaborating with Le Brun in decorating the Louvre (1663–71) and the Versailles gardens (1666–75), he executed on his own the tomb of Cardinal Richelieu (1675–94; Chapel of the Sorbonne, Paris), a three-figure composition of classical formalism. Thereafter he received many royal commissions, including his bronze equestrian statue *Louis XIV* (1683–99; destroyed 1792) and his famous *Rape of Proserpina* (1677–99), which was a baroque criticism of Giovanni da Bologna's Mannerist sculpture, the *Rape of the Sabine Women*.

Giraud, Henri Honoré [zhee-roh', ahn-ree' ohn-ohr-ay']

The French general Henri Honoré Giraud, b. Jan. 18, 1879, d. March 11, 1949, was cofounder with Gen. Charles DE GAULLE of the French Committee of National Liberation during World War II. After service in World War I, he was a commander in Morocco (1922–25, 1930–36). In 1942 he took part in the Allied invasion of North Africa and became commander in chief of French forces. After the assassination (December 1942) of Admiral Jean François DARLAN, he also became French high commissioner in Africa. Although he allied with de Gaulle in the French Committee, formed in June 1943, differences with de Gaulle forced his retirement in April 1944. Giraud served in the postwar Constituent Assembly in Paris.

Giraudoux, Jean [zhee-roh-doo']

Hippolyte Jean Giraudoux, b. Oct. 29, 1882, d. Jan. 31, 1944, was a French dramatist who wrote 15 plays, most initially staged by the actor-director Louis Jouvet and later inter-

The French writer Jean Giraudoux satirized society in novels, tragedies, and whimsical dramas. Many of his works use ancient or supernatural backgrounds to introduce the element of fantasy while voicing concern over the absence of human morality.

nationally acclaimed. Giraudoux was also a prose writer and served France as a diplomat and government official.

Giraudoux was born in the village of Bellac and studied at the École Normale Supérieure. In his youth he traveled extensively—to Germany, Italy, the Balkans, Canada, and the United States, where he spent a year (1906–07) as an instructor at Harvard. Returning to France, he served in World War I, was twice wounded, and became the first writer ever to be awarded the wartime Legion of Honor.

His worldwide importance rests on such plays as *Amphitryon 38* (1929; Eng. trans., 1938), *Judith* (1931), *Tiger at the Gates* (1935; Eng. adaptation of *La Guerre de Troie n'aura pas lieu*, 1955, by Christopher FRY), *Ondine* (1939; Eng. trans., 1961), and *The Madwoman of Chaillot* (1945; Eng. trans., 1949), which was published and produced posthumously. Giraudoux also wrote five novels, the best known being *My Friend from Limousin* (1922; Eng. trans., 1923) and *Bella* (1926; Eng. trans., 1927), and numerous short stories. He was one of France's outstanding essayists during the interwar years, acclaimed for such literary studies as *Racine* (1930) and such political studies as *Pleins Pouvoirs* (Full Powers, 1939). At the start of World War II he served as minister of information under Premier Édouard Daladier.

Girl Scouts of the U.S.A. see SCOUTING

Girondists [jir-ahn'-dists]

During the FRENCH REVOLUTION, the Girondists (properly, Girondins) were the deputies to the Legislative Assembly and the National Convention from the department of Gironde. Notable orators, these men were prominent as "patriots" in 1791–92 when they advocated war against Austria and expressed the general suspicion of the intentions of King LOUIS XVI. When the Republic was established, however, they sought to moderate the Revolution and to curb the power of Paris, which led to their downfall and execution in 1793. By extension, the name *Girondists* is often applied by historians to many others supposedly associated with them. Leaders of the group included Jacques Pierre Brissot de Warville and Jean Marie and Jeanne Manon Philipon ROLAND DE LA PLATIÈRE.

Girtin, Thomas [gurt'-in]

Thomas Girtin, b. Feb. 18, 1775, d. Nov. 9, 1802, together with J. M. W. Turner, revolutionized the art of WATERCOLOR and introduced the romantic style in English LANDSCAPE PAINTING. He was apprenticed to Edward Dayes in 1788, and from 1792 he produced topographical scenes for the antiquarian publisher James Moore. In about 1795 he began copying and studying the works of CANALETTO, John Robert Cozens (see COZENS family), Giovanni Battista PIRANESI, and Richard WILSON, which broadened the scope of his art and introduced a greater sense of atmosphere to his landscapes. From 1796 he traveled extensively in England, Scotland, and Wales in search of picturesque scenery, and in

1801–02 he visited Paris. On his return he exhibited an enormous panorama of London, *The Eidometropolis*. Girtin's final works, such as *The White House at Chelsea* (1800; Tate Gallery, London), introduced a personal note of tranquility into landscape painting, and his technique of broad washes and open compositions led the way to the poetic visions of the romantic era.

▬

Girty, Simon [gurt'-ee]   The American frontiersman Simon Girty, b. near present-day Harrisburg, Pa., 1741, d. Feb. 18, 1818, became known as the Great Renegade after transferring allegiance from the patriots to the British during the American Revolution. Girty, who had served (1759–74) as an Indian interpreter at Fort Pitt (Pittsburgh), joined the British at Fort Detroit in 1778. Thereafter he led Indian war parties against the Americans, reputedly encouraging the torture of prisoners. Following the Revolution he promoted Indian attacks on American pioneers in the Ohio country. He settled in Canada when the British abandoned Detroit in 1796.

▬

Giscard d'Estaing, Valéry [zhees-kahr' des-tan', vah-lay-ree']   Valéry Giscard d'Estaing, b. Feb. 2, 1926, was president of France from 1974 to 1981. He entered government service in 1952, in the Ministry of Finance. In 1956 he was elected to the National Assembly and in 1959 became secretary of state for finance.

Giscard founded (1962) the pro-Gaullist Independent Republican party (now the Republican party). From 1962 to 1966 he was minister of finance in Charles DE GAULLE's coalition cabinet, but he was dropped from the cabinet in 1967. After that year's March election, which returned him to the Assembly, he became more critical of some of de Gaulle's policies. He became minister of finance again in 1969 under de Gaulle's successor, Georges POMPIDOU.

As president, Giscard moved France toward fuller cooperation with other countries and reduced state controls on the economy. He also implemented an intensive nuclear-power program and built up France's independent nuclear deterrent. In the 1981 presidential election he was defeated by his Socialist rival, François MITTERRAND.

▬

Gish, Dorothy and Lillian [gish]   The Gish sisters (real name De Guiche) were among the earliest American film stars, especially known for their work in such D. W. GRIFFITH films as *Orphans of the Storm* (1922). Dorothy Gish, b. Massillon, Ohio, Mar. 11, 1898, d. June 4, 1968, made occasional talking films, such as *The Cardinal* (1963), but had a rather desultory career. Lillian Gish, b. Springfield, Ohio, Oct. 14, 1896, remained more in the public eye, from her early appearances in *Birth of a Nation* (1914), *Broken Blossoms* (1918), and *Way Down East* (1920) to such sound films as *Duel in the Sun* (1946), *Night of the Hunter* (1955), *The Comedians* (1967), *Poltergeist* (1982), and *The Whales of August* (1987). Through her eighties she starred in television movies and lectured in universities.

Lillian (left) *and Dorothy* (right) *Gish appear in a scene from one of their most important films,* Orphans of the Storm *(1922). The Gish sisters rose to stardom in silent films directed by D. W. Griffith.*

Valéry Giscard d'Estaing, president of France from 1974, was defeated in his bid to gain reelection in 1981. He had been criticized for the rates of unemployment and inflation, as well as for his aloof and aristocratic style.

▬

Gislebertus [jis-ul-bair'-tuhs]   The 12th-century French sculptor Gislebertus was the leader of an unusually homogenous group of sculptors that carved the figural capitals and the doorway sculpture of the cathedral of Saint Lazarus, at Autun in Burgundy, between about 1125 and 1135. Gislebertus's work represents a high point of Burgundian Romanesque sculpture (see ROMANESQUE ART AND ARCHITECTURE). His signature, *Gislebertus hoc fecit*, is found in the tympanum over the west entrance of the cathedral. The tympanum portrays in high relief the Last Judgment, with heaven and the saved to the left of the central figure of Christ, and hell and the damned to the right. The sculptural style is marked by a use of extraordinarily delicate linear patterns, an elongation of human body proportions, and the frequent use of fluttering drapery edges.

Gissing, George Robert [gis'-ing] George Robert Gissing, b. Nov. 22, 1857, d. Dec. 28, 1903, was an English novelist whose work marks the transition from Victorian melodrama to modern realism. His promising scholarly career was cut short when he was expelled from college and jailed for having stolen to support a prostitute whom he wished to marry and reform. A life of unremitting literary toil followed, often bordering on poverty, recorded in his popular novels *New Grub Street* (1891) and *The Nether World* (1889). From his first book, *Demos* (1886), the subjects of his 22 novels were the poor and the shabby genteel.

Gissing was influenced by French and Russian novelists, but English Victorian propriety denied him the freedom and honesty of European literary naturalists. His own ideal remained the life of classical scholarship and scholarly seclusion evoked in *By the Ionian Sea* (1901) and *The Private Papers of Henry Ryecroft* (1903).

Gist, Christopher [gist] Christopher Gist, b. near Baltimore, Md., c.1706, d. 1759, an American frontiersman, in 1750–51 became the first white man to carefully explore the Ohio River lands in southern Ohio and northeastern Kentucky. The following winter he explored the area between the Monongahela and Great Kanawha rivers. Gist accompanied George WASHINGTON as a guide on the latter's mission to the Forks of the Ohio in 1753–54 and twice saved his life. He was also the guide on Edward BRADDOCK's ill-fated expedition (1755) against Fort Duquesne.

Giulini, Carlo Maria [joo-lee'-nee] The Italian conductor Carlo Maria Giulini, b. May 9, 1914, began his career in radio and conducting opera. After graduating (1939) from the Conservatory of Music of Santa Cecilia in Rome, he studied conducting with Bernardino Molinari at the Accademia Musicale. Between 1946 and 1953, he was conductor of the orchestras of Radio Roma and Radio Milano. In 1951 he made his opera debut with *La Traviata* at La Scala, where he became principal conductor (1953–56). Invited by Fritz Reiner in 1955 to conduct the Chicago Symphony, he was principal guest conductor of that orchestra for nine seasons (1969–78). From 1978 to 1984 he was conductor and music director of the Los Angeles Philharmonic.

Giulio Romano [jool'-yoh roh-mah'-noh] The Italian architect and painter Giulio Romano, b. c.1499, d. Nov. 1, 1546, was a follower of RAPHAEL and one of the founders of MANNERISM. He began working in Raphael's workshop as a boy, and by the time of Raphael's death in 1520, he had become one of the leading artists working in Rome. He helped complete several projects begun by Raphael, among them the *Transfiguration* (1517–22) and the *Stanza dell'Incendio di Borgo* (1514–17) in the Vatican. Giulio's work cultivated Raphael's elegance and so-

Giulio Romano, one of Raphael's foremost students, painted The Bath of Cupid and Psyche *(1527–31) for Federigo II Gonzaga of Mantua. (Palazzo del Te, Mantua, Italy.)*

phistication and demonstrated the Mannerist tendency to strain and contradict classical principles of style. In 1524, Federigo II Gonzaga invited Giulio to Mantua, where he dominated the artistic life of the area as an architect and decorator until his death. His masterpiece is the Palazzo del Te (1527–34), designed for Federigo. The building's exterior exhibits the Mannerist characteristics of capriciousness and variety. The interior is equally ingenious: the beehive-shaped *Sala dei Giganti* is completely painted with a scene of Jupiter repulsing an attack of giants. After Federigo's death in 1540, Giulio began work on the rebuilding of the cathedral in Mantua.

Givenchy, Hubert de   SEE FASHION DESIGN

Giza [gee'-zuh] Giza is the administrative capital of Giza governorate, Egypt. It is located on the west bank of the Nile River opposite CAIRO, to which it is linked by bridges over the islands of Roda and Gezira. The population of Giza is 1,670,800 (1986 est.). A prosperous suburb of Cairo, Giza is noted for its shopping districts, zoological and botanical gardens, and museum of agriculture and has cotton-textile plants, breweries, and film studios. The University of Cairo (1924), the largest in Egypt, is also located there.

About 8 km (5 mi) southwest of Giza are the Great SPHINX and the three large PYRAMIDS of Khufu (Cheops), Khafre, and Menkaure, built between 2613 and 2494 BC. One of the Seven Wonders of the Ancient World, these monuments are a major tourist attraction in Egypt.

glaciers and glaciation A glacier is a large mass of mobile, permanent ice formed on land by the consolidation and recrystallization of snowflakes. It may move down a slope by gravity, or spread outward in all direc-

1. pyramid-shaped peak
2. nunatak, or lofty isolated peak
3. snow-covered basin
4. cirque (horseshoe like depression)
5. cirque lake
6. arête, or knife-edge ridge
7. crevasse
8. lateral moraine
9. seracs, or ice pinnacles
10. icebergs
11. medial moraine
12. terminal moraine
13. ice cave
14. till
15. ice front
16. end moraine
17. perched rock
18. roches moutonnées, or "sheep" rocks
19. drumlin
20. esker
21. glacial lake, or tarn
22. section of a drumlin
23. cliff lake
24. U-shaped valley
25. erratic boulders
26. truncated spur
27. alluvial fan
28. debris from slope
29. waterfall
30. hanging valley

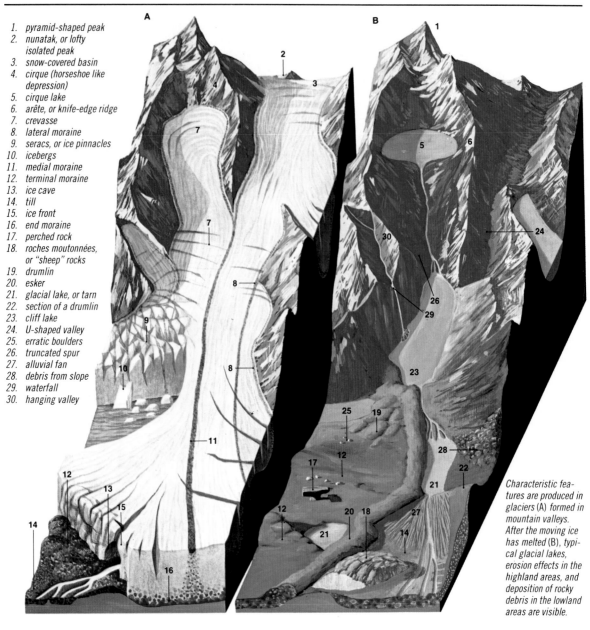

Characteristic features are produced in glaciers (A) formed in mountain valleys. After the moving ice has melted (B), typical glacial lakes, erosion effects in the highland areas, and deposition of rocky debris in the lowland areas are visible.

tions because of its own thickness. Glaciers may terminate on land, in the ocean, or in a lake. They vary in size from small features about 1 km (0.6 mi) long to the great Antarctic ice sheet, which covers 12,500,000 km^2 (4,826,000 m^2). They are found today in all of the great mountain ranges of the world, where they number in the tens of thousands, and on all of the continents except Australia. Glaciers store about 75 percent of the Earth's fresh water.

Ice Sheets

An ice sheet is a dome-shaped glacier covering an area of more than 50,000 km^2 (19,300 mi^2); an ice cap covers a smaller area. Ice sheets move outward in all directions and are not greatly impeded by topography. The Antarctic and Greenland ice sheets are the only ones now in existence, but during the Pleistocene Epoch (see ICE AGES) ice sheets covered the northern parts of both North America and Europe.

About 91 percent of the world's glacial ice is locked up in the ANTARCTIC ice sheet, which covers an area about 1½ times as large as the contiguous United States. The greatest thickness of ice measured in the Antarctic ice sheet is 4,300 m (14,000 ft); its average thickness is thought to be about 2,000 m (6,500 ft). If the Antarctic ice sheet were to melt completely, SEA LEVEL around the world would rise more than 60 m (200 ft).

Type of Glaciers

An ice shelf is an extensive, thick, flat, floating sheet of ice that is attached to the land on one or more sides and terminates in the ocean in a vertical ice cliff, generally 30 m (100 ft) high, from which many of the huge tabular ICEBERGS break off. Ice shelves are found mainly in Antarctica, although some occur in the Arctic. The Ross Ice Shelf in Antarctica is the best known. Nourished by snowfall, land ice, and perhaps by bottom freezing, it moves outward from the coast an average of 30 m/yr (100 ft/yr) and covers an area almost as large as Texas. Although appearing to be flat, it rises gently from the ocean inland, varying in total ice thickness from 100 m (330 ft) near the ocean to more than 700 m (2,300 ft) inland.

An alpine, mountain, or valley glacier flows down a valley. Tens of thousands of them exist at the present time. Fed by snow from one or more CIRQUES and confined by the walls of preexisting stream-cut valleys, they are much longer than they are wide. Some are less than a kilometer long, but the Hubbard Glacier in Yukon Territory and Alaska, one of the longest, is over 100 km (68 mi) in length. Most move less than a meter (3 ft) a day. The longer ones generally have tributaries.

A piedmont glacier is a thick, extensive sheet of ice formed on the lowlands at the foot of mountains where a valley glacier leaves the confines of its valley. Some of the larger piedmont glaciers are formed by the spreading out and coalescing of two or more valley glaciers. The best known is Alaska's Malaspina Glacier, which covers 4,200 km^2 (1,600 mi^2) and is about 600 m (2,000 ft) thick.

Outlet glaciers, found in Greenland, Iceland, and Antarctica, are fed from the margin of an ice sheet or ice cap and move through a pass in a coastal mountain range down into a preexisting valley. Tidewater glaciers, which occupy FJORDS in rugged coastal regions of high latitudes, are sources of icebergs.

Glacier Movement

It has long been known that glaciers move. Movement has been demonstrated by the invasion of ice onto ground earlier uncovered, by G. J. Hugi's observation that his hut on the Unteraar Glacier in Switzerland moved about a mile downstream between 1827 and 1840, and by the displacement of surface markers on glaciers. Pulled downhill by the force of gravity, a glacier slides over the bedrock beneath it, and internal deformation of the ice accommodates the motion.

The majority of valley glaciers move only a meter (3 ft) each day. Some valley glaciers in Alaska and elsewhere, called surging glaciers, however, can attain daily speeds of more than 60 m (200 ft). Ice sheets as a whole move much more slowly than valley glaciers.

Surface Features

A variety of features of different sizes form on the surface of a glacier. A medial MORAINE is a surface ridge of material near the middle of a glacier. It is aligned parallel to the flow lines of the glacier and moves down a valley with it. Medial moraines are formed immediately downstream from the point where the lateral moraines along the sides of two coalescing glaciers unite. A trunk glacier formed from a number of tributary flows will usually have as many medial moraines on it as it has tributary glaciers.

Crevasses, wedge-shaped cracks or fissures in the surface of an ice sheet or glacier, are formed by tensile stresses set up by ice movement. Though sometimes over 20 m (70 ft) wide and hundreds of meters long, they are usually less than 35 m (120 ft) deep. In winter they are often hidden by snow bridges, making travel dangerous.

A glacier table is a large block of stone resting on an ice pedestal, which may rise 3 m (10 ft) or more above the surface of a glacier. A glacier table is formed when the stone is large enough to insulate the ice immediately beneath it from the sun's radiation. The pedestal gets higher as the surface of the glacier is lowered by ablation.

Glaciation

The covering of the land by glacial ice is called glaciation, and the uncovering that results as glaciers retreat is called deglaciation. During either stage the processes of EROSION AND SEDIMENTATION operate to drastically modify the landscape. Glaciers and ice sheets erode by abrasion and quarrying. Abrasion occurs when the fine particles and fragments held at or near the base of a glacier are scraped across the bedrock immediately beneath. Quarrying, or plucking, is the removal by a glacier of blocks of rock from the bedrock over which it moves.

Striations, glacial polish, and grooves are small, surficial features resulting from abrasion. Roches moutonnées are larger features formed by both abrasion and quarrying. The largest topographic features resulting from glacial erosion are the U-shaped valleys formed by the deepening and widening of preexisting river valleys. These valleys, when deglaciated, are characterized by steep, high cliffs, tributary hanging valleys, truncated spurs, waterfalls, and other glacial features. They afford some of the most magnificent and spectacular scenery on earth; Yosemite Valley in California is a classic example. FJORDS are glaciated valleys invaded and drowned by the sea.

TILL, loose, unstratified glacial DRIFT, covers millions of square kilometers in North America and Europe and is being deposited now by modern glaciers. Till contains everything from clay-sized particles to large boulders, and varies in general from less than 1 m (3 ft) to more than 150 m (492 ft) in thickness. In New England, till contains so many boulders that it makes farming difficult, but in other regions good soil has developed on it.

When the terminus of a glacier neither advances nor retreats but remains more or less stationary for some time, a ridge of till called an end moraine is deposited along the ice margin, along with hills of stratified drift called kames. The moraine formed by glaciers at their farthest advance is called a terminal moraine. Valley glaciers may deposit terminal moraines hundreds of meters high. Some of the world's most beautiful lakes have formed behind moraine dams left by valley glaciers.

In the Alps, Scandinavia, and the Pacific Northwest,

glaciers supply great quantities of meltwater during the dry, warm summer months. This water is important for agricultural, industrial, and domestic use. Meltwater streams transport and deposit large quantities of sand and gravel, as well as very fine-grained sediment called rock flour. An outwash plain is formed by the coalescence of sand and gravel deposits from the many streams that issue from the margin of an ice sheet. LONG ISLAND, at the southern tip of New York State, is a Pleistocene outwash plain. Outwash deposits may bury blocks of ice, which long after burial are melted out, forming a hollow surrounded by sand and gravel. Called kettles, such hollows form ponds on Cape Cod, Mass. Glacial sand and gravel deposits are used to build roads and make concrete and are important sources of GROUNDWATER.

Glacier National Park   see NATIONAL PARKS

Glackens, William [glak'-enz]   A member of the ASHCAN SCHOOL, or The Eight, the American painter William James Glackens, b. Philadelphia, Mar. 13, 1870, d. May 22, 1938, was one of a group of artists whose search for realism challenged the genteel academicism of an

Chez Mouquin, *painted by William Glackens in 1905, evokes the gaiety of Parisian café life. After visiting France, Glackens abandoned his realistic style for a bright and colorful impressionism. (The Art Institute of Chicago.)*

earlier generation. With his friends John SLOAN, George LUKS, and Everett SHINN, Glackens worked as a newspaper artist. In 1908, in defiance of their rejection by the National Academy, Glackens, Robert HENRI, and six other artists participated in a counter-exhibition entitled "Eight Independent Painters," at New York's Macbeth Gallery.

As a realist, Glackens could not be considered innovative in his methods. His early works were painted in dark colors and with robust brushwork. After his travels in France introduced him to IMPRESSIONISM, his later paintings used the light, bright palette of Pierre Auguste RENOIR and a fragmented impressionist touch. Glackens was naturally drawn to society, and his most celebrated paintings are of fashionable life—festive café scenes, such as *Chez Mouquin* (1905; Art Institute of Chicago), or the cosmopolitan world of New York's Washington Square.

gladiators   In ancient Rome, gladiators—professional combatants drawn from the ranks of prisoners of war, criminals, slaves, and volunteer freedmen—competed as public entertainment at festival games. Such combats were held in Rome as early as 264 BC as part of memorial ceremonies. Although some gladiators fought wild animals, the combats generally featured a pair of human contenders. The gladiators fought in various styles, depending on their background and training. Unless the audience or emperor indicated that he should be spared, a defeated gladiator usually lost his life. Increasingly elaborate, the imperial games sometimes exhibited thousands of pairs of gladiators in a series lasting several months; some private individuals sponsored fights with as many as 100 pairs. Despite their condemnation by many observers, the gladiatorial contests persisted until the early 5th century AD.

gladiolus   Gladiolus, genus *Gladiolus*, is any of several corm-producing flowering plants that belong to the iris

Gladiolus species G. byzantinus (left) and G. hybrida (right) can be cross-pollinated to produce a surprisingly colorful crop of hybrids. The flowers are favorites of horticulturists and home gardeners.

family, Iridaceae. They produce swordlike leaves and spikes of funnel-shaped flowers. Most species are native to South Africa, but many new varieties and hybrids have been developed. Few other flowers thrive over such a wide geographic area. They are propagated primarily from corms.

Gladstone, William Ewart [glad'-stuhn]   William Ewart Gladstone, b. Dec. 23, 1809, d. May 19, 1898, four times Liberal prime minister of Britain, was an Olympian figure in 19th-century British politics. The son of a Liverpool merchant, he was educated at Eton and Oxford. He entered Parliament in 1832 as a Canningite Tory.

An erudite classicist and High Church Anglican given to soul-searching, Gladstone always sought to apply morality to politics. He became (1843) president of the Board of Trade under Sir Robert PEEL and with Peel began to support more liberal positions, including repeal of the CORN LAWS in 1846. After the ensuing split in the Tory party, Gladstone gradually moved into Liberal circles, finding much in common with Richard COBDEN and John BRIGHT. He served as chancellor of the exchequer in Lord ABERDEEN's coalition (1852–55) and by 1859 was ready to assume the same office as a Liberal under Viscount PALMERSTON, continuing tax reforms and securing a commercial treaty with France. By 1865 he had developed liberal views on the rights of nonconformists, disestablishment of the Church of Ireland, and electoral reform. He was well on the way to becoming "the people's William" when the death of Palmerston and resignation of Lord John RUSSELL gave him leadership of the Liberals in 1866.

Gladstone's first and most successful government (1868–74) was marked by disestablishment of the Irish church, the Irish Land Act (to protect the peasants against abuses by their landlords), abolition of religious tests in universities, open competition in the civil service, the Secret Ballot Act, and other reforms. However, a pro-Anglican bias in the Education Act of 1870 contributed to his electoral defeat in 1874.

Gladstone resigned the Liberal leadership in 1875,

William Ewart Gladstone, one of the outstanding statesmen of the Victorian age, served as prime minister of Great Britain four times between 1868 and 1894. As leader of the Liberal party, Gladstone campaigned for tax reforms, an end to Britain's colonial expansion, and the establishment of home rule in Ireland.

but he reentered the political arena to chastise (1876) his Conservative rival Benjamin DISRAELI for indifference to Turkish atrocities in the Balkans. After vigorous electioneering in the Midlothian campaign (1879–80)—the first such political campaign in British history—Gladstone returned to power in 1880. His second government carried (1884) the third REFORM ACT but was discredited by colonial setbacks, especially the failure to relieve Charles George GORDON at Khartoum, and fell in 1885.

In his third, short-lived ministry (1886) Gladstone attempted unsuccessfully to give Ireland home rule (see HOME RULE BILLS). Not always adept in handling colleagues and followers, he now split them on this issue; Joseph CHAMBERLAIN led the defection of the Liberal Unionists, who favored the continuing union of Britain and Ireland. The home rule issue also dominated Gladstone's fourth ministry (1892-94)—a second Home Rule Bill was defeated in 1893—and diverted the Liberals from constructive domestic policies. Gladstone finally resigned in 1894, however, in a dispute over the naval budget, peace and retrenchment remaining his strongest passions.

Gladstone died in 1898. Though he had failed in two ambitions—abolition of the income tax and settlement of the Irish question—and showed an uncertain touch in foreign and colonial affairs, the "Grand Old Man" had shaped the LIBERAL PARTY of the Victorian era.

Glamorgan [gluh-mohr'-guhn]   Glamorgan (also called Glamorganshire) was the most industrialized county in Wales, containing over half the population, until 1974, when the local government of Wales was reorganized. The region is located in the southeastern portion of Wales, bordered on the south by the Bristol Channel. CARDIFF is the former county seat and leading port.

The south of the region is a low, fertile plain where vegetables are grown and stock and dairy cattle are raised. The land gradually rises inland to mountains in the north. Coal resources located there attracted steel and iron manufacturing and tin-plating industries to urban centers, including SWANSEA, Caerphilly, and Port Talbot.

After the Normans conquered the region during the late 11th century, they organized it as a lordship. Beginning in the late 18th century Glamorgan became heavily industrialized. In 1974, Glamorgan was divided into the four counties of GWENT and Mid, South, and West Glamorgan.

---

gland   see HORMONE, ANIMAL

Glaser, Donald [glay'-zur]   The American physicist Donald Arthur Glaser, b. Cleveland, Ohio, Sept. 21, 1926, is known for his invention of the BUBBLE CHAMBER (1952), for which he received the 1960 Nobel Prize for physics. This device detects elementary atomic particles by photographing the vapor bubbles they leave when passing through a tank of heavy liquid maintained close to its boiling point.

Glasgow [glaz'-goh] Glasgow, the largest city and major port of Scotland, is situated on the River Clyde, in western Scotland, about 32 km (20 mi) inland, in a coal- and iron-mining area. The city has a population of 703,200 (1988 est.). Printing is an important industry, and the city produces ships, heavy machinery, chemicals, textiles, paper products, liquor, and foodstuffs. Glasgow's landmarks include the cathedral (12th–15th century), the Trades House (1794), the Kelvingrove Art Galleries and Museum, the Hunterian Museum, and the Burrell Collection (opened 1983). The University of Glasgow was established in 1451 and the University of Strathclyde in 1964.

About 550, Saint Kentigern (also known as Saint Mungo) reputedly founded a religious settlement on the site. A bridge across the Clyde was completed in 1350, and thereafter the city steadily grew as a market center. As trade with the New World developed, Glasgow rapidly became an important Atlantic port. Later, supplies of U.S. cotton led to the development of a textile industry. When the U.S. Civil War cut off the cotton supply the city developed varied industries. As new factories appeared, nearby residential sections turned into slums. Glasgow became notorious for its dreadful housing conditions in areas such as the Gorbals, but these conditions are being eliminated.

Glasgow, Ellen Ellen Glasgow, b. Richmond, Va., Apr. 22, 1874, d. Nov. 21, 1945, was a highly respected novelist whose best work concerns the reshaping of the South after the Civil War. *Barren Ground* (1925), generally considered her finest novel, deals with the survival strategies, both economic and emotional, of a young woman working a depleted farm. Her *Vein of Iron* (1935) was a fictional treatment of life during the Depression. She was an acute observer of manners and could be bitingly satiric, as in *They Stooped to Folly* (1929). Glasgow won a Pulitzer Prize for *In This Our Life* (1941). *The Woman Within* (1954), her posthumously published autobiography, describes her literary ascent and lifelong struggle with deafness.

Glashow, Sheldon American physicist Sheldon Lee Glashow, b. New York City, Dec. 5, 1932, shared the 1979 Nobel Prize for physics with Abdus Salam and Steven WEINBERG for their work leading to the development of the electroweak theory. This theory unites electromagnetism and the weak nuclear force, two of the FUNDAMENTAL INTERACTIONS of nature, into a single gauge theory (see UNIFIED FIELD THEORY). Glashow earned a Ph.D. from Harvard University in 1958 and later joined (1966) the faculty of Harvard, where he was named Higgins professor of physics in 1979. In 1983 he moved to the theoretical physics department of Texas A&M University.

glasnost [glahz'-nohst] *Glasnost* (Russian for "publicity" or "openness") is a word used by Soviet leader Mikhail GORBACHEV to describe his policy of disclosure. Until Gorbachev came to power in March 1985, the Soviet media had not reported candidly about activities of the government, foreign affairs, disasters, and shortcomings in the Soviet system. Gorbachev introduced a new tolerance for criticism, a broader range of opinions in the press and in the arts, and a more accurate rendering of Soviet history. The new freedom given to the media and to the intelligentsia has led to the rehabilitation and publication of formerly forbidden writers and suppressed works.

Glasnost was an essential first step in the carrying out of Gorbachev's economic and political reforms (PERESTROIKA), encouraging people to contribute to the debate on what kind of reform was needed. This allowed the expression, not only of liberal ideas, but also of conservative and extreme nationalist views. By 1990 this had resulted in the emergence of nationalist movements in most of the Soviet republics and helped to bring about dramatic changes in the Soviet-dominated countries of Eastern Europe. By 1991, however, under pressure from conservatives, Gorbachev seemed to be placing limits on his policy of *glasnost*.

Glaspell, Susan [glas'-pel] An American dramatist and novelist, Susan Glaspell, b. Davenport, Iowa, July 1, 1882, d. July 27, 1948, and her husband, George Cram Cook, founded (1915) the Provincetown Players in Provincetown, Mass. There they produced their joint one-act satire on psychoanalysis, *Suppressed Desires* (1915), and Glaspell's *Trifles* (1916). Her play *Alison's House* (1930) won the 1931 Pulitzer Prize. Other plays include *Inheritors* and *The Verge* (both 1921).

glass Glass is an amorphous substance made by heating a mixture of such materials as sand, sodium carbonate, and limestone to a temperature of about 1,300° C (2,400° F). It is made continuously in large tanks; powdered raw materials are fed in at one end, and molten glass emerges at the other end.

History of Glassmaking

Glass was used in Egypt for decorative objects, mainly as a colored glaze on stone or pottery beads, before 3000 BC. The art of making glass was perfected about 1500 BC in Egypt and the Near East. GLASSBLOWING, which was probably discovered about 50 BC in Phoenicia, greatly extended the types of objects that could be made of glass. It also made them easier to fabricate and more transparent. The art of glassblowing spread rapidly throughout the Roman Empire, and glassware (see GLASSWARE, DECORATIVE) became common and relatively inexpensive.

Beginning in the 11th century AD, several new centers of glassmaking arose in western Europe. In Bohemia, ash from plants (potash, which is high in potassium) was used as a raw material to make a glass with a lower melting point. The most important European center of glassmaking developed near Venice, where new compositions, colors, forming techniques, and artistic skills developed.

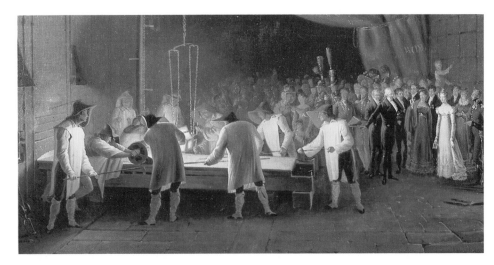

The first factory for producing cast plate glass was established in the late 17th century. In this painting (c. 1820), the duchesse de Berry watches as molten glass is poured onto an iron casting table. As the glass cooled, an iron roller pressed it to the desired thickness.

The Venetians added manganese to oxidize iron impurities in glass, clarifying the glass and removing the green or brown tint caused by the reduced state of iron.

So-called crystal was developed in England in the late 17th century to compete with Venetian *cristallo* glass. Purer raw materials, oxidation of iron, and addition of lead gave a more transparent glass.

In the 19th century techniques of glassmaking advanced rapidly. The growing need for improved optical glass stimulated the development of manufacturing processes that would strictly control bubbles, stria, refractive index, and color.

Clay pots heated by a wood fire were used to melt glass until about 1800, when coal and then oil and gas became the preferred fuels. Pot or batch melting of glass is used now only for specialty, laboratory, and some optical glasses.

Production of Flat Glass for Windows. Traditionally, window glass was made by hand by either the crown or cylinder process. In the crown process a gob of glass was blown out and one side of the resulting globe was flattened. A solid iron rod was attached to the flat part and the blowing pipe detached. The globe was then reheated and rotated until it formed a flat disk about 1 m (3 ft) in diameter. Panes of glass were cut from the disk after it had been slowly cooled. In the cylinder process the blower made a large cylinder that was then split open and flattened. Cylinder glass was also made by machine.

In the early part of the 20th century the Fourcault and Colburn processes for drawing sheet glass directly from the glass melt were developed. When used in conjunction with a continuous glass-melting furnace these processes are capable of producing large quantities of flat glass of reasonable quality. Until recently, plate glass of the highest quality was made by having the glass flow from the furnace through rollers. The rough-surfaced glass is then ground and polished by large automatic machines. This process requires a large capital investment but is economical since it produces large quantities of glass con-

tinuously. The ground and polished plate glass is very flat but is more costly than sheet glass that is drawn directly from the melt.

In the 1950s a new method of making relatively inexpensive flat glass of high quality was developed in England by Alistair Pilkington, of the Pilkington Glass Co. In this float process a continuous strip of glass from the melting furnace floats onto the surface of a molten metal, usually tin, at a carefully controlled temperature. The flat surface of the molten metal gives the glass a smooth surface as it cools. Today most flat glass is made by the float process.

Production of Glass for Other Uses. Glass containers such as BOTTLES and jars are made by blowing hot glass into a mold on a continuous machine. Light bulbs are also made by blowing hot glass into a mold.

Glass objects such as plates, tumblers, and vases can be made inexpensively by pressing hot glass in a mold. This pressed glass was popular in the United States in the 19th century because it was cheaper than imported crystal.

Types of Glass

The most important commercial glasses are the silicates, in which silica (SiO_2) sand is a major constituent. A variety of types of silicate glasses are produced for different uses.

Soda Lime. Because soda-lime glass can be melted at a relatively low temperature, is easy to form, has good chemical durability, and is inexpensive, it accounts for about 90% of all glass produced. A typical commercial soda-lime glass is composed of 72% silica, 15% soda (Na_2O), 5% lime (CaO), 4% magnesia (MgO), 2% alumina (Al_2O_3), and 1% boric oxide (B_2O_3). Also present are impurities in the raw materials and small amounts of special additives, such as antimony oxide to help remove bubbles from the glass melt. Soda-lime glass has a relatively high thermal expansion coefficient of 9.2×10^{-6} per degree Celsius and is thus easily subject to thermal shock.

Soda-lime glass is used for windows, mirrors, and flat

glass of all kinds; for containers such as bottles, jars, and tumblers; for light bulbs; and for many other purposes.

Pyrex. Pyrex (the most common brand of borosilicate glass) was developed at Corning Glass Works to provide thermal and chemical properties superior to those of soda-lime glass while retaining reasonably low melting temperatures (1,300–1,400° C/2,370–2,550° F). This kind of glass contains about 81% SiO_2, 13% B_2O_3, 4% Na_2O, and 2% Al_2O_3. It has a low thermal expansion coefficient of 3.3×10^{-6} per degree Celsius, giving it good resistance to thermal shock. It is more resistant to chemical attack than is soda-lime glass because it contains less alkali (sodium). Pyrex is more expensive than soda-lime glass because it must be melted at a higher temperature and the borate raw material is relatively expensive.

Pyrex borosilicate is used in cooking and laboratory ware, in automobile headlights, and in other applications requiring superior resistance to thermal shock and greater chemical durability.

Lead Silica. A variety of lead glasses are important as low-melting sealing and solder glasses and for use in lead crystal glassware. A typical sealing glass is composed of 77% SiO_2, 9% Na_2O, 5% K_2O, 8% PbO, and 1% CaO, giving a thermal expansion coefficient of 9.3×10^{-6} per degree Celsius.

Fused Silica. A glass of special interest is fused silica, which is pure SiO_2. Because the highest melting point of crystalline silica, cristobalite, is 1,710° C (3,110° F), fused silica must be melted at a higher temperature. Few materials are suitable as containers at such high temperatures; graphite and refractory metals such as tungsten, which are used commercially for this purpose, are expensive. Although fused silica is quite costly to produce, it is widely used because of its great purity, optical transparency, high temperature and chemical durability, and resistance to thermal shock—it has a thermal expansion coefficient of 0.5×10^{-6} per degree Celsius.

These properties make fused silica especially appropriate for use as arc tubes, crucibles, optical parts, containers, and as telescope mirrors.

Properties of Glass

Structure. Glass technology has traditionally defined glass as an inorganic product of fusion that has been cooled to a rigid condition without crystallization (see CRYSTAL). But it is also possible to make glass without cooling it from the molten state; for example, it may be deposited from vapor or from a liquid solution such as sodium silicate in water (water glass). Thus, it seems better to define glass as an amorphous solid.

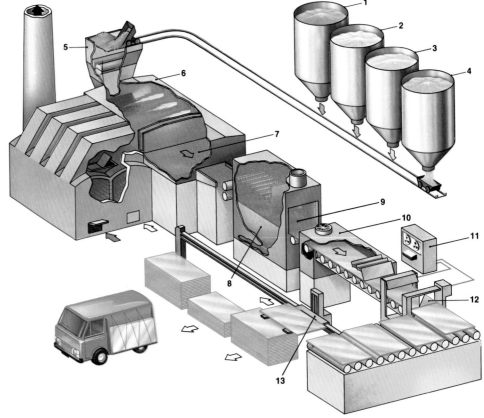

The float glass process is widely used to make flat, distortion-free plate glass. Weighed amounts of glass scrap (1), lime (2), sodium carbonate (3), and silica (4) are blended in a mixing hopper (5) and melted in an oil-fired regeneration furnace (6); high temperatures are attained when contact is made between incoming air (blue arrow) and the hot furnace brick. Molten glass (7) flows between rollers, then floats along the surface of a bath of molten tin (8) under a controlled temperature in the absence of oxygen. As the glass moves along the bath, it is gradually cooled and emerges as a uniformly thick, rigid, flat sheet (9), which is passed through a cooling unit, or annealing lehr (10), to relieve internal stresses. After annealing, a computer (11) controls the subsequent cutting (12) and stacking (13) of specified lengths of glass plate.

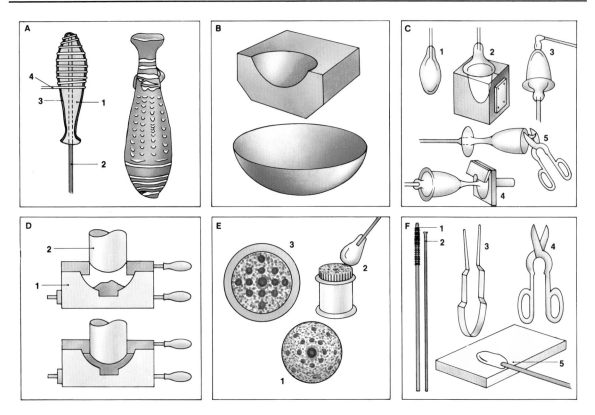

The glass-shaping techniques illustrated here have been in use for centuries, and many are still used in making fine glassware. (A) The ancient Egyptians used the sand-core method to make glass bottles. The sand core (1), supported on a copper or bronze rod (2), was dipped in molten glass (3) and then wrapped with threads of hot, softened glass (4). (B) Pressing molten glass into open molds produces cups, bowls, and dishes. (C) A wineglass is made by gathering a mass of molten glass at the end of a long, hollow blowpipe (1), shaping the mass by blowing it in a mold (2), adding a stem (3), shaping the foot (4), and trimming the rim (5). (D) In the relatively modern technique of press molding, a mass of molten glass is poured into a metal mold (1), and a metal plunger (2) presses the glass mass into the desired shape. (E) A decorative Millefiori paperweight (1) is made by filling a cylindrical mold with rods of colored glass (2) and incorporating them in a molten glass mass (3), which causes the rods to fuse, as well as surrounding them with a clear covering. (F) Glassworking tools include a blowpipe (1) and a pontil, or punt (2), a solid rod that is used to hold the molten glass mass; tongs (3); shears (4); and a marble slab (5), on which softened glass is smoothed.

To form glass a liquid must be cooled rapidly enough to prevent its crystallization. Thus, viscous liquids, which crystallize slowly, are more likely to form glasses than are fluid liquids. If cooled fast enough, materials not normally thought of as glassy, such as some metals and ALLOYS, can be made into glasses. Such amorphous metals were first made by "splat cooling," in which a globule of liquid metal is thrown against a rotating metal plate. The liquid is spread into a thin film that cools very rapidly.

The basic structural element of silicate glasses on the atomic level is a three-dimensional network of silicon-oxygen bonds (see SILICA MINERALS; SILICATE MINERALS).

Strength. Although the network structure of silicate glass is extremely strong, glass itself is very brittle. Brittle materials fracture more readily than their structure leads one to expect because of tiny flaws or cracks in their surfaces. When glass is loaded with a tensile (pulling) force, the force at the tips of these flaws is multiplied many times, and the flaw or crack grows until it breaks. Glass is also subject to fatigue; that is, it becomes weaker when it is loaded for a period of time, as a result of the reaction of water vapor with the glass.

Glass can be strengthened by a process called tempering. This is done by cooling the surface of the glass more rapidly than the interior. The surface becomes rigid first, and when the interior cools and contracts it pulls on the surface, causing a residual compressive stress.

Chemical tempering is another way to strengthen glass by developing a compressive stress in its surface. In this process smaller sodium ions in the glass are replaced by larger potassium ions. This "stuffing" of a larger ion into the glass causes a compressive stress in the glass surface.

Electrical Conductivity. The electrical conductivity of glass results from the motion of alkali ions, usually sodium, in the glass. These ions are the most mobile because they are the most loosely bonded in the glass structure.

Even pure fused silica, which has a concentration of alkali ions of less than one part per million, conducts electricity through the transport of sodium and lithium ions. At room temperature, however, these ions are not very mobile, so glass is a good insulator. At this temperature any electrical conductivity of bulk glass results from surface conductivity (see CONDUCTION, ELECTRIC).

Color. Glass can be colored by adding particular compounds: chromates for green, copper or cobalt for blue, copper or selenium for red, and manganese for purple. The common green of bottles results from the addition of oxidized iron, and brown is made by adding a combination of iron and sulfur. Very small metal particles in glass can color it deeply; for instance, the addition of gold produces ruby-colored glass.

Fluorescent glasses have recently been used in lasers and as optical elements for amplifying laser light; one type of fusion reactor being tested involves many fluorescent glass lenses.

The potential optical clarity of fused silica has led to its application as a transmission medium for optical signals in FIBER OPTICS. Glass thus used must have low optical absorption for lengths up to a mile, and fused silica fibers meeting these requirements are now being mass-produced.

Glass, Carter

Carter Glass, b. Lynchburg, Va., Jan. 4, 1858, d. May 28, 1946, was a U.S. legislator who sponsored some of the most important banking laws of the 20th century. A Virginia Democrat, Glass served in the House of Representatives from 1902 to 1918. In 1913 he wrote and sponsored the law setting up the Federal Reserve System. Glass was Woodrow Wilson's secretary of the treasury (1918–20). As U.S. senator (1920–46) he sponsored several banking acts, among them the GLASS-STEAGALL ACT (1933), which curbed bank speculation and established the FEDERAL DEPOSIT INSURANCE CORPORATION.

Glass, Philip

Philip Glass, b. Baltimore, Md., Jan. 31, 1937, is one of the leading avant-garde composers of his generation. After receiving traditional training at the University of Chicago and the Juilliard School, Glass became interested in synthesizing the musical traditions of East and West. Rhythm—rather than melody, harmony, and thematic development—forms the core of Glass's work, which is often characterized by the repetition of a small number of notes and note cycles. His many compositions include the instrumentals *Music in 5ths* (1969) and *Glassworks* (1982); the operas *Satyagraha* (1980) and *Akhnaten* (1984); and, in collaboration with Robert WILSON, the 4½-hour one-act opera *Einstein on the Beach* (1976) and the fifth act of the massive, multimedia *Civil Wars* (1984).

glass harmonica

The story of the glass harmonica, originally called "armonica," begins in the 17th century with tuned musical glasses, the results of centuries of experimenting with vessels of various materials. The actual instrument, however, originated in 1761 with Benjamin Franklin who, intrigued by the fashionable European craze, applied his ingenuity to inventing a more efficient mechanism. Threading a concentric series of glass bowls on a spindle and mounting them in a trough partially filled with water, he rotated them by means of a treadle. Sound was made by touching the moist rims of the rotating glasses with the fingertips; dynamics were controlled both by speed and pressure. The instrument had its virtuosos, notably Marianne Davies and Marianne Kirchgessner, and composers among whom were Johann Adolf Hasse, Jan Ladislav Dussek, and Wolfgang Amadeus Mozart. After the early decades of the 19th century, the instrument fell into disuse.

Glass-Steagall Acts

The Glass-Steagall Acts (1932, 1933) were among several pieces of legislation aimed at reforming the U.S. BANKING SYSTEM after its near collapse in the early years of the Great Depression. Both acts were sponsored by Sen. Carter GLASS—who in 1913 had been instrumental in establishing the FEDERAL RESERVE SYSTEM—and Rep. Henry B. Steagall. The 1932 act liberalized the terms under which member banks could borrow from the Federal Reserve. The 1933 act (also known as the Banking Act of 1933) established the FEDERAL DEPOSIT INSURANCE CORPORATION, which guaranteed the savings of bank depositors, separated commercial from investment banking, regulated the interest that banks could pay on time deposits, and increased the power of the Federal Reserve Board. Efforts to reform the banking-regulation system were undertaken by Congress in 1991 after the FDIC was forced to take over several large insolvent banks.

glassblowing

Glassblowing is a process in which glass objects are formed by forcing air into a gob of molten GLASS. Discovered in the 1st century BC in the Near

A two-piece iron mold is used for blowing large jars and bottles. A blown-glass blank (left) is inserted and reblown inside the mold (center). The finished bottle (right) has a smooth surface.

East, perhaps in Phoenicia, the process led to a great increase in the manufacture of useful glass articles. Before the invention of glassblowing, glass articles were made by covering a shaped core with a layer or coils of molten glass. Glassblowing was considerably quicker and simpler than this cumbersome process; it also facilitated the manufacture of thin and transparent glass.

In blowing glass a gob of molten glass is gathered on the end of a blowpipe, through which air is blown to form the glass into a hollow sphere. The size, shape, and wall thickness of the glass are controlled by the pressure of the air, the angle at which the pipe is held, and the speed at which the glass cools. The glass is formed into different shapes by the glassblower with simple tools as he or she twirls the pipe on a special bench. During this shaping process the glass is reheated as needed to allow easy forming. Air blown periodically into the object also helps to shape it. Many glass articles are manufactured continuously by the glassblowing process. Continuous BOTTLE-making machines and machines for jars and tumblers operate by blowing gobs of glass into a mold. The ribbon machine for making light bulbs is another example, in which glass from the ribbon is blown into molds at rates up to 2,000 bulbs per hour.

glassfish   see ICEFISH

---

glassware, decorative   Objects made of GLASS have been prized as ornaments and decorative ware from the time of the most ancient civilizations in Mesopotamia to the present. The inherent qualities of glass—lustrousness, beauty, color, and fragility—and its adaptability to numerous forms account for much of this popularity. Its most important application in the fine arts is STAINED GLASS.

Ancient Glass. Because glass objects are fragile, few have survived from ancient times. Among the earliest pieces of decorative glass from Egypt, dated to 2500 BC, are beads and unguent jars of dark blue glass with colored overlay designs in a zigzag pattern. These jars were not made from blown glass, but were built up around a core of sand. The technique of glassblowing is presumed to have been invented about the 1st century BC by the Phoenicians.

Although some glass was made during the Mycenaean period, most of the examples of glass found in Greece date from about 600 BC on. Hand-blown glass bottles made in Rome by the late 1st century BC were probably the work of glassblowers from Alexandria, Egypt, and Syria. (Syrian glassworkers are known to have traveled as far north as Reims, in France.)

Islamic Glass. Glass produced in Damascus and Aleppo beginning in the 9th century is generally classified as Islamic glassware. In the Middle East the art of enameling glass (see ENAMEL) was brought to its highest peak, with the glass itself serving merely as a base for the heavily enameled and gilded vases and mosque lamps.

Medieval European Glass. By the late 12th century, glassmaking was a thriving industry in Venice. Clear and colorless Venetian glass made with soda, called *cristallo*

By the 18th dynasty, (c.1500 BC), distinctive glassmaking techniques were developed by the Egyptians. The decorations on these Egyptian blue jars were produced by combing threads of glass into the jars. (Metropolitan Museum of Art, New York City.)

(crystal), was sparsely enameled or, in *lattimo*, also called *latticino* or *vetro di trina* (lace glass), alternate bands of opaque glass were drawn in wave patterns across the clear glass. The Venetians were the first to develop the stems of wine glasses.

During the Middle Ages in northern Europe, glass made with soda was largely superseded by Waldglas, made with potash. This glass tended to be yellow, green, or brown, depending on the impurities present in its molten state. Despite Venice's attempt to retain a monopoly on the production of glass, many Venetian glassblowers traveled northward, spreading the Venetian styles and technique. In Germany robust shapes were developed that have no resemblance to Venetian glass. By the 15th century a style of goblet called a *rümer* (or *roemer*) was used for white wines.

Northern Renaissance Glass. By the 16th century, glass was being produced in Silesia and Bohemia. Bohemian bottles, decanters, and goblets achieved an international popularity in the 19th century. They consisted of a clear base, on which designs in deep tones of red, green, and blue were overlaid, with gilding sometimes added as well.

A notable example of Roman reticulated glass is the 4th-century Lycurgus Cup. When viewed in reflected light, it is green (left), and when viewed in transmitted light, it is red (right). (British Museum, London.)

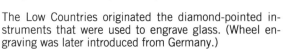

French luxury glass experienced its greatest period of development during the 19th century. This millefiori paperweight (above left) was created by the glasshouse of Baccarat. (Above right) This flask and pitcher are attributed to the Pennsylvania glasshouse of Henry Stiegel. Eighteenth-century Stiegel glassware was usually made of blue, amethyst, or clear lead glass. (Yale University Art Gallery.)

The Low Countries originated the diamond-pointed instruments that were used to engrave glass. (Wheel engraving was later introduced from Germany.)

English and Irish Glass. Most of the early glass factories in England employed Venetian workers or sent designs to Venice to be produced there, or to Holland to be diamond-engraved and diamond-stippled. By the 18th century both English and Irish glass became renowned for their brilliance, which was achieved by the addition of lead to the raw metal. To avoid the government excise tax (first imposed in 1745) that was placed upon prospering glass companies, several Englishmen started glass houses in Ireland, in Dublin, Cork, and Waterford.

French Glass. By the 19th century, French glass was noted for the quality of its cutting and engraving. Three centers that became famous for their paperweights were Clichy, St. Louis, and Baccarat. Emile Gallé, the famous French ART NOUVEAU designer, opened a glass house to produce his own creations in 1875. The foremost 20th-century designer of the ART DECO style was René LALIQUE, who used a heavy, molded glass. His lighting fixtures were especially designed for the modernistic interiors of the 1920s.

Swedish Glass. The earliest glassworks in Sweden were established at Kungsholm in 1676 and closed in 1815. In the 18th century the English influence became dominant. Beginning in 1917, with assistance from the Swedish Society of Arts and Crafts, the glassworks at Orrefors and Kosta began to employ artists in order to raise the quality of their products.

American Glass. Although several attempts were made to establish small glassworks in the colonies during the 17th century, the first successful glass factory in America was founded in 1739 by Caspar Wistar in Salem County, N.J. It produced a kind of glassware known as South Jersey-type glass—bottles and other utilitarian objects in green, brown, and an odd shade of terra-cotta. Two factories were established by Henry William STIEGEL in Pennsylvania in the 1760s; among his creations were amethyst-colored bottles that were dip molded and patterned,

(Above) *During the late 19th and early 20th century the Tiffany Glass Company originated the art nouveau style in American glassware. The Tiffany lamp combines a leaded glass shade and bronze base.* (Left) *This engraved Gazelle Bowl (1935) was designed by Sidney Waugh for the Steuben Glass Company.*

and cordial bottles in both clear and deep-blue glass that were decorated with colored enamel designs. In 1825 the Boston and Sandwich Glass Company was started by Deming Jarves, the inventor of press-molded glass.

Among the decorative types of glass produced from the 1880s were Satin glass, Amberina, Peach Blow, Burmese, and Favrile. Favrile, a glass with a metallic sheen, was the creation of Louis Comfort TIFFANY. The prestigious glass objects of the 20th century from the Steuben Glassworks (see STEUBEN GLASS) are made of wheel-engraved glass with a deep luster, individually designed by well-known artists. The Corning Museum of Glass, founded in 1951 in Corning, N.Y., has the most comprehensive historical collection in the world.

See also: ANTIQUE COLLECTING; ARCHAEOLOGY; CHANDELIER; EGYPTIAN ART AND ARCHITECTURE; ISLAMIC ART AND ARCHITECTURE; JEWELRY; MESOPOTAMIAN ART AND ARCHITECTURE; PERSIAN ART AND ARCHITECTURE; ROMAN ART AND ARCHITECTURE.

glassy state   The glassy, or vitreous, state of matter is exhibited by certain inorganic and organic substances. A GLASS appears solid, but its molecules are not arranged in crystalline form and it does not show the well-defined phase changes characteristic of solids. Instead it grows plastic and soft when heated and, on cooling, grows increasingly viscous until the limit of viscosity is reached and it appears solid again. Its molecules are randomly distributed, as in a LIQUID, and a glass may in fact be considered a supercooled liquid. If a glass is kept molten for a long time, crystals may form on its surface—a process called devitrification. The most useful glasses are the inorganic glasses, which generally are transparent, hard, and brittle and have a high shear strength, low thermal expansion, and low electrical and thermal conductivity. Nonflammable and inert to most chemicals, they are useful as containers, windows, lenses, mirrors, insulators, and dielectrics. Their main ingredient is silica, SiO_2; other oxides are added to modify the glass for a particular use.

---

glaucoma [glaw-koh'-muh]   Glaucoma is an EYE disease in which the optic nerve is damaged as a result of an imbalance between the production and draining of the watery fluid produced by cells behind the lens of the eye. Glaucoma is a major cause of BLINDNESS.

The normal eye continually produces a fluid that flows into the anterior chamber of the eyeball and eventually drains through tiny channels between the cornea and iris. A number of disease processes can cause these channels to become blocked. The fluid pressure then builds within the eyeball and, over a period of months or years, can damage the optic nerve. This condition, called chronic open-angle glaucoma, is the most common form of the disease; the risk of its onset increases from middle age onward. No pain is involved, and the loss of peripheral vision is so gradual that it may go unnoticed for a long time.

A less common condition, called acute narrow-angle glaucoma, results from a sudden and complete blockage of the drainage channels due to abnormal eye structure, injury to the eye, certain drugs, or systemic disorders such as diabetes. The risk of its onset also increases after middle age. The onset, sometimes preceded by preliminary attacks, is marked by pain, eye redness, blurred vision, and haziness of the cornea. Only one eye is usually affected at a time, but the other is likely to be affected later. Predisposition to both forms of glaucoma tends to run in families.

The peripheral vision lost in undetected chronic glaucoma cannot be restored. For this reason, regular examinations by an ophthalmologist are recommended for its early detection, especially after the age of 40. Chronic glaucoma is treated by drugs that increase fluid outflow or decrease fluid production. If drugs do not check the condition, surgery may be recommended to open drainage channels. Such surgery is essential following an attack of acute glaucoma, in order to prevent visual impairment. Drug therapies and modern surgical techniques, including the use of laser beams, have shown a high rate of success in treating the disease.

Glaucoma occurs when fluid pressure within the eye (A) *increases. Under normal conditions* (B), *aqueous fluid, which is produced by the ciliary body, flows into the anterior chamber and drains into blood vessels through the canal of Schlemm, located near the angle formed by the cornea and the iris* (arrow). *If the angle is narrow* (C), *the opening of the canal may become obstructed, resulting in acute-angle glaucoma. Pressure builds and is transmitted* (black arrows) *to the retina and the optic nerve. If the angle is wide* (D), *blockage may still occur in part of the drainage system; chronic open-angle glaucoma results, and peripheral vision* (E) *is gradually reduced.*

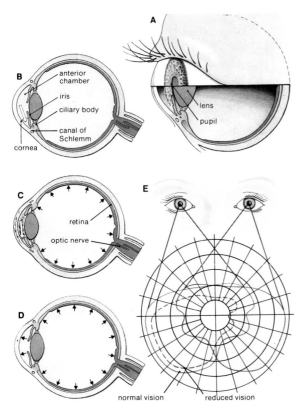

---

glaze   A glaze is a smooth, glassy coating applied to CERAMIC objects in order to add color and decoration to the surface or to vary its texture. The glaze forms a hard, nonporous surface that is easily cleaned.

Glazes are usually made from powdered glass combined with colored oxides of such elements as cobalt, manganese, or nickel. The mixture of powders is suspended in water and applied to the ceramic surface by spraying, brushing, or dipping. The glaze is then dried and fixed onto the ceramic surface by firing. During firing, the glass softens and flows over the ceramic surface to a greater or lesser extent, and reacts with the ceramic substrate to form a strong, adherent bond to it.

If a glaze is applied to a fired ceramic substrate, a second firing is necessary to melt and bond the glaze to the substrate. It is also possible to apply a glaze to an unfired ceramic, and fire both the glaze and substrate together.

The suspension, or slip, in which the glaze is applied to the ceramic surface must have particular properties to ensure that the glaze is easy to apply, does not run as it is

Colors obtained in glazing depend in part on the atmosphere within the kiln. A copper oxide glaze turns blue when fired in an oxidizing atmosphere (as on the base of the vase and at the left side of the plate); in a reducing atmosphere the same glaze becomes a brilliant red.

drying, and adheres well both when wet and after drying. These slip properties are often obtained by adding a small amount of clay to the suspension, and by controlling the amount of water in the slip and the size of the powder's particles.

Often fine crystals grow in the glaze, making it more translucent or opaque. Crystals also give a dull, or mat, surface finish. The crystals nucleate and grow in the glassy glaze in much the same way as they do in glass ceramics.

Glazes craze, or develop fine cracks, if the thermal expansion of the glaze varies significantly from that of the substrate. Thus, the glaze composition must be designed with an expansion coefficient close to that of the substrate. On the other hand, an artist may wish to induce crazing for its different appearance and texture (crackle glaze).

Colors in glazes are controlled by adding coloring agents to the glassy components of the glaze. A wide variety of colors is possible, depending on the agent added, the base composition of the glaze, the color of the substrate, and the state of oxidation in the kiln.

Glazer, Nathan [glayz'-ur]   Nathan Glazer, b. New York City, Feb. 25, 1923, is an American sociologist who specializes in ethnic studies and urban affairs. Glazer graduated from the City College of New York, worked as an editor for *Commentary* magazine, received his Ph.D. from Columbia University, and has been a professor at the University of California and at Harvard University. Much of his writing has been for magazines and deals with contemporary political and social issues.

With David Riesman and Reuel Denney, Glazer wrote *The Lonely Crowd: A Study of the Changing American Character* (1950), dealing with the effects of modern culture on personality. He collaborated with Daniel Patrick

Moynihan on *Beyond the Melting Pot* (1963; 2d ed., 1970) and wrote *Affirmative Discrimination* (1976) and *Ethnic Dilemmas, 1964–1982* (1983).

Glazunov, Aleksandr Konstantinovich [glah-zoo'-nawf]   Aleksandr Konstantinovich Glazunov, b. Aug. 10, 1865, d. Mar. 21, 1936, was a distinguished Russian composer of orchestral, chamber, and piano music. He was a child prodigy whose first teacher was his mother, a pianist. At age 15 he became a pupil of Rimsky-Korsakov, and at age 17 his first symphony was performed, conducted by Mily Balakirev. Glazunov taught at the St. Petersburg Conservatory from 1899, and was its director from 1905 until 1928; he then left Russia and settled in Paris. A master of orchestration, he composed several symphonic poems; nine symphonies, the last unfinished; two piano concertos; string quartets; and solo piano, organ, and vocal works. With Rimsky-Korsakov he completed Borodin's unfinished opera *Prince Igor.* His violin concerto in A minor and the ballets *Raymonda* (1898) and *The Seasons* (1899) have enjoyed considerable popularity.

Gleason, Jackie [glee'-suhn]   Herbert John "Jackie" Gleason, b. Brooklyn, N.Y., Feb. 26, 1916, d. June 24, 1987, was an entertainer and television producer. He began his career as an emcee in Brooklyn's Folly Theatre, and in 1949 he gained popularity in the television series "The Life of Riley." He headlined "The Jackie Gleason Show," which ran intermittently on television from 1952 to 1970, and achieved star status as Ralph Kramden, a bus driver in the weekly television show "The Honeymooners." In 1959, Gleason won a Tony Award for the musical comedy *Take Me Along.* He is also remembered for his performance as Minnesota Fats in the film *The Hustler* (1961) and for his later comedic roles in such films as *Smokey and the Bandit* (1977) and *Nothing in Common* (1986).

glee   A glee is a composition for unaccompanied male voices that flourished in England in the 18th and early 19th centuries. Normally a glee is comparatively short and contains several contrasting sections, mostly in a homophonic (chordal) style using short phrases and frequent changes of rhythm. The term *glee* comes from the Anglo-Saxon *gligge*, which means "music," and does not indicate that glees are necessarily gleeful. Several societies were formed in England for the performance of glees and other vocal part music. One of these was the Glee Club, founded in London in 1783. The term *glee club* is now used to describe choral groups that perform short works of various types.

Gleizes, Albert [glez]   The French painter Albert Gleizes, b. Paris, Dec. 8, 1881, d. June 23, 1953, was an influential proponent of CUBISM. Originally an industrial designer, Gleizes began painting impressionist-style works about 1900, but under the influence of Paul Cézanne he gradually began to simplify forms and colors. In 1912, Gleizes and Jean Metzinger published the important book *Du cubisme* (Eng. trans., 1913), which helped provide the movement with its theoretical foundations. Gleizes's own cubist paintings, of which *On Brooklyn Bridge* (1917; Guggenheim Museum, New York City) is representative, are marked by precise patterns of abstraction.

Glencoe, Massacre of

[glen-koh'] Glencoe, a valley in western Scotland, was the site of a massacre of members of the MacDonald clan in 1692. The MacDonald chief had failed, probably as a result of deliberate hindrance, to meet the deadline for the Highland clans to swear allegiance to the new king of England, WILLIAM III. As a result Sir John Dalrymple, a secretary of state for Scotland, sent a regiment of Campbells, a rival clan, to punish the MacDonalds. These troops lived among the MacDonalds in Glencoe for a week before attacking and killing 38 of them on Feb. 13, 1692. The massacre left deep anti-English and anti-Campbell feelings among the Scots.

Glendale

Glendale is a city in southwestern California, 13 km (8 mi) north of Los Angeles. It lies at the southeastern end of the San Fernando Valley in the Verdugo Hills. Primarily a residential community, it has a population of 180,038 (1990). The city's industries produce aircraft, pharmaceuticals, optical instruments, and films. Founded in 1886 on the former Rancho San Rafael, the first Spanish land grant in California (1784), the city was incorporated in 1906. Forest Lawn Memorial Park, a well-known cemetery, is located there.

Glendower, Owen

[glen-dow'-ur] Owen Glendower, c.1354–c.1416, was a Welsh prince who led the last major Welsh revolt against English rule. A dispute with an English neighbor touched off (1400) his revolt against HENRY IV, whom he had earlier supported. He first allied himself with Henry's enemies, the PERCY family, but after their defeat (1403) sought French aid. By 1404 he controlled most of Wales, but English forces under Prince Henry (later HENRY V) gradually captured his strongholds. By 1412, Glendower had disappeared into the Welsh mountains.

Glenn, John H., Jr.

The American astronaut and senator John Herschel Glenn, Jr., b. Cambridge, Ohio, July 18, 1921, was the first American to orbit the Earth. Glenn became a Marine Corps pilot in 1943 and flew in combat in World War II and the Korean War. In 1957 he became the first man to fly faster than sound from New York to Los Angeles, covering the distance in 3 hours, 23 minutes in an F8U Crusader. He was a test pilot when selected as one of the original seven astronauts in 1959.

John H. Glenn, Jr., a former military pilot, was chosen in 1959 as one of the original group of astronauts. On Feb. 20, 1962, he became the first American to orbit the Earth. Glenn has served as a Democratic senator from Ohio since 1975.

On Feb. 20, 1962, Glenn's 4-hour, 56-minute flight aboard *Friendship 7* (*Mercury-Atlas 6*), the third flight of the MERCURY PROGRAM, took him around the globe three times to a splashdown in the Atlantic Ocean. Although a signal during the flight indicated that *Friendship 7*'s heat shield was loose, the craft's retro-rockets were fired, and the reentry went without incident.

Deciding to enter politics, Glenn resigned from the space program (1964) and the Marine Corps (1965). In 1974 he was elected to the U.S. Senate as a Democrat from Ohio. He won easy reelection in 1980 and 1986. A prominent moderate, he was considered a serious potential presidential candidate when, in 1983, he announced his bid for the 1984 nomination. He suffered early losses in the primaries, however, and withdrew from the race in March 1984.

glider

A glider is a type of heavier-than-air AIRCRAFT that has no engine or has only a small auxiliary engine. Early gliders were not capable of sustained flight, but they did form a vital stepping-stone in the development of the airplane. Such pioneers as Otto LILIENTHAL, Octave Chanute, and Percy Pilcher had some early success with gliders, but their experiments (1893–99) pointed out fundamental problems involving stability and control. In 1900–02 Orville and Wilbur WRIGHT accomplished the vital process of learning how to fly a stable glider; they then fitted (1903) an engine onto their aircraft. With the development of the powered airplane, interest in gliders waned until the 1920s, when German glider designers created more efficient machines characterized by their extremely long-span slender wings (wings of high aspect ratio), which could produce greater lift at lower speeds, allowing the glider to travel further horizontally for a given drop in altitude. By finding and taking advantage of updrafts, a glider pilot could extend a flight and in some cases stay aloft almost indefinitely. Gliders have also been used by military forces landing invasion troops and supplies.

The long, thin wings of a glider, or sailplane, enable the craft to remain aloft by soaring on rising air currents.

Today's competition glider, or sailplane, is built to fit the rules of particular classes, which specify such things as the wing dimensions and equipment of the glider. The record for distance covered by a glider in a straight line is 1,460.7 km (907.7 mi), and the altitude record, set over California, is 14,938 m (49,009 ft), which is a respectable height even for powered aircraft.

Modern sailplanes are constructed chiefly from glass-fiber, often with carbon fiber to stiffen the wing spars. The pilot sits in a reclining position under a large transparent canopy. Wing flaps, airbrakes, water ballast, and a braking parachute are common features.

See also: AERIAL SPORTS; FLIGHT, HUMAN-POWERED.

gliding   see AERIAL SPORTS

gliding lemur   see COLUGO

Glière, Reinhold Moritzovich [glee-air']   Reinhold Moritzovich Glière, b. Jan. 11, 1875, d. June 23, 1956, was an eminent Russian composer and conductor. He studied (1891) violin and composition at the Kiev Music School and attended (1894–1900) the Moscow Conservatory. In 1914, Glière became director of the Conservatory in Kiev. From 1920 until his death he was professor of composition at the Moscow Conservatory. Glière traveled extensively in the Soviet Union, collecting folk melodies of the various European and Asiatic republics, and many of his works are based on the music of these cultures. He composed an opera, six ballets, orchestral and band music, chamber music, and songs.

Glinka, Mikhail Ivanovich [gleen'-kah]   Mikhail Ivanovich Glinka, b. June 1 (N.S.), 1804, d. Feb. 15 (N.S.), 1857, is universally considered the father of RUSSIAN MUSIC. He received desultory musical instruction, including piano lessons from John Field in St. Petersburg, and instruction in composition from Siegfried Dehn in

Berlin. His two major musical influences were Russian folk music and the operas of Bellini and Donizetti.

Inspired to create a true Russian opera, Glinka turned to a court official, Baron G. F. Rosen, who gave him the libretto of *Ivan Susanin; or, A Life for the Tsar,* a celebration of the Romanov dynasty and Russian patriotism in which Russian and Polish national music are vividly contrasted. First performed in 1836, the opera was an immediate success. For the first time, genuine Russian music was heard on the operatic stage with stunning effect, particularly in the choral scenes. This highly original music is interlarded, however, with set pieces in the ubiquitous Italian operatic style of the time. Glinka's second opera, *Ruslan and Lyudmila* (1842), based on a tale by Aleksandr Pushkin, was less successful, although it contains some striking and original scenes. Glinka again used Russian sources, but he also employed Oriental music, Viennese dance music, and Italian operatic conventions.

Glinka's orchestral works include the symphonic poem *Kamarinskaya* and two overtures, *Jota Aragonesa* and *Summer Night in Madrid,* inspired by a visit to Spain. In his many songs are combined a Russian character, a cosmopolitan polish, and a thorough knowledge of the voice.

globe   A globe is a three-dimensional cartographic representation of a sphere. Terrestrial globes, usually of the surface of the Earth or the Moon, give the user an image with equal distances, equal areas, and equal angles—characteristics impossible on a two-dimensional map. Celestial globes show the relative positions of heavenly bodies in the sky as seen by an observer from the surface of the sphere. The earliest globes were celestial, made of stone or copper by astronomers of ancient Mesopotamia, Egypt, and Greece. Crates of Mallus, a Greek astronomer, is thought to have made the first terrestrial globe in the 2d century BC. Martin Benhaim, a German, is credited with making the first modern globe in 1492.

Globe Theatre   see ELIZABETHAN PLAYHOUSE

globular cluster   see CLUSTER, STAR

globule [glahb'-uel]   A globule is the astronomical term for a relatively small, dense interstellar cloud that obscures optical light. It is thus a small galactic NEBULA. Many of these objects were discovered in the early days of astronomical photography by E. E. Barnard, who referred to them as dark nebulae or dark clouds. The extinction they produce is caused by the interstellar dust particles they contain. The density of atoms and molecules in these globules, estimated from the observed amounts of extinction, together with a reasonable assumption of the ratio of gas to dust, is often as high as 10^8 particles per cm^3.

glockenspiel [glahk'-en-speel]   The German word *Glockenspiel* translates as "bell chime" and has been

The glockenspiel is a percussion instrument in modern orchestras. It consists of a set of thin steel bars arranged in two rows in the manner of a keyboard and played with wooden mallets.

used to mean both a carillon and a set of small BELLS. The term now is generally restricted to tuned graduated metal bars that produce bright, silvery tones. The bars may be struck with a keyboard mechanism or, more commonly, by mallets; the latter allow a variety of tone quality regulated by the choice of beaters and the use of tuned resonators suspended on the underside of the instrument. A percussion instrument in modern orchestras, the glockenspiel was first used to major effect by Handel in his oratorio *Saul* in 1738. Another noteworthy early orchestral use occurs in Mozart's *The Magic Flute* (1791). Wagner and Tchaikovsky also wrote music for the instrument. The bell lyre is a portable and visually colorful form ubiquitous in marching bands.

Glorious Revolution   The Glorious Revolution is the name given to the overthrow in 1688 of the Roman Catholic JAMES II of England and the accession to the throne of his daughter MARY II and her Dutch Protestant husband, WILLIAM III. Invited to invade England by seven English noblemen, William hoped to bring England into the imminent War of the GRAND ALLIANCE against France. He feared that James would ally himself with the French king LOUIS XIV or that James's favoritism toward his Catholic subjects would so provoke the Protestant majority as to cause another civil war, thus making England impotent in Europe.

The invitation was sent to William on June 30, 1688; when he arrived in November, his partisans rose in rebellion in Yorkshire and elsewhere. William's triumph was bloodless; James's forces, under John Churchill, later duke of MARLBOROUGH, deserted, and James himself fled. When William and Mary were made joint sovereigns (1689), they acquiesced in a Declaration and BILL OF RIGHTS, which opened the road to constitutional monarchy.

glossolalia   see TONGUES, SPEAKING IN

Gloucester (England) [glahs'-tur]   Gloucester, in west central England on the River Severn, is the county seat of Gloucestershire. About 56 km (35 mi) northwest of Bristol, it is a major inland port linked to the Bristol Channel by the River Severn and a ship canal. Gloucester has a population of 92,133 (1981) and is a market center for a cattle- and grain-growing region. The city's industries manufacture airplanes, railroad cars, farm equipment, lumber, cutlery, and rope. Gloucester's magnificent cathedral, built mostly in the 11th century (the

68.6-m/225-ft tower was completed *c.*1450), contains the tomb of Edward II. Other landmarks include the churches of Saint Mary-de-Lode and Saint Mary-de-Cript (both 11th century). There are church schools and inns dating from the 15th to the 17th century and a notable folk museum.

The Britons established a settlement on the site, but the founding date is generally considered AD 97, when the Romans built Glevum where they bridged the Severn. As England became united the city became a royal residence, and it was incorporated in 1483.

Gloucester (Massachusetts)   Gloucester is a major fishing port and summer resort located on Cape Ann in northeastern Massachusetts. It has a population of 28,716 (1990). Since its settlement in 1623, its economy has been based on fishing. Henry Wadsworth Longfellow's *The Wreck of the Hesperus* concerns the nearby Reef of Norman's Woe. Rudyard Kipling's *Captains Courageous* tells of Gloucester fishermen, who are commemorated by Leonard Craske's statue, *The Man at the Wheel* (1923). With the declining numbers of haddock, halibut, and mackerel, the fishing catch now consists mainly of cod, whiting, lobster, and shrimp, much of which is frozen in Gloucester plants.

Gloucester, Humphrey, Duke of   Humphrey, duke of Gloucester, b. 1390, d. Feb. 23, 1447, was the younger brother of King HENRY V of England. During the minority of his nephew, HENRY VI, Humphrey was forced to share power with his brother John, duke of Bedford, and Cardinal Henry BEAUFORT. He was a disturbing political influence, defending the lands of his wife JACQUELINE OF HAINAUT against England's ally, PHILIP THE GOOD of Burgundy, and later championing a war policy in France against the peace efforts of Beaufort. Humphrey's enemies humiliated him by convicting (1441) his second wife, Eleanor Cobham, of sorcery. Humphrey died mysteriously after being arrested.

Gloucestershire [glahs'-tur-shir]   Gloucestershire, a county in west central England, is located immediately east of the border with Wales. The county covers an area of 2,643 km^2 (1,020 mi^2), and its population is 527,500 (1988 est.). The city and port of GLOUCESTER are the county seat and principal commercial center. Cheltenham is famous for its spa and private schools, most notably Cheltenham College (1841) and Cheltenham Ladies' College (1853).

Gloucestershire is bisected by the River SEVERN; in the fertile river valley wheat, barley, and fruits are grown, and dairy cattle are raised for milk and cheese production. In the east the beautiful Cotswold Hills support sheep and stock raising as well as tourism. The Forest of Dean is located in the west, where limestone is mined. The county has remains from the Iron Age, Roman (especially at Cirencester), Saxon, and Norman periods.

gloves Gloves are hand coverings with a separate sheath for each finger, unlike the simpler mitten. They can be made of fine leather or heavier hide, fur, knitted or woven cotton, silk, wool, or linen. Until the 19th century, when technology made possible machines that could mass-produce apparel, gloves were among the costliest items of clothing, and from early times they were associated with royalty and priests and were seen as symbolic of high rank or of religious purity.

Linen gloves were found in the tomb of the ancient Egyptian King Tutankhamen (14th century BC). Gloves are mentioned in the works of Homer and Herodotus and were worn by upper-class Romans. In the early Middle Ages, linen or silk gloves, embroidered and decorated with gems, were part of a bishop's liturgical costume.

The peak of ornateness in glove styles was reached in 16th- and 17th-century Europe, when glove cuffs became wide and heavily embroidered and were embellished with ribbon and lace. During the Renaissance the most elegant gloves were made in Spain, although France and Italy were also major glove-making centers.

In 1834 a French glover, Xavier Jouvin, invented a punch press that could cut out six gloves simultaneously. This press and a new machine for sewing glove seams were the foundation of an industry that was producing inexpensive cotton and leather gloves by the millions by the end of the 19th century.

See also: COSTUME.

glowworm [gloh'-wurm] Glowworm is the common name for the larvae and some adults of beetles of the family Phengodidae, a group of insects closely related to the fireflies, or lightning bugs. Glowworms live on the ground or under logs and bark, where they prey upon other insects. They have a row of light-producing organs along each side of the body, and these produce a luminous glow with almost no heat (see BIOLUMINESCENCE). It is not yet known whether the light serves any function.

Larvae and wingless adult females of some species of fireflies, and a few other light-producing insect larvae, are also popularly called glowworms.

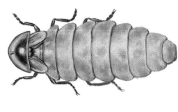

Some female adult glowworms, family Phengodidae, resemble glowworm larvae; both produce iridescent green light. Similar, wingless, luminescent females and larvae in the firefly family, Lampyridae, are also called glowworms.

gloxinia [glahk-sin'-ee-uh] Gloxinia, *Sinningia speciosa*, is a flowering plant belonging to the gesneriad

Gloxinia requires a warm, humid room in which to grow properly. The effort needed to nurture this plant is rewarded by a profusion of velvety flowers.

family, Gesneriaceae. It is Brazilian in origin and produces richly colored, showy, bell-shaped flowers that are violet, purple, white, or reddish, often marbled or spotted with darker shades.

Glubb, Sir John Bagot [gluhb] Sir John Bagot Glubb, b. Apr. 16, 1897, d. Mar. 17, 1986, was a British army officer who commanded the Arab Legion from 1939 to 1956. In 1930, Glubb was sent to the British mandate of Transjordan (now Jordan) as assistant commander of the Arab Legion. He became commander in 1939 and turned it into the best army in the area. Known as Glubb Pasha, he continued to head the army after Jordan became independent in 1946. In 1956, however, King Hussein I, bowing to Arab nationalist pressure, removed him from command. His writings include *The Story of the Arab Legion* (1948) and a three-volume history of the Arab world (1963–65).

glucagon see HORMONE, ANIMAL

Gluck, Alma [gluk] The American soprano Alma Gluck, b. Bucharest, Romania, May 11, 1884, d. Oct. 27, 1938, was brought to the United States as a child and attended public schools and college in New York State. She made her Metropolitan Opera debut (1909) as Sophie in Jules Massenet's *Werther*, and during her three years with the company she sang more than 20 roles. Gluck retired from opera in 1912 and embarked on a successful concert career. She gave her final concert at the Manhattan Opera House in 1925. Her second husband was the violinist Efrem Zimbalist.

Gluck, Christoph Willibald [gluk, kris'-tohf vil'-i-bahlt] Christoph Willibald Gluck, b. July 2, 1714, in Erasbach, near Nuremberg, Germany, was one of opera's most profound reformers. In Prague, Gluck learned to sing and play the violin, the cello, and the organ. While in Milan as a court musician he had his first instruction in

The German-born composer Christoph Willibald Gluck reformed baroque opera when he broke with the traditional Italian operatic form and rejected superfluous musical ornamentation. Gluck instead concentrated on a close integration of dramatic and musical elements.

music theory from Giovanni Battista Sammartini. In 1741, Gluck composed his first opera, *Artaserse*, to a text by Pietro METASTASIO.

Gluck later went to Paris, where he met Jean Philippe Rameau and heard some of his operas, and to London, where his own operas suffered by the public's comparisons with those of Handel. Gluck toured Europe for three years as conductor of an Italian opera company. In 1750 he married a wealthy Viennese heiress, Marianna Pergin.

He continued to compose, and by 1757 he was famous in Vienna and was knighted by the pope. Gluck admired the lifelike characters and situations in the new French plays and comic operas then in vogue in Vienna. His ballet *Don Juan* saw great success in 1761. Gluck renounced Metastasio's operatic conventions with *Orpheus and Eurydice* (1762). The libretto, by Ranieri Calzabigi, dealt with personal human conflicts and emotions, while Gluck's score contained unadorned melodies. The recitatives were orchestrally accompanied, and the chorus functioned as a corporate character.

With Gluck's *Alceste* (1767) opera finally became true music drama. For the Paris Opera, he composed *Iphigenia in Aulis* and revised *Orpheus*, with added numbers and a tenor as Orpheus instead of a contralto (which was unacceptable in Paris).

Armide (1777) and *Iphigenia in Tauris* (1779) were his last two successes in an output that included 29 Italian and 12 French operas. In 1779, Gluck stopped composing; he died of a stroke in Vienna on Nov. 15, 1787.

glucocorticoid see HORMONE, ANIMAL

glucose Glucose, $C_6H_{12}O_6$, is the most common MONOSACCHARIDE, or simple SUGAR. It is usually obtained from sugarcane or sugar beets, where, combined chemically with another monosaccharide, fructose, it forms the disaccharide sucrose. Synthesized in plants by the process of PHOTOSYNTHESIS, glucose (also called dextrose) is an energy-rich CARBOHYDRATE, important in human nutrition.

glucose tolerance test see DIABETES

glue see ADHESIVE

gluon Gluon is the whimsical name given to the subatomic particle held responsible for "gluing," or binding together, the QUARK constituents of protons and neutrons. Believed to be carriers of the strong nuclear force (much as photons are carriers of the electromagnetic force), gluons are theorized to exist in eight kinds, corresponding to the eight transformations that can change the "color" of quarks; the three noncolor transformations are accounted for by two gluons. Gluons also bind with each other to form particles called glueballs.

glycerol [glis'-ur-awl] Glycerol, or glycerin, a nontoxic liquid with a slightly sweet taste, is a commercially important alcohol. Its ability to absorb water makes it a valuable humectant (moisturizing agent) for tobacco and foods, which it also sweetens, and an emollient (softening agent) for skin conditioners. It is also used in the production of pharmaceuticals, plasticizers, alkyd resins, and the explosive nitroglycerin. Glycerin is derived from fats and vegetable oils as a by-product in soap manufacture and from propylene through chlorination and HYDROLYSIS. It is soluble in water and other polar solvents but insoluble in nonpolar organic solvents. Its chemical name is 1,2,3-propanetriol, and the structural formula is $CH_2OHCHOHCH_2OH$.

glycogen Glycogen, $(C_6H_{10}O_5)_n$, is a natural polymer made of many GLUCOSE molecules strung together. Also called animal starch, glycogen is an example of a POLYSACCHARIDE. Some glucose molecules, which provide the body with energy upon oxidation, are stored in the liver in the form of glycogen.

glycol [gly'-kawl] A glycol, also called a dihydric alcohol or diol, is a type of ALCOHOL that has two hydroxyl groups (OH), each bonded to different carbon atoms of an aliphatic carbon chain. The most common glycol is ethylene glycol, $(CH_2OH)_2$, used as an automotive antifreeze and in the production of polyester fibers, pharmaceuticals, and explosives.

Low-molecular-weight glycols are colorless, water-soluble liquids. As the molecular weight increases, the solubility in water decreases and the melting point, boiling point, and viscosity increase. Glycols undergo all of the reactions of alcohols. Simple glycols are usually synthesized from the corresponding unsaturated hydrocarbon.

glycolysis see METABOLISM

glycoside [gly'-kuh-syd] Glycoside compounds are a large family of plant chemicals composed of a sugar bonded to a nonsugar component called a glycon. The sugar generally is GLUCOSE. Long before anything was known about their chemistry, glycosides were used as natural dyes, drugs, and condiments. An ancient vegetable dye called madder, for example, was the first glycoside whose chemical structure was determined. Willow bark, which contains a glycon related to aspirin, was used to treat fever and acute rheumatism. Mustard seeds, long used as a pickling flavoring, contain a glycoside called sinigrin, and so on. The properties of glycosides—crystalline solids, bitter taste, and limited solubility in water—and their chemical makeup have led botanists to postulate that plants may use glycosides to store harmful substances.

Glyndebourne Opera Festival [glynd'-burn]

The Glyndebourne Festival in England was inaugurated in 1934 on the estate of John Christie and his wife, the singer Audrey Mildmay. This renowned summer opera festival opened with a production of Mozart's *The Marriage of Figaro*. Its founders included Fritz Busch as permanent conductor and Carl Ebert as stage director. Rudolf Bing became general manager in 1935, a post he held until 1948. An international roster of singers, conductors, and designers has participated each summer in a repertoire that includes traditional, rarely heard classical, and contemporary operas. Glyndebourne makes its own recordings, telecasts its productions, and has a touring company.

gnat see MIDGE

gnatcatcher [nat'-kech-ur] Gnatcatcher is the common name for the birds of the genus *Polioptila*, which is a New World group of the so-called Old World warbler family, Sylviidae; this family also includes the KINGLETS of North America. Gnatcatchers are tiny (9–13 cm/3.5–5 in), graceful, constantly active woodland dwellers that are given to aerial acrobatics in pursuit of flying insects. Most species are resident in small areas of tropical

The blue-gray gnatcatcher, a tiny bird of the warbler family, has a long, mobile tail. Gnatcatchers are insectivorous birds.

America, but the migratory blue gray gnatcatcher, *P. caerulea*, nests in the eastern and southwestern United States.

Gneisenau, August Wilhelm Anton, Graf Neithardt von [guh-ny'-zen-ow, grahf nyt'-hahrt fuhn]

August Wilhelm Anton Gneisenau, b. Oct. 27, 1760, d. Aug. 23, 1831, a Prussian field marshal, was one of the chief organizers of Napoleon I's final defeat. Joining the army in 1786, he achieved prominence as a result of his defense of Kolberg against the French (1807). After Prussia had accepted the harsh peace of Tilsit (1807), Gneisenau worked with General von SCHARNHORST to modernize the army. Succeeding Scharnhorst as chief of the general staff in June 1813, he was the principal strategist in the War of Liberation; the plan of the Battle of Leipzig (Oct. 16–19, 1813) was mostly his work.

gneiss [nys] Gneiss is a coarse- to medium-grained banded METAMORPHIC ROCK formed from igneous or sedimentary rocks during regional metamorphism. Rich in FELDSPARS and QUARTZ, gneisses also contain mica minerals and aluminous or ferromagnesian silicates. In some gneisses thin bands of quartz-feldspar minerals are separated by bands of micas; in others the mica is evenly distributed throughout. Gneisses formed from igneous rocks are similar in composition to GRANITE or granodiorite, and some may have originally been LAVA flows. The origin of a gneiss can usually be determined by its chemical composition and mineral content.

gnome see FAIRY

gnosticism [nahs'-ti-sizm] Gnosticism is a term derived from a Greek word for knowledge (*gnosis*) and applied to a philosophical and religious movement that influenced the Mediterranean world from the 1st century BC to the 3d century AD. It had a variety of pagan, Jewish, and Christian forms. Its name is derived from the fact that it promised salvation through a secret knowledge or understanding of reality possessed by its devotees. A collection of original gnostic documents were found near the Egyptian town of NAG HAMMADI in 1945.

A pervasive dualism underlay much of gnostic thought. Good and evil, light and darkness, truth and falsehood, spirit and matter were opposed to each other in human experience as being and non-being. The created universe and human experience were characterized by a radical disjunction between the spiritual, which was real, and the physical, which was illusory. This disjunction resulted from a cosmic tragedy, described in a variety of ways by gnostic mythology, as a consequence of which sparks of deity became entrapped in the physical world. These could be freed only by saving knowledge that was revealed to a spiritual elite by a transcendent messenger from the spirit world, variously identified as Seth (one of the sons of Adam), Jesus, or some other figure. Renunci-

Gnosticism was considered a heresy by orthodox Christians, and the Manichaeans, whose beliefs were influenced by it, were persecuted during the Middle Ages. Here Dominican inquisitors are shown burning books of the Albigenses, a Manichaean sect that attracted followers in France during the 12th and 13th centuries.

ation of physical desires and strict asceticism, combined with mystical rites of initiation and purification were thought to liberate the immortal souls of believers from the prison of physical existence. Reunion with divine reality was accomplished after a journey of the soul through intricate systems of hostile powers.

Associated in legend with SIMON MAGUS, a Samaritan sorcerer mentioned in Acts 8:9–24, gnosticism probably originated in the Near East as a synthesis of Oriental and Greek ideas before the advent of Christianity. It reached the height of its influence as a Christian sect in the middle of the 2d century AD, when it was represented by the Egyptian teachers Basilides and VALENTINUS. Some gnostic tendencies found their way into later Christian monasticism, while others survived among the MANDAEANS and adherents of MANICHAEISM.

GNP   see GROSS NATIONAL PRODUCT

gnu   see WILDEBEEST

go   Go is an oriental game played on a board marked with 361 points that are formed by the intersections of 19 horizontal and 19 vertical lines. The game also uses 361 pieces, called stones—181 black and 180 white. The rules of go are very simple, although the strategy is immensely complicated. Each player alternately places a stone on an empty intersection, trying either to control territory or to capture an opponent's stones. Stones are captured when they are completely surrounded by an opponent's stones and there are no unoccupied adjacent intersections. The player with more occupied intersections wins the game.

Go is known as I-go in Japan and *wiqi* in China, where an early version of the game, Yi, is mentioned in the entry for the year 546 BC in the Zuo Zhuan chronology. The game was introduced into Japan in AD 735. Go appeared in the United States as go-bang in the 19th century and enjoys a growing following in the West.

Goa   [goh'-uh]   Goa is a former Portuguese colony (1510–1961) located in west India between the Western Ghats and the Arabian Sea, about 400 km (250 mi) south of Bombay. It was part of the Union Territory of Goa, Daman, and Diu from 1961 to May 30, 1987, when Goa became the 25th state of India. Daman and Diu (1981 pop., 78,981; area 112 km^2/43 mi^2), tiny enclaves surrounded by Gujarat state, then became a separate union territory. Goa has a population of 1,007,749 (1981) and an area of 3,702 km^2 (1,430 mi^2). Panaji, the capital, retains a Portuguese colonial ambience. Its churches include the Basilica Bom Jesus, which contains the tomb and shrine of Saint FRANCIS XAVIER. The port of Marmagao exports a sizable amount of iron ore mined in Goa. Goa's tropical climate and picturesque coastal beaches make it a tourist center during the winter.

About 65% of the people of Goa are Hindus, and there is a substantial Roman Catholic minority. Official use of Konkani, the traditional language of Goa, was banned during Portuguese rule. India annexed Goa in 1961, ending 451 years of Portuguese rule. In 1966 its people rejected a merger with neighboring Maharashtra state.

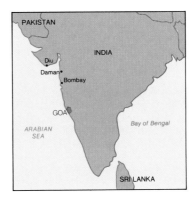

Goa, Daman, and Diu, three former Portuguese colonial possessions in western India, in 1961 formed a union territory with representation in the Indian parliament. In 1987, Goa became the 25th state of India; Daman and Diu became a separate union territory.

goat   The goat, genus *Capra*, is a mammal, related to the SHEEP, with backward-arching horns and a short tail. Goats have helped supply human needs since prehistoric times. The most important products that goats yield are milk, cheese, butter, mohair, and leather. Certain goat cheeses are highly prized, as is the leather made from the skin of young goats. Because they can feed by browsing, goats are valuable in some areas for brush control. Excessive browsing, particularly in arid lands, may lead to desertification, however.

Both milk goats, *C. hircus*, and mohair-producing goats, *C. angorensis*, were probably domesticated from the pasang, or Grecian ibex, found in Anatolia and Persia.

More than 200 breeds are recognized. The most important mohair-producer, the Angora, originated in Turkey. The average yield of mohair per goat is 3 kg (7 lb) annually.

The domestic goat, a member of the cattle family Bovidae and related to the sheep, serves as a source of milk, hair and wool, leather, and meat. Major U.S. dairy breeds include the Saanen (1), which yields high milk production over a long period, and the smaller Toggenburg (2). Both are sturdy, hornless varieties of Swiss origin. The British Alpine (3), a cross between the Saanen and the Toggenburg, is black with the Toggenburg's white markings; it is noted for its high milk output. A cross of Asian and British varieties, the Anglo-Nubian (4) gives milk with a high butterfat content. The Granada (5) is a black, hornless dairy breed raised in Spain. Mohair is made from the long, fine hair of the Angora goat (6), which was originally bred in Turkey and is now the single largest breed in the United States.

The principal breeds of milk goat in the United States are the Saanen, Toggenburg, Nubian, French Alpine, and La Mancha. The breeds vary in size and in the amount and quality of milk produced. A Saanen, for example, produces about 900 kg (2,000 lb) of 3.5 percent butterfat milk per year. Does weigh 61 kg (135 lb), and bucks 84 kg (185 lb) or more. In contrast, Toggenburgs typically give about 725 kg (1,600 lb) per year of 3 percent milk. Does weigh 57 kg (125 lb), and bucks 73 kg (168 lb) or more.

The Saanen, the largest breed of Swiss origin, is white or light cream with a flesh-colored muzzle. The Toggenburg, also a Swiss breed, is typically fawn to brown, with white stripes down the face and white on the legs and rump. The hair may be long, short, or curly, and wattles may or may not be present. The Nubian originated in England from native goats and importations from Egypt, India, and North Africa. They have short hair ranging from black through shades of red to white, with spotted or dappled patterns. They may be horned or hornless and have long, drooping ears.

French Alpine goats vary from pure white to shades of fawn, gray, red, brown, and black, plus combinations of these colors in the same animal. The America La Mancha was developed by crossing the La Mancha, a short-eared Spanish breed, with the dairy breeds. They may be any color, vary in size, and have very short ears or no external ears at all.

goatfish The goatfishes, or surmullets (family Mullidae, order Perciformes), are common fishes of warm seas. They have elongate and slightly compressed bodies with two widely separated dorsal fins. A small, ventrally placed mouth is well suited for obtaining food from sand or mud. A pair of barbels on the chin, having chemosensitive organs, serves to find crustaceans, worms, and small fish as the goatfish sweeps rapidly over the bottom or probes deeply into the sediments. The highly esteemed red mullet of Europe is a goatfish; it is the essential ingredient of the famous fish soups of many parts of the Mediterranean. Occasionally its flesh is poisonous.

The spotted goatfish, living inshore in the American Atlantic, drags its barbels along the bottom to find food.

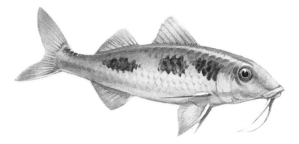

Gobbi, Tito [gohb'-bee, tee'-toh] The Italian operatic baritone, Tito Gobbi, b. Oct. 24, 1915, d. Mar. 5, 1984, mastered a repertoire of nearly 100 roles. He made his debut in Rome in 1938, and at La Scala in 1942. His American debut (1948) took place at the San Francisco Opera. In 1956 he began his long association with the Metropolitan Opera as Scarpia in Puccini's *Tosca*, to great acclaim. Known for his fine acting, he sang at most of the major opera houses in Europe and North and South America and had a parallel directing career.

Gobelins [gawb-lan'] The National Manufactory of Gobelins, the most important French tapestry factory, was founded on the outskirts of Paris as a dye works in the 15th century by Jean Gobelin. A tapestry-weaving workshop was added in 1601 by two Flemish artisans, and in 1662, Louis XIV purchased the manufactory, which then became a center for the production of tapestries and furniture for the royal palaces. Charles LE BRUN was director from 1663 until 1690, supervising a staff of weavers in low-warp and high-warp workshops. The factory was closed in 1694 because of the king's financial difficulties, and the weavers were dispersed. It was reopened in 1699 solely for the production of tapestries, and the first series woven there was the popular *Portières of the Gods*. The factory has survived to this day and since 1937 has functioned under the patronage of the state as a branch of the Mobilier National.

Gobi [goh'-bee] The Gobi, Asia's largest desert, covers an area of about 1,295,000 km² (500,000 mi²) in Mongolia and the Inner Mongolia region of China. The name is Mongolian for "place without water." The desert extends 1,600 km (1,000 mi) east to west, with a maximum north-to-south measurement of 966 km (600 mi). It is a region of plateaus averaging 900 m (3,500 ft) above sea

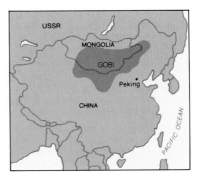

The Gobi Desert, which occupies portions of China and Mongolia, is a vast plateau bordered by mountain ranges. The Gobi experiences the most extreme range of temperatures of any of the world's deserts.

level, broken by hills and by the ALTAI MOUNTAINS, whose peaks exceed 3,700 m (12,000 ft).

The desert consists mostly of a shallow layer of gravel over granite, slate, and other rocks. Annual rainfall averages about 200 mm (8 in) in the east and fewer than 76 mm (3 in) in the west. The climate is continental, and temperatures range from highs of 50° C (113° F) in July to lows of –40° C (–40° F) in January. Small, brackish lakes exist, but wells and springs supply potable ground water. An ocean covered part of the area in the Permian Period (280 to 230 million years ago), but for the last 100 million years the Gobi has become increasingly dry. Vegetation is scarce and consists primarily of tough grasses, sage, and niter bush. The diverse wildlife includes gazelles, wild asses, jerboas, pit vipers, sandgrouse, and owls. The desert is home to scattered groups of Mongol nomads, who herd camels, goats, and sheep. The population density is fewer than 1 person per km² (3 per mi²).

The Gobi became widely known through the writings of Marco POLO, who reached it in the 13th century. For centuries it has been the site of numerous caravan routes, and today it is crossed by several railroads and highways. Sven HEDIN and Roy Chapman ANDREWS explored the Gobi

The Gobi Desert, extending across southern Mongolia into northern China, is one of the most sparsely populated areas on Earth. The prevailing winds have lifted the soil cover, resulting in the sand dunes and sparse grass cover.

in the 20th century, discovering artifacts of Bronze Age and earlier peoples, as well as fossilized dinosaur eggs of the Mesozoic Period (230 to 65 million years ago).

See also: DESERT; TAKLIMAKAN DESERT.

Gobineau, Joseph Arthur, Comte de [goh-bee-noh'] Joseph Arthur, comte de Gobineau, b. July 14, 1816, d. Oct. 13, 1882, was a French novelist, historian, and anthropologist best known for his racial theories, which are said to have influenced such major figures as Richard Wagner, Friedrich Nietzsche, and Adolf Hitler. Gobineau first attracted attention with his novel *Les Pléiades* (1874). While serving as a diplomat in Europe, Iran, and South America he wrote his *Essai sur l'inégalité des races humaines* (Essay on the Inequality of Human Races, 1853–55), setting forth his theory of the supremacy of the white race.

goblin   see FAIRY

goby [goh'-bee]   The gobies, family Gobiidae, order Perciformes, are abundant fishes that inhabit bottom, near-shore areas in tropical and temperate seas. Their pelvic fins are modified to form a suctorial disk. Gobies are small; one Philippine species is the smallest vertebrate known, reaching a length of 3 mm (0.12 in). The mudskippers, genus *Periophthalmus* and *Boleophthalmus*, are tropical gobies that spend most of their lives on land. The frilled goby, *Bathygobius sorporator*, exhibits remarkable learning ability. If trapped when the tide recedes, a fish that has been swimming over the area can jump unerringly from one pool to another.

The striped goby is a spiny-finned fish found in the waters off the coast of Southeast Asia.

God   In Western culture the word *God* generally refers to one supreme holy being who is believed to have created the entire universe, to rule over it, and to bring it to its fulfillment.

In the Old Testament, God was called YHWH, pronounced Yahweh by most scholars; the exact pronunciation of the name was lost because it was rarely enunciated. In its place was read Adonai ("Lord"). The written combination of the tetragrammation YHWH with the vowels of Adonai was traditionally rendered as Jehovah in English Bibles. YHWH is frequently translated as "He who is" and probably designates YHWH as creator. In ISLAM, ALLAH stands for a similar notion.

Thus, the word God refers to the object of WORSHIP, PRAYER, and religious MEDITATION. God also has been the object of religious and philosophical reflection, the su-preme object of THEOLOGY. In Jewish and Christian belief God is also in some way personal, righteous, or moral, concerned with people and their lives and therefore closely related to and active within the world and the course of history.

Variations in the Concept of God

Ideas of god vary widely from religion to religion and from culture to culture.

Many Gods. In primitive cultures that conceive of human life as totally upheld and threatened by (and thus subordinate to) strange and uncontrollable natural and social powers, all such powers and forces—in animals, totems, rivers, trees, mountains, kings and queens, tribes, ancestors, holy men and women—participate in and manifest holy power. Here the divine is undifferentiated; it is universally present in important objects and persons. In other ancient cultures that conceive of the person as unique and differentiated from natural and social forces and recognize the role of personal power in politics, these varied natural and cultural forces are personified or symbolized by gods and goddesses who control, work through, and manifest themselves in these powers. For example, ARES was the Greek god of thunder and of war; APHRODITE, the goddess of love and beauty; and APOLLO, the god of light and order. The worship of many gods, known as POLYTHEISM, characterized the religions of most of the ancient world. In every case, a deepening sense of unifying order in reality was accompanied by a drive toward a unity of these plural forces, toward MONOTHEISM.

Impersonal World Order. In many advanced civilizations, the divine appears, not as a person, but as order or harmony; it is thus impersonal, universal, and omnipresent. Clear examples of this view are the *Dao* of DAOISM and the notion of the LOGOS in STOICISM. Both are ultimately an impersonal and unifying principle of the world. Other forms of this view appear in the hymns to Indra in HINDUISM and in the worship of Ahura Mazda, the god of light, in ZOROASTRIANISM. In each of these religions, there is a dualistic principle: an impersonal order, harmony, or light represents the divine; but disorder, chaos, or matter represents the rest of reality.

Undifferentiated Unity. Some religions conceive of the divine as the undifferentiated unity of all, a unity in and beyond all manifestations, powers, and persons. The ultimate becomes not only the whole of reality as its unity and ground, but is so far beyond finite reality that it becomes relatively unintelligible and relatively unreal. In these cases, of course, the divine is thoroughly beyond ordinary speech and even beyond positive analogies. The clearest expression of this transcendence of all being and all thought is found in Mahayana BUDDHISM, which describes the ultimate principle in negative assertions and names it a Nothingness, or Voidness. In this notion of the divine the originating religious categories of power, person, and order are infinitely transcended as characteristics essentially related to finitude and therefore antithetical to the divine.

This 13th-century illustration portrays God as the architect of the universe. In the Judeo-Christian tradition, God is both a transcendent creator and a personal, moral force in history. In other cultures God is purely impersonal, an ultimate principle that defies definition.

Paradoxes of the Biblical Concept

The paradoxes or dialectical tensions characteristic of the Western understanding of God are derived from the Bible. In the Old Testament, God transcends all the limited and special forces and powers of the human experience. On the other hand, although God's power is manifested in nature, the main arena for divine activity is the sequence of historical events related to the calling, the establishment, and the protection of a chosen people. In this activity, moreover, God is revealed as moral or righteous, the source of the moral law, and is quick to punish those, even the chosen ones, who defy this law. God is, however, also a God of mercy, patience, faithfulness, and GRACE. This God of history, COVENANT, judgment, and promised redemption is assumed to be, and often clearly affirmed to be, the ruler of all events.

These aspects of the notion of God reappear, with some modification, in the New Testament. There the one God is also concerned with history, judgment, and redemption, but the central manifestation is JESUS CHRIST, through whom God's will for humankind is revealed, his judgments are made known, and his power to save is ef-

fected. The New Testament writers generally use the word *God* to designate the God of the Old Testament. Christ is understood as the fulfillment of the Messianic promise and as the Son, or Logos. His relation to God the Father and the HOLY SPIRIT led to the development of the Christian doctrine of the TRINITY. Both Jewish and Christian theology therefore display a dialectical tension between God's transcendence over nature and history as creator and ruler, and the personal, moral participation of God in history for the sake of humankind.

Philosophic Approaches

During the long period in which Western culture understood itself and the world largely through the framework of Greco-Roman philosophy (c.200–1400), the notion of God was shaped with the help first of Platonic and then of Aristotelian categories. Because of Greek philosophy's bias toward transcendent, changeless, eternal realms of being, this religious tradition greatly emphasized the absolute nature of God: God was understood as pure act, utterly independent, changeless, nontemporal, and unrelated. The active, related, personal aspects of God manifested themselves chiefly in piety and through numerous angelic and saintly representatives.

During the REFORMATION, which emphasized the primacy of Scripture, the personal, purposive, active side of the biblical God again achieved prominence, and the philosophical side receded: God's judgments and his mercy toward humans were considered his central attributes. The subsequent divergence of modern thought from Greco-Roman traditions led to the introduction of new philosophical options emphasizing change, process, and relatedness. They give expression to a new dynamic and immanent interpretation of God and can be found in systems such as PROCESS PHILOSOPHY.

Knowability of God. Those who argue that God can be known by reason offer one version or another of the classical proofs of God's existence: the cosmological proof from the existence of the world; the teleological proof from the order of the finite world; the ontological proof from the implications of the very concept of God as a perfect and necessary being; and the moral proof from the implications of moral experience. They argue that any theology intellectually respectable enough to speak to modern, intelligent men and women must be grounded in rational philosophy. Those who believe God can be known only by faith tend to be skeptical of such philosophical proofs. For them, the God of rational theology, proven and tailored by thinking processes, is merely the creature of humanity's own wayward wisdom. God himself must speak to humankind if he is to be known rightly, or even at all, and therefore faith, as a response to divine REVELATION, is the only path to a true knowledge of God. Finally, there are those who assert that God can be known neither by reason nor by faith but only by direct experience.

Reality of God. The appearance of the so-called death-of-God theologies in the 1960s introduced the issue of the reality of God into the Jewish and the Christian religious traditions themselves where it has been the subject of considerable debate: Is the notion of God, which correlates so closely with the self-understanding of humankind, merely a projection of humanity's self-consciousness onto an unresponding cosmos?

See also: CHRISTIANITY; JUDAISM; PRIMITIVE RELIGION; RELIGION.

Godard, Jean Luc [goh-dahr', zhawn luek] One of the most influential film directors of the 1960s, Jean Luc Godard, b. Paris, Dec. 3, 1930, of Swiss parents, is best known for his innovative NEW WAVE films and for his increasingly radical approaches to politics and art. His experimental use of the hand-held camera, jump cuts, and flash-shots; his disregard for cinematic continuity; and his recourse to question-and-answer sessions within films to illustrate philosophical dialectics have done much to revolutionize cinema.

A lively and controversial contributor to the journal *Cahiers du Cinéma* from 1952 on, Godard made several shorts before directing his first feature, *Breathless* (1959). In *Le Petit Soldat* (The Little Soldier, 1960), on the Algerian War, and other films, he combined documentary with fictional footage.

Godard's early films dealt with the nature and contradictions of modern society. Of particular interest to him was the place of women in society. *Une Femme est une femme* (A Woman is a Woman, 1961) was followed by *My Life to Live* (1962), on prostitution, *Une Femme mariée* (A Married Woman, 1964), *Masculin-Féminin* (1966), and *Two or Three Things I Know about Her* (1966). Their themes rested on the notion of woman as object, but his approach brought into question the entire commodity-advertising nexus of today's consumer society, as did *Alphaville* (1965) and *Weekend* (1968). In such films as *Made in USA* (1966), *La chinoise* (1967), and *Sympathy for the Devil* (1968), starring the Rolling Stones, Godard subordinated considerations of plot and pared down his visual imagery to a few static tableaux, becoming more overtly Marxist and didactic.

After a car accident in 1971, Godard produced the autobiographical *Tout va bien* (Everything's Fine, 1972). Other later films include *Numéro deux* (1975), *Every Man for Himself* (1980), *First Name: Carmen* (1983), and *Hail Mary* (1985).

Goddard, Robert The American physicist Robert Hutchings Goddard, b. Worcester, Mass., Oct. 5, 1882, d. Aug. 10, 1945, laid the foundations of modern rocket and astronautics technology. He earned his master's and doctoral degrees in physics at Clark University, in Worcester, Mass., where he later taught. On his own time and money, Goddard conducted research on improving solid-propellant rockets. Further experiments were conducted under a grant from the Smithsonian Institution, and in 1919 the Smithsonian published a 69-page summary of his results, entitled *A Method of Reaching Extreme Altitudes.*

The most noted milestone in Goddard's work came on Mar. 16, 1926, when he fired the world's first successful liquid-propellant rocket. A simple pressure-fed rocket that burned gasoline and liquid oxygen, it traveled only 56 m (184 ft) but proved that the principle was valid. Goddard's future work was dedicated to developing more powerful rockets and more complex systems. He later received grants from Harry F. Guggenheim and the Guggenheim Foundation that proved invaluable when he moved his work to Roswell, N. Mex. During World War II the U.S. government was unconvinced of the rocket's worth as a weapon and put Goddard to work on rocket-assisted-takeoff units for aircraft.

In 1951, Goddard's widow and the Guggenheim Foundation filed a joint patent-infringement claim against the U.S. government. In 1960 a $1 million settlement granted the government the rights to more than 200 patents covering "basic inventions in the field of rockets, guided missiles and space exploration." Goddard's records were later published as *The Papers of Robert H. Goddard* (1970). The National Aeronautics and Space

The French film director Jean Luc Godard became prominent during the late 1950s as a leading member of the New Wave cinema group. Godard is shown here directing actress Brigitte Bardot in Masculin-Féminin *(1966).*

Robert Goddard, an American physicist, pioneered research in rocketry that culminated in 1926 with the launching of the first successful liquid-fuel rocket.

Administration named its Goddard Space Flight Center in his honor.

See also: ROCKETS AND MISSILES.

Goddard College   Established in 1938, Goddard College is a private liberal arts college in Plainfield, Vt. It is a well-known experimental college, with a work-study program, no prescribed courses, and evaluations of student performance that are not reduced to numerical or alphabetical scales.

Goddard Space Flight Center   Goddard Space Flight Center, located in Greenbelt, Md., is the main U.S. facility for tracking and controlling unmanned spacecraft and for relaying data from manned spacecraft. It is also in charge of unmanned Earth-oriented missions and some astronomy missions. Goddard was established in 1958 shortly before the National Aeronautics and Space Administration (NASA) was formed, with the intention that it would become part of the new agency. The center is named in honor of Robert H. Goddard.

Godden, Rumer [gahd'-en, roo'-mur]   Rumer Godden, b. Sussex, England, Dec. 10, 1907, is known principally for her novels and children's stories. *Black Narcissus* (1939; film, 1947) concerns Anglican nuns in India and anticipated one of her best-known novels, *In This House of Brede* (1969), on life in a Benedictine convent. The Indian setting and Godden's recurrent theme of the mystery of childhood and the transition to adolescence are combined in *The River* (1946; film, 1951). Godden also wrote *Two under the Indian Sun* (1966), an autobiography coauthored by her sister Jon; many children's books; a biography of Hans Christian Andersen (1955); and a book of poems, *In Noah's Ark* (1949). Recent books include *Five for Sorrow, Ten for Joy* (1979) and *The Dark Horse* (1981).

Gödel, Kurt [gur'-dul]   Kurt Gödel, b. Apr. 28, 1906, d. Jan. 14, 1978, was a Czech-born American mathematician and logician. He is best known for his proof of Gödel's undecidability theorems, which state that any rigidly logical mathematical system contains questions that cannot be proved or disproved on the basis of the AXIOMS within the system. These results were an epochal landmark in 20th-century mathematics, indicating that mathematics is not a finished object, as was previously believed. Gödel's proof first appeared in a German technical journal in 1931. This paper ended nearly a century of attempts to establish axioms that would provide a rigorous basis for all mathematics. Gödel also helped develop geometric models for Einstein's theory of relativity. He became a member of the faculty of the University of Vienna in 1930, where he belonged to the school of logical positivism. In 1940 he immigrated to the United States; he was a professor at the Institute for Advanced Study, in Princeton, N.J., from 1953 to his death.

Godey, Louis Antoine [goh'-dee]   Louis Antoine Godey, b. New York City, June 6, 1804, d. Nov. 29, 1878, was an American publisher who cofounded (1830) the *Lady's Book*, later changing its name to *Godey's Lady's Book*. The leading American women's magazine of the 19th century, it dominated for more than 50 years under the guidance of Godey and Sarah Josepha Hale, his longtime coeditor. The magazine is best remembered for its richly illustrated fashion plates, but *Godey's Lady's Book* also published the works of leading writers and was an influential supporter of women's causes, including education.

Godfrey of Bouillon   Godfrey of Bouillon, b. c.1060, d. July 18, 1100, was a leader of the First CRUSADE and the first ruler of the Latin Kingdom of Jerusalem. Son of Count Eustace II of Boulogne and heir to the duchy of Lower Lorraine, Godfrey was excluded from his inheritance by Holy Roman Emperor Henry IV until 1082. In 1096, with his brothers, Godfrey joined the First Crusade. After the conquest of Jerusalem in 1099, he was elected ruler of the kingdom but took only the title of "Defender of the Holy Sepulcher." He repulsed an Egyptian incursion before his death at Jerusalem. His brother Baldwin I succeeded him.

See also: JERUSALEM, LATIN KINGDOM OF.

Godiva, Lady [guh-dy'-vuh]   Lady Godiva, fl. 1040–80, was an English noblewoman who, according to legend, rode naked through Coventry in order to persuade her husband, Earl Leofric of Mercia, to lighten the taxes on the townspeople. In one version, she was observed by only a tailor, the original Peeping Tom, who was struck blind.

Godoy, Manuel de [goh-doy']   Manuel de Godoy y Álvarez de Faria, b. May 12, 1767, d. Oct. 4, 1851, chief minister of Spain from 1792 to 1798 and from 1801 to 1808, led his country into disastrous wars. Joining the royal bodyguard in 1784, he became the lover of Maria Luisa, whose husband succeeded to the throne as CHARLES IV in 1788. Charles made Godoy chief minister in 1792.

Godoy's domestic policies were enlightened, for he weakened the Inquisition and supported education. Unfortunately he lacked talent for diplomacy. Spain entered the war against revolutionary France in 1793, but after a series of defeats Godoy concluded the Treaty of Basel (1795). In 1796, Godoy allied Spain with France and thus subjected his country to several defeats by the British; later, the Spanish fleet was destroyed at the Battle of TRAFALGAR (1805). In 1808 a popular uprising overthrew Charles in favor of his son FERDINAND VII. Godoy spent the rest of his life in Paris.

Godthåb [gawt'-hawp]   Godthåb (1989 pop., 11,957) is the capital and largest town of Greenland. Since

Greenland achieved home rule in 1979, the Greenlandic name Nuuk has been used increasingly for the town. It lies on an ice-free fjord and has large fishing and fish-processing industries. Greenland's legislature and a teachers college are there. The town was founded in 1721 by Hans Egede, a Norwegian missionary.

Godunov, Boris   see BORIS GODUNOV, TSAR OF RUSSIA

Godwin, Mary Wollstonecraft   see WOLLSTONE-CRAFT, MARY

Godwin, William [gahd'-win]   The English writer William Godwin, b. Mar. 3, 1756, d. Apr. 7, 1836, was the author of *An Enquiry Concerning Political Justice* (2 vols., 1793), an influential work of political and philosophical anarchism. Godwin stressed that humans, shaped by environment and governed by reason, are innately good and free to act without restraint (see ROMANTICISM). His novel *The Adventures of Caleb Williams* (1794) was both a psychological thriller and a social indictment. In 1797 he married Mary WOLLSTONECRAFT, who died giving birth to their daughter Mary Wollstonecraft SHELLEY.

Godwin Austen   see K2

Goebbels, Joseph [geb'-els]   Paul Joseph Goebbels, b. Oct. 29, 1897, d. May 1, 1945, was propaganda minister of the National Socialist regime in Germany. Reared a Roman Catholic, he received his doctorate in literature and history at Heidelberg in 1922, joined the National Socialist party the same year, and was elected to the Reichstag in 1928. Five years later, when Adolf HITLER came to power, Goebbels became minister of popular enlightenment and propaganda, with control over the press, radio, film, the theater, literature, and art. Goebbels did not simply block off undesirable information or commentary through censorship; he shrewdly exploited the media in an orchestrated campaign supporting the National Socialist party line.

A small man with a deformed foot, Goebbels did not measure up to the physical standards of the ideology he propagated. His virulent anti-Semitism and anti-intellectualism notwithstanding, he was a brilliant intellectual who had studied under the prominent Jewish scholar Friedrich Gundolf, and his wife, Magda, had been reared in a Jewish household. Moreover, contrary to his image as one of Hitler's earliest and most loyal stalwarts, Goebbels had actually demanded his expulsion from the party in 1926. But after Hitler had won him over and entrusted him with the party leadership in Berlin, Goebbels came to idolize his leader. He kept the faith until the end. When Hitler committed suicide at the end of World War II, Goebbels and his wife poisoned their six children and then took their own lives.

Goerdeler, Karl Friedrich [gur'-de-lur]   Karl Friedrich Goerdeler, b. July 31, 1884, d. Feb. 2, 1945, was a leader of the German resistance to Adolf HITLER. He was mayor of Leipzig (1930–37) before resigning to organize opposition to the Nazi regime. After the unsuccessful attempt to assassinate Hitler on July 20, 1944, Goerdeler, who was to have been chancellor in the new government, was executed.

Goering, Hermann [gur'-ing]   Hermann Wilhelm Goering (or Göring), b. Jan. 12, 1893, d. Oct. 19, 1946, was second only to Adolf HITLER in the German National Socialist regime and the one man in Hitler's inner circle with a distinguished social and military background. The son of the first German imperial commissioner of Southwest Africa, Goering was a highly decorated World War I flyer, having succeeded Manfred von RICHTHOFEN in command of the latter's famous air squadron.

Joseph Goebbels, Adolf Hitler's minister of propaganda, addresses a German Nazi party rally in 1937. A dynamic orator and highly efficient master of propaganda techniques, Goebbels orchestrated public opinion in order to favor and support Hitler's regime.

Hermann Goering, a German aviation hero during World War I, became one of the leaders of the Nazi party. As air minister (from 1933) he organized the Luftwaffe (German air force), and as plenipotentiary of the 4-year economic plan (from 1936) he directed the nation's economy.

The Portinari Altarpiece *(c.1476) is the masterpiece of the Flemish painter Hugo van der Goes. Admired for its realism, the painting also contains curious disjunctions in scale between the various figures. While the purpose of this triptych was religious, it also indicated the limitations of Flemish naturalism. (Uffizi Gallery, Florence.)*

Goering became a National Socialist in 1922 and took part in the abortive MUNICH PUTSCH of 1923. Elected to the Reichstag in 1928, he became its presiding officer in 1932, the year before Hitler came to power. During the 1930s he accrued enormous power as Prussian minister-president and minister of the interior; chief of the GESTAPO (secret police—with his ally Heinrich HIMMLER in operational control); minister of aviation and, with the rank of field marshal, commander in chief of the air force; and economic dictator of the Third Reich, directing the four-year plan (for economic mobilization).

Goering was ferociously efficient in his earlier years, but his personal vitality was later sapped by morphine addiction. During World War II his influence with Hitler was undermined by the failure of the air force (Luftwaffe), first against the British and then against the Soviets. Captured by the Allies in 1945, he was tried as a major war criminal at Nuremberg (see NUREMBERG TRIALS). He was condemned to execution but cheated the hangman by taking poison.

GOES   GOES (Geostationary Operational Environmental Satellites) is a series of meteorological satellites placed in geosynchronous orbits. It is a program of the U.S. National Oceanic and Atmospheric Administration (NOAA). The satellites provide pictures day and night at a rate of one every 30 minutes. *GOES 1* was launched on Oct. 16, 1975; *GOES 2*, on June 16, 1977; and *GOES 3*, on June 16, 1978. *GOES 4*, orbited on Sept. 9, 1980, also provides vertical water-vapor and temperature profiles of the atmosphere, as do subsequent entries in the series. *GOES 5, GOES 6,* and *GOES 7* were orbited on May 22, 1981, Apr. 28, 1983, and Feb. 26, 1987, respectively. *GOES 7*, which remains functional, is also the first geosynchronous weather satellite in SARSAT, the international satellite search and rescue service (see SARSAT).

Goes, Hugo van der [hoos]   The work of the Flemish painter Hugo van der Goes, b. c.1435–40, d. 1482, occupies an important position in the century-long transition between medievalism and humanism, which occurred in Northern European art between 1425 and 1525. Van der Goes explored the possibilities of portraying religious intensity through expressions of individual feeling—gestures and facial expressions—and far surpassed his predecessors in his ability to portray psychological complexities. The paintings attributed to him before 1474–76, when he painted his best-known work, the *Portinari Altarpiece* (Uffizi, Florence), were in the decorative, narrative Gothic style. In the *Portinari Altarpiece*, however, he introduced a distinction between the intellectual abstraction of the angels, which he painted in the Gothic style, and the human emotions exhibited by Saint Joseph, Mary, and the shepherds—the apprehensive Joseph; the sorrowing Mary; and the awestruck and wondering shepherds. It was enthusiastically received by contemporary Florentine painters, particularly Domenico GHIRLANDAIO.

About 1475, van der Goes entered the monastery of the Red Cloister near Brussels and became a lay brother. In his later years he became subject to increasingly severe attacks of depression, and his work took on a compulsive intensity, which can be seen in the *Death of the Virgin* (c.1480; Musée Communal, Bruges).

Goethals, George Washington   see PANAMA CANAL

Goethe, Johann Wolfgang von [gur'-te]   Generally recognized as one of the greatest writers and thinkers of modern times, Johann Wolfgang von Goethe, b. Aug.

Johann Wolfgang von Goethe, one of the greatest figures of German culture, encompassed literature, science, music, and philosophy within his work. His writings, culminating in Faust *(1808–32), superbly synthesize knowledge, philosophy, and art.*

28, 1749, d. Mar. 22, 1832, profoundly influenced the growth of ROMANTICISM. Best known for his lyrical poetry, his influential novels, and particularly his dramatic poem FAUST (Part 1, 1808; Part 2, 1832; Eng. trans., 1838), Goethe also made substantial contributions to science. For ten years a leading political figure, he was an acute observer of the social and intellectual revolutions of the late 18th century and one of the earliest thinkers to explore the implications of the Industrial Revolution. But Goethe's major significance is as a sensitive and vulnerable individual who struggled through a wide range of human crises and left a critical record of this experience.

Life. Goethe was born in Frankfurt am Main into a well-to-do middle-class family. His six-volume autobiography, *Aus meinem Leben: Dichtung und Wahrheit* (1811–22; trans. as *Memoirs of Goethe*, 1824), however, recalls his upbringing as chaotic.

At the age of 16, Goethe began his studies at the university in Leipzig, where he wrote his earliest poems and plays. In 1770 at the university in Strasbourg he came under the influence of Johann Gottfried von HERDER. In 1771, Goethe received a licentiate in law at Strasbourg and during the next four years practiced law with his father. In 1775 he was invited to the ducal court of Karl Augustus in Saxe-Weimar, where he held (1775–86) high offices and spent most of the rest of his life. During his early years there he also wrote the mysterious lyrics to Charlotte von Stein, a married woman seven years his senior.

During two years in Italy (1786–88), Goethe resolved to devote his life to writing. Many of his friends, however, were offended by his living with young Christiane Vulpius, who bore him a son in 1789, and whom he married in 1806.

Goethe spent much of his time in nearby Jena and from 1794 to 1805 collaborated intensely with Friedrich SCHILLER, a union that many regard as a high point in German letters. Goethe died in Weimar at the age of 82.

Works and Influences. In his early twenties Goethe achieved fame in Germany with the play *Goetz of Berlichingen* (written, 1771; publ., 1773; Eng. trans., 1799), which scorned fashionable literary correctness, formalism, and cosmopolitanism. Soon after, Goethe became famous throughout Europe with a sentimental and individualistic novel in the style of Jean Jacques Rousseau, *The Sorrows of Young Werther* (1774; Eng. trans., 1779).

During his first ten years in Weimar he also collected many previously published works in the eight-volume *Goethes Schriften* (Goethe's Writing, 1787–90). The highly lyrical BILDUNGSROMAN (developmental novel) that Goethe worked on for much of his life, *Wilhelm Meister's Apprenticeship* (1795; Eng. trans., 1824), was emulated by later German romantic writers as the exemplary form.

Most celebrated during his lifetime as the author of *Faust*, Goethe was also known for the satirical *Reynard the Fox* (1794; Eng. trans., 1855) and the rather saccharine epic *Hermann and Dorothea* (1798; Eng. trans., 1801), both written in hexameters. His so-called classical dramas, *Iphigenie auf Taurus* (final version, 1787; Eng. trans., 1793) and *Torquato Tasso* (1790; Eng. trans., 1827), were much admired, as were the ballads he wrote with Schiller.

Some of his mature works began to be appreciated only in the 20th century, including the second part of *Faust*, the ironical *Elective Affinities* (1809; Eng. trans., 1872), and the passionate lyrical cycle, *West-Eastern Divan* (1819; Eng. trans., 1877). Other works, such as the sensual *Roman Elegies* (1795; Eng. trans., 1876) and *Wilhelm Meister's Travels* (1821; Eng. trans., 1824), a discursive continuation of the earlier novel, are only now receiving recognition.

Goethe himself expected to be remembered as a scientist. Biology has long recognized its debt to him for the concept of morphology, fundamental to the theory of evolution. He thought his most important work was *Zur Farbenlehre* (3 vols., 1810; trans. as *Goethe's Theory of Colors*, 1840), in which he undertook to discredit Newtonian science.

Evaluation. Today Goethe is especially noted for recognizing the dehumanizing demands of the industrial epoch and for meeting them without forfeiting his humanity. Goethe was probably greatest as a lyric poet, however, and his other works often take their strength from lyricism. In the history of GERMAN LITERATURE he is credited with setting the tone for entire movements; for introducing new forms, such as the novella; and for profoundly influencing other forms, such as the novel. As determinism ceases to characterize science, it is finding greater tolerance for a Goethean world in which all phenomena tend to merge. To Goethe, poetry and science were one.

----

goethite [guh'-tyt]   The widespread iron ore mineral goethite, an iron hydroxide, FeO(OH), is a common WEATHERING product. It usually forms stalactitic masses with concentric or radiating internal structure. Color is yellowish to dark brown, hardness 5–5½, streak yellow, cleavage perfect, and specific gravity 3.3–4.3. Goethite is often associated with and indistinguishable from LIMONITE in the gossan of SULFIDE MINERAL deposits, in tropical LATERITE, and in bog deposits.

Gog and Magog [gahg, may'-gahg]   In the prophecy recorded in Ezekiel 38–39, Gog, ruler from the land of Magog, is to be destroyed when he attacks Israel. Symbolic of the conflict between good and evil, the theme reappears in Revelation 20:8, where both are agents of Satan.

Gogh, Vincent van   see VAN GOGH, VINCENT

—

Gogol, Nikolai [goh'-gul]   The novelist and short-story writer Nikolai Gogol, b. Mar. 31 (N.S.), 1809, d. Mar. 4 (N.S.), 1852, one of the most gifted Russian writers of his time, was a seminal force in 19th-century Russian literature. Celebrated above all for its bizarre comic vision, his work anticipates qualities in modern literature grouped under the label of ABSURDISM.

The son of a petty Ukrainian aristocrat, Gogol at age 19 moved to the capital, Saint Petersburg, where he published his narrative poem *Hans Küchelgarten* (1829). Disastrous reviews caused him to buy up and burn the unsold copies and to flee Russia briefly. His first success came with the story collection *Evenings on a Farm near Dikanka* (2 vols., 1831–32), for which the folklore of Ukraine provided most of the material. He then taught (1834) medieval history at St. Petersburg University before publishing more Ukrainian stories under the title *Mirgorod* (1835).

The conflict between Gogol's idealistic strivings and his sad cynicism became apparent in the stories "The Portrait" and "Nevsky Prospect" in *Arabesques* (1835). This dark vision shaped the trivia-ridden, sometimes phantasmagoric comic world of his greatest masterpieces—the drama *The Inspector General* (1836), the novel *Dead Souls* (1842), and the stories "The Nose" (1836) and "The Overcoat" (1842).

Gogol spent many of his productive years abroad, living in Rome, with interruptions, from 1836 to 1848. There he became ever more preoccupied with religion, coming to believe he had been called by God to reveal the path of righteousness. He resolved to make *Dead Souls* the first part of a contemporary *Divine Comedy*, but despite a decade of labor he believed he had failed, in part two, to give satisfactory expression to his positive religious ideas. This he did in *Selected Passages from Correspon-*

Nikolai Gogol, Russian author of the novel Dead Souls *(1842) and the play* The Inspector General *(1836), first gained success with* Evenings on a Farm near Dikanka *(1831–32), a collection of stories set in the Ukraine.*

dence with Friends (1847), which was, however, politically and socially reactionary. This work was strongly condemned by liberals, especially the influential critic Vissarion G. Belinsky, who had previously understood Gogol narrowly as a satirist of social abuses and injustice in autocratic Russia. After this Gogol gradually sank into the religious obsessions that darkened his last years. In a fit of despair, just ten days before his death, he burned the manuscript of the second part of *Dead Souls*.

—

goiter [goy'-tur]   Goiter is an enlargement of the THYROID GLAND, which produces the hormones thyroxine and triiodothyronine. These regulate the rate of METABOLISM in the body. Iodine is an essential part of the hormones' molecular structure. Simple goiter is an enlarged thyroid that occurs in reaction to insufficient iodine in the diet and is characterized by underproduction of the two hormones. It can be reversed or prevented by dietary iodine supplements such as iodized salt.

Exophthalmic goiter, due to unknown causes, is accompanied by excessive production of thyroxine. This causes a marked increase in the metabolic rate, nervousness, muscle weakness, rapid and irregular heartbeat, and, sometimes, protrusion of the eyeballs (exophthalmos). Tumors of the thyroid can produce similar effects if they involve the hormone-producing cells. Exophthalmic goiter is often treated with antithyroid drugs, radioiodine, or surgery.

See also: ENDOCRINE SYSTEM, DISEASES OF THE.

—

gold   The chemical element gold, atomic number 79, symbol Au (from the Latin *aurum*), is a soft, lustrous yellow, malleable metal. Its atomic weight is 196.967; it belongs to Group IB of the periodic table along with copper and silver.

Occurrence

Although the Earth's crust averages a mere 0.004 gram of gold per ton, commercial concentrations of gold are found in areas distributed widely over the globe. Gold occurs in association with ores of copper and lead, in quartz veins, in the gravel of stream beds, and with pyrites (iron sulfide, FeS_2). Seawater contains astonishing quantities of gold, but so much energy is required for its recovery that the process is not economical.

The greatest early surge in gold recovery followed the first voyage of Columbus. From 1492 to 1600, Central and South America, Mexico, and the islands of the Caribbean Sea contributed significant quantities of gold to world commerce. Following the discovery (1848) of gold in California, North America became the world's major supplier of the metal (see GOLD RUSH). By 1890 the gold fields of Alaska and the Yukon edged out those in the western United States, and soon the African Transvaal exceeded even these.

Because it is unreactive, gold is found uncombined and, along with copper and silver, was one of the first known metals. It was probably used in decorative arts before 9000 BC (see GOLD AND SILVER WORK).

Physical and Chemical Properties

Elemental gold has a melting point of 1,063°C and a boiling point of 2,966°C. In addition to its softness, it is both the most malleable and most ductile of all elements. This means, respectively, that gold can be hammered into extremely thin sheets (approaching a small number of atoms), and it can be drawn into extremely fine wires. Gold in the form of very thin sheets is called gold leaf, and it has many decorative uses. Elemental gold is an excellent conductor of electricity and heat, surpassed only by the other members of Group IB, copper and silver.

Gold usually forms compounds (and complexes) by giving up either one or three of its valence electrons. It is commonly alloyed with other metals, as in jewelry, in proportions that yield desired hardnesses and colors. An alloy of gold and nickel, for example, is called "white gold." The purity of alloyed gold is expressed by the karat system, where the percent of gold by weight is given as a fraction of 24. Therefore pure gold is 24 karat, whereas 18-karat gold is 18/24, or 75%, gold by weight. Gold dissolves in very few solvents, among them aqua regia and cyanide solutions (used in extraction).

Mining

Gold is obtained by two principal mining methods—placer and vein mining—and also as a by-product of the mining of other metals. Placer mining is used when the metal is found in unconsolidated deposits of sand and gravel from which gold can be easily separated due to its high density. The sand and gravel are suspended in moving water; the much heavier metal sinks to the bottom and is separated by hand. The simplest method, called panning, is to swirl the mixture in a pan rapidly enough to carry the water and most of the gravel and sand over the edge while the gold remains on the bottom. Panning is the classic method used by the forty-niners and is immortalized in story, art, and song.

Much more efficient is a sluice box, a U-shaped trough with a gentle slope and transverse bars firmly attached to the trough bottom. Sand and gravel are placed in the high end, the gate to a water supply is opened, and the lighter material is washed through the sluice box and out the lower end. The materials caught behind the bars are gleaned to recover the gold. A similar arrangement catches the metal on wool, and this may have been the origin of the legend of Jason's search for the GOLDEN FLEECE.

Another variation of the placer method is called hydraulic mining. A very strong stream of water is directed at natural sand and gravel banks, causing them to be washed away. The suspended materials are treated much as if they were in a giant sluice box. Vein, or lode mining, is the most important of all gold-recovery methods. Although each ounce of gold recovered requires the processing of about 100,000 ounces of ore, there is so much gold deposited in rock veins that this method accounts for more than half of the world's total gold production today. Gold is also obtained in significant amounts as a by-product of copper, lead, and zinc production.

Extraction and Refining

In obtaining gold from vein ore, the ore is first crushed in rod or ball mills. This process reduces the ore to a powdery substance from which the gold can be extracted by amalgamation with mercury or by placer procedures. About 70% is recovered at this point. The remainder is dissolved in dilute solutions of sodium cyanide, NaCN, or calcium cyanide, $Ca(CN)_2$. The addition of zinc causes metallic gold to precipitate. This precipitate is refined by smelting. The purification is completed by electrolysis similar to that used for COPPER.

Uses

One of the principal uses of gold today is as a currency reserve. Gold was for centuries used directly as currency along with silver. During the 19th century it assumed a role as the sole basis of the currencies of most nations; paper MONEY was directly convertible into gold. Since the 1970s gold has been bought and sold on the market, with widely fluctuating prices, and gold reserves maintain only

(Left) Gold bricks weighing 13 kg (35 troy lb) are used as currency reserves. Gold was first used for coins by the Lydians of Anatolia during the 7th century BC. (Center) Electrolytic refining purifies gold alloy. When electrolyzed in a chlorine solution by direct and alternating currents, the anode, silver-containing gold, dissolves and deposits 99.95% pure gold on the gold cathode. (Right) A jeweler creates a gold ring. Gold's extreme malleability makes possible simpler metalworking techniques.

a very indirect relationship with the values of currencies and economic systems.

There is a large and rapidly growing demand for gold in industrial processes. Its relatively high electrical conductivity and extremely high resistance to corrosion make the metal critically important in microelectrical circuits. Minute quantities dissolved in glass or plastic sheets prevent the passage of infrared radiation and make an efficient heat shield. Because of its chemical stability, gold is in demand for bearings used in corrosive atmospheres. It is also plated on surfaces exposed to corrosive fluids or vapors. Many other industrial uses demand the properties unique to gold. Its lack of toxicity and its compatability with living systems make it indispensable in dentistry and medicine, and its beauty has made it outstanding in the arts and crafts for at least 11 millennia.

Gold Coast see GHANA

George Northrup of Minnesota displays some of the equipment wielded by California gold prospectors in this daguerreotype (c.1860). The discovery of gold in California in 1848 touched off a massive rush, the first of its kind, into the western territories.

gold rush Although gold had been mined in western Georgia in the late 1830s, the greatest gold rush in the history of the United States began with the discovery of gold at Sutter's Mill on the American River in northern California on Jan. 24, 1848. When word reached San Francisco, thousands from that city and other parts of California flocked to the region. The great rush, however, began in 1849. California's population grew from about 14,000 in 1848 to 100,000 in 1850. That number increased to 250,000 by late 1852 and to 380,000 by 1860. While the majority of immigrants were from the United States, forty-niners also came from China, Australia, many Latin American nations, and all parts of Europe to prospectors' camps like Yreka, Spanish Bar, and Grass Valley.

Over the next decade, three mining regions developed in California. The first was in the mother-lode region of the Sierra Nevada from Sutter's Mill south to Mariposa. The second was to the north in Nevada County. The third area, in the northern coastal ranges west of Shasta, was never exploited fully because of its isolation and rough terrain.

The earliest placer miners sought the eroded gold in the form of dust, flakes, and nuggets. Found in stream beds and in gravels laid down by ancient rivers, this supply of gold was exhausted quickly, and miners were forced to turn to other techniques requiring greater cooperation, sophistication, and expenditure. Eventually deep mines were dug to tap the original deposits of gold. Rock was hauled to the surface, crushed, and treated to extract the precious dust. Such work, however, required huge amounts of capital, and the individual placer miner either went to work as a wage laborer, returned home, or wandered on to gold strikes in Colorado, Nevada, Idaho, Montana, and Arizona between 1859 and 1890. Subsequent gold strikes in Australia (1851), the TRANSVAAL (1886) in South Africa, the KLONDIKE (1896), and ALASKA (1898) produced similar sequences of events.

The gold rush drew not only fortune hunters but also merchants, artisans, and farmers to the American West. This boom in turn encouraged construction of wagon roads and railroads and attracted essential outside capital. Gold production provided wealth for an expanding American economy and stimulated technological advances later used elsewhere in the United States and the world.

gold and silver work Gold and silver were among the first metals to be worked and were prized by the earliest civilizations as tokens of wealth and symbols of power. Gold, which naturally occurs in a pure state, was made into ornaments as early as 3000 BC, but silver, which is usually found compounded with other substances, was not used until techniques of smelting were discovered during the BRONZE AGE. Gold and silver were first worked by hammering, and methods of decoration, such as embossing and engraving, followed quickly. Techniques of manipulating metal, which include CASTING, enameling, and WELDING AND SOLDERING, have changed little to this day.

The earliest surviving goldwork, made about 3000 BC, is simple Egyptian jewelry, but excavations at Ur (Iraq) have yielded sophisticated work made only 500 years later, which suggests that the Sumerians were the first goldsmiths. The influence of the Sumerian civilization (see MESOPOTAMIA) spread through western Asia and toward the Mediterranean, where, on the site of TROY, the archaeologist Heinrich Schliemann discovered a large hoard of gold jewelry dating from about 2500–2300 BC. During the Egyptian Middle Kingdom (c.2133–1786 BC) metalworkers attained a very high degree of skill, working in every decorative technique, including repoussé, ajouré, chasing and engraving, granulation, wirework, enameling, and lapidary work. The tomb of TUTANKHAMEN, who reigned during the Egyptian New Kingdom (1570–1085 BC), contained a wealth of fine gold ornaments.

The splendid *lunulae* (crescent-shaped neck ornaments) of the Irish Early Bronze Age were made during the period of about 1800 to 1500 BC, and the unique sheet gold cape with repoussé decoration found in Wales (British Museum, London) has been dated to about 1400 BC. The famous Celtic gold torcs, or neck rings, date from the 4th to the 1st century BC (see CELTIC ART).

The artistry attained in the metalwork of ancient cultures is seen in the decoration of this Egyptian throne (c.1350 BC) from the tomb of Tutankhamen. (Egyptian Museum, Cairo.)

From 850 to 700 BC, superb goldwork was produced in Greece, Anatolia, and Phoenicia (see PHOENICIAN ART). During the Hellenistic Age exceedingly fine and innovative jewelry was produced, and later Etruscan and Roman work was largely a continuation of these styles.

Outstanding goldwork and silverwork in other parts of the world include Persian artifacts of the 5th and 4th centuries BC, such as the Oxus treasure (British Museum) and the treasure from Susa (Louvre, Paris). There are numerous references to goldwork and jewelry in the literature of the Indo-Aryan civilization of northern India (c.1400–c.1000 BC), but the earliest surviving Indian piece of importance is the Bimaran gold reliquary (c.100 BC–AD c.100; British Museum), a superb example of repoussé work set with rubies. Very little early goldwork and silverwork from China has been discovered, but the Han dynasty (202 BC–AD 220) produced some refined gold jewelry.

The earliest gold artifacts in America, made by the primitive techniques of cold hammering and repoussé, were probably created in the Andean region of Peru about 2000 BC. It was not until a comparatively late date (AD c.300–800), however, that the INCAS acquired the important skill of casting. According to contemporary European descriptions, the 16th-century treasure of Montezuma, last ruler of the AZTECS, was filled with the finest goldwork. Unfortunately, none remains, for all of it was plundered by the Spanish and melted down.

Roman styles were adopted by Byzantine metalworkers (see BYZANTINE ART AND ARCHITECTURE) and even influenced the work of the SASSANIAN period in Persia (6th and 7th centuries). The *Antioch Chalice* (AD c.500; Cloisters, New York City), a silver-gilt cup thought at one time to incorporate the Holy Grail, marks a transition between late Roman and early Byzantine style. The *Reliquary of the True Cross* (AD c.930; Limburg Cathedral, Germany), made in the palace workshops at Constantinople (now Istanbul), is representative of Byzantine workmanship. Its configuration of rich enamels and precious stones is typical of a style that influenced much ecclesiastical goldsmiths' work in the centuries following.

During the Middle Ages most goldwork and silverwork was made for the church, and many goldsmiths were monks. The German Benedictine monk Theophilus wrote *De Diversis Artibus* (Of Many Arts, c.1110–40; Eng. trans., 1961), an important treatise on the craft. The churches of Western Europe abound in gold and silver reliquaries, crucifixes, chalices, and other sacred vessels. One of the few surviving pieces of secular work is the gold and enamel *Royal Cup of the Kings of France and England* (1380; British Museum).

During the Middle Ages and before, the goldsmith was the most highly honored of all artists, mainly because he worked with precious materials. This attitude gradually changed during the Renaissance (see RENAISSANCE ART AND ARCHITECTURE), when the artist's skill was valued more highly than his materials. Thus arose a distinction between the artist and the artisan that has persisted to this day.

Great artist-goldsmiths continued to flourish in the courts of Europe. Outstanding among these was Benvenuto CELLINI. The Flemish Van Vianen brothers (Adam,

Representative pieces of the metalwork of the Middle Ages are the 8th-century Ardagh Chalice (National Museum of Ireland, Dublin) and a French reliquary shrine (c.1340) (below). (Metropolitan Museum of Art, New York City.)

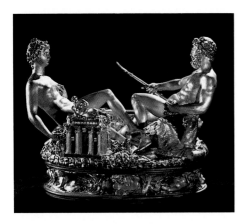

(Above) *The 16th-century saltcellar exemplifies the work of Benvenuto Cellini (Kunsthistorisches Museum, Vienna). Its ornate style contrasts with the functional designs of early-18th-century metalwork, typified by the silver teapot and stand* (right). *(Metropolitan Museum of Art, New York City.)*

(Above) *This silver and silver-gilt covered bowl (1930–40), created by the French silversmith Jean Puiforcat, reflects the elegant line and pure form that distinguish much of his work. (Metropolitan Museum of Art, New York City.)*

1565–1627, and Paul, 1568–1613) devised a curious auricular style of silversmithing, precursor of the ROCOCO STYLE. The last of the great court goldsmiths was Johann Melchior Dinglinger (1664–1731), whose patron was the extravagant Frederick Augustus I, elector of Saxony (Augustus II, King of Poland). Dinglinger's ingenious decorative fantasies are preserved in the "Green Vaults" of the palace treasury at Dresden.

Eighteenth-century goldsmithing and silversmithing became increasingly utilitarian and consisted largely of decorative articles for domestic use in palaces or middle-class households. A heavy neoclassical style with lavish classical motifs pervaded Europe in the early 19th century, when Napoleon I assumed Roman imperial grandeur.

The Industrial Revolution then began to affect metalworking techniques, and the goldsmith became an entrepreneur with a staff of designers and craftsmen. George Richards Elkington (1801–65) and Charles Christofle (1805–63) evolved methods of mass production in order to meet the growing needs of the middle class and employed the finest contemporary designers for more prestigious work.

In the later 19th century, the most important metalworker in the British ARTS AND CRAFTS MOVEMENT was the architect Charles Robert Ashbee (1863–1942), who sought to revive the skills of ancient craftsmanship. The artist-goldsmiths of today have continued this practice.

gold standard   The gold standard was an international monetary system in which the value of a currency was defined in terms of a fixed quantity of gold. Paper currency was freely convertible into gold, and both might circulate as money. The heyday of the gold standard was between 1870 and the outbreak of World War I in 1914, when the English pound dominated international trade, and prices

remained fairly stable. At the end of the war, however, the United States was the only Western country where paper money was still convertible into gold coins. European countries returned slowly to a modified gold standard, but by the mid-1930s, few central banks were required to hold stocks of gold in order to meet liabilities.

Because increases in the money supply were tied to the amount of gold held in national coffers, the gold standard enforced an inflexibility in EXCHANGE RATES, which had little reference to economic conditions. By the late 1950s, U.S. DOLLARS had almost entirely replaced gold in international transactions. While most countries continued to use gold as a reserve asset, its importance lessened until, by the 1970s, it was only one of several means of payment, which, in addition to dollars, also included such monetary mechanisms as the Special Drawing Rights, or "paper gold," issued by the INTERNATIONAL MONETARY FUND.

Goldberg, Arthur J.   Arthur Joseph Goldberg, b. Chicago, Aug. 8, 1908, d. Jan. 19, 1990, was a labor lawyer in Chicago and special counsel to the AFL-CIO when he was appointed secretary of labor by President John F. Kennedy in 1961. In 1962, Kennedy appointed him to the United States Supreme Court. He reluctantly resigned in 1965 when President Lyndon B. Johnson asked him to become U.S. ambassador to the United Nations. He resigned from that post in 1968 to return to private law practice. He was an unsuccessful New York gubernatorial candidate in 1970 and later was an ambassador-at-large in Jimmy Carter's administration.

Goldberg, Rube   The American cartoonist Reuben Lucius Goldberg, b. San Francisco, July 4, 1883, d. Dec. 7, 1970, created drawings of absurdly complex devices for performing simple tasks, designs that he attributed to the fictitious Professor Lucifer Gorgonzola Butts. The term *Rube Goldberg* is now part of the American idiom, denoting a complex or roundabout means of doing something that could be done more simply.

After receiving (1904) a degree in engineering, Goldberg began his career as a sportswriter and cartoonist. While working for the *New York Evening Mail* (1907–21), he created and began syndicating (1915) several series of cartoons including "Boob McNutt" and "Mike and Ike." He won (1948) the Pulitzer Prize for editorial cartooning while employed by the *New York Sun*. Goldberg's drawings are collected in such works as *Foolish Questions* (1909) and *Rube Goldberg vs. the Machine* (1968).

Golden Bough, The   see FRAZER, SIR JAMES

Golden Bull   A Golden Bull, from the Latin *bulla,* meaning "seal," was an important document with a gold seal attached, issued by a medieval ruler. The Golden Bull (1222) of King ANDREW II of Hungary enumerated the rights and privileges of the nobility. The Golden Bull (1356) of Emperor CHARLES IV served as a constitution for the HOLY ROMAN EMPIRE. The bull named seven electors: the archbishops of Mainz, Cologne, and Trier; the king of Bohemia; the count palatine of the Rhine; the margrave of Brandenburg; and the duke of Saxony. It defined their ceremonial functions, prescribed their judicial powers, and regulated succession in their principalities. No role was assigned to the popes, who were thus *de facto* excluded from a voice in imperial elections.

Golden Calf   In the Bible, the Golden Calf was an idol made by AARON for the Israelites while MOSES was on Mount Sinai receiving the TEN COMMANDMENTS. When Moses saw the idol, he was enraged and destroyed it (Exodus 32). Similar representations had a prominent place in other religions.

Golden Fleece   In Greek mythology the Golden Fleece was the treasure wrested from a dragon in Colchis by JASON and the Argonauts, after MEDEA had drugged the dragon. Jason and Medea then fled, carrying the fleece on Jason's ship, the Argo. Some ancient writers, for example, STRABO, believed that this fleece was covered with alluvial gold. Others held that what Jason sought was not gold, but amber. APOLLONIUS OF RHODES thought it was a ram's fleece used as a priest's costume, or the sign of Aries the Ram, or some other sacred cult object. After the Argo's return this prize was spread on the bridal couch of Jason and Medea, thus sanctifying their royal union.

Golden Gate   The Golden Gate is the strait linking San Francisco Bay with the Pacific Ocean. It is 5 km (3 mi) long, 1.6–3.2 km (1–2 mi) wide, and deep enough (90 m/300 ft) to accommodate large oceangoing vessels.

Sir Francis Drake may have landed in the area, but actual discovery of the strait is attributed to Francisco de Ortega in 1769.

Golden Gate Bridge   The Golden Gate Bridge (built 1933–37), with its span of 1,280 m (4,200 ft) at the entrance to San Francisco Bay, in the heart of the earthquake belt, is one of the world's most famous bridges (see BRIDGE, engineering). The two main cables, each 0.93 m (3 ft) in diameter, pass over the top of cellular steel towers 227 m (746 ft) high and support a six-lane roadway and two footpaths. Great difficulties were encountered in building the bridge foundations; one foundation had to be built inside a huge concrete cofferdam made on the ocean bed. The overall cost of the bridge was less than $35 million. Like many bridges, the Golden Gate attracts suicides.

Golden Horde, Khanate of the   The Khanate of the Golden Horde was the name given to the MONGOL state established in south Russia as a result of GENGHIS KHAN'S bestowal of that area on his son Juchi in 1223. Actual conquest of the area was undertaken by Juchi's son Batu Khan, who by 1240 had destroyed Kiev, the most important Russian state of that time. His conquest of Kievan Russia was the major factor in the decline of Russia from one of the most advanced to one of the most backward European nations in the succeeding centuries. The name *Golden Horde* is derived from the colorful tents of the Mongol encampments.

This group of Mongols merged with the TATARS and other Turkic peoples such as the CUMANS (or Kipchaks), adopting their language and their religion—Islam. As a result their state is also known as the Kipchak Khanate. Headquartered in the Lower Volga region, they imposed a system of strict vassalage on the Russian princes, who were forced to pay heavy tribute. Internal divisions—principally between the Blue (eastern) and White (western) hordes—weakened the khanate, enabling DIMITRY DONSKOI of Moscow to defeat the Mongols at Kulikovo in 1380, and TIMUR to conquer the state from 1389 to 1395. The Golden Horde then broke up into separate khanates of Astrakhan, Crimea, and Kazan.

Golden Notebook, The   see LESSING, DORIS

golden retriever   The golden retriever is a powerful dog with a dense, water-repellent coat that may range in color from light blond to a deep, lustrous, golden red. Males are about 61 cm (24 in) high at the shoulder and weigh up to 34 kg (75 lb); females are slightly smaller. Sir Dudley Marjoribanks played a significant role in the breed's development in the mid-19th century, when he bred a dog on his estate near Inverness, Scotland, to suit the local hunting conditions. The breed apparently derived from the yellow puppy that occasionally appeared in litters of the normally black, wavy-coated (or flat-coated) retriever. Initially the breed was called yellow retriever,

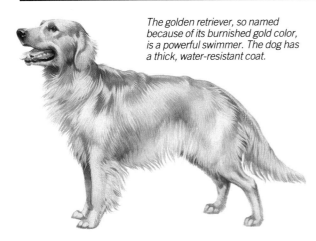

The golden retriever, so named because of its burnished gold color, is a powerful swimmer. The dog has a thick, water-resistant coat.

but in 1913 the dogs were separated as yellow, or golden, retrievers, and in 1920 the name *yellow* was dropped.

golden section A golden section is a line segment that has been divided into two parts in such a way that the ratio of the longer part (*a*) to the shorter part (*b*) is equal to the ratio of the entire segment (*a* + *b*) to the longer part (*a*). This can be indicated symbolically as $a/b = (a + b)/a = \phi$, and this ratio, ϕ, is called the *golden ratio*. The concept of a golden section is of historical importance in aesthetics, art, and architecture. It has often been thought that a form, including the human form, is most pleasing when its parts divide it in golden sections. A related concept is the *golden rectangle*, which is a rectangle that has adjacent sides with lengths in the golden ratio. The ancient Greeks felt that the golden rect-

Golden ratios are illustrated in this sequence of golden rectangles and corresponding golden sections. The three largest golden rectangles shown have sides a and b, a' and b', and a" and b", respectively.

angle had proportions that were the most aesthetically pleasing of all rectangles; the shape appears in many works from antiquity to the present. It is especially prevalent in RENAISSANCE ART AND ARCHITECTURE. A golden rectangle has the property such that if a square with sides equal to the rectangle's short side is marked off, the remaining figure will be another golden rectangle; this process can be repeated indefinitely.

goldenrain tree The goldenrain tree, *Koelreutria paniculata,* is a small deciduous tree of the family Sapindaceae. Native to China, Korea, Taiwan, and Fiji, it has been introduced into the United States and is widely planted in the Midwest. It is coarsely open-branched and flat-topped and has masses of upright, yellow, pyramidal blooms in midsummer.

goldenrod Goldenrod is a genus, *Solidago,* in the sunflower family, Compositae, of about 130 species of mostly North American hardy, perennial herbs that bloom in late summer or autumn. It is related to the aster and typically has a slender, unbranched stem with short-stalked or stalkless leaves and small, yellowish flower heads borne in complex clusters. Widespread throughout the United States, goldenrod has been erroneously blamed for the hayfever caused by ragweed (genus Ambrosia). Some species, however, are toxic because they contain high concentrations of nitrates or diterpenes or because of contamination with fungi. A yellow dye can be prepared from the flowers of some species.

Canada goldenrod, a perennial herb, is easily identified by its showy yellow flower clusters. Goldenrod is wrongly thought to be a cause of hay fever.

goldfinch Goldfinches are birds that include several species of the genus *Carduelis,* order Passeriformes, family Fringillidae, to which also belong SISKINS and greenfinches. They are sometimes placed in the genus *Spinus.* These birds are distributed throughout Europe and North America. They measure about 10–14 cm (4–5 in) and have short, notched tails. The American goldfinch, *C. tristis,* frequents bushes, trees, and fields and is

The American goldfinch, named for the male's distinctive yellow plumage, breeds from mid- to late summer, depending on the supply of thistle and other seeds.

fond of thistle and sunflower seeds. The male has breeding plumage that is bright yellow with a black cap, wings, and tail. The female, young, and male in winter have dull, olive brown plumage. In the lesser goldfinch, *C. psaltria,* of the southwestern states and Pacific coast, the male has a black or dark green back.

goldfish   The goldfish is a domesticated form of a carplike fish, *Carassius auratus,* native to East Asia. In the wild state, *C. auratus* is olive or dark brown, grows to a length of 30 cm (1 ft)—some have reportedly reached 60 cm (2 ft) in length—and weighs up to 4.5 kg (10 lb). When the reddish gold domesticated form escapes to the wild, it reverts in only a few generations to the original dull colors. In North America such reverted fish are called johnny carp or simply wild goldfish.

In North America, where they have been distributed widely, wild goldfish are found as far north as southern Canada. The domesticated variety appears to have originated about 1,000 years ago in China, where they were court pets of the Sung dynasty. They reached Japan about 1500 and Europe (Portugal) in the early 17th century. The most common color in goldfish is a brassy red or orange, but many others are known. Pink fish are often incorrectly called scaleless because the scales lack the amino acid guanine and are difficult to see. One officially recognized form, the shubunkin, does in fact lack scales; its skin color is a mixture of blue, red, white, black, and gold. Goldfish are hardy, peaceful aquarium fish that eat a variety of foods, but the fancier forms generally require warmer water, above 15° C (59° F), than the plainer forms. Hatching occurs in about 8 days in cool water, about 17° C (62° F). The newly hatched fish are nourished by their attached yolk sacs for the first 48 hours, after which they begin to feed on microscopic organisms. Goldfish have been known to live 30 or 40 years.

Golding, William   William Gerald Golding, b. Cornwall, Sept. 19, 1911, is a prominent English novelist, an essayist and a poet, and winner of the 1983 Nobel Prize for literature. Golding's often allegorical fiction makes broad use of allusions to classical literature, mythology, and Christian symbolism.

Golding's first novel, *Lord of the Flies* (1954; film, 1963), introduced one of the recurrent themes of his fiction—the conflict between humanity's innate barbarism and the civilizing influence of reason. *The Inheritors* (1955) reaches into prehistory, advancing the thesis that humankind's evolutionary ancestors, "the fire-builders,"

The goldfish has been bred in a variety of shapes and colors, all of which are considered variants of the original species, Carassius auratus. *The celestial goldfish is so named because its bulging, globular eyes are turned upward. The veiltail has a short, heavy body and a long, sheer, double tail. The lionhead has rounded, blisterlike growths on its head that form a "mane." The telescope black moor, a black goldfish, has large globular eyes that point forward.*

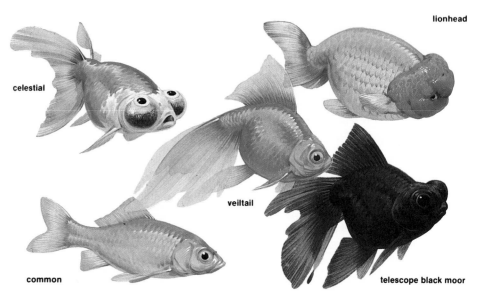

celestial

lionhead

veiltail

common

telescope black moor

William Golding, one of the most original post-World War II British writers, is best known for his allegorical novel Lord of the Flies *(1954), a bleak examination of human nature.*

triumphed over a gentler race as much by violence and deceit as by natural superiority. In *Pincher Martin* (1956) and *Free Fall* (1959), Golding explores fundamental problems of existence, such as survival and human freedom, using dreamlike narratives and flashbacks. *The Spire* (1964) is an allegory concerning the hero's obsessive determination to build a great cathedral spire regardless of the consequences. His later works include *The Scorpion God* (1971), a collection of three short novels; and two major novels, *Darkness Visible* (1979) and *A Moving Target* (1982). In addition to his novels, Golding has published a play, *The Brass Butterfly* (1958); a book of early verse, *Poems* (1934); and a collection of essays, *The Hot Gates and Other Occasional Pieces* (1966).

Goldman, Emma   Emma Goldman, b. Russia, June 27 (N.S.), 1869, d. May 14, 1940, was an American anarchist. During the HOMESTEAD STRIKE (1892), she and her companion anarchist Alexander Berkman (d. 1936) planned to start an uprising by assassinating the industrialist Henry Clay FRICK. Their plan failed and consequently

The American anarchist Emma Goldman infused her spirited lectures, publications, and demonstrations with a passionate belief in the freedom of the individual. Deported to the USSR in 1919, she continued her radical advocacy in Europe.

Goldman repudiated such acts. She rejected all institutions of force and exploitation: private property, wage slavery, religion, marriage, the state, and militarism. She envisioned a communist society of free individuals linked through federated association, contributing according to ability, and taking according to need.

Goldman was imprisoned for hindering conscription in 1917 and deported (1919) to the USSR. Disillusioned by Bolshevik repression, she left the Soviet Union in 1921 and became (1925) a British subject through a sham marriage. Her last crusade was to aid the Spanish anarchists during the Spanish Civil War (1936–39).

Goldmark, Peter Carl   The Hungarian-born American inventor Peter Carl Goldmark, b. Dec. 2, 1906, d. Dec. 7, 1977, invented the long-playing PHONOGRAPH record (LP) and developed systems for broadcasting color television and for viewing recorded film cassettes on television screens by using electronic video technology. After studying in Berlin and Vienna, Goldmark moved to England in 1931 and to the United States in 1933. He worked for the Columbia Broadcasting System from 1936 to 1971; after 1944 he was in charge of engineering research and development at CBS Laboratories. In 1940, Goldmark began work on color television broadcasting. He developed a rotating-disk method that was almost approved by the federal government in 1950. In 1948 he introduced the long-playing phonograph record, which revolutionized the recording industry. Goldmark's last major technological achievement was the development of an electronic video recording system that played video cartridges through a standard television receiver.

Goldoni, Carlo   [gohl-doh'-nee]   Carlo Goldoni, b. Venice, Feb. 25, 1707, d. Feb. 6, 1793, was an Italian dramatist whose plays completely reformed Italian comedy. After an unsuccessful first play, *Amalasunta* (1732), a tragedy, he turned to comedy. In 1734 he joined the Imer company of players at the San Samuele theater in Venice, for which he wrote the tragicomedy *Belisario* that year, as well as scenarios for the COMMEDIA DELL'ARTE.

Goldoni sought to reform traditional Italian comedy, in which masked figures presented stock characters in improvised farces. He believed comedy should reflect nature and, following Molière, depicted the foibles of the middle and lower-middle classes. He introduced this new style in his first successful play, *La Putta honorata* (The Respectable Girl, 1749). Other famous plays include *La Bottega del Caffè* (*The Coffee Shop*, 1750) and *The Mistress of the Inn* (1753; Eng. trans., 1958).

Goldsmith, Oliver   Oliver Goldsmith, b. Kilkenny West, Ireland, Nov. 10, 1730?, d. Apr. 4, 1774, was an Anglo-Irish author of prose, drama, and poetry, who achieved success with "The Traveller" (1764), a poem praising English freedom but attacking the social evils that concentrated wealth in the hands of a few. His greatest poetic triumph, "The Deserted Village" (1770), laments the passing of a simple rural life in the face of agricultural consolidation by the great landowners.

When Goldsmith arrived (1756) in London he became a versatile but improvident professional writer, constantly on the edge of poverty. His *Citizen of the World* (1762) is a collection of mildly satiric essays on English life as viewed by an imaginary Chinese visitor. He also wrote two successful plays, *The Good-Natured Man* (1768) and *She Stoops to Conquer* (1773), a witty attack on the sentimental drama of the day. *The Vicar of Wakefield* (1766), Goldsmith's only novel, is a mixture of humor, satire, and the melodrama and sentimentality that he deplored on the stage.

The American film producer Samuel Goldwyn, a founder of Goldwyn Pictures Corporation, later Metro-Goldwyn-Mayer, dominated the Hollywood film industry for more than 30 years.

Goldwater, Barry M.

U.S. Senator Barry Morris Goldwater, b. Phoenix, Ariz., Jan. 1, 1909, was the unsuccessful Republican presidential candidate in 1964. Goldwater was elected to the Senate from Arizona in 1952. A staunch conservative, he became a spokesman for right-wing Republicans in their campaign against big government, advocating instead greater state and local powers. He vigorously opposed federal welfare appropriations as socialistic and sought to curb public ownership of utilities. A strong anticommunist, Goldwater supported American military intervention in Vietnam and criticized efforts to achieve détente with the USSR. He was decisively defeated by Lyndon Johnson in the 1964 presidential election. Goldwater was reelected to the Senate in 1968, 1974, and 1980.

Barry Goldwater, a prominent U.S. senator from Arizona (1953–65, 1969–87), became a leader of the Republican party through his articulation of a conservative political philosophy. Running against Lyndon Johnson in the 1964 presidential election, Goldwater suffered one of the most decisive defeats in American history.

Goldwyn, Samuel

[gohld'-win]   Samuel Goldwyn, b. Warsaw, Aug. 27, 1882, d. Jan. 31, 1974, was considered Hollywood's greatest independent producer. A colorful figure known for his mangled but expressive syntax, Goldwyn translated his high technical and moral standards into the production of films that were admired.

An immigrant whose original name was Goldfisch, he joined his brother-in-law, Jesse Lasky, and Cecil B. De

Mille in founding (1913) the Lasky Feature Play Company. Their initial venture, *The Squaw Man* (1914), was one of the first feature-length films made in the United States. In 1916 he joined with Edgar and Arch Selwyn to establish Goldwyn Pictures Corporation; the corporate name, an amalgamation of Goldfisch and Selwyn, two years later became his own. In 1922 the Goldwyn company was merged into the Metro-Goldwyn-Mayer Corporation. Samuel Goldwyn sold his entire interest in 1924. Thereafter, as an independent producer, Goldwyn personally financed and supervised his films (made in his own studios with stars and other players contracted to him). The results included *Wuthering Heights* (1939), *The Little Foxes* (1941), and *The Best Years of Our Lives* (1946). Goldwyn retired in 1960 after his last film production, *Porgy and Bess* (1959).

golem

[goh'-luhm]   The Hebrew word *golem* means "unformed mass." It appears once in the Bible (Psalm 139:16) to refer to a human as an incomplete substance. The golem of medieval legend was a clay robot activated by magical words. In the famous tale of Rabbi Loew of Prague, the golem was a servant made of clay and brought to life by placing a piece of paper inscribed with the name of God under its tongue. Fearing that the creature, which had run amok, would desecrate the Sabbath, the rabbi destroyed it.

golf

Golf, a game of Scottish origin, is one of the most popular recreational and competitive sports in the world. Each participant uses a variety of clubs to drive a small ball into a succession of either 9 or 18 designated holes, over a course designed to present obstacles, in as few strokes as possible. In the United States alone more than 18 million people play golf, including 8,200 professional players. Golf tournaments in the United States and elsewhere are popular with spectators as well as with players and since the 1960s have received wide television coverage.

History. Roman emperors apparently played a relaxing game called *paganica*, using a bent stick to drive a soft, feather-stuffed ball. Over the next five centuries the game developed on several continents and eventually evolved into the popular Scottish game known as *golfe*. Various European countries had games somewhat similar to *paganica*—England's *cambuca*; France's *jeu de mail*; and the Netherlands' *het kolven*, which was played in the American colonies as early as 1657. The Scottish game, however, is the direct ancestor of the modern game. The first formal golf club, the Company of Gentlemen Golfers, now the Honourable Company of Edinburgh Golfers, was established in Edinburgh in 1744. The Honourable Company also codified the first set of rules, 13 in number, which helped eliminate local variations in play. The Royal and Ancient Golf Club, established 10 years later at Saint Andrews, Scotland, became the official ruling organization of the sport. The Royal and Ancient's rules committee, along with the United States Golf Association, still governs the sport.

Golf in the United States. The first golf club and course in the United States was the Saint Andrews Golf Club of Yonkers, established in Yonkers, N.Y., in 1888. The first national tournament in the United States was held in 1895. Through a succession of outstanding players, including Walter HAGEN, Bobby JONES, Ben HOGAN, Sam SNEAD, Arnold PALMER, and Jack NICKLAUS, the Americans assumed a dominant role in the sport. Before this long list of American champions began, however, an Englishman, Harry VARDON, helped popularize the sport in the United States. Vardon was a six-time British champion between 1896 and 1914. He made two extended tours of the United States in 1900 and 1913, winning the U.S. Open on his first tour and losing to a young American, Francis Ouimet, on his second. Americans marveled at his style and ability and began to copy him. Jones was one of those he influenced. Jones and Hagen became standouts that Americans could emulate in the era following Vardon's visit. For many years, however, golf was a sport played almost exclusively by the rich, even though many of the tournament golfers came from humble backgrounds. Not until the 1960s, when Arnold Palmer captured the imagination of the public, did golf become a game for all. Palmer's ascendancy paralleled the increased broadcasting coverage of sports on television. At the same time, the number of municipal golf courses was on the rise. By the end of the 1970s there were 12,500 golf courses, public and private, in the United States, which had become the largest training ground in the world for outstanding golfers. This fact was reflected in the professional standings, where young Americans, attracted by the popularity and large purses of major tournaments, each year dominated lists of the top 20 players. Among the major men's tournaments are the British Open, the U.S. Open, the Masters, and the Professional Golfers Association (PGA) tournaments. Women golfers have their own tour, sponsored by the Ladies Professional Golf Association, the governing body for about 450 women professionals. Their two major tournaments are the LPGA and the U.S. Women's Open. One or both of these

championships have been won by such outstanding golfers as Babe Didrikson ZAHARIAS, Mickey WRIGHT, Kathy WHITWORTH, and Nancy LOPEZ. Although professional golf has thoroughly overshadowed amateur competition since the retirement (1930) of Jones, the annual U.S. Amateur championships continue to be played, and intercollegiate play is widespread and governed by the National Collegiate Athletic Association (NCAA), which sponsors yearly national championship tournaments with both team and individual competition for both men and women.

International Play. Golf is played, to some extent, in most countries of the world. In Japan, for instance, golf is sometimes regarded as the national pastime. The World Cup (professional) and the World Amateur Team Champi-

(Left) *A golfer's equipment includes spiked shoes, a glove, and a golf bag* (1), *which may contain up to 14 clubs; woods* (2); *wedges and irons* (3); *a putter* (4); *tees* (5); *and golf balls* (6). *Woods are used to hit the ball great distances, and irons are used for accuracy and height. A putter is used to tap the ball into the hole.* (Center) *The golfer prepares to hit the ball.*

(Below) *To play a par-4 hole, the golfer assumes the correct grip* (1) *and drives from the tee* (2). *At 131 yd (120 m) from the hole, the golfer makes an approach shot* (3) *and lands in a sand trap, where he or she "explodes" the ball onto the green* (4) *then putts it into the hole* (5).

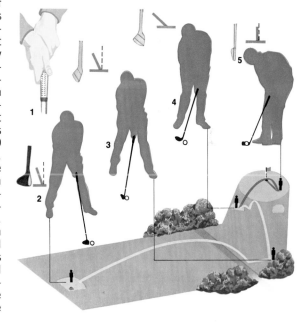

MASTERS CHAMPIONS

1934	Horton Smith	1948	Claude Harmon	1960	Arnold Palmer	1973	Tommy Aaron	1985	Bernhard Langer (Ger.)
1935	Gene Sarazen	1949	Sam Snead	1961	Gary Player (S.Afr.)	1974	Gary Player (S.Afr.)	1986	Jack Nicklaus
1936	Horton Smith	1950	Jimmy Demaret	1962	Arnold Palmer	1975	Jack Nicklaus	1987	Larry Mize
1937	Byron Nelson	1951	Ben Hogan	1963	Jack Nicklaus	1976	Ray Floyd	1988	Sandy Lyle (U.K.)
1938	Henry Picard	1952	Sam Snead	1964	Arnold Palmer	1977	Tom Watson	1989–90	Nick Faldo (U.K.)
1939	Ralph Guldahl	1953	Ben Hogan	1965–66	Jack Nicklaus	1978	Gary Player (S.Afr.)	1991	Ian Woosnam (U.K.)
1940	Jimmy Demaret	1954	Sam Snead	1967	Gay Brewer	1979	Fuzzy Zoeller	1992	Fred Couples
1941	Craig Wood	1955	Cary Middlecoff	1968	Bob Goalby	1980	Seve Ballesteros (Sp.)		
1942	Byron Nelson	1956	Jack Burke	1969	George Archer	1981	Tom Watson		
1943–45	No tournaments	1957	Doug Ford	1970	Billy Casper	1982	Craig Stadler		
1946	Herman Keiser	1958	Arnold Palmer	1971	Charles Coody	1983	Seve Ballesteros (Sp.)		
1947	Jimmy Demaret	1959	Art Wall, Jr.	1972	Jack Nicklaus	1984	Ben Crenshaw		

U.S. OPEN CHAMPIONS

1895	Horace Rawlins	1916	Charles Evans, Jr.	1936	Tony Manero	1959	Billy Casper	1977	Hubert Green
1896	James Foulis	1917–18	No tournaments	1937–38	Ralph Guldahl	1960	Arnold Palmer	1978	Andy North
1897	Joseph Lloyd	1919	Walter Hagen	1939	Byron Nelson	1961	Gene Littler	1979	Hale Irwin
1898	Fred Herd	1920	Edward Ray (U.K.)	1940	W. Lawson Little	1962	Jack Nicklaus	1980	Jack Nicklaus
1899	Willie Smith	1921	James M. Barnes	1941	Craig Wood	1963	Julius Boros	1981	David Graham (Aus.)
1900	Harry Vardon (U.K.)	1922	Gene Sarazen	1942–45	No tournaments	1964	Ken Venturi	1982	Tom Watson
1901	Willie Anderson	1923	Bobby Jones	1946	Lloyd Mangrum	1965	Gary Player (S.Afr.)	1983	Larry Nelson
1902	L. Auchterlonie	1924	Cyril Walker	1947	Lew Worsham	1966	Billy Casper	1984	Fuzzy Zoeller
1903–05	Willie Anderson	1925	William MacFarlane	1948	Ben Hogan	1967	Jack Nicklaus	1985	Andy North
1906	Alex Smith	1926	Bobby Jones	1949	Cary Middlecoff	1968	Lee Trevino	1986	Ray Floyd
1907	Alex Ross	1927	Tommy Armour	1950–51	Ben Hogan	1969	Orville Moody	1987	Scott Simpson
1908	Fred McLeod	1928	Johnny Farrell	1952	Julius Boros	1970	Tony Jacklin (U.K.)	1988–89	Curtis Strange
1909	George Sargent	1929–30	Bobby Jones	1953	Ben Hogan	1971	Lee Trevino	1990	Hale Irwin
1910	Alex Smith	1931	Billy Burke	1954	Ed Furgol	1972	Jack Nicklaus	1991	Payne Stewart
1911–12	John McDermott	1932	Gene Sarazen	1955	Jack Fleck	1973	Johnny Miller	1992	Tom Kite
1913	Francis Ouimet	1933	Johnny Goodman	1956	Cary Middlecoff	1974	Hale Irwin		
1914	Walter Hagen	1934	Olin Dutra	1957	Dick Mayer	1975	Lou Graham		
1915	Jerome D. Travers	1935	Sam Parks, Jr.	1958	Tommy Bolt	1976	Jerry Pate		

BRITISH OPEN CHAMPIONS

1860	Willie Park	1889	Willie Park, Jr.	1914	Harry Vardon	1947	Fred Daly (Irel.)	1974	Gary Player (S.Afr.)
1861–62	Tom Morris	1890	John Ball	1915–19	No tournaments	1948	T. Henry Cotton	1975	Tom Watson (U.S.)
1863	Willie Park	1891	Hugh Kirkaldy	1920	George Duncan	1949–50	Bobby Locke (S.Afr.)	1976	Johnny Miller (U.S.)
1864	Tom Morris	1892	Harold H. Hilton	1921	Jack Hutchison (U.S.)	1951	Max Faulkner	1977	Tom Watson (U.S.)
1865	A. L. Strath	1893	Willie Auchterlonie	1922	Walter Hagen (U.S.)	1952	Bobby Locke (S.Afr.)	1978	Jack Nicklaus (U.S.)
1866	Willie Park	1894–95	J. H. Taylor	1923	Arthur G. Havers	1953	Ben Hogan (U.S.)	1979	Seve Ballesteros (Sp.)
1867	Tom Morris	1896	Harry Vardon	1924	Walter Hagen (U.S.)	1954–56	Peter Thomson (Aus.)	1980	Tom Watson (U.S.)
1868–70	Tom Morris, Jr.	1897	Harold H. Hilton	1925	James Barnes (U.S.)	1957	Bobby Locke (S.Afr.)	1981	Bill Rogers (U.S.)
1871	No tournament	1898–99	Harry Vardon	1926–27	Bobby Jones (U.S.)	1958	Peter Thomson (Aus.)	1982–83	Tom Watson (U.S.)
1872	Tom Morris, Jr.	1900	J. H. Taylor	1928–29	Walter Hagen (U.S.)	1959	Gary Player (S. Afr.)	1984	Seve Ballesteros (Sp.)
1873	Tom Kidd	1901	James Braid	1930	Bobby Jones (U.S.)	1960	Kel Nagle (Aus.)	1985	Sandy Lyle
1874	Mungo Park	1902	Alex Herd	1931	Tommy Armour (U.S.)	1961–62	Arnold Palmer (U.S.)	1986	Greg Norman (Aus.)
1875	Willie Park	1903	Harry Vardon	1932	Gene Sarazen (U.S.)	1963	Bob Charles (N.Z.)	1987	Nick Faldo
1876	Bob Martin	1904	Jack White	1933	Denny Shute (U.S.)	1964	Tony Lema (U.S.)	1988	Seve Ballesteros (Sp.)
1877–79	J. Anderson	1905–06	James Braid	1934	T. Henry Cotton	1965	Peter Thomson (Aus.)	1989	Mark Calcavecchia (U.S.)
1880–82	Bob Ferguson	1907	Arnaud Massy (Fr.)	1935	Alfred Perry	1966	Jack Nicklaus (U.S.)	1990	Nick Faldo
1883	Willie L. Fernie	1908	James Braid	1936	Alfred H. Padgham	1967	Roberto de Vicenzo (Arg.)	1991	Ian Baker-Finch (Aus.)
1884	Jack Simpson	1909	J. H. Taylor	1937	T. Henry Cotton	1968	Gary Player (S.Afr.)	1992	Nick Faldo
1885	Bob Martin	1910	James Braid	1938	R. A. Whitcombe	1969	Tony Jacklin		
1886	D. L. Brown	1911	Harry Vardon	1939	Richard Burton	1970	Jack Nicklaus (U.S.)		
1887	Willie Park, Jr.	1912	Edward Ray	1940–45	No tournaments	1971–72	Lee Trevino (U.S.)		
1888	Jack Burns	1913	J. H. Taylor	1946	Sam Snead (U.S.)	1973	Tom Weiskopf (U.S.)		

onship are the most significant international tournaments. The former held annually since 1953, awards both a team and an individual prize. The latter, held biennially since 1958, is strictly a team competition and has been dominated by the United States. The Ryder Cup is a biennial men's professional competition between a U.S. team and one representing England, Scotland, and Ireland. The Ryder Cup, begun in 1927, has been won only three times by the Europeans. The Walker Cup and Curtis Cup are amateur competitions for men and women respectively, between teams from the United States and the British Isles (England, Scotland, and Ireland). The former began in 1922 and since 1947 has taken place in odd-numbered years. Curtis Cup competition began in 1932 and is held in even-numbered years. The U.S. teams have won the majority of both these matches.

PROFESSIONAL GOLFERS ASSOCIATION CHAMPIONS

1916	James M. Barnes	1938	Paul Runyan	1953	Walter Burkemo	1968	Julius Boros	1983	Hal Sutton
1917–18	No tournaments	1939	Henry Picard	1954	Chick Harbert	1969	Ray Floyd	1984	Lee Trevino
1919	James M. Barnes	1940	Byron Nelson	1955	Doug Ford	1970	Dave Stockton	1985	Hubert Green
1920	Jack Hutchison	1941	Vic Ghezzi	1956	Jack Burke	1971	Jack Nicklaus	1986	Bob Tway
1921	Walter Hagen	1942	Sam Snead	1957	Lionel Hebert	1972	Gary Player (S.Afr.)	1987	Larry Nelson
1922–23	Gene Sarazen	1943	No tournament	1958	Dow Finsterwald	1973	Jack Nicklaus	1988	Jeff Sluman
1924–27	Walter Hagen	1944	Bob Hamilton	1959	Bob Rosburg	1974	Lee Trevino	1989	Payne Stewart
1928–29	Leo Diegel	1945	Byron Nelson	1960	Jay Hebert	1975	Jack Nicklaus	1990	Wayne Grady
1930	Tommy Armour	1946	Ben Hogan	1961	Jerry Barber	1976	Dave Stockton	1991	John Daly
1931	Tom Creavy	1947	Jim Ferrier	1962	Gary Player (S.Afr.)	1977	Lanny Wadkins	1992	Nick Price (Zimb.)
1932	Olin Dutra	1948	Ben Hogan	1963	Jack Nicklaus	1978	John Mahaffe		
1933	Gene Sarazen	1949	Sam Snead	1964	Bobby Nichols	1979	David Graham		
1934	Paul Runyan	1950	Chandler Harper	1965	Dave Marr	1980	Jack Nicklaus		
1935	Johnny Revolta	1951	Sam Snead	1966	Al Geiberger	1981	Larry Nelson		
1936-37	Denny Shute	1952	Jim Turnesa	1967	Don January	1982	Ray Floyd		

Rules. The basic golf rules are internationally uniform for both men and women. A player is permitted to carry a selection of up to 14 clubs of varying shapes, sizes, and lengths. The U.S. golf ball is a minimum of 1.68 in. (4.26 cm) in diameter; the British ball is slightly smaller. The game changed considerably in the early 20th century when the B. F. Goodrich Company of Akron, Ohio, invented a lighter, tightly wound, rubber-threaded ball, which replaced the gutta-percha ball used in the 19th century.

A golf course generally has 18 holes spread over a landscaped area that customarily includes a number of hazards—water, rough, sand traps (also known as bunkers), trees—that are designed to make the game more difficult. Difficulty is also increased by the varying distances among holes. Play on each hole is begun at the tee area, from which players "tee off," or "drive" the ball into the fairway. At the end of the hole—which can vary in length from about 150 to 600 yd (135 to 550 m)—is the putting green, which surrounds the actual hole, or "cup," into which the ball must be putted in order to complete the hole. Saint Andrews in Scotland, Augusta National in Georgia (site of the annual Masters tournament), and Pebble Beach in California have some of the most famous and difficult courses.

Golf is usually played by groups of two to four people who move throughout the course together, each partici-

U.S. WOMEN'S OPEN CHAMPIONS

1946	Patty Berg	1956	Kathy Cornelius	1967	Catherine LaCoste (Fr.)	1980	Amy Alcott	1989–90	Betsy King
1947	Betty Jameson	1957	Betsy Rawls	1968	Susie Berning	1981	Pat Bradley	1991	Meg Mallon
1948	Babe Zaharias	1958–59	Mickey Wright	1969–70	Donna Caponi	1982	Janet Anderson	1992	Patty Sheehan
1949	Louise Suggs	1960	Betsy Rawls	1971	JoAnne Carner	1983	Jan Stephenson		
1950	Babe Zaharias	1961	Mickey Wright	1972–73	Susie Berning	1984	Hollis Stacy		
1951	Betsy Rawls	1962	Murle Breer	1974	Sandra Haynie	1985	Kathy Baker		
1952	Louise Suggs	1963	Mary Mills	1975	Sandra Palmer	1986	Jane Geddes		
1953	Betsy Rawls	1964	Mickey Wright	1976	JoAnne Carner	1987	Laura Davies (U.K.)		
1954	Babe Zaharias	1965	Carol Mann	1977–78	Hollis Stacy	1988	Liselotte Neumann		
1955	Fay Crocker	1966	Sandra Spuzich	1979	Jerilyn Britz		(Swed.)		

The world-famous Pebble Beach golf course in California regularly hosts professional tournaments. Three Grand Slam events are played annually in the United States. Whereas the sites of the PGA tournament and the U.S. Open vary from year to year, the Masters is always held at Augusta National golf course in Georgia.

Jack Nicklaus watches as his putt rolls toward the cup during a professional tournament. Nicklaus was the dominant figure on the men's tour from the mid-1960s into the 1980s.

pant taking a turn to play his or her ball. The ball must be played as it lies, except in unusual circumstances when the rules allow for the ball to be moved to a slightly better position. In stroke competition the total number of strokes used to move the ball from the tee to the hole is recorded as the player's score for that individual hole. The player who uses the fewest strokes to complete the course is the winner. In match play scores are compared after every hole, and a player wins, loses, or halves (ties) each hole.

As the game has developed, the courses have become more difficult to play, and the most successful players are those who are able to drive the ball more than 200 yd from the tee, approaching most holes with less than three shots. Each course has established an average number of shots (par) necessary to reach a hole (usually depending on length), and thus an average number of shots needed to complete the course. Most championship-caliber professionals score in the mid-60s to low 70s, depending on the tournament and course. Golfers use a peculiar and distinct language to describe their scoring—a birdie is a score on any one hole that is one stroke less than par; an eagle, two less than par; and a bogey, one more than par. A hole in one, the rarest of golfing events, is scored when a player drives the ball into the hole with only one stroke.

Golgi apparatus   see CELL

___

Goliath [guh-ly'-uhth]   In the Bible, Goliath was a Philistine warrior of great stature. When he challenged the Israelites to single combat, the youthful DAVID (later king) responded and vanquished him with a single stone from his sling (1 Sam. 17).

___

goliath frog   The shy and elusive goliath frog, *Conraua goliath,* family Ranidae, is the largest known frog. It reaches a body length of 30.5 cm (12 in) and overall length from nose to toe of about 91 cm (3 ft); specimens in excess of 3.2 kg (7 lb) have been collected. Goliath frogs inhabit cascading mountain streams in a restricted range in west central Africa (Mbini and Cameroon). They are prized as food by the Bayele, a tribe of pygmies, who also value the frog's thigh bones for their presumed power to bring good luck. The goliath frog is now protected by law.

The goliath frog is a giant frog measuring about 30.5 cm (12 in) in length. It is found only in the mountains of a small area in west central Africa.

___

Gombrowicz, Witold [gahm-broh'-vich, vee'-tohld]   The most distinguished Polish writer of the 20th century, Witold Gombrowicz, b. Aug. 4, 1904, d. July 25, 1969, revealed his iconoclasm in his first volume of short stories, *Pamiętnik z okresu dojrzewania* (Memoirs of Immaturity, 1933), when he wrote: "Wherever I see some mystique, be it virtue or family, faith or fatherland, there I must commit some indecent act." For Gombrowicz true humanity was achieved by breaking with the categories imposed by society, a feat he accomplished most dramatically in the brilliant comic novel *Ferdydurke* (1938; Eng. trans., 1961). A resident of Argentina from 1939 to 1963, Gombrowicz moved to France in 1964. His plays, especially *Yvonne, Princess of Burgundy* (1938; Eng. trans., 1969); his novels *Transatlantyk* (1953), *Pornography* (1960; Eng. trans., 1966), and *Cosmos* (1965; Eng. trans., 1967); and his essay-diaries for 1953–61 gradually won him recognition.

___

Gómez, Juan Vicente [goh'-mes, hwahn vee-sayn'-tay]   Juan Vicente Gómez, b. *c.*1857, d. Dec. 17, 1935, was dictator of Venezuela from 1908 to 1935. He joined Cipriano CASTRO's army of revolution in 1899 and, after Castro won control of Venezuela, was appointed vice-president in 1902. In 1908, while Castro was in Europe, Gómez seized control.

An uneducated but cunning man, Gómez controlled Venezuela's military forces. He served as the elected president in 1910–14, 1922–29, and 1931–35, and while out of office, he ruled through puppet presidents.

His administration suppressed all dissent, but the enforced stability helped Venezuela pay off its debts and encouraged foreign companies to develop a flourishing petroleum industry in the country. Gómez also instituted public works projects and at the same time amassed land and businesses for himself and his family.

Gompers, Samuel [gahm'-purz]   Samuel Gompers, b. London, Jan. 27, 1850, d. Dec. 13, 1924, was a U.S. labor leader who founded the American Federation of Labor (AFL). At the age of 14 he became a cigarmaker in New York City and joined the Cigarmakers' Union. He rose to become the first president of the American Federation of Labor in 1886—remaining in that position, except for the year 1895, until his death—and served as an advisor to the Council of National Defense during World War I. Gompers championed "business unionism," advising union leaders to build their unions and bargain with employers for economic gains. For Gompers the aims of labor were better wages, hours, and working conditions, not political reform. He was viewed as essentially conservative: opposed to industrial unions, government regulation, and the widening of the labor movement to include blacks, women, and unskilled workers. Although the powers of his position were limited, Gompers built the AFL into the largest labor organization in the country.
  See also: AMERICAN FEDERATION OF LABOR AND CONGRESS OF INDUSTRIAL ORGANIZATIONS.

The American labor leader Samuel Gompers organized (1886) the American Federation of Labor and served almost continuously as its president and chief spokesman until his death in 1924.

Gomułka, **Władysław** [guh-mul'-kuh, vlah-dis'-lahf] Władysław Gomułka, b. Feb. 6, 1905, d. Sept. 1, 1982, was a Polish Communist leader. He was born into a working-class family and trained as a mechanic. He became a Communist activist in 1926 and was imprisoned in 1932–34, and again in 1936–39.
  Gomułka's rise in Polish Communist ranks began during World War II. In December 1945 he became first secretary of the party, vice-premier, and minister of regained

territories—the Oder-Neisse lands acquired from Germany. He lost these positions in 1948 during a purge. After a period of imprisonment, Gomułka returned to power in October 1956, a time of political unrest. He was able to win popular support and Soviet approval of a somewhat more liberal "Polish road to socialism." Later, Gomułka's regime became increasingly repressive, anti-Semitic, and mired in economic problems. A drastic increase in food prices in December 1970 precipitated rioting by workers that led to Gomułka's resignation.

gonadotropin   see HORMONE, ANIMAL

Gonçalves, Nuno [gun-sahl'-vuhs, nun'-yoh]   Nuno Gonçalves, the greatest Portuguese painter of the 15th century, was active in Lisbon from about 1450 until his death, sometime before 1492. He was court painter to Alfonso V and is best known for his large altarpiece painted on six wood panels for São Vicente de Fora, Lisbon (National Museum, Lisbon). Represented on the panels are Saint Vincent, contemporary political and religious leaders, and other unidentified figures. Gonçalves's style is rooted in Flemish art and derives inspiration from Jan van EYCK and Dirk BOUTS, especially in the stark realism of facial detail in the panels.

Gonçalves Dias, Antônio   Antônio Gonçalves Dias, b. Aug. 10, 1823, d. Nov. 3, 1864, is regarded as Brazil's national poet, and his *Song of Exile* (1843), with its evocative first line, "My land has palm trees," is that country's best-known poem. Educated in Portugal, he wrote of love and his country in *Primeiros Cantos* (First Songs, 1846), *Segundos Cantos* (Second Songs, 1848), and *Ultimos Cantos* (Last Songs, 1851). The unfinished Indian epic *Os Tambiras* (1857) and a dictionary of the Tupi language (1858) reflect his interest in ethnology. He also surveyed the school system in North Brazil and participated in a scientific expedition to the Upper Amazon Valley. He was returning to Brazil from Europe when he died in a shipwreck.

Goncharov, Ivan Aleksandrovich [guhn-chuh-rawf']   Ivan Aleksandrovich Goncharov, b. June 18 (N.S.), 1812, d. Sept. 27 (N.S.), 1891, was a Russian novelist best known for his novel *Oblomov* (1859; Eng. trans., 1915). Oblómov has a keen mind and a worthy soul, but his incurable inertia causes him to while away his life. The term *Oblomovism* has since been used to describe mental apathy. Goncharov also wrote two other novels, *A Common Story* (1847; Eng. trans., 1917) and *The Precipice* (1869; Eng. trans., 1915), as well as poetry, short stories, critical essays, and memoirs.

Goncourt, Edmond de and Jules de [gohn-koor']   Frenchmen Edmond de Goncourt, b. May 26, 1822, d. July 16, 1896, and Jules de Goncourt, b. Dec.

17, 1830, d. June 20, 1870, were brothers who collaborated on writing social history and art criticism, a number of documentary novels, and from 1851 the *Journal des Goncourts* (9 vols., 1887–95; Eng. trans., 1937), still a valuable source for social and literary history. Their historical studies include *Histoire de la société française pendant la Révolution* (History of French Society during the Revolution, 1854), *Histoire de la société française pendant le Directoire* (History of French Society during the Directory, 1855), and *The Woman of the Eighteenth Century* (1862; Eng. trans., 1927). Studies of Watteau, Boucher, Fragonard, Greuze, Chardin, and others were collected in *French Eighteenth-Century Painters* (1859–75; Eng. trans., 1948). Later Edmond contributed to Western understanding of Japanese art with *Outamaro* (1891) and *Hokousaï* (1896). The Goncourts' novels include *Germinie Lacerteux* (1864; Eng. trans., 1955), a study of moral collapse, and *Madame Gervaisais* (1869), on religious mania, as well as Edmond's *La Fille Elisa* (1877; Eng. trans., 1959) on prostitution and *Les Frères Zemganno* (1879) on circus life.

gondola [gahn'-duh-luh] A gondola is a small, highly maneuverable boat used on the canals of Venice. Originally a much larger boat holding 12 oarsmen, by the 16th century the gondola had assumed the shape it still retains: long, narrow, keelless, with a tapered prow and stern that rise above the water. The single oarsman, or gondolier, propels the boat from a standing position near the stern. Gondolas average about 9 m (30 ft) in length and are slightly more than 1 m (3 ft) in width.

In the mid-19th century, before the era of steam power, Venice had a fleet of more than 10,000 gondolas. Today there are about 500, and their functions have largely been taken over by *vaporetti* (little steamers) and other powered boats.

Gondwanaland see CONTINENTAL DRIFT; PALEOGEOGRAPHY

Gone With the Wind *Gone With the Wind* (1936), a best-selling novel by Margaret MITCHELL, received the Pulitzer Prize in 1937 and inspired an enormously popular motion picture (1939). Set in Georgia during and after the Civil War, the novel follows the career of a self-centered belle, Scarlett O'Hara. Determined to regain the possessions her family lost during the war, she uses and discards men. Although she loves Ashley Wilkes, a genteel aristocrat, her real match is Rhett Butler, whose toughness equals her own. Such people, devoid of scruples, flourish in the postwar era, while the gentler ones, like Ashley, belong to a society that is "gone with the wind."

gong A circular percussion instrument, the gong may be tuned or of indefinite PITCH; it is common in Oriental and Asian musical life but relatively specialized in Western music. Gongs are suspended or cradled on cords, and

The gong is thought to have originated in China, where it was known by the 6th century AD. Unlike the bell, which vibrates most strongly at its rim, the gong resonates at its center, with vibrations diminishing toward the edge of the rim.

they must be struck in the center because they lack resonance at the edges. They were known in China before the 6th century, and spread through Asia and Africa before being introduced into Europe. Gongs are important components of the Javanese gamelan and the gagaku, the Japanese court orchestra. By the end of the 18th century, Western composers had begun to introduce gongs into concert music.

Góngora y Argote, Luis de [gohn'-goh-rah ee ahr-goh'-tay] Luis de Góngora y Argote, b. July 11, 1561, d. May 23, 1627, was one of the most important representatives of the baroque movement in Spanish literature and the eponym of *Gongorism*, an affected poetic style full of neologisms, Latinate and Greek diction, and dislocated word order.

Góngora's poetry was not directed toward the masses, and he did not seek publication; as a result all his major works were published posthumously. These include the *Fable of Poliphemus and Galatea* (1613; Eng. trans., 1961), a retelling of the story, from Ovid, about the love of Galatea by the cyclops Polyphemus, and a burlesque version of the classical story of *Píramo y Tisbe* (Pyramus and Thisbe, 1618). Góngora's most important work is the unfinished *Solitudes* (1613; Eng. trans., 1931), a lengthy lyric poem of which only one of the projected four

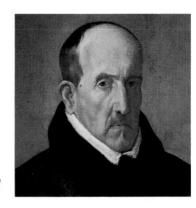

The Spanish poet Luis de Góngora y Argote's baroque and deliberately obscure style gave rise to the term Gongorism. This portrait of Góngora is by Velázquez. (Museum of Fine Arts, Boston.)

sections had been completed at his death. It consists of descriptions of the persons and natural phenomena seen by a lovelorn youth shipwrecked on the shore of a strange land. Prominent among Góngora's critics were QUEVEDO Y VILLEGAS and Lope de VEGA. Although Góngora had important 17th-century followers and was praised by Cervantes, his poetry was subsequently held in little esteem. His works, collected in a modern edition in 1921, a few years before the tercentenary of his death, had a profound influence on Spanish poetry in the early 20th century.

Gongorism   see GÓNGORA Y ARGOTE, LUIS DE

gonorrhea [gahn-uh-ree'-uh]   Gonorrhea is a specific infection caused by the bacterium *Neisseria gonorrhoeae*, commonly called gonococcus. It is one of the most common VENEREAL DISEASES. The bacterium can primarily infect only certain parts of the body: the urethra, uterine cervix, rectum, throat, and eyes. The vast majority of cases are acquired by sexual contact.

Initial symptoms of gonococcal urethritis appear an average of 2 to 10 days after a person becomes infected. The urethra is the site most often infected in men. Most men develop a combination of burning on urination and a thick, pus-laden discharge from the tip of the penis. Three percent of men show no symptoms at all. Women are usually infected in the uterine cervix, but only a minority experience burning on urination or a vaginal discharge. Infection in the throat or rectum almost never produces symptoms, and infection of the eyes results in pain, redness, and discharge.

If the infection is untreated in women, it can lead to pelvic inflammatory disease (see UROGENITAL DISEASES), and subsequently some of these women have difficulty becoming pregnant. The disease may result in infection of the joints (arthritis). During birth, babies may contract gonococcal eye disease from an infected mother; silver nitrate drops placed into the eyes of newborns kill the gonococcus if present. Treatment with antibiotics is usually highly effective. Both sexual partners must be treated. The gonococcus has become increasingly resistant to commonly used antibiotics, however. In 1985 a potential gonorrhea vaccine was developed that showed promise in early clinical testing.

Gonzaga (family) [gohn-tsah'-guh]   The Gonzaga family ruled MANTUA, Italy, from the early 14th century to 1707 and Montferrato from 1536 to 1707. **Luigi Gonzaga**, *c.*1268–1360, inaugurated the family's rule in Mantua by wresting control from the Bonacolsi family in 1328. **Gian Francesco Gonzaga**, 1394–1444, an astute diplomat and soldier, was also the patron of Vittorino da Feltre, the creator of humanistic educational ideals. **Francesco II**, 1466–1519, a leader against the French at the beginning of the ITALIAN WARS, made Mantua a cultural center. The Gonzagas were dukes of Mantua from 1530 and of Montferrato from 1575. The extinction (1627) of

the direct line led to the War of the Mantuan Succession (1628–31), in which France and Spain backed rival claimants. The French branch of Gonzaga-Nevers won and ruled both duchies until it died out in 1707.

Gonzales, Pancho [gahn-zahl'-es, pahn'-choh]   Richard Alonzo Gonzales, b. Los Angeles, May 9, 1928, is an American tennis champion. A fierce, volatile player, Gonzales often played his most breathtaking tennis after losing his temper. Respected for his powerful first serves, he captured the U.S. singles championship in 1948 and 1949, two U.S. Clay Court championships, and the U.S. Indoor title in 1949. Gonzales dominated professional tennis in the 1950s. In 1958, at his peak, he played a series of challenge matches in the United States against highly ranked Lew Hoad of Australia and defeated Hoad by a wide margin.

Pancho Gonzales, playing at the age of 43, makes a backhand return during a match in 1971 at Wimbledon, which he won. Gonzales won the U.S. professional men's singles championship eight times between 1953 and 1961, and remained active on the pro tour well into the 1970s.

González Márquez, Felipe   Felipe González Márquez, b. Mar. 5, 1942, became prime minister of Spain in December 1982. After studying at the University of Louvain in Belgium, he joined the clandestine Socialist party, outlawed under the dictatorship of Francisco Franco. He became the party's leader in 1974 and emerged as a popular political figure when democratic rule was reestablished after Franco's death. As premier, González pursued a moderate leftist policy, leading Spain into the European Community and maintaining its ties with NATO.

Good Friday   Good Friday is the Christian commemoration of the death of JESUS CHRIST, observed on the Friday before EASTER. Originally, it was a day of fasting in preparation for the unitive celebration of the death-resurrection-exaltation of Jesus; no liturgy was held on that day. In the 4th century, at Jerusalem, a procession was staged from Gethsemane to the sanctuary of the cross, followed by readings about the passion. This was the beginning of the Good Friday observance as it is now known.

In the Catholic tradition, the liturgy of the day consists of reading the passion, the ceremony of the veneration of the cross, and communion from the sacrament consecrated the day before. The service of preaching on the seven last words, of Jesuit origin, has become popular in Protestantism.

Good Hope, Cape of

The Cape of Good Hope is a small, rocky peninsula jutting into the Atlantic Ocean near the southern tip of Africa in Cape Province of South Africa. The tip of the cape rises in a sheer cliff to a peak 260 m (850 ft) above the ocean. Thought by early sailors to be the extreme southern point of the continent, the cape is noted for winds and currents that are more dangerous than those off Cape Agulhas (the true southern tip), slightly to the southwest. Called the Cape of Storms by Bartolomeu DIAS, who first sighted it in 1488, it was renamed by King John II of Portugal when the riches of Oriental trade flowed around it. The Cape of Good Hope Nature Reserve was established on the cape in 1939.

Good Neighbor Policy

The Good Neighbor Policy describes the efforts that Pres. Franklin D. ROOSEVELT made to improve relations with Latin America. The phrase became linked to his American policy in the Western Hemisphere. At the Pan American Conference in Montevideo, Uruguay, in December 1933, the United States signed a convention forbidding intervention by one state in another's affairs. The following year Roosevelt ended the 19-year occupation of Haiti by U.S. Marines and abrogated the PLATT AMENDMENT, which had made Cuba a virtual U.S. dependent. The Good Neighbor Policy also encouraged cultural exchange programs.

Goodall, Jane

Jane Goodall, b. Apr. 3, 1934, is a British animal behaviorist best known for her long-term observations of chimpanzees in the wild. She is associated with both the Gombé Stream Research Center in Tanzania and Stanford University. Her work has led to an appreciation of individual differences among nonhuman primates and the discovery of tool use and man eating among chimpanzees. Goodall's writings include *My Friends the Wild Chimpanzees* (1967), *In the Shadow of Man* (1971), and *The Chimpanzees of Gombé: Patterns of Behavior* (1986), a summary of her research.

Goodbye, Mr. Chips

Goodbye, Mr. Chips (1933; film, 1939; musical film, 1969), a short sentimental novel about an English schoolmaster by the English author James HILTON, was an immediate best-seller when it first became available in the United States in 1934. The book consists of flashbacks over a long life of quiet dignity, humor, and richness of experience loyally spent in the service of the boys, World War I, and a new educational outlook that threatens to displace Mr. Chipping.

Goodman, Benny

The "King of Swing" during the SWING era of the 1930s and '40s, the clarinetist Benjamin David Goodman, b. Chicago, May 30, 1909, d. June 13, 1986, led one of the greatest of the big bands. Although Fletcher Henderson's band had been playing swing for several years (and Goodman used many Henderson arrangements), from the mid-1930s, Americans danced to Goodman's music. In addition to his band, the Benny Goodman Trio, with drummer Gene KRUPA and pianist Teddy Wilson—the first black musician to be featured with a popular white group—was formed in 1935. It soon expanded to include vibraphonist Lionel HAMPTON, guitarist Charlie CHRISTIAN, and many other jazz greats. After 1945, Goodman played almost exclusively with small groups. He also played as a soloist with classical orchestras.

Goodnight, Charles

Charles Goodnight, b. Macoupin County, Ill., Mar. 5, 1836, d. Dec. 12, 1929, was a Texas Ranger, cattle rancher, and powerful figure in the Texas Panhandle. He lived an active life from his early years, when he fought Indians on the frontier. Goodnight established ranches and cattle trails in New Mexico Wyoming, and Colorado and in 1876 started a ranch in Texas that eventually covered nearly 400,000 ha (1,000,000 acres) of range. He organized a stockmen's association to pacify the Panhandle and was also a breeder of Angus cattle, crossing them with buffalo to produce the cattalo.

Goodrich, Benjamin F.

Benjamin Franklin Goodrich, b. Ripley, N.Y., Nov. 4, 1841, d. Aug. 3, 1888, founded the B.F. Goodrich Company. Having been a medical student, he served as an army surgeon during the Civil War. Then Goodrich went into the real-estate business, which led him and a partner into buying a rubber-goods factory. After an initial failure they moved to Akron, Ohio, and established (1870) Goodrich, Tew & Company, which manufactured various rubber products and was the predecessor of the present firm.

Goodyear, Charles

Charles Goodyear, b. New Haven, Conn., Dec. 29, 1800, d. July 1, 1860, was an American inventor who developed the vulcanization of RUBBER. In 1830 he began a determined search to improve Brazilian gum rubber, which turned sticky when hot and brittle when cold. He accidentally found that a heated mixture of rubber and sulfur gave the desired properties: improved strength, stability, and elasticity. This discovery came in 1839, but Goodyear did not obtain a U.S. patent until 1844; by then, Thomas Hancock had studied Goodyear's samples and received a British patent.

The Canada goose (left), a favorite North American game bird, is easily recognized by its black head and white cheeks. The snow goose (center) and the white-fronted goose (right) inhabit subarctic and Arctic regions.

goose   The goose is a web-footed water bird of the family Anatidae, which also includes the duck and swan. Geese find much of their food on land, browsing on grasses and eating various grains. Male geese are referred to as ganders, the female is the goose, and young are called goslings. The plumage of the sexes is alike. Geese are monogamous and pair for life; usually both sexes care for the young.

Geese have played an important role in the lives of humans. They were hunted as an important source of food, for both meat and eggs. They also serve as food today, more commonly in Europe than in North America. Goose feathers have been used as ornaments of dress as well as for insulation. Goose down is used widely in quilts, jackets, and other items for comfort and warmth. Domestic geese are also sometimes used as "watchdogs" because they hiss and honk at strangers.

Among wild geese the Canada goose, *Branta canadensis*, is probably the best known. As the human population has grown and destroyed former breeding grounds, the Canada goose has been breeding in larger numbers along streams, lakes, and ponds closer to urban centers. Such adaptations may assure the continuation of the species. Other well-known wild species are brant, snow geese, and blue geese. The more common domesticated varieties are the Toulouse, Emden, African, and Chinese.

Goose Bay   Goose Bay is a village and the site of a large air force base at the western end of Lake Melville in Labrador, Canada. The base was built in 1941 by the Canadian government, and during World War II, it was used by the U.S. and Canadian air forces. It is now a U.S.-Canada early-warning-detection site.

gooseberry   Gooseberry is the common name for several low, spiny shrubs that, together with CURRANTS, con-stitute the genus *Ribes* of the family Saxifragaceae, and for the edible red or green fruit that they bear. Gooseberries are native to the temperate Northern Hemisphere, extending into the South American Andes; because they are hosts to white pine blister rust, they are prohibited in some areas of the United States. They are widely grown as garden fruit but are not commercially important. The name is also applied to a number of mainly tropical, edible fruits of different genera. The KIWI fruit is sometimes called the Chinese gooseberry.

Goossens, Sir Eugene [gaw'-senz]   Eugene Goossens, b. May 26, 1893, d. June 13, 1962, was a distinguished English conductor and composer. He played violin in the Queen's Hall Orchestra (1911–15) and was assistant to Thomas Beecham (1916–20). In 1921 he formed his own orchestra and also conducted opera and the Russian Ballet at Covent Garden. From 1923 to 1931 he conducted the Rochester (N.Y.) Philharmonic Orchestra and then succeeded Fritz Reiner as conductor of the Cincinnati Symphony (1931–46). He was conductor of the Sydney Symphony and director of the New South Wales Conservatorium in Australia from 1947 to 1956. A prolific composer, Goossens was knighted in 1955.

GOP   see REPUBLICAN PARTY

gopher [goh'-fur]   Gophers are burrowing rodents of North and Central America that belong to the family Geomyidae. They are sometimes called pocket gophers because they have cheek pouches for carrying food. There are 5 genera and about 25 species. The animals have stout, heavyset bodies with short necks, legs, and tails. Gophers are 13 to 45 cm (5 to 18 in) long. The coat varies from whitish or brown through black. The eyes and ears are small. The lips can be closed behind the incisors,

The plains pocket gopher is found on prairies of the U.S. Midwest. Its forelimbs' ten strong claws enable it to dig rapidly.

enabling the gopher to gnaw dirt without getting it into the mouth. Gophers destroy crops by tunneling under growing plants and eating the roots.

Gorbachev, Mikhail [gahr-bah-chawf'] Mikhail Sergeyevich Gorbachev, b. Mar. 2, 1931, general secretary of the Soviet Communist party (1985–91) and president of the USSR (1988–91), was that nation's last leader. By his reform programs, Gorbachev hoped to revive the stagnant Soviet system. Instead, by removing the rigid controls that had kept the system together for decades, he brought about its dissolution, the end of the cold war, and the virtual elimination of Communism as a dominant influence in world affairs.

Born and raised on a collective farm in the Stavropol region, Gorbachev studied law at Moscow University and joined the Communist party in 1952. Rising in the ranks, he became party leader of the Stavropol region in 1970. A protégé of KGB chief Yuri ANDROPOV, Gorbachev was elected to the party's Central Committee in 1971. In 1978 he was brought to Moscow, and when Andropov was chosen head of the party in 1982, Gorbachev aided the ailing leader in his reform efforts. After the deaths of Andropov and his short-lived successor, Konstantin CHERNENKO, Gorbachev was elevated to the top party position in March 1985.

Gorbachev immediately embarked on a sweeping program of economic and political reforms (PERESTROIKA) and announced a new policy of openness in the media (GLASNOST). He advocated greater initiative from below, less direction by the bureaucracy, and more reliance on market forces. Gorbachev dealt confidently with the nuclear accident at CHERNOBYL (1986), a devastating earthquake in Armenia (1988), and nationalist unrest in the Baltic and elsewhere. His popularity, however, was undermined by the disruptions resulting from his economic reforms, which led to strikes and chronic shortages of consumer goods. By 1990 his leadership was being challenged by the more radical Boris YELTSIN, president of the Russian Republic.

Gorbachev restored friendly relations with the West, disengaged the USSR from its war in Afghanistan, and ended its long-standing quarrel with China. In 1989 he renounced the "Brezhnev doctrine" by which the Soviets had claimed the right to intervene militarily in Warsaw Pact countries. This quickly led to the fall of the Eastern European Communist regimes. At home he was forced to renegotiate Moscow's relations with the Soviet republics, all of which declared themselves either sovereign or independent in 1990.

Gorbachev reorganized the Soviet government into a presidential system headed by himself and persuaded the Communist party to give up its constitutional monopoly of power and compete with other political forces for the support of the people. By the end of 1990, however, Gorbachev slowed the pace of reforms in the face of strong conservative opposition. His popularity at home was eroded as the USSR faced increasing economic and political problems

In August 1991, Gorbachev survived a coup attempt by Communist hard-liners, foiled after three days of massive popular opposition. In the aftermath, Gorbachev resigned (December 25), ceasing to be active in public affairs and devoting his time instead to writing and lecturing, both in Russia and abroad.

Soviet president Mikhail Gorbachev, won worldwide acclaim by ending the cold war and renouncing Soviet control over Eastern Europe. For his foreign-policy initiatives he was awarded the Nobel Peace Prize in 1990. He was unable to control the reforms he instituted within the USSR, however.

Gordian knot [gohr'-dee-uhn] In Greek legend the Gordian knot was an intricate knot tied by Gordius, king of Phrygia. An oracle foretold that he who untied the knot would rule all of Asia. According to the story, Alexander the Great cut the knot with his sword. Thus "cutting the Gordian knot" came to mean solving a difficult problem by forceful action.

Gordimer, Nadine [gohr'-di-mur, nay-deen'] Nadine Gordimer, b. Nov. 20, 1923, is a highly praised South African writer who has written novels and short stories about the tensions of life under apartheid. Among her best novels are *The Lying Days* (1953), *The Late Bourgeois World* (1966), *A Guest of Honour* (1970), and *Burger's Daughter* (1979). *My Son's Story* (1990) deals with the destructive effects of political struggle on a South African family. Gordimer's short-story collections include *Six Feet of the Country* (1956), *Livingstone's Companions* (1971), and *Something Out There* (1984). Gordimer won the 1991 Nobel Prize for literature.

Gordin, Jacob [gohr'-din, yah'-kuhb]   Jacob Gordin, b. May 1, 1853, d. 1909, was a Russian-born playwright whose plays ushered in the golden age of Yiddish theater after his immigration to America in 1891. Among the more than 70 plays that Gordin wrote, adapted, or translated are *The Jewish King Lear* (1892), *God, Man, and the Devil* (1900), and *The Kreutzer Sonata* (1902).

Gordon, Charles George   Charles George Gordon, b. Jan. 28, 1833, d. Jan. 26, 1885, was a British general who won renown for his dramatic but unsuccessful defense of KHARTOUM (1884–85) against the Sudanese rebels led by the MAHDI.

Born near London, Gordon was commissioned in the British Army in 1852 and fought in the Crimean War (1853–56). In 1860, during the Second OPIUM WAR, he joined the British forces in China, taking part in the capture of Beijing. The Chinese government later (1863) made him commander of the peasant force known as the Ever-Victorious Army, which helped to suppress the TAI-PING REBELLION. He returned (1865) to London a famous figure, popularly known as "Chinese Gordon."

In 1873, Gordon became governor of the province of Equatoria, on the upper Nile. From 1877 to 1880 he was also governor-general of the Sudan and was active in suppressing the slave trade and putting down revolts. Four years later he was sent back to the Sudan to evacuate Egyptian forces from Khartoum, then threatened by the Mahdi's army. Disobeying the orders to evacuate, Gordon defended the city against siege from March 1884 until Jan. 26, 1885, when the rebels broke through and massacred the entire garrison. Two days later a British relief force reached the city.

Gordon, John Brown   The American military and political leader John Brown Gordon, b. Upson County, Ga., Feb. 6, 1832, d. Jan. 9, 1904, was a distinguished Confederate general and later an important and revered political figure in Georgia. After practicing law and working as a mine developer, he joined Robert E. Lee's Confederate army in Virginia at the outbreak of the Civil War in 1861. He fought well in every campaign, rising to head a brigade in 1862, a division in May 1864 under Jubal A. Early, and finally, in the winter of 1864 as a lieutenant general, he commanded Stonewall Jackson's old II Corps.

Gordon was a brilliant orator, and after the war he served as U.S. senator from Georgia (1873–80, 1891–97) and governor of Georgia (1886–90). He headed the United Confederate Veterans from 1890 until his death.

Gordon, Ruth   The American actress Ruth Gordon, b. Wallaston, Mass., Oct. 30, 1896, d. Aug. 28, 1985, also achieved success as a writer of drama and television plays. She won an Academy Award (1969) as best supporting actress for her role in *Rosemary's Baby* (1968).

Gordon, who made her stage debut in 1915, is the author of such plays as *Leading Lady* (1948) and *A Very Rich Woman* (1965), as well as the autobiographical *Myself among Others* (1971), *My Side* (1976), *An Open Book* (1980), and *Shady Lady* (1981).

Gordon setter   The Gordon setter is a breed of dog similar to the English setter and the Irish setter. It is black with distinctive tan markings about 2.5 cm (1 in) in diameter over the eyes, on the sides of the muzzle, on the throat, chest, the inside of the hind legs, the forelegs from the carpus to the toes, and around the anus.

Popular with hunters in Scotland for years, the Gordon setter is somewhat more thickset than the Irish setter and, consequently, a slower worker. This is largely a result of the effort of Alexander, fourth duke of Gordon, in the late 1700s. The Gordon setter is the least popular of the three setter breeds.

The Gordon setter displays the smooth, flowing gait and stamina of other setters but works closer to the hunter. Its dark color makes it unfavorable for hunting in the woods.

Gore, Al   Albert Gore, Jr., b. Washington, D.C., Mar. 31, 1948, a U.S. representative (1977–85) and senator (1985–92) from Tennessee, was elected to the U.S. vice-presidency on a Democratic ticket with Gov. Bill Clinton of Arkansas in 1992. He is the son of Albert Gore, Sr., who was also a congressman (1934–44, 1945–53) and senator (1953–71). After graduation (1969) from Harvard, Gore served (1969-71) in the army, with a tour of duty in Vietnam, then attended divinity school and law school at Vanderbilt. His expertise as a moderate liberal ranges from foreign policy and health-related issues in general to arms control and environmentalism in particular. Gore ran unsuccessfully in the 1988 presidential primaries. He wrote *Earth in the Balance: Ecology and the Human Spirit* (1992).

Gore, Thomas P. Thomas Pryor Gore, b. Choctaw (now Webster) County, Miss., Dec. 10, 1870, d. Mar. 16, 1949, was a U.S. senator from Oklahoma for many years (1907–21, 1931–37). Totally blind by 1890, he was known as "the Blind Orator." A leading Democrat in Oklahoma Territory from 1901, he entered the Senate when Oklahoma became a state in 1907 and was a major spokesman for farmers' interests.

Goren, Charles H. Charles Henry Goren, b. Philadelphia, Mar. 4, 1901, d. Apr. 3, 1991, was an American expert on the card game BRIDGE. In 1949 he introduced a point-count system of bridge bidding that became nearly universal nationwide. Goren wrote over 50 books on the game, the first of which was *Winning Bridge Made Easy* (1936). Another, *Contract Bridge Complete* (1951), was a best seller. In these works he presented his system of allocating points for honor cards and suit distribution in a bridge hand and for determining the correct bids from the sum of points. Goren also wrote daily and weekly bridge columns and presented bridge shows on radio and television.

Gorey, Edward Edward Gorey, b. Chicago, Feb. 22, 1925, a well-known author and illustrator, is largely a self-taught artist. In the early 1950s he founded the Poet's Theater in Boston, with Frank O'Hara and V. R. Lang. Since the publication of his first book in 1953, Gorey has found an appreciative audience among both children and adults. Combining a gloomy severity with a sly, sinister wit, his drawings portray eccentric individuals in genteel, often Victorian, settings. His stories and poems give a macabre flavor to the most innocent literary traditions. He designed the sets for the Broadway production of *Dracula* (1977).

Gorges, Sir Ferdinando [gohr'-jez] Sir Ferdinando Gorges, b. 1568, d. May 24, 1647, played an important role in the early English development of New England, although he himself never visited America. In 1620, Gorges obtained a royal charter for the Council for New England, a company that received land rights to all of North America from Philadelphia to the Gaspé Peninsula. During its 15-year history it issued large and overlapping land grants that became the basis of five New England colonies: Plymouth, Massachusetts Bay, New Hampshire, Maine, and part of Connecticut. One of the grants (1622), a huge tract between the Merrimack and Kennebec rivers, went to Gorges and his chief associate, John MASON. In 1629 they divided the area, Gorges receiving the region between the Piscataqua and Kennebec rivers; a royal charter later confirmed (1639) Gorges's title and made him lord proprietor of Maine.

Gorgias [gohr'-jee-uhs] Gorgias of Leontini (Sicily), *c*.480–380 BC, was a Greek SOPHIST philosopher famous in his time as a teacher of rhetoric. He led a diplomatic delegation from Leontini to Athens in 427 BC, and figures prominently in Plato's dialogue *Gorgias*, where he is a foil for Socrates. Gorgias is best known for his treatise *On Nature or the Nonexistent*, in which he argued that (1) nothing exists; (2) if anything exists, it cannot be known; and (3) if it can be known, it cannot be communicated to others. It is not certain whether he meant this extreme skeptical position to be taken literally, or whether his arguments were intended as a demonstration of rhetorical skill. Most of his works are known only from the writings of others, the originals having been lost. Two rhetorical exercises, *Helen* and *Palamedes*, survive.

Gorgon [gohr'-guhn] In early Greek mythology the Gorgon was a monster of the underworld. In later tradition, the Gorgons were the three daughters of sea-god Phorcys and Ceto: Stheno, Euryale, and MEDUSA. They had writhing snakes for hair and were so ugly that the sight of them turned beholders into stone.

gorilla [guh-ril'-uh] The gorilla, genus *Gorilla*, is a member of the family Pongidae, or great APES, which also includes the chimpanzee and orangutan. Together with the lesser apes—a group that includes the gibbon and the siamang—the great apes are close relatives of monkeys and humans; all belong to the order PRIMATES.

The gorilla is the largest living primate: males sometimes reach 180 cm (6 ft) in height and in nature weigh between 135 and 180 kg (300 and 400 lb). Females are shorter and weigh about half as much as the males.

A silverback gorilla is an adult male whose hair on its back has turned from black to silver gray. A silverback is the dominant male of its troop and defends females and infants from intruders.

Gorillas become sexually mature at 6–9 years of age and live about half as long as a human. Single infants are born following a pregnancy of 8½ months, are partially weaned by 1 year, but remain with the mother for at least 3 years. The hair on the male's back turns silver gray with maturity, giving rise to the term "silverback" for adult males.

Gorillas are the most terrestrial of the great apes, their bulky size making them ill-suited to tree dwelling. Locomotion on the ground is quadrupedal, and the knuckles of the hands are used to support the upper body. Youngsters and females with infants demonstrate their arboreal heritage, however, by building sleeping nests in trees each night.

Gorillas live in family groups that consist of a single male leader, or silverback; some younger, black-backed males, possibly sons of the silverback; several adult females; and varied numbers of juvenile and infant offspring. Group size varies with geographic location and food availability.

Gorillas are rather amiable vegetarians. They spend most of their day foraging for food. When gorilla groups meet, fighting is rare. When tension does develop between silverbacks of two groups, it is generally relieved in nonaggressive ways such as impressive displays of chest beating.

There are three geographic variants, or races, of gorilla, all of which are found in the African rain forest: the western lowland gorilla (*Gorilla gorilla gorilla*), the mountain gorilla (*G. gorilla beringei*), and the eastern lowland gorilla (*G. gorilla graueri*). The gorilla is threatened with extinction in its natural habitat by various human activities, and its last chances for survival may be a few gorilla sanctuaries in Africa and the zoos and other captive environments that maintain gorillas in other parts of the world.

Göring, Hermann   see GOERING, HERMANN

Gorky [gohr'-kee]   Gorky is the capital of Gorky oblast in the Russian republic of the USSR. It is situated on the Volga River, at the mouth of the Oka, a tributary. The city has a population of 1,438,000 (1990). Originally named Nizhni Novgorod, it was the site of Russia's largest annual trade fair in the 19th century. Gorky is one of the USSR's largest industrial cities, known mainly for its automotive and shipbuilding industries. It also has a wide range of machine-manufacturing, apparel, and food-processing factories.

The city is divided into an old town, which is located on high ground on the right bank of the Oka, and newer sections on the lower, left bank of the Oka. Noteworthy in the old town is a kremlin, or fortress, dating from the 16th century, which overlooks the Oka-Volga confluence. The kremlin contains the Cathedral of the Archangel Michael, which was completed in 1631 and is now a museum. Most residential and industrial areas are on the low bank, where the old fairground was located. The Gorky auto plant is southwest of the old town, and the shipyards are at Sormovo, northwest of the old town. Because of its defense industries, Gorky is closed to foreign tourists.

One of the oldest Russian cities, Nizhni Novgorod was founded in 1221. It was annexed to Moscow in 1392 but plundered by the Tatars in 1520 and 1536. Because of its favorable location on important waterways, it developed into a major commercial center. In 1932 the city was renamed for the writer Maksim Gorky, who was born there in 1868.

Gorky, Arshile   Arshile Gorky, b. Armenia, Oct. 25, 1904, d. July 21, 1948, is best known for his postsurrealist abstract paintings of the 1940s, which were an important contribution to the first generation of American ABSTRACT EXPRESSIONISM. Gorky came to the United States in 1920. He painted *The Artist and His Mother* in 1926, a work in which he began his process of abstraction and individuation that led him from the styles of Paul Cézanne, Pablo Picasso, Wassily Kandinsky, and Joan Miró to his original brand of biomorphism, a sensuously symbolic multiple imagery derived from his intimate study of nature. His biomorphic abstraction began with his series *Image in Xhorkam* (from 1936). Important for Gorky were his friendships with Willem de Kooning and John Graham. Chief among his works of the 1940s are *The Liver Is the Cock's Comb* (1944; Albright-Knox Gallery, Buffalo, N.Y.) and *The Bethrothal II* (1947; Whitney Museum, New York City). Gorky committed suicide following several tragedies in his personal life.

The biomorphic imagery of Arshile Gorky's The Liver Is the Cock's Comb *(1944) points to the inspiration of surrealism in early abstract expressionism. (The Albright-Knox Art Gallery, Buffalo.)*

Gorky, Maksim   The Russian writer Maksim Gorky, pseudonym of Aleksei Maksimovich Peshkov, b. Mar. 28 (N.S.), 1868, d. June 18, 1936, gained worldwide renown as a spokesman for the downtrodden through his novels, stories, dramas, and memoirs. This, together with involvement in the revolutionary movement, friendship with Lenin, and leadership in establishing SOCIALIST REALISM, ensured his canonization in the USSR as "the great proletarian writer."

The Soviet writer Maksim Gorky exercised considerable influence in post-revolutionary Russia because of the proletarian themes of his works. He became a confidant of Lenin and served Stalin as a propagandist. Since his death, Gorky has been recognized as the founder of socialist realism.

Gorky (meaning "the bitter") was born into an impoverished middle-class family of Nizhni Novgorod (renamed Gorky). At five, after the death of his father, he went to live with his maternal grandparents; the harshness of that household was captured in *My Childhood* (1913–14; Eng. trans., 1915), the brilliant first part of Gorky's autobiographical trilogy that also includes *In the World* (1915; Eng. trans., 1917) and *My Universities* (1923; Eng. trans., 1952).

Sent to work at age 8, Gorky for many years led a difficult, penurious, increasingly aimless life, finally becoming a hobo. Rebellious, freedom-loving tramps, in fact, became the heroes of Gorky's early stories. It was, in turn, the success of these stories, including "Makar Chudra" (1892) and "Chelkash" (1895), that ended his own vagabondage. Although Gorky later rejected the hoboes' antisocial nihilism, he remained attracted to the personalities of willful men who had the strength to shape life. This is evident in his novels about Russian merchants, *Foma Gordeyev* (1899; Eng. trans., 1955) and *The Artamonov Business* (1925; Eng. trans., 1948), as well as in his memoir *V. I. Lenin* (1924).

Gorky's youthful contacts with radicals brought him to the attention of the police, and because of his association with Russian Marxists his election to the Russian Academy of Sciences was annulled (1902). He was later imprisoned for participation in the revolutionary events of 1905 and released only after foreign luminaries, in response to the international success of his powerful drama *The Lower Depths* (1902; Eng. trans., 1906), made formal protests to the tsar. A trip to the United States in 1906 to raise funds for the revolutionary movement failed in part because of his insistence on traveling with his mistress. After completing *Mother* (1906; Eng. trans., 1911), a crude but still widely read revolutionary novel, and *City of the Yellow Devil* (1906), an attack on the United States, he settled in Capri, where he remained until 1913. There he wrote some of his best works, including *The Small Town Okurov* (1909), *The Life of Mat-*

thew Kozhemyakin (1910; Eng. trans., c.1960), and *My Childhood*.

Gorky's assertive nonconformity again surfaced after the Bolshevik coup in 1917, when his outspoken criticism of party leadership led to suppression of his newspaper *New Life*. Suffering anew from pulmonary tuberculosis and dissatisfied with political developments, Gorky again left (1921) the USSR to settle in Sorrento. The Bolsheviks, however, desired his return, and in 1928 he responded to their urgings. Thereafter he increasingly became the chief literary propagandist for Stalin's hardening dictatorship and the socialist realism subsequently imposed on creative artists, although he continued to protect individual writers. Some mystery surrounds his sudden death in 1936 while under medical treatment. He was at work on a multivolume novel of Russian life over four decades, *The Life of Klim Samgin*, at the time of his death.

Gorton, John Grey   John Grey Gorton, b. Sept. 9, 1911, was prime minister of Australia from 1968 to 1971. He belonged to the left wing of the basically conservative Liberal party. Gorton was elected to the Senate for Victoria in 1949. He served as minister of the navy (1958–63), minister of works (1963–66), and minister for education and science (1966–68). He became prime minister in 1968 on the death of Harold Holt. In that position Gorton tried to strengthen the Australian alliance with the United States. One of his major problems was the independence movement in Papua New Guinea, a territory administered under United Nations charter, and his handling of it led to his removal from office by his colleagues. He was successful, however, in winning better opportunities for the Aborigines of Australia. After losing a Liberal party vote of confidence, Gorton resigned in March 1971. He served for a time as minister of defense in 1971 and retired from politics in 1975.

Gorton, Samuel   Samuel Gorton, c.1592–1677, was the Anglo-American founder of a religious sect known as the Gortonites. Gorton denied belief in a Trinity, claiming that only Jesus Christ was divine and that union with him would make an individual perfect. He emigrated to America in 1637 and immediately offended both the clergy and civil officials of Massachusetts by criticizing their control over religious affairs. Within a year he moved to Rhode Island, where he established (1632) the settlement later called WARWICK. The Gortonites remained an active sect for about a century.

Gosford, Archibald Acheson, 2d Earl of [gahz'-fohrd]   Lord Gosford, b. Aug. 1, 1776, d. Mar. 27, 1849, was governor in chief (1835–37) of British North America. He sat in the British House of Commons before inheriting his title (1807) and from 1811 was a representative Irish peer in the House of Lords. As governor in chief of Canada,

Gosford was ordered to report on conditions in Lower Canada (Quebec). He recommended "conciliation without concession" toward the French Canadians, a policy that pleased neither the French nor the English. He resigned only days before the REBELLIONS OF 1837.

gospel music   The term *gospel music* embraces several types of song, all of which share an emotional, personal identification with the biblical text and a rich musical vocabulary. Of the various types, the gospel music sung in black Baptist churches is perhaps the most important, because it has influenced not only white gospel forms but also certain styles of popular music. Unlike the SPIRITUAL, which is rooted in the formal Protestant hymn, black gospel music is extemporaneous, highly emotional, and joyful. Based on a sung dialogue between congregation and preacher, with the preacher setting the text and the congregation supplying musical affirmation, gospel music inspires a "fire and excitement that sometimes, without warning, fill a church, causing [it] to `rock't" (James Baldwin, *The Fire Next Time*). In the 1940s, Mahalia JACKSON, Clara Ward, and Sister Rosetta Tharpe began recording gospel-style music. In the 1950s and '60s, church-trained musicians took the style into popular music. Singers like Aretha FRANKLIN and James BROWN recorded what came to be known as SOUL, a style that reproduces the vocal devices of gospel: use of falsetto, bent and sliding tones, shouts, and the stretching-out of a single sung syllable over many notes.

White gospel music, sung at Protestant revival meetings, was similar to black gospel music in its spontaneity and emotional fervor. A popular offshoot of white revivals was the gospel hymn, which can be traced to evangelists Dwight L. MOODY and Ira D. Sankey, who exposed large audiences to such hymns and composed many others. White quartet and family gospel groups now dominate this genre; in addition, a youth-music movement, largely in the South, has developed a repertoire of pop-gospel music.

Gospels   see BIBLE

Gossaert, Jan [gohs'-airt]   Jan Gossaert, called Mabuse, *c.*1478–*c.*1533, was one of the earliest Northern Renaissance painters to popularize the Italianate style in the Low Countries. By 1503 he was classified as a free master in the Antwerp painters' guild, and about 1507 he entered the service of Philip, duke of Burgundy. His earliest Mannerist paintings (see MANNERISM), such as the *Holy Family* altarpiece (*c.*1505; Museum National de Arte Antiga, Lisbon), are richly detailed, ornate, and somewhat crowded. Gossaert's early influences were Gerard DAVID, Albrecht DÜRER, Jan van EYCK, and Hugo van der GOES. In 1508–09 he traveled to Italy and was much impressed by what he saw there, which complemented by his later study of prints by Jacopo de' Barbari and Marcantonio Raimondi. His many nudes, including *Venus and Cupid* (*c.*1521; Musées Royaux des Beaux-Arts, Brussels),

were greatly influenced by his Italian experience. Gossaert was also known for his sober, realistic portraits, such as the *Merchant* (Philadelphia Museum of Art).

Göteborg [yuh-te-bawr']   Göteborg, the seat of Göteborg och Bohus county in southwestern Sweden, is that country's second largest city and chief seaport. The population is 430,763 (1989 est.). Located on the Göta River near where it empties into the Kattegat, the port has direct access to the Atlantic. The Göta Canal runs between Stockholm and Göteborg, and the city is connected to most parts of Sweden by rail lines and domestic air service. Nearby shipbuilding facilities are the largest in the country, and the industries in Göteborg produce automobiles, office machines, textiles, foodstuffs, paper, leather, and wood products.

The old parts of the city contain the cathedral (1633), Kristine Church (1648), the law courts (1672), the town hall (1750), and the opera house (1859). There are art, natural-history, and folk museums; botanical and amusement parks; and a university (1891); as well as technical and other schools.

In 1619, King Gustav II Adolf founded Göteborg on the site of a previous settlement, giving Sweden a port on its southwest coast. The city prospered, especially during the Napoleonic Wars, when Göteborg remained open while many European ports were blockaded by France.

Gotha (city) [goh'-tah]   Gotha (1983 est. pop., 57,662) is a city in central Germany, situated on the Leine Canal. It is a rail junction and its industries produce transportation equipment, precision instruments, chemicals, and textiles. Publishing has been an important industry since the 18th century, when the famous publishing house of Justus Perthes (now Hermann Haack) was established. Many historic landmarks are there, including Saint Margaret's Church (first built in the 12th century, rebuilt in 1652), the town hall (begun 1567), and 16th-, 17th-, and 18th-century palaces.

By 775 a Frankish settlement was established there. Much of the city was destroyed (1567) during the religious wars of the Reformation. The city became the residence of the dukes of Saxe-Gotha in 1639; from 1826 to 1918 it served as the residence of the dukes of Saxe-Coburg-Gotha.

Gothic art and architecture   The term *Gothic* was first used during the Italian Renaissance to characterize all the monuments of the Middle Ages because they were contemptuously regarded as the products of barbarian Goths and therefore utterly lacking in artistic merit. Subsequently, however, the term was restricted to the art and architecture of those centuries immediately following the Romanesque period and preceding the Renaissance. As the last medieval period, the Gothic age has now also come to be regarded as one of Europe's outstanding artistic eras.

The Cathedral of Notre Dame (1163– c.1250), located on Paris's Île de la Cité, is a magnificent amalgam of Gothic elements that developed during the more than 150 years of its construction and renovation. Such features as the rib-vaulted nave, flying buttresses, clerestory windows, and delicate stone tracery create a quality of weightless verticality.

Early and High Gothic Architecture

Gothic architecture, arising out of the 12th-century heyday of the Romanesque (see ROMANESQUE ART AND ARCHITECTURE), remained the dominant expresssion of the Gothic period and outlasted all of the other Gothic arts well into the 16th century. It was in the service of the church, the most prolific builder of the Middle Ages, that the new architectural ideas were formulated and brought to their fullest fruition. Although by 1400, Gothic architecture had become international in scope, its creative heartland was in northern France in an area stretching from the royal domain around Paris, including Saint-Denis and Chartres, to the region of the Champagne in the east and southward to Bourges. Within this restricted area, in the series of cathedrals erected in the course of the 12th and 13th centuries, the major innovations of Gothic architecture took place.

Gothic architecture is not easily defined. Rib vaulting and the pointed arch (see ARCH AND VAULT), its most characteristic features, both were widely used in Romanesque churches. Only when diagonal ribs are used in direct conjunction with pointed transverse arches in the vaulting of an interior can a structure be identified as Gothic. The outward thrusts of the vaults—deflected downward by the pointed transverse arches—is counteracted by narrow buttresses and by external arches, or flying buttresses, invented at NOTRE DAME DE PARIS sometime after 1163.

With these structural advantages, the thick Romanesque walls could be replaced with translucent walls of STAINED GLASS, and builders were able to erect vaulted interiors of unprecedented heights.

Early Gothic Architecture. The creative phase of Gothic architecture that was to lead to the building of the great northern cathedrals began in 1144 with the completion, under the patronage of Abbot SUGER, of the ambulatory (aisle circling the apse) and radiating chapels of the royal abbey of SAINT-DENIS just outside Paris. Instead of being separated in Romanesque fashion, the chapels now opened out into each other, forming a single flowing space called a chevet, while the slender supports of the vaults and the expansive windows further de-emphasize the solids. The innovations at Saint-Denis led in the 1160s to a series of bold experiments. Still adhering to the general features of the French Romanesque churches—a three-aisled nave, a transept, and a semicircular chevet, with a three-story elevation consisting of a groundfloor arcade, a gallery over the side aisles and a clerestory—the architects of the Early Gothic cathedrals sought, often in complicated ways, to open up the solid walls and to attain added height by inserting still another story between the galleries and the clerestory. Known as a triforium, this additional story is nothing more than a narrow passageway contrived in the thickness of the wall immediately below the clerestory windows and faced on the open inner side with a small arcade. The triforium was to become a standard feature in later Gothic churches.

Notre Dame de Paris, in its original unremodeled form (with circular openings instead of a triforium), and the five-towered Cathedral of Laon, both begun in the 1160s, are two of the most successful of these experiments in four-story elevation; the interior of Notre Dame de Paris attained a height of 35 m (115 ft), unprecedented for its time. These results, however, involved complexities that demanded a solution, and it was in the rebuilding of CHARTRES CATHEDRAL, begun immediately following a catastrophic fire in 1194, that they were resolved. Retaining the narrow band of the triforium, Chartres returned to a simpler three-story design. Height was achieved by the creation of a huge clerestory as tall as the ground-floor arcade and, in each bay, embracing two large lancet windows surmounted by a ROSE WINDOW. In one stroke the architect of Chartres had created a clarified and integrated formula for the elevation of a Gothic interior that, in spite of all subsequent changes in style, was to be endlessly repeated in the later churches.

High Gothic Architecture. Chartres inaugurated the High Gothic period; it culminated in the great Coronation Cathedral of REIMS, begun in 1210. Somewhat cold and intellectual in design, overwhelming in scale, and, like Chartres, ponderous in its masonry structure, the internal proportions of Reims are as classical in their way as those

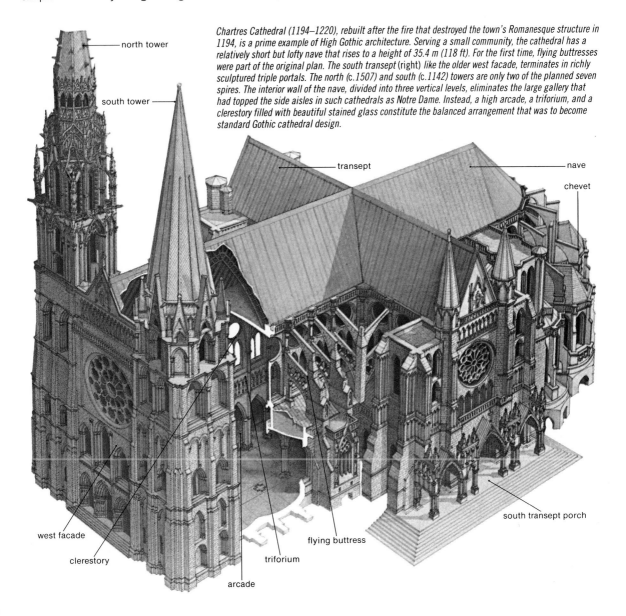

Chartres Cathedral (1194–1220), rebuilt after the fire that destroyed the town's Romanesque structure in 1194, is a prime example of High Gothic architecture. Serving a small community, the cathedral has a relatively short but lofty nave that rises to a height of 35.4 m (118 ft). For the first time, flying buttresses were part of the original plan. The south transept (right) like the older west facade, terminates in richly sculptured triple portals. The north (c.1507) and south (c.1142) towers are only two of the planned seven spires. The interior wall of the nave, divided into three vertical levels, eliminates the large gallery that had topped the side aisles in such cathedrals as Notre Dame. Instead, a high arcade, a triforium, and a clerestory filled with beautiful stained glass constitute the balanced arrangement that was to become standard Gothic cathedral design.

north tower

south tower

transept

nave

chevet

west facade

clerestory

triforium

arcade

flying buttress

south transept porch

The south transept of Reims Cathedral (1211–90) contains one of the magnificent rose windows for which this coronation cathedral is noted.

of the Parthenon. A notable contribution of Reims to the development of later Gothic architecture was bar tracery, or stone framework of a Gothic window. The earlier plate tracery, such as that in the clerestory of Chartres, consists essentially of a series of openings in a masonry wall constructed in horizontal courses. In bar tracery these separate openings are absorbed into a single large window, which is then subdivided into tall lancets by thin upright monoliths, or mullions.

The Cathedral of Bourges, begun in 1195, rivals Chartres and Reims in providing a High Gothic solution to the problems of church design. Here height is achieved from below by means of an extraordinarily lofty ground-floor arcade, thus reducing the dimensions of the clerestory to approximately those of the triforium. The soaring 42-m (138-ft) nave of Amiens Cathedral (begun 1220), chronologically following Reims, represents a transitional stage in which attenuation and aspiring verticality are again stressed, while the tracery of the large clerestory windows is a further elaboration of the simpler design of Reims.

Rayonnant or Late Gothic Architecture. The last of the great cathedrals, Beauvais, was begun the year before

Louis IX came to the throne in 1226. Early in his long reign there emerged a new phase of Gothic architecture known as Rayonnant, a term derived from the radiating spokes of the immense rose windows that form an important feature of this new style. Height was no longer the dominant goal. Rather, the aim of Rayonnant architecture was the further elimination of solid masonry by piercing the triforium wall with traceried windows. A more unified internal effect was achieved by continuing the vaulting shafts uninterruptedly from pavement to vault and by linking the clerestory windows and the triforium arcade into one interrelated design.

The rebuilding (1232) of Saint-Denis was the first major undertaking in the Rayonnant, but the structure that best epitomizes the spirit of the style is the SAINTE-CHAPELLE, the shrinelike chapel erected (1246–48) on the Parisian Île de la Cité. It was commissioned by Louis IX as a fitting receptacle for the Crown of Thorns he had acquired from the Latin emperor Baldwin II of Constantinople. Piers, arches, and tracery formed a delicate armature for the jeweled medallions of the stained-glass windows that completely fill the spaces between the slender vaulting shafts.

Stained-Glass Windows. The windows of Gothic churches were progressively enlarged—not to allow more light to penetrate into the interior, but to increase the areas reserved for the stained glass.

The subject matter of stained-glass windows can be divided into two categories. The lancets of the clerestory are generally occupied by large figures of saints and prophets, sometimes of immense size and thus easily distinguishable from below. The more detailed episodes from the Bible and the legends of the saints, rendered with an effective economy in design, are illustrated in small medallions in the windows of the aisles and of the ambulatory chapels that are nearer to the observer. Throughout the first half of the 13th century the color

The intricate facade of Amiens Cathedral (1220–88), completed during the 15th century, combines the structure of the earlier facade with the ornamentation and abundant sculpture typical of late Gothic design.

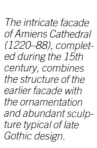

(Above) *The upper chapel of La Sainte Chapelle, Paris (1246–48), a reliquary shrine built by King Louis IX, is the culmination of Gothic attempts to replace heavy walls with radiant stained glass.*

(Left) Notre Dame de la Belle Verrière, *one of the most magnificent examples of mid-12th-century stained glass, is in the cathedral of Chartres.*

scheme was dominated by a brilliant ruby red and a dark saturated blue. With the lighter tonality of the later glass and with the introduction of grisaille glass—white glass infused with gray patterns—the earlier mystic darkness was dispelled.

Influence of French Gothic Architecture. The impact of French Gothic architecture on much of continental Europe was profound. The scheme of Bourges, with its gigantic arcade and short clerestory, was repeated only once in France, at Le Mans, but it served as the direct model for the Spanish cathedrals of Toledo (begun 1227) and Burgos (begun 1221). The giant arcade and the French semicircular chevet were used in the cathedrals of Palma de Mallorca (begun 1306), Barcelona (begun 1298), and Gerona (begun 1312). The nave of Amiens served as the inspiration for the Cathedral of León (begun c.1255). In Germany the towers of Laon were copied at Bamberg (c.1237) and Naumburg (c.1237) and its four-story elevation emulated in the Cathedral of Limburg-an-der-Lahn (begun 1211). French High Gothic forms appear throughout Saint Elizabeth's Church (begun 1235) at Marburg. Cologne Cathedral (begun 1248), rivaling Beauvais in height, adapts the Rayonnant choir of Amiens.

England and Italy were the exceptions to this pervasive influence across the continent. The Gothic churches of Florence, in a uniquely Italianate style, and the facades at Siena (begun 1284) and Orvieto (begun 1290) were but stages of the progression toward the Renaissance of Filippo BRUNELLESCHI. In England, French Gothic intrudes decisively only twice: once in the 1170s at Canterbury Cathedral and again in Henry III's rebuilding of WESTMINSTER ABBEY (begun 1245). Eschewing the emphasis on height and the logical constructionalism of French Gothic, the English churches stressed horizontality in the elevation and an extreme elongation in plan. Double transepts were sometimes included, and a square east end was usually substituted for the French polygonal chevet. Typically English as well was the multiplication in the number of vaulting ribs, some purely decorative.

Early and High Gothic Sculpture

Like its Romanesque antecedents, Gothic sculpture was

The Cathedral of Siena (c.1226–1380), like other structures of central and southern Italy, incorporates Gothic elements in a strongly Mediterranean design. The heavy walls and flat roof, requiring no buttresses, are given horizontal emphasis by the alternating white and black marble. The campanile, domed crossing, and relatively few windows further accentuate Romanesque traditions.

at first predominantly an architectural adornment on church portals. It can also be said to have originated at Saint-Denis, in the triple portals of the west facade, consecrated in 1140, but at Saint-Denis the sculpture was still overwhelmingly Romanesque in character. In the tympanum of the west portals of Chartres (about 1155; they survive from the older cathedral), the Romanesque theme of the Apocalyptic Christ surrounded by symbols of the four Evangelists was reinterpreted in boldly conceived plastic forms, while a new human quality pervaded the benign figure of the blessing Savior. The major innovation of this Proto-Gothic style was the so-called statue-columns in the lateral embrasures of the portal. Eventually the statue-column led to the freestanding monumental statue, a form of sculpture hitherto unknown in the Middle Ages.

The west portals of Chartres inspired a host of similar portals with statue-columns in France and also gave rise to one of the outstanding creations of medieval Spain—the sculptural ensemble of the cathedral at Santiago da Compostela, appropriately known as the Pórtico de la Gloria (1168–88). In the 1180s, however, in northern Europe as well as in England, a more relaxed period in all the arts began; the Romanesque figure style was replaced by a feeling of grace, sinuosity, and freedom of movement. The classical quality of this phase of Gothic sculpture is clearly seen in the group of the *Visitation*, of about 1230, on the west central portal of Reims cathedral.

It was in Germany that Gothic statuary achieved its fullest plastic expression. The *Bamberg Rider* (c.1240) was the first truly monumental equestrian statue of the later Middle Ages. Although the identity of the regal horseman remains unknown, no other work so impressively embodies the chivalrous ideal of the medieval ruler.

The stylistic evolution of Gothic sculpture reflected the growing intensification of the cult of the Virgin Mary. In the 1170s, for the first time on a cathedral portal, her death, her assumption, and her crowning by Christ in Heaven are represented on the tympanum of the main doorway of the Cathedral of Senlis near Paris. From then on a coronation portal was included among the doorways of the major Gothic cathedrals. A new type of cult statue of the Virgin, standing and holding the Christ Child, was introduced between 1215 and 1220 on the central pier of the coronation portal on the west facade of Notre Dame de Paris.

Decorative Arts

In Paris during the reign of Louis IX the decorative arts tended to emulate the arts of the churches. In the 1260s the large metal shrines, or reliquaries (see RELIQUARY), of the saints assumed the aspect of diminutive Rayonnant churches, and the decorative gables surmounting the traceried roses of the windows on the exterior of the Sainte-Chapelle were copied in the miniatures of the *Psalter of Louis IX* (1253–70; Bibliothèque Nationale, Paris). From this same period the delicate ivory of the *Virgin with the Christ Child* (c.1260; Louvre, Paris) from

Jamb statues (c.1225–45) from the west portal of Reims Cathedral, the Annunciation *(left) and the earlier* Visitation *(right), illustrate the change in Gothic sculpture from the stiff* Visitation *figures to the graceful smiling angel in the* Annunciation.

The Virgin of Paris, early-13th-century sculpture from the coronation portal of Notre Dame, embodies the mannered elegance characteristic of the late High Gothic.

The German statue Bamberg Rider (c.1230–40), the earliest surviving equestrian statue since those of classical Rome, transforms the knightly ideal seen in French sculpture into an intensely expressive and realistic style.

the Sainte-Chapelle was directly inspired by a large statue formerly on one of the portals of the chapel, now preserved in a modern Parisian church.

The expressionistic tendencies in Germany resulted in the creation of devotional works of extraordinary pathos. In about 1300 the misnamed Plague Crosses of polychromed wood displayed the emaciated, broken body of the Savior as in the *Forked Cross* (c.1304; Santa Maria im Kapitol) in Cologne. A new type of the mourning Virgin, seated and holding the dead body of Christ across her lap—the so-called *Pietà*—was given its most harrowing evocation.

In Parisian ILLUMINATED MANUSCRIPTS, as illustrated in a page from the *Belleville Breviary* (1323–26; Bibliothèque Nationale, Paris; MS Lat. 10488), decorated by Jean Pucelle in the 1320s, the lettering, the vignette at the beginning of the text, the vine borders with their butterflies and other creatures, and the little scenes at the bottom of the page all contribute to a totally integrated effect that established an enduring precedent for later illuminators. More significant for the future, however, was the rendering of the little barrel-vaulted room in the vignette. Here Pucelle used the new art of linear PERSPECTIVE borrowed from the contemporaneous illusionistic painting (see ILLUSIONISM) of the Italian Proto-Renaissance.

Late Gothic Period

Although Paris had been the leading artistic center of northern Europe since the 1230s, the ravages of the Black Death and the outbreak of the Hundred Years' War in the middle of the 14th century drastically changed the situation. Paris became only one among several artistic centers; the most talented artists were imported from French and Belgian Flanders.

The International Style. As a result of this dissemination of artistic currents a new pictorial style emerged in which Gothic elements were combined with the developing illusionistic art of the Italian painters. This "International Style" in art has sometimes been described as Gothic. In this context, however, the term can only be understood as a qualitative adjective, because by definition illusionistic painting lies outside the medieval artistic conceptions of the Gothic period. Gothic sculpture remained unaffected by the Italian Renaissance. In Paris around 1387 the lifelike figures of Charles V and his queen (Louvre, Paris) from the Hospice Chapel of the Quinze-Vingts herald the revival of the standing-portrait statue, a form of sculpture unknown in the West after late Roman times.

Late Gothic Sculpture. The most momentous works were those produced for Philip the Bold, duke of Burgundy, by the Flemish sculptor Claus SLUTER, whose art culminates in the series of prophets surrounding the so-called *Well of Moses*, created between 1395 and 1404 at the Chartreuse de Champmol in Dijon. Breaking away entirely from the soft, pliant aristocratic types current in the 14th century, Sluter conceived his prophets in terms of rugged Flemish patriarchs. In the Moses he emphasized enormous breadth in the voluminous folds of the cape, and in the bald-headed Isaiah he created a highly individualized figure worthy of Donatello. The influence of Sluter expanded over much of Europe, but by 1500 the era of Gothic sculpture was drawing to its close.

Late Gothic Churches. The last phase of French Gothic architecture was the Flamboyant, so named for the flamelike quality of its intricate curvilinear decoration. Among its new decorative motifs was the acutely pointed ogee arch, formed of two double curves. The interior of the churches underwent a drastic simplification by eliminating the capitals of all the piers, which were reduced to plain masonry supports from which the moldings of the vaulting ribs gradually emerge. These features are also observable in the German churches, as in the interior of the Lorenzkirche (1439–77) in Nuremberg. Although it was already underway by the 1380s, the great flowering

Claus Sluter's figure of Moses, part of the Well of Moses (1395–1404) in the Carthusian monastery of Champmol, Dijon, represents the late-Gothic return to robust, realistic sculpture.

of Flamboyant architecture did not occur in France until the first half of the 16th century.

Never prone to imitation, the English builders devised their own Late Gothic style—the PERPENDICULAR GOTHIC STYLE—using a traceried rectangular panel as a module for both window tracery and wall decoration and even, in modified shapes, for the new type of fan vaulting that reached its apogee in the Chapel (1502–12) of Henry VII at Westminster Abbey, where it is combined with gravity-defying pendentives.

Late Gothic Secular Buildings. Late Gothic architecture is not confined to churches. The roster of important secular buildings is almost endless. In Belgium the series of civic halls began very early with the huge belfried Cloth Hall (1304–80; destroyed 1915) of Ypres and continued to the apogee of Late Gothic, the Hôtel de Ville (1448–63) of Louvain. In France the civic buildings culminated in the vast Flamboyant Gothic Palais de Justice (1499; damaged 1944) at Rouen. In the earlier periods the austere castles had been little affected by developments in ecclesiastical architecture, but in the 1380s the grim fortresses began to be transformed into pleasure palaces.

The 15th-century castellated House of Jacques Coeur (1443–51) at Bourges is the grandest of the many Late Gothic town mansions, including the elegant Hôtel de

This full-page illumination from the Psalter of Paris (c. 1223), produced during a period of flourishing stained-glass design, reflects the influence of this art in its heavy lines and dominant hues of red, blue, and green. (Bibliothèque de l'Arsenal, Paris.)

(Left) The intricate fan vaults of King Henry VII's chapel (1502–12), Westminster Abbey, are some of the most elaborate extensions of Gothic stone tracery produced in the English Perpendicular style.

Cluny (1485) in Paris, now appropriately transformed into a museum for the arts of the Middle Ages. All over France, from Josselin (early 16th century) in Brittany to Amboise (1483–1501) and BLOIS (1498–1515) on the Loire, new châteaux were being erected in the Flamboyant style. Late Gothic secular architecture also developed its own vernacular, from the Venetian Gothic of the Ca d'Oro (Golden House; c.1430) and the Doge's Palace (1424–1529) to the Tudor Gothic of HAMPTON COURT (1515–36) on the Thames and the Collegiate Gothic of Oxford and Cambridge (15th and 16th centuries). The GOTHIC REVIVAL brought a great resurgence in the 19th century.

See also: ARCHITECTURE; ART; CATHEDRALS AND CHURCHES; ENGLISH ART AND ARCHITECTURE; FLEMISH ART AND ARCHITECTURE; FRENCH ART AND ARCHITECTURE; GERMAN ART AND ARCHITECTURE; ITALIAN ART AND ARCHITECTURE; MONASTIC ART AND ARCHITECTURE; PAINTING; SCANDINAVIAN ART AND ARCHITECTURE; SCULPTURE; SPANISH ART AND ARCHITECTURE.

Gothic Revival The Gothic Revival style of architecture, which dominated much of the building activity of mid-19th-century Europe and the United States, originated in the mid-18th-century vogue for "gothick" architectural fantasies. Essentially a part of the romantic movement, this dilettante preference for Gothic picturesqueness, epitomized by Horace WALPOLE's villa at Strawberry Hill (1770), outside London, was transformed in the 1830s into a serious moral crusade for the supposedly superior Christian virtues represented by medieval Gothic art and architecture. The standard-bearers of the ideological phase of the Gothic Revival were John RUSKIN and Augustus PUGIN, whose book Contrasts (1836) became the manifesto of the movement.

Significantly, the building in which the revivalists' as-

The intricate decoration and soaring design of the Albert Memorial (1864–72; London) exemplifies Gothic Revival architecture. The Albert Memorial was created by Sir George Gilbert Scott, a leading figure of the movement.

pirations were first embodied was also England's foremost national monument—the new Houses of Parliament, or WESTMINSTER PALACE, designed in 1836 by Sir Charles BARRY with Pugin's assistance. This immense project included all the interior furnishings and decoration. The enthusiasm engendered by the Houses of Parliament elicited a tremendous spate of neo-Gothic building activity, particularly by Sir George Gilbert SCOTT, who designed 39 cathedrals and minsters, in addition to numerous smaller buildings in the Gothic mold, including the Albert Memorial (1864–72) in London.

In Germany, the centerpiece of the revival was the completion of Cologne Cathedral (1842–80). In the United States, where the new architectural vogue was enthusiastically received, New York City alone possesses three important early landmarks of the revival: Richard UP-JOHN's famous Trinity Church (1840–46), James REN-

WICK's ensemble of Grace Church and its parish buildings (1843–46), and Renwick's ambitious design for SAINT PATRICK'S CATHEDRAL (1858–79).

The revival as a coherent movement had largely spent itself by the late 19th century, its momentum slowed by the fantastic cost of medieval-type craftsmanship, and its aesthetic program undermined by more forward-looking artistic movements.

Gothic romance The earliest Gothic romance, a class of novel dealing in the mysterious and supernatural, was Horace WALPOLE's *Castle of Otranto* (1764). Reacting against the literalism and confined domesticity of Samuel RICHARDSON, Walpole indulged a contemporary taste for the "Gothic," which for the 18th-century reader conjured up a medieval world of barbarous passions enacted in melodramatic settings of ruined castles, ancient monasteries, and wild landscapes. Within a plot designed for suspense, a delicate feminine sensibility is subjected to the onslaught of elemental forces of good and evil. Sanity and chastity are constantly threatened, and over all looms the suggestion that evil and irrationality will destroy civilization. Walpole's invention, inspired by a general awakening of interest in the past, brought the subconscious within the range of the novel and implicitly challenged the rational confidence of his time (see ROMANTICISM).

The Gothic romance flourished in its original form until 1820 and produced, besides many minor novelists, three writers of considerable stature. Ann RADCLIFFE's *Mysteries of Udolpho* (1794) typifies one style of gothic narrative in which a persecuted heroine survives numerous assaults to arrive at last at a happy ending in the arms of a handsome young man. Matthew Gregory LEWIS added a stronger content of terror in *The Monk* (1796), but the finest work in this genre was *Melmoth the Wanderer* (1820), a Faustian novel by the Irish clergyman Charles Robert Maturin. Other notable Gothic works include William BECKFORD's *Vathek* (1786), William GODWIN's *Caleb Williams* (1794), Mary SHELLEY's *FRANKENSTEIN* (1818), and the Waverley novels of Sir Walter SCOTT.

The Gothic strain also appears in the work of Nathaniel HAWTHORNE, Edgar Allan POE, and Henry JAMES, as well as in that of contemporary writers such as John HAWKES. The "Gothic" paperback novels popular since the 1970s owe much to the plots devised by the English novelist Daphne DU MAURIER.

Goths The Goths were a GERMANIC PEOPLE who probably migrated from southern Scandinavia sometime before the time of Christ. By the 3d century the Goths had settled in the areas around the Black Sea and were staging periodic raids on Roman territory. Those who settled in the area of the modern Ukraine came to be known as Ostrogoths. Those who settled in the region of the Danube were called Visigoths.

During the 4th century the Visigoths coexisted peacefully with the Romans, farming and trading agricultural products and slaves for luxury goods. The Visigoths adopted many elements of Roman culture. Some of them became literate in Latin. In the middle of the century substantial numbers of the Visigoths accepted ARIANISM.

The Huns' drive westward pushed the Visigoths into territory controlled by the Roman Empire. The resulting conflict culminated in a great Visigothic victory at Adrianople in 378 and led to an alliance with the empire. But the Visigoths were fickle allies; under ALARIC I they sacked Rome in 410 and in 418 settled in Aquitaine in southwestern France. During the last half of the 5th century the Visigoths expanded their control to Spain, but in 507–08 the Franks under CLOVIS drove them from most of Aquitaine.

The Visigoths in Spain conquered (585) the Suevi and drove out (629) the Byzantines. In 589, King Reccared converted the Visigoths to orthodox Christianity, and King Reccesvinth tried (c.654) to unite the various inhabitants of Spain under a single law (see GERMANIC LAW). Social, political, religious, and regional differences in Visigothic Spain, however, led to frequent regicide and to civil war. Spain came under the domination of the Muslims in 711.

Conquered (c.370) by the Huns, the Ostrogoths moved west, led by THEODORIC THE GREAT, who became king of Italy (493–526). He was succeeded by his daughter Amalasuntha, who was murdered in 535 by her husband and co-ruler, Theodahad. Her allies, the Byzantines, soon attacked Italy, but the Ostrogoth forces held out until 553. The Byzantines, and later the LOMBARDS, took control of Italy.

Gotland [gaht'-luhnd] Gotland, the largest island (3,023 km²/1,167 mi²) in the Baltic Sea, lies 80 km (50 mi) off the Swedish coast. Together with the smaller islands of Fårön, Gotska Sandön, and Karlsö, it constitutes a county of Sweden. The island has a population of 56,383 (1989 est.), and Visby is the administrative center. Gotland is a low, undulating limestone plateau, where sugar beets, cereals, and sheep are raised. Tourism, fishing, and stone quarrying are important.

Settled during the Stone Age, Gotland early developed extensive trade with the people of northern Europe. By the 12th century Visby was an important town of the Hanseatic League. Beginning in 1361, when Denmark captured it, control of Gotland was disputed by several nations. Trade routes shifted, however, and by the time Sweden gained lasting control in 1645, it was impoverished.

Gottfried von Strassburg [gawt'-freet fuhn shtrahs' boork] Gottfried von Strassburg, c.1170–c.1215, was a medieval German poet whose incomplete version of the TRISTAN AND ISOLDE legend, *Tristan* (c.1210), was one of the most influential poems of the period. It is particularly significant for the mystically tinged conception of love it advances, which marks a departure from the troubadours' conception of courtly love. Gottfried's idealization of Tristan's love is conveyed sometimes by explicit statement, sometimes by subtle modification of his immediate source, Thomas of Britain. Thus the lovers' retreat in the forest becomes an idyllic temple of love from which the rightful husband is allegorically and practically excluded. This scene is the culmination of Gottfried's decorative yet lucid style, which became a model for authors of the next generation.

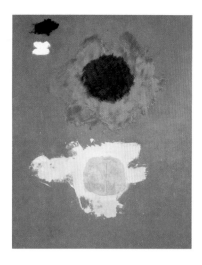

Adolph Gottlieb was a leading figure of American abstract expressionism when he painted Etendue Rouge (1960). (Sydney Janis Gallery, New York City.)

Gottheil, Gustav [gaht'-hyl, gus'-tahv] Gustav Gottheil, b. Prussia, May 28, 1827, d. Apr. 15, 1903, was a leader of American Reform Judaism. Educated in Berlin and Halle, he served as rabbi in Manchester, England, and lectured at the university there from 1860 to 1873. Upon invitation from Temple Emanu-El in New York City, Gottheil immigrated to the United States in 1873 and served as senior rabbi of that synagogue until 1899. He prepared (1886) the first Jewish hymnbook in the United States, founded the Association of Eastern Rabbis, helped establish the Jewish Publication Society of America, and was one of the founders of the Federation of American Zionists, later known as the Zionist Organization of America.

Göttingen [gurt'-ing-en] Göttingen, a city in central Germany in Lower Saxony state, is situated along the Leine River. Its population is 132,454 (1984 est.). Manufactures include precision instruments, pharmaceuticals, electrical equipment, and processed foods. The University of Göttingen (1737) and research institutes of the Max Planck Scientific Society are there. Among Göttingen's many historic landmarks are the Rathaus, or town hall, and the Church of Saint John, both dating from the 14th century, as well as medieval fortifications.

By 953 a village called Gutingi existed on the site. In the 14th century Göttingen joined the Hanseatic League and prospered as a trade center. During the Reformation, Göttingen accepted Protestantism and suffered heavy damage during the ensuing religious wars of the 16th century. The establishment of the university during the 18th century ushered in a new growth period.

Gottlieb, Adolph [gaht'-leeb] Adolph Gottlieb, b. New York City, Mar. 4, 1903, d. Mar. 4, 1974, was a prominent member of the abstract expressionist group of artists (see ABSTRACT EXPRESSIONISM). After studying painting in New York City with John Sloan and Robert Henri, and in Europe, Gottlieb exhibited regularly in the 1930s with the avant-garde artists Ilya Bolotowsky and Mark Rothko. From 1941 to 1951, Gottlieb painted several "pictographs"—monochromatic paintings composed of abstract symbols arranged on a grid understructure. In the early 1950s he explored the relationship between floating forms and dense masses in a series of imaginary landscapes. Gottlieb's interest in object placement and his growing emphasis on expressive color led to his "Burst" paintings. In Burst (1957; Collection of Ben

Heller), he reduced the imagery to two shapes on a white ground, without reference to the canvas edge. Although extremely large, Gottlieb's "Burst" paintings are poetic and intimate works that present a subtle interplay of colors, shapes, and density.

Gottschalk, Louis Moreau [gaht'-shawk] Louis Moreau Gottschalk, b. New Orleans, May 8, 1829, d. Dec. 18, 1869, was a celebrated American composer, pianist, and conductor. His German-English father and French mother were well educated and socially prominent. At the age of 12 Gottschalk was sent to study in Paris, where he made his professional debut as a pianist in 1849. He embarked on concert tours of France and Switzerland (1850) and Spain (1851–52), winning great acclaim both for performance and composition. He made his American debut in New York in 1853, then conducted his orchestral works at mammoth music festivals. He spent the years 1856–62 wandering about the Caribbean islands. In 1865 he performed in California, after which he lived and performed for a few years in South America. An attack of yellow fever caused his death in Rio de Janeiro at the height of his fame.

Gottschalk's character pieces for piano blend Creole and American Negro idioms. Many of his orchestral works are inspired by Spanish subject matter. Long neglected, Gottschalk's music has been revived in recent years.

Gottwald, Klement [gawt'-vahlt, klay'-ment] Klement Gottwald, b. Nov. 23, 1896, d. Mar. 14, 1953, was the Czech Communist leader who established Czechoslovakia's Communist regime in 1948. A Communist party member from 1921 and party secretary from 1929, he spent the years of World War II in the USSR. He returned to Prague to become deputy premier (1945) and then premier (July 1946) in the postwar coalition government of Eduard BENEŠ. On June 14, 1948, after the forced resignation of Beneš, Gottwald became president of the now de facto single-party state. He was responsible for a major purge of Communist party members, including Rudolf Slánský, the party's secretary general, who was executed with ten others in November 1952.

gouache [goo-ahsh'] Gouache is paint made from opaque water color but with the addition of white pigment and a higher proportion of binder, such as gum arabic. The presence of a larger quantity of vehicle (the liquid in which pigments are mixed) creates the opaque effect, while the white pigment produces the characteristic brilliant, light-reflecting quality, as opposed to the luminosity of watercolors. Gouache paintings are commonly executed on paper in a spontaneous, *alla prima* manner. The technique has frequently been used for making preliminary studies for large oil paintings.

Goujon, Jean [goo-zhohn'] Jean Goujon, c.1510–c.1568, was the most accomplished sculptor of the French Renaissance. His first documented work, the Corinthian columns of the organ loft in the Church of Saint Maclou, Rouen (1541), demonstrate that Goujon had a profound knowledge of classical architecture and may have been trained as an architect. In 1544 he collaborated with Pierre Lescot on the rood screen of Saint Germain l'Auxerrois, Paris. The central panel, a Pietà (Louvre, Paris), is an entirely personal synthesis of classical Renaissance motifs. In mid-century he executed his finest work, including the sculptures for the *Fountain of the Innocents* (1547–49; Louvre, Paris), which are figures carved in shallow relief within an architectural framework. Goujon's depictions of human figures in motion recall classical Greek sculpture.

Goulart, João [goo-lahr', zhwow] João Belchior Marques Goulart, b. Mar. 1, 1918, d. Dec. 6, 1976, was president of Brazil from 1961 to 1964. A protégé of Getúlio Dornelles VARGAS, Goulart served (1953–54) as Vargas's minister of labor, industry, and commerce and was vice-president (1956–61), first under Juscelino KUBITSCHEK and then under Jânio Quadros. After Quadros's resignation in August 1961, Goulart became president. His reputed Communist leanings led the military to insist on restricting his presidential powers, but a plebiscite in 1963 restored them. Goulart's administration was marked by inflation and labor unrest. He was ousted by a military coup in April 1964.

Gould, Chester The American cartoonist Chester Gould, b. Pawnee, Okla., Nov. 20, 1900, d. May 11, 1985, helped introduce the adventure comic strip by creating *Dick Tracy* in 1931. The strip, which first appeared in the *Chicago Tribune* and was later widely syndicated, portrays explicit violence but always stresses that crime does not pay. Gould's characters, such as Pruneface, B.

O. Plenty, and Gravel Gertie, are highly imaginative. The strip's hero, Dick Tracy, is thought to have been inspired by J. Edgar Hoover.

Gould, Glenn The brilliant Canadian pianist Glenn Gould, b. Toronto, Sept. 25, 1932, d. Oct. 4, 1982, retired from concertizing at the peak of his success in 1964. He made his professional debut (1946) as soloist with the Toronto Symphony. In 1955 he gave his first U.S. recitals in Washington, D.C., and New York City, and in 1957 he made his European debut in Berlin. Gould was the first North American pianist invited (1957) by the Soviet government to perform in the USSR. After leaving the concert stage, he concentrated on making recordings, which he considered a distinct art form. Often cited for his creative, if not always popular, interpretations, Gould was best known for his playing of J. S. Bach.

Gould, Gordon Gordon Gould, b. New York City, July 17, 1920, is credited with conceptualizing the LASER in 1957. Independent of Gould, Charles Hard TOWNES realized the same idea in 1958. Because Gould had not immediately applied for patents (as Townes had), Townes was long given credit for the idea. Gould finally won laser patents in 1977, 1979, and 1987.

Gould, Jay The railroad builder and speculator Jay Gould, b. Roxbury, N.Y., May 27, 1836, d. Dec. 2, 1892, was one of the most successful and notorious "robber barons" of the 19th century. He was the son of a poor farmer and went to work early in his life. At age 21, with savings of $5,000, he invested in the leather business and began speculating in railroad stocks. By age 31 he was a director of the Erie Railroad. With Daniel DREW and James FISK he waged the "Erie war" to prevent Cornelius Vanderbilt (see VANDERBILT family) from gaining control of the railroad. They issued illegal stock and bribed state legislators, making fortunes in the process. Gould became president of the Erie and continued to speculate in its stock. In 1869, Gould and Fisk almost cornered the gold market until the U.S. Treasury released some of its own gold stocks, leading to the BLACK FRIDAY panic of Sept. 24, 1869. The resulting public indignation forced Gould to resign (1872) as director of the Erie.

Gould, Morton The American pianist, composer, and conductor Morton Gould, b. Richmond Hill, N.Y., Dec. 10, 1913, blends popular and serious music in compositions that emphasize American themes. Much of Gould's professional experience has been in radio: he conducted (1934–43) a program of contemporary American music on station WOR, and he was a staff musician and conductor at NBC and CBS. In 1965 he was engaged by Radio City Music Hall as composer and conductor. Among his compositions are scores for Broadway musicals, films, ballets (including *Fall River Legend*), and symphonic works with American themes such as *Symphony of Spirituals* and *Cowboy Rhapsody*.

Gould, Stephen Jay

American paleontologist Stephen Jay Gould, b. New York City, Sept. 10, 1941, is an evolutionary theorist and a writer of popular works on natural history and the role of science in society. Obtaining his Ph.D. from Columbia University in 1967, Gould joined and has remained on the staff of Harvard University. With others, he has advanced the debated concept that major evolutionary changes take place in sudden bursts (see EVOLUTION). Among his award-winning books are *The Panda's Thumb* (1980) and *The Mismeasure of Man* (1981); the latter traces the historical development and social misuse of supposed intelligence-measuring techniques.

Gounod, Charles

[goo-noh'] Charles François Gounod, b. Paris, June 17, 1818, d. Oct. 18, 1893, was the composer of *Faust*, one of the most popular operas in the repertoire. Gounod's father was a painter, his mother a pianist. Gounod entered (1836) the Paris Conservatory, won (1839) the Prix de Rome, and spent two and a half years in Italy, where he studied church music and composed a mass. From 1852 to 1860 he was director of the choral society Orphéon, for which he wrote choral music.

The premiere of *Faust* at the Théâtre-Lyrique in Paris in 1859 was only moderately successful. Ten years later, however, after Gounod had made revisions in the score and added a ballet, the work was produced at the Paris Opera to acclaim. Since then *Faust* has been performed in virtually every opera house in the world. Gounod's operas *Roméo et Juliette* (1867) and *Mireille* (1864) are also frequently performed; his 10 other operas (one incomplete) were unsuccessful. His most popular short piece is his "Ave Maria"; for its accompaniment he used a keyboard prelude by Johann Sebastian Bach—thus it is also known as the Bach-Gounod "Ave Maria." (Gounod referred to it as a prank and was said to have deplored its popularity.) Also popular is the whimsical *Funeral March of a Marionette*. Gounod had a deep understanding of the voice and was a skillful orchestrator. His works include 23 masses, 6 oratorios (including *The Redemption*), 2 symphonies, 3 string quartets, piano pieces, and incidental music for plays.

Charles Gounod, a 19th-century French composer, achieved fame with his lyrical opera Faust, *first performed in 1859. Although Gounod was best known for his popular operas, he also wrote numerous sacred compositions.*

---

gourd

[gohrd] Gourds are a large and diverse group of plants belonging to the family Cucurbitaceae and related to pumpkin and squash. They are grown for their fruits, which occur in a great variety of sizes, shapes, and colors. Many gourds are raised as ornamentals, and the hard shells of some are used for making utensils such as dippers. The yellow-flowered gourd, *Cucurbita pepo*, the most common American type, produces small, smooth or knobby fruits in several shapes and colors. Bottle gourds, genus *Lagenaria*, may reach a length of 1.5 m (5 ft) and are used in India as sounding boxes for certain musical instruments. Gourds of the genus *Luffa* have a spongelike interior that, when dried, can be used as a dishcloth. Some gourds are edible.

Gourds are used primarily for decoration, although some hard-shelled varieties are turned into drinking cups. Their long vines bear broad palmate leaves and yellow flowers. They are harvested in autumn and waxed or varnished for preservation.

---

gout

[gowt] Gout is a disease marked by recurrent acute attacks of ARTHRITIS, the result of deposits of monosodium-urate crystals around the joints and tendons. These crystals occur when abnormally high amounts of uric acid are present in the body (hyperuricemia). Hyperuricemia distinguishes gout from other forms of arthritis because more than 95 percent of persons with gout are hyperuricemic; it is not, however, the sole cause.

Almost all gouty patients are men, usually over 30 years old. Primary gout appears to involve a heredity factor. A genetically sex-linked defect in purine metabolism leads to increased purine production, called the Lesch-Nyhan syndrome, resulting in a high uric acid concentration. Secondary gout develops as a result of other causes, such as another disease. Excessive cell breakdown, as in hemolytic anemia, results in overproduction of urate. Diuretic drugs used to treat high blood pressure can induce hyperuricemia and result in clinical gout.

Gout usually begins with pain and inflammation of a joint, often the big toe. Acute attacks are treated with the drug colchicine. One treatment is aimed at preventing crystal deposits of urate. Excretion of urate by the kidney is aided by uricosuric drugs along with high fluid intake, which increases the urine output.

---

government   Government comprises the set of legal and political institutions that regulate the relationships among members of a society and between the society and outsiders. These institutions have the authority to make decisions for the society on policies affecting the maintenance of order and the achievement of certain societal goals. This article provides an overview of the types of government, the ways authority can be distributed, the divisions of government, and the functions of government. Separate articles deal with the origins and development of the concept of the STATE, the theoretical and practical development of REPRESENTATION, LAW, and the study of government (see POLITICAL SCIENCE).

The power of a government over its own citizens varies, depending on the degree to which it is free of limitations and restraints. The power of a government abroad also varies, depending on the human and material resources with which it can support its FOREIGN POLICY. Governments range in size and scope from clans, tribes, and the shires of early times to the superpowers and international governments of today. Within the modern nation-state, government operates at many different levels, ranging from villages to cities, counties, provinces, and states.

Types of Government

ARISTOTLE, a Greek political philosopher of the 3d century BC, distinguished three principal kinds of government: MONARCHY, ARISTOCRACY, and polity (a kind of enlightened DEMOCRACY). The differences among them chiefly concerned whether power was held by one, by a few, or by many. Aristotle thought that the selfish abuse of power caused each type to become perverted, respectively, into tyranny, OLIGARCHY, and a lower form of democracy characterized by mob rule. Monarchy tended to become tyrannical because it vested authority in a single ruler. Aristocracy, a government based on birth and privilege, in which the rulers governed for the good of the whole society, tended to become oligarchy as a consequence of restricting political power to a special social and economic class; only a few members of the class would have enough drive and ability to acquire the power to govern. The polity, likewise, would deteriorate into ochlocracy, or mob rule, if the citizens pursued only their selfish interests.

Modern writers have developed a variety of schemes for classifying governments, based on the nature of the ruling class, the economic system, the government's political institutions, the principles of authority, the acquisition and exercise of power, and other factors. Some influential writers on government include Thomas HOBBES, Baron de MONTESQUIEU, Jean Jacques ROUSSEAU, Karl MARX, Gaetano MOSCA, Vilfredo PARETO, and the sociologist Max WEBER.

Monarchy. The most common form of government from medieval times to the early part of the 20th century was monarchy, or rule by a hereditary king or queen. Monarchy passed through three basic stages, varying according to the nation and the political and economic climate. The first stage was that of the absolute monarch, in which some kings proclaimed that God had given them the DIVINE RIGHT to rule.

Limited monarchy was the second stage. Kings depended on the support of the most powerful members of the nobility to retain their thrones. In England and some other Western European countries the nobility placed limits on the power of the ruler to govern. Threatened with the loss of political and financial support, even the strongest kings and emperors had to accept a system of laws that protected the rights and privileges of powerful social and economic classes.

The third stage in the evolution of monarchy was the constitutional monarchy. Present-day monarchs are nearly all symbolic rather than actual rulers of their countries. In such monarchies as Great Britain, the Netherlands, and Sweden, governing power is now in the hands of the national parliaments.

Constitutional Government. Today most governments derive their legitimacy from national CONSTITUTIONS that provide a legal framework for their rule and specify how power is to be exercised and controlled. Even one-party states have found it necessary to establish formal constitutions. In democratic countries the constitution can be amended or replaced. In authoritarian one-party systems, however, all political power, including that of revising the constitution, resides with the leaders of the party. The constitution may thus be only a paper facade, and in order to understand how the country is governed one must examine the actual political process.

Democracy. Representative government in the modern world is based not only on a constitution that provides for it but on the actual rule of law—the assurance that provisions of the constitution will be enforced. It requires that citizens be free to organize competing POLITICAL PARTIES, engage in POLITICAL CAMPAIGNS, and hold ELECTIONS according to agreed-upon rules. Democratic governments vary in structure. Two common forms are the parliamentary and the presidential. In the parliamentary form of government, as in Australia, Britain, Canada, and India, all political power is concentrated in the parliament or LEGISLATURE. The prime minister or premier and the officers of the cabinet are members of the parliament. They continue in office only as long as parliament supports—or has "confidence" in—their policies. In the presidential form of government, as in France and the United States, the voters elect a powerful chief executive who is independent of the legislature but whose actions are delimited by constitutional and other legal restraints.

Dictatorship. As a form of government, DICTATORSHIP is principally a 20th-century phenomenon. The dictator, often a military leader, concentrates political power in himself or herself and his or her clique. There is no effective rule of law. The regime may or may not have a distinctive political IDEOLOGY and may or may not allow token opposition. The primary function of a dictatorship is to maintain control of all governmental operations.

The totalitarian dictatorship, as in Nazi Germany or Communist China, is much more thoroughgoing. It seeks to control all aspects of national life, including the beliefs and attitudes of its people. It has a set of ideas that everyone is expected to embrace, such as revolutionary MARXISM or counterrevolutionary FASCISM.

Distributions of Authority

Effective government in any form requires a workable method for distributing authority within the country. The larger and more diverse the jurisdiction of the government, the stronger the tendency toward a federal system in which authority is "layered" or distributed among different levels, as in the United States or Canada. In countries with a relatively homogeneous population and with a common tradition, language, and sense of national history, the central governments may not be federal but unitary—that is, they may retain most of the administrative power at the center, as in France. Loosely allied autonomous states sometimes join together to create a type of central government known as a confederation, in which the central government exists only at the pleasure of the sovereign members—as in the United States under the ARTICLES OF CONFEDERATION of 1781.

Federal Systems. The United States and India with their state governments and Canada and China with their provincial governments are examples of workable federal systems in large nations with very diverse populations. Other federal states include Argentina, Australia, Brazil, Czechoslovakia, Mexico, Nigeria, and Germany. The national governments of these countries are clearly more powerful than those of their subdivisions, even though the constitutions delegate many powers and responsibilities to the subnational units. In certain prescribed policy areas a state government may have a high degree of autonomy. In the United States, for example, state legislatures pass laws having to do with state affairs, state administrators carry them out, and state judiciaries interpret them. Federal systems also include autonomous local governments, such as county governments and MUNICIPAL GOVERNMENTS—in cities, boroughs, townships, and villages.

The layers of government in a federal system may not be clearly defined in practice. Often the different levels compete for control of functions and programs. In the United States and other countries the tendency over the years has been for the national government to become much more involved in areas that once were the exclusive domain of state or regional governments. Cooperative interaction between state and federal governments has become common, leading to a complex, interlocking relationship. In the United States, for example, national and state governments both appropriate funds for cities, with the consequence that the affairs of a large city such as New York or Chicago are partly determined by political decisions made in the national capital at Washington, D.C., and in the state capital at Albany or Springfield.

Unitary States. In unitary states the national government performs all the governmental functions. Subnational national units administer matters within their jurisdiction, but their powers are set and delegated by the national authority. The national government retains the police power—the inherent power of a government to provide for the health, safety, and welfare of its citizens. The power to tax also rests almost entirely with the national government. Likewise, all significant laws are national in scope.

Most nations are unitary states, but their institutions and processes may differ markedly. Great Britain, for example, is considered a unitary system, yet a certain degree of regional autonomy exists in Northern Ireland, Scotland, and Wales, and local county governments perform certain fairly autonomous functions. In France, however, strict control over the administrative territorial subdivisions called *départements* and *arrondissements* is exercised by the national government.

Confederations. Confederation produces the weakest central government. Member states in a confederation retain their sovereignty, delegating to the central government only those powers which are essential for its maintenance. The individual states jealously guard their power to tax and to make their own laws. The central government serves as a coordinating instrument to protect the interests of all its members. It also represents the confederation in dealings with outside governments, but its actions are subject to the review and approval of the confederated states. The weakness of the confederate form of government led the United States to abandon that system in 1789 after only eight years, although the South attempted to adopt such a system during the U.S. Civil War (see CONFEDERATE STATES OF AMERICA). Confederations, however, have also served other nations—Germany and Switzerland, for example—as a preliminary step toward a more unified government. No modern nation-state is organized along confederate lines.

Divisions of Government

Various political thinkers have distinguished types of government activity. Montesquieu was the first, however, to urge the creation of three separate institutions or divisions of government—the executive, legislative, and judicial—a distinction that became common in almost all modern constitutions. Some governmental structures, notably the United States, are based on the principle of SEPARATION OF POWERS. Executive, legislative, and judicial powers are divided into three branches of government, creating a system of checks and balances among them. This separation of powers has helped to protect citizens from arbitrary and capricious actions on the part of any of the three branches. It has also diminished the influence of SPECIAL-INTEREST GROUPS, or factions, over any one branch of government or over the government as a whole.

Not all states, of course, have such clear divisions of government, nor do divisions necessarily guarantee personal liberties. Parliamentary democratic systems, for example, tend to merge legislative and executive functions yet control the exercise of power by constitutional methods of sharing it. Authoritarian states may, however, be constitutionally bound to have separate organs of government yet actually concentrate power in the executive.

Functions of Government

Maintenance of Authority. One of the principal functions of government is to remain in power. Governments do not relinquish their authority unless compelled to do so. Every government strives to increase its legitimacy in the eyes of the people. It may identify itself with ancient traditions, with hope for the future, or with fear of a common enemy. Some governments employ repression, never relaxing their vigils against real or imagined opponents. Even democracies, when threatened, are likely to engage in a search for subversives and "enemies of the people."

When a regime draws its main support from a privileged class or group that decreases in numbers and strength, when a government becomes ineffective, or when a society's consensus on the principles and goals of government evaporates, a government tends to lose authority. The French monarchy in the 18th century and the Russian monarchy in the 20th were based on aristocracies that had lost much of their legitimacy in the eyes of the people. Eventually they were unable to enforce their laws, and REVOLUTIONS swept them from power. The Weimar Republic of Germany and France's Third and Fourth republics lost authority largely because of their ineffectiveness. Governments tend, therefore, to foster widespread ideological commitment to the nation through patriotic ceremonies, propaganda, and civic education; they employ armed forces and intelligence-gathering organizations for national defense; they maintain police and prison systems to ensure domestic order; and they undertake the administration of supervisory, regulatory, and entrepreneurial functions to carry out national goals by establishing various bureaucracies to handle the complexities of each function.

Administration. All governments recognize the principle that the public must be protected and served. The citizen, in effect, surrenders a degree of individual sovereignty to the government in return for protection of life and property and the delivery of essential services. Governments supervise the resolution of conflicting interests, the workings of the political process, the enforcement of laws and rights, and the monitoring of national income (see INCOME, NATIONAL) and INTERNATIONAL TRADE; they regulate economic and social relationships among individuals and organizations, especially private business firms (see GOVERNMENT REGULATION); and they carry out enterprises such as production of military goods, provision of postal services, and ownership of power utilities and public works. Among the most basic services provided by government are the printing and coining of MONEY and the provision of roads, sewers, water, education, and SOCIAL AND WELFARE SERVICES. With the growth of the WELFARE STATE, governments began to provide services such as SOCIAL SECURITY and health insurance.

Federal, state, and local governments in the United States also engage directly in economic activity. They are involved in TAXATION, formulate budgets, produce and consume goods, sell electric power, lend money to farmers and exporters, and insure bank deposits.

In other countries governments intrude even farther into the workings of the economy. In Western Europe governments own and operate telephone, radio, and television services, railroads, coal mines, and aircraft companies. In some countries, such as Sweden and Great Britain, the entire health system is also run by the state. In countries with Communist governments, the state controls the entire economic life of the nation.

International Government

In modern times national governments have become increasingly involved with one another in supranational systems. The LEAGUE OF NATIONS, established in 1919, grew to include 94 members. It collapsed in World War II but was succeeded by the UNITED NATIONS (UN), which had 159 members in 1991. The UN, like the League, is a voluntary association generally without power to act unless the five permanent members of the Security Council agree. It has, however, served as a forum for international debate and a convenient meeting ground for negotiations.

Government Printing Office, United States

The Government Printing Office (GPO) was established by the U.S. Congress in 1860 to print and distribute federal government publications. These now include the CONGRESSIONAL RECORD, covering the business of Congress, and more than 25,000 publications of government agencies. The GPO prints pamphlets explaining social security and other governmental benefits, as well as publications on subjects of interest to homemakers and farmers. Lists of its publications may be obtained from the Superintendent of Documents, Government Printing Office, Washington, D.C., 20402.

---

government regulation Regulation is the practice in which governments seek to influence the behavior of individuals or organizations, especially private business firms, by imposing and enforcing legal obligations. As a method of economic intervention, regulation is intended to serve governmental goals, such as protecting the public from various harms, while leaving most business decisions to the discretion of management and the test of the market. It is a kind of halfway house between unfettered private enterprise on the one hand and public ownership or detailed ECONOMIC PLANNING on the other.

In the United States several industries have been heavily regulated by the federal government—including agriculture, banking, securities, telecommunications, radio and television broadcasting, energy, and transportation. In some cases this regulation has been reduced or was eliminated in the 1970s and '80s. Besides regulating particular industries, the federal government also regulates many or all industries with respect to certain aspects of business performance; these include wages and hours, labor relations, employment discrimination, environmental pollution, workplace safety, product safety, trade practices, and industry structure.

State governments play a role in implementing some federal regulatory programs, and states act on their own authority to regulate certain industries (such as insurance) and occupations (from electricians to bartenders to medical doctors). Finally, there is considerable regulation in the form of local ordinances, much of it concerned with building practices, health and sanitation, and land-use planning.

Government control is even more extensive in many other developed economies. Typically, outside the United States, the gas, electric-power, telephone, and railroad industries and at least one of the major television networks are publicly owned. Some countries, such as Sweden and Germany, have regulations requiring that labor representatives participate formally in corporate policy-making. In Japan, the ministry of trade and industry plays a large role in planning industrial development. In the so-called command economies of Communist countries, of course, the state owns and directly operates all of the significant enterprises.

The Controversial Role of Regulation

The proper role for government regulation has long been controversial. Under the policies of MERCANTILISM dominant in Europe in the 16th, 17th, and 18th centuries, governments attempted to control manufacturing, trade, and shipping to achieve a favorable balance of trade and increase national wealth. Mercantilist doctrines were discredited by 18th-century economists such as Adam SMITH, who proposed that governments should refrain from interfering with the market. The resulting ideology of LAISSEZ-FAIRE liberalism was dominant in Great Britain and the United States during the 19th century. Some regulation was introduced, however, and in the 20th century it was expanded greatly.

Today's liberals (unlike the bearers of that label in the 19th century) often advocate regulation to mitigate social and economic problems they associate with unregulated private enterprise. Conservatives usually oppose such plans—arguing that regulation merely diminishes freedom and makes the economy less efficient. Taking a kind of middle position, many economists argue that markets are "imperfect" and government intervention may be appropriate in several well-defined circumstances: (1) if there is a monopoly (see MONOPOLY AND COMPETITION); (2) if the cost of obtaining and using information (say, about food additives) prevents consumers or others from choosing intelligently; (3) if economic activities affect third parties (for example, by pollution); or (4) if certain goods (such as police service or local parks) are by their nature consumed collectively and hence cannot be sold successfully to individuals.

Early Regulation

Throughout American history, as the scholars Merle Fainsod and Lincoln Gordon have observed, regulation has been "initiated by particular groups to deal with specific evils as they arose, rather than inspired by any general philosophy of governmental control." The first significant regulatory programs were adopted, at the state level, to control businesses in a position to exercise arbitrary power. In Massachusetts, for example, a bank commission was created in 1838, direct supervision by the legislature having been tried and judged inadequate. The state also regulated railroads to prevent excessive rates. As in much of the U.S. regulatory experience, these Massachusetts programs generally lacked the resources and legal powers needed for effective enforcement.

The federal government first assumed a major regulatory function to deal with railroads. In the Interstate Commerce Act of 1887, Congress created the INTERSTATE COMMERCE COMMISSION (ICC) and gave it modest authority to oversee the industry. Congress was also given authority to regulate trusts and monopolies in the SHERMAN ANTI-TRUST ACT of 1890.

The ICC is an independent regulatory commission, a type of administrative agency used earlier by the states and subsequently in much federal regulation. Designed to be independent of the executive branch, such agencies are headed by a commission whose members are appointed by the president. These commissions have been given "quasi-legislative" powers to determine policy and "quasi-judicial" ones to decide cases. Besides the ICC, the principal independent regulatory commissions now in existence are the CONSUMER PRODUCT SAFETY COMMISSION (1972), the FEDERAL COMMUNICATIONS COMMISSION (1934), the Federal Reserve Board (1913; see FEDERAL RESERVE SYSTEM), the FEDERAL TRADE COMMISSION (1914), the National Labor Relations Board (1935), the NUCLEAR REGULATORY COMMISSION (1975), and the SECURITIES AND EXCHANGE COMMISSION (1934). Other regulatory programs are administered by agencies located in the executive branch, such as the Antitrust Division of the Justice Department; the FOOD AND DRUG ADMINISTRATION (1931), in the Department of Health and Human Services; the OCCUPATIONAL SAFETY AND HEALTH ADMINISTRATION (1970), in the Department of Labor; the National Highway Traffic Safety Administration, in the Department of Transportation; and the ENVIRONMENTAL PROTECTION AGENCY (1970), which is independent of any cabinet department.

Regulation and the Court

The growth of regulation occasioned a half-century of eventful debate over the interpretation of the U.S. Constitution. In 1877 the Supreme Court upheld the states' authority to regulate industries, such as railroads and grain elevators, that are "affected with a public interest." For much of the period from the 1880s to the 1930s, however, the Court vetoed numerous regulatory laws, both state and federal, as unconstitutional. In 1895 and 1918 it held that federal authority to "regulate interstate commerce" did not extend to production. In other cases it used the due-process clauses of the 5th and 14th amendments to invalidate regulatory measures as "unreasonable" or "arbitrary and capricious."

The Court's assertiveness ended abruptly in 1937, as

a result of confrontation with President Franklin D. Roosevelt's program to end the Depression. After the Court had struck down major parts of Roosevelt's NEW DEAL and this had led to an escalating conflict with the president, one of the conservative justices switched his position, and the Court removed itself as an obstacle to regulation. Since then, the Court has prohibited state regulation only if it conflicted with federal responsibility and has enforced no limits to federal control. The federal courts still review the actions of regulatory agencies on statutory grounds, exhibiting a new activism in recent years. In many of these cases they have demanded more regulation.

The Expansion of Federal Regulation

Most of the expansion of the federal regulatory role took place in three waves, each occurring during a period of general political ferment and governmental activism. The Democratic party, which has been more liberal and less responsive to business than the Republican party, has controlled Congress in each of these periods; much of the time a Democrat also occupied the White House. Several major regulatory acts, the first wave of expansion, owed their impetus largely to the Progressive movement from 1900 to World War I. These include the Pure Food and Drug Act of 1906 (see PURE FOOD AND DRUG LAWS), the Hepburn Act of 1906 (which strengthened railroad regulation), and several major laws adopted in President Woodrow Wilson's highly productive first term: the Federal Reserve Act (1913), the Clayton Anti-Trust Act (1914), and the Federal Trade Commission Act (1914).

A second wave emerged from the economic chaos of the Depression of the 1930s, which led to widespread distrust of the unregulated workings of capitalism. Regulation was created or expanded for industries that were held responsible for the Depression (banking and the stock exchanges); that seemed to be victims of it (agriculture, coal, airlines, trucking); or for which regulation had previously been sought on other grounds (radio, telephone, food, drugs). In the NATIONAL LABOR RELATIONS ACT, or Wagner Act (1935), labor unions won a long-sought federal guarantee of a right to collective bargaining.

Much of the New Deal regulation, like the earlier regulation of railroads, was PUBLIC UTILITY–type regulation of prices and service. Versions of such regulation were also extended during the 1930s to transportation industries— described as "sick" or "infant" industries—whose structure was highly competitive.

The third, and most consequential, expansion was largely a product of the liberal activism and skepticism toward business of the 1960s and '70s. Promoted by a network of citizens' organizations, whose most prominent spokesman was Ralph NADER, the measures of this period often sought "social" objectives (such as health or racial equality) instead of the "economic" objectives (reasonable rates or stable service) more characteristic of earlier regulation. In numerous laws, Congress established or expanded regulatory programs in four areas of social concern: CONSUMER PROTECTION, environmental protection, workplace safety, and civil rights. In contrast to previous regulation, which usually covered a single industry, some

of the recent social regulation has broad scope—affecting a large part of the economy. It has been correspondingly difficult to administer and expensive to comply with.

Deregulation and Regulatory Reform

Since the mid-1970s the dominant trend in regulatory policy has been to prune away some of the excesses of existing programs. Besides a generally conservative trend in politics, this reflects a broader concern that existing regulatory programs may be hindering the overall performance of the economy. They probably do so—but not to a great extent.

The most successful reform effort has been to cut back price and entry regulation in industries where regulation has merely suppressed competition. Procompetitive reform began administratively as early as the late 1960s, with relaxation of controls on stock brokerage commissions and telecommunications services. It became a force to be reckoned with as of 1978—when the Air Transportation Deregulation Act completely removed price and entry controls in the airline industry and ordered the abolition, by 1985, of the CIVIL AERONAUTICS BOARD (CAB). (The air lines are still regulated with respect to safety by the FEDERAL AVIATION ADMINISTRATION.) Subsequent legislation substantially reduced anticompetitive regulation in the trucking, bus, railroad, and banking industries. In the same period the rather different form of regulation that held energy prices below market levels in the middle and late 1970s was also largely eliminated.

The effects of deregulation have caused at least temporary instability in some industries such as the airlines. On the whole, however, deregulation has had precisely the effects its advocates had promised. In several industries it has demonstrably pushed down average prices, forced improvement in efficiency, and promoted innovation.

A less successful effort has been made to control the costs of health, safety, and environmental regulation. Presidents Gerald Ford, Jimmy Carter, and Ronald Reagan made efforts to create pressure to limit costs, and cost-conscious reformers have proposed to amend statutes that instruct agencies to pursue a primary goal, such as protection of health, and give them no mandate to weigh the costs. There has been no significant progress on such amendments—nor on other legislation to make regulation more efficient. The Reagan administration's main impact on regulatory policy has been to loosen some regulations administratively and to weaken enforcement by sharply cutting agency budgets.

The post-Reagan period seems to promise a return to more balanced regulatory politics. To be sure, there will be continued efforts to limit costs, but there will also be intensified regulatory effort to deal with serious problems—such as acid rain and toxic chemicals—that have not yet been adequately addressed.

———

governor   In the United States a governor is the elected chief executive of a state. The office evolved from the post held in prerevolutionary times by the royal governor appointed by the British crown to administer a colony.

The chief task of a modern governor is to formulate and execute state policy. As leader of his or her party the governor can influence legislation, and through the preparation of the budget, one of the main gubernatorial functions, he or she establishes state priorities. A governor also has the power to summon special sessions of the legislature, to veto legislation (except in the state of North Carolina), and to issue pardons and commute sentences in cases that do not involve treason or impeachment. In addition, the governor acts as commander in chief of the state militia. Most governors serve 4-year terms, although about a fifth of the states have 2-year terms. Many states set no limit on the number of terms a governor may serve; some stipulate a limit of one term or two successive terms. Governors may be removed from office through IMPEACHMENT by the state legislature and, in 12 states, by RECALL. Because of the political power wielded by the governor, the position has been one of the traditional stepping-stones to the presidency.

governor-general Governor-general is the name sometimes given to the chief executive of a country's present or former territorial possessions, colonies, or dependent areas. Governors-general under a monarchy personally represent the crown; in other systems they represent the government. They may be either selected by the people of the area in which they serve or appointed by the government of the mother country.

Governors-general have been responsible for administering the possessions of Great Britain, the Netherlands, Portugal, and Spain, and the overseas territories and departments of France. The post has frequently been retained even after an area has achieved independence and the governor-general no longer represents a controlling government. In the British COMMONWEALTH OF NATIONS, for example, Australia, Canada, and New Zealand are among the countries that have governors-general. The powers of the office of governor-general vary. In Canada, for instance, the governor-general has little real authority. In dependent territories the governor-general has more extensive executive authority, and in some possessions or colonies, governors-general have ruled autocratically.

Gower, John [gow'-ur] John Gower, c.1330–1408, was an English poet whose work, although largely neglected today, was once favorably compared with that of his friend Geoffrey Chaucer. Gower wrote in Latin and French, but his masterpiece is the long poem in English, *Confessio Amantis* (c.1390). Mixing medieval learning with classical stories often taken from the Latin poet Ovid, it discusses the Seven Deadly Sins and also develops the theme of courtly love with considerable rhetorical skill and delicacy.

Gowon, Yakubu [goh'-wahn, yah-koo'-boo] Yakubu Danjuma Gowon, b. Oct. 19, 1934, led Nigeria's government during the Nigerian civil war of 1967–70. Gowon was educated at the Government College at Zaria, Nigeria, and in England. A career officer, he became the Nigerian army's chief of staff after the coup of January 1966; following the countercoup of July 1966, Gowon became head of the military government. The next year, the IBOS of the eastern region formed the secessionist state of BIAFRA under Chukwuemeka OJUKWU, and Gowon led the war against them. Following the Nigerian government's victory in 1970, Gowon initiated a policy of reconciliation. In 1975 he was deposed by a bloodless coup. His generalship was restored in 1987, effective 1986.

Goya, Francisco de [goy'-ah, frahn-thees'-koh] Francisco José de Goya y Lucientes, b. Mar. 31, 1746, d. Apr. 16, 1828, was a brilliantly imaginative Spanish painter and engraver. After studying in Saragossa he established himself about 1774 in Madrid, where his brother-in-law, the painter Francisco Bayeu (1734–95), helped him obtain commissions from the royal tapestry manufactory. For his tapestry cartoons (see CARTOON, art), executed between 1775 and 1792, Goya rejected the customary mythological scenes, adopting instead the genre subjects (see GENRE PAINTING) that Jean Honoré FRAGONARD was establishing in France. Goya depicted the open-air amusements attended by Madrid's upper classes, who often appeared dressed as majos and majas, Madrid's popular types. In *The Picnic* (1776; Prado, Madrid) he used the luminous colors, subtle gradations, and undulating rhythms characteristic of the ROCOCO STYLE, to make natural objects more graceful and harmonious. His juxtaposition of light and shade demonstrates that the baroque painters Diego VELÁZQUEZ and REMBRANDT van Rijn were the masters Goya acknowledged after nature itself.

Goya's keen observation of nature is revealed in his portraits, which were in great demand following his appointment in 1786 as court painter to Charles III. Unlike Velázquez, whose luminous paint spiritualized Philip IV, king by divine right to the 17th-century mind, Goya did not idealize his royal and upper-class subjects, especially after a near-fatal illness in 1792–93 left him totally deaf and less impressed with the world. His later portraits, such as *The Duchess of Alba* in the costume of a maja (1797; Hispanic Society Museum, New York City), are remarkable for their acute observation of personality, their social implications, and their new, striking color. Goya's sympathy with liberal reform movements may have prompted his unflattering depictions of the corrupt and reactionary Spanish royal family. In *The Family of Charles IV* (1800; Prado), the awkward poses and fatuous features of the royal persons contrast oddly with their brilliantly painted, splendid costumes, a disparity that makes the painting satirical.

After Napoleon's invasion of Spain in 1808, and the savage guerrilla warfare that followed, Goya executed two large canvases representing tragic events of the war. In his passionate and monumental *The Third of May, 1808* (1814; Prado), the horror and cruelty of war are evoked by the stark image of a group of Spaniards about to be shot by

Francisco de Goya's painting The Third of May, 1808 *(1814–15) memorializes the execution of Madrid citizens by Napoleon's occupational forces. The intense drama and brutality of the act is depicted in glowing color and nocturnal light. (Prado, Madrid.)*

shot by a French firing squad. The victims are differentiated by writhing gestures and grimaces of despair, but the faceless soldiers, who are seen from behind, are lined up like automatons, denoting the inhuman nature of their task.

Goya's reaction to war led him to invent macabre caricatures of the irrational bestiality of human behavior, something he had already begun in a series of etchings, *Los caprichos* (1796–98), that are ironic treatments of familiar social events. The French occupation of his country brought this side of Goya's artistic vision to full realization in *The Disasters of War*, a series of etchings made between 1810 and 1814. These were followed by *Bullfighting* (1815–16) and finally by *Los proverbios* (c.1813–18), in which Goya offered a vision of the world populated by monstrous personifications of evil. These last etchings have counterparts in the paintings that Goya executed on the walls of a house near Madrid that he bought in 1819. These black paintings, now in the Prado, are nightmarish images prompted by the aging painter's reflections on human nature.

To avoid the repressions of the restored monarchy, Goya lived in voluntary exile in Bordeaux, France, from 1824 until his death. He executed such portraits as that of his liberal friend, Don Tiburcio Pérez (1820; Metropolitan Museum of Art, New York City), in which the subject is portrayed with simple human dignity against a background of neutral color. Goya had many outspoken admirers among early-19th-century French romantic painters and writers, and his art contributed to the formation of the French impressionist style.

Goyen, Jan van [goy'-en]   Jan van Goyen, b. Jan. 13, 1596, d. Apr. 27, 1656, was a prolific Dutch landscape painter and etcher. About 1630, atmospheric tonality began to dominate over color in van Goyen's paintings, leading to nearly monochromatic landscapes in tones of gray or brown. During this period his work had an affinity with that of contemporaries Salomon van Ruisdael and Pieter de Molyn. His paintings of dunes (for example,

Village and Dunes, 1647; Allen Memorial Museum, Oberlin College, Ohio), river landscapes, and views of Leiden and The Hague place van Goyen as a leader in bringing atmosphere to Dutch LANDSCAPE PAINTING. In the 1640s van Goyen became more concerned with color, and a full chromatic range is present in his later pictures. About 1,200 of his paintings survive, and van Goyen is represented in most of the world's major museums and collections.

Goytisolo, Juan [goy-tee-soh'-loh]   The contemporary Spanish novelist Juan Goytisolo, b. 1931, has lived in exile in France, the United States, and Mexico since 1957. His early novels deal with post–Spanish Civil War society in an almost documentary fashion. His more recent works abandon realism and traditional novelistic form. *Marks of Identity* (1966; Eng. trans., 1969), *Count Julian* (1970; Eng. trans., 1974)—ranked as his masterpiece—and *Juan the Landless* (1975; Eng. trans., 1977) are stylistically experimental diatribes against the traditions of his estranged homeland.

Gozzi, Carlo, Conte [goht'-tsee]   The Italian dramatist Carlo Gozzi, b. Dec. 13, 1720, d. Apr. 4, 1806, was a traditionalist who opposed the philosophical and scientific thought of the Enlightenment and was a founding member of the conservative Accademia dei Granelleschi. Gozzi rejected Carlo GOLDONI's theatrical innovations by returning to the improvisational scenarios of the COMMEDIA DELL'ARTE. His ten important satirical and moralistic plays, collectively called *Fiabe* (Fables, 1761–65), were based on Oriental and popular grotesque stories. *Re Turandot,* perhaps the most famous fable, was transformed into operas by Carl Maria von Weber, Ferruccio Busoni, and Giacomo Puccini; *L'Amore delle tre melarance* was the basis for Sergei Prokofiev's opera *The Love of Three Oranges.*

Gozzoli, Benozzo [goht-tsoh'-lee, bay-noht'-tsoh] Benozzo Gozzoli (Benozzo di Lese, di Sandro), 1420–97, was an Italian Renaissance fresco painter. From 1450 to 1452 he worked in the churches of San Fortunato and San Francesco in Montefalco, in Umbria. In 1459, Piero de'Medici commissioned him to decorate the walls of the chapel of the Medici-Riccardi palace in Florence. Here, in his best-known work, Benozzo painted on three walls a *Procession of the Magi* in which the three Magi and their attendants ride toward a Nativity scene by Fra Filippo Lippi, on the fourth wall. From 1463 to 1467, Gozzoli worked in the Church of Sant' Agostino in San Gimignano, and from 1468 to 1485 he painted Old Testament scenes in the Campo Santo in Pisa.

graben   see HORST AND GRABEN

Gracchus (family) [grak'-uhs]   The Roman tribunes Tiberius Sempronius Gracchus and Gaius Sempronius Gracchus are famous for their radical reform program. They were the sons of Tiberius, a plebeian noble who served as consul (177 BC) and censor (169), and of Cornelia, a daughter of SCIPIO AFRICANUS MAJOR; their sister Sempronia married SCIPIO AFRICANUS MINOR.

Tiberius Sempronius Gracchus, b. *c.*164 BC, d. 133 BC, served (146) with the younger Scipio at Carthage but later clashed with him over foreign policy. Supported by his father-in-law, Scipio's rival Appius Claudius Pulcher, Tiberius was elected tribune for 133; he sponsored legislation to redistribute public lands held by the rich to poorer citizens. Opposition from rivals and vested interests, however, forced him into blatant violation of political customs. A mob led by fellow senators killed Tiberius as he sought a second tribunate.

Gaius Sempronius Gracchus, b. *c.*154 BC, d. 122 BC, became tribune ten years after his brother's death and promoted further reforms: grain subsidies, public-works employment, and additional distribution of land to the poor; citizenship for Rome's Italian allies; and increased power for the wealthy, nonsenatorial class of equestrians. When he failed to win election to a third tribunate, Gaius gathered armed followers to oppose the repeal of his legislation. A murder resulted, and the Senate for the first time declared a state of emergency. Gaius died in the subsequent violence.

grace   Grace, a central concept in Christian THEOLOGY, refers to God's granting SALVATION not in reward for the moral worth of the human but as a free and undeserved gift of love, as opposed to any notion that salvation can be earned by human effort apart from God's help.

The Old Testament contains important themes related to God's undeserved love for his people, Israel. The chief architect of the early Christian church's theology of grace, however, was Saint Paul; *charis,* the Greek word for "grace," is infrequent in the non-Pauline writings of the New Testament. For Paul, grace means the free gift of salvation by which God liberates humans from SIN and frees them from death "through the redemption which is in Christ Jesus" (Romans 3:24). Paul deliberately sets grace in contrast to all human efforts to achieve favor with God.

Medieval Christianity and much Roman Catholic theology has treated grace as a divine power that enters a person and, in cooperation with the person's own will, transforms him or her into one who loves God and is loved by God. This grace is transmitted especially, perhaps exclusively, through the church's SACRAMENTS (the "means of grace"); and it allows some room for human merit because the one who receives grace must also cooperate with it in the process of transformation.

Protestant theologians have insisted that grace is given where God wills and is not conditional on a person's receptivity. Thus the sacraments are signs of grace, but do not impart it, and salvation depends entirely on God, not at all on human will—a theme close to the idea of PREDESTINATION. This grace is not a power that transforms a person; it is a love that receives a person directly into God's favor.

Grace, W. R. The founder of the Grace shipping lines, William Russell Grace, b. Ireland, May 10, 1832, d. Mar. 21, 1904, ran away to sea at age 14. After working as a clerk in New York City, he eventually moved to Peru, where he entered the shipping business with a brother. Eventually, this enterprise became (1865) W. R. Grace & Company and dominated merchant shipping between the United States and Latin America after 1895. By helping to underwrite Peru's national debt, the company acquired huge mineral, land, and railroad concessions there. Grace also served two terms (1880–88) as mayor of New York City. Running on a reform, anti-Tammany ticket, he was the first Roman Catholic to be elected mayor.

Graces   In Greek mythology the Graces were beautiful sister goddesses, most often represented as three in number. Their names are synonymous with their attributes: Aglaia ("brilliance"), Euphrosyne ("joy"), and Thalia ("bloom"). Their charm and winning manner made them welcome as the companions of the MUSES and the attendants of APHRODITE, EROS, and DIONYSUS.

grackle [grak'-ul]   Grackle is the common name for several species of New World blackbirds in the family Icteridae. Grackles are typically black. Males often have an iridescent sheen and have very long tails. Females are generally smaller, with shorter tails and little or no iridescence. Grackles have an extremely varied diet, feeding on insects, fruit, grain, and even crayfish, lizards, and the eggs and young of other birds.

The common grackle, *Quiscalus quiscula*, found in North America east of the Rocky Mountains, is about 30 cm (1 ft) in overall length. It has a long, wedge-shaped tail, which the male often "keels" while in flight by depressing the central feathers. The common grackle is black with a blue, purple, green, or bronze iridescent sheen and has bright yellow eyes. Females are smaller

The common grackle, a blackbird native to eastern and central North America, is considered an agricultural pest; large flocks descend on a wide variety of crops.

and duller in color. Common grackles feed on open ground, favoring wet areas. Most nesting is in colonies of up to 25 pairs of birds.

graduate education   Graduate education is rigorous, specialized training in particular academic and professional fields and is generally considered to include all postbaccalaureate programs with the exception of the first professional degree programs in medicine, veterinary medicine, dentistry, law, and theology. Traditional graduate-education programs culminate with the award of a doctor's or master's degree (see DEGREE, ACADEMIC). Admission to graduate-degree programs in the United States is usually based on students' undergraduate records, recommendations by professors, and scores on the GRADUATE RECORD EXAMINATION.

Development of Graduate Education.   Modern graduate education, emphasizing scientific research, began in Germany in the early 19th century, and German universities remained preeminent until the 1890s. A few colleges in the United States experimented with graduate education before the Civil War, and Yale University awarded the first doctor of philosophy (Ph.D.) degree in the country in 1861. The continuous growth of graduate education in the United States, however, dates from the founding of The Johns Hopkins University in Baltimore in 1876. By then a national elite had emerged, secular in outlook and eager to foster German scholarly ideals.

Soon other leading colleges and universities established similar graduate programs. Most early graduate schools were part of privately endowed universities. Only in Michigan, Wisconsin, and California did state universities initially try to compete in this area. Among U.S. universities offering high-quality graduate education by 1900, 14—Catholic University of America, Clark, Columbia, Cornell, Harvard, Johns Hopkins, Princeton, Stanford, and Yale universities, and the universities of California, Chicago, Michigan, Pennsylvania, and Wisconsin—founded the Association of American Universities to coordinate mutual concerns. Graduate education grew rapidly during the 20th century, and today more than 300 universities in the United States award Ph.D. degrees.

Doctorate.   In general, doctoral programs in the United States consist of three stages. After completing a specified number of advanced courses in their fields of study, students prepare for and must pass an oral or written qualifying examination. A period of supervised research then follows and culminates with the submission and defense of a research dissertation, a book-length, scholarly work. In European universities doctoral programs generally consist of supervised individual study and research and the completion of a dissertation.

While the Ph.D. is the dominant doctoral degree associated with graduate education, other doctoral degrees are also awarded. For the most part, they are professionally oriented: doctor of education (Ed.D.), doctor of business administration (D.B.A.), and doctor of psychology (D. Psych.). The doctor of arts (D.A.) degree was introduced in the 1960s. It emphasizes college-teacher preparation and requires the writing of an expository thesis instead of the traditional research dissertation.

The great advances in knowledge, especially in the sciences, have made it desirable for individuals to continue highly specialized study upon receiving the doctorate. Postdoctoral positions were created to accommodate this need. Such appointments, which have been funded primarily by government and industry, provide individuals with the experience of concentrated and sophisticated research.

Master's Degree. The achievement represented by the master's degree has long been a subject of controversy. Nevertheless, the master's degree has survived, in various forms, for eight centuries, and it is today the most widely awarded degree on the graduate level.

The University of Paris awarded the first master of arts (M.A.) degree in the 12th century. As the most advanced degree then offered by the faculty of arts, it entitled holders to join that faculty and also to pursue doctoral studies in medicine, law, or theology. Whereas in Europe the master's degree was gradually discontinued, in the United States, where for a time it remained the ultimate degree, the master's was more highly regarded. The degree represented exacting academic achievement—comprising three years of postbachelor's study—when it was first awarded by Harvard University in the 1640s. By the early 19th century, however, the degree's significance lessened in the United States as well.

The revival of the master's degree is often credited to a program established by the University of Michigan in 1858. It required the holder of a bachelor's degree to complete two courses in each of two semesters, to pass examinations in three of the four courses, and to submit a thesis. Those requirements characterized master's degree programs at most institutions by the beginning of the 20th century.

Recognition of the master's degree as distinct from the doctorate increased as colleges and universities admitted greater numbers of students, especially women, and expanded their offerings in the field of education. From 1939 to 1959, when approximately 75 percent of liberal arts master's degrees were awarded to public school teachers, growth of master's-degree education was notably tied to the expansion of elementary and secondary education. An increase in career-oriented graduate education also contributed to the growth of master's-degree programs and to the proliferation of degree titles, such as master of business administration (M.B.A.), master of social work (M.S.W.), master of library science (M.L.S.), and master of education (M.Ed.).

In 1975 the Council of Graduate Schools in the United States characterized the master's degree as indicating that the holder has mastered a program in a particular field sufficiently to pursue creative projects in that specialty. The degree should be awarded for completion of a coherent program rather than for the random accumulation of a certain number of course credits after attaining the baccalaureate.

See also: UNIVERSITY.

Graduate Record Examination The Graduate Record Examination (GRE) is a series of aptitude and achievement tests taken by applicants for admission to programs of GRADUATE EDUCATION and widely used by graduate schools in the selection of graduate students. The tests are administered by the EDUCATIONAL TESTING SERVICE (ETS) at many sites in the United States on six dates each year. The tests also are administered at less frequent intervals in major cities throughout the world.

All students who register for the examination must take three tests, the morning tests of the GRE, measuring verbal aptitude, quantitative aptitude, and analytical aptitude. In addition, students may elect an afternoon test designed to assess achievement in their major field of undergraduate study. Test scores are reported by the ETS to the student and to admissions offices of graduate schools designated by the student.

The GRE program was established in 1948. Since 1966 it has been supervised by the GRE Board, which is responsible for all aspects of the testing program and supports research to improve the validity of the tests.

See also: EDUCATIONAL MEASUREMENT AND TESTING.

Graf, Steffi German tennis star Steffi Graf, b. June 14, 1969, was the world's top-ranked woman player in 1987–89. Armed with a powerful forehand, Graf won 11 of 13 tournaments, 75 of 77 matches, and the French Open in 1987. In 1988 she became only the 3d woman ever to win the tennis Grand Slam—the Australian, French, Wimbledon, and U.S. Open singles titles—earning the Olympic gold medal as well. In 1989 she repeated her Australian, Wimbledon, and U.S. victories, but in 1990, only her Australian.

Graf Zeppelin see AIRSHIP

graffiti [gruh-fee'-tee] In contemporary usage, *graffiti* (singular *graffito*, from the Italian *graffio*, a "scratch") refers to handwriting or images on the walls or surfaces of a public area, such as buildings, parks, toilets, and trains; they are usually political or sexual in content: a lover's pledge, a proposition, or obscene words. The word was originally used by archaeologists to describe drawings and inscriptions scratched on walls and other surfaces in ancient Pompeii and Rome.

Graffiti are ubiquitous, appearing in many places and times, including the walls and pillars of medieval churches. Some graffiti preserved today, such as those in churches around Cambridge, England, were wrought with great care and intricacy of pattern. Graffiti are characteristically urban, and today especially embody a reaction against the featureless, depersonalized character of modern architecture. The term also refers to an ancient technique of decorating architectural plaster or pottery surfaces, in which patterns are produced by incising a top layer of plaster or glaze to reveal a contrasting undercoat.

graft Something of value given to, and accepted by, public officials for dishonest or illegal purposes is commonly called graft. The practice may also involve corrupt officials directing the fraudulent expenditure of public funds for private benefit. In order for graft to be present in a transaction, one of the parties must occupy a position of public trust. The word probably reflects the idea that extra or illegal profits are something grafted onto a legitimate transaction. "Graft" is usually considered synonymous with "political corruption."

In its least offensive form, graft merely involves favored treatment or unfairness. It usually extends, however, to criminal activity such as blackmail, theft, fraud, and swindling. Whatever its form, graft is usually secretive and is almost always regarded as morally repugnant.

grafting Grafting is a method of plant propagation in which a scion (a bud or a stem containing several buds) of one plant is inserted into the stock (root, stem, or branch) of another plant so that they unite and grow as one plant. This technique of propagation is ordinarily used for biennial or perennial woody plants, not for annuals or soft succulent plants.

Purposes. Grafting is done to increase the numbers of plants of a desired variety when it is difficult or impossible to do so by seed germination; to adapt desired varieties to soil or climatic conditions that normally would be unsatisfactory for good growth; to increase a plant's resistance to insects and diseases; to control the size of a plant; to facilitate pollination; to repair damaged plants; to change the form of the plant; and to transmit diseases for purposes of research.

Principles and Methods. Grafting is not difficult if certain principles are followed. First, the cambium, or inner bark, of both the stock and the scion must be in contact to allow the tissues to knit together. Second, the cut surfaces must be protected from excessive moisture loss. Last, the stock and the scion must be compatible, or closely related; for example, a pear can be grafted to a pear or to a quince.

Various grafting methods are available. The whip graft is used with stocks 2 cm (0.8 in) or less in diameter. It is often used to propagate new woody ornamental plants and pear and apple trees. Other methods depend on the size of the scion. The cleft graft is often used on large apple trees to change one variety to another. A bridge graft may be used to repair plant damage known as girdling, in which the conducting tissues of the tree are cut apart by rodents or deer.

Budding is a specialized grafting method in which only one bud is used rather than a shoot with several buds. A detached bud of the desired variety is placed under the bark of the stock. Natural grafting is also possible. Adjacent branches are tied so that they will grow naturally together and strengthen the top of the tree.

Graham, Billy [gray'-uhm] William Franklin (Billy) Graham, Jr., b. Charlotte, N.C., Nov. 7, 1918, is an American religious leader with a worldwide reputation for charismatic preaching and evangelistic crusades. After graduating from Wheaton College, Ill., in 1943, he en-

A whip graft (A) is formed by making a slanted, notched cut on both the scion and stock, and then fitting and tying them together. In a cleft graft (B), the scion, with a wedge-shaped lower end, is inserted into a split in the sawed-off end of the stock. Bridge grafting (C) reconnects conducting tissues between the stem and root of a girdled plant; scions reach from the lower to upper end of the wound. Inarching (D) involves the grafting of a rooted sucker or seedling onto the stem of another plant. T-budding (E) is done by inserting a bud into a T-shaped cut in the bark of the stock. In any graft, the cambium layer of stock and scion should be in close contact.

A

B

C

D

E

The American evangelist Billy Graham has conducted revivalist crusades all over the world. Preaching to thousands at a time, with radio and television broadcasts reaching millions, he exhorts his listeners to make a life-changing commitment to Christ.

tered the ministry as pastor of the First Baptist Church of Western Springs, Ill., and became a leader in the Youth for Christ movement.

In 1947 Graham organized a revival team in the style of Billy Sunday, and this group, which included George Beverly Shea as singer, began a series of revivals. His first big success came in Los Angeles in 1949, when several prominent Hollywood personalities were converted to Christianity.

The Billy Graham Evangelistic Association, founded in 1950, has promoted crusades, developed radio and television programs (including *The Hour of Decision*), and produced films. In 1969, Graham gave a prayer at the inauguration of President Richard Nixon, and he subsequently became a close advisor to the president.

Graham, Katharine   Katharine Meyer Graham, b. New York City, June 16, 1917, is owner and chairwoman of the board of the WASHINGTON POST. The daughter of Eugene Meyer, who in 1933 purchased the newspaper, Graham learned newspaper management from him. When her husband, Philip L. Graham, committed suicide in 1963, she became president, with control over the *Post, Newsweek* magazine, and several television stations. Under Graham's direction, the *Post* supported John F. Kennedy and Lyndon B. Johnson, employed more blacks than any other U.S. newspaper, and in 1971 won a battle for freedom of the press when the Supreme Court supported the *Post*'s publication of the PENTAGON PAPERS. The *Post* gained world attention in 1972 by exposing the WATERGATE scandals.

Graham, Martha   More than any other individual, Martha Graham, b. Pittsburgh, Pa., May 11, 1894, d. Apr. 1, 1991, created the image and substance of the art form called MODERN DANCE. She developed a new vocabulary of movement and from it created a body of powerfully expressive dances.

From 1919 to 1923, Graham toured with the DENISHAWN troupe. After dancing in vaudeville and teaching at

the Eastman School of Music in Rochester, N.Y., she opened her own studio in New York City in 1927. She discarded the serpentine flourishes of Denishawn dancing and evolved a language of angular, percussive gestures originating in the contraction and release of the muscles of the lower torso. Body weight was emphasized; dancers moved on the floor and in space, using an unconcealed tension and effort that added to the impact of the dance.

In *Primitive Mysteries* (1931), Graham explored the individual's relation to the universe and society in a ritualized, austere, quasi-religious ceremony. Later she adopted specifically American themes, illustrating the bold pioneering spirit in *Frontier* (1935) and *Appalachian Spring* (1944), the New England heritage and art of Emily Dickinson in *Letter to the World* (1940), and the Southwestern culture in *El Penitente* (1940). Next, Graham explored universal psychological problems as they were expressed in mythology. *Cave of the Heart* (1946) embodied Medea's overwhelming hate; in *Errand into the Maze* (1947), the Minotaur legend suggested the conquest of fear.

As she grew older, Graham was reluctant to preserve her dances or pass on her roles, and in the early 1970s her company almost collapsed. She relented, however, and revivals of Graham classics, as well as new works, including *Acts of Light* (1981), *Andromache's Lament* (1982), and *Song* (1985), brought her fresh acclaim.

Martha Graham was one of the most innovative and influential American dancers and choreographers of the 20th century.

Graham, Otto   Otto Everett Graham, b. Waukegan, Ill., Dec. 6, 1921, was an American professional football player who played quarterback for the Cleveland Browns for 10 years (1946–55). During this period the Browns won four All-America Football Conference championships and, after joining the National Football League, six division titles and three league championships. Graham was known for his passing (he threw 174 touchdown passes in his career), but he also ran for 46 touchdowns. He retired from professional football in 1955 and was elected to the

Hall of Fame in 1965. He coached briefly (1966–68) for the Washington Redskins.

Graham, Thomas   The Scottish inorganic and physical chemist Thomas Graham, b. Dec. 21, 1805, d. Sept. 16, 1869, was the founder of colloid chemistry and also a founder of physical chemistry. He became professor of chemistry at Anderson's College in Glasgow (1830–37) and at University College, London (1837–54), and finally Master of the Mint (1854–69). From 1828 to 1833 he studied diffusion of gases and in 1833 proposed Graham's law, which states that the rate of diffusion of a gas is inversely proportional to the square root of its molecular weight. In his work on colloids (1849–61) he distinguished between crystalloids and colloids as different states of matter (see COLLOIDAL STATE) and devised a method for their dialysis (separation) by osmosis (both of these terms were coined by Graham).

Grahame, Kenneth [gray'-uhm]   Kenneth Grahame, b. Mar. 8, 1859, d. July 6, 1932, was a Scottish author best known for his juvenile classic THE WIND IN THE WILLOWS (1908). The book was written for his only son, Alastair, while Grahame served (1897–1908) as a secretary of the Bank of England. He wrote only three other books: *Pagan Papers* (1893), personal essays that reflect his private frustrations, and the short-story collections *The Golden Age* (1895) and *Dream Days* (1898). Although his works are noted for their graceful charm, the conflict between Grahame's aristocratic background and new social concerns lies just beneath the surface of his mythic tales. He also compiled the *Cambridge Book of Poetry for Children* (1916).

Grail, Holy [grayl]   The Holy Grail, a symbolic talisman around which numerous medieval legends and poems revolve, probably originated in Celtic pagan tradition but later became associated with the cup used at the Last Supper, in which Joseph of Arimathea gathered blood from Christ's wounds. The Grail was sought by the knights of King Arthur in several medieval romances, the earliest of which was the late-12th-century *Perceval* by CHRÉTIEN DE TROYES. The quest for the Grail, which can be found only by a hero free from sin, is treated at great length in Sir Thomas MALORY's *Morte Darthur* (c.1469) and in Wolfram von Eschenbach's epic, *Parzifal* (c.1210), which inspired Richard Wagner's opera *Parsifal* (1877–82).

    See also: ARTHUR AND ARTHURIAN LEGEND.

grain   Grain is the seed or fruit of various cereal grasses of the family Gramineae. The principal grain crops are WHEAT, CORN (or maize), RICE, BARLEY, OATS, RYE, SORGHUM, and MILLET. Sometimes seeds other than grasses, such as BUCKWHEAT, WILD RICE, and SOYBEANS, are characterized as grains. Grains are grown under a wide range of environmental conditions from the equator to close to the Arctic

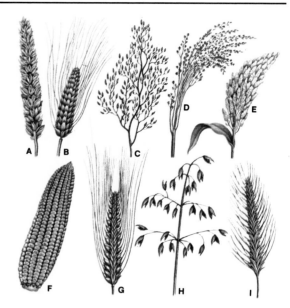

Grains, or cereal grasses, the most important of all food crops, are grown in almost every agricultural region. The chief grain crops are wheat, including Triticum vulgare (A) and Triticum durham (B); rice (C); millet (D); sorghum (E); corn (F); barley (G); oats (H); and rye (I).

Circle in the Northern Hemisphere and to the 40th parallel in the Southern Hemisphere. They can be grown with little labor, and in comparison to other crops, returns are high for the work required. Cereal grasses were among the first domesticated plants, and today grains are a mainstay of agricultural production.

Grainger, Percy [grayn'-jur]   Percy Aldridge Grainger, b. Melbourne, Australia, July 8, 1882, d. Feb. 20, 1961, was a composer and pianist so thoroughly absorbed in folk music that it colored nearly every one of his compositions. He began (1901) his concert career in England, then settled (1914) in the United States and taught at various academic institutions. Grainger tried to give his music the spontaneity of folk song and experimented with unorthodox scales and polyrhythmic combinations. His works include *Irish Tunes from County Derry* (1909) and *Harvest Hymn* (1933) for orchestra; *Tribute to Foster* (1932) for chorus and orchestra; and *Handel in the Strand* (1913) and *Spoon River* (1922), and *Free Music* (1935) for chamber groups.

grammar [gram'-ur]   Grammar is the study of the structure and meaning of human language; the term is also applied to books that set out rules governing a language's use. Grammar may be understood either in a traditional sense, designating an unbroken chain of theories about language extending back to ancient Greece, or in a more modern way. In current LINGUISTICS, grammar is defined as the body of tacit knowledge that constitutes a speaker's grasp of his language.

Grammar includes such specific subtopics as morphology (the principles of word formation; see PHONOLOGY AND MORPHOLOGY), SYNTAX (the principles of sentence structure), and the PARTS OF SPEECH. Descriptive grammar is observational and attempts to characterize the principles of word and sentence formation that speakers actually follow in using their language. On the other hand, prescriptive grammar, also called normative grammar, formulates rules about how people ought to speak or write.

Traditional Grammar. Traditional grammar isolates and identifies language units of various sizes and develops rules for combining them into larger structures. A properly constituted structure—one formed according to the rules—is called grammatical; ungrammatical structures are those that violate the rules. For example, a morphological rule for English is that nouns but not verbs can end in the suffix *-ness*. Forms such as *quickness, fastness*, and *presentness* may or may not be nouns in English, but they cannot be verbs. A syntactic rule is that singular subjects take singular verbs.

The root of a word is its core—a minimal meaningful unit to which prefixes and suffixes can be progressively added to create larger forms. *Beat* can be expanded into *beatable*, which in turn can be enlarged to *unbeatable*. In the domain of sentence structure, words are traditionally divided into classes—the parts of speech—whose members perform similar grammatical functions. In accordance with rules specifying their order, form, and allowable combinations, words can be grouped into larger expressions such as phrases, clauses, and sentences.

Linguistic Competence and Performance. Following the lead of Noam CHOMSKY, modern linguists tend to emphasize the status of language structure as a facet of human psychological organization. Linguistic competence is the subconscious ability to string words into grammatical sentences; linguistic performance can be measured by how grammatical the resulting sentences are. To be understood, successful speakers must pair a meaning and a pronunciation. For example, to express the two different concepts, a speaker subconsciously learns to say *he runs* but *they run*.

Grammy Award [gram'-ee] The National Academy of Recording Arts and Sciences established the Grammy Award in 1958 to give public recognition to creative achievement in about 70 categories of recording. Awards are given for virtually every type of recorded music from rock and jazz to opera.

Grampian [gram'-pee-uhn] Grampian is an administrative region in northeastern Scotland bounded by the North Sea on the east and north. The region covers an area of 8,702 km^2 (3,360 mi^2) and has a population of 501,400 (1988 est.). Grampian's economy is based on agriculture, fishing, distilling, and textile and paper manufacturing. ABERDEEN, the largest city, is the center of the North Sea oil industry. Grampian was created in 1975 from the former counties of Aberdeen, BANFF, KINCARDINE, and part of MORAY.

Gran Chaco see CHACO

Granada (city in Nicaragua) [grah-nah'-dah] Granada (1985 est. pop., 88,636), the capital of Granada department in southwestern Nicaragua, is situated beside Lake Nicaragua at the foot of Mombacho Volcano. It is an industrial center, and its chief products are furniture, soap, clothing, oil, rum, hides, coffee, and sugar. Granada, the oldest city in Nicaragua, was founded in 1523 by Francisco Fernández de Córdoba. In the 17th century pirates from the Caribbean raided Granada frequently. In 1857 the U.S. filibusterer William Walker sacked the city. Granada is Spanish in style, with many old mansions and churches remaining from its early days.

Granada (city in Spain) Granada, a city in southern Spain, is the capital of the province of Granada. It is located on the Genil River, a tributary of the Guadalquivir, in a small but intensively cultivated plain. The city has a population of 256,800 (1987 est.). The province of Granada, which has a population of 803,810 (1988 est.) and an area of 12,531 km^2 (4,838 mi^2), is part of the historical region of Granada, which also includes the provinces of Almería and Málaga.

Granada's industries include sugar refining, tanning, iron and copper working, and textile manufacturing. The city's great architectural treasures make it one of Spain's most visited tourist centers. The most famous site is the Alhambra, a fortified Moorish palace built between the 13th and 14th centuries. Now extensively restored, the beautifully decorated palace and surrounding gardens give a vivid impression of the artistry of the last flowering of Moorish civilization in Spain. Other notable sites include several Moorish villas, the Renaissance cathedral (begun 1523), which contains the tombs of Ferdinand II of Aragon and Isabella I of Castile, and the unfinished palace of Charles V (begun 16th century). The University of Granada was chartered in 1531.

The old city is spread around two steep hills and is divided into two quarters by the Darro River. The Albaicín was the residence of the Moorish aristocracy. The Antequeruela was founded in the 15th century by refugees from Antequera.

Granada first rose to prominence under the Moors. After the breakup of the Moorish caliphate in 1002, it became the seat of a kingdom (1031–90) ruled by the Banu Ziri, or Zirids, a local Muslim dynasty. After a period of Almoravid and Almohad domination, another local dynasty, the Nasrids, came to power in the 13th century. During the more than 250 years of Nasrid rule, Granada was a flourishing commercial and artistic center. The city fell to Christian forces in 1492, ending Moorish power in Spain. In the 17th century, after the Jews and the Moriscos (Muslim converts to Christianity) had been expelled, it entered a period of decline.

Granados, Enrique [grah-nah'-dohs, ayn-ree'-kay]
Enrique Granados, b. July 27, 1867, d. Mar. 24, 1916, was a Spanish composer and pianist. After piano studies at the Barcelona Conservatory, he studied composition in Madrid with Felipe Pedrell. From 1889 he lived in Barcelona, where he established his own academy of music. The 12 *Spanish Dances* for piano (1892) have remained his most popular pieces, especially No. 5, *Andaluza*. On a larger scale is the suite for piano, *Goyescas* (2 vols., 1912–14), inspired by the paintings and tapestries of the Spanish artist Francisco Goya. Granados's last opera, also titled *Goyescas*, was based on the music and the scenes represented in the piano suite. It was produced (1916) at the Metropolitan Opera with the composer present. On the homeward voyage Granados and his wife perished when their ship was torpedoed by a German submarine.

Grand Alliance, War of the   The War of the Grand Alliance, 1688–97, was the first war in which LOUIS XIV of France was confronted by a major European coalition. The latter, called initially the League of Augsburg, became known as the Grand Alliance in 1689; it included the Holy Roman Empire, the United Provinces, England, Spain, and Savoy.

The war began (September 1688) when Louis invaded the Palatinate, thus uniting the other powers against himself. Louis provided support to the deposed English king JAMES II in Ireland, but the latter's forces were defeated by the new king WILLIAM III at the Battle of the Boyne in 1690. At sea, too, although defeated by the French at Beachy Head (1690), the English were ultimately victorious in the Battle of La Hogue (1692). On the Continent the French were more successful. They won a series of victories, including Steenkerke (1692) and Neerwinden (1693), in the Low Countries. The French also defeated Duke VICTOR AMADEUS II of Savoy at Marsaglia (1693) and invaded Catalonia. Subsequent action was indecisive, and the war ended inconclusively in the Treaty of Ryswick (1697). Louis recognized William III as king of England and gave up most of his post-1679 conquests. The question of the succession to the Spanish throne remained a major issue in European affairs, however, and led directly to the War of the SPANISH SUCCESSION.

Grand Army of the Republic   The Grand Army of the Republic (GAR), founded in Springfield, Ill., in April 1866, was the largest organization of Union veterans of the Civil War. Organized under the leadership of Dr. Benjamin F. Stephenson, a former army surgeon, the GAR sought to promote comradeship among veterans, to extend pension rights, to provide relief for war widows and orphans, and to maintain homes for old soldiers. In 1868, GAR commander in chief John A. LOGAN inaugurated the observance of MEMORIAL DAY in honor of fallen soldiers. Membership in the staunchly Republican organization peaked at more than 400,000 in 1890. The GAR was dissolved in 1956.

Grand Banks   The Grand Banks is a large (93,000 km²/36,000 mi²) area of submerged highlands located in the North Atlantic Ocean off the southeastern coast of Newfoundland and east of the Laurentian Channel. Noted for its thick fogs and hazardous icebergs, the area also has the reputation of being the world's best fishing grounds. The waters over the banks are relatively shallow, and sunlight penetrates to the seabed, where small marine life thrives. In addition, the warm GULF STREAM, which meets the cold Labrador Current, deposits sea plants, crabs, worms, and shrimp in the area, attracting cod, haddock, mackerel, herring, and flatfish. In 1929 a severe submarine earthquake shattered a large area of the fishing grounds, snapping transatlantic cables, and sending TSUNAMIS washing over Newfoundland's Burin Peninsula.

The map indicates the approximate boundaries of the Grand Banks, a portion of the North American continental shelf lying southeast of Newfoundland.

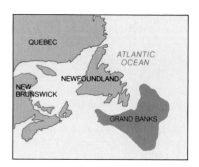

Grand Canal   The Grand Canal is an ancient Chinese waterway that extends for about 1,600 km (1,000 mi) from BEIJING to HANGZHOU, roughly parallel to the coast of the Yellow Sea. Called the *Yunliang He* ("transport river") in Chinese, it is still used to transport cargoes of coal, grain, lumber, and cotton.

The canal was dug in three stages. In the 6th century BC a prince of the later Zhou dynasty began constructing a waterway 225 km (140 mi) long that would link the Chang Jiang (Yangtze) and the Huai He. Approximately 1,200 years later, Emperor Yang Ti extended the canal southward 400 km (250 mi) to Hangzhou. Kubla Khan further extended the canal to his capital city, Cambaluc (Beijing), during the 13th century.

The growth of coastal shipping and the construction of railroads in the 19th century lessened the canal's importance. A plan to divert water from the Chang Jiang to the arid north along the Grand Canal was announced in 1986.

Grand Canyon   The Grand Canyon, located in northwestern Arizona, is a spectacular gorge carved by the COLORADO RIVER into rocks that represent over a billion years of Earth history. Its total length, from the Little Colorado River to Lake Mead, is 349 km (217 mi), of which 169 km (105 mi) is in Grand Canyon National Park.

The canyon is more than 1.6 km (1 mi) deep in places and from 6 to 29 km (4 to 18 mi) wide. Plateaus to the

The Grand Canyon, in northwestern Arizona, was designated a national park in 1919. The formations within the canyon are remnants of a plateau from which the gorge was carved by the Colorado River over millions of years.

north and south rise 1,520 to 2,740 m (5,000 to 9,000 ft) above sea level, partly as a result of regional uplift, which left the North Rim more than 305 m (1,000 ft) higher than the South Rim in places. On the bare walls, strata of limestone, sandstone, lava, and other rocks can be seen; they change color as the day passes.

García López de Cárdenas, a Spanish explorer, discovered the canyon in 1540, but systematic exploration did not begin until 1850. John Wesley Powell was the first to travel (1869) through the canyon by boat. The national park, created in 1919, has an area of 4,931 km^2 (1,904 mi^2).

Grand Central Terminal New York City's Grand Central Terminal, a notable example of the Beaux-Arts style, was designed by Whitney Warren and constructed in 1907–13. Once the rival of New York's even more grandiose Pennsylvania Station (demolished in 1963), Grand Central still functions as a major railroad terminus and has been designated a landmark structure.

Grand Coulee Dam [koo'-lee] The most massive concrete structure in the world when opened in 1942, Grand Coulee Dam on the Columbia River in Washington State contains more than 7.6 million m^3 (10 million yd^3) of concrete. The 1.3-km-long (0.8-mi), 168-m-high (550-ft) gravity DAM served the world's largest hydroelectric complex. Although recently enlarged to 9.7 million kilowatts, the capacity of the Grand Coulee Dam has been exceeded (1982) by Itaipú Dam, on the boundary between Brazil and Paraguay, with an installed capacity of 12.6 million kilowatts.

Grand Forks Grand Forks (1990 pop., 49,425) is the seat of Grand Forks County in eastern North Dakota. It is located at the junction of the Red River of the North and Red Lake River, 145 km (90 mi) south of the Canadian border. The city is the center of trade and processing for an agricultural region where wheat, potatoes, sugar beets, and livestock are produced. The University of North Dakota (1883), an air force base, and a Minuteman missile complex are located in or near the city. Grand Forks was settled in 1871 and incorporated in 1881.

Grand Island Located in southern Nebraska on the Platte River, Grand Island (1990 pop., 39,386) is the seat of Hall County. It is a rail, shipping, and manufacturing center. Grand Island was settled in 1857 by Germans and laid out in 1866, when the Union Pacific Railroad arrived.

grand jury A grand JURY, a body of from 12 to 23 private citizens, hears accusations of crimes committed in a district or county. After hearing the evidence submitted by the prosecutor (it seldom hears the accused), the grand jury decides whether the evidence is sufficient to hold the accused for trial. If so, it authorizes an INDICTMENT that carefully spells out the charges against the accused so that a defense may be prepared. A grand jury may also initiate its own investigation and subpoena witnesses. Grand juries are often chosen by lot, and the process of selection must be fair.

The grand jury is part of the jury institution developed in Anglo-American common law, although England abolished the grand jury in 1933. In the United States grand jury protection was guaranteed by the 5th Amendment of the Bill of Rights. In recent years the use of the grand jury has declined. The U.S. Supreme Court had ruled in *Hurtado* v. *California* (1884) that grand jury indictments were not required of the states, and prosecutors have increasingly presented accusations in the form of an information, a formal accusation that does not have to be made by a grand jury.

See also: POWELL V. ALABAMA.

Grand Old Party see REPUBLICAN PARTY

Grand Ole Opry [ohl ahp'ree] The Grand Ole Opry's rise from one among many square dance radio shows to an international musical and tourist institution parallels COUNTRY AND WESTERN MUSIC's climb to national eminence. In 1925 radio station WSM in Nashville, Tenn., began broadcasting hillbilly music weekly. At first, the mostly amateur musicians presented authentic regional music. The first star of the show—banjoist and singer "Uncle" Dave Macon, whose style reached back into the 19th century—achieved national acclaim during the 1930s.

The Grand Ole Opry's growth began when Roy Acuff joined the show in 1938 as its first singing star. During the 1940s the show was broadcast nationally over NBC radio and began to send out auxiliary touring companies.

By 1950 the Grand Ole Opry had become a supershow with a cast of about 120 performers. It was largely responsible for the growth of Nashville as the center of the country music recording industry and became the city's most famous tourist attraction. By this time the Opry had long since lost its regional, down-home quality, and in 1974 the last link with the past was cut when it moved to a new multimillion-dollar Opryland concert center on the outskirts of the city.

Grand Rapids   A furniture-manufacturing center and the second largest city in Michigan, Grand Rapids is situated at the rapids (now largely dredged) of the Grand River in west central Michigan. Grand Rapids is the seat of Kent County and has a population of 189,126 (1990) within the city limits and 688,399 in the metropolitan area. In addition to furniture production, the city has several hundred diversified industries; it is the distribution, trade, and cultural focus for much of western Michigan. It is also the gateway to fishing and recreational areas. Several colleges are located there.

The city was established (1827) as a fur-trading post on the site of an Indian village. Abundant forests and waterpower fostered a thriving lumber industry, which led (by 1859) to furniture making; the many new Dutch immigrants excelled at this craft.

Grand Teton National Park   see NATIONAL PARKS

grand unification theories   In theoretical physics, grand unification theories (GUTs) are attempts to describe three of the fundamental forces of nature—the strong, weak, and electromagnetic forces—as aspects of a single interaction (see FUNDAMENTAL INTERACTIONS). Grand unification theories also describe the two primary constituents of matter, QUARKS and LEPTONS, as manifestations of a single type of subatomic particle.

According to current theory, forces between subatomic particles are transmitted via the emission and absorption of vector BOSONS, particles with one unit of intrinsic angular momentum. Theorists use a mathematical structure known as a gauge field to describe these fundamental interactions. The weak, strong, and electromagnetic interactions differ mainly in their strengths, as measured by the rest energies of their bosons, and by the probability of boson emissions. In order of decreasing strength, the individual bosons are GLUONS (the strong force), PHOTONS (the electromagnetic force), and W and Z particles (the weak force).

In GUTs the differences between fundamental forces are seen to be the result of the fact that particles are observed at relatively low energies. If particles could be observed at very high energies, the three types of interaction would be found to have equal strength. In addition, quarks and leptons would behave similarly under those conditions. The energy at which this unification is expected is about 10^{14} GeV (giga electron volts), a trillion times higher than the energies of present-day experiments. While it may never be possible to examine such high-energy processes in the laboratory, it is thought that in the very early universe a small fraction of a second after the big bang (see COSMOLOGY) the average energy of all particles was high enough for these particles to behave in the manner described by GUTs.

One startling prediction of GUTs is that new interactions may exist, involving vector bosons whose rest energy is 10^{14} GeV. These interactions would allow three quarks to convert into a lepton, inducing the decay of protons and neutrons into leptons. The result of such decays would be a proton lifetime of 10^{31} years, and evidence for this would defeat the long-held notion of the eternal stability of the proton. Experiments designed to detect these rare proton decays are being carried out, but no conclusive evidence has been obtained.

Although the validity of GUTs is not yet established, physicists are developing theories that will link the fourth force, gravitation (and its boson, the graviton), with the other three forces. These models are referred to as supersymmetry theories.

See also: SYMMETRY (PHYSICS); UNIFIED FIELD THEORY.

grandfather clause   A grandfather clause exempts certain people from specific requirements in laws or regulations that normally have to be fulfilled in order to enter into an occupation, start a business, or assume a right. People who are declared exempt by a grandfather clause are privileged because of their status or their ancestors' status prior to enactment of the requirements. In 1895 several Southern states began to pass laws with grandfather clauses to allow whites to vote, in spite of the fact that they failed to meet literacy or poll-tax requirements, if they themselves, or their fathers or grandfathers, had been entitled to vote on Jan. 1, 1867. Such laws, designed to keep blacks from voting, were declared unconstitutional under the 15th Amendment in *Guinn & Beal* v. *United States* (1915).

Grandma Moses   see MOSES, GRANDMA

Grange, National   The National Grange is the popular name of the Order of the Patrons of Husbandry, the oldest general farm organization in the United States. It was established in Washington, D.C., on Dec. 4, 1867, largely through the efforts of Oliver Hudson Kelley, a Minnesota farmer who was deeply affected by the poverty and isolation of the farmers he saw while inspecting farm areas in the South for the U.S. Department of Agriculture in 1866. Kelley felt they had to unite and promote their interests collectively. The organization, which acquired the character of a FRATERNAL SOCIETY, provided lectures and entertainment for farm men and women. It also experimented in COOPERATIVE buying and selling of farm products and supplies and carried on educational programs, setting up Grange units for children as well as adults.

In the 1870s the Grange was prominent in the broader Granger movement, which campaigned against extortionate charges by monopolistic railroads and warehouses and helped bring about laws regulating these charges in some states in the upper Mississippi Valley. Although challenged, the constitutionality of such laws was upheld by the U.S. Supreme Court in *Munn* v. *Illinois* (1876).

Grange, Red   Harold Edward Grange, b. Forksville, Pa., June 13, 1903, d. Jan. 28, 1991, was a legendary American football player. Red Grange became nationally known at the University of Illinois (1923–25) as he rushed for 3,637 yards and scored 31 touchdowns. In his most famous game, against the University of Michigan in 1924, Grange scored five touchdowns and set up a sixth in a 39–14 upset. Grange joined the professional ranks after his last college game in 1925 and went on a 19-game tour in which he drew record-breaking professional crowds in many cities. He is credited with making professional football a major spectator sport. Grange played with the New York Yankees of the American Football League and the Chicago Bears of the National Football League until 1934. He was a brilliant broken-field runner and was thus nicknamed (by sportswriter Grantland Rice) "The Galloping Ghost."

Red Grange, one of the outstanding running backs in the history of collegiate football, led the University of Illinois to a national championship during his first season with the varsity squad and won All-American honors three times (1923–25). Grange left school to play professional football for the Chicago Bears.

Granger movement   see GRANGE, NATIONAL

granite [gran'-it]   Granite is a light-colored plutonic rock found throughout the continental crust, most commonly in mountainous areas (see IGNEOUS ROCK). It consists of coarse grains of QUARTZ (10–50%), potassium FELDSPAR, and sodium feldspar. These minerals make up more than 80% of the rock. Other common minerals include MICA (muscovite and biotite) and hornblende (see AMPHIBOLE). The chemical composition of granite is typi-

cally 70–77% SiO_2, 11–13% Al_2O_3, 3–5% K_2O, 3–5% Na_2O, 1% CaO, 2–3% total iron, and less than 1% MgO and TiO_2. Volcanic rock of equivalent chemical composition and mineralogy is called RHYOLITE.

Granites are the most abundant plutonic rocks of mountain belts and CONTINENTAL SHIELD areas. They form vast bodies called batholiths that may occupy thousands of square kilometers and are usually closely associated with quartz monzonite, granodiorite, DIORITE, and GABBRO.

Granite was once thought to form mainly from magmatic differentiation of basaltic MAGMA, but geologists now believe there is simply too much of it for it to have formed this way, except locally. Most granite seems to have formed either by melting, partial melting, or metamorphism of deeply buried shale and sandstone. Granite DIKES are clearly igneous, and granite emplaced in the upper few kilometers of the Earth's crust may also show evidence of forceful intrusion; but where evidence of either a magma chamber or of fluidity is lacking, a metamorphic origin must be considered.

Granite is used as a building and ornamental stone. Many ORE DEPOSITS (copper, lead, zinc, gold, and silver, for example) were produced by hydrothermal solutions created during late stages of cooling of granite bodies. These may be emplaced around the peripheries or related to fissures and fractures within bodies of granite.

Grant, Cary   Cary Grant was the professional name of English-born Archibald Alexander Leach, b. Jan. 18, 1904, d. Nov. 29, 1986, who won world fame in dozens of Hollywood movies as the quintessentially debonair, self-confident sophisticate. Appearing in films from 1932 on, he played roles particularly suited to his talents in *The Awful Truth* (1937) and *My Favorite Wife* (1940) opposite Irene Dunne, in *The Philadelphia Story* (1940) with Katharine Hepburn, and in such Alfred Hitchcock thrillers as *Suspicion* (1941), *Notorious* (1946), *To Catch a Thief* (1955), and *North by Northwest* (1959). Grant retired in 1970.

Cary Grant shares a romantic moment with leading lady Ingrid Bergman in this scene from the spy drama Notorious *(1946).*

AT A GLANCE

ULYSSES SIMPSON GRANT
18th President of the United States (1869–77)

Nickname: "Hero of Appomattox"

Born: Apr. 27, 1822, Point Pleasant, Ohio

Education: U.S. Military Academy, West Point, N.Y. (graduated 1843)

Profession: Soldier

Religious Affiliation: Methodist

Marriage: Aug. 22, 1848, to Julia Boggs Dent (1826–1902)

Children: Frederick Dent Grant (1850–1912); Ulysses Simpson Grant (1852–1929); Ellen Wrenshall Grant (1855–1922); Jesse Root Grant (1858–1934)

Political Affiliation: Republican

Writings: *Personal Memoirs* (2 vols., 1885–86); Papers (4 vols., 1967–), ed. by John Y. Simon

Died: July 23, 1885, Mount McGregor, N.Y.

Buried: Grant's Tomb, New York City

Vice-Presidents: Schuyler Colfax (1869–73); Henry Wilson (1873–75)

Grant, Ulysses S.   Ulysses Simpson Grant, the best-known Federal general in the CIVIL WAR, served also as 18th president of the United States. He was born in the Ohio River village of Point Pleasant, Ohio, on Apr. 27, 1822, the son of a tanner. Although baptized Hiram Ulysses, Grant was listed by the congressman who secured his appointment to West Point as Ulysses Simpson, the latter being his mother's maiden name. Grant graduated from West Point in 1843, but his performance there was undistinguished; he graduated 21st in a class of 39.

In the Mexican War, Grant served effectively with Zachary Taylor's army at Monterey and then with Winfield Scott's army in the campaign for Mexico City. He won two brevets for meritorious conduct at Molino del Rey and Chapultepec.

After the war, Grant was assigned to garrison duty. His early postings in the Great Lakes region were happy because he was with his new wife, Julia Dent Grant (1826–1902), whom he married on Aug. 22, 1848. In 1852, however, he was sent to the Pacific Northwest, where he was unable to have his family with him. He apparently so overindulged in alcohol that he was impelled to resign from the army in 1854. For six years he struggled in Missouri as a farmer, real estate salesman, unsuccessful candidate for county engineer, and agent in a custom-house. In 1860 he was obliged to accept a clerkship in his brothers' leather-goods store in Galena, Ill.

Civil War. After the outbreak of the Civil War, Grant tried in vain to obtain a position on the staff of Gen. George B. McCLELLAN. He initially received the colonelcy of an Illinois regiment, but his effective leadership of that soon brought him appointment (Aug. 7, 1861) as a brigadier general of volunteers. His capture of FORT HENRY AND FORT DONELSON on the Tennessee and Cumberland rivers, respectively, in February 1862 brought him new prominence, and he was advanced to major general.

In early April, Grant moved incautiously southward along the Tennessee River to Pittsburg Landing, or SHILOH, Tenn. There his carelessly disposed army was surprised by a sudden and shattering attack by Albert Sidney JOHNSTON, who was mortally wounded at the height of the Confederate advance. Near defeat on the first day of battle, Grant was reinforced by Maj. Gen. Don Carlos BUELL and counterattacked the following day with moderate success. Grant was subsequently shelved for several months as unfounded rumors to the effect that he was again drinking caused several of his superiors to hesitate in giving him another important command.

On Oct. 25, 1862, Grant was restored to a vital position. Appointed commander of the Department of Tennessee, he was instructed to take Vicksburg, Miss., the great enemy bastion on the east bank of the Mississippi River. The VICKSBURG CAMPAIGN began badly for Grant, but later, in a masterpiece of planning and bold execution, he fought five victorious battles. This permitted his investiture of Vicksburg, which, after a stern 47-day siege, capitulated on July 4, 1863.

In September 1863, Grant went to the rescue of the beleaguered Union army under William ROSECRANS at Chattanooga. He reinforced this army, replacing Rosecrans with George H. THOMAS, and opened up new lines of supply and communication. Then, in battles at Lookout Mountain and Missionary Ridge in November 1863, he defeated Braxton BRAGG and opened the way toward Dalton, Ga., and eventually for William T. SHERMAN's advance on Atlanta and Savannah. (See CHATTANOOGA, BATTLES OF.)

President Abraham LINCOLN became impressed with Grant's self-reliance, bulldog tenacity, and confidence in final victory; so early in 1864 Lincoln promoted him to lieutenant general and named him general in chief of all the Federal armies. Leaving Sherman in command in the West, Grant established his headquarters with George G. MEADE's Army of the Potomac in the East. In effect, he commanded that army in its driving campaigns of 1864 against Robert E. LEE's army in Virginia.

With troops outnumbering Lee's almost two to one, Grant launched the so-called WILDERNESS CAMPAIGN in early May 1864. He tried to bludgeon his way through the Virginia Wilderness, but was checked and forced to sidestep toward Spotsylvania Court House. Here, in several days of desperate fighting, Grant's gains were negligible and he suffered numerous casualties. At Cold Harbor he was massively repulsed, again with high losses, as morale sagged in the Army of the Potomac. Finally outguessing Lee and stealing a march on him across the James River (June 12–18), Grant and his subordinate generals missed an opportunity to take Petersburg, the railroad key to Richmond, by surprise. After the 9-month PETERSBURG CAMPAIGN (June 18, 1864, to Apr. 2, 1865), conducted while Philip SHERIDAN cleared the Shenandoah Valley of Jubal EARLY's forces, Grant was finally able to force Lee back from Petersburg and Richmond. A 142-km (88-mi) pursuit to the west-southwest ended in final triumph when Lee was obliged to surrender to Grant at APPOMATTOX COURT HOUSE on Apr. 9, 1865. Grant's generous terms were accepted immediately by Lee.

Presidency. After the war Grant was advanced to full general and served not only as general in chief but also, briefly, as President Johnson's interim secretary of war. In 1867, Grant's attempts to protect the army of occupation in the South deflected him from Johnson's policy and toward the Radical Republicans with their more rigorous RECONSTRUCTION policies. This helped secure for him the Republican presidential nomination in 1868. In the election of that year he defeated the Democrat Horatio SEYMOUR and began the first of his two terms in the White House.

As president, Grant seemed at times torpid and irresolute, and many of his appointments left much to be de-

sired. Despite campaign pledges for civil-service reform, Grant was largely responsible for scuttling such a program. He did relentlessly oppose the KU KLUX KLAN, however, in which he was aided when Congress passed the so-called Force Acts of 1870–71.

Grant's hard-money stand delighted business and banking interests and helped him win reelection over Horace GREELEY in 1872. Although at first slow to react, he had been able in 1869 to block the attempts of Jay GOULD and James FISK to corner the gold market. However, his second term came under a cloud of graft, scandal, and corruption. The scandal that came closest to the White House itself was that of the WHISKEY RING, in which Grant's private secretary, Orville Babcock, was implicated. Grant's chief successes, due largely to his capable secretary of state, Hamilton Fish (see FISH family), were scored in the field of foreign affairs. They included favorable settlement of the Alabama Claims dispute with Britain.

Later Years. After leaving office, Grant was exploited in a business venture and failed. To get his family out of debt he undertook to write his memoirs. These were completed while he was dying of throat cancer and were published in two volumes as the *Personal Memoirs of U. S. Grant* (1885–86). Not only were they profitable, netting his family $450,000, but they also have become an American classic. Grant died at Mount McGregor, N.Y., on July 23, 1885, and his body was finally laid to rest in an imposing tomb on Riverside Drive in New York City.

◼

Granville-Barker, Harley [gran-vil-bar'-kur, har'-lee] Harley Granville-Barker, b. London, Nov. 25, 1877, d. Aug. 31, 1946, was an English actor, dramatist, producer, and critic whose work invigorated English theater during the Edwardian period. As manager of London's Royal Court Theatre (1904–07), he developed a progressive repertoire that included many of the first English stage productions of George Bernard Shaw, Maurice Maeterlinck, and Henrik Ibsen. Granville-Barker's own plays, including *The Voysey Inheritance* (1905), *Waste* (1907), and *The Madras House* (1910), supported the new realism in early 20th-century English drama. His six-volume work, *Prefaces to Shakespeare* (1927–47), is still considered an important critical study of Shakespearean theater.

◼

grape The grape is the fruit of vines of the genus *Vitis* of the family Vitaceae; the genera *Cissus* and *Rhoicissus* also belong to this family. Classified botanically as berries, domesticated grapes grow in clusters, range in color from pale green to black, and contain sugar in varying quantities. Grapes with about 20 percent sugar are used to make WINE. Other types are eaten fresh, dried as raisins, or canned. Unfermented grape juice is processed for drinking or for use in jellies. More than 90 percent of all cultivated grapes are varieties of *V. vinifera*, the Old World or European grape. Originating in Anatolia, this species has been spread by humans into all temperate regions and recently into subtropical areas. At least 5,000 variet-

Pictured here are two important varieties of the Old World wine grape: the white Pinot Chardonnay and the red Pinot Noir. Native American species, such as the Concord, are generally less sweet and, unlike the grapes shown here, their skins slip readily from the pulp.

The grapefruit was first cultivated in the West Indies and introduced into the Florida area in the 1820s. Only in the 1900s, however, did the fruit become commercially significant, and among citrus fruits it now ranks fourth in the world in economic importance.

The globular fruit usually grows in clusters somewhat like bunches of grapes, although some grapefruit are borne singly. Mature grapefruits reach 8 to 15 cm (3 to 6 in) in diameter, with a pale yellow rind and pale yellow or yellow-pink pulp. Juice content ranges from 35 to 50 percent, with more acid and slightly less vitamin C than orange juice. More than half the U.S. production is processed into canned and frozen fruit or juice. Processing residues are used to produce peel oil, cattle feed, and various chemicals.

The grapefruit tree, a member of the orange family, was so named because of the grapelike clusters in which its large fruit grows.

ies of grapes have been derived from this species.

Whereas European grapes derive exclusively from *V. vinifera*, native American grapes come from many wild species of *Vitis*. These grapes are characterized by their musky, or "foxy," odor and flavor, and by the fact that, unlike *V. vinifera*, their skins slip from the fruit pulp.

Specimens of the European grape were brought by the Spanish into areas of present-day California and Mexico and by the English to settlements along the Atlantic seaboard. The latter plantings failed mainly because of climatic extremes; fungal diseases that thrive in the hot, humid summers; and the plant's susceptibility to root aphids *(Phylloxera)* that are less harmful to native American grapes. *Phylloxera* were accidentally introduced into Europe in the mid-19th century, almost completely destroying vineyards in France, Germany, and Italy. Most wine grapes in Europe and America are grown on vines grafted onto resistant rootstocks.

Derivations of American species or hybrids of American grapes and *V. vinifera* are cultivated throughout the United States. They fall into three broad categories: American cultivars, the most important of which are varieties with *V. labrusca* as one parent, including Catawba, Niagara, and Concord grapes; the Muscadine cultivars, from the American *V. rotundifolia*; and "French hybrids," crosses of *V. vinifera* and native American species.

grapefruit The grapefruit is an evergreen tree, *Citrus paradisi*, of the Rutaceae family, and its fruit is the largest of the commercially grown CITRUS FRUITS. A descendant of the pomelo—a citrus species that grows in Southeast Asia and was brought to the West Indies in the 17th century—the grapefruit is believed to be either a pomelo mutant or a hybrid resulting from crossing the pomelo with the sweet orange.

Grapes of Wrath, The *The Grapes of Wrath* (1939) by U.S. novelist John STEINBECK is one of the most powerful chronicles in American literature of the Depression of the 1930s. It deals with the Joads, a family that loses its farm through foreclosure and leaves the Oklahoma Dust Bowl for California in the hope of finding work. The eldest generation has the comfort of religion, the next one has a dogged perseverance, but the youngest has little to believe in. Embittered by the brutal exploitation of migrant workers, Tom, who had been jailed for murder and who later kills again, becomes a labor organizer. In this Pulitzer Prize–winning (1940) novel, Steinbeck alternates his narrative with serious discussion of the problems of migrant laborers.

graph A graph is a pictorial representation of numerical data. It is a diagram representing interrelationships between two, three, or more quantities by the use of a number of distinctive features such as points, lines, and bars. Types of graphs include HISTOGRAMS (bar graphs),

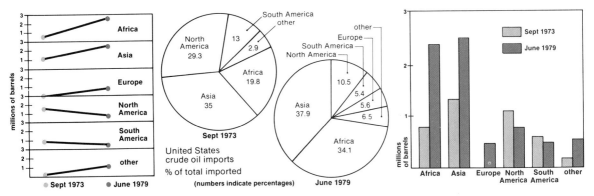

Bar, pie, and line graphs indicate amount of U.S. crude oil imports from various areas in September 1973 and June 1979.

circular (pie) graphs, and line graphs. A histogram consists of a series of bars or rectangles, the lengths of which are proportional to the data being presented. In a line graph the data are represented by points that are joined by straight-line segments. A "pie" graph presents data in the form of slices of a pie, with the size, or angle, of each slice proportional to the quantity it represents. A pictorial representation displays at a glance much of the quantitative behavior of the variables involved; at times graphs can be misleading, and care must be used in interpreting them. Branches of mathematics such as ANALYTIC GEOMETRY, STATISTICS, and TRIGONOMETRY deal with the study of various graphs.

The graph of an EQUATION in two variables is the set of points in a plane whose coordinates satisfy the equation. The graphic representation of an equation in three variables is a surface in space.

—

graphic arts In a general sense, the term *graphic arts* includes all forms of artistic visual representation executed on a two-dimensional surface by such means as painting, drawing, or photography. More specifically, the term is a synonym for printmaking. In this application, the graphic arts include all works of art that begin with an original impression of any kind of imagery or design executed by the artist and intended to be reproduced by any one of a number of printing processes.

Among the many reproduction processes used by artists, those involving intaglio techniques, where the design is cut into the surface of a metal plate or wood block, are among the most important. In ENGRAVING, the design is cut directly into the surface of a copper or zinc plate, using a tool called a burin, which leaves a minute shaving along both sides of the line it cuts. The shaving may be brushed away. Prints made from plates where the shavings have been deliberately created and left on the plate surface are called DRYPOINT engravings. They have a generally softer, more shaded line. In ETCHING, the plate is first covered with a "ground," usually a wax mixture, and the artist draws the design through the ground with etching needles of various sizes, exposing the metal underneath. The plate is then immersed in acid, and where the ground

has been scratched away, the acid eats into the exposed metal, leaving the design etched below the plate surface.

The three processes—engraving, drypoint, and etching—are very often used together, and sometimes in conjunction with other intaglio processes. With AQUATINT, which is used to create greater tonal gradation or to add color, a layer of rosin is poured on the plate and then heated, so that the grains fuse to the surface. When immersed in acid, the metal between the grains is eaten away, forming tiny holes which print as a soft-toned background. The MEZZOTINT has even softer, more shaded qualities, produced by first pitting the entire plate surface with a "rocker," then scraping and burnishing where the design is to appear.

Wood blocks can also be carved with intaglio designs, although more commonly the blocks are carved in relief: that is, the design stands up from the surface of the block, all nondesign areas having been cut away (see WOODCUTS AND WOOD ENGRAVINGS).

In lithography, an oily paint is used to draw on a smooth stone surface. An acid treatment leaves the design area capable of holding and printing ink. (See LITHOGRAPH.) The silk-screen printing process involves cutting the design out of fine silk stretched within a frame, and then squeezing paint through the open portions of the silk onto the surface to be printed (see SILK-SCREEN PRINTING).

Woodcut. The woodcut is the oldest form of printmaking. In the 2d century AD paper was developed in China, and wood blocks were used to create book illustrations. Japanese woodcuts achieved their greatest refinement in the masterful, multicolored 18th- and 19th-century *ukiyo-e* prints that depict landscapes and scenes of everyday life by such masters as HIROSHIGE, HOKUSAI, and UTAMARO (see also JAPANESE ART AND ARCHITECTURE).

The woodcut was developed as a pictorial art in Europe at the end of the 14th century, when the process was used to make simple religious pictures for mass distribution. They were executed by skilled craftsmen after original designs by painters and sculptors. With the mid-15th century invention of the printing press, woodcuts were used for BOOK ILLUSTRATIONS.

Among the first great European artists to use the woodcut were the German Renaissance masters Albrecht

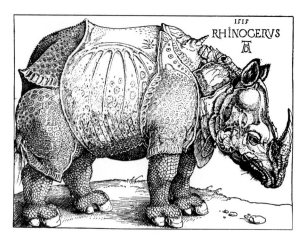

Albrecht Dürer's minutely detailed engraving of a rhinoceros (1515) shows the naturalism characteristic of his work. Dürer was one of the most eminent German artists of the Renaissance. (British Museum, London.)

Dürer and Hans HOLBEIN the Younger. Hans BURGKMAIR experimented with woodcut *chiaroscuro*, which created contrasts of light and shade by using several blocks.

Woodcut declined as a fine art after the mid-16th century, when it was replaced by line engraving and etching. During the late 19th century, however, it had its greatest revival, chiefly in the works of Frenchmen Paul GAUGUIN and Félix VALLOTTON and the Norwegian artist Edvard MUNCH. Unlike most previous woodcuts—which had been reproductions of the drawings of the masters by craftsmen—these were executed by the artists themselves.

Related to the art of woodcut are Pablo PICASSO's linocuts (using linoleum blocks) of the 1950s, the wood engravings of the American Leonard BASKIN, and the cellocuts (using plastic plates) developed by Boris Margo. New techniques and forms have kept woodcut a vital medium in contemporary art.

Engraving and Etching. The technique of engraving metal surfaces with pictorial designs dates back to classical antiquity and was practiced continually throughout the Middle Ages by such skilled craftsmen as goldsmiths and armorers.

The earliest datable engravings on paper are from about 1430 and show the influence of the Flemish master painters of the period. The German artist Martin SCHONGAUER was the first printmaker (he was also a painter) to gain international acclaim for his finely detailed, late-Gothic engravings. Of the same period was the Master of the Housebook, who pioneered the technique known as drypoint.

The greatest etcher of the 17th century, and perhaps the greatest in the entire history of art, was the Dutch master REMBRANDT van Rijn. His style of dramatic chiaroscuro—in rich, dark tones executed with a vigorous spontaneity—is exemplified in his almost 300 etchings of landscapes. Another important 17th-century graphic artist was the innovative French printmaker Jacques CALLOT,

who developed the hard-varnish ground technique.

During the 18th century outstanding etchings were produced by three Italian artists—Giovanni Battista Tiepolo (see TIEPOLO family), CANALETTO, and Giovanni Battista PIRANESI—and the English painter William HOGARTH, who engraved series of biting, satirical paintings—*The Harlot's Progress* (1732) and *The Rake's Progress* (1735).

During the late 18th and early 19th centuries, the great Spanish painter Francisco de GOYA produced several series of powerful black-and-white etchings of grotesque figures that satirized the contemporary social situation. More than 400 plates remain of the etchings of James McNeill WHISTLER, who was perhaps the most innovative of the graphic artists during the late 19th century. His delicate, summary impressions exemplify his technical mastery of the medium.

James ENSOR and Edvard Munch are among the many artists who used etching as part of their oeuvres during the early 20th century. The etchings of Paul KLEE were a major part of his multimedia work, rich in technique and texture. The graphic designs of M. C. ESCHER are especially notable for their creation of unusual perspectives and optical illusions.

Related to the history of etching is the inventive exploration of new intaglio techniques by Stanley William Hayter's Atelier 17 in pre–World War II Paris, in New York City during the 1940s, and in Paris during the 1950s and '60s.

Lithography. The earliest lithographic process was developed (1796–98) by the German playwright Aloys Senefelder, whose main objective was the inexpensive duplication of his works. His partners, Philipp and Johann André, introduced the technique in England, where linear works on the lithographic stone were done by William BLAKE, Henry FUSELI, and Benjamin WEST. The ability of lithography to reproduce a more expressive line was used to its best advantage in the 19th century by the French,

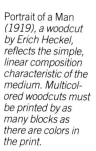

Portrait of a Man *(1919), a woodcut by Erich Heckel, reflects the simple, linear composition characteristic of the medium. Multicolored woodcuts must be printed by as many blocks as there are colors in the print.*

"Can Nobody Liberate Us?" is one of Francisco Goya's series of 80 bitterly satirical etchings, Los Caprichos (1797–98), executed on an aquatint ground. The aquatint technique uses a granular plate to create a solid, textured background. (Rijksmuseum, Amsterdam.)

Rembrandt's etching The Three Crosses (c.1661) displays the control of line and light and the powerful evocation of atmosphere that made him one of the greatest masters of the graphic arts. (Rijksprentenkabinet, Amsterdam.)

first by Théodore GÉRICAULT and Eugène DELACROIX and later by Honoré DAUMIER. Daumier produced about 4,000 lithographs, boldly personal caricatures of the lower and middle classes that grew out of Daumier's early political cartoons. The celebrated posters of Henri de TOULOUSE-LAUTREC are among the finest examples of 19th-century French lithography. Also of note are Odilon REDON's symbolist lithographs, such as his series dedicated to Edgar Allan Poe (1882).

Early-20th-century accomplishments in European lithography include those by the German expressionists Karl SCHMIDT-ROTTLUFF, Emil Nolde, and Ernst Kirchner (all members of Die BRÜCKE) and by Edvard Munch and the Austrian artist Oskar KOKOSCHKA.

In the United States CURRIER AND IVES and Joseph Pennell are outstanding in the area of 19th-century lithography, followed by such 20th-century artists as Arthur B. DAVIES and George BELLOWS. The lithograph was widely used by New York painters of the 1960s, including Jasper JOHNS and James ROSENQUIST. The lithographic process has been employed in recent years to record body prints.

Silk-Screen Printing. The technique of silk-screen printing originated during the Middle Ages in the art of stencil printing of China and Japan, where it was practiced with great delicacy and intricacy. Until the 20th century, screen printing was a decorative and commercial medium, used to enhance fabrics, wallpaper, furnishings, and advertising.

In 1936 screen printing was seen as a means of artis-tic expression by a group of American artists working on the Works Progress Administration (WPA) under the leadership of Anthony Velonis. The art historian Carl Zigrosser coined the term serigraph to identify the new screen prints as a fine art.

Op artists of the 1960s, such as Richard ANUSZKIEWICZ and Victor VASARELY, have used silk-screen printing in their style of precise form and color. The two most impor-

In works such as Marcelle Lender (1895) Henri de Toulouse-Lautrec exploited the possibilities of color lithography, elevating a commercial printing technique to an art form. (Musée Toulouse-Lautrec, Albi, France.)

Andy Warhol's screen-printed Flowers *(1964) shows how much fine detail is possible in modern methods of silk screening. Silk screening, printing from a stencil and mesh screen, permits numerous duplications. (Private collection.)*

tant artists of the 1960s to use silk-screen printing as a major medium were Robert Rauschenberg and Andy WARHOL, both of whom used screen printing in combination with photographic processes.

See also: PRINTING.

graphite   see CARBON

graptolite [grap'-tuh-lyt]   Graptolites are the remains of extinct, colonial invertebrate animals that inhabited a number of marine habitats and were especially abundant during the early Paleozoic Era (see GEOLOGIC TIME). The most common fossils superficially resemble small hacksaw blades impressed in rock. Others appear as small, bushy structures pressed onto the rock matrix. Those resembling hacksaw blades are commonly about 15 to 44 mm (½ to 1½ in) long; the smallest of the bushlike structures are about 25 mm (1 in) across; larger ones are several centimeters across.

The floating, planktonic graptolites have been useful in correlating stratigraphic units because they have wide geographic distribution. Since the floating graptolite colonies changed shape rapidly, they are also particularly valuable as index fossils, or indicators of geologic age (see FOSSIL RECORD). Graptolites are among the few fossils that may be preserved in METAMORPHIC ROCKS and thus can be used to date terrains of otherwise undatable rock.

Graptolites lived from the middle of the Cambrian Period into the Carboniferous, some 200 million years. The biological relationships of graptolites are uncertain. They most closely resemble shells of the modern rhabdopleurans, tiny colonial marine animals belonging to the phylum Hemichordata.

grass   Grasses, family Gramineae, are the most variable, widespread, and useful plant groups and comprise more than 600 genera and 7,500 species. The soft, velvety turf plants that form lawns bear little resemblance to the huge, woody bamboos towering 40 m (132 ft) or more in height. Submerged aquatic plants growing in the sea seem quite different from the small, tender shoots emerging from a snowbank in the alpine tundra above the timberline. Yet all these may be grasses.

To the average urban dweller, grass may mean only the green carpet covering a lawn or courtyard. To a farmer in the Great Plains, on the other hand, grass cereal grains such as wheat may be the major cash crop. Grasses produce the bulk of forage for the world's livestock industry, and they provide building materials for houses in tropical areas.

Grasses grow on all continents. They are found in the sea, in freshwater marshes, in deserts, above the treeline on high mountains, and in arctic areas. In some regions grasses constitute the dominant vegetation type. As a group, grasses are among the most successful and actively evolving of all plants. Their great flexibility and adaptability permit them to live in most situations. Their adaptive radiation has evolved treelike forms, intermediate tufts that compete with understory in forests and savanna, and horizontally spreading perennials that form either dense sod or loose ground cover.

Structure

Stems. The grass plant is composed of stems, leaves, roots, and fruiting structures. Stems of grasses have two parts: nodes and internodes. The node is a joint in the stem at the place where leaves are attached. The internode, or area between where leaves are attached, may be either pithy, hollow, or solid. The erect stem of a grass is called a culm. Lateral shoots immediately above the ground may produce creeping prostrate stems called stolons. Stoloniferous grasses may reproduce asexually by stolons growing into new territory and establishing roots at the nodes.

Lateral buds immediately below the ground may produce subterranean stems called rhizomes. Rhizomes are a major source of asexual reproduction and allow a plant to persist even under heavy defoliation. Lateral shoots of cultivated grasses may be called tillers (usually in wheat, oats, and other cereals) or suckers (in maize and sorghum).

Most perennial grasses have herbaceous culms that die back each year and are replaced by new shoots. The resulting colony of individual grass shoots is often called a "plant" or a clone. The clone grows from the center outward, with the older plants in the center becoming weakened from competition. In extreme cases the "plant" may actually develop into a ring of healthy plants with a dead open center. Not all perennial grasses die back each year; some have a woody stem that stores nutrients, and they behave much like a woody shrub. Bamboos are the most common woody grasses.

Leaves. The leaves of grasses are two-ranked, a char-

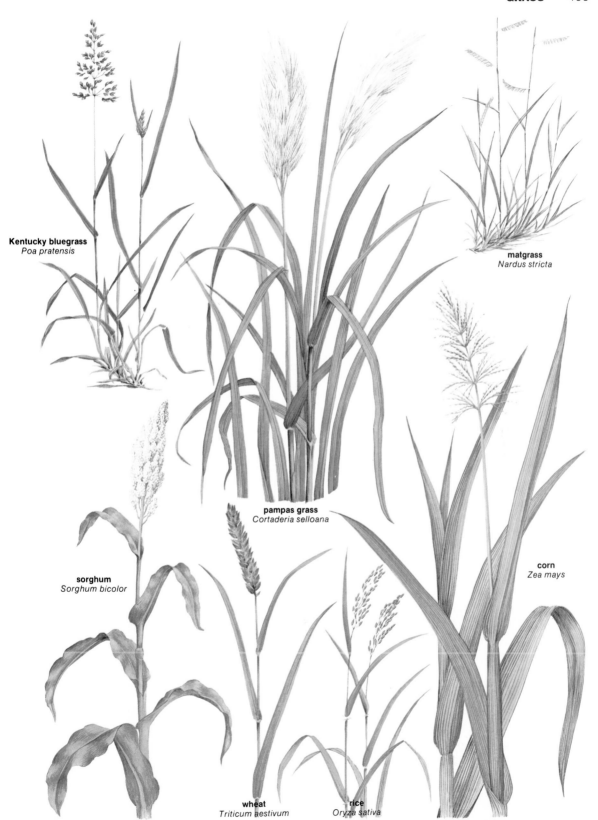

Kentucky bluegrass
Poa pratensis

matgrass
Nardus stricta

pampas grass
Cortaderia selloana

sorghum
Sorghum bicolor

corn
Zea mays

wheat
Triticum aestivum

rice
Oryza sativa

acteristic that separates grasses from other families that they closely resemble, such as sedges (Cyperaceae) with three-ranked leaves. The grass blade itself consists of a sheath and a blade, or lamina. The sheath, the lower portion of the leaf, tightly enfolds the culm from its attachment at the node almost to the next node. The blade is the flattened, elongated portion of the leaf that extends away from the culm. A membranous or hairy structure on the leaf at the side toward the axis where the sheath and blade come together is called a ligule. Lateral projections at the base of the leaf or the apex of the sheath are auricles. Photosynthesis and respiration are carried out in both the sheath and the blade. The growing point of the new shoot, the apical meristem, is usually enclosed by several older leaves that give the new shoot some protection from the extremes of a harsh environment.

Roots. Most grass roots are fibrous. When the seed first sprouts it produces primary, or seminal, roots. These roots are usually of little importance after the first few weeks. Early in the development of the grass plant, adventitious roots (roots growing from stems or leaves) are produced at the lower nodes of the shoot. The root systems of most native grass plants are almost entirely adventitious. The size of the root system is usually related to the amount of shoot growth. Plants with large root-to-shoot ratios appear to be more drought-tolerant than those with smaller ratios.

Fruiting Structures. The flowering and fruiting structure of a grass is called the inflorescence. Its basic unit is the spikelet, which may contain one or more flowers, or florets, on a shortened stem axis, or rachilla, enclosed by two flora, or "empty," bracts called glumes.

There are three basic types of inflorescences: spikes, racemes, and panicles. A spike is an inflorescence in which all spikelets are attached directly to the main axis. Wheat and rye are good examples of this type. In a raceme, the florets are borne on short flower stalks, or pedicels, on the major axis; barley is an example. When the flower stalk branches, as in oats, it is called a panicle. Grasses have wind-pollinated flowers. The grass fruit varies greatly in size, from the very small grains of *Sporobolus* and *Muhlenbergia* to common grains of corn, wheat, and rice. Regardless of size, all have a high percentage of stored nutrients, making them attractive to insects, birds, and mammals.

Some species of grass produce large amounts of highly fertile seeds that can quickly colonize disturbed areas. Other species rely on rhizomes or stolons to move the plants into new environments.

Uses

Human Consumption. Grass seeds have a large quantity of nutrients stored in them that allow new shoots and roots to develop quickly upon germination. These large, nutritious seeds are ideally suited as food for animals and human beings alike. Grass seed, or GRAIN, is grown on about three-fourths of the world's arable land. Three species of cereal grass—WHEAT, RICE, and maize (CORN)—form the basis of the staple human food for most of the world. Many specialized varieties of each have been developed through controlled breeding. Wheat is a grass of temperate origin, ideally suited to the cooler climates of the

world. Rice is of tropical origin; its grain probably feeds more people than does any other plant. Maize probably originated in Mexico from tropical grasses.

Cereal grasses such as BARLEY, OATS, and RYE are cool-season species that are important grain crops in temperate regions of the world. Tropical cereals such as SORGHUM and pearl MILLET form the basis of human diets in much of Africa and other tropical areas. Sugarcane produces much of the world's refined SUGAR and molasses. It is cultivated in tropical areas throughout the world.

Animal Feed. Although grasses produce a large part of the world's diet, only relatively small amounts are consumed directly by humans. Most grasses are used as animal feed. Whereas animals are fed some grain, the bulk of animal feed comes from specialized varieties of grass that are not very palatable to human beings. In addition, grass varieties such as sorghum and maize are raised as fodder crops.

Native grasses provide a major source of feed for domestic livestock on all continents. The species of grass growing in each area varies, but a sustained yield of products from these lands depends on the application of the rules of ecology to perpetuate healthy populations of both plants and animals. The science of managing plants while observing ecological principles is called range management. Almost 30 percent of the Earth's land surface is grazed by animals: grazing is the most widespread of all land uses.

Some grasses are grown under cultivation and grazed by animals. These cultivated pastures are managed as farms. In cool temperate areas species of *Poa* (bluegrass), *Festuca*, *Phleum* (timothy), and *Dactylis* (orchard grass) are the most common forage plants. In tropical climates *Sorghum*, *Paspalum*, *Panicum*, and *Cynodon* are more important.

Turf. Turf for aesthetic and recreation purposes is a major use of grass. Most lawns are of grass. The cool regions of the world regularly use plants of the genera *Poa* and *Agrostis* for turf. Kentucky bluegrass (*Poa pratensis*) is by far the most widely used lawn grass in the northern United States. Creeping bent grass (*Agrostis palustris*) is also used, but it is more popular for golf greens and specialty turfs than for home lawns. Bermuda grass is the popular lawn in much of the warm temperate to tropical areas. In hot areas Saint Augustine grass (*Stenotaphrum secundatum*) is a popular grass, but because of its coarse leaves and high water use it has not challenged the finer-leaved varieties in areas where they can be grown. Some native sod-forming grasses such as buffalo grass (*Buchloë dactyloides*) and curly mesquite grass (*Hilaria belangeri*) are used as minimum-maintenance turfs in the drier portions of the U.S. Great Plains.

Other Uses. There are many nonfood or nonfeed uses of grasses. Grass is used for skirts in the South Pacific Islands and for huts in many tropical regions. Some grasses, particularly bamboos, are used in construction and industry. Houses, bridges, and boat masts are sometimes constructed from the poles and posts of large bamboos. Furniture, window shades, mats and floor coverings, water pipes, and cooking utensils made from grass are found in homes throughout the world. In addition, recreational equipment such as fishing poles, musical instruments, toys, and pipes have been made of grass.

Grasses as Weeds

Grasses that invade new habitats and spread rapidly may become unwanted plants, or weeds. Crabgrass (*Digitaria sanguinalis, D. adscendens*) and quack grass (*Agropyron repens*) are major weeds throughout temperate areas.

Many of the annual grasses become weeds on overgrazed rangeland. Cheatgrass (*Bromus tectorum*), for example, is an aggressive annual from the European area that has invaded the dry ranges of the western United States wherever fire or heavy grazing has left the soil bare.

See also: GRASSLANDS; individual articles on grass species.

Grass, Günter [grahs, gun'-tur]   The German writer Günter Wilhelm Grass, b. Danzig (now Gdańsk, Poland), Oct. 16, 1927, has been called the conscience of his country's postwar generation. Drafted into the Labor Service toward the end of World War II, he was wounded and taken prisoner in 1945. After the war he moved (1947) to Düsseldorf, where he studied sculpture and painting. In 1953, Grass settled in Berlin, where he has since devoted himself to writing, the graphic arts, and socialist politics.

Grass's first novel, *The Tin Drum* (1959; Eng. trans., 1962; film, 1980), earned the 1958 prize of GRUPPE 47. Its complex and self-contradictory narrator, the dwarf drummer Oskar, is an amoral, picaresque hero who narrates the events of the war and postwar eras through a distorted and exaggerated perspective. Together with *Cat and Mouse* (1961; Eng. trans., 1963) and *Dog Years* (1963; Eng. trans., 1965) it forms the Danzig Trilogy. Grass's poetry has been translated in *Selected Poems* (1966) and *In the Egg and Other Poems* (1977).

Grass's dramatic works reveal the influence of the THEATER OF THE ABSURD and the EPIC THEATER of Bertolt Brecht. The grotesque is dominant in *Mister, Mister* (1957; Eng. trans., 1967), *Only Ten Minutes to Buffalo*

Günter Grass, here addressing a political rally, is considered one of the foremost literary figures of postwar Germany. His commitment to political ideals is manifested in satiric novels and plays. The Tin Drum (1959) and The Flounder (1977) are among his most acclaimed works.

(1959; Eng. trans., 1967), and *The Wicked Cooks* (1957; Eng. trans., 1967). In *Flood* (1957; Eng. trans., 1967), Grass depicts the varied reactions and decisions of representatives of two generations as they watch the floodwaters rise around them. In his most controversial play, *The Plebeians Rehearse the Uprising: A German Tragedy* (1965; Eng. trans., 1967), Grass points an ironically critical finger at Brecht. The play concerns the role of the committed artist vis-à-vis society, a question that led in the 1960s to Grass's support of leftist politician Willy Brandt.

Grass's political activities and his sense of commitment inform his later works as well. *From the Diary of a Snail* (1972; Eng. trans., 1978) is a fictionalized account of his involvement with Brandt's 1969 campaign. *The Flounder* (1977; Eng. trans., 1978) is simultaneously novel, fairy tale, diary, political commentary, and a history of women's emancipation. The satire *Headbirths; or, The Germans Are Dying Out* (1980; Eng. trans., 1983), the historical novel *The Meeting at Telgte* (1979; Eng. trans., 1981), and the apocalyptic fiction *The Rat* (1986; Eng. trans., 1987) contribute to Grass's vision of a world that, because it is not better, is inevitably going to be worse.

Grasse, François Joseph Paul, Comte de [grahs]   The comte de Grasse, b. Sept. 13, 1722, d. Jan. 14, 1788, was a French naval officer who commanded the French Atlantic fleet during the AMERICAN REVOLUTION. He won a series of battles against British Caribbean fleets in 1781 before going north to ensure the Franco-American victory against Charles CORNWALLIS in the YORKTOWN CAMPAIGN by turning back a British relief fleet in the Battle of Chesapeake Bay (Sept. 5–9, 1781). Resuming Caribbean duties, de Grasse was soundly defeated and captured by the British in 1782. After his release he was court-martialed in 1784; although acquitted, he did not recover his command.

---

grasshopper   Grasshoppers are members of two different superfamilies in the order Orthoptera characterized by long, slender bodies; hind legs specialized for jumping; chewing mouthparts; and production of sound, or singing, typically only in the males. When four wings are present, the front pair, called tegmina (singular, tegmen), are usually somewhat thickened, long, and slender. The hind wings are wide and membranous.

The superfamily Acridoidea, or short-horned grasshoppers, includes the LOCUSTS. These have antennae shorter than the body, and ears (tympana) set in the abdominal wall. The male's song is generally produced by rubbing a row of stubby comblike teeth on the inside of the hind leg against a hardened edge on the front wing. One group, however, the band-winged grasshoppers (Oedipodinae), sings by snapping the hind wings while in flight. The second superfamily is the Tettigonioidea, the long-horned grasshoppers (KATYDIDS), which have antennae longer than the body, the ears in the front legs, and a bladelike extension (ovipositor) of the female's abdomen. In this

A grasshopper has large compound eyes, leathery forewings that protect its membranous hind wings, and long, powerful hind legs used for jumping. Its coloration enables the grasshopper to blend into its habitat, mainly bushes and grass.

group, the males sing by rubbing a scraper on the base of one front wing against a filelike ridge on the underside of the other front wing.

A female short-horned grasshopper lays her eggs in the soil, a few dozen at a time, and embeds them in froth as an egg pod. The newly hatched larva is wormlike and inches its way to the soil surface, where it quickly molts to become a hopper. It then passes through approximately five or six larval, or nymph, stages and becomes progressively more like the adult, which is readily distinguished only by the complete wings and genitalia. Growth continues for some time in the adult stage, especially in the exoskeleton and muscles, before sexual maturation begins. Mating occurs with the male riding the female and curling his abdomen tip beneath hers to insert the spermatophore, a specially secreted package containing

the sperm. One such insemination suffices to fertilize all the eggs the female will lay in her lifetime, which may total more than a thousand but usually is much less.

Development may be suspended in any stage of the life history, for weeks or months, in unfavorable seasons. The egg stage usually continues through cold winters, and in continental climates the eggs may remain dormant from the start of the hot, dry season until the following spring. Where winters are milder, hibernation occurs in the hopper or adult stage. In the dry tropics the adults remain sexually immature through the dry season, and sexual development proceeds only when, or just before, the rains come. Night migrations by winged adults to extend their geographical range is another way many grasshoppers escape unfavorable conditions and gain access to favorable ones.

Short-horned grasshoppers have adapted to a great range of habitats, but the great majority of species inhabit arid and semiarid regions. Some of them are liable to become pests, when forest or bush is cleared for farms and when grasslands are overgrazed. Among the thousands of species only a few—such as the swarming locusts—are pests, but these can cause severe damage.

---

grasslands Grasslands, a major world BIOME of Earth, are characterized by the dominance of grasses, the smooth cover they provide, and the monotony of flat to rolling terrain. Trees and shrubs occur as scattered individuals or are concentrated along streams or in low areas. Resident wildlife must be adapted to distinct wet and dry seasons, temperature extremes, drying winds, and prolonged droughts.

The fluctuating conditions ensure that grasslands change in the abundance and distribution of wildlife. Plants become dormant in the dry seasons or develop ex-

Grassland vegetation reduces competition between species for water and nutrients by concentrating each species' roots and foliage at different, noncompetitive levels (called layering). In root layering, for example, some species have short, surface root systems that exploit only precipitation, and others have extremely long taproots that may absorb no precipitation (taking water only from underground sources). Grassland soils, in order of depth, are litter (yellow), fine loam (dark brown), two layers of dense loam (light brown and gray brown), calcerous loam (light gray brown to yellow brown), and sandy clay (light gray to yellow).

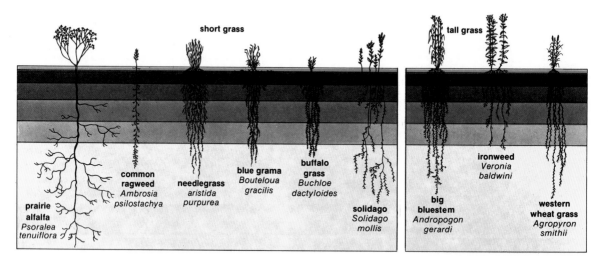

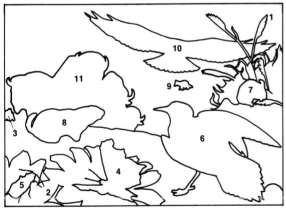

The varied species of plants and animals inhabiting the North American prairies all contribute to the ecological balance of this grassland ecosystem. Grasses, the climax vegetation of the prairies, have evolved to take full advantage of the moderately dry climate. The narrow leaves and short stems of such species as buffalo grass (1) minimize loss of moisture, and their small flowers are readily pollinated by the winds. Plants such as sunflowers (2) and the leguminous Lambert crazyweed (3) develop colorful blossoms that attract the insects that pollinate them, including the fritillary butterfly (4) and the cucumber beetle (5). These insects, in turn, provide the diet of such birds as the killdeer (6), which nests in small depressions of the prairie soil. The seeds and stems of prairie grasses and plants are consumed by insects and such rodents as the deer mouse (7) and the prairie dog (8). Predators such as the coyote (9) and scavengers such as the red-tailed hawk (10) scour the plains for these smaller prey. Large grazing animals such as the North American bison (11) were once abundant in these regions. The migratory habits of the bison prevented overgrazing and subsequent erosion of the land. Insects and burrowing rodents play a vital role in improving drainage and restoring fertility to the soil.

tensive root systems that can tap water at greater depths. With drought, grass cover, flowering, and seed production decline, and drought-tolerant plants spread; most animals migrate in search of food and water. With rainfall, recovery is rapid; dormant plants resume growth, and animals have more food available.

Periodic fires are common and play an important role in the maintenance and character of grasslands. Most growing parts of the grasses are below ground and survive the fires.

Shrubs, trees, and herbs are eliminated temporarily, and browsing animals must look elsewhere for food. Release of nutrients by burning soon stimulates grass growth.

Underground stems and dense, fibrous root systems may constitute one-half or more of a grassland's living plant matter. This mass of plant material and the activity of microbes, invertebrates and burrowing rodents account for a dynamic portion of the grasslands. They ensure availability of water and nutrients to above-ground vegetation.

Temperate Grasslands. The temperate central North American grasslands are rich in warm-season grasses and broad-leaved herbs; during summer months more than 70 species may be flowering at any one time. Major herbivores are pronghorn, rodents, and rabbits. Coyotes, bobcats, badgers, and snakes prey on the rodents. Birds include lark buntings, meadowlarks, plovers, and predatory hawks and owls. Marshes, sloughs, and potholes (poorly drained depressions) provide essential habitats for ducks, geese, and other waterfowl.

The temperate grasslands of Argentina (pampas), the USSR, China, and Siberia (steppes) are also rich in plant species. Large herds of grazing ungulates (hoofed animals) are absent in South America and Australia, but they are important to the maintenance of the Asian steppe, where gazelles and antelopes are numerous and widely distributed. Burrowing rodents, such as marmots and ground squirrels, affect the steppe vegetation with their consumptive grazing and underground activity, and they provide food for predatory birds and mammals. Locusts and grasshoppers provide food for the flocks of cranes, starlings, and bustards (see STEPPE LIFE). The kangaroos and wallabies of Australia are ecological equivalents of the ungulates of Asia.

Tropical Grasslands. Plants and animals of tropical grasslands are adapted to longer growing seasons. The greatest concentration of mixed plains wildlife in the world exists on the Serengeti Plains of Africa, where more than 100 large species plus other plants support wildebeests, gazelles, impalas, zebras, and about 25 other species; predatory lions, hyenas, cheetahs, leopards, and other carnivores; and numerous species of birds, rodents, and insects. The ungulates move in large herds across the plains on the basis of grass palatability and dry seasons.

Tundra Grasslands. The treeless polar and alpine tundras are characterized by plants and animals that must survive short growing seasons, low temperatures, and drying winds. Many of these habitats have an abundance of broad-leaved herbs associated with grasses. Herbivores of the polar tundra include rodents, caribou, and reindeer, which are prey to wolves, foxes, and eagles. In mountainous areas, sheep, goats, and rodents provide food for predator cats and wolves.

Human Influence. Human use of grasslands for cropland, livestock grazing, and living space places considerable pressure on grassland life. Several species of plants and animals are threatened with extinction as habitats critical to their survival decline and illegal collecting continues. Conversion of the perennial grass cover into row crops elimates wildlife habitats and accelerates soil erosion. Overgrazing reduces vegetative cover, and under prolonged drought desertlike conditions may spread. Overgrazing also permits invasion of unpalatable species and nonnative weeds. As grazers avoid them, these plants begin to dominate and exclude the original species, which contributes to a drop in grazing and wildlife potential.

Grasso, Ella T. [gras'-oh] Ella Tambussi Grasso, b. Windsor Locks, Conn., May 10, 1919, d. Feb. 5, 1981, became governor of Connecticut in 1975, the first woman to be elected a state governor in her own right. A Democrat, she held other state elective offices (1952–70) and served in the U.S. House of Representatives (1971–75). She was reelected governor in 1978 but resigned at the end of 1980 because of ill health.

Grateful Dead, The The Grateful Dead, one of America's most enduring rock-music bands, helped create the "acid-rock" sound of the 1960s and later pioneered "country rock." Their free San Francisco concerts were among the first of the giant, multimedia rock happenings. The Dead's first album, *The Grateful Dead*, was released in 1967. Two 1970 albums, *Workingman's Dead* and *American Beauty*, along with the 1987 album *In the Dark*, are rated among their best works. Original members still with the group are Jerry Garcia, b. San Francisco, Aug. 1, 1942, and Bob Weir, b. San Francisco, Oct. 16, 1947, guitars and vocals; Phil Lesh, b. Berkeley, Calif., Mar. 15, 1940, bass; and Bill Kreutzmann, b. Palo Alto, Calif., June 7, 1946, drums.

Gratian [gray'-shuhn] Gratian, a 12th-century Italian monk and legal scholar, is considered the father of CANON LAW. Very few details of his life are known other than that he taught at the Camaldolese monastery in Bologna and was a consultant to a papal judge in 1143. His greatest work is the *Concordia discordantium canonum*, commonly known as the *Decretum Gratiani*, a collection of canon law. This was not the first such compilation, but it was the most original in its attempt to analyze conflicting authorities and arrive at some specific conclusion in the case of each question at issue. His collection quickly became standard, was taught in the law schools by the end of the 12th century, and became the manual used in the papal curia under the pontificate of Pope Alexander III.

Gratian, Roman Emperor in the West Flavius Gratianus, AD 359–383, was Roman emperor of the West from 367 to 383. He was coemperor with his father, VALENTINIAN I, until the latter's death (375); then he divided his father's empire with his young half-brother, VALENTINIAN II. Gratian ruled over Gaul, Spain, and Britain and successfully defended Gaul against barbarian invaders. He was a devout Christian and relied upon Saint AMBROSE as one of his chief advisors. He declined the title of *pontifex maximus* and removed the statue of Victory from the Senate. His power declined, and he was assassinated by the supporters of Magnus Maximus.

Grau, Shirley Ann [grow] The novelist and short-story writer Shirley Ann Grau, b. New Orleans, La., July 8, 1928, writes tough, realistic stories about the American South. *The Black Prince and Other Stories* (1955), her first collection, has been described as "Southern Gothic." *The Hard Blue Sky* (1958), a novel, was praised for its view of a Gulf Coast Cajun community. *The Keepers of the House* (1964), a powerful story of a Southern dynasty with a history of miscegenation, won a 1965 Pulitzer Prize and led critics to compare Grau with William Faulkner. Later works include the novels *The Condor Passes* (1971) and *Evidence of Love* (1977) and the short-story collections *The Wind Shifting West* (1973) and *Nine Women* (1985).

Grau San Martín, Ramón [grow sahn mar-teen', rah-mohn'] Ramón Grau San Martín, b. Sept. 13, 1887, d. July 28, 1969, was twice president of Cuba. A professor of medicine at the University of Havana and a political progressive, he participated in the overthrow of dictator Gerardo MACHADO in August 1933. A month later, after Fulgencio BATISTA's sergeants' revolt had driven out President Carlos Manuel de CÉSPEDES, Grau San Martín became provisional president. The United States refused to recognize his government, however, and Grau was forced to resign in January 1934.

Leading Cuba's non-Communist left, Grau lost the 1940 presidential election to Batista but won in 1944. Widespread corruption within his government hampered implementation of promised social reforms. In 1954, Grau ran again for the presidency, but withdrew before the election.

gravel [grav'-ul] In geology, any loose, or unconsolidated, natural accumulation of rounded rock fragments with individual sizes greater than 2 mm (0.08 in) in diameter is called gravel. The size distribution of the fragments is not necessarily uniform; pebbles, cobbles, and boulders may predominate, and fragments of intermediate size may not occur. Sand, which is less coarse than gravel, often fills the spaces between pebbles.

Graves, Michael [grayvz] Michael Graves, b. Indianapolis, Ind., July 9, 1934, is a leading theorist and practitioner of POSTMODERN ARCHITECTURE. He studied at the University of Cincinnati and Harvard University before becoming one of the New York Five group of architects. His work has always stressed the historical continuity of architecture and preserves close relationships with traditional modes of design and decoration. He has taught at Princeton University since 1962. His major buildings include the San Juan Capistrano, Calif., public library (1983) and the Humana Building (1985) in Louisville, Ky.

The Portland Building (1982), with its cube shape and colored facade, exemplifies the style of Michael Graves, a leading exponent of postmodern architecture. This controversial structure, containing the municipal offices of the city of Portland, Oreg., was Graves's first major public building.

Graves, Morris The American painter Morris Graves, b. Fox Valley, Oreg., Aug. 28, 1910, works in a highly individual vein expressive of the values of Oriental philosophy, particularly Zen Buddhism and Taoism. In cultivating his interest in these philosophies he made three trips to the Orient. The artist who influenced Graves most strongly was the American painter Mark TOBEY. From Tobey he derived the mode of "white writing," a kind of calligraphy as fine in its touch as filigree, which he used with striking effect in *Bird Singing in the Moonlight* (1938–40) and *Blind Bird* (1940), both in the Museum of Modern Art, New York City. Graves never tires of painting birds, which have been recognized as symbols of this extremely private, introspective artist who leads a rather isolated life in the woods north of Seattle, Wash.

Graves, Nancy The American artist Nancy Stevenson Graves, b. Pittsfield, Mass., Dec. 23, 1940, first established her reputation with sculptures of Bactrian camels (1966–71) in a variety of materials; some sculptures resembled ancient camel bones (such as the 36-piece *Variability of Similar Forms*, 1970). Her paintings of the 1970s, first inspired by maps (of Mars, of the ocean floor), evolved to complete abstraction. In the 1980s Graves concentrated on bronze sculptures, based on direct casts of natural objects and specimens.

Graves, Robert The novelist, poet, and scholar Robert Ranke Graves, b. Wimbledon, Greater London, July 24, 1895, d. Dec. 7, 1985, went straight from Charterhouse School to the horrors of trench warfare. Seriously wounded during the first Battle of the Somme, he wrote poetry during his convalesence to identify his feelings about the war. After earning a degree (1926) at Oxford, Graves devoted his life to writing, study, and teaching. Prose works range from his autobiography, *Goodbye to All That* (1929), and a critical study, *The White Goddess* (1948), which sets forth his theory of poetry and poetic inspiration, to a series of historical novels, notably *I, Claudius* (1934), *Claudius the God* (1934), and *King Jesus* (1946). He taught English literature at Cairo University (1926-27) and was professor of poetry at Oxford (1961-66).

During the 1930s, Graves worked closely with the

American poet Laura Riding, collaborating with her on the influential *Survey of Modernist Poetry* (1927). Graves published more than 15 volumes of poetry, but *Collected Poems, 1959* represents what he wished to preserve. His *Greek Myths* (1955) contains translations and commentary; and with Omar Ali-Shah he translated the *Rubaiyat of Omar Khayyam* in 1967. Graves lived for most of his life on Majorca.

gravimeter [gruh-vim'-uht-ur]   Gravimeters measure differences in the magnitude of the Earth's gravity field. Measurement of gravity involves balancing the gravity force on a so-called proof mass contained in the meter against the force exerted by a spring. Such a force on a mass is called the acceleration of gravity. The net acceleration that the meter feels is the sum of the effects of all surrounding masses.

The unit of gravity measurement is the milligal (mgal), named after Galileo. One mgal is equivalent to an acceleration of 0.001 cm/sec^2, or 0.001 dyn/gm. Sometimes a "gravity unit," equal to 0.1 mgal, is used. The attraction of the Earth as a whole is about $980,000$ mgal, and a typical gravity meter can be read to 0.01 mgal. Thus a gravimeter measures to about 1 part in 100 million.

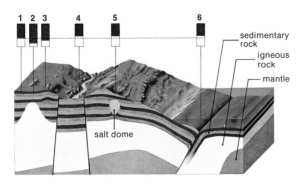

Gravimetric readings are often compared to a "normal" value (1). Higher readings indicate a stronger gravitational pull from regions of heavy igneous rock (2) or from an anticline (3), an arch of stratified rock. Lower readings occur above a rift valley (4), where lighter sedimentary rocks reach a greater depth; a salt dome (5), a mass of relatively light material; and an oceanic trough (6), where the Earth's crust extends into the mantle.

gravitation   Gravitation, or gravity, is a force that attracts all objects in the universe; it is the most familiar of the four FUNDAMENTAL INTERACTIONS of matter. Gravitation has several basic characteristics that distinguish it from the other fundamental interactions. First, it is universal, affecting all forms of matter and energy in essentially the same way, whereas all the other interactions directly affect only certain types of particles; the electromagnetic force, for example, affects only charged particles. Sec-

ond, gravity is always attractive, since it interacts with mass-energy, which is always positive; in electromagnetism, on the other hand, charges can either attract or repel. Third, gravitation is a long-range interaction; electromagnetism is also long-range, but the strong and weak nuclear forces generally operate only within a distance the size of an atomic nucleus. Fourth, gravity is the weakest of the four fundamental forces. It has a negligible effect on elementary particles; the electromagnetic attractive force between a proton and an electron is nearly 10^{40} times greater than the gravitational force at the same separation. Because gravity is a long-range attractive force affecting all matter, however, it is the dominant force in the universe.

Historical Theories

Throughout history there have been many attempts to describe or explain gravitation. Sir Isaac NEWTON made the most significant contribution to gravitational theory when he perceived (1666) that the orbit of the Moon depended on the same type of force that causes an apple to fall on Earth. This proposition required that the magnitude of the force decrease in inverse proportion to the square of the distance from the Earth's center. Newton combined the inverse-square law with his three LAWS OF MOTION to formulate a theory of universal gravitation, which stated that there is a gravitational attraction between every pair of objects, directly proportional to the square of the distance between them. Newton's description was sufficient to deduce KEPLER'S LAWS of planetary motion, the oceanic TIDES, and the PRECESSION OF THE EQUINOXES. In 1846 it was used to predict and discover a new planet, Neptune. Thus Newton's theory of gravitation stands as one of the greatest advancements of scientific knowledge.

Expressed mathematically, Newton's theory states that there is an attractive force F, given by $F = Gm_1m_2/r^2$, between two particles having masses m_1 and m_2 and separation distance r. G is the gravitational constant of proportionality, an unknown quantity that could not be determined by solar-system observations, which give only ratios of masses and thus the product of G and some mass. The value of G was first determined in 1798 by Henry Cavendish, who measured the force of gravitational attraction between two spheres of known mass. This experiment has come to be known as "weighing the Earth," because once G was determined, the Earth's mass, m_e, could be determined from the astronomically known value for Gm_e. The experiment has been repeated many times with increasing precision; the currently accepted value of G is 6.67259×10^{-8} cm^3/g sec^2.

Modern Theories

In 1905, Albert EINSTEIN developed his theory of special RELATIVITY, which modified Newton's theory of gravitation. Seeking to describe gravitation in a way that was independent of the motion of observers and of the coordinates chosen to label events, Einstein's work led him to describe gravity purely by the structure of the SPACE-TIME CONTINUUM. According to this geometrical theory, gravity affects all forms of matter and energy, all of which move in space-time. Thus this theory obeys the weak-equivalence principle and gives the same gravitational acceleration for all freely falling objects.

In addition to describing the effect of gravity on matter, Einstein described the effect of matter on gravity. This theory, completed in 1915, is called general relativity. Although Einstein's theory is much different from Newton's, it predicts nearly the same effects in systems in which gravitational fields are weak and velocities are slow compared with the velocity of light. Einstein's theory, however, accounts for some solar-system phenomena not considered by Newton, including the perihelion precession of Mercury, the bending of light rays by the Sun's gravitational field, and the gravitational RED SHIFT. All of these effects have been confirmed by scientific observation.

In addition, Einstein's theory of general relativity predicts several qualitatively new effects in other systems and is especially useful in dealing with COSMOLOGY. Relativity asserts that the universe must be either expanding or contracting. General relativity also predicts GRAVITATIONAL WAVES from masses in nonuniform motion, but these waves are so weak that they have not yet been definitely detected. The theory predicts gravitational collapse

of sufficiently massive objects into BLACK HOLES.

Einstein's general relativity is not the only 20th-century theory of gravity, though it is perhaps the simplest and most elegant. All viable theories of gravity must, like Einstein's, be complete, self-consistent, and relativistic, and predict the same Einstein shift as measured by all ideal clocks at the same position. There is strong experimental evidence for accepting these criteria as fundamental, and L. I. Schiff has conjectured that they can be satisfied only by geometrical, or metric, theories.

The strongest rival theory has been the Brans-Dicke theory. Like general relativity, it is a geometrical theory that satisfies the fundamental criteria. Its field equations are different, however, and it claims that the geometry of space-time is affected not only by matter but also by an additional scalar field. Unlike Einstein's calculations, the Brans-Dicke theory cannot predict the perihelion shift of Mercury.

Some recent theories attempt to explain gravitation nongeometrically, proposing instead that particles called gravitons are responsible. These so-called supersymmetry theories place gravitational phenomena within the realm of quantum physics. They are part of an attempt to show that the four fundamental interactions of nature are related, and that they were a single, united force at the birth

According to Newton's law of universal gravitation (A), all bodies attract each other with a force that varies inversely as the square of the distance between them (1). Thus a planet (2) that is one astronomical unit (AU) away from the Sun, S, is attracted by a force that is four times as great as that experienced by a planet (3) two AUs away. A planet near the Sun moves faster than one farther away, as indicated by the length of the arrows; increasing length corresponds to increasing velocity. The orbit (B) of an artificial satellite at a given height above the Earth is dependent on the relationship between the Earth's gravitational field and the satellite's inertial or centrifugal reaction force resulting from its velocity, v, at that point. A circular orbit (1) results at a critical velocity, v_1. A slightly greater velocity, v_2, produces an elliptical orbit (2). At a specific higher velocity, v_3, called the escape velocity, the orbit is a parabola (3) with the Earth at one focus, and the satellite will escape the Earth's gravity. The orbit becomes hyperbolic (4) at any velocity, v_4, greater than the escape velocity. Newton's laws of gravity and mechanics also explain Kepler's laws of planetary motion (C); the equatorial bulging (D) of rotating planets, such as Jupiter; the parabolic paths (E) of ballistic missiles on Earth; and the hyperbolic paths (F) of nonrecurring comets.

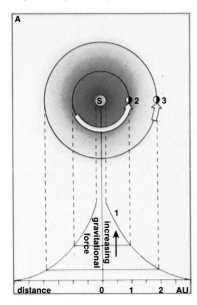

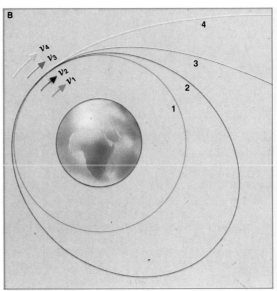

of the universe (see GRAND UNIFICATION THEORIES; UNIFIED FIELD THEORY).

Multidimensional analysis has also raised the issue of the constancy of the gravitational constant G. This idea was proposed earlier by British physicist Paul Dirac in his so-called "large numbers" hypothesis. If G were decreasing, however, gravitational time would change with respect to atomic time; thus far, experiments have not shown this to be happening.

gravitational collapse Gravitational collapse is the catastrophic fate that befalls a massive object when its own gravity completely overwhelms all other forces. During most of a star's lifetime, its tendency to contract as a result of its gravity is balanced by the outward pressure produced by the heat of its nuclear reactions. Eventually, however, the nuclear fuel will be exhausted. If the star's mass is less than about 3 solar masses, it will eventually contract to a stable configuration as either a WHITE DWARF (about the size of the Earth but hundreds of thousands times denser) or a NEUTRON STAR (a similar mass compressed into a sphere only a few miles across). More massive stars, however, will continue to shrink even further when their thermal and rotational energy are exhausted. Unless the star sheds its excess mass, gravity will overcome all conceivable pressure forces, and gravitational collapse will occur.

Once gravity exceeds the other forces, the star will fall in on itself in a few hours. When the size of the collapsing star falls below what is called the Schwarzschild radius, the escape velocity becomes equal to the velocity of light. When not even light can escape from the surface, the star is said to be inside a BLACK HOLE. Theorems by Roger PENROSE and Stephen HAWKING show that, according to general RELATIVITY and similar theories of GRAVITATION, a singularity, or edge to the space-time continuum must then occur. The universe as a whole may also undergo gravitational collapse. The universe is presently expanding as distant galaxies move apart, but, if they do not have escape velocity relative to each other, they will eventually fall back together and bring the universe to an end. Whether this will happen depends on the density of matter in the universe, which is not precisely known.

gravitational lens Albert Einstein's theory of general RELATIVITY predicts that starlight is deflected by the gravitational field of an intermediate massive body. A predicted deflection of 1.75 seconds of arc at the Sun's edge has been observed at numerous solar eclipses since 1919. Einstein's theory also predicted that a massive intervening body, such as the nucleus of a galaxy, would tend to deflect the light from a more distant object and act as a gravitational lens. An "Einstein ring" of light could be produced by a precise alignment of objects. Much more likely would be the observation of one or more distorted images of the more distant object lying to one side or another of the intervening mass.

A gravitational lens was first identified in 1979, when two nearly identical quasar images were observed lying only about 6 seconds of arc apart in the sky. The intervening galaxy producing these images was later also identified. A number of other lens effects have since been observed. In 1987 luminous arcs were sighted in distant galaxy clusters, the arcs apparently being distortions of still more distant clusters. In 1988 an apparent Einstein ring produced by perfectly aligned objects was observed. In 1989 astronomers detected the first example of a "microlens"—a single star or other intervening object apparently focusing the light of a more distant quasar.

gravitational waves Gravitational waves are theoretical perturbations in a gravitational field. According to the theory of general RELATIVITY, when an object changes its configuration, its gravitational field changes; because nothing can travel faster than light, the gravitational field cannot change instantaneously over all space. Instead, the changes in the field spread out from the source in the form of gravitational waves. The strongest waves should come from massive objects changing configuration at high velocity, as during the GRAVITATIONAL COLLAPSE into BLACK HOLES of stars, star clusters, the central regions of galaxies, and matter that condensed before galaxy formation. Even these strongest waves, however, are predicted to be very weak by the time they reach the Earth and would produce distortion amplitudes of less than one part per 10^{15}.

American physicist Joseph Weber built the first gravitational-wave detectors in the 1960s. They consisted of massive aluminum cylinders, cooled to low temperatures, that were expected to oscillate in response to the waves. The gravitational-wave detectors built since then have been either of this type (sometimes using niobium instead of aluminum) or separated-mass instruments that extend over distances of several kilometers. Thus far no conclusive evidence for gravitational waves has been found.

To detect low-frequency waves from massive black-hole events, scientists have suggested using the Earth and interplanetary spacecraft as free particles. An observer would look for oscillations in the time radio signals take to travel between them.

gravity see GRAVITATION

gravity, center of see CENTER OF GRAVITY

Gravity's Rainbow see PYNCHON, THOMAS

gravure see PLATE MAKING; PRINTING; ROTOGRAVURE

Gray, Elisha The American inventor Elisha Gray, b. Barnesville, Ohio, Aug. 2, 1835, d. Jan. 21, 1901, contested the invention of the TELEPHONE in a famous patent litigation suit against Alexander Graham BELL. Gray was interested in electricity and in 1867 received a patent for a self-adjusting telegraph relay. In 1888 he invented the telautograph, an electrical device for reproducing and transmitting handwriting and line drawing. On Feb. 14, 1876, Gray filed with the U.S. Patent Office a caveat announcing his intention to file a patent for a telephone. A few hours earlier, Bell had filed just such a patent. Extensive patent litigation followed and was brought to an end only when the U.S. Supreme Court ruled that Bell was the inventor. Trial testimony showed, however, that Bell's first transmission of the human voice could not have taken place with the device that he patented, whereas the device that Gray intended to patent was workable.

Gray, Francine du Plessix

An American essayist and novelist, Francine du Plessix Gray, b. France, Sept. 25, 1930, has written widely. The essays in *Divine Disobedience: Profiles in Catholic Radicalism* (1970) are based on her Catholic background. *Hawaii: The Sugar-Coated Fortress* (1977) deals with militarism and racism, and *Adam and Eve and the City* (1987) is a collection of her writings for journals. *Soviet Women: Walking the Tightrope* (1990) exposes the myth of sexual equality in the USSR. Her fiction includes *Lovers and Tyrants* (1976), *World without End* (1981), and *October Blood* (1985).

Gray, Robert

The American navigator Robert Gray, b. Tiverton, R.I., May 10, 1755, d. 1806, was the first seaman to carry the U.S. flag around the world—on a 35-month voyage ending in 1790. In May 1792, Gray sailed his ship, the *Columbia*, into the mouth of what came to be called the Columbia River, his discovery forming the basis of the U.S. claim to the Oregon Territory.

Gray, Thomas

Of all English poets to achieve greatness, Thomas Gray, b. Dec. 26, 1716, d. July 30, 1771, was the least productive, yet his Elegy Written in a Country Churchyard (1751), his Pindaric odes (1757), and

The lyricism, wit, and intensity of the British poet Thomas Gray place him in the vanguard of the 18th-century romantic movement. A refined, disciplined style characterizes Gray's work, the best known of which is "Elegy Written in a Country Churchyard" (1751). (National Portrait Gallery, London.)

"Ode on the Death of a Favorite Cat, Drowned in a Tub of Gold Fishes" (1748) are all the finest of their kind.

Gray entered Eton College at eight, where he met Horace Walpole and Richard West. He attended (1734–38) Cambridge University, then toured Europe with Walpole. Cambridge was his home from 1742, and he became Regius Professor of Modern History in 1768. There he began to write poems, among them "Ode on a Distant Prospect of Eton College" and "Sonnet on the Death of Mr. Richard West," both occasioned by the death of his friend in 1742. Gray's later Pindaric odes "The Bard" and "The Progress of Poesy" exploit a taste for picturesque imagery and historical allusion anticipating the romantic movement. Gray turned his prodigious learning to lighter purposes in the mock-heroic ode on the death of Walpole's cat, and in his somber but witty denunciation of a venal politician, "On Lord Holland's Seat near Margate, Kent," he recalled the brilliance of Alexander Pope's satiric verses.

Gray Panthers

The Gray Panthers is a U.S. organization that seeks to combat discrimination against people on the basis of age. Founded in 1971, the group, which includes both old and young members, conducts discussions, does research, lobbies local, state, and federal governments, and maintains an information and referral service. The headquarters of the Gray Panthers is in Philadelphia.

Graz

[grahts] Graz is the capital of Styria province in southeastern Austria. Situated on the Mur River at the foot of the Styrian Alps, it is Austria's second largest city, with a population of 241,437 (1986 est.). It is a rail, cultural, and industrial center with iron and steel works and breweries. Graz manufactures machinery, paper, leather, and optical instruments. Its name is derived from the fortress that was located on top of the Schlossberg (475 m/1,558 ft high), a defensive site since ancient times. During the Middle Ages, Graz became the principal city of Styria, and the Leopoldine Habsburgs made it their seat (1379). Noted for its clock tower (1561) and belfry (1588), Graz was founded in 1586.

Graziani, Rodolfo

[graht-see-ahn'-ee] Rodolfo Graziani, b. Aug. 11, 1882, d. Jan. 11, 1955, was an Italian field marshal and supporter of Benito Mussolini. He was commander of the Italian forces in Libya (1930–34), governor of Somaliland (1935–36), viceroy of Ethiopia (1936–37), and governor of Italian East Africa (1938). Commanding Italian forces in Libya in 1940, he advanced into Egypt but soon resigned (March 1941) when defeated by the British under Archibald Wavell. After the Italian armistice of 1943, Graziani became defense minister in Mussolini's northern Italian Republic. Sentenced to prison after World War II, he was granted amnesty in 1950 and later headed Italy's neo-Fascist movement.

ILLUSTRATION CREDITS

The following list credits or acknowledges, by page, the source of illustrations used in this volume. When two or more illustrations appear on one page, they are credited individually left to right, top to bottom; their credits are separated by semicolons. When both the photographer or artist and an agency or other source are given for an illustration, they are usually separated by a slash. Those illustrations not cited below are credited on the page on which they appear, either in the caption or alongside the illustration itself.

3 Geocom BV
7 Michael Gray
15 The Bettmann Archive
20 Rand McNally & Company
21 Uniphoto/Janice Blumhern; Sem Presser
22 Agence de Presse Photographique Rapho
23 Agence de Presse Photographique Rapho
24 Picturepoint, London; Sem Presser
25 Inter Nationes
26 Lothar Roth & Associates; Biliothèque Nationale
27 Sem Presser; Sem Presser
28 Lothar Roth & Associates; Lothar Roth & Associates
30 Photographie Giraudon
31 Photographie Giraudon
32 Lothar Roth & Associates; The Bettmann Archive
34 Photographie Giraudon; Sem Presser
35 The Bettmann Archive; Scala, Florence
37 The Bettmann Archive
38 Lothar Roth & Associates
41 Photo Researchers/Fritz Henle; UPI/Bettmann Newsphotos
42 National Portrait Gallery, London
43 Courtesy Library of Congress
44 The Bettmann Archive
45 Photographie Giraudon
46 The Bettmann Archive; UPI/Bettmann Newsphotos
49 Hessische Landesbibliothek
50 Scala, Florence
51 The Bettmann Archive
52 The Bettmann Archive
54 The Bettmann Archive
58 The Bettmann Archive
60 The Bettmann Archive
61 Sandak, Inc.
63 Photographie Giraudon
64 Photographie Giraudon
65 Photographie Giraudon; Scala, Florence
69 Rand McNally & Company
71 Lothar Roth & Associates
72 Yale University Art Gallery
74 The Bettmann Archive; The Bettmann Archive; The Bettmann Archive
75 The Bettmann Archive; The Bettmann Archive; The Bettmann Archive
76 The Bettmann Archive; The Bettmann Archive; Het Spectrum
77 The Bettmann Archive; Wide World Photos; The Bettmann Archive
78 The Bettmann Archive; Photographie Giraudon
79 The Bettmann Archive; Wide World Photos
80 Photographie Giraudon
81 Photographie Giraudon; Photographie Giraudon
82 Photographie Giraudon; Photographie Giraudon; Photographie Giraudon
83 Photographie Giraudon
84 Lothar Roth & Associates
87 Sigmund Freud Copyrights Ltd.; Sigmund Freud Copyrights Ltd.
89 The Bettmann Archive
90 UPI/Bettmann Newsphotos; Ralph Kleinhempel
96 The Bettmann Archive; Courtesy Amon Carter Museum/Fort Worth, Tex.
98 The New York Public Library Astor, Lenox, and Tilden Foundations; California State Library; University of Chicago Library, The Reuben T. Durrett Collection, Department of Special Collections

99 Nebraska State Historical Society Salomon D. Butcher Collection; James Jerome Hill Reference Library, St. Paul, Minn.
100 The New York Public Library Astor, Lenox, and Tilden Foundations; ANP—Photo
102 Superstock/Shostal/Leahey
103 Superstock/Shostal/Upitis
106 The Bettmann Archive
108 Gisèle Freund
110 UPI/Bettmann Newsphotos
111 Wide World Photos
117 Het Spectrum
118 Photo Researchers/Arthur Tress
119 Centraal Bureau Voor Schimmelcultures
121 Centraal Bureau Voor Schimmelcultures; Heinz Schrempp; Heinz Schrempp
125 Metropolitan Museum of Art, New York, Rogers Fund
126 Nelson Gallery–Atkins Museum/Kansas City, Mo., Nelson Fund; Photographie Giraudon
127 Philadelphia Museum of Art, Foule Collection; The Frick Collection, New York
128 National Gallery of Art, Washington, D.C., Widener Collection; National Gallery of Art, Washington, D.C., Widener Collection
129 Collections of Greenfield Village and the Henry Ford Museum, Dearborn, Mich.; Metropolitan Museum of Art, New York; Courtesy Museum of Modern Art, New York, Gift of Mme Hector Guimard
130 Brooklyn Museum, New York
131 Thonet/York, Pa.; Thonet/York, PA; Carl Ruff Associates; © Andrew Garn; © American Craft Council
137 Het Spectrum
138 Stedejilk Museum, Amsterdam; Rand McNally & Company
141 UPI/Bettmann Newsphotos
145 Lund Observatory. Reprinted by permission
146 Camera Press Ltd./Crane
147 Het Spectrum
148 The Bettmann Archive
149 The Bettmann Archive
153 The Bettmann Archive; The Bettmann Archive
155 The Bettmann Archive
156 Rand McNally & Company
159 Cameramann International Ltd.
161 S.P.L./Photo Researchers
162 UPI/Bettmann Newsphotos
163 Wide World Photos; Magnum Photos/Raghu Rai
164 Rand McNally & Company
165 The Bettmann Archive
166 AGE/World Photo Service
167 Photographie Giraudon; Bruce Coleman Inc./Eric Crichton
168 Photo Researchers/H. W. Silvester
169 Superstock/Shostal/Carle
170 Webb Photos
172 White House Historical Society
173 The Bettmann Archive
174 Brown Brothers
175 Photo Researchers/Russ Kinne
176 Brown Brothers; The Bettmann Archive
177 UPI/Bettmann Newsphotos
181 The Bettmann Archive
182 Mas Ampliaciones y Reproducciones
184 Bildarchiv Preussischer Kulturbesitz
185 BBC–Hulton Picture Library
191 California Institute of Technology

192 NASA
199 IBM Research, Zurich; IBM Research, Zurich
203 H. Roger Viollet
209 Oakland Tribune © Lonni Wilson
210 Monsanto; Gamma Liaison/Jim Bourg
211 Rainbow/Dan McCoy
212 Katholicke Universiteit/Zoölogisch Laboratorium
217 Picturepoint, London
218 National Palace Museum, Taipei
219 Photo Researchers/Gianni Tortoli
224 Photo Researchers/Russ Kinne; Photo Researchers/Russ Kinne
225 Lothar Roth & Associates
227 The British Museum
228 The British Museum
229 NASA
232 Black Star/Ken Sakamoto
233 Aretê Archives; USGS Eros Data Center
237 All pictures—Art Matrix/Cornell, National Supercomputer Facility
238 The Bettmann Archive
240 The Bettmann Archive; The Bettmann Archive
241 The Bettmann Archive; The Bettmann Archive; UPI/Bettmann Newsphotos
244 Rand McNally & Company
245 Courtesy Tourist Division Georgia Bureau of Industry
246 Photo Researchers/George Thompson; Photo Researchers/Russ Kinne
247 Courtesy Tourist Division, Georgia Bureau of Industry; Photo Researchers/Kelly Dean
248 Courtesy Tourist Division, Georgia Bureau of Industry
254 Scala, Florence
255 © Hirmer Verlag München
256 Foto: Fagus-Grecon
257 The Granger Collection; The Granger Collection; The Granger Collection
258 H. Roger Viollet
259 Osterreichische Nationalbibliothek; The Bettmann Archive
260 The Bettmann Archive
261 Goethe Institute, London; The Bettmann Archive
262 The Bettmann Archive; The Bettmann Archive; The Bettmann Archive; Culver Pictures
267 Rand McNally & Company
269 Photo Researchers/John Verde; Inter Nationes
270 Photo Researchers/Bernard Pierre Wolff
271 Vereniging Nederland-DDR
272 Zentrale Farbbild Agentur Zefa; Photo Researchers/David Cain
273 Picturepoint, London; Inter Nationes; Inter Nationes
274 Inter Nationes; Vereniging Nederland-DDR
275 Photographie Giraudon; Metropolitan Museum of Art, New York, Gift of George Blumenthal
276 Art Resource; Lothar Roth & Associates
277 The Bettmann Archive; The Mansell Collection
278 Lothar Roth & Associates
279 The Bettmann Archive; Mary Evans Picture Library
280 Lothar Roth & Associates
281 Bildarchiv Preussischer Kulturbesitz; The Bettmann Archive; The Bettmann Archive
282 Bildarchiv Preussischer Kulturbesitz
283 Lothar Roth & Associates; The Bettmann Archive; The Bettmann Archive
285 The Bettmann Archive
286 The New York Public Library Astor, Lenox, and Tilden Foundations: Rare Book Division; Wide World Photos
289 The Bettmann Archive

290 Photo Researchers/Porterfield-Chickering
292 Rand McNally & Company
293 Picturepoint, London
297 Paul C. Pet
298 Vandaag BV
299 National Portrait Gallery, London; The Bettmann Archive
301 AGE/G. Franco; Rand McNally & Company
302 Photographie Giraudon
303 The Bettmann Archive
304 The Bettmann Archive
309 Scala, Florence
310 Photographie Giraudon
312 UPI/Bettmann Newsphotos; The Hark Group Ltd./Slidemakers
317 National Portrait Gallery, London
319 Saint Gobain, France: Photo Belzeaux Rapho
322 Photo Jobling
323 Metropolitan Museum of Art, New York, Gift of Edward S. Harkness; The British Museum
324 Yale University Art Gallery, Mabel Brady Garvan Collection; Metropolitan Museum of Art, New York; Steuben Glass Company
326 Royal Doulton Ltd.
327 NASA
328 The Image Bank/J. L. Stage
331 The Bettmann Archive
333 The Bettmann Archive
335 Photo Researchers/Paolo Koch
337 Bildarchiv der Oestrerreichischen National Bibliotheek, Vienna
338 Peter Hunter; Culver Pictures
340 The Bettmann Archive; The Bettmann Archive
341 Scala, Florence
342 Servizio Editoriale Fotografico
343 Sovfoto
344 ABC Press; Courtesy South African Tourist Corporation; Courtesy South African Tourist Corporation
345 The Bettmann Archive
346 John G. Ross; Lee Boltin; Metropolitan Museum of Art, New York, Gift of H. L. Bache Foundation, 1969
347 Bruce Coleman Inc./J. Wright; Metropolitan Museum of Art, New York Purchase, Edgar Kaufmann, Jr., Gift 1972.
351 Mark Gerson; The Bettmann Archive
352 Wide World Photos; UPI/Bettmann Newsphotos
355 © David Madison/Duomo
356 UPI/Bettmann Newsphotos
357 The Bettmann Archive
358 Mas Ampliaciones y Reproducciones
359 Popperfoto/Paul Popper
362 Black Star/Bryn Colton
366 Brown Brothers
368 A. F. Kersting
370 Scala, Florence; Photographie Giraudon
371 Photographie Giraudon
372 Scala, Florence
373 Scala, Florence; Sem Presser; Art Resource
375 A. F. Kersting; Picturepoint, London
379 The Bettmann Archive
391 UPI/Bettmann Newsphotos; Martha Swope Assoc.
395 Photo Researchers/D. Zirinsky
397 Wide World Photos; The Hark Group Ltd./Slidemakers
398 White House Historical Society
402 Het Spectrum; Stedelijk Museum, Amsterdam
403 Het Spectrum
407 Steve Raviez
411 Greg Hursley
415 National Portrait Gallery, London